DISRAELI, GLADSTONE

AND

THE EASTERN QUESTION

DISRAELI, GLADSTONE

AND

THE EASTERN QUESTION

A STUDY IN DIPLOMACY
AND PARTY POLITICS

BY

R. W. SETON-WATSON

FRANK CASS AND CO. LTD

1971

First published by Macmillan and Co. Ltd

This Edition published by Frank Cass and Co. Ltd
67 Great Russell St., London, WC 1

ISBN   0   7146   1513   7

First Edition   1935
Reprinted   1962
New Impression 1971

Printed in the United States of America

TO
BERNARD PARES

PREFACE

THE present volume forms a sequel to a book (still unpublished) entitled *Britain in Europe*, in which I attempt to give a connected survey of British foreign policy in the nineteenth century: and the germ of both is to be found in a course of lectures delivered at the University of London, King's College, in 1927 and again in 1930. When I reached the year 1874, a double motive led me to adopt new methods and an altogether larger scale. In the first place, the Eastern crisis of the seventies, to an even greater degree than the Crimean War, illustrates the essential interaction of home and foreign policy, the bearings of remote happenings in eastern Europe upon British party government, and the resultant dangers for the peace of the nation and the world: and yet its history has remained unwritten for over fifty years. In the second place, a happy chance enabled me to obtain access to a mass of unpublished Russian correspondence and thus to study those innermost secrets of the Tsar, his Chancellor and his Ambassadors, which were denied to contemporary Englishmen. The Disraeli and Salisbury Papers have already been made accessible, but in each case the aim was to interpret the standpoint of a single man and a single country, rather than to correlate or compare that standpoint with foreign sources. And yet it may reasonably be claimed that if Lords Beaconsfield, Salisbury and Derby could in 1875–8 have seen into the cards which I am now placing upon the table for the first time, their outlook towards Russia, and so towards the Eastern Question, would have been radically different.

I was thus led by gradual stages to attempt to construct a narrative in which not only the statesmen in whose hands British policy lay, but also their political opponents, the diplomatists with whom they had to deal and the foreign statesmen whose policies they sought to counter or whose alliance they courted, would all figure, and their relative importance at each stage of the crisis would be revealed, so far as possible from their own words or from the comments of their contemporaries. The major parts in the drama belong as of right to Disraeli and Gladstone, to Derby, Salisbury and Queen Victoria, but the key to the plot will often be found to lie with Shuvalov and Gorchakov, with Bismarck and Andrássy, with Elliot and Layard, with Hartington and Granville, with Northcote and Hardy, while many minor characters provide an occasional spice.

The execution of my plan has involved close attention on the one hand to diplomatic sources, on the other to the columns of Hansard, to the outpourings of the press and to masses of ephemeral literature, often of a most violent and partisan character. Whether I have avoided the twin dangers of overloading the text with quotations and of tipping the scales by tendencious selection, is for the reader to judge. On the whole, I have preferred what may be called the cumulative method, which has obvious drawbacks, but seems to me both safer and fairer than any known alternative. I can at least claim never to have consciously suppressed any material facts or arguments: and if my own very definite views occasionally intrude, the reader is always free to discard them if he is not convinced. Indeed it has always seemed to me far more honest for an author to reveal his considered opinions on the subject of which he is treating, rather than to affect an entirely non-committal attitude which can hardly represent his real views if he has fully mastered the facts.

This is the point at which to express my very special debt to Mr. Buckle's masterly *Life of Disraeli*. It is, however, based mainly upon the Disraeli Papers, to the virtual exclusion of Continental sources: and I have therefore endeavoured to provide a new perspective by interweaving the letters of Disraeli, Salisbury and the Queen with much hitherto unknown material from other sources, alike British, Russian, German and Austrian. Mr. Buckle regards Disraeli's "management of the Eastern Question" as "the most outstanding feature of his great Administration": but to me, on the basis of this mass of new evidence (which I trust the reader will regard as conclusive), the only fitting word is "mismanagement". Disraeli as a master of foreign policy belongs to the myths of history.

It is none the less necessary to enter a special caveat with regard both to Disraeli and the Queen, as two of the central figures in the drama. I can honestly affirm that my study of British foreign policy has led me to an almost unstinted admiration of Queen Victoria: and this will be apparent in my forthcoming book on foreign policy from 1815 to 1874, of which the present volume is really a sequel, written on an extended scale. The Queen's attitude towards the Eastern crisis of the seventies is to be regarded as a mere passing aberration, in striking contrast to her wise and balanced judgment in the earlier period. In a somewhat different way my criticism of Disraeli's foreign policy must not be construed as a root-and-branch condemnation of that statesman. The whole subsequent history of the Near East bears witness to the prophetic vision of Gladstone, and no less prophetic and enduring was his famous Midlothian statement of the principles of foreign policy. The greatness of Disraeli is to be sought in the sphere of Imperial politics, and it ought to be possible at this distance of time to feel appreciation for both the great rivals, whatever may be our political, religious or social preferences. In my interpretation Salisbury provides the synthesis between Disraeli and Gladstone; while Derby (to change the metaphor) is the brake on every wheel.

In this volume two currents meet from two very different fields which have always fascinated me. The study of the Eastern Question in its various phases, historical and political, has occupied me ever since I first visited the Near East in 1900. On the other hand, the rivalry of those political titans Disraeli and Gladstone was an intense and living memory to those from whom I learnt the political alphabet, and still makes an extraordinarily vivid appeal. I grew up in a household where the portraits of Disraeli, Gladstone and Bright hung side by side upon the wall. One member of it was an ardent Tory and carried his admiration of Disraeli to the length of appearing on Midlothian Tory platforms to the detriment of his own official career: while the other, a no less ardent Gladstonian, retained a certain hero-worship for the old chief, even though he followed Chamberlain in 1886. Many a crude, contemporary gibe against the rival statesmen came my way and still lingers shamefacedly in my memory, with the result that in the decade before the War the animosities that centred round Limehouse sounded like mere harmless squibs after the infernal machines of the Victorian era. If these early memories have served me at all, it has been in the sense of a warning not to treat this great controversy on party lines, but rather to judge it in its European aspects and in the light of subsequent events.

It may be claimed that the new material provided throws an entirely new light upon British policy in the seventies—in particular, upon the two secret overtures made by Disraeli to Russia in June 1876 and March 1877; upon Salisbury's relations with Ignatyev during and after his Constantinople mission; upon Disraeli's relations with Layard behind the back of Derby; upon the secret Austro-Russian convention and the various British overtures to Vienna; upon the relations of Shuvalov with Derby on the one hand and with the Liberal Opposition on the other; upon Layard's close relations with Abdul Hamid; upon the inner reasons of Derby's second and final resignation and of his joining the Liberals; upon the mutual relations of Gladstone, Granville, Hartington, Harcourt and Chamberlain; upon Salisbury's triple parallel negotiations with Russia, Austria and Turkey and upon the inner history of the Berlin Congress.

I owe a very special debt of gratitude to Mr. M. Sablin, Chargé d'Affaires of the former Imperial Russian Embassy in London, and to my former colleague, Baron Alexander F. Meyendorff, for granting me full access to the secret correspondence between Count Shuvalov, Prince Gorchakov and Tsar Alexander throughout the crisis of the seventies. Thanks to this, it becomes possible for the first time to compare the realities of Russian policy with the estimates formed of it by contemporary British statesmen. I also desire to express my warm thanks to Lady Gwendolen Cecil for allowing me access to certain documents in the Salisbury Papers and thus clearing up an important point in the relations of Lords Salisbury and Beaconsfield with the Russian Ambassador; to Lord Gladstone, for access to the Gladstone Papers, and to Mr. Tilney Bassett, for his constant and ready assistance while I was consulting them; to Lord Granville, for access to the later papers of his father at the Public Record Office; to Lord Harcourt, for access to the correspondence between Lord Granville and Sir William Harcourt; to Mr. Stephen Gaselee, Librarian of the Foreign Office, and to the officials of the Public Record Office and the MS. Department of the British Museum, for their extremely kind assistance: to Dr. Ludwig Bittner, Director of the Staats-, Haus- und Hof-Archiv in Vienna, and to his colleagues for the great facilities which they extended to me during two visits to the archives; to Sir Arthur Evans for access to material relating to his experiences in Bosnia during the seventies; to Professor Ferdo Šišić of Zagreb University, for hitherto unprinted letters of Canon Liddon to Bishop Strossmayer, in the Jugoslav Academy of Sciences; to Mr. Ivan Švegel, late Jugoslav Minister to the Argentine, for access to certain papers of his uncle Baron Schwegel; to Mr. B. H. Sumner of Balliol College, Oxford; to Mr. Dwight Lee; and finally to my colleague Sir Bernard Pares, to Professor L. B. Namier, to my former pupil Dr. Winifred Taffs, and not least of all to my wife, for constant detailed criticism and encouragement.

R. W. SETON-WATSON

School of Slavonic and East European Studies
University of London   1935

CONTENTS

CHAPTER V

CHAPTER VI

CHAPTER VII

CHAPTER VIII

CHAPTER IX

CHAPTER X

CHAPTER XI

CHAPTER XII

EPILOGUE

MAP

Abbreviations

G.P.	= *Die Grosse Politik der europäischen Kabinette* (1871–1914).
D.D.F.	= *Documents Diplomatiques Français* (1871–1914). 1ᵉʳ série.
R.B.D.	= *Russo-British Documents*, series i.-vii. (Slavonic Reviews).
U.R.B.D.	= Unprinted Russo-British Documents (hitherto unpublished, sequence to R.B.D.).
Buckle	= G. E. Buckle, *Life of Disraeli*, vol. vi.
Life	= Lady Gwendolen Cecil, *Life of Robert Marquis of Salisbury*, vol. ii.

Italics in quotations have been added by the Author, unless the contrary is stated.

Nichts Bessers weiss ich mir an Sonn- und Feiertagen,
Als ein Gespräch von Krieg und Kriegsgeschrei,
Wenn hinten, weit, in der Türkei,
Die Völker auf einander schlagen.

GOETHE, Faust

CHAPTER I

DISRAELI AND THE NEW IMPERIALISM

FOUR times in the last hundred years has the so-called Eastern Question involved Europe in a crisis of the first magnitude. In 1854 it led to a war of the three Western Powers and Turkey against Russia—a war which the allies did everything in their power to make universal by involving Austria and Prussia also, and which only remained localised because of the hesitant policy of Vienna and Berlin. Twenty years later troubles in Bosnia involved first Serbia, then Russia, in conflict with Turkey, and more than once a general war seemed imminent. In 1908 the Bosnian question again became a European issue, and war between the Triple Alliance and the Triple Entente was only narrowly averted. Finally in 1912 and 1914 there were fresh turns of the Balkan kaleidoscope, and the catastrophe so long feared was precipitated by a quarrel which centred in the Near East. Four years of a World War altered the Eastern Question out of all recognition, but even to-day some of the poison engendered by it is still working in the veins of Europe.

There are many aspects from which these tragedies can be considered, but there are two which deserve especial attention. The more closely they are studied, the more conscious do we become of the extent to which the political, racial and economic issues of the modern world have become interwoven and interlocked, until it is scarcely possible to name any question, seemingly, of internal politics in one country which may not, under force of circumstances, become a cause of international complications. Early in the Great War the late Lord Morley expressed to me his grief and horror at the idea that Lancashire lads should die in Flanders and Thrace because a Bosnian Serb had murdered an Austrian Archduke: and even then it seemed to me strange that a philosopher and historian of his calibre should have been so blind to a process which has been increasingly at work for a whole century, and to which the railway, the telegraph, the telephone, the motor-car and the airship have given added impulse. Horrible indeed it is that the sons of one nation should perish in a quarrel which was perhaps started in another hemisphere, which in no

1

way concerned them, and of which they did not know the very elements. In 1934 there are many who loudly asseverate that the Austrian, or Danubian, or Polish or Ukrainian question in no way concerns the British Empire and may be ignored by it. Yet at any moment one of these questions, or others not yet even visible on the horizon, may swiftly and inexorably involve Europe, against its will and without all possibility of choice. For that is "the way of the world", and will continue to be so until mankind consents to apply religion or ethics to politics and can find a substitute for war.

A second and still more practical aspect is the extent to which these issues are determined by public opinion, elemental, unreasoning, sweeping away the leaders of a nation and raising new idols to power. In the first of the four instances quoted, the Crimean War, public opinion in Britain radically misjudged the facts and was positively hysterical in its outbursts: and the result was a war which posterity agrees in regarding as the most superfluous in our modern annals. New classes of the nation, vocal for the first time and incapable of judging the niceties of foreign policy, swept the Government and the Crown off their feet: and in the process men like Cobden and Bright, who a few years earlier had won an overwhelming popular victory, found themselves isolated and exposed to fierce obloquy. In the second instance, the Eastern crisis of the seventies, it was again public opinion which exercised the decisive influence, but this time it was split into two closely balanced sections which neutralised one another, and in the end the Government, which had sometimes fanned opinion into flame, hesitated and drew back from the very brink of war.

These two classic instances should provide us to all time with a warning against the dangers of allowing foreign policy to become a catchword of internal party politics. Lord Salisbury was not exaggerating when he pointed out, on his return from the Congress of Berlin, that no question had within the memory of man "so deeply excited the English people, moved their passions so thoroughly and produced such profound divisions and such rancorous animosity". Even after the lapse of half a century it should be profitable to explore this field and to examine the theses of rival statesmen and propagandists. The path is strewn with warnings which may still be taken to heart.

The Return of the Conservatives

The advent of the Conservatives to power in 1874, as the result of a decisive victory at the polls, forms a landmark in foreign policy. It ends the long and not very edifying period of isolation and non-intervention during which immense changes took place on the Continent, without this country seeming able to exercise any very noticeable influence in one direction or the other. This deliberate abstention from Continental affairs had since 1865 been equally the policy of both the great political parties. At earlier periods each in turn had pursued an active policy in Europe, though the methods adopted to this end had varied very greatly under Castlereagh, under Canning and under Palmerston. Since the Crimean War, the responsibility for which must be shared by every section of political opinion, it was the Tories who had been most chary of anything savouring of intervention. That it was the Conservatives who now broke away from their former traditions and entered for a time upon what in our own day is sometimes labelled as "activism", was above all due to the personality of Benjamin Disraeli, who had at length overcome the suspicious reserves of the Tory aristocracy, and stood forth as their acknowledged leader, displaying qualities of restless energy and still more of vivid imagination, such as differentiated him from most British statesmen. These he unquestionably owed to his Jewish blood, from which only too often spiteful deductions have been drawn, but whose significance can scarcely be exaggerated, even if we do not accept the deliberate overstatement of one of his novels, "Race is everything, there is no other truth". In his first elation and surprise he himself described the new Government as "the strongest since Pitt": [1] but he was now in his seventieth year, racked with gout and asthma, and he pathetically reminded his admirers: "Power has come to me too late. There were days when on waking I felt I could move dynasties and governments: but that has passed away." [2]

It is a commonplace of history that Disraeli introduced the Imperial conception of affairs and assigned to our expanding Empire for the first time the attention and sympathy that were its due. The international situation which confronted him was radically different from that which prevailed when he first became Prime Minister. The old balance on the Continent had been overthrown, France was

---

[1] To Lady Bradford, 6 Feb. 1874—Buckle, v. p. 283.   [2] *Ibid.* p. 299.

under temporary eclipse, Italy was still a negligible quantity. Germany was not merely preponderant, but more closely allied than ever to the other two Imperial Courts: and thus Britain found herself in a position of uncomfortable isolation, faced by what some regarded as the old Holy Alliance in a thinly disguised form.

Britain and Russia in Central Asia

Meanwhile our eastern policy was suffering a sea change in more than one direction. The great transformation wrought in sea communications gave a growing importance to Egypt as the key to the nearest route to India, and it was no longer possible to be indifferent —or even hostile, as Palmerston had been to the last, and Disraeli as a younger man—to the achievement of the Suez Canal and its control by a French company. At the same time the steady advance of Russia in Central Asia was regarded with grave anxiety both by students of Indian affairs and by members of the Viceroy's Council. The vast regions stretching from the Caspian to the Tian Shan and Pamir ranges were inhabited by backward and fanatical Turkoman tribes, professing Islam and governed by rival Khans and Emirs. General Kauffmann, the most famous of Russia's military administrators, was appointed Governor of Turkestan in 1867, and already in the following year reduced Samarkand and Bokhara to submission, thus making Russia the immediate neighbour of Afghanistan on the south-east. In 1873 the advance was resumed by the subjection of Khiva, and two years later the fall of Khokand marked the final stage. Thus within a quarter of a century Russia had pushed forward her frontiers 700 miles to the south and 900 miles to the south-east![1]

To-day it is no longer possible to deny that the Russian advance ended a corrupt and altogether effete régime, and, by letting air and light into regions that had been hermetically sealed for centuries, was a real gain for civilisation. This was treated as incontrovertible even by that noted Russophobe, Arminius Vámbéry, who, disguised as a Moslem pilgrim, saw with his own eyes the hideous cruelties practised by the native rulers of Khiva and Samarkand. But to many contemporaries this fact was still obscured by all too recent memories of Russian repression in Poland and intervention in Hungary and by ugly tales of religious persecution. To those again who looked through Anglo-Indian eyes the advance seemed a serious menace to India, not so

[1] See "Russian Advances in Central Asia", *Quarterly Review*, April 1874, p. 431.

much directly—for the idea that the Russians could invade India with adequate, or even inadequate, forces, by such a route as Kashgar and the high Pamirs, was really too grotesque for all but monomaniacs —but indirectly by reducing Persia and Afghanistan to the position of vassal or dependent states. Afghanistan in particular, lacked clearly defined frontiers, and after the death of Dost Mohammed in 1865 fell into a state of latent disorder which seemed to foreshadow dissolution. Lawrence, who was Viceroy till 1868, consistently upheld the view that the establishment of order and culture by Russia was preferable to the survival of unrest and anarchy in such wide regions: and both he and his successor, Lord Mayo, would have welcomed a definite understanding between the two countries as to their respect-ive spheres of influence. Conversations took place in 1869 between Clarendon and Brunnov, and resulted in a suggestion from Prince Gorchakov that a neutral zone should be formed between the two Empires, and an assurance that the Tsar himself regarded Afghan-istan as "completely outside the sphere" of Russian influence. Early in 1873 it was agreed that the Oxus should form the northern line, and the Tsar denied any intention of taking Khiva. But he had under-taken more than he could fulfil. Khiva under its Khan was no better than a den of robbers and a centre of slavery: occupation was well-nigh inevitable, and even so prominent a Russophobe as Sir Henry Rawlinson proclaimed the impossibility of subsequent withdrawal, without endangering the whole achievement of the preceding decades. It was the same inevitable process which had determined the piece-meal advance of the British in India. Indeed, it was pointed out at the time, that Napier's conquest of Scinde was carried out under almost identical conditions, for it took place in spite of the unanimous disapproval of Sir Robert Peel and his Cabinet (of which Gladstone was then a member), but it created a situation which it was found impossible to reverse.

The fact, then, that Khiva was annexed within less than a year of the assurance referred to above was not merely a striking proof that two rival currents existed at the Russian Court, but provided con-siderable excuse for the suspicions which now began to dominate the Viceroy's Council. One of its most active members, Sir Bartle Frere, was thoroughly infected by the Russophobia which Sir Henry Rawlinson had learnt as envoy to Persia and lost no chance of preaching to the authorities at home. Meanwhile the fall of Khiva had a magical effect upon the Amir, Shere Ali, who gravitated more and more towards Russia: and the wild language used by certain Russian officers in books[1] and even in French review articles, increased the uneasiness. Frere put forward his views in June 1874, scouting the danger of actual invasion, but arguing that a Russian Minister, if once admitted to Kabul while Britain had no representative there, would find it very easy "to impel upon us hordes of Asiatic barbarians".[2] Lord Salisbury, as Disraeli's Secretary for India, accepted this view and wrote to the retiring Viceroy, Lord Northbrook: "I agree with you in thinking that a Russian advance upon India is a chimaera. But I am by no means sure that an attempt to throw the Afghans upon us is impossible."[3] It was therefore decided to appoint a British Agent to the Amir, with instructions to visit Kabul from time to time, but to make his headquarters at Khelat.[4]

Despite these grounds for mutual distrust in Asia, there had been a genuine effort towards *rapprochement* on the part of the two home Governments, influenced by motives of central European policy. The outward signs of this were the marriage of the Duke of Edinburgh to the Tsar's only daughter, Marie, on 7 March 1874, and the state visit of Alexander II. to Windsor in May. The new Prime Minister, who was struck by the "mournfulness" of the Tsar's expression—"whether it is satiety, or the loneliness of despotism, or the fear of a violent death, I know not"[5]—was as yet quite receptive to the proposal of "a frank exchange of ideas at all times", but confided to Salisbury a certain scepticism as to reaching "a real understanding".

"EMPRESS OF INDIA"

This incident doubtless served to stimulate still further Disraeli's interest in India. There were many even in the inner councils of his party who continued to regard him as an exotic figure: yet that very interest in the East which was a tradition in his blood may fairly be claimed as a proof of his patriotic zeal and imagination. He strongly encouraged the visit of the Prince of Wales to India in 1875, and then,

---

[1] *E.g.* Colonel Terentiev, who accused Britain of distributing rifles among the Turkomans and asserted that Lord Lawrence had been recalled because he was not Russophobe enough.

[2] John Martineau, *Life and Correspondence of Frere*, i. p. 497.

[3] 19 Feb. 1875—Lady G. Cecil, *Life of Lord Salisbury*, ii. p. 72.

[4] *Ibid.* p. 75: cf. Frere's letter to Salisbury from Lahore, 3 March 1876—Martineau, *op. cit.* ii. p. 136.

[5] To Lady Chesterfield, 16 May 1874—Buckle, v. p. 416.

realising the effect of pageantry and titular rank upon the Oriental mind, pushed through Parliament, in the face of very considerable opposition, the adoption by the Queen of the title of Empress of India. In his conception this was intended to appeal to the peoples of India and to counteract the effect of rumours concerning a distant Emperor from the north, who was slowly extending his frontiers in their direction and eclipsed in rank their own sovereign. In the words of a writer in the *Quarterly Review*, the new title "declares to all the world that she is the personal head of a great Asiatic Empire and that the position is emphatically one which can never with honour be abandoned".[1]

The Bill was only passed after the Queen had definitely disclaimed all idea of drowning the ancient royal title in the new imperial, which, despite the recent triumph of the Hohenzollern, was still a little tarnished by Maximilian's misadventure in Mexico and the short-lived glories of Napoleon III. There seems to be little doubt that the contrast between the attitude of Disraeli and Gladstone in this question strengthened that bias in favour of the former and against the latter, which was to grow upon Queen Victoria with every year. The Liberal party resented what it regarded as a breach of precedent in Disraeli's omission to consult the Opposition: but it seems to have forgotten that the Crown was worn by a woman. She herself treated them as "factious" and even "unpatriotic".[2]

The strong personal sympathy which by now existed between the Prime Minister and the Queen played a decisive part in the politics of the next six years. That Disraeli felt for her the most genuine personal affection, no fair-minded man can deny: that he strengthened his influence upon her by fulsome flattery, bordering upon adulation, is no less certain. "With other women", he once said, "I employ a camel's hair brush, with the Queen I lay it with a trowel."[3]

Already within the first year we find him writing as follows: "Were he Your Majesty's Grand Vizier instead of Prime Minister, he should be content to pass his remaining years in accomplishing every-thing Your Majesty wished: but alas, it is not so":[4] and there is much more in a similar strain in the years that follow. Yet it may well be that the decisive factor was the new note of imperialism sounded in many of his speeches and the skill with which he identified Crown

---

[1] April 1876—*Kashgar, Pamir and Tibet*, p. 443.
[2] 15 June 1876, Queen to Lord Lytton—*Letters*, ii. p. 464.
[3] *Personal Papers of Lord Rendel*, p. 49.
[4] 23 April 1875—*Letters*, ii. p. 385.

and Empire and at the same time (quite unfairly) denounced "the attempts of Liberalism to effect the disintegration of the Empire".[1]

LORD DERBY AT THE FOREIGN OFFICE

Disraeli entrusted foreign affairs to Lord Stanley, who had in the interval succeeded his father as fifteenth Earl of Derby. At this time the intimacy and mutual confidence of the two men were still unclouded, their views on general policy agreed at every point, and they were in the habit of taking joint action without consulting their colleagues in the Cabinet. But Lord Derby, as he grew older, showed a certain apathy or immovability which led his chief to assume the initiative more and more: while he did not possess to anything like the same degree the confidence of the Queen and had to appeal periodically to Disraeli for help in dealing with her. We find her writing of "that very peculiar person Lord D.", who was "very difficult to manage", and complaining that he was "so terribly impartial that he will never express interest one way or the other".[2]

THE WAR SCARE OF 1875

The preoccupations caused by Russia's Asiatic policy were suddenly driven into the background by the famous "War Scare" of 1875, which has ever since been a subject of controversy, and in which there still lingers just enough obscurity to make a final verdict dependent upon a reading of psychology.[3] Early in 1875 the inspired German press began to denounce the alleged warlike preparations of France, and the campaign culminated in an article published in the Berlin *Post* of 9 April, under the title "Is War in Sight?"—which at once reverberated across Europe.

Undoubtedly the most remarkable feature of the early seventies had been the rapid recovery of France from her crushing defeat. "La France se relève trop vite à ses yeux," wrote M. Gabriac, the first French Chargé d'Affaires in Berlin after the war, after his first conversation with Bismarck. "He thought he was done with her for twenty years."[4] But on the contrary, the French Republic consoli-

---

[1] 24 June 1874—Buckle, v. p. 194.   [2] *Ibid.* v. pp. 416-17.
[3] The fullest and most reliable survey of the whole incident will be found in two articles by Miss Winifred Taffs, "The War Scare of 1875", in *Slavonic Review*, nos. 26 and 27—a preliminary study to her forthcoming Life of Lord Odo Russell, based on the unprinted British and German documents.
[4] *Documents Diplomatiques Français*, 1st Series, i. no. 42, 14 Aug. 1871.

dated its position, returned a conservative, not to say reactionary, majority to power, succeeded in paying off its indemnity at the earliest possible moment, and engaged in a thorough reorganisation of the army. The intense feeling kindled between France and Germany by the annexation of Alsace-Lorraine had not even begun to die down when Bismarck's conflict with the Vatican roused fresh antagonism among the Clericals of France and Belgium also, at a moment when the French Right had forced Thiers to give way to Macmahon. Bismarck was suspicious of the Broglie Cabinet, and scarcely less so of Duke Decazes, who became Foreign Minister after its reconstruction in November 1874 and retained the post after its fall: and he showed a somewhat nasty temper in connection with the pastoral letters of certain French Bishops, virtually espousing the cause of their German colleagues in the *Kulturkampf*: that of the Bishop of Nancy was especially resented, owing to his proximity to the conquered provinces. Decazes met Bismarck's protests by suspending the chief Catholic journal and made pacific declarations in the Chamber: but his secret fear that Germany meant to pick a fresh quarrel was confirmed by Moltke's Reichstag speech on the new army Bill, in which he spoke of "a savage cry of revenge from beyond the Vosges".[1] It was only too clear that there were many in Germany who held that they had committed a grave blunder in not bleeding France still further, and that some, even in high authority, favoured drastic measures to prevent her from resuming her former position in Europe. The Tsar, it is true, assured General Le Flô very positively that no one, not even Bismarck, wanted war:[2] but the effect of this was destroyed by a remark of Count Andrássy, who told Le Flô that Bismarck "a perdu tout sangfroid et ne se connaît plus".[3] In England the whole affair was taken equally seriously by Derby and by Granville, and if Decazes was accurately informed, a specially strong impression was produced by a recent outburst of Bismarck to Lord Odo Russell, to the effect that "he wanted to finish with France, that Russia could not put any obstacle in his way, and that in agreement with her he would partition Austria if she tried to oppose him".[4] The best proof that London took the matter seriously is the letter addressed by Queen Victoria to the German Emperor, expressing her

---

[1] Hanotaux, *Hist. de la France contemp.* ii. p. 402.

[2] *D.D.F.* i. no. 278—Le Flô to Decazes, 29 Jan. 1874.

[3] *Ibid.* no. 284; do. 17 Feb.

[4] A private letter of Decazes, 9 March 1874, quoted by Hanotaux, *op. cit.* iii. p. 79.

personal attachment to him and to Germany and her joy at its
unification, and underlining the Protestant sympathies of England,
but also alluding to the persistent rumours of war and of "a disposition on the part of Germany to avail herself of her greatly
superior force to crush and annihilate a beaten foe". Though disclaiming all belief in any such design, she ended by urging "magnanimity" and "generosity" as the wisest policy which Germany could
follow, and argued that the peace of Europe was "guaranteed for a
considerable time by the exhaustion of France".[1] William I., who was
undoubtedly pacific, replied a fortnight later at considerable length,
laying emphasis upon the Ultramontane danger and the Catholic
tendency to create a state within the state, but deploring that "the
desire for another war is constantly imputed to me" and denying all
idea of aggression against France.[2] Bismarck found it wise to draw
back and in May spoke to Odo Russell of the importance for Europe
of "a strong France".

London, however, remained suspicious. Lord Derby, answering
a question in the House of Lords in July, used curiously guarded
language as to the prospects of European peace, and at the Guildhall
banquet in November the Premier paid a marked compliment to the
new French Ambassador, M. de Jarnac, and to "the elasticity, nerve
and resource" by which his country had extricated itself from its
difficulties. Meanwhile Jarnac's Russian colleague, Count Shuvalov,
sought to reassure him by drawing a distinction between the "*grossièreté*" which was natural to the Prussian, and "premeditated
aggression", which he was confident was not in Bismarck's mind.[3]
Bismarck was no coward, but despite his strong physique he was at
this time a bundle of nerves, and the attempt on his life in July 1874
and the alleged Duchesne plot in December may well have stiffened
his attitude. During the following winter, while the German press
was full of allegations as to the purchase of horses for the French
army, Bismarck made formal representations in Brussels owing to the
attitude of the Belgian Catholics and communicated the Note to all
European Governments. He then took somewhat similar steps at the
Quirinal, with the result that Decazes remained on tenterhooks and
warned his Ambassadors to expect trouble.[4] Gavard, writing from
London, lamented the optimism and lack of foresight of the British
Government and summed up: "Lord Derby agrees with Mr. Gladstone

---

[1] 10 Feb. 1874—*Letters*, 2nd Series, ii. p. 314.   [2] 26 Feb.—*ibid.* p. 325.
[3] 28 Oct.—*D.D.F.* no. 339.   [4] *Ibid.* no. 375, April 3.

in summing up political wisdom in the doctrine of non-intervention".[1]
That Disraeli himself had at this time no clear idea of Continental
issues is shown by the fact that barely three months after his Guildhall compliments to the French, he assured Count Münster, the
German Ambassador in London, that he had never believed in
France as a sincere ally of England and that "the only people who
could go hand in hand were Germany and England".[2] Derby, it is
true, expressed his fears to Münster, but was reassured both by him
and by Lord Odo Russell from Berlin. But nothing would convince
Decazes.

It was at this juncture that the famous *Post* article appeared, and
the atmosphere at once became electric, for other newspapers swelled
the strain, and as the French Ambassador, M. Gontaut-Biron, reminded his chief, "everyone in Berlin knows the empire exercised by
Bismarck" over the German press. He was, however, able to report
a friendly conversation with Herr von Bülow at the Foreign Office
and a specially gracious mood of the Emperor:[3] and the whole
incident was already taking its place as yet another storm in a tea-
cup, when it was revived and even accentuated by an after-dinner
conversation at the British Embassy between Gontaut-Biron and
Radowitz, Bismarck's able diplomatic understudy. "Can you assure
us", Radowitz said in a seemingly half-reflective vein, "that France,
regaining her ancient prosperity, having reorganised her military
forces, will not find the alliances she lacks to-day and that the resentment she cannot but nourish owing to the loss of her two provinces, will not push her invincibly to declare war on Germany? If
revanche is France's intimate thought, why wait to attack her till
she has recovered her strength and formed alliances? Politically,
philosophically, even from the Christian point of view, these deductions are well grounded."[4]

It is not surprising that this should have made a deep impression
on the doctrinaire and jumpy Decazes, who used it as the basis of an
elaborate disquisition to all his ambassadors.[5] Radowitz's notes on
the conversation—written, however, three weeks later, when its exact
course was already a matter of dispute—do not contain the crucial

---

[1] *Ibid.* no. 377, 8 April.
[2] Münster to Bismarck, 28 Feb. 1875—cit. W. Taffs, *The War Scare*, i. p. 341. On
6 January 1875 Disraeli wrote to Derby: "I begin to think Bismarck means business,
and if so the future may be less difficult"—Buckle, v. p. 420.
[3] "On a voulu nous brouiller: maintenant tout est terminé" (G.-Biron to Decazes,
17 April—*D.D.F.* no. 392).
[4] Report of 21 April to Decazes—*ibid.* no. 295.   [5] *Ibid.* no. 399, 29 April.

phrases quoted above: the German historians are entitled to argue that their use has not been proved or that they were a mere soliloquy rather than a considered official utterance. But it is now known that Bismarck himself used almost identical language to Károlyi only a week later: "If the French continued their preparations on the present scale and their intentions of attacking Germany admitted no further doubt, it would manifestly be the duty of the German Government to take the initiative so as to put a stop to war by energetic measures".[1]

Russell was further alarmed by a conversation with Moltke, and confided to Lord Lyons his fear that neither William I. nor the Crown Prince had the strength of character to resist Bismarck's designs for a fresh war.[2] This alarm was endorsed by General Walker, our Military Attaché, while the Belgian Minister reported a warning from Bismarck that Belgium might ere long have to defend her neutrality.[3] Early in May Bülow assured Russell that his Government possessed secret information as to ultramontane plots directed from France, Belgium, and Italy against the new Empire, and it seems probable that Bismarck, with whom Rome had become such an obsession that his health was seriously affected, was genuinely convinced of dangers sufficiently serious to justify a policy of forestallment.

In London both the Foreign Office and the press were very seriously alarmed. Lord Derby admitted to M. Gavard his belief that "Bismarck either wishes war or wants to be thought to wish it": he had told Count Münster, he added, that German talk of French armaments seemed to him a mere pretext, and that he could not understand why he "thus keeps up the general unrest".[4] The crisis may be said to have reached its height on the day of this conversation, thanks to the sensational article of M. de Blowitz in *The Times*.[5] On the same day Baron Nothomb reported conversations with Bismarck and Moltke, both of which rested on the assumption that the new French military burdens were too heavy to bear and must make a *coup de tête* inevitable.[6]

Meanwhile the Tsar had as early as 15 April spoken very openly

[1] F.O. Berlin, reported by Russell to Derby, 27 April—cit. W. Taffs, *The War Scare*, ii. p. 633.
[2] Newton, *Lord Lyons*, p. 333, 24 April 1875.
[3] Russell to Derby—cit. Taffs, p. 634; Newton, *op. cit.* p. 333.
[4] *D.D.F.* no. 403, 6 May, Gavard to Decazes.   [5] "A French Scare."
[6] *Ibid.* no. 406, 7 May, Biron to Decazes.

to General Le Flô, assuring him that French interests were identical
with those of Russia and that if they should be threatened, "you will
know it very quickly—*through me*".[1] A week later, referring to his
own impending visit to Berlin, he told the Ambassador, "I shall most
certainly be a calming element there",[2] and now on 7 May he
deliberately recalled to Le Flô their previous conversation and
promised to keep his word—thus leaving Le Flô with the absolute
conviction of "Russia's energetic intervention in case of conflict with
Germany".[3] Immediately afterwards the Tsar and Prince Gorchakov
started for Berlin, *en route* for a cure at Ems, and threw their whole
weight with William I. and his Government into the scale of peace.
Almost at the same time Derby had reported to Queen Victoria the
language used by Bismarck and Moltke and described "the prevalence
of such ideas, if they do prevail in Germany" as "a serious danger to
Europe".[4] Thereupon the Queen talked to Disraeli, and as a result
Russell received instructions to intervene with Bismarck, to quote
the British Government's firm conviction that France had no "design
of making war for the recovery of the lost provinces", and to support
the pacific efforts of the Tsar.[5] At the same time Derby invited the
Italian Government to take similar action in Berlin.[6] Moreover, the
Queen wrote to the Tsar begging him to use his great influence to
maintain peace and dissipate the profound alarm excited throughout
Europe by the language of Berlin".[7]

The convergence of peace efforts from all parts of Europe forced
Bismarck to beat a retreat. The decisive factor was undoubtedly
the meeting between Alexander II. and his uncle William I., but
Gorchakov, with his colossal vanity, could not resist issuing a circular
which culminated in the winged phrase, "Maintenant la paix est
assurée", and Blowitz gave full advertisement to the story, both then
and later. Whether Gorchakov really believed in his own decisive
rôle, it is not easy to determine: and the Tsar himself appears to have
assured the German authorities of his belief in their "conciliatory
disposition".[8] But none the less a public affront had been administered
to Bismarck in his own capital, in a manner which the German
Chancellor never forgave. To Russell, on the other hand—one of the
few foreign diplomats to whom he was either accessible or gracious—

---

[1] *Ibid.* no. 388, 15 April, Le Flô to Decazes.   [2] *Ibid.* no. 396, 23 April.
[3] *Ibid.* no. 404, 6 May.   [4] 5 May—*Letters*, 2nd Series, ii. p. 389.
[5] 9 May—*ibid.* p. 394.   [6] *Grosse Politik*, i. no. 179, Bülow to Reuss, 14 May.
[7] 10 May—*D.D.F.* p. 396. The Tsar replied on 18 May in very confident terms
(p. 398).   [8] *G.P.* i. no. 182.

Bismarck expressed his gratitude for Derby's good offices, but professed himself entirely unable to understand how London came to credit him with warlike designs.[1] His own notes show that he assumed British suspicion of Germany not to have been fed by Russell, whereas a letter of Russell to Derby shows the Ambassador to have successfully concealed his own mind, without swallowing the Chancellor's assurances. "Although Bismarck is as civil, confidential and amiable to me as ever," he wrote on 15 May, "I fancy he must be frantic at our combined action with Russia in favour of peace, which took him by surprise. However . . . he will get over it, as he wishes to keep well with us. But he will seek an opportunity of paying out Gorchakov for having come the Peacemaker and Dictator over Germany again."[2]

How far Bismarck was pursuing the subordinate aim of sowing discord between Russia and Britain, must remain in doubt. It was alleged to Russell by Shuvalov, who on a summons from the Tsar played a not unimportant part as intermediary between St. Petersburg and London: but Russell remained only half convinced and thought that the Russian was drawing the long-bow. On the other hand, Russell caught out Gorchakov definitely trying to produce bad blood between Britain and Germany. In this complicated pattern of intrigue and counter-intrigue Austria-Hungary gave steady support to Germany and declined any part in a joint *démarche*: and as Andrássy's calculation that the crisis would not end in war proved correct, his general attitude marked a new stage in the friendship of Vienna and Berlin.

So far as England was concerned, the final stage in the crisis were the profuse assurances given to Queen Victoria by the Emperor and Crown Prince, coupled with regrets that Blowitz's sensational articles in *The Times* should have "so lamentably overstepped all bounds".[3] After a further exchange of letters the Emperor promised to be more watchful and to preach prudence on every side.[4] Bismarck withdrew to his country house at Varzin for six months, and the incident died

[1] Miss Taffs would seem to be right in rejecting Saburov's account of recriminations between Bismarck and Russell—see *op. cit.* ii. p. 647. To Münster meanwhile Bismarck took the line that if England had in 1870 shown but one-tenth part of the zeal displayed during the present crisis, war would have been altogether averted. For French reactions see *D.D.F.* no. 420, 12 May, Gavard to Decazes.
[2] Newton, *Lord Lyons*, p. 338.
[3] William I. to Queen, 3 June—*Letters*, ii. pp. 400-404. For her reply of 20 June see *ibid.* p. 408, and *G.P.* i. no. 189. According to Shuvalov (unpublished letter of 23 June to Jomini—Russian Archives), the British Ministers were "*froissés*" at the tone of the Emperor's reply.   [4] 23 June—*ibid.* p. 410.

down almost as quickly as it had arisen. But London did not throw off its suspicions, and the Queen wrote to her daughter the Crown Princess: "No one wishes more than I do for England and Germany to go together: but Bismarck is so overbearing, violent and unprincipled, that *no one* can stand it, and *all* agreed that he was becoming like the first Napoleon, whom Europe had to join in putting down".[1] In the words of Lord Derby, "it is really imposing on our supposed credulity to tell us now that our ears have deceived us and that nothing was said or meant against France".[2] To Gavard Derby even committed himself to the view that Bismarck had wanted war and prepared everything for the explosion.[3]

The War Scare is still surrounded by a halo of uncertainty, and this will always be so, for its history is very largely compounded of *imponderabilia*, of suspicions, guesses and surmises, which are capable of an infinite variety of interpretations. But it is one of the most characteristic and instructive episodes in the diplomatic history of the Armed Peace and had very definite effects upon the grouping of the Powers in the next great European crisis. It thus forms the necessary background without which that crisis cannot be understood.

---

[1] 8 June—*Letters*, ii. pp. 404-5.
[2] 14 June—*ibid*. p. 407, Derby to Gen. Ponsonby.
[3] *D.D.F.* no. 437, 5 June.

CHAPTER II

THE EASTERN CRISIS

If the integrity of the Sultan's dominions be formally secured, there is but too much reason to fear that the Porte will give way to its natural indolence and leave the firman of reform a lifeless paper, valuable only as a record of sound principles.
        LORD STRATFORD DE REDCLIFFE, as Ambassador
        in Constantinople, to Lord Clarendon, 3 Feb. 1856

Wherever Turkey is sufficiently predominant to be implicitly obeyed, laziness, corruption, extravagance and penury mark his rule: and wherever he is too feeble to exert more than a doubtful and nominal authority, the system of government which prevails is that of the Arab robber and the lawless Highland chief.
        SIR HENRY BULWER, as Ambassador
        in Constantinople, 24 April 1860

The open bribery and corruption, the invariable and unjust favour shown to Mussulmans in all cases between Turks and Christians.
        W. R. HOLMES, H.M. Consul at Sarajevo, 24 Feb. 1871

There are not a dozen Turks in the Empire who see the necessity of reform. There is nobody to carry out reforms.   J. A. MACGAHAN, 10 Aug. 1876

This absolute want of statesmen is one of the worst symptoms of the declining state of the Empire.
        H. A. LAYARD, as Ambassador, 25 July 1877

THE BOSNIAN INSURRECTION

THE unrest which the famous War Scare had provoked all over Europe had scarcely died down when the Eastern Question once more became acute and gave rise to yet another long and dangerous international crisis. The original cause of the trouble was the rising in Hercegovina; but this was of course merely symptomatic of the untenable conditions which prevailed throughout the Ottoman Empire, but especially in its European provinces. Since 1856 Turkey had enjoyed a period of unusual internal calm. It is true that the liquidation of the Roumanian question had lasted three years and for a time endangered the peace of Europe, that the Lebanon massacres of 1860 and the Cretan troubles of 1867 had led to partial intervention, and that Turkey had twice been engaged in hostilities with Montenegro. None the less, her new status as a member of the Concert of Europe had given her relative freedom from interference,

16

and the inveterate Turcophils of the West had assumed that the reforms proclaimed with such a flourish of trumpets in 1856 were being put into effect, and that Palmerston's belief in her regeneration would be justified by twenty years of peace. In reality the cancer of corruption and misgovernment had only eaten deeper still: the harem had prematurely ended the worthless Abdul Medjid, and his successor Abdul Aziz was a vicious and incompetent Oriental tyrant, who kept 900 concubines, squandered vast sums on ballets, menageries, astrologers and cockfights, and allowed the finances to plunge year by year into greater disorder, while the few reputable statesmen whom Turkey possessed—such men as Fuad and Ali—died and were replaced by men of a lower calibre. The attempts to establish foreign control proved ineffective. The Loan of 1854 had been officially recommended to the western public by the French and British Foreign Secretaries and guaranteed by the Egyptian tribute, and that of 1871 was in the same position. A series of eight further loans between the years 1858 and 1875 had only been raised on the security of the Constantinople customs, the tobacco, salt and stamp taxes, the sheep tax first of Roumelia and then of Anatolia, and numerous other sources of revenue: and the creditors enjoyed an interest of $9\frac{1}{2}$ per cent. Officials were unpaid and recouped themselves by squeezing the population, justice was venal to the last degree, the word of a Christian was not accepted in a Moslem court, and the state of the peasantry beggared all description. The inevitable bankruptcy was near at hand. For the Christians redress was impossible, and revolt offered the only hope of betterment.

In Hercegovina, and in Bosnia, to which the revolt speedily spread, unrest had been chronic since the beginning of the century. The two provinces had been hermetically sealed from the outside world ever since the final Turkish conquest in 1483. Of purest Serbian blood, the population was divided between Moslem, Orthodox and Catholic, the big feudal lords having in the first instance accepted Islam to save their lands and having imposed their new religion upon a certain section of their serfs. Power had remained in the hands of a small landed oligarchy, mercilessly exploiting the masses, impervious to all new ideas and intensely hostile to the innovations of Sultan Mahmud. In 1831 their dissatisfaction had found expression in a formidable revolt under Hussein Kapetan, known as "the Dragon of Bosnia", which could only be repressed with great difficulty. Two decades later the power of the Begs was broken by the famous Croat renegade Omer

Pasha as Bosnian Vizier: but in the chamber which he left swept and garnished, the seven devils of extortion and venality drove the peasantry to despair, and the malcontents saw a triple source of help in Montenegro, which in 1858, and again in 1862, resisted the whole force of Turkey: in Serbia, which in the sixties under Prince Michael was preparing herself for the leadership of the Southern Slavs; and in Croatia and Dalmatia, where the movement for Jugoslav unity under the Habsburgs was steadily gaining ground. In Vienna the military party favoured the occupation of Bosnia, with the double object of strengthening Austria's strategic hold on Dalmatia and Istria and of securing the direction of the Jugoslav movement: and one of its leaders, Baron Rodić, the Governor of Dalmatia and himself a zealous Jugoslav, induced Francis Joseph to pay his first visit to that province in 1875, and was meanwhile in secret contact with the Bosnian leaders. When, then, the first revolt broke out in Hercegovina almost immediately after the journey, it was widely supposed that Rodić had been prompted by Andrássy: but in reality the Foreign Minister held quite other views, looked upon a weak Turkey as a convenient neighbour, wished to prevent its break-up as long as possible, and was only resolved that if the Turks could not maintain their hold upon Bosnia and Hercegovina, no other Power than Austria-Hungary should have them, and least of all Serbia or Montenegro, whose expansion into a large Balkan state he regarded as a danger to the Habsburg Monarchy. It was at this point that he came into conflict with Serbia, whose national aspirations had for a generation past been directed towards Bosnia: as his own Diplomatic Agent in Belgrade, Benjamin Kállay, so effectively pointed out, Bosnia was "the sensitive point for all Serbian politicians, the centre round which all their desires and hopes have long turned".[1] The insurgents for their part turned naturally to their free kinsmen beyond the border, and the appeal of the insurgent chiefs—while couched in the phrase with which the Croat patriot Jelačić launched his attack on Hungary in 1848, on behalf of the Habsburgs[2]—was specially directed to Serbia and Montenegro, for "what they do for us, they do for themselves and their future". It was therefore only natural that the movement should kindle intense sympathy and excitement throughout the two Serb Principalities and should serve

[1] Kállay to Beust, 6 July 1870—*Austrian Archives*. See my "Les Relations de l'Autriche-Hongrie et de la Serbie" in *Le Monde Slave* and my *The Rôle of Bosnia in International Politics* (Raleigh Lecture, 1931), p. 13.

[2] "Što Bog dade i sreća junačka" ("What God gives and a hero's fate").

as a stimulus to the radical movement, known as the Omladina, among the Serbian youth. Shortly before Kállay left his Belgrade post in the previous February, he had reported Serbia to be "in a state of latent revolution",[1] and by the summer Prince Milan found himself faced by a popular clamour for war against Turkey and by a constant change of ministers, till with every month it became more difficult for him to hold back without risking his throne and with it the dynasty of which he was the last survivor.

Meanwhile, as the insurrection dragged on, Russian public opinion was strongly and genuinely stirred by the sufferings and discontents of their Slav kinsmen and Orthodox co-religionists in Turkish territory, and the Slav societies of Moscow began to agitate in their favour. Suspicion of Russia blinded Western opinion to this aspect of affairs, and it was quite erroneously assumed that the insurrection was due to a deep-seated Russian conspiracy. In actual fact the Tsar and his Government disapproved of the rising, laid the chief blame upon the Omladina, and regarding it as revolutionary and subversive, frowned upon Prince Milan and most of his ministers as in sympathy or collusion with it. It is, however, true that in the Russian diplomatic and consular service there were individuals whose Slavonic zeal far outstripped the instructions or policy of head-quarters, and among them were the consuls at Belgrade and Ragusa, Kartsev and Yonin, of whom the latter was in direct contact with the insurgent chiefs. Above all, General Ignatyev, since 1864 Russian Ambassador at the Porte, was credited with a "forward" policy, resting upon widespread secret propaganda, and was colloquially known as "Mentir Pasha" or in his own country as "the Father of Lies". The commonplace Lord Augustus Loftus gives as good a summary as any, of Ignatyev's character.[2] "A man of pleasing manners, of considerable ability and of endless resource: of indefatigable mental and bodily energy and of a sanguine temperament in all he undertook." It is but fair to quote the testimony of Sir Edwin Pears, deliberately recorded after thirty years in the Near East, that he "never knew a false statement brought home to Ignatyev, and that the Ambassador himself bragged about deceiving diplomats by telling them the simple truth".[3] But another story told by Pears provides the real clue to Ignatyev's remarkable position, which had earned

---

[1] *Austrian Archives*, Kállay to Andrássy, 22 Feb. 1875, no. 10.
[2] *Reminiscences*, iv. p. 30.
[3] *Turkey and its People*, p. 217.

him the reputation of an arch-intriguer. One day he entered the
Grand Vizier's room while his Russophobe rival Sir Henry Elliot was
there, and was met with the remark "that he had just heard that
Russia had spies all over the Empire. 'Yes,' said Ignatyev, 'wherever
there is a Christian, he is ready to bring his complaint to our notice.
They are all spies for Russia.'"[1] And therein lay the undoubted
advantage enjoyed by Russia—which rested on ties of blood and
religion, strengthened by the fact that despite many faults and
ambitions, she had repeatedly made sacrifices for the Christians of the
East, such as no other Power had made and was therefore regarded
as their natural champion and liberator.

It is necessary at the very outset to dwell upon this aspect of the
question, for a failure to grasp it distorted the whole attitude of a
large section of British opinion, and of no one more than the Prime
Minister himself, and is even noticeable among the few modern
writers who have dealt with the subject. The argument that only
Russia would gain by the emancipation of the Christians, and that
therefore Turkish integrity must be upheld at all costs, was not
merely based upon a fundamental misreading of what was possible
and impossible in Turkey: it also involved a false estimate of the
Balkan peoples, as the history of Bulgaria in the eighties was to
demonstrate in the most striking way. As an anonymous Serbian
statesman had argued in a little-known English pamphlet of the
sixties, none of these peoples had the slightest desire for union with
Russia, and simply looked to the Tsar "because they think they have
found in him the enemy of their oppressors and the protector of their
nationality and their faith". England, he held, could adjourn, but
not prevent the final catastrophe of Turkey, and the alternative to
partition among the Great Powers was "to leave it to its natural
heirs", the Slavs, Greeks and Roumanians.[2] As an independent M.P.,
Mr. Forsyth, very pertinently put it in one of the many debates of
1876, "the strength of Russia in this matter arises from the oppression
of the Slavonic people: and she has always a reason for interfering
as the champion of humanity and the redresser of their wrongs".[3]

---

[1] *Turkey and its People*, p. 92. According to W. T. Stead, Ignatyev made very much
the same remark to Salisbury at the Conference of Constantinople: "Paid agents I
have not: not one rouble do I need to pay for help. But you will find that everyone
who fights for his country and faith . . . is my friend and agent. I have thousands of
these, and they are my strength. But you are the support of the savagery and tyranny
of the Turks" (*The M.P. for Russia*, i. p. 307).

[2] *The Case of Servia*, by a Servian (London, 1863).

[3] Hansard, ccxxxi., 31 July 1876.

But unhappily this was a truth to which the great majority of parliamentarians were still quite impervious.

So far, however, from the Russian Government having instigated the rising of 1876, it is known that Prince Milan of Serbia had informed St. Petersburg of impending trouble in Bosnia, and enquired whether he could count on Russian help if he went to war with Turkey. Not merely did Russia send a negative reply, but passed on the information to Andrássy and suggested a joint *démarche* of the three Imperial Powers at Belgrade.[1]

CONSULAR INTERVENTION

It was perfectly natural that the first active proposals for dealing with the Bosnian crisis should have come from the three Imperial Courts, which saw in its prolongation a possible danger to their new alliance. It was therefore proposed that the Consuls of the Great Powers should be authorised to meet and confer with the insurgent chiefs, and to this the Porte consented, for reasons which soon became apparent. Lord Derby was at first disposed to refuse co-operation, but consented at the express request of the Porte itself, and W. J. Holmes, our consul at Sarajevo, a notorious Turcophil, was instructed to join his colleagues. But the Turks used the meeting as a trap, and while the consuls were conferring, sent to the spot two battalions of troops, who massacred [2] some of the insurgents and very nearly succeeded in waylaying the chiefs. This was described as "clever strategy" by Shevket Pasha, who six months later was to organise the Bulgarian atrocities: and Rashid Pasha, the Turkish Foreign Minister, had the effrontery, or naïvety, to send a formal expression of thanks to the British Government for the "friendly disposition" and "perfect tact" of Mr. Holmes during the whole incident! [3]

It is not surprising that the negotiations proved altogether abortive, for the Turks were not ready for serious concessions, while the Bosnians, quite apart from such flagrant proof of Turkish bad faith, hoped to exploit in their own favour the interest, or perhaps the discords, of the Powers.

Andrássy meanwhile warned the Serbs that military action on

[1] Details will be found in the forthcoming book of Mr. B. H. Sumner on Russian foreign policy.

[2] The word is Consul Holmes's own.   [3] *Turkey No. I.* (1877).

their part might lead to an Austrian occupation of Belgrade: but he persuaded Francis Joseph to reject Rodic's project for marching into Bosnia. In a nutshell, his view was that Serbia and Montenegro could be forced to heel and that the main problem was agreement with Europe and especially Russia, in which case the Triple League would remain intact and there would be no danger of an "Oriental Piedmont" on the Austrian frontiers.[1] Perhaps the prime difficulty of the situation was that neither side was amenable to advice. The Bosnians wanted to embroil Europe, the Serbs were bent on helping them, the Turks were full of prevarication and arrogance. As the Sultan said to Ignatyev, he could not accept foreign intervention, for "that would be suicide, and I prefer to die on my throne".[2]

This joint initiative at once aroused distrust in London, which was also annoyed to notice a tendency of the French to favour co-opera-tion with the Russians. Disraeli and Derby were equally indifferent to the cause of the Christians in Turkey, the former telling Lady Chesterfield that "this dreadful Herzegovinian affair . . . might have been settled in a week . . . had there been common energy, or perhaps pocket money even, among the Turks",[3] while the latter, in conver-sation with Count Shuvalov, treated the agitation in Serbia and Montenegro—"petit peuple à demi barbare"—as a mere manœuvre.[4] Both were strongly opposed to autonomy for Bosnia, with its mixed population: "autonomy for Ireland", wrote Disraeli, "would be less absurd",[5] and it appears that his nervousness towards the programme of the insurgents, in which of course land reform figured prominently, was partly due to the possibility of precedents being created for the Irish agrarian campaign.[6]

Yet the files of the consular service would have provided Derby and Disraeli with overwhelming evidence of the untenable position of the Christians in European Turkey, and perhaps particularly in Bosnia. Indeed, within two years of the Treaty of Paris, Lord Clarendon, one of its principal authors, was writing to the redoubt-able Lord Stratford de Redcliffe on the ill-treatment of the Bosnian Christians: "Her Majesty's Government know by experience the utter futility of appealing on such matters, but the Turkish Government

[1] Wertheimer, *Graf Andrássy*, ii. pp. 265-7.
[2] Lord A. Loftus, *Diplomatic Reminiscences*, iv. p. 142.
[3] 21 August—Buckle, vi. p. 13.
[4] 14 October, Shuvalov to Jomini—*Russo-British Documents*, i. p. 428.
[5] 1 Oct., to Lady Bradford—Buckle, vi. p. 13.
[6] Shuvalov to Gorchakov, 12 Jan. 1876—*R.B.D.* ii. pp. 658-9.

should be made aware that if this system of misgovernment and persecution of Christians and violations of engagements continue, it will be impossible to arrest the progress of opinion . . ., that Mohammedan rule is incompatible with civilisation and humanity and can no longer be endured".[1]

Even Consul Holmes, whom we have just quoted, had, as recently as 24 February 1871, written of "the open bribery and corruption, the invariable and unjust favour shown to Mussulmans in all cases between Turks and Christians", and declared that without the Capitulations the position of foreign residents would be intolerable —an argument *a fortiori* which, after the inevitable rising had occurred, he was unwilling to apply to the native victims of the system.

The British Cabinet, then, adopted a negative and waiting attitude. Disraeli lamented that "since the fall of France, who used to give us so much alarm and trouble, the conduct of foreign affairs for England has become infinitely more difficult. *There is no balance, and unless we go out of our way to act with the three Northern Powers, they can act without us*, which is not agreeable for a state like England."[2] Active co-operation meant, in one form or another, help for the Christians against Turkey, while abstention meant inglorious inaction.[3] As, however, France was in eclipse and Italy scarcely counted, the triumvirate was the only solid political combination in Europe, and Disraeli had no choice between following its lead or endeavouring to break up its unity. After the May intervention he congratulated Derby on his "very popular and very successful policy" and wrote to Lady Bradford: "Since Pam. we have never been so energetic and in a year's time we shall be more so".[4]

Disraeli's policy at this early stage of the crisis can only be explained by a desire to extricate Britain from her isolation and to find a Continental ally. France could no longer (or not yet again) serve this purpose. Germany, or at least Bismarck, did not inspire confidence after the events of the previous spring. Austria-Hungary also seemed open to objection: for Disraeli, utterly misjudging Andrássy's character and aims, fondly imagined him to be "quite undecided or playing a double game, perhaps both", and again "changing his mind every week or day", with "half a dozen intrigues at work, which will defeat each other", and again even to require "a guide—a man

[1] Clarendon to Stratford de R., 30 June 1857.
[2] 6 Sept. 1875, to Lady Bradford—Buckle, vi. p. 13.
[3] See Shuvalov's very interesting and sound estimate in *R.B.D.* i. pp. 427-9.
[4] 18 and 14 May—Buckle, v. pp. 423-4.

of quick perceptions and iron will".[1] There remained Russia: and the best proof of Disraeli's opportunism lies in his initial attitude to Russia. In May 1875 he expressed himself to the Queen as in favour of "alliance with Russia, as we know the Tsar's pacific feelings".[2] At the same time Shuvalov reported to the Tsar at Ems "a very marked current of public opinion . . . in favour of drawing still closer the *bonne entente* between Russia and England": Disraeli himself expressed himself in this sense, and Derby wrote his gratitude and "high appreciation".[3] But as the summer advanced, the idea of any actual alliance was dropped, and London remained negative, even when Gorchakov, on the Tsar's instructions, emphasised his desire for "a complete *entente* with England for the regulation of all difficulties in the East".[4] Shuvalov's reading of the situation was that London realised its isolation and consequent impotence, but would at once try to profit by any divergence of views between the three allied Cabinets.[5]

Meanwhile, though Russia's official attitude was still cautious and tentative, Jomini, who was acting for Gorchakov during the late autumn and noted Vienna's growing reserve, made a first overture to the French Chargé d'Affaires, in which the problem of Turkey's "succession" is faintly envisaged, and the idea of a federalised Balkan Peninsula is held out. But though this was scarcely even a *ballon d'essai*, a clear note was sounded as to Russia's special "moral obligation" towards the Christians of Turkey,[6] and this was fundamental in her position, being compounded of that strongest of all amalgams, religious and national sentiment and imperialistic and economic expansion.

RUSSIA AND THE "STANDARD"

It was at this moment that a mysterious incident occurred which remained entirely unknown until some years after the Great War. In October 1875 the editor-proprietor of the *Standard* appears to have made a secret overture to the Russian Government in the hope of selling that newspaper for the sum of £250,000! He had employed as intermediary a certain Mr. Machin, a Russian subject of British

[1] Disraeli to Lady Bradford, 6 Sept. and 3 Nov. 1875, and to Lord Derby, 15 Aug. 1876—Buckle, vi. pp. 13, 15, 49.
[2] Queen's Journal for 6 May—*Letters*, 2nd Series, ii. p. 392.
[3] 13 and 17 May, Shuvalov to Tsar—*R.B.D.* i. pp. 424-6.
[4] 14 Oct., Shuvalov to Jomini—*ibid.* p. 427.
[5] 11 Nov., to Jomini—*ibid.* p. 431.
[6] Hanotaux, *op. cit.* iv. p. 70.

origin who was attached to the Grand Dukes Sergius and Paul, and who, after accompanying them to the Crimea, got into touch first with Count Adlerberg, the Court Chamberlain, then with General Potopov, one of the Tsar's aide-de-camps, and finally with Baron Jomini, of the Russian Foreign Office, to whom the Tsar himself had spoken on the subject. Jomini now wrote to the Ambassador in London, opposing any action on three grounds—firstly, that the price was altogether excessive; secondly, that the sale could not be permanently kept secret, and the circulation—which was at the moment represented as bringing in an annual profit of £25,000— would be bound to drop to zero; and thirdly, that the son of the proprietor (presumably the then editor, James Johnstone, junior) had already informed his father that in that event he would withdraw, which would in itself presumably lead to exposure. Jomini, therefore, expressed to Shuvalov the view that at the most there should be an annual subsidy. No definite figure is suggested, and as there is no further record in the archives of proceedings in the matter, it is probable that Shuvalov decided to take no action. It is interesting to note that Jomini's letter alludes to the fact of a similar proposal having already been made from the same quarter as long ago as 1863, though without result.[1]

It is impossible to express any opinion upon this mysterious incident, as we do not possess, and are not likely to possess, the English end of it. From the *Dictionary of National Biography*[2] we learn that the *Standard* was purchased in 1852 from Charles Baldwin by James Johnstone for the low sum of £16,500, and issued for the first time in that year as a morning paper; its circulation having by that date fallen to 700; that the new owner reduced the price to one penny in 1858; that his son James Johnstone was editor from 1872 to 1877, when he was succeeded by W. H. Mudford: and that Mr. Johnstone, senior, when he died in 1878, left a fortune of £500,000.

The Turkish Default and the Suez Canal Coup

The mediation of the Consuls was a complete failure, but the insurrection continued and the Turks seemed quite incapable of suppressing it. Early in October their internal difficulties culminated in what amounted to a declaration of bankruptcy, the interest on

[1] Secret autograph letter of Jomini to Shuvalov, 16 Oct. 1875—summarised in *R.B.D.* i. p. 430.   [2] See article on James Johnstone, by G. C. Boase.

all foreign loans save those contracted during the Crimean War being suddenly reduced by one-half, but the 144,000,000 francs of State papers held by the Sultan being specially exempted! This step, which appears to have taken the British Government entirely by surprise,[1] naturally produced a most unfavourable impression in the City of London, and shook the confidence of many in Turkey's solidity. It led Disraeli himself to believe—as he confided to Lady Bradford—that "the Eastern question, that has haunted Europe for a century, and which I thought the Crimean War had adjourned for half another, will fall to my lot to encounter—dare I say, to settle?"[2] Decazes suspected him of "dreaming of Palmerstonian glories".[3]

It was at this moment that Disraeli learned of negotiations between the Khedive Ismail of Egypt and a French syndicate for the sale of his holding of 177,000 shares in the Suez Canal. Ismail, like Abdul Aziz, was faced by the nemesis of years of gross extravagance and by the end of November 1875 had about a fortnight in which to find nearly £4,000,000 or to follow his suzerain into bankruptcy. Mortgage or sale were his only alternatives, and the conditions laid down for the former by the French seemed exorbitant. Disraeli at once grasped the significance of the whole affair, induced a somewhat reluctant Cabinet to accept his idea and addressed a memorandum to the Queen, arguing that "it is vital to Your Majesty's authority and power at this critical moment, that the Canal should belong to England", and that not a day was to be lost, since it was "doubtful whether a financial catastrophe can be avoided" in Egypt.[4] For a short time the Khedive seemed reluctant to place himself in the hands of London, but it proved difficult to raise the purchase money in Paris in face of British opposition, and the French syndicate demanded a rate of 18 per cent before it would make its first advance upon a mortgage, while the Duke Decazes, fearful of losing the political support which had stood him in such good stead in the spring, hesitated to intervene on behalf of the syndicate. Lord Derby appears to have made it clear to M. Gavard that the British Government had hitherto regarded the Khedive's interest in the Canal Company as one of our main safeguards in dealing with M. de Lesseps and would be opposed to its falling into the hands of another French company:[5] to the Ambassador a few days later he admitted very

[1] "This quite unforeseen bankruptcy of the Porte" (Disraeli to Lady Bradford, 3 Nov.—Buckle, vi. p. 14).   [2] *Ibid.*
[3] Hanotaux, *op. cit.* ii. p. 415.   [4] 18 Nov.—Buckle, v. p. 443.
[5] See Buckle, *op. cit.* v. p. 445, whose narrative has in the main been followed.

frankly that our attitude to Lesseps in the past had been unfair, but now, he insisted, British action was "purely defensive".[1] The final transaction rested on a verbal agreement between the Prime Minister and the Rothschilds, who advanced the necessary £4,000,000 almost at a moment's notice: and within ten days of the first overture the Khedive's shares were made over to the British Government. Small wonder that Disraeli wrote with some elation to Lady Bradford: "We have had all the gamblers, capitalists, financiers of the world, organised and platooned in bands of plunderers, arrayed against us, and secret emissaries in every corner and have baffled them all, and have never been suspected. The day before yesterday Lesseps, whose company has the remaining shares, backed by the French Government, whose agent he was, made a great offer. Had it succeeded, the whole of the Suez Canal would have belonged to France, and they would have shut it up!"[2] "The Fairy", he added, "is in ecstasies" at what King Leopold called "the greatest event of modern politics".

The coup made a profound impression throughout Europe and was accepted as a proof that Britain had definitely abandoned her passivity and was embarking upon a "spirited foreign policy". But while the Queen greeted it as "a blow at Bismarck" and "his insolent declarations that England had ceased to be a political power",[3] no one in reality was more pleased than Bismarck himself, who saw that it led logically to British intervention in Egypt and was henceforth constantly recommending this to London, not of course without a certain ulterior hope of embroiling Britain and France.[4]

THE ANDRÁSSY NOTE

With this singular exploit to his credit, Disraeli could afford to adopt a waiting attitude in the Eastern crisis, but both Austria-Hungary and Russia were driven to action, the former because of the unrest along her southern borders, across which thousands of destitute Serbo-Croat refugees were flying, the latter because of the growth of Panslav sentiment in Moscow, expressing itself in Red Cross committees and infecting the Empress and her *entourage*. Towards the close

---

[1] *D.D.F.* ii. no. 17, 27 Nov.: cf. also Lord Newton, *Lord Lyons*, p. 343, for Derby's letter of 17 Nov. to Lyons.
[2] 25 Nov.—Buckle, v. p. 449.   [3] 26 Nov.—*ibid.* v. p. 450.
[4] Bismarck's attitude is brought out fully in Miss Taffs's forthcoming Life of Lord Odo Russell. Russell reported Bismarck's very cordial congratulations, in a dispatch of 29 November—F.O. 64: 831, no. 488.

of the year Count Andrássy, with the full backing of Bismarck, took the initiative in pressing for collective action at the Porte: his aim was to isolate the Bosnian question, to appease the two provinces, and avert the danger of Russia acquiring a sort of moral protectorate over the Slavs. It may be quite positively affirmed that at this stage Andrássy had no desire whatsoever to annex Bosnia, regarding it as "an unproductive and ruined country, where everything has to be created anew".[1]

The Porte in vain tried to forestall him by an Irade of 12 December, promising certain paper reforms, not merely for the two provinces but for the whole Empire. This deceived no one, and on 30 December 1875 Andrássy addressed a Note to the Powers, outlining the minimum reforms which seemed to him necessary—equality of religions, abolition of tax-farming, restriction of taxes to the use of the province in which they were raised, various improvements in the lot of the peasantry, and a European commission of supervision. In this he had the other Powers behind him, but Britain held back for some weeks, until the Porte itself, under pressure from Vienna, requested London to adhere. One reason for the delay was the absence of ministers from London at the turn of the year, Lord Derby being at Knowsley and pleading as an excuse to the three Ambassadors his duties as a colonel of volunteers and other local business![2] Even after adherence Disraeli in his own mind was definitely hostile, and in a letter to Derby went so far as to describe Austria's action as "an act of imbecility or treachery"—an unwarranted remark which shows him to have been out of touch with the realities of the Balkan situation. In his view Andrássy had no right to advise the Porte to take measures already announced, some of which "so far as they are intelligible, would appear to be erroneous in principle and pernicious in practice": and he was especially nervous on such points as "the apportionment of local taxation to local purposes[3] and the right of the peasantry to the soil", lest he should be committing himself to "principles which may soon be matter of controversy in our own country".[4]

If the Government was indifferent to the fate of Bosnia and

[1] This telling phrase is quoted by the French Ambassador Vogüé, in a dispatch to Decazes, 28 Dec. 1875—*D.D.F.* ii. no. 25.

[2] Count Shuvalov, in his report home, is sarcastic about this and the "week-end habit" of Ministers.

[3] In the House of Lords on 26 June 1876 Lord Campbell treated this proposal of Andrássy as "astounding"—Hansard, ccxxx. p. 396.

[4] 9 Jan. 1876—Buckle, vi. pp. 18-19.

unfamiliar with the true situation in the Near East, this was no less true of the Opposition. Indeed, so little did the Liberal leaders realise the importance of the Eastern Question, that we find Lord Hartington writing to Lord Granville, within a few days of the Cabinet's tardy adhesion to the Andrássy Note: "I had much talk in London with James and Harcourt about the *new Slave Circular*, and we thought it gave a good opening for attack".[1] Gladstone was of course in retirement at Hawarden, and even Harcourt, whose later pronouncements on the Eastern Question were perhaps the most trenchant of all, seems not yet to have thought of it as a weapon with which to belabour Tories. Even ten months later, after he had himself visited Constantinople, Hartington wrote to Granville— apparently without provoking any challenge—that "the provinces of Bosnia, Hercegovina and Bulgaria are not Christian" and Bosnia "more than half Mussulman".[2]

It is but fair at this stage to point out that much of the scepticism of the Government towards the Bosnian rising was due to the consistently Turcophil reports of Sir Henry Elliot from Constantinople, and that he in his turn was influenced by the views of our Consul in Sarajevo, Mr. Holmes. The latter upheld the thesis that "the so-called insurrection in Bosnia might be better termed an invasion of bands openly formed in Austria, Croatia and Serbia",[3] and again that "the revolt was assuredly arranged by Serbian agitators"; that there was no desire whatever for union either with Serbia, Montenegro or Austria, and that all the Christians of the two provinces asked was "to be Turkish subjects, but governed with justice and placed on an equality in law with their Mussulman compatriots". There was "no particular reason or any excess of oppression", he contended, "to justify a rising in 1875, beyond what has existed any time since 1860". With this last phrase, however, Holmes gave his whole case away, to all save the officials who were impervious to facts: for only four years before he had written from the same post (though this had been already forgotten, if ever noted): "The universal ignorance, corruption and fanaticism of all classes precludes all hope of an efficient administration of justice for at least a generation"[4]—a view which might serve as an argument against autonomy, but even more

---

[1] By which escaped slaves, once on board a British vessel, were not to be surrendered—*Granville Papers*, Hart. to Gran., 19 Jan. 1876.
[2] *Ibid.* 26 Nov. 1876, printed in *Life of Duke of Devonshire*, i. p. 184.
[3] *Turkey No. III.* (1876), p. 40.
[4] 24 Feb. 1871—cit. Drummond Wolff in the House, 7 May 1877.

so against Turkish rule. Meanwhile his ignorance of conditions in the two provinces which were his special concern is shown by his description of Nevesinje, the scene of the first outbreak, as "the richest and most prosperous district of Herzegovina", whereas in reality, as Mr. Forsyth pointed out in the House of Commons a year later, it was "one of the poorest and most barren", and indeed is so to this day.[1] Yet Lord Campbell in the House of Lords was able to base his denial of the genuine character of the whole insurrection on another preposterous phrase of Holmes—"the undue liberality of the Porte was the immediate cause of the explosion".[2]

The plain fact is that Consul Holmes was content to remain in Sarajevo and to accept almost at their face value the lying reports of the Bosnian Vali, Dervish Pasha, and his incompetent officials. Yet even at that early stage there were Englishmen who were studying the real situation at first hand and whose testimony in the long run was to prove unchallengeable. Arthur Evans, who was travelling through Bosnia when the rising actually broke out, published his first impressions in an attractive book of travel[3] and then became correspondent of the *Manchester Guardian*, with his headquarters at Ragusa. W. J. Stillman, who had been through the Cretan rising of 1866 as correspondent of *The Times* and had thus acquired a practical knowledge of Turkish methods of government and of warfare, now visited Hercegovina and expressed the view that "the condition of the Christian Herzegovinian was the most intolerable of all the subjects of Turkey", and that Turkish rule was "an old bottle which will not hold a new wine".[4] But though his exposure of a massacre at Popovo led Holmes to press the Vali for an enquiry, the report eventually submitted by Constant Pasha simply denied the whole story, and this was enough for the Consul.

Among those who upheld the credit of the British name, special mention must be made of Miss Paulina Irby and Miss Muir-Mackenzie, joint authors of a remarkable book of travel republished during the crisis, with a preface by Mr. Gladstone. Miss Irby, after her companion's premature death, continued to take so lively an interest in the oppressed Christians of Turkey, that in 1865 she settled in

---

[1] 31 July 1876—Hansard, ccxxxi. p. 147: cf. with this the first-hand description of the "terrible poverty" of this "limestone desert", in Arthur Evans' *Through Bosnia and Herzegovina on Foot* (1876), pp. 329-32. "Mainly an agrarian war" is one of his phrases.   [2] 26 June 1876—*ibid*. ccxxx. p. 395.
[3] *Through Bosnia and Herzegovina on Foot* (1876).
[4] *Herzegovina and the Late Uprising* (1877).

Sarajevo and, with another friend, Miss Johnston, devoted herself to the education of Christian girls in Bosnia. When the rising interrupted their normal work, they transferred their headquarters to Knin in the Dalmatian highlands, and for the next three years organised relief work among the thousands of destitute refugees in Austrian territory. When the two provinces fell under Habsburg rule, Miss Irby resumed her work in Sarajevo and devoted the rest of her life to it, dying on the eve of the Great War.

The Andrássy Note, like the consular action, was a complete failure, and for three reasons. The Porte had not the slightest intention of carrying out reforms, the insurgents saw no adequate guarantee of improvement and set their hopes on international complications, while the lukewarm attitude of Britain towards identical action robbed it of most of its sting at Constantinople. France gave its full backing to Andrássy, and Decazes intimated to the Marquis d'Harcourt in London, "what a price we attach to the British Government making its voice heard in the European concert".[1] But Derby's attitude was tersely summed up in a letter at this very time to Lord Lyons in Paris: "One can trust none of these Governments".[2]

For the first four months of 1876 the deadlock was complete. The insurgents held their own, the number of refugees in Croatia, Dalmatia and Montenegro grew steadily, and with this the excitement in all the Southern Slav lands. In Serbia popular feeling was unanimous in favour of the Bosnians: each change of Government, in August and in October, strengthened the hands of the Omladina, and Prince Milan was on the horns of a dilemma. By consenting to military preparations he exposed himself to repeated remonstrances and warnings from all the Powers, not least of all from Russia, who suspected his ministers of revolutionary views: yet to resist the currents leading to war was to risk his throne, not merely because he was already intensely unpopular, but because he had not one, but two rivals for popular favour. Prince Nicholas of Montenegro was of purest Serbian blood, the son of the hero of Grahovo: he carried on his family tradition as a poet of nationalism,[3] and he was in close contact with the Hercegovinian chiefs and enjoyed their confidence. But even he was outbid by the heir to the exiled dynasty, Prince

[1] 21 Jan. 1876, Decazes to Harcourt—*D.D.F.* ii. no. 32.
[2] Jan. 1876—Newton, *op. cit.* p. 349.
[3] His grand-uncle Peter II. (Petrović Njegoš) is generally recognised as the greatest of Serbian poets.

Peter Karagjorgjević, who had in 1870 fought as a volunteer in the French army and who now joined an insurgent band in north-west Bosnia, where his fame still lingers under the pseudonym of "Peter Mrkonjić". Special stress deserves to be laid upon this triangular competition, of which contemporary British statesmen seem to have been entirely ignorant: for it meant that the initiative lay, not with the Great Powers, but with those lesser actors in the play, at Belgrade, Cetinje and in the remote Bosnian mountains, whom fate was forcing to outbid each other.

While Serbian opinion strained at the leash, the Turks not un-naturally assumed a menacing attitude towards their obstreperous vassals, and Russian opinion also grew restless. But the official attitude of St. Petersburg is as yet summed up in the remark of Giers to the German Ambassador on 18 April—"Nous n'avons pas de programme si ce n'est la paix, mais nous ne pouvons pas laisser écraser la Serbie".[1]

THE BERLIN MEMORANDUM

As the crisis seemed likely to drag on indefinitely, Tsar Alexander, towards the end of April, suggested, in view of his approaching annual cure at Ems, that the three Foreign Ministers of the Northern Courts should meet in Berlin in May and concert a joint policy. Before, however, this meeting could take place, the pace was hastened by disorders at Salonica, resulting in the murder of the French and German Consuls by the mob (6 May), and four days later, by a riot in Constantinople, which led to the overthrow of the Grand Vizier. The three Imperial Powers can hardly be blamed for thinking that no time was to be lost, and for refusing to wait till England could be roused from her dilatory and lethargic attitude. On 12 May 1876, therefore, Bismarck, Andrássy and Gorchakov drew up the famous Berlin Memorandum, which proposed an armistice of two months, both sides retaining their arms meanwhile, the Turkish Government undertaking to assist the rebuilding of ruined houses and to provide temporary relief, and the supervision of these measures being placed in the hands of a consular commission. If, however, the armistice should expire before an agreement as to the necessary reforms, it

[1] Schweinitz, *Denkwürdigkeiten*, i. p. 321. When these memoirs appeared in 1927, Prince Lichnowsky—German Ambassador in London in 1914—in his *Auf dem Wege zum Abgrund* (i. p. 170), quoted this phrase of Giers and compared it with Sazonov's exactly similar attitude in the Serbian question in July 1914.

would be necessary to take "efficacious measures in the interests of peace". This proposal was transmitted to the three Western Govern-ments and at once accepted by France and Italy. But it met with a hostile reception in London, where the week-end—that bugbear of Count Shuvalov—had suspended all political activity and made impossible any telegraphic exchange of views before Gorchakov and Andrássy left Berlin.[1] Disraeli himself showed his first reactions by a brusque encounter with Shuvalov at a levee of the Prince of Wales: "They are beginning to treat England as if we were Montenegro or Bosnia":[2] and Derby recounted to the Ambassador his detailed objections. Could Turkey afford the sums necessary for reconstruc-tion, and "was it a good principle to insist that a regular Government should pay the expenses of an insurrection, and not those who pro-voked it"? It might well lead to massacres between Christians and Moslems, while the final clause was "equivalent to advice to the insurgents not to lay down their arms".[3] Derby was ready to consider separating the principle of an armistice from the conditions suggested, but even this was rejected by the Cabinet, to which Disraeli argued that participation in such a scheme "must end very soon in the disintegration of Turkey". He picked holes in each of the five pro-posals, treating the distribution of relief as "a huge system of indiscriminate almsgiving, totally beyond the power of the Porte to effect, and utterly demoralising to any country", and consular supervision as "reducing the authority of the Porte to a nullity": and he even went so far as to give his "opinion that it would be far better for Turkey to give up Bosnia and Herzegovina altogether, as Austria gave up Italy, than to acquiesce in the new proposals".[4] He would consent to "an armistice and an European Conference based upon the territorial *status quo*", but only if Turkey agreed, and till her views were known, the Imperial Powers must be told that "a general concert cannot be attained by the course they are adopting". The Cabinet unanimously refused adherence to the Berlin Memoran-dum, on the assumption that Russia had her two allies in tow and

---

[1] Disraeli actually complained to Derby of the mismanagement at the Foreign Office, which delayed sending him information as to the whole affair—Buckle, vi. p. 23.

[2] General von Schweinitz, the German Ambassador at St. Petersburg, records the phrase as "Montenegro or Monaco", which suggests that Disraeli expressed himself more than once in this sense—Schweinitz, *Denkwürdigkeiten*, i. p. 330: cf. also Prince Hohenlohe, *Denkwürdigkeiten*, ii. p. 189 (21 May 1876).

[3] 19 May, Shuvalov to Gorchakov—*R.B.D.* ii. p. 666.

[4] 16 May—Buckle, vi. p. 25.

aimed at dragging all Europe in her wake: and Shuvalov with not unpardonable annoyance reported to Gorchakov: "a little more, and the insurgents are non-existent, and it is Russians in disguise who are fighting in Herzegovina". He was really not so far off the mark as he imagined!

From two quarters only came doubts as to the wisdom of our course. The wise Lord Odo Russell wrote from Berlin, urging "the serious consequences" which would follow rejection, while the Queen reminded the Prime Minister that the three Northern Powers were "more intimately and vitally connected with the welfare of Turkey" than the three Western Powers, and added: "The Queen's dislike to our separating ourselves from the rest arises from the fear that Turkey will look to us to help her against the rest of Europe and that we shall thus precipitate rather than prevent the catastrophe".[1] Never did the Queen show a surer or more prophetic instinct, though later it was to fail her lamentably.

Disraeli's brusque assumption that Britain was being ignored at Berlin was by no means justified: for the three Foreign Ministers, before taking action, had had a full discussion with the Ambassadors of Britain, France and Italy, at which Gorchakov gave an *exposé* of the joint policy proposed—the aim being defined as the *"statu quo amélioré"*, in other words, a combination of Turkish integrity with effective internal reforms. The Ambassadors only took this statement *ad referendum*, but each of the three expressed the hope and belief that his Government would give its approval. When on the contrary London declined, Gontaut-Biron reported home that Lord Odo did not share his Government's views and had expressed to Lord Derby his readiness to resign his post.[2]

Meanwhile Lord Granville, in the name of the Opposition, expressly associated himself with the Government's attitude, when the question first came before Parliament a month later,[3] and the first real public criticism came from Mr. Gladstone on 31 July, when the Bulgarian affair was already giving an entirely new complexion to the whole affair. Already at the end of June, however, Gladstone was seriously perturbed at the official British attitude towards the memorandum and found that his views were fully shared by Lord Stratford de Redcliffe and by Lord Hammond (who had been Permanent Under-Secretary at the Foreign Office from 1854 to 1866). They

---

[1] 16 May—*Letters*, ii. p. 453.   [2] *D.D.F.* ii. nos. 51 (13 May) and 76 (18 July).
[3] 26 June—Hansard, ccxxx. p. 416.

were all agreed, so Gladstone wrote to Granville,[1] "that Lord Derby was wrong in saying this [*i.e.* the Bosnian rising] was a civil war and we had no more business with it than any other civil war, referring apparently to Austria and Hungary as an example. *Because* this civil war arises out of the alleged non-fulfilment of engagements taken by the Sultan in 1855–6 to his own subjects, which we, apart from our interests, are under obligation, in common with the rest of Europe, to promote the fulfilment of." Here, as so often, Gladstone lays his finger on one of the essential points: Turkey had broken her pledges to Europe, and we had the clearest moral obligations towards her victims.

None the less, there can be no possible doubt that it was the British refusal of co-operation, and still more the failure to put forward any concrete alternative, that made joint action by Europe impossible[2] and actually precipitated events in Eastern Europe. To this the Queen was fully alive, even before the German Emperor expressed his regret at the absence of a "counter-proposal".[3] When Disraeli—on the advice of Elliot, who feared disturbances in the Turkish capital—ordered the British fleet to Besika Bay (24 May), the Queen remained sceptical and insisted most strongly upon the danger of "letting the Porte believe that we advised" rejection.[4] To this the unrepentant Disraeli replied in very self-revealing terms: "Your Majesty's fleet has not been ordered to the Mediterranean to protect Christians or Turks, but to uphold Your Majesty's Empire. Had Your Majesty sanctioned the Berlin Memorandum, Constantinople would at this moment have been garrisoned by Russia, and the Turkish fleet placed under Russian protection."[5] No attempt is made to provide proof for this wildly exaggerated assertion, and it is clear that the Queen's nervousness was not dispelled. The arrival of the fleet was greeted by the Turks as a proof that Britain was on their side and encouraged them in their rigid attitude.

THE TURKISH REVOLUTION

Events were now free to take their course. On 30 May—the very day on which the Ambassadors of the three Powers were about to

---

[1] *Granville Papers*, 27 June 1876.
[2] Gontaut-Biron reported from Berlin to Paris: "On est généralement affligé et contrarié de la réponse anglaise" (20 May, *D.D.F.* ii. no. 55).
[3] William I. to Empress, 3 June, for transmission to Queen—*Letters*, ii. pp. 459-60.
[4] *Ibid.* p. 455, 27 May.   [5] *Ibid.* pp. 455-6, 29 May.

present the memorandum on their own account—the unrest which had long pervaded the Turkish capital culminated in a palace revolution. The liberal Midhat joined hands with the masterful Hussein Avni, the wretched Sultan, who as long ago as 1862 had shown signs of mental aberration and had been declared by the chief doctor of an asylum as "suffering from mania, with paroxysms of fury", was now forced to abdicate and was replaced on the throne by the phantom Murad V., who greeted the change with terror and only too soon developed in his turn all the symptoms of a deranged and decaying intellect. A few days later Abdul Aziz was found dead, with the arteries of his arm cut by scissors: and it will probably always remain uncertain whether he was murdered or committed suicide.[1] Then, on 14 June, before the new situation could consolidate, an officer of the Guard forced his way into the council chamber and shot down the Ministers of War and Foreign Affairs, the fanatical Hussein Avni Pasha and the more colourless Rashid Pasha. Turkish authority seemed on the point of dissolution.

So long as there seemed some prospect of the Powers assuming the initiative in the Bosnian dispute and imposing a settlement, it was still possible to check the growing war-fever in Serbia and Montenegro, and in actual fact more than one warning came from both St. Petersburg and Vienna. When, however, England was seen to be opposing any intervention between Turks and insurgents, and when events in Constantinople made Turkish resistance problematical, Prince Milan found it quite impossible to stand out against excited public opinion. The Serbian Foreign Minister, Jovan Ristić, told the German Agent that the one remaining means of averting war was that the Porte should entrust to Serbia the administration of Bosnia for an annual tribute.[2] The Russian Agent, Kartsev, it is true, on orders from his Government, publicly announced that Russia would leave Serbia to her fate if she broke the peace. But the general public might be excused for relying less on this official utterance than upon Kartsev's own marked sympathy for the Serbian cause. Moreover, it was known that the Moscow Slavophils were full of enthusiasm, and the arrival in Belgrade of their agent General Cherniayev, the hero of Samarkand, had a magical effect

---

[1] Dr. E. D. Dickson, physician to the British Embassy, published in the *British Medical Journal* for July 1876 a detailed description of his examination of the Sultan's body, and dismissed all possibility of suicide, on the basis of "a mass of evidence which no sophistic subtilties can shake". See *The Times*, 7 July 1876.

[2] *Austrian Archives*, Wrede to Andrássy, 30 May (unpublished).

upon opinion. The last straw was provided by the news—now constant and indisputable, and of course more accessible than in the West—of hideous atrocities perpetrated by the Turks just beyond Serbia's eastern frontier, and of the simultaneous massing of the Turkish troops. On 30 June, then, the Serbian Government, in defiance of all advice, declared war upon Turkey and was joined the next day by Montenegro.

The general situation at midsummer 1876 was as follows. The three Northern Powers were blamed by the London Cabinet for their precipitate action at Berlin, but they could rejoin that they had waited for nearly nine months since the rising broke out, that London's attitude had been consistently negative and that they could wait no longer; that the murders in Salonica made action imperative and that the British Ambassador's fears of possible massacre at Constantinople had been the excuse for sending the British fleet to Besika Bay. Above all, they could criticise the negative attitude of London in refusing co-operation but offering no alternative suggestion. But the Turkish Revolution suddenly transformed the situation and seemed after all to justify the British Cabinet, who could now argue that the new Sultan and his reforming ministers must be given the necessary breathing-space in which to carry out their programme. The desirability of this was really felt in London, but it drove the Balkan nations to desperation. They had with difficulty been restrained by the prospect of European action: its failure convinced them that they must act for themselves, while the events in Constantinople encouraged them to hope that a bold offensive might lead to Turkey's overthrow. For the moment, then, London seemed to be right and the others wrong, until the revelations from Bulgaria brought another swift transformation of the situation, in which an outburst of British public opinion played a leading part.

Meanwhile the presence of the British fleet greatly stiffened the attitude of the Porte. As Gallenga, the able *Times* correspondent at Constantinople, explained, the Turks "overlook the fact that the ships are there as a demonstration of England's displeasure at the Salonica massacre. They think that the British flag is there as a harbinger of a British alliance such as twenty years ago led to the Crimean War, and there is no doubt that this fond conceit to a great extent contributes to deepen their resentment at what they consider Russian treachery and emboldens them to assume a defiant attitude towards the Powers" (8 June).

He was also one of the first men on the spot to warn against exaggerated belief in Turkish reforms. The projected constitution of Midhat and his friends will, he argued, "hold aloft the flag of 'Turkey for the Turks' and will allow the Christians simply what a conquered race may exact from the sense of justice and clemency of the conquerors, and no more": to create constitutional government in Turkey was "something like weaving ropes of sand" (21 June). Unhappily there was an influential section of opinion in England which remained to the very end impervious to this truth, and its obtuseness cost Europe dear. *The Times* itself was an honourable exception and steered a sober middle course, pointing out as early as 10 June 1876 that pacification was perfectly impossible without the grant of self-government in one form or another.

DISRAELI'S FIRST OVERTURE TO RUSSIA

Both Derby and Andrássy warned Serbia beforehand that by attacking Turkey she would forfeit her guarantee under the Treaty of Paris, and Disraeli actually argued that one of the "legitimate consequences" of Turkish victory would be "the restoration of Belgrade" to the Turks—in other words, the abolition of Serbian autonomy—and that Russia should be told that in such circumstances England would object to her interference.[1] At this stage Disraeli believed—and in July still upheld the argument in the House of Commons—that Britain by declining the Berlin Memorandum had enforced her policy of "non-intervention" and ended her isolation in the most effectual way, in that "the five Powers have come over to us".[2] His motive is clearly revealed in a special memorandum for the Queen, which defines the rejection of the Berlin Note, the dispatch of the fleet and the friendly warning to the Powers as "forming together a policy of determination" such as will preserve peace "and at the same time restore Your Majesty's influence in the general councils, which for some years has not been so marked as could be desired. To escape isolation by consenting to play a secondary part does not become Your Majesty and is a short-sighted policy, for, leading to frequent humiliation, it ultimately occasions wars which are neither just nor necessary. Mr. Disraeli looks upon the Tripartite understanding between the three Imperial Powers of the Continent

---

[1] *Austrian Archives*, Andrássy to Wrede, 28 June (unpublished).
[2] Hansard, ccxxx. p. 207.

as virtually extinct, as extinct as the Roman triumvirate, and that no leading step will in future be taken without first consulting Your Majesty."[1] On the same day he told Lord John Manners that "the tripartite confederacy" was "at an end". It was an unnatural alliance and never would have occurred had England maintained of late years her just position in public affairs.[2]

Disraeli's calculations were wrong, and the alliance was still to resist many growing causes of internal friction. His main aim was to split its unity, in the presumed interests of British power and prestige, and the above extracts go far to prove this contention. But the final proof lies in an incident of which neither Mr. Buckle's *Life of Disraeli* nor his edition of the Queen's letters give any inkling.

On 9 June Disraeli made a somewhat calming speech in the House. While announcing the definite withdrawal of the Berlin Memorandum owing to "the remarkable events" at Constantinople, he affirmed that Britain's refusal of co-operation had been "received in no unfriendly spirit by any of the Powers that we had to address", even though they expressed "great regret"—and further, that there was "a complete understanding between us and the Great Powers that there should be no undue pressure put upon the new sovereign of Turkey" until he and his ministers had time to concert a policy. He also laid stress on the joint representations made by Austria, Russia and Britain at Belgrade in favour of "counsels of moderation", and denounced with marked fervour as "a forgery" a letter which the Vienna press had published on the previous day as written by himself, and which "spoke with unpardonable disrespect of a Great Power which is the ally of our Sovereign".[3] This obvious reference to Russia, and indeed the whole tenour of the speech, left it to be inferred that the Prime Minister was ready for some kind of co-operation after all: and *The Times*, struck by his "hopeful tone", put in a plea for common action, arguing that "there has not yet been anything to emphasise antagonism".

The speech was made in answer to Lord Hartington's request for information on the Eastern Question, but the Leader of the Opposition

[1] 7 June—*Letters*, ii. p. 457. [2] Buckle, *op. cit.* vi. p. 31.
[3] The essential passage from the forged letter runs thus: "You see that we know how to protect our rights when they are threatened by Muscovite ambition. A few months ago I said that England is better able now than in the days of Pitt to face an European coalition. To-day I can add that England will have no lack of allies. The strong never have." These phrases were, however, so much in keeping with the Prime Minister's outlook, that we need not be surprised at its having found credence.

at this stage disclaimed all "desire to press for any explanation that might cause the Government any embarrassment" and was quite ready to believe "that there exists in the country" no distrust of the Government's action. Public opinion, as voiced in the press, took the quite reasonable view that a breathing-space should be accorded to the new régime in Constantinople and that diplomatic negotiations might also take a new departure.

The mild tones of this speech find their explanation in the secret overture made by the Prime Minister on the very same evening to the Russian Ambassador, at a dinner of Baron Rothschild, and repeated in greater detail the following day.

Count Peter Shuvalov was one of the most marked personalities of his day. With good connections at court, a fascinating presence and a reputation for mildly liberal principles, he held the appointment of Governor-General of the Baltic Provinces, when in 1866 chance led the Tsar to select him for one of the key posts of the old Empire. From 1866 to 1874 he was head of the "third division" of the police, and thus held in his hands the threads of political administration and all measures for the protection of the Tsar and the Government. He speedily restored the falling credit of his department, which had been shaken by Karakosov's attempt on the Tsar's life, and held his own so successfully against all intrigues—alike from the extreme reactionaries and Panslavists and from his quondam Liberal friends— as to earn the nickname of "Peter IV.". He was even sent abroad by the Tsar on a delicate mission connected with a liaison of the Grand Duke Alexis, which at one time threatened to complicate the succession. His selection for the post of Ambassador in London at first caused some surprise, though it was really a sign of the importance attached by the Tsar to Russo-British relations, that he sent one who still enjoyed his close personal confidence. By his social gifts and versatility Shuvalov soon justified the choice and from the first filled a foremost place in the diplomatic world of London. His dispatches afford ample proof that this man, who knew the innermost secrets of St. Petersburg, was quick to acquire equal knowledge and discernment in the radically different *milieu* of London.

Shuvalov was taken entirely by surprise by Disraeli's overture, but hastened to report it in full detail to the Chancellor and the Tsar. In the opening conversation Disraeli said to him, "If Russia would tell us at this moment what she wants, we could still arrange with her: but let her tell us direct, and not through the intermediacy of the Harcourts, Münsters and Beusts"—meaning Shuvalov's French, German and Austro-Hungarian colleagues. Next day he was more precise. "Yesterday you spoke of our suspicion towards Russia and of the *arrière pensées* which you ascribe to us. Please get this out of your head. Neither I nor my Government distrust a Great Power which is governed by wise men and on conservative principles. I distrust you neither in Asia nor in Turkey. As for Asia, I recently spoke in a sense which inaugurates a new policy: I don't wish to suspect your action in Asia or to check the development of your power: we only ask you to do nothing which could react upon Afghanistan—which would threaten our Asiatic possessions. In the same way I do not suspect your policy in Turkey. I understand that a wise and strong Government like yours does not wish to precipitate matters and is waiting for the nature of things to let Turkey disappear from the map of Europe, which may happen sooner or later, but is inevitable."

He went on to blame General Ignatyev and Count Andrássy for the embroilment of affairs—the former by his intrigues among the Christians, the latter by Francis Joseph's Dalmatian journey[1] and by the Note of 30 December. "We have lost all confidence in this statesman and will no longer follow him." Shuvalov had reproached him for not making clear "what we want. Well, here is my mind. The insurgents are not fighting for reforms, and nothing will satisfy them, since they aim at independence. In that case neither you nor we can prevent bloodshed. You have been wrong to hold back Serbia and Montenegro, for the conflict is imminent and on its issue the solution will depend. We think blood-letting to be necessary and will consult together. If the Christians get the upper hand, we shall only have to register accomplished facts: if Turkey crushes the Christians and the repression becomes tyrannous, it will be the turn of all the Great Powers to interpose in the name of humanity."

In reply to this cynical view Shuvalov cogently urged that Russia's aim was to improve the lot of the Christians without raising the whole Eastern Question, whereas this was exactly what the Prime Minister's method would involve: for if the Turks were beaten their Empire would collapse, whereas if they were victorious only intervention would prevent reprisals and massacres. Disraeli closed the conversation by affirming his desire to eliminate Decazes and "his

---

[1] In reality Andrássy disapproved of and tried to prevent it. See Wertheimer, *Graf Andrássy*, ii. pp. 257-8.

bête noir of the moment", Andrássy—Bismarck's name does not seem
to have been mentioned—and to establish direct contact between
Britain and Russia. To his no small embarrassment Shuvalov was
pledged to secrecy towards his diplomatic colleagues, and was left
speculating as to the real motive of the advance. "Does he want to
separate us from Count Andrássy? . . . Knowing the sincerity of our
relations with Berlin, would he like to eject Austria and occupy her
place in the Concert of three? Does he simply want to draw near
to Russia and have with her a strong hand in ultimate decisions?
Or—and this seems the most probable—does he want, after gathering the fruits of popularity due to refusing the Note and sending
the fleet, to return to a wiser policy, one more likely to assure
the peace of Europe, and is he choosing as the best means a direct
entente with Russia?" [1]

On Disraeli's suggestion Shuvalov also talked to Derby, who denied
that Britain was following a policy of isolation, expressed readiness
to co-operate with the three courts, but favoured abstention from
any fresh proposals for another three or four weeks, in order to give
the new Sultan a chance of pacification. [2] Gorchakov was by no means
edified at the overture, suspected an attempt to break Russia's
"entente with Austria and France" and announced the Tsar's
"immutable" adherence to the League of Three. [3] At the same time he
wished to avoid recriminations, "since the mere indication of a fissure
in the entente of the Great Powers had produced such terrible results": [4] in other words, he revealed his own conviction that Britain's
negative attitude had unchained events.

During the next week Gorchakov insisted, with growing urgency,
that only energetic joint action at the Porte by Britain and the
Powers could avert "imminent explosion". [5] Kartsev was again
ordered to warn the Serbs, but by this time it was obvious that
Prince Milan was "*débordé*" and could no longer draw back without
risking expulsion. [6] Nor was it possible to galvanise Lord Derby in
time. His main anxiety was to avoid "appearing as the supporters of
Turks against Christians": but he agreed "that we ought to have no
antagonism with Russia" and did not believe that the Tsar desired

---

[1] Shuvalov to Gorchakov, 11 June—no. 38 of my *Russo-British Documents*, ii.
pp. 672-5; nos. 33-7 (telegrams and letters). The references are to a series of
seven articles in the *Slavonic Review*.
[2] *Ibid.* no. 41, Shuvalov to Tsar, 14 June.
[3] *Ibid.* no. 43, Gorchakov to Shuvalov, 14 June.   [4] *Ibid.* no. 44, 17 June.
[5] *Ibid.* no. 56, 28 June.   [6] *Ibid.* no. 53, 27 June.

to break up Turkey.[1] The Queen, too, at this stage still realised the danger that our exaggerated Turcophilism merely forced the Christians into the arms of Russia, and held that Turkey should be made to understand very clearly "that we have no intention of making the state of the Ottoman Empire a cause of quarrel with Russia" and "that the interests of Russia and England are not antagonistic".[2]

Disraeli, however, was already blowing cold again towards Russia, and Shuvalov, during his next conversation on 24 June, could extract nothing definite from the Prime Minister, save a strong disclaimer of any desire to annex Egypt, which the Russian skilfully countered with the argument that it was equally absurd to suspect Russia of designs on Serbia or a future outlet on the Adriatic through the medium of Montenegro.[3] He interpreted British policy as "hesitating, tortuous, but not warlike. England feels isolated and dares not admit her solidarity with Turkey. This solidarity is a fact, and one of Mr. Disraeli's confidants told me quite recently that the Porte had asked England's protection in exchange for its submission to all advice she might give. The British Government *wishes an agreement with someone and cannot find anyone.* Count Andrássy is in its eyes the author of all evil, Duke Decazes the representative of an enfeebled nation eager to place itself on the pedestal of a conciliator, Prince Bismarck a trickster who would gladly see the cards muddled up, in order to have more elbow room against Catholicism and France. There remain ourselves, but England cannot escape from her secular suspicions or seek a peaceful solution in agreement with those who are in her eyes the future masters of Constantinople and the Slav Empire. Thus it is not a bellicose *élan*, but fear of us, which prompts British armaments and naval demonstrations. It may be positively affirmed that no one here wants war, but it is a question whether Mr. Disraeli's policy is not unconsciously leading up to it."[4]

This acute estimate was to be justified by events. The first proof was provided by Queen Victoria's frigid reply to the Tsar's appeal for co-operation. "It may be", she was made to say, "that the six Great Powers intervened a little prematurely in Turkish affairs, but the course of events has extricated them from a difficult position and allowed them to revert to the principle of non-intervention, the

[1] Derby to General Ponsonby, 20 June—Buckle, vi. p. 33.
[2] Ponsonby to Derby, 18 June—*Letters*, ii. p. 465.
[3] *R.B.D.* no. 52, Shuvalov to Tsar, 24 June.
[4] *Ibid.* no. 57, 2 July.

consequence of which is general neutrality, which will, I hope, be strictly observed by all."[1]

In other words, the Government had fallen back upon the negative policy of waiting upon events, Disraeli himself being "sanguine enough to believe that before the month terminates, the infamous invasion of the Servians will have been properly punished", and "the insurrection soon subdued" [2] Derby also disapproved of the Serbs, failing to realise the irresistible force of popular sympathy with the Bosnians, but he did not go nearly so far in his friendly feelings towards Turkey, and to a deputation introduced to him at the Foreign Office by John Bright on 14 July, denied any ulterior motive in rejecting the Berlin Memorandum, explained the dispatch of the fleet solely by "fear of sanguinary civil war and massacre of foreigners" and defined his general policy towards Turkey in the anything but complimentary phrase: "We undertook undoubtedly twenty years ago to guarantee the Sick Man against murder, but we never undertook to guarantee him against suicide or sudden death".[3] How vague and inaccurate were the Prime Minister's ideas of the true situation in the Near East is shown by a memorandum addressed to the Queen on 29 June, in which he maintained that "the so-called insurgents are not natives of any Turkish province, but are simply an invasion of revolutionary bands, whose strength lay in the support afforded to them by Servia and Montenegro, acting on the instigation of foreign agents and foreign committees". Almost in the same breath he challenged the suggestion that Sir Henry Elliot was "extremely anti-Russian", while confessing that he had till recently imagined him to maintain "confidential relations" with his Russian colleague General Ignatyev.[4] These two passages throw a vivid light upon Disraeli's sources of information.

DISRAELI'S PERSONAL VERDICTS

This is the moment at which to note the consistently poor opinion and sweeping judgments of Disraeli with regard to almost all his

---

[1] *R.B.D.* nos. 60 and 61, Tsar to Queen, 4 July; Queen to Tsar, 9 July—*Letters*, ii. pp. 468-70.

[2] 9 and 13 July, to Ladies Chesterfield and Bradford, vi. p. 37. Contrast *The Times* of 10 August 1876: "It was a great gain to Europe when the Turks withdrew from Belgrade, and to allow them to come back again would simply be to bring two sets of explosive materials close together".

[3] *Speeches of Fifteenth Earl of Derby*, ed. W. H. Lecky, ii. p. 289.

[4] Buckle, *op. cit.* vi. p. 35.

own diplomatic representatives abroad, as well as the foreign Ambassadors whom he met in London and their chiefs in Europe. Lord Augustus Loftus at St. Petersburg he dismisses as "a mere Polonius" or again "Pomposo", or worse still "a mere Livadian parasite, afraid even of Gorchakov's shadow",[1] and to the Queen, "he is not only absurd, he is mischievous"[2]—all grossly unfair over-statements about a man of admittedly light calibre. Sir Andrew Buchanan at Vienna he calls "a hopeless case" and "a hopeless mediocrity".[3] Of Lord Odo Russell at Berlin, beyond all doubt one of our greatest Ambassadors in the nineteenth century, he said that "he might as well be at Bagdad" for all the use he was in influencing Bismarck, though it was even then notorious both that Bismarck rarely allowed himself to be influenced by foreigners and that Russell was one of the very few foreigners to whom he listened and attached any value.[4] When warned by Russell of the effect that rejection would have upon Berlin, Disraeli merely wrote to Derby: "I do not like Lord Odo's letter or anything he has done. . . . He does not seem to comprehend the situation":[5] and even as late as December 1876 he could coin such an absurdity as "the Russian courtier Odo"![6] Even Sir Henry Elliot at Constantinople—the man who eventually proved to be most after his own heart—he denounced for his "stupidity"[7] and "a lamentable want of energy and deficiency of information" about the Turkish Revolution.[8] Of Henry Layard a year earlier at Madrid he had written to Derby that "though of unquestionable talents", he was "prejudiced and passionate, and always—I will not say, misleads, but certainly misinforms us".[9] But when early in 1877 Disraeli changed his opinion of Layard and sent him to succeed Elliot at Constantinople, as "a man of the necessary experience and commanding mind . . . and not too scrupulous",[10] Layard displayed his good judgment by setting himself to gain the Sultan's confidence and was "continually representing" Abdul Hamid to the Prime Minister "as one of the most amiable men he ever knew, with nothing but good impulses".[11]

---

[1] 20 April, 28 Dec., 4 Nov. 1876, to Derby—Buckle, vi. pp. 23, 111, 89.
[2] To Queen, 10 Sept. 1876—*Letters*, ii. p. 478.
[3] 15 August, to Derby—Buckle, vi. p. 49.
[4] 17 Oct.—*ibid.* p. 81: cf. letter of 10 Sept. to Queen—*Letters*, ii. p. 478.
[5] 29 May—*ibid.* p. 28.   [6] 28 Dec., to Derby—Buckle, vi. p. 112.
[7] 2 Sept., to Northcote—*ibid.* p. 51.   [8] 7 Aug., to Derby—*ibid.* p. 46.
[9] *Ibid.* v. p. 417.   [10] 10 April 1877, to Lady Bradford—*ibid.* vi. p. 179.
[11] 6 Sept. 1877, to Lady Bradford—*ibid.* p. 179. Salisbury, on the other hand—so wrote Derby to Russell—"reports ill of the new Sultan, calls him a poor weak creature from whom no help is to be expected. But his judgment is the result of a single interview"—Newton, *Lord Lyons*, p. 358. See *infra*, pp. 207, 354, 406.

It is only too probable that these very wholesale, and very erratic, strictures upon all and sundry[1] were largely the result of Disraeli's growing ill-health and testiness of temper: it is in any case necessary to refer to them here, as showing the mentality with which he looked upon Europe.

THE REICHSTADT CONVENTION

The Imperial Powers, meanwhile, were under no illusions as to the gravity of the situation, and, in despair at Britain's negative attitude, decided to make their own plans. The Tsar, who was now about to return home from his cure at Ems, expressed his desire for a personal exchange of views with Francis Joseph, and on 8 July the two sovereigns met at Reichstadt, accompanied by their Foreign Ministers, Gorchakov and Andrássy. Complete and cordial agreement was reached, on the basis of non-intervention in the first instance, but prompt and close co-operation under the impulse of fresh events. Two contingencies were considered—the victory of the Turks, in which case Serbia and Montenegro were to be saved from the consequences of their rashness and the territorial *status quo* was to be upheld; and a Turkish defeat, in which case (1) Serbia was to extend her frontiers both on the Drina and the Lim, and Montenegro to receive a portion of Hercegovina and "the harbour of Spizza",[2] the Lim henceforth forming a common frontier between them; (2) the remainder of Bosnia-Hercegovina was to fall to Austria-Hungary; (3) Russia was to reannex southern Bessarabia and round off her Asiatic territories; and (4) Bulgaria, Roumelia and Albania "may" become autonomous states, and Constantinople a free city, while Thessaly and Crete would be united to Greece.[3] It is clear that the two Powers had regarded the second alternative as the more probable, but, as so often in Balkan wars, events falsified the forecasts of Europe. During July and August the Turks rapidly asserted their military superiority over the Serbs, and it soon became obvious that even the *status quo* would take some saving. Thus the Convention of Reichstadt was

[1] For similar criticisms of Münster see *ibid.* p. 81; of Beust, p. 15; of Andrássy, pp. 15, 21, 49, 89, 186, 317. Of Waddington he wrote to Salisbury: "I have not the slightest confidence in him: he is feeble and sly, which feeble men often are", and again, "W. looks like an *épicier* and I think his looks do not belie his mind and general intelligence" (vi. p. 327).

[2] Five miles south of the Bocche di Cattaro.

[3] *Austrian Archives*, "Teschenberg Dossier"—"Von welcher Seite ist die Initiative zur Entrevue von Reichstadt ausgegangen?" (unpublished).

stillborn: but its real importance lay in the fact that if Turkey had been defeated, the two Powers, with the backing of a more than benevolent Germany, would almost certainly have been able to impose some such settlement very rapidly upon the Porte, and London would have found itself completely isolated and scarcely able to prevent it.

The Convention was shrouded in extreme secrecy, mainly at the instance of Andrássy, and indeed its contents did not become generally known till after the Great War. Even Bismarck was at first only informed as to the general lines, not the details, of agreement, though Francis Joseph confided in William I. a month later at their meeting in Salzburg, and Gorchakov assured the German Ambassador that he had no secrets from Berlin.[1] But from London Andrássy carefully concealed the facts, apparently for the double reason that he repaid Disraeli's suspicion of himself with interest, and that he did not wish to initiate his own Ambassador there, Count Beust, whom he rightly suspected of intriguing to oust him from office. "Tell Lord Derby confidentially", he wired to Beust, "that the result of the Reichstadt meeting was very satisfactory: we agreed to adhere to non-intervention under present circumstances"[2]—a highly misleading interpretation of the facts. When Beust communicated to him a London version of certain alleged decisions, he wired back: "There were no written agreements whatsoever. . . . It is very important that the British Government should not regard these points as final arrangements, but only as what they are, *namely a verbal exchange of opinion, which might in time serve as a basis for an agreement between the Great Powers.*" In other words, he deliberately misrepresented what had actually occurred, both to Derby and to Beust: and the fact that Beust believed it—perhaps because his colossal vanity did not permit him to imagine himself excluded from the secret—materially helped to mislead the British Government for over a year to come.

The Convention of Reichstadt was an attempt to revert to the old tradition—dating back as far as Catherine and even Peter—of parallel Russo-Austrian action for the solution of the Eastern Question. In its essence it rested upon a partition of the whole Balkan Peninsula into two spheres of influence—the eastern, Russian; the western, Austrian: and this involved momentous consequences

---

[1] Schweinitz, *Denkwürdigkeiten*, i. p. 335.
[2] *Austrian Archives*, "Teschenberg Dossier", 9, 10 and 14 July, Andrássy to Beust; 12 July, Beust to Andrássy.

for the Southern Slav race, since it meant Russia sanctioning the Austrian claim to the purest of Slav provinces. It was dictated in the first instance by strategic considerations, but also by the Tsar's suspicions of Serbia as a revolutionary centre.

THE SERBIAN WAR

Serbia's disastrous plunge into war had been very largely determined by the dubious rôle of the Russian Consul in Belgrade, Kartsev, who officially repeated the perfectly genuine warnings of his Government, but privately played the game of the Moscow Slavophils, and knowing that the Empress and the Heir Apparent—the future Alexander III.—both favoured intervention, encouraged his Serbian friends to believe that in the end they could rely on active Russian help. Their conviction became universal among the population, when General Cherniayev, already famous for his exploits in Central Asia, came to Belgrade as the emissary of the Moscow committees and was almost at once given the rank of a General in the Prince's army. This brave if bombastic knight-errant had taken Tashkent against orders, and true to his past, now openly defied the Tsar's public disapproval of his action, thus encouraging many hundreds of other Russian volunteers to take service under him in Serbia. The part played by these volunteers in the Serbo-Turkish War was, perhaps not unnaturally, treated by suspicious public opinion in London as a proof of Russian official duplicity. But the realities of the Russian situation were imperfectly understood in the West. The Tsar's pacifism was perfectly genuine and was fortified by his distrust of Balkan revolutionaries, and above all by the internal situation of Russia itself, its precarious finance and the spread of nihilism and terrorism. He had either to lean upon the Right or to find alternative support from the Left: but the latter was irreconcilable, even if he could have brought himself to work with it, while with the former two of the main motives were Orthodoxy and Slavdom. In a word, he could only disinterest himself in the fate of the Balkan Christians by flouting the main pillars of the dynasty and of the existing order, and in a certain sense he may be said to have been the prisoner of Moscow opinion—actively supported, moreover, by his wife, his son and most of the imperial family, under whose influence the ladies of the court collected subscriptions for the Serbs on the streets of St. Petersburg and the Metropolitan of Moscow offered special prayers for a Serbian victory.

In London, however, the Tsar's difficulties were not appreciated, and his failure to prohibit his subjects from joining the Serbian army was treated as a proof of bad faith. The Prince of Wales took the line that the Tsar was "about the only sovereign who can prevent his subjects from leaving their country without his consent":[1] and Derby, when he asked Shuvalov to procure such a prohibition, was not convinced by the reply—unquestionably justified though it was—that his master could not risk the intense unpopularity which such a step would arouse. When, however, the German Emperor of all men sent the Queen a memorandum arguing that the Tsar "could not act otherwise", she seems at last to have been convinced.[2]

Serbia entered the war ill-led, badly equipped and without adequate preparation, alike from the diplomatic and the military point of view: and impartial observers, while utterly refusing to blame the gallant Serbian peasantry, held that a properly led and equipped European army could easily have routed Abdul Kerim. One army failed in its attempt to establish contact with the Montenegrins through Novipazar, and within three weeks the main forces under Cherniayev were forced to withdraw from Turkish territory. Early in August the advancing Turks captured Knjaževac and Zaječar and began to concentrate in the Morava valley, the backbone of the little Principality. Dr. Sandwith, who visited Turkish headquarters under a flag of truce from the Serbs, records that "the war is a thorough war of the time of Genghis Khan. As the Turkish army advances, a desert is left behind."[3] The Serbs held their own in six days of fighting at Aleksinac, but they were henceforth on the defensive, and the successes of the Montenegrins could not of course retrieve the situation, since their numbers were small and they could be isolated and contained by superior forces. By the end of August Prince Milan was secretly inviting the mediation of the guarantor Powers, and was relieved to find that Andrássy was ready to protest against the Porte's desire for his deposition, in the calculation that his future line would inevitably be Austrophil.[4] By the middle of September even Ristić realised that the game was up, and desired peace: but the army was now out of hand, and at the instance of Cherniayev and the Russian volunteers, who presumably hoped that Russia might be led

[1] 2 Oct., to Queen—*Letters*, ii. p. 481.
[2] 8 and 17 Oct.—*ibid.* pp. 485, 488: cf. Derby's view in letter of 29 Sept. to Queen—Buckle, vi. p. 75.
[3] 15 Aug. 1876, to Dr. Allon—*Letters to a Victorian Editor*, p. 56.
[4] *Austrian Archives*, Andrássy to Wrede.

to intervene, proclaimed Milan as King (16 September). The Prince felt himself to be ridiculous before Europe and refused even to receive the deputation which offered him the crown—the more so as Andrássy had at once warned him that under no circumstances need he look for recognition by Vienna. In any case, as the autumn advanced, there was a growing danger that the Turks would occupy the whole of Serbia and reimpose the old system of garrisons.

Moreover, Turkish self-confidence had received a natural stimulus, and one notable result was a fresh palace revolution on 31 August. A contemporary describes the wretched Murad "as one possessed, sitting on his sofa, motionless and speechless, smoothing his thin moustaches and beardless chin with his right hand hour after hour the livelong day, meditating on his abdication and only wondering on which of his reluctant brothers may devolve the burden which is too much for his shoulders".[1] According to Elliot's information, Murad, on first hearing of his uncle's death, had fallen down in a faint and had a fit of vomiting which lasted thirty-six hours. The Viennese specialist who was eventually called in certified him to be "suffering from chronic alcoholism aggravated by the emotions he has gone through", and a month after his fall a panel of seven doctors reported a hopeless case of "monomania of the suicidal type".[2] It was intolerable that the supreme power should remain in the hands of such a phantom, and on 30 August Murad was replaced by his brother Abdul Hamid. The statesmen in control were less inclined than before to adopt serious internal reforms, and the only terms which they were prepared to offer to Serbia would have involved serious curtailment of her autonomy.

Already, before the change occurred, an overture had been made by Abdul Hamid to Elliot through "an Englishman" of his acquaintance, whom he assured of his determination to win back the lost sympathies of the West by establishing "a totally new era", by "rigorous economy" and by finding new and more competent ministers.[3] Elliot wisely refused to commit himself, but a fortnight later, while referring to the new Sultan's "kindliness of disposition and enlightened views", doubted "whether he will accept restrictions which the reforming party thinks necessary".[4]

[1] *The Times*, 3 Aug. 1876, dated Therapia, 25 July.
[2] F.O. 78/2462, no. 867, 17 Aug.; 78/2464, 25 Sept.
[3] F.O. 78/2462, no. 915, 27 Aug.   [4] F.O. 78/2463, no. 1016, 15 Sept.

CHAPTER III

THE BULGARIAN ATROCITIES

A tale far more bloody than that of Cawnpore. . . . The atrocities were clearly unnecessary for the suppression of the insurrection, for it was an insignificant rebellion at the best.

Report of EUGENE SCHUYLER, 10 Aug. 1876

To Ahmed Aga and his men belongs the distinction of having committed perhaps the most heinous crime of the present century, Nana Sahib alone having rivalled their deeds.

Report of WALTER BARING, 1 Sept. 1876

We are the trustees of the settlement under which these Bosnians and Bulgarians live.

The Times, 5 Sept. 1876

How the Rising began

EVEN before the Serbs plunged into war, news was slowly trickling westwards, which was soon to transform the situation in England and range public opinion in two passionately opposed camps. The sixties had witnessed a steady growth of national feeling even in Bulgaria, the most down-trodden of all Turkey's European provinces. Under the more efficient rule of Midhat Pasha as Governor of "Roumelia", there were stirrings of educational and literary effort, and a first abortive rising, most cruelly suppressed: and Turkish recognition of the Bulgarian Exarchate in 1870—though mainly intended to sow discord between Slav and Hellene—was a real stimulus to the national cause. Revolutionary committees already existed in Belgrade and Bucarest, and indeed an early statute of one of them proclaimed as its goal a federal Serbo-Bulgar state under the leadership of Michael Obrenović. Levski, the first Bulgarian leader of note, was captured and executed at Sofia in 1873, but in the summer and autumn of 1875 a new central committee was formed at Giurgiu, led by Botjov, Zaimov and Stambulov, and inspired by Bosnia's example, decided to organise an insurrection in Bulgaria. The first attempt, at Stara Zagora in September, was a complete failure: but at the end of April and in the first week of May 1876 there were fresh outbreaks in various villages of the Rhodope mountains and a plot to burn down Philippopolis. The depredations of Turkish irregulars and the intoler-

51

able method of tax collecting had rendered the population desperate
and ready to follow even the foolhardiest leaders: but to-day it is
obvious that the Bulgarians were from the outset foredoomed to utter
failure, since they possessed far fewer resources and an infinitely less
favourable strategic position than that of Bosnia. Within a very few
days it was crushed out with hideous barbarity by hordes of "bashibazuks" and Circassian immigrants who had been settled in Bulgaria
after the Crimean War and had remained a fanatically Moslem and
disturbing element. The last resistance ended with the death of
Hristo Botjev on 19 May and the dispersal of his gallant but quite
unpractical band.[1] Contemporary friends of Turkey, and notably
Sir Henry Elliot, made great play with the fact that it was the
Bulgars who began, and this is undoubtedly true. But if ever there
was a case of "C'est le lapin qui a commencé", it was this, and the
real point is whether gross misgovernment does not render revolt
sooner or later inevitable, and whether a ruling race is justified in
maintaining its rule by wholesale massacre and crime.

London was first roused to a knowledge of these happenings by
three articles published in the *Daily News*,[2] then the leading Liberal
organ and specially famous for its foreign service. In view of the
contemptuous attitude adopted by official spokesmen towards these
revelations, it is necessary to say a few words at the very outset on
the two men with whom they originated. Edwin Pears, who was the
regular correspondent of the *Daily News*, was then a young lawyer
practising at the Constantinople bar, and eventually acquired a high
repute as a writer on Turkish and Near Eastern affairs.[3] MacGahan
was a young Irish American journalist, whom his friend and colleague
Archibald Forbes—himself almost without a peer in his profession—
has deliberately described as "the most brilliant of all war corre-
pondents". He was already the hero of a famous lonely ride to over-
take the army of General Kauffmann in its march across the desert

[1] The best modern account is to be found in Alois Hajek, *Bulgarien unter der
Türkenherrschaft*, pp. 220-92, and in the older Jireček, *Geschichte der Bulgaren*.

[2] 8, 23 and 30 June. The honour of first alluding to the facts, however, belongs to
the *Spectator*, in its article of 3 June entitled "The Bulgarian Insurrection".

[3] See his volumes *Turkey and its People* (1908), *Abdul Hamid* (1917), *Forty Years
in Constantinople* (1916) and his chapters in the *Cambridge Medieval History*. He
was knighted in 1909. In *Forty Years* he writes as follows: "There was no one among
us who hated the Turk as a private man. We all recognised that he had traits of
kindliness, simplicity and generosity which made him lovable. It was only when he
was acting as one in authority, and when the damnable spirit of fanaticism took
possession of him, that he became a savage beast. Even when such spirit was
rampant, it was well under control by the Government" (*op. cit.* p. 60).

to Khiva, and had told the story in his book *Campaigning on the Oxus*. In the next two years he was to cross the Balkans with Gurko, and again with Skobelev, this time in defiance of a broken ankle-bone. Before the war was out, he died at the age of thirty-two, "a martyr of duty and friendship"—these again are the words of Forbes—by nursing an American officer laid up with typhus in a Bulgarian hovel. This Galahad of journalism is assured of his own niche in the history of Balkan liberation.

Needless to say, Disraeli and his colleagues are not to be blamed for not knowing the horoscope of these two men: but stress is laid upon their record, as upon that of Eugene Schuyler later, so that the modern reader may be in no manner of doubt as to the seriousness of the *Daily News* sources. Pears obtained his first information from American missionaries and others connected with Robert College— some of whom were none the less Turcophil enough to regret the publicity which he had given them: while Gallenga, the *Times* corre- spondent in Constantinople, dispatched an identical account of the atrocities to his paper on the very same day, but this was for some reason withheld from publication. It may well be that the Editor's subsequent discovery that the facts which he had suppressed were only too accurate was a potent factor in the noticeable change of opinion in *The Times* that summer and autumn.

Robert College had already begun to play its great part in Near Eastern education, and as a high proportion of its pupils were Bulgarian, information came to its staff—Cyrus Hamlin, Albert Long and George Washburn, men of rare character and energy—such as no other Europeans could have obtained. As Dr. Washburn himself put it, "It was the most natural thing in the world that in their terror and helplessness the Bulgarians should have thought of us, who had no political interests at stake, as friends whom they could trust to help them".[1] They handed on this information in the first instance to Sir Henry Elliot as "a warm personal friend",[2] hoping that he might be able to bring the Turks to reason. But they soon found it necessary to turn to Pears and Gallenga, and publicity followed.

---

[1] *Fifty Years in Constantinople*, pp. 103-4.

[2] This is confirmed by Elliot, who wrote to Derby on 19 July 1876 that "the statements in the *Daily News* have been taken principally from information furnished by the American missionaries" (F.O. 78/2461, no. 757). To Lord Tenterden he wrote of this information as "beyond all question immensely exaggerated" (*ibid*. 20 July). On the other hand, it is well to quote the remark of Walter Baring, in his own defence: "Except the American missionaries, I know no foreigners who speak Bulgarian"—F.O. 78/2463, no. 965, 5 Sept.

DISCUSSIONS IN THE HOUSE OF COMMONS

Disraeli, when questioned in the House of Commons on 26 June, denied the accuracy of the stories and simply assumed that "their object is to create a cry against the Government".[1] But the stream of revelations flowed on both in the *Daily News* and in other newspapers: and on 10 July, in reply to W. E. Forster, he was obliged to admit that there had been "proceedings of an atrocious character in Bulgaria". But he refused to believe that as many as 10,000 persons had been thrown into prison: "In fact, I doubt whether there is prison accommodation for so many, or that torture has been practised on a great scale among an oriental people who seldom, I believe, resort to torture, but generally terminate their connection with culprits in a more expeditious manner".[2]

A week later, abandoning this flippant tone, he gave full quotations from the official correspondence with Sir Henry Elliot: but his bias was apparent from the fact that he warmly defended the Circassians against the name of "irregulars",[3] spoke of the admirable discipline of the Turkish troops, declared that there was "no doubt from the evidence before the House that acts on both sides were equally terrible and atrocious", and quoted Elliot as to "the almost unanimous loyalty shown by the Christians" of Turkey and their "hostility against Serbian aggression". It is to be noted that in the interval between these two discussions Disraeli complained bitterly to Derby of the failure of the Foreign Office to supply him with the necessary accurate information before so critical a debate.

The Opposition were now pressing hotly for further details, Lord Hartington declaring that there was "a strong feeling of the deepest anxiety" in the country:[4] and the question was debated at some length in the House of Commons on 31 July and on 7 and 11 August. On the first of these occasions Gladstone intervened, as the only active survivor of the ministers responsible for the Crimean War, and at once struck a new note. He claimed that that war had substituted

---

[1] Buckle, *op. cit.* vi. p. 43.

[2] Hansard, ccxxxi. p. 1182. The grammar is as in Hansard.

[3] "The men, or the descendants of the men, who twenty years ago commanded the sympathy and admiration of the House of Commons" and who had "lived peaceably for twenty years" on their farms (8 and 17 July—*ibid.* p. 1488). Yet a little later he was quoting Elliot's "evidence that the employment of Circassians and Bashibazuks has led to atrocities which were to be expected" (16 June, to Derby)—*ibid.* p. 1490.   [4] 3 July—Hansard, ccxxx. p. 878.

"a European conscience, expressed by collective guarantee and the concerted and general action of the European Powers, for the sole and individual action of one of them" and had destroyed "the dangerous prerogative" of Russia. On the other hand, he contended that while Russia under an enlightened Tsar—responsible for the emancipation of the serfs—"is not where she stood in 1853". Turkey had not fulfilled her engagements, despite twenty years of unusual calm and had fallen under "a moral blight". For this he quoted "the sorrowful conviction" of no other than Stratford de Redcliffe. He ridiculed the charge that the revolts in Turkey were merely due to foreign instigation ("it is always the foreigner who does it: it was so in Italy"): on the contrary, they were "the reflection of popular opinion". Moreover, it was absurd to deny the possibility of Bosnian autonomy, with a whole series of successful examples before us in Greece, Lebanon, Samos, Serbia, Crete and Roumania. He still desired "if possible the maintenance of Turkish integrity", because "a Southern Slav state is much more easily said than done".

The main stress of the speech was laid upon "the European Concert"—"the greatest of all the results achieved by the Crimean War"—as the sole alternative to "European convulsion"—its unwise abandonment at Berlin being directly responsible for Serbian intervention.[1] It was only as a side issue that he urged a full enquiry, not a sham one, into the alleged atrocities, though he gave some prominence to the story of twelve Hercegovinian refugees who had returned home at the request of the Turkish Government and were then treacherously murdered.

Disraeli at once replied in a tone of some irritation, declining to "enter the politics of the Crimean War" and challenging Gladstone's story of the refugees: and while for the first time admitting any official confirmation of the atrocities—in a dispatch from the British consul at Rushchuk—he now boldly maintained that he "was not justified for a moment to adopt (*sic*) that coffee-house babble brought by an anonymous Bulgarian to a consul".[2] He then went on to justify the Government's objections alike to the action of the six Consuls, to the Andrássy Note and to the Berlin Memorandum, denied that the Serbs had any grievances whatsoever against the Turks—"Serbia required no redress: what Serbia wanted was Provinces, a very differ-

[1] *Ibid.* pp. 174-201.

[2] It does seem extraordinary that so admirable a biographer as Mr. Buckle should, in his zeal for Disraeli, add the comment, "Disraeli was right: it *was* coffee-house babble" (vi. p. 45).

ent thing"—and ended by claiming that the British fleet, whose dispatch was so much criticised, had been sent "to maintain the interests of England and the British Empire, not to bolster up any Power that was falling into decrepitude from its own weakness", and that the other Powers had all ended by adopting our policy of non-intervention.[1]

In the final debate Lord Derby's Under-Secretary, Robert Bourke, made a fairly effective defence of Elliot, but Sir William Harcourt drove him on to the defensive by telling quotations from Elliot, and his consular subordinates Dupuis and Reade, proving excesses by the Circassian irregulars, the terror into which the Balkan villages had been thrown and the intense provocation thereby aroused. He then proceeded to mock at the Prime Minister's "unrivalled powers of humour and sarcasm" as to the absence of Turkish torture; he declared that "they all knew there had been a deliberate plan to exterminate the Christians of Bulgaria", and he denounced the Turkish Government as a "Government tempered by assassination and maintained by massacre".[2] Disraeli was obliged to confess that "on the score of my multifarious duties" he had only seen Reade's dispatch ten days after its arrival,[3] and made the most of the difference between the original rumour of "30,000 slain, 10,000 in prison" —not of course an accurate version of the essential messages of Pears and MacGahan—and "cartloads of heads" and "1000 girls sold as slaves", and the final authenticated figure of 12,000 victims, which, though "a horrible event", could not, even by "a most extravagant abuse of rhetoric", be described as "the depopulation of a province" of 3,700,000 inhabitants. He then reverted to his former note, of our engagements towards Turkey and of the dangers of intervention, claimed that Turkey was "never misled" by the arrival of the fleet, that there was "nothing to justify us in talking in such a vein of Turkey" as in the present debate, and that "our duty at this critical moment is to maintain the Empire of England".[4]

Disraeli admitted privately to Derby that the debate had been "very damaging" for the Government, and that it was "lucky for us ... that the session is dying":[5] and on another occasion, in criticising

---

[1] 3 July—Hansard, ccxxx. pp. 203-14   [2] *Ibid.* pp. 1129, 1135.
[3] He offered to explain privately to W. E. Forster—*ibid.* p. 1096. The decisive dispatch of Reade will be found as no. 500 (18 June) in *Turkey No. III.* (1876). Other alarming dispatches of his, of 25 and 27 May, together with others of 9, 16, 30 May and 9 June, are given as nos. 346, 382, and again 273, 315, 383 and 458.
[4] Hansard, p. 1146.   [5] 7 Aug.—Buckle, vi. p. 46.

the incompetence of the Foreign Office, he told Derby that "had I seen that dispatch of Consul Reade, which never reached me, I would never have made those answers".[1] By February 1877 he was ready to confess publicly that there was "not the slightest doubt that Her Majesty's Government was ill served on that occasion".[2] It seems legitimate to conclude that Disraeli, led away by his Turcophil bias, the existence of which cannot be contested, interpreted the apparent silence of diplomatic and consular agents as conclusive proof that the massacres were a mere mare's nest invented by a factious Opposition, and therefore committed himself to an attitude from which it was difficult to recede and which laid him open to cheap and unjustified charges of inhumanity. Thanks to this deplorable accident the Bulgarian atrocities became—what they never ought to or need have become—a burning issue between the two great parties in the state, with the result that for the next two years major issues of foreign policy came to be considered not on their merits, but from the angle of party prejudice and with a passion and bias such as is almost unequalled in our history since the days of Queen Anne.

It would be easy to devote a whole volume to the Bulgarian controversy, but it must suffice here to summarise as briefly as possible the main facts. During the summer a further mass of details slowly accumulated, and could no longer be ignored. Edwin Pears, the original correspondent whose information Disraeli had so summarily rejected, was reinforced by his American colleague on the *Daily News*, J. A. MacGahan, by the American Consul-General Eugene Schuyler, by Dr. Washburn, of Robert College in Constantinople, Dr. Humphrey Sandwith (one of the British defenders of Kars in 1855), and various American missionaries and other private correspondents of W. E. Forster, Mundella, Evelyn Ashley and other M.P.'s. Finally, on instructions from the Foreign Office, Walter Baring was sent from the Constantinople Embassy to conduct a detailed enquiry on the spot, but it was the original intention of his chief Sir Henry Elliot to send him without any interpreter and to leave him entirely dependent on the good offices of the Turkish authorities. Dr. Washburn, learning this and failing to move Elliot by his remonstrances, went to the American Minister, Maynard, and induced him to dispatch Schuyler on a similar mission.[3] Thus Schuyler and MacGahan arrived on the scene while Baring was still

---

[1] 14 July—*ibid.* p. 44. [2] Hansard, ccxxxii. p. 801.
[3] Washburn, *Fifty Years*, p. 109.

there, and the two enquiries, though quite distinct, supplemented each other.

Schuyler, in his official report to Washington, gave full details as to the burnt villages and estimated the number of victims in the districts he had visited at not less than 15,000. He described "the indiscriminate slaughter" at Batak by bashibazuks under Ahmed Aga: "fully 5000, a very large proportion of them women and children, perished here", most of them being shut up in the village church and burnt alive. "I saw their bones, some with the flesh still clinging to them." Of Panagurishte he says, "this scene of rapine, lust and murder was continued for three days". On the other hand, "no Turkish women or children were killed in cold blood, no Mussulman women violated, no Mussulmans tortured, no purely Turkish village attacked or burnt, no mosque desecrated or destroyed" (Baring, however, saw one burnt Turkish village and mosque).[1] The report of the Turkish commissioner he dismissed as "a tissue of falsehoods".[2] His general verdict was, "a tale far more bloody than that of Cawnpore". What makes Schuyler's evidence all the more weighty is, that he was a man with a long experience of Eastern affairs, the author of an important book on Turkestan, in which Russian practices in Central Asia were very frankly criticised, and that he could not therefore by any stretch of imagination be dismissed as a Russophil or as a mere ignoramus.[3] But it is characteristic of the extreme Turcophils, that while exploiting to the full his strictures on the barbarous Russians in Asia, they poohpooed or discredited his exposure of the civilised Turks in Europe.

One passage in particular deserves to be quoted from Schuyler's book: "It is practically impossible for Russia to withdraw from her position in Central Asia. . . . On the contrary, she will be compelled to advance still further. . . . Notwithstanding the many faults which may be found in the administration, the Russian rule is on the whole beneficial to the natives, and it would be manifestly unjust to them to withdraw her protection and leave them to anarchy and to the unbridled rule of fanatical despots."[4] Several months later he wrote to Mr. Gladstone to express his annoyance

[1] Baring Report—no. 220 of *Turkey No. I.* (1877), p. 164.
[2] Schuyler's Report is printed as Appendix to no. 220 in *op. cit.* and reprinted in *The Turkish Atrocities in Bulgaria*, by J. A. MacGahan (1876).
[3] The *Spectator* (5 Aug. 1876) called him "a man known to all Europe as exceptionally a speaker of truth, a keen observer and one of the extremely limited class allowed, even in America, to be 'aristocrats' ".   [4] *Turkistan*, ii. pp. 388-9.

"that the acts of one man should have been used by unfair writers to bring an accusation against a whole nation. Had I known what subsequent events would be, I should have tried to make it more clear—though I hardly know how I could—that I accused General Kauffmann alone and not Russia." [1]

MacGahan, who accompanied Schuyler on his tour of inspection, flatly challenged Lord Derby's assertion in the House of Lords, that both sides were equally guilty, and wanted to know on what authority he said so, since no agent of the British Government "capable of giving information" had been on the spot till Baring arrived. He insisted that there was no evidence whatever—apart from the impudent inventions of Edib—that "the insurrection was fomented from without", save by the Bulgarian committee at Bucarest: and this is the verdict of modern Bulgarian historians who have collected and sifted the facts. He maintained that "Midhat Pasha and his associates are still hanging and imprisoning these poor people" and that "the Turkish authorities do not even pretend that the inhabitants offered any resistance whatever". [2] As an American and a journalist, he evidently enjoyed making a frontal attack upon Disraeli and Elliot, and argued that the great crime in their eyes "was not to have killed many thousands of innocent people, but to have said there were 30,000 killed when there were only 25,000. . . . It was not much matter to have cut off the heads of a great many people: but to have said that these heads were carried through the streets of Philippopolis, when in reality they were carried in bags and rolled down a street before the house of the Italian Consul in a very different place, is a kind of crime" that they "cannot easily forgive". [3]

Meanwhile Baring, who visited the scene of the massacres with his father-in-law Guarracino, a prominent Levantine—for thirty years in the British consular service, [4] knowing Turkish but no Bulgarian, and known as a philo-Turk—handed in an elaborate report in which every allowance is made for the Turks. None the less, he estimated the number of Bulgarian victims at about 12,000 and of Moslems at 163, and described in all its grisly details the Batak

---

[1] *Gladstone Papers*, 9 Jan. 1877. Layard speaks of Schuyler as a habitual correspondent of Mr. Gladstone: but in reality this was Schuyler's first letter to him, and the *Gladstone Papers* contain only two other letters of his, of 9 March and of 16 May 1877. In the former he writes, "Your kind mention of me in your Taunton speech was the cause of complaint at Washington, and I received a severe reprimand for the liberty of my correspondence". The second is mainly an acknowledgment of *Lessons in Massacre*.   [2] MacGahan, *op. cit.* pp. 25, 37, 84.
[3] *Ibid.* p. 63.   [4] F.O. 78/2461, no. 841, 9 Aug., Elliot to Derby.

massacre, where Ahmed Aga induced the villagers to surrender their
weapons and then set his bashibazuks to "slaughter them like sheep"
and burnt a thousand of them in the church. "I visited this valley
of the shadow of death on 31 July, more than $2\frac{1}{2}$ months after the
massacre, but still the stench was so overpowering that one could
hardly force one's way into the churchyard." [1]

In a private letter to the Ambassador he told how he had seen
"twenty or thirty dogs devouring human bodies" and had counted
sixty-two skulls in about twenty yards—many of them "severed by
hatchets or yataghans". "The whole of the main street was a mass
of human remains, but the most fearful spectacle was the church and
its enceinte: here the corpses lay so thick that one could hardly avoid
treading on them. . . . Altogether I can hardly describe the horror
of the scene." [2] This roused Elliot to declare that Batak "equals or
exceeds in horror" any previous allegations, though he still insisted
that the number of victims was exaggerated. [3] Scepticism was no
longer possible, and Baring, like Schuyler, dismissed the Turkish
official reports as "entirely untrustworthy". [4]

Baring was unfairly attacked by MacGahan for his Turcophil
views and linguistic deficiencies, and defended himself in a vigorous
and convincing statement to his chief. [5] After his official report was
published, criticism was silenced.

In the final debate Evelyn Ashley, on the basis of direct information
from Constantinople, had asserted that the Porte had distributed
fifty decorations among the organisers of the massacre, that Shevket
Pasha, who had ordered the sack of Bazardžik, had been appointed
commander of the Palace Guard, while the humane governor of
Philippopolis had been dismissed: and Baring, while confirming
the Porte's policy of decorations and promotions, pointed out that
Ahmed Aga—whom he compares with Nana Sahib as author of "the
most heinous crime" of the century—had received the Order of the
Medjidieh. [6]

The first attempt at an independent private enquiry into Bulgarian
conditions after the Schuyler and Baring reports was made by
Robert Jasper More in *Under the Balkans*. This describes in very

---

[1] *Turkey No. I.* (1876), no. 220, enclosing Baring's, Schuyler's and 3 Turkish
reports. See esp. pp. 150, 155.
[2] F.O. 78/2461, Baring's letter of 1 Aug. enclosed in no. 840 of Elliot.
[3] *Ibid.* no. 964.   [4] F.O. 78/2463, no. 1071.
[5] *Ibid.* no. 965, 5 Sept., enclosure. But his claim to have started "without pre-
conceived ideas" will not hold water, for he begins his report by assuming that the
rising was fomented by "schemers in Moscow".   [6] *Turkey No. I.* (1876), p. 155.

sober language a visit to the district of Philippopolis in the autumn
of 1876, summarises the various relief work undertaken there,
criticises Mr. Layard's attempt to minimise the outrages and confirms the general conclusions of Baring, declaring that he had "heard
of two men only who differed" from Baring, and both had spent only
a single night in Roumelia! A later chapter describes, on the basis of
information obtained on the spot, the sack of Batak by Ahmed Aga
and his bashibazuks, and closes with his own experiences in one
village after another where massacres had occurred. It is curious that
this book should not have obtained greater publicity at the time.

Lord Derby and Sir Henry Elliot

Disraeli's speech on the atrocities was his last appearance in the
House of Commons. His health could no longer stand the strain, and
after a vain attempt to induce Lord Derby to take over the Premiership,[1] he accepted a peerage and on 12 August entered the Lords as
Earl of Beaconsfield. After Parliament had risen, he strongly urged
upon Derby the advisability of recalling Elliot, who "has many
excellent qualities both moral and intellectual, but no energy", and
whom "as a public servant the nation has utterly condemned".[2]
This view was shared by Lord Salisbury, and by the Queen herself,
who was horrified by the news from Bulgaria and "repeatedly spoke,
wrote and telegraphed on the subject".[3] Derby, however, could not
be won for this step,[4] and Elliot was allowed to remain. But it was
obvious that the country was by now thoroughly roused, and despite
his sluggishness and powers of obstruction—Salisbury said of him
that "making a feather-bed walk is nothing to the difficulty of
making an irresolute man look two inches into the future"[5]—Derby
was peculiarly sensitive to popular opinion.[6] Towards the end of
August, then, he took action which amounted to a distinct modification of policy towards Turkey—an assertion vigorously denied at the

---

[1] See Buckle, v. pp. 492-5.   [2] 15 Aug., to Derby—Buckle, vi. p. 49.
[3] Memo. of Gen. Ponsonby, 8 July—*Letters*, ii. p. 470: "I cannot rest quiet without trying to do something to prevent further atrocities" (Queen to Disraeli, 10 Aug.,
ibid. p. 474).
[4] Professor Temperley, in his interesting pamphlet *The Bulgarian and other
Atrocities* (British Academy, vol. xvii), p. 15, refers to further letters on this point,
in addition to those printed by Mr. Buckle.
[5] Sept. 1876—Lady G. Cecil, *Life of Salisbury*, ii. p. 89.
[6] That keen observer of our affairs, M. Gavard, had on 10 April 1875 written of
him as "cet homme d'état essentiellement attentif à l'expression de l'opinion du
pays" (*D.D.F.* i. no. 380).

time, but proved up to the hilt by the documents. He warned Elliot, first by wire on 22 August and then more fully on 5 September, that "any sympathy previously felt in England towards Turkey has been completely destroyed by the lamentable occurrences in Bulgaria . . . and to such a pitch has indignation in all classes of English society risen . . . that in the extreme case of Russia declaring war against Turkey, H.M.G. would find it practically impossible to interfere in defence of the Ottoman Empire".

Such an event, by which the nation's sympathies would be brought into direct opposition to its treaty engagements, "would place England in a most unsatisfactory and even humiliating position", but the contingency might arise.[1] Of this dispatch Derby wrote on the same day to his chief, "I have warned the Turk in plain terms". It is clear that Derby's own feelings were outraged by the revelations, whereas the Prime Minister, as late as 2 September, was writing of the "atrocities" in inverted commas and regarded them mainly as something that "will permit us to dictate to the Porte", enable Britain to take the lead in peacemaking and so "make the excited 'Public' forget or condone the Elliotiana".[2] His own utmost concession to public opinion was to publish a brief letter in *The Times* of 7 September: "I was perfectly grave when I replied that I was sceptical as to such occurrences" [as the charge of 10,000 Bulgarians "submitted to torture"], "as massacre, not torture, was the custom of an oriental[3] people". This had evoked "a single laugh" in the House: "I hope the misplaced laughter of another is no proof of the levity of your obedient servant".

Derby seems to have warmed to his work, for his first telegram was followed by two others, on 25 and 28 August, in which he warned the Porte to make peace speedily, in order to avert intervention by the Powers, "the consequences of which might be fatal to Turkey", and then went on to protest "against the cruelty displayed" in the execution of Bulgarian insurgents.[4] All this, be it noted, on the very eve of the second Turkish Revolution.

Meanwhile the earlier wire evoked a reply from Elliot which illustrates perhaps better than any contemporary document the mentality not only of our Ambassador, but of the average British Turcophil. After assuring Lord Derby that he had "over and over

---

[1] *Turkey No. I.* (1877), no. 159.   [2] To Northcote—Buckle, vi. p. 51.
[3] He had, he said, used the adjective "oriental", not "historical", as was usually quoted in the press. Hansard, however, gives the correct version.
[4] *Turkey No. I.* (1877), nos. 78 and 105.

again" entered strong protests at the Porte, he continued: "To the accusation of being a blind partisan of the Turks, I will only answer that my conduct here has never been guided by any sentimental affection for them, but by a firm determination to uphold the interests of Great Britain to the utmost of my power; and that those interests are deeply engaged in preventing the disruption of the Turkish Empire is a conviction which I share in common with the most eminent statesmen who have directed our foreign policy, but which appears now to be abandoned by shallow politicians or persons who have allowed their feelings of revolted humanity to make them forget the capital interests involved in the question. We may and must feel indignant at the needless and monstrous severity with which the Bulgarian insurrection was put down, but the necessity which exists for England to prevent changes from occurring here which would be most detrimental to ourselves, *is not affected by the question whether it was 10,000 or 20,000 persons who perished in the suppression. We have been upholding what we know to be a semicivilised nation,* liable under certain circumstances to be carried into fearful excesses: but the fact of this having just now been strikingly brought home to us all cannot be a sufficient reason for abandoning a policy which is the only one that can be followed with a due regard to our own interests."[1]

This was too much for Derby, who replied that "the Porte cannot afford to contend with the public opinion of other countries", and "no political considerations would justify the toleration of such acts": "ample reparation" must therefore be made.[2] But Elliot was incorrigible and in a letter to Lord Granville pushed the argument even further: "While execrating the atrocities as much as anyone, I confess that I very greatly regret the tone in which the question has been taken up in England, for it is impossible to calculate the evil that must result from it. If our traditional policy towards this country had been dictated by a mere sentimental affection for the Turks, what has just occurred might be sufficient reason for changing it, but if, as I hold in common with all Foreign Ministers up to the present time, it was the policy which a consideration of our own interests renders imperative, it cannot be abandoned without sacrificing them."[3]

[1] *Ibid.* no. 221, 4 Sept.   [2] *Ibid.* no. 316, 21 Sept.
[3] 29 Sept. 1876—cit. Temperley, *op. cit.* p. 25. This passage was quoted in the House of Commons during the debate of 23 March 1877 upon Sir Henry Elliot, and was undoubtedly one of the main grounds for his not returning to the Constantinople post.

The question of Elliot's attitude to the atrocities was raised in the House of Commons and debated in considerable detail: and as it was made clear that the Opposition would actively protest against his returning to his post at Constantinople, he was allowed to succeed Sir Andrew Buchanan at Vienna, and Mr. Layard, an even more pronounced Turcophil, was sent in his place. A comparison of the facts known to contemporaries with what only became known in our own day leads to the very definite conclusion that his official defender Robert Bourke, the Under-Secretary, confused two charges which should really be kept quite distinct—first, that he showed callousness towards the atrocities; second, that he openly took the Turkish side on the major issues. The first can be definitely dismissed, for the second there is overwhelming proof: in other words, his personal honour is not in question, but his political bias must be admitted.

The first hint of excesses in Bulgaria came in a dispatch of Hutton Dupuis, British Vice-Consul at Philippopolis, dated 9 May,[1] and this was sent home by Elliot. On 24 May he reported having made "strong representations" to the Porte against the use of bashibazuks.[2] On 8 June he reported that the rising had been suppressed "with cruelty and in some places brutality" and again blamed the bashibazuks.[3] On 19 June he reported having again complained to the Grand Vizier as to "an unarmed population at the mercy of hordes of those savages".[4] On 6 July he reported having made constant remonstrances "for weeks past" and added a warning as to the danger of fresh barbarities in Serbia. These facts were laid before the House by Bourke and not challenged, and Elliot's two dispatches had been quoted by Disraeli at an earlier debate and were eventually published.[5]

On the other hand, certain passages from two dispatches of Dupuis, throwing doubt on the statements of a Turkish commander and hinting at designs of deliberate extermination, were omitted from the Blue Books, though initialled and even underlined by Elliot when he transmitted them. The responsibility for this would seem to lie with Lord Tenterden, the Permanent Under-Secretary. Elliot also toned down many of the consular reports before publication, and notably the account of the gross treachery of the Bosnian Vizier towards the insurgent chiefs at the time of their negotiations with the six consuls;

[1] See *Turkey No. III.* (1876). See also Disraeli's statement on 17 July—Hansard, ccxxx. p. 1487.　　　　[2] *Ibid.* p. 212.　　　　[3] *Ibid.* p. 267.
[4] *Ibid.* p. 344.　　　　[5] 6 and 14 July.

the worst details of the Popovo massacre, and the fact that Elliot in so many words ascribed to the Sultan himself the orders for the employment of bashibazuks and a refusal to consider foreign remonstrances.[1]

The main criticism against Elliot has centred round his alleged suppression of Dupuis' dispatch of 23 June, containing the essential passage: "It is estimated that some 12,000 innocent men, women and children have been massacred, hundreds of young women carried off and dishonoured and some 60 villages more or less completely burnt, and the country between Philippopolis and Tatar Bazardzik plundered".

Dupuis sent this in duplicate to the Ambassador and to his own immediate chief, the Consul-General Sir Philip Francis, and Elliot at a later date maintained that this was "improperly withheld" from him "and given to the correspondent of the *Daily News*":[2] in a minute addressed to the Foreign Office in 1879 he formally denied having seen the document at the time. Both he and Layard suspected Francis of a conspiracy against him, and it seems to be true that Francis was in sympathy and close contact with Pears, Schuyler, MacGahan and Gallenga, the leaders of the atrocity campaign in Constantinople itself. None the less, Mr. E. B. Malet, the Embassy official who was instructed by the Foreign Office to enquire into the whole matter, reached the conclusion that the suppression was accidental, and that Francis had assumed Elliot to be in possession of a duplicate or of similar intelligence. The evidence for malicious suppression is not convincing, for Elliot is seen to have been in possession of all the essential facts, even if that one dispatch did not reach him. Special weight attaches to the opinion of Dr. Washburn, who went to Pears because he regarded Elliot as too inactive. On 10 September Washburn spontaneously assured the Ambassador that "the vigorous protests which you made at the time saved the greater part of the Tuna vilayet from the same fate as the province of Philippopolis" and that he was "entitled to gratitude rather than abuse".[3]

Meanwhile Professor Temperley has succeeded in showing that Elliot received two other dispatches from Dupuis, of 7 May and

---

[1] This was in a telegram of 29 January 1876. These and similar details are summarised for the first time, very clearly and succinctly, by Professor Temperley, *op. cit.* App. I. pp. 27-32.

[2] Elliot, *Some Revolutions*, p. 260.

[3] F.O. 78/2464, enclosure in no. 1048, 23 Sept.

12 June, stating that the Turks were "hunting down and shooting all Bulgarians indiscriminately" and that "human nature recoils at the barbarities" recounted, but that he omitted to send either of these to London, or again Brophy's dispatch from Burgas early in June, reporting a massacre of 2000. Quite apart from these, however, a perusal of the Blue Books themselves proves that Consul Reade sent warnings on 25 and 27 May as to the arming of the Circassians and their notoriously lawless character[1]—received in London on 2 and 7 June—and a further warning on 18 June as to "atrocities" (the actual word) by these Circassians, "a state of greatest terror" in the Balkan villages and the boasts of irregulars—overhead, it is true, in cafés, but accepted by Reade as true.[2] This only reached London on 28 June, but even then was admittedly not acted upon till 13 July. It is also quite clear that Pears sent his first decisive information to the *Daily News* a whole week before Dupuis' dispatch of 23 June, and that he obtained it from two American missionaries, and not from Dupuis.[3] Hence the importance of what is sometimes called "the missing dispatch of Dupuis" would seem to have been much exaggerated,[4] especially as there are passages from other dispatches no less incriminating for the Porte. On 9 July he wrote to Elliot: "Edib Effendi expressed to Bulgarian notables of Philippopolis his astonishment at the fact that so few atrocities were committed by his countrymen during the recent troubles, considering the great excitement produced among them by the Bulgarian movement. What are the horrors he expected to witness, it is difficult to understand."[5] In passing Dupuis refers to "judicial torture" as "a common practice against Bulgarian political prisoners". On 20 July he reported that "many Bulgarians were hanged for defending their homes and families against the bashibazuks", but that "not one of the latter was punished for the atrocities committed on innocent men, women and children".[6]

At the time Sir Henry Elliot undoubtedly had to submit to much unfair criticism: Freeman's wild language is an extreme instance. But the account which he himself has left us of these happenings

[1] *Turkey No. II.* (1876), nos. 346, 382.   [2] *Ibid.* no. 500.
[3] Pears, *Forty Years in Constantinople*, pp. 16-21.
[4] All that can be said on this whole incident will be found in Appendix II. of *Bulgarian and Other Atrocities*, by H. W. V. Temperley, pp. 32-6; and in *Vice-Consul Dupuis' "Missing" Dispatch of 23 June 1876*, by W. N. Medlicott (*Journal of Modern History*, vol. iv. no. 1).
[5] F.O. 78/1461, enclosed in no. 757, Elliot to Derby.
[6] *Ibid.* enclosed in no. 801, 30 July, Elliot to Derby.

reveals its bias and prejudice on every page, and nothing is more unjust than his assumption that "Gladstone's conscience was not tender" and "his language on the subject altogether unscrupulous". He misunderstood Disraeli no less seriously: for long afterwards he told Dr. Washburn that "on one occasion the Prime Minister produced what appeared like a telegram in the House of Commons and declared that he had a telegram from Sir Henry Elliot, saying that the alleged atrocities were gross exaggerations, and adding words which created the impression that Sir Henry was the defender of the abomination of the Turks and the Circassians".

Elliot warmly denied ever having sent such a telegram and said "that the importance which the public attached to this imaginary telegram placed him in the difficulty of deciding whether he should remain under the imputation . . . or should state the fact and thus throw the responsibility upon Mr. Disraeli".[1]

This almost certainly rested on a misapprehension, for there is no evidence whatsoever of Disraeli having played such a trick. The worst that can be said of him, as of Elliot himself in this connection, is that they were openly and incurably predisposed in favour of the Turks. That Elliot was very credulous, and at the same time very obstinate, is shown by the fact that to the end of his life he believed the fable that the insurrection "had been planned and fomented by Russian agents", and that Baring had proved this in his report.[2] Elliot was in poor health throughout 1876, and it may well be that the anxieties of the situation and the often unfair criticism to which he was subjected got upon his nerves and led him into imaginary grievances against his chief and his opponents alike.

His reaction against the charges of indifference, however, was very strong. On 9 August he assured Derby, "It is impossible for me to use stronger language than I have employed about the atrocities in Bulgaria".[3] He keenly resented "the insinuation that H.M.'s Embassy did nothing to prevent these atrocities. . . . A fouler calumny was never invented. . . . From the very first moment of the employment of bashibazuks and of the arming of the Mussulman populations, I protested against the measure. . . . Over and over again I called the attention of the Turkish ministers to them, and sometimes did so in language much stronger than is common in diplomatic usage, and I confess that I have felt a certain indignation at finding myself

[1] Pears, *Forty Years*, p. 21, and *Turkey and its People*, pp. 211-12.
[2] Elliot, *Some Revolutions*, p. 267.   [3] F.O. 78/1461, no. 839.

represented as personally responsible for them, as though Turkey was a British colony and I was the Governor of it. . . ."[1]

But while giving vent to his just indignation, the Ambassador continued to warn his Government against those who advocated British protection of "Christians against their oppressors". "I must", he wrote, "be allowed to repeat that any attempt to drive the Turks back will prove the utter destruction of whole Christian populations. Their expulsion could be readily effected by large European armies, but those little know the character of this people who can suppose that they would retire without massacring every man, woman and child and reducing the whole country to a desert. It is easy enough to say that the Turks must be driven out of such and such a province, but if those who advocate it were at all aware of what it would entail upon the Christians both in Europe and Asiatic Turkey, they would hardly speak of it so lightly."[2]

He firmly opposed autonomy for Bosnia: "nothing could be more chimerical than the supposition that Mussulmans and Christians—the latter being divided between Catholic and Orthodox and animated by feelings of jealousy and aversion—should live in harmony under an automatic system". But he was equally opposed to autonomy for Bulgaria, pointing out that the outrages had for the most part taken place south of the Balkan range, but that "south of the Balkans no natural line could be found, and the large Bulgarian populations would be left in a state of perpetual discontent at their exclusion from the autonomic arrangements made in favour of their country-men north of the mountains. The Turks will never entertain the idea of granting an independent administration to a province over which, with a view to the defence of their Danubian frontier, it is essential for them to have direct control, and if the question should unfortunately be raised by persons of influence in England, the future tranquillity of the province will be rendered more precarious than ever."[3] In a word, Elliot was opposed to the only solution which could bring appeasement, yet had no remedy of his own to suggest: he strongly deprecated violent criticism of the Turks, yet himself credited the Turks with a mentality which might be said to justify the more extreme critics.

Gladstone, for his part, persistently refrained from attacking Elliot. On 31 July 1876 in the House he declared the Ambassador to have

---

[1] F.O. 78/2463, no. 966, 4 Sept.   [2] *Ibid.* no. 1008, 14 Sept.
[3] *Ibid.* no. 999, 13 Sept.

"discharged his duties, as he always does, in the spirit of an honourable and enlightened Christian diplomatist".[1] In the debate of 27 March 1877 he again paid tribute to Elliot's high character, declined to charge him with "misconduct", and fully agreed that he made "constant, earnest and forcible representations" to the Porte, "when he became conscious of the facts" (this last being doubtless intended as a qualifying phrase).

In the interval there had been a sharp passage of arms between the two men, Gladstone resenting Elliot's inferences from the famous Bulgarian pamphlet, and when he got no satisfaction, sending the letters to the press. "I then understand you [wrote Mr. Gladstone] to charge upon me the idiotic proposal that the civil and military servants of the Porte should be corporally ejected from Bulgaria, without any provision against their going into Macedonia or Thessaly or other neighbouring provinces of Turkey. I cannot but be grateful for the distinguished compliment you have thus paid to my understanding."[2]

Elliot gracefully redeemed the situation by writing on the day after publication, "I can assure you that I have been throughout sensible of the manner in which, while criticising as you were entitled to do the course followed by the Government and myself in the affairs of Turkey, you have avoided everything of a personal nature or that implied any reflection upon my character".[3] But the extract already quoted from his memoirs suggests that Elliot none the less continued to bear a grudge: and it may well be that he was influenced by the anti-Gladstonian obsession of his friend and successor Layard, in making so uncalled-for a statement.[4]

Gladstone, then, while sparing Elliot's person, adhered all the more firmly to the view that "the opinions which he holds" unfitted him to represent Britain at Constantinople, and that those opinions, as expressed in his famous dispatch of 4 September,[5] were "a precise contradiction of the position of Lord Derby". In this Gladstone was unquestionably right, and as on previous occasions he raised the discussion to an altogether higher plane when he asked, "What is to be the consequence to civilisation and humanity, to public order, if British interests are to be the rule for British agents all over the world, and are to be for them the measure of right or wrong?"

[1] Hansard, ccxxx. p. 189.
[2] Letters of 26, 27 and 28 Feb. in *The Times* of 1 March.
[3] 2 March, Elliot to Gladstone—*Gladstone Papers.*
[4] See *infra*, pp. 207, 213, 355, 359.   [5] Quoted *supra*, p. 63.

Every other Power would naturally be free to take the same line, and "I, sir, will not lose the right to protest against the assertion of such a doctrine by France, Austria, Germany or Russia".

It would be well if we could leave the whole deplorable controversy on this note: but it is now necessary to trace the course of the unparalleled agitation in the country.

THE ATROCITY AGITATION

The revelations of Edwin Pears and MacGahan came as a severe shock to public opinion in England; the seeming indifference of the Government and the long delay in providing official information had an even more disturbing effect: and the debates of 31 July and 7 and 11 August may be said to have roused the whole country. The *Spectator* as early as 15 July had foretold that as the result of Disraeli's levity "England will be all aflame". The state of feeling is admirably reflected in the rising crescendo of *The Times*, which as early as the 2nd agreed with Mr. Gladstone that Turkey was suffering from "impotence" and described it as "the most hopeless of all political maladies". Quoting the American missionaries as impartial witnesses in the matter of the atrocities, it affirmed that "doubt prevails only in those minds which will admit no fact of which there is not official evidence, and which instinctively reject all extraneous testimony as 'coffee-house babble'".[1] Six days later it dismissed the official Turkish report of Edib Effendi as "vague and evasive" and as "an impudent romance", and blamed the Constantinople Embassy for its credulity. It declared that "in our own age we must turn to Ashantee or Dahomey for anything similar" to the Bulgarian outrages. "It is time", it warned Mr. Bourke, "that the Government should be made aware that the more worthy part of English society was deeply pained by the frivolity of the Prime Minister's speech, as well as by the evident desire to diminish or excuse what had happened." It described Disraeli's attack on Serbia as "more epigrammatic than exhaustive", drew for the first time a comparison between Serbia and Piedmont and challenged the view that the Turks should be allowed to return there. It is most significant that on the very day when Mr. Disraeli's peerage formed the subject of the first leader, a second should have declared it impossible to reconcile the Prime Minister's language "with the facts on record", and should have preferred "the

[1] *The Times*, 2 Aug. 1876.

Under-Secretary in his agreement with facts to the Prime Minister in contradiction with them". The atrocities had "deprived the Porte of the good will of England", and "if the maintenance of Turkish integrity means a grant of licensed impunity to bashibazuks . . . our efforts cannot be directed to uphold it". A few days later it was comparing events in Bulgaria with the massacres of Chios in 1822 and of Syria in 1860, and declaring that "Turkey still remains the same". A later leader insisted quite logically on the impossibility of putting her victims back under the yoke, and added, "It is better at once to recognise that this grand theory about the necessity of repressing the Slavic nationality is unsound in policy as it is cynically selfish".

Opinion all over the country was moving rapidly on similar lines. The evidence adduced in Parliament was already sufficient and was now supplemented by circumstantial statements from Bulgaria itself, made public by Sir Charles Dilke,[1] and later in the month by Mr. Schuyler's first report. A few voices were raised, arguing that the Porte "had neither the leisure nor the means to be scrupulous in its choice of agents", and that the prompt stamping out of the rising had averted "a war of races, intensified by religious rancour". This plea was openly put forward in *The Times* by Admiral Sir Adolphus Slade, who till 1868 had been naval adviser to the Turks.[2]

Public opinion in the seventies, however, had not been glutted with such horrors as the wholesale Armenian massacres of the nineties or of the Great War, and reacted keenly to the irrefutable evidence before it. Lord Salisbury freely admitted that "the country was roused", and the Queen records in her diary on 23 August "the dreadful excitement and indignation" kindled by the clamour in the press. But the opportunist attitude of the Government deprived the country of a clear lead, there was a chorus of conflicting views in the daily press and in the vast stream of pamphlet literature, often of the most vituperative or emotional nature, and Lord Granville could ask himself which force was strongest, "hatred of Russia or of Turkey".[3]

[1] *The Times*, 16 Aug.
[2] See his letter in *The Times* of 22 Aug. and rejoinder of "Constantinopolitan" on 25 Aug. As a young naval lieutenant on 4 Oct. 1834, Slade had submitted to Lord Palmerston a report on the fortifications of the Bosphorus, assuming *the near dissolution of Turkey and advocating a British seizure of the Chersonese (i.e.* the Crimea) as "a share of the wreck"!! See V. J. Puryear, *England, Russia and the Straits Question*, p. 113.
Slade was succeeded as naval adviser by Hobart Pasha, who had had an adventurous career hunting slave-traders on the African coast and running the American blockade on behalf of the Confederates.
[3] Fitzmaurice, *Life of Granville*, i. p. 165.

A perusal of the contemporary press shows that the first reaction of opinion in August was a greatly increased support for the humanitarian societies already engaged in Balkan relief work: and a fresh staff of surgeons and doctors from St. Thomas's left for Belgrade under Colonel Loyd-Lindsay,[1] with the open approval of Florence Nightingale. Nor is it possible to study the press without realising that the agitation far transcended any party lines, and that though nothing could have brought the two front benches together at this stage, Liberals and Conservatives in almost every town and borough of the United Kingdom vied with each other in repudiating Turkey and all her works.

It has been repeatedly asserted that the whole agitation was the work of Gladstone and was ruthlessly exploited by him for mere party ends: but in actual fact he remained quite in the background during July and August; in his speech of 31 July he treated the massacres as an entirely subordinate question and expressly declined to attack Elliot: and Derby's dispatches, above quoted, had already been sent off and the campaign of public meetings was in full swing before he entered the lists in earnest.

Apart from isolated meetings at Darlington, the home of W. T. Stead and the *Northern Echo*, the real campaign started with a working men's meeting at Hackney on 29 August, and that in the eight days between the publication of Gladstone's famous pamphlet meetings of protest were held in the following places—Nottingham, Stoke, Norwich, Halifax, Woolwich, Sunderland, Birmingham, Rochdale, Sheffield, Mile End, Brighton, Devonport, Hartlepool, Aston, Oldham, Dundee, Bangor, Burnley, Leicester, Wolverhampton, Plymouth, Newport, Newark, Leeds, Southampton—in addition to others in Scotland and lesser meetings not reported in the press. W. T. Stead, who first came into prominence at this time as a fervent Turcophobe agitator, has described what followed with all his habitual over-emphasis and shrillness of note. It was, he affirmed, "the first agitation in the long annals of England, in which the Democracy sprang to its feet by an instantaneous impulse, without waiting for the guidance of its leaders, in order to compel a reluctant and hostile administration to repudiate the traditional policy of the Empire".[2] Stripped of rhetoric, this means that the Government was faced by a

[1] M.P. and chairman of National Society for Aid to Sick and Wounded in War. Miss Emily Guest and two doctors from Bart.'s went out for the League in Aid of the Christians of Turkey.
[2] *The M.P. for Russia*, i. p. 247.

spontaneous outburst of indignation throughout Britain, and this stands beyond all question, to the eternal credit of the country.

The first Liberal statesman who openly called for action would appear to have been the veteran Lord Russell—long since in retirement—who in a letter to Lord Granville, written for publication, urged that we ought, *through the British fleet*, "to insist on instant termination to the atrocities". "Ultimately, if we cannot keep the Turks from being barbarous and cruel, we might ally ourselves with Russia and concert means to accomplish our objects."[1]

Of the active Liberal leaders, Lord Hartington had been most cautious and faint-hearted in his criticism of Disraeli, and Sir Charles Dilke's speech of 16 August stood almost alone, until supplemented a fortnight later by the invective of Mr. Mundella at Sheffield.[2]

GLADSTONE INTERVENES

It none the less remains true that though Gladstone did not enter the lists till the crowd was already swaying with excitement, it was his pamphlet on *Bulgarian Horrors*, published on 6 September, which acted as a clarion call to the movement: it appeared at the exact psychological moment, and though hurriedly written during a fit of lumbago and full of rhetoric and guess-work, it rested on the solid foundation of fact provided by Pears and MacGahan, and when hot upon it came the Baring Report—which he had *not* seen—its effect was naturally all the greater, and it gave the lead for which men were waiting.

That Gladstone acted on his own responsibility, though he was in close touch with his friend and acknowledged chief Granville, is clearly shown in one of his letters to the latter, prompted by the *Spectator's* demand that the Bulgarian massacres should be made an issue at the Bucks bye-election, created by Disraeli's withdrawal to the Lords. "Good ends", he writes in highly characteristic vein, "can rarely be attained in politics without passion, and there is now, the first time for a good many years, a virtuous passion. I am much struck with the indications of feeling that the post (as well as the newspapers) brings me daily. . . . I am in half, perhaps a little more

[1] *The Times*, 4 Aug.
[2] Disraeli, he declared, had "demoralised English politics": he was "unequalled as a satirist and an epigrammatist, unrivalled in audacity and tergiversation"— "the parent of that elastic Toryism which was as bewildering to friends as to opponents"—*Ibid*. 16 Aug.

than half, a mind to write a pamphlet: mainly on the ground that parliamentary action was all but ousted. Does this shock you?"[1] This was as late as 29 August: then spurred into action by overflowing feeling, "with some difficulty on account of lumbago, which made my body creak as I tried to write, but at length I performed the task in bed with pillow-props, in two or three days".

Presumably Lord Granville was *not* shocked, for he contented himself with advising against a dedication of the pamphlet to Lord Russell as "too late"—doubtless in the knowledge that the veteran statesman might die at any moment.[2] "Pray be merciful to Elliot," he added as an afterthought, and at this stage Gladstone respected his wish.

Passages from the pamphlet have often been quoted, yet a summary of its main arguments cannot be omitted from the present narrative. The nation, he contended, had for a whole year been kept without adequate information as to Eastern events, despite constant appeals in Parliament: "it will now have to speak through its Government, but . . . it must first teach its Government, almost as it would a lisping child, what to say". In face of the Bulgarian horrors, the great question is, "what can be done to punish or to brand or to prevent". He then proceeded to sketch "what the Turkish race was and is"—"a tremendous incarnation of military power", resting on force and leaving "a broad line of blood . . . wherever they went, but now suffering from a decay of martial energy": and here he took care to distinguish between Islam as a whole and the Turks in particular. The Crimean War had given Turkey twenty years of repose, but the insurrection of 1875 "disclosed the total failure of the Porte to fulfil its engagements". The British Government had been very remiss, its information "deplorably inefficient", and the effect of the Prime Minister's pronouncements was to lay the responsibility for events upon "certain invaders of Bulgaria", to suggest that the atrocities were "fairly divided" between Christians and Circassians, to absolve the Turkish Government from all share, and to "mitigate and soften as much as possible . . . the whole devilish enginery of crime". In such circumstances the *Daily News* had rendered a great service, and the Schuyler report had clinched matters.

One very common argument used by Disraeli and his supporters —that Serbia had no direct grievance against Turkey and had no

[1] *Granville Papers*—29 Aug. 1876, Gladstone to Granville.
[2] *Gladstone Papers*—1 Sept., Granville to Gladstone.

business to concern herself with the rising next door—was most effectively refuted by Gladstone. "It would have been as reasonable for the thirteen colonies of America in 1782 to negotiate separately for peace with Great Britain, as it would be for Europe in 1876 to allow that in a settlement with Turkey the five cases of Servia, Bosnia, Herzegovina, Montenegro and Bulgaria should be dealt with otherwise than as the connected limbs of one and the same transaction."

Gladstone laid down three great aims, "to put a stop to the anarchical misrule", to prevent "the recurrence of outrages" by administrative reform, and "to redeem the honour of the British name, which in the deplorable events of the year has been more gravely compromised than I have known it to be at any former period". He still desired to uphold the territorial integrity of Turkey, but protested against Disraeli's pleas for the *status quo* and Bourke's "trumpet-tongued silence" on reform ("Indignation is froth, except as it leads to action") and advocated pressure upon Turkey by "United Europe", as something which Turkey had never in modern times been able to resist. And then came the famous peroration which has been so often quoted and yet cannot well be omitted here, if only as a specimen of Gladstonian eloquence. "An old servant of the Crown and State, I entreat my countrymen, upon whom far more than perhaps any other people of Europe it depends, to require and insist that our Government, which has been working in one direction, shall work in the other, and shall apply all its vigour to concur with other states of Europe in obtaining the extinction of the Turkish executive power in Bulgaria. Let the Turks now carry away their abuses in the only possible manner, namely by carrying off themselves. Their Zaptiehs and their Mudirs, their Bimbashis and their Yuzbachis, their Kaimakams and their Pashas, one and all, bag and baggage, shall, I hope, clear out from the province they have desolated and profaned. This thorough riddance, this most blessed deliverance, is the only reparation we can make to the memory of those heaps on heaps of dead; to the violated purity alike of matron, of maiden and of child; to the civilisation which has been affronted and shamed; to the laws of God, or if you like, of Allah; to the moral sense of mankind at large. There is not a criminal in an European gaol, there is not a cannibal in the South Sea Islands, whose indignation would not arise and overboil at the recital of that which has been done, which has too late been examined, but which remains unavenged; which has left behind all the foul and all the fierce passions that produced it, and which may again spring up in another murderous harvest, from the soil soaked and reeking with blood and in the air tainted with every imaginable deed of crime and shame. That such things should be done once, is a damning disgrace to the portion of our race which did them; that a door should be left open for their repetition would spread that shame over the whole. Better, we may justly tell the Sultan, almost any inconvenience, difficulty or loss associated with Bulgaria,

> Than thou reseated in thy place of light,
> The mockery of thy people and their bane.

We may ransack the annals of the world, but I know not what research can furnish us with so portentous an example of the fiendish misuse of the powers established by God 'for the punishment of evil-doers and for the encouragement of them that do well'. No Government ever has so sinned; none has so proved itself incorrigible in sin, or which is the same, so impotent for reformation. If it be allowable that the executive power of Turkey should renew at this great crisis, by permission or authority of Europe, the charter of its existence in Bulgaria, then there is not on record since the beginnings of political society a protest that man has lodged against intolerable misgovernment, or a stroke he has dealt at loathsome tyranny, that ought not henceforward to be branded as a crime."

It is a curious fact that the phrase which of all others caught the public ear—"bag and baggage"—was not Gladstone's own, but was borrowed from an early dispatch of no other than the redoubtable Stratford Canning,[1] whose Crimean record has obscured the fact that he rose to fame as an ardent Philhellene and played a decisive part in the emancipation of Greece. This, it may be presumed, was not a pure accident: for the pamphlet was dedicated to no other than the Great Eltchi himself, now an octogenarian and crippled with gout, but still clear in intellect and able to write to *The Times*. That he of all men was proud to associate himself with Mr. Gladstone was specially galling to the Turcophils. "My feelings naturally go with yours", Stratford wrote to Gladstone, "on the subject of Turkish misrule. Whatever shades of difference appear in our opinions may be traced to your having made Bulgaria the main object of your

---

[1] In a letter to his cousin, George Canning, 29 Sept. 1821. See Lane Poole, *Life of Stratford de Redcliffe*, i. p. 307.

appeal, whereas the whole Eastern Question was my theme, and
the Bulgarian atrocities, execrable as they were, only a part of it. My
diplomatic habits may also have led me to shed a few drops of oil on
the angry surges of indignation which were roaring on every side,
to the credit no doubt of our noble-hearted people, but not without
danger to the adoption of practicable remedies. I believe you are
aware of my impression that the present formidable crisis would not
have arisen had England in the first instance taken part with the
other Powers. Not that I conceive Russia to be *always* and *fully*
trustworthy, but it seems to me that she was so circumstanced then
as to be open to the full bearing of our moral influence." [1]

Lord Stratford simultaneously wrote a letter to *The Times*,
advocating joint pressure by the Powers, a mixed commission to
superintend reforms and the formation of a chain of tributary
provinces from the Black Sea to the Adriatic.[2] *The Times* in its
comments claimed that Lord Stratford "only fulfilled the spirit of
his chief" Lord Palmerston, "in declaring that the time has come
when another point of departure must be taken in the Eastern
Question". Even if this is to be regarded as an attempt to "save the
face" of British policy during the previous fifty years, it is certainly
a remarkable sign of the changed course of central opinion in England,
under stress of the "Bulgarian horrors".

The Times in criticising Mr. Gladstone's indictment of Turkey, as
"precipitating what is perhaps the most extraordinary issue ever
presented for the decision of statesmanship", asked whether it was
"prudent to frame such tremendous premisses": and this evoked a
letter of Mr. Gladstone himself,[3] explaining that his plea for the
expulsion of the Turks was "*strictly limited to military and official
Turks*" (hence the list of offices such as Zaptiehs and Bimbashis), and
that in his view the Moslems had exactly the same rights as the
Christians.

Even Gladstone's declared enemies could not deny that there was
a certain crusading trait in his character, and the spirit which had
inspired his exposure of Neapolitan prisons now kindled in the cause
of the downtrodden Christians of the East. The great Blackheath
speech with which he followed up his pamphlet reflected the same
spirit: and behind all the eloquence—his critics called it verbosity—

---

[1] *Gladstone Papers*, Stratford de Redcliffe to Gladstone, 10 Sept. 1876.   See also
Morley, *Life of Gladstone*, ii. p. 555.   [2] *The Times*, 9 Sept. 1876.
[3] *Ibid.* 9 Sept.

there was now a concrete demand for "the extinction of the Turkish executive power in Bulgaria". Nor were Bosnia and Montenegro forgotten, and two months later he devoted a special essay to "The Hellenic Factor in the Eastern Problem".

While then "a burning and innate hatred of all cruelty and oppression"[1] was the chief motive in Gladstone and blended with a fuller insight into Near Eastern problems than was possessed by his opponents, personal animosity towards Disraeli also played its part. He confessed to his friend the Duke of Argyll a suspicion "that Dizzy's crypto-Judaism has had to do with his policy".[2] When Disraeli went to the Lords, Gladstone felt that he "had better be mute about him and his influence generally, except as to a full acknowledgment of his genius and his good points of character", and wrote to Argyll, on the occasion of the Turkish debate, "He is not quite such a Turk as I had thought: what he hates is Christian liberty and reconstruction".[3]

Long afterwards, in cold blood, Gladstone assured his close friend Lord Rendel, that he had never felt any "personal animosity to Disraeli and felt sure Disraeli never had to him"—a sentiment highly creditable to the veteran statesman, on which the reader may be left to judge. He admired, but intensely disapproved of Disraeli, he went on, for "he corrupted the great political class": and indeed he "had never regarded Disraeli as serious or sincere in any of his utterances, however vehement".[4] This would seem to be withdrawing with one hand what he gave with the other. At an interval of three years he expressed a similar verdict to the same friend. "In past times the Tory party had principles by which it would and did stand for bad and for good. All this Dizzy destroyed."[5] Whether just or unjust, this was probably Gladstone's considered and deliberate verdict of his great rival.[6]

The animus was mutual, and Disraeli returned Gladstone's distrust with liberal interest. "Posterity will do justice to that unprincipled maniac Gladstone—extraordinary mixture of envy, vindictiveness, hypocrisy and superstition—whether Prime Minister or Leader of

---

[1] Morley's phrase—*Life*, ii. p. 555.   [2] *Ibid.* p. 552.
[3] *Ibid.* p. 550.   [4] 29 May 1892—*Personal Papers of Lord Rendel*, p. 100.
[5] 14 Jan. 1895—*ibid.* p. 108.
[6] An anecdote recorded by Mr. Buckle (vi. p. 644, note) brings out the differing mentalities of the two men. At a reception in honour of a famous foreign diplomatist, Disraeli remarked to one of Gladstone's daughters, "That is the most dangerous statesman in Europe—except, as your father would say, myself, or, as I should prefer to put it, your father".

Opposition—whether preaching, praying, speechifying or scribbling—never a gentleman!"—this to Derby in October 1876.[1] And a year later he told Lady Bradford, "My theory about him is unchanged: a ceaseless Tartuffe from the beginning. That sort of man does not get mad at seventy."[2]

It may well be that literary jealousy played its part. Neither could abide the other's writings, and *Punch* hit the nail on the head with its famous cartoon of the bookseller's shop, with the two rivals dipping into each other's latest publications and exclaiming, "H'm, prosy", and "Ha, flippant". Gladstone's diary records his impression of *Vivian Grey*: "The first quarter extremely clever, the rest trash".[3] And Disraeli wrote: "Gladstone, like Richelieu, can't write. Nothing can be more unmusical, more involved or more uncouth than all his scribblement": and again "I think his usual style the worst I know of any public man".[4] Mr. Buckle endorses Mr. Monypenny's approval of Disraeli's own estimate of his rival's literary achievements: "Mr. Gladstone is an excellent writer, but nothing that he writes is literature".[5] But to-day it may safely be affirmed that this merely betrays the prejudices of all three, and that, if we want the golden mean of truth, we must apply the original verdict equally to Gladstone and to Disraeli himself. *Tancred* and *Coningsby* will always find curious readers, but they too, like the manifold *Gleanings* of Hawarden, scarcely deserve the name of "literature".

He would be a bold man who would attempt to disentangle the relative effects of personal and party feeling. Disraeli was actually the older man by five years, yet if his rise to power was for many obvious reasons slower, it was all the more dramatic and aggressive when it came, and there is evidence that Gladstone greeted his rival's exultant moods with positive dismay. In 1867 Bishop Wilberforce writes that Disraeli "has been able to teach the House of Commons almost to ignore Gladstone, and at present lords it over him and, I am told, says that he will hold him down for twenty years":[6] while Lord Houghton recorded in the same year that Gladstone "seems quite awed by the diabolical cleverness of Dizzy".[7] All this helps to explain the mentality of the man who after retiring from public life

---

[1] Buckle, *op. cit.* vi. p. 67.   [2] 3 Oct. 1877—*ibid.* p. 181.
[3] 20 March 1874—Morley, *op. cit.* ii. p. 499.
[4] Buckle, vi. p. 181 (3 Oct. 1877) and v. p. 274 (27 Jan. 1874).
[5] *Ibid.* vi. p. 644.   [6] *Life of Wilberforce*, iii. p. 227.
[7] Cit. Morley, *op. cit.* ii. p. 230: "Awe, by no means the right word, I fancy," comments the ardent Morley.

and immersing himself, as it seemed permanently, in country pursuits well blended with theology and classics, now emerged once more from his lair—"like the Dragon of Wantley breathing fire and fury", said his incensed rival[1]—and proceeded to develop a demagogic activity unequalled in the history of Britain.

Disraeli was not unnaturally furious with Gladstone's "vindictive and ill-written" pamphlet,[2] of which 200,000 copies were sold, and still more embarrassed at the series of public meetings held throughout the country. To the Queen he argued that "when the country goes mad on any subject . . . explanation is hopeless, for a time", but that the month of September was a propitious moment for working off the frenzy.[3] He was as yet ready to "leave everything" to Derby's "consummate tact":[4] and Derby, in receiving a deputation at the Foreign Office at this very moment, utterly denied "that we have been in favour of the Turks against the Christians: we have been in favour of the territorial integrity of Turkey". He dismissed as equally impracticable Mr. Lowe's plan—"to wash our hands of the whole affair and let Turkey drift where it pleases"—and Mr. Gladstone's plan of ejecting the Turks as a governing force. On the other hand, "local or administrative autonomy", of which so much was heard, was not an English phrase and indeed was "very vague and elastic in meaning", but it offered "a possible and practical solution". In the Serbo-Turkish conflict he openly favoured "a return to the *status quo*".

Ten days earlier he had told another deputation—consisting of working men and headed by John Bright—that Elliot had "repeatedly warned the Porte of the extreme danger from the employment of irregular troops", but admitted that the massacres took place at a moment when there was "entire anarchy" at Constantinople[5]—thus indirectly proving the Opposition contention that the Turks were incapable of effective reforms. Many people, Lord Derby complained, seemed to think that Lord Beaconsfield was Sultan and he himself Grand Vizier. "The last word of the Eastern question is this: Who is to have Constantinople?" It could not be allowed to fall into the hands of a Great Power: but the relations of the various races had been frequently modified and could be again. Here already was a very different note from that of the early summer.

Bulgarian Horrors was followed within the week by Gladstone's

[1] Buckle, vi. p. 56.   [2] *Ibid.* p. 60, 8 Sept., to Derby.
[3] *Letters*, ii. p. 476.   [4] 23 Sept.—Buckle, vi. p. 68.
[5] 23 Sept.—*Speeches of Fifteenth Earl of Derby*, ii. pp. 295, 302, 303.

great philippic at Blackheath, which marks an era in his political career, as the first step to the resumption of power. From the outset he struck a new note: "The Crimean War entailed on us most solemn obligations, and it is for their fulfilment that I am here to-day": for the Schuyler report had convinced him that the time had come to speak out, "as one of the authors of the Crimean War". The movement of protest he described as a national, not a party one, and he rejoiced that the working men had been the first to raise the flag. The *Daily News* remained unrefuted, and the Turkish reports were "the greatest aggravation of the case". The Turkish Government itself was clearly implicated: it knew the men it was employing, it took every possible step to conceal the truth and punished all who tried to divulge it or who wrote officially of "pretended excesses". Honour, then, "to the Power, whatsoever its name, that first steps in to stop them", and the simplest course was "to recommend that all Turkish authorities should walk out of the place", as in Roumania at an earlier date.

If asked how the spoils were to be distributed, "I would not distribute them at all", but would assign the territory concerned, not to Russia, or Austria or England, but to the inhabitants themselves, leaving titular Turkish sovereignty and a tribute, but no control. "I am not such a dreamer", he declared, "as to suppose that Russia more than other countries is exempt from selfish ambitions", but the animosity felt for her was no better grounded than that which once led Fox to call France "our natural enemy". "Never have I known a great object so pressing in its urgency, upon which the Powers and the peoples of Europe were so cordially united as upon this." "Twenty-six years ago I endeavoured to stir you up with respect to the abuses of government in Italy: but let me render this justice to defunct dynasties, that it would be a cruel sin and shame to compare for one moment that government of the Bourbon dynasty in Naples with the atrocious system that has been devastating Bulgaria." His dominant note, then, was responsibility and the need for European co-operation, if war was to be averted.

A week later, another of the few survivors of the Crimean Cabinet, the Duke of Argyll, sounded a similar note of responsibility at Glasgow, arguing with great force that the object of that war had been, "not to support the Turks, but to put the fate of Turkey in the hands of united Europe, and take it out of the solitary hands of Russia".

Amid the rising tide of popular anxiety and indignation *Punch* once more stands out—as in the Crimean War and during the Risorgimento—as the mouthpiece of sane, middle-class unpolitical sentiment. It is amazing, after a lapse of sixty years, to note the sureness of instinct with which Tenniel's cartoons depict the essence of a changing situation. His treatment of the Andrássy Note and the Berlin Memorandum had already been particularly felicitous: and now on 15 July "The Sphinx is Silent" appeared. Needless to say, the face of the sphinx is the face of Disraeli: while all around a crowd of pygmy figures clamours "Speak, speak". A fortnight later the cartoon is entitled "Neutrality under Difficulties": the Prime Minister is impatiently exclaiming, "Bulgarian atrocities! I can't find them in the Official Reports!" Next week we find "Augurs at Fault", and a poem entitled, "A Word in Season: from Bull to Benjamin"—which is almost anything but poetry, but provides a valuable clue to contemporary reactions.

> "Coffee-house babble?" Benjamin, my boy,
>   That sounds a very pat and pithy summary,
> Nor do I quite expect you to employ
>   The hot philanthropist's effusive flummery;
> But though of fuss I'm far from being fond,
>   The news I'm getting now my dander raises
> To heat that's just a little bit beyond
>   The chilling power of cool official phrases.
>
> Moslem and Christian! Blood both flags must drench,
>   When Crescent flies on Cross and Cross on Crescent!
> But not the coldest Derby douche can quench
>   Wrath at some wrongs to coolness acquiescent:
> Fire, plunder, prison, butchery, bestial lust,
>   Are things to mix hot rage my scalding shame with,
> Which no snow-blooded policy, I trust,
>   Will ever load my soul or stain my name with.

By 9 September the note has risen by several octaves. The Turk appeals to Britannia: "Will you not still befriend me?": and Britannia draws sternly back. "Befriend you?—Not with your hands of that colour!" On 16 September there is another poem, no less outspoken though even less inspired, entitled "England Aroused": and the contemporary Dutch celebrations of independence are ingeniously connected with Gladstone's Bulgarian pamphlet. "William of Orange was celebrated as William the Silent, whereas William of Hawarden is distinguished by speaking out." Disraeli is depicted as "The Drowsy Pointsman", asleep outside the Eastern Line signal-box, while John Bull warns him of an approaching train and the prospect of a still bigger smash. A fortnight later there is "A Call for the Manager": Mr. Punch draws aside the curtain for Disraeli to address the excited audience from the front of the stage, with the words, "I'll say what I can to quiet them!"[1]

THE ATTITUDE OF THE CHURCHES

It is not surprising that on such an issue the voice of the Churches should have made itself heard. Not merely were the clergy prominent at countless meetings, but men who differed as widely as the Archbishop of York, the Bishop of Manchester, Dean Church, Cardinal Manning, Dr. Dale and Mr. Spurgeon, were loud in their protests, the first of them denouncing "the tottering throne whose feet are planted in corruption and blood", and the last praying openly at the City Temple for the defeat of the Turks. The Bishop of Exeter (Dr. Temple) wrote to the press insisting that it was not a party question, but that at all costs it was necessary "to stop this wickedness", lest England should seem to have been "accessory after the fact". The Bishop of Oxford at an uproarious meeting moved a resolution of "horror and indignation". The Bishops of Ely and Norwich invited intercession and active sympathy for the sufferers, and the Primate recommended his clergy to appeal for collections in aid of the Eastern Christians. Among the very numerous clergy who were stirred into protest an honourable place belongs to William Denton, vicar of St. Bartholomew's, Cripplegate, who had already published one of the first serious English books on Serbia and had many personal connections with Orthodox churchmen in the Near East. The clearest note of all was struck by Bishop Fraser of Manchester, who as early as 9 August demanded "a policy of intervention in concert with the other great Christian Powers".[2]

---

[1] Incidentally, it is interesting to note the reaction of German public opinion in a poem addressed "An England", by Kladderadatsch, of 17 September 1876, in the sense that statesmen will hesitate to flout the popular feelings, for "Ein Volk auch lebt in Land der Briten, Und dieses Volk hat auch ein Herz". The "auch" needs no commentary.

[2] It is here necessary to pillory the Protestant *Rock*, which on 8 September wrote: "It is one thing in God's sight to 'avenge his saints', and quite another to avenge the worshippers of the wafer-God".

It is necessary to stress these activities of the Anglican Church, because there was a loose tendency, both then and later, to treat the agitation as one with which only the Nonconformists sympathised —an entire misrepresentation of the facts.

One of the most notable Nonconformist pronouncements at this early stage was that of R. W. Dale, the famous Congregationalist leader, who reminded a Birmingham audience that Cromwell had prescribed a day of humiliation after the massacre of the Piedmontese Protestants and the collection of money for the victims, and who now exhorted the Queen to follow the Protector's good example.

There was perhaps no churchman whose attitude produced a deeper effect than Canon Liddon, then at the zenith of his powers as a preacher, and the recognised upholder of the Puseyite tradition. Certain passages from a memorable sermon delivered at St. Paul's on the Sunday following the atrocity debate in the House will serve to reveal the profound impression left upon religious and intellectual circles by events in Bulgaria.

"As a rule", he said, "it is undoubtedly better for us, the ministers of Christ, to avoid reference to topics connected with the public action of the country. . . . But there are times when silence is impossible without manifest disloyalty to the cause of Christ. . . . Such a time is surely upon us now, when we as a nation are slowly awakening to a true estimate of recent events in Eastern Europe and of our involuntary share in them. Day by day we English are learning that this year of grace 1876 has been signalised by a public tragedy, which I firmly believe is without parallel in modern times. . . . People now scarcely mutter the word 'exaggeration'. They know that when all that must be deducted has been deducted on this score, the remainder of solid unassailable fact is unspeakably horrible.

"It may fairly be pleaded for the Power which has perpetrated these acts that it knows not the name of Christ, and that its proceedings are not to be judged by the standard of a European and Christian civilisation. Be it so: but that which makes the voice falter as we say it is that, through whatever misunderstanding, the Government which is immediately responsible for acts like these has turned for sympathy, for encouragement, not to any of the historical houses of despotism or oppression, not to any other European Power, but alas to England—to free, humane Christian England. The Turk has, not altogether without reason, believed himself, amid these scenes of cruelty, to be sure of her smile, or at least of her acquiescence." [1]

Canon Liddon followed up this sermon by a visit to the Balkans, with the object of establishing personal contacts with the Eastern Christians. He was accompanied by another remarkable cleric, the Rev. Malcolm MacColl, who through the common link of Glenalmond had already been in relations with Gladstone for the past fifteen years, and who as an ardent Gladstonian in politics now urged him to make a pronouncement on the Eastern Question. "The country is evidently thoroughly roused, but it wants guidance," he wrote, and his appeal was doubtless a contributory cause of Gladstone's intervention. [2]

The two clergymen went out together to Belgrade, Liddon giving as his motive "to assure leading Servians of the change which has happily come over English sympathies": and his enthusiasm is revealed in the phrase: "These Christian races of the Balkans are the predestined heirs of the future". They met Ristić and others, and Dr. Sandwith showed them authentic hospital cases of men mutilated by the Turks. On their way home they visited the great Croat patriot, Bishop Strossmayer of Djakovo, whose diocese nominally included Bosnia, and to whom they had an introduction from Döllinger. [3] Liddon duly reported to Gladstone the Bishop's view that Turkish reform was quite illusory, that Bosnia-Hercegovina should be united with Serbia and Montenegro, and that this would do more than anything else to "create a barrier against Russian ambition and to endear England to the South Sclavonic populations". Never in all history was there a war undertaken from nobler motives: this was Strossmayer's considered view, and Liddon endorsed it without reserve. At the latter's instance Bishop Strossmayer commenced a private correspondence with Mr. Gladstone, which had a marked influence in shaping that statesman's views on the Eastern Question. [4] Unfortunately the Bishop, owing to his exposed and delicate political position towards the strongly Turcophil Government of Budapest, felt bound to refuse Gladstone's urgent request for permission to publish his letters in the press.

---

[1] J. O. Johnston, *Life of H. P. Liddon*, p. 206.

[2] 1 Sept. 1876—MacColl, *Memories and Corresp.*, ed. G. W. E. Russell, p. 47.

[3] Formerly his comrade in the struggle against infallibility during the Vatican Council of 1870, but now severed from the Roman Church.

[4] The full correspondence was first published by me as Appendix to my book *The Southern Slav Question* (1911), by kind permission of the Gladstone Trustees. The Bishop's two first letters are of 1 and 24 October 1876, and were written at the instance of Liddon and MacColl.

THE IMPALEMENT INCIDENT

It was on their homeward journey that an incident[1] occurred to Canon Liddon and Mr. MacColl, which attained great notoriety at the time and roused the Turcophils to positive frenzy. Travelling on a small steamer down the river Save—then the frontier between Austria-Hungary and Turkey—they passed a number of Turkish military blockhouses, with stakes "about the height of a lamp-post" outside them, on one of which a man was impaled. They claimed to have seen this at a distance of less than a hundred yards, and at several angles, as the river at that point followed an extremely winding course. They were given grisly particulars as to this practice, not only by the steward of the steamer, but by a Croat Catholic priest, Father Odžić, a member of the Croatian Diet, who was their fellow-passenger and assured them that there had been other cases during the previous months. When MacColl told this story in *The Times*,[2] a "categorical denial" was issued by the Turkish Embassy, which had not long before denied the whole story of Bulgarian atrocities: and the Turcophil press, in particular the *Daily Telegraph*, fell upon the two clerics for their "credulity" and boldly maintained that two centuries had passed since impalement was practised by the Turks. Our Consul in Sarajevo, Mr. W. R. Holmes, duly reported that the Turkish authorities knew nothing of such happenings, treated the "reverend gentlemen" as "the victims of a monstrous joke" and suggested that what they had really seen was a stake with haricot beans fixed up to dry! Impalement, he added, was thirty or forty years ago a very common mode of execution, "but for the last twenty years, not even in the wilds of Mesopotamia, much less in Europe, have I ever heard of a single instance of this old barbarous custom."[3]

This did not, however, silence the combative Highlander, who was able to show that Consul Holmes himself, as recently as 18 October 1875, had forwarded unchallenged to London a document including impalement as one of the charges put forward by the Bosnian insurgents. He was able to quote cases of impalement from the reports both of Baring and Schuyler, from the experience of Miss Irby in Bosnia, of Dr. Sandwith in Serbia, to say nothing of notorious

---

[1] For a detailed account see MacColl, *The Eastern Question*, pp. 358-92.
[2] 28 Sept. 1876.
[3] 5 Oct. and 3 Nov. to Elliot—nos. 687 and 961, *Turkey No. I.* (1877).

cases during the Lebanon troubles of 1860. Finally he showed that
Holmes's own subordinate, Vice-Consul Freeman, had reported
another case of impalement, of a smith called Rade Buić, near Novi
on the Bosnian frontier in February 1876, and that this was confirmed
by a special correspondent of the Russian *Golos*, by several Austrian
regimental officers and by the Corps Command in Zagreb. But all
this was of no avail, and for a long time ardent Turcophils like Lord
Elcho or the Duke of Sutherland held up Liddon and MacColl to
public ridicule as unable to distinguish between a Christian martyr
and a faggot of beans. Mr. Lowther, Under-Secretary for the Colonies,
went so far as to describe them as "carried away by their sympathy
for the idolatrous form of so-called Christianity which prevails in the
East".[1]

A similar incident aroused considerable controversy some nine
months later. In May 1877 Mr. Arthur Evans reported to the
Manchester Guardian that a certain Jovan Dunjelović had been
impaled and then roasted to death on 23 April at Gabella, near
Metković in Hercegovina. This story was duly challenged by Consul
Freeman, who quoted the denials of a neighbouring Catholic priest:
but Evans was able to show that this priest had not merely written
no such letter, but had affirmed his belief in the outrage "to more
than one acquaintance of mine at Metković". He further produced a
signed statement by the Mayor of Metković, appending the deposition
of an eye-witness, and evidence given by two further witnesses whose
names he knew. Here the matter rested, but the honours obviously
did not lie with the consular service.[2]

DISRAELI, DERBY AND THE ARMISTICE QUESTION

While Gladstone, Argyll, Lowe, Fawcett and a crowd of minor
luminaries headed the campaign of protest in the country, it is
abundantly clear that Beaconsfield had no illusions about Turkey and
fully realised that if no solution were found during the winter for
the conflict between the Porte, its rebel subjects and its ambitious
vassals, "Russia and Austria will march their armies into the
Balkans" in the spring. And he goes on to discuss with Derby the
possibility of "a division of the Balkan spoil" between these two
Powers, "under the friendly auspices of England", who might be

[1] At Southsea, *Standard*, 1 March 1877.
[2] *M.G.* 13 Aug. 1877, "Vice-Consul Freeman and the Bosnian Outrages".

appeased by "the custody and guardianship" of Constantinople as a neutralised free port.[1] His bile rises at the thought of acting "under the pressure of this Hudibrastic crew of High Ritualists, Dissenting ministers and 'the great Liberal party'", but in opening his mind to his chief colleague in office he claims that "all this tumult is on a false assumption, that we have been or are upholding Turkey. All the Turks may be in the Propontis so far as I am concerned, and the first thing, after we had declined the Berlin memorandum, that you did, was to tell Musurus so."[2] This last phrase is doubtless an over-statement, but it proves that the Prime Minister's attitude in the Eastern Question rested in no way upon principle, but on a purely opportunist searching for some formula which would increase British prestige and weaken the coalition of the Eastern Powers. "There is nothing between our plan and partition," he again told Derby at the end of the month.[3] On the other hand, he resisted the Queen's suggestion that he should give public expression to his horror at the atrocities:[4] and in a speech delivered to his late constituents at Aylesbury on 20 September he struck an aggressive and unrepentant note.

Unquestionably, he said, there was in England "a large party whose thoughts and sentiments are absorbed by other things than the maintenance of the permanent interests of the country or the main-tenance of peace". The British nation could always be roused by tales of injustice, and there was a "danger that designing politicians might take advantage of such sublime sentiments and apply them for the furtherance of sinister ends". "In the general havoc and ruin" that might result, "it may fairly be described as worse than any of the Bulgarian atrocities." After this hit at Gladstone, he vigorously denied the suggestion that at the time of the Berlin Memorandum Britain and Russia were in acute conflict: on the contrary, *"by no Power have we been met so cordially as by Russia"*. What prevented a satisfactory settlement during the summer was the fact that "Serbia declared war on Turkey, *that is to say, the secret societies of Europe declared war on Turkey"*—"societies", he added, warming to his task, "which have regular agents everywhere, which countenance assassina-tion and which, if necessary, could produce a massacre". Not content with this grotesque confusion of Russian Nihilists, Russian Slavophils,

---

[1] 4 and 6 Sept.—Buckle, vi. pp. 52-3.
[2] *Ibid.* p. 52.   [3] 23 Sept.—*ibid.* p. 62.
[4] On the ground that he would lose his self-respect if he yielded to public clamour —10 Sept. to Queen, and 28 Sept. Queen's reply, *Letters*, ii. pp. 476-80.

Serbian nationalists and Bulgarian or Bosnian insurgents—and only a very imperfectly informed public even in 1876 could have swallowed what every student of Balkan history in 1934 knows to be pitiable nonsense—he went on to denounce Serbia as guilty of an "outrageous and wicked war", which violated "every principle of public morality and honour".[1] He was more successful in defending Derby against the charge of doing nothing, but then resumed his attack on Gladstone and his pamphlet: "humanitarian politicians", he said, "do not look before they leap", thus deliberately repudiating his own claim to such an adjective.

Next morning *The Times* took the Prime Minister to task for "a negligence astonishing in so great a master of language", hinting that if his phrases meant anything, they involved "one of the gravest charges ever made by one eminent English statesman against another". Nor was the "diabolical craft" of secret societies needed to light a flame in Turkey: "detestable misgovernment" was the real cause, without which all the secret societies in Christendom would not avail. Moreover, "Serbia", it declared, with a perception all too rare in those days, "saw people of her own race struggling to free themselves from a yoke which she as well as they had felt". The most that can now be said for Beaconsfield is that the disturbing effects of the agitation upon internal affairs had blinded him to the elements of the situation. All that he saw in a war of national liberation and in the uprising of subject races was "the Servian conspiracy, carried on entirely now by Russian men and Russian money".[2] All that he saw in Gladstone was that "we have been stabbed in the back, and the very lowest arts of faction, abusing the notable enthusiasm of a great portion of the people, have endangered our highest national interests and European peace". He failed to see that first Serbian and then Russian intervention were absolutely inevitable, unless Turkey could be forced to adopt reforms such as he and his Government had consistently rendered nugatory for over a year past.

[1] With all respect to Mr. Buckle, whose brilliant book on Disraeli deserves special praise for the admirable frankness of its quotations, it is impossible to refrain from criticising him for the omission of these very vital sentences in the Aylesbury speech. Without them, his extracts on pp. 65-6 convey a very creditable general effect, whereas with them the reader, whatever his political views may be, is bound to form a radically different estimate of Disraeli's competence on the main problems before Europe. Mr. Buckle even goes so far as to treat Gladstone's policy in 1876 as one "which gratuitously provoked the 'havoc and ruin' of a general European war" (vi. p. 66). There could hardly be a more fundamental misconception of the European situation!

[2] Beaconsfield to Hardy, 30 Sept.—*Life of Gathorne Hardy*, i. p. 373.

It cannot be too strongly emphasised that Disraeli's Aylesbury speech was based upon a fundamental misconception of the Russian situation. The "Slav Benevolent Society" of Moscow, which was the moving force of the Serbophil volunteer movement, so far from being either secret or revolutionary, was public, strongly conservative and Orthodox, and the organ of circles which believed in the mission of "Holy Russia" against the subversive and "rotten West". It had played a prominent rôle since the sixties, it was "duly authorised by the Government, held its meetings with open doors and published periodically a report of its proceedings".[1] In strongest contrast to these Slavophil currents there was a secret revolutionary current, based upon a repudiation of Orthodoxy and even of Slav nationalism, in favour of the extremer western social panaceas; and inside this current there was the undoubted tendency to regard war as the best means of precipitating revolution and social upheaval. But the two were as incapable of blending as oil and water, and both were suspect, in varying degrees, to the cautious bureaucracy of St. Petersburg and to the Tsar's diplomatic confidants.

It was the first of these currents that responded to the Slav call in 1912 and 1914, and the second that effected the Bolshevik Revolution of November 1917, while some of the young idealists who fought for Serbia in 1876 lived to share in the short-lived Liberal Revolution of March 1917, only to find themselves swept aside by the extremists and ruthlessly classed with those reactionaries whom they had combated all their lives.

The first beginnings of dissension within the Cabinet date from this period, many of Beaconsfield's colleagues resenting the extravagance of tone often adopted by the Liberal leaders, but also and no less, the idea that Britain might be dragged into a quarrel on the Turkish side. "The first to take serious alarm" was Lord Salisbury,[2] who told his special friend Lord Carnarvon, the Colonial Secretary, that Turkey's "alliance and friendship is a reproach to us. The Turk's teeth must be drawn, even if he be allowed to live."[3] He wrote to his chief immediately after the Aylesbury speech, declaring that "the

---

[1] This phrase is quoted from Donald Mackenzie Wallace's *Russia*, which appeared in 1877 and did more than any other book in English to correct false estimates of Russian conditions. The influence which its author gradually won in court circles, and not least with the Prince of Wales, undoubtedly contributed to the marked contrast between the latter's wild views in 1877 and his eminently sane views as King Edward from 1905 onwards.

[2] Words of Lord Carnarvon's memorandum, quoted by Hardinge, *Life of Carnarvon*, ii. p. 340.   [3] *Life of Salisbury*, ii. p. 84.

traditional Palmerstonian policy is at an end", congratulating him on his "cordial language towards Russia" and arguing that "our best chance" of peace was in "an early understanding" with that Power. "I deplored the Crimean War," he wrote on another occasion, "and I heartily wish the Turks were out of Europe." But he held the difficulties to be insuperable, and looked upon Austria as "the obstacle to any reasonable arrangement", owing to her suspicions of "the small Slav states as Russian outposts": hence Britain must avoid "hanging on to the coat-tails of Austria", whose "existence is no longer of such importance to us" and whose "vocation in Europe has gone"—a verdict which riper reflections was to modify.[1] Inside the Cabinet there were still men who unreservedly endorsed their chief's extreme view—Lord Cairns, Lord John Manners, Gathorne Hardy, who records in his diary on 5 October: "On Gladstone and others rests the bloodshed".[2] Others too were torn between the two extremes.

The plain truth is that there was now an acute division of opinion between those who approved or resented the introduction of a moral issue into the solution of international problems: for it was in this that Gladstone's great enormity consisted. The wild language of the Prime Minister at Aylesbury unquestionably "added to the excitement of the public mind", and there were many who argued that its "evident animus" more than justified all the criticism to which the Bulgarian revelations had given rise.[3]

The division of opinion ran across both parties. Among the Liberals Sir William Harcourt was very critical of Gladstone, who, he held, was "*more suo*, exaggerating the situation". He warned Granville that "Chamberlain, Fawcett and the extreme section are making use of the occasion to demand the deposition of Hartington and the return of Gladstone. I do not for a moment suppose that this is what Mr. G. himself means, but the mischief is none the less serious on that account."[4]

Meanwhile, on the advice of the Powers, the Turkish and Serbian Governments consented to a temporary suspension of hostilities.[5] But the peace terms submitted by the Porte—personal homage of

---

[1] 23 Sept.—*ibid*. pp. 85-6; Buckle, vi. pp. 70-71.
[2] *Life of Gathorne Hardy*, i. p. 374.
[3] George Potter, writing in the *Contemp. Rev.* (Oct. 1876), p. 865, on "Working Men and the Eastern Question". He went on, "but surely there cannot be a man in the Empire that can believe it (*i.e.* the story of secret societies). . . . No madness of Lord George Gordon or Mr. Whalley ever went beyond this."
[4] *Granville Papers*, Harcourt to Granville, 10 Oct. 1876.
[5] From 15 to 25 Sept.

Prince Milan, the restoration of Turkish garrisons in Serbia, a drastic
reduction of the Serbian army and militia, an increased tribute and
control of the future railway through Serbia—were of the kind only
accepted after utter defeat, and some of them were at once described
as "quite inadmissible" even by the British Government.[1]

THE SUMAROKOV MISSION

It was during this brief but not very promising interlude that Lord
Derby, somewhat reluctantly, formulated his idea of a settlement—
the *status quo* for the two Serbian states and local autonomy for the
insurgent provinces, defined as "some voice in the management of
their local affairs" and "protection against arbitrary acts".[2] This
very qualified initiative of London appears to have encouraged the
Tsar to send Count Sumarokov to Vienna, with concrete proposals.
Starting from the assumption that Austria and Russia had identical
interests and were directly concerned in escaping from the present
impasse, he assured Francis Joseph that he shared his "repugnance
for the formation of a large Serbian state" and would oppose it.[3]
Force was inevitable, but only joint intervention could avert European complications, and he therefore suggested a simultaneous
occupation of Bosnia by Austria-Hungary and of Bulgaria by Russia,
while the fleets of the Powers entered the Bosphorus "to protect
the lives of the Christians, . . . shatter the arrogance of the Turks
and force them to submit to the decisions of Europe". Gorchakov,
realising that the secret could not be kept from London, instructed
Shuvalov to lay the proposal in its main lines before Derby.[4] General
von Schweinitz, one of the acutest and best-informed observers in
any capital, accepted the Tsar's suggestion of joint *naval* action as
proving both that he was thoroughly in earnest and that he had no
separate designs.[5] But both Britain and Austria found it too drastic
and declined, Francis Joseph arguing that joint intervention would
provoke anarchy and opposing the permanent occupation of Bulgaria.
Andrássy wrote to Gorchakov of "the traditional error of a crass
conflict of interest between Austria-Hungary and Russia",[6] but in
urging further insistence upon an armistice, but no action unless the

---

[1] *Turkey No. I.* (1877), no 236, Elliot to Derby, 15 Sept., no. 247, Derby to
Elliot, 16 Sept.
[2] *Ibid.* no. 282, 18 Sept.   [3] *R.B.D.* iii. no. 79, 23 Sept., full text.
[4] *Ibid.* no. 83.   [5] Schweinitz, *Denkwürdigkeiten*, i. p. 352.
[6] 2 Oct. 1876—Wertheimer, *Graf Andrássy*, ii. p. 344.

Porte refused or fresh outrages occurred, he in effect laid the main onus and all the risks upon Russia, and this was presumably why the Tsar was so annoyed at the answer which Sumarokov brought back.

To his Ambassador at St. Petersburg, Baron Langenau, who added to an extreme Russophilism a marked hostility to Bismarck, Andrássy said some two months later that he would never imitate Buol's policy towards Russia during the Crimean War—"If I once bark, I would almost sooner bite".[1]

BISMARCK AND RUSSIA

This was the occasion for a curious incident between Russia and Germany, which provides a key to the inner workings of Bismarck's mind. The Tsar, first in conversation with General von Manteuffel, then through his own Ambassador in Berlin, Oubril, and finally through the German Military Attaché in Russia, General von Werder, tried to sound Germany as to her probable attitude in the event of his being forced into a war with Austria. The enquiry was all the more embarrassing because in each case he raised the memory of his own benevolent neutrality in 1870 towards Germany, to whom he had indeed made an informal offer of 300,000 men, contingent upon Austria-Hungary moving. Bismarck, who distrusted Gorchakov and Oubril almost equally, suspected a trap, to be exploited later in Vienna: he therefore declined to be drawn and kept up the pretence that the Tsar's reference was to war with *Turkey*, not Austria, and must have been mangled in transmission. But he committed to paper his own confidential view that "a war between Russia and Austria is for us and our future an extraordinarily difficult and dangerous dilemma: and we cannot be expected to make it easier so long as it is not absolutely inevitable".[2]

That there was nothing new in this attitude, and that it represents the real Bismarck, is sufficiently shown by an earlier instruction to Count Münster in London on 6 July 1876. "War between England and Russia", he wrote, "would be a great calamity and a European misfortune: but for us war between Austria and Russia would be even more dangerous." The Emperor, therefore, wished Münster to do what he could to "calm down" England, "whose war-lust appears to

[1] Wertheimer, "Neues zur Orientpolitik des Grafen Andrássy", *Historische Blätter*, ii. 1921, p. 269.   [2] *G.P.* no. 241, 2 Oct., Diktat of Bismarck.

His Majesty analogous to that of Napoleon in 1870" (!). There is an amusing sting in the tail of this dispatch: for Bismarck recommends his ambassador, in making representations to the British Cabinet, to take as his model the British Circular of May 1875, urging calm upon Germany.[1]

Our interpretation is further borne out by the record of a conversation between Bismarck and Baron Münch, an official sent by Andrássy to report at Berlin upon the Sumarokov mission and Austrian policy in general. On this occasion Bismarck referred quite freely to the recent Werder incident, explaining his refusal to reply on the ground that it would involve "a point hostile to Austria". He then turned to Münch's own enquiry as to Germany's attitude towards an Austro-Italian war, and declined to answer on exactly similar grounds, since that would involve "a point hostile to Russia". By this he meant that Germany's own possible contribution to such a war would be to attack Russia and so prevent her from taking Austria in the rear: and any commitment in this sense would, of course, be regarded by Gorchakov as "a provocation".[2] This incident not only clinches the argument in favour of Bismarck's balancing between Russia and Austria, but affords admirable proof of his skill in complicated *combinazioni*—keeping five balls in the air at once, as was said of his policy. He closed his talks with Münch by the classic dictum, "A rogue gives more than he has": in other words, he himself declines to promise what he cannot fulfil.

In consequence of this incident, Bismarck gave very careful instructions to Schweinitz, declining to give any pledge in advance, because that would rob Germany of her freedom of action. But he laid down as axiomatic that it would suit Germany, *neither* to see Russia beaten by an European coalition, *nor* to see Austria endangered in her existence as an European Great Power.[3] He got the old Emperor to tell Alexander II. that he would understand, even while regretting, any action of the Tsar to prevent an indefinite prolongation of such disastrous conditions and that he would do his utmost to keep Britain and Austria-Hungary neutral.[4] In a word, next to the necessity of averting a Franco-Russian combination such

[1] *Aus Bismarcks Briefwechsel*, no. 304.

[2] Wertheimer, *Neues zur Orientpolitik*, i. pp. 271-3.

[3] It is impossible to admit the highly tendencious interpretation of this incident by M. Hanotaux: "Gorchakov était payé de ses politesses de 1870. On lui disait tout aussi poliment, qu'en cas de conflit on prendrait parti pour l'Autriche"—Hanotaux, *op. cit.* iv. p. 116.

[4] *Ibid.* no. 251, 23 Oct., Bülow to Schweinitz.

as would threaten Germany on both flanks, the capital aim of Bismarck's policy was to avoid the necessity of choosing between Russia and Austria-Hungary.

It may well be questioned whether the Tsar's enquiry represented a real change of policy, for he speedily resumed his secret negotiations with Vienna. But it is hardly possible to determine with exactitude how much was due to the momentary exasperation of the Tsar himself, whose nerves were already seriously affected, and how much to the tactical manœuvres of Prince Gorchakov and of Milyutin, the Minister of War.

BRITAIN AND THE RUSSIAN ULTIMATUM TO TURKEY

Meanwhile Russian volunteers continued to pour into Serbia[1] and exercised virtual control of the army—the Foreign Minister, Jovan Ristić, complaining bitterly to Prince Wrede that they were prolonging the war and that Russia, if she wished to help the Serbs, would do better to declare war herself.[2] Under their influence, Serbia had unwisely resumed hostilities on 28 September, only to meet with a series of severe checks. Her defeat at Aleksinac on 17 October was decisive, her forces being cut into two and the road being opened to a Turkish advance upon Belgrade itself. Cherniayev immediately resigned the supreme command and withdrew with most of his compatriots, amid mutual recriminations of inadequate measures of defence and actual cowardice. Turkish arrogance knew no bounds and found fresh encouragement in the strong Turcophil demonstrations organised in Budapest as a counterblast to Panslav activities.[3] The Porte then stubbornly held out for a six months' armistice, which of course meant in practice a prolonged Turkish occupation of Serbia, with all its objectionable consequences. The peace conditions hinted at to Elliot even before the victory were personal homage by Prince Milan to the Sultan, restoration of four Turkish garrisons in Serbia, reduction of the Serbian army to 10,000, razing

---

[1] In all, more Russian officers came than the entire Serbian officers' corps, but of privates only two battalions. Slobodan Jovanović, *Vlada Milana*, p. 350.

[2] *Austrian Archives*—19 Sept. 1876, no. 151, Wrede to Andrássy.

[3] Later in the winter a deputation of 100 Magyar students visited Constantinople in order to present a sword of honour to Abdul Kerim, the victor over the Serbs. The reprisals against the Serbs of Hungary had already begun in July 1876, with the arrest, on the orders of Koloman Tisza, of Svetozar Miletić, the leader of the Omladina movement. He was eventually sentenced to four years' imprisonment for high treason, lost his reason in prison and never recovered.

of all recent fortifications and an increased tribute in lieu of indemnity. The ministers warned Elliot that "the day may come that before the Powers are in time to pour in their armies, not a Christian may be found surviving".[1] In such a mood they, of course, would not hear of autonomy.

At this stage there is a noticeable difference between the attitude of Beaconsfield and Derby, though they themselves as yet seem hardly aware of the fact. At the end of September the Prime Minister congratulated the Foreign Secretary on his speech to the deputation, "which was perfect",[2] told him that he had shown some of the highest qualities of public life and went still further in writing to Sir Stafford Northcote, the new Leader of the House of Commons. "Derby has shown throughout the negotiations the utmost energy and resource. A clear head and a sound judgment I always gave him credit for: but I feel I never did him sufficient justice—much and long as I have appreciated him—for his vigour, action and fertility."[3] The Queen also was still ready to praise Derby for his "admirable and energetic" conduct of affairs.[4] It is important to bear these tributes in mind, in view of the striking change in their attitude which events were soon to produce.

While, however, Beaconsfield treated the Russian proposals as "a real Bulgarian atrocity"—in itself a phrase full of implications—assuming them to be "a false move", due to Gorchakov being "misled by Gladstone and Co.", and exultingly told Lady Bradford that he had "sent Shuvalov off with a flea in his ear"[5]—in other words, while he wrecked the only concrete peace proposals rather than seem to yield to his hated party rival—Derby was pursuing a much more moderate line. In the first place, he had instructed Elliot on 21 September to ask for a personal audience with the new Sultan, communicate the substance of Walter Baring's enquiries (and incidentally he accepts Baring's definition of the massacres as "the most heinous crime" of the century), to protest vigorously against the failure to punish the guilty parties, and also to insist on "ample reparation" and a

---

[1] F.O. 78/2464, no. 1016, Elliot to Derby.
[2] Buckle, vi. p. 74.
[3] 30 Sept.—*ibid.* p. 77. To Hardy on the same day in almost identical terms—*Life of Gathorne Hardy,* i. p. 372.
[4] Queen to Beaconsfield, 28 Sept.—*Letters,* ii. p. 480. Lord Cairns, on the other hand, writing to Gathorne Hardy on 16 September, complained of Derby as "negative . . . sadly deficient in sentiment or suggestion"—*Life of Gathorne Hardy,* i. p. 370.
[5] 5 Oct.—Buckle, vi. p. 79.

guarantee of "future security" for the Bulgarians.[1] This audience actually took place on 7 October, and the Sultan gave the necessary promises, but nothing was done, and on 21 October Elliot reported a most unsatisfactory answer of the Grand Vizier to his further demand for punishment.[2]

Already on 5 October, however, Derby told Elliot to press an armistice upon the Turks and expressed the Government's view that an armistice should at once be followed by a conference.[3] They went even further and warned the Porte that "the recommendation of the armistice was England's last step; that if refused she should attempt no longer to arrest the destruction of the Turkish Empire, but leave her to her fate; and that our Ambassador would leave Constantinople".[4] The Porte, however, countered with the suggestion of five or six months as the proper term of an armistice and also objected to a conference:[5] and when not merely Serbia but also Russia quite naturally objected, London expressed itself as unable to understand the reasons for this and spoke of the "grave responsibility" which any Power neglecting the longer term would incur.[6]

Beaconsfield's acute distrust of Russia led him to suggest to Derby the possibility of a treaty with Germany "for the maintenance of the *status quo*":[7] he entirely failed to realise that for Bismarck the survival of Turkey was almost a matter of indifference, whereas Germany's good relations with Russia were fundamental.[8] He dimly perceived that William I. attached great value to the friendship of his nephew the Tsar, and for that reason he petulantly wished him "in the same cave as Friedrich Barbarossa": but he quite unfairly blamed Lord Odo Russell for failure to win Bismarck to an impossible attitude, declaring that the Ambassador "might as well be at Bagdad" as Berlin, and that Münster in London was "suspicious and stupid"[9]— suspicious of the Prime Minister's policy, but, as his reports and diaries show, by no means stupid. The Queen was, of course, better informed as to German policy, but Beaconsfield persisted in the quite erroneous view that Bismarck "maintains a rigid silence,

---

[1] *Turkey No. I.* (1877), no 316.   [2] *Ibid.* no. 847, 21 Oct.
[3] *Ibid.* no. 536, 6 Oct.   [4] 12 Oct., to Lady Bradford—Buckle, vi. p. 80.
[5] *Turkey No. I.* (1877), nos. 611-12.
[6] 14 Oct., Derby to Malet for Italian Government, repeated to other Embassies—*ibid.* no. 635.   [7] 17 Oct.—Buckle, vi. p. 81.
[8] Cf. Diktat of 14 Oct.—*G.P.* no. 246. At this stage popular German opinion is reflected in *Kladderadatsch's* comment upon "the hundred years' armistice, with ten years' notice", while Serbian women are being driven away with bound hands by Turkish soldiery.
[9] Diktat of 20 Oct.—*G.P.* no. 250.

because he really has no opinions on the matter" and "has only one object and wish—to prevent the renewal of the Anglo-Franco alliance".[1] In reality, of course, Bismarck trusted Russell, but not Russell's chiefs, and had shown a natural reserve towards London since what he regarded as its wrecking tactics towards the Memorandum. It is on record that at this stage he declined Russell's efforts to elicit a proposal from him, on the ground that he knew of nothing which England, Austria and Russia alike would accept without annoyance. At the same time he confided to Russell his own private view that "the whole of Turkey, including all its various races, is not, as a political institution, worth great wars between the Great Powers": that Austria-Hungary was quite wise to remain neutral towards Russia, reserving the power to occupy Bosnia as a *pis-aller*: and that England meanwhile would be wise to take Suez and Egypt—her weak spot (*wunde Stelle*)—while extracting from Russia a pledge to leave the Turks in Constantinople and perhaps making concessions to France in Syria.[2]

That considerations such as these were passing through Lord Beaconsfield's mind is revealed by a memorandum of Lord Barrington, with whom he discussed the view that Russia might be allowed to take Constantinople, if we took Egypt and thus "secured our highway to India". "The answer is obvious," said Lord Beaconsfield. "If the Russians had Constantinople, they could at any time march their army through Syria to the mouth of the Nile, and then what would be the use of our holding Egypt? Not even the command of the sea could help us under such circumstances. People who talk in this manner must be utterly ignorant of geography. Our strength is on the sea. Constantinople is the key of India, and not Egypt and the Suez Canal."[3]

Almost at the same time he told Derby, "As for compensation to England by having Egypt and Crete, this is moonshine. If Constantinople is Russian, they would only be an expensive encumbrance."[4] This view, fantastic as it may seem in these days of vastly improved communications, seems to have been very widely held at that time, and only yielded very gradually to the saner view expounded by Lord Salisbury, that the practice of looking at problems of the Middle East in the light of small-scale maps caused a lack of focus and led to highly fallacious conclusions. Beaconsfield's imagination,

[1] 10. Sept.—*Letters*, ii. p. 478.   [2] 20 Oct.—*G.P.* ii. no. 250.
[3] 23 Oct.—Buckle, vi. p. 84.   [4] 21 Oct.—*ibid.* p. 100.

which had stood him in such good stead in the question of the Canal, became mere fantasy when the prospects of invasion were considered: if he could have seen into the secret correspondence of Gorchakov and Shuvalov, he would have realised how little they thought about Egypt, and how absurd they held his suspicions to be. But his fantasy ran on while Serbia's danger grew acute and Russia was obviously preparing to save her from ruin: and he actually told the Cabinet that "he would like to buy a port in the Black Sea from the Porte—Batum . . . or Sinope. . . . What he wants is a Malta or Gibraltar which would prevent the Black Sea being a constant threat to our maritime power in the Mediterranean." [1] Well might Carnarvon anxiously write of his chief a few weeks later: "His mind is full of strange projects, and if he had been ten years younger he might have risked splitting the Cabinet in order to achieve them". [2]

The Tsar, though discouraged by Austria-Hungary's reserved attitude, had sent another friendly message to Francis Joseph, explaining that if Turkey remained recalcitrant, he must recall his Ambassador from Constantinople, that the Reichstadt Agreement would then acquire renewed importance and that he was ready to negotiate joint Austro-Russian action against Turkey. The Turkish victory over Serbia forced him to act hurriedly, and on 31 October a Russian ultimatum was presented to the Porte, imposing an armistice of two instead of six months.

It has generally been assumed that Serbia was only saved at the last moment by this ultimatum. If, however, the memoirs of General Ignatyev are to be believed, he himself had already on 30 October obtained from the Turks the acceptance of an armistice, and the cessation of hostilities had been fixed for three days later. But suddenly that evening he received orders from the Tsar to impose it by ultimatum. This, Ignatyev tells us, roused Elliot's indignation ("He suspected the sincerity of my actions"), convinced the Turks that Russia meant war and drove the Sultan away from the Russophil party and into the arms of Midhat. He ascribes it to a sudden impulse on the part of the nerve-racked and sentimental Tsar, for the moment influenced by the Moscow Committee. [3]

It is by no means improbable that a Turkish refusal would have been followed by an European war: but the Sultan found it advisable

---

[1] Hardy's Memo. of 28 Nov.—*Life of Gathorne Hardy*, i. p. 377.
[2] Hardinge, *Life of Carnarvon*, ii. p. 349.
[3] Onou, *Memoirs of Ignatyev*, i. pp. 20-21.

to yield, and the Tsar hastened to issue a fresh appeal to Francis Joseph for co-operation and to reassure the British Government. To Lord Augustus Loftus he expressed "his anxious desire" for an understanding with England and "pledged his honour that he had no views of conquest or of Constantinople",[1] adding that the British should dismiss from their minds this and two other bogies, the so-called will of Peter the Great and the alleged designs for the conquest of India. "One must be mad to think of a march upon India across those mountain ranges!"[2] "All he required was the amelioration of the position of the Christians, but not resting on Turkish promises, but on real efficient guarantees." That such were the sentiments, not merely of the autocrat himself, but also of his responsible ministers, is amply confirmed by the confidential correspondence of Prince Gorchakov with Count Shuvalov during the critical period of October and November 1876.[3] In a letter of 3 November the Chancellor expressed "profound surprise" at British suspicions, based on the will of Peter the Great. "I thought such old wives' tales (*vieilleries*) were discredited and relegated, with the conquest of India by Russia, to the domain of political mythology." The Tsars had repeatedly renounced such ambitions, and their word was something better than "a parliamentary declaration revocable at the will of a majority". They had proved the honesty of their professions in 1829, in 1848 and in 1870, when Europe was absorbed elsewhere and Russia had her chance. "The only rational combination for Russian interests", he proceeded to argue, "was to leave the keys of the Black Sea in hands too feeble to be able to close this trade outlet to Russia and menace her security. Turkish rule responded to this programme: is it our fault if the Turks abused it by making their rule insupportable to their Christian subjects? . . . It is really painful to see two great states which united could regulate European affairs to their mutual advantage and to the advantage of all, troubling themselves and the world by an antagonism resting on prejudices and misunderstandings. . . . The Eastern Question is not a purely Russian question, it affects the peace and prosperity of Europe and Christian

---

[1] *Turkey No. I.* (1877), no. 835, Loftus to Derby, 2 Nov.

[2] *G.P.* no. 253, Schweinitz to Bülow, 2 Nov.; and Schweinitz, *Denkwürdigkeiten*, i. p. 363.

[3] In 1924, through the kindness of MM. Sablin and Meyendorff, I obtained access to the archives of the Russian Embassy in London and copied the entire correspondence for the years 1874–8. The essential material was published in seven series of articles in the *Slavonic Review*, entitled "Russo-British Relations during the Eastern Crisis", down to January 1878.

civilisation. Is there not room enough for England to put herself at Russia's side? Have we not invited her to do so by inviting her squadrons to the Straits? What additional gage must we give, to show that we have no claim to the exclusive possession of Constantinople?" [1]

"But to conquer English prejudices, absurd as they may be," so he lamented in his next letter, "is a task beyond human powers." His only consolation was that Germany and Austria-Hungary were too well disposed towards Russia for London to be able to win them for any anti-Russian coalition, and that the worst that it could do was to exploit "the force of inertia which the Treaty of Paris created in favour of the Turks, by stipulating for the need of an agreement '*à six*' before any action can be taken in the Eastern Question". [2] At the same time Gorchakov showed intense irritation against Sir Henry Elliot for his Turcophil attitude. He told Shuvalov on 3 October that he had "unhappily positive proofs of his pernicious influence" at the Porte, and three weeks later declared that his "attitude and language exceed all limits". [3] On 15 November the Tsar himself, in conversation with the French Ambassador, openly accused Elliot of deterring the Turks from accepting the Conference which Derby was pressing on them. [4] Though this must, of course, be discounted as a Russian view, there can be no doubt whatever that Elliot had long been regarded at Constantinople as a main bulwark of the Turkish point of view.

[1] *R.B.D.* iii. no. 91 (3 Nov.).   [2] *Ibid.* no. 92.   [3] *Ibid.* nos. 84 and 90.
[4] *D.D.F.* ii. no. 113, Le Flô to Decazes, 15 Nov.

CHAPTER IV

THE CONFERENCE OF CONSTANTINOPLE

Lift up thy brow, renownéd Salisbury
And with a great heart heave away this storm.

KING JOHN, v. ii.

There was one force which Sir Henry Elliot resolutely ignored, and that was
the public opinion, the sympathies of the Christian world.

GEORGE WASHBURN, of Robert College

DERBY'S CONFERENCE PROPOSAL

FORTUNATELY the news of Loftus's conversation with the Tsar, received by telegram on 2 November, greatly reassured Derby, and it was at once decided by the Cabinet to accept the new situation created by the Porte's submission to the ultimatum, but to take the initiative in inviting the Powers to an European Conference. Fortunately, too, it was also decided that Lord Salisbury should be the chief British delegate—an appointment which both home and foreign opinion at once greeted as an ideal compromise, and indeed in a certain sense as the synthesis of two opposite extremes. Of special interest is Mr. Gladstone's reaction. Writing to Madame Novikov, he described it as "the best thing the Government has yet done in the Eastern Question". "Salisbury," he added, "has little foreign or eastern knowledge, and little craft. He is rough of tongue in public debate, but a great gentleman in private society. He is very remarkably clever, of unsure judgment, but is above everything that is mean: has no Disraelite prejudices, keeps a conscience and has plenty of manhood and character."[1] The essence of the matter could hardly have been summed up better. John Bright was more reserved, but publicly expressed the hope that Salisbury's "liberality, justice and strong intellect" would "have fair play" at the impending Conference.[2]

Derby urged Salisbury to go, "because as a leading member of the Cabinet", he would speak "as one having authority and not as the diplomatists", because the public did not regard him as "Turkish",

[1] W. T. Stead, *The M.P. for Russia*, i. p. 272.
[2] Speech of 4 Dec. 1876, Birmingham.

and because he would be able to defend his own acts in Parliament afterwards.[1] Beaconsfield strongly pressed acceptance on him and it is highly significant of the situation that Salisbury in consenting, added the phrase, *"But it is essential that your policy should be settled first"*,[2] and warned Derby that it was necessary "to determine, at least roughly", beforehand what was "the minimum of security for the Christians" and "the maximum of interference" with Turkish independence. On the very same day Beaconsfield tried at some length to "impress upon" Derby "the importance, if we wish to secure a long peace, of *coming to some understanding with some European Power*"—if not Germany, then Austria and perhaps France.[3] In other words, Salisbury's inference that the Prime Minister's policy was entirely opportunist would seem to be fully justified. How could he expect to reach a satisfactory result with statesmen whom he contemptuously described as "the old coxcomb at Livadia" and "the fox at Varzin"[4] or with others whom he despised as much as Andrássy or Decazes?

Beaconsfield's famous speech at the Guildhall on 9 November reflects his undoubted irritation. In it he laid down as his Government's twofold aim, the maintenance of peace, through the upholding of existing treaties, and the amelioration of internal conditions in Turkey. These treaties were "not antique and dusty obsolete documents", but had been revised by all Europe as recently as 1871. The Andrássy Note had had the "fatal fault" of being "inopportune": the Berlin Memorandum had been rejected because it summoned Turkey to perform impossible tasks which would have led to military occupation, while the later proposal for triple parallel action [the Sumarokov Mission] was a violation of the most solemn treaties. Peace had almost been achieved in September, all the Powers had "acceded, no Power with more readiness and cordiality than Russia": but "the indignant burst of feeling" at the atrocities led the Serbs to renew war. In other words, he tried indirectly to lay the main blame upon the Opposition for the events leading to the Russian ultimatum. After expressing confidence in "the abilities, grasp of subject, tact and firmness of character" of Lord Salisbury, he concluded with a peroration which aroused many protests in the country and some alarm on the Continent. "Peace", he said, "is especially

[1] 3 Nov.—*Life of Salisbury*, ii. p. 90.
[2] *Ibid.* p. 91; Buckle, vi. p. 87. [3] *Ibid.* p. 88.
[4] Livadia was the Tsar's "Balmoral" in the Crimea, where Gorchakov then was: Varzin was a country-house of Bismarck's.

an English policy. She is not an aggressive Power. . . . She covets no cities and no provinces. What she wishes is to maintain and enjoy the unexampled Empire which she has built up and which it is her pride to remember exists as much on sympathy as on force. But, though the policy of England is peace, there is no country so well prepared for war as our own. If she enters into conflict in a righteous cause . . ., if the contest is one which concerns her liberty or her Empire, her resources are, I feel, inexhaustible. She is not a country that, when she enters into a campaign, has to ask herself whether she can support a second or a third campaign. She enters into a campaign which she will not terminate till right is done."[1]

As *The Times* somewhat caustically remarked, he had enveloped his subject "in a haze of grandiloquent mystery".[2]   Robert Lowe replied in a most aggressive speech at Bristol, but hit the nail on the head when he represented the Prime Minister as saying in effect to Lord Salisbury, "Go, my son, relieve the Turkish rayahs from their miseries, but mind you don't give up the independence of Turkey!" "I say he cannot do both," added Lowe: "it is beyond the power of human nature."

The very next day after the Guildhall speech, but, of course, before its text had reached him, Tsar Alexander addressed the nobles of Moscow in sensational terms. "In this unequal struggle the Montenegrins have, as on all previous occasions, shown themselves to be real heroes. Unfortunately the same cannot be said of the Serbs, notwithstanding the presence of our volunteers in their ranks, many of whom have shed their blood for the Slav cause. I know that all Russia most warmly sympathises with me in the sufferings of our brethren and co-religionists." After this very pointed differentiation between the two Serb states—which is to be noted as a turning-point of policy, fraught with many future consequences—he went on to express his efforts for the preservation of peace and his "most ardent wish" for the success of the Conference. "Should this, however, not be achieved, and should I see that we cannot obtain such guarantees as are necessary for carrying out what we have a right to demand of the Porte, I am firmly determined to act independently, and I am convinced that in this case all Russia will respond to my summons, should I consider it necessary and should the honour of

[1] *The Times*, 10 Nov. 1876.
[2] *Ibid.* leader of 10 Nov. "Why", it pertinently asked, "was the Andrássy Note inopportune? Because we were about three months in arrear in appreciating the conflict."

Russia require it." In a certain sense the Tsar may be said to have killed two birds with one stone: for he associated himself with the most ardent aspirations of the Slavophils, while at the same time throwing over the Serbs by a gesture which Vienna was meant to take as a fresh recognition of Reichstadt.

The two speeches were quite independent of each other, but in the general nervousness of Europe they were widely interpreted as leading towards war, and Decazes described them as having "clouded the horizon".[1] On the other hand, the Chancellor of the Exchequer, Sir Stafford Northcote, made a really conciliatory speech, in which, while upholding his chief's main thesis, he declined to see any cause for alarm in the Tsar's phrases. He frankly admitted the weakness of the Turkish central government, and the "impossibility of securing the peace of Europe unless we take steps also for the improved administration of the provinces of Turkey".[2]

On the very day of the Guildhall speech Stratford de Redcliffe received a visit from Algernon Borthwick, of the *Morning Post*, who maintained that the Government was "fully prepared for war—ships, troops, gunboats, artillery and everything".[3] But the "Eltchi" in his old age no longer responded as in Crimean days, and sent on the news to Gladstone, adding the hope that Derby's proposals would avert war. This time he could see no other course save "that of taking Bruin by the paw and going with him as far as we reasonably and honourably can, . . . at the same time striving by diplomatic action to *keep him within bounds*!!"[4]

LORD SALISBURY'S MISSION

It was arranged that the Conference should be held at Constantinople in the second half of December, but that there should be preliminary discussions between the six Ambassadors. On the initiative of the Prince of Wales, Lord Salisbury left England early, in order to exchange views with the statesmen of the Continent on his way. It is highly significant that the future King Edward should have stressed the extreme value of these personal contacts, that the Foreign Office officials should have opposed anything so unconventional and intelligent, and that Beaconsfield should have sided

---

[1] *D.D.F.* no. 110, Decazes to Gontaut-Biron, 14 Nov.
[2] This Sir William Harcourt described as "a piece of sticking plaster put over a wound while there is festering matter still below"—Hansard, ccxxxiii. p. 112.
[3] *Gladstone Papers*, Stratford to Gladstone, 10 Nov. 1876.   [4] *Ibid.* 14 Nov.

strongly with the Prince and denounced "Tenterdenism—a dusty affair, not suited to the time and things we have to grapple with".[1] "You must remember", wrote the Prime Minister to Salisbury, *"we suffer from a feeble and formal diplomacy*, and there has been little real interchange of thought between the English Government and foreign Powers. . . . You should personally know the men who are governing the world, and . . . under circumstances which will allow you to gauge their character, strength and infirmities." It was here that he himself was most at fault, but that he had the imagination to see what was needed and thus gave the first incentive to the diplomatic career of one of our greatest Foreign Secretaries.

Salisbury appears to have accepted the mission, not so much out of enthusiasm as from a sense of duty, foreseeing that it might resolve itself into "seasickness, much French and failure". He went first to Paris, and talked with the Duke Decazes, who was already nervously speculating on a series of territorial adjustments and compensations and now vaguely hinted at the occupation of Bosnia, Bulgaria and Macedonia by Austria, Russia and Britain respectively, while at the back of his mind he was afraid of Italy claiming Tunis.[2] Salisbury escaped with vague phrases about misgovernment and guarantees.[3]

In Berlin he had a very frank conversation with Bismarck, and as the record left of it by the two statesmen is almost identical, we are safe in assuming its general accuracy. Bismarck's "view of the prospects of peace was very gloomy", nor did he believe that German intervention would help matters. Germany was not much interested in the fate of Turkey, but very much interested in Britain, Russia and Austria remaining friends: he therefore urged Britain not to start "a precipitate (*übereilt*) war": for though the failure of the Conference, for which he was prepared, would probably lead to a Russo-Turkish war, this need not involve Russia and Britain, in view of the Tsar's explicit pledge regarding Constantinople, and besides there would be plenty of time to negotiate between the crossing of the Danube and any danger to the capital. His concrete suggestion was that Austria-Hungary should occupy Bosnia and Britain Egypt, and when Salisbury promptly protested at this idea, he at once changed his ground and suggested Constantinople itself: the three Powers could then easily come to terms, the more so as Russia was

---

[1] Lord Tenterden was then Permanent Under-Secretary. *Life of Salisbury*, ii. p. 95, 10 Nov., Beaconsfield to Salisbury.
[2] *D.D.F.* ii. no. 116.   [3] *Life of Salisbury*, ii. p. 96.

likely to meet with more resistance from Turkey than she bargained for. Bismarck's main object was to dispel Salisbury's suspicions of Russia, to convince him that she had no cut-and-dried plan and to make it clear that Germany was bound to use every effort to avert an Austro-Russian war, while relatively indifferent to a mere Russo-Turkish war, as not endangering German interests (and indeed, he might have added, even serving the convenient medical purpose of blood-letting in the Near East). Salisbury's net impression was that Bismarck would help him at the Conference, but "does not believe in a solution and is only occupied with settling what shall be done when the Turkish Empire comes in pieces".[1] He reached the same general conclusion as Lord Odo Russell, that Bismarck, though "doubtless Machiavellian", genuinely desired to maintain peace between Russia and Britain, or he could not have used the arguments which he did: and he was confirmed in this by his conversations with the Emperor William and, above all, with the Crown Princess, who "hates Bismarck like poison", but was most emphatic as to his pacific aims.

His next stage was Vienna. He found Andrássy scarcely less sceptical than Bismarck as to the issue of the Conference, but anxious to co-operate with his two allies, and only prepared to occupy Bosnia in case of real necessity. Above all, Andrássy was eager to know how far Britain would go in opposition to Russia: the scepticism which all along inspired his attitude towards London, at the initial stages of consular intervention and his own Note no less than during the secret overtures of June 1877 and January 1878, was now only too apparent: and Salisbury's cautious answers probably only served to increase his resolve not to pull chestnuts out of the fire for Britain.

Two not unimportant details in the conversation were the almost morbid stress laid by Andrássy upon secrecy—he insisted on a pledge that his words should not figure in a British Blue Book—and his anxiety that Count Beust, his own Ambassador in London, should not be admitted to the inner secrets. This attitude—which materially contributed towards confusing the issue—was due to the undoubted fact that Beust, Andrássy's predecessor in office and once the champion of a French rather than a German orientation, had by no

[1] G.P. ii. no. 263, 27 Nov., Bülow to Münster; no. 264, 29 Nov., Bülow to Schweinitz; and Life of Salisbury, ii. pp. 96-9, Salisbury to Derby, 23 and 25 Nov. Bismarck allowed Count Stolberg to inform Andrássy of his talk with Salisbury—Wertheimer, op. cit. ii. p. 363.

means abandoned all hope of returning to the Ballplatz and did not scruple to intrigue against his chief when occasion arose.

In Rome Salisbury found a Russophil current at the Court, but a natural resolve to avoid any rash intervention. One result of his journey he promptly reported to Derby: "In the course of my travels I have not succeeded in finding the friend of the Turk. He does not exist. Most believe his hour is come."[1]

Shuvalov, who reported home what he could glean, described Salisbury as "singularly emancipated from the central Government" and as pushing his silence (*mutisme*) so far as to embarrass his chiefs. He telegraphed "neither from Berlin, Vienna nor Rome", sent no special messenger and after ten days' delay sent a statement "so succinct . . . that his colleagues accuse Derby of concealing the results of Salisbury's visits".[2]

Lord Salisbury was furnished by the Government with very full instructions for the Conference—its aims being defined as (1) the independence and territorial integrity of Turkey; (2) a renunciation by the Powers of "any territorial advantage, any exclusive influence" or any special commercial concession; and (3) peace on the basis of the *status quo* towards Serbia and Montenegro, "a system of local or administrative autonomy" for Bosnia—but "there is to be no question of a tributary state"—and similar guarantees against maladministration in Bulgaria. An interesting distinction was drawn between Serbia and Montenegro, the opinion being expressed "that it would be politic on the part of the Porte" to cede to the latter certain adjacent districts, together with "the port" of Spizza, which are of no sort of value to Turkey, but rather "a cause of embarrassment". The Porte's objections to "the diplomatic discussion" of autonomy were squarely challenged, and the reforms recommended in the Andrássy Note—so grudgingly accepted by London in the previous January—now accepted as "a useful starting point" of negotiation. After a lengthy disquisition on the various measures of reform put forward in Turkey during the previous forty years, the instructions conclude with a two-edged affirmation of policy: "Her Majesty's Government cannot countenance proposals, however plausible or well-intentioned, which would bring foreign armies into Turkish territory", but is "at the same time . . . resolved not to sanction misgovernment and oppression, and if the Porte by ob-

[1] 30 Nov.—*Life of Salisbury*, ii. p. 107.
[2] *R.B.D.* iv. no. 108, Shuvalov to Gorchakov, 23 Nov./5 Dec. 1876.

stinacy or apathy opposes the efforts which are now making to place the Ottoman Empire on a more secure basis, the responsibility of the consequences which may ensue will rest solely with the Sultan and his advisers".[1] This final phrase was reported by Count Münster to Berlin as "the main point", but he added that Lord Derby, in conversation with him and Beust, had insisted upon his desire to leave the Porte an entirely free hand and disclaimed all idea of coercion on the part of England—a passage which drew from the Emperor William the terse comment, "That is to say, he is *not* willing to avert war".[2]

In a further dispatch Lord Salisbury was requested to enter further protests at the Porte for its failure to punish those guilty of atrocities and to point out that "even if the dictates of humanity may have no influence" with the Government, it might be affected by "the most ordinary considerations of policy".[3]

There is a very different note in the private letters addressed by Beaconsfield himself to Salisbury after his departure. He, too, is sceptical as to the Conference, unless "Russia may wish honourably to avoid a struggle which the state of her finances, the unpreparedness of her armies and her want of naval power, may make her desirous to postpone"—here we see into the somewhat dangerous calculations which underlay his policy. He thinks it "wise to assume" that Russia will invade Turkey, and Austria "seek consolation" not only in Bosnia, but Hercegovina and Serbia also: and so England must prepare to send troops for the defence of Constantinople. And now his imagination runs riot. "It is a most critical moment in European politics. If Russia is not checked, the Holy Alliance will be revived in aggravated form and force. Germany will have Holland: and France, Belgium and England will be in a position I trust I shall never live to witness. If we act in the manner I have generally indicated, we shall probably in conclusion obtain some commanding stronghold in Turkey from which we need never recede. It will be for the interest of the Porte itself that we should, and if they would sell to us, for instance, Varna, the supremacy of Russia might for ever be arrested. I am surprised that Bismarck should go on harping about Egypt. Its occupation by us would embitter France, and I don't see it would at all benefit us, if Russia possessed Constantinople. I would sooner we had Asia Minor than Egypt."

[1] *Turkey No. II.* (1877)—no. 1, 20 Nov., p. 9.
[2] "!! d.h. den Krieg *nicht* verhüten wollen"—*G.P.* no. 268, 20 Dec.
[3] *Ibid.* no. 18, 24 Nov.

He was ready to propose to the Cabinet this idea of occupation, subject to the consent of the Porte and to a pretence at great reluctance,[1] and he rashly assumed that "40,000 English troops would be ample for European Turkey". Above all, the Russian idea of triple occupation—which had underlain the Sumarokov Mission—must be resisted absolutely, for "it would insure another Navarino".[2]

THE "NATIONAL CONVENTION" AT THE ST. JAMES'S HALL

Meanwhile the excitement throughout the country had grown steadily in volume and intensity. As has already been pointed out, Gladstone's famous pamphlet was only the match that kindled the flame: it had already been preceded by a spontaneous outburst of feeling, especially in the north of England, on a scale hitherto unknown in our history. Men like Edward Freeman and Sir George Cox, while duly grateful to Gladstone for his intervention, were naturally enough annoyed that there should still be so little recognition of views which they had consistently pressed since before the Crimean War.

At first opposition to Disraeli's policy was general in the Liberal party, which unanimously approved Hartington's demand for an autumn session, but a gradual divergence of opinion arose between those who desired close co-operation with Russia in bringing the Turks to reason and those who were content with shaking off the entanglements of the Turkish alliance—in a word, between the rival advocates of "coercion" and "abstention". Detestation of Turkey was not, of course, confined to the Liberals, but was shared by large sections of the Tories: but extreme distrust of Russia, in view of her recent record in Poland, Hungary and Central Asia, had a paralysing effect in many quarters, and was felt by none more strongly than by the Radical group of Dilke and Chamberlain.

At the end of September a meeting of northern Liberals was held at Darlington, to organise fresh protests on a really representative basis, and the eventual result was the formation of a "National Convention on the Eastern Question", sponsored by many men of great prominence in church and state. It was inaugurated on 8 December by a double meeting at the St. James's Hall, Piccadilly, its two chairmen being the Duke of Westminster and Lord Shaftes-

[1] "It must be so done that we must seem almost unwilling to consent."
[2] 29 Nov. and 1 Dec.—Buckle, vi. pp. 103-6.

bury: and among the many speakers were the Bishop of Oxford, Canon Liddon, the Rev. W. Denton (author of one of the first English books on Serbia), Dr. Allon (a prominent Nonconformist divine and editor of the *British Quarterly*), James Bryce, Freeman, Anthony Trollope, and out of a band of thirty M.P.s, Evelyn Ashley, George Trevelyan, Fawcett, Lord Arthur Russell and Sir George Campbell, ex-Governor of Bengal. Among those present on the platform were William Morris, J. R. Green, Lecky, Ruskin, Burne-Jones, Stopford Brooke and Mark Pattison. A fiery letter of Carlyle was read out, and Darwin, Herbert Spencer and Browning conveyed their active sympathy. At the time there was a great deal of mocking criticism levelled at the motley array of clergymen of all persuasions who attended the meeting. But as Freeman effectively pointed out, "what stronger argument can there be in favour of a certain object than that it commends itself alike to High Church and Broad Church, to Nonconformists of every sect, to men of no special religious creed at all?" [1]

Gladstone explained to Granville his motive in coming specially from Hawarden to attend. "I came to the conclusion after much consideration that it was desirable for me to make a further utterance. It is anything but a pleasant task, for the 'situation', which some months ago was in my judgment comparatively easy, has become enormously difficult. In this difficult situation we send a clever but raw man to face much low cunning—of the Turk—and much astuteness—of the Russian—without, so far as I know, anything to lean upon but his own good intentions and natural talents, for not one of all the Powers is entirely trustworthy. . . . I need hardly say that I shall do nothing intentionally to perplex Salisbury: poor fellow, he will, unless I am mistaken, have in all likelihood quite enough to perplex him already. . . . So far as I can forecast the probable matter of my speech, I do not think it will be disagreeable to you." [2]

Needless to say, however, his speech was the sensation of the meeting. He proclaimed that "the power and influence and reputation of England were being employed for a purpose directly at variance with the convictions of the country", but supported the appointment of Lord Salisbury as British delegate and insisted that every effort must be made to strengthen his hands. The Prime Minister's speech of 31 July, with its references to "imaginary atrocities" and its

[1] *Contemp. Rev.* Feb. 1877, "The English People in relation to the Eastern Question".   [2] *Granville Papers*, 6 Dec. 1876, Gladstone to Granville.

claim that the Powers had come over to the British side, would no longer be possible to-day, and his Guildhall speech, with its insistence upon those treaties which the Porte had "broken and trampled under foot", was also open to challenge. "We want to cut him adrift from that speech": for its effect upon Russia and upon Turkey had been equally mischievous. "Constantinople", he added, "is described by all who know it as a paradise of nature. . . . There is also such a thing as a paradise of fools."

Gladstone admitted that both Russia and Austria required watching, but flatly denied Disraeli's contentions that the Serbian war was the wickedest on record, or that the Bosnian rising was the work of foreign emissaries. The present policy of Britain was simply driving the Christians of Turkey into the arms of Russia, and stood in strong contrast with that of Canning, whose initiative first won the confidence of the Greeks, then invoked the aid of Russia and finally, hand in hand with her, solicited the aid of Europe. In a word, "the traditional policy of England was not complicity with guilty power but sympathy with suffering weakness".[1]

The meeting unquestionably made a deep impression upon the country, and *The Times* of that morning freely admitted, "we have never known any association for a political object which has obtained support over so large a part of the scale of English society". Next day it added that "to all save the wilfully blind it is clear that the agitation of August and September was no transient flash of emotion, but expressed a profound and fixed determination". But it was perhaps not unnatural that the Turcophils should have taken especial exception to the speech of E. A. Freeman and concentrated much of their criticism upon certain phrases pitched on the top-note of aggression and overstatement, and of distinctly questionable taste. Not content with denouncing "our barbarous ally" Turkey, he took as his motto *fiat justitia, ruat coelum*[2] and made a frontal attack upon the Guildhall pronouncement: "From amid the clatter of winecups a voice of defiance went forth, conveying the brag . . . that England would fight a first and a second and a third campaign rather than permit another Power to do the work which she herself ought to accomplish". Would they, he asked, fight to uphold *the integrity and independence of Sodom*? And then followed the culminating phrase:

[1] *The Times*, 8 and 9 Dec. 1876, reports and leaders.
[2] It is surely well to record Lord Selborne's comment on this much misrepresented speech of Freeman. By this Latin quotation "he does not mean he *wishes* the heavens to fall"—Selborne, *Memorials*, iii. p. 457.

"We are told that English interests demand it, that our dominion in India will be imperilled, that the civilised world will crumble into atoms, if a Russian ship should be seen in the Mediterranean. If it be so, then I say, perish the interests of England, perish our dominion in India, rather than that we should strike a blow or speak a word on behalf of the wrong against the right. But I need hardly answer fallacies which have been answered a thousand times already. *Look at the map: the path to India does not lie by Constantinople.*"[1]

At the time this crude overstatement of a good case tended to obscure the undoubted fact that Freeman—best known for his reconstruction of the Saxon and Norman past of his own country—had made many valuable contributions to the history of the Near East alike in ancient and in modern times and knew more of the Eastern Question than almost any person in England. His studies of that fascinating Illyrian borderland between East and West which bred so many of the later Emperors and which has always possessed a strange complex dual character of its own, are equally original from the purely historical and from the architectural point of view.[2] How prophetic he could be on occasion, may be shown by a single passage written in 1877: "We do not presume to say what the final solution ought to be, whether it is to be sought in empire or federation, in founding new states or in enlarging old ones. . . . But we do lay it down as a principle that no settlement of these lands will be wholesome or lasting which does not make the coast and the land behind it, in some shape or another, parts of one political whole."[3]

Unfortunately Freeman did not always rise to this level, and had already imparted to the controversy a violent personal animus against Disraeli. Writing in November of public meetings at Exeter and Manchester, he declared: "Whether we are a majority, I cannot tell: but I am sure we are a large enough part of the English people to make even the Jew in his drunken insolence think twice before he goes to war in our teeth".[4] Far from being an isolated phrase, this was entirely characteristic of Freeman's utterances throughout the long crisis and illustrates only too well the extraordinary acrimony which Disraeli inspired in many quarters and which was fully reciprocated

[1] The controversy was further complicated by misquotation. The above passage is Freeman's own version, as admitted in his letter to *The Times* of 16 Dec., defending himself against the strictures of Sir Stafford Northcote and others.
[2] Notably *Subject and Neighbour Lands of Venice*, and *Historical Essays*, 3rd Series.
[3] *Op. cit.* iii. p. 421, "The Southern Slaves".
[4] 27 Nov.—*The M.P. for Russia*, i. p. 265.

towards Gladstone by Tory fanatics, of the stamp of Henry Chaplin, Lord Stanley of Alderley or Lord Elcho.

Though the St. James's Hall meeting aroused great indignation among the extreme Turcophils and led the Queen to wish that the Attorney-General "could be set at these men",[1] it met with approval in many unexpected quarters: and on 11 December we find Lord Granville writing to Mr. Gladstone that Lady Derby had expressed satisfaction at the holding of the meeting, and "that Lady Salisbury had said that Paris and Berlin had opened her and Salisbury's eyes very much".[2] Meanwhile the rabidly Protestant *Rock*, undeterred by the fact that Lords Acton and Camoys alone represented the Catholics and that the Nonconformists were already to the fore, denounced the whole agitation as "a Ritualist conspiracy".

On the other hand, Lord Hartington remained not merely unimpressed, but positively hostile. He had opposed its being held, because it would get "into the hands of men of extreme opinions", like Freeman, Liddon and "the innumerable parsons" on the prospectus of the meeting. "The number of the latter on the list is quite enough for me": and he was "in daily dread" of seeing Gladstone's name added.[3] After the meeting had been held, he was "rather surprised" at Granville's view that it had been a success.[4] He himself saw in it nothing "either new or useful. All the old anti-Turk abuse was warmed up again, a good deal of unnecessary confidence in Russia expressed and all the difficulties carefully ignored." Gladstone, he went on, half soliloquising, "might be supported in the country at a general election, though I doubt it: but I feel certain that the Whigs and moderate Liberals in the House are a good deal disgusted, and I am much afraid that if he goes on much further, nothing can prevent a break-up of the party." He was averse to helping the Turks and afraid of the Government giving them undue encouragement, but at the same time "I don't feel the slightest confidence in Russia and think it would be a mistake to base our policy in any degree on Russian assurances", especially as there was no security against the seizure of Constantinople beyond the Tsar's bare word. "The Conference people", he concluded, not without much show of reason, "appear to be so anxious to get rid of the Turks and so confident in the good intentions of Russia, that they don't care to look at what

[1] 18 Dec., to Beaconsfield—*Letters*, ii. p. 504.
[2] *Gladstone Papers*, 11 Dec., Granville to Gladstone.
[3] 26 Nov.—*Life of Duke of Devonshire*, i. pp. 183-4.
[4] *Ibid.* pp. 185-6, 18 Dec.

may follow the destruction of the Turkish Government."[1] It is abundantly clear from this and other letters that Hartington was much more interested in Liberal unity than in a solution of the Eastern Question, and there is a curious parallel between his attitude and that of Salisbury, who certainly cared more for the merits of the case, but was constantly held back by regard for the interests of his party.[2]

OLGA NOVIKOV

At the close of the meeting Mr. Gladstone offered his arm to Madame Novikov and ostentatiously escorted her from the platform to the door. The controversy that has raged round this altogether trifling incident speaks volumes for the intensity of feeling aroused by the Eastern controversy. But in any case the narrative would not be complete without some account of this remarkable woman, whose personal influence upon Russo-British relations was a very real one, even though it has been grossly exaggerated alike by friend and by foe. Olga Kireyev was the daughter of a Russian officer of good family, her husband, General Alexander Novikov, held a post in the General Staff, while his brother Eugene was for many years Russian Ambassador at Vienna, where he enjoyed the special confidence of Count Andrássy and followed a strongly Austrophil policy, in sharp contrast to the Slavophil circles to which his family belonged. Olga and her brothers were partly educated by a Scottish tutor, and after 1873 she paid several prolonged visits to London, where she was introduced by the veteran Ambassador Baron Brunnov, won many friends by her vivacity, charm and breadth of interest, and held a small salon of her own at Claridge's, to which she attracted men as different as Kinglake, Froude and Freeman; Tyndall, Gladstone and Carlyle ; Charles Villiers, Hayward and Lord Napier.

It was not, however, till the autumn of 1876 that Madame Novikov assumed an active political rôle, and the decisive factor was the heroic death of her brother Nicholas Kireyev, the first of the Russian volunteers to fall in the Serbian war. He had been a popular figure in Moscow society, and his gallantry and the rumour—probably false—that his body had been mutilated, caused great excitement in Russia and led the Slavophil group to redouble its agitation. A regular legend gathered round him, and this is reflected in Kinglake's almost mystical allusions in the new preface to his famous *History of*

---

[1] *Life of Granville*, ii. p. 167.   [2] See *infra*, p. 157.

the Crimean War,[1] but also in the more sober pages of Mackenzie Wallace's book on Russia, and again in the rambling reminiscences of Philip Salusbury, one of the few Englishmen who fought in the Serbian ranks.[2]

Her brother's memory roused Madame Novikov to action, and in a series of somewhat emotional letters, published under the title of *Is Russia Wrong?* she set herself to refute Lord Beaconsfield's preposterous legend of the "secret societies" and to defend and justify the Slavophil policy of "emancipation", as "due to the same benevolent spirit which leads English people to send tracts to Fiji cannibals". At the same time she drew an emphatic distinction between the two Russias, "official and national", St. Petersburg and Moscow. "*St. Petersburg, thank God, is not Russian, any more than the West-end of London is English*": and "I grieve to say Russia has its Beaconsfields".[3]

The Turcophils seem never to have stopped to consider how distasteful such language was to official Russia and its diplomatic representatives, or perhaps sometimes assumed a skilful division of the rôles between the two currents: but in actual fact, while Beaconsfield coined for her the nickname "Member for Russia"—which W. T. Stead's interesting literary extravaganza has perpetuated—and while the Jingo press was denouncing her as an agent of the Tsar, she was all the time virtually boycotted by her own Embassy. In all the hundreds of telegrams and confidential letters that passed between Count Shuvalov and St. Petersburg from 1875 to 1878, I have not found one single reference, direct or indirect, to Madame Novikov: and it is not too much to say that both Shuvalov and her own brother-in-law Eugene Novikov at the Vienna Embassy found her activities most embarrassing.

Her true importance was entirely misjudged at the time: it lay

[1] Sixth ed., published in Jan. 1877. Lecky told Mme. Novikov that this would make her brother's name "a household word in England" (*The M.P. for Russia*, i. p. 210).

[2] See *Two Months with Tchernaieff in Servia* (1877), p. 194. This book is a delightful illustration of the complete ignorance of Balkan affairs then prevalent in England. Salusbury, who was only twenty-one and a lieutenant in the Cheshire Light Infantry, went out to Belgrade with an introduction from a mutual friend to "Prince Karageorgevitch" (then Pretender to the throne and afterwards King Peter of Jugoslavia) and sent it in to the palace, in the fond belief that he and Prince Milan Obrenović were identical!! (see p. 23). And afterwards, in his book, he was not ashamed to describe the incident in detail! Eventually the Prince sent Salusbury the Order of Takovo for his gallantry.

[3] The preface to the second edition was written by no other than Froude, who assumed that public opinion had "already decided that English bayonets shall not be stained again in defence of Turkish tyranny".

in her influence, not with her own Government, which regarded her as a mischievous busy-body, but with some of the foremost writers, politicians and publicists of Britain, and in the indirect contacts which she contrived to maintain between them and opinion in Moscow. At a later stage she established a fighting alliance with W. T. Stead, who, as editor of the *Northern Echo*, was the outrider and trumpeter of the twin cause of Balkan liberation and Anglo-Russian friendship—a cause to which he remained consistently true till the Hague Peace Conference and the *rapprochement* of 1907. After Madame Novikov's return to Russia in the autumn of 1877, Stead corresponded with her almost daily, keeping her informed of every phase of the agitation against war and thus providing for her Moscow friends the proof that British idealism was still a force with which to reckon.

The picture would not be complete without a few illustrations.

Side by side with these scurrilities let us place some of the comments of *Punch* and of that inspired caricaturist Tenniel. On 21 October Dr. Bull administers a "A Pill in Time"—labelled "armistice"—to the Sick Man of Europe. On 28 October "A Break in the Game" is depicted—John Bull throws up his hand. The outcome of the Russian ultimatum is represented as "Doubtful Diplomacy" on the part of Britain: a crowd of Balkan children are seen running to the Russian Bear, while John Bull asks Lord Derby, "Is *that* what you've been driving at?"[1] A fortnight later we see a football team gathering on the field for "A Fresh Kick-Off", the ball being "the Eastern Question": and Captain Beaconsfield, pointing to the burly Salisbury, calls out, "There, stand out of the way, Elliot, we've got a stronger man".[2]

Next week again the British Lion addresses Beaconsfield with vigorous bluntness: "Look here, I don't understand *you*! But it's right you should understand *me*! *I don't fight to uphold what's going on yonder!*" Early in December the Russian Bear and the British Lion, both in soldiers' uniform, meet at a cross-road where one signpost is marked Bulgaria and Bosnia, the other Constantinople. "*That's* my road," says the Bear, pointing to the former. "It's mine too," says the Lion. "Let's go together. When we can't, it will be time enough to quarrel."[3]

Salisbury's arrival at Constantinople is greeted with the apt and graceful quotation from Shakespeare's *King John* which forms the

[1] 4 Nov.   [2] 18 Nov.   [3] 25 Nov.

motto for this chapter. The Christmas number reveals the Great
Powers stirring a vast pudding for Dame Europa's dinner. The
Turk, as a small obstreperous boy, is seen thrusting in his scimitar
and is held back by Salisbury with the words, "No, my little man,
you mustn't stir it. You'll only make a mess and spoil the pudding".
The first number of the New Year depicts a fat old Turk with his
hookah, blowing bubbles of constitution—"One Bubble more!"

HUMPHREY SANDWITH

Among the lesser figures on the stage, none more fully deserves a
niche of honour than Humphrey Sandwith,[1] who as a young doctor
had worked under Stratford de Redcliffe at Constantinople, accompanied Layard to Nineveh, organised the medical service at Kars
in 1855 during its famous defence by Fenwick Williams, and thus
had an intimate personal knowledge of Turkey and the Balkans,
extending over twenty-five years. During the war of 1876 he was in
Serbia,[2] visiting the Drina army with Colonel Mure, the member for
Renfrewshire,[3] advising the Serbian authorities on medical matters
and launching an appeal in England on behalf of the wounded
and refugees. The extent to which the Serbian Government trusted
him—despite Prince Milan's not unnatural hostility to Britain—is
shown by the mission with which Jovan Ristić wished to entrust him
early in August, with the private approval of the brilliant British
Agent-General, Mr. White. He was to visit Constantinople secretly,
put out a feeler for peace and suggest an alliance with Turkey
against both Austria and Russia, in return for a Serbian mandate in
Bosnia. It may well be doubted whether this could have led anywhere, but in any case it was nipped in the bud by the hostility of
the Russian Agent.

Early in 1877 Sandwith was back in England, lecturing and
writing on the Eastern Question, supplying information to the

---

[1] For details see a not very adequate *Memoir* by his nephew Thomas Humphrey
Ward (1884) and a number of his letters in *Letters to a Victorian Editor: Henry
Allon* (ed. Dr. Albert Peel, 1929). His articles, published mainly in the *British
Quarterly Review* (January and July 1876, January 1877 and October 1878) are still
worth reading.

[2] It is interesting to note that as early as 1865—in a preface to *Notes on the South
Slavonic Countries* (a paper prepared for the British Association by Miss Mackenzie
and Miss Irby) he insisted on the spelling "Serbia" not "Servia"—a change not
generally accepted in England till August 1914.

[3] Mure afterwards pled the cause of Serbia before an unsympathetic House of
Commons, coining the phrase of her "mad chivalry".

Liberal leaders, openly criticising the Disraelian policy and collecting funds for a hospital which he was able to open at Bucarest on the outbreak of the Russo-Turkish War. The tribute eventually paid by Canon Liddon to this man with "the head of a man and the heart of a woman" has stood the test of history and comes from one who, like Sandwith, had helped to vindicate the honour of Britain. "Of Englishmen who sympathised with the subject races in European Turkey, some fought, some spoke, some wrote: Dr. Sandwith did all three. The misery of the Christian population in Turkey was only rendered possible by the ignorance or the incredulity of Europe. . . . Sandwith was resolved that this ignorance, sometimes involuntary, sometimes voluntary, should cease."[1]

The Queen's View of Patriotism

Meanwhile the Queen, throwing her wonted restraint to the winds, and at the same time begging the whole question, complained to Disraeli of "the unpatriotic and disloyal conduct . . . of public men who would hand over the interests and honour of their country to Russia".[2] A few weeks earlier she had told her son-in-law Lord Lorne —obviously with the intention that he should repeat it to his father the Duke of Argyll, now and later a consistent Gladstonian—that in her view Gladstone seemed to have taken leave of his reason and to have "done irreparable mischief in encouraging Russia and people abroad to think that we shall never fight or resist their encroachments and arrogance".[3] The plain fact is that Russia and Turkey had become bugbears to the two rival factions, and that few on either side could see the whole question in perspective. Gladstone was one of the rare exceptions who saw the enormity of Turkish rule, yet had no intention of giving Russia a free hand. Lord Carnarvon, who as yet occupied a middle position, as an influential member of the Cabinet, but keenly sympathising with the Eastern Christians, was quite right in describing the rising feeling in the country as "violent and unreasonable, but founded in a righteous indignation".[4] An acute foreign observer wrote at the turn of the year: "England, the land with the strongest nervous system, has at last got a fit of nerves."[5] It was by now obvious that British policy in

---

[1] 5 June 1884, to Ward—T. H. Ward, *op. cit.* p. 250.
[2] 18 Dec.—*Letters*, ii. p. 504.   [3] *Ibid.* p. 499.   [4] *Life of Carnarvon*, ii. p. 341.
[5] Count Wolkenstein, Austro-Hungarian Chargé, 29 Dec. 1876. See Wertheimer, *Neues zur Orientpolitik*, i. p. 275.

the East was no longer in unison with the march of events and required revision.

BISMARCK AND THE EASTERN QUESTION

At this juncture Bismarck, who had already tried to clear up his relations with Russia, found it advisable to explain to Andrássy, both through Stolberg in Vienna and through Károlyi in Berlin, that it was his ardent desire to remain on good terms with both Russia and Austria. At a parliamentary dinner in Berlin on 1 December he made a somewhat unconventional speech. If asked what Germany wanted in the Eastern Question, he felt bound to give the same answer as he gave to his wife when she asked him what he wanted for Christmas— "He could not think of anything" (*Es fiele ihm nichts ein*). He anticipated three stages in the quarrel: neither the first—war between Russia and Turkey—nor the second—British intervention—would force Germany out of her reserve. But if Austria-Hungary became involved, that would concern Germany more closely, for her integrity was an European necessity, which corresponded to the traditions of the German nation, and Germany could not allow her to be fatally wounded.[1]

A few days later he struck a somewhat different note before the Reichstag, pointedly reviving memories of the "War Scare" by the phrase that eighteen months earlier his Government was being unjustly reproached with seeking war and quarrels, whereas now it was being blamed for its unduly pacific attitude. He openly paraded the goodwill of German policy towards Russia, defended the Tsar and his pledges against conquest and expressed the conviction that Russia's chief aim at the Conference was co-operation "to prevent fresh massacres by the Circassians in Bulgaria" and to assure the lot of the Christians in Turkey. All she asked of Germany was neutrality, and this was entirely a German interest. The Three Emperors' League deserved its name and was still in full force, but had no point against England. But good relations could only be injured "if one of our friends asked that we should treat the other friend as an enemy . . . and prove our stronger love to the one by hatred to the other". The speech culminated in the famous assertion that Germany would take no active part, "so long as I can see in the whole affair no interest for Germany which would be worth the

[1] Wertheimer, *op. cit.* ii. pp. 367-8.

healthy bones of a single Pomeranian musketeer".[1] In all this
Bismarck, with his usual consummate skill behind a blunt exterior,
was dealing side-hits in all directions and enabling the fully initiated
to estimate exactly how far they might reckon upon his support. For
instance, to the Tsar and Gorchakov this pronouncement, following
so soon upon the Werder incident, was a very definite warning
against an Austrophobe policy, and yet a public assurance of German
loyalty to the traditional Eastern alliance so dear to the heart of his
imperial master. In the same way it was a hint to Vienna that
Berlin desired an Austro-Russian agreement, and to London that the
three Powers had no intention of allowing Beaconsfield to divide
them, and yet that Germany would welcome English friendship.
Whether London at this time was capable of perceiving all its
subtleties is quite another question, and indeed this would perhaps
have been impossible, in view of the secrecy which then enveloped
so much of European diplomacy, even among friends.

THE CONFERENCE AND THE TURKISH CONSTITUTION

On reaching Constantinople Lord Salisbury soon found that everything centred round his relations with the Russian Ambassador,
General Ignatyev, who stood in acute rivalry towards Sir Henry
Elliot. To his no small surprise Salisbury found Ignatyev most
amenable in their preliminary conversations, and was soon informing
Derby that he did not share Elliot's distrust and had found it quite
possible to negotiate on all points of detail.[2] This does not mean that
he discarded his original suspicion of Ignatyev's motives and tactics
(there was a curious incident about two maps with divergent frontier
markings, which Salisbury used to recount to his daughter and future
biographer): but he none the less found no great difficulty in reaching a general agreement on the programme to be pressed upon the
Turks. In actual fact, Ignatyev had received instructions from the
Tsar and Gorchakov, emphasising their strong preference for a peaceful solution and their desire to negotiate "without any *arrière-pensée*
whatever".[3]

A series of discussions followed between Salisbury and the Ambassadors of the other five Great Powers—Baron Werther, Count Zichy

[1] The usual translation is "grenadier": but "Musketier" was the word used.
[2] *R.B.D.* iv. nos. 130, 133, 7 and 8 Dec., Shuvalov to Gorchakov.
[3] *Ibid.* no. 127, 27 Nov., Gorchakov to Ignatyev.

and Baron Calice, M. de Bourgoing and Count Chaudordy, Count Corti, and General Ignatyev—who on 21 December unanimously signed proposals to be laid before the Conference itself: (1) on peace terms between the Porte and the two Serb Principalities; (2) on the future autonomy of Bosnia and Bulgaria; and (3) on the sphere of action of the international commissions to be entrusted with its enforcement. Though the *status quo* was in the main upheld, Serbia was to receive the long-coveted strategic point of Mali Zvornik on the Drina, and Montenegro certain small districts of Hercegovina and free navigation on the lake of Skutari and the river Bojana. One of the guarantees suggested was the employment of a Belgian *gendarmerie*.

It is not, however, proposed to dwell upon the arid, and in the end quite futile, details of these discussions, or even of the Conference itself, for the issue was decided by entirely extraneous events. In the first place, the Turks, who never had the slightest desire that the Conference should succeed and were, as usual, playing for time, resolved to place their unwelcome visitors before an accomplished fact. Accordingly, on the very day before the Conference was to open, Midhat Pasha was proclaimed Grand Vizier, and on 23 December, while the plenipotentiaries were engaged upon the initial formalities, the thunder of cannon announced to the capital the proclamation of a new Turkish constitution of the most elaborate kind, so framed as to provide an excuse for the argument that the Porte was now actively embarking upon far-reaching reforms and could dispense with the proferred assistance of the Powers. It is quite probable that Midhat, who had acquired certain Western allures, genuinely aimed at a limitation of the Sultan's autocratic powers: but it is certain that he looked with the eyes of a Turkish nationalist on any attempts at external dictation, and that though he himself had a relatively high record as an efficient administrator, he had been known to express regret that the Christians of European Turkey had not been forcibly Moslemised early in the century, when drastic assimilation was still a possibility. He was once indiscreet enough to confide to the Italian Ambassador that he would put down the Bulgarian insurrection by *le système par terreur*.[1] Midhat—himself a "Pomak" or Moslemised

---

[1] This "tremendous fact" W. E. Forster records as given to him by Count Corti himself during his visit to Constantinople—*Life of Forster*, i. p. 137. In 1876 Consul-General White (afterwards the famous Ambassador) described Midhat to MacColl as "one of the most cruel and unscrupulous men in the Turkish Empire"—M. Mac-Coll, "Midhat Pasha on Turkish History and Reform" (*Gentleman's Magazine*, July

Bulgar—had all the astuteness of the *faux bonhomme*, but his vanity misjudged the silent, catlike plotter Abdul Hamid, and he imagined himself to have full control of a sovereign who never had the slightest use for representative government and who simply regarded the constitution as a temporary device to checkmate foreign interference.

On paper the charter looked well enough, and indeed was almost overwhelming in its detail, but it never had the slightest prospect of becoming a reality. Elliot, however, had complete confidence in Midhat, whereas Salisbury reported his frank impression of Midhat and Ignatyev, that they were "the biggest pair of liars to be found in Europe, but I am inclined (though with much diffidence) to think that Midhat is the falser of the two".[1] To the German diplomat Clemens Busch he also "spoke of the Turkish Ministers, and especially of Midhat, with contemptuous scorn",[2] and on a second occasion as "intrigants" and "venal".

Salisbury's belief in the venality of Midhat is worth underlining. The charge was often put forward, but of course the Young Turk leader had a crowd of unscrupulous enemies, only too prone to accuse him of their own vices, in a country where incorruptibility was very rare in an official. Midhat's standards of truth may be gathered from an article which he subsequently contributed to the *Nineteenth Century*.[3] Here he actually claimed that "in Islam the principle of government rests upon bases essentially democratic, inasmuch as the sovereignty of the people is therein recognised": and as if this were not enough, he went on to argue that the Christians of Turkey enjoyed perfect equality and had never been oppressed by the Moslems: nay, that the Porte "had granted the Christians more liberty and more means of instruction than it allowed to Mussulmans". Englishmen who accepted this—and there were still many sufficiently naïve or blinded by party prejudice to do so—were obviously immune against fact or argument.

Already on his way eastwards, Salisbury had voiced to Derby his fear that "the ditch into which the Conference will tumble, will be the obstinacy, not of the Russian, but the Turk".[4] The soundness of his instinct was now to be proved, for he had to report every possible

1878, p. 46) and *The Eastern Question* (1877), p. 157. Midhat once suspended the *Courier d'Orient* for three months for charges of corruption against him: but the matter was never cleared up (*ibid.* pp. 162-3).

[1] *Life of Salisbury*, ii. p. 112.

[2] 12 and 18 Jan. 1877, in Busch's diary, "Die Botschafter-Konferenz in Konstantinopel" (*Deutsche Rundschau*, Oct. 1909, p. 22).

[3] June 1878.   [4] Florence, 26 Nov.—*Life*, p. 102.

prevarication, excuse and delay from the Turkish side. The main cause of this he very soon discovered to be "the belief that England will fight for them in the long run"[1]—a belief which was maintained and deepened by the strongly Turcophil attitude of Sir Henry Elliot, and the growing conviction of those in power that Elliot, not Salisbury, really represented the views and enjoyed the confidence of the London Cabinet. Not that there was ever any question of Elliot consciously working against his colleague, as some partisans alleged at the time: Salisbury made it quite clear that he did not believe this, and proved it at a later date by the confidence which as Foreign Secretary he accorded to Elliot in Vienna. But he felt bound to warn London that Elliot "allows it to be seen that his sympathies are with the Turks and against the proposals of the Powers" and "makes Midhat believe that England is not in earnest. This impression, unless it is removed, must lead to war".[2] And again, "my power of negotiation with the Turks is almost *nil* so long as he stays".[3] Once convinced of this, he was logically bound to press for Elliot's recall, "as the most important addition to our chances of peace", and this view was shared not merely by Elliot's enemy, Ignatyev, but also by the other four Ambassadors, French, German, Austrian and Italian.[4] In short, Elliot was in a minority of one against five—a fact which far outweighs his own private opinion that Zichy and Werther were dominated by Ignatyev.[5]

THE SECRET CORRESPONDENCE OF SHUVALOV AND IGNATYEV

Gorchakov, realising the dangers of the situation, had authorised direct communication between his Ambassadors in Constantinople and London: and the telegrams exchanged by Ignatyev and Shuvalov before and during the Conference throw a valuable light upon the innermost aims of Russian policy and upon the *coulisses* in more than one capital. Ignatyev's statements are obviously full of bias, but they give a vivid picture of the situation as he really saw it, and of his reactions to the positive instructions of his chief and to the warnings of his London colleague. They therefore deserve some prominence in the present narrative.[6]

The original motive of this direct correspondence is clearly revealed

---

[1] To Derby, 29 Dec.—*Life*, p. 117.
[2] *Ibid.* p. 119.
[3] To Carnarvon, 5 Jan.—*ibid.* p. 120.
[4] 29 Dec.—*ibid.* p. 118.
[5] Elliot, *Some Revolutions*, pp. 205-6.
[6] The full text was published by me in *R.B.D.* iv. nos. 109-64.

in Shuvalov's first telegram to Ignatyev as early as 23 October—"Elliot's credit with Derby is shaken: I can counteract it if you keep me *au courant*".[1] Shuvalov, in announcing the selection of Salisbury, talks of "the dominant English preoccupation not to ask for the Christian population of the three provinces more than the Porte could grant to the whole Empire",[2] and rejoices at the appointment on the ground that Salisbury had already "constantly demanded Elliot's removal".[3] On 10 November Ignatyev reports that "Elliot, in order to induce the Turks to accept the Conference, tells them that the chief aim is to control and reduce our (Russia's) demands, and that England will combat them at the meetings. . . . His language is warlike, approves Turkish preparations for war, as being provoked by measures taken at Odessa."[4] A week later he promises to do his best to agree with Salisbury: "But don't forget that from Livadia I am enjoined to insist on military occupation as indispensable guarantee. Elliot, desiring war, will try to rouse Salisbury indirectly against Russia, profiting by his Indian doubts. News spread here of English military preparations have intoxicating effect and lead Porte to believe it can count boldly on material support . . . Midhat, assuming English aid, speaks openly of war with us."[5] Shuvalov was able to contradict the report of British military preparations, but Ignatyev continued to report the encouragement given by Elliot to the Turks and the admissions made by Turkish ministers to his diplomatic colleagues, "based on Elliot's attitude and the language of Byzantine English" (that is, the British Levantine colony).[6]

At this stage Ignatyev received precise instructions from the Russian Chancellor. "Present first the maximum project: if it meets with strong opposition, produce the minimum. That will show that we were not aiming at dictating [terms], as we are accused of doing. It is not impossible that the minimum project may rally the majority in view of its moderation—perhaps even Salisbury, who has gathered at Paris, and will gather at Berlin, impressions favourable to us. According to you, who are the best judge, the minimum already assures to Bulgaria a satisfactory and attainable autonomy, being based on the elements which the country offers. If your two projects are ruled out, you will enter your opinion in the minutes and will reiterate it at the Conference, from which, in my view, you must not hold aloof. If in the preliminary discussions the project of

[1] *Ibid.* no. 109.   [2] *Ibid.* no. 116.   [3] *Ibid.* no. 117.
[4] *Ibid.* no. 119.   [5] *Ibid.* no. 122, 18 Nov.   [6] *Ibid.* no. 124, 22 Nov

Salisbury or others offers serious guarantees, you will not reject it forthwith and will take it *ad referendum. . . . Even if our minimum prevails, it would be a great result which would spare us the military campaign, which would be risky both politically and materially and would above all bear heavily on our financial position.* If we can avoid it, while maintaining intact the honour and dignity of the Empire, I should applaud loudly and our country would gain. You see the fine task allotted to you." [1]

This was still not sufficiently precise for Ignatyev, who replied: "Profoundly touched by proof of confidence, without having any illusions as to the immense difficulties of the task, I deduct that so far as possible I am to reserve our declaration *in extremis* for the plenary conference with the Turks. Is this so? It would be important to know in advance, (1) if I am to insist on military occupation of Bulgaria by us, or not? (2) if you are disposed to prolong the armistice or not? and for how long, for it is to be expected that the question of prolongation will soon arise. Our answer will be significant. It is further necessary to know forthwith the view of the War Minister and the Commanders-in-Chief, *whether they prefer in the event of failure of Conference, rupture in December, January or towards the spring, so as to conduct negotiations accordingly,* by prolonging or accelerating them. I venture to beg telegraphic orders." [2]

Gorchakov's answer came next day. "I confirm the Emperor's orders as received by you. In the preliminary conferences produce your maximum, then your minimum. . . . If minimum, which does not contain our military occupation, is accepted, then all is said. If not and another project with guarantees is proposed, *don't reject it,* take it *ad referendum.* We shall weigh here the value of the guarantees. You will say in the preliminary conferences that, being convinced that Europe wishes with us a real achievement, we must insist on guarantees, and if others are not offered, it would be difficult for us to escape the duty of a temporary military occupation. Once the discussion is opened, keep a quick pace. One could not at the outset demand prorogation, which we desire to avoid. The Emperor wishes our rôle in the Conference to bear a character of complete frankness and loyalty, without any *arrière-pensée* whatever. We have nothing to conceal. *His Majesty prefers above all a pacific solution and would rejoice exceedingly if military demonstration is not imposed on us by our dignity.* Imbue yourself (*pénétrez-vous*) with these principles."[1]

These three telegrams leave no possible room for doubt as to the pacific intentions of the Tsar and his Government, and their readiness to agree with Britain and accept any such compromise as would ensure to the Balkan Christians a minimum of protection against Turkish misrule. We are now looking into the Tsar's own cards, and it is difficult to believe that even the most confirmed Russophobe in the British Cabinet of those days could have failed to be reassured if it had been possible for him to do the same.

There is a lull in the correspondence till Salisbury arrived on 5 December, on which day Ignatyev telegraphed that the impression of Bismarck's speech was unfavourable, and that Constantinople no longer believed in the entente of the three Empires.[2] Two days later Shuvalov announced that Derby was "very perplexed" at a telegram from Salisbury sounding his Government as to the possible occupation of Constantinople by 20,000 men in agreement with Russia. "Salisbury adds that he does not share Elliot's distrust of Ignatyev and is inclined to accord him his confidence" (this must have been quoted to the Ambassador by Derby himself).[3] Shuvalov had, however, been misinformed: for next day he wired that Salisbury had merely enquired whether the Government thought of ensuring the safety of Constantinople by introducing foreign troops.[4]

Meanwhile Salisbury had telegraphed home the result of his first discussion with Ignatyev as to the details of a settlement: and Shuvalov found Derby alarmed at such ideas as the election of local officials or the restriction of Turkish troops to certain garrisons or the transfer of Circassian settlers to Asia.[5] Ignatyev in a series of telegrams reports "excellent personal relations" established with Salisbury. "We confer daily *tête à tête* and have agreed on conditions of peace and Bulgarian autonomy." Salisbury recognised the need of guarantees and the use of some force, but still opposed a Russian occupation and insisted on the division of Bulgaria into two provinces, an eastern and a western. "Elliot continues to plot with Midhat, hoping to counteract our efforts with Salisbury: Chaudordy has notified his incorrect attitude."[6]

At the preliminary meeting of Ambassadors on 15 December 1876

[1] *Ibid.* no. 127, 15/27 Nov., Gorchakov to Ignatyev.
[2] *Ibid.* no. 129.   [3] *Ibid.* no. 130.   [4] *Ibid.* no. 133, 8 Dec.
[5] *Ibid.* no. 135, 9 Dec.   [6] *Ibid.* nos. 136, 137, 9 Dec.; no. 138, 12 Dec.

Bulgarian autonomy was accepted in principle, and it was agreed by all save Elliot that the commission to supervise it must have some kind of force behind it. As, however, Salisbury on the one side objected to a Russian occupation, while Ignatyev on the other ridiculed an Ottoman corps under European officers, various suggestions were put forward by the French and Italian members, as to a Roumanian or Belgian militia or an European *gendarmerie*.[1]

By the 18th the idea of a Belgian *gendarmerie* seemed to hold the field, but Ignatyev reported that "the Turks, seeing European inaction, are very bellicose. . . . Will only accept proposals of Conference if they lose all hope of creating general quarrel (*zizanie*) between England and Russia and are menaced by a general diplomatic rupture."[2]

Still further light is thrown upon Russian official policy by a secret letter addressed by Gorchakov to Ignatyev on 11 December discussing "various hypotheses".[3] If the Porte accepts "the irreducible minimum put forward as the firm and unanimous wish of Europe, . . . then there is no more to be said. If without formally declining it pleads its general constitution, it could be told that it is free to do as it thinks fit in the other provinces of the Empire, but that in Bosnia, Hercegovina and Bulgaria Europe will not admit other arrangements. . . . If the Porte refuses, the dignity of the Great Powers obviously won't allow them to submit to this refusal. The recall of the Ambassadors seems the first step to be taken unanimously. It would also be opportune to prolong the armistice till 1 April. . . . This is indispensable to save Serbia and even in the interest of possible military operations on our part, otherwise our right flank would remain exposed. As for us, we shall remain with shouldered arms without reducing our active forces. We have no intention of giving up this attitude unless the Porte forces us by massacres, hostile demonstrations, etc. We retain our liberty of military action. At this season or at the beginning of spring a campaign would offer great difficulties and in any case would involve inevitable delays. It may be that by April political complications unfavourable to us may arise. That will partly depend on our attitude. If we preserve that adopted by Our August Master, by which at the price of some concessions we reach *the main aim of maintaining agreement between the Christian Powers*, it will be difficult to attack us on grounds of logic and good faith". Gorchakov, how-

---

[1] *R.B.D.* iv. 140, 15 Dec.   [2] *Ibid.* no. 141, 18 Dec.

[3] *Ibid.* no. 143, 11 Dec.

ever, closes with words that showed how precarious he felt the situation to be, warning Ignatyev that all he had written was "conjectural" and might be upset by events at any moment.

AN EMISSARY OF DISRAELI IN TURKEY

In the background there were other minor influences. The British colony at Pera, containing many very mixed elements, was, apart from a fervent and active minority, very definitely Turkish, for obvious business reasons: and the *Levant Herald*, edited by Whitaker, was accused of being subsidised by the Porte, and certainly backed it blindly through thick and thin. An Armenian agent of Midhat, Odian Effendi, was sent to London to supplement the action of the Ambassador, Musurus Pasha, against Salisbury,[1] and to work for a new loan and the neutralisation of Roumania in the event of war. But more important, though little known, were the activities of Mr. Butler-Johnstone, Conservative member for Canterbury,[2] who visited Constantinople and gave himself out as a confidant of Beaconsfield "and the representative of his real mind".[3]

During his visit Butler-Johnstone was the guest of Ali Suavi, then director of the Imperial Lyceum of Galata Serai—a Young Turk of visionary and unbalanced character, who less than eighteen months later perished in a mad attempt to seize the Palace and replace poor mad Murad on the throne.[4]

Evidently he was one of those persons of whom Salisbury telegraphed home, as trying to deceive the Grand Vizier by convincing him that "whatever I might say, he could count on the assistance of Lord Derby and Lord Beaconsfield".[5] Derby, who was energetic enough on paper, wired back next day that he had warned Musurus "in the strongest terms to the contrary". "It is not in my power to speak more plainly than I have done on this subject: and I am satis-

---

[1] *Ibid.* no. 149, 2 Jan. 1877.

[2] Henry Alexander Munro Butler-Johnstone, grandson of the 22nd Lord Dunboyne, inherited through his mother the Scottish estates of Corehead and Auchen, and sat for Canterbury from 1862 to 1878.

[3] *R.B.D.* iv. no. 142, Ignatyev to Shuvalov, 23 Dec. Lord Salisbury reports the same story to Lord Derby (*Life*, ii. p. 111—21 Dec.): "The talk runs that he professes to be the secret emissary of the Prime Minister. He can hardly be so impudent as that, but in whosoever's name he affects to talk, he is doing a deal of harm." Cf. Wertheimer, ii. p. 380.

[4] He was shot down by the loyal guards, while Murad himself—far too insane to be Ali's accomplice—cowered and gibbered behind the divan. See *The Times* of 24 May 1878. See also *infra*, p. 427.

[5] 8 Jan., Salisbury to Derby, F.O. 78/2678.

fied that no person connected with the Government is holding different language." [1] It is, however, more than doubtful whether Beaconsfield told Derby of his relations with Butler-Johnstone, and in any case the mischief had already been done in Constantinople.

The mentality of this man is sufficiently revealed by his two contemporary pamphlets, designed to prove "the vital importance of maintaining the Ottoman Empire", and to represent the Turks as "the most polite, cleanly, respectful, disciplined and just race under the sun"—"justice and legality" being "of the essence of the Ottoman mind".[2] Even he admitted that Turkey was in a desperate financial plight, and that "corruption and decay will have prepared the work of destruction and slight external pressure will complete it": but none the less "we cannot afford to let Turkey destroy herself: she is too necessary for us, and her salvation is identified with our own imperial interests".[3]

All this reads to-day as arrant nonsense, but in its day it had a potent effect in encouraging the Porte to believe that Beaconsfield was on their side. Indeed even the Turcophil Layard, when he took over the Embassy in April 1877 and found Butler-Johnstone back at the Galata Lyceum, hobnobbing with the wild Softas, writes of him with disapproval, as a fanatic who was encouraging the Turks in their intransigeance, on the ground that though official London might refuse them its help, "the English people were favourable to Turkey . . . and in the event of war England would be compelled sooner or later to interfere". "This", adds Layard, "has no doubt been the cause of a great deal of mischief." [4]

Butler-Johnstone thus stands condemned from the mouth of a foremost protagonist on his own side. He appears to have stayed on in Constantinople during the early summer of 1877, working with Admiral Selwyn at the mining of the Bosphorus,[5] and according to the Ambassador, he left early in July, "with one Captain Applin, on a secret mission", having promised to get the Turks a loan from some mysterious quarter.[6]

---

[1] 9 Jan., Derby to Salisbury, F.O. 78/2674.
[2] *The Eastern Question*, reprinted from *Pall Mall Gazette* (1875), p. 5, and *The Turks* (1876), H. A. M. Butler-Johnstone, pp. 23, 47.
[3] *The Eastern Question*, pp. 45, 48.
[4] Add. MSS. *Layard Papers*, British Museum—Layard to Derby, 30 April 1877.
[5] "I hope", wrote Layard to Derby (*Layard Papers*, 23 May), "they will render the Turks better service by their infernal machines than by their political advice."
[6] *Ibid.* 4 July, Layard to Derby.

BEACONSFIELD DECLINES TO RECALL ELLIOT

It is perfectly possible that Butler-Johnstone himself exaggerated his influence upon Beaconsfield, and quite certain that Turkish fantasy magnified it tenfold. But there can be no doubt whatever that, from whatever cause, Beaconsfield's attitude stiffened noticeably towards the end of December 1876. The Cabinet met on the 23rd and unanimously decided in favour of "strong moral pressure" upon Turkey—"no coercion by arms, no assistance in case of war", but withdrawal of Salisbury and even Elliot[1]—in other words, a momentary reversion to the October policy of leaving the obstinate Turks to their fate. But deeper insight into Cabinet secrets is given by the letter which Lord Carnarvon wrote out to Salisbury on Christmas Day, warning his friend that the Prime Minister "as far as it depends on him, intends us to take part in the war, and on behalf of Turkey. He hardly indeed makes any secret of this: in the last Cabinet he spoke of the difficulty of distinguishing between British interests and support of Turkey."[2]

By the turn of the year Beaconsfield was disposed to "fear that Salisbury is much duped by Ignatyev" and wrote in irritation to Derby: "He seems most prejudiced and not to be aware that his principal object in being sent to Constantinople is to keep the Russians out of Turkey, *not to create an ideal existence for Turkish Christians. He is more Russian than Ignatyev*: plus arabe que l'Arabie." Doubtless, if Gladstone could have read this phrase, his worst suspicions would have been confirmed.

In this mood Beaconsfield was obviously indisposed to listen to Salisbury's urgent request for the recall of Elliot, on which it is not too much to say that the success or failure of the whole Conference depended. It might none the less have been impossible to refuse the request, but for a false step taken by Shuvalov at the critical moment. On December 29 Ignatyev wired to Shuvalov: "Language and attitude of Salisbury leave nothing to be desired, but the retention of Elliot here undermines him (*le mine*) with the Turks, who believe that once Salisbury leaves, the old policy will be resumed. Elliot had already announced his departure, but to-day wants to stay to end of Conference, by agreement with Midhat."[3]

---

[1] Diary for 23 Dec.—*Life of Gathorne Hardy*, i. p. 481: cf. Buckle, vi. p. 109.
[2] Sir A. Hardinge, *Life of Carnarvon*, ii. p. 347.
[3] *R.B.D.* iv. no. 146, Ignatyev to Shuvalov, 29 Dec.

Next day Shuvalov appears to have called on Derby at the Foreign Office and read him Ignatyev's telegram. A memorandum of the conversation was submitted by Derby to Beaconsfield,[1] but the mere fact that their colleague Salisbury's proposal was favoured by Ignatyev seems to have decided both statesmen to refuse it! On 1 January 1877 the Prime Minister telegraphed to Salisbury: "Ignatyev through Shuvalov has counselled the withdrawal of Elliot. If this gets out—and everything does get out at Constantinople—and Elliot withdraws, we shall be turned out the first day of the Session by our own men."[2]

It is difficult to avoid the conclusion that Beaconsfield, who definitely took Elliot's part against Salisbury, won the naturally suspicious Derby's alarmed consent by an appeal to party prejudice. His support of Elliot was a fatal blow to the Conference and so rendered war inevitable in the long run. But his whole attitude during the previous eighteen months shows that Disraeli was much less interested in preventing war than in bolstering up Turkey.

A curious sequel to this incident is to be found in the Shuvalov correspondence. Lord Salisbury, who did not reach London till 6 February, was met at the station by his stepmother and close friend Lady Derby,—who had already by this time convinced herself that Count Shuvalov was no less bent upon peace than herself and her husband and was therefore in constant communication with him. She immediately recounted to him her conversation with Lord Salisbury. Shuvalov, in a report to his chief, gives his own version of what followed and reveals a strong animus against the Prime Minister. "One of the first things which he (Lord Salisbury) said to Lady Derby disclosed a new lie of Lord Beaconsfield. 'What seems to have irritated the Prime Minister, he said, is the ill-considered *démarche* of Count Shuvalov, who urged on Derby . . . the immediate recall of

---

[1] I am exceedingly indebted to Lady Gwendolen Cecil, who kindly gave me a copy of this memorandum and of Beaconsfield's telegram, both from the *Salisbury Papers*. The memo. runs as follows: "Count Schouvaloff read to Lord Derby this afternoon privately and confidentially a second telegram from General Ignatieff stating that the language and attitude of Lord Salisbury leave nothing to be desired. But the attitude of Sir H. Elliot weakens his position (*le mine*) with the Turks, who believe that when Lord Salisbury is gone, Sir H. Elliot will return to his former line. Sir H. Elliot had announced his departure, but now says that he wishes to stay till the end of the Conference. This General Ignatieff says is in accordance with the wish of Midhat Pasha."

This will be seen to fit in exactly with Ignatyev's telegram to Shuvalov, quoted above.

Beaconsfield's telegram is quoted in the *Life of Salisbury*, ii. p. 120: but there is no indication that it was addressed to Salisbury himself.

Sir Henry Elliot.' 'But that is false', was the reply to him [*i.e.* by Lady Derby]. 'No such thing occurred. Where did you get this absurdity from?' 'I got it from Beaconsfield, who communicated it to me in a private letter,[1] asking me to retain Elliot in view of this interference of a foreign ambassador.' This little manœuvre requires no commentary." [2]

It is quite clear from this passage that neither Lady Derby—who doubtless knew of the earlier incident—nor Count Shuvalov, regarded his action in reading Ignatyev's telegram to Derby as anything which could fairly be treated as a diplomatic *démarche*. Lady Gwendolen Cecil, in her brilliant Life of her father, rightly describes the incident as "an interesting example of the reaction of representative institutions on the workings of diplomacy": but she seems to overstate what happened, when she says that "General Ignatyev, whether from ignorance or malice, had just tendered similar advice to the British Cabinet". What actually happened—and the issue proves it to have been a blunder—was that the Russian Ambassador informed the British Foreign Secretary that the Russian Ambassador to the Porte agreed with the British Plenipotentiary (the Foreign Secretary's own colleague in the Cabinet) in thinking that the continued presence of Sir Henry Elliot would prejudice the issue of the Conference. This was not so much advice as the broadest of hints that Elliot's removal would lead to the surrender of the Turks and an Anglo-Russian agreement. The root fact of the situation was that Beaconsfield and Derby were agreed in their refusal to apply coercion to the Turks, whereas Salisbury, on the spot, saw that in coercion lay the only hope and that the Turks would not yield so long as Elliot remained. Events completely justified Salisbury's contention.

THE CONFERENCE FAILS

Under these circumstances it would be quite unprofitable to dwell upon the barren details of the Conference itself. After holding nine formal meetings, it broke up on 20 January 1877, without achieving anything, the Porte having resolutely declined to give the required guarantees and basing its refusal upon the views expressed by a Council of Notables convoked in Constantinople on 18 January by

[1] Lady Gwendolen Cecil was kind enough to look for this letter among her father's papers, but failed to find it and draws the very natural inference that "my father, in his conversation with Lady Derby, must have been thinking of the telegram".
[2] *R.B.D.* v. no. 173, 7 Feb. 1877.

imperial decree. The members of this Council were chosen by the Sultan and his ministers and their decisions were therefore a foregone conclusion. According to Ignatyev's report home, Salisbury shared his colleagues' indignation at "an unworthy comedy staged beforehand by Midhat" and serving as "a slap in the face of Europe, and especially of England".[1]

To Dr. Busch, whom Bismarck had sent out to act as Chargé in the event of the Ambassador having to withdraw, and who had a long previous experience of the Turkish capital, Salisbury spoke with surprising frankness of the Turkish ministers, as men "incapable of serious political action, and only bent on extricating themselves by wretched tricks and insincere concessions". Could Europe have any interest in prolonging such a régime? Unhappily England, he added, still believed in Turkey as a "British interest": for "in England public opinion required to have a bogey—formerly it was the Pope, now it was Russophobia". But he himself did not share this view or believe that the road to India lay through Constantinople: for India was sufficiently protected against Russia by her own natural frontiers.[2] This, from the Secretary for India, may well have impressed the German: unhappily its sound common sense was not shared by many in England, including his own chief. As an amusing instance of oriental imagination, it may be added that Busch records the widespread belief that Lady Salisbury was the daughter of a Protestant missionary and had accompanied him in order to influence him in favour of the Christians of the East!

At the closing session Salisbury uttered an impressive warning as to the changed and perilous "position of Turkey before Europe . . . if after having enjoyed for twenty years the security assured to her by the accord of the Christian Powers, she now refuses to listen to their complaints. The whole feeling of Europe will be excited by the conviction that she no longer exercises any influence in the counsels of the Porte and that she can no longer relieve herself of the responsibility imposed upon her by the efforts she has made for the protection of Turkey." Britain in particular, he declared, was "resolved not to give her sanction either to maladministration or to oppression", and if the Porte, "from obstinacy or inactivity", resisted Europe's proposals, "the responsibility of the consequences will rest solely on the Sultan and his advisers"[3] Ignatyev added the warning

[1] *R.B.D.* iv. no. 162, Ignatyev to Shuvalov, 19 Jan.

[2] Busch, *Nachlass*, already quoted (*Deutsche Rundschau*, Oct. 1909, pp. 22, 25).

[3] *Turkey No. II.* (1877), pp. 362, 376.

that his Government would regard this attitude "as a defiance of Europe".

As a sign of their displeasure, the six Powers at once withdrew their ambassadors: but even this lost much of its effect, when Elliot delayed his departure for some days after all the others, thereby confirming the Turks in their belief that his influence outweighed that of his combined colleagues.[1] During a private audience in December the Sultan had persisted, in the teeth of Salisbury's disclaimers, in the conviction that the agitation in England "was due rather to the repudiation of the Turkish debt than to the atrocities in Bulgaria":[2] and this cynical attitude was maintained throughout the Conference, no serious attempt being ever made to punish the criminals, despite the periodical remonstrances of Baring. Ignatyev was certainly right in reporting that Midhat's whole calculation rested on dissensions among the Powers: "Salisbury will be disavowed, the Turcophil current will get the upper hand and Austria's defection is certain".[3] (Ignatyev's notorious hatred of Austria discounts the last phrase.)

It is no exaggeration to say that the main causes of the failure were the two voices with which Britain spoke and the conclusions drawn from this by the Porte. This was not accepted at the time by official British opinion, but it is the verdict of history. It was quite obvious to most continental diplomatists—to the Ballplatz, to the Wilhelmstrasse, to the Quai d'Orsay, to Prince Hohenlohe, then German Ambassador in Paris,[4] to General Le Flô in St. Petersburg,[5] and others. But for proof it is not necessary to go farther than the Blue Books which the Beaconsfield Government itself published: for already on 22 December Derby had wired to Salisbury the Cabinet decision "that England will not assent to, or assist in, coercive measures, military or naval, against the Porte",[6] and two days later Safvet Pasha told Musurus to inform Lord Derby that the Porte "reckons more than ever on the kind support of Her Majesty's Government".[7]

One highly practical reason for Turkish reliance upon London has

[1] Cf. *R.B.D.* iv. no. 163, Ignatyev to Shuvalov, 20 Jan. According to Shuvalov (*ibid.* no. 165, 22 Jan. to Gorchakov), Elliot's delay was "contrary to the orders of the Foreign Office".
[2] *Turkey No. II.* (1877), no. 138, 26 Dec., Salisbury to Derby.
[3] *R.B.D.* iv. no. 150, 3 Jan.
[4] *G.P.* ii. no. 269, Hohenlohe to Bismarck, 8 Jan. 1877.
[5] *D.D.F.* ii. no. 129, Le Flô to Decazes, 3 Jan.
[6] *Turkey No. II.* (1876), no. 78.   [7] *Ibid.* nos. 87 and 134.

still to be mentioned. In the autumn Disraeli had sent out British engineering officers, under Colonel Home, to work at the fortifications of Constantinople, to examine the Turkish ports and "to survey the ground behind Constantinople" and evolve plans for its defence in the event of war: and their presence in the Turkish capital during the Conference was not a good augury. They continued to provide information to the War Office and the Prime Minister for some months afterwards, and this was critically considered by such experts as General Sir Lintorn Simmons.[1] In his view the defence of the Tchekmedje lines would require at least 65,000 men and 120 guns, and a British expeditionary force of 50,000 men would be quite inadequate. He therefore suggested the use of Mohammedan troops from India—this is probably the germ of the subsequent decision to bring Indian troops to Malta—and raised as an urgent subject of enquiry, "what effective force Great Britain can bring into and sustain in the field?"

Salisbury himself was under no illusions: and the keenness and accuracy with which he penetrated the Turkish situation is as striking as the blindness of his colleagues in London. Towards the end he unbosomed himself to his friend Carnarvon. "Our influence here is at a very low ebb" (this would have been flouted at the time, but it was the brutal truth, and the Turcophil Layard's experience was to prove it within the next two years): "They know that they have nothing to fear from us, and if they think they have anything to hope, they believe that our aid will not be conditional on their good conduct. The character of our Ambassador has no doubt done something to ruin our influence, but the character of our policy has done more."[2]

His final warning to Derby is acute and prophetic. "Your future policy will require the gravest consideration. You will have to choose between: (1) helping to coerce; which would give you a voice in the ultimate disposal—but that you will not do. (2) Allowing Russia to do her worst, and if she attacks and wins, coming in to regulate her demands when peace is talked of. This would be the easiest way, if practicable. But it is very possible that she may refuse to let you

[1] Buckle, vi. pp. 100, 117, 136. Vol. 232 of the *Layard Papers* (Brit. Mus. Add. MSS. 39162) contains these confidential reports and memoranda by Lt.-Col. R. Home, R.E., of 15, 16, 18, 25 Nov., 11 and 12 Dec. 1876 and a report by Capt. Ardagh, R.E., on such matters as the defence of the Tchekmedje lines, railway, harbour and landing facilities, quartering of troops, communications, trenches, etc., and also on the port of Rodosto and the lines of Bulair.

[2] *Life*, ii. p. 121, 11 Jan.

have your word at the end, and that you may have to content yourself with writing a pathetic despatch on the model of Lord Aberdeen's after the peace of Adrianople. (3) You may come to terms with Andrássy and Gorchakov for a regulated occupation of Bulgaria and Bosnia: providing for evacuation after a certain date, and securing an indemnity to the occupying Powers out of the revenues of the provinces, of which Bulgaria at least is very rich. This could only end in the creation of two tributary states, but I believe it to be the safest course. That the machine here can stand very long I believe to be impossible. Even if Russia does not invade, it will crumble of itself: and the Russian Embassy has in its hands the threads of a vast network of intrigue, by which it can, if it will, aggravate enormously any natural causes of anarchy."[1]

It is only necessary to compare this with the ultimate settlement in Berlin and Disraeli's original aims, to obtain the measure of Salisbury as a practical statesman.

IGNATYEV'S REPORT UPON SALISBURY

Of quite exceptional interest is the confidential report sent home to St. Petersburg by Ignatyev on his relations with Salisbury during the Conference. It is clear from this document that Ignatyev, whatever view we may take of his character, was genuinely attracted by Salisbury and that "the relations of mutual confidence" between them, of which he wrote, were more than a mere phrase. His estimate of Salisbury only confirms what is already known from British sources, but it has a certain piquancy and originality of its own. Salisbury, then, appears to have agreed quite frankly that the choice of Constantinople for the Conference was a grave blunder, that the proclamation of a new constitution—"under the patronage of Sir Henry Elliot and the British colony"—was designed to compromise the Conference's success, but that it had at least, thanks to the friendly preliminary discussions, averted a general war. "He recognises openly that the present Grand Vizier, far from being the saviour of the Empire, is leading it straight to ruin, and that he should be removed. I have the satisfaction of having pointed out Midhat Pasha as a dangerous man ever since 1867, and of having then been alone

---

[1] *Ibid.* p. 124. Lady Gwendolen Cecil may be excused for not underlining the contrast between her father's foresight and his chief's utter cynicism and lack of directive: I have the historian's duty of outspoken interpretation.

in my opinion." This fits in exactly with Werther's account of how Salisbury, before all his colleagues, criticised Midhat for his ignorance and how Elliot "listened in pained silence".[1]

Lord Salisbury, Ignatyev continues, "has carried away the worst impression of the political field of Constantinople . . . as a centre of intrigue and a refuge of ill-intentioned persons, who are mainly furnished by the European colonies and above all the British. The local activities of an Embassy, plunged in this obnoxious milieu, must be highly embarrassing for him, and he deplores that the British Cabinet should be so little informed as to the situation.

"He recognises that Sir Henry Elliot has constantly misled his Government by false information and by presenting things in a false light. He would like to see a British representative who, without being hostile to the Turks, might inspire the Christians with confidence and co-operate with Russia. He regrets that Lord Lytton's present position makes it impossible to send him. Taking advantage of the intimate and friendly nature of our conversation, I thought it possible to warn him against the candidature of Mr. Layard. Having connections with Turkey and being mixed up in its financial affairs, he did not in my eyes offer the necessary guarantees of impartiality.

"As far as I could judge, Lord Salisbury has been converted to the idea of intimate alliance with us for Eastern affairs. While hedging in his confidences with prudent reservations, he did not conceal from me that he would work for the adoption of this line of conduct, at the risk of breaking with Lord Beaconsfield and causing a new alignment of parties. He would not be far from letting us act alone in the east, subject to safeguarding British interests, and would even go the length of thinking that in certain circumstances agreement with us and material help from Great Britain would be possible. He confessed to me that he personally would prefer the Slav races to the Greeks, whom he thinks too undisciplined and too imbued with constitutional theories to be able to play a useful rôle amid the primitive populations of Turkey. It remains to be seen whether this estimate will withstand the impressions he will gather at Athens.

"In any case these dispositions of the English statesman cannot but be favourable to our own political intentions, and it would be in every way desirable that he should be in a position to enforce them among his compatriots and in his party. But he will have many struggles to surmount and adversaries to combat: his parliamentary

[1] G.P. ii. no. 271, Werther to Bülow, 14 Jan.

experience and political skill will show him the propitious moment
for commencing work in the sense of these ideas, after sufficiently
preparing the ground with public opinion."[1]

While it is highly regrettable that in the memoirs left by Ignatyev
there should be an almost complete blank with regard to the Conference and his relations with Salisbury, the above document gives a
vivid insight into his mind and explains why he was so much more
anxious than Salisbury himself to renew the acquaintance.[2] It is not
any the less instructive because Ignatyev naturally had only the very
slightest conception of parliamentary conditions in England.

Salisbury returned home by slow stages, not a little sore and disappointed at his failure. He received quite an enthusiastic welcome
from his colleagues, the Queen was "very civil", and he confessed
himself quite unable to find "a clue to the mysteries of Disraeli's
conduct".[3] And indeed it is impossible to detect any principle in the
Prime Minister's Turkish policy—anything beyond sheer negation.
His first reaction to the Queen's private secretary, General Ponsonby,
on the news that the Conference had failed, was that we should do
nothing and "were called upon to do nothing".[4] And almost his
first greeting to Salisbury was to declare that he felt *"stronger than
ever*, that all that is occurring *portends, and that not remotely, partition".*[5] To Derby he also expressed his belief in "Partition" and argued
that "in that case we must have a decided course and seize at the
fitting moment what is necessary for the security of our Empire"—a
phrase from which it would appear that as yet he neither had a
decided course nor knew exactly what was necessary.

Meanwhile he seems to have convinced himself that Bismarck was
"resolved that Russia shall go to war or that Gorchakov, whom he
hates, shall endure ineffable mortifications by retreating":[6] and
Salisbury shared this distrust of Bismarck. On this occasion, however,
they had not gauged the inner mind of Bismarck, who told Schweinitz
for his confidential guidance, that he would not actually prevent
Russia from war, but would try to ensure its being localised. "The
basis of our policy", he added, "remains our lively wish to preserve
our two close friends Russia and Austria from differences and at the
same time to maintain our good relations with England."[7] The former
point, it cannot be too often repeated, is the foundation of Bismarck's

[1] *R.B.D.* iv. no. 165, Ignatyev to Gorchakov, 22 Jan.
[2] See *infra*, p. 161.   [3] *Life*, ii. p. 127.   [4] 19 Jan.—*Letters*, ii. p. 519.
[5] 6 Feb.—Buckle, vi. p. 114.   [6] 8 Jan.—*ibid.* vi. p. 113.
[7] *G.P.* ii. no. 270, 13 Jan.

policy throughout his career, parallel with his fear of a Franco-Russian combination.

THE SECRET AUSTRO-RUSSIAN AGREEMENT

Meanwhile, Russia had fully realised that if the Conference failed war with Turkey was virtually inevitable, and in view of the equivocal attitude of Britain, thought it wiser to conduct parallel negotiations with Austria-Hungary behind the back of Europe. That the Tsar and his immediate counsellors were sincerely desirous of avoiding war is beyond doubt, and it is curious to note that even those whose suspicions of Russia were most profound, took into their calculations the financial weakness, military unpreparedness and internal revolutionary ferment of Russia. But the Tsar was on the horns of a dilemma: pacific though he was, he could not abandon the cause of his Christian kith and kin without alienating those upon whose support his throne rested, and he recognised that after eighteen months of crisis drastic steps were needed to terminate the uncertainty and unrest which affected Russia scarcely less than the Balkan Peninsula.

If, however, war should come, it was even more essential than in 1854 to know what Austria-Hungary would do: for she could once more threaten Russian communications from Galicia towards Odessa and perhaps also through the Transylvanian passes, while Russia was engaged with the Turks in Bulgaria, and these land communications were all-important, since the Crimean War had destroyed Russia's naval power in the Black Sea and placed its waters at the mercy of a British fleet in alliance with Turkey. Ever since the failure of the Sumarokov mission there had been discussions between Andrássy and Novikov, the Russian Ambassador in Vienna: and a curious difference of opinion had arisen as to the exact nature of the agreement reached at Reichstadt, both Gorchakov and the Tsar professing their inability to remember having committed themselves to Hercegovina as well as Bosnia, as Austria-Hungary's share of the spoils,[1] while Andrássy remained adamant on this point, which reflected Russia's desire to compensate Montenegro after its victories. The misunderstanding seems to have first arisen in the instructions sent by Gorchakov to Novikov on 2 November 1876. This document, which virtually assumes war to be coming and is concerned with Austro-Russian relations in

[1] Wertheimer, *op. cit.* ii. p. 384.

that event, leaves entirely to the judgment of Vienna "the moment and the manner" of occupying Bosnia, but urges that Austria-Hungary must "engage not to extend the sphere of its military influence to Roumania, Serbia, *Hercegovina* or Montenegro", since these countries "must form a continuous zone destined to preserve the armies of the two Empires from contact".[1] The fact that the instructions were communicated by Novikov to Andrássy[2] suggests that, this time at any rate, Gorchakov was in perfectly good faith and not trying to steal a march upon Vienna. None the less, the suspicious Andrássy attributed to him the desire to send Russian troops to Serbia, though not merely Novikov's instructions but the Tsar's whole attitude towards the Serbs both before and after this date render this most improbable. Archduke Albrecht, whom Andrássy naturally enough consulted, held that to tolerate the Russians in the Morava valley would be contrary not merely to the dignity but to the life interests of the Habsburg Monarchy, for it would mean looking on while Russia placed herself at the head of a crusade of the Balkan peoples against Turkey. "Co-operation with Serbia and Montenegro", Andrássy himself argued, and this shows how seriously he took the matter, "makes out of the European action a Slav movement, out of the Christian humanitarian tendency a one-sided Orthodox movement and out of war a revolution".[3] Reasons of internal politics in both halves of the Monarchy made him reluctant to occupy Turkish territory unless the collapse of Turkey seemed imminent, and he knew that public opinion among the two dominant races, the Germans and Magyars, would still less tolerate a campaign against Turkey at the side of Russia.

In view of Andrássy's firmness Gorchakov gave way and told Novikov to raise no objection to the occupation of Hercegovina, "except the portion separating Serbia from Montenegro".[4] (this suggests imperfect acquaintance with geography). Thus reassured, Andrássy expressed to Gorchakov "our perfect accord as to the nature of the Reichstadt arrangements", which he had never regarded as more than "contingent" (*éventuels*), and further, his especial pride at having taken the initiative on that occasion.[5] He

[1] 21 Oct./2 Nov. 1876, Gorchakov to Novikov—*Austrian Archives*.
[2] My quotations are made from the copy in the *Austrian Archives*.
[3] Wertheimer, *op. cit.* iii. p. 386.
[4] Gorchakov to Novikov, 5 Dec.—*Austrian Archives*.
[5] "J'accepte volontiers l'honneur que me fait le Prince Gorchakov de m'en attribuer l'initiative."

assumed that there had been a misunderstanding with regard to Hercegovina, without attempting to explore its origin, and in conclusion laid fresh emphasis on the resolve of the two sovereigns to avoid "the establishment of a large and compact Slav state" (*"slave ou autre"* was the exact phrase). Throughout the negotiations much depended upon the person of Novikov, who enjoyed Andrássy's close confidence and indeed had been left by the Tsar at the Vienna Embassy at the urgent request of Francis Joseph and his Foreign Minister. Novikov was a strong opponent of Panslav tendencies and did not conceal his disapproval of his colleague Ignatyev. His outlook is revealed in a letter to the Chancellor: "Politically it seems to me a matter of indifference that a few 100,000 Bosnians—for the most part Catholics and Moslems—should obey the law of natural attraction towards the neighbouring Monarchy".[1]

While the Conference was sitting, discussions continued between Russia and Austria-Hungary, but in order doubly to ensure their secrecy, they were conducted, no longer through a special envoy, nor at the Ballplatz, but simply through Novikov and at Budapest, where Andrássy was spending the Christmas vacation. On 15 January 1877, then, the secret Convention of Budapest was concluded, expressly framed to avert "a collision of interests" in the event of a Russo-Turkish rupture. The first clause laid down that owing to the mixed character of the population in Bosnia-Hercegovina the autonomy to be demanded for the two provinces should not greatly (*pas trop*) exceed the lines of the Andrássy Note and the Berlin Memorandum, whereas Bulgaria, "being placed in more favourable conditions", should receive a larger measure of autonomy. Secondly, Austria-Hungary formally undertook, in the event of a Russo-Turkish war, to observe benevolent neutrality and "to paralyse so far as possible by her diplomatic action any attempts of the other Powers at intervention or collective mediation". She is to decline to act upon Article VIII. of the Treaty of Paris or upon the Franco-Austro-British Treaty of 15 April 1856—the instrument upon which the unwitting Lord Derby had laid such reiterated stress in the earlier stages of the crisis. Under Clause VII. Francis Joseph reserved the right "to choose the moment and manner of occupying Bosnia-Hercegovina by his troops", and this was not to be regarded as in any way an act of hostility towards Russia. Serbia, Montenegro and the territory between them were to form the subject of a special

[1] 2 Oct.—Goriainov, *Le Bosphore et les Dardanelles*, p. 323.

convention.[1] Great emphasis was laid upon secrecy, and in point of fact the very existence of the agreement was concealed from many of the ambassadors of the two Powers concerned. Andrássy himself, only a few days before the signature of the first convention, informed Buchanan that no understanding existed between Austria and Russia.[2] This denial was of course deliberately intended to mislead, for the negotiations were almost concluded, and the Reichstadt Agreement, never actually abrogated, was on the point of being reaffirmed.

The Budapest Convention represented a definite *détente* between the two Powers, but conversations continued for another two months with regard to action in so obviously obscure a future. At last on 18 March an "Additional Convention" was signed, bearing the original date, and reaffirming the arrangements of Reichstadt as the basis of their future joint policy. A separate clause specially confirmed Austria-Hungary's right to Bosnia-Hercegovina, "except that part of the latter embraced (*umfasst*) by Serbia and Montenegro", which is left to a later agreement: Russia has a free hand in Bessarabia,[3] and a clause relating to territorial changes in Asia is omitted as a final concession to Russian *amour propre*.

A despatch of Andrássy to his Ambassador at St. Petersburg, Baron Langenau, makes his attitude abundantly clear. He wished Russia to realise that "so long as the maintenance of Turkish territorial integrity is possible, we have no interest in or desire for annexations. Any change in the *status quo*, however, might affect the balance and security of the Monarchy. Several of our provinces, especially Dalmatia, would feel the effect. Only such an eventuality, and not the desire of aggrandisement, could lead us, as a safeguard to our interests in the east, to annex Bosnia-Hercegovina. After fulfilling her mission in Bulgaria, pacifying the province and endowing it with national institutions, Russia could evacuate it without affecting her authority. Bulgaria possesses the conditions necessary to independent existence, and under a new form would always remain Bulgaria.

"Not so with Bosnia and Hercegovina. The elements necessary to a life of their own are lacking. Left to themselves, they would become on the one hand an object of desire, on the other a centre of competition and rivalry for the formation of a large Southern Slav state,

[1] Text in *G.P.* ii. no. 265.
[2] Derby evidently accepted this statement, for he telegraphed it to Salisbury on 15 Jan. 1877—F.O. 78/2674.
[3] *G.P.* no. 266.

and finally a permanent hotbed of revolutionary intrigue. If Austria-Hungary, interested above all as a bordering Power, occupied these countries without establishing a definitive state of things, she would seem to admit as legitimate aspirations for the creation of a compact Slav state and to regard such a result as the only possible outcome."

According to his argument it did not absolutely follow that a Russo-Turkish war would compel him to action, but on the other hand he could not consent to limit that action to the sole event of Turkish dissolution. "It is like the case of baldness. When does it begin? When does it end? An Empire does not dissolve in a day. How then to define the degree of decomposition at which dissolution takes place? One person might consider it effective at the *first*, another at the *last* blow directed against the *status quo*."[1]

Meanwhile an undated *aide-memoire* of Gorchakov[2] was sent to Vienna, enclosing a map of the Balkan Peninsula, assigning to Austria-Hungary the whole of the two provinces, but not the territory separating Serbia and Montenegro, admitting that she "would thus dominate the Adriatic and the outlets of Serbia and Montenegro to the sea", and therefore arguing that it would be only fair to divide "the rest of Hercegovina" between them—it is clear that in all this what is actually meant is "the Sandjak of Novipazar", which was to acquire a certain international notoriety from 1878 to 1909. Andrássy expressed himself as ready to accept this division, but insisted on the need of special agreements to ensure against Austrian trade being cut off from its eastward outlet—in other words, towards Salonica and the Aegean. To this Gorchakov in his turn consented in principle, while putting up a special plea for Montenegro—"ces braves montagnards"—and even recommending an extension of their territory, on the ground that "this country possesses the necessary elements of order and discipline". The contrast between this and his complete silence regarding Serbia is ominous: it fits in with the Tsar's alienation from Serbia and Shuvalov's consistent indifference to her interests, and already foreshadows her virtual abandonment by Russia at the Congress of Berlin.

In a narrow sense, these Russo-Austrian discussions have nothing to do with British policy in the Near East, and remained shrouded in mystery for another thirty years. But they provide the real clue to much that was unexplained at the time.

[1] *Austrian Archives* (unpublished)—Andrássy to Langenau, 28 Feb. 1877.
[2] *Ibid.*—"Teschenberg Dossier", with note, "unzweifelhaft hier übergeben 15/27 Feb.".

Russia, for the same strategic reasons which compelled her to evacuate the Roumanian Principalities on the eve of the Crimean War, could not risk being involved in war with Turkey while Austria-Hungary was free to mobilise on her Galician flank and so threaten her land communications. Hence, the very Power which stood forward as a champion of Slavdom and Orthodoxy, saw herself obliged to concede to Austria as the price of neutrality the very two Slav provinces where the trouble had originated. This accorded with the Tsar's pacific outlook and his knowledge of Russia's internal weakness, but would, had it become known publicly, have been denounced as arrant treachery to the Slav cause by the whole Slavophil party and its adherents at court.

The Tsar's attitude towards Austria-Hungary is best revealed in an official memorandum of the following July. After warmly thanking Andrássy for certain recent assurances, he insists that "our Entente is as much monarchical as political", that Vienna can rely implicitly upon his word, and that "there is no longer a Europe with whom to treat: there is only Austria-Hungary, with which he has precise engagements, and Germany who has adhered to them. He will be faithful to their letter and spirit: he has no intention of decreeing of his own accord a definitive order: he leaves the interests of other Powers to assert themselves at the end of the struggle. He does not desire a permanent occupation of Bulgaria, and no democratic element will be introduced there. . . . In a word, he will in no way depart from the ideas of Reichstadt." [1]

During 1877, then, there was an agreement in principle between Russia and Austria, but with a difference in emphasis: for the former, partition was the aim, while for the latter it was a *pis-aller*, and it was impossible for anyone to foresee in advance how and when the memorable Reichstadt clauses were to come into operation.

The Deadlock in Europe

With the failure of the Conference, a deadlock had been reached in the European situation. While negotiating secretly with Austria-Hungary for that very eventuality of failure, Russia endeavoured to represent the question as "not a Russo-Turkish or Slav question, but one of humanity and Christendom"—those were the words of the

---

[1] *Austrian Archives* (unpublished)—Russian "communicat", très confidentiel. 14/26 July 1877, no. 20 in Teschenberg Dossier.

Tsar to Schweinitz.[1] All Europe had been rebuffed by Turkey, and the next step ought therefore to be taken in common. Such was the sense of the Circular addressed by Prince Gorchakov to the Powers on 31 January. Bismarck warned his Ambassador that the Tsar must always be treated like a lady: there must be no answering back. But in his view the Turkish calculations that Russia was averse to war had had even more to do with the failure of the Conference than the attitude of Elliot and Calice.[2]

In London, meanwhile, Disraeli already favoured a *rapprochement* with Austria-Hungary, but failed because Andrássy preferred to deal directly with Russia. Derby, so Shuvalov learned from a highly confidential source, was not eager for these overtures:[3] and indeed the general attitude in London at this juncture may be described as equally negative towards Russia and towards Turkey.

The lack of directive in British policy is admirably depicted in the columns of *Punch*. On the failure of the Conference Mr. Punch pointedly asks the British Lion, "If you didn't mean to back him (Salisbury) up, why did you send him?"[4] After the Gorchakov Circular he asks, "What Next?" The Russian Bear, dressed as a soldier, addresses the British Lion in sailor's kit: "You've read my Circular. You know my intentions are strictly honourable! What are *you* going to do?", to which the puzzled Lion replies, scratching his head, "Blest if I know! Ask the Government, and if they can't tell you, try the Opposition!"[5]

Punch's reactions to the warring parties are even more sarcastic: for on 24 February "Sergeant Derby" is seen drilling "The Awkward Squad" of the Cabinet, who are all at sixes and sevens, while a week later John Bull shows equal disinclination for the rival beers which they offer him and treats them as "Much of a Muchness".

The Government's negative tendency was increased when on the very eve of Parliament reopening, news came that a palace intrigue had overthrown the reforming Grand Vizier Midhat Pasha. Nothing could be more unconstitutional than the manner of his fall: for on the morning of 5 February, when he called for his usual audience with the Sultan, he was detained without any explanation in an ante-

---

[1] *G.P.* no. 272, Schweinitz to Foreign Office, 17 Jan.
[2] *Ibid.* no. 273, Bismarck to Schweinitz, 24 Jan.
[3] *R.B.D.* v. no. 166, postscript of 17 Jan.   [4] 27 Jan. 1877.
[5] 17 March. On 10 March Tenniel produced the more famous, but much more questionable cartoon called "Phoebus questions Phaeton", in which the new leader of the Commons is being advised by the old chief how to drive the four awkward steeds, Bunkum, Banter, Management and Mystery.

chamber, then after a couple of hours hurried straight on board the Sultan's private yacht, which lay under steam off the palace, and forthwith deported to Brindisi, without being allowed to communicate with family or friends. With a superb insolence his fall was notified to foreign Powers as having been carried out under paragraph 113 of the new constitution, which gave the Sultan the right to banish persons dangerous to the state! The Moor had done his duty of wrecking the foreign reform project; the Moor could now go.

Not a single protest was raised, the constitutional party submitted in utter helplessness, and Midhat's successor, the reactionary Edhem Pasha, found it perfectly safe to let the general election take place, amid popular indifference. Few save official candidates were elected, there was a small sprinkling of venal and subservient Christians, and a Senate of 25 members was nominated from among the higher officials. The Sultan found it convenient to open the new Parliament in person on 19 March. It served on the one hand as a sign that his Empire was rallying against Russia, for it promptly voted a state of siege and whatever laws were required: while on the other hand it strengthened the illusions of western Turcophils, who fondly contrasted the Liberal allures of Abdul Hamid with the evil despotism of the Tsar! The farce was prolonged into the following winter, until Abdul Hamid, firm in the saddle, sent Parliament about its business and proceeded to govern Turkey by a despotic system of corruption and espionage peculiarly his own. Looking back to-day, it is easy to realise the incredible naïvety of Turkey's advocates, but at the time it was with many a solemn article of faith. None the less, the fall of Midhat was, as Harcourt exultantly wrote to Granville, "a tremendous blow to the Anglo-Turks who have laid all their money on him".[1]

The one good piece of news that came from Turkey was that negotiations were set on foot with Serbia, and eventually led on 28 February to the conclusion of peace on a basis of the *status quo*. With Montenegro, however, who claimed an accession of territory, peace could not be arranged.

The Porte was very noticeably stiffening its back and showed but little disposition to accept any of the details of reform so laboriously put forward from London. This was doubtless why Beaconsfield on the eve of Parliament declared that "we are now indeed as free as air".[2]

---

[1] *Granville Papers*, 6 Feb. 1877, Harcourt to Granville.
[2] Buckle, *op. cit.* vi. p. 117.

CHAPTER V

THE BATTLE IN PARLIAMENT

Nothing could justify any member of either House in joining such an agitation, except the conviction that the attitude of the Government has been fundamentally wrong on some matter of justice and the national honour.

DUKE OF ARGYLL, Sept. 1876

Mr. Gladstone may not succeed in carrying the House or reuniting his party, or even winning the solid support of the British people, but his work will stand and bear fruit if he has disabused England of her old Turkish prepossessions and delivered her soul from one of its most evil, most unprofitable and most dishonourable illusions.

The Times, 18 May 1877

THE OPPOSITION OPENS FIRE

THE Queen in opening Parliament on 8 February 1877 was made to say, "My object throughout has been to maintain the peace of Europe and bring about the better government of the disturbed provinces, without infringing upon the independence and integrity of the Ottoman Empire". Lord Granville at once opened fire, in the name of the Opposition, flatly denying the view that the Turks were now in the same position with respect to the Treaty of Paris as when it was made, and adding that he himself as Foreign Secretary in 1871 had warned Turkey against the delusion that she could rely on British support, "whatever she did".[1] Derby in his reply argued that the original insurrection in Hercegovina had been a very unimportant affair, which might have been easily suppressed, but it had been fanned by sympathy from outside, by "the almost incredible apathy of the Turkish authorities and by the bankruptcy of Turkey". This evoked a lively protest from the Duke of Argyll, against the Foreign Secretary's obvious regret that Bosnia had not been reconquered. "I say distinctly in this high place, every insurrection against that Government is a legitimate insurrection," and "you will have no peace in Europe till the well-being of the Christian subjects of the Porte has been secured by the united action of the European Powers."[2]

Derby's concluding phrases were much less contentious: he denied

[1] Hansard, ccxxxii. pp. 20-21.　　　　[2] *Ibid*. p. 49.

that menace should fairly be read into the much criticised Guildhall speech and gladly accepted the Tsar's pacific assurances, while entering the caveat that even a Tsar was not all-powerful and "events may be too strong for him".[1] Beaconsfield intervened with the brief but highly characteristic argument that a bigger question was at issue than the "mere amelioration" of the Christians' lot—a question "in which is involved the existence of Empires". Salisbury ended the debate with a warning that "no threat of coercion should be made unless the Government were absolutely prepared to follow up the menace". He denied with equal vigour the charge of "lack of friendliness" towards "the deeply suffering Christians" of Turkey, and on the other hand, the doctrine of legitimate insurrection advanced by one whose ancestors had led resistance to the royal power in our own island.

In the Commons on the same day there was a similar preliminary skirmish. Lord Hartington attacked the Prime Minister for his Aylesbury speech, with its monstrous reference to the secret societies of Europe. He had "denounced everybody and everything except the Turkish Government", yet "after a few months all Europe saw the Serbian cause was not merely the cause of an ambitious petty state, but the cause of the oppressed nationalities of Turkey". As leader of the Opposition he condemned the Premier's Guildhall "taunts towards Russia" and contrasted his "menaces" and "imprudence" with the pacific assurances of the Tsar.[2] The Chancellor of the Exchequer countered by denying any lack or shifting of policy during "these transactions", and by claiming that the Government was just as bent as the Opposition on securing improved government in the Turkish provinces and had always made it clear that England would not go to war on behalf of Turkey. He was on fairly strong ground when quoting the Cabinet's instructions to Lord Salisbury. He would not even admit that the Conference had been a failure, and while confessing a lack of confidence in the new Turkish constitution, he hugged a belief in "Turkey's willingness to reform herself".[3] Gladstone was unusually brief. After defending his pamphlet, he complained that Northcote was "still involved in the old labyrinth of persuasions to Turkey to set about the work of self-reform". If the Government had denied any change of policy, it had at least made "an acknowledgement of responsibility". He ended with an eulogy of Salisbury's conduct at Constantinople and a warning that if the Porte refused

[1] *Ibid.* p. 42.   [2] *Ibid.* pp. 78, 87.   [3] *Ibid.* pp. 97, 102, 104.

further proposals of the Powers, her position before Europe would be totally changed.[1]

A week later feeling flared up in the House of Commons, when Gladstone quoted Derby's now famous dispatch of 5 September to Elliot[2] and challenged the Ambassador's contention that the protocol of internal reforms would be an infringement of the Treaty of Paris. He reinforced his own view by Palmerston's definition of the guarantees to Turkey as "to give the right of interference, but not to impose an obligation of interference". The Treaty of 1856 had been replaced by that of 1871—after the repudiation of the Black Sea clauses: did Her Majesty's Government then consider itself absolved from the obligations of 1856 and "free to act as policy, justice and humanity may seem to direct and require"?[3] Gathorne Hardy's answer came straight from the shoulder. "We do not." If Turkey was bound to Europe by 1856 and 1871, then Europe was bound to her. The latter clearly reaffirmed the earlier, and when did Turkey forfeit her rights? He quoted a Liberal Under-Secretary, Lord Enfield, who had admitted as recently as 1871 that till then the Turkish firmans of reform had been "fairly fulfilled"—here Gladstone loudly protested—and he went on to quote a famous saying of the Duke of Wellington in 1829: "The Ottoman Empire stands for the benefit not of the Turks but of Christian Europe, not to preserve Mohammedans in power, but to save Christians from a war".[4] "I could not", he added, "express myself in any shorter or better language."[5] This was nothing if not candid. He perhaps toned down the effect a little by denying that the Treaty bound us to "go to war" or that the Government lacked sympathy for the Christians, even though it did not favour autonomy. But he harped in a curious way upon the triple treaty of April 1856 and "the great humiliation" to this country, if being called upon by France and Austria to fulfil our obligation . . . we were unable to have regard to it". It is quite clear that he did not realise how little prospect there was of either France or Austria claiming such fulfilment: and his argument shows how little the Government speakers were in touch with the realities of the situation.

Much the most notable contribution to the debate came from a

---

[1] Hansard, ccxxxii. pp. 114, 119.   [2] See *supra*, p. 63.
[3] Hansard, ccxxxii. pp. 476, 486.
[4] The Duke of Westminster countered in the House of Lords on 20 February by a rival quotation from the Duke of Wellington in the same year 1829—"It would no doubt have been more fortunate if the Russians had entered Constantinople and the Turkish Empire had been dissolved".   [5] Hansard, ccxxxii. pp. 488-91.

little-known member, P. J. Smyth, who rarely intervened, though he
was one of the very few able to speak from first-hand knowledge, and
not out of a mere sea of ignorance and prejudice. Smyth maintained
—what none would now attempt to deny—that the Hatti Humayun
of 1856 had from the very first been "a dead letter". He reminded
the House of what even Gladstone had not made clear, and what was
not always clearly understood even during the Great War—that "the
Bosnians and Herzegovinese are one in race, in faith, in language and
in history with the Montenegrins and Serbians: why should they not
be one in freedom?" Self-government and foreign domination in
south-eastern Europe had borne respectively their natural fruits:
"Roumania, Montenegro and Serbia are comparatively prosperous
and progressive, because of their freedom: Bosnia, Herzegovina and
Bulgaria are withered and decrepit because of their servitude". The
real issue was "not the constitutionalism of Midhat Pasha, the sun-
burst of the Guildhall or the humanitarianism of St. James's Hall:
it is simply national independence as represented by Serbia and
Montenegro, against foreign domination as represented by Turkey".
To give his speech its true balance, he took care to insist that the
Eastern Question "has also an Hellenic aspect", and that even though
the revival of Byzantium might be a delusion, the enlargement of the
Greek Kingdom was "an aspiration which must be satisfied before
there can be a settlement of the Eastern Question". A free Bulgaria,
a free Thessaly, Epirus, and Macedonia, would be "a surer and more
becoming defence of legitimate interests than Turkish forts on the
Danube, or fortified passes in the Balkans". He disclaimed the title
of Russophil, "but when Russia is in the right, as by the admission
of Europe she now is, she is entitled to the sympathy, respect and
support of Europe". England "stood benevolently neutral" while the
Poles were conquered, the Duchies wrested from Denmark, and
Alsace-Lorraine torn from France: he hoped that "should a similar
ignominious policy now prevail, she may be debarred from appearing
even as a gleaner on the harvest-field of the Danube". He "never
could discover what danger the west has to apprehend from Russia.
Her destiny impels her eastward and there her mission must necessarily be one of civilisation."[1] Here spoke the voice of the future,
though its echoes were drowned at the time.

No contrast could be greater than the speech that followed from
Henry Chaplin, who made a frontal attack on Gladstone, denounced the

[1] *Ibid.* pp. 537, 542-5.

St. James's Hall demonstration as "a packed meeting, . . . a barefaced audacious sham and imposture, so far as its national character and name were concerned", and interpreted him to desire the coercion of Turkey and therefore war. This grotesque inversion brought Gladstone to his feet in a stormy House and led him to claim that the Bulgarian agitation was "an almost unexampled national and popular feeling" which he had done nothing to set in motion. He had only "entered the arena most reluctantly and very late", but "with the deep conviction that . . . the Government had unintentionally" [the adverb was probably inserted *pro forma*] "misrepresented the sentiment of the country and were using its power and influence for purposes which were in direct antagonism to the best and deepest wishes of its heart". He again quoted Derby's much debated dispatch, as confirming the impossibility of intervening on behalf of Turkey, pleaded for "a great watchfulness" regarding British policy and ended on the warning note, "We are those who gave her the strength which has been exhibited in the Bulgarian massacres".[1] But though all this was effective enough from the debating point of view, the Chancellor of the Exchequer held his ground and boldly invited a vote of censure, which he well knew the Opposition to be too disunited to put forward.

The whole question was again formally raised on 20 February in the House of Lords by the Duke of Argyll, perhaps the most advanced in his views of all Gladstone's leading colleagues in the Liberal party. On this occasion he took a skilful middle course, treating the instructions to Lord Salisbury as "common ground" between the rival views, and paying tribute to Derby's speeches as "always more or less philosophical, bearing the impress of careful thought and the calmest judgment", but insisting that the Government as a whole, so far from being impartial, were "active partisans of Turkey against the insurgents", although the Bosnian rising was quite demonstrably "not instigated by foreign agents, but was the natural consequence of abominable oppression". The Turks, he argued, had since 1856 been engaged in committing suicide: their Government was "nothing better than a permanent Government by bashibazuks", and there was no hope of redress. "Russophobia", on the other hand, was the cause "that humane and honourable men came to justify themselves in acting on such a cruel and unjust policy". This telling phrase was followed by a comparison—fully justified by a perusal of the lucubrations of Butler-Johnstone, Augustus Daly and other rampart Turco-

[1] Hansard, ccxxxii. pp. 554-8.

phils of the day—with the mania against the First Napoleon, referred to in *Rejected Addresses*: "Who fills the butchers' shops with large blue flies?" At last, however, there had come a tardy repentance of public opinion, due to the perpetration of "the horrid cruelties of Genghis Khan in the days of Queen Victoria". But though this involved a certain change of policy after September, the papers issued by the Government made it quite evident that the Salisbury mission was "foredoomed to failure", since the Porte knew Britain to be opposed to coercion, and even calculated on her active support. The Duke concluded with a personal appeal to Beaconsfield to consider practical measures for the protection of the Christians, "not only against the odious barbarism of the Turks, but also the crushing autocracy of the Tsars".[1]

This speech evoked interesting rejoinders from Derby, Salisbury and the Prime Minister himself, which already throw light upon the great difference in mentality and outlook between the three men. The Foreign Secretary was mainly concerned to deny the charge of feebleness and even of failure to attain the two cardinal objects of European peace and Turkish reform. The flow of European capital into Turkey had, he frankly admitted, "done more harm than good", and "independence", he agreed with his friend Salisbury, was "a very relative term". But he tried to justify his attitude towards the rising in its early stages, pointed out that the Russian consulate in Ragusa was "the headquarters of the insurgent chiefs" and "every Serbian defeat was felt in Russia as a Russian defeat". None the less, we had "gained our object" and had clearly warned the Porte that it "must not look to England for assistance or protection", if its *non possumus* attitude "resulted in a war with other countries".[2]

Salisbury took quite a different line. "This country works in a glass hive: all the sentiments of its public men are well known", and it was "now reaping the harvest" sown in the Crimean War. An attempt had been made to achieve the impossible, to place the subject population of Turkey under the tutelage of the six Powers: it had been made because Palmerston and Clarendon had "an entirely false idea of the probable reform and progress of the Ottoman Empire". "Long experience", however, "has proved that Turkey will not reform herself." But though it was "evident that the sanguine hopes of 1856 would not be realised", that was not a reason for turning round and tearing up the treaty, and the Conference, though it sought to restore

[1] *Ibid.* pp. 640, 645-6, 648, 659.   [2] *Ibid.* pp. 660-69.

peace between Turkey and her vassals and to obtain good government for the Christians, had found its "motive force" in "the fear of a breach with Russia". The refusal of the Porte to accept the terms of Europe was a mystery, "a tremendous infatuation", and the internal Turkish situation was one of "tremendous danger" for a country which had "no aristocracy, no governing class, no organised democracy, no representative government and two foundations only— religion and the Sultan". The value of all these admissions from the standpoint of the Opposition was seriously discounted by Lord Salisbury's blunt insistence on the impossibility of extracting from the other side of the House "any statement of their opinion or their desires", any clear definition of coercion and its probable consequences.[1]

Much the most important contribution, however, was the concluding speech of Lord Beaconsfield. Faced by the question whether Turkey "can maintain itself or is doomed to partition", Europe, he contended, must cling to the policy of territorial integrity, as "almost traditional" and as the sole means of averting "great wars". "Depart from the principle, and we leave the ship without a rudder in our discussions." He then proceeded to vindicate the Government's course from the beginning of the crisis, in terms which conveyed a thinly veiled criticism of the other Powers. Britain had associated herself with the consular action, because the Porte had given its sanction: she had for the sake of peace and unity adhered to the Andrássy Note, though regarding it as "essentially an inopportune move" and its efforts at social reform as "perfectly idle": she had resisted the Berlin Memorandum, because "it would obviously and inevitably lead to the military occupation of European Turkey". It was unjust to say that "we took no steps" afterwards, because the Turkish revolution had quite transformed the situation. Two policies were now before us, the Russian and the British. The former, "deserving of all respect", was to establish a chain of autonomous states, "tributary, but in every other sense independent". The Turks, he reminded the House, had only very gradually established themselves in Europe and had "remained for some time in company with" a number of independent and autonomous states: "there was of course an Emperor at Constantinople, a King of Bulgaria, a King of Servia, a Hospodar of Wallachia, a Duke of Athens, a Prince of Corinth".

---

[1] Hansard, ccxxxii. pp. 689-97. Shuvalov reported home on this speech that it was "perhaps a parliamentary manœuvre to bring back the Prime Minister to less Turkish points of view"—*R.B.D.* v. no. 179, 21 Feb. This shows that the Russians were still hoping on the lines of Ignatyev's confidential dispatch—see *supra*, p. 138.

These were gradually absorbed and conquered, till the Empire, "limited to its matchless city and to what in modern diplomatic language is called a cabbage garden, was invested and fell. And it did occur to us that if there were a chain of autonomous states and the possessors of Constantinople were again limited to a cabbage garden, probably the same result might occur." The alternative was "administrative autonomy", defined as "institutions that would secure to the Christian subjects of the Porte some control over their local affairs and some security against the excesses of arbitrary power": and in due course the Russian Government "gave up their views and adopted those of England"—"very cordially", he added. What prevented a peaceable *dénouement* had been the Serbian war.

Turning to the recent Conference, he praised Lord Salisbury and poured scorn on the theory that he had not enjoyed the confidence of the Cabinet because he was not defended by his colleagues: he himself had had "many vituperative articles" against him, but no colleague defended him. In his opinion the only error of Salisbury had been that "he gave too much credit to the Turks for common sense" —certainly a rude enough rebuff to the friends of the Porte. He defended the much-challenged phrases of his Guildhall speech: "They were no sneer: I was unconscious of any sarcasm". And he ended as ever on the note, that deep as might be the humanitarian feelings of the nation, deeper still was "the determination to maintain the Empire of England".[1]

A week later Lord Derby made a most illuminating statement in the House. After distinguishing between the various forms of "local or administrative autonomy", he added—and quoted Hungarian and Canadian analogies—"I do not believe the administration can be held together except by the introduction of the principle of self-government to a considerable extent". He denied "that mythical change of policy attributed to us" and met the criticism that the Government failed to prevent a coalition of the three Imperial Powers or to secure continental alliances for Britain, in the following passage. "We stand in a very different position from the other Governments. . . . We can keep back nothing from the public, we can give no pledge, we can enter into no secret alliances, we can hold out no inducement to any state to join us, except our well-known desire for peace and our friendly intentions towards all Powers, and that of course is not enough to offer, when you are competing with Governments who

[1] *Ibid.* pp. 713, 718, 721-2, 725.

are able to hold out offers of alliances offensive and defensive."
Here Lord Derby put his finger on one of the fundamental causes of
British isolation in the era of the old diplomacy, the main reason
why Bismarck's series of overtures to this country were all more or
less half-hearted and led to nothing, the reason why other Powers
also looked with scepticism upon the prospects of a British alliance.

It is not the least instructive feature of this great crisis of the
seventies, that it presented this peculiar issue in a specially acute form
and accentuated the contrast with the three other Powers which then
counted most in the counsels of Europe and in each of which the
control of foreign policy by the Crown secured a continuity unknown
on this side of the Channel. Here foreign policy remained as before in
the hands of the Crown, the Prime Minister, and the Foreign Secretary,
though the relative weight of each may have varied considerably: but
on the major issues endorsement by the Cabinet had become a tacit
necessity, and this in turn involved ratification by a strong parliamentary majority. And what guarantee was there, asked our continental neighbours, that a policy canvassed with such fervent passion,
but such indifference to hard facts, between the two great parties in
the state, might not be utterly reversed when the electoral kaleidoscope was reversed?

SALISBURY AND PARTITION

Lord Salisbury after his return was full of anxiety and perplexity.
His intimate discussions with Carnarvon revealed "a rooted belief
in Disraeli's untrustworthiness".[1] In his daughter's words, "The
memory of '67 weighed heavily upon them both: they had known
betrayal and they dreaded a repetition of the experience".[2] While
quite out of sympathy with "Gladstone's abominable agitation" and
laying on it the blame for the Tsar's "unlucky Moscow speech",[3] he
felt that "the old policy of defending English interests by sustaining
the Ottoman dynasty has become impracticable", and the time had
come for "some territorial rearrangement". He treats British loss of
influence at Constantinople as "infallible" and fears "the development of Germany into a naval power".[4] He could not bring himself
as yet to trust Austria or to believe in her future, and he shared one

[1] Carnarvon's diary, 8 Feb.—*Life of Carnarvon*, ii. p. 352.
[2] *Life of Salisbury*, ii. p. 137.
[3] 16 Feb. to Lytton—*ibid*. p. 128.   [4] 9 March—*ibid*. p. 130.

prejudice of his chief, distrust of Bismarck. With such views, he was led to make definite proposals to the Cabinet for the abandonment of the old Palmerstonian policy and "the substitution for it" of what his daughter calls "a bold initiative in partition",[1] arguing quite fairly that Turkey's attitude at the Conference had freed the Powers from all treaty obligations. In this, however, he failed to carry the majority of his colleagues: indeed Lord Carnarvon was probably the only one who would have followed him with enthusiasm. He was thus faced by the difficult choice of foregoing or postponing a policy which seemed to him necessary for the welfare of the Near East and sooner or later inevitable, or of risking a split in the Conservative ranks, which in the prevailing state of party passion and excitement might have produced a deplorable situation at home just when a united front seemed more than usually desirable. We may assume that the choice was not easy, but that his lifelong belief in conservative statesmanship outweighed the drawbacks of which he was only too conscious, and that the knowledge of his inability ever to co-operate, much less coalesce, with Gladstone was stronger than his undoubted suspicions of Beaconsfield.

None the less the result of his acquiescence must have been galling. "English policy", he told Lytton, "is to float lazily down stream, occasionally putting out a diplomatic boat-hook to avoid collisions":[2] and two months later, when war had come very largely as the result of British negation, he wrote of our foreign policy to the same correspondent "with sadness and apprehension". "The system of never making a plan beyond the next move is bearing its natural fruits. I trust we may avoid any great disaster."[3]

BEACONSFIELD'S FRESH OVERTURE TO RUSSIA

Meanwhile Europe had its eyes fixed upon the proceedings in the British Parliament. Turkish obstinacy was still further encouraged by the passages in the Queen's speech and the Premier's speeches and by the strength of the Conservative battalions. The London Cabinet's weak attitude with regard to the punishment of those guilty of excesses in Bulgaria (despite Baring's repeated exposure of the facts, despite Elliot's official remonstrances to the Grand Vizier and Salisbury's complaints to the Sultan, almost a year had passed, yet no serious step had been taken) increased the reliance of the Turks in

[1] *Ibid.* p. 134.   [2] 9 March—*ibid.* p. 130.   [3] 4 May—*ibid.* p. 135.

their powers of diplomatic bluff. Moreover, the appointment of Mr. Layard as Ambassador at Constantinople far outweighed any regrets at the decision against Elliot's return: and Gladstone, who remembered him as "the chief advocate of Turkey in the House of Commons"—in days when he was an outrider of the great Stratford de Redcliffe—was fully entitled to describe his selection now as "a delicate attention" to "a Government which has made itself responsible in full from first to last for the massacres of Bulgaria".[1] Among other Turkish calculations were undoubtedly the knowledge that official Russia hesitated before the final arbitrament of war, and, fantastic as it may sound, the hope of complications in Hungary and Poland.[2] One further detail is worth mentioning: Baron Werther, the somewhat ineffective German Ambassador at the Porte, was replaced by Prince Reuss, which apparently caused considerable annoyance both to the Tsar and to Gorchakov[3]—though his Russophil outlook soon proved their fears to be groundless.

Russia, on her side, was still playing for time. Not merely were the decisive negotiations with Vienna still incomplete, but the financial and military situation was by no means brilliant and required a certain preparation. The High Command, which had already concentrated over 300,000 men on the Bessarabian frontier and 100,000 more in the Caucasus, were anxious to avoid hostilities until the melting of the Balkan snows increased the chances of a rapid campaign. Gorchakov told Shuvalov quite categorically that the Tsar "preferred a pacific solution, but on condition of a serious and real improvement in the lot of the Eastern Christians":[4] and to this attitude he consistently adhered throughout.

It was at this moment that Count Shuvalov, who was on the friendliest terms with the German Chancellor, wrote to him in favour of a Russo-German alliance—whether as a mere feeler on his own initiative or at the instance of his master the Tsar is uncertain. Bismarck, while reaffirming his belief in the maintenance of the traditional ties between the two countries, declined, as always throughout his career, to commit himself unreservedly to one of his two allies. In passing, he struck an almost prophetic note, when he hinted that the old friendship "will perhaps be easier to destroy than it was to create", if his successors lacked his experience and patience

[1] 7 May 1877—Hansard, ccxxxiv. p. 407.
[2] *G.P.* ii. no. 271, Werther to Bülow, 14 Jan.
[3] Schweinitz, *Denkwürdigkeiten*, i. p. 420.
[4] *R.B.D.* v. no. 184, 25 Feb.

and his constant resolve to "subordinate personal susceptibilities to great monarchical interests"[1]—yet another proof that he could never resist a side hit at the detested Gorchakov. Shuvalov saw that it was useless to press him, though later on he returned more than once to the charge: but the incident illustrates what the Werder affair has already shown, that Bismarck had resolutely set his face against "opting" for either Russia or Austria, unless driven to it by dire necessity.

Towards the end of February, Beaconsfield, wavering as ever and apparently overcome by sudden and almost certainly groundless fears of fresh aggressive designs of Bismarck upon France, made one of his periodic private overtures to Shuvalov, and argued to him that Russia and Britain were equally interested in preventing the reduction of France to the rank of a second-rate Power. The Prime Minister then plunged into a fresh proposal, which is here given in the *ipsissima verba* used by Shuvalov to the Chancellor on the same day. The colours may be too vivid, but they clearly represent Shuvalov's personal impression at its very height.

"After the indispensable 'my dear friend', Lord Beaconsfield expressed himself thus: 'Let us begin by eliminating an error. I know that bellicose sentiments towards Russia are attributed to me . . . and you believe them. Well, I assure you it is a pure calumny propagated by my enemies: I am not only pacific, but I am your friend and want to work together with you. Last summer we were on the point of agreeing, and this would have forestalled many things. You know as well as I who it was who prevented our Entente. I told you at the same time what I thought of the Ottoman Empire, *whose days are numbered*: one must not precipitate its fall, but consider seriously what will happen after and prepare ourselves for it. I also told you that we are not prepared, and that its collapse at that moment would provoke a war, soon involving all Europe and England in her turn. As the Tsar desires peace, I shall second his intentions, but there is no other pacific solution than to grant the Porte a lapse of time necessary to execute its reforms. To make war is not to provoke reform, but to produce the collapse of Turkey. . . . The first condition for the execution of reforms is the disarmament of Turkey. It is not for me to reply to you point by point. . . . What I can say is that I want to agree with you and satisfy the Tsar. I realise the difficulties of the situation. My talk with Salisbury is complete on all points: that should satisfy you, because he in turn was in agreement

[1] Letter of 15 Feb. 1877, cit. in chap. xxviii. of *Reflections and Reminiscences*.

with your ambassador in Constantinople. *When I chose Salisbury as special envoy of the Queen, I selected him as the man most favourable to the* entente *with Russia.* I shall use all my influence to make the reply to your Circular satisfying to Prince Gorchakov and I should like it to be not only that golden bridge of which so much has recently been said, but *a bridge of diamonds and rubies.* I promise you this, and you can count on it.' "

The Ambassador in reply stressed Russia's difficulties in waiting very much longer, with 500,000 men under arms, and argued that if reform were postponed, there must be a "declaration that Europe upholds its demands and will know how to make Turkey respect them". Such a declaration, however, "infallibly brings us to the coercion which the British Cabinet has erased from its programme. The Prime Minister must therefore choose one of two dangers—to warn Turkey that coercion would follow her failure to enforce reform, or to permit isolated action by Russia, which probably would mean war. Shuvalov had expected, he writes, a strong protest from Beaconsfield, but on the contrary the latter reaffirmed his appreciation of Russia's difficulties and ended on a light note: "I want peace and hope we shall soon drink a glass of wine to celebrate its conclusion. But when all is over, we shall have to agree upon a pacific solution for the moment of the Sick Man's death." [1] Small wonder that the Ambassador was left wondering whether Beaconsfield was preparing to abandon his Turcophil policy, but afraid to draw any firm conclusion in either direction. The reader may be left to draw the obvious contrast between Disraeli's overture to Russia in 1877 and Tsar Nicholas's famous overture to the British Ambassador in 1853.

The Russian Circular referred to, addressed to the five Powers, was simply an attempt to convert Europe to the necessity for a joint front towards the Porte, or rather to obtain sanction for Russia as "the mandatory of Europe"—on the plausible but somewhat naïve ground that its rejection of the unanimous recommendation of the Conference had really been an affront and a *soufflet* to all alike.

The Ignatyev Mission

The news of Beaconsfield's fresh overture excited both Gorchakov and the Tsar and prompted them to a step of doubtful wisdom. General Ignatyev was sent upon a special mission to the West, with

[1] *R.B.D.* v. no. 179, 20 Feb. 1877.

the childishly transparent camouflage of a visit to a London oculist![1]
Shuvalov at once warned his chief that the name of Ignatyev might
well rouse in London "a storm such as Elliot's would have roused in
Russia", and that the British Cabinet, in the face of press recriminations, would be more suspicious than ever. He stood before English
opinion—quite unfairly, and immensely to his own credit, his colleague was very careful to add—as the man above all responsible
for the Porte's declaration of bankruptcy, for opposition to British
policy in Turkey, for the fall of Midhat and as leader of the Russian
war party. But the Chancellor, who did not know London, upheld the
decision, arguing that Ignatyev was bringing "such moderate explanations that the exaggerated terror was bound to disperse before
the reality", and that the British Cabinet would be relieved from "a
very heavy burden", whatever that might mean. The aim of the
mission was to provide, through a man possessing an unrivalled
knowledge of the Turkish situation, a full explanation of Russian
aims, and so to secure a favourable answer to his Circular, as the basis
of "a pacific solution".[2]

Before reporting to Lord Derby the impending visit, Shuvalov
called on Lady Derby, with whom he had for some months past been
in close and constant consultation on all political questions. "She
showed alarm" at the news, and Lord Salisbury, whom on her advice
he also consulted before going to her husband, was no less urgent
for a postponement, on the ground that Ignatyev's arrival at this
particular juncture might easily "provoke a sudden *revirement* in
England and a return of Turkish sympathies".[3] Salisbury even sent
a private telegram of his own to Ignatyev, in this same sense,
advising him to wait in Paris in the first instance.[4]

As a result, Ignatyev, who on his way through Berlin had a
conversation of five hours with Bismarck and an audience with the
Emperor, waited in Paris until Shuvalov could join him. He had laid
before the German Government "the first draft of a protocol, intended
to be signed by the Powers"[5] and at the same time confided to them

---

[1] *R.B.D.* v. no. 179.   [2] *Ibid.* no. 191, 1 March.   [3] *Ibid.* nos. 192 and 193.
[4] "Charmed to see you, but if possible postpone your arrival till crisis is past.
English opinion vacillating and distrustful. Special mission of so celebrated a man
will arouse suspicions. Cabinet will be accused of leaning too much towards Russia,
thus leading to reaction in favour of Turkey. Stop in Paris to inform yourself"—*ibid.*
no. 194.
[5] Russell to Derby, 7 March (F.O. 64,877, no. 82), and Derby to Russell, 6 March
(F.O. 64,874, no. 77). I am indebted to Miss W. Taffs for this evidence that the
Protocol originated with Ignatyev, though subsequently drafted out of recognition
by Shuvalov.

the Tsar's view that within five or six weeks at latest there must be
a certainty of joint diplomatic action, or else war was inevitable.[1]
Bismarck's own reaction was that England would again not join the
other Powers and that Russia, despite all her professions, had by now
made up her mind to war. None the less William I. at once notified to
St. Petersburg, London and Vienna his Government's acceptance of
the Russian Protocol, and this was not without effect. Shuvalov came
straight back to London and communicated to Lord Derby what
Ignatyev had told him of the Tsar's view. The discussion now centred
round the specification of reforms and the means of securing demobil-
isation, Gorchakov insisting that Turkey must take the first step in
disarming. Shuvalov in his reports shows considerable nervousness as
to lack of support from his German and Austrian colleagues and fears
lest Russia might be forced into undue concessions, in order to secure
a free hand against Turkey. "I do not know the part of the booty reserved to herself by Russia"—the Budapest negotiations were as yet
unknown to him—"but even were it the lion's share, the history of
our country would inscribe on one of its blackest pages the cession of
Slav provinces to Austria and the establishment of the English in
the Straits":[2] and the former, he learns from Ignatyev, is Vienna's
price, while the latter is widely favoured in England.

The next fortnight was filled with lengthy negotiations between
Shuvalov and the Foreign Office: and on 17 March Ignatyev arrived
in London and went to stay with Lord Salisbury at Hatfield, where
Hartington and W. E. Forster were specially invited to meet him.
The Prime Minister, who received the news of his arrival as "a
thunderbolt—nothing could be more inopportune",[3] ended by showing him every courtesy and entertaining him at an official dinner. The
wording of the draft Protocol was submitted to almost microscopic
examination at the Foreign Office, and the two Russians acquired the
impression that "England's sole objective in signing the Protocol was
to obtain from Russia an engagement, in whatever form, of demobil-
isation after Turkish initiative in disarming. On this point Whigs and
Tories are of the same opinion."[4] Derby assured them that he personally did not doubt "the loyal intentions" of Russia, but he was "a
minister responsible to the country" and found it impossible to cure
public opinion of its suspicions. It is quite impossible to read

---

[1] *G.P.* no. 276, Bismarck to William I., 4 March, and no. 278, note of William I.
("Ignatyev spoke a great deal, I very little").
[2] 2/14 March—*R.B.D.* v. no. 200.
[3] 14 March—Buckle, vi. p. 127.   [4] *R.B.D.* v. p. 756.

Shuvalov's very full correspondence with his Government without reaching the conclusion that he was desperately anxious to avert war, that he clutched at the (from his point of view) rather colourless Protocol as a last straw, and that even the normally far more bellicose Ignatyev was at this time working on absolutely parallel lines. In the last few days his efforts were stimulated by Gorchakov's confidential warning that unless the Porte yielded by 13 April, at latest, Russian troops would cross the frontier.[1]

That Ignatyev worked in genuine accord with Shuvalov for an arrangement with England may be regarded as certain: but his visit was none the less a failure. Even on W. E. Forster, who was predisposed in his favour, he seems to have left an impression of shiftiness and insincerity. Their very frank conversation, recorded in Forster's diary, culminated in a brief passage of arms. "Your Government", said the General, "will be in an awkward position. Your refusal to sign the Berlin Memorandum brought on the Serbian war: and now, when we are willing to make great concessions to save the peace of Europe, your Government would make them useless by obliging us to leave the Christians to be massacred." "Very clever of you to have brought it to this!" replied the unimpressed Radical: "at which he [Ignatyev] grinned complacently".[2] And we find Forster quoting Congreve's lines,

> No mark like open talk to cover lies,
> As to go naked is the best disguise.

No less enlightening is Count Münster's comment on Ignatyev, written from Hatfield on the same occasion. "His coming was a mistake. Liars—and that he is to the full—make nothing of it here in the long run, and he not even in a short time, for his reputation is too firmly established."[3]

If the British Government eventually accepted the Protocol, it was very largely owing to the urgent efforts of Lord Salisbury, who warned his chief of the dangers of isolation at such a moment. "If we reject the Note", he argued, "it is pretty clear the Tsar must go to war. We shall then come before Parliament under these conditions. We shall be alone against the other five Powers. We shall have brought on a war by this isolation. And we shall have done this to avoid accepting a Note which pledges us to hardly anything to which

[1] *Ibid.* no. 204, 26 March, Gorchakov to Shuvalov.
[2] T. Wemyss Reid, *Life of W. E. Forster*, ii. p. 171.
[3] "Aus den Briefen Bennigsens", *Deutsche Revue*, Sept. 1907, p. 310.

we are not already pledged, and which can at all events be plausibly described as a Note of extreme moderation."[1] These arguments were already sufficiently unanswerable, but he showed his keenness of perception still further. "Shuvalov tells me that they [*i.e.* Russia] have squared Vienna. I believe it, not so much because he tells me, but because I believe Andrássy to be for the present in Bismarck's pocket"—here of course he was going too far—"and Bismarck's consent implies Andrássy's. But what does the assent of Vienna to a Turkish campaign mean? It is ominous to England. It means that Russia will not threaten Constantinople, and will not permanently occupy Bulgaria. But the national feeling will insist on some territorial result. She can only find it on the side of Asia." The result of isolation, then, would be that "we should have restored the alliance of the three Empires, established Russia on the Armenian hills, lost all hold on Turkey—and got nothing whatever in compensation".[2]

At this critical juncture letters passed between Carnarvon and Salisbury which reveal the doubts surrounding Beaconsfield's attitude to the last moment. Carnarvon has placed on record that the Prime Minister, on 23 March, used language at a Cabinet meeting "which pointed in no doubtful way to Salisbury and Carnarvon as disturbers of the peace", but that, on the other hand, he was not sure of the support of the House of Commons.[3] He warned Salisbury that the Prime Minister was scheming to compel their resignations. The cooler Salisbury, without actually dismissing the possibility, found it difficult to believe in "any course so violent". "I admit that if he means war with Russia, it is his interest to get rid of us now rather than when the crisis comes. But he can get rid of us in one of two ways. He must dismiss us, or he must pick a quarrel and provoke us to resign." In neither case would it be possible for him to come before Parliament and the country with an adequate explanation: and as "it takes two to make a quarrel", due caution on their part should make any such plot impossible.[4] The event proved him to have taken the saner view.

GLADSTONE AND HARTINGTON

In March Mr. Gladstone decided to publish a further pamphlet entitled *Lessons in Massacre*, which was mainly devoted to showing that the Turkish Government, so far from punishing those guilty of

[1] *Life of Salisbury*, ii. 131, 12 March.   [2] *Ibid.*
[3] *Life of Carnarvon*, ii. p. 353.   [4] 26 March—*Life of Salisbury*, ii. pp. 138-9.

the Bulgarian atrocities, had protected and even promoted and decorated them, while dismissing more than one official who had shown a humane temper.[1] Before publishing it, he appears to have consulted Lord Granville, who then discussed the matter with Lord Hartington.

A letter addressed by Hartington to Gladstone direct on this occasion shows how very differently they regarded the burning problem of the day. After conversation with the Liberal Whip, Adam, and others, Hartington remained "as strongly persuaded as ever, that there exists on our side of the House no disposition to raise, at the present time, any definite issue relating to the Eastern Question, and further that if it were considered necessary to raise such an issue, the Bulgarian case would not be considered the best ground on which to raise it". Referring to Granville's expression of opinion that the objections to such a pamphlet no longer existed, Hartington went on: "I should like to guard myself from any, even the slightest, responsibility for such an opinion. The probable effect of either a motion or a pamphlet from you, on the Bulgarian case, would be the revival of the feeling of horror and detestation of the Turkish Government which existed last autumn. I do not see at this moment what evil this is intended to avert, or what good it is to effect. I see no danger of our going to war for *Turkey*, on the other hand there seems to be no prospect of securing collective European action to enforce the Conference proposals. A renewed agitation might tend to lead Russia to act alone. In such a case it would be the duty of our Government with other European Governments to watch and prevent Russia turning the opportunity to her sole advantage: and I should be sorry to see a state of public opinion in which horror of the crimes of the Turkish Government would overpower every other consideration." [2]

Hartington's estimate of party opinion was confirmed to Gladstone by Granville, with whom he was of course on far more intimate terms than with his official successor in the Commons. "There is the greatest apathy in the House of Commons on the Eastern Question", he wrote, quoting his own brother "Freddy Leveson".[3] As for the motion

---

[1] He wrote to Madame Novikov that his object was to show that the Porte, ever since the massacres, "has acted to the utmost of its power and daring, with a view to teaching its people to *repeat them* when they have an opportunity"—2 March 1877, *The M.P. for Russia*, i. p. 332.

[2] *Gladstone Papers*, 3 March 1877, Hartington to Gladstone.

[3] *Ibid.* 7 March, Granville to Gladstone.

in the House for which Gladstone was already pressing, Granville was frankly opposed: but, he added, "as you think it a necessity, Hartington believes it unavoidable in some way or other, and Forster, Lowe, Harcourt, Charles Howard, Freddy Leveson and, I am told, Bright and Goschen, approve of it, there only remains to discuss to-morrow what will be the best way of bringing it on".[1] This shows only too clearly how little the new leaders were masters in their own house so long as the shadow of the old leader fell across the threshold.

THE MARCH PROTOCOL

The Protocol signed in London in the name of the six Powers, by Lord Derby and the five Ambassadors, on 31 March, reaffirmed their "common interest in the amelioration of the lot of the Christians of Turkey", took note of the peace with Serbia, recommended a rectification of frontier in favour of Montenegro and advised the Porte to "consolidate itself" by putting its armies on a peace footing and promptly instituting internal reforms—thus taking care to assume good dispositions on its part. In conclusion, they warned Turkey that a continuance of unrest would be regarded as "incompatible with their interests and those of Europe in general", and they would in that case discuss common action in the interest of the Christians. Count Shuvalov created a favourable impression by proposing that if peace between Turkey and Montenegro were once concluded and the Porte accepted the advice of Europe, it should then send an envoy to St. Petersburg, to discuss measures for a simultaneous return of Russia and Turkey to a peace footing. Lord Derby, however, signed a special declaration, declaring that the Protocol would be null and void unless this parallel disarmament were achieved:[2] and it transpired only too soon that this reservation had taken the edge off the new-found unity of the Powers.

"So the Protocol is signed", wrote Beaconsfield next day to Salisbury, "and everybody writes to me about our triumph and the humiliation of Russia. *I can't yet quite make head or tail of it.*"[3]

Shuvalov meanwhile had but few illusions. He had, "by the most secret ways", been enabled to read a secret dispatch of the Porte to Musurus Pasha and its other ambassadors, written "in the most abrupt (*cassant*) and imperative tone":[4] and he soon learned that

[1]
Gladstone Papers, 18 March, Granville to Gladstone.   [2] Text in *G.P.* ii. no. 282.
     [3] Buckle, vi. p. 131.   [4] *R.B.D.* v. no. 293, 25 March.

Musurus was treating the Protocol as "annulling the Treaty of Paris" and denouncing his own statement as arrogant and offensive.[1] Musurus, in talking to Derby, took the haughty line that it would be better for the Sultan to lose one or two provinces rather than his prestige and independence, to which Derby rejoined that it was no longer a question of one or two provinces, but of the existence of the whole Empire.[2] The Turks, however, were in no yielding mood, and on 9 April, in the teeth of British advice, rejected the Protocol and appealed past it to the provisions of 1856. They appear to have specially resented the idea of ceding Nikšić to the Montenegrins. It is generally acknowledged that the appointment of Layard to the Constantinople Embassy, which took effect at this moment, led them to assume a reversion of Britain to the standpoint of Elliot: and the plain speech of a few leading English journals—*The Times*, for instance, advised acceptance, on the ground that they must observe "the elementary necessities of prudence"—made but little impression on the Turkish Embassy in London and was barely regarded at the Porte itself.

Since the fall of Midhat the short-lived Turkish constitution had become a complete farce, and just as its first function had been to undermine the Conference of Constantinople, so its last was to secure "parliamentary" rejection of the Protocol. Then the twilight and night of the Hamidian despotism settled upon Turkey for over thirty years.

[1] *Ibid.* vi. no. 205, 3 April.   [2] *Ibid.* no. 210, 11 April.

CHAPTER VI

THE RUSSO-TURKISH WAR

I adhere to our old view that whilst Russia is a real agent of civilisation in Asia, she has *nothing* to give us in Europe—except the help of her sword to do what others ought to do also.

Duke of Argyll to W. E. Gladstone, 15 Dec. 1876

I am not such a dreamer as to suppose that Russia more than other countries is exempt from selfish ambition.

W. E. Gladstone at Blackheath, 11 Sept. 1876

It has been generally acknowledged to be madness to go to war for an idea, but it is yet more unsatisfactory to go to war against a nightmare.

Lord Salisbury at Merchant Taylors, 23 June 1877

Turkish Calculations

There is not much doubt that the Turks on their side calculated that Russia at the last moment would hesitate and draw back. They were doubtless well aware that Russia was faced by grave financial difficulties, that her Finance Minister, Reutern, protested against war to the very last moment and, again, that the reorganisation of the Russian army, undertaken in 1874 under the auspices of Milyutin, was as yet far from complete, and inspired many of the army leaders with doubt and misgivings.

The plain fact is that war, when it came, was due not to any Government initiative, but to a spontaneous outburst of nationalist feeling, which was doubtless confined to the narrow ranks of the intelligentsia, but for a time swept the masses with it. There were indeed three radically different currents of opinion in Russia. Official circles in St. Petersburg were content to defer to the Tsar's wishes, in so far as all these were well defined, and had a sufficiently European outlook to realise the dangers of adventure. The Slavophils of Moscow—centring round Prince Cherkasky and Ivan Aksakov, President of the Slav Benevolent Society, and possessing a powerful focus of opinion in the *Moscow Gazette*, so brilliantly edited by Katkov—were distrustful of Europe, confident in Russia's own resources and no less confident that they could force the hands of the Tsar in the cause of Slavdom and Orthodoxy. The Social Revolutionaries also dreamt of Slav emancipation, but to them Russian, not Balkan, liberty was the objective, and their outlook was still summed up in Herzen's phrase, "When the Imperial Eagle of Byzantium returns to its fatherland, it will disappear from Russia". There were even some who occupied an intermediate position, such as we should be tempted to call Liberal, who hoped that a constitution for Russia could be won on Balkan battle-fields.

A speech delivered by Aksakov in March 1877 before the Benevolent Society provides the key to the prevailing nationalism. There was already an underlying note of pessimism in his references to the martyrdom of Bulgaria and to the still unavenged blood poured out by Russia for the Serbian cause, and in the admission that the crusading fervour of the previous summer seemed to be abating. But he quoted with all the greater fervour the Tsar's famous Kremlin speech of November 1876, with its pledge of Slav liberation: "The historical conscience of Russia spoke from the lips of the Tsar. . . . He spoke as the successor of the Orthodox Grand Dukes, as the descendant of Ivan III., who received from the Paleologi the Byzantine arms and combined them with the arms of Moscow, and as the descendant of Peter and Catherine, and the crowned protector of ancient traditions. . . . In the grey joyless twilight . . . these words alone shine as a star to encourage and guide us . . . —these words and the unanimous spontaneous popular expression of fraternal love for the oppressed Slavs."

This speech would seem to have been interpreted at the Porte as a sign of diminishing war-fever, and when the *Moscow Gazette* was actually confiscated for reproducing it, there was perhaps some excuse for assuming that the Russian Government had turned against the war-mongers. But the Turkish rejection of the Protocol at once stiffened the back of St. Petersburg. Gorchakov told the German Ambassador that the Turks had gone mad, and warned Loftus that if it came to war, the main responsibility would rest with England—a standpoint which the reader must never forget, as explaining the Russian official outlook during the next eighteen months. Schweinitz strongly urged Loftus to bring home to Derby the fact that Russia was now really in earnest: but his private comment on his British colleague was that though he always did his best, he carried but little weight either in London or St. Petersburg.[1]

On 13 April the Russian Council of Ministers, presided over by

[1] Schweinitz, *Denkwürdigkeiten*, i. p. 409.

the Tsar in person, ordered general mobilisation and other military measures, and on the 24th a formal declaration of war upon Turkey followed. Never had Russia begun a Turkish war under such favourable circumstances. She had a secret arrangement with Austria-Hungary, she was assured of the benevolence of Germany, she could rule out any action on the part of France or Italy, and finally she had Roumania openly in arms on her side and Serbia waiting to resume the campaign if desired. The only serious challenge could come from Britain: but Britain could scarcely act alone without an ally, and such an ally was not forthcoming. Shuvalov, who took a highly realist and indeed somewhat gloomy view of the situation, reported home exactly in this sense: "if England did not feel so isolated, if she could assure herself of an ally, she would not be slow to join in".[1] According to his information the Cabinet was already discussing such eventualities as "the occupation of Gallipoli and Crete, and the transformation of Egypt into a British tributary".[2] He warned Chancellor and Tsar that Lord Derby was "the only British Minister who is thoroughly opposed to every kind of British intervention", and that "his personality offers us no guarantee, for whether he gives in or resigns, his policy will not prevail. The rest of the Cabinet share Lord Beaconsfield's views, that is to say, they do not admit that any question connected with the East should be dealt with or solved without the direct and preponderant participation of their country. Their opinions only vary as to the moment and means of safeguarding 'British interests'."

"British Interests"

How, then, asks Shuvalov, is this vague phrase "British interests" to be defined? Firstly, he argues, they involve a friendly attitude towards the Sultan, as Caliph of forty million Indian Moslems. Secondly, it is assumed in London that the Russian armies will only require ten weeks to reach Constantinople, and that the crossing of the Balkans will be a threat to Britain. But above all, there is great nervousness as to a possible advance on the Caucasian frontier, since Russia might then extend her influence in Asia Minor and threaten Suez and the route to India. Rightly or wrongly, these views are strongly held, and a few Russian victories might easily rouse England to frenzy and provoke a conflict. The Ambassador therefore advises

[1] *R.B.D.* vi. no. 226, 25 April.   [2] *Ibid.* no. 213, 19 April.

his Government to forestall this danger by confidential negotiations, in which it would indicate to London in precise terms what concessions it intends to demand for the Christians, what it will ask for itself and what limitations it would accept for the sake of benevolent neutrality on the part of Britain. This course, though open to obvious objections, was in his opinion the only means of keeping Britain neutral and preventing some *coup de tête* of Lord Beaconsfield, perhaps even the seizure of the Dardanelles.[1]

Shuvalov was only too well informed. On 21 April Beaconsfield proposed to the Cabinet the occupation of the Dardanelles, "as material guarantee against Russia seizing Constantinople".[2] He was opposed by Derby, who insisted on the preliminary consent of the Porte, and by Salisbury, who argued that this would place us in the rôle of allies of the Turks. Salisbury reported to Carnarvon that Beaconsfield's "real intention" was to help Turkey in defence of Bulgaria, and that even a few days earlier he had been "almost rude" when confronted with Salisbury's opposition.[3] The Prime Minister had a powerful ally in the Queen, who expressed her fear of receiving "a slap in the face from these false Russians", and sent him a message to be read to the Cabinet, to the effect that "if England is to kiss Russia's feet, she will not be a party to the humiliation of England and would lay down her crown". She appealed to "the feelings of patriotism" of her ministers—which for some months past she had contrasted with "the wildness, folly and fury" of Mr. Gladstone [4]—and declared that "it is not the question of upholding Turkey: it is the question of Russian or British supremacy in the world".[5] That Beaconsfield was not alone in his bellicose outlook is shown by two speeches by the First Lord, Ward Hunt, and by the Irish Secretary, Hicks Beach, both delivered on 4 April and both arguing that for the last few months the three great military Powers of the East, which had a year earlier signed a memorandum "without even the ceremony of previous consultation", had found it necessary to give way, and that England was now "the leader of the nations of Europe".[6]

How the stalwarts of the other side interpreted the Premier's tactics may be seen from a letter of Edward Freeman, who bluntly assumed that it had been "his policy all along to let Russia go to war

---

[1] *Ibid.* no. 214, Shuvalov to Gorchakov, 20 April.
[2] 23 April—*Letters*, ii. p. 530.   [3] *Life of Salisbury*, ii. p. 140.
[4] 14 Feb.—Buckle, vi. p. 122.   [5] 19 April—*ibid.* p. 133.
[6] Cit. by Lord Granville in House of Lords, 16 April 1877—Hansard, ccxxxiii. p. 1185: *not reported in "The Times"*.

with the Turk and then to pick some quarrel with her. I don't suppose he tells this either to Lord Derby, who is too stupid, or to Lord Salisbury, who is too honest: but that is clearly his game. And we must speak against it in time."[1]

The attitude of official London was in no way shared by Germany: indeed William I. was definitely of opinion that all the trouble was originally due to England's separate action at the time of the Berlin Memorandum,[2] and was quite indignant at the Turkish circular (rejecting the Protocol), "which makes the impression that an unjustly accused civilised state is defending itself, whereas an uncivilised state has by centuries of oppression driven its Christian subjects to revolt".[3] He therefore sent a message to St. Petersburg, that he could only sympathise with Prussia's old comrades-in-arms, and looked eagerly to an improvement in the lot of the Christians:[4] and he assured the Tsar most warmly of German neutrality.[5]

Lord Derby for a time favoured a joint reply to the Turkish circular, but both Vienna and Berlin declined, and he was therefore not prepared to consider mediation, as requested by the Porte. He anxiously enquired of Shuvalov whether Russia intended to blockade Egypt, and was only partially reassured by the Ambassador's reply, endorsed by a telegram of Gorchakov, that this was "pure phantasy".[6]

At this juncture a former Egyptian Minister, Nubar Pasha, visited London with the object of preparing a British protectorate in Egypt, and rumours actually circulated as to Germany taking Holland as compensation for this.[7] But official circles were extremely reserved and definitely disinclined to commit themselves in Egypt, realising that it might easily embroil us with France. This was undoubtedly one reason why Bismarck favoured the idea of a British occupation, just as a few years later he encouraged the French to enter Tunis and so alienate Italian sympathies. But his main motive in reverting to it at this juncture was the genuine desire to promote an agreement between Britain and Russia, which he regarded as in the interest of Germany.[8]

LORD DERBY'S NOTE OF 6 MAY

A new phase was reached at a Cabinet meeting of 1 May, which might have gone further but for the sudden illness of the Prime

---

[1] 22 April—*The M.P. for Russia*, i. p. 352. [2] *G.P.* no. 286, 13 April.
[3] *Ibid.* no. 287, 14 April. [4] *Ibid.* no. 288, 15 April.
[5] *Ibid.* no. 292, 28 April. [6] *R.B.D.* vi. nos. 216, 217, 25 and 26 April.
[7] *G.P.* nos. 289, 290, 293, 295. [8] *Ibid.* no. 284, 15 June.

Minister. The result was Lord Derby's Note of 6 May to Russia, explaining with admirable lucidity the points on which Britain desires to be reassured and on which she could not make concessions. He made it clear that Britain was prepared to remain neutral, but only on condition that certain specifically British interests were not imperilled. First came "the necessity of keeping open . . . the communication between Europe and the East by the Suez Canal: an attempt to blockade or otherwise interfere with the Canal or its approaches would be regarded as a menace to India and a grave injury to the commerce of the world". Secondly, Britain could not "witness with indifference the fate of Constantinople or the passing into other hands than those of its present possessors, of a capital holding so peculiar and commanding a position", and it also considered "the existing arrangements" for the navigation of the Straits as "wise and salutary" and not requiring alteration. Thirdly, "the course of events might show that there were still other interests, as for instance on the Persian Gulf, which it would be their duty to protect". He closed with the hope that the Tsar would "appreciate their desire to make their political understanding at the outset of the war", thereby responding to his assurances, given to Loftus and since published, against any permanent occupation of either Constantinople or Bulgaria.

This unusual diplomatic candour represents the last occasion of cordial co-operation between Foreign Secretary and Prime Minister. Both were agreed as to the need of clear definitions towards Russia, but as the summer passed, they were to diverge more and more both as to the tactics to be followed in enforcing them and the amount of trust to be reposed in Russian promises. The Note of 6 May may fairly be regarded as a turning-point in Anglo-Russian relations, and as time passed, it became the rallying ground of "centre" opinion in England, until at the height of the crisis in the following winter it was described, not without justice, as " the charter of England's policy". For the moment it decided Shuvalov to visit St. Petersburg, in order to inform Tsar and Chancellor as to the British situation, with all its *imponderabilia* and psychological riddles. But it is characteristic of the acute distrust which had arisen between the two Courts, that his departure was delayed by a most unfortunate personal incident. The Tsar requested that his only daughter, the Duchess of Edinburgh, to whom he was much attached, should be allowed to go to her mother in

Russia while he himself was absent with the army. But to this Queen Victoria most strongly demurred—undoubtedly because she already regarded war with Russia as only a matter of time and did not wish her daughter-in-law to be in the camp of the enemy when the time came! The Queen's irritation was not diminished by the fact that the British Military Attaché in Russia, Colonel Wellesley, was not granted the same facilities as his German, Austrian and French colleagues—it being thus tacitly implied that Britain and her sovereign were relatively less friendly than the others and therefore less worthy of confidential treatment in a moment of crisis. It was doubtless an answer on the part of the Tsar to the action of the British Government in issuing, in a Blue Book of 14 April, an exposure of Russian ill-treatment of the Uniates. The matter was made still worse, first by a provocative speech in the House of Lords by Lord Stanley of Alderley, and then by an answer from Lord Derby. For though the latter deprecated all idea of "a Great Power setting the example of interfering by official representations in the internal affairs of others", it was sufficiently obvious to everyone that this was precisely what he had just done. His attempt to justify such action must have been keenly resented. "Some said that the Russian Government were merely using the Eastern Question as a means to its own aggrandisement, while others said that Russia was the champion of religious freedom and was defending an oppressed race against religious persecution. That is a very fair controversy on both sides", and it was quite natural that those who took the first view should wish to know Russia's record of religious toleration towards her own subjects.[1] Though he took care to argue that there was no parallel between the case of the Uniates and that of "the Bulgarian atrocities" or of "the Polish War" (this latter phrase of course spoilt the effect of the former), the Blue Book clearly had no object whatsoever, unless to confuse the issue and rouse public hostility towards Russia. The Russian record towards the Uniates was execrable, both then and much later, but then as now two blacks did not make a white, nor even two whites a black.

OPPOSITION TACTICS

The Russian declaration of war produced a tense situation in England, where public opinion was more acutely divided over a

[1] Hansard, ccxxxiv. pp. 1822-5, 15 June 1877.

question of foreign policy than at any time since the French Revolution. The issue between Turk and Russian became a predominant issue, and for the time suspended personal intercourse between the warring factions and even divided families among themselves. The animosity between the two great statesmen now reached its height and infected to an almost incredible degree the outlook of their adherents, until it became more and more difficult to find anyone capable of judging the Eastern Question upon its merits.

If the seeds of acute dissension had already been sown within the Cabinet—though as yet concealed from outer view—the Opposition was scarcely less divided. The return of Gladstone from his Homeric and Scriptural studies and his resumption of a gladiatorial rôle in the political arena, was bound to upset all the calculations of his successor in the Liberal leadership, Lord Hartington, who was not merely far less emotional by nature, but was far from taking the same keen interest in foreign problems, though by no means indifferent to them. Both he and Lord Granville, who led the party in the House of Lords, had at the time definitely approved the Government's reserved attitude towards the Andrássy Note and even the Berlin Memorandum, and Granville himself had publicly endorsed its policy and "views", though criticising "the measures adopted" to enforce that policy. When Gladstone first sounded the trumpet in his speech of 31 July, Hartington had slightly raised his note,[1] but a week later insisted that he and his friends had "no disposition to make this in any degree a party question".[2] Though he possessed many high qualities, imagination and fire were not among them. It is recorded that he "yawned in the middle of his maiden speech",[3] and Gladstone once in cold blood described him as "densely ignorant as to any history beyond his experience".[4]

The atrocity campaign that followed left Hartington breathless and far behind his former leader. During September he paid a short visit to Vienna, Budapest and Constantinople, but modestly confessed on his return that he had reached no very clear conclusions on the Eastern Question. During the winter he and Granville nervously compared notes at intervals as to Gladstone's crusading activities: unlike him, they declined to take part in the St. James's

[1] *Ibid.* ccxxxi. p. 89, 31 July, House of Lords.
[2] *Ibid.* p. 744, 7 August.
[3] Holland, *Life of Duke of Devonshire,* i. p. 289.
[4] 24 Jan. 1892, to Rendel—*Papers of Lord Rendel,* p. 86.

Hall demonstration, and remained entirely unimpressed by the speeches or the speakers. Through his brother, Lord Frederick Cavendish, a whole-hearted Gladstonian, Hartington even entered a mild protest against such proceedings,[1] being quite genuinely afraid that Gladstone might split the Liberal party in two.[2] But the longer the crisis continued and the deeper the agitation struck roots in the country, the more embarrassing became Hartington's position, disapproving the exaggerated Turcophilism of Beaconsfield, but unable to endorse the extravagances of Gladstone, Fawcett or the High Church group. A letter of Lord Spencer to Lord Hartington shows that the latter feared that he might lose control of the Liberal party: it also contains a penetrating criticism of Gladstone from one who did not take the great plunge of 1885 and to the end retained the highest regard and affection for his chief: "It is useless to try and gauge Mr. Gladstone's conduct by any ordinary tests. He is governed by the most intense impulsiveness and enthusiasm, and when once his indignation is roused, he cannot be guided by the prudence which would no doubt better become the position of a retired Premier. . . . No doubt he went on too far, and I think . . . his last war with the *Pall Mall Gazette* exceedingly injudicious. But Gladstone, altogether judicious, when once launched in a movement without the check of colleagues, would not be Gladstone as he exists."[3]

In a word, Lord Hartington was unreservedly opposed to war upon the side of Turkey, but he had "not the slightest confidence" in Russia and her assurances, and doubtless as a partial corollary to this, was suspicious of what was so often called the "bag and baggage" policy against Turkey. Lord Granville, on his side, torn between an almost unlimited personal devotion to Gladstone and a very clear perception of the awkward plight in which Hartington was placed through no fault of his own and the generous forbearance which he displayed, devoted his main efforts to preventing a split in the party. The mixed feelings of the rank and file are best illustrated by the attitude of Sir William Harcourt, who, though himself a most outspoken critic of Turkey, confided to Dilke his view that "Gladstone and Dizzy seem to cap one another in folly and imprudence, and I don't know which has made the greatest ass of himself. . . . There is no fear of a return from Elba. He is *played out*. His recent conduct

---

[1] B. Holland, *Life of Duke of Devonshire*, i. p. 186.   [2] See *supra*, pp. 114, 165.
[3] 16 Nov.—Fitzmaurice, *Life of Granville*, ii. p. 190.

has made all sober people more than ever distrust him. He has done
two good things: he has damaged the Government much, and himself still more." [1] Yet, speaking to his Oxford constituents in January
1877, he defended Gladstone against the common charge of being
the author of the whole agitation. "He approved it after it had
spontaneously arisen, and his spirit could not but give it a gigantic
impulse. . . . He dragged back a misguiding and misguided administration from the brink of the abyss into which they had all but
precipitated the fortunes and the reputation of England." [2] But this
did not in the least mean that he approved of Gladstone's full policy,
still less his tactics, and he urged on Hartington "the adoption
en bloc" of Salisbury's views at the Conference of Constantinople.

Even in the Radical wing there was by no means unity of opinion.
Sir Charles Dilke, then still its most distinguished member and
already a recognised authority on foreign affairs, had been one of the
first to condemn our attitude to the Berlin Memorandum and to
quote Eugene Schuyler's exposure of Bulgarian horrors, disapproved
strongly of Gladstone's agitation, and told Harcourt, "If Gladstone
goes on much longer, I shall turn Turk". [3] He evidently did not relish
the fact that the London mob nicknamed the Opposition Front Bench
"Bag and baggage Billy and his long-eared crew". [4] In his view
Hartington was "the best man for us Radicals": his strong distrust
of Russia outweighed even his detestation of Turkey, and he was
genuinely afraid that the continuance of such a campaign might
prove fatal to the Liberal party. [5] In other words, the reactions of
party loyalty upon him were not altogether dissimilar to those of
Salisbury among the Conservatives: each valued party unity higher
than his personal views upon the Eastern Question.

Mr. Chamberlain, on the other hand, regarded Gladstone as "our
best card". If he "could be induced formally to resume the reins",
he wrote to Dilke, "it would be almost equivalent to a victory and
would stir what Bright calls 'the masses of my countrymen' to the
depths". [6] It would seem that in Chamberlain's case a deep-rooted
distrust of Disraeli dominated all other feelings. Meanwhile John
Bright, who though far from inactive was by now too old for the heat
of the battle, but had presided over the party meeting which selected
Hartington as Gladstone's successor, resolutely set his face against

---

[1] 10 Oct. 1876—A. G. Gardiner, *Life of Harcourt*, i. p. 312.
[2] *Ibid.* p. 314.   [3] Gwynn and Tuckwell, *Sir Charles Dilke*, i. p. 209.
[4] *Ibid.* p. 216.   [5] *Ibid.* p. 217.   [6] *Ibid.* p. 210.

any movement for "restoration" and refused to admit the contention that "Harcourt and Co." were unjustifiably trying to keep their chief in the cold.[1]

Such were the currents in the Liberal party, when Mr. Fawcett, one of the stalwarts of the atrocity campaign, moved a resolution declaring that "misrule and misery will continue" in Turkey, unless the Powers "obtain some such guarantees for improved administration as they agreed on at the Conference". After contending that the House of Commons merely neutralised the public opinion of the country, he contrasted Lord Derby's dispatches of May and of November, the one in a tone of "friendly advice", the other of "absolute command", and ascribed this to the working of public opinion upon the Government's policy. But from this he went on to an open condemnation of non-intervention. Ample quotations were brought from the Blue Books of the last sixteen years, and from such first-hand testimony as Mr. Arthur Evans and Miss Irby, to prove that absolute misgovernment was no new thing in Turkey, and that the new paper reforms were utterly inadequate. This was too much for Hartington, who declared the motion to be "most inopportune" and preferred to wait for further information.

Gladstone then intervened, taking the highly characteristic, and to his adversaries more than usually irritating, line that he could neither support the motion nor join in censure of Fawcett. But his arguments were more than usually cogent. He contrasted the "paper currency" of Turkish promises of reform with the guarantees which were so "absolutely indispensable"—adding that "without guarantees from without" all the projects of forty years past were "so much trash". He protested against three doctrines propounded by Mr. Gathorne Hardy, the Secretary for War—that if Turkey's rights had lapsed, then her obligations had lapsed also; that we were not authorised to construe the Tripartite Treaty of 1856; and that if France or Austria summoned us to join in the defence of Turkey, we should be in a humiliating position. "That miserable and dastardly creature called prestige is too much in favour among us"—so ran one of his most eloquent if declamatory phrases. Reverting to the Crimean War, he contended that our action then had given Turkey "a lease of peaceful and independent life" and that we could not possibly wash our hands of the question now. It was quite untrue that the war had been fought exclusively for the sake of British interests: the much quoted

[1] G. M. Trevelyan, *Life of Bright*, p. 416.

Tripartite Treaty of 9 April 1854 definitely referred to the double object of maintaining territorial integrity and "consolidating . . . the civil and religious rights of the Christian subjects of the Porte".[1] By destroying the undeniable right of interference possessed by Russia under the Treaty of Kainardji (1774), we made the Concert of Europe responsible for the maintenance of Christian rights, and could henceforth no longer evade a share of the responsibility. Such events as the Bosnian and Bulgarian risings made a return to the past impossible, and "every day added to the long list" of outrages which mark Turkish rule.[2]

Gladstone was followed by Butler-Johnstone, who established a fresh record in grotesque statement. He thanked God for our refusal to coerce Turkey, defended the arming of the Moslem population, declared the new Ottoman constitution to be "certainly the most democratic in the whole world", prophesied success for it (though it was ceasing to exist almost as he spoke!) and foretold that Turkey would "outlast many other Empires of Europe". His speech culminated in the double claim that England and Turkey were "the only two nations that had the spirit of wise compromise and patriotism", and that the Turkish army was "the vanguard of the British army".[3] It might be argued that it is superfluous to disinter such rhapsodies from the neglected sepulchre of Hansard: but it would be quite a mistake to treat as negligible the views of one who appears to have possessed the ear of the Prime Minister himself.

The rest of the debate need not detain us long. A well-known northern Liberal member, Mr. Rylands, in a closely reasoned speech, based on extensive quotations, led up to the argument that Salisbury's mission was a change of policy, welcomed by the country at large; that it failed because the Prime Minister adhered to his former views and intended his Guildhall speech "as an impediment to Salisbury's success", and that Britain had now drifted back to the old position during the Andrássy Note of over a year earlier.[4] It is characteristic of the feeling in the House that Colonel Mure, who had recently visited Serbia and ventured to describe her as "very hardly dealt with, much maligned" and "signally misunderstood",[5] was constantly interrupted from the other side, and that the Chancellor of the Exchequer, generally so moderate in language, expressed himself as not surprised at this reception, because Mure's remarks were

---

[1] *Eastern Papers* (1854), no. 8.   [2] Hansard, ccxxxiii. pp. 418-34.
[3] *Ibid.* pp. 437-41.   [4] *Ibid.* p. 454.   [5] *Ibid.* p. 459.

"not cognate to the subject". Sir Stafford Northcote was on firmer ground when he complained that the Government was "continually harassed and tortured by honourable gentlemen opposite who will not give us battle", and had to meet "direct negative taunts for not plunging Europe into war". His version of policy—hardly in keeping with the inner mind of Beaconsfield—was the triple desire to maintain a concert with the Powers, to uphold British interests and to improve the lot of Turkey and her Christians.[1] On a division Fawcett's motion was defeated by 242 to 71.

On 27 March there was a further discussion in the House, this time centring round the question of Elliot's return to the Constantinople post, and the weighty criticisms advanced by Rylands, Forster, and finally by Gladstone on this occasion [2] undoubtedly influenced the decision to send him to Vienna and replace him by Layard. About the same time a distinctly left-handed compliment was paid to Elliot by *Vanity Fair*, which described him as "a pattern Foreign Office creation, thoroughly versed in the official methods and governed in all his acts by the traditional official policy".[3]

In April the public excitement was more intense than ever, and Hartington and Granville decided to make formal motions for papers in both Houses. The fairly lively debates that followed give a certain impression of manœuvring for position. Hartington treated the Protocol of 31 March as "almost for the first time a direct acknowledgement of the duty which Her Majesty's Government have undertaken . . . in common with the other Powers", namely, "the pacification of the East". Did this mean coercion, he asked, and what alternative was there? "Have you in your minds any other means, less objectionable, less drastic, equally efficacious?"[4] Gathorne Hardy in reply admitted the Porte's answer to be "an unconciliatory document", which "does not ring of peace", but challenged the view that the treaties of 1856 had ceased to exist, or that coercion or "armed interference" could provide a remedy.

Harcourt quoted a speech of Northcote in the previous November, to the effect that the only hope for the peace of Europe lay in

[1] Hansard, ccxxxiii. pp. 462-5.
[2] See *supra*, p. 69. On 17 March Gladstone had written to Granville: "Forster spoke to us the other day about Elliot, and said *he* could not stand his going back. This I heard with pleasure and understood to mean that others with him would resist it. Nothing can please me so much as to walk in the rear: but I think I ought to make known to you that my patience cannot stretch over this point, and that if nobody objects to Elliot, I must"—*Granville Papers*, 17 March 1877.
[3] *Vanity Fair* of 17 March 1877.   [4] Hansard, pp. 1083-7.

securing better administration for the Turkish provinces. He defended the agitation of the autumn and argued most effectively
that while it was the fashion to distrust Russia—a just penalty
which she had to pay for many acts of insincerity—we had been
betrayed by that very distrust into playing her game, by allowing
her to become the champion of the oppressed Christians.[1] Later on,
Dilke took a somewhat similar line, confessing to "a great suspicion
of Russian policy", yet driven to admit that "the only Power that
would fight was Russia, and in future the Christians would not forget
their obligation to that nation".[2] After a series of minor speeches
the debate was closed by the Chancellor of the Exchequer, who denied
the alleged "gospel of selfishness", adhered to the original instructions to Salisbury, and defended Derby's declaration on the Protocol, as prompted by a desire to keep our hands free.

In the Lords, meanwhile, the debate was little more than a brief
passage of arms between Granville and Derby, the latter defending
the Protocol and contesting his opponent's suggested resemblance
between it and that Berlin Memorandum which the Government
had so summarily rejected.[3] Beaconsfield himself did not intervene,
and expressed himself to Lady Bradford as highly satisfied with
the result of both debates. Harcourt he described as breaking down
"quite demoralised", and Derby as demolishing Granville so completely "that it was impossible to sustain the debate, which after
some ordinary remarks of Lord Lansdowne and some nonsense from
that maniac Dudley, like the Rhine never reached the sea, but
vanished in mud".[4] Without accepting this as an impartial version,
it is safe to assume that the weight of opinion still lay with the
Government.

THE GLADSTONE RESOLUTIONS

It was under the sting of Northcote's and Hardy's reproaches, and
amid the excitement of the outbreak of war, that Gladstone decided
that the time had come "for raising the rather stiff question whether
a policy, or a substantive motion, is to be submitted to Parliament". He proceeded to draft five resolutions, to be laid before
the House of Commons, whose sense may be briefly summarised as
follows :

1. The House finds just cause of dissatisfaction in the conduct

---

[1] *Ibid.* pp. 112, 1117.   [2] *Ibid.* p. 1148.   [3] *Ibid.* pp. 1184, 1197.
[4] 14 and 17 April—Buckle, vi. pp. 136-7.

of the Porte towards Lord Derby's dispatch of 21 September 1876.

2. "Till such conduct is essentially changed" and till "the guarantees on behalf of the subject populations, other than the promises or ostensible measures of the Porte", have been carried out, the Turkish Government "will be deemed by this House to have lost all claim to receive either the material or the moral support of the British Crown".

3. The third recommended that British influence should be used for "early and effectual development of local liberty and practical self-government" in the disturbed provinces, "without the imposition of any other foreign domination".

4. The fourth, opening with a reference to "the wise and honest policy" of Canning in the Protocol of 1826 and the Treaty of 1827, recommended a European concert to exact "by their united authority . . . changes in the Government of Turkey". The fifth was merely formal, recommending an address in the above sense to Her Majesty.

These resolutions had a curious effect upon the two parties. Harcourt, on the strength of "pretty safe philo-Turc" information, reported to Hartington that there was "civil war in the Cabinet"; [1] and Carnarvon's papers show that the tension was extreme and felt as such even by the moderate Northcote.[2] But the resolutions rallied the Conservatives again round their chief, while at the same time they brought to a head the growing divergence of view within the Opposition ranks. Granville and Hartington both protested against them as "inopportune" [3] and took the line that Gladstone, by persisting in bringing them forward, would "give Dizzy a decisive advantage over his peaceful colleagues". The Radical group, under Chamberlain and Dilke, was strongly in their favour, but Dilke found Harcourt "boiling over with rage at Gladstone" [4] and was seriously afraid of a split in the party. That this was not exaggerated is shown by Harcourt's letter to Hartington, declaring that "the thing really in its mischievous egoism and folly is past endurance". "There never was a leader of a party placed in a more incessant series of awkward and disagreeable situations." [5] Yet Gladstone was clearly right when in his diary he wrote of the official leaders having

[1] 30 April—A. G. Gardiner, *Life of Harcourt*, i. p. 318.
[2] Harding, *Life of Carnarvon*, ii. pp. 353-4.
[3] *Life of Granville*, ii. p. 169; *Life of Devonshire*, i. p. 194.
[4] Dilke's diary for 29 April—Gwynn and Tuckwell, *Life of Dilke*, i. p. 216.
[5] 30 April—*Life of Devonshire*, i. p. 196; *Life of Dilke*, i. p. 318.

been "in truth awakened as from a slumber by the extraordinary demonstrations in the country".[1]

Finding the two Whig leaders actually ready to move "the previous question" in the two Houses, Gladstone reluctantly yielded to pressure and consented to withdraw the last three resolutions and restrict himself to the two first, which did not raise the direct issue of coercion of the Turks. But as this only happened at the very last moment, Hartington's threatened "previous question" had already been entered on the paper and had to be formally withdrawn, thus revealing to the Government and its supporters the acute dissensions in the Liberal ranks. When the debate at last opened on 7 May, a large part of the initial effect was destroyed by a technical discussion on interminable points of order, which gave free play to Mr. Gladstone's dialectical powers, but left the House completely in a maze as to what had or had not been withdrawn or modified. That this is no exaggeration is shown by the sarcastic remark of the Chancellor of the Exchequer—"I hope the House understands all these explanations",[2] and by Chaplin's later contention that the third and fourth resolutions had been "morally, if not materially, withdrawn"[3]—a remark which would have been entirely pointless, even from so extreme a partisan, unless the House had been obviously puzzled.

After this inauspicious beginning and the frank admission that such discussions "must have had a dissipating effect on the mind of the House", Gladstone launched upon what was to be one of his greatest oratorical triumphs. That night he recorded in his diary, "For over two hours I was assaulted from every quarter, except the Opposition bench, which was virtually silent. Such a sense of solitary struggle I never remember."[1] Yet, in Forster's words, he looked "like an inspired man", and though as usual he spoke too long, he carried even that unsympathetic audience away upon the rushing stream of his eloquence. At the outset he stressed his approval of the Salisbury mission, handicapped though it was by the Guildhall speech and the attitude of Elliot. After the Conference Her Majesty's Government had become "the sole obstacle" to the aims so gallantly promoted by Salisbury, and was "playing the evil genius of Europe": and Layard's appointment as Ambassador—"a delicate attention to the Government which has made

---

[1] Morley, *Life of Gladstone*, ii. p. 565.   [2] Hansard, ccxxxiv. p. 382.
[3] *Ibid.* p. 642.

itself responsible from first to last for the massacres of Bulgaria"—
was now having "the same effect". The rôle of the British fleet
was one of "material as well as moral support" to Turkey, by over-
awing the coast provinces of Turkey and Greece and preventing
any movement in sympathy with the Slav provinces. In short, there
was definite "retrogression in British policy", together with a strong
conflict of views inside the Government—instanced not only by
the well-known views of Salisbury and Carnarvon, but also by the
Tory criticism of Northcote.

This brought him to a discussion of "British interests"—a phrase
"the most elastic in the world". "We are endowed with a superiority
of character, a noble selflessness, an inflexible integrity which the
other nations of the world are too slow to recognise: and they are
stupid enough to think that we superior beings are to be bound by
the same vulgar rules that might be justly applicable to the ordinary
sons of Adam. We have improperly allowed the vindication of the
great cause in the East to pass into the hands of a single Power."

Derby's stiff dispatch to the Porte either ought to have been
followed up, "or else was a gross and unwarrantable insult to
Turkey". Nothing had been done for almost a year to punish those
responsible for the atrocities: Shavket, Tusun, Ahmed Aga were still
unpunished, the Moslems were armed, the commission of enquiry
was a packed body, prisoners were tortured to secure favourable
evidence before it—this on the authority of Eugene Schuyler. He
himself had once believed, on the authority of Palmerston and
Stratford, that the Turkish Government could be improved: but
"some men with deeper insight than that possessed at the time by
any politician, knew that the case was hopeless", and the situation
was now far worse than then.

He did not commit himself to unreserved approval of Russia,
whose policy towards Hungary and Poland could not possibly be
justified. But though these cruelties were constantly being quoted
by Tory members, they had *at the time* declined to back up the
enquiries raised in the House from the Liberal side. He was fully
within his rights in contrasting the Government's attitude to Bulgaria with that of the Liberal Government in 1860 towards the
Lebanon massacres: but he no doubt antagonised many of his
audience by the phrase, "The West End of London does not express
the true sentiments of England".

"There is before us not one controversy, but two—between Russia and Turkey, between Turkey and her revolted subjects: and the Government make the mistake of addressing themselves only to one." "You talk to me of established tradition and policy in regard to Turkey. I appeal to an established tradition older, wider, nobler far—a tradition not which disregards British interests, but which teaches you to seek the promotion of those interests in obeying the dictates of honour and justice." The root fact was that "it is the populations of those countries that will ultimately possess them". Bosnia, Montenegro, Bulgaria "do not seek alliance with Russia or any foreign Power . . . but to be delivered from an intolerable burden of woe and shame. . . . I believe that the knell of Turkish tyranny in those provinces has sounded. The destruction may not come in the way or by the means that we should choose: but come this boon from what hands it may, it will be a noble boon, and as a noble boon will gladly be accepted by Christendom and the world."

Joseph Chamberlain at once associated himself with this "magnificent speech" and maintained that the resolutions fully represented "the great mass" of unrepresented opinion, and that the Government had been driven to change its policy "in deference to the public agitation". He was careful to disclaim sympathy with Russia and proclaimed as his aim "to take the matter out of the hands of Russia and put it in the hands of united Europe".

After Gladstone's great effort, however, the rest of the debate, which dragged on for five whole nights, was somewhat in the nature of an anticlimax. No fewer than fifty-one other speeches were delivered, the chief protagonists on the Conservative side being the Home Secretary, Assheton Cross, Drummond Wolff, Chaplin, Bourke and Northcote, on the Liberal, Childers, Lowe, Courtney, Forster, Harcourt, and in a very lukewarm fashion Hartington. But it would scarcely serve any useful purpose to re-echo these much attenuated thunders: indeed the most striking feature of the whole debate is its remoteness from the essential facts of the Eastern situation. It is perhaps worth recording W. E. Forster's prophecy that there was no danger of Bulgaria becoming Russian,[1] and Jacob Bright's phrase: "We have failed in the affairs of Turkey and have retired, acknowledging our impotence. Russia has taken our place."[2] Sir Robert Anstruther was alone in pointing out that feeling for the Slavonic cause was so strong in Russia "that the Tsar could not risk any opposition".[3] Sir William Harcourt was alone in warning

[1] Hansard, ccxxxiv. p. 694.   [2] *Ibid.* p. 671.   [3] *Ibid.* p. 754.

the House not to disregard "those great principles of nationality which for the last ten or twenty years had been reconstituting Europe".[1] The lengths to which even the saner apologists for the Government were prepared to go are shown in Robert Bourke's incursion into history. There was no proof, he solemnly contended, that Canning ever contemplated the use of force: indeed there was "reason to think that Canning, if he had lived, would have agreed with the Duke of Wellington in characterising the battle of Navarino as an untoward event".[2] Meanwhile Henry Chaplin vigorously protested against "the insinuations of discord inside the Cabinet".[3] But it was reserved for Lord Elcho to minimise the Bulgarian atrocities and defend the Turkish Government for its attitude towards the criminals: Shavket Pasha, he argued in all seriousness, had not, it is true, been executed, but he had been sent to Bagdad, and when his words evoked a sally of laughter, he solemnly added that this was no laughing matter, for the plague was at Bagdad! He went on to accuse Lord Salisbury and his friends of being "entirely ignorant of the character of the Turkish mind", and illustrated his own knowledge of Turkish affairs by asserting —on the authority of Laurence Oliphant—that there were eleven races and religions in Bulgaria, all hating each other!—the inference apparently being that Turkish rule was their only salvation. He attacked the Liberals for sneering at the gift of a constitution by the Sultan, such as the Tsar dared not grant—this at a time when Abdul Hamid had already torn his paper constitution to shreds: and he concluded by denying the Turk to be "unspeakable" and defending, nay, glorying in, Elliot's unhappy phrases about British interests outweighing the slaughter. By way of counter-provocation Robert Lowe accused the Government's supporters, in the old phrase of Sidney Smith, of "having sung the wrong song, drunk the wrong beer, made the wrong speech and cracked the wrong heads".[4]

The House was already worn out by its own eloquence when late on the fifth night Sir Stafford Northcote put forward an effective case for neutrality, in contrast to Gladstone's policy of coercion by "British ships and Russian troops". He freely admitted the errors of Turkey at the Conference and ridiculed the confusion that surrounded the resolutions.

[1] Hansard, ccxxxiv. p. 885.   [2] *Ibid*. p. 748.   [3] *Ibid*. p. 643.
[4] *Ibid*. pp. 940-52.

> The first that died was Number Three,
> Then followed Four and Five,
> And nought but their vacuity
> Has kept the two alive.

Obviously, when the Leader of the House could sound such a Carollian note, after four days of battle, victory was not far off: and he ably summed up the main interests at stake—free trade and navigation, which affected all Europe, and those on which we laid special stress, the protection of Suez and Egypt and the route to India. "We have kept ourselves perfectly free", in order to act as circumstances require.[1]

The last word was with Gladstone, who laid a debater's stress on the conflict between Derby and Elliot, on the divergent speeches of Beaconsfield and Salisbury, and on "Turkey's belief that she might rely on England in the last resort". "I withdraw nothing and I alter nothing." His excursions into history were far more effective than those of his opponents: for he was able to adduce the examples of Navarino, the Scheldt blockade, the Lebanon, and even the two unjust blockades of Greece in 1850 and 1853, as proving "that coercion, adequately supported and in a good cause, need not be followed by war". Again he brought the analogies of Spain during the war against Napoleon, of Portugal in 1826, of Greece in 1827, of Belgium in 1830, and of Italy in the middle of the century, to show that "few nations have in modern times established their own liberties without foreign aid". On Russia he spoke with surprising balance, making all due reserves as to its "military and ruling classes", but describing the Tsar as "a Christian gentleman and a great benefactor to his people" and that people "as capable of noble sentiments as any people in Europe". At last, turning to his opponents, he declared, "Your majority is powerful, but not omnipotent", and "the longer you delay, the less in all likelihood you will be able to save from the wreck of the integrity and independence of the Turkish Empire". If Russia succeeds, "*as an Englishman I shall hide my head, but as a man I shall rejoice.* Nevertheless, to my latest day I shall exclaim—'Would God that in this crisis the voice of the nation had been suffered to prevail: would God that in this great, this holy deed England had not been refused her share'."

Gladstone's oratorical effort during the prolonged debate has been

---

[1] *Ibid.* p. 571.

described by one present as "perhaps the greatest triumph of irrepressible moral and physical vitality over depressing conditions that
was ever won in the House of Commons": and long afterwards Arthur
Balfour, in his tribute to the dead titan, spoke of its lasting impression upon his mind. "As a mere feat of physical endurance it was
almost unsurpassed: as a feat of parliamentary courage, parliamentary skill, parliamentary endurance, and parliamentary eloquence, I
believe it will always be unequalled." [1]

On 14 May, then, the resolutions were lost by 223 to 354. *The
Times* [2] had already asked why Mr. Gladstone thundered and
lightened, but cast no bolt. W. T. Stead, a strenuous contemporary
worker, was probably quite right in asserting thirty years later his
doubt "whether there were at any time more than sixty or seventy
avowed coercionists in a House of 658": [3] and it was only thanks to
the strict discipline imposed by Hartington upon his rank and file,
after the withdrawal of the later resolutions, that Gladstone received
even such support as he did. At first Gladstone was soothed by the
argument that the debate had brought home to the Government the
country's resolve not to be embroiled on the Turkish side, and had
therefore ensured a policy of neutrality as the next best thing to
some form of coercion. But it soon became apparent that the aggressive elements in the Government had been encouraged by the demonstration of their own strength: and the open divergence between the
views expressed by Gladstone and by Hartington served as a further
encouragement. [4] Hartington's own considered view of the crisis, as
expressed in a letter to Granville, was that a split could not have been
avoided, "unless we were prepared to follow instead of to lead". [5]
Granville himself took an intermediate position, telling Gladstone,
"I admit that good has been done by the debate", but adding significantly, "Of course, if you had gone on alone, you would only have
either more or less than half the Liberal party". [6] Even the fervid
Argyll had not been happy about the form of motion adopted by
Gladstone and wrote to him beforehand, "I assume that defeat is
certain": [7] while Stratford de Redcliffe ventured to express doubts

---

[1] Morley, *Life of Gladstone*, ii. p. 566.   [2] 10 May 1877.
[3] *The M.P. for Russia*, i. p. 352.
[4] Mr. Herbert Paul is hardly exaggerating when he writes in his epigrammatic
way, "Against such a heterogeneous combination, so unskilfully led, the Government were perfectly safe, whatever they did, or failed to do" (*Hist. of Modern
England*, iv. p. 27).   [5] 25 May—*Life of Devonshire*, i. p. 199.
[6] *Gladstone Papers*, Granville to Gladstone, 16 May 1877.
[7] *Ibid.* Argyll to Gladstone, 27 April 1877.

as to the effect of the resolutions upon Gladstone's own "political position and the continental mind".[1]

Gladstone was genuinely desirous not to embarrass his successor in the leadership and as yet disclaimed all idea of resuming it: but inexorable fate was drawing him in that direction. Here again Hartington hit the nail on the head. "He does not cease to be the leader of the party by merely saying that he will not be the leader. If, as he has done since the autumn, he takes the lead, he *is* the leader, and all that he can do is to disclaim . . . the responsibility which naturally attends upon leadership."[2] The fact that the Radical wing preferred the impulsive Gladstone to the more cautious Whig peers did not make the situation easier: and the intense feeling of the Midlands and the North kept Gladstone at white heat.

The long-suffering Hartington put the dilemma very clearly to his colleague in the Lords: "So long as you and I have any responsibility for the management of the party, I think we cannot altogether submit our judgment to his, and in that case some will follow him and some us. Hence the split in the party, and here are the materials for more splits in the future. Can nothing be done to make him see this and let us understand where we are?"[3] Harcourt meanwhile ascribed to Granville the chief credit for averting an open breach and wrote congratulating him on having "saved the party from the greatest scrape they ever were in, by a miracle of skill".[4]

Yet however much we may criticise Gladstone's tactics, however negative the result of the debate may have been, and however open to criticism from a narrow party standpoint, it is none the less not too much to claim for the famous Resolutions that they played a real part in holding back the nation from rash action at a critical juncture. For the moment the Cabinet had found it necessary to abandon the idea of an active alliance with Turkey, though the Prime Minister and some of his colleagues were already searching for other possibilities. But a position had now been reached which was far from satisfactory—the two extremes of Turcophil and Russophil neutralising each other and leaving Russia, as both Gladstone and Salisbury saw clearly from their very different angles, in a position of the foremost, if not the sole, champion of a cause on whose side the stars in their calm slow courses were also fighting.

---

[1] *Ibid.* Stratford de Redcliffe to Gladstone, 3 May.
[2] *Life of Devonshire*, i. p. 200.
[3] 25 May 1877—*Life of Granville*, ii. p. 172.
[4] *Granville Papers*, 9 May, Hartington to Granville.

GLADSTONE AND CHAMBERLAIN

An interesting sequel to these debates was the visit paid by Gladstone to Birmingham at the end of May, where as the guest of Joseph
Chamberlain he received the welcome of a king and addressed Liberal
delegates from all over the kingdom at a mass meeting of 30,000
people in Bingley Hall. The occasion was the founding of the National
Liberal Federation, of which Chamberlain wished Birmingham, not
London, to be the centre. Hartington was highly suspicious of what
was often spoken of as an attempt to introduce "Caucus government" into England and to capture the old leader for a Radical
Fronde.[1] But Granville took a calmer view, agreed that the Liberal
central organisation "requires great improvement" and assumed that
"Chamberlain's object is not to reorganise the whole Liberal party,
but to strengthen the young Liberal and more advanced portion of
it and to secure you willing or unwilling as its leader".[2] Harcourt,
who disapproved almost equally of Gladstone and of Birmingham,
told Granville, on Dilke's authority, that Chamberlain, after Gladstone had withdrawn his third and fourth resolutions, "would gladly
have got out of the Birmingham meeting, but could not".[3] But this
does not fit in with Chamberlain's own version, that Gladstone had
been "induced to cave in", as the result of a "conspiracy".[4]

Gladstone on his side was absolutely frank, and his explanatory
letters before the meeting reveal the absolute confidence between
him and Granville. Moreover, they are such a revelation of character
as to deserve quotation here, especially as showing the extent to
which in Gladstone's mind at this stage home and foreign policy
were intertwined.

"The Government will only be kept even decently straight by
continuous effort and pressure from without. The 'agitation' worked
them up to the point of the Salisbury mission. Even all through that
mission Dizzy showed his teeth, as in the Guildhall speech: but it is
the high-water mark of the better influences. With it, and mainly by
it, the agitation was effectually suspended. In the St. James's Hall
meeting we frankly accepted it as a new point of departure. From
that time the agitation being still, the Government had you steadily

[1] As late as 27 Nov. he wrote to Granville of "what is considered Birmingham
dictation".   [2] *Gladstone Papers*, 21 May, Granville to Gladstone.
[3] *Granville Papers*, 1 June, Harcourt to Granville.
[4] Chamb. to Bunce and Collings, cit. Garvin, *Life of Chamberlain*, i. p. 243.

backwards until Cross's speech. They are now held pressed up to a certain height, but the 'seven devils' are not exorcised: I believe B. is waiting for his opportunity, and the last state may be worse than the first. From the Birmingham meeting there will be a ramification through the Liberal delegates assembled there, stretching all through the country. . . ." [1] The last phrase gives the clue to Gladstone's eagerness to visit Birmingham: he hoped to permeate the Liberal organisations with his views on the foreign situation.

Two days later, he wrote again. "My opinion is and has long been that the vital principle of the Liberal party, like that of Greek art [how typical of the Homeric student turning back in his old age to politics], is *action*, and that nothing but action will ever make it worthy of the name of a party. You can muster them for wars of religious liberalism (so to call it) and for little else. And the party lukewarmness on the aristocratic side is about as injurious as, and less excusable than, the rampant disorderliness on the radical side. You are not on a bed of roses, or if you are, they are roses with the thorns, and I do not know whether my sermonising will much mend it. However, it grew out of my desire to know your mind on the meaning of 'reorganising the Liberal party'." [2]

His next letter indicates the line he intends to take at Birmingham. "I shall, I hope, effectually steer clear of any plan for the reconstruction of policy, though I may be tempted to carp, in a sentence, about economy, and cannot avoid perhaps saying something about reliance on the Liberal party for the promotion of the Eastern cause. The reorganisation of party machinery will of course deserve a compliment from me. In all this I do not see any difficulty, but it may be there without my seeing it. If there is anything prophylactic which it occurs to you that I might say, pray let me know before the time, for you have a discerning eye.

"What I of course regret is that the action of the party as a whole within the House does not come up to its action and feeling in the country at large. While there was a hope that the Tories would run true upon it, I for one could have no wish to make it a party question. But nothing is to be hoped from them, and as in so many other cases, the Liberal party alone is the instrument by which a great work is to be carried on. In my opinion, to carry it on freely would have been very beneficial to the party as such, but of this I am not the judge.

---

[1] *Granville Papers*, 17 May 1877, Gladstone to Granville.
[2] *Ibid.* 19 May.

I could wish that there were some other question of real magnitude likely to reunite them: but I do not see any. On disestablishment they perhaps will be united some day, but plainly not yet. On the Eastern Question I feel that it is only by an unremitted action that we can in any degree keep Dizzy's hands from mischief."[1]

Of especial interest is the brief impression penned by Gladstone to Granville on the morning after the meeting, from Chamberlain's own house: it affords yet another proof, if any were needed, that his nature had a touch of the prophetic. "My host . . . had a reception uniting the freshness of one arrived from a distance and the familiarity of one well known. He certainly endeavoured to turn the occasion to account in favour of an advanced policy generally, and his reference to Hartington, though guarded, was not entirely genial. He is a man worth watching and studying: of strong self-consciousness under most pleasing manners, and I should think of great tenacity of purpose: expecting to play an historical part, and probably destined to it. . . ."

And after this prophetic passage he proves himself a mortal of limited vision after all: for he adds, "My earnest hope is that this Eastern Question is to reach a close or a resting-place during the summer, and that then I shall be a free man again".[2]

Here we have clear proof[3] that Gladstone throughout the long crisis continued to regard Granville as the future Liberal Premier and his own re-emergence as a temporary measure, dictated by a passing crisis.

SHUVALOV AND RUSSIAN POLICY

Meanwhile the Russian Ambassador—devoted to the cause of peace, both because he desired to promote Russo-British friendship and because he took a somewhat gloomy view of Russian internal conditions—had taken alarm at the attitude of the Prime Minister and his group and hastened to St. Petersburg, in order to lay before the Tsar and the Chancellor his own detailed interpretation of the situation created by the Derby Note of 6 May. His time was not wasted, and on 8 June he again reached London, bearing with him a long memorandum for submission to Lord Derby, but also highly confidential instructions for his own use. This document enables us to see into the Russian cards, and indeed it is probable that if Beaconsfield, Derby, and even the Queen, could have had access to it at the time, their fears would have been very greatly assuaged. In

[1] *Granville Papers*, 23 May.   [2] *Ibid.* 1 June.   [3] See *infra*, p. 537.

it Gorchakov, on the Tsar's instructions and in view of Shuvalov's "vivid picture (*tableau saisissant*) of the grave situation in London", set himself to "sketch more precisely the contours of our policy". Russia cannot stop on her present path, but greatly desires that England should meet her half-way.

"As to Suez and Egypt, we shall not touch these two points: we have neither the interest, the desire, nor the means, to do so." As to Constantinople, Russia can only give assurances as to permanent annexation: a pledge against temporary occupation would, if it became known, only encourage the Turks in their obstinacy. But "once the British Ministers are fully assured that we shall in no case remain at Constantinople, it depends on them to save us from the need of going near to it", by exerting due pressure at the Porte. As to the Straits, the existing regulations ought to be "revised in a spirit of equity" and "by common agreement".

As regards British fears of Russian action on the Euphrates and the Persian Gulf or at Erzerum, and its effects on the route to India, "our position is simple and clear. We have no interest to injure England in this direction, but we may be forced to seek measures of defence against her hostility. Our attitude depends entirely upon hers. It is natural that Persia should be roused by events in her neighbourhood and should try to profit by them at Turkey's expense. That is partly due to the rivalry created there by British policy through its distrust of us. If the London Cabinet had responded to our sincere desire for a joint agreement on Persian affairs . . . the situation would be different. As matters stand, we have tried to moderate the Shah's aspirations towards an official and definite alliance with us . . . but we could not altogether rebut him, if only because we should have risked throwing him, *par dépit*, into the arms of the very active British Legation. . . . We are quite disposed to come to terms frankly and loyally on all these questions with the London Cabinet: we believe such an entente to be possible and more advantageous than mutual distrust and suspicion. In general, we have no interest in troubling England in her Indian possessions nor in her communications. The present war does not demand this, for its aim is clearly defined and it would only be complicated by so vast an extension of the struggle. You can give categorical assurances on this point. But we must reserve our absolute right to defend ourselves by every means against English hostility, so long as we have not the certitude of being able to avoid it."

Gorchakov then turns to consider "the essential aim of the war". *"The English"*, he says, *"find it hard to understand a war of religious and national sentiment, and being incapable of one themselves, they consequently look for arrières pensées.* But they should at least be accessible to the material side of the question and recognise that Our August Master can no longer tolerate a state of affairs which may at any moment affect the peaceful development of Russia and precipitate her in her own despite into disastrous crises and wars. This situation must cease or be improved so far as possible. For two years we have sought this improvement in an European agreement. Sad experience has abundantly proved that what has upset the Concert of the Powers is the lack of guarantees and material sanction. They have drawn up programmes of the reforms to be imposed upon the Porte without effective means of coercion or control. They should, on the contrary, have left to the Porte the initiative of improvements, but imposed upon it the control of Europe and the material sanction of her power.

"To-day we [*i.e.* Russia] have to fulfil this double task. It is a question of finding the limits within which it can be reconciled with British interests or scruples. We do not regard this as impossible. What is absolutely necessary for us is to put an end to permanent crises in the East—on the one hand by asserting our military superiority in such a way that the Turks should not in future be tempted to defy us lightly, on the other by putting the Christians, above all of Bulgaria, in a situation effectually guaranteed against the incorrigible abuses of the Turkish administration. What England needs is the maintenance in principle of the Ottoman Empire and the inviolability of Constantinople and the Straits. *These views are not irreconcilable.*"

This first section of the dispatch, read in the light of subsequent events, is absolutely unanswerable, and as it was intended for no other eyes save Shuvalov's, there is every reason to suppose that it represented the true inner mind of the autocrat and his chief minister. But it must be added that it was a point of view which the British Cabinet was never really able to grasp.   So little was it capable of throwing off its *arrière pensées*, that, as we shall soon see, it could not bring itself to believe the truth when it came to it through the mouth of a Russian diplomatist.

In the later portion of the dispatch Gorchakov points out that there is a third factor of great importance, namely, Austria-Hungary.

"Lord Beaconsfield has given you to understand that the destinies of the East ought to be regulated between England and Russia. Formerly it was with Austria that the British Government sought to settle them. We think that the question can best be solved by an accord between the three Powers, based on a just appreciation of their mutual interest. This is what led us to agree in the first instance with the Court of Vienna." He then assumes Shuvalov to know the contents of the Austro-Russian conventions, though he carefully avoids quoting them, and proceeds to indicate the general terms on which the Tsar would conclude peace if the Porte made overtures before his armies had crossed the Balkans—making it clear, however, that Russia could not accept any restriction of her military operations. The terms comprised the following main points: (1) Bulgaria as a vassal state under European guarantee, with a national militia and without Turkish garrisons; (2) administrative guarantees for Bulgaria south of the Balkans and the other Christian provinces of Turkey; (3) "an augmentation of territory" for Serbia and Montenegro; (4) autonomy for Bosnia-Hercegovina; (5) regulation by Europe of the relations between Serbia, Bulgaria, Roumania and the Porte. The Powers, if they accepted these terms, could exercise joint pressure upon the Turks, and if the latter proved refractory, Russia would have no choice but to continue the war until it could force its terms upon them. Russia would, however, in the event of acceptance, be entitled to demand the cession of southern Bessarabia and of Batum, and Roumania could receive compensation in the Dobrogea. Nor would Russia oppose Austria-Hungary "seeking compensations in Bosnia and partially in Hercegovina". Apart from this last clause, which can scarcely be described as honest in view of Gorchakov's recent commitments towards Vienna, the general programme was distinctly moderate, and justifies the Chancellor's claim that his master desired "to re-establish the understanding with England and Europe and reach a peace equitable and satisfactory to all". Shuvalov was authorised to assure London that the Tsar would keep his armies to the north of the Balkans, if the Porte would consent to negotiate on the basis indicated.[1]

These proposals represent a supreme effort on the part of Shuvalov to persuade the Tsar in favour of *la petite guerre* and an early and moderate peace, forestalling British intervention, in contrast to the Slavophil programme of a knock-out blow to Turkey and the emanci-

[1] *R.B.D.* vi. no. 228, 30 May, Gorchakov to Shuvalov (*réservée*).

pation of the whole Christian East by Holy Russia. Shuvalov, in his first conversation with Derby after his return, argued that the Tsar's proposal "offered the means of localising the war and preventing the dissolution of Turkey. But the Tsar must know whether, within the limits indicated, he can be sure of the neutrality of England—which would exclude any occupation, even temporary, of Constantinople and the Straits by her." Lord Derby replied that so serious a question must be referred to the Cabinet. Shuvalov's skilful presentation of the Russian case was, it is true, considerably marred when on 14 June he received orders from home to insist on autonomy for southern as well as northern Bulgaria: this was interpreted in London, not without some show of reason, as meaning that two currents were contending for the mastery in St. Petersburg, a civilian and a military.

At this juncture, when a real arrangement might have been reached, the British Cabinet was profoundly divided, and Northcote has left a vivid picture of its situation. The peace party inside it at first consisted of Derby, Cairns, Cross, Richmond, Salisbury, Carnarvon and himself. "As time wore on, Cairns, Cross and Richmond seemed somewhat to modify their views. I was much in communication with Salisbury and Carnarvon, and . . . also with Derby, between whom and the other two there was some coldness. Carnarvon was strongly impressed with the belief that the Prime Minister was desirous of war. Derby, judging more correctly, said to me: 'I don't think he desires war: he desires to place England in a "commanding position"'. The Prime Minister himself said to me more than once that his great fear was that Derby's policy would lead us to war: and looking back, I am more and more convinced that there was much ground for the apprehension."[1]

Every Cabinet in a crisis is bound to have a certain number of cross-currents, but on this occasion it is clear that the most important members of the Government did not know each others' minds and were simply groping in the dark. Worse still, the Prime Minister and Foreign Secretary were now rapidly drifting apart, the former feeling that Derby was increasingly negative in outlook, the latter as ever mainly concerned with sentiment in the country and warning his chief that "the middle class" was "strong against war".[2] The Queen, too, was rapidly losing confidence in him. "Lord Derby must be *made* to move", she wrote to Beaconsfield, with a special request for secrecy. "The Queen feels horribly anxious about this."[3] Next day

[1] Buckle, *op. cit.* vi. p. 139.   [2] 24 May—*ibid.* p. 141.   [3] *Ibid.* p. 144.

she sent a personal appeal to Derby, in view of Russia's steady advance, despite all her profuse promises. His reply, however, only incensed her still further, as showing that his eyes were turned mainly towards England. "Feeling", he submitted, "is much divided", but war would be thoroughly unpopular. "He well remembers the Crimean War, and has never seen so near an approach to a really revolutionary condition of public feeling as after the first failures and disasters of that struggle. He does not believe that England could now reckon on any European ally, and has no doubt as to there being an understanding between the three Empires."[1] This exchange of letters seems to have decided the Queen against Derby: the next, we shall see, was an actual passage of arms,[2] and henceforth she never dealt with him if she could avoid it.

THE QUEEN'S ATTITUDE

It is necessary at this stage to devote special attention to the attitude of Queen Victoria, who for the first and last time in her long career threw off the wise restraint which had so often saved a difficult situation. Instead of endeavouring to hold back her ministers and exercise her influence with her fellow-sovereigns in Europe—as she had done so effectually during such crises as the Spanish Marriages, the Duchies dispute or even the War Scare of 1875—she now pressed Beaconsfield more and more to extreme measures. Her indignation at the Bulgarian massacres seems to have evaporated in proportion as the campaign of protest gained volume in this country and soon her violent distrust and resentment towards Russia obscured every other sentiment—even gratitude towards the Tsar for his rôle in 1875, and even her deep-seated suspicions of Bismarck.

By March 1877 she was denouncing to Beaconsfield "this mawkish sentimentality for people who hardly deserve the name of real Christians ... and forgetting the great interests of this great country." Her dislike of Russia and of Gladstone blended, and she argued that[3] we could never allow the Russians to occupy Constantinople. "To let it be thought that we shall never fight and that England will submit to Egypt being under Russia" (once more this curious assumption that Constantinople is the key to Egypt) "would be to abdicate the position of Great Britain as one of the Great Powers—to which

---

[1] 11 June, Derby to Queen—*Letters*, ii. pp. 541-3.
[2] *Infra*, p. 221.   [3] 21 March, to Beaconsfield—*Letters*, ii. p. 130.

she will never submit, and another must wear the crown if this is
intended".[1] Gladstone she regarded as having "entirely forgotten . . .
the vital interests of this country".[2] By the middle of June she even
went so far as to threaten that "another sovereign must be got to
carry out Lord Derby's policy".[3] "Such a Foreign Minister", she told
the Prime Minister, "the Queen never remembers", and she spoke in
favour of fetching Lord Lyons from Paris to replace him.[4]

"Be bold," she wrote two days later. "If the Russians reach Constantinople, the Queen would be so humiliated that she thinks she
would abdicate at once."[5] The heights to which her excitement had
risen are reflected in the phrase of Beaconsfield to Lady Bradford:
"The Faery writes every day and telegraphs every hour: this is
almost literally the case".[6] But even in September he was still complaining that "it rains telegrams morn, noon and night, and Balmoral
is really ceaseless".[7]

The Queen's anger against Russia was greatly increased by the
hostile reception of Colonel Wellesley, the British Military Attaché.
In the words of Shuvalov himself to Schweinitz, Russian military
circles were simply "foaming at the mouth" against England for her
Turcophil attitude, and the Grand Duke Nicholas, still further incensed at Wellesley's disparaging reports of the Russian mobilisation
—which had come back to him through Berlin—informed him to
his face in front of several staff officers, that he had only received
him at army headquarters on express orders from the Tsar himself,
that he would have him strictly watched and would instantly expel
him if he wrote anything objectionable. Wellesley not unnaturally
went straight back to Bucarest, put on civilian clothes and reported
home by telegraph. The incident was ended by an invitation from
the Tsar to join his personal staff, and by a frank apology from the
Grand Duke, and Wellesley by his tact eventually won the confidence
of the Russians and was able to play a most useful part.

THE BRITISH OVERTURE TO AUSTRIA-HUNGARY

The Queen's special gravamen against Derby in June 1877 was
his reluctance to make fresh overtures to Vienna. She was, it is
true, more inclined than Beaconsfield—and here history has shown

[1] 25 April—*Letters*, ii. p. 133.
[2] *Ibid.* p. 135.
[3] 14 June, Beaconsfield to Salisbury—*ibid.* p. 145.
[4] 25 June—*ibid.* pp. 147-8.
[5] 27 June—*ibid.* p. 148.
[6] *Ibid.* p. 150.
[7] *Ibid.* p. 177.

her to be right—to suspect the existence of an Austro-Russian agreement. But none the less the impossibility of challenging Russia without first finding some European ally, pointed by an obvious process of exclusion to Austria-Hungary.

The first step was taken on 19 May, when it was feared that Russia's advance might be very rapid and that Constantinople, once occupied, might not be so readily evacuated: Derby, assuming the two Powers to have a common interest in Constantinople and the Straits, invited Count Beust to "discuss a plan of joint action" in the event of "a Russian march" on the capital.[1] After an interval of ten days, which was already significant, Andrássy sent a lengthy statement of his views, making it clear that he had no objection to "Russia deciding her quarrel by arms", and admitting the Treaty of Paris to be "capable of modification", but giving a list of seven points which he could not accept—namely, any exclusive protectorate over the Balkan Christians, any settlement dictated by a single Power, Russia's acquisition of either Roumania or territory south of the Danube, the erection of a "secundogeniture", whether Russian or Austrian, in those countries, a Russian occupation of Constantinople or "the erection of a large Slav state at the expense of the non-Slav elements of the Peninsula". To prevent the realisation of any such aim, he would be ready to risk war: but he denied any ground for nervousness, both because the Tsar had given satisfactory assurances and had "a full knowledge of our interests", and above all because Russia had "placed herself in a military position which she would certainly have avoided if she had not intended to abstain from injuring" those interests.[2] In the light of our present knowledge of the Austro-Russian agreement, this answer can only be described as highly disingenuous and misleading: for there is not the slightest indication that he was in any way tied to Russia, still less that he had definitely pledged himself to hinder diplomatic intervention by other Powers.

Andrássy, then, though distrustful of Russia, thought that he had her as yet under the necessary control, but he felt an equal distrust towards England, based first and foremost upon the memory of her cavalier attitude to his own Note, but also on the uncertain quantities in her political life, on a sceptical attitude towards the persons of Beaconsfield and Derby, and on a firm belief that England wished

[1] Dwight Lee, *The Anglo-Austrian Understanding of 1877*, i. no. 1 (*Slavonic Review*, no. 28). [2] *Ibid.* no. 3, 29 May.

him to pull the chestnuts out of the fire for her, by providing a large army against Russia, such as she herself did not possess. His private view was that the main responsibility for the war lay with England. He therefore told Beust to "do nothing which might create the impression that we wished to evade an understanding with England",[1] but a few weeks later made it clear to the Ambassador that "joint diplomatic action against St. Petersburg had been made impossible from the outset (*im vorhinein*) by England's attitude".[2]

Moreover, he soon received what struck him as satisfactory proof that Russia was playing the game towards Austria-Hungary: for Novikov, on Gorchakov's orders, communicated to him the essence of the instructions with which Shuvalov had just returned to London.[3]

As a matter of fact Gorchakov was not playing the game quite as strictly as this communication suggested. Much the simplest illustration of this is to place in parallel columns the phrases relating to Bosnia, as supplied to Shuvalov himself and to Novikov for transmission to Andrássy.

(To Shuvalov)	(To Novikov)
Bosnia and Hercegovina would be endowed with institutions judged by common accord as compatible with their internal state and apt to assure to them a good native administration.[4]	Bosnia and Hercegovina would be endowed with institutions judged by common accord as compatible with their internal state and apt to assure to them a good native administration. But if Austria-Hungary on her side claimed compensation, whether for the acquisitions made by Russia, or as a gauge of security against the territorial and political rearrangements in favour of the above mentioned Christian Principalities of the Balkan Peninsula, Russia would not oppose her seeking such compensation in Bosnia and in part in Hercegovina."[5]

---

[1] 11 May to Beust—Wertheimer, *op. cit.* iii. p. 29.
[2] 29 May—*ibid.* iii. p. 30.   [3] See *supra*, pp. 193-4.
[4] *R.B.D.* vi. no. 228, 18/30 May, Gorchakov to Shuvalov.
[5] *Austrian Archives*, Notice très Secrète, 31 May/12 June, Gorchakov to Novikov

It is clear that Gorchakov's first aim was to conceal the actual terms of the Budapest Convention even from Shuvalov, but that a document so mangled could not be submitted to Vienna as fully covering the ground. It is of course just possible that Novikov explained this verbally to Andrássy: but it certainly seems more likely that Gorchakov still entertained hopes of at least partial evasion of his pledge towards Vienna.

The reader may well exclaim in impatience at these intricate contortions of the old diplomacy: but it is really most instructive to dwell upon such an admirable series of lessons in the mischief of being too clever and the rude art of being hoist with one's own petard.

Andrássy's desire to negotiate with London and yet conceal from it not only the terms, but the very existence, of his bargain with Russia, placed him in a somewhat embarrassing situation, which was increased by his resolve that even his own ambassador Beust should not be admitted to the secret—a crowning proof of the distrust between the two rivals. He therefore resorted to the extraordinary course of requesting his personal friend Novikov to warn Shuvalov by telegram, to breathe no word of the conventions to Beust, "who is not initiated".[1]

This naturally misled London still further. On 11 June Beaconsfield made a personal overture to Beust, and after expressing his regret that he has in Vienna "a perfectly useless" ambassador—Sir Andrew Buchanan—spoke of "an entente with Austria-Hungary as the question which comes before all others". "If once I am sure that Count Andrássy is willing to engage himself with us in whatever action, *I promise you that I control the Cabinet* and that there will no longer be the least difficulty in our path."[2]

On the top of this Derby addressed to Austria-Hungary the enquiry whether "they would in case of need join England to prevent" the occupation of Constantinople:[3] and on 14 June he put forward a proposal of "active alliance" with Austria, which the Cabinet had already sanctioned.[4] Some days later he pressed very strongly upon Beust the view that a semi-independent Bulgarian state—"which

("Aus den Papieren S.E. Grafen Andrássy in Oktober 1879 erhalten"), in other words, one of the documents which he left behind him at the Ballplatz on leaving office.

[1] *R.B.D.* vi. no. 230 (10 June), Novikov to Shuvalov; no. 231 (11 June), Shuvalov to Novikov; no. 232 (15 June), Novikov to Shuvalov.

[2] Lee, *op. cit.* no. 5, 11 June, Beust to Andrássy (*Austrian Archives*); Wertheimer, *op. cit.* iii. pp. 30-31.   [3] Lee, *op. cit.* no. 7, 13 June.

[4] 14 June, Beaconsfield to Salisbury—Buckle, vi. p. 144.

would be a Russian dependency"—would be a danger for Austria; that Britain might hesitate to act alone: but that in the event of joint Austro-British action "there was not only no doubt of success, but no danger of war", since Russia would have to give way.[1] Andrássy replied on 22 June by a lengthy dispatch which shows him to be really playing for time. Britain, he argued, might occupy Gallipoli without risking very much, for she and Russia were "like the shark and the wolf, who can show one another their teeth, . . . but in the end each retires again to its own native element and the whole thing is at an end". But the occupation of Serbia or Roumania by Austria-Hungary would be a far more serious affair and might lead to "a death struggle". He was therefore not prepared to oppose the Russians crossing the Balkans, but merely insisted on the results of the war being subjected to "European approval", and co-operation if any mutual interest were endangered[2]—in other words, a very vague programme.

As Andrássy became vaguer, Derby grew still more precise and proposed a secret Austro-British convention: but to this Andrássy found it necessary to reply that under no circumstances could he allow any public reference in Parliament to "an understanding hostile to Russia" between London and Vienna.[3] To-day this is obvious enough, for we know that he could not thus perjure himself towards Russia. At the time it must have been puzzling to the London Cabinet. The Queen recorded in her journal that Beust was quoting Andrássy's positive denials of any secret understanding with Russia, whereas Shuvalov affirmed its existence:[4] yet such was the distrust of official Russia, that Beust was believed and not Shuvalov.

It was certainly just as well for Andrássy's own reputation with his ally, that he played a straighter game with St. Petersburg than with London. For while Shuvalov was keeping Beust successfully in the dark about the agreement between their two countries, he had contrived to see the text of Andrássy's *refus* to London, within a very short time of its arrival, and to summarise it for the benefit of the Russian Government.[5] His inside source of information, of which we shall have to speak later, provided him at this time with almost every phase of British official policy. Thus he was able to report that Derby

[1] Lee, *op. cit.* i. no. 11, memo. of 19 June.
[2] *Ibid.* ii. no. 12, 22 June, Andrássy to Beust.
[3] *Ibid.* no. 16, 12 July, Andrássy to Beust.   [4] *Letters*, ii. p. 551.
[5] *R.B.D.* vi. pp. 428-30, telegram of 27 June and letter of 3 July, Shuvalov to Gorchakov.

"had not shared the illusions of his colleagues and had warned them of the uselessness of the *démarche*" at Vienna, and again that the "warlike ardour" of the Queen was growing even stronger.[1] Her correspondence with the Prime Minister, he was informed, no longer passed through her private secretary, but "through female hands". "The other ministers do not look favourably on *this conspiracy of a half-mad woman with a minister who once had genius but has degenerated into a political clown*"—here for almost the only time in his long correspondence Shuvalov exceeds the bounds of reason and restraint. "They apprehend some warlike extravagance which might be transmitted to them any day as expression of her sovereign will, and whose acceptance their chief would make a question of confidence." In view of the numerous extracts, already quoted and still to be quoted, from her correspondence with Beaconsfield—on the subject of Russia and her own abdication—these fears cannot be dismissed as in any way exaggerated or groundless.

LAYARD AND THE TURKS

At this point it is necessary to emphasise the peculiar rôle of Mr. Layard, as successor to Sir Henry Elliot at the Constantinople Embassy. Certainly no other Englishman could have been found who possessed the same intimate knowledge of Turkish affairs, for his experience dated back to the forties, when as a young man he undertook his famous excavations at Nineveh and was employed by Stratford Canning on informal missions, first in Mesopotamia, then in Serbia after the expulsion of the Obrenović (when he rode with messages from Belgrade to Constantinople in the record time of six days!) and then as a regular "go-between" to Reshid and other Turkish ministers. In the years preceding the Crimean War he also acted as Stratford's intermediary with the British press. It was at this time, when the Assyrian discoveries won him an honorary degree at Oxford and the freedom of the City of London, that Lady Palmerston coined the unkind phrase, "We are grateful to Mr. Layard for bringing Nineveh to light, but not at all to Nineveh for bringing Mr. Layard to light". It was at this time that he acquired a definite liking for the individual Turk. In 1851 he returned to England and next year became Liberal member for Aylesbury and for a few months Foreign Under-Secretary under Malmesbury. He was one of the most

[1] *Ibid.* 7 and 10 July.

active advocates of the Crimean War. At the Liberal *débâcle* of 1857 he lost his seat, but was elected in 1860 for Southwark and now held the post of Under-Secretary for five years under Russell and Clarendon. In Gladstone's first Cabinet he was made Chief Commissioner of Works, but resigned that post in 1869 in order to become British Minister in Madrid, where he remained till 1877. This thumb-nail sketch was necessary to show that he was one of the most arresting and original figures of the period. It is also worth noting that Layard's aunt, Mrs. Austen, had been one of the closest friends of the young Disraeli, and there was thus a personal link between the two men.

There can be no question that Disraeli deliberately selected Layard as a strong Turcophil and a man of energy and initiative who might be trusted to follow in the footsteps of Stratford and Elliot, and that the appointment was, in the words of Gladstone, regarded by the Turks as "a delicate attention". There was moreover a certain picquancy in the selection of one who had held office under Gladstone himself, and who was still remembered in the House of Commons for his Turcophil sallies, as the protagonist of anti-Gladstonian policy on the Golden Horn. In January 1877 the *Quarterly Review* published an unsigned article on "The Eastern Question and the Conference", which is now known to be from the pen of Layard:[1] and it may be assumed that Disraeli studied its contents and that it encouraged him in his choice. It in any case deserves special attention, not merely as the considered view of Disraeli's chief exponent in the East, but also as the ablest and most reasoned contemporary statement of the Turcophil position.

The article starts by regretfully noting the lack of any balance of power in Europe and assuming as a cardinal principle of British foreign policy "the maintenance of Constantinople and the Dardanelles in the hands of a Power from whose hostility and ambition England had nothing to fear. We supported the Turks because they were there, and we had nothing to put in their stead which would be equally safe and advantageous for us or for the peace of Europe and the world." No British statesman was Turcophil for the Turk's sake (here we find the same note as in Elliot's notorious dispatch to Derby). "The real problem was, who was to take Turkey's place? Would it be better to break up the Ottoman Empire suddenly and

---

[1] See list of his anonymous articles, in appendix to Sir Henry Layard's *Autobiography*.

to leave the Powers without and the Christians within to fight and
scramble for its debris? or to tolerate it for some time yet, to allow
Ottoman rule to expire of itself and to give the Christians time and
opportunity to improve themselves?" The former was the policy of
Russia, the latter had been that of Palmerston.

It was utterly untrue that no improvement had taken place in
Turkey. Despite the abuses of tax-farming, there had been a steady
growth of wealth, schools and agriculture: and the most real grievance of the Christians was "the ignorance, rapacity and corruption
of their own clergy". "It cannot be too often repeated that neither
Servia nor Roumania had any grievances whatever against Turkey."
Why then was there no progress?—"Because Russia has willed it so",
and because "it is her policy to prevent the development of education
and liberal institutions among the Slavs of Turkey and assert her
own control of them". Ignatyev's definite aim was "to end the Ottoman dominion by constant incitement of the Christians": he it was
who advised the Porte to declare bankruptcy, and—it could also be
"stated on no mean authority"—had even advised the repressive
measures adopted in Bulgaria. Disraeli was quite right in attributing
the insurrection to secret societies: it was "part and parcel of a carefully prepared plot and of a distinct policy".

The problem was whether Russia shall or shall not be allowed to
establish her influence in Bulgaria, so as to be "eventually the complete mistress of Turkey in Europe". "To make Serbia the nucleus
of a great Slav state to replace Turkey is out of the question": even
some of their admirers "now denounce the Serbs as cowardly,
treacherous and wanting in the qualities necessary to a great independent nation". Then comes a side-appeal to religious prejudice:
"There is not a Bulgarian priest who does not offer up his daily
prayer for the Emperor of Russia" (surely a virtual admission of
the Slav case), and Russia's first act when she possessed herself
of Bulgaria would be to put an end to all Protestant missions (an
obvious appeal to Victorian Protestant prejudices.)

Russia's possession of the Straits would serve aggressive purposes
and endanger India: since "at any moment her fleet issuing from the
Dardanelles might make a dash at Suez". "Russian policy is mainly
Asiatic, and Constantinople is the indispensable key to the Empire
of the East": Mesopotamia and Syria will follow Asia Minor, *unless
England were prepared to reject the counsels of politicians of Mr. Gladstone's school and were to go to war with Russia. . . .* We are all agreed

that the rule of the Turk is bad and oppressive and must be abolished, if it cannot be fundamentally reformed. No one worth alluding to has ever wished to fight for the Turk." The real problem is, however, how to ensure reform. To this the author attempts a constructive answer. There must be firm and constant pressure at Constantinople, such as was formerly applied by Stratford de Redcliffe or Ponsonby: corruption must be rooted out of the provinces, equality for all citizens must be enforced by the Powers, a new code on Indian lines, a cadastral survey and a reform of taxation must be introduced, and training colleges for officials must be established. But all depends on pressure by the foreign Ambassadors. Meanwhile, "Turkey has tyranny enough to answer for: but she has neither a Poland nor a Siberia".

In conclusion, the alternatives are summed up as follows: "To destroy Turkey, that her government may be replaced by Russia or Chaos, or rather by both, or to maintain her independence and integrity consistently with internal reform and the stern suppression of injustice, disorder and misgovernment. This is the steady English policy, consecrated by the Treaty of Paris as part of the public law of Europe: and it underlies every line of Lord Derby's dispatches." [1]

In its April number the *Quarterly* published a further article on Turkish affairs, underlining Layard's argument and insisting that "it cannot be too often repeated that self-government is not at present the cure for Turkish disorders. The materials for it do not exist. The idea of the Mussulman is complete domination over the Christian." It endorsed the claim of Consul Holmes that "a paternal despotism is the only possible government". It warmly greeted the appointment of Layard and stressed his special qualifications. "Trained in the school of Stratford de Redcliffe, possessing an intimate knowledge of the Turks and other races, with a long experience in Spain of a disorganised society and of government scarcely able to cope with the perplexities of administration, possessing great energy and decision of character, he will not condone the faults and offences of the ruling classes, while his appreciation of what is really good in the Turkish character will cause his advice to be accepted and his remonstrances heeded. The appointment is a sign that there is no shadow of wavering in the policy of the Cabinet."

From the first Layard sought to emulate his great predecessors in office and took as strongly Russophobe and Turcophil a line as the

[1] Main quotations, in their order, pp. 280, 298, 303, 314, 320.

Prime Minister himself. Within a fortnight of arrival at the Golden
Horn we find him reporting to Derby his attempts to establish his
personal influence over the Sultan—"a man out of whom much
might be made"[1]—and to secure the dismissal of two leading
ministers, Mahmud Damad and Redif Pashas. He appears to have
told the latter to their face that "through the evil counsels they had
given and the way in which they had shielded the authors of the
Bulgarian outrages, they had sacrificed the friendship and alliance
of England and plunged their country into what might prove a fatal
war".[2] Whether language so reminiscent of the Great Eltchi was
calculated to increase the new Ambassador's popularity at the Porte
is at least open to question. It certainly confirms the estimate of
Lord Granville, under whom Layard had served—"He was a philo-
Turk, but *he is a very strong man with orientals*, and"—he added the
somewhat qualified conviction, which events were to justify—"I
think he will be faithful to instructions, if the latter are of the right
sort".[3]

At his second audience with Abdul Hamid he was "even more
favourably impressed" than at the first: "I fancy that no ambassador
has ever had such a conversation with a Sultan as I had with H.M.",
and it was indeed "unprecedented" that Mrs. Layard should have
been allowed to be present at the audience.[4] Redif, he writes, "well
aware that it depends upon me, whether he shall go or not, has become abject like such Turks usually are under such circumstances".[5]
He at once used his influence to press for the punishment of those
guilty of the Bulgarian atrocities, but had to report "the perfect
infatuation" of the Turks in refusing to impose the death sentence
on the notorious Ahmed Aga.[6]

Layard had the most decided opinions, and attributed "this
shocking and unjustifiable war almost entirely to the Gladstonian
agitation".[7] He ascribed the intractable attitude of the Turks to
their conviction that England had abandoned them, and warned
London that his position was "an extremely difficult and delicate
one. I have much to ask and nothing to offer in return", and "there
is already a very bitter feeling springing up against England". At
the same time, with all his zeal for British support for Turkey, every

[1] *Layard Papers* (British Museum), 30 April, to Derby.
[2] *Ibid.* 4 May, to Derby.
[3] *Gladstone Papers*, Granville to Gladstone, 20 March 1877.
[4] *Layard Papers*, 18 May, to Derby.   [5] *Ibid.* 23 May, to Derby.
[6] *Ibid.* 30 April, to Derby.   [7] *Ibid.* 1 May, to Sir Andrew Buchanan.

dispatch reiterates the refrain that the Turkish statesmen are "poor creatures", and that much as he desires their removal, he cannot see a man of whom a decent Grand Vizier could be made".[1] No worse indictment of his own policy could be imagined.

His attitude is clearly revealed in two official dispatches written in June 1877, when Derby sent him the Russian terms as communicated by Shuvalov, and enquired whether in his view the Porte would be likely to consider them. Layard at once replied with a vigorous survey of the Turkish view—that to make Bulgaria autonomous would be to lay the foundations for its complete independence and union with Serbia "and the *inevitable extension* of Russian influence and rule over the whole Slav Christian populations of Turkey in Europe": that to destroy the Turkish fortresses on the Danube or to grant Bulgaria self-government and a national militia, would be to place Turkey and Constantinople at the mercy of Russia, and would probably lead to a Greek invasion of Thessaly and Epirus; that to cede Batum would be "to hand over the key of Armenia"; and that the Porte might consent to Roumanian independence, but was far too exasperated against Serbia, and too confident of ultimate victory over Montenegro, to cede any territory to either. "Nothing but the direst necessity would induce the Porte even to listen to these conditions", and though far from being an alarmist, he believed that the resistance of the Turkish fanatics and of "a powerful party in the Palace . . . would end in frightful massacre". For Britain to recommend such terms would be to destroy "any influence we may still possess here".[2]

After six days' reflection Layard sounded an even more alarmist note. "The formation of the provinces north and south of the Balkans into one vassal autonomous province, with the withdrawal from them of the Turkish troops and functionaries and the abandonment and destruction of the Turkish fortresses on the Danube, *would be in fact the end* of the Ottoman Empire in Europe": and he earnestly begged the Government "not to be the medium" of such proposals, which were "simply dictation". "It is vital to our gravest interests", he continued in phrases reminiscent of Elliot, "that we should be ready to interpose to save the Turkish Empire from complete dissolution. . . . Surely the policy which has hitherto made us support Turkey for our own purposes and safety, and for no abstract love

[1] *Layard Papers*, 30 May, to Derby.
[2] *Turkey No. XV.* (1878), Affairs of Turkey, no. 8, Layard to Derby, 13 June.

of the Turks or their faith, a policy approved and adopted by the greatest statesmen that England has produced, is not one which the events of the last few months . . . are sufficient to reverse. That policy was partly based on the belief that Turkey is a barrier to the ambitious designs of Russia in the East, and that the Sultan, the acknowledged head of the Mohammedan faith, is a useful if not necessary ally to England, who has millions of Mussulmans among her subjects." "The establishment of a vast military Slav Empire in Eastern Europe" would have fatal effects upon the Balance of Power and upon liberty and civilisation, and if Her Majesty's Government could do nothing "to oppose Russian designs", it should at least be prepared to mediate in order to secure "justice and moderation" for Moslems and Christians alike. "It is the only course left to us if we are not prepared to give Turkey even such indirect aid as the preservation and maintenance of our own national and imperial interests may render necessary. By following it we may recover and maintain a part of that great and preponderating influence . . . which England once enjoyed among the Mussulmans." As a Parthian shot, he emphasised the enormous difficulties in the way of Bulgarian union, and hinted that it might sow "the seeds of inevitable discord, wars and maybe massacres".[1]

LAYARD AND DISRAELI

These views, however, outspoken as they were, are mild in comparison with his private letters to the Prime Minister and the Foreign Secretary, though to the latter he is more reserved than to the former. He set himself to convince Beaconsfield that the only means of maintaining the *status quo* "is by telling Russia distinctly and decidedly what we shall allow her to do", and that the creation of an autonomous Bulgaria "will inevitably lead to the dismemberment of Turkey, not only in Europe, but in Asia and Africa". He therefore suggested a British occupation of the Peninsula of Gallipoli, "as a material guarantee, to be restored at the end of the war", and the sending of the fleet to Constantinople—in the belief that such action would lead Russia to draw back. He made four further concrete suggestions, such as must, if adopted, inevitably have involved us in hostilities—(*a*) "to assist the Turks actively by money and officers and by troops"; (*b*) "to incite the Hungarians and Galician Poles to take part against

[1] *Ibid.* no. 10, 19 June.

Russia"; (c) "to raise the Mohammedan states in Central Asia" against Russia and to use the Sultan's influence in this sense; and (d) to inform Greece "that we will not permit her to move against the Turks or promote insurrections", and to send ships to the Piraeus to enforce this view.[1]

Subsequent events completely justified the importance attached by the Ambassador to Gallipoli, as the key to the defences of Constantinople: for his correspondence with Admiral Hornby brings out very clearly the dangers of entering the Straits without securing the peninsula,[2] while on the other side we shall see the Grand Duke Nicholas and his staff declining to commit themselves to the occupation of the capital so long as the Tsar's veto upon the seizure of Gallipoli was upheld in deference to British wishes.[3] In view of the precedent of Admiral Duckworth's fleet in 1806 and of our still more memorable experiences in 1915, it is surprising to find the difficulty which the truculent, but in this instance very clear-sighted, Layard experienced in convincing the Turks of the value of Gallipoli. It was not until he had direct recourse to the Sultan that the necessary orders for fortifications were given, and the Grand Vizier, Edhem Pasha, "alluding angrily to the Sultan's order, which was too decided to be evaded, said that it was only given to please me (Layard)".[4]

Layard, then, on 1 August, warned the Prime Minister against sending in the fleet "unless its retreat is absolutely secure". The Turks could not be trusted, he argued. "Their feelings against us are such that they might go over to the Russians 'bag and baggage', if the Russians made it worth their while. If the fleet is sent up to Constantinople, it must be in the interests of the Turkish Empire, and the Turks must understand that it is done for their protection against the designs and ambitions of Russia. *We cannot tell them that it is entirely and exclusively in our own interests*, nor could we, I believe, induce them to ask us to send the fleet for the protection of the lives and property of Europeans and Christians." [5]

Here we are at last on bedrock, and the professions in favour of

---

[1] *Layard Papers*, Layard to Beaconsfield, 20 June.

[2] *E.g.* Layard to Hornby, 25 and 30 Jan. and 6 Feb. 1878.

[3] See *infra*, p. 265.

[4] *Layard Papers*, 25 July 1877, Layard to Beaconsfield, and 20 July to Derby, *re* Edhem's outburst to Sir Collingwood Dickson, to the effect that "the Turkish Government cared nothing for the Dardanelles, the Russians might have them if they chose. The Porte was going to fortify the Gallipoli Peninsula to please Mr. Layard, and what had the British Government done for Turkey?"

[5] *Ibid.* 1 Aug., Layard to Beaconsfield.

Turkish regeneration are seen to be merely the husk covering a kernel of exclusively British interests. A month later Layard stated even more clearly the dilemma with which the British Cabinet was confronted throughout the crisis. "Unless we come as an ally and a friend to 'help the Turk', we cannot come at all, or only at the risk of driving Turkey into a peace and alliance with Russia, which would make matters even worse than they are." [1]

There are two other highly interesting features of Layard's private correspondence with his chiefs—namely, his unrestrained criticism of all Turkish statesmen, which was certainly well-grounded, and his wholesale attacks upon all his diplomatic colleagues, which was no less certainly exaggerated and helps to explain British isolation at the Porte. He constantly emphasises the incompetence of such generals as Abdul Kerim or Suleiman, of the Minister of War, Redif, of such ministers as Damad, Server, and even Midhat. But he always reaches the same conclusion—that he has no alternative recommendations! "There is such an absolute want of statesmen, that *I really know no man who is capable* of filling this high and responsible office" of Grand Vizier.[2] Or again, "This absolute want of statesmen is one of the worst symptoms of the declining state of the Empire".[3] Or again, "If only there were one or two Turkish statesmen who could control and guide the Sultan, something might be done for this unhappy country. But I search in vain for the man." [4] In a word, we have the most damaging admissions of Turkish failure and decay from the mouth, not of the "unpatriotic" Gladstone, but of his chief denunciator, the greatest Turcophil of his time—who did not hesitate at the same time to denounce the Bulgars and Serbs as cowardly and degraded races, or to describe the Turkish race as "far superior to the Greek in all those qualities which form the nobler part of the human character".[5]

No less sweeping are his attacks upon his colleagues. Almost from the first he seems to have fallen foul of the German Ambassador, Prince Reuss, whom he accused of extreme Russophil tendencies, partly perhaps owing to the relationship of his wife, a princess of Saxe Weimar, with the Russian Court. One of Layard's private letters to Derby records a small scene between the two colleagues, which suggests complete incompatibility of temper. "Reuss asked me why we

[1] *Ibid.* 23 Aug.   [2] *Ibid.* 1 Aug., Layard to Beaconsfield.
[3] *Ibid.* 25 July, to Derby.
[4] *Ibid.* 12 Sept. and 10 Oct., to Derby: cf. *infra*, p. 406.
[5] *Ibid.* Layard to Childers, 25 Jan. 1878.

were pushing the Turks on to war. I replied that so far from England pushing Turkey to war, rumour attributed that intention to another Power. He understood of course what I meant."[1] Henceforth Layard is never tired of repeating that Reuss's aim is "to make the Turks believe that Germany will make peace between them and Russia",[2] and "to make them suspicious of us and to play the game of Russia".[3] If the Russians cross the Balkans, "we must be prepared for a peace made under the pressure or dictation of Germany, and without consulting us or reference to our interests".[4] Reuss is cynical, he told Derby on another occasion, "and in the habit of saying very disagreeable things which it requires some command of temper not to resent. However, socially we are on very good terms."[5] To Beaconsfield he wrote, "Germany as represented here is absolutely Russian. Zichy [the Austrian] is a mere appendage to Reuss. The Italian [Corti] does 'his little best' against us. The French Chargé d'Affaires has little weight; what he has is thrown in the balance against us. They all nourish the suspicion of the Porte as to our intentions. Prince Reuss openly declares that Russia must dictate terms of peace at Constantinople . . . Andrássy cannot be depended upon."[6] To Derby he quotes the rumour that Reuss is candidate "for the Bulgarian throne or whatever it is"—thereby again betraying both his personal animus and his profound hostility to Bulgarian liberation.[7]

It was a repetition of Stratford de Redcliffe, who fought with an almost endless series of French Ambassadors and Chargés even during the height of the Franco-British alliance and joint war, and of Elliot, who found all the other five Ambassadors united against him and consoled himself by treating some of them as Ignatyev's tools. Numbers are of course not conclusive, but there is, to say the least, a presumption that isolation was the result of an impracticable or mistaken policy, and it is easy enough for our generation to see the extent to which Turkey failed to justify the hopes of its Victorian advocates. There seems to be no doubt as to Zichy's inconstant and unreliable character: for after being very much under the influence of Ignatyev, he was ere long denouncing him "as a devil incarnate".[8] After Reuss's arrival Zichy and he were inseparable for some months, but by the end of 1877 Zichy drew back again and began to attach

---

[1] *Layard Papers*, 27 June, to Derby.   [2] *Ibid.* 4 July, to Derby.
[3] *Ibid.* 11 July, to Derby.   [4] *Ibid.* 11 July, Layard to Beaconsfield.
[5] *Ibid.* 29 Aug., Layard to Derby.   [6] *Ibid.* 1 Aug., Layard to Beaconsfield.
[7] *Ibid.* 15 Aug., Layard to Derby.   [8] *Ibid.* 28 Nov., Layard to Beaconsfield.

himself to Layard to a degree which the latter found most embarrassing. Shortly before this occurred, Layard was lamenting that he stood alone and could "neither expect support nor sympathy from any of my colleagues who have a voice in the fate of Turkey". Yet "I do not despair of holding my own and maintaining the honour and interests of England, *if I could only know what the intentions and objects of my Government really were*".[1] What more impressive commentary could be obtained as to the internal dissensions and paralysis of the Cabinet at home, than that the "key" Ambassador should write thus to the Prime Minister!

It will be seen that in Layard's list of likes and dislikes the latter far outweighed the former. But his main antipathy was reserved for his old party, and, in particular, for Mr. Gladstone, to whose agitation "I attribute almost entirely this shocking and unjustifiable war!".[2]

CONSUL HOLMES AND ARTHUR EVANS

Like master, like man. While Amurath to Amurath succeeded, in the shape of one Ambassador more Turcophil than the last, it would have been too much to expect that those consular officials who already shared such views should modify them now: and we find Consul Holmes reporting steadily in the old sense. But early in 1877 Mr. Arthur Evans began to publish in the *Manchester Guardian* a fresh series of sensational articles, describing the pitiable plight of the Bosnian refugees in Dalmatia and his own impressions of a visit to the mountain fastnesses of the insurgents. On the basis of enquiries on both sides of the frontier he estimated the number of fugitives at 200,000 (including 40,000 in Serbia and about as many in Montenegro), the number of burnt villages in south Bosnia alone at 145, and the number of "old men, women and children butchered in cold blood" at over 6000. He described very vividly the farcical nature of "elections" to the Turkish Chamber and instanced the manner in which the new constitution had recently been proclaimed at Kulen Vakuf—"The Emperor of Emperors had called together the seven subject kings of Europe [who was the seventh, Mr. Evans

[1] *Ibid.* 28 Nov., Layard to Beaconsfield.
[2] *Ibid.* 1 May 1877, to Buchanan. Cf. 12 July to Lytton—"Gladstone and those who encouraged Russia to enter upon this iniquitous war". Such extracts could be continued indefinitely, for this point of view became a real obsession with Layard.

irreverently but very pertinently enquired] to Stambul to signify to them his sovereign will and pleasure", and so on.

Evans entered "the strongest possible protest against the consular reports received by our Government from the capital of Bosnia" and made it very clear that Sarajevo was quite alienated from "free Bosnia" and Holmes himself cut off from all relations with the "rayah" and dependent on official information. "It was perfectly natural", he added, with more than a touch of sarcasm, "that Sir Henry Elliot should remain in ignorance of the extent and enormity of the Bulgarian massacres, and it is equally unreasonable and ungenerous to blame Mr. Holmes because he was not informed by the Turks themselves and their friends of the horrors which have desolated the greater part of Bosnia, and that he was humanely loath to accept the first accounts of impalements and other atrocities, on the real occurrence of which I for one am prepared to supply overwhelming evidence".[1]

These revelations led to questions in Parliament from Mr. Jenkins and Sir George Campbell, but Mr. Bourke denied all knowledge of the alleged massacres and pinned his faith on Holmes. One of the latter's reports, read aloud to the House, assumed that "all the unemployed and needy Slav patriots, aided and encouraged by Slav committees, will find their way into Bosnia and cause a renewal of the brigandage on a large scale which . . . it has pleased Slav sympathisers to call 'insurrection' ". His truly agnostic attitude was revealed in a later dispatch, which said of a particular story that it "may or may not be true, . . . like everything else in this land of lies".[2]

Mr. Evans, however, was irrepressible and in the *Manchester Guardian* denounced Holmes's dispatches as "surpassing any I have ever seen in perverse ignorance and unconscious partisanship". He upheld his previous assertions regarding the situation in Sarajevo (which Holmes had challenged), as coming from "an European resident who knows the language, which Mr. Holmes does not": and he persisted—as we now know, quite correctly—in treating the rising as due, not to outside intrigues, but to "the flagrant and unendurable tyranny of the Begs and their aiders and abettors the Osmanli officials". Holmes had expressed his intention to urge the Vali "if possible to sweep these bands of brigands out of Bosnia". "Well", wrote Evans, "I have visited seven insurgent camps, I have seen

[1] *M.G.*, 9 March 1877, "Further Experiences of 'Free Bosnia' ".
[2] Hansard, ccxxxiii, p. 840: *M.G.* 10 April.

mountain strongholds from which disciplined armies might recoil,
I have seen freemen in their thousands not ill-supplied with arms and
inspired with the enthusiasm of a just cause: and I return from the
mountains of free Bosnia to find that it was all an ocular illusion. . . ."
The *Manchester Guardian* associated itself with its correspondent and
quoted damning passages from earlier dispatches of Holmes himself,
admitting all officials in Bosnia to be corrupt and the country to be
"relapsing into a new era of disorganisation and neglect".[1]

As a result of public criticism Vice-Consul Freeman was sent to
investigate the massacre at Očevo in Hercegovina, and produced
a very sceptical report, declaring that he was "more disinclined than
ever to put faith in the stories of Turkish outrage and violence".
This was very different from his private admissions to Miss Irby,
when he visited her refugee camp on his way to Očevo. "He is fully
aware of the impossibility of an English Consul getting information
from the terrified Christians in Bosnia", so she writes to Mr. Gladstone: "I begged him to mention this disadvantage in his reports".[2]

Stung by the injustice of such a *volte-face*, Evans sent to his paper
a detailed rejoinder[3] to Freeman's report, pointing out that Freeman
had not visited the actual scene of the outrages, and Miss Irby
backed him up in a letter which made it quite clear that most of the
survivors had long since fled across the Austrian border, and that no
Orthodox on Turkish soil could give evidence against a Turk, save
at the risk of his life. It was only too obvious that the Vice-Consul's
views had been toned down for publication by his chief in Sarajevo,
whose main connections were with the Turkish authorities.

Evans, however, was a hard fighter, and in a fresh article on "The
Reign of Terror in Bosnia" reminded his readers that the Vali had
"yielded to the pressing solicitations of a consul more actively
Turkish than the Turks themselves, and let loose his dogs of war",
with the result that there was a fresh exodus of Christian refugees
into Austrian territory. There followed a long series of vivid articles
from August to December 1877, describing the country as "little
better than a desert", and insisting that if there had been "no holo-
causts to compare with Batak", still "the sum total of horror and
devastation can fall little short".[4]

[1] Leader of 15 May 1877.
[2] 5 May 1877—*Gladstone Papers*, general correspondence.
[3] *M.G.*, 11 July, dated from Knin, in Dalmatia, "Vice-Consul Freeman's Report
Examined" and letter of 26 July.
[4] *Ibid.* 27 Nov., "Town and Country in Bosnia".

No amount of facts could change the official attitude. In July Mr. Bourke defended Consul Holmes against the strictures of Mr. Shaw Lefevre: he had been forty-one years in the consular service, to his chiefs' entire satisfaction. Finally, by way of emphasising their disregard of all criticism and their devotion to Turcophil principles, the Government conferred a knighthood on Holmes—then a very unusual step, whose significance was not wasted in the Near East. In view of the constant objections raised by the Queen to honours of this kind—as repeatedly revealed in her published *Letters*—it is hardly too much to infer that this act was meant by her and the Prime Minister as an open rebuke to the critics of Turkey. We may perhaps be excused for adding Freeman's smashing commentary: "Holmes, who urges the suppression of insurrections, and Shefket, who himself suppresses them, receive that honour from their superiors, which according to the standard of their superiors they so thoroughly deserve".[1]

Beaconsfield risks War

The Queen was highly alarmed at Layard's Constantinople reports and incensed at the calmness with which Derby received them. "Such a Foreign Minister the Queen really never remembers." [2] She would have liked to see him replaced by Lord Lyons, and was not deterred by the danger of Salisbury also resigning. "Be bold," she besought Beaconsfield, "call your followers together . . . tell them that the interests of Great Britain are at stake, that it is not for the Christians . . . but for conquest that this cruel wicked war is waged, that Russia is as barbarous and tyrannical as the Turks. Tell them this, and that they should rally round their sovereign and country." [3]

The Prime Minister on his side made it clear that he sympathised entirely with her views, but warned her of the difficulties of obtaining a vote of men and money from Parliament, and even then of using them "without the permission of the Porte". "All these difficulties would be removed, if we declared war against Russia: but there are not three men in the Cabinet who are prepared to advise that step." [4]

Here was the crux of the whole matter. Beaconsfield, as he informed the Queen, had braced himself to let Derby and Salisbury

---

[1] *Contemp. Rev.*, Oct. 1877, "Neutrality Real or Pretended".
[2] Buckle, vi. p. 147, 25 June.   [3] 27 June—*ibid*. p. 148.
[4] 28 June—*ibid*. p. 149.

resign, "had they alone been the obstacles", and to "attempt to guide a discordant and unwilling Cabinet".[1] But he soon found that not even Lord Cairns and the Duke of Richmond could be relied upon, and that only Lord John Manners and Hicks Beach were ready to back him through thick and thin.[2]

On 18 July Derby informed the Russian Ambassador confidentially that any occupation of Constantinople, "even if temporary and dictated by military necessity, would threaten the good relations of the two countries".[3] Shuvalov replied that Russia desired an understanding with England, and would prefer to attain her aim without occupying Constantinople, but could not possibly give an undertaking, least of all a public one, not to do so.[4] It ought to have been sufficiently obvious that such a step would have been intensely resented by Russian public opinion, and would also have served as a direct encouragement to the Porte. On the other hand, the Turcophils could advance the strong argument that even with the most honourable intentions, it would be far easier to occupy Constantinople than to evacuate it afterwards, in view of what might happen to Turkey as the result of so utter a defeat. Lord Derby quoted a very apt analogy in the occupation of Rome by the French, which was prolonged far longer than had ever been foreseen or intended by Napoleon III.

The refusal of such a pledge gave Beaconsfield his chance, and on 21 July he extracted from the Cabinet the unanimous decision to declare war upon Russia, if she occupied the Turkish capital and did not arrange for her immediate retirement from it.[5] Orders were given to strengthen the Mediterranean garrisons.

How dangerous the Prime Minister's mentality had by this time become, is revealed by his letter of the next day to the Queen. In the event of war, he wrote, "*Russia must be attacked from Asia*, troops should be sent to the Persian Gulf, *and the Empress of India should order her armies to clear Central Asia of the Muscovites and drive them into the Caspian*. We have a good instrument for this purpose in Lord Lytton, and indeed he was placed there with that view." [6] This last phrase is especially illuminating. That it was not a mere isolated flash of imagination on the part of Beaconsfield was shown at a Cabinet meeting on 15 August,[7] when Derby reminded him that "we

---

[1] 12 July—*ibid.* p. 151.   [2] Journal of 17 July—*Letters*, ii. p. 550.
[3] *R.B.D.*, 18 July, Shuvalov to Gorchakov.   [4] *Ibid.* 19 July.
[5] Buckle, vi. p. 154.   [6] 22 July—*ibid.* p. 155.
[7] Contrast other passages in Buckle, *op. cit.* vi. pp. 172, 178, 199.

have no allies". To this he rejoined that no other ally than Turkey was required, that it was not for us to conquer Bulgaria, "that we were masters of the sea and could send a British force to Batum, march without difficulty through Armenia and menace the Asiatic possessions of Russia".[1] And a fortnight later he was still harping on the same line, to Derby himself. "An English army, 40,000 men, with the Black Sea and Batum at our command, *could march to Tiflis*. We want no allies. We are not going to fight in Bulgaria. The situation is much the same as when Wellington went to the Peninsula, except that a Turk as a soldier is worth twenty Spaniards. What allies had we then?" [2] Anything more reckless it is difficult to imagine: the only possible parallel is provided by Palmerston's fire-eating programme towards the close of the Crimean War. It is indeed evident that the Prime Minister had not assimilated the warnings of Lord Salisbury as to the danger of using and arguing from small scale maps of distant and unfamiliar tracts of territory.

There can be little doubt that Beaconsfield was very materially influenced by Layard's alarmist and inflammatory letters,[3] and that the two encouraged each other in a fantastic forward policy, which fortunately did not appeal to the Cabinet as a whole. Beaconsfield's inner mind is revealed by his "secret" letter of 6 August.[4]

"I regret the suspicions in the mind of the Sultan as regards our intentions. I admit they are reasonable, but they are not true—at least so far as I am concerned, being resolved to maintain if possible 'the integrity and independence' of the Ottoman Empire.

"The Turks have proved their independence, for without allies they have gallantly, and I think successfully, defended their country, and I still hope to see, at the conclusion of the war, the Porte a recognised Power, and no despicable one, in Europe.

"If there is 'a second campaign', I have the greatest hopes this country will interfere and pronounce its veto against a war of extermination, and the dark designs of a secret partition, from which the spirit of the nineteenth century recoils. As we have command of the sea, why should not a British *corps d'armée* (via Batum) march into Armenia and even occupy Tiflis? We might send another to Varna and act on the Russian flank.

"But all this requires time. The Turks gain victories, but don't

---

[1] Cabinet notes, 15 Aug.—Buckle, *op. cit.* vi. p. 172.
[2] 13 Sept.—*ibid.* pp. 178-9.   [3] See *supra*, p. 208-10.
[4] *Layard Papers*, 6 Aug. 1877, Layard to Beaconsfield.

follow them up. After Plevna, they should have driven the Russians across the Danube, destroyed the bridge and taken the Emperor prisoner. Wellesley tells me that might have been done.

"The thing is—to secure another campaign, or rather the necessity for one, for if Russia is told by England that 'another campaign' will be a *casus belli*, she may be inclined to make what Prince Gorchakov calls *une paix boiteuse*.

"The danger is, if the Russians rally, again successfully advance and reach Adrianople this autumn. What then is to be done? With her suspicions of England, Turkey would be ruined. *That is why I should like to see our fleet in her immediate waters, and Gallipoli in our possession as a material guarantee*, and with her full sanction. We should then be able to save Turkey."

After this letter it is finally impossible to maintain that Disraeli was not contemplating war in the summer of 1877—unless, as he still hoped in his dreams, the Turks unaided overcame the Russians.

The Prime Minister was undoubtedly affected by the alarm of the Anglo-Indians, military and civil, round the Viceroy, regarding Russia's advance in Asia: this may be studied in the correspondence of Salisbury and Lytton, which contains more than one highly interesting passage. "The commonest error in politics is sticking to the carcasses of dead policies", Salisbury wrote in May, meaning that it was no longer possible to adhere rigidly to the idea of Turkish territorial integrity. "Our foreign policy", he told Lytton, "has lacked a bold initiative and a settled plan." [1] His own idea would have been "to secure the water-way to India, by the acquisition of Egypt or Crete", and "in no way to discourage the obliteration of Turkey". It was on this occasion that he expressed opinions peculiarly characteristic of the man and of the methods which he followed throughout his political career. "I think you listen too much to the soldiers. . . . *You should never trust experts*. If you believe the doctors, nothing is wholesome: if you believe the theologians, nothing is innocent: if you believe the soldiers, nothing is safe. They all require to have their strong wine diluted by a very large admixture of insipid common sense." [2] And so Salisbury very wisely set himself against the Indian Council's panic-stricken demand for immediate action in Central Asia, and begged Lytton not to let "the military men become practically the arbiters" of peace or war. He refused

[1] *Life of Salisbury,* ii. p. 146.   [2] *Ibid.* p. 153.

to be involved in the dispute of what he called "Quettites and Anti-Quettites".[1]

The foremost exponents of the Russian danger were Sir Bartle Frere and Sir Henry Rawlinson, whose outlook was excusably coloured by long residence at such a hotbed of Russian intrigue as Teheran, and who also suffered from an excess of fantasy in European questions.[2] There were, however, many others, both military and civil—such men as Sir John Adye and Sir Lepel Griffin—who knew "what the invasion of Khiva cost Russia", and how infinitely more difficult was the invasion of India. "Herat, Kabul, Khelat, Yarkund", wrote the latter, "are names which may frighten children. . . . To move from our strong position which Nature herself has fortified, into barren and hostile regions, every step in which must take us farther from our base of operations, our railways and magazines, would be an act of madness which only our worst enemies and Sir Henry Rawlinson could seriously approve."[3]

The excitement was of course fanned by events at the seat of war. It was not until the second half of June that the Russians crossed the Danube in force, at Galatz, in the Delta, and soon afterwards at Sistova. Then after a short interval Nicopolis was captured, while General Gurko occupied the northern section of the Shipka Pass and seemed on the point of pressing through to the undefended plains. There was panic in Constantinople: Abdul Kerim and Redif Pashas were hastily dismissed, and the more energetic Mehemed Ali Pasha and Suleiman Pasha put in their place. But what turned the scale was the unexpected and heroic resistance of Plevna under Osman Pasha, which the Russians twice failed to take by storm on 20 and 30 July, and which soon had to be subjected to a long and difficult investment.

On 28 July the Queen made a final appeal to Derby, excitedly hinting that there might be "a horrible massacre" of Christians in Turkey, unless the Russians were prevented from occupying Constantinople. This may be regarded as thoroughly typical of the pre-

---

[1] *Life of Salisbury*, ii. p. 160.

[2] Rawlinson at this time feared a Russo-German alliance against England! Lytton appears to have sent a copy of his reply to Layard, who considered the Viceroy's arguments to be "unanswerable" and added, "Between ourselves I had never a high opinion of Rawlinson's judgment on political questions. He has not the class of mind to deal with such questions" (*Layard Papers*, 6 Sept. 1877, Layard to Lytton). A few months later he refers to Rawlinson's "statement about Russo-French policy" as "a mare's nest. He is rather given to their discovery" (*ibid.* 21 Nov., Layard to Lytton).

[3] Sir L. Griffin, *Our North-West Frontier*, p. 10.

vailing mentality: in order to hold back the Turks from killing whole-sale the subjects whom they were incapable of governing or control-ling, it was solemnly proposed that Britain should risk war with the greatest Christian Power in the East, thereby frustrating the libera-tion of the victims and reimposing Turkish rule. Lord Derby in reply expressed the frank opinion that the war party was "small in num-bers, though loud and active", and that "the great bulk of the nation desires nothing so much as the maintenance of peace".[1] This earned the Foreign Secretary an unusually severe snub, which, as Mr. Buckle shows, was actually drafted by the Prime Minister and passed by the Queen as "admirable". In it she regretted Lord Derby's opposition to an expedition to Gallipoli, when proposed by Beaconsfield, ap-proved by herself and generally concurred in by all parties. "The Queen does not know from what sources Lord Derby gathers his opinion that the British people are in favour of Russian supremacy. She is convinced of the contrary and believes there will soon be no controversy on the subject" [2]—a *non sequitur* of the most feminine quality.

This incident would in itself justify Shuvalov's statement of the extent to which the Prime Minister and the Queen were working together without reference to any of his colleagues. He even went so far as to telegraph secretly from Osborne to Layard in Constantinople, behind the back of the Foreign Office, in so vital a question as the dispatch of the British fleet to Turkish waters.[3] This shows drastic-ally enough that the old confidence between Beaconsfield and Derby, of which their exchange of letters on 17 June still bore evidence, had by this time broken down altogether. But for Derby's resistance —if Shuvalov is to be believed on a point for which, for once, we lack corroborative evidence—the Prime Minister might have rushed the Cabinet into threatening a rupture with Russia if she marched on Constantinople. Meanwhile the Queen had summoned Salisbury to Osborne, in the hope of converting him, and was fairly satisfied with his "sensible views": Lady Salisbury explained to Count Shuvalov that the Queen "has lost control of herself, badgers her ministers and pushes them towards war".[4]

The essential difference of outlook at this stage of the crisis be-tween the Prime Minister and Lord Salisbury is revealed in a speech of the latter at the Merchant Taylors on 11 June. He quoted a

---

[1] Buckle, vi. p. 158.   [2] 29 July—*ibid*. p. 159.
[3] *Ibid*. p. 160.   [4] *R.B.D.* no. 243, 26 July.

Colonel friend who had demonstrated to him "that Russia was in Armenia, that Armenia is the key to Syria, that Syria is the key to Egypt, and that anyone advancing into Egypt has the key to Africa. By this list of keys long drawn out, he shows that the present victories of Russia seriously menace South Africa." That—he added, with a sting for those who knew how to read between the lines, "is characteristic of the apprehensions I hear around me". And he then coined the admirable phrase, "It has generally been acknowledged to be madness to go to war for an idea, but if anything is more unsatisfactory, it is to go to war against a nightmare".

Punch's comment on this was a cartoon entitled "Disturbed Dreamers". Three children are tossing in bed—the *Morning Post*, *Pall Mall Gazette* and *Daily Telegraph*—while the hideous nightmare of a Cossack is riding to India across their stomachs: and at the bedside the calm figure of Lord Salisbury is saying, "Wake up, my little men, don't make such a horrible noise: it is only a nightmare".

The informed reader will feel no surprise at such constant quotations from *Punch*, for it may in all seriousness be affirmed that no newspaper throughout the long crisis so repeatedly touches the heart of the problem. And indeed, amid the scare about Central Asia, no popular presentment could be better than the following brief passage from a quizzical preface to volume lxxii.

" 'Do you not fear what Russia can do to endanger our rule in India?'

" 'No: for I think our basis of defence about the strongest, her basis of attack about the weakest, in the world. If a thousand miles of waterless deserts and impassable mountains, and more than that distance between even the border of these and the sources from which all Russia's supplies must be drawn,—and that by a nation whose European credit, as I am assured by those who are loudest in their fear of her, is exhausted, and whose internal system is honeycombed by the secret workings of discontent and disloyalty—be not sufficient defence of a power rooted as England is in India, with her communications secured by her command of the sea, her soldiers and sailors well-trained, well-officered and animated by the high courage of our race, and the wealth and credit of Great Britain's vast empire and world-wide commerce at their back, then facts and fancies are one, and *Punch* has read history in vain.' "

" 'And worse still, has studied in my schools and worked in my service to no purpose', exclaimed Common Sense, as with a sudden explosion of impatience, he shut down with a snap the Russian Old Bogey into his Box. . . ."

COUNT ANDRÁSSY'S RESERVES

In the first week of August Shuvalov again proved the extreme accuracy of his inside information by reporting the details of further discussions between London and Vienna—and this despite Andrássy's complaint, as voiced by Beust, that whatever he said to London "was immediately known in St. Petersburg and earned him reproaches of treachery".[1] In actual fact, a series of "Declarations" were at last agreed upon between the two Cabinets, but they gave Beaconsfield but little satisfaction. They reiterated the seven points already laid down by Andrássy at the very outset, and now accepted by Derby, and to this was added a further reservation regarding the Straits, whose status could only be altered by general consent among the Powers: while it was specifically stated that in the view of Vienna "the best method of guaranteeing" these interests "would consist in parallel and independent action" by the two Powers.[2] In a word, Andrássy had no intention of being used as a "scarecrow" against Russia[3] and contended that the points formulated could not be regarded as objectionable by Russia so long as she adhered to her public professions. At the same time he insisted on absolute secrecy, on the pretext that publication might seem an attempt to dictate to Russia before the peace. Moreover, if the French Ambassador, Marquis d'Harcourt, was correctly informed, Andrássy was once more assuring Derby confidentially that no arrangement had been concluded between Austria and Russia.[4] This was typical of his tortuous course between Russia and England: and Beaconsfield had to be contented with what he vaguely called "a moral understanding".[5] It was at this stage that the Tsar sent further assurances to Vienna,[6] stressing the monarchical and undemocratic character of their co-operation, announcing the suspension of negotiations with

[1] *R.B.D.* vi., 5 Aug.

[2] Lee, *op. cit.* ii. no. 25, draft approved by Cabinet and Queen, 13 Aug.

[3] 11 July, Andrássy to Beust—Wertheimer, iii. p. 38. Granville judged the situation with singular accuracy when he wrote to Gladstone, "Austria has not the slightest intention of moving"—6 Aug. 1877 (*Gladstone Papers*).

[4] *D.D.F.* ii. no. 191, Harcourt to Decazes, 18 July.

[5] 13 July, Beust to Andrássy—Wertheimer, *op. cit.* iii. p. 39.

[6] Already quoted in another connection, *supra*, p. 92. Russian Communicat of 26 July (*Austrian Archives*).

London, and reaffirming his engagements with Austria-Hungary and through her with Germany.

This time, if he had only known, Andrássy's extreme methods of secrecy were being reduced to an absurdity: for Shuvalov in reporting to St. Petersburg "the seven points" of Austria-Hungary, was able to announce that he had copied them from the original text—which forces us to conclude that he had been shown them by no other than Lord or Lady Derby, or that he had a very skilful thief employed within the Foreign Office itself.[1]

A few weeks later Layard writes to Derby: "I may mention that almost everything that passes in London, even of the most secret nature, is known at once to my German and Austrian colleagues, and if known to Prince Reuss, is, of course, known at St. Petersburg"— here, of course, his personal animus against Reuss makes him jump to conclusions. "Your communications with Count Andrássy, for instance, were known to him and Zichy before probably they were known to me." [2]

Meanwhile Andrássy concealed the negotiations even from Bismarck, until the latter came to see him at Salzburg on 18 September, and then only mentioned them under seal of direst secrecy. Bismarck promised nót even to tell the Emperor William, adding significantly, "for he is the most indiscreet man in the world ": [3] but his main motive was doubtless the knowledge that his master leaned more to Russia than to Austria and might discuss it with his nephew Alexander. The confidence displayed in him by the notoriously discreet Andrássy appears to have flattered Bismarck, for it was on this occasion that he coined the memorable phrase: "They treat me like a fox, a cunning fellow (*Schlaukopf*) of the first rank. But the truth is that with a gentleman I am always a gentleman and a half, and *when I have to do with a pirate, I try to be a pirate and a half.*" [4] The two ministers parted with mutual congratulations that Russia was encountering such great difficulties in the Balkans.

In his unprinted memoirs Shuvalov has placed on record his opinion that "the lack of agreement between Austria-Hungary and England had a great influence on the whole course of the crisis", and that "if London and Vienna had been able to agree at the outset and had declared that they would not tolerate war, war would have

---

[1] *R.B.D.* vi., 5 Aug. [2] *Layard Papers*, 29 Aug., Layard to Derby.
[3] Wertheimer, *op. cit.* iii. p. 43. [4] *Ibid.* p. 42.

been quite impossible".[1] This is only one of many proofs of Shuvalov's acute and accurate judgment. We have Lord Salisbury's authority for the statement that Andrássy, at the Congress of Berlin, made it quite clear that he could not afford to "remain in the air".

The situation at the height of the summer was really only saved by a combination of circumstances—first and foremost the Russian reverses before Plevna in the first week of August, which seriously delayed her advance southwards and forced her to call out the Guards and apply for the once despised Roumanian help ; secondly, Andrássy's reluctance to become the cat's-paw of Britain ; thirdly, the acute disagreement inside the British Cabinet, together with the precarious health of Beaconsfield and the steadying influence of Derby. Mr. Buckle says of this period that "Beaconsfield was never far from the border of physical collapse":[2] what commitments he might have imposed upon the country but for the constant reactions of gout and asthma, it is not easy to say. Public opinion, meanwhile, was inclined to assume that Russia, for good or for bad, had failed in her objective, and was correspondingly relieved.

BRITAIN AND EGYPT

At this period the idea of a British occupation of Egypt was again put forward. On 11 July 1877 the Crown Princess wrote to her mother, Queen Victoria, "All lovers of England are so anxious that this opportunity should not pass by, of gaining a firm footing in Egypt",[3] and the same week [4] Beaconsfield reported to the Queen that an offer had come from the Porte to sell its suzerainty of Egypt, Crete and Cyprus—not formal, he added, "but of the fact there is no doubt". The atmosphere in London was still unfavourable for this. When Bismarck in November 1876 had suggested to Salisbury that Britain should take Egypt as her share of a Turkish partition,[5] Salisbury had not responded, and Beaconsfield when this was reported to him had at once dismissed it as merely likely to embroil us with France, modestly adding, "I would sooner we had Asia Minor than Egypt".[6] In July 1877 he still seems to have been of the same opinion, and the Queen asked her enthusiastic daughter why we should

---

[1] Cit. Hanotaux, *La France Contemp.*, iv. p. 314.
[2] Buckle, vi. p. 167. [3] *Letters*, ii. p. 547.
[4] 16 July—*ibid*. p. 549. [5] *Supra*, p. 106.
[6] 29 Nov. 1876, Beaconsfield to Salisbury—Buckle, vi. p. 104.

"make a wanton aggression, such as the taking of Egypt would be".[1] She, Beaconsfield and Derby were, from three somewhat different angles, almost equally suspicious of Bismarck, and in September and October seem to have been confirmed in this view by Lord Odo Russell, who "reported all Bismarck's cynical bravadoes",[2] and by Lord Lyons, who was afraid of Germany promising Egypt to France "as compensation for Alsace-Lorraine".[3] Later on, in December, Derby sent the most emphatic denials to Lyons for transmission to the French.[4]

In reality they were all doing Bismarck an injustice: for on 15 June he had dictated to his son Herbert a memorandum in which he laid it down as a German interest "to promote an agreement between England and Russia", and treated a British occupation of Egypt as the easiest means to that end. If a Russo-British war should prove inevitable, he added, Germany's rôle should be "mediation at the expense of Turkey".[5] In July he carries his train of thought further, by urging upon Oubril, the Russian Ambassador in Berlin, the desirability of Britain and Russia coming to terms at Turkey's expense: "Our understanding with the Polish and Papal Austria was always difficult: there is nothing against an intimacy between us, you and England".[6] It is, of course, possible to argue that there was some hidden motive in this overture: for its form was anything but tactful towards a man whom Bismarck himself detested for his "Papal" sympathies and connected with Ultramontane intrigue against himself.

In this connection it may be added that already on 27 May Lord Odo had reported to Lord Derby a strong overture from Bismarck in favour of an Anglo-Russian entente. After expressing his own gratitude to Russia, he declared that "he would give his last effort to bring about a cordial and intimate understanding between England and Russia, to which Germany would become a party". It may be that Lord Odo did not believe him and discouraged Beaconsfield, though there is no actual trace of this. But it is still more likely that Beaconsfield never read the dispatch at all, or put it down to the "sycophancy" of Lord Odo, whom he utterly misjudged and periodically abused throughout this period.

---

[1] *Letters*, ii. p. 550.

[2] *Ibid.* p. 178, Beaconsfield to Derby, 13 Sept. He again does Lord Odo great injustice by adding, "which he evidently listens to in an ecstasy of sycophantic wonder"—vi. p. 178. The Prime Minister cannot have read Russell's dispatches at all regularly, as Miss Taffs's forthcoming biography is likely to show.

[3] 10 Oct., Beaconsfield to Queen—*ibid.* p. 188.

[4] 21 Dec.—*Life of Lyons*, p. 365.   [5] *G.P.* no. 294, Diktat of Bismarck.

[6] Rachfahl, *Deutschland und die Weltpolitik*, p. 181.

Layard's appeal for the occupation of Gallipoli greatly impressed the Queen and was laid before the Cabinet, but Derby insisted, to her great annoyance, that "it would be too late to occupy, even if that step were desirable", [1] and telegraphed in this sense to the Ambassador. Next day, however, the Prime Minister himself telegraphed from Osborne direct to Layard: "The telegram sent to you yesterday from the Cabinet opens a prospect of recurring to the wise and ancient policy of England. The British Fleet in the Turkish waters with the consent of the Sultan may be the first step in the virtual preservation of his Empire. I much depend upon your energy and skill, in both of which I have the utmost confidence." [2] His motives are revealed in a letter to the Queen. "Great care must be taken, lest we be accused of changing our policy without due public notice. The state of neutrality . . . renders the conduct of affairs extremely delicate and difficult": but he "has much confidence in the secret telegram".

In other words, he has intervention in his mind and is already acquiring the habit of going behind the back of the Foreign Secretary, with the Queen's active connivance. Public opinion, both inside and outside the Cabinet, was slowly beginning to calm down, as the immense obstacles which still lay across the path of Russia became apparent, and the fear of an imminent fall of Constantinople faded. But these very obstacles encouraged Beaconsfield to assume a new tactical position, and at the last Cabinet meeting before ministers parted for the vacation, he argued that if the Russians could not complete their military task before the winter, it must be Britain's aim to prevent a second campaign: "his own opinion", he said, "was strong,—that we, and Europe, ought not to tolerate another campaign".[3] It must have been obvious that this was to risk war: and it was on this occasion that Derby reminded him of our lack of allies, and that he talked wildly of marching through Armenia and found his views "favourably received" by his other colleagues. Or was it merely that silence seemed to give consent, and that they hoped that no such situation would arise?

COLONEL WELLESLEY'S MISSION

At this time the Prime Minister, in agreement with the Queen, took the highly questionable step of entrusting Colonel Wellesley

[1] Buckle, vi. pp. 157-8.
[2] Quoted *ibid.* p. 160, note; see also *Layard Papers*, Beaconsfield to Layard, 29 July.   [3] 15 Aug.—Buckle, vi. p. 172.

with a direct mission to the Tsar, behind the back of the Foreign Secretary, thereby showing their complete loss of confidence in the latter. Wellesley had by his tactful behaviour reinstated himself in the good graces of the Tsar, who genuinely desired a *détente* with England. The War Minister, Milyutin, had, with Alexander II.'s approval, made a tentative overture for mediation, and Wellesley had at once offered to take a message to London, where his relations with the Court were known to be very close. Wellesley travelled day and night to Osborne and laid before the Queen the Tsar's earnest assurances, contrived to explain the prevailing view that she and the Prince of Wales were anti-Russian ("which I said was not untrue, for we felt strongly the way in which Russia had behaved all along and . . . had instigated the Bulgarian insurrection which had led to the massacres"—such is her own comment) and urged that a firm line on the part of Britain would enable the Tsar to escape from a difficult dilemma. The Queen recorded in her journal the original if somewhat incoherent opinion that "this war would ruin Russia and paralyse her for fifty years. . . . Failure was impossible, ruin was preferable to that, for Democracy would be worse in Russia than in any other country, the whole of it being mined by it."[1] The Queen then urged on the Prime Minister that Wellesley should be sent back with the confidential message for the Tsar, "that we will not allow him to go to Constantinople, and that that would be a *casus belli*".[2] She fully realised "the almost insuperable difficulties" of concealing such a mission from Lord Derby, fearing that these tactics might easily lead the Tsar to discover "that there is a division in the Cabinet".[3] But this did not worry the Prime Minister, and the whole affair was deliberately concealed from Foreign Secretary and Foreign Office.

This fact and the instructions given to him are made absolutely clear in Colonel Wellesley's own memorandum, as submitted to and approved by Beaconsfield.[4] He was to assure the Tsar of Britain's desire to promote speedy peace "on terms honourable to Russia". "Should, however, the war be prolonged and a second campaign undertaken, the neutrality of England could not be maintained, and she would take her part as a belligerent." The general argument was reinforced by two highly questionable statements, which do not

[1] Journal for 8 Aug.—*Letters*, ii. pp. 560-61.
[2] 9 Aug., to Beaconsfield—*ibid.* p. 562.
[3] 17 Aug., published *in extenso* by Mr. Buckle, vi. pp. 174-7.
[4] 14 Aug., to Beaconsfield—*Letters*, ii. p. 564.

redound to the credit of any of those concerned. In the first place, he was to deny the existence of "dissensions in the Cabinet, which would prevent active intervention. This is entirely false. The Cabinet is led by *one mind and has the entire support of the sovereign.*" This can hardly have deceived the Tsar, in view of Shuvalov's detailed and accurate reports of the true situation, and must have shown him both Queen and Premier in a somewhat equivocal light. In the second place, a rather crude attempt was made to hold Bismarck responsible for having driven Russia into war, in contrast to Beaconsfield, "who has endeavoured to save her from it". Here again the Tsar cannot have been deceived for a moment, for he knew better the real mind of Bismarck and William I.

Wellesley performed his mission with success and contrived to avoid giving personal offence to the Tsar. But it may be said to have spurred the latter on to all the greater efforts to finish the war before the winter checked operations, and thus to avert the dangers inseparable from a second campaign. Meanwhile the Queen's zeal continued unabated and she repeatedly denounced this "iniquitous war of extermination", in which Russia merely used "the cloak of religion" to secure concessions for "the so-called 'Christians' of the Principalities, but who are far worse than the Mussulmans". By this time she had learned from her Prime Minister to refer to "the so-called 'Bulgarian atrocities' " in inverted commas![1]

It has already been shown that the designs for preventing a second campaign against Turkey originated with Layard, and the latter's stocks rose during August, both at home and abroad, as the result of a sudden and severe reverse at Plevna, following upon a period of very real panic at the Porte. By the end of the month Layard was able to report, "our influence here is now re-established beyond what I could possibly have hoped": and he and his wife were invited "to dine in a quiet way" with Abdul Hamid—a complete "departure from Imperial and Mussulman etiquette".[2]

Serbia again prepares for War

Osman Pasha's heroic defence of Plevna definitely held up the Russian advance and produced a certain lull in Europe. A fresh assault on 11 September—St. Alexander Nevski, the Tsar's name-day

---

[1] Memo. of 7 Sept.—*Letters*, ii. p. 567.
[2] *Layard Papers*, 29 Aug., Layard to Beaconsfield.

—was repelled with a loss of 30,000 men, and the situation was increasingly saved by the hitherto despised Roumanians and the military qualities of Prince Charles.

The increasingly important part played by Roumania in the crisis was not unnaturally viewed with mixed feelings in Serbia, who, since the Skupština accepted peace on the basis of the *status quo* on 28 February, had been condemned to a precarious, almost humiliating, neutrality and began to fear that she might be omitted or neglected in the final settlement. When Russia declared war, the Tsar, true to his unfavourable verdict on the Serbs, warned Belgrade that he expected strict neutrality on their part. In June Prince Milan and Jovan Ristić paid a visit of courtesy to the Tsar at his headquarters in Roumania, in the hope that Serbia might be allowed to resume hostilities in the direction of Vidin and Sofia. But they were given to understand that they must keep the peace, and above all do nothing to offend Austria-Hungary: indeed the Tsar used a high tone towards Milan, and his categorical phrase—"*Il ne me convient point, entendez-moi bien, que la Serbie poursuive une politique d'action*"— was repeated by Colonel Mansfield, the British Agent in Bucarest, to his Austrian colleague in Belgrade, Prince Wrede, and reported with much satisfaction to Vienna.[1] Wrede had the impression that Milan had been "browbeaten" by the Tsar,[2] and in his next audience found him employing cautious language about the paternal advice which he had received and "the folly and presumption" of any Serbian action without full Russian sanction.[3] But as a result his position in the country was once more exceedingly difficult, there were stormy scenes in Parliament, and the Government actually took the drastic step of cutting the communications between the capital and Kragujevac—the little provincial town where the session was being held— in order to prevent public knowledge of what was occurring.[4] Meanwhile the Conservative leader Marinović took the extraordinary step of a direct appeal to Andrássy, arguing that it would suffice for Austria-Hungary to make it known that she would not permit the renewal of hostilities by Serbia, in order to stop the ferment.[5] Andrássy and Wrede were at one in disregarding this, feeling that they could adopt a passive and waiting attitude, so long as the Tsar

---

[1] *Austrian Archives* (unpublished), no. 62, 28 June, Wrede to Andrássy.
[2] "Quelque peu malmené."   [3] *Austrian Archives*, no. 63.
[4] *Ibid.* nos. 67 (9 July) and 68 (14 July).
[5] *Ibid. lettre particulière* of Wrede to Andrássy, 15 Aug., enclosing letter of Marinović to Andrássy.

played their game by discouraging the Serbs. Meanwhile the jumpiness of such public opinion as existed in Serbia compelled the Government to continue certain military preparations, and the British Agent-General, Mr. William White, came to suspect Russia of changing her tactics and, after the third repulse before Plevna, of welcoming Serbian co-operation. On 25 August, therefore, on Lord Derby's orders, he communicated to Ristić the British Government's view that Serbia, if she resumed hostilities, would be committing a breach of faith towards both the Porte and the guaranteeing Powers, and need expect no further help from Britain.[1] Meanwhile the Prince's uncle, Colonel Catargiu, a Roumanian in the Russian service, was negotiating at the headquarters of the Grand Duke Nicholas, but found it difficult to extract any commitments or even to arouse much active interest, and was consumed with jealousy at the contrast with the position acquired by Prince Charles of Roumania.

Meanwhile Derby asked Andrássy whether he was disposed to hold back Serbia, and received the equivocal answer that if Serbia began "a revolutionary war", he would occupy Bosnia, and that he had told Russia that the entry of her troops into Serbia would be "a breach of the treaties".[2] Derby doubtless understood this (as Andrássy had intended) to be a reference to the settlement of 1856, whereas of course it was really a subtle invocation of Reichstadt and Budapest, of which Derby knew nothing.

The Serbian situation may be summed up very briefly. It was generally felt that Russia's entry had transformed the whole Eastern problem beyond recognition; that in view of Serbia's vital interests and after all her initial sacrifices the settlement could not be allowed to take place without her; that further inaction might easily cost Prince Milan his throne: and that as a Russian victory was now almost certain, intervention was less of a gamble than at any previous stage. Wrede regarded Milan as ready to become "a Russian satrap", and had undoubtedly taken his measure when reporting that his attachment to his native land was not unbounded, and that he would soon console himself with life on the boulevards of Paris and other European capitals. Anti-dynastic feeling was rife, and there was even wild talk of Serbia's absorption in the neighbouring monarchy.

Neither the internal situation nor the foreign policy of Serbia were clearly understood in London. Layard in his letters home fulminated

---

[1] *Ibid.* no. 89.
[2] *R.B.D.* vii. no. 246, Shuvalov to Gorchakov, 14 Aug.

against "those faithless little states" Serbia and Greece [1] and, assuming quite correctly that Prince Milan wished to join the Russians, told Beaconsfield that *"the only thing to be done is to get up a revolution in the Principality and to put Karageorge against Milan,* promising the former Little Zvornik and other concessions if he prove successful. This the Grand Vizier is ready to do, but he wants some money. If the Turks could only get a loan, they could do much, and would fight Russia with her own weapons." [2]

Meanwhile Lord Beaconsfield expressed to Count Beust his annoyance at Andrássy not ordering mobilisation against the Serbs, and told him bluntly: "If you let the Russians march through Serbia, I regard our mutual agreement at an end and shall go my own way". [3] Needless to say, this attitude did not disturb Andrássy, who knew the Tsar's real sentiments and had in his pocket the secret convention, one of whose clauses expressly debarred both Austria-Hungary and Russia from sending troops to Serbia. [4]

During this same conversation Beaconsfield committed himself to several remarkable statements. Doubtless realising Beust's ancient hostility to Bismarck, he confessed his own conviction that the latter had encouraged Russia to make war, in order to leave Germany free for an attack upon France. Finally, losing all restraint, he treated Beust to the following amazing outburst. *"I find Bismarck everywhere in my way.* What does this fancied omnipotence mean? *The man is an European pest.* I have far less against Russia than against Bismarck, and I am determined to oppose him." [5] It is safe to assume that this greatly strengthened Andrássy in his extreme reserve towards London.

---

[1] *Layard Papers,* 29 Aug., to Derby.   [2] *Ibid.* 29 Aug., to Beaconsfield.
[3] Wertheimer, *Graf Andrássy,* iii. p. 48.
[4] On 5 June we find M. de Ring, French Chargé in Vienna, informing his Government of the existence of an Austro-Russian Convention containing a mutual pledge not to occupy Serbian territory—*D.D.F.* ii. no. 181.
[5] 15 Aug., Beust to Andrássy—Wertheimer, *op. cit.* iii. pp. 49-50.

CHAPTER VII

THE GROWTH OF CABINET DISSENSIONS

"Through the official system of suppressing all information until it is useless, England happily knows not what end he [Count Shuvalov] is pursuing, or what fatal Anglo-Russian understanding he is maturing with the amiable co-operation of our Foreign Office. But some day this also will be known, and it will be seen that the advent and maintenance of Count Schouvaloff as Ambassador from Russia was a turning-point in English history."

JEHU JUNIOR, in *Vanity Fair*, 13 Feb. 1875

THROUGHOUT September the Prime Minister, egged on by Layard[1] and encouraged by Turkish resistance, continued to press for action. "The country", he told Lord Derby, "is every day getting more Turkish", events were proving Turkey's right to "remain among the sovereign Powers of the world", and there was "no clear evidence that a better government than the Ottoman can be established in the regions in question"[2]—a remark signally disproved by the subsequent course of history.

Granville's estimate of opinion was not dissimilar: "I am afraid Chauvinism is rampant at this moment," he wrote to Gladstone, "and I believe if the Russians had been more successful, Dizzy might possibly have had his way".[3]

Beaconsfield, then, summoned the Cabinet for 5 October and laid before it a concrete proposal of intervention. His main object being to prevent at all costs a second campaign, he suggested that "the settlement of Bulgaria, on the basis of the Protocol of London" and the restoration of southern Bessarabia to Russia would be sufficient concessions to the latter, and that if Turkey accepted and Russia then rejected them, "we should depart from our present position of neutrality and inform Russia that if Constantinople be menaced, England would afford material assistance to Turkey to prevent its seizure".[4] He was fully justified in describing this as "a clear and precise policy", but it would almost certainly have involved war and hence met with definite opposition from Derby, Salisbury, Carnarvon

---

[1] He told Lady Bradford of his "secret correspondence" with Layard, but warned her not to mention the fact. 6 Sept.—Buckle, vi. p. 179.

[2] *Ibid.* p. 177, 1 Sept.   [3] *Gladstone Papers*, 7 Sept., Granville to Gladstone.

[4] 28 Sept., to Derby—Buckle, p. 182.

and Northcote: and it was eventually decided that no "active step" could be taken "while the campaign was not concluded".[1] Both Beaconsfield and the Queen were much disappointed, but there was now little or nothing to be done save to await military developments in the Near East. During October Beaconsfield felt "very ill",[2] and told Lady Bradford that "if it were not for the Faery", he "certainly would at once retire".[3]

Beaconsfield's hesitations at this time are clearly reflected in the letter which he addressed to Layard on 11 October.[4] He doubts the utility of an appeal by the Sultan to the signatories of 1856, on the ground that "no power is for peace except England". He feels that England "cannot offer to mediate unless solicited by one of the belligerents", but he is ready to consider an "outline of terms", sketched by Turkey, approved by England and recommended by her to Russia. "If Russia refused, she would put herself much more in the wrong, and if the terms were publicly acknowledged by England as just and satisfactory, *it would be very difficult for us to adhere to our present neutrality*. Opinion at home would force us to action."

He recognises, however, that such terms "must to a certain degree study the *amour-propre* of Russia" and asks Layard's opinion on possible Turkish concessions, such as the restoration of "the Bessarabian bit" to Russia, and the transfer of the suzerainty of Roumania to Austria! This is as far as he can bring himself to go. "Servia must be left alone, she deserves no consideration", and "as for Montenegro, the *uti possidetis* might be accepted." The Sultan must have "the complete military command of Bulgaria", and all provinces must be "governed by his nominees". "Great as the struggle and effort have been for him, it is fortunate that he had no allies. He has proved his independence and may yet secure the integrity of his dominions."

Beaconsfield is careful to insist that this is "not the letter of a Minister so much as of an individual who sympathises with your views and entirely approves of your conduct": but he is ready to recommend these suggestions to the Cabinet, if Layard finds them "feasible".

Layard replied that the Prime Minister's letter was a great comfort to him. "An acquaintance with even your personal opinions cannot be but of immense advantage to me, *as I am without general in-*

---

[1] Beaconsfield to Queen, 6 Oct.—Buckle, p. 184.
[2] 23 Oct.—*ibid.* p. 190.   [3] 25 Oct.—*ibid.* p. 191.
[4] *Layard Papers*, 11 Oct., Beaconsfield to Layard.

structions for my guidance." He feared that the Turks, left to themselves, might be forced into "a direct understanding with Russia", and suspected his German colleague of working for this. But he thought that the Sultan might not be indisposed to restore Bessarabia, and quoted the Grand Vizier as favouring the transfer of Roumania to Austria: "but would Russia consent to the placing of such a barrier between herself and her prey?"[1] This was in no sense a concrete programme, and as the winter drew in and the Russian grip upon Plevna tightened, Beaconsfield remained as Turcophil as ever, but could not stand up alone against a lethargic or doubting Cabinet, an excited Opposition, and a deeply suspicious public opinion.

BEACONSFIELD AND SHUVALOV

A small incident at this time admirably illustrates the profound distrust with which every Russian statement was regarded. Beaconsfield during a week-end at Brighton met Shuvalov and duly reported to the Queen the stress which the ambassador laid on the existence of a secret Austro-Russian convention, despite Andrássy's formal denial through Beust. "He had seen it. He had been severely called to account on his last fruitless visit to St. Petersburg for having let the cat out of the bag, as it was agreed that it should be kept a secret from Beust": and he appears to have justified this calculated indiscretion "on the ground that it was only by such a communication he could induce the English Government to act with energy on Turkey".[2] The Prime Minister summarised Shuvalov's "singular monologue", but obviously remained unconvinced and preferred to believe Beust, who continued to uphold his denial of "any convention between the three Empires"—for instance to Gathorne Hardy at the end of October.[3]

It is but fair to add that there was one Englishman who penetrated Andrássy's mind, but whose violent manner of presenting the facts may have had the same negative effect as the distrust felt towards Shuvalov's calculated indiscretions. A few months later Layard wrote to Derby of Andrássy's "double and dishonest game. I cannot resist the conviction that he looks to the annexation of Bosnia and Herzegovina, and that he has a secret understanding on the subject with the Russians. He is afraid to show his game too soon for fear of

[1] *Ibid.* 31 Oct.   [2] 10 Oct., to Queen—Buckle, vi. p. 186.
[3] Diary, 29 Oct.—*Life of Gathorne Hardy*, ii. p. 34.

the Hungarians. He will not declare himself until it is too late for them to interfere. . . . If Austria, cowardly and short-sighted, is ready to hold her tongue and to gnaw the bone which will be thrown to her, there will be no means of preventing the Turks acceding to anything."[1] But Layard, despite such shrewd guesses at a carefully guarded truth, often went off the rails in his verdicts, and in particular completely misjudged Bismarck's policy, telling Beaconsfield that his bugbear Reuss was "as much a Russian agent as Ignatyev was".

"Seven Parties" in a Cabinet of Twelve

The classic illustration of the divisions that now riddled the Cabinet and kept it upon mainly negative lines is provided by Beaconsfield's astonishing memorandum of 3 November, in which he confessed to the Queen that *"in a Cabinet of twelve members there are seven parties or policies"*. These he proceeded to define as follows: (1) "The war party pure and simple", which favoured immediate material help to the Turks—Gathorne Hardy, Manners, Hicks Beach, and Ward Hunt, who died soon after; (2) those ready to make war "if Russia will not engage not to occupy Constantinople"—Cairns, Cross, W. H. Smith, and the Duke of Richmond; (3) the party prepared for war "if after the signature of peace the Russians will not evacuate Constantinople"—Salisbury; (4) "the party of peace at any price"— Derby; (5) "the party which disapproves of any policy avowedly resting on what are called 'British interests', which is considered 'a selfish policy' "—this, the view of Sir Stafford Northcote, is dismissed by Beaconsfield as "utterly futile" and "approaching silliness"; (6) the party of "Constantinople for Russia", led by Carnarvon, Liddon, Freeman and "other priests and professors".

"The seventh policy", he went on, "is that of Your Majesty, and which will be introduced and enforced to his utmost by the Prime Minister—viz. that *in the first place, the Cabinet shall decide upon something*, and, if so, that the something shall consist of a notification to Russia, that . . . British neutrality cannot be depended on for another campaign, unless Your Majesty's Government receives a written engagement from Russia, that under no circumstances will

---

[1] *Layard Papers*, Layard to Derby, 14 Nov. 1877. On 21 Nov. he wrote to Lyons, "Andrássy's conduct is inexplicable except on the supposition that he has a secret understanding with Russia": and on 28 Nov. he repeated this view in a letter to Derby (*ibid.*). He also realised that "Andrássy does not trust Beust and is afraid that anything confided to him may leak out in England" (*ibid.* 17 Oct., to Derby).

she occupy Constantinople or the Dardanelles"—this pledge to be secret.[1]

It is amusing to compare Beaconsfield's summary for the private eye of the Queen with a contemporary version which he appears to have given to Sir Stafford Northcote. In this latter there are only six parties. Northcote's own "utterly futile" party is naturally omitted, and Northcote is now honourably grouped with the Prime Minister himself as one of the two "who desire to see something done, but don't know exactly what"![2]

The Cabinet appears to have accepted Beaconsfield's proposal in theory, but he dared not press for definite action in the event of a Russian refusal, as that "would at once break up the Cabinet". Small wonder, then, if the decision remained merely on paper, though the Queen demanded that Derby and Northcote should be overruled, and that "No Second Campaign" must remain "the Shibboleth of England".[3]

Lord Derby kept his hands firmly on the brakes, hoping, as his wife confided to Lord Carnarvon, "that a kind of dogged resistance will prevail against his wonderful chief".[4] Throughout this time Lady Derby played a decisive rôle behind the scenes, encouraging him in his pacific attitude and collaborating with all who shared it. Montagu Corry, the Premier's private secretary, saw this in a somewhat different light and reported to his chief, "I gather from my lady D[erby]. that our friend is as resolute as ever to keep his hands in his pockets".[5]

Meanwhile Gladstone made periodic, if less frequent, orations, but they made no impression upon the Gallio-like Hartington, who wrote impatiently to Granville: "He never will be made to understand that people who listen to him and admire his speeches do not necessarily agree with him".[6] His own lukewarm and negative attitude is revealed in a later letter: "As to the East, I suppose I must defend what we have done: maintain our position that integrity of Turkey is not necessary to British interests: but is there any policy except that of neutrality (which the Government accept) which can be indicated?"[7] This is not leadership.

The annual Guildhall banquet revealed only too clearly the direction in which the Premier's mind was moving. While almost every

[1] 8 Nov., to Queen—Buckle, vi. pp. 194-5.
[2] A. Lang, *Life of Northcote*, ii. p. 106. [3] 5 Nov.—*Letters*, ii. p. 570.
[4] 8 Oct.—*Life of Carnarvon*, ii. p. 363. [5] 31 Oct.—Buckle, vi. p. 195.
[6] *Granville Papers*, 13 Oct. 1877, Hartington to Granville.
[7] *Ibid.* 29 Oct., Hartington to Granville.

member of the Cabinet attended, the Ambassadors of the five great Powers were conspicuous by their absence—so conspicuous that the Lord Mayor alluded somewhat naïvely to the fact: and thus it was left to the Turkish Ambassador, Musurus Pasha, to respond as doyen of the diplomatic corps, and to claim that Turkey was following England's example by establishing "a complete liberal constitution, based on free representation of all its peoples". His reception was an ominous feature of the evening and was followed by Beaconsfield's own speech, stressing the policy of "a conditional neutrality", which must cease if British interests were menaced. "Cosmopolitan critics," he said sneeringly, with an obvious hit at his party rival, "men who are friends of every country save their own, have denounced this as a selfish policy. . . . It is as selfish as patriotism." He then indulged in a warm tribute to Turkey. "For some years it had been a dogma of diplomacy that Turkey was a phrase and not a fact—its Government a phantom, its people effete. . . . In that case a repetition of what occurred in the Crimea would have been the greatest error. If a people is effete and a Government a mere fiction, why, the sooner that is proved in the eyes of the civilised world the better. You know what proof has been given on these subjects during the last year. The independence of Turkey is not doubted now." If the obvious inference was that a renewal of the Crimean experiment would no longer be such an error, he took care that his concluding phrases should be studiously vague. He laid strong emphasis on the Tsar's disclaimer of territorial conquest, paid a two-edged compliment to the feats of valour performed by the Russian army "even in defeat" and used the argument that the military prestige of Russia was not injured, in order to imply that the war might end without decisive victory. As to the issue of the war, Her Majesty's Government had "both hope and patience", which might mean almost anything. His real inner mind was revealed to Lady Bradford a few days earlier, when he wrote, "Plevna is our only chance".[1]

The press comments were not altogether reassuring, and the Continent showed its nervousness. The *Daily Telegraph*, as the most ardent of the Turcophil organs, held "that Turkey must feel animated by such powerful praise". Of special interest are the somewhat trenchant phrases of *The Times*. "If he thinks that because Osman Pasha has valiantly defended Plevna, the Turks have refuted the charges brought against their treatment of the Christian population, the

[1] 6 Nov.—Buckle, vi. p. 192.

opinion is interesting, but it can scarcely be commended as a specimen of sound political reasoning." "The Turks . . . are unchanged
amid universal change . . . wolves among sheep. . . . The domination
of the strong man has become intolerable and therefore impossible."

Gladstone, who had been on a visit to Ireland, voiced Liberal
opinion in a speech at Holyhead, pointing out that while the Guildhall pronouncement "represents Turkism in a very developed form",
its most notable feature is that it "drops entirely the integrity of the
Ottoman Empire". It was in this speech that he first declared publicly
—speaking as a devoted Anglican—that the cause of justice and
humanity had on this occasion "found its best supporters in the
Nonconformists".[1]

At the time nothing caused greater annoyance to supporters of
the Government than the suggestion that its members differed in
their views and outlook: but as we study their utterances in cold
blood after an interval of half a century, this profound divergence is
one of the outstanding factors. Nothing could be more unlike the
Prime Minister's pronouncements than those of Derby, Salisbury
and Carnarvon: and Derby's speech of 28 November was as reassuring as that of the Guildhall had been disturbing. He had to answer
a deputation from such bodies as the "Society for the Protection
of British Interests against Russian Aggression in the East", the
"Turkish Defence Association", and the Polish "Society of the White
Eagle", whose leaders, Lord Campbell, Sir Henry Hoare and others,
urged "a bold course at a critical moment", and disregard for "the
ravings of fanatics". Derby poured a surprising amount of cold water
on the successive theories that the true route to India lies through
the Euphrates valley, that Suez would be endangered by a Russian
occupation of Trebizond, that if the Afghans turned against us, all
the Moslems of India would join them, that Austria was "ready to
do something or other—it is not quite clear what", or finally, that
Constantinople was in immediate danger and that the fleet could be
sent there without the consent of the Porte. He ended as he had
begun, by denying any deviation, or intention of deviation, from the
original policy of "conditional neutrality". It is only necessary to
compare this with the quotations already given from the Prime
Minister, to realise how distasteful Derby's attitude must have been
to him and to the Queen.

Here, again, it is well worth quoting the comment of *The Times*

[1] *The Times,* 13 Nov. 1877.

next morning, which hits off to a nicety the whole Eastern agitation. "India depends on the command of the sea. As a way to India, the Euphrates is useless to any Power which does not hold the Persian Gulf. So long as we can close that narrow outlet, a Russian army might as well march towards our eastern Empire through the desert of the Sahara as along the Euphrates valley. Indeed it is difficult to speak with courtesy of the extravagances which are talked and written about the strategical importance of that road to the Persian Gulf." Yet this language was not a whit more extravagant than the phrases of the Prime Minister himself, as to the possibilities of warfare in Central Asia.

PLEVNA AND ITS REACTIONS

Meanwhile events were moving to a crisis. On 11 November came the fall of Kars, which was the end of serious Turkish resistance on the Asiatic front—"a great blow", Beaconsfield wrote to Lady Bradford: and though Suleiman Pasha inflicted one last check upon the Russians near Gorni Dubnik and so for a moment revived Beaconsfield's fading hope that Plevna might still be saved, it was by now obvious that the end could not be very long averted. The Tsar, forewarned by Shuvalov and indeed by Beaconsfield himself through Wellesley, was now resolved to avert the complications incident upon "a second campaign", by pushing the first to a victorious conclusion, if neces- sary in midwinter. It is probable that Beaconsfield realised by this time his tactical error, but it was only to the Queen that he could seriously advance the argument that "the whole of the Ottoman Empire is a British Interest", with a capital I.[1] Even he, however, seems to have felt that the country could hardly commit itself to the expulsion of Russia from Armenia.

Yet if Granville was rightly informed—and his source would seem to have been the French Ambassador—"Dizzy has been using the most violent language, telling the Ambassadors that he is desirous of peace, but that his hand will be forced by national feeling and that he will have to land 300,000 men in Turkey!!!"[2] And only a few weeks later Beaconsfield's ally Layard unburdened himself in a letter to the Viceroy in these modest terms: "If we lived in the days of Chatham or Pitt, I should say, if Russia attempts to annex Batum

[1] 7 Nov.—*Letters*, ii. p. 572.
[2] *Gladstone Papers*, 21 Nov. 1877, Granville to Gladstone.

or any part of Armenia, let England at once take possession of that port and of the Dardanelles and of the mouth of the Bosphorus, and hold them until Russia is driven back over the Caucasus and an independent state is formed between her and Persia. But in these days I fear that such heroic measures will not suit the spirit of Birmingham and Manchester."[1]

On 4 December the Cabinet met, and Lord Derby was asked to draft a Note to Russia, inviting her to give "a definite answer to our conditions of neutrality as to Constantinople and the Dardanelles".[2] But when the Prime Minister wished to make "the occupation, or rather *the menaced occupation*, of Constantinople a *casus belli*", Derby definitely demurred and was not in the least impressed by his chief's argument that Turkey was still "a powerful ally", with 400,000 well-armed men in the field and fair prospects of a loan from India.[3]

Plevna fell on 10 December, and the public excitement in England, which had died down during the summer deadlock, again rose to fever pitch. On the one side Osman Pasha's stubborn defence exalted him into a hero of the moment, though his treatment of wounded prisoners was the reverse of heroic, and Sandwith, who had exceptionable means for judging, spoke of him as "a great ruffian" and "a sulky savage".[4] On the other side the end of Turkish resistance, however gallant, was rightly hailed as the dawn of liberation for half the Balkan Peninsula and its completion for the rest.

On 13 December the much delayed Note to Russia was handed by Derby to Shuvalov, expressing the hope that neither Constantinople nor the Dardanelles would be occupied, since such a step would alarm British public opinion and "seriously endanger the good relations happily maintained between the two countries" (is it possible that no sarcasm was intended?) and Great Britain would then feel free to consult her own interests.[5] To this Gorchakov promptly and very convincingly replied that to let the Turks know of such a veto would be equivalent to encouraging them in their resistance, and thus might very easily force Russia into that very occupation of the capital which London was so anxious to avoid.

---

[1] *Layard Papers* (Add. MS. 39131), 2 Jan. 1878, Layard to Lytton.
[2] Lord John Manners to Queen, 4 Dec.—Buckle, vi. p. 198.
[3] Beaconsfield to Derby, 5 Dec.—*ibid.* p. 199.
[4] T. H. Ward, *Humphrey Sandwith*, p. 244.
[5] *R.B.D.* vii. no. 257, Shuvalov to Gorchakov, 29 Nov./11 Dec. Derby quoted this passage in the House of Lords, 4 Feb. 1878—Hansard, ccxxxvii. p. 919.

If, on the other hand, London made it clear to the Porte that no out-side help could be expected, it would accept the inevitable and submit.[1]

Before this answer could arrive, the Cabinet again met twice. Beaconsfield, without previous warning to any of his colleagues, proposed that Parliament should be summoned forthwith, "a con-siderable increase" in the army voted, and steps taken to mediate between the belligerents. This was opposed first by Carnarvon, then by Salisbury, who "could not assent" to the alliance with Turkey which such a proposal involved, and finally by Derby, who "entirely disapproved", complained that "he had been taken by surprise" and "was not prepared to look upon the occupation of Constantinople by the Russians as a *casus belli*".[2] When the discussion was resumed three days later, the Prime Minister "found half his Cabinet arrayed against him" and greatly alarmed the Queen by talking of resig-nation.[3]

At this point Sir Stafford Northcote set himself to mediate between the two Cabinet groups. "We cannot", he told Salisbury, "go on without a policy, with nothing but a *non possumus*, and a break-up . . . may lead to chaos and war."[4] To this Salisbury replied, "An active policy is only possible under one of two conditions—that you shall help the Turks or coerce them". He would accept the second method, or the two combined, but not the first alone, whereas the Queen and Prime Minister would not hear of the second and obvi-ously favoured the first. Derby's resignation at such a juncture, he contended, would cause "the utmost consternation", and while uniting the Opposition, would divide the nation into two camps.[5]

For the last time as it proved, Derby and Beaconsfield tried hard to reach a personal agreement, the latter writing a little note to express his dismay at the danger of being separated from his "old friend and teacher in public life".[6] When, then, the Cabinet met again on 17 December, a temporary compromise was reached: Parlia-ment was to be summoned for 17 January and to be asked for "a large increase of force", and the principle of mediation, at first opposed, was ultimately accepted even by Lord Derby.[7] The Prime Minister was exultant and told Lady Bradford: "On Monday night there was virtually no Government, but on Tuesday the recusants

[1] *R.B.D.* vii. no. 260, Gorchakov to Shuvalov, 16 Dec.
[2] Memo. of 14 Dec., for Queen—Buckle, p. 201.
[3] 17 Dec., to Queen—*ibid.* pp. 204-5.   [4] *Life of Salisbury*, ii. p. 163.
[5] Memo. reproduced in full—*ibid.* pp. 165-6.   [6] 17 or 18 Dec.—Buckle, p. 205.
[7] Memo. of 18 and letter of 19 Dec.—*ibid.* p. 206.

fell upon their knees and surrendered at discretion".[1] According to Granville, Salisbury was "in high spirits and considers the position to be exactly in accordance with his views".[2]

LAYARD'S DELICATE POSITION

While the fate of Plevna still hung in the balance, Layard wrote in a panic to his friend the Viceroy. "I am in very great anxiety. It is almost evident that the three Northern Empires have come to an understanding for the breaking-up and partition of Turkey. Italy has been offered and is ready to take her share in the spoils, and the jackals Roumania, Servia, Greece and Montenegro are waiting for the offal. England looks on hopeless and helpless. We have no policy, no definite views, consequently no influence, no power. We are reduced to this position by the unpatriotic and insensate conduct of Mr. Gladstone and the Liberal party. It has been said of Mr. Gladstone that after destroying his party he would destroy his country, and the prophecy may be verified."[3] To Derby he denounced a recent speech of Gladstone at Hawarden as "the most untruthful and discreditable utterance that ever came from an English statesman".[4]

After Plevna the Turkish Ambassador, Musurus Pasha, went to Beaconsfield and appealed for a loan to enable Turkey to enter upon a second campaign: and the Prime Minister "hinted at some territorial concession" as a guarantee. This was reported by the Foreign Minister, Server Pasha, to Layard, and the possibility of a British administration in Crete was discussed. Layard in a long secret letter to Beaconsfield discusses one by one the possibilities of territorial concession. "Neither Batum nor any other port in the Black Sea would be of much use to any Power that had not the permanent command of the Straits, except Russia": but Batum's conversion into a free port under guarantee of the Powers might provide a solution.

As for "a commanding position in the Persian Gulf" (Disraeli's own phrase) Layard could think of nothing answering that descrip-

[1] Buckle, vi. p. 207, 19 Dec., to Lady Bradford.
[2] *Gladstone Papers*, Granville to Gladstone, 25 Dec. 1877. On the 20th the French Ambassador gave to Granville an interesting version of what had happened. "D'Harcourt tells me that the belief of the Corps Diplomatique is that Dizzy proposed an ultimatum dispatch to Russia a fortnight ago, that it was rejected, that he pressed it again, with august support, this week, that it was still rejected, but the moderate members made a compromise of the meeting on the 17th and a demand for money"—*ibid.* Granville to Gladstone, 20 Dec. 1877.
[3] *Layard Papers*, 5 Dec., Layard to Lytton.
[4] *Ibid.* 5 Dec., Layard to Derby.

tion on Turkish territory. The island of Mohammorah, near the mouth of the Euphrates, would be suitable, but unluckily it belonged to Persia.

In his view "the Porte would not cede Crete, Cyprus or any other island. Crete has a splendid harbour, Suda, but would yield little or no revenue. Cyprus would be even of less use to us by all accounts. If we only want a good harbour, one can be found in the small island of Spadalia, which has been visited by some of our officers with that view."

Layard "quite agrees" with his chief "in thinking that if the Porte could be enabled to enter upon a second campaign and we could help it to get money to do so and could combine with it the presence of the English fleet in the Bosphorus and *a British army corps at Gallipoli and Derkos*, the result as to after negotiations might be great. But in order to accomplish this, we ought to abandon at once a hesitating and undefined policy. The Turks do not know what to make of us: we seem to them to blow hot and cold. They think that we take an interest in them and advise them for their good, but will abandon them at once, should Russia decline to listen to us, and that we are not ready even to make an effort in support of the most vital English interests. This language has been held to me by the Grand Vizier and Server Pasha and other Turks of high station." He again reverts to his suspicions against Reuss, whom he accuses of "seeking a kind of Monroe doctrine for the three Empires in Turkey". But "a firm and decisive policy on our part would scatter this kind of conspiracy against us to the winds: for it is founded on the presumption that England will resign herself to anything rather than run the risk of war".[1]

Layard by now was quite beside himself, and gave his undiluted views to Lytton. "It is the most monstrous piece of folly that we should be ready to sacrifice the most vital interests of our country, India, our position as a first-class Power, the influence that we have hitherto exercised in the cause of human liberty and civilisation, rather than stand shoulder to shoulder with the Turks, *because some Bashibazuks have murdered some worthless and unfortunate Bulgarians!*"[2] This is the old argument[3] of Elliot, which had roused Derby's ire in the autumn of 1876, but restated in a still more reckless form.

[1] *Layard Papers*, 26 Dec., Layard to Derby.
[2] *Ibid.* 2 Jan. 1878.   [3] *Supra*, p. 63.

So completely had prejudice ousted logic in Layard's mind that he complains of Derby's indifference to the alternative route to India, "when a ship sunk in the waterway, or a few pounds of dynamite judiciously placed in the banks might completely close the Suez Canal before we could hold up a finger to prevent it. And then where would we be?"[1] Did he in all seriousness mean that if a Russian spy had blown up the Canal, it would be possible for us to substitute a connection with India *via* Van? It was a poor compliment to Lytton that he should have been thought capable of swallowing such nonsense.

Beaconsfield continued to show the fullest sympathy for Layard's views. "If the Russians find a Plevna in Adrianople or anything like it, the Ottoman Empire may yet be saved. At the same time, although most anxious to effect that object, I strongly and earnestly recommend the Porte not to lose the opportunity of concluding a peace consistent with their existence as an independent Power of some importance. I have confidence in you at this trying moment, the most searching since 1815."[2]

Derby at once intimated to Layard the decision regarding Parliament, but at the same time bade him explain to the Turks that this "did not imply any intention to depart from the policy of conditional neutrality". At almost the same moment, however, Layard learned from the Sultan that Lord Beaconsfield "had himself suggested to Musurus Pasha an appeal from the Porte to the British Government for their mediation, hinting they would be prepared to offer mediation, even if left alone by the other Powers, and that if Russia refused the offer, and persisted in continuing the war, England would then proceed to take other measures to bring it to an end. The difference between this and the official communication which I was authorised by Lord Derby to make to the Porte with respect to the early meeting of Parliament was a sufficient proof, if any further proof were required, of the *divergence of opinion which existed between the two leading members of the Cabinet* and perplexed me not a little as to the course I should pursue. *The Sultan was greatly delighted* with Lord Beaconsfield's language and *at once counted upon armed support* from England at no very distant period."[3]

In transmitting to the Prime Minister the Sultan's gratitude for the suggestions to Musurus, Layard pointedly added: "I did not like

[1] *Layard Papers*, 2 Jan. 1878, Layard to Lytton.
[2] *Ibid.* 20 Dec., Beaconsfield to Layard.
[3] *Ibid.* (Br. Mus. Add. MSS. 38935), Memoirs, vol. v. p. 308.

to raise hopes that might not be fulfilled, and confined myself to acquainting him with Lord Derby's telegram". On the same day he wrote to the Foreign Secretary begging for "any private hint that may guide me in the very difficult and anxious task that I have before me. It is not easy to avoid the dangers which I have to contend with, in not encouraging or discouraging the Turks too much. To encourage them might lead to hopes which may end in bitter disappointment or might commit H.M.G. To discourage them at this moment might seriously compromise our interests and even the peace of Europe, by driving them into the arms of Russia." [1] This proves two things—the extent to which our Ambassador at the key position in Europe was left in the dark as to his Government's policy, and—in common fairness be it added—his own genuine desire neither to mislead the Turks nor to outrun his orders.

No wonder that Layard—as he tells us in his unpublished Memoirs —should at this juncture have entertained doubts as to his own mission. "Without definite instructions, knowing that a grave division of opinion existed in the Cabinet, unacquainted except through what I could gather from a few private letters from Lord Beaconsfield, my task was a most arduous and delicate one. An enormous amount of personal responsibility was thrown upon me. . . . I had to encourage the Turks without encouraging them, to lead the Porte (to think) that it could expect no help from us, whilst leading it to believe that we were determined to step in when our interests were seriously threatened, to maintain my personal influence over the Sultan and his advisers whilst almost every communication I was instructed to make to them tended to destroy it." [2]

ATTEMPTS AT MEDIATION

The situation was still further complicated when on 14 December Serbia declared war upon Turkey for the second time, and Prince Milan, in his proclamation to the nation made a flimsy pretence at shifting the onus of violation on to Turkish shoulders, and openly put forward a programme of liberation and independence. This natur-

[1] *Layard Papers*, Layard to Derby, 26 Dec.
[2] *Ibid.* Memoirs, vol. v. He adds: "I cannot complain of any want of support from H.M.G. or from Lord Derby. My action in all the intricate important and delicate matters with which I had to deal was without one exception fully approved. I received from them publicly and privately the handsomest testimony to the value they attached to my services. . . . And nevertheless my position was by no means an enviable one."

ally made a disingenuous impression upon those Powers who a year earlier had held back the Turks from imposing their will upon helpless Serbia: but it could not justify the violent language of Layard, who denounced the Serbian attack as "the most dastardly and villainous act ever committed by a people—one who had been treated with unheard-of kindness and generosity by the Turks".[1] In reality the facts of the situation had not changed, and the national motives of the Serbs were overwhelming. Their Bosnian kinsmen were still holding out in the mountains, the Montenegrins were successfully holding the Turks at bay, Prince Nicholas was in a fair way to outtrumping his Obrenović rival, and there was imminent danger of the Bosnian question, on which Serbia's whole future was felt to depend, being settled without her and against her. But to such considerations neither Layard nor his chief were amenable.

Meanwhile the Porte had appealed for the intervention of the Powers, and when this had been rejected by Germany and Austria-Hungary—the latter in pursuance of her secret pledge at Budapest —the Sultan addressed himself to Great Britain, and the appeal was not merely instantly accepted, but also made public in the press. On the 24th Derby informed Layard that the hope of joint mediation had been spoilt by Germany, and this dispatch was published in the second of the twenty or thirty Blue Books issued during 1878.

Bismarck's attitude all this time was perfectly simple. He told Russell that Germany could not mediate at the suggestion of *one* belligerent, but he placed on record his private view that he could not mediate on behalf of Turkey, because Russia as a neighbour was so infinitely more important to Germany.[2]

The Queen's old frenzy now revived: she bade the Prime Minister be "very firm and decided" and not give way even if Derby resigned: for "England will *never* stand (not to speak of her sovereign) to become subservient to Russia, for she would then fall down from her high position and become a second-rate Power".[3] Beaconsfield's closing message for the year was that he "adopts Your Majesty's motto, BE FIRM".[4]

On 27 December Derby, fortified by the Sultan's sanction, instructed Lord Augustus Loftus to offer Britain's good offices, in the hope that Russia "will see a proof of her sincere desire to prevent

---

[1] *Ibid.* 19 Dec., Layard to Admiral Hornby.
[2] *G.P.* ii. nos. 298 (25 Nov.), 299 (15 Dec.) and 300 (3 Jan.).
[3] 13 Dec.—*Letters*, ii. p. 576.   [4] *Ibid.* p. 582.

further bloodshed". Gorchakov replied with studied politeness, that Russia desired nothing better than to arrive at peace, but that for this purpose "the Porte must address itself to the Imperial Commanders-in-Chief in Europe and Asia".[1]

The decision to summon Parliament earlier than usual was criticised somewhat captiously by the Opposition, as liable to be misconstrued abroad and to increase the risk of war : while supporters of the Government argued that it would have been more logical to demand an early summons, so that the voice of the nation might express itself through the constitutional channel. Both sides were a little insincere in this: for the reason of their respective eagerness and reluctance lay in the fact that the Liberals were far weaker and more divided inside the House than on the hustings! Meanwhile the Liberals openly rejoiced at Turkey's defeat. "I wish Turkey *down*, and no patching", wrote Argyll to Gladstone.[2]

Gladstone expressed to Granville the fear that the Prime Minister "will renew his machinations in the worst form of which circumstances, as then developed, may admit", and will secure "huge votes of men and money to back our mediating character". He was even prepared "for the contingency of a dissolution if the House of Commons does not fully support the Government. B. if he is to disappear, would rather disappear in flame and stench, and I agree in thinking he would have a chance, though not a very good one if every man does his duty."[3]

THE BREACH BETWEEN DERBY AND DISRAELI

It was at this critical moment that the breach between Foreign Secretary and Prime Minister became irreparable, and that each made a separate appeal to Lord Salisbury, who had come to occupy what may be called the central key position in the Cabinet, and now found himself faced by a choice momentous no less from the political than from the personal point of view. Derby, not without abundant reason, by this time suspected his chief of warlike designs and was alarmed at the phrase which he had let fall in the Cabinet itself— "The country is asleep and I want to wake it". His main concern was

[1] *Turkey No. II.* (1878), Correspondence *re* Overtures for Peace, nos. 11 and 15. On 21 Dec. Musurus to Derby "referred more than once to the possibility of British intervention" (*ibid.* p. 3.)
[2] *Gladstone Papers*, 19 Dec. 1877.
[3] *Granville Papers*, 19 Dec., Gladstone to Granville.

to ensure "that nothing shall be done without the Cabinet being consulted", and to "keep military preparations within bounds". He complained that the Prime Minister "believes thoroughly in 'prestige'—as all foreigners do, and would think it quite sincerely in the interests of the country to spend two hundred millions on a war, if the result of it was to make foreign states think more highly of us as a military power".[1] Such an outlook he assumed to conform as little to Salisbury's as to his own. There is a special piquancy in the phrase "as all foreigners do": it shows the breach to be final between this typical English aristocrat and his enigmatic and brilliant, but essentially un-English chief.

Salisbury wrote a brief, impersonal and guarded reply, not responding to the appeal and not even mentioning Beaconsfield's name.[2] The explanation doubtless lies in his equivocal position between two fires: for though the Prime Minister's overture to him only took place two days later, it could not have been made at all, if he had not realised that the distance between himself and Salisbury was steadily diminishing. On Christmas Eve, then, Beaconsfield sent on to him a letter of Colonel Wellesley, containing the warning that the Tsar was being kept fully informed of the innermost secrets of the British Cabinet, and urging that a favourable moment had arrived for the "inevitable" war with Russia. The Prime Minister was obviously disconcerted at this news of leakage, and starting from the assumption that "every resolution of every council is regularly reported by Count Shuvalov", proceeded to argue that "we must put an end to all this gossip about war parties and peace parties in the Cabinet, and must come to decisions which may be, and will be, betrayed, but which may convince Russia that we are agreed and determined. You and I must go together into the depth of the affair and settle what we are prepared to do."

Salisbury in his reply challenged Wellesley's theory of an inevitable war. Russia, he contended, was not so exhausted as to be unable to resist England, Turkey was now of little value as an ally, the Indian army was not ready, industry was "depressed and profoundly averse to war", Austria "our natural ally, has been seduced from us", with the result that war would be "unpopular and unprofitable". The whole tone shows readiness to co-operate, but far greater restraint and grasp of the decisive facts, and it leaves the direct appeal unanswered.

[1] 23 Dec.—*Life of Salisbury*, ii. pp. 170-71.   [2] *Ibid.* p. 172.

The key probably lies in the delicate question of leakage. Both men must for a long time past have been aware that Shuvalov drew much of his inside information from no other source than Lord and Lady Derby, with whom his relations had grown steadily closer during 1877. Under no circumstances would the historian be justified in passing this over in silence: for whatever view may be taken of their action, and of the grave responsibility which they incurred, it was beyond all question an important factor in averting disaster and was prompted by the most honourable and patriotic motives. But nothing illustrates better the abnormal situation which had grown up during the closing months of 1877, and the deep cleavage wrought by the Eastern controversy, not merely between the rival parties, but even between old associates within each party. Apart from a close political partnership of many years between the three Conservative leaders, Lady Derby was the stepmother of Lord Salisbury: she had in former days often been Disraeli's hostess at Hatfield and was in the inner councils of the party.[1] She, perhaps even more than her husband, had become convinced of the dangers involved in Beaconsfield's policy, and at the same time realised that Shuvalov, for a whole number of motives, was straining every nerve for peace and earnestly working to promote Russo-British friendship. She was probably strengthened in this attitude by Lord Carnarvon, who put to her the argument that a firm alliance between the three friends—her husband, Salisbury and himself—would checkmate even a majority in the Cabinet.[2] With the Cabinet meeting following upon the fall of Plevna, both were agreed that at last a critical point had been reached, especially after "the unparalleled communication from the Queen": and Lady Derby wrote her view, which gives us a clue to her and her husband's action throughout the winter: "I believe Lord Derby *holds the key of the position and can save the country from war by remaining*".[3]

SALISBURY AND CARNARVON

Salisbury, then, still occupies a middle position, and we may assume is torn by rival loyalties, complicated by the inevitable

[1] Cf. Buckle, v. pp. 455, 495, and *R.B.D.* ii. no. 55, "une femme politique qui discute les affaires avec M. Disraeli et son mari", is Shuvalov's description when he begins to obtain information from Lady Derby.

[2] 18 Oct.—*Life of Carnarvon*, ii. p. 363.　　　[3] 15 Dec.—*ibid*. p. 365.

perception that the issue must in large part depend upon him. He is drawing steadily away not only from Derby, but from his more intimate associate Carnarvon, whose distrust of Beaconsfield, already acute in the previous March, has now reached a note of shrill hostility. On 2 January, when receiving a deputation at the Colonial Office, he publicly referred to the manner in which the country had drifted into the Crimean War, as something which few could now regard with satisfaction. "And I am confident", he added, "that there is nobody insane enough to desire a repetition of it"—though it was by now only too notorious that both the Prime Minister and the Queen were perfectly ready to risk it. Carnarvon himself has placed on record that such a speech was only justified by the conviction of himself "and *many of my colleagues*, that Disraeli was determined to force us into an alliance with Turkey and a war with Russia, and that there-fore almost any sacrifice was worth making to avoid an act of in-justice, immorality and grave impolicy".[1]

Next day Carnarvon was received at the Cabinet with "black looks from all except Derby", and strongly censured by the Prime Minister, though still defended by Salisbury. "A terrible escapade —a speech worthy of Gladstone", was Beaconsfield's characteristic comment, and to the Queen he went so far as to write of "his disloyal colleague".[2] The Queen, however, required no prompting. She had already in November expressed herself as shocked at Carnarvon's views, wondering how he "*can* think true religion and civilisation can be advanced by Russians who are more barbarous and cruel almost than the Turks".[3] She now proceeded to lecture him at some length upon his "lamentable" behaviour and "extreme imprudence", and ended by informing him that the line of policy which he advo-cated was "*most* detrimental to the position of her great Empire . . . and calculated to prevent peace by encouraging Russia, our worst enemy, in her policy of ambitious aggression and duplicity".[4]

Very different, of course, was the view of the Opposition leaders, and Granville wrote to Gladstone that Carnarvon's speech "came in the nick of time", and that "Dizzy is furious with him".[5] Lord

[1] *Life of Carnarvon*, ii. pp. 369-71.   [2] 4 Jan.—*Letters*, ii. p. 587.
[3] 5 Nov., to Beaconsfield—*ibid.* p. 569.
[4] 4 Jan., Queen to Carnarvon—*ibid.* pp. 588-9.
[5] *Gladstone Papers*, Granville to Gladstone, 7 Jan. 1878. Harcourt, writing to Granville a day earlier, used this very phrase: "The Carnarvon incident came in the very nick of time. It has, I think, decided *The Times* on the right side, and has given heart to many others who were wavering."—*Granville Papers*, 6 Jan. Harcourt to Granville.

Bath interpreted the speech as "a cry of alarm, intended to explain that there is a party inside the Cabinet resisting evil and asking for support. . . . I have repeated assurances that the Cabinet as a whole are opposed to war. Yet there can be little doubt that they had consented to proceedings that brought the danger of war nearer."[1]

How little even the Conservative rank and file realised what was happening behind the scenes is shown by the strong approval bestowed upon Carnarvon's "timely speech" by such organs as the *Standard*[2] and the *Globe*.[3] Clearly, they had no inkling of Beaconsfield's and the Queen's fury with Carnarvon. Yet there was a deep division of opinion inside the Cabinet, and Lady Gwendolen Cecil in no way exaggerates when she describes it as having "paralysed action".[4]

The confusion inside the Cabinet was indeed greater than ever. Salisbury begged Carnarvon not to resign—as Beaconsfield definitely hoped he would—except "on a broad issue of policy clearly raised", and not to act upon "a rude phrase by a man whose insolence is proverbial".[5] For the moment, then, the quarrel was patched up, and Beaconsfield, relapsing into the style of Tancred or Coningsby, announced to the Queen that "except brave John Manners and haughty Sir Michael . . . all his colleagues are on their knees to Lord Carnarvon to stay. The Cabinet wants a little of Your Majesty's fire."[6]

From 4 January onwards there were constant meetings of the Cabinet—"it really sits *en permanence*", he told Lady Chesterfield on the 22nd[7]—and it was only with the utmost difficulty that agreement could be reached as to the text of the impending Speech from the Throne.

SHUVALOV AND THE OPPOSITION

It was at this stage that an incident occurred which throws most valuable light upon the attitude of the Opposition leaders. They had by now fallen into three main groups. The Radicals kept to themselves, and though tempted to rally round Gladstone as leader, were doubtful as to his Whig propensities. Gladstone remained at Hawarden, somewhat out of touch with events and in no way contemplating

---

[1] *Gladstone Papers*, Bath to Gladstone, 6 Jan. [2] 5 Jan.   [3] 3 and 5 Jan.
[4] *Life of Salisbury*, ii. p. 171.   [5] 8 Jan.—*ibid.*, ii. p. 175.
[6] Buckle, vi. p. 215.   [7] *Ibid.* p. 216.

his return to power.[1] Granville and Hartington were increasingly negative in their attitude to the Eastern Question, and embarrassed by the activities of Gladstone, to whom, however, Granville retained far more cordial relations than his colleagues in the Commons.

The most confident and active of them all at this time was Sir William Harcourt, who was in closest touch with the two Whig leaders, but disapproved of Gladstone, although of all the public utterances of 1878, his own coincide most closely with those of Gladstone.[2] On Christmas Eve he expressed to Granville the view that the Government's position was daily becoming more impossible, and that "before long they will be driven like wild duck in a decoy into an inextricable impasse". He based this undue optimism on talks with Borthwick of the *Morning Post* (who was "in a state of condign and most satisfactory dissatisfaction with the Cabinet" and accused them of having "no policy but to stave off the difficulty from day to day"), and on news brought by Dean Stanley from Hatfield as to Salisbury's "high spirits at having got his own way". The meeting of Parliament Harcourt treated as "only an expedient to give an empty satisfaction to H.M. and her Vizier".[3]

Granville in his reply was distinctly less optimistic and disbelieved in "an immediate break-up of the Ministry, as the pear is certainly not yet ripe for us. But it will take a long course of discredit really to break up the Conservative party, and Dizzy, if he fails in carrying whatever views he may have, will gracefully retreat from everything except the Treasury."[4]

Harcourt, undeterred, recounted to Hartington his talk with Borthwick and treated the meeting of Parliament as "only a tail to the luncheon party of Hughenden" (a reference to the Queen's recent visit). "I very much agree with you as to the impossibility and impolicy of strongly resisting a moderate proposal for increased armaments: though to increase the Navy would be ridiculous against Powers which have none, and as to a land campaign an English force would be useless if Austria does not move, and superfluous if she does. My conclusion is that the country will do anything for the Turks except fight *for*, and everything against the Russians except go to

[1] On the first news of Parliament meeting, he wrote hot foot to Granville, "To you as leader, I give my first hasty construction of this proceeding"—*Granville Papers*, 19 Dec., Gladstone to Granville.
[2] There are, throughout the Eastern crisis, no letters of Sir W. Harcourt to Mr. Gladstone in the *Gladstone Papers*.
[3] *Granville Papers*, 24 Dec., Harcourt to Granville.
[4] *Harcourt Papers*, 25 Dec., Granville to Harcourt.

war *with* them. I have no doubt that Layard is doing all he knows to harden Pharaoh's heart, but to me who desire to see that gentleman with his horse and his rider cast into the sea, his obstinate determination to be destroyed is rather satisfactory than otherwise."[1]

On 30 December 1877 Harcourt, by a pure accident, met Shuvalov in the street and had a long conversation with him, which on reflection seemed to him to be so important that he reported it in very great detail to Granville. Shuvalov on his side thought it so important that he called at Harcourt's house and had a further conversation of two hours:[2] Harcourt then "read him what I have written and he confirms its accuracy".

Harcourt made it clear to him that the Opposition was "in the dark" as to the situation, and "that the task of maintaining the cause of peace, which was our chief object, was very difficult without knowing what the attitude of Russia was to be in respect to a settlement with Turkey". Shuvalov complained that the British offer of mediation "could only be intended to place his Government in a false position", and that it was "altogether inadmissible" to ask Russia to treat with England alone, or to accept Lord Beaconsfield's Government as the sole mediator between Russia and Turkey, though "if Mr. Gladstone's Government had made such a proposal, it would have been another matter". He affirmed Russia's desire for peace and "vehemently repudiated" the idea of occupying Constantinople, pointing to the Tsar's pledge and adding that South Bessarabia was the only territory in Europe which Russia desired for herself.

Harcourt urged that such assurances could not be too often repeated, and "that the disclaimer of acquisition of Constantinople should be attached in the most conspicuous manner to the refusal of English mediation. He said, 'We have already promised it'. I replied, 'Well, promise it over again and promise it in a way which will appear in the papers presented to Parliament'. He seemed cordially to assent to this, and said he would telegraph for instructions to renew their assurances. He then added, 'The English Government are not satisfied with the promise not to acquire Constantinople, they demand that we shall neither occupy nor even approach it'. He did not exactly define the word 'approach', but said, 'If we take Adrianople, the Turks will retire upon Constantinople and refuse to

---

[1] *Harcourt Papers*, 27 Dec., Harcourt to Hartington.
[2] The bare fact is recorded in A. G. Gardiner, *Life of Harcourt*, i. p. 321, but the quotations in the text are now printed for the first time.

make peace'. I replied, 'Surely once at Adrianople, you could stay there and reorganise Turkey as you pleased'. He demurred to this and said, 'We have not the money to keep up a regular army of occupation'. I laughed and said, 'On mange assez bien en Bulgarie'. He said, 'Yes, on mange très bien en France, but the Germans could not stay there indefinitely'."

The Ambassador took the line that if Russia promised not merely not to annex, but not even to occupy, all the Turks need do was "to withdraw before the Russian arms, secure that at Constantinople they will find an ally in England. Once certain of this, they will do all they can to provoke a conflict with England."

Harcourt tried to "draw" him on the subject of terms, but was more successful when he suggested that the final result would depend on whether London "could secure the co-operation of Vienna. On that point Count Shuvalov spoke with great confidence. He said that the Government had tried Austria in every form and had altogether failed. That Austria was bound by engagements to Russia from which she could not escape. I said I understood there are limits which Austria has placed on her inaction. He replied, 'Mais ces limites, nous ne les dépasserons pas'."

Next day nothing new emerged save Shuvalov's obvious alarm and his insistence upon the irritation at St. Petersburg. When Harcourt expressed the view that Bismarck desired a Russo-British war—perhaps again partly in order to "draw" the Ambassador—Shuvalov gave it as his personal opinion "that Bismarck would be glad to see a declaration of war by England against Russia, that then he would step in as mediator and give peace to Europe and settle the Eastern Question, that he would in fact seek to overtrump Dizzy by a great *coup de théâtre* in his old age. But when I pressed him he admitted that Germany would not act *by force* against Austria if she turned against Russia."[1]

Granville acknowledged Harcourt's "deeply and painfully interesting" letter, and at once took it to Hartington. At the same time he wished "some of our friends would not threaten dissolution. I do not see a chance of it until after action has been taken on our part, and that action failing, which I believe it would, the notion of our settling the Eastern Question without France and against Russia, Germany and Austria appears to me absurd."[2]

[1] *Granville Papers*, 31 Dec. 1877, Harcourt to Granville.
[2] *Harcourt Papers*, 1 Jan. 1878, Granville to Harcourt.

Harcourt had meanwhile reached the conclusion that the situation was "as grave as it can be", and that "we need all our counsel and prudence".[1] "Dizzy is driving his parallels slowly but surely up to the breach." During a flying visit to his Oxford constituents he found "the anti-Russian sentiment tremendously strong", extending to all classes and parties: and a local Liberal bigwig at his own meeting made a tirade against Russia and was "rapturously applauded amidst cries of 'That's the true voice of England' ". "There can be no doubt we are in the presence of a rising gale on a lee shore. We have but one anchor to ride by, and that is the moderates in the Cabinet. If that parts, it is all over. A dissolution would destroy us as it did the Peelites and Cobdenites on the China vote.[2] Nevertheless if we are driven to the position of the Rockingham Whigs in the early days of the American War, I am all for standing to our guns and resisting the modern Lord North."

Harcourt's main anxiety was to get the Russian terms of peace published, in the belief that public opinion would be "surprised at their moderation". "Shuvalov was very anxious to impress upon me that Russia was nearly *au bout* of her resources, that she could get no money, and he said expressly that she could not get any considerable increase of her men. His view was if she could not get peace in a few months she would have to give up the attempt. In fact he admitted that if England went to Gallipoli and encouraged the Turks to wait for a year, Russia must throw up the sponge. They could not find the means to go on. Dizzy knows this probably as well as Shuvalov. Of course it would be a great triumph for D. to compel the retreat of Russia. But then his difficulties would begin, he would have got rid of Russia and lost the support of Russophobia and he would have to settle Turkey."

"I asked Shuvalov point-blank, 'If Austria was to declare war against you, would Bismarck use force to restrain her and help you?' He answered quite frankly, 'No'. I said, 'then you must give it up and go back'. He replied equally frankly, 'Yes'. My impression, though not equally decisive, is from what he said, that if England were to declare war, Russia would succumb without fighting. This I take to be the meaning of a significant sentence of his, 'I think there will be rupture, but no war'. Russia would cast upon us the responsi-

---

[1] *Granville Papers*, 1 Jan. 1878, Harcourt to Granville.
[2] This one sentence, but without its context, is quoted in *Life of Harcourt*, i. p. 321.

bility of her failure and throw the fate of the Christians on our hands.

"Shuvalov insisted over and over again that the occupation of Gallipoli would be fatal to their finances by destroying their southern trade. Of course it is destroyed now, but they hope in a few months to recover it by peace, but the occupation by England would prolong their ruin till they could not endure it. He said, 'The occupation of Gallipoli would be more serious than 200,000 men in Bulgaria'. All this satisfied me that the one object of Russia is to get out on the easiest terms possible, if Dizzy will let them. If they cannot make a peace of some sort in six months, they are done and they know it." [1]

On 6 January Harcourt had another long conversation with Shuvalov, who gave him an account, doubtless based on the information which we have already seen in his secret dispatches—of what had passed in the Cabinet. "I could see the trace of great uneasiness in my informant as to the future, which he did not explain and which I endeavoured to fathom. I reverted to the terms of Russia and said if they were what had been stated in our last conversation, there was not much to fear, as I thought they could be regarded as not unreasonable. I saw at once that I had touched the sore point. He admitted that if Turkey applied for the armistice, the general terms of peace demanded by Russia would have to be stated. He then began to guard himself and to hint that the terms might no longer be those which had been previously proposed. He pretended not to know what they were *now*, and said he did not believe they were settled *yet*. I drew my own conclusions and felt sure there was something he did not think it well to reveal, and the consequences of which he dreaded. I tried to get to the bottom of it, but only with partial success."

Shuvalov may possibly have realised that he was creating an impression of evasion: in any case he found a field where he could become expansive and gave Harcourt the inner history of the terms offered by Russia in June 1877 in response to the Derby Circular of 6 May. "In June he went to Derby and said, 'You accuse us of making arrangements with Germany and Austria: well, we have made arrangements with them and we offer to make arrangements with you also; here are our terms, we don't ask you to agree to them *en bloc*, but at least discuss them with us, and we shall see if we cannot come to an accord'. The Government refused even to discuss, and therefore he says we have not to consult them in any alterations we may make

[1] *Granville Papers*, 2 Jan. Harcourt to Granville.

now. If they had been accepted, then we should have been bound. Now we have only to ask the assent of Germany and Austria to alter them, and we shall of course ask nothing to which those Powers have not assented."

This evidently reassured Harcourt as to Shuvalov's good faith and good intentions, but he warned him very flatly, "that if Russia advanced new terms which would be generally regarded as excessive, I could not answer for the consequences, as every Englishman might be bound to resist them".[1] Next day Harcourt summed up the general impression left upon his mind by these talks. It was that Shuvalov "knew things are changed since he had spoken to me the Sunday before, that Russia was more confident in her strength and that she would be more *exigeante* than he had previously led me to suppose. He evidently spoke with much more reserve than before. He could not and would not tell me what he knew and what he pretended not to know, but he felt that he might be reproached as having misled us by assurances of moderation which did not turn out to be fulfilled. Indeed he expressed himself to me almost in these words." Here, and in the suspicion that Bosnia was "the price of Andrássy's obstinate neutrality", Harcourt hit the nail straight on the head.

The whole correspondence reveals his frank and earnest tone: there is not one trace of that subservience to Russia of which the Jingoes were accusing their opponents. Granville on his side, speaking for Hartington as well as himself, had no objection to his "stating that the Liberal leaders are strongly for neutrality and peace",[2] but naturally enough assumed that "of course you will not let it be known that you have been in such close communication with Shuvalov and have suggested moves to Russia. But the suggestions have been most judicious and the information you have extracted is most useful."[3]

Granville summed up very acutely the situation of the moment. "The Russians see that the Government is not heartily supported in a war policy—they know that Dizzy is opposed in his own Cabinet, as well as by the leaders of the Opposition. They know that they can rely on Austria, and that the language of the Prime Minister as well as of the Ministers there has exceedingly irritated Bismarck as well as the Russian nation. In a military sense they are carrying everything before them. They also know probably better than laymen,

---

[1] *Granville Papers*, Sunday, 6 Jan., Harcourt to Granville.
[2] *Harcourt Papers*, 2 Jan., Granville to Harcourt. This phrase is quoted in *Life of Harcourt*, i. p. 323.
[3] *Ibid.* 7 Jan.

and the majority of the army know that we are utterly unprepared for war. Why should they be so polite to us, when we snub all their overtures and insist upon treating them as outlaws. I can only explain Shuvalov's language about Gallipoli by a wish on his part to encourage us, if there be a rupture, to do the foolishest thing we can think of.

"The majority of the Cabinet, I am assured on good authority, is strongly against war, but some of them see they have made foolish concessions. I suppose it is true that the clamour for war is really based upon enormous Turkish speculations."[1] Hartington on his side was puzzled and suspicious. "I don't believe", he told Granville, "in Russia being in such straits or so much afraid of us. Shuvalov must have some object in telling Harcourt all this: but what can it be?"[2]

On the 8th Shuvalov sent Hartington fresh information,[3] which led him to conclude that "for the present the Peace Party are clearly in the ascendant, and Dizzy has probably learnt that the disposition of the country would not support him in breaking the windows and so has drawn in his horns. But *sic notus Ulixes*: when baffled in one direction, he will 'try it on' in another, and he generally gets his own way. However, we are over the first fence, viz. the principle of separate negotiations between Turkey and Russia."[3]

This represents the culminating point of the relations between Shuvalov and the Opposition: but it is better to forestall events and give the sequel here. It is curious that Shuvalov on his side scarcely ever refers to these relations, in writing home: and this can hardly have been due to distrust of Gorchakov's discretion, for his secret reports at this time are fuller than ever before or after. It was much more probably due to the belief that his relations with Lord Derby were worth all the other cards in his hand and might only be jeopardised by what would, if discovered, be wildly denounced as intrigue with the rival party.

None the less, towards the end of January, when Derby's resignation seemed for the moment to be an accomplished fact, the gravity of the situation forced him to modify his tactics, and on 28 January he wrote home as follows:

"I felt it indispensable to renounce the reserve which I have

---

[1] *Harcourt Papers*, 8 Jan.   [2] *Granville Papers*, 4 Jan., Hartington to Granville.
[3] *Ibid.* 8 Jan., Harcourt to Granville. The letter of Shuvalov here referred to is not to be found among the *Harcourt Papers*: it may possibly have been sent to Lords Granville and Hartington and not returned.

hitherto maintained and to play counter with the Whigs. It would have been injurious to our cause to keep them in ignorance of what is happening between the Government and us, and to expose them to possible surprise in the course of the parliamentary debates. Consequently I have put myself into daily relations with the leaders of the Opposition and keep them confidentially informed of my different discussions with members of the Cabinet. The point on which they are feeblest and most divided is the question of armaments: many of them do not want to become unpopular by refusing to the nation the means of preparing for future eventualities, others share the view that England's position at the future Conference would be pitiable if Europe did not know her to be ready for action." [1]

It is clear from this letter that Shuvalov only regarded his relations with the Opposition as a last resort: and this explains why, having originated through an accident and continued intensively during the first week of the year, they then again languished till the middle of February. There is a letter of Harcourt to Granville, dated 18 February, which shows that the former had not met the Ambassador for six weeks, and that at the moment he was mainly interested in the newly published correspondence of Derby and Layard from the previous summer, as showing that Russia "did not act to us in a spirit of dissimulation or reserve, but on the contrary with great frankness, and that the Government and Layard between them did all they could to prevent the Turks from accepting a moderate settlement". [2] Harcourt does not appear to have met Shuvalov again till 4 March, when they discussed the proposed Russian terms of peace. The conversation was again extremely frank: the Ambassador hoped that England would not pit Greek against Slav, since "that would be to complete the destruction of Turkey", to which Harcourt replied, "Tant mieux, we do not want to leave you a serviceable slave". [3]

It can hardly be doubted that Shuvalov relied very little upon the Opposition—which in his opinion "at the moment no longer exists" [4] —and therefore put his main effort into co-operation with Derby,

[1] *U.R.B.D.* letter of Shuvalov to Gorchakov, 16/28 Jan. 1878.
[2] *Granville Papers,* 18 Feb., cit. *Life of Harcourt,* i. 327. He asks, "What on earth has induced Derby to publish Layard's dispatches at this moment? It seems insanity". Is it possible that it was a deliberate attempt of Derby to discredit the war party? [3] Harcourt to Granville—*Life of Harcourt,* i. p. 328.
[4] "Actuellement n'existe plus"—*U.R.B.D.* 10 Feb. Shuvalov to Gorchakov.

and after Derby's fall, with his successor Salisbury. The Opposition, though able to stage a final peace agitation in the country during April, was virtually reduced to impotence inside Parliament, and in Shuvalov's view was during May and June simply waiting on events. This helps to explain why the conversations between Shuvalov and Harcourt were not renewed after 3 March: and it is important to add that there was never any contact between Shuvalov and Gladstone throughout the long crisis—doubtless for tactical reasons on both sides. Indeed the only exchange of letters between the two men—in July 1877—is of the most formal character and reveals great hesitation on Gladstone's part at having written at all.[1] It is of course possible that Shuvalov, knowing the influence which Madame Novikov exercised over Mr. Gladstone and many prominent Liberals, was content to leave the advocacy of the Russian cause in her hands and thus to avoid the risks of direct intercourse. But this does not altogether fit the facts: for her whole outlook as a Moscow Slavophil was antipathetic to him as the mouthpiece of official St. Petersburg.

There is a certain piquancy in the final incident. When Shuvalov finally took leave of Lord Derby at the Foreign Office, he went out of his way to deny the report "that he had been in the habit of talking over official matters with members of the Opposition, especially Harcourt. He denies having ever held any private conversations with them or having talked about pending negotiations with anyone except members of the Government."[2] At his special request Derby transmitted the denial to Beaconsfield, but without comment, and there is nothing to show how far either statesman accepted these assurances.

In the light of the correspondence published above there is no escape from the conclusion that Shuvalov was this time deliberately lying. The most that can be said is that it is the only instance throughout the long crisis in which such a charge can be brought home to him, and that this secret correspondence shows him in a strictly honourable and pacific light. It may well be that he knew the Prime Minister to suspect him of direct contacts with Gladstone, Hartington and Granville, whereas in reality he never met or corresponded with any of the three during all this critical time, while his contacts

---

[1] *Gladstone Papers*, Gladstone to Shuvalov and Shuvalov to Gladstone, both dated 20 July. Mr. Gladstone urged the Ambassador if possible to refute publicly certain concrete charges of "atrocity" ascribed by *The Times* to the Russian forces in Bulgaria.   [2] 3 April—Buckle, vi. p. 272.

with Harcourt were due in the first instance to an accident, were narrowly circumscribed in time, and were soon abandoned. He must of course have long ere this been well aware that the Prime Minister never believed anything he said, and we know that he fully returned the compliment: and this makes the incident all the more puzzling. In any case the conversations themselves deserve to be placed on record in any full account of the Eastern crisis, both as showing the far-sighted, frank and courageous attitude of Harcourt, and as proving, no less clearly than his conversations with Derby, Shuvalov's desire for peace between Russia and Britain.

Russian Plans

In order to understand events in England in the early part of 1878, it is now necessary to be clear as to the course of events in eastern Europe—the more so as the full facts have not hitherto been accessible to Western readers. The memoirs of Ignatyev, and still more the secret correspondence of Shuvalov and Gorchakov, enable us to reconstruct the story, and to see into the Russian hand. We shall then be better able to estimate the fluctuating aims and fears of the British Cabinet, and to compare them with the views which actuated Vienna and Berlin at the same time and created the basis on which Europe was eventually to reach a compromise.

The fall of Plevna had broken Turkish resistance and produced boundless confusion at the Porte: but Russia also was not very far from the end of her offensive powers, and there was already a strong current at army headquarters in favour of reducing the fortress of Rushchuk before advancing any farther. This time it was the rear that was more aggressive than the front—the Tsar and the Minister of War rather than the Grand Duke Nicholas: and the more adventurous policy was resolved upon—based, after all, upon the perfectly sound calculation that the Balkans were *not* impassable in winter, even though no less an authority than Moltke thought so. In the first week of 1878, then, General Gurko routed the western Turkish army and occupied Sofia. Meanwhile the Serbs, to whom Andrássy made it quite clear that he would not tolerate any interference in Bosnia, concentrated their main efforts upon Niš, which fell on 10 January —the Turks having been forced by the fall of Plevna to withdraw most of their forces in the west and centre of the Peninsula. Serbia's action was much resented in London, and as usual—though this time without much ground—the main blame was laid upon Russian shoulders.

Again, on the 9th the Shipka Pass was triumphantly forced by Radetzky and Skobelev, and the Turks definitely routed. Panic reigned at Constantinople, and the Sultan had no course save to ask for an armistice. The Grand Duke Nicholas replied that he must await instructions from his brother the Tsar, and in due course came the latter's intimation that a courier was being dispatched with full powers, but that in the interval military measures must not be discontinued. The Tsar not unnaturally took the line that there could be no armistice without acceptance of certain preliminary conditions of peace, or otherwise Russia might easily be robbed of the fruits of victory by foreign interference. It was therefore his aim to occupy as much territory as possible before the actual signature, in order to have more to bargain with afterwards, and hence not to reveal his conditions prematurely, since the Turks might be expected to make them known in London. He therefore ordered the advance to continue "till all our demands have been unconditionally accepted by the Porte".[1]

It was at this time that Archibald Forbes, the war correspondent of the *Daily News*, made his famous ride from Shipka and brought to the Tsar the first authentic accounts of victory. Forbes has left a vivid description of Tsar Alexander as "gaunt, worn and haggard, his voice broken by nervousness and by the asthma that afflicted him, with an expression in his eyes as of a hunted deer": and he put this down, not without good reason, to "the bitterest consciousness" of the many abuses in the Russian army which even an autocrat was powerless to overcome.[2]

A real panic now reigned in Constantinople: the ministers accused England of betraying Turkey, and some favoured throwing themselves into the arms of Russia, as in 1833 before Unkiar Skelessi. The Sultan himself was afraid for his throne and his life and even entertained the idea of retiring to England,[3] intimating for this purpose his desire that a British ship should be at his disposal. Layard was full of warnings that "no promise or pledge given by Russia can be trusted", and that her conduct was "more worthy of the brutal conquerors of the tenth and eleventh centuries".[4]

---

[1] 14 Jan.—Onou, *Memoirs of Ignatyev*, ii. p. 633: "La Guerre russo-turque", ii. (*Nouvelle Revue*, iv. 1880—esp. pp. 761-3).
[2] *Memories and Studies of War and Peace*, pp. 34-7.
[3] Tel. of 19 and letters of 23 and 30 Jan., Layard to Derby—*Layard Papers*.
[4] *Ibid.* 6 Feb., Layard to Hornby.

Negotiations opened on 19 January at Kazanlik, on the southern slope of the Balkans, between the Russian commander-in-chief, assisted by the diplomatist Nelidov, Ignatyev's former secretary at Constantinople, and the Turkish plenipotentiaries Server and Namik Pashas. The first delay was caused by a telegram from Gorchakov, bidding the Grand Duke not state his demands to the Turks, but gain time by asking what they offered. But when Namik gave him the message that the Sultan threw himself on his mercy, the Grand Duke—already resentful and suspicious towards Gorchakov, and feeling that he could not in honour refuse to communicate the Russian terms—did so with the frank assurance that the Tsar had no idea of ejecting the Turks from their capital, adding that England was to blame for all their misfortunes and that their sole hope lay in close friendship with Russia.[1]

While, however, the Turks were throwing themselves upon the magnanimity of the Tsar, Gurko had pressed on from Sofia to Philippopolis: on the 29th even Adrianople fell, and the Grand Duke at once transferred his headquarters there. The Turks found it necessary to apply for fresh instructions, which involved further delays: and when discussions could be resumed, on the 24th, the Grand Duke on his side insisted on waiting for a final message from St. Petersburg, which only reached the Russian headquarters on the 29th, after an unaccountable interval of four days. Meanwhile the Sultan, in terror at the prospect of a final advance on the capital, sent a series of telegraphic appeals to the Tsar for the cessation of military operations, and ended by ordering his envoys to make the best terms they could. After two days of final haggling the armistice protocol was signed on the 31st.

At the time and long afterwards it was widely supposed that the Grand Duke and his staff were the leaders of the forward policy and deliberately cut the cables, in order to keep all news not only from the outside world and from Constantinople itself, but even from the more pacific Tsar. But the publication of Ignatyev's memoirs has made it clear beyond all possibility of doubt that at the close of the campaign the two groups had exchanged rôles, and that it was the Tsar and his immediate advisers who now held out for stiffer terms and were prepared to take the risks involved in occupying Constantinople, whereas the high command, realising the exhaustion of the troops and the precarious situation of supplies and communica-

[1] *Nouvelle Revue*, iv. p. 764.

tions, was eager to conclude peace at the earliest possible date. This change of feeling was not unconnected with Ignatyev himself, who had been under an eclipse since the relative failure of his mission in March 1877, but who had rapidly recovered influence with the Tsar after the fall of Plevna. While Gorchakov, impressed by Shuvalov's rain of telegrams and dispatches, was eager to find a compromise such as would satisfy Britain and Austria, and to that end would have accepted a preliminary protocol with Turkey, leaving the details to be reconsidered by an European conference, Ignatyev, on the contrary, favoured direct and final peace negotiations, either at Odessa or in some suburb of Constantinople, in which case representatives of the Powers could have been called in to resume the inconclusive conference of the previous winter. By these tactics he hoped to avoid a full-fledged conference such as that of 1856, and to reduce to a minimum outside interference with Russia's demands.

Overruled in this, Ignatyev strongly urged that the advance should be continued as far as the heights above the Bosphorus, and on the 24th the Tsar sent orders in this sense to the Grand Duke. The troops were, however, not to enter the capital, and if disorders should break out, or if the fleets should enter the Straits, the Grand Duke was to "enter into friendly agreement with their commanders, *in order to re-establish order by their united forces.*" [1] In this connection it came to a sharp passage of arms between Ignatyev and Gorchakov in presence of the Tsar, the former demanding the occupation of the heights of Bulair, behind Gallipoli, whereas the latter argued that this would involve perjury towards both Britain and Austria-Hungary. The Tsar, backed by Milyutin, evidently leaned towards Ignatyev, and ordered that he should proceed at once to headquarters, with full powers to negotiate—at the same time giving him only twenty-four hours to prepare a draft of the future peace treaty for submission to the Tsar and his Council. Ignatyev apparently did not trust the officials and clerks of the Foreign Office, and with his wife's help worked all through the night in order to complete the draft. On 24 January, then, it was unanimously approved by the Tsar, Gorchakov, Milyutin, Giers and Jomini, with an overflow of complimentary phrases, and Ignatyev left hot-haste for the south, only stopping in Bucarest to lay before Prince Charles the first official intimation that Russia intended to reannex southern Bessarabia,

[1] Onou, *op. cit.* ii. p. 634.

and to throw out a cautious hint that compensation might be found in the Prince's election to the future throne of Bulgaria.[1] Ignatyev's draft was fatally vitiated by the fact that he knew what had been agreed at Reichstadt, but not the contents of the essential convention of Budapest. He was already strongly predisposed against Austria-Hungary, disliked the idea of her receiving Bosnia-Hercegovina for her neutrality and wished to assign territory in due proportion to Serbia and Montenegro, and indeed to Greece and Roumania also. In other words, the assumption accepted by all historians for the last half-century—that the one-sided solution of San Stefano was due to Ignatyev's fanatical interest in the Bulgarians and relative indifference to all the other Balkan races—is a travesty of the actual facts. In his own words, the first draft "included the full independence of Greater Bulgaria, a great augmentation of Montenegro and Serbia, the union of Crete and parts of Epirus and Thessaly with Greece",[2] but he was forced by Gorchakov's unanswerable objections to modify his original maximum and prepare a new minimum.

From Bucarest Ignatyev travelled over Balkan roads—never too good in winter, but now cut to pieces by the movement of large masses of troops: his carriage was thrown over a ravine, he lost his baggage and was fortunate to escape with his life, and at last reached Adrianople on 8 February, only to find that the Grand Duke had already concluded the armistice a whole week earlier, on terms differing widely from those at which he aimed.

This was due on the one hand to the growing anxiety of G.H.Q., and on the other to the pressure of external events upon the Tsar and his Chancellor, which will become clear when we turn to the reactions of London, Vienna and Berlin.

ORDERS TO THE FLEET

The Carnarvon incident was only followed by the briefest possible lull, and on 9 January renewed dissensions broke out in the Cabinet when it came to drafting the Speech from the Throne. The Prime Minister reported to the Queen with "consternation", that his own draft was condemned by Derby and Salisbury as "a menace to Russia"; that the Lord Chancellor, hitherto a tower of strength, "too much agreed with them"; that the Home Secretary, Assheton

[1] *Aus dem Leben*, iii. pp. 456-60.   [2] Onou, *op. cit.* ii. p. 636-7.

Cross, was alarmed at the decline in trade and revenue: and that he himself was "nearly alone in the Cabinet", Manners and Northcote alone supporting him.[1] The Queen was more indignant than ever. "She feels she cannot, as she said before, remain the sovereign of *a country that is letting itself down to kiss the feet of the great barbarians*, the retarders of all liberty and civilisation that exists. Her son feels more strongly than herself even. She is utterly ashamed of the Cabinet, but delighted to see and hear Sir Stafford is right and sound. . . . *Oh, if the Queen were a man, she would like to go and give those Russians*, whose word one cannot believe, *such a beating*! We shall never be friends again till we have it out." [2]

Evidently Shuvalov was not exaggerating when he reported to his chief the Queen's "extreme animation and passion" in pushing a policy which might be "summed up in the two words 'war or dissolution'. . . . Her daily and persistent intervention in all details of the present crisis is a new feature of this reign. It is beginning to cause anxiety and forms the object of unfavourable comments. This direct participation of the Sovereign is disapproved even by Ministers, who find that Her Majesty is leaving the limits prescribed by the constitution and encroaching on their duties and prerogatives."[3] This from the representative of the Russian autocrat! But the only answer that Beaconsfield had for the Queen's outburst was, "It is something to serve such a sovereign!"[4]

Next day the Cabinet sat for three "most stormy" hours, to consider its chief's proposal to send the fleet to the Dardanelles and land forces to hold Gallipoli, subject to permission from the Sultan: but rather than consent to this both Derby and Salisbury threatened resignation.[5] The heat engendered in discussion may be gathered from Beaconsfield's report to the Queen, which shows him to have charged the dissentient ministers with having "deceived the Queen" and accused Carnarvon of "impertinence". Finally it was agreed as a compromise that the Russian Government should be invited to explain whether the Tsar's pledge not to occupy Constantinople except under military necessity applied to the Dardanelles also, and that, pending an answer, the fleet should be sent to Besika Bay. As meanwhile the Sultan sent a personal appeal to the Queen,[6] it was

[1] 9 Jan.—Buckle, vi. p. 216.   [2] 10 Jan.—*ibid.* p. 217.
[3] 8 Jan. 1878—*R.B.D.* vii. no. 269.
[4] Buckle, vi. p. 218. "Spirited" appears to be Mr. Buckle's word.
[5] 12 Jan., to Queen—*ibid.* p. 219.
[6] *U.R.B.D.* "Un télégramme éploré", reports Shuvalov to Gorchakov, 2/14 Jan.

268 THE GROWTH OF CABINET DISSENSIONS CHAP.

decided that she should transmit this to the Tsar direct and urge
him to accelerate the negotiations. His answer was brief, but to the
point: though desirous of peace, he wished it "to be serious and
lasting", and the commander of his armies knew the terms on which
the Sultan could obtain it. The Queen in her turn felt "much
affronted" at such an answer, and Beaconsfield agreed with her that
it was "rude" and "vulgar":[1] it confirmed her in the view that this
was "the *last* moment" for rallying "all true Englishmen" round
him.

A minor incident throws a highly significant light upon the attitude
of both Queen and Premier. Colonel Wellesley had again reached
London, and, after telling Her Majesty that the Russians were in a
wretched plight and really a most despicable military Power, was
privately received by Beaconsfield and asked whether he could
guarantee that the Russian army would not reach Adrianople within
the next six weeks, as in that case "I see my way". Wellesley, who
at once understood the question to refer to the moving of British and
Indian troops from Malta to Constantinople, could not give the
required pledge and said it was quite possible that they might be
there in less [2] (Adrianople was actually occupied on 20 January).
This conversation appears to have had a decisive influence: for if once
that view were accepted, it became obvious that Britain alone could
not hold back Russia, and that all depended on the impending
negotiations with Austria-Hungary.

It is instructive to note Shuvalov's day-to-day comments on the
situation. "*The Cabinet is in extremities (aux abois)*", he wrote on
14 January, "and caught in the net of its own policy", changing
intermittently from morning till evening from a pacific to a bellicose
tone. He warned Gorchakov, however, that the Grand Duke's refusal
to negotiate without instructions from the Tsar was regarded in
London as a mere excuse for taking Adrianople and making a
definitive peace under the pseudonym of an armistice. In talking to
both Derby and Disraeli he attempted to refute this argument on
the ground that the urgency of the signature was being exaggerated
by the Porte for motives of its own, and that Russia must insist upon
preliminary acceptance of the main lines, as otherwise she would be
risking the possibility of having to start pourparlers all over again.
This was too obvious to admit of refutation, and both statesmen

[1] *Letters*, ii. p. 595; Buckle, vi. p. 220.
[2] F. A. Wellesley, *With the Russians in Peace and War*, p. 283.

accepted it, subject to the reserve that for peace to be final it must have the approval of England.[1]

The very next day (15 January), while Derby was ill in bed, the Prime Minister induced the Cabinet to order the fleet to the Dardanelles and to make overtures to Vienna, but as Derby and Carnarvon protested vigorously, the order was again suspended. Little wonder that Gorchakov, at the St. Petersburg end, wrote cuttingly to his ambassador, whose almost daily reports kept him and the Tsar in a state of bewilderment: "We cannot follow the fluctuations of this policy, at once hesitating and surly". The only possibility at this stage, he argued, was a preliminary peace: "the collective examination of questions of general interest *can come later*. But it is clear that a discussion *à six* of the preliminary conditions would be utterly impracticable and would lead, not to peace, but to general war." He urged Shuvalov to use these arguments, adding, "With the English it is difficult to find the measure between the conciliation which emboldens and the firmness which offends them". In his view the decisive factor for Russia was her negotiation with Austria and Germany.[2] Meanwhile he acted on Shuvalov's telegraphic advice and postponed sending any further answer to British enquiries until he could be sure that it could not affect the wording of the Queen's Speech.

The Tsar and Francis Joseph

Meanwhile the Russian advance had thrown Count Andrássy into a state of some excitement, which was doubtless influenced by the strong Turcophil agitation in Budapest and its reactions upon Serbo-Magyar relations in the south. As early as 9 December—the day before the fall of Plevna—the Tsar had sent from his headquarters at Poradim a provisional outline of the peace terms which were in his mind, together with an appeal for co-operation, both to his uncle William I. and to Francis Joseph. To this the Austrian Emperor took a whole month to reply, and the answer when it came, though couched in a friendly form, made no concealment of his "apprehension" as to the new situation, which, he feared, was "not yet ripe for the definite rearrangement of the Balkans forecast at Reichstadt". Public opinion in his own country, and this was for him decisive, could not be made to believe in Turkey's "natural death". It is interesting to note in passing that he blames "the vacillating

[1] *U.R.B.D.* 2/14 Jan. 1878.   [2] *Ibid.* 4/16 Jan., Gorchakov to Shuvalov.

policy of England" for creating the Bulgarian Question, while at the same time encouraging Turkish resistance.[1] A note annexed to the letter made it clear that Austria-Hungary could not approve the creation of a Big Bulgaria, or its occupation by Russian troops after peace was signed, and added a pointed reminder of Austria's right to annex Bosnia.[2]

Tsar Alexander replied immediately, making it clear that he desired an *entente* under all circumstances, but striking a high and unwonted note which may well have caused some alarm at Vienna. "Turkish bravery", he contended, was not a sign of vitality: "it only proves that the Turks preserve even in decadence their original qualities, but it does not prove their aptitude for governing conquered peoples". There could be no question of replacing Christian populations under Turkish rule: hence "any other solution" save complete Bulgarian autonomy, "would be bastard, lying, illusory". Nor could Bulgaria be left at once to her own resources: without some temporary occupation "sanguinary anarchy" would result. In asking for Bessarabia he was merely asking for "restitution", but this had "a moral value for Russia".

The passage relating to Austria-Hungary deserves full quotation. "The acquisitions reserved for her in principle under certain circumstances remain intact despite the turn which affairs have taken. In offering you latitude to occupy Bosnia and Hercegovina temporarily, as I have Bulgaria, I had in view to leave you the option of transforming this temporary occupation into an annexation later on, if you found it necessary for your security—even if my troops had evacuated Bulgaria. I am told that this occupation was offered you by the Porte, and that you rejected it. But this offer could only be made voluntarily (*à titre gratuit*). If it aimed at an alliance with Turkey, it was an insult to your loyalty, and I can conceive your refusing it. In actual fact *you are the sole judge of the right moment* (*de l'opportunité*). But if you renounced the advantage reserved to you by our arrangements and adhered to by me, you will, I hope,

---

[1] *U.R.B.D.* 8 Jan., Francis Joseph to Alexander II. His *exposé* of his reasons for remaining inactive while Russia felt constrained to act is highly interesting. "Intervention he thought unnecessary: it was enough to demand reforms from Turkey. The Porte could not have realised its promises, . . . the incompatibility of the Turkish régime with the needs of Christian civilisation would have become self-evident, the dissolution of the Empire through intrinsic causes would have forced itself upon everyone as an inevitable fatality, and Europe would have come to welcome the intervention it had always distrusted as a deliverance from anarchy."

[2] *Observations sur les Notices*, cit. Wertheimer, iii. p. 59.

understand that I could not subordinate what is for me a necessity to what is for you only a matter of convenience. In any case, any scheme or compensation which you may think likely to conciliate your interests with mine will be examined by me in the same spirit which has hitherto presided over our *entente.*" He concluded his appeal by insisting on a preliminary peace, negotiated direct, but declared that he had never thought of withdrawing "questions of European interest" from "a collective examination".[1]

The Tsar's desire for peace is further shown by the fact that he at once communicated his correspondence with Francis Joseph to his other ally and uncle, William I.: and the latter expressed himself, not only as flattered by this mark of confidence, but as convinced that there was no "essential divergence which could not be smoothed over" between Russia and Austria-Hungary, and as anxious to do all in his own and his Government's power to mediate.[2] In reply Alexander II. cordially thanked his uncle for his firm attitude regarding the occupation of Bulgaria and his "sentiments of equity: for it is impossible for me to understand how I could be asked to abandon a work for which Russia has shed her purest blood", and yet on this Francis Joseph was "insisting absolutely". He relied upon William I.'s personal influence to maintain the *entente* of the three courts, "now more necessary than ever".[3] There can be no doubt that the old Emperor's Russophil outlook was one of the determining factors in the situation.

---

[1] *U.R.B.D.*, 16 Jan. 1878, Alexander II. to Francis Joseph; summarised in Wertheimer, *op. cit.* iii. p. 63.
[2] *Ibid.* 23 Jan., William I. to Alexander II.
[3] *U.R.B.D.* 3 Feb., Alexander II. to William I.

CHAPTER VIII

THE FINAL BREACH

The decisions of the Cabinet were absolutely unanimous. They had never swerved from the policy to which they had agreed with one mind.
DISRAELI, 17 Jan. 1878

Three times within a few weeks it has been my misfortune to be at variance with other members of the Cabinet on matters of the highest importance.
CARNARVON, 25 Jan. 1878

THE OPPOSITION CAMPAIGN

DURING the month of January the agitation in the country may be said to have reached its culminating point. Rarely, if ever, has opinion been so keenly roused, and so deeply divided, on a question of foreign policy: and though such speculations are always open to challenge—if only because they are incapable of positive proof—it seems highly probable that a plebiscite at this moment would have given the Prime Minister a rousing victory in England south of the Trent and a yet more crushing defeat throughout the industrial centres of the north and in Scotland.

Day by day the columns of the press were filled with reports of monster meetings, demonstrations, resolutions and counter-resolutions: and the number of rival societies steadily grew. "The National Society for Resistance of Russian Aggression and Protection of British Interests" addressed a solemn memorandum to the Foreign Secretary, opposing an armistice because "under its shelter the Russian army will escape the destruction that awaits it", urging the need for immediate diplomatic intervention, and asserting that Austria, "tortured by the fear of a revolution in Hungary, would gladly escape from the Triple Alliance under the protection of England and France", and that in Germany a formidable working-class movement had been inaugurated to prevent Bismarck's attempt to make of his country the ally of Russia! In contrast to this crazy stuff must be placed the work of such bodies as the Eastern Question Association, the City Neutrality and Peace Committee, the Workmen's Neutrality Committee, the Nonconformist Committee of Vigilance on the Eastern Question, the Midland Arbitration Union, and so on. The National Federation of Liberal Associations, under the presidency of Joseph Chamberlain, issued a fighting circular, which argued that "the Premier never speaks but to eulogise Turkey, to menace Russia and to magnify without defining those British interests which he insinuates rather than alleges to be in danger".[1] At the same time a representative meeting of Nonconformist leaders was held in London to organise resistance to a Turkish policy, and at it a letter of Gladstone was read aloud. Meanwhile a "Committee for the free navigation of the Straits" was formed by Freeman, Liddon, Sandwith and Auberon Herbert, and secured the open support of Carlyle, Froude, Browning and John Morley.

Humanitarian interest was represented by the Russian Sick and Wounded Fund, of which Malcolm MacColl was honorary secretary, by the Serbian Relief Fund and kindred committees for the relief of the Bosnian refugees, by Lady Strangford's committee at Philippopolis, by the Mansion House Relief Committee, the Central Relief Committee at Constantinople (in which Dr. Long, of Robert College, Edwin Pears and Eugene Schuyler were the moving spirits) and the Manchester Relief Fund, mainly organised by the Society of Friends.

Early in the year Joseph Chamberlain gave to the press a letter which he had received from Gladstone, who declared that he had "felt it my duty to remain silent in the face of many solicitations, for fear I should unintentionally contribute to throw the question into the arena of party", but added the warning that "we know not what a day may bring forth".[2] That this feeling of nervous uncertainty was shared not merely by most Liberals, but also by many of Gladstone's Conservative critics, is illustrated by a *Times* leader of the same date, which argued that "there cannot but be danger, so long as an active and passionate party, with representatives in high places, are struggling, not to keep this country out of war . . ., but to make it intervene . . . and assume . . . the character of a Turkish ally". Such designs had been repudiated by Derby and Carnarvon, but ought to be repudiated by the Cabinet as a whole, for "great doubt prevails throughout Europe".

It might perhaps be said that the reopening of Opposition fire on a grand scale dated from a letter of John Bright in *The Times* of 29 December. "I do not think we shall have war," he wrote, "for the country is for peace, and the Government has no ally. The

[1] *The Times*, 5 Jan. 1878.   [2] *Ibid.* 8 Jan.

administration may not be a wise one, but it must bend to circumstances. It has, as a Government, no interest in war: for war would
soon destroy it." Nothing is more characteristic of the deep gulf that
divided public opinion than this letter and the fierce comment upon
it in no less weighty an organ than the *Quarterly Review*: "It would
be difficult to find, in all the bitter annals of political controversy,
words more unscrupulous and violent, and more unworthy than
these, in the mouth of any statesman who has a reputation to
preserve".[1]

During January, then, the whole Opposition opened vigorous fire
in every part of the country. W. E. Forster at Bradford denounced
the war panic, reminded the Government that the persistent rumours
of dissension had been set on foot by their own side, and not by the
Liberals, and while confessing his belief "in the duty and necessity
of war on occasions", declined to admit that England could suffer
harm if the Balkan states achieved independence, or that Russia
could possibly acquire Constantinople, in the face of all Europe's
opposition. Sir Henry James at Taunton compared the attitude of
the Government to that of a farmer who shot a boy for stealing his
apples and was acquitted on the plea that he "shot at nothing
and missed it". Sir William Harcourt at the Liberal Club in Oxford
struck his usual aggressive note. There could be no greater crime
than an unrighteous or unnecessary war, yet the country was daily
threatened with this: some "sinister influence" was at work, and the
only antidote was an appeal to public opinion. The policy of the
Crimean War had been "condemned, exploded and abandoned",
even by the Government itself: and why? Because the nation, when
it heard that policy expounded in the words of Sir Henry Elliot's
famous dispatch,[2] strongly repudiated it, in the knowledge that we
could not fight against the Russians without fighting for the Turks.
He then poured ridicule on the official assumption that Russia had
designs on Egypt and Suez, pointed out that the Russian armies in
Armenia had been led by an Armenian General, Loris Melikov, and
crowned his references to the Russian advance in central Asia by an
effective quotation from a speech of Disraeli as recent as 5 May 1876:
"The idea that Britain and Russia agreed to establish a neutral zone,
and that Russia has been systematically violating it, is one of those
delusions which, having once got possession of the public mind, is

---

[1] *Q.R.*, "The Meeting of Parliament" (Jan. 1878).
[2] A reference to the dispatch of 4 Sept. 1876, see *supra*, p. 63.

very difficult to terminate". He reminded the ministerial press that less than two years earlier it had boasted of the very isolation which now caused it such regret, but that obviously "a Government, which bawls about the streets that it consults no interests but its own, will find, as H.M.G. have found, that they have no allies".

This frontal attack upon a favourite doctrine of the Prime Minister was reinforced by further blows at his last Guildhall speech and at the Secretary for War, his most bellicose supporter. "To identify selfishness with patriotism is not to exalt selfishness, but to degrade patriotism: the gospel of selfishness, as preached by Mr. Hardy in the House of Commons, is the chief cause of our isolation in Europe." [1]

At a huge meeting in Birmingham John Bright and Joseph Chamberlain drew further lessons from the Crimean War, the former reminding his audience that that war had been fought "unwisely, as I thought then, and as most people think now", and that the arguments against it were now as strong as ever. He quoted a *Times* leader of February 1854—"To destroy Sebastopol is nothing less than to demolish the entire fabric of Russian ambition in those very regions where it is most dangerous to Europe"—and then pointed out that every aim of those days had failed, that Russia was far stronger, her fleet no longer limited, Turkey in greater danger than ever, France no longer in favour of war, while "we are alone, . . . yet constantly meddling". The only real point of British interest was the free maintenance of Suez, and as all Europe was interested in the Canal, it was unnecessary to connect this question with Russia. He quoted David Urquhart, "so possessed of certain notions" as to suspect Palmerston of being bribed by Russia and of planning the Crimean War "not to save Turkey, but to place Turkey in the hands of Russia". But "the heart of the nation is gradually changing. Now a man may have an opinion in favour of peace, and the dogs of war will scarcely bark at him." Yet how easy to stir up a war by some such futile phrase as the Balance of Power or "British interests".

> Religion, freedom, vengeance, what you will—
> A word's enough to rouse mankind to kill.

Chamberlain struck a louder note, appealing to somewhat different sentiments. Behind Derby and Carnarvon, he said, stood the Prime Minister, "and behind the Prime Minister there stood—he knew not what. This isle was full of noises, and there were rumours of uncon-

[1] 9 Jan. 1878.

stitutional interference, of which he would only say that it would be
wiser to believe none of them until they knew more." This scarcely
veiled allusion to the Queen and her entourage was not without
significance, in the mouth of the foremost Radical of those days.
The policy of the Prime Minister, he went on, "was to juggle into
war. The powder was to be brought a little nearer to the candle, and
then an accident would do the rest." Distrust of Russia was not confined to the Conservatives: but the Russia of 1878 was not the Russia
of 1853, and in any case, how would Poland be benefited "by keeping
Bulgaria in servitude", and why help the Turks who had "sought
to put down rebellion by extermination", and whose doom was now
sealed?

Meanwhile Sir Charles Dilke addressed his constituents at Ken-
sington, in a reasoned survey of the Eastern Question which aroused
much attention at the time and revealed him as a Liberal Foreign
Secretary *in posse*. He pointed out that the promises which Turkey
had made in 1875 were as much a dead letter as those of 1839 and
1856, sketched the "reluctance" with which the British Government
had adhered to the consular mission, its "hesitation" to sign the
Andrássy Note, its refusal of the Berlin Memorandum, though adherence would have averted war: its failure to press home its demand
for the punishment of Turkish criminals, and its fatal encouragement
to the Turks by Derby's addendum to the Protocol of March 1877
and by the selection of Layard for the Constantinople Embassy.
"On at least twelve occasions", he boldly claimed, "the European
Concert was violated by our Government", yet it had failed, "with
danger and with loss of dignity to England", to prevent war.

Dilke was careful to guard himself against the Jingo reproach of
Russophilism. "My want of confidence in Russia is nothing new",
for Russia is "a pure autocracy, . . . the great Tory power." But
though the war must be regarded as "a conflict between two corrupt
and cruel Governments, with neither of which can Liberals feel
sympathy", yet one stands for "a nation in decay", whose "promises
are on paper", while behind the other "are ranged powerful forces
of the future". And Britain, so far from having "taken the lead in
a spirited foreign policy", as the Tories alleged—"Why, we stand
absolutely alone, in face of terms of peace which we dislike, but
cannot resist", while "Turkey is crushed, about whose integrity the
Tory party raved. . . . England can do nothing but hold five Cabinets
in a week and so proclaim her isolation to the world." And he drew

an effective comparison with the situation in 1828, when Wellington and Aberdeen reversed the policy of Canning in the Eastern Question, and, without an active ally in Europe, had to look on while Russia dictated peace to Turkey at Adrianople.

There are several almost prophetic phrases in this speech. He leans quite frankly towards friendship with France and Austria, but says of the latter that she "will have to accelerate her conversion into a Slav state by accepting the fatal gift of Bosnia, an increase of territory which may destroy that unhappy hybrid power". Of Egypt he says that the only real alternatives are the independence of the Khedive—"perhaps the greatest robber that ever sat upon a throne"—or annexation by Great Britain: and "I am as convinced that Egypt ought to be acquired as I am that India must be retained". Finally he declared, "This Europe is probably mined beneath our feet with secret treaties"—perhaps without fully realising how sure had been his aim and how that isolation which he and his colleagues criticised so strongly was essentially due to the secret arrangements of Reichstadt and Budapest.[1] "The day may come", he said, "when England will have to fight for her existence, but for Heaven's sake let us not commit the folly of plunging into war at a moment when *all Europe would be hostile to our arms*—not one Power allied to the English cause."

Rival Literature

Apart from this fresh outburst of platform agitation, the issue had for months past been envenomed and confused by a great mass of pamphlet literature. Gladstone's two pamphlets—*Bulgarian Horrors* and *Lessons in Massacre* — not unnaturally attained the widest circulation. That of Butler-Johnstone, already quoted, is a good specimen of the ultra-Turkish standpoint. But others which met with a passing success reveal the depths to which controversy could sink. In *Bulgarian Horrors! and Mr. Gladstone's Eastern Policy*[2] a certain Mr. S. G. B. St. Clair argues in all seriousness that Gladstone's aim is to save, not England, but "Russian finance and Bulgarian banditti", and that he "does not even now know that he is the tool of Russia". St. Clair's own recipe for a settlement is that Montenegro and Serbia should be disarmed and forced to accept Turkish garrisons, that Bosnia and Bulgaria should be organised on the lines of

---

[1] This speech was published in pamphlet form, *The Eastern Question* (1878); see especially for above quotations pp. 16, 35, 43, 49, 53, 56.   [2] *Ibid.* pp. 3, 12, 22.

the Austrian Military Frontiers, and that "rayahs and Turks" alike should be obliged to serve three years in the regular Turkish army and seventeen years in the militia!

An even wilder note is struck in two pamphlets by Augustus Daly. In the first, *The Duty of Civilised Europe on the Settlement of the Eastern Question*,[1] Russia, who is at one point described as "the yelping northern mongrel", is denounced as "the prime instigator" of the Bulgarian atrocities, whose great aim for twenty years past has been to alienate English sympathy from Turkey. Perhaps its culminating phrase is "the innumerable hordes of spies whom Russia has scattered broadcast throughout Europe in general and England in particular". In a second and longer effusion, *Greater Lessons in Massacre*,[2] Daly concentrates his attack upon "this sanguinary hypocrite" Gladstone, who "howled treason and yelled nonsense" about atrocities, of whose immediate causes the Turks were "perfectly innocent", and in which the Russians were "the chief criminals". "The Turk", he maintained, "is a lover of order and will have his laws obeyed", whereas the Russians have been guilty of endless horrors in Siberia, Poland and central Asia and are false to the interests of Christianity. "When the Russians have murdered, burnt, destroyed and devastated, it has been from a natural love of rapine and greed of gain. The Turks on the contrary have been driven to massacre through adhering to the first law of nature—self-preservation". There is an ascending scale to the argument that if the Russians take Constantinople, *"India will be irretrievably lost"*, and there is a final call to arms "to prevent the Tsar from teaching even greater lessons in massacres".

If lucubrations of this sort were possible in England, it may be imagined that in the East of Europe further records were established. *The Times* correspondent in Constantinople reported articles in the Turkish press, solemnly affirming that Gladstone was in reality the illegitimate son of a Bulgarian named Demitri, servant to a pigmerchant at Kustendil; that at the age of sixteen he had betrayed his master's daughter, fled to England and there made an unexpected career: and finally that "his gluttony for gold makes him look yellow". All this in a leading organ of the Turkish Government gave Gladstone himself great cause for merriment at a lecture which he delivered at Hawarden in November 1877.[3]

---

[1] *The Eastern Question*, pp. 17, 9, 10, 6.   [2] *Ibid*. pp. 6, 27, 25, 46, 33, 54-6.
[3] *The Times*, 13 and 24 Nov.

At the turn of the year there appeared a pamphlet under the grandiloquent title *Russian Imperial Freedom versus Turkish Constitutional Liberty*, by Captain St. Clair, who had formerly been consul in Bulgaria and Moldavia. Undeterred by the thoroughness with which his forecasts were being falsified, he had just time to add a postscript affirming that the victory of the Russian arms at Kars and elsewhere in no way affected his conclusions. It may be thought that such an effusion is too absurd to deserve mention: but coming from a man who knew the Near East, it found readers and is typical of a form of literature that long confused the public mind.

A strangely arresting note is struck by an article in the December *Contemporary Review*, by the exiled "Governor of Hungary", Louis Kossuth, defining the Eastern Question as "a question of Russian power". In his fear of a Russo-Austrian bargain, he utters a warning not devoid of prophetic quality: "What the Viennese Cabinet would pilfer, under the shadow of the Russian highwayman, from the Turkish Empire, would only weaken us and become eventually our death. . . . If St. Petersburg and Vienna should divide the rags of the torn Turkish Empire, twenty-five years would not elapse before the Russians, Prussians and Italians would divide Austria and Hungary among themselves, perhaps leaving some of the booty to Wallachia, as the reward of subserviency to Russia."

By way of contrast, two books deserve very special mention, as vindicating the national reputation for sanity in this question: for though they did not appear till after the actual crisis was over, they strongly influenced the flow of public opinion in 1879 and are still worth reading to-day by those who desire a sane and generally accurate survey of contemporary facts. The first of these is *The Eastern Question*,[1] by the Duke of Argyll, who was, after Gladstone himself, the principal survivor from the Crimean Cabinet, who like Gladstone felt that this imposed upon him a very special responsibility, and whose periodical pronouncements on this question have not received the attention which they merit. There is no doubt that they played a great part in winning Scotland for the cause of the Christians of the East and caused special annoyance to Queen Victoria.

Still more valuable, because based upon first-hand information, is *Some Observations on Bulgarian Affairs*, by the Marquis of Bath,

[1] Two vols. 1879.

which unfortunately did not appear till 1880. It is the result of a prolonged visit to the Balkans, in which he was accompanied by Humphrey Sandwith, a man with linguistic knowledge and the experience
of a quarter of a century, to whom all doors were open. This very
able and moderate survey provides evidence on a number of points
hitherto misunderstood in England: (1) That the Circassian settlers
were *deliberately* introduced into Bulgaria, in order to strengthen
Moslem predominance, and drove the Christian peasantry to desperation; (2) that the Bashibazuks were in the main Turkish peasants,
undisciplined, but armed against their Christian neighbours; (3) that
the "liberal" Midhat Pasha during three terms of office in Bulgaria
"suppressed with a strong hand all national currents"; (4) that
throughout the war the Turks were constantly executing Bulgarian
intellectuals at Sofia and Plovdiv[1] and that in certain towns and
villages—notably Karlovo, Kalofer, Kazanlik, Nova and Stara Zagora
(which in June 1879 they still found "like a charnel-house"[2])
there was a general massacre of Bulgarians after the first Russian
retreat; (5) that the fearful sufferings of the Turkish population,
which fled before the final Russian advance, were due hardly at all
to the Bulgarians, and still less to the Russians, but in the main to
the ravages of typhus and to the Porte's utter lack of any means for
dealing with them; and (6) that the alleged ill-treatment of Moslems
by the new Bulgarian authorities was in the main confined to the
attempt to prevent the return of those guilty of massacre. The general
conclusion, based on the progress already evident in the brief space
of time since the fall of Turkish rule, was that despite every horror,
liberty had been well purchased.[3]

It would indeed be difficult to exaggerate the public excitement:
for it was a time of trade depression, finding vent in such riots as
those at Blackburn; of music-hall demagogy in its most blatant and
vulgar form and of the organised rowdyism that broke up Liberal
meetings and smashed the windows of "the bloody woodchopper"
in Harley Street. It was a time when the Duke of Sutherland, pre-
siding at a lecture of Mr. Algernon Borthwick, could boldly declare
that "Russia's principal agents were Mr. Gladstone and General

---

[1] "When Ahmed Vefik Pasha sent, at the request of the Ambassadors, to Plovdiv
to stop the executions, Suleiman Pasha celebrated his arrival by hanging five or
six Bulgarians before his Konak and boasted that he had orders from Constantinople
in justification of his conduct"—*Observations*, p. 29.
[2] *Ibid*. p. 35.   [3] *Ibid*. p. 42.

Ignatyev, and of course with the former he included the names of a couple of dukes, a marquis, an officer in the army and two clergymen who apparently travelled about with their eyes in their pockets".[1] It was a time when Freeman penned an outrageous phrase about the Queen "going ostentatiously to eat with Disraeli in his ghetto",[2] when Froude spoke of Disraeli as "a mountebank from the beginning",[3] when even John Bright arraigned him for his alien blood, and when his old friend Lord Derby discovered, after thirty years of close co-operation, that his mental processes were after all those of a "foreigner".[4] Sir Wilfrid Lawson at Carlisle quoted the Hebrew prophet, "Benjamin shall rave as a wolf". Sir George Campbell denounced "the genteel snobocracy" of the West End and contrasted it with Lord Carnarvon, on whom Mr. Mundella, at a meeting of working-men, bestowed the endearing but embarrassing epithet of "our watch-dog in the Cabinet". Another hard hitter, Professor Goldwin Smith, writing on "The Slave-owner and the Turk", foretold, not quite accurately, that if Russia should win, "it will be as difficult to find a Turcophil in the clubs and drawing-rooms of London as it was to find a Secessionist after the surrender of Lee".[5]

The "priests and professors" whom Disraeli had scornfully denounced for their opposition to his Eastern policy were in danger of being hooted down at the crisis, but perhaps the most effective answer to the gibe is merely to recite some of their names—Liddon, Church, Dale, Spurgeon, Freeman, Froude, Kinglake, Carlyle, J. R. Green, Stubbs, Bryce, Goldwin Smith, George Cox, Thorold Rogers— and to ask what men of equal eminence supported the Turkish cause.

Meanwhile the Jingo press, led by the *Pall Mall Gazette* and the *Morning Post*, was more violent than ever, and *Punch*, after

[1] *Globe*, 11 Jan. 1878. The sneer is at the Dukes of Argyll and Westminster, Lord Bath, Canon Liddon and Mr. MacColl. It drew from the Labour Representation League a strong protest against "a want of decency and a depth of meanness which would shame one in the humblest walk of life"—*Gladstone Papers*, general correspondence, 14 Jan. The incident hurt Mr. Gladstone more than any other insult of the period: for the Duke's mother had been a very close personal friend. There are no fewer than 900 letters from her among the *Gladstone Papers*!

[2] Dec. 1877—*The M.P. for Russia*, i. p. 419.

[3] 22 June 1878—*ibid.* p. 508. "Dizzy", wrote Froude in May 1878, "grudges the enlargement of the space within which men cannot be impaled." There is some piquancy in Freeman's comments upon Froude, whom he detested. He could not understand how they came to be on the same side: "the apologist of Henry VIII. and Flogging Fitzgerald ought to go in for Midhat and Shafket"—*ibid.* p. 419.

[4] *The Times*, 9 and 17 Jan.

[5] *Contemp. Review*, Dec. 1877.

depicting it in Tenniel's famous cartoon "The Ass in the Lion's Skin", took off its sentiment in the poem:

> I am a wholehog Turcophil,
> Hold History and its teachings *nil*:
> Downtrodden tribes that won't keep still
> I'd stifle.[1]

THE CAMPAIGN AGAINST "RUSSIAN ATROCITIES"

Ever since the first crossing of the Balkans by Gurko the Turcophil press in London had brought forward periodical counter-charges of "atrocities" against the Russians and Bulgarians: and a new fillip was given to this campaign by the publication of an immense Blue Book of 600 documents, consisting mainly of dispatches from Layard and his subordinates on this question.[2] These dispatches, but still more Layard's unpublished correspondence from the same period, prove his keen bias in favour of the Turks and a predisposition to believe any report about the Russians. Already in July 1877 he reported to Beaconsfield and Derby, without a shadow of proof, a deliberate design on the part of Russia, "to exterminate and drive out the Mohammedan population of Bulgaria. A mixed Mussulman and Christian population would give too much trouble."[3] His motive in writing thus is sufficiently transparent: for he goes on to suggest that such incidents "may *have the same effect upon the public mind and our policy as the massacre of Sinope*"—an allusion to an incident which stamped British opinion into the Crimean War, though it was really not a "massacre" at all, but an action between the navies of two belligerents, in which, it is true, one was almost wiped out owing to its own incompetence.

Layard's information conflicted absolutely with that of other Embassies, notably the German, whom he therefore denounced in a private letter to Beaconsfield as "little better than a Russian Agency". To Consul Blunt he wrote that "the old 'atrocity party' here" [by which he means Pears, Schuyler and the American missionaries] "and the German Embassy deny absolutely that there have been any Russian or Bulgarian atrocities, and maintain that they have all been committed by the Turks".[4] In the same breath he had to admit that "owing to the absence of police and troops in the pro-

---

[1] *Punch*, 12 Jan. and 2 Feb. 1878.   [2] *Turkey No. I.* (1878).
[3] *Layard Papers*, 18 July, Layard to Beaconsfield.   [4] *Ibid.* 2 Aug., to Blunt.

vinces, whence they have been removed to the seat of war, Kurds,
Circassians, Tatars and robbers of all kinds and religions [*sic*] are
devastating the country": [1] and again, that "the anarchy caused by
the war leads to great misery on the part of the Christians, who are
robbed and harassed by the marauding Circassians and others, but
not as yet by the Turks, who are, if left alone, quiet and inoffensive
people". [2]

On 8 August, in reporting the Russian retreat from Shipka, he
announces "a complete massacre of all the male Bulgarians who have
been found in Eski Zagora, Kazanlik and other places" [3] and speaks
of "a war of extermination on both sides", in which, however,
"Russia set the example". He had talked with the Grand Vizier, who
"cried like a child" in recounting the horrors. Soon after, however,
he had to report evidence of Colonel Lennox as to fresh massacres
by Circassians in Bulgarian villages: [4] and he warned Said Pasha at
the Palace of the infinite harm which such incidents would do to the
Turkish cause in England. [5] Once more he revealed his bias by assuring Lord Derby that "pro-Russian newspapers, *The Times* included",
were exaggerating the Turkish atrocities, and that "Bulgarians
incited and protected by the Russians are worse than the Turkish
irregulars", and by insinuating that Prince Reuss was a candidate
"for the Bulgarian throne or whatever it is to be". [6] A week later he
gives away his case by writing that he has tried to check the excesses
of the Circassians—and this was perfectly true—but "it is difficult
to restrain men who are not amenable to discipline". [7]

By this time military operations had produced terrible devastation
and suffering for all races throughout Bulgaria, though it may be
doubted whether Layard's constant comparisons with the ravages
of Genghis Khan and even with the Thirty Years' War [8] were not
much exaggerated. What he certainly failed to realise was that if
the Turkish population fled in large numbers before the advancing
Russians, it was from fear lest the Bulgarians might wreak vengeance
for the horrors of the previous year; that the horrors inevitable to
war in an Eastern country could not be reasonably put on the same
footing as the outrages of soldiery upon a defenceless population in

[1] *Layard Papers*, 11 July, Layard to Beaconsfield.
[2] *Ibid.* 1 Aug., Layard to Beaconsfield.   [3] *Ibid.* 8 Aug., to Derby.
[4] *Turkey No. I.* (1878), no. 225, 12 Aug.; no. 251, 18 Aug. His protests to the
Grand Vizier are in nos. 255 and 288, 20 and 24 Aug.
[5] *Layard Papers*, 11 Aug., to Said.   [6] *Ibid.* 15 Aug., to Derby.
[7] *Ibid.* 22 Aug., to Derby.   [8] *Ibid.* 22 Aug., Layard to Beaconsfield.

time of peace: and again that on the Turkish side there was a lack of discipline among the irregular and even the regular troops, and a break-down of administrative machinery, for which no parallel could be found among the advancing Russians. But when he found that Colonel Wellesley, now once more with the Russian army, admitted that quarter was "neither given nor asked", yet strongly defended the Russians from all charge of atrocities, Layard receded somewhat, and wrote to Derby, "The truth is that one side is as barbarous as the other, but that there is really more excuse for the Turk who sees his country wantonly invaded and his wives and children outraged and massacred".[1]

Early in September news began to reach Constantinople of Turkish reprisals against the Bulgarians. Layard instructed Blunt that prudence and caution were necessary on behalf of Bulgarian prisoners, but assumed severity to be inevitable. "Remember", he significantly added, "what has taken place in Poland."[2] At the same time he told Derby that the executions of Bulgarians "don't appear to me to have been excessive". He turned to the Indian Mutiny for a parallel and asked, "If the Turks were daily blowing Bulgarians from the guns in the public squares of Constantinople, what would not Europe say?" Yet he added the admission that "even the most exaggerated accounts circulated in 1876 were absolutely nothing in comparison with what is now taking place". It had of course been "begun by the Bulgarians, perhaps at the instigation, certainly with the connivance and under the protection, of a party in Russia".[3] Nor had he any illusions as to Turkish policy. The Bulgarian villages would, he believed, be handed over to the Circassians, and "the Porte will do its best to dechristianise Bulgaria and have there a well-armed and powerful Mohammedan population".[4]

At Philippopolis the executions were "recklessly persisted in", the court-martial being presided over by Ibrahim Pasha, "a cruel fanatic", but brother-in-law of the Sultan, and therefore hard to move. "It is despairing work dealing with these people," groans Layard in a moment of candour; "corruption and intrigue are doing more to ruin the Empire than even the Russians."[5] Among many Bulgarian victims special attention was aroused by the case of the brothers

---

[1] *Layard Papers*, 5 Sept., to Derby.   [2] *Ibid*. 30 Aug., to Blunt.
[3] *Ibid*. 29 Aug., to Derby.   [4] *Ibid*. 19 Sept., to Derby.
[5] *Ibid*. 10 Oct., to Derby.

Geshov, described in the Blue Book as "Gueshoglu": petitions from Manchester and Leeds, where they had business connections, led Derby to make special enquiries.[1] Layard held out little hope of saving two men "most deeply compromised in the insurrection": and "as thousands of poor ignorant wretches who have been misled by them have suffered, it is but just that they should not escape". In the end, however, his intervention with the Grand Vizier was successful, and the brothers were deported to Aleppo, one of them living to be Bulgarian Premier during the Balkan War of 1912.

During the autumn Layard, in his defence of Turk against Russian, was caused fresh embarrassment by the reports of Zohrab, the British Consul at Erzerum, and his co-operation with *The Times* correspondent, Captain Norman, and Dr. Casson, the representative of the "Turkish Sick and Wounded Fund", who after what they had seen on that front were agreed in hoping that Armenia would pass out of Turkish hands and were indiscreet enough to write to that effect in *The Times*. He remonstrated with Zohrab for his "readiness to believe anything he hears against the Turks", and requested him "not to send me mere bazaar reports without taking the trouble to verify them".[2] "One would have thought a feeling of honour, if not of decency, would have prevented them abusing those whose hospitality and protection they were enjoying." But then *The Times* was guilty of "deliberate and malicious misrepresentation in all things Turkish", while Murray of the *Scotsman* was "a violent and unscrupulous hater of the Turks".[3] Meanwhile the Ambassador quarrelled with Colonel Lennox, characterised the tone of his dispatches as "improper and disrespectful"[4] and forbade him to go to Plevna, on the ground that he had "neither tact nor temper".

The fact is that Layard can be constantly refuted out of his own mouth. On one occasion he informs Lord Derby that consular reports, reaching him from all parts of Turkey, "prove the anarchy and utter disorganisation which the Russian invasion has brought upon it, and the effects of which it will take many generations to repair".[5] This is but one of many admissions of anarchy and disorder, which the Turkish authorities were powerless to repress, even had they possessed the necessary zeal. There can be little doubt that this outcry against the Russians was an attempt to forestall and destroy the

---

[1] *Turkey No. I.* (1878), nos. 326, 382, 435, 540, 566.
[2] *Layard Papers*, 14 Sept., to Lord Tenterden, and 24 Sept. and 30 Nov., to Sir A. Kemball.   [3] *Ibid.* 21 Nov., to Sanderson.
[4] *Ibid.* 24 Oct., to Tenterden, and 21 Nov., to Derby.   [5] *Ibid.* 31 Oct.

effect of the wholesale ill-treatment of Bulgarians after the Russian retreat. It may be taken for granted that there were many cases of reprisals and excess against the Moslems, but against Layard's reckless accusations of the Russians—based mainly on the same sources as produced the farcical and lying official Turkish reports of the previous year—must be set the evidence not only of the "atrocity gang"—in reality men of proved value and accuracy—but also of Americans and Germans who had no axe to grind, and also of Greek sources—doubtless more suspect, but very definitely anti-Slav. Moreover, such men as Colonel Wellesley, who had not hesitated to criticise the Russians on more than one point, and Archibald Forbes, who had quite exceptional means of observation and who did not conceal his dislike of the Bulgarians, were emphatic in absolving Russians and Bulgarians alike from charges of atrocity.

The fall of Plevna and the rapid advance of the Russians naturally produced a panic among the Moslem population of Bulgaria and Thrace, where the long series of executions of Bulgarian patriots since the summer had aroused keen exasperation and might well be expected to provoke reprisals. Moreover, Layard's bugbear Suleiman Pasha increased the panic by encouraging evacuation. The result was that the Thracian roads were blocked with pitiable processions of Moslem refugees, carrying with them the last scanty fragments of their household goods: and not merely did this prove a grave handicap to military operations, by stopping the movement of Turkish troops,[1] but it caused fearful hardships and loss of life, since the Turkish administration, even in the capital itself, was utterly incapable of providing either accommodation, work or even food for the victims. The Treasury was empty, and indeed by May it was no longer able to find proper rations for the troops.[2] So these poor people died like flies, and the only real help came from British relief organisations, such as those of Lady Strangford and Baroness Burdett-Coutts.

At this stage Layard was still desperately apologising for the Turk and expressed to Derby his doubts regarding the massacres ascribed to the Circassians! "The tendency to exaggerate among the Christians

[1] *Turkey No. I.* 23 Jan. 1878, to Derby, "general exodus" is one phrase used. Cf. Dr. George Washburn's account in *Fifty Years in Constantinople*, pp. 128-9. He accepts 100,000 as a reasonable estimate of those who died in this panic retreat and afterwards on the streets of the capital. He does not even hint at Russian atrocities, but describes how the Russian soldiers rescued derelict Turkish babies. The horrors are also fully described by Archibald Forbes in *Daily News*.

[2] *Layard Papers*, tel. of 19 May, most secret and personal, Layard to Salisbury.

and Europeans in this country is the source of infinite mischief: *it is impossible to get at the real truth*." [1] "You must not", he wrote on the same day to Childers, "confound the Turkish race, as some have unhappily done, with the bastard semi-Byzantine Greek governing class or the wild tribes who form bashibazuks and are no more Turks than you or I are. A Turk might just as well take a St. Giles rough as the model of an English gentleman or a pirate as the type of a civilised Christian." [2]

There seems to have been no limit to Layard's recklessness of statement. Without any evidence he now accused Russia of demanding the removal of the entire Moslem population from the new Bulgaria. "Such horrible relentless barbarity, such an extermination of a race for the purposes of greed and ambition and under the cloak of humanity and religion, has not been seen since the time when the hordes of Asia crossed the Danube in the Middle Ages." [3] This legend was of course emphatically denied from St. Petersburg, but Layard, writing to Derby, treated "the audacious denial" as "on a par with all the Russian proceedings". [4] As ever, he laid the chief blame upon "an unprincipled faction led by Gladstone". [5]

By the end of March his efforts were concentrated in three main directions—to prevent Russia from regaining influence with the Sultan, to prejudice his home Government against any projects of autonomy, and to work up a counter-agitation against Russian and Bulgarian "atrocities" and denounce "the shocking and heart-rending state of affairs which already prevails under Russo-Bulgarian rule". [6]

Parliament Meets

Pending the assembling of Parliament, the public agitation knew no bounds, in view of the obscurity in which the Eastern front was now involved. It was only natural that the silence of official Russia as to the terms about to be imposed should have been regarded as ominous, and her Ambassador repeatedly appealed to St. Petersburg for their speedy definition if calm was to be restored in London. None the less his German colleague, Count Münster, was not far wrong in his diagnosis. "England cannot bear that Russia should be making peace with the Turks without her having a word in the matter: for

---

[1] *Turkey No. I.* 23 Jan. to Derby.   [2] *Ibid.* 25 Jan.
[3] *Layard Papers*, 20 Feb., to Lytton.   [4] *Ibid.* 27 Feb., to Derby.
[5] *Ibid.* 20 Feb., to Lytton.   [6] *Ibid.* 20 March, Layard to Beaconsfield.

a peace without alteration of the guarantee treaties and without injuring English interests in the East is inconceivable. . . . The old British lion has slept a long time and is now wide awake and angry."[1]

On 14 January, then, Lord Derby sent a firm telegram to Loftus, bidding him inform the Russian Government that "any treaty between Russia and Turkey affecting the treaties of 1856 and 1871, must be an European treaty and would not be valid without the assent of the Powers who were parties to those treaties".[2] The very next day Gorchakov telegraphed the assurance that Russia had no intention of moving against Gallipoli unless the Turkish regulars should concentrate there, and the hope that England on her side did not contemplate landing there, as this would be a breach of neutrality and could only encourage the Porte to resist.[3]

On 17 January the British Parliament met, and the Queen's Speech, after summarising the Government's efforts to promote a speedy peace, culminated in the following phrase: "Hitherto neither belligerent has infringed the conditions on which my neutrality is founded", and so long as this is so, "my neutrality will continue the same. But I cannot conceal from myself that should hostilities be unfortunately prolonged, some unexpected occurrence may render it incumbent on me to adopt measures of precaution." On this rested the appeal to the liberality of Parliament.

Lord Granville for the Opposition threw doubt on the motives for calling Parliament and contrasted "the anything but reassuring effect" of the Guildhall speech with more recent pronouncements of Carnarvon and Derby, the latter "the embodiment of good sense". He was very sarcastic about the Turkish constitution and expressed his conviction that it was "to the unfortunate mode of dealing with the Berlin Memorandum that most of the subsequent misfortunes" were due.[4] Beaconsfield replied with some signs of irritation, claiming that British policy might have been "erroneous" or "infirm" but not "vacillating", that the Government had been unanimous as to neutrality and that "from that policy we have never swerved". He keenly resented Granville's taunts of isolation, and argued not very convincingly that the much canvassed Berlin Memorandum "was a document which ceased to exist before England refused to sanction it: that does not look like isolation or want of influence": while to-day

---

[1] Münster to Bennigsen, written during a visit to Lord Derby at Knowsley, 1 Jan. 1878—*Deutsche Revue*, Oct. 1909 p. 314.
[2] *Turkey No.* III. (1878), no. 6.   [3] *Ibid.* No. 8, Loftus to Derby, 15 Jan.
[4] Hansard, ccxxxvii. pp. 19-24.

all the other Powers had declined mediation, England alone had acted. There was not isolation. "England never quitted the European concert": only Turkey and Russia had done so.

"There are two kinds of isolation," he continued. "There is an isolation that comes from decay, from infirmity, that is a sign of impending insignificance. . . . But there is also an isolation which may arise from qualities very different—from self-confidence, from extreme energy, from abounding resources and, above all, from the inspiration of a great cause." Early in the century England was isolated "because among the craven communities of Europe it alone asserted and vindicated the cause of national independence".

From insulting, his language became menacing. "It may be your duty to follow in their footsteps. If that cause were again at stake, if there were a Power that threatened the peace of the world with a predominance fatal to public liberty and national independence, I feel confident that your Lordships would not be afraid of the charge of being isolated, if you stood alone in maintaining such a cause and in fighting for such precious interests." "We have never swerved from our original conception and determination," he added, and turned to attack Granville for his "sneers against British interests", claiming that British influence would be "exercised for the greatest interests of humanity" and for peace. "But if we are called upon to vindicate our rights and to defend the interests of this country, if our present hopes and prospects are baffled"—then he was convinced that he would not appeal to Parliament in vain.

The Duke of Argyll was quite impenitent, and expressed his disappointment at the Prime Minister's answer to "accusations which were never made". He "has only filled our ears with the east wind". He made havoc of the Government's denial of internal dissensions, pointing to the "violent abuse" of Salisbury in the leading Conservative organs and contrasting his and Carnarvon's speeches with "the drums and fifes" of Gathorne Hardy[1] at Edinburgh and Lord John Manners's "laurel of unquestioned victory, intertwined with the lily of lasting peace". He concurred "most cordially" with Derby's definition of British interests in the decisive dispatch of 6 May 1877, emphasising the fact that in it there was no mention of the integrity and independence of Turkey": and he sought to prove Britain's isolation in Europe by quoting the words in which Derby had rejected the Berlin Memorandum. "Her Majesty's Government have

---

[1] The Secretary for War.

since the outbreak of the insurrection deprecated the diplomatic intervention of other Powers in the affairs of the Ottoman Empire": but this diplomatic interference, he very pertinently added, was the sole object of the European Concert in Eastern affairs. Parliament had heard "an elaborate defence of selfish motives" from the head of the Government: what if Russia avowed the same? But Russia's main motive lay in the impossibility of putting off indefinitely the vindication of her co-religionists. "Call it sentimental, humanitarian, illogical, what you will, nevertheless this was one of the most powerful motive forces in the history of the world." He himself, as a survivor of the Crimean Cabinet, would continue to maintain that Britain had "undertaken obligations to the subject populations" which she could never repudiate, and that it was useless to "attempt to prop up the phantom of the Turkish Empire": far rather let us devise "some scheme for the just government of its subject populations", and recognise frankly that the cruelties of the war were due to "the barbarism of the Government with which Russia is fighting", and that the true solution was to put an end to "the ruling classes" of Turkey.

The debate closed with a speech of Lord Salisbury, who, while declaring, "I heartily and deeply sympathise with the subject races in the East", doubted whether nine months of war "had not accumulated more misery than would result from generations of Turkish government" and feared lest Argyll's policy of evicting the Turks might drive them to "absolute desperation". He endorsed the Government's measures of precaution, "not in any spirit of despair of peace. . . . The duties of humanity I am very far from disputing, but I am not prepared to accept the new gospel which I understand is preached—that it is our business for the sake of any populations whatever, to disregard the trusts which the people of this country and our sovereign have reposed in our hands." This open challenge to Mr. Gladstone is a fair measure of the difference of mentality between two men whose views on the Eastern Question were not really so very far apart. The speech concluded with high praise of the Tsar, tempered by a hint that even an autocratic sovereign was not always able "to control the caprice of armies in the flush of victory".[1]

Meanwhile in the House of Commons, Egerton, the mover of the Address, struck a somewhat curious note, freely admitting that the

---

[1] Hansard, ccxxxvii. pp. 54-6.

Turks, "by their gross misrule have brought on themselves their present calamities", but warning Russia that if "in the elation of triumph, false to her solemn promises and deaf to our appeals, she should drive those wretched people to desperation", there would be in England "an irresistible reaction of feeling". Lord Hartington as usual assumed a half-way-house position, contrasting the language of the Prime Minister with the tranquillising phrases of the Foreign Secretary and insisting upon "the moderation of language" at the Opposition's public meetings. The situation, he argued, had greatly altered since the rejection of the Berlin Memorandum, but though perhaps in its new phase "mortifying to the statesmen who have taken a particular view of the Eastern Question", it could not be regarded as "humiliating to this country"—a reference to the phrases constantly reiterated at this time in the Jingo press. The Opposition he declared to be equally against alliance with either Turkey or Russia. Meanwhile, "every fact points to the conclusion that preparation is less required now than last autumn", yet the Government appears to have come to "a directly opposite conclusion". Its action suggested "want of foresight", and would only encourage the Turks —which was no kindness to them themselves, since it was "certain that Russia will respect your conditions of neutrality, . . . and you will therefore have no opportunity of quarrelling with her".[1]

Northcote was as conciliatory as ever, but complained of misrepresentation as regards the Berlin Memorandum, and scouted all idea of either "humiliation" or "isolation". The position was "one of considerable delicacy and anxiety", but there was every hope of localising and ending the war. "We have no secret intentions to play the country false, or our allies false, or Turkey false. . . . We desire to promote the cause of freedom, of liberty and of peace, upon the largest and highest scale. . . . Until we know what the Russian conditions are, we have no proposals to make."

This last phrase was at once caught up by Gladstone, as having "immensely relieved" the minds of the Opposition: but he was careful to add that an increase of the army would be "in high degree dangerous and in glaring contradiction to the expressed wishes of the country".[2] The debate tapered off into the Irish question, and was not even rekindled when Lord Robert Montagu—one of the most uncompromising "Die Hards" of his day—bade the Government fear isolation more than war and declared it to have been "cajoled,

[1] *Ibid.* pp. 79-86.   [2] *Ibid.* p. 106.

bamboozled, outwitted in diplomacy". On the 18th the Address was carried by 301 to 253, the real struggle being left to the debate upon Army Estimates at the end of the month. *The Times* made the sarcastic comment "that so far Parliament has only been called together to prove that there was no very urgent need for summoning it".

Behind the scenes the Prime Minister remained warlike, and was obviously influenced by Layard's letters and dispatches. On 9 January in particular the Ambassador wrote, warning him that the Turkish situation was "extremely critical", that the Turks were "greatly disappointed at what they call our 'desertion' of them and very bitter at the advice to make terms with Russia. Their complaint is no doubt unreasonable, but I cannot but feel for them, for since the partition of Poland no nation has been so cruelly and iniquitously treated." He again urgently repeated his previous advice: "Let us at all costs secure the Gallipoli Lines". In the meantime, he did not hesitate to write to the Sultan's master of ceremonies, Said Pasha, denouncing Suleiman Pasha as "the primary cause of all the misfortunes that have befallen your gallant troops":[1] and he was able to report home that he had "prevailed on the Sultan, notwithstanding the opposition of the Grand Vizier, to give the command in Roumelia to Mehemed Ali Pasha".[2] To such lengths was his policy of interference pushed: yet in the same breath he is again lamenting that "it would require a genius such as the world has rarely produced to set this unhappy country right".

At this very moment Musurus reported to the Porte a talk with Beaconsfield, who lamented the Shipka defeat, but assumed that the Turks could rally 100,000 men round Adrianople and took the line that his Government, sure of the Queen's support, would be very strong in Parliament, and that very favourable results would ensue for the Turkish cause.[3]

It is thus quite impossible to absolve the Premier and his Ambassador from encouraging Turkish illusions to the last and thus postponing the inevitable capitulation. Layard's language during this critical period was so open as to become the gossip of the Turkish capital and the subject of comment at all the Embassies. His German colleague, Prince Reuss, reported to Berlin on 15 January, that Layard

---

[1] *Layard Papers*, 10 Jan., Layard to Said. To Derby he wrote of Suleiman's "shameful mismanagement, if not something worse"—*ibid.* 11 Jan.

[2] *Ibid.* 9 Jan., Layard to Beaconsfield.

[3] *Ibid.* 10 Jan., Musurus to Server (copy).

for a month past had not ceased dissuading the Turks from direct overtures to Russia and urging upon his own Government a still more Turcophil attitude—thereby rousing false hopes in the Turkish ministers and delaying the final settlement.[1]

There is a certain piquancy in Reuss's considered opinion of Layard, addressed to Radowitz, one of Bismarck's confidants in Eastern affairs and soon afterwards the organiser of the Berlin Congress. "He [Layard] is still more unreliable and mendacious than Ignatyev. The Turks cannot bear him, and he abuses them, so that they will no longer do what he advises. It is really difficult for me, much as I try to maintain good relations with him. There is not one among our colleagues who has not caught him out in palpable and very clumsy insincerities. Ignatyev at least deceives his fellow-men with ingratiating elegance."[2]

BEACONSFIELD'S SECOND OVERTURE TO AUSTRIA

The Prime Minister's warlike attitude is revealed in his report to the Queen upon the successful turn of the debate. In it he interpreted Northcote's speech to her as meaning that "we should be prepared to go to war" if the Russian peace terms were not such as England "had a right to expect".[3] Next day he tried to prepare her for "the disruption of the Cabinet, *inevitable war with Russia, though not without allies*, and many other trials".[4] She replied with an embarrassing offer of the Garter, which Beaconsfield had some difficulty in postponing, and she went on to declare, "*War with Russia is, the Queen believes, inevitable now or later*. Let Lord Derby and Lord Carnarvon go, and be very firm. A divided Cabinet is of no use."[5] Great importance attaches to this interchange of views, which was promptly followed by a series of aggressive steps on the part of Lord Beaconsfield.

How utterly at sea he was as to the fundamentals of the continental situation, is best shown by his illusions of an Austro-British alliance.

[1] *G.P.* no. 301, Reuss to Bülow.
[2] Radowitz, *Denkwürdigkeiten*, i. p. 367. It is strange that these memoirs should not yet have attracted the attention of any English writer.
[3] 18 Jan.—Buckle, vi. p. 225.   [4] *Letters*, ii. p. 596, 19 Jan.
[5] This letter is quoted by Mr. Buckle (vi. p. 225), but the first sentence, as italicised above, has been omitted, with the result that the significance of the whole incident is more than half lost. In vol. ii. of Queen Victoria's *Letters*, 2nd Series, p. 597, the full text is reproduced by Mr. Buckle, together with Beaconsfield's letter of the 19th, from which we quote the earlier italicised passage above. It is not clear how he came to omit such vital passages in the earlier volume.

It is true that Andrássy was increasingly alarmed at the Russian advance and at the tone of the Tsar's communications, and that a Crown Council held in Vienna on 15 January discussed the eventuality of war, Archduke Albrecht and Count Beck agreeing that it would be quite feasible to cut Russia's forces into two and compel her to evacuate Roumania, as in 1854. But when Beust reported a blunt enquiry from Beaconsfield, as to whether Andrássy would "make the *grand coup*"—in other words, mobilise—a prompt answer came from Vienna in the negative, "unless, as is not impossible, Russia forces us to do so". The fact is that the military chiefs, though agreed on the broad lines, differed as to tactical details, Beck insisting upon the need for a rapid advance through the Transylvanian passes, while the Archduke held that Transylvania could not support the large armies that would be required.[1]

For our present purpose, however, it is more important to note another of Andrássy's reactions. The British Speech from the Throne made upon him—and in his opinion, upon all Europe [2]—"a very unfavourable impression": once more he felt that Britain, with its inscrutable and ignorant Prime Minister, its divided Cabinet, its incalculable Opposition and its half-hysterical public opinion, would be a highly dangerous and doubtful ally. He therefore preferred to deal direct with St. Petersburg and appealed to Gorchakov not to create an accomplished fact: but in his mind the Russian Chancellor's reply that there was no question of ignoring Austria-Hungary, was offset by the steady advance of the Russian army and the knowledge that two parties were contending for the Tsar's favour, and that the more chauvinistic and anti-Austrian, under Ignatyev, might easily win.

Meanwhile Beaconsfield on the first day of the Session reported to the Queen "constant and promising" communications with Vienna, and next day wrote again: "Austria is thoroughly alarmed and appears really to have been duped. Nothing but a secret treaty, or formulated understanding with Russia, could have authorised her conduct throughout these transactions, and she appears now to have nothing of the kind." [3] It is easy for us, looking over the shoulders of the players, to see that Beaconsfield had misjudged his opponents' and his partners' hands: but at the time he was deaf to every hint of an Austro-Russian agreement, whether it came from Russell or

[1] Wertheimer, *op. cit.* iii. pp. 61-3.   [2] *Ibid.* p. 66.
[3] 19 Jan., to Queen—*Letters*, ii. p. 596.

Shuvalov or Layard, and he was inevitably misled by the ignorance in which Beust himself was kept by his own chief. On 21 January, then, he proposed to the Cabinet overtures for a "defensive alliance" with Austria-Hungary, and this was "warmly adopted", in spite of "fierce opposition" from Lord Derby. But nothing came of this, for the simple reason that neither Government completely trusted the other.

Dispatches written towards the end of January give us the clue to Andrássy's attitude, but it can scarcely have been clear to London at the time. On the 28th he enquired of Elliot—since the autumn our Ambassador in Vienna—whether England was ready for joint armed intervention, but in his tortuous way insisted that there must be no public admission of alliance till the final moment for action came. "If we act separately, but in agreement, our attitude will seem an European one, and the other signatory Powers cannot very well reject it." [1] In a word, he was not willing to proclaim an alliance with Britain until the latter had actually gone to war, while London wanted to be sure of the alliance first. This was natural enough, since he seems to have been uncertain how long the Conservatives would survive, and not without reason doubtful of a *rapprochement* with the Liberals. The foundations of his policy are to be found, not in any perfunctory "sounding" of London, but in his message to Bismarck, [2] that *"we shall do our utmost not to bring him into the dilemma of a choice between us and Russia"*. Incidentally, this phrase shows how clearly Andrássy understood the foundations of German policy under Bismarck, and how events were ripening towards a closer friendship between Vienna and Berlin.

None the less, when next day he received from Novikov the Russian terms of armistice, he wrote in real panic to Károlyi: *"So Russia has played us false.* Gorchakov seems to wish to settle the whole Eastern Question with a *coup* such as that of 1871 in the Black Sea affair." This forces him to declare that Turkey may renounce her own rights, but that European treaties cannot be dissolved by individual Powers, and that Austria-Hungary will regard the settlement as invalid "until we are in a position to enforce our equal vote in the remoulding of conditions". [3] The only alternatives were a conflict with Russia or a Conference such as would restore Austria's loss

[1] Wertheimer, iii. p. 70.
[2] Through Count Károlyi, his Ambassador in Berlin, 25 Jan.—*ibid*. p. 72.
[3] "Bei Neukreierung der Zustände", 28 Jan.—*G.P.* ii. no. 303.

of prestige before public opinion. Meanwhile, at his instance, the Emperor replied to the Tsar's letter, affirming that "our chief task as friends and sovereigns is not to sacrifice to the impressions of the moment the great interests of the future", but at once adding that it was "absolutely impossible" for him to consent to a military occupation of Bulgaria after the signature of peace, "for then all efforts could not avert a collision of our interests". On the other hand he accepted the cession of Bessarabia and would refuse an autonomous Bulgaria, even though this had only been intended in the event of Turkish dissolution, and though it would offend public opinion.[1]

That Russia had no desire to alienate Austria-Hungary is amply demonstrated by the secret memorandum addressed by Gorchakov to his two allies in Vienna and Berlin,[2] with the object of elucidating the terms imposed upon the Turks. As regards Bulgaria, Russia felt bound to insist upon full autonomy, without any Turkish garrisons, and to oppose its artificial division into two sections—on the very convincing ground that the two would gravitate towards each other, like Moldavia and Wallachia. "The objections to a compact Slav state had been removed by force of circumstances", and a Big Bulgaria "would actually be a guarantee for the maintenance of Ottoman rule in Europe". In drawing the frontiers "the principle of nationality" must be applied. Meanwhile Russia had no objection to Austria-Hungary taking possession of Bosnia-Hercegovina, "even though the Reichstadt conditions had not arisen". As regards the Straits, she was ready to leave this question to the decision of Europe, but held that it would be more dangerous to make of Constantinople a free port, than to leave the Turks as "mandatories of Europe for the protection of the Straits".[3]

Bismarck at this juncture was seriously disturbed at Andrássy's violent reactions, and though careful not to raise objections to a Conference demanded "with such liveliness" by Andrássy, entirely failed to see what the latter could hope to gain by it.[4] He continued to charge Gorchakov with "insincerity" and even bad faith, and

[1] Francis Joseph to Alexander II., 26 Jan.—*U.R.B.D.*
[2] Russian Memoire, 31 Jan. 1878 ("bloss an uns und Deutschland gerichtet")—"Teschenberg Dossier", *Austrian Archives*.
[3] "Constantinople, ville libre, serait le receptacle de tous les aventuriers de l'Europe, le théâtre incessant des luttes de race et probablement aussi des rivalités politiques parmi les Grandes Puissances protectrices, tandis que la proximité des Turcs, à portée de canon sur la rive asiatique, y rendrait impossible le maintien de l'ordre et de la tranquillité"—*ibid.*
[4] *G.P.* ii. no. 304, 29 Jan., Herbert Bismarck to Bülow; no. 305, 30 Jan., Diktat of Bismarck.

never lost an opportunity of speaking ill of him, even in confidential documents for the use of the office: but he also continued to believe in the maintenance of the Three Emperors' League and laid it down that Germany's main interest was an understanding between Petersburg and Vienna.[1]

Soon after this Lord Odo Russell reports a conversation with the German Chancellor, who complained that "the three Emperors were in frequent personal correspondence with each other, without the knowledge and behind the backs of their ministers, and the difficulty of finding out what Their Majesties were settling among themselves was often very great. He never would cease to remonstrate against a practice so fraught with danger to the public service." The only explanation which could be extracted from him was their habit of unreserved comment upon their ministers![2]

DERBY AND CARNARVON RESIGN

We are now in a better position to understand events in London. On 23 January Beaconsfield went to the Cabinet, fortified with the Queen's authority to accept possible resignations, and evidently assuming that Andrássy's response to his overtures would be favourable. He won a majority of his colleagues for the proposal that the fleet should proceed through the Dardanelles to Constantinople itself, and that the House of Commons should be asked for a Vote of Credit. Derby and Carnarvon at once resigned—the former expressing his pain at severing a connection of thirty years, and confessing, with exaggerated, but obviously sincere, modesty, that he had long doubted his capacity of "even moderately efficient service":[3] t'·e latter writing an unequivocal refusal "to agree to any armed intervention" and persisting in his resignation when it was not at fir.. accepted.[4] The Queen lost no time in expressing "her immense satis faction and relief. . . . To the last she feared Lord Derby would stay", though "his inaction and delay on every occasion and total want c' energy and purpose have been such that he had become totally unfit to be Foreign Secretary".[5]

Shuvalov was by now acutely anxious and wired to his Government on the 24th that it was no longer a question of the fleet or of

[1] *Ibid.* nos. 308 and 310, memorandum of Bülow and Bismarck.
[2] Odo Russell to Derby, 17 Feb.—F.O. 64912, no. 119.
[3] 23 Jan.—Buckle, vi. p. 228.
[4] Hansard, ccxxxvii., 25 Jan. pp. 440-41.   [5] 24 Jan.—Buckle, vi. p. 229.

Gallipoli, "but of immediate rupture" with Russia.[1] News of the Cabinet's decision was instantly sent to him, presumably by Lady Derby,[2] "who implored me to use every means" to avert the crisis. He took so grave a view of the situation that he hurriedly asked to see Derby before he went to the House of Lords, and gave him, on his own responsibility, an assurance that the Straits question would be reserved for general discussion. When asked as to Russia's intentions for Bulgaria, he replied, autonomy and unity, with tribute as the sole link with Turkey: and when Derby frankly assumed that Austria would never consent to such a solution, he retorted, "I have not come to discuss Austria, but to prove that Russia is not threatening 'British interests', and to stop you on the slippery incline". Only on one point did he hedge, namely, a Russian occupation of Bulgaria after the peace: and here he was skilful enough to quote no less a witness than Colonel Wellesley for the impossibility of abandoning Bulgaria "to her own resources" without an intermediary stage.

Following on this conversation, Sir Stafford Northcote as Leader of the Commons announced that as a whole week had elapsed without the Russian peace terms being communicated, and as the Russian armies continued their rapid advance, the Government felt it impossible to delay any longer and gave notice that a supplementary estimate of £6,000,000 for military expenditure would be laid before Parliament in a week's time. This action Shuvalov quite accurately ascribed to Austria's attitude and London's "fear of losing an ally who was awaiting a sign of energy on England's part, before pronouncing herself".

Instructions were at once telegraphed to the fleet—then at Smyrna under Admiral Hornby—to proceed through the Dardanelles to the Turkish capital, in order "to keep open the waterway and protect British life and property in the event of tumults at Constantinople".[3] But scarcely had these orders been dispatched when news came from Layard in Constantinople that the Turks had accepted the Russian armistice terms and incidentally that the question of the Straits was reserved for settlement "between the Congress and the Tsar". Northcote has left a memorandum recording the "bombshell" effect which this made upon the Cabinet, who not un-

[1] *U.R.B.D.* 12/24 Jan., Shuvalov to Gorchakov (tel.).
[2] "La source bienveillante d'où je la tenais me conjurait d'employer tous les moyens pour l'écarter."
[3] Northcote's quotation in House of Commons, 25 Jan.—Hansard, p. 468.

naturally felt that it robbed them of all excuse for immediate naval and military action. A telegram was therefore sent to the Admiral, ordering him not to enter the Straits after all, and to remain at Besika Bay until further instructions.[1] What really made this decision inevitable was an urgent telegraphic appeal from the Sultan to the British Government, insisting that to send the fleet might be regarded by Russia as a threat and would give her an excuse for breaking off negotiations and seizing the capital, and that if England was none the less bent on action, she must announce publicly that she was acting against his express wishes.[2] Obviously such a step would have been quite impossible in the excited state of British public opinion and would have made the breach with Derby irrevocable.

There is a certain mystery about this famous revocation of orders. It is quite clear that Northcote believed it to have been mainly due to Layard's report that the Straits question was to be referred to a future Congress, and that he was correspondingly annoyed next day, when it transpired that the true version was "between *Sultan* and Tsar, not between Congress and Tsar".[3] Mr. Buckle not only accepts Northcote's version as the whole truth, but appears to know nothing about the Sultan's personal appeal. Quite apart, however, from the decisive character of that appeal—all the more decisive on the very day when the Leader of the Opposition was arguing in the House of Commons that to enter the Dardanelles without the consent of the Porte would be an infraction of the Treaties of 1856,[4] on which the Government were so constantly harping—Northcote's version assumes an entirely different complexion when pieced together with the correspondence of the Russian Ambassador and Chancellor, hitherto unpublished.

The fact is that Shuvalov, who had been clamouring for information from his home Government, at last received an official summary of the Russian terms on 25 January, and at once hastened with it to Lord Derby. They at once compared the two texts as sent by

[1] Buckle, vi. pp. 230-31.
[2] *U.R.B.D.* 13/25 Jan., Shuvalov to Gorchakov (tel.).
[3] Buckle, vi. p. 231. The relevant portion of Layard's telegram of 24 Jan. (F.O. 78/2809, no. 102) runs as follows: "Sixth. The question of the Bosphorus and Dardanelles to be settled between the Congress and the Emperor of Russia." At the word "Congress" on the original document there is a marginal note stating, "Alteration of one figure in the group makes Sultan". Next day, 25 Jan., Layard telegraphed (*ibid*. no. 109): "In my telegram no. 102 read 'Sultan' not 'Congress' ".
[4] 25 Jan.—Hansard, ccxxxvii. p. 470.

Gorchakov and by Layard, and Shuvalov reports home that the crucial point made by Derby ran, "The question of the Dardanelles shall be decided in a conference between Russia and Turkey"—a version which only differs in wording, but not in sense,[1] from the text on which Northcote's memorandum is based. Shuvalov, however, having his chief's authority to show Derby the actual terms submitted by the Grand Duke to the Turks—expressly telegraphed, in Gorchakov's own words, *"in case of their being distorted by Layard"* [2]— was able to convince Derby that this very case had arisen, and that the phrase about the Straits ran in the much more harmless form, "subsequent agreement to safeguard Russian rights and interests in the Straits".[3] After this rectification he repeated to Derby "the assurance included in your [Gorchakov's] telegram, that we would not solve European questions by ourselves [*isolément*]".

Obviously, if Tsar and Chancellor had no longer adhered to this pledge, they would at once have challenged Shuvalov, and probably pretty sharply, as peace and war hung upon the issue. So far from this, Gorchakov wired four days later, "If they question you further on the *vague phrase* concerning the Straits in our conditions of preliminary peace, you can positively affirm that we persist in regarding the passage through Bosphorus and Dardanelles *as a question reserved for an European agreement. You know that my opinion, to which His Majesty leans, is for a* mare clausum, *forbidding passage to warships of every nationality."* [4] This may or may not have been a practical solution, but it makes it quite clear that the alarm of the British Cabinet on that particular question was unfounded. Yet so little were they reassured by Shuvalov's explanation—even though it robbed them for the moment of the excuse for action—that they credited an insidious rumour that peace was to be signed at Sebastopol—"a choice", Shuvalov reported, "interpreted as a provocation to the Powers which made the Crimean War".[5] Gorchakov at once replied that the preliminaries would be signed at Adrianople: [6] and as we now know, there had never been any other intention.

This incident has been dealt with in extreme detail, because it

[1] Shuvalov doubtless wrote from memory, on getting home from the Foreign Office.

[2] "Vous les envoie pour le cas ou défigurées par Layard": "Alors en ferez usage" —*U.R.B.D.* tel. of 12/24 Jan.

[3] *Ibid.*: "Entente ultérieure pour sauvegarder droits et intérêts russes dans Détroits".   [4] *Ibid.* Gorchakov to Shuvalov, tel. of 17/29 Jan.

[5] *Ibid.* Shuvalov to Gorchakov, tel. of 16/28 Jan.

[6] *Ibid.* Gorchakov to Shuvalov, tel. of 17/29 Jan.

represents perhaps the most dangerous moment in the whole crisis, when war was on a razor's edge. Rarely has an error in the deciphering of a single word had so vital an effect on a major issue of international politics!

DERBY IS REINSTATED

The Queen's exultation had been premature. Lord Carnarvon was allowed to go, in view of his obvious "personal feeling against the Prime Minister": but there was a consensus of opinion inside the Cabinet that Derby must be retained at all costs. Northcote told the Queen that his secession "would shake our Lancashire members to the centre" and greatly strengthen Gladstone.[1] Shuvalov, as uncannily well informed as ever, was at the same time reporting home that by disembarking Derby the war party "will have thrown off its chief obstacle", but that the Cabinet would "lose in vitality", because of his great influence and the certain loss of many county constituencies.[2] Even Hardy noted that "Derby's name carries weight from the prudence of his words—the world does not know his inability to act".[3] Beaconsfield himself reluctantly recognised this and told Salisbury that "at this juncture his secession would have exposed us to all kinds of wild suspicions and added to the difficulties".[4] Thus there was nothing for it but to write a letter to the Queen, addressed "Madam and most beloved Sovereign", and appealing to her "infinite indulgence". The retirement of Lord Derby, he assured her, was "producing disastrous results on the Conservative party, both in Parliament and out of doors: a general *disintegration is taking place*", the manufacturing centres could no longer be relied upon, and almost every member of the Cabinet was clamouring for his retention.[5]

The Queen yielded to his "agitation and disquietude", simply because she had no other course: but she made no concealment of her regret and complained that the Foreign Secretary's "great dilatoriness was one of the most alarming features in his very peculiar character".[6] Northcote was entrusted with the task of bringing the disgruntled Derby back to the fold, and had some difficulty in insuring him against "fresh *coups de tête* on the part of his chief".[7] Henceforth

[1] 26 Jan.—*Letters*, ii. p. 599.   [2] *U.R.B.D.* 13/25 Jan.
[3] Diary, 26 Jan.—*Life of Gathorne Hardy*, ii. p. 49.
[4] *Life of Salisbury*, ii. p. 194.   [5] 26 Jan.—Buckle, vi. p. 234.
[6] 27 Jan.—*ibid.* p. 235.
[7] *U.R.B.D.* 15/27 Jan., Shuvalov to Gorchakov (letter).

the old intimacy between Derby and Disraeli was entirely at an end, and Derby on his side recorded in his Diary that he remained in office "rather in the hope of preventing mischief as long as I can, than from sympathising with the views of my colleagues".[1] In the House of Lords he admitted his "dissent from an important step by the Cabinet", but "before many hours the circumstances of the case had entirely altered", and he had "no hesitation or difficulty" in remaining. More than one of his colleagues must have winced when he laid renewed stress on the conditions of neutrality laid down by him on 6 May 1877 and declared that "we have not varied and do not intend to depart from them now", and still more when he denied that any encouragement had been given to the Turks "to persevere in a hopeless struggle, by holding out to them fallacious expectations".[2] But this brief statement undoubtedly had a reassuring effect in very wide circles, and it was no accident that *The Times*, true to its middle course throughout the long crisis, should have referred to Derby as "the Minister whose calm and consistent conduct of foreign affairs has throughout this difficult period been one of the chief sources of public confidence, and who was author of the famous dispatch defining our neutrality".[3]

When the Cabinet next met, Lord Derby no longer resumed "his usual seat" next to the Prime Minister, but "sate far apart in the vacant seat of Lord Carnarvon. This was very marked. He is evidently in a dark temper, but all must be borne at this moment."[4] The plain fact is that the Premier's warlike designs were hardly in question, but he lacked the power to enforce them, without endangering the unity, and the very future, of his party.

Meanwhile his public attitude to Lord Carnarvon was somewhat equivocal. Though a meeting of working-men at Exeter Hall had recently thanked Carnarvon as "our watchdog",[5] and though his conduct of the Colonial Office had won general recognition, it was obvious that, unlike Derby, he stood mainly for himself and could probably be dropped with impunity. He could not, however, be prevented from reading in the House of Lords the formal letter in which he explained his resignation to his chief, and went on to describe

---

[1] Diary, cit. Buckle, vi. p. 237. This document is probably the only political document of the first importance from the period of the seventies which has not yet seen the light. Its publication would almost certainly enhance Lord Derby's reputation and is really due to his memory.

[2] Hansard, ccxxxvii. pp. 521-3.   [3] Leader of 25 Jan. 1878.

[4] 27 Jan. to Queen—Buckle, vi. p. 238.   [5] *The Times*, 17 Jan. 1878.

Derby's policy as "wise and consistent" and to refer to the "wide divergences of opinion as to the principles on which our foreign policy should be conducted". Indeed, he felt that "we were exchanging the position of a neutral for that of a belligerent". To this the Prime Minister himself replied that he failed to "comprehend a sufficient reason", and maintained that since the dispatch of 6 May 1877 "British policy has never changed, and there never has been the slightest division in the Cabinet respecting it".[1] In view of what we now know of the Government *coulisses*, this assertion can only be regarded as intended to mislead contemporary opinion.

Shuvalov's comments upon the Sunday Cabinet that followed, are worth quoting. While fearing that Derby would be "garlanded and forced to make concessions", he felt that "from the standpoint of European peace it is desirable to keep Lord Derby, even at this price". But he was still seriously alarmed, for while in his view the Government was "quite discredited by its tergiversations" and the Opposition was rubbing its hands, there was a danger lest Beaconsfield, "baffled in his policy, might try to escape from ridicule by winning fame such as that of Herostratus, who burned the temple of Ephesus".[2]

A FIVE NIGHTS' DEBATE

The tension and excitement in the country were extreme, when on 28 January the Chancellor of the Exchequer introduced a motion for an additional sum of £6,000,000 on the Army and Navy Estimates. In 1878 such a sum was still regarded as worthy of serious challenge by our parliamentarians, though it was admittedly a mere inadequate trifle if there was to be a new Crimean War.

Sir Stafford Northcote's statement was alternately alarmist and reassuring. He freely admitted Russia's right to advance, and deprecated any advice to the Porte—"absolute silence is our duty". But he made it quite clear that the Government was alarmed at the simultaneous delay in signature and the advance of the Russian armies. The terms communicated by Shuvalov to Derby were of "a very sweeping character": and while the status of Serbia, Montenegro, Roumania and even Bulgaria were admittedly of only secondary interest to us, the question of the Straits was "a matter of European concern, . . . not a British interest only". Turkey was

---

[1] Hansard, ccxxxvii. pp. 442, 448.
[2] *U.R.B.D.* 15/27 Jan., Shuvalov to Gorchakov (letter).

"in danger of being dismembered", and Britain could not be indifferent to such drastic changes in a state of things which she had upheld for a century. He was careful to "make no complaint" as to the Tsar's refusal [1] to renounce the right of occupation, but added that "it may become the duty of England to watch over the action of Russia with regard to Constantinople". He went on to express himself as satisfied with Gorchakov's assurance to Loftus that Russia had no intention of occupying Gallipoli "unless the Turks concentrated there", and added that Britain on her side had no such intention. He even explained that the orders to the fleet had been rescinded, "because we understood that satisfactory terms had been offered and accepted". Indeed he made what many of his audience must have taken for a side-hit at the Queen, when he deprecated as mischievous the loose language current about the "humiliation of England". But he at once toned this down by an attack upon "those among us who decry and make light of the power and spirit of the country", and concluded by appealing to Parliament "to enable us to use the force of England" in case of need. [2]

The debate that followed lasted for five nights, and took on a note of personal passion, and indeed at times of vituperation, such as only marks the stormiest periods of parliamentary history. The long series of Liberal demonstrations had naturally stung the Conservative majority into active protest. Specially resented was a speech of Mr. George Trevelyan at Selkirk, in which he described the Prime Minister as "the most strong-willed, audacious and pertinacious of all his colleagues", who "has never disguised his desire to plunge the nation into war": [3] and now the Secretary for War, Mr. Gathorne Hardy, after a violent passage of arms, denounced this attitude as "a criminal state of mind" and "one which is of itself a disgrace". But the outspoken Trevelyan was completely eclipsed by Gladstone himself, who on 30 January delivered at Oxford one of his most famous fighting speeches. This, he declared, was no ordinary crisis. In the Eastern Question, "when you speak of the Government, you mean Lord Beaconsfield": for "not one man in the Government has a tenth part of his tenacity of will and patient purpose". Referring to the Cabinet as a bag in which "all the warring winds of heaven are shut up", he quoted Brougham's gibe against the Iron Duke's Cabinet of ten men—"one and a nought: the Duke of Wellington is

<hr>

[1] In answer to Derby's Note of 13 December to Shuvalov.
[2] Hansard, ccxxxvii. pp. 541-60.   [3] *The Times*, 12 Jan.

the one and the other nine the nought". At the same time he contrasted "the astonishing discipline of the Tory party" with his own party, "where we give too much weight to our own individual peculiarities". He denounced the sending of the fleet as "an act of war, a breach of European law". He argued that by strengthening the garrison at Malta, by sending the fleet to Besika, by appointing such an Ambassador as Layard, and now by the Vote in Parliament, we had roused "false hopes" in the Turks, encouraged them "to prolong the war" and so "used them cruelly". He expressed keen regret that the liberation of the Balkans should have been achieved, not by the state "which has achieved freedom for herself, but by that state in Europe which perhaps was the least fit of all to do it". Of himself he confessed, and this was the phrase which stuck—that he had been driven to play "the part of an agitator. My purpose has been . . . to the best of my power, for the last eighteen months, day and night, week by week, month by month, to counterwork as well as I could, what I believe to be the purpose of Lord Beaconsfield." [1]

The Prime Minister's own comment upon these phrases is to be found in a letter to Lady Bradford: "The mask has fallen, and instead of a pious Christian, we find a vindictive fiend, who confesses he has, for a year and a half, been dodging and manoeuvring against an individual—because he was his successful rival".[2] The incident illustrates only too clearly the acute personal animus between the two men. Gladstone was ready to believe anything of his rival, while passion blinded Disraeli to the fact that daily opposition is the obvious duty of any Opposition leader, especially in a great international crisis, and not the mark of a vindictive fiend.

By this speech Gladstone had presumably let off the necessary steam, for when he intervened in the Commons debate, he was far more moderate in tone,[3] and while he opposed the Vote as

[1] *Ibid.* 31 Jan. We understand all the better the pent-up feeling behind this outburst, when we compare its words with a letter written by Mr. Gladstone to Lord Bath on 4 January (*Gladstone Papers*): "I hang back and decline public action on the principle on which I have acted throughout. I could not speak without more or less censuring the Government: without censuring its head, more and not less. This I think *from me a great evil and a bad precedent in foreign policy.* I have done it in what seemed to me a case of necessity: and I am prepared to do it again if such a case arises. I wait therefore for positive indications of mischief. Such action from *others* as has taken place I think very advantageous."

[2] 1 Feb.—Buckle, vi. p. 239. Mr. Buckle wisely avoids all comment on this outburst.

[3] *The Times* was fully entitled to contrast his mildness inside the House with his "previous ferocity"—see leader of 5 Feb.

"perfectly unreal" and "contrary to all the rules", he disclaimed all intention of "arraigning keenly the past policy of the Government", and frankly regretted that the form in which they had clothed their proposals rendered impossible any "united expression of opinion" by Parliament. None the less he adhered to his Oxford attack on the Premier, on the ground that the latter's utterances "form a perfectly consistent whole", containing "nothing ambiguous or uncertain".[1] This roused Gathorne Hardy to a defence of his chief. Till recently there had been "a little oozing of lava from the cracks in the mountain, but at length it poured forth in pent-up force at Oxford on the devoted head" of the Prime Minister. No one complained of objections directed against a Government's foreign policy: all Oppositions had done so: "what we do object to is an Opposition attempting to stop supplies".[2] The fact that the withholding of supplies was the most effective, if not the only effective, means of checking an objectionable policy does not seem to have occurred to him.

Once more *The Times* struck the just balance between the rival athletes, openly questioning the wisdom of Gladstone's tactics and adding the side-hit, that as "the professed enemy of Lord Beaconsfield" he "will perhaps not be expected to judge of affairs in the same way as other people", but none the less insisting that "in his firm determination to do nothing to help Turkey, to leave her to bear the consequences of her own misdeeds and perversity, he has the voice of the country with him. The course of events has by this time shown sufficiently that he was right."[3]

The best proof of the extreme tension on both sides is to be found, not in the habitual violence of Henry Chaplin — who inveighed against "a factious and unscrupulous Opposition" and would not accept even the Duke of Wellington as a witness against the Turks— but rather in the speech of the Home Secretary, Assheton Cross, whose moderation had been a striking feature of the debate on the Gladstone Resolutions a year earlier, but who now spoke of "a lying spirit abroad" and taunted the Opposition with having very little to say "for your friends the Russians".[4] On the other side a no less aggressive temper was revealed. Sir Wilfrid Lawson was fully entitled to contrast the violence of a Jingo mob in London with the series of Tory reverses at the by-elections of Perth, Leith and

---

[1] Hansard, *op. cit.* p. 934.
[2] *Ibid.* p. 967.
[3] Leader of 31 Jan.
[4] Hansard, pp. 760, 764.

Greenock: but he became merely fatuous when he drew comparisons
between the war tactics of the barbarian, the bully and the snob.[1]
John Bright had every right to insist on the two voices in the Cabinet,
as exemplified by Disraeli at Aylesbury and the Guildhall and by
"the three Lords", Salisbury, Derby and Carnarvon: but he was not
at his best when he affected to be thankful that the Government was
"not involved in the raving lunacy of the *Pall Mall Gazette* and the
delirium tremens (d.t.) of the *Daily Telegraph*".[2] Childers declined
to follow Chaplin in "vituperation of his opponent", but he only
added fresh fuel to the flame when he described a Conservative meeting at Sheffield as inspired by "a policy of more armour-plates".[3] A
word must, however, be found for a memorable phrase of Sir William
Harcourt, which history has long since endorsed, but which was far
ahead of his time. The Treaty of Vienna, he contended, had "gone
to pieces . . . because it was founded on principles radically false—to
suit the ambition of rulers—and neglected the interests and sympathies of nationalities and populations".

There are not many debates whose faded eloquence and storms of
passion stand the test of being exhumed after fifty years: but these
five nights were singularly barren and leave a deplorable impression.
I am tempted once more to lay stress upon the forgotten speech of
a private member, P. J. Smyth who almost alone struck a note
based upon personal knowledge of the Eastern situation. He disapproved equally the negative policy of the Opposition and the
"joint-stock Do-Nothing Co., Ltd. by British Interests" of the
Government. Britain should have been belligerent from the beginning,
not for Russian, Turkish or British interests, "but for justice, truth
and right": for the real cause at issue was "not Russian versus
Turkish rule, but liberty or slavery, life or death for Christian peoples,
and so a policy of neutrality is a policy of effacement and desertion".
He flatly denied the danger to India and pleaded again for "the
legitimate aspirations" of Roumania, Bulgaria, Montenegro, Serbia
and Greece. War on the Turkish side "would degrade the sword of
Wellington and Napier to the level of the yataghan of the Circassian
and the Kurd. It would be a war against nationality, liberty and
law." Here was a note, undoubtedly pitched too high and scarcely
noticed amid the contemporary din, but one whose memory may
atone for much sound and fury and serve to remind the Balkan

---

[1] *Ibid.* p. 770. He was the first to quote the "Jingo" music-hall song on the floor
of the House.   [2] *Ibid.* p. 790.   [3] *Ibid.* p. 1012.

nations that their cause was not without its minor champions, even in the House of Commons.

Not the least curious feature was the equivocal attitude of Lord Hartington, who pointedly moved the adjournment on the last night and eventually abstained from voting. The fine frenzies of his followers and the war fever of the Jingoes left him equally cold. He regarded the Eastern Question as merely jeopardising other things that meant far more to him. He had no great confidence in Gladstone's tactics, and he probably felt as Harcourt when he wrote that "a dissolution would destroy us, as it did the Peelites and Cobdenites on the China Vote".[1] His inner mind is revealed in a letter to Lord Granville, in which he definitely approved the Government formula of "conditional neutrality" and declared himself "not able to condemn altogether" its general policy. "I am aware that I disagree with almost the whole of my late colleagues and also the great majority of the party. . . . I cannot conceal from myself that I have not been able in this question to lead, but have rather followed a long way behind." He was therefore ready to restore the leadership into the hands of Gladstone, as the man who had "formed and guided the opinion of the Liberal party throughout these transactions".[2] Clearly the party was in a parlous state, and neither Hartington nor Granville were equal to the occasion.

In the end a meeting at Lord Hartington's house decided to withdraw the Forster amendment, in view of the conflicting news and hourly changing situation, and as a result only ninety-five Liberals voted with Gladstone in an uncompromising minority. Goschen, then one of the ablest of the Liberal second line, feared a schism to be inevitable and wrote in his diary: "We cannot be dragged any further by Gladstone and Bright. We are compromised by them every moment. This is my ruling idea. We have no opportunity of showing our anti-Russian policy." [3] This, from the man who two years later was sent by Gladstone to reverse the Layard policy at Constantinople, reveals the perplexity of the rank and file.

EGYPTIAN RUMOURS

We have already seen that the idea of a British occupation of Egypt had cropped up from time to time since the autumn of 1876,

---

[1] 2 Jan. 1878—A. G. Gardiner, *Life of Harcourt*, i. p. 321. A reference to 1858.
[2] 29 Jan., Hartington to Granville—*Granville Papers*.
[3] A. D. Elliot, *Life of Goschen*, i. p. 187.

and that Bismarck in particular favoured it as an admirable method of killing two birds with one stone—providing Britain with compensation for Russian aggrandisement at the expense of Turkey, and alienating France from Britain. Curiously enough, a similar proposal came from the Khedive himself—already gravely embarrassed by his incredible extravagance and squandering of public funds. As early as April 1877 his former Foreign Minister, Nubar Pasha, came to London in the hope of preparing a British protectorate, but confided to the German Ambassador that he found British statesmen extremely reserved.[1] Two months later he complained that though he had been well received in the City, at the India Office and the Treasury, Lord Derby was impervious to his advances, arguing that if England added to her possessions, she could not blame Russia for doing the same.[2]

Nubar's central idea had been that England should in effect purchase Egypt from the Turks, by making herself responsible for the annual tribute: and in the autumn this proposal assumed a new and ingenious form. A Levantine Englishman named Bright, and a certain Colonel Gordon in the War Office, were used as informal intermediaries between the Grand Vizier and the British Cabinet, the motive being to raise money on a large scale for Turkey, by the sale of Crete or Egypt,[3] and thereby to provide the sinews of war for a second campaign against Russia. Nothing came of this, but rumours began to circulate:[4] the French Government grew nervous, while Lord Lyons feared that Bismarck might encourage France to occupy Egypt, and Beaconsfield, reporting this to the Queen, took the view that it might be necessary for us to forestall any such move.[5] But Paris still required to be reassured, and on 21 December Derby instructed Lyons to use "the most decided language" and to declare that "we want nothing and will take nothing from Egypt, except what we have already and what other Powers share equally with us".[6] A week later he gave even more explicit assurances to the French Ambassador, that "our sole desire was to continue the *entente* which had subsisted for almost forty years in Egypt between France and ourselves".[7]

---

[1] *G.P.* no. 289, 24 April, Münster to Bülow; no. 290, Herbert Bismarck to Bülow.
[2] *Ibid.* no. 295, 28 June.   [3] 22 Nov., Disraeli to Layard—Buckle, vi. p. 252.
[4] The *Quarterly Review* for Jan. 1878 condemned the scheme in these words: "The offer to purchase sovereign rights at a moment of defeat comes amazingly near a sharing of the spoil".
[5] 18 Oct.—*ibid.* p. 188.   [6] Newton, *Lord Lyons,* p. 365.
[7] *D.D.F.* ii. no. 221, 28 Dec., Harcourt to Waddington.

It is characteristic of Gladstone's profound distrust of Beaconsfield, that he too should have believed the rumoured designs upon Egypt. In the Russian Embassy Papers I found among the dossier of letters to Prince Gorchakov, without any indication of how it came there, an extract from one of Mr. Gladstone's letters—evidently written to a colleague and then copied for the use of Count Shuvalov.

"I am inclined to suspect that Lord Beaconsfield will endeavour to take us in flank. I am afraid, not of any majority for war, but of a majority for getting hold of Egypt by giving ten millions to Turkey for the suzerainty of Egypt. This will be an effective subsidy of that amount to Turkey. It would justify Russia in making war, though she probably would not do it. It will probably embroil us with France. But I am not without uneasiness on this head. I fear Lord Salisbury might be entrapped."[1]

"Dizzy", he wrote to Granville in the same connection, "is of course looking for the weak side of the English people, on which he has thriven so long, and he must feel encouraged by the decided way in which they accepted his tomfoolery in the affair of the Suez Canal. This purchase of the suzerainty would in my opinion be most unwise and would probably embroil us both with Russia and with France: but it might succeed. The nation may be better or may be worse: we are governed on Asiatic principles."[2]

Granville, in response to these fears, wrote very sensibly, "I do not believe in Egypt. Dizzy does not wish for it. He told Münster last year that he would not take it as a gift. There are a great many foolish people who do wish for it."[3] How little could the two friends foresee their own future rôle in Egypt!

[1] *U.R.B.D.* The document is undated, but was almost certainly written in the first few days of 1878. For on 4 January he wrote the very same thing, though in other words, to Lord Bath: "I am driven to suspect that Beaconsfield will despair of taking the country in front and will try it in flank. Supposing he starts the purchase of the suzerainty of Egypt. This I think and I fear the majority might approve. Supposing this is to be done, by paying 8 or 10 millions down to Turkey, this is in effect a subsidy for the prosecution of the war, and it would justify, though it might not produce, a declaration of war against us from Russia" (*Gladstone Papers*).

Lord Bath replied: "I confess to having been rather in favour of the acquisition of Egypt, but your observation that the purchase of the suzerainty will be a form of subsidising the Porte puts the matter in a new light and brings out objections I had not before seen. I much fear the proposal may meet with considerable support. Salisbury, I believe, favoured it last summer, though Lord B. and Derby opposed it, and the Crown Princess suggested the measure to the Queen" (*ibid.*). For this last statement, which shows how well informed Lord Bath was, see *Letters of Queen Victoria*, 2nd Series, ii. pp. 546, 553.

[2] *Granville Papers*, 5 Jan. 1878, Gladstone to Granville.

[3] *Gladstone Papers*, Granville to Gladstone, 7 Jan. 1878. This almost certainly relates to the extract in the Russian Embassy Papers (see previous note).

In this particular instance Gladstone did his rival an injustice (quite apart from his own failure to appreciate the Suez *coup*). But though Beaconsfield was undoubtedly deterred from the occupation of Egypt by the fear of offending France, he was prepared to contemplate designs infinitely more foolhardy.

THE SENDING OF THE FLEET

The issue was a foregone conclusion. On 7 February the Government had a majority of 295 to 96, and next day in Committee carried the vote by 328 to 124. In the interval news had come from the Near East which revived the public excitement inside and outside the House and led W. E. Forster to withdraw the motion.

On 31 January the armistice protocol was signed at Adrianople between the Grand Duke and the Turks. Its terms may be summarised in briefest outline as follows: (1) Bulgarian autonomy, with annual tribute, a national militia and frontiers not narrower than those proposed at the Conference of Constantinople; (2) independence of Montenegro, Serbia and Roumania; (3) autonomy for Bosnia-Hercegovina; (4) reforms in other provinces; (5) a war indemnity; (6) an agreement regarding the Straits to follow; (7) immediate negotiations for peace preliminaries; and (8) Turkish evacuation of Vidin, Rushchuk, Silistria and Erzerum.

Severe as these terms were, it was at least reassuring that there was no word of the occupation of Constantinople. But it soon transpired that the Russian advance had not been countermanded, and while the House of Commons was discussing the supplementary vote, Rodosto, on the Sea of Marmora, the Danubian key-fortress of Silistria and the lines of Tchatalja, outside Constantinople itself, were successively occupied on 2, 4 and 6 February. Layard, who a fortnight earlier had sent alarmist telegrams reporting "the whole Mohammedan population" to be "flying before the Russians"[1] and had added to his summary of peace terms the comment, "It is scarcely necessary to say this amounts to the destruction of the Turkish Empire in Europe",[2] now wrote privately to the Prime Minister: "Russia has indeed played her game with wonderful skill and audacity. She has succeeded in checkmating us, and in pretty nearly exterminating the Mussulman population in Roumelia and

---

[1] *Turkey No. III.* (1878): *Affairs of Turkey*, no. 17, Layard to Derby, 19 Jan.
[2] *Ibid.* no. 40, Layard to Derby, 28 Jan.

Thrace, so that almost nothing but a Christian Bulgaria now re-mains." [1] It was widely reported in the press that the Turkish Government might abandon the capital—*"rebrousser chemin"* to Broussa, according to a contemporary diplomatic pun—and it was even alleged that the Sultan kept his best ironclad moored off the palace in case of emergencies. Meanwhile the Russian Court was naturally elated and less conciliatory than before.

The news of the Russian advance caused something very like panic in London, both in the general public and on the Stock Exchange: and Shuvalov warned his Government that "extreme measures" might be taken. Indeed, for a moment he was afraid that the credits might be voted by acclamation, but saved the situation by com-municating to Derby an explicit telegraphic assurance of Gorchakov that orders had been given to the military commanders to stop their advance "along the whole line in Europe and Asia".[2] None the less, the discovery that all the cables connecting Constantinople with Europe had been cut and that Layard's messages now had to come via Bombay, not unnaturally caused great alarm, and fresh orders were given to the fleet to enter the Dardanelles. In the Commons Northcote gave as the motive the Government's fear of disturbances in the Turkish capital, while Derby in the Lords tried to tone down the effect by declaring that the dispatch of the fleet was no longer open to the same objections since the cessation of military opera-tions, and that "if we had intended war, it would have been not merely impolicy but madness to wait until the forces of Turkey were crushed, in order to enter on it".[3]

Hereupon Hartington, declaring that the sending of the fleet could not be regarded as "a menace to any Power", and that the Tsar's pledge was sure to be maintained, withdrew any further opposition to the credits, especially since the Secretary for War had repudiated warlike designs "with such vehemence". He further assumed that the task of the Conference would be "to assist at the revision, from top to bottom, of the settlement of 1856".[4] Even Gladstone, while declining to support the Vote, refrained from opposing the sending of the fleet and declared himself "perfectly willing, on intelligible bases, to give every constitutional support to

[1] *Layard Papers*, 5 Feb. 1878, Layard to Beaconsfield.
[2] *U.R.B.D.* tels. of 26 Jan./7 Feb., from Gorchakov to Shuvalov and from Shuvalov to Gorchakov.
[3] Hansard, ccxxxvii. pp. 1320 and 1328.
[4] *Ibid*. p. 1347.

the Government during these negotiations". But not, he added, on
the basis—

> Yours not to reason why,
> Ours not to make reply,
> Ours but to say, "You lie,
> Vote the Six Millions".

Nor could he resist reminding the House that "the heart and root
of the matter" was the fate of twelve or fifteen million people in
European Turkey, and that the terms of the armistice had been
received on the benches behind him in "a silence profound and almost
lugubrious". He added a plea for "a vigilant eye on Austria", who
"for sixty years has taken the wrong side", and a cordial eulogy on
the independence of Roumania, as a future "home of freedom" and
the Belgium of the East: and he ended by denouncing the view that
in questions of foreign policy we are to have no regard to right or
wrong as "shallow in philosophy and unwise in policy".[1]

Gladstone described the Vote to Madame Novikov as "a silly, misleading and mischievous measure" and regretted the abstention of
his Liberal colleagues, but he contended that as a result of the agitation in the country the Government was growing "not only more
peaceful, but more favourable to the great emancipation" worked
by Russia. His courageous and far-sighted attitude to the projected
settlement is shown by his uncompromising regret at Russia robbing
"gallant Roumania" of southern Bessarabia.[2]

There were eight more speakers in the debate, but the Opposition
had already given up the game, and at the end of the evening the
Government had its majority of 204. Shuvalov reported home that
"many of its most influential members have frankly turned their
coat, while others suspect us of a secret treaty with Turkey, and
accuse us of throwing over our English friends by making so prolonged a mystery of the peace terms. Useless to depict the sentiments
of the Queen and royal family: they are intoxicated by the Government's success and its immense majority, and greet the sending of
the fleet as the first step towards collision. If I were susceptible, I
should feel that one of the Princes talks too loudly of rupture and
war in my neighbourhood. . . ."[3]

Shuvalov was not exaggerating. The Queen wrote three letters to
the Prime Minister on a single day, denouncing Russia's "monstrous

---

[1] *Ibid.* pp. 1365-77.   [2] 11 Feb.—*The M.P. for Russia*, i. p. 457.
[3] *U.R.B.D.* 29 Jan./10 Feb., Shuvalov to Gorchakov.

treachery" and "false hypocritical intrigues", demanding "strong measures", and arguing that the very contingency had now arisen which in the previous July and November he had treated as justifying war with Russia.[1] His rejoinder was to "call upon the Cabinet to fulfil their engagement to their sovereign" and to express to her his regret that we had not "a *corps d'armée* at Gallipoli".[2]

That the Queen definitely wanted war cannot be questioned. When Lord Derby wrote to her, hoping that the order to the fleet "will do much to satisfy the feeling of those who are complaining of inaction", she bluntly replied that she did not feel "this satisfaction, but a painful humiliation", since *"we have by our forced neutrality cruelly abandoned . . . our former faithful ally Turkey . . . to a most unscrupulous, aggressive and cruel foe".*[3] "Her own first impulse", she told Beaconsfield, "would be to throw everything up and to lay down the thorny crown", but she consoled herself by the hope that "in the Conference we may reassert our position".[4]

This attitude was too much even for Beaconsfield, who, while expressing "deep distress" and "real unhappiness" at her criticism, explained at some length that "the present no doubt lamentable state of affairs" was due, not merely to Derby or Carnarvon, but was "a necessary consequence of a policy of neutrality", which made alliance with Turkey impossible. At the same time he took the extraordinary line of argument that though the Government could not "as men of honour resign" in so difficult a situation, yet "Your Majesty has the clear constitutional right to dismiss them".[5] Of course the veteran strategist knew perfectly well that she could not possibly do any such thing, and was obviously playing with "a sovereign whom he adores"—another phrase from the same letter. But even as a manœuvre, it was highly heterodox doctrine for a British Prime Minister.

In this connection it is worth referring to a secret memorandum written by Mr. Gladstone some months later [6] and published long afterwards by his son. It relates to information supplied by Lord Carnarvon, after his resignation, as to the attempts of the Queen to impose a veto upon the discussion of certain subjects by the Cabinet, and also the reckless remark of the Prince of Wales to Lord Carrington, that when he came to the throne he intended to be his own

---

[1] 7 Feb., quoting Beaconsfield's letters of 22 July and 16 Nov.—Buckle, vi. p. 243.
[2] 9 Feb., to Queen—*ibid.* p. 244.   [3] 8 and 10 Feb.—*Letters*, ii. pp. 604-5.
[4] 9 Feb.—Buckle, vi. p. 245.   [5] 10 Feb.—*ibid.* p. 246.
[6] 28 May—Viscount Gladstone, *After Thirty Years*, p. 141: see *infra*, pp. 402-4.

Foreign Minister. Gladstone replied that "it recalled James II. and the Bill of Rights" and was "at any rate a position much more advanced than that of George III., who limited himself to a case of consistency with the Coronation Oath". Here, apart from the riddles of personal sympathy and antipathy, lies one of the secrets of Queen Victoria's preference for Disraeli rather than Gladstone—namely, that the latter, though equally devoted to the Crown, assigned much stricter limits to its prerogative in foreign affairs.

There was yet another slip twixt cup and lip. The orders to the British fleet to enter the Straits were promptly countered by an announcement from the Grand Duke Nicholas that in that case Russian troops would at once occupy the Turkish capital. The Sultan appealed through Layard, and with the Ambassador's strong backing, for a reversal of the orders, and Admiral Hornby, learning that the Turks might resist, telegraphed for further instructions.

This time it was Lord Salisbury who reacted most strongly and urged upon his chief that unless we were to make ourselves "utterly ridiculous" and "lose all weight in Europe", the fleet "ought to force its way in without delay".[1] Or in the words of Shuvalov, "English pride does not permit a second recoil in the space of a fortnight". The last straw seems to have been a report from Loftus that the Tsar has authorised the Grand Duke to occupy Constantinople with the consent of the Sultan—a rumour which soon proved groundless.

On 13 February, then, definite orders were sent to Admiral Hornby to enter the Straits, with or without the necessary firman from the Porte: and that afternoon the squadron duly reached the Sea of Marmora without the Turks daring to oppose resistance. As a slight concession it cast anchor not off the city itself, but off the Princes Islands at a distance of some ten miles along the Asiatic coast, and then at Mudania, considerably to the west of Broussa. France, Italy and Austria had also applied a week earlier for permission to send ships, but all three backed down at the last moment, and Britain was left alone.[2]

The Cabinet's position had been rendered still more perplexing by the Sultan's imploring message to the Queen to withhold the fleet, and by Shuvalov's frank warning that its arrival off the Golden Horn would release Russia from all her pledges not to occupy. Indeed, the

---

[1] 10 Feb.—*Life of Salisbury*, ii. pp. 197-8.
[2] Dwight Lee, Proposed Mediterranean League of 1878 (*Journal of Modern History*, March 1931, p. 39).

Ambassador, who had hitherto shown the utmost forbearance, now encouraged his Government to take a stiff attitude, and to threaten immediate occupation of Constantinople if the British landed a single man. Such a line, he telegraphed, "far from causing a rupture, would avert it by holding back the English from the dangerous incline", and would also revive the Opposition—*qui actuellement n'existe plus* —by showing that the Government's measures have produced the opposite effect from that intended.[1] Gorchakov's answer followed the line suggested, but was couched in disingenuous phrases. The British Government was sending ships to protect the lives and property of its subjects, Russia then would enter Constantinople "with the same object, but with the nuance that our protection would extend to all Christians. Thus the two Governments would fulfil a common duty of humanity. It seems to us difficult to understand how this work, pacific in its nature, could possibly assume a character of hostility."[2] It may be presumed that Shuvalov kept to himself these laboured and unconvincing sentiments.

Gorchakov's sarcasm finds its excuse in the knowledge that while the Sultan was telegraphing to the Queen for a revocation of the orders to the fleet, and to the Tsar to suspend action till her answer came, he was at the same time consulting Layard as to the wisdom of resisting a Russian occupation.[3] Derby, when this enquiry was referred to him, at once replied, "without consulting his colleagues", that in his view resistance was impossible and would only do harm by creating fresh complications. "The attitude of Derby", Shuvalov reported, "is very correct, but his situation is compromised and hangs by a thread."[4] Strangely enough, he was unable to learn anything of a telegram of the Sultan to the Queen, and wired to his chief the highly significant comment, "*unless she is concealing it, in order to attain her aim, which is rupture with us*".[5] And indeed this would seem to be the true explanation why his "source" was for once without information which probably only went to Windsor and to the triumvirate now working behind Derby's back.

The fleet was sent because the Cabinet felt that it could not draw back again in the eyes of all Europe. But it was sent in complete disregard not merely for Turkish wishes, but this time even for the advice of the trusted Layard. One of Layard's letters to Derby paints a vivid

[1] *U.R.B.D.* Shuvalov to Gorchakov, 3 tels. of 29 Jan./10 Feb.

[2] *Ibid.* Gorchakov to Shuvalov, tel. of 31 Jan./12 Feb.

[3] *Ibid.* Shuvalov to Gorchakov, 2 tels. of 1/13 Feb., and Gorchakov to Shuvalov tel. of 2/14.   [4] *Ibid.* third wire of 1/13.   [5] *Ibid.* third wire of 2/14.

picture of the situation in Constantinople. "The Sultan appears to have made up his mind that the entry of our fleet will lead to the loss of his life or at least of his throne, as it will bring the Russians into his capital, and a general massacre of the Mussulmans and destruction of their property will ensue. I have scarcely been one hour, day and night, without having one of his Ministers in the house, or receiving a letter from them. They implore me to stop the approach of the fleet. . . . It is useless to argue with persons who are seized with a panic, but it is most painful to go through such scenes as I have witnessed during the last few days." The treasury, he adds, is empty, the fugitives are starving by the thousand, "the Sultan cannot make up his mind, and constantly sends for my advice, but I have none to give".[1]

Layard's view of the Cabinet's policy is summed up most tersely in a single sentence to Admiral Hornby, who shared his opinion: "Under present circumstances how can we bring the fleet up to Constantinople, with the chance of being cut off by the Russians? We should be putting ourselves still more at their mercy."[2] And to the Viceroy he wrote no less bluntly: "Our ships were sent up here to protect the lives and property of British subjects which required no protection. But we gave the Russians a pretext for entering the capital and causing the very danger apprehended."[3] No more damning criticism can well be found than this from the lips of Turkey's most ardent champion.

Meanwhile some idea of the prevalent hysteria and violence of statement at this time in England—alternately urging the Cabinet forward and reining it back—may be gathered from the speech of that Radical stalwart Joseph Cowen, who attacked the Russians as "the sanguinary apostles of Orthodoxy", declared that there was "no justification for the northern vulture preying on Turkey's yet quivering carcass", and asked whether "Turkey was to be strangled and annihilated by those who murdered for the love of God".[4]

Derby and Shuvalov

At this juncture both Derby and Shuvalov were searching eagerly for a compromise such as would avert a rupture. Derby appealed to

---

[1] *Layard Papers*, 15 Feb., Layard to Derby.
[2] *Ibid.* 6 Feb., Layard to Hornby.
[3] *Ibid.* 20 Feb., Layard to Lytton.   [4] *The Times,* 12 Feb. 1878.

Russia not to move upon Gallipoli or to take any step that would endanger the communications of the fleet, and postponed any statement in Parliament in order to give Gorchakov time to send assurances in this sense. Shuvalov's interpretation is interesting—"being unable in view of their own presence at Constantinople to uphold a veto on the entry of our troops, the English Ministers are now adopting a veto regarding Gallipoli", in other words, "a new safety-valve to avert explosion": and he added, "If you want to prevent Derby's fall, give a favourable reply". Then as an afterthought, "It seems to me that the Emperor has so fully attained his object, thanks to the last mistakes of the English, that it would be a useless risk to refuse".[1]

Shuvalov's genuine desire for peace is revealed still more clearly in a temperamental dispatch of the 14th. "Confusion générale, totale, absolue! is the right word, and one might ask whether we are in London under a regular Government or under a 'Convention'. The Queen and the Princes intervene in public affairs: they cry loudly that if England's humiliation should last a few days longer, they would hang Lord Derby on the first tree of Hyde Park. The clubs are signing petitions for his dismissal. . . . Meanwhile the mistake, or rather folly, of sending the fleet is revealed to its full extent: Constantinople had been definitely preserved from a Russian occupation, and here we are, about to enter. . . . At great crises nations need expiatory victims, and it is Lord Derby who has been chosen for this rôle: he is held responsible for not having been at war for the last six months. It is he whose imbecile confidence I have deceived, it is his obstinate resistance which has exposed England, disarmed and powerless, to the insults of Russia. Gladstone can no longer show himself and demands police protection for his 'life and property'. Opposition has ceased in face of the general hatred evoked by the name of 'Russian'. . . .

"In these circumstances Lord Derby appears to me, I must admit, in a new light. No more hesitation or falterings (*défaillances*): he is calm, resists the passionate incitements of public opinion, and still believes an arrangement possible. Very few people in London share his hope, and even my colleagues describe this calm by quite another name. It is none the less true that Lord Derby by his present attitude *is rendering great services to the cause of peace.* . . . Are his days in office numbered? That is the question."[2]

---

[1] *U.R.B.D.* fifth tel. of 1/13 and first tel. of 2/14 Feb., Shuvalov to Gorchakov.
[2] *Ibid.* Shuvalov to Gorchakov, *lettre particulière* of 2/14 Feb.

On the previous day (13 February) he had called on Derby at the Foreign Office while the newsboys were shouting on the streets the false report of his resignation, and found him ready to admit that "the demonstration of the fleet" had in a sense brought the Russians to Constantinople, though in its turn rendered necessary by the "regrettable silence" in which the peace terms had been shrouded. Derby was very frank and urged the Ambassador to warn Gorchakov that the last hope of peace depended upon Russia keeping her hands off Gallipoli. Shuvalov was on tenterhooks until he at last obtained the Tsar's sanction to an explicit pledge not to occupy either Galli- poli or the lines of Bulair, on condition that no British troops should be landed on either side of the Straits. It is clear that the Tsar was putting no little restraint upon himself, for to the German military attaché he described the sending of the fleet as a "box on the ears".[1]

Meanwhile no clearer proof can be found of the jumpy and sus- picious attitude of the British Cabinet than the emphasis which it laid upon a Russian undertaking not to place troops on the Asiatic as well as the European side of the Straits. As Shuvalov argued with some impatience, how could the Russians be so mad as to send troops to the Asiatic side, when they had no fleet of their own and both the British and Turkish fleets lay between them and Asia! His impression of one such conversation was that the British Government was "so *dérayé* and helpless before the irresistible force of events that it no longer knows what it is saying or asking".[2]

At this point of high tension there is a mysterious and inexplicable gap of nearly a fortnight in the Disraeli Papers:[3] but fortunately Shuvalov's very full correspondence gives a real insight into the missing facts. "*My sole occupation for the last three days*", he writes,[4] "*is to postpone an explosion on the part of the British Ministers. To gain a day, an hour, is perhaps to avert rupture between the two coun- tries.*" Is there any possible inference from this, save that the Am- bassador was working for peace, and in so doing had the approval of his correspondent, the Chancellor, and of his master the Tsar? "Lord Derby's attitude", he goes on, "the personal *rapprochement* which has come about between him and me in these last grave

[1] Wertheimer, *Andrássy*, iii. p. 76, 16 Feb., Gen. v. Werther to William I.
[2] *U.R.B.D.* second addendum of 8/20, to letter of 5/17 Feb. See also F.O. memo- randum of 19 Feb. and Shuvalov's memo. of 9/21 in answer.
[3] Mr. Buckle jumps suddenly from 16 Feb. (p. 248) to 28 Feb. (p. 249), merely quoting two phrases from letters of 13th and 17th: and for the first three weeks of March the narrative is again very incomplete.
[4] *U.R.B.D.* letter of 5/17 Feb.

circumstances, are the sole means of which I dispose, and I use them to the full. Knowing his meticulous and hesitating temperament, I try to see him daily, twice rather than once: I raise his fallen courage, sustain his force of resistance when almost exhausted, and assure him that a pacific solution is still possible. There is even something infantile in the promise I extract from him every time on leaving, that of doing nothing, or rather allowing nothing to be done, till our next meeting. So for three days I have not left him without receiving a sort of *casus belli*, very friendly it is true, and depicting anguish rather than determination."

THE PRIME MINISTER'S PLANS

While, then, Derby was working day and night for peace, the Prime Minister, finding it politically unsafe to eliminate him altogether, was devising means for acting without him: and during February and March the real control of foreign affairs was in the hands of a secret unofficial committee, consisting of Beaconsfield, Salisbury and Lord Cairns, a colleague with whom Disraeli had long been specially intimate.[1] It was an utterly anomalous position, which could not be reconciled with constitutional procedure, and led inevitably to great bitterness between the former friends. Major decisions had of course in the last issue to go before the Cabinet, but till that final stage Derby was virtually never consulted and then generally found his hand forced. He on his side swallowed the affronts and set himself deliberately to act as a brake upon his colleagues, most of whom were chafing for his dismissal. Salisbury was in a specially delicate, not to say equivocal position, for it was increasingly obvious that he was the only possible successor to Derby's office: and he was undoubtedly torn between personal loyalty and the honest conviction that he himself could not merely do better, but perhaps save a desperate situation. He never shared Beaconsfield's readiness for war: he believed that "one hour of frankness on Russia's part would have avoided the whole imbroglio", and felt that "we should trouble ourselves neither about the Turks nor Austria".[2] But he was driven to despair by the Government's alternating moods and exclaimed, "We shall be handed down in history as the Government which

---

[1] For instance, when Lady Beaconsfield died in 1872, he wrote to Cairns: "You are the one whom I should wish first and most to see"—Buckle, v. p. 232.

[2] 31 Jan., to Lord Bath—*Life*, ii. p. 200.

through sheer incompetence plunged Europe into the greatest war of the century".[1]

Beaconsfield alone was ready to go to the uttermost, as is shown by his reports to the Queen. On the 16th he told her that Layard had been authorised by the Cabinet "to purchase, if possible, the chief ships of the Turkish fleet", and even to welcome the Sultan on the British flagship if he should find final flight advisable. Within two days, Gorchakov had learned of the project, either from his spies in Stambul or still more probably from one of the Turkish Ministers, and was telegraphing to Shuvalov for further information.[2] The latter went with the story to Derby, who frankly admitted the purchase of three Turkish cruisers which had been under construction in English dockyards when war broke out, and on whose departure from a neutral country the Ambassador had succeeded in obtaining a veto. Derby even admitted that further purchases had been under discussion, but positively denied that Layard had any authority to act in the matter. Gorchakov, on receipt of this version, adhered to the story as coming from absolutely certain secret sources:[3] but Shuvalov was no less positive, in view of "Derby's explanations, confirmed by my other confidential information", and was therefore "inclined to believe" that Layard was "pursuing a personal policy of his own. . . . It is also possible that he is in secret correspondence with the Prime Minister and inspired by him. This was believed to be the case more than once in Sir Henry Elliot's time. If so, these intrigues take place without the knowledge of Lord Derby and the majority of members of the Government."[4] Our periodical extracts from the secret correspondence of Layard and Disraeli are the best proofs of Shuvalov's astonishing *flair*, and on this occasion, as on others, Derby does not seem to have been let into the secret.

Gorchakov was for once even better informed than his ambassador in London. For on 14 February the following "most secret" telegram had duly been dispatched to Layard: "H.M.G. desire you to acquire secretly by purchase four best Turkish ships of war. Admiral has been instructed to assist you in this, but not to prevent by force the transfer of the Turkish fleet to the Russian flag, unless specially

---

[1] *Ibid.* p. 211.   [2] *U.R.B.D.* Gorchakov to Shuvalov, tel. of 6/18 Feb.
[3] He also expressed regret that Shuvalov should have shown his knowledge of such information: "Cela peut faire deviner la source et la tarir". To which Shuvalov replied, on the same day: "Ne craignez rien: source ne peut être deviné, car Derby croit que cela m'a été insinué à Londres par des Anglais. Fallait élucider pour votre gouverne" (*ibid.* two tels. of 21 Feb.).   [4] *Ibid.* tel. of 7/19 Feb.

instructed from here. H.M.G. know perfectly these ships if you will report their names. Should you succeed, you might suggest that means should be found to send the ships away on a mission or special service, with secret orders to go to Malta, where the money would be paid on transfer."[1]

The reader must be left to draw one of two conclusions from the above facts. Either Derby denied or toned down what he knew to be true, taking the view which nine Foreign Ministers out of ten in every country would take—that Shuvalov's direct and searching question went beyond the limits permitted to a foreign diplomat and justified an evasive answer.[2] Or alternately the message of "H.M.G." was sent by the Premier and his Committee of three, with the knowledge of the Queen—in which case Derby may have been telling Shuvalov the literal truth as to what he knew. The second is at least as probable as the first.

Meanwhile the Prime Minister was also negotiating for an Austrian alliance, and led the Queen to expect at least 300,000 Austrians "put into the field immediately", to force Russia to withdraw from Constantinople and Gallipoli.[3] The bait was Britain's guarantee for an Austrian loan:[4] but—as Shuvalov was able to report home within a very few days—Andrássy once more boggled over an arrangement which left Austria-Hungary to do most of the fighting, and the loan remained suspended. There was the double difficulty that Andrássy insisted on utter secrecy, whereas such a loan required the sanction of Parliament, and that this aroused in London the suspicion that Andrássy could not secure the Emperor's approval.

Shuvalov reports a most significant incident on the 17th. That afternoon Beust had a long interview with Derby, and when Shuvalov was received in his turn, the Foreign Secretary took his hand on leaving and said, "I conjure you to do your utmost to avert an European war. *To-day* I can tell you not to trust Austria, for in the event of war, she will be against you."[5] The Ambassador countered very neatly by bidding Derby in his turn not trust Austria too far, since Austrian and British interests were by no means identical.

On the 21st the second reading of the supplementary vote was

---

[1] *Layard Papers*, vol. cci. 14 Feb., Derby to Layard (tel.); *U.R.B.D.* third addendum (of 8/20) to letter of 5/17 Feb.
[2] Cf. Lord Salisbury's attitude to press revelations of state secrets.
[3] 16 Feb.—Buckle, vi. p. 248.
[4] *U.R.B.D.* Shuvalov to Gorchakov, tel. 6/18 Feb. (very secret).
[5] *Ibid.* Shuvalov to Gorchakov, 5/17 Feb. (letter).

moved in the House of Lords by Beaconsfield himself, in anything but reassuring language. "Every nation in Europe is armed to the teeth," he reminded the House, and Britain, "whether so fortunate as to contribute to an honourable and durable peace"—an aim towards which she was "ardently and arduously labouring"—"or whether those efforts may fail and the war may be extended . . . should be in a position to make her word respected".[1] On the same day a Foreign Office memorandum was handed to Shuvalov, intimating that if the Russians occupied Constantinople without the Sultan's consent, the British Ambassador would be withdrawn from St. Petersburg.[2] Gorchakov complained that it was utterly illogical of a Power which had sent its own fleet against the express wishes of the Sultan to insist that Russia should not take a similar step without the Sultan's approval.[3] But he took the hint and used his influence with the Tsar against occupation.

It is probable that the speech delivered by Lord Derby four days later in the same place was intended to counteract the effect of this language: for though he threw out to Russia some fairly obvious hints as to questions that exercised British public opinion,[4] he laid his main stress on the argument that there were only three possible policies before Britain—to join Russia, which was not serious; to remain neutral; or to maintain the treaties of 1856 and 1871 by open war. As, however, "the great majority of the nation held that adherence to the policy which led to the Crimean War was no longer desirable", the second course became inevitable.[5] Derby must of course have been fully aware how distasteful such language would be to his chief and to the Queen, and how isolated he was in his own party. Indeed, the strength of Tory feeling is vividly illustrated by a speech delivered during the same debate by Lord Campbell, who ventured to apply to Lord Derby the drastic lines of "Coriolanus",

He's a disease which must be cut away.[6]

It seemed, however, as though open insult was dispelling Derby's irresolution and justifying the Duke of Argyll's subsequent tribute

[1] Hansard, ccxxxviii. pp. 46-7.   [2] Cf. *G.P.* no. 323.
[3] *G.P.* no. 324, 23 Feb. Cf. *U.R.B.D.*, Gorchakov's pompous telegram to Shuvalov of 10/22 Feb.—"Il [the British Gov.] fera ce qu'il voudra. L'histoire et peutêtre même les contemporains porteront leur verdit sur cette conduite complètement illogique et sur ce dédain pour la paix générale".
[4] *E.g.* the allegations that Russia was claiming the surrender of the entire Turkish fleet, the earmarking of the Egyptian tribute for her indemnity and the expulsion of the whole Moslem population from Bulgaria.
[5] *Ibid.* p. 289, 25 Feb.   [6] 7 March—Hansard, ccxxxviii. p. 831.

to "a calm and philosophic manner that was all his own". The Queen's view is sufficiently shown by her letter of 5 March to the Prime Minister—"Lord Derby *must* go, for he is believed abroad to be THE person who *acts* and NO ONE trusts him".[1]

Meanwhile the Cabinet authorised considerable preparations for a military expedition to be commanded by Lord Napier of Magdala, with Garnet Wolseley as Chief of Staff.

Throughout this period of suspense the capital blunder of the Russians was to shroud in utter mystery their whole negotiations, first for an armistice and then for a preliminary peace, thereby causing intense irritation in England and giving the extremists a most plausible case for beating the big drum. This was fully realised by Shuvalov, who urged upon his Government the need for a prompt communication of terms.[2] But the Russian Government on its side was no less exasperated, and had good reason for suspecting Layard of such misrepresentation and active intrigue as rendered a maximum of secrecy advisable.[3]

THE SEARCH FOR A "PLACE OF ARMS"

During February and March the Prime Minister's fertile mind was full of plans. Having resolved upon action, he found that Malta was inconveniently far from Constantinople or Egypt, and began to revert to his idea of the previous summer, of acquiring "some territorial station conducive to British interests". Since the Russian victories Varna and Batum no longer seemed practicable, and he felt that Egypt would be dearly bought at the expense of French friendship. But after privately sounding Layard, he made a perfectly concrete proposal to the Cabinet on 2 March, indicating "Mytilene, Acre and a post on the Persian Gulf" as alternatives for discussion.[4] The object was defined as "securing the trade and communications of Europe with the East from the overshadowing interference of Russia".[5] No one appears to have objected except Derby: and he

---

[1] *Letters*, ii. p. 607.

[2] *U.R.B.D.* Shuvalov to Gorchakov, second tel. of 15/27 Feb.

[3] For instance, Layard reported that Russia was demanding the expulsion of the entire Moslem population of Bulgaria. Gorchakov indignantly pointed out that it was only a question of the Turkish troops and functionaries. Shuvalov and the Grand Duke were in direct telegraphic communication as to "the constant lies of Layard" (*ibid.* tel. of 14/26 Feb.): and Nelidov, on the latter's behalf, complained that the Russian terms were being "sciemment mutilées et défigurées" by Layard (*ibid.* Nelidov to Shuvalov, tel. of 17 Feb./1 March).

[4] Northcote to Queen—Buckle, vi. p. 253.

[5] Beaconsfield to Queen, 2 March—*ibid.* p. 253.

would probably retire during the next week, so Beaconsfield confided to the Queen. The need for extreme secrecy was obvious: for as early as 27 February Shuvalov had heard rumours of the occupation of Mytilene and Crete and duly protested to Derby.[1]

A further suggestion for the occupation of Cyprus appears to have originated with Colonel Home, one of the officers whom the Government had sent out eighteen months earlier to examine the defences of Constantinople, and who since his return had held a post at the War Office. Home's advice appears also to have turned the scale against Crete and Alexandretta.[2] His memorandum on the strategic aspects of the Eastern Question was eventually taken to the Berlin Congress by our military adviser Sir Lintorn Simmons and has only very recently been published for the first time.[3] It starts from the assumption that "if England does acquire any territory in the East, it should be sufficiently large, possessed of sufficient material resources and inhabited by such races of people as shall allow the experiment of what good government will do being fairly tried". It examines Gallipoli, Lemnos and Mytilene, only to dismiss them as too far out of the way of our Indian trade route, and the first also as constituting "a standing menace to Russia and Turkey, nay even to Austria and Italy". Acre and Haifa are treated as inadequate, Alexandria is dismissed as involving the occupation of Egypt, Stampalia because it offers "a coaling and naval station and nothing more".[4] Crete, though too far from the Syrian coast, "offers enormous advantages", but as its people have always sought union with Greece, its occupation "would infallibly produce political trouble". Scanderoon "has at all times been deemed the gate of Asia, the way by which the valleys of the Euphrates and Tigris have been approached": but once established there, we should find it very difficult to know where to stop, and might "have to take possession of the whole country up to the Euphrates", including Aleppo.

The ten possible choices were thus narrowed down to Cyprus, which was, in Home's view, of the right size and resources, "easily defended" and well suited for "an experiment in treating the Eastern Question fairly" (*sic*). Moreover, "whoever holds Cyprus, potentially

---

[1] *U.R.B.D.* first telegram of 15/27 Feb., Shuvalov to Gorchakov.

[2] *Life of Salisbury*, ii. p. 215.

[3] Dwight E. Lee, "A memorandum concerning Cyprus" in *Journal of Modern History*, June 1931, pp. 236-41. See also H. W. V. Temperley, "Further Evidence on Disraeli and Cyprus" (*E.H.R.* xlvi. p. 457), who quotes from the Simmons Papers an opinion in favour of Stampalia, 2 March 1878.

[4] Since 1912 Italy's naval station in the Dodecanese.

holds Scanderoon". "Militarily speaking, it affords ample space for forming an army and possesses large quantities of mules, oxen and supplies of all kinds." From a naval point of view, "the harbour is deficient, but there are facilities for making a harbour", such as "would be far superior to any in the Levant".

THE MEDITERRANEAN LEAGUE

As Beaconsfield explained to the Queen, these measures were "not sufficiently matured" to be revealed to the Cabinet, and were concealed from Derby, on the assumption that he would retire rather than give his consent.[1] Yet another project—"a secret of secrets", as he confided to the Queen—was a League of Mediterranean Powers, which for a brief space of time took shape as the result of conversations between Sir Augustus Paget and the Italian Premier Depretis. The idea appears to have been to begin with Italy and Greece, and then to secure the adherence of Austria and France:[2] it was closely linked up with the less creditable, but much more practical idea of territorial compensation for Russian aggrandisement. Austria obviously could not be prevented from taking Bosnia, though Italy already disliked the thought of any Habsburg extension on the eastern Adriatic: so Italy might perhaps occupy Albania, and France's name was already coupled with Tunis, probably under Bismarck's inspiration.[3]

Beaconsfield was quite unduly optimistic as regards Italy, where the situation was somewhat fluid owing to the deaths of Victor Emmanuel and Pius IX. within a few weeks of each other: and just at the critical moment the fall of Depretis paralysed the negotiations. Meanwhile Lord Lyons, with his intimate experience of the French, was opposed to the League and reminded his chiefs "that the English view of what is for the general commercial and political interest in the Mediterranean is seldom if ever shared by all or even the majority of the Powers".[4] At home Lord Tenterden, and of course Lord Derby, shared his scepticism. The "inner Cabinet" none the less persisted, and in the middle of March a rough proposal was transmitted to Rome for submission to the new Foreign Minister, Count Corti. He and his colleagues were afraid that such a combination might draw them into war, and gave a definite refusal, in conformity with their

---

[1] March, to Queen—Buckle, vi. p. 254.
[3] Dwight Lee, *op. cit.* p. 41.
[2] 8 March—*ibid.* p. 255.
[4] *Ibid.* p. 42.

policy of strict neutrality in Europe.[1] The project was thus stillborn, and Beaconsfield concentrated more and more upon his search for a new Gibraltar in the Near East.

There can be no doubt that at this stage there were many currents —not least of all in the City—setting strongly in favour of war, as the only means of recovering prestige and silencing the scoffing voices that echoed from the Continent. This was the considered view of the German Ambassador, who wrote that "it was impossible to conduct matters more clumsily, and a parliamentary leader said to me recently, 'The worst of it is that our parliamentary and constitutional régime should have suffered such thorough fiasco'. This is quite true, but the fault lies in the lack of a really *leading* statesman. Beaconsfield is not a leader—a clever parliamentarian and intriguer." [2] His further comment is patently unfair: "Out of a Jew one can never make a statesman: when it comes to taking great responsibility, the Jew at the last moment shifts it on to a colleague"—for if there is one thing for which Disraeli will be remembered, it is his power of initiative and readiness to accept responsibility. None the less Münster was right in his earlier phrases: and it may well be that Beaconsfield felt the danger of a fiasco, and that his warlike designs were intended to provide an outlet from the blind alley.

BISMARCK AS HONEST BROKER

While to the Continental mind British policy was uncertain and distracted by hysteria, while France nervously awaited the repercussions of the impending conflict, and while in Vienna Andrássy was suffering from a sharp attack of Russophobia, Bismarck braced himself for the difficult and bruising function of a buffer between opposing forces. On 19 February he delivered a weighty speech in the Reichstag, in answer to an interpellation of the National Liberal leader Bennigsen—believed by many to have been arranged between them, though this he strenuously denied. Starting from the premiss that the recent debates in the British Parliament saved him from dealing with many points, and that the armistice gave Russia the uncontested control of the Danubian frontiers, he declared that "the chief German interest in the East is that the waterways—the Straits and

---

[1] Telegrams of Paget—*ibid.* p. 43. "Italy declining, the scheme collapsed. Foolish Italy!" is the comment of Sir Charles Dilke—*Life of Dilke*, i. p. 249.
[2] 2 March 1878—"Aus den Briefen Bennigsens" (*Deutsche Revue*, Sept. 1907, p. 314).

the Danube—should remain free as hitherto", and that the certainty
of this was now assured: Germany's interest in "the better government of the Christians", he added, was less direct. Any change in the
existing treaties would "require sanction", failing which there would
either be a new war or "a waterlogging (*Versumpfung*) of the question". He regarded it as improbable that Russia would insist to the
point of war, but in any case what was to happen to these countries?
Was the simple restoration of Turkish rule a solution?

Germany, then, readily accepted the idea of a Conference, either
at Baden-Baden or any other place that met with general approval.
But she found it almost impossible to "fix her attitude in advance":
for "that would make impossible our rôle of mediation at the Conference—to which I attach the greatest importance—because everyone would have the menu of German policy in his hand". Broadly
speaking, he conceived that rôle "as that of an honest broker, who
really wants to do business". There was no conflict of interests with
England, "and I flatter myself we could be as good a confidential
agent between England and Russia as we certainly can be between
Austria and Russia". The League of the Three Emperors rested not
on written obligations, but on the personal sympathy of the three
monarchs and the old relations of their ministers. Germany had
always avoided taking sides in the differences of opinion between
Russia and Austria: she could not imitate Napoleon in the desire to
be "if not the arbiter, then the schoolmaster in Europe". He could
not accept the proposal of a leading journal, that Germany should
ally herself with England and Austria, for by Russia that would be
regarded as "a stab in the back", and Germany could not play the
part of "substitute at a duel" (*auf der Mensur*).

The Catholic leader Windhorst, treating Austria as duped by
Russia, made the comment that the real issue in the Eastern Question was "whether the Teutonic or the Slav element should rule the
world", and that this would be decided by the possession of Constantinople and the Dardanelles. Bismarck at once took his chance
against the hated Centre and with biting sarcasm accepted Windhorst's assurance that "the Sultan has hitherto ruled the world!" At
present certainly Russia had no such aim, the Tsar's own word was
the guarantee, and there was no truth in the duping of Austria by
Russia. He concluded in phrases which were to be very variously
interpreted for some time to come. "Our relations to Austria are
those of reciprocity, entire frankness and mutual confidence . . . not

only from monarch to monarch and Government to Government, but in the friendly relation to Count Andrássy, which enables him to put openly every question he thinks necessary in the interest of Austria, and he is convinced that I give a true answer, and I am convinced that he tells me the truth about Austria's intentions." [1]

This was a daring attempt to square the political circle, and is only to be explained by the most imperative motive of the whole Bismarckian policy, the desire to escape from the necessity of choosing between his two traditional allies.

THE TREATY OF SAN STEFANO

That an interval of over four weeks elapsed between the armistice and the final signature of peace, with lamentable effects upon the nerves of Europe, was due to a combination of circumstances. Not the least remarkable feature of the long crisis is the lack of contact between the various centres of activity. Not merely was telegraphic communication interrupted between Constantinople and the rest of Europe, with the result that news arrived most irregularly in London or Paris and the press was full of uncontrolled rumours, but there was an almost equal lack of connections between the Porte and its plenipotentiaries at the Russian headquarters, and even between the Russian high command and the Government of St. Petersburg. Moreover, the Porte pursued its usual dilatory tactics and was encouraged in this by the prospect of British, and perhaps even Austrian, intervention, and by the active partisanship of Layard and Zichy. Namik and Server were at once recalled after signing the armistice, and the new plenipotentiary, Safvet Pasha, who did not even arrive at Adrianople till 11 February, continued to prevaricate and play for time till the last possible moment.

Even more paralysing was the conflict between the two schools of thought among the Russians themselves. Ignatyev only reached Adrianople some days after the armistice had been signed, and at once became involved in acute controversy with the Grand Duke Nicholas, whom he found eager for peace and roundly accused of disregarding the Tsar's express orders to advance as far as the heights commanding the Bosphorus. After some careful enquiries at the field telegraph, Ignatyev elicited the fact that the Tsar's telegram had actually arrived on the morning before the armistice: but

---

[1] *Politische Reden Bismarcks*, ed. Horst Kohl, vii. pp. 85-105.

he was not able to discover how a message of such importance, from such a source, had taken eight days on the way, and there can be but little doubt that it was deliberately suppressed until, as the Grand Duke himself contended, his deputy Nelidov had already come to terms with the Turks and the agreement could be represented as definitive. Ignatyev's reproaches greatly incensed the Grand Duke, who "almost shouted: 'Are you going to saddle us with another war with England? It is time to stop all military operations and go home'." [1] Finding himself on the defensive, he went on to explain that the troops were tired, without boots and with their clothes in rags, that the supply of ammunition and shell was running short, and that the roads were impassable with mud. Above all, he justified himself by a reference to Shuvalov's urgent telegraphic warnings that any further advance, and above all the occupation of Gallipoli and Bulair, would provoke a rupture with England, which Russia would be mad to risk. Both he and Nelidov also tried to convince Ignatyev that through Namik and Server they had won over the Porte to a Russophil attitude. But here the former Ambássador was justly sceptical, for he not only knew that the two Pashas counted for little in the counsels of the Sultan, but he was very soon in receipt of detailed reports from his former dragoman, M. K. Onou, whom he had sent to Constantinople to study the Turkish situation.

There seems but little doubt that a further motive with the Grand Duke and his staff was friction with the Bulgarians, of whom he is alleged to have said: "Ce sont des brutes".[2] While, however, certain Russian military circles disapproved the whole Balkan enterprise and frowned upon Bulgar, Serb and Greek alike as democratic and revolutionary, there were on the other hand numerous Russian officers who established the most cordial relations with the populations whose liberation they were effecting, and afterwards left their mark in devoted work for Bulgaria.

At the time the West seems to have remained in complete ignorance of the inner history of these rivalries, and until Ignatyev's own memoirs and Tatishchev's documentary history of Alexander II. became available a whole generation later, it was invariably assumed that the Grand Duke cut the cables in order to steal a march upon Europe and occupy Constantinople in defiance of his pacific brother. In reality it seems pretty well established that his telegraphic difficulties were due almost equally to climatic and technical reasons and

[1] Onou, *op. cit.* iii. p. 110.   [2] Wertheimer, *op. cit.* iii. p. 103.

to Turkish tampering with the wires, and that in so far as he tampered with them at all—and this is not definitely proved—his motive was to protect himself from the insistence of the Tsar and Milyutin, to isolate the bellicose Ignatyev, and so to escape from the embarrassing necessity of occupation. His pacific tendencies, based above all on necessity and the precarious state of feeling in the army, is confirmed by the German military attaché, General von Lignitz,[1] by Prince Alexander of Battenberg—the future Prince of Bulgaria, then a young officer attached to the army of his uncle the Tsar—and other foreign observers.[2]

Incensed by the first news that the British fleet had been ordered to enter the Straits, the Tsar on 11 February sent further instructions to his brother, to arrange for the occupation of Constantinople, "with or without the agreement of the Turks".[3] According to Ignatyev's own account of what followed, the Grand Duke was once more evasive, and after waiting four or five days wired back to the Tsar that occupation was no longer "so easy and possible as it was two weeks ago"[4]—thereby directly contradicting his former contentions. More convincing, however, is the version supplied anonymously by Nelidov, at the instance of the Grand Duke himself, to a French review, and challenged only in its deductions, but not in its facts, by the official Russian apologist who replied.[5] It seems certain that the only two cables accessible to the Grand Duke at Adrianople —the one via Constantinople, the other via Dedeagach, Gallipoli and Trieste—were both controlled by the Turks, and that they held back the Tsar's instructions to his brother. When these failed to arrive, the Grand Duke wired urgently for them to be sent and received the petulant answer, "I understand neither your questions nor your hesitations, for I have sent detailed instructions for the event of England entering the Bosphorus".

This delay of three or four days in the arrival of the original instructions was decisive, for they ordered the *immediate* occupation of Constantinople, *but not of Gallipoli*—in the event of the British

---

[1] *Aus drei Kriegen*, with interesting diaries.

[2] Corti, *Alexander von Bulgarien*, pp. 26-8: see also Prince Charles of Roumania's *Aus meinem Leben*, iii. p. 476.

[3] Onou, *ibid.* iii. p. 113. Here Ignatyev is confirmed by the telegrams published by Tatishchev in his Life of Alexander II.   [4] *Ibid.* p. 113.

[5] See *Nouvelle Revue*, iv. (1880), "La Guerre Russo-Turque, d'après des Documents Inédits", pp. 473-506, 738-73, and a reply under the same title, vi. pp. 721-64. The former was the work of Elie Cyon, the well-known writer on Franco-Russian relations, while the latter was by Baron Jomini, the ablest of the Russian permanent officials under Gorchakov.

entering *the Bosphorus*. When the telegram was at last in the Grand Duke's hands, he was faced by a double ambiguity: for the British fleet had not only by now withdrawn to Mudania, but had never entered the *Bosphorus*, but only the Dardanelles and the Marmora—and again, the Staff firmly upheld the view that the occupation of Gallipoli must precede that of Constantinople. We are left with the doubt whether "Bosphorus" was a mere *lapsus linguae* for the "Straits", whether Gorchakov was deliberately ambiguous in referring to the Bosphorus, or whether his geography was so shaky that he imagined the Princes Islands, to which the British fleet first went, to be actually situated in the Bosphorus.

In any case the Grand Duke, in adopting a negative attitude, had the full support of the General Staff, led by General Nepokoyichitsky, though the two fighting generals, Gurko and Skobelev, sided with Ignatyev and inveighed against "headquarters". Curiously enough, this was the moment when Shuvalov, after consistently urging moderation on his home Government, took for a brief space the view that to meet British naval threats by immediate military occupation would have a deterrent rather than a provocative effect upon London. No actual step was taken, but it is quite probable that the daily expectation of a Russian entry had a sobering influence upon the Sultan, who was exceedingly displeased at the coming of the fleet and kept appealing to Queen Victoria for its withdrawal. The Tsar continued to urge the occupation of Constantinople, peaceably if possible, but if necessary "even by force": [1] but the Grand Duke affected to regard the order as only conditional, and gained time by negotiating with the Turks for occupation by consent. But when at last the Porte merely notified its consent to a garrison of 1000 men at San Stefano—a little village on the Sea of Marmora, eight miles west of the capital—the Grand Duke lost all patience, and on the 24th himself occupied San Stefano with considerable advanced forces, and kept the Tsar quiet by describing it as a "suburb".

During the final negotiations strained relations continued between the Grand Duke and Ignatyev, especially when on 28 February the Turkish delegates threatened a rupture over the proposed Albanian and Serbian frontier, and Ignatyev was eager to take them at their word, since this would afford an admirable excuse for occupying Constantinople after all. But the Grand Duke and his staff were insistent that at all costs "some kind of peace treaty should be signed

[1] *Nouvelle Revue*, iv. (1880), p. 117.

not later than 3 March", which was the anniversary of the Tsar's accession amid the disasters of the Crimean War: and Ignatyev's appeal, "It depends upon Your Highness to erect the Cross on St. Sofia to-morrow", fell upon deaf ears.[1]

A detailed account of these negotiations lies quite beyond the scope of this volume.[2] The Turks bargained up to the very last moment, but the point on which they were most obstinate, and upon which Gorchakov very wisely compelled Ignatyev to yield, was a demand for the surrender of the Turkish fleet. Onou reported that the Sultan threatened to sink every vessel in the Bosphorus rather than see the Cross of St. Andrew hoisted on them, and that there was even talk of transferring the seat of government to Broussa, where the Russians "might go and look for them". At the final stage the Tsar, cured of his momentary bellicose fit and entirely reconciled to the more moderate views of Gorchakov and Shuvalov, sent a personal telegram to Ignatyev, "Fais vite", and the Grand Duke was so impatient that he could not await the final drafting and paraded his troops outside San Stefano in honour of peace, before the final signatures had been appended.[3]

In the opinion of Bismarck Ignatyev allowed himself at the last moment to be duped by Safvet, in respect of the military clauses: for, if he had insisted upon the surrender of the Bulgarian quadrilateral and Russia had once had the four fortresses in her hands, she would have been almost unassailable and could safely have risked a fresh war.[4]

Stripped of unessential details, the results of the Treaty of San Stefano were as follows:

The independence of Montenegro, Serbia and Roumania was successively proclaimed, while Bulgaria became an autonomous tributary Principality, with a Christian Government and a national militia. Her Prince was to be freely elected, and "confirmed by the Porte with the assent of the Powers", no member of any reigning dynasty of the Great Powers being eligible, and the new constitution

---

[1] The appeal, Ignatyev records, was made "half in jest"—Onou, *op. cit.* iii. p. 120.
[2] For this the reader must be referred to the full series of Ignatyev's Memoirs—"San Stefano"—six articles in *Istorichestvy Vestnik*, republished in book form in 1917 (of which there is no copy in the British Museum, nor apparently in Great Britain, as Mr. Onou had to borrow a rare copy from the National Library in Sofia before writing his articles in the *Slavonic Review*); to Tatishchev, *Alexander II.*—both in Russian only, but above all to Mr. B. H. Sumner's forthcoming book on Russian foreign policy.   [3] Onou, *op. cit.* iii. p. 122.
[4] Conversation of 26 August 1878, between Bismarck and General von Lignitz at Gastein—Lignitz, *Aus drei Kriegen*, p. 301.

was to be drawn up by an Assembly of Notables, "under surveillance of a Russian, and in presence of a Turkish, commissary", on lines following the Roumanian precedent of 1830.

Russia claimed for herself southern Bessarabia, which she had been forced to cede to Turkey in 1856, and in Asia the Armenian districts of Ardahan, Kars and Bayazid, with the port of Batum. In return for these cessions she reduced the indemnity demanded of Turkey from a nominal 1,410,000,000 to an actual 300,000,000 roubles.

Roumania, as compensation for the loss of southern Bessarabia, was to receive the Dobrogea, a non-Roumanian territory south of the Danube delta, including the future port of Constanza. Montenegro roughly doubled its territory, obtaining access to the Adriatic at Antivari and Dulcigno, and advancing as far as the Drina river on the north. Serbia received the coveted outpost of Zvornik on the west and Niš and Leskovac on the south-east, but not Pirot or Mitrovica, and did not obtain a common frontier with Montenegro.

The most sensational territorial change, however, was the inordinate frontier assigned to "Big Bulgaria", including 163,000 square kilometres, or only 5000 sq. m. less than all the remaining Turkish territory in Europe. On the south Bulgaria was to obtain access to the Aegean from a point well east of Thasos to the gulf of Rendina, and again close to Salonica itself, with the result that that city would become a port without a hinterland, while Constantinople lost all land connection with all its western possessions in Europe. On the west Bulgaria was to be extended far into the heart of Albania, to include not only Skoplje, Prizren, Monastir, but even the lakes of Prespa and Ohrid—in other words, at the expense of Greek, Serb and Albanian alike.

Portions on each side of the Sandjak of Novipazar were to be assigned to Montenegro and Serbia, but they were not made contiguous, a narrow funnel of territory being left between them, in order to connect Turkish territory in Albania with Bosnia-Hercegovina—in short, combining every possible disadvantage for Turkey, the Serb states and Bosnia alike, and only explicable on the assumption that its authors were ignorant of the mountainous terrain and the great strategic difficulties involved.

The most that was done for the Greeks was to insist on a strict fulfilment of the Cretan Règlement of 1868 and to demand similar constitutions for Epirus, Thessaly and the remaining provinces of

European Turkey—in other words, not assigning any fresh territory to Greece.

As regards Bosnia-Hercegovina, the proposals of the Conference of Constantinople were to be applied—in other words, Russia's solemn pledge to Austria-Hungary was completely overlooked. This is only explicable in one of two ways: either the Tsar kept his plenipotentiary Ignatyev in ignorance of his commitments towards Vienna, or he permitted him to ignore them, in the calculation that Vienna could be "bounced" later: and this is hardly compatible with the honourable character of Alexander II., though many contemporaries regarded it as typical of Ignatyev.

Finally, there were other clauses pledging Turkey to introduce reforms in Armenia and to raze the Danubian fortresses, maintaining the Danubian Commission unimpaired and making special provision for the monastic republic of Mount Athos and for Russian pilgrims to Palestine. The last clause laid down that "the Bosphorus and Dardanelles shall remain open in war time as in peace time to the merchant vessels of neutral states arriving from or destined to Russian ports". The Tsar thus made it clear that he had no intention of breaking his pledges to Europe in the delicate Straits Question.

It is only necessary to read the terms of San Stefano to realise that the treaty was foredoomed to failure, as a combination of geographical impossibilities and of racial favouritism. As every advocate of the San Stefano settlement from 1878 down to our own day has relied on varying degree upon the maps of Kiepert, the well-known German geographer, it is not without importance to note that he, when requested by Clemens Busch to prepare a Balkan map for official use, expressed the view that the frontiers of San Stefano had been drawn "with great carelessness and without regard for topographical conditions".[1] Infinitely stronger were the objections on ethnographic grounds: and it is not surprising that five out of the six chief Balkan races have denounced it ever since.

CONFERENCE PROJECTS

Throughout February, while Europe waited impatiently for news of a peace settlement which seemed indefinitely prolonged, there was a constant exchange of diplomatic views between the various capitals.

[1] See Clemens Busch's diary for 10 March 1878—*Deutsche Rundschau*, cxli. p. 220.

The first initiative for a conference came from Count Andrássy, who in his first anger at the Russian armistice terms, notified Berlin that in his view a Conference was the sole means of averting a conflict. Bismarck was not at all enamoured of the proposal, but as his main object was to preserve peace between his two Imperial allies, he concealed his annoyance and decided to humour Vienna.[1] Gorchakov on his side at once accepted the Austrian suggestion, but announced his objection to its being held either in London or Vienna,[2] and favoured a small neutral town, such as Brussels, Dresden or Baden-Baden, while at the same time he set himself to woo Bismarck and expressed his grief at finding himself "so misjudged".[3] His main objections to Vienna were that Andrássy would inevitably preside there, that Novikov was too much under Andrássy's influence, and that his former bugbear Elliot, now ambassador to Austria-Hungary, would still further weigh down the scales against Russia.[4] But he took away much of the sting of his refusal by cordially consenting to "preliminary discussions" (*pourparlers préalables à trois*) at Vienna, between Novikov, Stolberg and Andrássy, in the hope that the three Imperial Courts might reach a private understanding such as would render the conference little more than a formality.[5]

Bismarck at once consented, but the suspicious Andrássy warned him that the conversation might only serve to reveal the difficulties of agreement and so increase the danger of war. At the same time Andrássy disclaimed all idea of following a Turkish policy and insisted that he too desired the liberation of the Christian races, but not the creation of a large Slav state which would become a centre of attraction for the restless Slavs of the Dual Monarchy. He therefore could not accept too big a Bulgaria, or a Russian occupation of it, but on all other points was ready for the widest concessions.[6]

Andrássy's attitude was in great measure determined by the international situation of the Monarchy and his parliamentary difficulties both in Vienna and Budapest, owing to the wildly Turcophil and Slavophobe sentiments of the Magyar public and the meddlesome nervousness of the German Liberals. Francis Joseph, who was very sensitive towards any sign of interference with his foreign or military

---

[1] *G.P.* no. 305—30 Jan. 1878.
[2] *U.R.B.D.* Gorchakov to Novikov, tel. of 21 Jan./2 Feb.
[3] Oubril's communication to Bülow, in *G.P.* no. 308.   [4] *Ibid.* no. 313.
[5] *Ibid.* no. 315, 8 Feb.; *U.R.B.D.* Gorchakov to Shuvalov, tel. of 24 Jan./5 Feb. For once Shuvalov was misinformed when he reported that Andrássy's proposal of Vienna had been inspired by the London Cabinet—*ibid.* Shuvalov to Gorchakov, tel. of 25 Jan./6 Feb.   [6] *G.P.* nos. 318 and 319, Stolberg to Bülow, 12 Feb.

policy, and was indeed eventually led to the decisive breach with the Liberals owing to their maladroit tactics during the Eastern crisis, was averse to war with Russia: and both he and the military chiefs were much influenced by the Military Attaché in St. Petersburg, Baron Bechtolsheim—like the Ambassador, Baron Langenau, a strong and very active Russophil.[1] At the very end of February Andrássy strengthened his position at home by the somewhat risky expedient of offering to resign office, which evidently alarmed the Emperor and drew him once more closer. The minister's confidential secretary Baron Orczy has recorded his belief that the Tsar had demanded of Francis Joseph the dismissal of Andrássy as "a disturber of the peace": and though no evidence seems to have survived, it is conceivable that some such "feeler" was made, and that Andrássy knew his master well enough to realise that an offer to resign, following on such a step, was likely to have the very opposite effect.

All this played its part in reconciling Andrássy to discussions *à trois*, and these took place in the last week of February. Beaconsfield, as so often before, misjudged Andrássy, whom he portrayed to the Queen as "on his knees to us to agree to Berlin, giving the most solemn assurance that she has no secret treaty or understanding with Russia".[2] This persistent denial seems to have been still believed in London, but not so much from reliance upon Andrássy's word as from utter distrust of Russia.

On the very eve of these negotiations Oubril, on instructions, had communicated in Berlin his home Government's view that the principles accepted by the Conference of Constantinople for the regulation of the Bulgarian problem—two separate provinces under a Turkish Governor, with a Belgian militia—were no longer tenable, and again that it was better to leave the Sultan in Constantinople than to make it into a free city. At the same time, though not admitting that the contingency provided for at Reichstadt—namely, the dissolution of Turkey—had actually arisen, it would not oppose Austria-Hungary taking Bosnia.[3] At the discussions *à trois* Andrássy concentrated on two points. He was ready to go further than Russia in the matter of *independence* for Bulgaria, but was very emphatic that the southern half was Greek and should be detached, and above all that the projected frontiers conflicted with the Reichstadt veto

[1] Wertheimer, *op. cit.* iii. p. 77.
[2] 8 May, to Queen—Buckle, vi. p. 256.   [3] *G.P.* no. 320, 15 Feb.

upon a large Slav state. On the other hand, he insisted upon restricting to a minimum the period of Russian occupation after
peace.[1]

Meanwhile London pressed for a decision as to the Congress, and
there was much hairsplitting in Europe as to the distinction between
a conference conducted by ambassadors and special diplomatic
envoys, and a congress at which the heads of governments were
present. Beaconsfield, however, when asked in Parliament, declared
himself unable to recognise any difference between the two.[2] In any
case opinion both in London and in St. Petersburg moved in favour
of major representation. Bismarck, for his part, though not at all
anxious to assume the exposed position of chairman, gradually came
to realise that Berlin was the almost inevitable place of meeting. By
the beginning of March this was virtually recognised by everyone:
when Gorchakov sounded the German Government, he received the
answer that the Emperor William would consent but would not take
the initiative.[3] Andrássy at once consented in cordial terms,[4] but
Derby was far from pleased, because he never ceased to distrust
Bismarck.[5] Indeed he argued to Shuvalov in all seriousness that
since the beginning of the crisis Bismarck had steadily pushed
Russia into war, and that he was now trying to involve her in a
second. "Russia permanently at war—that is what the German
Chancellor wants. He will keep Russia out of war with Austria, but
he will throw her against us." This *"marotte"* of Derby, as Shuvalov
very aptly called it, undoubtedly influenced other members of the
Cabinet, and Beaconsfield himself had been led to suspect that the
German and Austrian Governments had only accepted Berlin "in
order to be agreeable to the Tsar"—which was in itself a reason for
objecting—and to fear that Bismarck might surrender the chair-
manship to Gorchakov.[6] The Cabinet took three long sittings to come
to a decision, but in the end it hesitated to reject Berlin, if only not
to revive memories of the ill-omened Berlin Memorandum, and also
out of fear that this might bring the three Imperial Courts together
again. After all, the initiative of the invitation had been claimed by

[1] *G.P.* nos. 326, 328, 330, 331.
[2] Hansard, ccxxx. p. 265 (House of Lords, 25 Feb.).
[3] *G.P.* no. 333, Stolberg to Berlin, 14 March.
[4] *Ibid.* no. 334, Münster to Bülow, 6 March.
[5] *U.R.B.D.* Shuvalov to Gorchakov, tel. of 22 Feb./6 March.
[6] *Ibid.* Shuvalov to Gorchakov, letter of 23 Feb./7 March. On the other hand, Gorchakov, in a tel. of 21 Feb./5 March to Shuvalov, stated that Germany and Austria-Hungary both accepted Berlin "avec empressement".

Andrássy, and hence the first formal step came through Beust.[1] On the 8th, then, Derby formally instructed Odo Russell to accept Berlin, and he may have been somewhat reassured by Bismarck's message that he himself had only accepted reluctantly, feeling that refusal would expose him to the charge of not doing all in his power for peace.[2]

At the same time Derby made a pronouncement in Parliament which can hardly have been palatable to Beaconsfield and other war-like colleagues. Speaking of the treaties of 1856, he claimed that they contained an obligation towards Turkey, but not to the extent of making war. It had been an attempt to see whether by a question of peace and security from outward attack Turkey could be made really independent and self-supporting. The Government's chief aims at the future Congress he summarised as a desire for an European rather than a Russian settlement, and for one which should be durable and hold the balance fairly between races and creeds.[3]

LONDON IS KEPT WAITING

The place of meeting was now settled, but it was far more difficult to reach agreement as to the scope of the discussion: for the British Government laid down as preliminary conditions of its attending any Congress whatsoever, "that all questions dealt with in the Treaty should be considered as subject to be discussed in the Congress, and that no alteration in the condition of things previously established by treaty should be acknowledged as valid until it has received the consent of the Powers". These conditions were now to be the subject of an unprofitable and highly dangerous haggling for many weeks to come.

Mutual suspicion between the two countries surpassed all reasonable bounds. On the one hand Shuvalov reported, not unfairly, that the situation in England now "defies all logical appreciation: it has latterly become no longer political, but psychological, dependent not on events but on the temperament of the English and on that anonymous thing called public opinion, guided by an anti-Russian press".[4] On the other hand, no one was more conscious than the Ambassador himself of the fatal effects of the secrecy practised by his own Govern-

---

[1] *Ibid.* tel. of Gorchakov to Shuvalov and Shuvalov to Gorchakov, both of 2¹ Feb./5 March.   [2] *G.P.* nos. 339 and 342, 9 and 11 March.
[3] Hansard, ccxxxviii. pp. 866-9.
[4] *U.R.B.D.* Shuvalov to Gorchakov, dispatch of 20/4 March.

ment. The mystery in which Russia had veiled the whole course of
negotiations with the Turks was still maintained after the signature
of peace: and it was not till 23 March that the official text became
known in London. This silence, Shuvalov urged, had "increased to
paroxysm" the prevailing animosity against Russia: it was regarded
as nothing short of a "conspiracy", with the one hand to propose
a Congress and with the other, so to speak, to withhold the facts upon
which the work of that Congress must rest.[1] Gorchakov in reply gave
the unsatisfactory excuse that he would gladly have helped Shuvalov
to end the uncertainty and irritation in England, but nothing could
be done until St. Petersburg itself had received the full text, as it
would be highly dangerous to communicate an incomplete or premature version.[2] And indeed Ignatyev after the signature had proceeded to Constantinople, and on obtaining formal ratification from
the Sultan, set sail for Odessa and only reached St. Petersburg on
17 March.

Technically no doubt Gorchakov was entirely within his rights in
arguing that the Tsar himself must see and sanction the official document before any further use could be made of it. But the real fact is
that Gorchakov, on his side, as a result of British opposition to his
policy for the past two years, was scarcely open to persuasion: his
colossal vanity, his fears and ambitions were alike roused, and his
love of pompous and redundant argument had developed into a
positively mulish obstinacy that parried all Shuvalov's efforts at
compromise. The argument that the text could not be submitted to
other Powers till the Russian Government itself had seen it might
seem plausible to Gorchakov, but in London it suggested bad faith
or extraordinary ineptitude, for though Ignatyev was known to
have had full powers to negotiate, it was obvious that he was tied
down on all essential points and unthinkable that all the main provisions (apart from minor nuances) should not have been instantly
telegraphed to St. Petersburg. In any case the bare possibility that
wider latitude had been left to him increased the concern of the
British Government, who distrusted him more profoundly than any
of his compatriots—even *The Times* writing of him as "one of those
eminently unwise people who risk the whole future for the sake of
speedy triumphs".[3] Moreover, as early as 8 March Count Münster

---

[1] *U.R.B.D.* Shuvalov to Gorchakov, letter of 23 Feb,/7 March.
[2] *Ibid.* Gorchakov to Shuvalov, letter of 21 Feb./5 March:
[3] Leader of 8 March 1878.

received details of the settlement from his own Government, thereby exploding Gorchakov's main argument and showing his readiness to draw distinctions between "friendly" and "unfriendly" Powers. In point of fact, the unreasonableness of Gorchakov's contention is best proved by the fact that Nelidov and Ignatyev themselves, on the very day of signature at San Stefano, sent to Shuvalov direct a telegraphic survey of all essential points,[1] and if only Shuvalov had been authorised to communicate this promptly to Derby, infinite mischief might have been avoided.

Two diplomatic details at this stage are worthy of passing notice. While the ambassadors of the three Imperial Courts continued to co-operate closely, there was a great difference between the frank exchange of secrets between Münster and Shuvalov[2] and their joint reserve towards the vain and perfidious Beust, who constantly played into Beaconsfield's hands and, in Shuvalov's phrase, "mingled in his *rancunes*, not to say hatred, Russia and Germany, Bismarck and Andrássy".[3] Meanwhile in Berlin Bismarck's bugbear, M. de Gontaut-Biron, had been replaced by M. de St. Vallier, who from the first established surprisingly cordial relations with the Wilhelmstrasse: and Bismarck was all the more mollified when the new French Foreign Minister, M. Waddington, not only accepted Berlin but welcomed the Chancellor as President of the Congress.[4] Paris had, it is true, an ulterior motive, which was to secure a veto upon the raising of such questions as Egypt, Syria, Palestine and the Holy Places—the first of these being, as Bismarck at once perceived, the only one likely to be raised and the only one about which France felt keenly at this time.[5]

The condition that all clauses of the Treaty must be submitted to the Congress was resented not only by Gorchakov, but by Shuvalov also, who would have liked to see the other Powers hold the Congress even without England—or in his phrase, *passer outre*.[6] This idea was

---

[1] *U.R.B.D.* tel. of 19 Feb./3 March.

[2] A trifling but very good example of this is to be found in their reports of the Prince of Wales's *levé* of 11 March. Münster reports (*G.P.* no. 343): "The Prime Minister said to me, the Congress seems a dream to him, and dreams are seldom fulfilled". Shuvalov reports (*U.R.B.D.* tel. of 27 Feb./11 March): "The Prime Minister called the Congress a dream. 'A beautiful dream, I hope,' said Münster." Obviously the two had compared notes.

[3] *Ibid.* Shuvalov to Gorchakov, letter of 23 Feb./7 March.

[4] *G.P.* no. 339.   [5] *G.P.* no. 354, Bülow to Hohenlohe, 17 March.

[6] *U.R.B.D.* addendum of 25 Feb./9 March to letter of 23 Feb./7 March, Shuvalov to Gorchakov. Gorchakov in his reply (*ibid.* letter of 6/18 March) doubted the possibility of *passer outre*, for "history shows us that it is the constant falterings (*défaillances*) of the Continent which cause the arrogance of England".

very speedily killed by Bismarck, who wisely took the line that a
Congress without British participation was out of the question.[1]
Bismarck also made it clear that he could not consent to a majority
vote as binding upon the Congress, and that a free agreement between all the Powers was the only possible method.[2]

Gorchakov remained adamant, and on the 14th telegraphed to his
Ambassador: "If at the Congress plenipotentiaries raise questions of
European interest, we could not prevent them, but in no case could
we engage to accept them without knowing what they are".[3] Derby
continued to press for a definite undertaking from Russia, and
refused the Preliminary Conference to prepare the ground which
Bismarck now proposed. There were no divergences to regulate, he
argued, save the solitary question to which the answer was "yes" or
"no": if yes, then there were no further obstacles to the Congress;
if no, England would enter neither Congress nor Conference.[4]

Gorchakov was still not to be moved. On the 16th he telegraphed
to Shuvalov: "The entire Treaty—and we have no secret engagement
—will be communicated to the Powers before the Congress: all will
enter with full liberty of action, and we claim the same right".[5] Next
day he wired again: "Must answer flatly [*nettement*]. We grant to
others full liberty of action, and claim for ourselves same liberty.
We do not understand the imperative English Yes or No. If that
means that we accept in advance any decision taken by the plenipotentiaries, it would be a Caudine Fork under which Russia would
never pass."

There was no precedent in former Congresses for the principle of a
majority vote, and it was clear that the British Cabinet, having gone
off the lines (*fourvoyé*), " would like to re-establish its prestige on
the ruins of our consideration, forgetting what we have been doing
and are".[6]

In a long letter of the next day he defined his attitude still further:
"The hostility to us is growing: and it is no longer interests, but
questions of amour propre and prestige that are at stake. We shall

---

[1] *G.P.* no. 342, Bülow to Münster, 11 March.   [2] *Ibid.* no. 346, 15 March.
[3] *U.R.B.D.* Gorchakov to Shuvalov, second tel. of 2/14 March.
[4] *Ibid.* Shuvalov to Gorchakov, letter of 4/16; *G.P.* no. 356, Schweinitz to Berlin,
17 March. According to Münster (*ibid.* no. 358) Gorchakov, in his eagerness to evade
a direct answer, chose the roundabout route via Langenau, the Austro-Hungarian
Ambassador in St. Petersburg, Andrássy in Vienna and Beust in London, and this
increased both the confusion and London's distrust.
[5] *U.R.B.D.* Gorchakov to Shuvalov, tel. of 4/16 March.
[6] *Ibid.* Gorchakov to Shuvalov, tel. of 5/17 March.

remain polite and even conciliatory in form, but firm in substance. In 1871 we agreed to give London the satisfaction of saving its amour propre, the essential thing for us being to obtain the substance, viz. abrogation of the Black Sea clauses of 1856. To-day after a bloody and victorious war we could not even for the form debase the dignity of Russia before the prestige of England." He further made it clear that he was ceasing to regret the failure of the Congress, that he regarded an *entente* of the three Empires or direct correspondence between the Powers as the only hope, and that he had warned Langenau of "the possibility of war, not only with England, but also with Austria-Hungary": he protested, but was impressed.[1]

At this stage fresh nervousness was caused in London by the double news that the Russians were moving upon the Bosphorus—which was false—and that they were about to embark troops for home at Buyukdere. Layard at once protested and inspired his Austrian and French colleagues with his own alarm: and Gorchakov, believing him to be "aiming at rupture", countermanded the decision, but told Shuvalov that if the British Government should ask him for explanations, he should limit himself to replying that it was rather Russia who had to interpellate them as to the presence of their squadron in the Sea of Marmora "in violation of treaties and despite the Porte's protest".[2] Shuvalov persuaded Derby not to insist on a written remonstrance,[3] and meanwhile suppressed his chief's message, fearing that it would provoke the war which he was straining every nerve to prevent: but as Münster wrote home, "this shows how irritated St. Petersburg is".[4] This incident led the Emperor William to enquire how Britain could justify the threatening action of her fleet, while objecting to Russia sending her troops home by sea on unarmed transports.[5]

The much-maligned Derby was hardly less persistent than the Russian Chancellor. Shuvalov's formal answer ran as follows: "Her Majesty's Government like other Governments reserve to themselves the full liberty of appreciation and of action at the Congress. This same liberty, which Russia does not contest to others, she claims for herself: and it would be to restrict it if alone of all the Powers Russia

[1] *Ibid.* Gorchakov to Shuvalov, letter of 6/18 March.
[2] *Ibid.* Gorchakov to Shuvalov, tel. of 7/19 and 8/20 March.
[3] *Ibid.* Shuvalov to Gorchakov, tel. of 9/21 March.
[4] *G.P.* no. 363, 21 March. It is a further proof of mutual confidence that Shuvalov told his German colleague of Gorchakov's tactless message.
[5] *Ibid.* note on no. 363.

contracted a preliminary engagement." On 21 March Derby formally declared himself unable to admit that Russia would be more restricted in her "liberty of opinion and action" as the result of a preliminary undertaking.[1] But Gorchakov took the rigid view that if England was not satisfied with *"liberté d'appréciation et d'action pour tous"*, it was "a proof that she only seeks our humiliation" and wishes to "force us to undertake accepting in advance decisions taken at the Congress by other Cabinets on European questions".[2]

The British Cabinet, however exaggerated its distrust of Russia may have been, can hardly be blamed for wishing some further definition of Gorchakov's typically pompous and nebulous phrase. The unhappy Shuvalov, finding himself hard pressed by more than one member of the Cabinet, did his best to give a tactful interpretation and then referred it anxiously to his chief.[3] When finally cornered by Derby on 25 March, he gave the following definition: "We leave to others liberty to raise at the Congress such questions as they think fit, while reserving to ourselves the right to accept or refuse discussion".[4]

Shuvalov had by now no illusions as to the gravity of the situation. He reported home that the Queen at her two Drawing Rooms addressed neither him nor Musurus, and that at the Prince of Wales's ball none of the Ambassadors were placed at the tables occupied by royalty: "the exclusion was aimed only at me, the plague-stricken, beside whom no member of the royal family would have been willing to dine". "All that is most hostile to Russia was invited to this ball, even to the most cross-grained newspaper scribblers (*jusqu'aux folliculaires les plus hargneux*) who at other times would never have crossed the threshold of Marlborough House." Neither Lord nor Lady Derby were there. "The Queen", he added, "continues to do what she can (*à faire des siennes*). 'She is mad,' Lady Waldegrave said to me. 'She makes of it a personal question between her and your Empire.'"[5] And again, the Prime Minister's "unparliamentary tone towards me at the first Levee has forced me to cease all relations with

[1] Cf. *G.P.* no. 367, Münster to Bülow, 22 March.
[2] *U.R.B.D.* Gorchakov to Shuvalov, tels. of 9/21 and 10/22 March.
[3] *Ibid.* letter of 11/23 March. "It means that we cannot prevent you from raising discussion on any question that seems to you European. If you don't abuse this, we shall always accept frankly. But if you raised a question to which we cannot attribute common interests, and especially if others supported you, we should then reserve liberty to refuse this discussion and should leave the Congress."
[4] *Ibid.* Shuvalov to Gorchakov, tel. of 13/25 March.
[5] *Ibid.* Shuvalov to Gorchakov, letter of 10/22 March.

him", for he could not allow him "to pour out with impunity on the
Emperor's representative all the bile he has accumulated against
Russia". One of Beaconsfield's "intimates", unfortunately not
named, told Shuvalov that in his chief's view the only course, if the
Congress was abandoned, would be to inform both Russia and Turkey
that London regarded San Stefano as null and void and to recall
Loftus. Shuvalov with great verve replied, "Lord Beaconsfield has
too much *esprit* to commit such a bloomer (*bévue*). It would be like
declaring after a day of rain, that this rain was regarded as null and
void, and if it had fertilised the soil and produced fresh vegetation,
that that too was null and void."[1]

At last on the 22nd the full text of San Stefano was published in
the London press.

BRITISH COMMENT ON THE TREATY

Though certain special features of the treaty had been slowly
leaking out for some weeks past, the document as a whole came like
a clap of thunder to many. British opinion may be divided into
three main groups—the Jingoes who denounced Russia in the shrillest
tones and whose extreme wing would inevitably have plunged the
country into war within a week, if they had been left uncontrolled;
the Liberals, who openly welcomed the downfall of Turkey and regarded war with Russia as altogether unjustified; and a middle group,
recruited from both parties, which insisted upon the European aspect
of the dispute and the possibility of a fair compromise with Russia,
but endorsed the preparations of the Government as a warning that
there did exist "British interests" for which in the last resort the
country might really have to fight. The point of contact on which
all save fanatics could rally, was insistence upon the Congress. It
may be useful to summarise the arguments of these three groups,
as expressed in three representative journals, the *Daily Telegraph*,
the *Daily News* and *The Times*.

The *Daily Telegraph*—generally regarded as the Prime Minister's
own organ—instantly launched out against "the inadmissible character" of the Treaty, in the eyes of "all reasonable Englishmen".
It provides for "the rapid and easy conversion of this Big Bulgaria
into a Little Russia", and there is "not a single British interest
reserved under [the Derby dispatch of] 6 May 1877, which is not

[1] *Ibid.* Shuvalov to Gorchakov, second letter of 11/23 March.

directly or indirectly assailed". "Russia on her own responsibility has broken up and redistributed the territories formerly known as Turkey-in-Europe, has laid hands on a large cantle of Armenia, has confiscated the revenues of the Porte, has sought to recover the control of the Danube, has reduced the Sultan to a state of vassalage, has placed the freedom of the Straits at her future mercy and has effaced, so far as England and the Powers may permit, the Treaties of 1856 and 1871. The states substituted for the Europe of those years are Russia, Austria, Turkey, Roumania, Servia, Montenegro, Bulgaria—no mention is made anywhere of France, Italy, England or even of Austria" (*sic!*—the cloven hoof of territorial compensation is already visible). "None can now doubt that spoliation, not redemption or reform, was from the first the object" of Russia. "But her most fortunate exploit was the creation of an English party as zealous as suicidal in forwarding Russian designs. . . . It is they who, taking in vain the most sacred names, have sanctioned the revival of marauding on a grand scale, identifying their party fatally with that of a barbaric, aggressive, intolerant and despotic Power" (the very language of Windsor!) [1] "which for half a century has been openly and by stealth engaged in the 'holy' work of undermining their own country while conspiring against Turkey".[2]

After an interval of two days the note grew even shriller. Mr. Gladstone was accused of "working incessantly" in Russia's interest: "what are the 'trumpery interests' of England when weighed in the scale against the triumphs of the Blackheath policy?[3] But the British public is in neither a craven nor a credulous mood. It understands that these San Stefano conditions *must be altered root and branch for the future safety of our Empire.*" When the war began, no notice was given "that the sanguinary crusade was undertaken for *the overthrow of a great historical Empire*". "Russia", it goes on, "will soon extirpate all Mussulmans from Bulgaria and create a vast corrupt Muscovite Slavonia, centuries behind the Turkish rule in civilisation and tolerance." "The savage and bigoted Bulgar will persecute Muslim, Catholic, Jew, Greek and Protestant missionary." It contrasted the Russian autocracy with "that spontaneous initiation of western systems by Sultan Abdul Hamid, *which to all who know the East was the most hopeful of modern experiments*", and warned its

[1] See *supra*, pp. 251, 267.
[2] *D.T.* leader of 23 March. In the same issue its Paris correspondent reports "a secret agreement" forced upon Turkey by Russia, and two columns of a letter by "Anglophil", headed "Ought We to occupy Egypt?" [3] See *supra*, p. 81.

readers that Russia, if abetted by Austria and Germany, will "in a few years be mistress of Constantinople and the Straits, and the Ottoman Empire will have ceased to exist, with consequences to Great Britain worse than many single-handed campaigns fought against the broken forces and embarrassed finances of St. Petersburg". "We've got the money too," came in faint echo as the phrase was penned.

The violence of the ministerial press may be contrasted with the moderation of the *Daily News*, as the leading Liberal organ and the special champion of the Bulgarian cause. In successive leading articles, while accepting the treaty as "likely to be the beginning of a new era in the East", it insisted upon "the necessity of frank and full discussion by the Great Powers" and treated the arguments in favour of a Congress as "irresistible". It entered a caveat against Gladstone's view that Bulgaria had been given too much, and concentrated its main criticism upon the "loose and inadequate" character of the promised reforms, freely recognising that "the treaty does too much for the Sclavs and too little for the Greeks". But it treated as "a fatality" the presence of Layard and Elliot in two key embassies "at such a crisis", and warned against a definite conspiracy in Constantinople, of which "the British Ambassador is too probably the dupe", to embroil England and Russia. Its main emphasis, however, was laid upon the Congress, and it fully shared the view of that other Liberal stalwart the *Spectator*, that "there is nothing in the treaty which can afford this country ground for war".

The central position was occupied by *The Times*, which was henceforth more and more representative of saner opinion in the country. Its first reaction was that the Russian proposals, "while offering abundant materials for objection, tend to increase the general wish that the way should be cleared for the Congress. . . . Many people may not like the fall of Turkey . . . but regrets cannot change the fact that it has fallen", and that it is no more possible to restore the Porte to its old position than to restore the Temporal Power of the Pope. "There is much to criticise, much to resist, but there is nothing absolutely beyond the pale of discussion. . . ." The main points of the treaty are then subjected to a detailed but temperate criticism, special exception is taken to the treatment of Roumania and Greece, the "delicate" question of Asia is treated with reserve, and the boundaries of Bulgaria are described as "the gravest question". It is held that "specially British interests" are affected by the question of a right-of-way through the Straits and by the temporary Russian military occupation, but there is "no cause for immediate alarm", since the Straits question is specifically left to the Congress. In a second leader it is frankly admitted that Russia's "reserve" towards the proposed Congress "has arisen mainly from a feeling of ill-humour and irritation, and no similar reserve has been shown towards other Powers".[1] Returning to the subject next day, *The Times* treated "sweeping changes of some kind" as inevitable, but declined to be thrown off its balance by the news of a Big Bulgaria, a heavy indemnity or a Russian Armenia. Then, settling down to a very acute analysis of the new boundaries, it recalled the old story of the division of the oyster: "the whole flat centre of the Peninsula" was assigned to the Bulgarians, while "a thin shell, which itself is shattered by the force of the opening knife, remains to unhappy Turkey". Constantinople was cut off in an impossible manner, not only from Bosnia, but from Thessaly and Albania: the Greek claims were unduly passed over, Bulgaria's extension to the Aegean could not be justified on ethnic grounds, and the new state thus constituted "would easily become a kind of Russian province and all the minor states in the Peninsula would simply cluster round". In short, the demand for Bulgarian autonomy was "incontestable", but "such changes are matters of degree". "Europe cannot avoid very grave doubts", and must insist on fair play for all the races of the Near East.[2] This was followed by a succession of leaders,[3] voicing the desire "to maintain the European character of the Eastern question", pleading that war "would be a scandal to our age and a step backwards in European civilisation" and declining to surrender "the hope of a Congress", since in that case "discussion would leave the region of reason and self-control" for that of "passion and mere prestige".

A DISTRACTED OPPOSITION

That the attitude thus taken up by *The Times* was not only most reasonable, but tactically wise, and prepared a way for the rallying of "central" opinion round the Government after its impending reconstruction, may be deduced from the perplexed attitude of the Opposition leaders during these critical weeks. It so happened that Mr. Gladstone had chosen 23 March to make his farewell speech to

---

[1] *The Times*, two leaders of 22 March.   [2] Leader of 23 March.
[3] 25, 26, 27 March.

his Greenwich electors, and his reactions to San Stefano are most instructive. He reproached the Government for not warning Turkey in the autumn of 1876 that "the European fleets would not allow the passage of a single soldier from Asia to Europe to maintain her iniquitous dominion": that, he argued, would have settled the question, and there would probably have been no war. "But it seems to have been the will of the Almighty to apply a more searching, more drastic, more pungent remedy to this great historical calamity and problem of Christendom. . . . That terrible war has produced great results. You know I am no lover of war, but looking at the wars of recent times, I am constrained to say, speaking not of the efforts of human agents, but of the aims and purposes of Providence, that I know of none that has produced results more glorious than the one which has so recently been brought to a conclusion. A great and iniquitous domination has been brought to the ground." He noted, however, "in European politics a swell like that on the ocean after the winds have ceased to blow". He disliked military preparations and the presence of the fleet "in defiance of those very treaties which we have been told all along it was our business to uphold", and he failed to understand the delay of the Congress. On the other hand, "I see various things which ought to be altered. *I cannot justify the immense extension westwards which has been given to Bulgaria. . . .* I cannot justify the taking away from the gallant Roumanians" of Bessarabia. He was not prejudicing these questions, but since neither Constantinople nor the Straits were to be Russian, there was "nothing in the treaty to justify war", and war without just cause was the greatest of all possible crimes. In a word, despite a difference of emphasis and tone, he seemed to join with *The Times* in advocating revision and a reference to the European forum (25 March).

Only a few days later, in receiving a deputation of northern Liberals, he denounced very strongly the idea of intervention on behalf of Turkey, as openly urged by Layard—the only argument for war being "the vague idea that 'Russia is too powerful' ". He insisted on the advantages of a Congress, at which "we bring the whole pressure of Europe to bear upon Russia", protested against British isolation and the extent to which public opinion was "kept in the dark", and urged "the pursuit of objects which are European by means which are European, in concert with the mind of the rest of Europe and supported by its authority" (29 March).

How essentially unfair it was to represent Gladstone as a mere mouthpiece of Russia—and this was the Jingo parrot cry—may be seen from his letters of protest to Madame Novikov regarding Bessarabia and his still more outspoken criticism in the *Nineteenth Century*, where he pointed out how greatly this gross injustice to Roumania had weakened the Tsar's moral position before Europe.

No greater contrast can be imagined than that between Gladstone's high tension and the utter flatness of view of the official leaders: and if we wish to understand the undoubted set-back to the Liberal cause in the weeks following Lord Derby's fall, we cannot do better than study the speeches delivered by Granville and Hartington on 3 April to a deputation of northern Liberals, introduced by John Bright— Joseph Chamberlain being in the chair. Granville began with a reference to "those persons who are in perfect ecstasy with the warlike measures" of the Government, and made the very effective point that if those measures could be justified at all, they clearly should have been taken nine months, if not a year, earlier. But he then proceeded to elaborate the argument that any Government which wished to do so could "drag the country into war upon almost any cause", thanks to "the power they have, by adopting step after step which it is difficult to retrace and the power of exciting feeling in the country—sometimes of a very noble, sometimes of a very low character—which seems from time to time to take possession of the most civilised as of the most barbarous nations. With the one exception of Fox, who had prevented war with Russia, he failed to remember any case of an Opposition having prevented war. The Tahiti incident in 1843, he argued, would certainly have ended in war, if Peel and Aberdeen had not wished peace: while all the efforts of Bright and Cobden were powerless to avert the Chinese war in 1857, despite the strength of Opposition feeling. In the same way Palmerston, if he had wished it, could easily have involved us in war either over the incident of the French colonels or during the struggle of North and South in America. And even in 1870, when he himself was Foreign Secretary, the Government "could so easily have slid from neutrality to war", if it had followed Disraeli's advice of "an intimate neutral but armed alliance with Russia to maintain the peace of Europe". In a word, wars were "generally prevented by the prudence of the Government and not by the power of the Opposition", and "it would be deceiving ourselves, Europe and especially Russia, if we were to pretend that we have power to control the Government, if they are determined— which I still trust they are not—to drag this country into a war for which at present I cannot see any real justification". Hartington confined himself to regrets that the Congress was not meeting, the dangers of collision owing to some "trifling and unforeseen accident" and a cautious criticism of the Salisbury circular, as offering no alternative policy, but yet "as the beginning of clear and plain speaking".[1]

The speech of Granville and its indirect endorsement by Hartington amounted to nothing less than a public admission of impotence and a virtual abdication of leadership. Henceforth it must have been finally clear that the return of Gladstone was only a question of time, if initiative and weight were to be restored to the Liberal counsels: and indeed henceforth the Liberal rank and file acknowledged their allegiance to the old leader in an increasingly marked way. Especially was this the case among the Nonconformists. Within the next fortnight the United Methodists at their annual meeting protested against the "rowdyism" which insulted "one of the noblest of statesmen", and against "the political sleight of hand" which had "grasped the destinies of the nation": while a deputation of 400 Nonconformist ministers from the London radius alone [2] thanked him for "his noble courage" in defiance of "malignant opposition", and denounced war as an "act of criminal folly".

Another no less curious feature of the situation was a growing cleavage between north and south. On 30 March a bye-election at Worcester, fought mainly on the Eastern Question, brought a Conservative victory. But in Scotland the tide was already running strongly in the other direction, and Lord Rosebery told Stead that opinion was so unanimous north of the Tweed, that it was unnecessary to distribute Lord Derby's speech there. The Jingo outbursts in the metropolis were impossible in the north, except on certain rare and well-staged occasions. This was perhaps above all because the stronghold of jingoism was to be found in Pall Mall and Piccadilly and in the drawing-rooms of Mayfair: and this was clearly reflected in the *Morning Post*, in *Vanity Fair* and in the *Pall Mall Gazette*.

The outlook of Clubland and Society was curiously reflected in the music-halls, which thundered out the great refrain:

> We've got the ships, we've got the men, we've got the money too . . .
> The Russians shall not have Constantinople.

In April Charles Williams, then a popular favourite, sent "the

---

[1] *The Times*, 4 April.
[2] Led by Mr. Guinness Rogers and Dr. Allon—*The Times*, 19 April.

greatest war-song on record" for august approval: and Sir T. M. Biddulph received the Queen's command to thank him for "the appropriate verses", and to inform him that "H.M. fully appreciates his motives". Among other appropriate phrases were the following:

> Bruin thinks we've been asleep, but a watch we've had to keep,
>   Knowing well the value of his word . . .
> For every British heart would burn to take a part,
>   To fling the Russian lies back in their face. . . .[1]

LAYARD AND THE SULTAN

Meanwhile the situation in Constantinople itself was very peculiar. Galvanised into action by the feverish anxieties of defeat and invasion, the new Turkish Chamber, which had been "elected" amid general public indifference and had hitherto shown complete subservience, now suddenly attempted to intervene in public affairs and to launch unwonted philippics at the head of ministers. Unhappily the Opposition had neither leaders nor plan and was crushed by a single blow. On 12 February Abdul Hamid, uncomfortably balanced between hesitant England at a distance and victorious Russia on the spot, appointed as Grand Vizier—but with the new title of Premier for foreign consumption—Ahmed Vefik Pasha, a Liberal of honest reputation who had been President of the Chamber. How skin-deep was his Liberalism, however, became apparent two days later, when the Chamber was dissolved. It was destined not to meet again for thirty years. In the words of an acute French eyewitness, "the constitution fell of itself, having no root": [2] not a hand was raised in its defence. The Sultan, having publicly asserted his autocratic position, found it good tactics to retain Ahmed Vefik in power, as a close personal friend of Layard: but he already had feelers out towards Russia, to whom Osman Pasha, the hero of Plevna, and Reouf Pasha, now Minister of War, both increasingly inclined.

Layard, indeed, was more active than ever in his efforts to influence the Sultan, to counter Russophil tendencies among the Turkish ministers and to inculcate firmer views in the Cabinet at home, through the medium of the Prime Minister.

On 5 March—the very day of San Stefano—we find him dining privately with Abdul Hamid, who was "very anxious to know whether a war in which England would be engaged was probable. If

---

[1] *Spectator*, 27 April 1878.   [2] Mouy, *Souvenirs*, p. 73.

it were, he could keep up his army and be prepared to place it at our disposal. But he could not do so for long, as the expense was beyond what the country could bear." Layard very properly pointed out that he could only submit the question to the British Prime Minister, "without holding out any hopes whatever". The Sultan, however, returned to the charge, arguing that "he had still a fine army, which, supplied with English officers and helped with English money, might be sufficient to drive the Russians across the Balkans". Layard tried to divert his mind from the prospect of recovering his European provinces and insisted on the common interests of Turkey and Britain in Asia Minor and Mesopotamia. By promoting our interests in that direction, "he would secure the support and sympathy of England and would best be able to hold his own against Russia".

A fortnight later Layard had another intimate conversation with Abdul Hamid in the garden of Yildiz Kiosk and pronounced him to be "anti-Russian to the very bottom of his heart". "He still looks to England and is disposed to go with us in everything. If we desert him altogether, he may not be able to continue in this frame of mind, surrounded as he soon would be by men entirely gained over to Russia, and exposed to every manner of threat and intrigue against his person. It appears to me that we should take into very serious consideration the present state of affairs here. Supposing that . . . we have to accept the Russian treaty, disastrous as its terms are, . . . are we prepared to abdicate our position as an Asiatic Power? If we are not, Turkey may still be of the utmost use to us, and it will be to our interest to save and keep together what we can of the Asiatic dominions of the Sultan and to have him as our ally in Asia. The treaty, unless greatly modified in some of its terms, will not only completely destroy the Turkish Empire in Europe, but threatens to undermine it in Asia and consequently in Africa too."

Layard, finding that the force of events has overborne his resistance to autonomous states in European Turkey, now concentrates on the view that "to constitute anything like really independent self-governing states" out of such "Asiatic fragments" as Syria or Bagdad "is out of the question" and would mean "the general and complete break-up of the Ottoman Empire". "We must be ready for confusion and anarchy, which must lead to annexation by some Power, if the Sultan can no longer rule. The whole of Asia Minor would no doubt pass into Russian hands, and *if the old English spirit remained, we should possess ourselves of the Pashalic of Bagdad and the mouth of the Euphrates.* France would have a word to say for Syria, and Egypt would become a bone of contention. These events, although possible, are remote and consequently not within the sphere of 'practical politics', until the conclusion of preliminaries of peace. That they would amount to a total upsetting of the political system in the East, no one can doubt. It remains to be considered whether such a catastrophe would suit us. I venture to believe that it would not, and that we should do all in our power to prevent it. If my opinion be well-founded, the only course that we can pursue is to uphold the power of the Sultan in Asia, if we can do nothing for him elsewhere, and to make him feel that on that continent his interests and ours are identical."

It was during this audience, at which Mrs. Layard was present, that Abdul Hamid spoke "with the greatest admiration and affection of the Queen, and in a curious conversation Mrs. Layard and I had with him about marriage, of which he spoke like an enlightened Christian, he referred more than once to Prince Albert and H.M.'s married life". It is safe to assume that Layard suspected his letters to the Prime Minister of finding their way to Windsor, and he was probably not far wrong.

The personal influence over Abdul Hamid, which these audiences show Layard to have enjoyed, had already been illustrated in the most practical of all ways, by the substitution, at the Ambassador's instance, of Mehemed Ali Pasha for Suleiman Pasha as commander in Thrace, and by the selection of Ahmed Vefik Pasha as Prime Minister early in February—mainly because he was "known to be my intimate friend", as Layard confidentially reported to Beaconsfield.[1] Only a few weeks later Layard succeeded in ousting Server Pasha from the position of Foreign Minister, in which the less Russophil Safvet Pasha took his place.

The case of Server admirably illustrates the struggle of Britain and Russia—now again represented by an ambassador, the tactful and moderate Prince Lobanov—for influence over the beaten and despondent Porte. On 7 February the *Daily News* published an interview with Server, in which he declared that he had believed in England and an Anglo-Turkish alliance, but now saw his mistake and accepted "the Russian policy and alliance" instead. This was quoted on the same day in the House of Commons by Mr. Rylands, who showed himself remarkably well informed and alluded to the en-

---

[1] *Layard Papers*, 5 Feb., Layard to Beaconsfield (Most Confidential).

couragement given by Layard to Server and by Beaconsfield to
Musurus.[1] Later in the evening the Chancellor of the Exchequer gave
a message from the Prime Minister as to "an infamous fabrication"
on the part of the *Daily News*. A week later Derby announced in the
Lords that not merely Server but the Sultan himself had expressed
regret to the Ambassador and given "an absolute denial" to the
Daily News.[2] How much this was worth is revealed by Layard's
private correspondence with Derby, which takes the original facts
for granted. "After the disgraceful conduct of Server Pasha in sending his declaration of hostility to England and her interests ... *I could
not do less than demand his dismissal*. I had another reason—to test
the sincerity of the Sultan and his principal advisers." [3]

In a word, Layard is attempting to play the dictator on the Golden
Horn, in a style altogether worthy of Ponsonby and Stratford de
Redcliffe. This rivalry of the two Powers at Constantinople—in
which Vienna, Berlin, Paris and Rome played the part of nervous
onlookers, rightly or wrongly blaming Layard as a war-monger—is
exemplified in the overture of the Grand Duke Nicholas for an audience with the Sultan. This is described by Layard as an "ungenerous
and barbaric demand", on the part of a man "evidently determined
to exercise all the rights of the conqueror".[4] But we now know that
the Grand Duke's main aim was peace: and as for his desire to restore
Russian influence to its position in 1833 or in 1872, this was presumably as legitimate as the rival ambition to establish exclusive British
influence.

Incidentally Layard never lost a chance of denouncing all and
sundry who held different views from himself. His correspondence
shows that Mr. Gladstone had become a positive obsession, and that
no terms were too severe to describe his "unpatriotic" conduct and
his primary responsibility for the Russo-Turkish war![5] Of all the
Christian nationalities of Turkey, in his opinion, one is more despicable than the other, and the Bulgarians in particular are "at present

[1] Hansard, vol. ccxxxvii. pp. 1249-51 and 1303. A member of Server's staff assured
the correspondent that Layard had used these words to him: "Do you think that I,
as a friend of Turkey, was sent here for nothing? ... It was to encourage you and
offend Russia. Believe me. Have courage. Make no peace. Fight to the end"
(dated 28 Jan., Adrianople).
[2] *Ibid.* p. 1842.
[3] *Layard Papers*, 20 Feb., Layard to Derby.
[4] *Ibid.* 13 March, Layard to Derby.
[5] *E.g.* "That man has been the cause of infinite calamities and he appears to be
insensible to all the mischief he has done and to glory in it" (Layard to Lytton,
20 Feb., *Layard Papers*).

a sordid, cowardly and cruel race",[1] who "have shown themselves utterly unfit for self-government, as even their Russian friends admit. They may become so in time, although I doubt whether the race is capable of it, but they certainly will not under Russian administration".[2] In another letter to his chief he wrote: "Though not on the whole an admirer of the Greek character, I consider it very far superior to the Slav, and especially to the Bulgarian, the Bulgarian being by the way no Slav at all, but of Tatar or Mongol origin. If anything really good and stable and independent is to rise out of the ruins of the Turkish Empire in Europe and Asia Minor, we must expect it from the Greeks and not the Bulgarians." [3]

Of his diplomatic colleagues, the German is more of a Russian than Ignatyev, the Austrian is double-dealing and cannot be trusted, the Italian makes fair professions but works secretly against them: the French Chargé—the well-informed Mouy—is little better, and only his successor Fournier is at all acceptable—seemingly because, as a new arrival, little acquainted with local conditions, he almost at once surrendered himself to Layard's influence.

LAYARD AND GLADSTONE

It was at this stage that Layard's activities formed the subject of a debate in the House of Commons, whose course illustrates the intensity of feeling between the contending factions while waiting for the text of San Stefano.

Simultaneously with the formal *démenti* of Server Pasha's state-to the *Daily News*—a *démenti* invented by the Porte for the occasion —Lord Derby on 18 February read out in the House of Lords a telegram from Layard, which ran as follows: "I deny that I ever encouraged the Turks to go to war or continue the war, or ever promised or encouraged them to expect material aid from England. On the contrary I have always striven for peace. If sympathy for human suffering, a desire to uphold the interests and dignity of my country and efforts to promote the cause of religious and civil

[1] *Layard Papers*, 1 May, Layard to Salisbury. This may fairly be compared with the very different verdict of Consul Blunt, long resident in Philippopolis, and not anti-Turk: "The Bulgarians on the whole are a shrewd, active and industrious people, ranking in capacity and intelligence with any other of the European races. They require only the full development of their good qualities, for attaining a high accomplishment in modern civilisation" (Blue Book of 1867, pp. 35, 44).
[2] *Ibid.* 27 March, Layard to Derby.   [3] *Ibid.* 13 March, Layard to Derby.

liberty are considered offences, I confess to having been guilty of them." [1]

Such assurances did not, however, avail to dispel the widespread suspicion with which the Ambassador was regarded, and the Opposition, which blamed him very specially for what W. T. Stead has called "the Layard-begotten panic", [2] took advantage of the so-called "Negroponte Affair" to make very searching criticism of the Ambassador during the debate of 12 March. Some weeks later Gladstone did not hesitate to speak publicly of Layard as "holding a diplomatic war, while the Government at home have been neutral". [3]

A year earlier Gladstone had been in correspondence with a certain Levantine Greek merchant named Negroponte, and had argued to him that an understanding between Greeks and Slavs was an essential feature of any settlement. "For me", he wrote, "the question of the East is not a question of Christianity against Islamism: it is, however, a question of the Christians against the Porte and the governing Ottomans", and if their relations could once be solved, the grievances of Moslem and Jew would also disappear. In a second letter he refused to pronounce as between Greek and Slav, but insisted on "the policy and duty of treating the Christian cause as one" and regretted the Greek tendency to stand aloof from the Slavs. Negroponte had a conversation with the Ambassador during the summer of 1877, and was quoted by him a few days later to the correspondent of the *Daily Telegraph*—the most emphatic of the Turcophil organs—to the effect that Gladstone had been urging the Greeks to join the Slavs in an attack upon the Turks: whereupon the *Daily Telegraph* published a violent onslaught upon Gladstone, which caused no small sensation in England and was used by his enemies as a proof of his unscrupulous and irresponsible attitude.

After an interval Negroponte sent a denial to *The Times*, and Gladstone himself circulated a statement in the press, describing the correspondent as "a dupe": but the paper itself refused to retract information derived from "several distinguished persons". Layard made no attempt to put matters right, and as the incident soon became a staple of public controversy, Gladstone pressed the Foreign Office for satisfaction. At last on 29 October Layard admitted having mentioned "the contents of the letter to a gentleman connected with the Embassy", with leave to mention it to the correspondent, but

[1] Hansard, ccxxxvii. p. 1843.   [2] *The M.P. for Russia*, i. p. 458.
[3] *The Times*, 29 March, speech to Leeds deputation to Harley Street.

went on to accuse Gladstone of suppressing certain letters which he had received from Negroponte, and expressed not a word of regret.[1]

Early in January 1878 Gladstone, finding that the story was still being exploited against him, made a further complaint to the Foreign Office, and this, when transmitted to Layard, only elicited the airy statement, "I have not thought it necessary to continue the controversy with Mr. Gladstone".[2] In his final statement Layard utterly denied having been "a party to any attack on the character of Mr. Gladstone" and admitted that he "may, perhaps indiscreetly, have called the attention of a newspaper correspondent to a letter which was already public property"—a highly misleading version of the affair. But he ended on a high and aggressive note—"my view of the duty of an Ambassador is that he should faithfully and fearlessly serve the interests of his sovereign and his country, and not those of a faction or of an individual. I do not know whether this is the view of Mr. Gladstone." Thus to the end there was no pretence at apology.[3]

These facts were the subject of a long and acrimonious debate in the House, in which the Under-Secretary, Robert Bourke, summed up Layard's defence "in one single sentence"—that he was not responsible for the *Daily Telegraph* telegram—and tried to shift some of the blame on to Negroponte for giving the Ambassador "a totally erroneous view" of Gladstone's letters.[4] Northcote turned the tables on the Opposition by arguing that Layard was accused not only of indiscretion but of "a wicked and deliberate conspiracy", and excused the silence of the *Daily Telegraph* correspondent by explaining that he was shut up in Plevna and so could not deal with the matter —though how this explained his attitude in the three months since Plevna's fall was not stated.[5] Some of the Opposition were indeed violent, and Sullivan aggressively recalled the fact that Layard had once been rebuked by Palmerston for calumniating Lord Hardinge and refusing to retract, and added, "He is at the same game still".[6] Their excuse for such strong feeling, however, was obvious: their leader had been scurrilously abused as a traitor, until it was necessary

[1] Letters of 9 Jan. and 21 July 1877, quoted by Evelyn Ashley in House of Commons, 12 March 1878—Hansard, ccxxxvii. pp. 1158-9.   [2] 17 Jan. 1878.
[3] See the two Blue Books on the subject—*Turkey No. X.* (1878) and *No. XVIII.* (1878), esp. dispatch of 19 Feb.   [4] Hansard, *ibid.* p. 1173.
[5] The correspondence was in Greek handwriting, which the correspondent could not read, at any rate, with facility: and Edwin Pears charitably puts forward this excuse for him (*Forty Years in Constantinople*, p. 77). Gladstone had unwisely not kept a copy of his answer.   [6] Hansard, p. 1191.

for the police to guard his house and person. Indeed it is essential to
remember that this discussion took place at a moment when Dilke
could record in his diary: "A great mob going to howl at Mr. Gladstone—at this time, the ordinary Sunday afternoon diversion of the
London rough".[1]

The *juste milieu* of the debate was provided by Hartington, who
disclaimed all charges of "conspiracy", but pointed out that Layard
must have read the *Daily Telegraph* and realised the full implication
of its charges, and yet had not taken the course "obvious to most
gentlemen", but on the contrary "argues and fences". Here he had
the Government in a dilemma from which there was no escape.

No less interesting was the attitude of Lord Granville, who after
perusing the correspondence, returned it with the comment, "I am
really sorry that an old friend, as Layard is of mine, should have
written such a dispatch. You have almost wasted too much ink upon
him."[2]

Layard himself put a bold face upon it to the last, and wrote to
the Under-Secretary, Robert Bourke: "I had no explanation or
apology to give to Mr. Gladstone as to the accusations made against
him, as I had nothing to do with it". Yet he persisted in arguing that
"the Greeks here unquestionably did believe that Gladstone advised
them to unite with the Slavs in war against Turkey", and that Gladstone's attitude had been "disingenuous" and "wanting in discretion".[3] To Childers, an old Liberal colleague, he assumed an aggrieved
tone: "I had no conception that the *Daily Telegraph* would make use of
the information in the way he [*sic*] did.... I never desired to make an
injurious accusation against Mr. Gladstone. . . . Both Mr. Gladstone
and I have been the victim of an unscrupulous lying Greek who
inveigled Mr. Gladstone into a correspondence and then used the
letters for his own purposes. . . . Mr. Gladstone has not behaved well
to me. . . . From the day of my appointment here he has openly or
covertly sought to injure my position, and his charge against me of
want of neutrality was unfounded and unjust to a public servant
whom he had himself trusted, and whose conduct he had fully approved
under very difficult circumstances in Spain."[4] These excuses do not
ring true and make unpleasant reading, especially by contrast with a
private letter to Lord Beaconsfield, in which he says: "Mr. Gladstone

[1] *Life of Dilke*, i. p. 249.
[2] *Gladstone Papers*, 5 Dec. 1877, Granville to Gladstone.
[3] *Layard Papers*, 26 Feb., Layard to Bourke.
[4] *Ibid.* 26 Feb., to Childers.

is doing his best to incite the Greeks to rise. His letters to a Mr. Negro-ponte, a well-known Greek intriguer and conspirator here, are shown about. I have seen them . . . one could have believed that the course taken by Mr. Gladstone last year had cost carnage and misery enough without adding a Greek rebellion to it."[1] This is downright denunciation.

The Times, commenting on the published correspondence, treated Layard's attitude as "strange and incredible", completely absolved Gladstone from all blame and described his treatment as "far from creditable to his accusers".[2] After the debate it went still further: referred to Layard's "very improper step", and while acquitting him of "deliberately setting on foot a calumny", declared itself unable to acquit him of "most indecorous readiness to believe disparaging stories and to assist in their further dispersion".[3] In a word, the net result of the debate was to reveal Layard as a more thorough-going partisan than any of his predecessors in an office which seems to have carried the taint of partisanship with it.

Very soon afterwards Layard's German colleague, Prince Reuss, was writing home about "the three War Ambassadors", Layard, Zichy and Fournier, of whom the second was now as much under the influence of Layard as formerly under that of Ignatyev in 1876 (and it might pertinently be added, of Reuss himself in 1877).[4] Another good illustration of what acute foreign observers thought of Layard is to be found in Münster's very interesting report on Derby's resignation, where he compares the position of the Russians and British to "two powder-casks between which some children (the Turks) and *a very dangerous boy* (Mr. Layard) are playing about with sulphur matches".[5]

It is perhaps not altogether surprising, in view of the public controversy evoked by the Negroponte affair, that the press should have earned Layard's special anathema. He complained bitterly of successive *Times* correspondents—Gallenga, Helbert, Norman, Austen—and did not hesitate to describe *The Times* and *Daily News* as "anti-English papers", whose strings were pulled by "Mr. Gladstone's friend and correspondent, Mr. Schuyler, the U.S. Consul-General".[6] To Derby he wrote of the "deliberate misrepresentations and suppressions of truth" of *The Times*, and declared that its correspondent

---

[1] *Layard Papers*, 22 Aug. 1877.   [2] Leader of 11 Feb.   [3] Leader of 13 March.
[4] 2 April—Wertheimer, *op. cit.* iii. p. 96: see *supra*, pp. 124, 224.
[5] *G.P.* no. 375, Münster to Bülow, 29 March.
[6] *Layard Papers*, 6 March, Layard to Beaconsfield.

and one or two others "hesitate at nothing, as in the time of Elliot, to discredit the English Embassy and promote the interests of Russia".[1]

The long smouldering feud between Layard and *The Times* flared up towards the end of March, owing to their very different interpretations of the Buyükdere incident. It had been the Grand Duke's intention to use this place on the Bosphorus for the embarkation of troops returning to Russia, thus avoiding a march across the quagmires of Thrace to Bourgas or Varna. This was at once denounced by the Jingoes as an insidious attempt to gain possession of the Straits, and the rumour was put about that the Russians intended laying torpedoes secretly by night in the Bosphorus, though this would obviously have endangered their own transports more than any other shipping. The Grand Duke was naturally enough furious at the outcry, but at once abandoned his intention—the only result being that as San Stefano at that season of the year was far too exposed for embarkation purposes, the withdrawal of troops was indefinitely delayed.

According to *The Times* correspondent, the whole incident had been deliberately puffed up by the war party, "who would rather see England go to war on any grounds, however trivial, than not at all". And he added his "belief, shared by Philo-Turks as well as Philo-Russians, that this party is headed by the English Ambassador. Even those who approve his conduct admit this view of it. . . . I have no doubt his motives are genuinely . . . patriotic and public-spirited, and that he is sincerely convinced that England ought to go to war with Russia to avert what he regards as the grave danger of Russian aggrandisement, and that if she does not go to war now, she will be throwing away a favourable opportunity of doing what she will otherwise have to do later at still greater cost. But he is so carried away by his dread and hatred of the Russians and a lifelong sympathy with his friends the Turks, to the overthrow of whose Empire, as a Philo-Turk of the old school, he cannot reconcile himself, that he is in constant danger of deceiving himself and then his Government."[2] The publication of so outspoken a verdict in such a journal as *The Times* sufficiently proves how far Layard had exposed himself on the

[1] *Ibid.* 13 March, Layard to Derby. On 9 January he had already complained of "innumerable misstatements of the gossiping and ill-informed" *Times* correspondent, who was "completely in the hands of a few designing Greeks". How the Greeks, to a man anti-Russian, influenced him in favour of Russia, Layard does not explain.
[2] *The Times*, 25 March (dated Pera 22).

Turkish side. It suggests that Gladstone was not far wrong in speaking of Layard as "holding a diplomatic war, while the Government at home have been neutral".[1]

Austen was also perfectly right in warning his readers that Ahmed Vefik had but little influence outside the Palace, and that "if one of the court intrigues so common in Turkey destroyed his momentary ascendancy over the Sultan", Turkish policy might suddenly turn from England to Russia once more. Only a week later a practical illustration of this danger was provided by the markedly cordial reception of the Grand Duke Nicholas by the Sultan. The Grand Duke granted a very frank interview to Austen, in which he disclaimed all idea of seizing Constantinople, expelling the Turks or altering the status of the Straits, and while stressing Bulgarian autonomy and Christian equality, declared that the actual boundaries were "not the essential condition". He added the pointed remark—doubtless addressed as much to Abdul Hamid as to British opinion—that the Sultan was disturbed at the growth of·British sympathies for Greece and would remain neutral in any Russo-British conflict, since his main wish was to see Turkish territory freed as soon as possible from both Russian and British forces![2] Only the most obtuse could fail to read between the lines.

Such a declaration meant open war, and Layard's anger knew no bounds. But by April he carried the feud further than ever before. Another correspondent of *The Times*, Ogle, had been murdered by the Turks in Thessaly, owing to his association with the Greek insurgents, and his body had been mutilated. Layard, with an equal lack of restraint and humour, wrote of this incident to Wyndham, the British Minister to Greece[3]—himself a "Greek-eater", according to his Austrian colleague[4]—"*It was a great misfortune that Mr. Ogle's head was cut off.* Some people suspect it was done by the Greeks themselves, in order to create a misunderstanding between England and Turkey." Ogle, the Ambassador added, was a revolutionary and would certainly have been shot by the Yankees under similar circumstances! It was a pity that the captain of H.M.S. *Wizard* should have been "made an accomplice in the matter"—in other words, should have objected to and interested himself in the murder of a British citizen: and he was complaining to the Admiral about this.

---

[1] *The Times*, 29 March, to Leeds deputation at Harley Street.   [2] *Ibid.* 3 April.
[3] *Layard Papers*, 24 April, Layard to Wyndham.
[4] "Un hellènophage"—22 Feb., Austrian report to Vienna, cit. Lhéritier, *Hist. diplom. de la Grèce*, iii. p. 470.

"It now appears", he wrote in the same letter, "to be the fashion for a *Times* correspondent to be a revolutionary agent", and to invent "stories of murders and outrages without end": and he urged on Wyndham the removal of his *bête noire*, the "unscrupulous and mischievous"[1] Gallenga, whom *The Times* sent to replace the murdered man.

A further clue to the incorrigibly Turcophil attitude of Layard is provided by two of his private letters to Mr. White, then Diplomatic Agent at Belgrade and eventually one of his successors at the Constantinople Embassy. Writing of the provisions of the armistice, signed on the previous day but not yet known in every detail, he declared that "if they are carried out, there is an end to Turkish rule in Europe and to our influence in the East. They are scarcely less disastrous to Austria than to Turkey, for it is difficult to see how the Austro-Hungarian Empire (*sic*) can hold together when the greater part of Turkey in Europe is formed into a great Slav state, entirely dependent upon Russia if it be not speedily annexed to her." He admits the need for "fundamental reforms" in Turkey, to repair "the utter rottenness of the present system", but somewhat unfairly lays the entire blame upon Suleiman Pasha.[2] Writing again on the very eve of San Stefano, he again assumes "the end of the Turkish rule in Europe"—"no bad thing if it could be replaced by any other that suits the interests of peace, humanity and civilisation": and he, of course, assumes further that Bulgaria will be "a mere Russian dependency", on bad terms with a number of other "small Slav states".[3]

How little his mind had accepted the transformation of the Balkan Peninsula since his younger days is shown by his insistence to White on the importance of Turkish rather than the various Slav languages as a study for ambitious young diplomatists. The comic element is provided by the fact that White himself owed much of his reputation in the past and the future to a thorough knowledge of Polish, Russian and the minor Slav tongues, and thus possessed the key to many Danubian and Balkan secrets which the versatile Layard never grasped.

In a word, Layard was the most thorough-going partisan whom a British Government had ever sent to the Golden Horn, but his violent phrases came in large measure from a consciousness that he

[1] *Layard Papers*, 24 April, Layard to Salisbury.
[2] H. Sutherland Edwards, *Sir William White*, p. 127.   [3] *Ibid.* p. 129.

was playing a losing game. Edward Freeman, despite all his violence of statement, was on firm ground when he referred to Layard as "a Liberal of that singular class whose Liberalism is geographical": for with all his sympathy for Italian liberty, he had on the east of the Adriatic "ever been the most zealous champion of tyranny, the bitterest enemy of freedom".[1]

LORD DERBY'S FINAL RESIGNATION

The impression of the peace terms and Gorchakov's obstinate refusal of the British conditions combined to convince Beaconsfield that the time had come for action. "Rest assured", he wrote to his special confidant Hardy, "the critical time has arrived when we must declare the emergency. *We are drifting into war.* If we are bold and determined, we shall secure peace and dictate its conditions to Europe."[2] On 24 March he informed the Queen that he knew—from a source so secret that it could not even be revealed to his colleagues, but "he can have no secrets from his beloved sovereign"—that the Russian answer had already arrived and was "a categorical refusal".[3] There is no evidence as to this secret source, but there are some just grounds for the conjecture that it was Beust, who was distrusted equally by Shuvalov and Münster, by Andrássy and Bismarck, and who seems to have been in specially close touch with the Prime Minister at this time.

Beaconsfield's concrete proposals were laid before the Cabinet on 27 March. The reserves were to be called out—thus placing "two *corps d'armée* immediately at our command" for an expeditionary force—and Indian troops were to be brought through the Suez Canal, "to occupy two important posts in the Levant, which will command the Persian Gulf and all the country round Bagdad, and entirely neutralise the Russian conquests and influence in Armenia".[4] Derby was not prepared to consent to these measures and at once handed in his resignation, which the Queen "without a moment's hesitation" accepted, as "an unmixed blessing".[5]

Derby had of course long been prepared for this step, and on the

---

[1] *Contemp. Review*, Oct. 1877, "Neutrality Real or Pretended". Meanwhile *Punch* was depicting Layard as the "Nineveh bull in the Stambul china-shop" (2 March 1878). [2] *Life of Gathorne Hardy*, ii. p. 36.
[3] 24 and 26 March—Buckle, vi. pp. 260, 262.
[4] 27 March, to Queen—*ibid.* p. 262.
[5] Queen to Beaconsfield, 27 March—*ibid.* p. 263.

eve of the critical meeting he confided to Shuvalov, *à titre d'ami*, his intention of resigning. The talk began with a characteristic *malentendu*, Derby remarking, "I must tell you that to-day is our last conversation", and the Ambassador, who had for some days been prepared for receiving his papers, accepting the remark in this sense and to Derby's no small surprise replying, "I have long been expecting it". Derby's explanation of his step, as reported to St. Petersburg, is of high interest, though of course it is only half the truth. He laid upon himself as Foreign Secretary the chief blame for formulating the demand for a discussion of the whole treaty in Congress: and yet "I had no intention whatever of wounding Russia or restricting her liberty of opinions, on the contrary it would serve to smooth the difficulties by avoiding the need for other conditions. But I see that I was mistaken and that you regard our condition as wounding. I made a second mistake in thinking Europe would share our view, whereas she pronounces in your favour. I regret not opposing those colleagues who wished to formulate this condition before entering the Congress. If we had to start again, we should have accepted the Congress without this reservation: but I repeat I had no intention of wounding Russia." A further reason for resigning, he added, was that he could not approve the measures resolved on by the Government, but on this he must preserve absolute secrecy.[1]

When Shuvalov expressed his keen regret and his fear that all Europe, and especially Russia, would regard the resignation "as a symptom of war", Derby agreed and said that this thought had more than once held him back. But, he added, in half-contemplative mood, "my colleagues never would understand what harm there was in the heap of petty questions and chicanes which they raised towards you. They knew I was very cautious [2] and eager to smooth edges, and so counted upon me unduly. When I am gone, they will use more Vigilance:[2] for despite the excited state of feeling in England, my colleagues do not really want war." [3]

---

[1] That this accurately reproduces Derby's discreet language, is confirmed by a letter from Malcolm MacColl to the Editor of the *Daily News*, on 30 March: "I have ascertained at the Russian Embassy that it was not the calling out of the Reserves, merely or chiefly, that made Lord Derby resign, but a *coup* upon which the Government have decided. They do not know at the Embassy what this *coup* is—whether the seizure of Gallipoli or Mitylene or some other strategic point on Turkish territory. They only know—I believe from Lord Derby—that the Government have decided on some action behind the calling out of the Reserves"—G. W. E. Russell, *Malcolm MacColl: Memories and Correspondence*, p. 57.

[2] These words are quoted in the original English.

[3] *U.R.B.D.* Shuvalov to Gorchakov, second letter of 16/28 March.

In his very next letter Shuvalov reported an incident which throws
fresh light upon Beaconsfield and his sources of information. Beust—
speaking, Shuvalov sarcastically writes, "*en bon* [sic] *collègue* to
render me more prudent"—repeated to him a conversation with the
Prime Minister, who declared the bad relations between London
and St. Petersburg to be due to "the monstrous proceedings" of the
Russian Ambassador, and accused him of showing the text of the
Russian official answer to the Opposition three days sooner than to
the Government. "Is it necessary", Shuvalov indignantly asks his
chief, "to say that the fact alleged by Lord Beaconsfield is absolutely
false?"[1] For in actual fact he had kept back the answer till the final
authorisation came from Gorchakov, and within an hour of its arrival
had handed it to Derby and to no one else. He at once complained
to Derby as to this allegation, and found that the Foreign Secretary
"attaches no credit to the inventions of his colleagues and disdains
this kind of political gossip [*commérage*] with which Beaconsfield tries
to complicate the situation still further. I took care to assure him
that I had no complaint as to the conduct of any of the ministers
towards me—*à l'exception toutefois d'un seul qui confondait deux
choses très distinctes—l'esprit belliqueux et la grossièreté.*"[2]

Gorchakov's comment on Derby's resignation was as pompous as
usual, and far from friendly. Though regretting the loss of "the sole
pacific element" in the British Cabinet, he compared his rôle to that
of Aberdeen in 1853: "despite the best intentions, he prevented
nothing and after making us descend the scale of free concessions, he
has ended by being carried away by the torrent".[3]

Shuvalov's estimate of Derby is of quite exceptional interest.
"His resignation, if it had come a few months or weeks earlier, would
perhaps have compromised the existence of the Tory Cabinet, and
his colleagues would have made great concessions to keep him.
To-day all is changed: the majority of the ministers no longer trouble
about Derby, who has lost his popularity by an attitude lacking in
firmness in both directions. His real friends must regret for him that
his decision came so late.

"I need not say to what degree this crisis will paralyse my action.
A daily contact of two years with this man, honourable [*loyal*], ultra-

---

[1] On 26 March Beaconsfield told the Queen: "The Russian reply has been seen
by some members of the Opposition" (Buckle, vi. p. 262). Obviously then he believed this. Can it be that Beust deliberately, or unconsciously, misled him?

[2] *U.R.B.D.* Shuvalov to Gorchakov, letter of 17/29 March.

[3] *Ibid.* Gorchakov to Shuvalov, letter of 17/29 March.

pacific, but not equal to the events which he was called to direct, gave me the possibility of averting many catastrophes. Now that he is 'dead', I can affirm that it is thanks to the efforts of Lord Derby *alone*, that peace has been maintained up till now, *and that we could crush Turkey before England interfered.*[1] This last result is the real cause of Derby's fall."

The resemblance between this passage and the comments of Count Münster is striking. "Shuvalov", he wrote to Berlin,[2] "has lost very much through the departure of Derby. He had quite a remarkable influence on this otherwise so suspicious statesman. His intimate relation with Lord and Lady Derby caused much gossip and was exploited in a very spiteful way by the war party. Yet even Lord Beaconsfield, who does not at all like Count Shuvalov, recognises that he always genuinely endeavoured to preserve peace between England and Russia and is even now tirelessly working in this sense at St. Petersburg." Then referring to a rumour, unhappily false, that Shuvalov was to replace Gorchakov as Chancellor, he qualified him as "one of the few Russians who realise the mischief which a war with England will bring about, he knows England well and sets a high value on her financial and even military forces". In another place he recognised that Derby had found his position untenable, having been attacked in a ruthless manner by the war party, the royal family and all connected with the Court and by a strange anomaly finding his only defenders in the Opposition.[3]

Lord Derby may not have been a man of powerful calibre, but as a typically English *grand seigneur*, possessed of many of the solid qualities ascribed to John Bull, his presence in the Government had had a soothing and reassuring effect in all sorts of unexpected quarters. "While Lord Derby is at the Foreign Office", wrote Mr. Punch in his "Essence of Parliament"—a most efficient barometer of opinion, we would again remind the reader—"the country feels assurance that the sword will not be lightly or needlessly drawn", and there follows an ominous allusion to "the war-bellows of the *Telegraph* and the *Pall Mall*". "A week of shipwrecks", the same journal wrote after his final resignation, "first of the *Eurydice* [a reference to a famous naval disaster], next of the hopes of peace, founded on Lord Derby's presence in the Cabinet." The *Daily News* openly expressed its regret, since it had always recognised Derby's "sincerity, the calmness of his judgment, his curiously un-Torylike

[1] Italics in original.   [2] *G.P.* no. 379, 2 April.   [3] *Ibid.* no. 375, 29 March.

propensity for ascertaining facts before forming opinions, and his superiority to the vulgar influences of mere partisan interest". The *Spectator* made the interesting comment: "That capacity for fighting hard, for being indiscreet if driven too far, for making himself dangerous when needful, was just what the country in its heart was denying Lord Derby".

An even more striking instance of his hold upon "Centre" opinion is to be found in the full-dress leader with which *The Times* subsequently welcomed Beaconsfield and Salisbury back in triumph from Berlin. "At certain periods during the last six months", was its pointed comment, "a single untoward occurrence might have precipitated us into war. Lord Derby's and Lord Carnarvon's services at this juncture ought not to be forgotten."

The fact is that though slow to move and somewhat suspicious, both of men and of clear-cut theories, he could present a case and defend it with equal ability, and only extreme provocation could turn him from the even tenor of his way. Both by temperament and from practical memories of the Crimean years, he was a convinced advocate of peace, not at any price, but if humanly possible. The closeness of his co-operation with Shuvalov—in which Lady Derby so ardently encouraged him—was due simply and solely to a perception of the fact—proved up to the hilt by the Russian correspondence published above—that Shuvalov, for his own reasons (some no less ideal than Derby's own, some doubtless of a more opportunist character, connected with Russian internal politics), was also straining every nerve for peace. It seems difficult to escape from the conclusion that this alliance, however open to criticism on abstract grounds, was in practice the most powerful factor in saving the country from war, and that without it not all the agitation of a divided Opposition would have held back the Prime Minister and the Queen from what *Punch* punningly called the "Dizzy brink" of war.

IGNATYEV'S MISSION TO VIENNA

One reason for Gorchakov's rigid refusal to concede the British demands was that he was engaged in a by no means unpromising attempt to isolate London. General Ignatyev, who as the chief negotiator of San Stefano was in higher favour than ever with the Tsar, was now sent on a special mission to Vienna, which Gorchakov himself described as "a supreme effort to reanimate and fortify [*reserrer*] the entente of the three courts, which is to-day the sole chance of preserving general peace and checking English preponderance".[1] The Tsar's autograph letter which Ignatyev handed to Francis Joseph, assumed that England was bent on humiliating Russia and that further negotiations were pointless.[2] It was hoped that the way had already been prepared by the Tsar's brother-in-law, Prince Alexander of Hesse, in a series of conversations at Vienna.

Ignatyev was a highly inept choice for Vienna, where he was even more distrusted than in London, and with greater reason, since like all true Panslavs he was strongly Austrophobe and indeed in his heart of hearts inclined to General Fadeyev's view that Russia's road to Constantinople lay through Vienna. Still, he of course possessed the qualifications mentioned in the Tsar's letter, of knowing more than any other man of the details of the treaty, and of his master's mind respecting it. He soon got to grips with Andrássy, when he advanced the more than doubtful claim that there was nothing in San Stefano which in any way conflicted with Austro-Hungarian interests. Andrássy retorted by reading the clause from the secret Budapest Convention, imposing a veto upon a large Slav state in the Balkans: but Ignatyev had a most plausible explanation which was accepted but doubtless not believed. In framing the San Stefano frontiers, he said, he had been guided by a map given to him by Novikov, which he had assumed to have received the sanction of Andrássy. On this map there was a red line indicating the new Serbian and Montenegrin frontiers and prolonged southwards towards the Pindus: its lower section Ignatyev had interpreted as the western frontier of Bulgaria, while Andrássy, who had to admit having had it before him, had supposed it to be the eastern boundary of an autonomous Albania and a new northern frontier for Greece, but had hardly taken note of these, having only been interested in the provisions relating to Serbia and Montenegro, for which the map had really been prepared.[3] Ignatyev, however, had a better argument than the map: for he was able to point out that the definition given to Bulgaria at San Stefano did not greatly differ from that accepted by the six Powers at the abortive Conference of Constantinople.

Andrássy then pitched his claims pretty high—so high that the German Ambassador assumed him to be using Russia's fears of an

---

[1] *U.R.B.D.* Gorchakov to Shuvalov, letter of 17/29 March, with enclosure, Gorchakov to Novikov, *lettre particulière* of 11/23.   [2] *G.P.* no. 371.
[3] *G.P.* nos. 376 and 377, Stolberg to Berlin, 1 April (tel. and letter) based on detailed oral information from Andrássy himself.

Austro-British entente as a lever for extracting a maximum of concessions. Foremost among his demands was a virtual veto upon Montenegro obtaining either a coast-line which might some day give Russia a foothold on the Adriatic, or a common frontier with Serbia. He wished to have Spizza and Antivari [1] for Austria, partly with a view to extending his influence over the Catholic Albanian tribes, and to unite the Sandjak of Novipazar with Bosnia, thereby retaining control of any future railway from Sarajevo to Salonica or from the Danube to the Adriatic, and especially of Mitrovica, where two such lines were almost bound to cross.

The impression of vagueness and vacillation which Andrássy left upon some of his contemporaries is quite unfounded. In reality he knew very well what he wanted and has left it on record: and the memorandum which he sent to Beust and Karolyi for submission to the British and German Governments, supplemented by his confidences to the French Ambassador, ought to have left Salisbury in no manner of doubt.[2] His central argument was that Austria-Hungary could not tolerate the formation of any new state such as would affect her frontier provinces, and especially Dalmatia, which he aptly compared to "a fairly weak pallisade", already cut at two points.[3] He would actually prefer autonomy for Bosnia and Hercegovina, but in his view it would be equally impracticable for the two together or separately, and would only be a temporary experiment, soon leading to union with some neighbouring state. It was useless to suppose that after such a war the Porte could ever fulfil promises of reform, still less undertake the repatriation of 150,000 refugees and the introduction of land reform: and in that case unrest would continue. There remained the possibility of their union with Serbia and Montenegro, which would place Austria-Hungary before "the highly awkward alternative" of annexing the whole complex or risking the new state's growing powers of attraction upon the Serbo-Croat population inside the Monarchy itself. This line of argument led Andrássy to the conclusion that such a development must be prevented at all costs, and that annexation, little as he desired it and unpopular as it was in Vienna or Budapest, was the lesser of two evils,

---

[1] To the French Ambassador he described Antivari and Dulcigno as "le point de mire des agitateurs panslavistes"—D.D.F. no. 295, Vogüé to Waddington, 30 April.

[2] Ibid. and G.P. no. 400, 21 April.

[3] Hercegovina touches the sea at the mouth of the Neretva (Narenta) and just inside the Bay of Kotor (Cattaro)—the northern and southern extremities of the former territory of the Republic of Dubrovnik (Ragusa).

and that only a strong state could restore order after so long a period of anarchy. To M. de Vogüé he defined the problem even more bluntly: it was a choice of "losing Dalmatia or taking Bosnia". He added the highly plausible arguments that Turkey also would gain by the loss of the two provinces, just as Austria-Hungary was the stronger for the cession of Lombardy and Venice, and again that it was in the interest of Europe, since it not merely meant pacification, but provided a counterweight to the growth of Slav influence in the Balkan Peninsula.[1]

In actual fact, Austria-Hungary was at the parting of the ways: for the occupation of Bosnia-Hercegovina had a fatal effect upon her relations both with Serbia and Montenegro and with her own Jugoslav provinces, and in the end the Southern Slav question was to prove the undoing of the Dual Monarchy. None the less Andrássy's outlook and motives may be favourably contrasted with those of his successors Aehrenthal and Berchtold. In his anxiety to control future railway development in the western Peninsula we may detect the germ of the impracticable Sandjak Railway scheme, which Aehrenthal propounded, and then dropped, in 1906: but we must also contrast Andrássy's eventual acquisition of the Sandjak in 1878 with Aehrenthal's inept evacuation in 1908, which alone made it possible for Serbia and Montenegro to acquire a common frontier in 1912. Again Andrássy insisted to Ignatyev that the valley of the Vardar, down which the main line from Central Europe to Salonica and Athens was bound to pass, must not be assigned to Bulgaria—thereby anticipating the Serbo-Greek standpoint in the internecine Balkan conflict on 1913, in which Berchtold supported the aspirations for a "Big Bulgaria" extending far to the west of the Vardar valley and linking up with a new Albania to shut off Serbia from access to the Aegean.

It is curious to note that Ignatyev's resistance was concentrated against the curtailment of Montenegro—which the German Government also regarded as objectionable—and that he was not unready to renounce western Bulgaria. An interesting feature of the Russian mentality is this constant enthusiasm for Montenegro and its Prince, in contrast to the disillusionment about the Serbs, and a little later the irritation against the Bulgarians. Even Shuvalov, who cared far less about the fate of the Slav minor brethren than about Russia's relations with the Great Powers, had a warm side for Montenegro

[1] *D.D.F.* i. no. 295.

and did what he could for her, while ready to throw Serbia to the
Austrian wolves.

Andrássy for his part appears to have wished an autonomous
Macedonia with Salonica as its capital,[1] and hereupon Ignatyev actually suggested—can he have had his tongue in his cheek?—that this
should be placed under General Rodić, who of course, as an ardent
Croat patriot and advocate of Jugoslav union under the Habsburg
sceptre, was decidedly suspect to the Magyar statesman. Andrássy
told Vogüé a few days later that Ignatyev had offered him not only
Bosnia-Hercegovina, but even Albania and Macedonia with Salonica,
while he himself favoured autonomy for both, disclaimed all desire
to annex them or Serbia, refused to follow him into such fantasies
as the Rodić scheme, and treated Thessaly and Epirus as bound to
fall to Greece.[2] In other words, he seemed to lean towards thorough-
going partition of European Turkey.

Finally Andrássy readily conceded Bessarabia to Russia and raised
no objection to Bulgaria extending to the Aegean, doubtless in the
idea that the Mediterranean would draw her away from the Russian
magnet.[3]

On the basis of the above facts it is difficult to avoid the double
conclusion that the claim commonly made out for Ignatyev as the
whole-hearted advocate of the extreme Bulgarian claim cannot be
upheld, and that Andrássy wasted a great opportunity and could
have extorted very far-reaching concessions from Ignatyev, at a
moment when the latter was in a position to implement them
through the Tsar's favour. But the news of Derby's fall and the
calling of the Reserves, while causing a panic on the Viennese Bourse,
abruptly ended the effort to find a compromise. Ignatyev, on the
eve of departure, gave an interview on 29 March, to the *Daily
Telegraph* of all papers, laying the greatest stress on Russia's desire
to preserve peace and avoid anything that might affect British
or Austrian interests. The Straits, he said, must remain open, for
if England took the Dardanelles, Russia would have to take the
Bosphorus: but England might take any island outside the narrows,
for instance Mytilene, if she so wished. This reads like a "feeler",

---

[1] Wertheimer, *op. cit.* iii. p. 95: cf. Bareilles, *Rapport secret de Carathéodory Pacha.*
[2] *D.D.F.* ii. no. 295. It is interesting to note that the *Daily Telegraph* in a leader
of 27 March assigned to Ignatyev the aim of bribing Austria-Hungary not only with
Bosnia but "a vast tract to Salonica", adding that this was first suggested by
Bismarck and revived by Prince Alexander of Hesse (the Tsar's brother-in-law and
father of the future Prince Alexander of Bulgaria).
[3] *G.P.* no. 380, Schweinitz to Bülow, 4 April.

based upon some rumour of Beaconsfield's search for a "place of arms".[1] Another point on which he laid great stress in the Turcophil and philo-Moslem journal, was Russia's respect for the Moslem population, which was now cursing Suleiman Pasha for his folly in destroying 140 villages during the final retreat.

Ignatyev's inconclusive mission to Vienna was the culminating point of his influence with the Tsar. Powerful currents—backed even by Prince Reuss, the Russophil German Ambassador to the Porte—worked to prevent his reappointment to the Constantinople Embassy: and the Sultan naturally was not eager for his return and showed great relief at the selection of the Turcophil Prince Lobanov-Rostovsky.[2] Finally, when it came to selecting delegates for the Congress, Ignatyev was again passed over, though at first the Tsar had thought of him in the leading rôle. His apologists maintain that he was not really in favour of war with England, but believed that a firm attitude on Russia's part would produce a compromise: and it certainly seems true that his Panslavist proclivities made Austria rather than England the bugbear.[3]

Early in April the Grand Duke Nicholas was also recalled from the Near East—though without real reluctance on his part—and General Todleben was appointed to the supreme command, in the calculation that his great engineering gifts, first revealed at the defence of Sebastopol, would enable the Russians, if necessary, to block the Bosphorus to the British fleet and so secure their communications across the Black Sea.

GORCHAKOV'S REAL MIND

Meanwhile, Gorchakov, on the news of Derby's impending resignation,[4] had telegraphed his conviction that "the Congress could not lead to any satisfactory result. Our interest is that it should not be realised, but this point of view must be carefully dissimulated. What matters to us is that the refusal of the Congress should come from the side of England. It would isolate her from the other Great Powers which desire peace, and would give us chances of strengthening

---

[1] See *supra*, p. 325.
[2] A *Times* leader (of 3 May) openly expressed relief at the selection of Lobanov, a man with a "clean reputation", instead of Ignatyev, "for years the evil genius of his country", and described San Stefano as "not an isolated blunder, but merely the last link in a long series of brilliant mistakes".   [3] Cf. Onou, *op. cit.* iii. p. 122.
[4] *U.R.B.D.* Gorchakov to Shuvalov, tel. of 15/27 March (Very Secret).

the *entente* of the three Imperial Courts."[1] We seem to read between the lines Gorchakov's genuine belief that England was bent on picking a quarrel.

This telegram was warmly welcomed by Shuvalov, who wrote back that though he had worked hard to save the Congress, he had never acted so much à *contrecœur*. "It was clear to me that to meet in Congress was to offer the British Cabinet table, ink and paper to facilitate its reaching what the *maladresse* of its diplomatic correspondence with Vienna had failed to obtain—viz. an Anglo-Austrian *entente*." But unless Andrássy contrives to resuscitate it, the Congress is "*bien mort*".[2] In a word, Derby's instinct had been quite sound, when he confessed to Münster his doubts as to whether Russia really wanted the Congress.[3] And yet this attitude on the part of Gorchakov was not permanent and was at least partially compounded of pique. He unquestionably did not want war and he would gladly have ended his career by a fresh diplomatic triumph in Berlin: and even if it was not to be a complete triumph, it was likely to be far less risky than a fresh war. Hence in the end he reverted to the Congress as the lesser evil.

Meanwhile the immediate reaction of Turkey to Lord Derby's resignation was a secret message from the Sultan to Lord Beaconsfield,[4] asking to be informed "as soon as possible if war between England and Russia were imminent", and holding out the hope of massing over 100,000 troops within a fortnight for the defence of the Bosphorus. Layard added his own belief that the Sultan was "fully to be depended upon", but refused to "give any encouragement without positive instruction from H.M.G."

---

[1] *U.R.B.D.* Gorchakov to Shuvalov, tel. of 16/28.
[2] *Ibid.* Shuvalov to Gorchakov, tel. of 16/28.   [3] *G.P.* no. 367.
[4] *Layard Papers.* Transmitted by Layard to Lord Tenterden, 30 March, 9.30 P.M., no. 341.

CHAPTER IX

SALISBURY AT THE FOREIGN OFFICE

My object has throughout been to maintain the peace of Europe and to bring about the better government of the disturbed provinces, without infringing upon the independence and integrity of the Ottoman Empire.

THE QUEEN'S SPEECH, 8 Feb. 1877

Turkey's maintenance can only avert great wars. . . . Depart from that principle [territorial integrity] and we leave the ship without a rudder in our discussion.

LORD BEACONSFIELD, 20 Feb. 1877

We have never swerved from our original conception and determination.

LORD BEACONSFIELD, 17 Jan. 1878

The policy has never changed, and there never has been the slightest division in the Cabinet respecting it.

LORD BEACONSFIELD, 25 Jan. 1878

The time is passed for talking about independence and integrity.

LORD SALISBURY to Mr. Layard, 4 April 1878

For a quarter of a century English politics had been obsessed by the antagonism between two remarkable men, and this agitation was the last and most violent manifestation of its power. Viewed in the light of this obsession, Lord Salisbury's consistency admitted of no defence.

LADY GWENDOLEN CECIL, ii. p. 201

LORD DERBY'S resignation caused a profound sensation in the country: and the Opposition, full of suspicion as to the Prime Minister's aims, was naturally much alarmed. The *Daily News* greeted the news with "profound emotion"; the *Manchester Guardian* "with the shock of a great and unwelcome surprise", while the *Spectator* treated it as "a catastrophe", removing "the last mainstay of a prudent and patriotic policy". The pronouncements in Parliament made a good impression, but threw little or no light upon the causes. Only a week earlier Derby had, very loyally but very misleadingly, challenged the very idea of "duality" or "differences" inside the Cabinet.[1] He now simply stated that it was neither possible nor desirable, in the public interest, to explain the nature of their differences. "We agree as to the end, but unhappily differ as to the means." The obstacles to the Congress were not due to England. There were no personal motives, he added: indeed, he had "few political or personal ties closer and older than those with the Prime Minister". Beaconsfield, on his side, paid a high tribute to his old friend's

[1] Hansard, ccxxxix., 21 March.

"capacity for affairs, the penetrating power of his intelligence and the judicial impartiality of his general conduct": and he spoke with genuine emotion of "these wrenches of feeling" which are "among the most terrible trials of public life. . . . I have felt of late that the political ties between us must soon terminate: but I believed they would terminate in a very different and a more natural manner—that I should disappear from the scene, and that he would remain in the maturity of manhood, with his great talents and experience, to take that leading part in public affairs for which he is so well qualified." [1]

At the same time the Prime Minister announced, what could hardly be concealed, that it had been decided to call out the Reserve: but the coming of the Indian troops and the project of a *place d'armes* remained a jealous secret.

The Queen wrote a gracious letter to Derby, but pointedly assumed that he would "never join in any factious opposition to the Government". [2] Beaconsfield generously offered him the vacant Garter, but on reflection Derby decided to refuse, though still in really cordial terms.

LORD DERBY'S SUCCESSOR

During February and March 1878 foreign affairs had been conducted by a Cabinet Committee of three—Beaconsfield, Cairns and Salisbury—behind the back of Derby, who was left to discuss with Ambassadors while ultra-secret plans were being hatched elsewhere. The first outsider to obtain a real inkling of this extraordinary position before Mr. Buckle and Lady Gwendolen Cecil published much of the documentary proof, was Sir Charles Dilke, who, as Under-Secretary to the Foreign Office in 1881, undertook researches into the origins of the Tunis dispute.

As time passed, however, Lord Salisbury became more and more the driving force of this "inner Cabinet", and Beaconsfield came to lean upon him and to accept his directive. Their relations at the final crisis which produced Derby's resignation would seem to afford definite proof that the Prime Minister had no rooted principles in the Eastern Question like some of his fanatical admirers, and followed an entirely opportunist policy of prestige. On 11 March he wrote to the Queen: [3] "A policy of partition is very simple and does not require

---

[1] Hansard, ccxxxix., 28 March, pp. 101-4.   [2] Buckle, vi. p. 271.
[3] Cf. *supra*, p. 139.

much genius to devise. It is not impossible that eventually it may be inevitable, but it is not for Your Majesty to set such an example."[1] In other words, he had lost faith, if he ever possessed it, in the complete maintenance of the old Turkey.

While in this mood, he received a most weighty letter from Lord Salisbury, urging that "it would be doubtful policy" to object to every article of the Treaty, and that it would be wiser to concentrate against "those articles which menace the balance of power in the Aegean . . . and threaten the Greek race in the Balkan Peninsula with extinction", and against those which "threaten the free passage of the Straits" and therefore "English interests". "*I am, as you know*, not a believer in the possibility of setting the Turkish Government on its legs again, as a genuine reliable Power: and unless you have a *distinct belief the other way*, I think you should be cautious about adopting any line of policy which may stake England's security in those seas on Turkish efficiency." He then defined British aims under four heads: (1) "Driving back the Slav state to the Balkans and substituting a Greek province"; (2) "effective securities for the free passage of the Straits; (3) two naval stations for England—say, Lemnos and Cyprus, with an occupation, at least temporary, of some place like Scanderoon, for the sake of moral effect"; and (4) perhaps "reduction of indemnity".[2] Thus Beaconsfield, in appointing the author of this letter to Derby's post, was acting with his eyes wide open, and thereby acknowledged his own much vaunted policy of "Turkish integrity" to be dead.

That shrewd observer Count Münster, who had never formed a very high estimate of Disraeli's energy or clarity of thought on foreign questions, saw that Salisbury would from the first assume the lead. "Lord Salisbury," he reported to Berlin, "owing to his whole Christian and anti-Turkish tendency, will give the war another direction: he will not (even if he could) re-establish the Turkish Empire and will not form an alliance with the Turks, whom he despises. He is one of the very few English statesmen who under circumstances would go so far as to share the booty with Russia—which would not work if England made common cause with Turkey."[3] Small wonder, then, that during April and May it took a good deal of correspondence in order to reconcile Layard to a policy that no longer deserved the name of Turcophil. The Ambassador must have bitterly regretted

---

[1] *Letters*, ii. p. 608.   [2] 21 March 1878—*Life*, ii. p. 214.
[3] *G.P.* no. 378, Münster to Bülow, 2 April.

his recent unnatural monopoly of a Prime Minister as Turcophil as himself, but less stubbornly grounded in principle.

The change seems to have been at once felt in the diplomatic corps, for within ten days Münster was confiding to his Hanoverian ally Bennigsen, that "conditions have very much altered here, the leading man is now Lord Salisbury *alone*, and an energetic man he is, who in the position which he has adopted stands up even to the danger of a war". He added characteristically, "England will hardly feel the war, while it will ruin Russia and throw back for at least a quarter of a century the development of this half-barbaric state".[1]

Shuvalov, on the other hand, definitely disapproved of the appointment as "a bad choice: his hatred of the Turks has been appeased by their defeat, and he has returned entirely to his former anti-Russian sentiments".[2] Meanwhile he transmitted the wise advice given by Derby at their farewell official talk. "Advise your Government to remain calm and conciliatory in face of the various measures taken, which I disapprove. I know my colleagues well: they do not want war, but to satisfy their party by demonstrations. Then propose direct negotiations: our only real objections to the Treaty are the excessive extension of Bulgaria westwards, and the fear of your influence replacing ours in the future at Constantinople. Find compensation for us—not Egypt, but a naval station, even outside the Dardanelles: and an agreement will soon be reached—though I personally should oppose, because I regard it as dishonest to take compensation from the property of others, without a war"[3]—a nasty indirect hit at Andrássy!

Shuvalov in his telegram expressly dissociated himself from these views, but a night's reflection made him less sceptical, and next day he wired, "Derby may be right. If we keep calm, ignore the demonstrations which are coming, and above all refrain from advancing on Buyukdere and Gallipoli, we may obtain our aim without war. The desire for a direct *entente* with us is gaining ground here."[4] Gorchakov, it is true, bluntly replied that he had "no confidence in direct *entente* with England: the recent past has taught us harsh lessons. The sole service which the British Cabinet can render us is to refuse the Congress: if it suspected this, it would not do so."[5]

[1] 11 April—"Aus den Briefen R. von Bennigsen", ed. H. Oncken (*Deutsche Revue*, Sept. 1907, p. 316).   [2] *U.R.B.D.* Shuvalov to Gorchakov, first tel. of 16/28 March.
[3] *Ibid.* Shuvalov to Gorchakov, tel. of 17/29.
[4] *Ibid.* Shuvalov to Gorchakov, 2 tels. of 19/31 March.
[5] *Ibid.* Gorchakov to Shuvalov, tel. of 19/31 March.

But Shuvalov continued to urge that if the Russian press could be kept quiet and nothing happened in Turkey, there might be a *revirement*, and the Opposition would revive its efforts for a peaceful settlement. "If", he added, with an unwontedly Machiavellian touch, "I hold out to Ministers the prospect of a direct *entente*, it is to maintain them in their refusal of the Congress, which Vienna is trying to resuscitate."[1] This is suspiciously like the tactics of the Irishman whose pig thought he was going to Limerick, not Cork!

Beaconsfield's choice of Salisbury would seem to have rested on a triple basis. In his own precarious state of health he felt the need for assigning foreign affairs to a man of energy and constructive ideas: he felt that if after the loss of Carnarvon and Derby Salisbury also was allowed to drift away, the break-up of the Cabinet and perhaps of the party was wellnigh inevitable, and he also realised that this choice was the best means of covering up his own strategic retreat from high Palmerstonian doctrine to a restatement of policy. Nothing illustrates better the extent to which passion obscured the facts than the contemporary failure to realise that Disraeli's and Salisbury's policies were quite different, though thrown together, as in a dissolving view, on the same canvas; that what Salisbury eventually put through at Berlin was—with the important exception of the Turkish Convention—far nearer to Gladstone than to Disraeli: and that where he differed from the Liberal statesman was not so much in opinion, as in emphasis, in mentality, in tactics, in sense of proportion, in his view of what should be said and what suppressed.

THE SALISBURY CIRCULAR OF 1 APRIL

Lady Gwendolen Cecil has described how her father, on the very day of his appointment as Foreign Secretary, returned home late from a dinner-party, shut himself up in his study and worked till three in the morning at a statement of policy for submission to the Cabinet. This was the famous Salisbury Circular of 1 April, which won the immediate approval of his colleagues, was at once telegraphed all over Europe and demonstrated the fact that the conduct of policy had passed into energetic hands and was losing its character of negation.

It began by recapitulating, succinctly but clearly, the various diplomatic negotiations, from the British Note of 14 January, making

---

[1] *Ibid*. Shuvalov to Gorchakov, 2 tels. of 19/31.

the validity of the future treaty dependent on the assent of the Powers, to the Russian Note of 26 March, containing Gorchakov's final interpretation of the much vexed phrase "liberty of appreciation and action". It expressed "deep regret" at this decision, since Her Majesty's Government could not acquiesce in the withholding from the Congress of articles which modified existing treaties— especially in view of the declaration of 1871.

It then passed in review the Treaty of San Stefano and argued that its most important consequences came from "its action as a whole on the nations of South-East Europe". The future Bulgaria would be "a strong Slav state . . . under the auspices and control of Russia, . . . so constituted as to merge in the dominant Slav majority a considerable mass of population which is Greek in race and sympathy". The provisions regarding Thessaly and Epirus were good in themselves, but their framing was left to the supervision of Russia. "The territorial severance from Constantinople of the Greek, Albanian and Slav provinces still left under the Porte" would cause serious embarrassment. The "compulsory alienation of Bessarabia", the creation of Bulgaria and cession of Batum and Armenia would make Russia dominant along all the coasts of the Black Sea. The indemnity, far beyond Turkey's means, would become "an instrument of formidable efficacy for the coercion" of the Porte.

"The combined effect" of these provisions, "in addition to the results on the Greek population and on the balance of maritime power, is to suppress, almost to the point of entire subjection, the political independence of the Government of Constantinople. . . . It is in the power of the Ottoman Government to close or open the Straits which form the natural highway of nations between the Aegean Sea and the Euxine. Its dominion is recognised at the head of the Persian Gulf, on the shores of the Levant, and in the immediate neighbourhood of the Suez Canal. It cannot be otherwise than a matter of extreme solicitude to this country, that the Government to which this jurisdiction belongs should be so closely pressed by the political outposts of a greatly superior Power, that its independent action and even free existence is almost impossible. These results arise not so much from the language of any single article in the treaty as from the operation of the instrument as a whole."

The British Government's aim at the Conference of Constantinople —to give effect to the policy of reform and render the different populations contented—had been frustrated by the unfortunate resistance of the Porte: and now "large changes may and no doubt will be requisite in the Treaties. But good government, assured peace and freedom, for populations to whom those blessings have been strange, are still the objects which this country earnestly desires to secure." Britain, it concluded, could not enter a Congress whose deliberations were subject to such reservations.[1]

The Circular was on the whole well received in the country. The moderate *Times* praised the clearness with which it defined policy, denied that it contained any menace, and expected that it would "on the whole be firmly supported by public opinion": while the *Daily Telegraph* affirmed its "reasonings . . . to be as irrefragable as its tone is dignified, resolute and honest". The *Pall Mall Gazette* printed the whole dispatch in place of a leader, which led the *Spectator* to remark that in that position it was "in place", but that as an official manifesto it was "a fatal blunder". The Radicals meanwhile denounced the Circular as "incendiary":[2] and Madame Novikov wrote of it as "appalling by its cynicism". But the *Daily News*, the leading Liberal organ, accepted it as setting out "with great force and considerable minuteness the objections to the Treaty".

That this saner view was held by the official Opposition leaders is shown by a letter of Hartington, when the Circular was expected at any moment, but not yet ready. "I think if this Circular is a moderate one and takes a reasonable view of things", so he wrote to Granville, "*it may very much assist us* in abstaining from direct opposition: and at all events, we ought to have time to consider it before we decide what we shall do."[3] Clearly he was in no fighting mood, once more following not leading, and evidently not unconscious of the fact.

Even the more sober Shuvalov in his first interview with the new Foreign Secretary referred to it as "an instrument of war": but on this its author showed surprise and begged him to regard it as "an instrument of peace", adding somewhat cryptically, "there must be modifications in the treaty, but perhaps what we shall ask concerns us more than it interests you".[4] Next day he reiterated "with vivacity" his desire for a pacific solution.[5]

On the Continent it was welcomed as a step towards ending the

---

[1] Published as separate Blue Book—*Turkey No. XXV.* (1878).
[2] *Life of Salisbury*, ii. p. 230.
[3] *Granville Papers*, 31 March, Hartington to Granville.
[4] *U.R.B.D.* Shuvalov to Gorchakov, tel. of 22 March/3 April.
[5] *Ibid.* tel. of 23 March/4 April.

uncertainty in which British intentions had hitherto been veiled. In Paris, for instance, where there had been a growing tendency to regard war as inevitable, the press changed its tone and became more hopeful. In Vienna there was a chorus of welcome to Salisbury and his new confession of faith: and this of course reflected Andrássy's own feelings, for the press of Budapest was already rabidly Turcophil and preaching an alliance with England against the Slav danger, while that of Vienna was all the more amenable to the influence of the Ballplatz because its chief exponents were Jews and therefore uniformly Russophobe and suspicious of the Monarchy's own Slavs. To Drummond Wolff Andrássy expressed "the pleasure felt throughout the Continent *at the recent change of policy in England*". "For months England had been nowhere: no answer could be obtained, and her policy seemed to be one of indecision, vacillation and tergiversation. Now all was altered, and everyone must admire Salisbury's brilliant dispatch." [1]

In Berlin there was less restraint of the press, though not less possibility of judicious control, but on the other hand more indifference and therefore far greater caution in utterance. Meanwhile Clemens Busch, whose powers of observation were sharpened by close personal knowledge of Turkey, interpreted the British attitude as one of "stepping over the Turks as over a dead body, and it seems everywhere to be taken for granted that their succession is now open", and that England no longer contemplates a restoration of the Balkan *status quo*. [2]

In point of fact, Salisbury, though prepared to risk war as an ultimate necessity, definitely did not desire it, and the best proof of this lies in the prompt means that he took to extricate himself from the deadlock which he saw to have arisen between Britain and Russia. As early as 6 April he requested Lord Odo Russell to sound Bismarck and see whether he could be induced to father a proposal for the simultaneous withdrawal of the British fleet from the Straits and of the Russian army from their positions before Constantinople. Bismarck, who sarcastically remarked of Beaconsfield that he had led his country gallantly to the brink of war, [3] was relieved at the advent of Salisbury, and at once fell in with the suggestion, which

---

[1] Wolff, *Rambling Recollections*, ii. p. 171. Here Wolff forgets that at home he was one of those Conservatives who always denied the idea of a change and claimed continuity.

[2] Busch, *op. cit.* iii. p. 363.

[3] *Life of Duke of Devonshire*, i. p. 209.

Russell presented as a mere informal idea of his own.[1] On 9 April, then, with the approval of the Emperor William, Bismarck made a formal overture both to London and St. Petersburg, arguing that the juxtaposition of armed forces was a permanent danger, and that their withdrawal would produce a calmer atmosphere in which negotiations could be resumed. He obviously regarded the proposal as entirely his own, and Shuvalov, who at once learned of it from some secret source,[2] accepted it as such. But Gorchakov, while accepting the mediation and even the German condition of secrecy towards Vienna, learned that the Sultan had confided to the Grand Duke Nicholas—an interesting proof of the improvement in Russo-Turkish relations—that "the same idea had been communicated direct to him in Queen Victoria's name".[3]

Salisbury on his side concealed his extreme satisfaction by a tactical reference to the Cabinet, and there followed a somewhat minute bargaining between London and St. Petersburg, through Berlin as intermediary, as to the relative distance to which the land and sea forces should retire and the rapidity with which they could resume their old positions if one side denounced the arrangement. The Tsar did not believe in the sincerity of London, whom he suspected of not being ready and wishing to gain time: but he none the less, with the approval of the War Minister, requested Bismarck to continue his good offices.[4] Münster won the very definite impression that Salisbury wished to avoid war,[5] though he was constantly demanding fresh safeguards against Russia securing "a start in the race" back. Eventually by the 19th a satisfactory formula had been found: the details are too barren and technical to detain us. The worst obstacle was now surmounted, and the holding of a Congress again became a practical possibility.

Nothing of course was known of these negotiations at the time, and early in April the agitation in the country and the cleavage between the war and peace parties became more acute than ever.

---

[1] 6 and 7 April—*Letters of Queen Victoria*, ii. pp. 613-15. Lady Gwendolen Cecil fails to lay due emphasis on her father's initiative in this matter (cf. *Life*, pp. 239-42) while the German editors of *Die Grosse Politik* have overlooked it altogether (cf. *G.P.* ii. no. 381, *sqq.*). Strangest of all, Mr. Buckle is unaware of it in vol. vi. of his *Life of Disraeli*, though a few years later he publishes the essential letters between Salisbury and Russell, in *Letters of Queen Victoria*, ii. p. 613.
[2] *U.R.B.D.* Shuvalov to Gorchakov, tel. of 29 March/10 April.
[3] *Ibid.* Gorchakov to Shuvalov, tel. of 30 March/11 April.
[4] *G.P.* nos. 387 and 388, Schweinitz to Bismarck, 13 and 14 April.
[5] *Ibid.* nos. 392 and 396, Münster to Bismarck, 15 and 17 April.

BEACONSFIELD AND DERBY

On 8 April, in the House of Lords, the Prime Minister moved an Address to the Queen, accepting the calling out of the Reserve. His whole tone was unconciliatory and menacing. In a masterly summary of the diplomatic negotiations between the two countries, he no longer took as his point of departure the Derby Note of 6 May 1877—hitherto treated by all Government spokesmen as the basis of their policy, but now presumably avoided as an uncomfortable reminder that the terms of San Stefano were almost identical with those accepted by the Government as a definition of Russian war aims and not incompatible with its own definition of "British interests"—but Derby's earlier dispatch of 1 May 1877, characterising the war as a contravention of the Treaty of Paris. This, Beaconsfield now claimed, somewhat late in the day, had been "the keynote of our policy". He showed in great detail that the Government had throughout insisted that "any Russo-Turkish treaty" was "invalid without the assent of the Powers", and ended by claiming that Gorchakov's famous phrase—"liberty of appreciation and action" —was "not a clear conception. Delphi itself could hardly have been more perplexing and more august."

Then he turned to San Stefano. "I do not say that every article would be a violation of the treaties of 1856 and 1871, because that would be a harsh phrase." But it "completely abrogates what is known as Turkey-in-Europe" and substitutes the power of Russia for that of Turkey in Bulgaria. *It would "make the Black Sea as much a Russian lake as the Caspian"*. He reminded the House that Palmerston had "placed the utmost stress on Bessarabia, as involving the freedom of the Danube". As regards the Straits, the Sultan had been "reduced to a state of absolute subjection to Russia". Indeed in the east of Europe there was "only one step between collapse and convulsion: and but for the British fleet the chief highway between Europe and Asia might have been seized". Playing upon the momentary prejudices and illusions of the mob, he reminded the House that within living memory "armies marched through Syria and Asia without firing a shot and held Constantinople in a state of trepidation": why then should not the same fate befall Egypt and Suez?

He then referred to the contingency of England being "involved in a great war" and to the need of adequate military preparation, and turned upon his late colleague with the biting phrase: "I cannot conceive that any person with a sense of responsibility in the conduct of affairs could for a moment pretend that when all are armed, England alone should be unarmed. I am sure my noble friend whose loss I so much deplore, would never uphold that doctrine. . . . No, I cannot think such things of him: for to the individual of whom I did, I should say, *Naviget Anticyram:*[1] only I trust for heaven's sake that his lunacy might not imperil the British Empire." This enabled him to close on the favourite note of Empire. "No Caesar or Charlemagne", he declared, "ever presided over a dominion so peculiar. Its flag floats on many waters: it has provinces in every zone: they are inhabited by persons of different races, religions, laws, manners and customs. Some of these are bound to us by the ties of liberty, fully conscious that without their connection with the metropolis they have no security for public freedom and self-government: others are bound to us by flesh and blood and by material as well as moral considerations. There are millions who are bound to us by our military sway, and they bow to that sway because they know that they are indebted to it for order and justice. All these communities agree in recognising the commanding spirit of these islands, that has formed and fashioned in such a manner so great a portion of the globe. . . . That Empire is no mean heritage: but . . . it can only be maintained by the same qualities that created it—by courage, by discipline, by patience, by determination, and by a reverence for public law and respect for national rights. My Lords, in the east of Europe at this moment some securities of that Empire are imperilled. I never can believe that at such a moment it is the Peers of England who will be wanting to uphold the cause of their country."[2]

This eloquent conclusion made a deep impression upon his audience, but so far from helping to elucidate the Eastern Question, it confused the issue still further by staking the Prime Minister's great authority upon the opposition to San Stefano as an infringement of ill-defined British interests. It suggests that Beaconsfield was still blind to the fact bluntly stated in the House of Lords by Lord Hammond, that "for all practical purposes the Treaty of 1856 is dead",[3] and with it the old policy of Turkish territorial integrity.

A weighty debate followed, in which Lord Granville took the

[1] The island to which the lunatics of ancient Rome were sent.
[2] Hansard, ccxxx. pp. 761-77. Mr. Buckle quotes this "purple passage" in full, but then says that "the speech need not detain us", and omits the more threatening phrases quoted above, which were its real point.   [3] 7 March—*ibid.* p. 851.

ineffective line of disapproving, yet not opposing, the measure proposed: and it was left to the Duke of Argyll to declare the simple truth that the issue of peace and war was in the balance, and that the Prime Minister had "advised a warlike measure and introduced it in a corresponding tone", with "a distinct appeal to passion and prejudice". The maintenance of Turkish independence he described as "unattainable", and "rejoiced that such was the case": for "the sooner the Porte is dead and buried as an European Power, the better".[1]

The sensation of the evening, however, was the speech of Lord Derby. On retiring from office he had carried to the lengths of mystery his discretion as to motives: but he had been intensely annoyed by his old chief's transparent attempt to isolate him and save Lancashire and "the Stanley interest" by including his brother Colonel Frederick Stanley in the Cabinet as Secretary for War.[2] His irritation was increased by the unjust and even scathing criticism in the press, which assumed his resignation to be due solely to the calling out of the Reserve, which many moderate men approved. In the circumstances Beaconsfield's aggressive pronouncement was the last straw, and Derby—who had in his pocket the Queen's explicit sanction for explaining his motives *"at such a time as he in his discretion might think fit"*[3]—now spoke with a force and frankness all the more impressive from one habitually so calm. He would have preferred to remain silent, if he "could in honour do so", despite "the many reproaches" levelled at his "indecision, vacillation, even cowardice". "But it requires infinitely more courage for a man to stand up in his place and express views which he knows are unpopular among the great body of his friends, than to sit at a desk in Downing Street and thence issue orders which bring to him no danger and no unpopularity, but upon the giving of which may devolve the responsibility of a European War."

He went on to state that the calling of the Reserves was "not the sole, nor indeed the principal, reason for differences" with the Cabinet, and that other weighty reasons existed which he could not as yet divulge: and he revealed the further facts that he "did not willingly acquiesce in the summons of Parliament", that he had "ex-

---

[1] Hansard, ccxxx. pp. 824-8.

[2] The *Daily Telegraph* in its leader of 2 April was indiscreet enough to declare that this appointment "brings back into the Cabinet the influence and prestige of the great House of Knowsley".

[3] Quoted from Queen's letter—Buckle, vi. p. 268.

pressed grave doubts as to the necessity for this Vote of £6,000,000",
and indeed that "when that question came forward, he had temporarily retired from the Cabinet". It is difficult to see what just
exception can be taken to this statement, even without regard to the
keen provocation under which it was made: indeed his critics, who
sheltered themselves behind the doctrine of Cabinet secrecy in its
most "high and dry form", were, as it seems to us to-day, only too
obviously attempting to "have their cake and eat it", to reduce to
silence one of the very few men whose disapproval of their policy was
fortified by knowledge of their innermost purposes.

Moreover, by concentrating on this single point of Derby's speech,
his critics evaded the many powerful arguments which it contained.
He frankly regretted the objections raised by the Government to
provisions of San Stefano, the haste with which they were pressing
forward and their disregard for the natural irritation thus caused in
Russia. He refused to believe "that there is any very strong ground
for irritation on either side". He failed to understand the panic-
stricken assumption that the Russian army could march through
Syria before the British fleet could reach Alexandria, and he went
on to ask what were the Government's means of fighting, who were
its allies and what it was fighting for. He reminded them that it
was easy to determine who would *not* be our allies—Germany, who
showed undisguised sympathy for Russia; France, where no one
would accept the policy of another Crimean War; Italy, who would
not move under any circumstances. There remained that very
"doubtful ally" Austria-Hungary, who would in the end be deterred
by the ties between the three Emperors and by its own mixed population, since it was "a country which a single unsuccessful campaign
might not impossibly break up". And what would be the result of
such a war? "You cannot now restore Turkey": and he asked the
English people "how they can expect to have a foreign policy—I do
not say far-sighted, but even consistent and intelligent—if within
eighteen months the great majority of them are found asking for
things directly contradictory?" He clinched his argument for posterity, though not for the deaf ears of many hysterical contemporaries, by insisting that Russia's influence in Bulgaria rested, not
on her military successes, but *"on what you cannot take away—
identity of race, community of religion, traditional historical sympathies
and the common hatred felt against a common enemy. . . . I say, therefore, if you go to war for the sake of influence over these populations,*

you are fighting for a shadow, and even that shadow you will not secure."

His obvious alarm and indignation culminated in the phrase, "I am compelled to ask if we are—*I do not say drifting, but rushing into war*"—to ask, what it is we are going to fight for, and what would be the result even of its successful conclusion. With the utmost emphasis he denied that a *casus belli* existed, or that diplomatic means were exhausted, and he declared that war, if it came, would be "a war without necessity, without a clear and defined object, with a divided country, and in all probability without an ally".[1] All this from the late Foreign Secretary was extremely unpalatable and not a little damaging.

Meanwhile in the House of Commons Sir Stafford Northcote took a strangely different line from his chief in the Lords. He argued that the calling out of the Reserve was simply "a measure of precaution", not due to an emergency such as the presence of Napoleon at Boulogne or the Indian Mutiny. He claimed for Britain a voice in the final settlement, but was most anxious "to avoid language irritating or offensive to Russia"—an anxiety of which there was no sign in Beaconsfield himself or in the ministerial press—and he believed that "the sentiment of Europe" was in accord with the British view that the treaty showed "an absence of consideration for all save the Slavs". The sweet reasonableness of Northcote is throughout one of the saving graces of a dangerous situation.

Gladstone in his reply referred to the "ominous declarations elsewhere", minimised the emergency and insisted upon the country's alarm at the Government's increasingly "warlike frame of mind". He expressed satisfaction at the promises to Greece contained in Lord Salisbury's Circular, while refuting its "mis-statements" regarding the Russian Church and the rumour of a Russian Prince for Bulgaria. Turning to the details of San Stefano, he described Russia's demand for Bessarabia as "*impolitic and culpable spoliation*", quite unworthy of her, but the clauses relating to Armenia as "fair and moderate", and a large Bulgaria as less liable to Russian influence than a small one—a point which scarcely seems to have occurred to anyone else. But his main point was a reminder that the terms imposed at San Stefano scarcely differed from those which Russia had frankly intimated before ever she crossed the Danube.[2]

Two nights were occupied in ineffective discussion of Sir Wilfrid

[1] Hansard, vi. pp. 789-801.   [2] *Ibid.* pp. 877-86.

Lawson's amendment opposing the calling out of the Reserve: and it is characteristic of the confusion in the Opposition ranks that Chamberlain balanced the nation's dislike of Turkey against its suspicions of Russia and advocated the revival of a Greek Empire, while Dilke expressed satisfaction at Derby's resignation, ascribed a "European character" to Salisbury's policy and endorsed his support of the Greeks. Hartington as Leader dissented from the amendment, but asked the Government whether it was prepared to go to war against Russia, with Turkey as an ally. To him there was almost equal danger in the language of the Government, rendering Russian concessions impossible, and in the language of its rivals, which might encourage Russia in her refusal. In the end Hartington again abstained from voting, and with him even the stalwart Forster: and Gladstone found himself, on a division, in a minority of 64 to 319! In a word, the Opposition remained as divided as ever, while the ranks of the Government were closing. Granville and Hartington were agreed that Lawson's insubordination was fatal to party discipline, but were seemingly incapable of enforcing it.[1]

Lord Derby's resignation had been greeted with glee by the Jingo press, but with restraint and appreciation in the more responsible organs. Even the *Daily Telegraph* paid its "tribute of personal respect and regret" and described the manner of his going as "in all points worthy of his character". None the less it hinted that Russian intrigues had been "notoriously encouraged by Lord Derby's honourable clinging to peace", and urged that the Government "must now follow up their defence of the public law and of the national safety" as "the only and best road to peace"[2]—a clumsy paraphrase of *Si vis pacem, para bellum. The Times* was cautious, but openly regretful, alluding to certain "malicious and unjustifiable attacks" and asserting that "except among a clique unworthy of the nation" there were no two opinions regarding Derby's "ability, patience and self-sacrificing labour".[3] Outside the innermost ring of the initiated there was still but little perception of the depth of cleavage inside the Cabinet itself: unity had been so often and so vehemently proclaimed, and the rank and file had not doubted the good faith of their leaders. But the debate of 8 April was full of startling revelations and hints

---

[1] "I considered the proceedings of last night one of the heaviest possible blows to the discipline of a party I had ever remembered" (Granville, writing to Hartington on 10 April 1878, quotes himself as having spoken to Gladstone in the above sense)—Fitzmaurice, *Life of Granville*, ii. p. 176.

[2] *D.T.* leader of 29 March.   [3] *The Times* leader of 29 March.

of many yet unexplored recesses: and the Lawson amendment, inept
though it might be, was none the less an index of public excitement,
which now flared up once more in a long series of public meetings and
protests. Lord Derby's speech was reprinted by the *Northern Echo*,
and close upon half a million copies of it were sold. Even after an
interval of thirty years W. T. Stead described it, not without his
habitual over-emphasis, as "the blast of a trumpet to the sane and
sober portion of the nation".[1] Froude's contemporary verdict, that
it was "felt throughout the country", was undoubtedly correct. "If
Beaconsfield can be kept from going to war for another month," he
wrote, "the reaction will have gathered force", and Layard's intrigues in Constantinople would fail: "once let the congress meet,
and all is safe".[2]

The shock to public confidence was very great, and the Jingo
press could not conceal its rage at the exposure of acute disagree-
ments in the innermost councils of the Crown. As so often during the
crisis, the attitude of *The Times* is specially enlightening: even it
betrays surprise on learning that Cabinet differences had been of
such "long standing", and at the same time it contains perhaps the
weightiest and most permanent of contemporary criticism. It finds
it "hard to understand how Lord Derby can have continued so long
the colleague of a Prime Minister from whom his foreign policy differs
so completely"; it points out Derby's failure to "defend his own
passive reception" in the summer of 1877 "of what amounted to a
draft of the Treaty of San Stefano":[3] and it makes clear that this
reflects upon the whole Cabinet and that the *apologia* put forward by
Cairns and Hardy was "very inadequate". For "if as ministerial
policy assumes, San Stefano be matter for war when the Russians
are at Constantinople, it would have been more judicious to have
thought of protest at an earlier period". It even reminded Hardy
that in stressing Derby's concurrence in the Vote of Credit when in
reality (though the public had not yet learned the fact) Derby actually resigned for forty-eight hours on that very issue, he had allowed
his zeal to "outstrip his argumentative force". But the main point
of its criticism was directed against the Lord Chancellor's unconvincing plea that the Russian terms communicated by Shuvalov had
been treated by the Cabinet "as of merely theoretical interest",
since the Porte could not be expected to accede to them, unless

---

[1] *The M.P. for Russia*, i. p. 479.   [2] 13 April—*ibid.* p. 496.
[3] *I.e.* the Russian terms, as notified by Shuvalov in June 1877—see *supra*, p. 193.

"reduced to the last extremity". That meant that, as so often in the past, official and public opinion profoundly misjudged both Turkey's "inherent strength" and powers of resistance, and "the difficulties of the Russian enterprise". This verdict has been amply endorsed by history.

GATHORNE HARDY AND CROSS VERSUS JOHN BRIGHT AND CHAMBERLAIN

The public controversy reached its height in the last days of April and early May, with the rival pronouncements of Hardy and Bright, of Chamberlain and Cross: and a few extracts may serve to bring home to the modern reader the intensity of feeling that prevailed on both sides, and the vituperative powers which it provoked. In the words of *The Times* (3 May), "the whole country is in debate on the Eastern Question and the attitude of the Government", and "each side taunts the other with a plentiful lack of logic and a copious flow of passion".

Gathorne Hardy at Bradford laid the main stress on "public faith and honesty", or, in other words, the sanctity of the treaties of 1856 and 1871, reminding his Liberal critics that in the latter year, when they had been in power and had effected a revision of the Paris settlement, not a voice had been raised about the Christian nationalities. He admitted the horrible character of the Bulgarian massacres, but argued, like Elliot, that "the policy of a great contract is not to be destroyed by an incident, however horrible or disastrous". He then put forward the claim that England, as one of the co-signatories of the Treaty of Paris, had the right "to appear in the Sea of Marmora in force"—of course a direct negative to the view of Gladstone and the Opposition. He defined the alternatives that faced the nation as peace at any price, or a new crusade, and added, " I hope the sword of England will never be drawn against freedom or liberty anywhere. ... But are we to proclaim ourselves the knights-errant of the world?" We would, he declared, never become "the military gladiators of the world". Before he closed, however, he tried to rouse his audience by a fantastic estimate of 500,000 Moslems dead by famine or the sword, and while vigorously denying the existence of a "War Government" and hoping for durable peace through a Congress, spoke of England being able to put 70,000 men into the field. Incidentally, this figure, quoted so confidently by the late Secretary for War, as presumably adequate for a struggle with a huge military Empire of almost boundless man-power, is a measure of the dangers which confronted the country from leaders whom history may perhaps acquit of deliberate war-mongering, but certainly not of extreme and aggressive recklessness.

The Times in its comment on Hardy's "strong incisive style and sturdy manner", held that "Mr. Hardy seems to speak naturally in the accents of a born warrior", and treated the speech as "a good party manifesto, but scarcely an impartial or exhaustive record" (30 April).

If Hardy pushed self-confidence to its limit, John Bright, speaking at the Liberal Conference in Manchester two days later, went further and pitched a fiercer note than ever before or after, and in due course, on leaving the hall, had his hat smashed over his head by indignant Jingoes. From the outset he treated "the near approach of war" as certain, ridiculed Hardy's denial of a war party in "a speech of boisterous recklessness and want of logic", and after quoting the Prince Consort's remark upon Stratford de Redcliffe on the eve of the Crimean War—"he fulfils instructions to the letter, but he so contrives that we are constantly getting deeper into a war policy"—applied it openly to the case of Beaconsfield and "that war section of the Government which looks to him as representative of their views". Speaking deliberately within a few miles of Knowsley, he drew a contrast with Lord Derby, who "went out from among them, declaring by his act that he would not be in any degree a participator in the great crime they meditated against the true interests of his country". He then challenged Hardy's claim that the entry of the fleet did not violate the treaties: for in that case why had the Sultan's permission been asked? The motive put forward by Northcote in the Commons—the protection of British lives and property—was one which no one believed, and in its new form, as explained by Hardy—such protection in the event of a Russian occupation—was even more flimsy, first because in that event British lives would be perfectly safe, and everyone knew it, and above all because the only reason for fearing a Russian occupation was the very presence of our fleet! He was no longer in a mood to condone the more moderate Northcote, whose "smooth and consoling words" in the Commons had been uttered when all the time he knew that Indian troops had been summoned to Europe. "We might", cried the orator, "be living under the great despotism which we exercise in India, or the much smaller despotism which the Tsar exercises in Russia", and such secretiveness was "humiliating to the House and insulting to the nation". "The 'British interest' dodge had been dropped", and the country was now summoned "in defence of what they call European law", of "that very old hobgoblin", the balance of power in the Mediterranean, and of "that multitudinous crime which we call the Ottoman Government".

By this time his pacifist zeal had overcome his self-restraint. He attacked the policy of the Prime Minister as "wicked and shameful in the sight of Heaven": he even denounced "the betrayal of a Minister who has not one single drop of English blood in his veins". He spoke of "the suspension for an indefinite period not only of the Ten Commandments, but also of the Sermon on the Mount", and then recovered his logical balance in a final phrase, "Let us get rid of our Christianity or get rid of our tendency and willingness to go to war"—a sentiment more likely to win approval in 1935 than in 1878 (1 May).

On the same day Joseph Chamberlain, while repudiating "the ignoble doctrine of peace at any price", vigorously denied that war could be justified under present circumstances, when Egypt and Suez were in no way menaced, and even a Russian Constantinople— which he opposed and did not admit to be in prospect—would not be as dangerous to British interests as the unquestioned possession of Mediterranean ports and arsenals by France, Austria and Italy. He made effective use of Bismarck's phrase about the Pomeranian musketeer, objected to a war which could only result in restoring "the fabric of iniquity" of Turkey and concluded by insisting that the necessary changes in San Stefano could be achieved by diplomacy.

The Home Secretary, Assheton Cross, was generally regarded as one of the most reasonable and persuasive members of the Government, only breaking silence at intervals: and he now appears to have been selected as the apologist of official policy in the north of England. Speaking at Preston on successive days, he endorsed his colleague Hardy's remarks, but took care to follow entirely different lines himself. He challenged the whole theory of the Prime Minister's wickedness, of Northcote's deception of the House and of the rest of the Cabinet as mere dummies: he submitted that it was quite unfair to accuse the Government of a secretive policy, in view of the very explicit terms of the Derby Note of 6 May 1877 and of the Salisbury Circular of 1 April 1878. He disclaimed all desire for war, merely pleading that "the loss of national honour" was even worse, that "this tearing up of treaties is an unhappy doctrine", and that no unilateral change in the public law of Europe could be tolerated. He defended the military and naval measures with varying degrees of success: for it can only be presumed that when he reminded Bright that the fleet entered the Marmora *with the firman of the Porte*, he did not know the true facts of the Sultan's protest to the Queen and of Salisbury's agreement with Beaconsfield that it must enter "firman or no firman".[1] He was on stronger ground in arguing that but for the Liberal Cardwell's Army Act (which he was careful not to condemn) an army corps could have been sent to Malta without reference to Parliament and without any need for calling out the Reserve. But the essential point of his speech was to admit that "great alterations must undoubtedly be made in the Treaties of 1856 and 1871. The object of Her Majesty's Government *is not the independence and integrity of the Ottoman Empire, as has been stated*"—not a reversal of the whole treaty from beginning to end, but "the good government and assured peace of those populations of Turkey".

Public opinion at once settled on this pronouncement, as an abandonment of the extreme Turcophil point of view. *The Times*, for instance, assumed that "the Government repudiates through Mr. Cross any wish for war or intention of undertaking it, if its legitimate purposes can be attained by other means".[2] This undoubtedly had a reassuring effect in many quarters, and though the situation remained tense until 3 June, when the Congress was at last officially announced, there was through May a certain feeling of expectancy and suspended judgment, while diplomatic negotiations of which we have yet to write were known to be proceeding.

Indian Troops in Europe

On 17 April the Government had taken advantage of the Easter Recess to reveal their closely guarded secret of the dispatch of 7000 Indian troops to Malta. Nothing shows more clearly our insular outlook than the sensation which this news caused at home, as compared with the openly scoffing attitude of Continental opinion at the grotesque inadequacy of our military forces for a great war. That the decision took most people by surprise is shown by Mr. Gladstone's public comment next day. He had been "much puzzled for a time to

---

[1] See *supra*, pp. 267 and 315.   [2] Second leader of 3 May.

know to what Lord Derby was alluding" when he spoke of *other* vital
grounds of disagreement with the Cabinet, which he could not as yet
reveal: yesterday's announcement "told you part of it. Rely upon it,
there is more behind", for Lord Derby "knows more of his colleagues
than we do", and "of the floating intentions" of the Prime Minister.[1]
This means that the secret had been jealously guarded, and that
even the leaders of the Opposition had remained for some weeks
utterly in the dark. Hartington greeted the announcement as "rather
audacious" after Northcote's attitude in the House, and wrote to
Granville, "I really begin to think that Lord B." [no longer "Dizzy"]
"means war".[2]

It is small wonder that this secrecy impressed them more forcibly
than ever with the danger of their hands being suddenly forced, and
led them to organise a strong critical assault upon the Government's
action, alike on political and on constitutional grounds. But here
again Hartington and Granville hesitated between two courses and
thus gave the debate on 7 May a certain unreality. It opened on an
acrid note, when Fawcett bluntly accused Northcote of misleading
the House after Derby's resignation, by his assurance that there was
"no change in our policy". The use of Indian troops behind the back
of Parliament was a momentous change in our policy, for which
there was no precedent.   In 1863 the project of employing them in
New Zealand was abandoned for this very reason: their use in
Abyssinia in 1867, and again at Singapore and Hongkong, had been
formally sanctioned beforehand. The latest method, if unchallenged,
would invest the home Government with new powers, the more so
as the expenses could be defrayed out of the revenues of India and
therefore not submitted to Parliament. These and similar arguments
were urged by Sir George Campbell, a former Governor of Bengal,
and by Mr. Laing, once Indian Financial Secretary to Lord Canning,
who, he argued, would never have given his consent to such a thing.
Sir Stafford Northcote retorted that it lay within the undoubted
prerogative of the Crown, that Malta was not the same thing as the
United Kingdom, and that Parliament would be asked to bear the
entire cost. It was left to Sir John Hay to argue that Malta was really
in Africa, not in Europe, and to Sir Robert Peel and Mr. Baillie-
Cochrane to denounce the critics as inspired by "a spirit of faction".

Ten days later the question was still more solemnly debated in

---

[1] *The Times*, 19 April 1878.
[2] *Granville Papers*, 20 April, Hartington to Granville.

both Houses, Lord Hartington moved that no forces may be raised or kept by the Crown in peace time without consent of Parliament, except those serving inside India itself: and Sir M. Hicks Beach moved as an amendment, that the constitutional control of Parliament over military forces was fully secured by the existing law and by the Commons' power to grant or refuse supplies, and that the motion was therefore unnecessary and inexpedient. Thus, while the Government was content with a half-hearted defence of its policy, the Opposition again fell into two groups, those who wished to strike home, and those who tried to eliminate all criticism of policy and concentrate on the constitutional issue, which, in the words of *The Times*, was "magnificent, but not parliamentary warfare".

There followed a portentous legal duel between Lord Selborne and Lord Cairns, in which every ambiguity in the Bill of Rights was argued at length: but in the end it all boiled down to the question whether the times were normal, or whether a sudden emergency existed, such as would justify the Government in thus anticipating Parliament. *The Times* was again undoubtedly right when it argued that if there were no real danger from San Stefano, then secret orders were not only unnecessary but a menace to the peace of Europe, but that if this question of "urgent necessity" were once eliminated, the constitutional question was "little better than an academical exercise".[1] And so after some nights of sound and fury there was a truce on this issue: but "the lack of vigour" displayed by Granville and Hartington was again apparent to all eyes and again contrasted with Gladstone's frontal attack upon "the extraordinary rashness of H.M.G. in employing for the first time Indian troops not under parliamentary control, in the conduct of European wars".[2]

This whole incident is a remarkable illustration of our insular outlook upon public affairs: for the mere sending of 7000 troops would have been wellnigh worthless if it had really come to war. John Bright's phrase—that "Russia is not invading India, India is preparing to invade Russia"—was little better than a catchword. The Continental outlook is seen in Count Münster's assumption that the move was more *political* than military in intention—for home quite as much as for foreign consumption. Mr. Buckle is entitled to argue that the solidarity of imperial defence was thus established as a principle, but when he goes on to deduce that it was this which

[1] *The Times*, 7, 9, 20 and 21 May.
[2] 8 May, to Welsh deputation at Hawarden.

convinced Russia that England was in earnest, and so led to a *détente*, he misjudges Russian motives.[1] Russia could at this moment unquestionably have seized Constantinople, blocked the Bosphorus and made any British military advance impossible. She did not underestimate British financial resources, but what decided her to compromise was her own precarious internal position and her distrust of Austria-Hungary on her flank.

The plain fact is that Beaconsfield was really receding from his advanced position, and some dramatic action, preferably of not too ambitious a character, was needed to conceal his retreat and pacify the impatient Jingoes. Kinglake sarcastically accused him of "imitating Canning. Canning said, I call the new world into existence to redress the balance of the old. Beaconsfield by bringing the Sepoys says, I bring the brown world into existence to redress the balance of the white." [2] The Prime Minister's own strongest argument doubtless was that the real stakes in the conflict were Asiatic and that Indian troops would be suitably employed in holding back a Russian advance in Asia, such as might ultimately endanger the safety of India. But here we find ourselves in the old controversy which had long divided the Indian Council and leads far beyond our present subject.

GLADSTONE AND THE CROWN

The excitement with regard to the Indian troops gave rise to a curious incident, which throws light upon the rival mentality of the two sides and perhaps helps to explain the personal attitude of Queen Victoria during the succeeding decade. Reference has already been made to Gladstone's anxiety as to the personal intervention of the Crown in the whole controversy: and this anxiety was now heightened by an extraordinary article in the *Quarterly Review*, which it is safe to describe at that epoch as the supreme repository of Tory doctrine, enjoying direct ministerial inspiration.

The third volume of Theodore Martin's remarkable *Life of the Prince Consort*—covering the stormy period of the Crimean War— had just appeared and had aroused no small sensation, because its publication of state papers and confidential memoranda, then infinitely more unusual than now, was known to have been directly ordered by the Queen, as a vindication of her beloved husband's

---

[1] Buckle, vi. p. 290. [2] *The M.P. for Russia*, i. p. 477.

memory. It was upon this volume and a series of articles published in a Manchester Radical organ under the title of "The Crown and the Cabinet",[1] that the anonymous *Quarterly* reviewer based his argument. He plunged straight into the fray by vindicating the Queen from the charge of aggressive aims or of collecting a party of "Queen's friends", and denounced as "dangerous fallacies" the attempt of Verax to represent Martin's *Life* as "a message from the Crown, sent straight to the nation over the heads of ministers". He then proceeded to moralise on constitutional practice, enouncing such seductive axioms as "All government is founded partly on force, partly on opinion", and "Human nature is perpetually driving monarchy towards despotism and democracy towards anarchy". Government by party, he argued, arose from "the unnatural conduct of the sovereign" before 1688: from 1702 to 1832 "the various elements of the constitution were more evenly balanced than ever before or after": 1832 produced "a revolution in the political balance of power", and "the sovereign was once more in direct personal contact with his subjects in a Government resting almost entirely on public opinion". This leads up to the claim that "strong monarchs have always been popular in England", that the Crown "must be allowed a large personal share in the control of our foreign policy, and that the House of Commons was "utterly unqualified" for such functions. "The ordinary Englishman is ignorant of elementary geography, still more ignorant of history, unacquainted with foreign languages, manners and modes of thought, and peculiarly susceptible of insular prejudice": how, then, can he "judge with sagacity of imperial questions"? Since 1789 the main question in Europe had lain between Authority on the one side and Liberty and Equality on the other— a question almost decided in England by the compromise of 1688. A policy of intervention on behalf of a new doctrine of "nationality" —here he stops to condemn Sir William Harcourt's vindication of oppressed races in a recent speech—had been successively repudiated by Canning, Aberdeen and Peel: and now "the only way of steering between the Scylla of absolutism and the Charybdis of anarchy" was "by leaving the executive (we will go further and add the Sovereign herself) just liberty in the conduct of foreign affairs".

There follows a highly ingenious argument, based on the not unjust theory that public sentiment was blended of "love of freedom and national pride" ("it pleased popular imagination to think of

[1] By Verax. Reprinted from *Manchester Weekly Times*.

England as the leader of European freedom, and to hear of foreign nations adopting constitutional government, because the notion was English"); on the increasing difficulty of "a just application of the principle of non-intervention" as the century advanced and as wars became increasingly inspired by "democratic motives"; on the constant difficulties in which Palmerston involved the nation "by the ardour with which he pushed his constitutional propaganda", and by contrast, on the beneficial effect of the personal influence of the Crown, especially during the forties and fifties. After the Crimean War, "the policy of non-intervention grew into a confirmed habit of abstention from Continental quarrels": but though the Eastern Question was "specially unsuited to be dealt with by public opinion", the Bulgarian atrocities sent "an electric current" across the kingdom, such as once led an Asiatic mob to shout for two hours "Great is Diana of the Ephesians". "Throughout the country poets, historians, professors, High Churchmen and Dissenters appeared on public platforms, denouncing with equal vigour the unspeakable Turk and the bloodthirsty Premier." He then jumps to the paradoxical conclusion, "Our Empire rests upon Opinion, and the Crown is the centre to which all sound opinion, independently of party, should gravitate". This is backed up by a reference to Lord Derby, who in 1876 assured a deputation of his anxiety "to meet the wishes of his employers". At the time the reviewer had regarded this merely as "a vein of pleasantry", but as it was being taken seriously, "we desire to record our hearty protest against the unconstitutional principle implied. . . . Lord Derby is the servant, not of the people, but of the Crown. He is responsible to the people for the conduct of affairs, whereas, if his words were to be taken seriously, his responsibility would obviously cease." The Englishman "is apt to be carried away by a rush of opinion which deprives him of all sense of justice and wisdom. . . . There is only one quarter in which the knowledge exists, in which the unity and continuity of England's policy is kept ever clearly in view apart from the illusions of party warfare. That quarter is the Crown, represented by the Ministry." The article closes in the ominous phrase: "The Queen may be assured that, should she be unfortunately called upon to exercise her prerogative of declaring war, her subjects will spare no sacrifices to maintain the safety of her Empire and the honour of her Crown".

It is not surprising that such bold doctrines were not allowed to pass unchallenged. The rival "great gun" of the press, the *Edinburgh*

Review, under the inverted title of "The Constitution and the Crown",
devoted the first article of its next issue [1] to a frontal attack upon the
Quarterly and incidentally upon some of the theories propounded by
Baron Stockmar to the Prince Consort and first printed in Martin's
Life. Not content with exposing certain gross errors in the *Quarterly*
reviewer's chronology with regard to the conquest of Canada, India
and Malta, it accused him of "mis-statements and misapprehensions
of English constitutional history such as have not been seen in print
since the times of the Stuarts". The British constitution, he very
aptly pointed out, "has a theory, but the practice is the reverse of
the theory", in so far as the respective powers of Crown and Parliament are concerned. "The pretensions set up on behalf of the
sovereign to direct foreign policy are wholly incompatible" with the
existing constitutional relations between the two: and if the incompetence of the House of Commons in that sphere were to be
admitted, there would follow the necessary inference that party
government should be abolished. He dismissed as unlikely "any
direct attempt" to assert such doctrine, but would not rule out the
possibility of "some secret adviser—a consort or perhaps a mistress,
a foreigner, a friend, a tutor or even a body physician": and to drive
home his point, he boldly affirmed that the Prince Consort "took a
more active part in public affairs than was convenient or becoming",
and that Stockmar, clever and experienced though he was, never
managed to understand the British constitution.

Feeling, perhaps, that he was proving too much, he denied any
desire "to reduce the Crown to a cipher" and went on: "The control
of foreign policy is at present exercised by Parliament: it cannot be
exercised by the Crown and Parliament conjointly. . . . We do not
wish to see the constitution shaken to its foundations by a collision
between Crown and people: but this would be, sooner or later, the
certain result of shifting responsibility from the executive Government to the Crown." Speaking now openly as a party politician, he
reproached the Tories with a desire "to exalt prerogative on the
ruins of parliamentary government", and with being "in spirit, and so
far as times permit, in action, the same" as "fifty years ago": and he
affirmed that it would be a grave error to treat the article as "the
rhodomontade of a crazy fanatic", in view of the *Quarterly's* close
connection with the party in power.

The writer's main object is to warn that the advocacy of such
subversive doctrines "coincides with a remarkable act of state",

namely, the calling out of military forces not sanctioned by Parliament and the announcement of this fact on the day after the adjournment, with the result that "we suddenly learn that engagements have been entered into by the ministers of the Crown, entirely without the knowledge of Parliament". This leads him to accept the challenge contained in the *Life of the Prince Consort*, and to claim the theories propounded by the *Quarterly Review* as virtually modelled on Bolingbroke's *Patriot King* and, above all, as identical with those of Stockmar, which were "not the rambling of a distempered brain, nor the fulsome adulation of a silly courtier, but the deliberate counsel of a man of mature years and good understanding, who wrote essays on the British constitution and was honoured with the entire confidence—nay, the respectful deference—of the Queen and her consort". In direct contradiction to Stockmar, the *Edinburgh* reviewer contends that "wise and good kings are only happy accidents", and asks whether in the century and a half following the Revolution there was "any sovereign except William III. capable of being permanent Prime Minister and directing foreign policy".

The article closes with a warning against Lord Beaconsfield, whose "dazzling qualities are not those of an English statesman", as the contents of *Coningsby* amply demonstrate. "Having mystified his intellect in penning original theories of the constitution and fantastic histories of party until his perception of the difference between truth and fiction has become confused, it is possible that he may have brought himself to entertain" some such idea as "the supplanting of parliamentary government by prerogative". It was, at any rate, certain that the House of Commons had "sunk in public confidence and respect under his administration". The writer thus ended with a more personal note than his rival: the issue was fairly joined between the two camps.

This personal note was no accident. The *Edinburgh's* allusion to *Coningsby* must have automatically turned many of his readers to the pages of that volume, and it is only necessary to compare certain passages in it with the original offending article, in order to recognise the similarity of ideas and the extent to which the anonymous writer was expounding a theme dear not merely to the long dead Bolingbroke, but to the present Prime Minister himself. "The tendency of advanced civilisation is in truth to pure Monarchy." "The House of Commons, that has absorbed all other powers in the state, will in all probability fall more rapidly than it rose." "The House of Commons is the house of a few, the Sovereign is the sovereign of all. The proper leader of the people is the individual who sits upon the throne." "Opinion is now supreme, and Opinion speaks in print." "Let us propose to our consideration the idea of a free monarchy, established on fundamental laws, itself the apex of a vast pile of municipal and local government, ruling an educated people, represented by a free and intellectual press. Before such a royal authority, supported by such a national opinion, the sectional anomalies of our country would disappear. Under such a system, where qualification would not be parliamentary but personal, even statesmen would be educated; we should have no more diplomatists who could not speak French, no more bishops ignorant of theology, no more generals-in-chief who never saw a field."

The coincidence is too striking to require much emphasis. So long as these sentiments were expressed through a character in fiction, there was no need to take them all too seriously, even if they seemed to betray a tendency or attitude of mind in their author. But when voiced in the leading organ of the Tory Government, and fortified by quotations from Tory thinkers of the past, they assumed a new significance.

Hence, long before the *Edinburgh* rejoinder could appear, the original article had awakened a lively echo in political circles, and on 8 May Gladstone himself, in replying at Hawarden to a "national memorial" from Wales, roundly denounced what he called a feeler, "very clever and crafty", whose purposes were "disloyal to the Crown and dangerous to public liberty. . . . The object is carefully to confound the Sovereign and the Crown and to shift about from the one to the other, and to establish the doctrine that the Sovereign personally should direct the policy of the country in peace or war." There was thus "a direct tendency to bring the sovereign personally into the arena of politics, to render her liable to questions, and to direct against her personally the discontent and dissatisfaction which political miscarriage will bring about". "Quite as good productions", he added, "have been burnt by the common hangman."

It is impossible to dismiss this as mere sound and fury: for in the same breath Gladstone, with all the weight of an ex-Premier who was obviously on the eve of resuming his leadership, denounced "the extraordinary rashness of H.M.G. in employing for the first time Indian troops not under parliamentary control in the conduct of European wars". Beaconsfield was evidently stung by this speech of Gladstone, for to Lady Bradford he wrote that it "exceeds any of his previous performances":[1] but it may well have served as a warning "hands off". For it is difficult not to read into the *Quarterly* article exactly what Gladstone affirmed—a feeler, intended to prepare public opinion for action corresponding to the notoriously bellicose sentiments of the Queen and her entourage.[2]

In September, when the echoes of Berlin were dying away, Gladstone gave a calmer and more considered verdict on this delicate controversy in an article for American consumption.[3] Taking William IV.'s coup of 1834 as the last example of "a very real exercise of personal power", he argued that as the monarch is permanent while ministers are "fugitive", "he may be a weighty factor in all deliberations of the state", but his influence is "moral, not coercive", and "it would be an evil and perilous day for the monarch, were any prospective possessor of the Crown to assume or claim for himself final, or preponderating, or even independent power in any one department of the state. . . . The ideas and practice of the time of George III., whose will in certain matters limited the action of the ministers, cannot be revived otherwise than by what would be, on their part, nothing less than a base compliance, a shameful subserviency, dangerous to the public weal and in the highest degree disloyal to the dynasty. . . . Sole action, for the sovereign, would mean . . . unprotected action, . . . a head would project beyond the awning and would invite a sunstroke. . . . No distinction is more vital to the practice of the British constitution than the distinction between the Sovereign and the Crown. . . . It is a cardinal axiom of the modern constitution that the House of Commons is the greatest of the powers of the state."

"The Crown is entitled to make a thousand peers to-day and as many to-morrow: it may dissolve all and every Parliament before it proceeds to business: may pardon the most atrocious crimes, may declare war against all the world, may conclude treaties involving unlimited responsibility and even vast expenditure, without consent, nay without the knowledge of Parliament. . . . But the assumption is that the depositaries of power will all respect one another,

---

[1] Buckle, *op. cit.* vi. p. 304.

[2] In October another writer in the *Edinburgh* ("England in the Levant"), commenting most adversely upon our policy in Cyprus, declared that "the spirit of his [Beaconsfield's] policy would have made him a Strafford under Charles I. and a Bolingbroke under Queen Anne".

[3] *North American Review*, Sept. 1878; *Gleanings*, i. p. 230 *sqq.*

will evince a consciousness that they are working in a common interest for a common end, that they will be possessed, together with not less than an average intelligence, of not less than an average sense of equity and of the public interest and rights. When these reasonable expectations fail, then it must be admitted the British Constitution will be in danger."

Seldom have the doctrines expounded by Bagehot been more aptly stated by a political leader, and though they may sound almost commonplace to-day and seem to have held the field at the time, it is well to remember that they were an answer to one of the last serious attempts to put forward the rival doctrine, and that while Gladstone himself did more than most statesmen to crystallise their form, they have been, at any rate since the fall of Beaconsfield, the common property of all parties in the state. On the other hand, the *North American* article filled Beaconsfield "with amazement" and was denounced by him to the Queen:[1] and Mr. Buckle holds that his famous speech at the Guildhall in November 1878 was an answer to its evil doctrine. No better example could be found in our recent history of the warping effect of the party outlook upon even the greatest minds: for a judicious interweaving of the best passages in Gladstone's article and Disraeli's speech would make an affirmation such as all but the decadent or the defeatist could endorse.

SALISBURY AND LAYARD

One of Salisbury's first steps on taking office was to establish close contact with Layard, who henceforth discontinues his secret letters to the Prime Minister and turns all his guns upon the Foreign Secretary, thereby tacitly revealing his different verdict upon Derby and Salisbury. The Ambassador's private views on his new chief's rôle in the Eastern Question are to be found in two letters of the previous year to Lord Lytton.

"The whole of this Turkish question was a series of blunders, the greatest of which was the line taken at the Conferences. Nothing could have been more unwise than the selection of a Representative at it, both on public and private grounds. I have always been against employing amateur diplomatists,[2] but when the one selected is a member of the Cabinet, the danger and inconvenience are increased a thousandfold. We have now placed ourselves in this undignified

[1] Buckle, vi. p. 392.
[2] Layard had himself begun as a diplomatic "amateur" under Stratford.

and fatal position, that knowing that Turkey is really fighting our battle, we leave her to her fate, rejoicing when she wins because we profit, seeing her exposed to every injustice, violence and wrong without lifting a finger or saying a word in her defence, conniving at the violation of the most solemn treaties and allowing Russia to do that which we know is undermining our influence and our interests, *and all this because some passionate and irregular minds discovered a year ago that a semibarbarous Government permits semibarbarous things.*" [1]

A fortnight later he wrote even more bluntly—and it is Lord Lytton's own chief, the Secretary for India, of whom he is writing. "Lord Salisbury has, I fear, exercised a very fatal influence over the Cabinet. He is a strong man of a decided will, which makes up two-thirds of the receipt of one who can govern others. I have never been able to understand the course he pursued here. He set at nought the most elementary rules of diplomacy by showing his hand at starting. Whatever may have been his instructions or his individual opinions, this was not the way of entering upon most delicate and important negotiations with such an antagonist as Ignatyev to deal with. Lady Salisbury and himself threw themselves in open enmity to Elliot and the policy he had pursued. Ignatyev with all his craft and skill could not have devised a more effective measure to destroy all our influence with the Turks and to render all our efforts to induce them to listen to our advice useless. It will be very long before we can recover from the fatal results of his proceedings, if we ever do. He and others who think with him forget that by maintaining our influence, which he might have done while rendering every justice to the Russians, he might have guided the Turks for good, and without any sacrifice of principle or even of opinion have maintained and promoted the interest of England and of humanity. We recklessly threw away all our power for good, to obtain nothing in return, except the cynical contempt of Russia and other Powers.

"What Turkey has been able to do shows how completely ignorant Lord Salisbury and others of his school were of her resources and of the vitality which still existed in her people. They were equally ignorant of the true condition of the Bulgarians, whose wrongs these humane and sentimental politicians goaded Russia into a war to redress. It is now found that the Turkish population is superior in every respect to the Bulgarian." [2]

[1] *Layard Papers*, 9 Aug. 1877, Layard to Lytton.
[2] *Ibid.* 23 Aug. 1877, Layard to Lytton.

It may be assumed that the author of such sentiments was not without misgivings as to the appointment of Lord Salisbury, but he was at least partially reassured, first by the energetic Circular of 1 April, and then by Salisbury's frank and cordial overture, making it clear that though he had "not invariably concurred in all the views" expressed by Layard, he had "much admired the skill and the unsparing energy" with which he had performed his "very arduous functions". "You have hitherto laboured", he went on, "to prevent Russian preponderance by sustaining the Turkish breakwater. But the breakwater is now shattered, I fear, beyond repair, and the flood is pouring over it. Another dyke may have to be established behind it, which possibly must be constructed from the material of the first. To us the idea of additional territory is repellent, and if we are forced at any time to strengthen ourselves, our wish will be to reduce any acquisition to the smallest dimensions." [1]

The extent to which Layard regarded Abdul Hamid as his trump card in Turkey is shown by his first letter to Salisbury as his chief. In this he recalls a conversation which they had had in London after the failure of the Conference of Constantinople, and in which Salisbury had approved "his design of obtaining a personal influence over the Sultan. . . . When you saw the Sultan, he was labouring under the greatest possible disadvantages. He is naturally timid and his manner did not make a favourable impression on you. But the more I see of him, the more I am satisfied that he is a man of very sound judgment, excellent intentions and a just and humane disposition, and that at the same time he has much firmness of character and is not to be led if he is on his guard. . . . No foreigner has seen so much of a Sultan as I have of the present sovereign. I constantly dine or breakfast with him or meet him in his garden. . . . It appears to me of the highest importance that the influence I possess over the Sultan should be maintained. *It is through it alone that we may hope to effect any real improvement in this country*." [2] But a week later he reverts to his old theme of the "lamentable want of men". "The Turkish population, with the exception of course of Kurds, Circassians and such like, are docile and easily governed. They have very great and noble qualities. But the governing class is as bad and incapable as possible." [3]

In other words, the Turkish ruling class is rotten to the core, there

---

[1] *Layard Papers*, 4 April, Salisbury to Layard—cit. *Life of Salisbury*, ii. p. 264.
[2] *Ibid*. 3 April, Layard to Salisbury.　　　[3] *Ibid*. 10 April, Layard to Salisbury.

are no leaders on whom to fall back, and all depends on the sovereign himself. Little did Layard foresee the extent of his miscalculation, which was to become apparent within the next two months. The more balanced Salisbury seems to have remained unconvinced, and looked upon Layard as a vigorous instrument of policy, but one which required cautious handling.

The real direction of Layard's mind is revealed in a secret letter to the Prime Minister, written on the very same day as his first letter to Salisbury. "I hear from all sides that the Turks are most ready to go with us in making a great effort to free themselves from the terms which Russia has imposed upon them. I believe that in a very short space of time we might get together an army of 150 or 200,000 men, who, partly officered by Englishmen and paid by us, would be equal to any work. I have Turkish gentlemen of influence and officers constantly coming to me, to offer to raise men or to serve under us. I do not of course give any encouragement to such overtures, nor have I in any way whatever committed H.M.G. to any line of action, or held out any hopes to the Sultan or his ministers, that England may interfere to check the pretensions of Russia. But I think it right that you should know the actual state of things. People in England are too much inclined to underrate the strength still left to the Sultan. If we were compelled by circumstances to go to war with Russia and were to treat, as it deserves, the foolish cry of our humanitarians that even for the highest interests of England we could never fight with the Turk, we should still find in the Turkish Empire materials with which we could prevent the accomplishment of the designs against Turkey and ultimately against England."[1]

That Beaconsfield henceforth renounced his secret correspondence with Layard is the best proof both of his tendency to work behind the back of Derby and of his readiness to leave the details of policy in the hands of Derby's successor, and it may be also of his feeling that Layard had at last gone a little too far. Layard on his side was slowly resigning himself to the inevitable loss of large territories in Europe and concentrating his attention upon Turkey-in-Asia: and a natural compromise was found between his own views and Salisbury's, when the latter announced as the Cabinet view, that the only way of checking Russia's disintegrating influence upon Turkey was "by establishing ourselves at some strong place either in the Persian Gulf or the Aegean coast, which shall make it our interest as well as

[1] *Ibid.* 3 April. Layard to Beaconsfield.

place it in our power to sustain his authority and uphold the integrity of his remaining dominions".[1]

The grounds on which he seeks to justify such a policy throw a flood of light upon the Conservative statesman, reluctantly compelled to reckon with democratic forces. "The point to which your attention should be most distinctly drawn is that this country, which is popularly governed and cannot therefore be counted on to act on any uniform or consistent system of policy, would probably abandon the task of resisting any further Russian advance to the southward in Asia, if no other but speculative arguments can be advanced in favour of action. But it will cling to any military post occupied by England as tenaciously as it has clung to Gibraltar: and if any movements were made which would threaten it while attacking the Ottoman dominions, its actions might be counted on."[2]

SALISBURY AND SHUVALOV

The relations between the new Foreign Secretary and the Russian Ambassador were at first extremely cold and formal: and Shuvalov was doubtless right in ascribing this partly to his own known intimacy with Derby[3] and to a certain fear on Salisbury's part, lest his former Russophil attitude at Constantinople should now be thrown up against him. Moreover, Shuvalov noted, not without anxiety, that Salisbury seemed to be entirely free from the rooted distrust so long displayed by Derby towards both Bismarck and Andrássy. This anxiety was doubtless illogical in one who prided himself on Bismarck's confidence, but it reflects his general nervousness at the change. The Circular made a hostile impression upon him,[4] and this was strengthened by Salisbury's speech in the debate of 9 April, which he described as "the worst of all" and "full of hostility" to Russia.[5] But by the middle of April the mutual distrust of the two men was slowly beginning to thaw. Salisbury used pacific language in their conversations, and was "very conciliatory" in tone:[5] while he sent Colonel Wellesley to Prince Gorchakov, to convey his extreme desire for peace and a congress, if only Russia would consent to the discussion of all questions.[6]

[1] *Layard Papers*, 18 April, Salisbury to Layard.
[2] *Ibid.* 18 April, Salisbury to Layard.
[3] *U.R.B.D.* Shuvalov to Gorchakov, tels. of 27 March/8 and 7/19 April. This intimacy makes Salisbury *"plus raide à mon égard"*.   [4] *Ibid.* letter of 16/28 March.
[5] *Ibid.* Shuvalov to Gorchakov, tels. of 4/16 and 6/18 April.
[6] *Ibid.* Gorchakov to Shuvalov, tel. of 3/15 April.

Salisbury was obviously feeling his way and testing the men with whom he had to work, though well aware that no time was to be lost. In retrospect he declined to admit that his conduct of foreign policy during these months deserved special praise, and indeed claimed, most unjustly, that he was "only picking up the china that Derby had broken", and with much more justice, that he "had to do in three months what ought to have taken three years".[1] His daughter, in one of the many psychological sketches with which her biography is studded, has shown that he was at one and the same time extremely reserved, not to say secretive, reluctant to delegate responsibility and "persistently sceptical as to his powers of personal influence".[2] Indeed, his dislike of publicity and his ultra-conservative views as to the sacrosanct nature of affairs of state, led him to take a very high line towards what he regarded as "indiscretion", even in a colleague such as Lord Derby: and this, as we shall see, sometimes landed him in statements and denials for which it was hard to find any excuse.

Meanwhile Salisbury felt, very wisely, that in so strained a situation it would do more harm than good to enter a congress without some preliminary agreement as to essentials: and he was already preparing the way for direct conversations with Russia. On 22 April Loftus called upon Gorchakov, to assure him of his Government's pacific sentiments and its eagerness for discussions either direct or through Bismarck.[3] The Chancellor favoured the latter method,[4] and Münster's efforts at mediation continued. Beaconsfield on his side assumed that Bismarck's mediation "would never have been made, unless the Tsar was determined on peace": yet he could not help doubting whether Bismarck could "withstand the temptation of embroiling and exhausting both Great Britain and Russia"[5]—a calculation almost certainly unjustified.

Beaconsfield and Salisbury were by this time agreed upon laying the main stress of their demands in two directions: (1) free Bulgaria must not be allowed to extend further south than the Balkan range, Greek influence being encouraged in the southern province; and (2) if Russia was to retain her conquests in Asia, Britain must acquire "some post which would safeguard her Asiatic interests".[6] Salisbury's letters of this period show beyond all manner of doubt that

---

[1] *Life*, ii. p. 232.   [2] *Ibid.* pp. 233-6.
[3] *U.R.B.D.* Gorchakov to Shuvalov, 11/23 April.
[4] Giers to Shuvalov, 12/24 April, no. 16.
[5] 19 April, to Queen—Buckle, vi. p. 289.
[6] Salisbury to Russell, 10 April—*Life*, ii. p. 242.

he had almost ceased to reckon with Turkey, that he would have liked to find a substitute in an expanding Greece, and that he sometimes speculated upon Austria following in the path of Turkey.[1] He was quite frankly of the opinion that "the Turkish breakwater" was "now shattered beyond repair", that "any return to the position of 1856" could only lead to the "dissolution of the whole Empire, followed by endless anarchy", and that the main problem for the Turk was "how to keep his Asiatic Empire together": for "sooner or later the greater part of his European Empire must go", and "Bosnia and Bulgaria are as good as gone".[2] These views were with Salisbury a perfectly natural evolution, whereas their acceptance by Beaconsfield represented a complete departure from his original policy. Of his former zeal for Turkish territorial integrity nothing more is heard: he too is ready to accept the Balkans as Turkey's northern frontier, and to concede Kars to Russia. But if Batum also is to be Russian, he tells the Queen, "we must occupy some island or station on the coast of Asia Minor, which will neutralise the presence of Russia in Armenia".[3] This only confirms the view, already demonstrated by earlier evidence,[4] that Beaconsfield had no fixed principles or scruples in the Eastern Question, and that to him it was simply and solely a "Machtfrage"—in the fullest sense of the German phrase—from which to extract a maximum of profit for England.

Meanwhile Salisbury was in steady contact with Vienna and grew increasingly dissatisfied with Andrássy, whom he misjudged only less than his chief had done earlier. While exaggerating the uncertainty of survival of such an "ill-compacted structure" as Austria-Hungary,[5] he underestimated the internal difficulties resulting from Magyar hostility to the Slavs and from the restlessness of the German Liberals. Andrássy knew his own mind perfectly well,[6] but more than ever he lacked confidence in England, in view of her very limited military resources,[7] and was resolved not to be used as the instrument to pull England's chestnuts out of the fire: Francis Joseph, in writing to the Tsar, even went so far as to lay the chief blame for the European misunderstanding upon "the ill grounded (*si peu justifiée*) attitude of England".[8]

---

[1] Cf. *supra*, p. 386, Derby's speech of 8 April.
[2] 4 April and 9 May 1878, Salisbury to Layard—*Life*, ii. pp. 264-7.
[3] 21 April—Buckle, vi. p. 290.   [4] See *supra*, pp. 43, 103, 137, 213, 241.
[5] 10 April to Elliot—*Life*, ii. p. 245.   [6] See *supra*, pp. 92, 141, 201, 224.
[7] Andrássy to Langenau, 2 April—cit. Wertheimer, *op. cit.* iii.
[8] *G.P.* no. 393—enclosure in minute of Bülow for William I., 15 April.

A minor obstacle to understanding lay in the personality of Beust, who had lost the confidence alike of the British ministers and of his colleague Münster, had never possessed that of Shuvalov and was so distrusted by Andrássy himself, that the latter sent his own private emissary, Count Montgelas, to the Embassy, to serve as a means of direct communication with Beaconsfield.[1]

The difficulty of inducing Andrássy to commit himself led Salisbury more and more to the perception that the real exit from the *impasse* lay through direct negotiations with Russia, and that for this Shuvalov was an ideal instrument, owing to his knowledge, influence and earnest desire for peace. The Ambassador at once profited by this mood, to point out that the negotiations for withdrawal were a mere preliminary, that the crux lay in the discussion of the chief clauses of San Stefano, and that in his view, while the former were safe in Bismarck's hands, only the two principals could deal with the latter. Salisbury agreed unreservedly and spoke of the need for eliminating "telegraphic misunderstandings and false interpretation of dispatches": and this gave Shuvalov the opportunity of expressing his readiness to go himself to St. Petersburg with "the English *sine qua non* and the arguments in support, and to return with the reply of the Imperial Cabinet"—a suggestion which was also accepted "with warmth". In reporting this conversation to his chief, he argued that further discussion by telegram would only increase the difficulties, whereas the whole matter could be settled verbally in a fortnight.

According to Shuvalov, Salisbury put to him the "infantile" wish that the Russians should themselves state to which clauses they attached a capital importance and for which they would fight. "You are joking, my dear Marquis," replied Shuvalov, "in making such a proposal. You know what we want, since you have the treaty in your hands. It is for you to say what you do not want. The fact that we consent to discuss the treaty proves that we are ready if possible to admit certain modifications, but one can't demand of us indiscreet confessions, or to annul our own work by abjuring it ourselves."

"Salisbury has the bad habit of laughing as uproariously (*bruyamment*) as *mal à propos*, and it was with one of these outbursts that he answered: 'That's extraordinary! It is you then who are provoking an ultimatum from me!'

---

[1] *U.R.B.D.* Shuvalov to Gorchakov, 31 March. According to the omniscient Shuvalov, Montgelas was very intimate with Montagu Corry, the Prime Minister's private secretary, and was notoriously Russophobe and Ultramontane.

" 'No,' I replied. 'It is you on the contrary, who have said that the Congress, if it met without preliminary agreement between us, must infallibly fail, that then war was imminent and that to avoid it you insist on a preliminary agreement. It is for you, then, to formulate your *sine qua non*, and for us to examine it and reply.' The Marquis ended by concurring: it would have been difficult to continue to uphold the contrary thesis." [1]

There is a witty passage in Shuvalov's—still unhappily unpublished—memoirs, which the subsequent course of Balkan history was amply to justify:—"I remember that while Lord Salisbury was looking for names for these two Bulgarias, I proposed to him that one should be called 'Satisfied Bulgaria', and the other 'Discontented Bulgaria' ".[2] Perhaps in 1885, when Britain had become the chief supporter of union, Lord Salisbury may have remembered this sally with embarrassed amusement.

SHUVALOV'S MISSION TO ST. PETERSBURG

It is quite clear that both sides were by now equally eager for a *détente*—the more so as Salisbury was steadily losing the very limited confidence which he had ever reposed in Andrássy. The very next day Beaconsfield and Salisbury informed the ambassador of their readiness to initiate him confidentially into the British objections to the treaty, if he would consent to carry them to St. Petersburg, explain them there and bring back the Russian reply, adding that "they would trust to the spirit of conciliation which I should bring into these negotiations".[3] By 3 May Shuvalov had received the Tsar's authorisation,[4] and after three further discussions—"the first very bad, with inacceptable proposals, the third better and much more conciliatory" [5]—and after attending the Queen's Drawing Room by special permission, he left on the 7th, visited Bismarck on his way, spent six days (12-18 May) in St. Petersburg, paid a second visit to Bismarck at Friedrichsruh on the return journey, and was back in London on the 22nd with the Russian answer.

The rapid growth of confidence is reflected in Salisbury's request

---

[1] *U.R.B.D.* Shuvalov to Gorchakov, *lettre très confidentielle*, 18/30 April.
[2] Cit. Hanotaux, *op. cit.* iv. p. 339.
[3] *U.R.B.D.* Shuvalov to Gorchakov, tel. of 19 April/1 May, no. 25.
[4] *Ibid.* tel. of 3 May, Giers to Shuvalov: "Your idea of seeing Bismarck and coming here to give account of the confidences which you expect from the British Ministers, *a été très goutée en haut lieu*. It is the best, perhaps the only exit from the imbroglio." [5] *Ibid.* tel. of 23 April/5 May, no. 30.

to Shuvalov "to tell all that we have spoken of together to Prince Bismarck".[1] According to Shuvalov's own account—and there is nothing to suggest its inaccuracy[2]—Bismarck was "very surprised" at what Shuvalov told him, "and at first showed great preoccupation at our having negotiated with England, instead of treating with Austria. . . . I replied that it was our obvious interest to negotiate with that one of the Powers which was most disposed to declare war on us and whose fleet was ready. Moreover, it was not Austria but England which contested our possession of Kars and Batum: and public sentiment in Russia favoured the annexation of these two points with as much ardour as in Germany in 1870 it had demanded the annexation of Alsace." Bismarck showed "extreme surprise" on learning that England had conceded Kars and Batum, and when at last convinced on the point, remarked "Well, in that case you are right to negotiate with England. She would have gone to war alone, whereas Austria would only have made war *if she had allies*."[3] He then promised Shuvalov Germany's "sincere and loyal support" for the solution aimed at.

Of what passed at St. Petersburg itself we possess no actual record, but special interest attaches to a report of the German Ambassador, General von Schweinitz, on whom Shuvalov called as an old acquaintance, and who expressed astonishment at the traces which three years of an English *milieu* had left upon him. In many points the German—himself to some extent a victim to his own Russian *milieu*—found that Shuvalov was "not Russian enough" and passed unduly severe verdicts upon the political blunders of St. Petersburg. We do not need Schweinitz's evidence to assume that Shuvalov's main aim was to counteract Ignatyev's influence with the Tsar, and that in this he was successful: yet, as Schweinitz pertinently observes,

---

[1] These are Salisbury's own words in a letter of 4 May to Lord Odo Russell— *Life*, ii. p. 255.

[2] Here I venture to differ from Lady Gwendolen Cecil, who seems to think that the extract given by Hanotaux proves that "Shuvalov's memory was not to be trusted" (p. 255). The two accounts can be reconciled by the very reasonable assumption that Bismarck affected surprise at British concessions in Asia, in order not to betray the fact that he was already prepared for it. As for Salisbury's account of a later conversation (3 Nov. 1879) with Shuvalov (who quoted Bismarck as saying that Russia was right to settle with England rather than with Austria, because Austria's military power was worthless—she *could* not fight—p. 256) it seems pretty clear that *Salisbury* misunderstood *Shuvalov*, and that the phrase actually used by Bismarck is that given above. This is surely proved by internal evidence: for the one phrase is as impossible in Bismarck's mouth as the other is possible and probable. How could Bismarck have described Austria's military power as "worthless" so short a time before he concluded the German-Austrian alliance?

[3] Cit. Hanotaux, iv. p. 341.

Ignatyev was "the one-eyed among the blind" and put up a strong fight, owing to his intimate knowledge of Turkish affairs and of all the geographical and racial points at issue.

In his efforts to achieve a practical result, Shuvalov was undoubtedly assisted by the fact that Gorchakov was temporarily in eclipse—too ill to conduct affairs, though not ill enough to hand them over finally to another—that Giers lacked the energy and prestige to assert himself and in any case shared most of Shuvalov's views, and that the War Minister, Milyutin, was urging upon his master that Russia could not stand the strain of a fresh war and must somehow or other reach a compromise. This attitude was due not merely to the exhausted and diseased state of the army and to the outbreak of typhus in the capital, but to the unsound position of Russian finances and to the alarming recrudescence of Nihilist and subversive tendencies. The attempt on the life of General Trepov, head of the notorious Third Division of the Police (specially concerned with the safety of Tsar and Government and forerunner of Okhrana, Cheka and Ogpu), had been an ominous sign in the previous March: and now the acquittal of the would-be assassin, Vera Zasulich, by a Petersburg jury, had caused a profound sensation. Like Schweinitz, we are so accustomed to think of Shuvalov as the enlightened and westernised diplomatist, that it is almost a shock to recall the fact that he had been Trepov's predecessor in that all-important office, and indeed bore the nickname of "Peter IV." in view of the omnipotence which it seemed to confer. But this renders all the more impressive the entry in Schweinitz's diary which records Shuvalov's gloomy verdict that "the organs of government were no longer capable of maintaining order". The General shuddered at this confession "from such a quarter", and could only ask himself whether it was the result of long residence in England or a sound estimate of the real situation in Russia.[1] It is interesting to note in passing that Shuvalov, once a decided reactionary, now favoured the extension of the Zemstvo principle of self-government in Russia.

To use Lord Salisbury's own phrase, "everybody seems to be holding their breath during Shuvalov's *dernier essai*",[2] and his return was awaited with real anxiety. Meanwhile Andrássy, after two months' of haggling with all parties to the dispute, at last awoke to the danger of finding himself isolated, instead of England, and

---

[1] *G.P.* no. 407, Schweinitz to Bülow, 19 May; Schweinitz, *Denkwürdigkeiten*, ii. p. 28.   [2] 15 May, to Lord Odo Russell—*Life*, ii. p. 256.

on 22 May sent concrete proposals to Salisbury.[1] But the latter was by now thoroughly disgusted with what he interpreted as "intense irresolution" and possible proof of a "death agony", and commiserated with Sir Henry Elliot on his "task of inducing this insincere, unready Government to pledge itself to some definite line of action".[2] He disagreed with Andrássy's veto upon a Montenegrin access to the sea and at this stage was only ready to approve the occupation, not annexation, of Bosnia.[3] He was therefore not in the least disposed to close with Vienna until quite certain that the proposals which Shuvalov was bringing back with him were quite inacceptable: and indeed Münster reported Salisbury to be "very bitter against Austria", to resent her attitude towards Greece and Montenegro, and to distrust her all the more that he had previously sought her alliance.[4] Meanwhile Bismarck, who had made such genuine efforts at mediation, was now positively disconcerted at the approaching *détente* between London and St. Petersburg and urged Stolberg in Vienna to promote that Russo-Austrian agreement which he considered to be distinctly more a German interest than even a Russo-British.[5] At the same time he could not but be flattered at Shuvalov's obvious reliance upon him, still more at the request that he should draft the magic "formula" for the final negotiations in London.[6]

Andrássy's biographer treats the direct negotiations as aimed mainly at Austria-Hungary, but this merely reflects a permanent bias against Britain characteristic of one whose relations with the Ballplatz were very close during the decade preceding the Great War. In actual fact Andrássy was constantly kept informed by the German Government of the course of the negotiations and declared himself in agreement.[7] The plain truth is that Andrássy had overreached himself by his tortuous, secretive and exacting tactics, for he had kindled in Salisbury the very distrust which he himself felt, and could neither induce England to expose herself against Russia nor bring himself to bear the brunt of war, as would now have been inevitable.

Moreover, there is evidence that at this moment he was doing Russia a real injustice. For on 8 May a new Russian Mémoire was

---

[1] 22 May, Salisbury to Queen—*Letters*, ii. p. 619.
[2] 10 and 24 April—*Life*, pp. 245-6.
[3] *U.R.B.D.* Shuvalov to Gorchakov, tel. of 13/25 May, no..36.
[4] *G.P.* no. 417, Münster to Bülow, 25 May.
[5] *Ibid.* no. 410, Bismarck to Stolberg, 23 May.·
[6] *Ibid.* no. 408, Bülow to Bismarck, 20 May.
[7] Busch's Nachlass, iii. p. 366 (*Deutsche Rundschau*, Dec. 1909).

handed in at Vienna, consenting to the division of Bulgaria into a western and an eastern province, within the bounds laid down at the Conference of Constantinople, with a native militia and under a joint guarantee of the Powers, and to the *occupation and annexation* of Bosnia-Hercegovina by Austria-Hungary.[1] That he did not respond to this was perhaps due to a fact which Andrássy saw more clearly than any other statesman in Europe: he warned Berlin that to divide Bulgaria into two, without leaving Turkish troops in the province nearest Constantinople, was quite futile, and that it would be better to allow at once with a good grace the union which in that case would only be a matter of time.[2] Bismarck on his side made it clear to Andrássy that in his view it would be wise to occupy Bosnia without waiting for the Congress's sanction, and that German backing in this question was certain, but only up to the point of "no breach with Russia".[3]

THE SECRET PROTOCOL OF 30 MAY

The last week of May saw the final trial of strength. On the 23rd Salisbury and Shuvalov had two long interviews, and began the task of drafting "a memorandum to serve as mutual engagement for the Congress", which, in deference to Andrássy, was not to meet before 11 June. Shuvalov appears to have found Salisbury more rigid regarding Russia's Asiatic conquests and feared an attempt to extract fresh concessions at the last moment.[4] The fact is that Salisbury on his side met with considerable resistance inside the Cabinet, and also had to reckon with the Queen, who expressed to Beaconsfield "the greatest suspicions of the Russian proposals", and refused to believe "in any permanent settlement *until we have fought and beaten the Russians*".[5]

The point on which Shuvalov encountered most resistance was the demand for the withdrawal of Turkish troops from southern Bulgaria: this was only conceded when he made of it a *conditio sine qua non*, and even then Britain reserved to the Congress power to discuss the

---

[1] *Austrian Archives*—"Teschenberg Dossier". Two other clauses, providing for the partition of the Sandjak of Novipazar between Montenegro and Serbia, and for Montenegro's retention of the boundaries laid down at San Stefano, were doubtless objectionable to Andrássy, but the general effect was most conciliatory.

[2] *G.P.* no. 413, Stolberg to Bülow, 23 May.

[3] *Ibid.* no. 415, Herbert Bismarck to Bülow, 25 May.

[4] *U.R.B.D.* Shuvalov to Gorchakov, 11/23 May, no. 32.

[5] 23 and 31 May, Queen to Beaconsfield—*Letters*, ii. pp. 622 and 626.

Sultan's right of defending the frontiers of the new province or sending troops to repress insurrection, and again insisted that the heads of the Bulgarian national militia should be nominated by the Porte. Other points which Britain insisted on leaving open for the Congress were the duration and conditions of Russian occupation in Bulgaria, the lines on which the administration of both Bulgarias was to be framed, the name of the southern province, the future of Danubian navigation, and the pledges of Armenian reform.[1] Shuvalov on his side found the Tsar still hesitating to withdraw his armies without a Turkish evacuation of Shumla and Varna, and therefore did all in his power to separate the military question from that of the Congress, while at the same time begging his master to leave him a free hand on this point.[2] It is quite evident that he was thoroughly nervous. "I beg the Emperor to rely on me," he telegraphed on the 26th. "I shall not compromise anything that can be saved, and shall do my best, but every minute is precious, for the *English are beginning to understand that they have conceded too much to us.* The situation is critical, and I must sign at any moment or risk seeing the promises withdrawn. The results are unexpected . . . but if we delay, the Congress would be compromised and war imminent." Next day he was clamorous in the same sense and reported Austrian intrigues in London, great impatience on the part of Bismarck and alarm of the Cabinet at their surrender of Batum and Kars leaking out. He was also afraid of the Turks provoking a collision in order to ruin the prospects of a Congress and "drive England into war".[3] It is not too much to say that Shuvalov was staking his whole future career upon achieving a *détente*.

A final delay occurred because the Tsar insisted upon the full text of the agreement being submitted to him by telegram,[4] but at last on the 29th his full authorisation was dispatched, and on 30 May the Protocol was signed by Salisbury and Shuvalov at the Foreign Office. Even then Salisbury held in suspense his acceptance of the German invitation to the Congress—which had for days past been burning Münster's pocket—until Russia consented to the withdrawal of forces as a preliminary step.[5] For this the Tsar could not be won,

[1] *U.R.B.D.* Shuvalov to Gorchakov, tel. of 12/24 May, no. 35: cf. also *G.P.* no. 427, Münster to Bismarck, 2 June.
[2] *Ibid.* 3 tels. of 14/26 May, nos. 37, 38, 39.
[3] *Ibid.* 2 tels. of 15/27 May, nos. 40 and 41.
[4] *Ibid.* Giers to Shuvalov, 14/26 May, no. 24.
[5] *Ibid.* tels. of 18/30 May, nos. 47 and 48.

and Shuvalov was again summoned to St. Petersburg, having "after long efforts" induced Salisbury not to insist on instant withdrawal, but to rely upon his verbal explanations to the Tsar[1]—a sterling proof of the extent to which the Ambassador had convinced yet another Foreign Secretary of his earnest desire for peace and of his capacity for playing the game. Salisbury did all he could to encourage this second journey, because from his private information he feared that the war party in St. Petersburg was again raising its head for a final effort. By a fortunate accident Count Münster was on a brief visit to Hatfield with the German Crown Prince and Princess, and was able to hand to his host Prince Bismarck's formal invitation to the Congress to open in Berlin on 13 June. Salisbury, in accepting, told Münster that in going farther to meet Shuvalov than he could have wished, he was partly influenced by the hope of seeing him at the head of the Russian Foreign Office.

The Protocol opens with a definition of the Tsar's essential war aims—security and good government for the Balkan Christians—and then proceeds to marshal under eleven heads the various mutual concessions and reservations of the two Governments. Its essence may be briefly summarised as follows.

Russia consents to the division of Bulgaria into two provinces—a northern, enjoying "political autonomy" under a Prince of its own, and a southern, with "a wide administrative autonomy", under a Christian Governor. She also accepts a drastic modification of the Bulgarian frontiers—exclusion from the Aegean and restriction to a line east of the Vardar valley, with a view to eliminating so far as possible the non-Bulgar populations. No Turkish troops are to be allowed in the southern province, the Tsar attaching special importance to this provision, without which there could in his view be no security or guarantee for the Bulgarians. It is, however, left to the Congress to settle the methods by which Turkey should protect the frontiers of South Bulgaria or quell possible insurrection inside it.

Britain having expressed her special interest in the Greeks, it is laid down that the Powers shall have a consultative voice in the future organisation of Epirus, Thessaly *"and the other Christian provinces left under the Porte"*. This principle was unhappily not fully upheld at the Congress, with the result that a new and festering sore soon formed upon the Turkish body politic—this time in Macedonia—

[1] *U.R.B.D.* tel. of 21 May/2 June, no. 50; cf. *G.P.* no. 426—Münster to Bismarck, enclosing Salisbury's acceptance.

and Europe paid dearly for its neglect, in the upheavals of 1903, 1908, 1912 and 1914.

Britain expressed her "profound regret" at Russia's claim upon Bessarabia, but weakly added that as she found the other signatory Powers not disposed to uphold the existing status by force of arms, she herself was "not so immediately interested" as to insist.

In Asia Russia undertook to restore Bayazid, but retained her other conquests in Armenia and the port of Batum: and to this Britain consented, "despite the grave dangers menacing the peace of the populations of Turkey-in-Asia" which might result. "But Her Majesty's Government are of opinion that the duty of protecting the Ottoman Empire from this danger, which henceforth will rest in a special measure upon England, can be effected without exposing England to the calamities of a fresh war." The British Cabinet accepted this phrase with a very definite *arrière pensée* which events were soon to reveal.

The concession was further toned down by a personal assurance from the Tsar that Russia would not again extend her frontier in this direction, though it may be assumed that little more than a platonic value was attached to this phrase.[1]

Apart from the eleven specific points enumerated, Britain was content to leave the rump of San Stefano uncarved.

A private letter to Sir Henry Elliot [2] supplies a clue to the main motives of the Foreign Secretary. Realising that Austria-Hungary would not fight either for Bessarabia or Armenia, and taking the line that "the Montenegrin and Servian question does not interest us in the least", he found himself "forced to face the question whether we were prepared to go to war for Kars and Batum alone", and drew the wise conclusion that the country would not endorse such a policy, and that it would be far preferable to extract Russian concessions in Europe by relative complaisance in Asia.

Though Lord Salisbury attached the greatest possible importance to secrecy, a summary of the contents of the Protocol, under ten heads, was published in the *Globe* only twenty-four hours later! While deploring the retrocession of Bessarabia and regretting the surrender of Batum—"the Belfort of Turkey", according to its extravagant phrase—it took the view that Russia's renunciation of Bayazid would "secure our central Asian trade through Armenia".

[1] Full text in Martens, *Nouveau Recueil*, 2nd Series, iii. p. 269.
[2] 3 June—*Life*, ii. pp. 260-61.

Above all, it exulted over the destruction of "the preposterous New Bulgaria imagined by General Ignatyev". There was considerable outcry in the Jingo press at what seemed a betrayal of Turkey. In answer to questions in Parliament, Salisbury roundly declared the *Globe's* summary to be "wholly unauthentic and not deserving of the confidence of Your Lordships' House":[1] and almost at the same time Andrássy expressed his entire scepticism to the Hungarian Delegation. The *Globe*, however, upheld the accuracy of information which "neither Government ever intended should be laid before the public", and continued its discussion of details, arguing that though the Bessarabian settlement was "peculiarly repugnant" and the fate of Batum regrettable, none the less all the main points raised in the Salisbury Circular—the two Bulgarias, the Danube, Greek interests, the route to Persia—had been duly safeguarded.[2]

Salisbury's secretive policy was doomed to failure, for a fortnight later the same newspaper—thanks to the venality of Charles Marvin, an underpaid temporary clerk in the Foreign Office—was able to publish the full text of the Protocol.[3] By this time Salisbury himself was in Berlin, and Northcote, on behalf of the Government, described the publications "not only unauthorised, but surreptitious, and as a statement of their policy incomplete and therefore inaccurate".[4] But this pitiable subterfuge, so unworthy of the two men, deceived no one, for the accuracy of the text could no longer be challenged, and the facts spoke for themselves.

Lady Gwendolen Cecil, in an admirably judicious passage, defends her father's view "that when a Minister's confidence is being forced, no one has a right to read more than verbal accuracy into his reply".[5] Here we are transported from the sphere of politics to that of casuistry: but while every such case must be judged on its own merits, this was an obvious example when so emphatic a denial went far beyond the right of defence, and created a deliberately misleading impression in the country.[6]

There were still many who, as in earlier stages of the crisis, clung to the impossible position that no change of policy had taken place.

---

[1] 3 June—Hansard, ccxl. p. 1061.   [2] *Globe*, leaders of 4 and 5 June.
[3] *Ibid.* 14 June.   [4] 17 June—Hansard, p. 1614.   [5] *Life*, ii. p. 262.
[6] The *Globe* itself on 13 June said of "the guarded disclaimer" that it "strained very far the right of public men to produce misleading impressions by means of equivocal denials", and this was probably the contemporary verdict.
On 31 May Salisbury sent a warning telegram to Layard, to the effect that Musurus, the Turkish Ambassador, was alarmed at the *Globe* revelation. "*If questioned, you say information is quite inexact.*"

But the Duke of Argyll rightly argued that the Protocol abandoned four of the main positions upheld in the Circular of 1 April, respecting Bessarabia, Batum, Armenia, and Bulgarian access to the Black Sea; that it abandoned the old military frontier of Turkey on the Danube, which Layard had always claimed as essential to her survival in Europe, and that it merely concentrated on reducing the size of the new Bulgaria. "Under this agreement the British plenipotentiaries went into Congress with their hands bound and with their tongues only untied for the purpose of keeping up an appearance of freedom", while Russia "had secured that her principal demands in the treaty were not to be seriously contested".[1]

THE ANGLO-TURKISH CONVENTION

The history of the Eastern crisis is an object lesson in the infinite complications and eventual futility of ultra-secretive methods: and the two most striking instances are Andrássy's concealment of his successive conventions with Russia, and Salisbury's secret parallel negotiations with Russia, Austria and Turkey. But while in the first case the facts remained unknown for a whole generation and the documents were not made public till after the Great War,[2] in the latter a series of accidents threw light into dark places and dislocated the Government's calculations.

Meanwhile, there can be little doubt that a stimulus to agreement was provided by the growing evidences of internal unrest in Russia, by the Socialist effervescence in Germany, by the attempt on the life of William I. on 13 May, followed by the far more serious and indeed very nearly successful attempt of Nobiling on 3 June, and again in this country by the persistence of trade depression.

On 3 June it was announced in Parliament that the Government had accepted Bismarck's invitation to the Congress, and that Beaconsfield and Salisbury were to be the British delegates. Beaconsfield himself admitted that there was no precedent for both the Prime Minister and the Foreign Secretary going, but very rightly added, "in matters of this kind we must not be guided merely by precedents".[3] Britain, and Europe, were duly impressed at a decision

[1] Argyll, *The Eastern Question*, ii. pp. 130-35.
[2] The first faint outline is given by A. Fournier, *Wie wir zu Bosnien kamen* (1909), much fuller details came in Wertheimer's big Life of Andrássy (1910–13), while the treaties were first published by A. F. Pribram, *The Secret Treaties* (1919): but many of the relevant documents are quoted for the first time in the present volume.
[3] Hansard, ccxl. p. 1058.

which showed the immense importance which the Government attached to the impending settlement. Beaconsfield's somewhat precarious health militated against his going, and the Queen was distinctly nervous. But he himself was bent upon the great adventure, feeling quite naturally that he had the right, perhaps even the duty, to pit himself against the other foremost statesmen of Europe, and that his prestige and resolution would render him a match for them all. The Prince of Wales showed less than his usual acumen in arguing that Salisbury had suffered a "fiasco" at Constantinople and would therefore not be equal to this occasion: but he was of course right in thinking that the presence of the Prime Minister "would show Russia that we were really in earnest".[1]

The Government now stood irremediably committed to the Congress, but up to the very last moment it had been engaged in what amounted to a gamble with Turkey: for if the Porte had refused its consent to what both Beaconsfield and Salisbury appear to have regarded as a vital factor in the settlement as a whole, the undertakings given to Shuvalov would presumably have had to be withdrawn, and a public *blâmage* could hardly have been avoided.

The essence of their argument would seem to have been the following. Russia could only be induced to accept the curtailment of "Big Bulgaria" in return for cessions of territory in Bessarabia and Armenia. The former presented little difficulty, as the brunt of concession would be borne by the luckless Roumanians: but the latter, it was assumed, involved a grave menace to the Asiatic dominions of Turkey, and therefore could only be conceded if the integrity of those dominions could be guaranteed from the outside. Britain was the only Power in the least likely to give such a guarantee, but her Government's inclination to do so was whetted by the argument that a *quid pro quo* might reasonably be demanded, and that it would take the obvious form of the much coveted "place of arms" in the eastern Mediterranean.

The Prime Minister's fancy had ranged from Varna to Batum, from Mitylene to Crete and Basrah:[2] but as the impossibility of evicting Russia from the greater part of her Armenian conquests became increasingly evident, the British Cabinet's appetite gradually concentrated itself upon Cyprus, and it was definitely suggested on 2 May that in return for the cession of that island Britain should enter upon a defensive alliance with the Porte, "guaranteeing Asiatic

---

[1] 28 May, to Queen—Buckle, vi. p. 306.   [2] *Supra*, p. 325.

Turkey from Russian invasion". Beaconsfield justified this scheme
to the Queen by the utterly untenable theory that "Cyprus is the
key to Western Asia", that such an arrangement would make of
Turkey "a stronger barrier against Russia than she was before the
war", and that then "the Queen need fear no coalition of Emperors".[1]
"Under the protection of England" Turkey would be "the most
effective and indeed the only possible barrier against an aggressive
Russia".[2]

The arguments which swayed the Cabinet are fully set out in Lord
Salisbury's letters to Mr. Layard during May, and show how far
they have already moved from Disraeli's original policy. Any return
to the Treaty of 1856 he dismissed as hopeless, adding that "the
time has passed for talking about 'independence and integrity'. It
was something of a sham in 1856, as events have proved. But it
would be a mere mockery now. The Porte must recognise that it
needs protection. . . ."

"As a governor of European Christians the Porte has failed", and
its jurisdiction must be considerably restricted. "In Asia it is otherwise. Its Government there has been as good as that of any other
Government except England. And from Asia it will continue to
draw that which is its real strength, the magnificent Mussulman
material of its armies. If we can protect the Asiatic Empire from
disintegration and procure a more reasonable frontier in Europe,
there will be a fair chance of the Ottoman Empire retaining Constantinople for a considerable period. . . ."

"The mere presence of the Russians at Kars will cause Persia,
Mesopotamia and Syria to turn their faces northward." Chaos would
follow, and these provinces would become "Russian satrapies".
"The presence of England is the only remedy which can prevent this
process of destruction", and this means "a defensive alliance with
the Porte, undertaking to join in defending her Asiatic Empire from
any attacks of Russia"—a policy for which he already hopes Cabinet
sanction. For this end "some port in the Levant would be an absolute
necessity":[3] for indeed "a port that is four days' sail from the scene
of action", like Malta, is useless for "efficient and prompt military
action", since "the first blows at least have always to be struck
suddenly and secretly".[4]

---

[1] 5 May—Buckle, vi. p. 291; *Life of Salisbury*, ii. p. 265.
[2] 23 May, to Queen—Buckle, vi. p. 294.
[3] *Layard Papers*—2 May, Salisbury to Layard, partially quoted in *Life of Salisbury*, ii. pp. 266-7.   [4] *Ibid.* 9 May, Salisbury to Layard.

Layard replied to this letter—with what may have been quite unintentional sarcasm—that it "has given me some distinct idea of a policy". This he sums up under five main heads—(1) The Balkan chain as Turkey's essential frontier to the north : (2) an alliance between Turkey and Greece (on which he has no illusions): (3) and most essential, "that good government should be secured to the populations which had remained under the direct rule of the Porte": (4) a defensive alliance with Turkey in Asia, on condition of "some direct control over Turkish administration": and (5) the acquisition of a port in the Levant. Arguing quite justly that government in Asia and in Europe must follow quite different lines, he jumps with characteristic exaggeration to the assertions that San Stefano "places Asia Minor absolutely at the mercy of Russia", and that "autonomy for Armenia is an absurdity, and probably a Russian intrigue. The Armenians of Armenia are utterly incapable of self-government. They are not the bankers of Constantinople. . . . Autonomous Armenia could not hold its own against the Kurds for a month" and would then call for Russian help. On the other hand the establishment of real order "would soon lead to a vast development of agricultural and other resources", while "the alternative route to India and our colonies" which is so "absolutely necessary" can only go "through North Syria and the valley of the Tigris and Euphrates".

He hesitates to give an opinion as to which port "would suit us best". "The question must be decided on military and naval as well as political considerations. High authorities advocate Mitylene as a fine island with two excellent harbours near the entrance to the Dardanelles, and in a position which would enable the British fleet to command the east end of the Mediterranean. Others suggest Crete, but there appears to me to be a strong objection to the possession of that island in consequence of the Greek population which would constantly be kept in a state of agitation through Greek intrigue. No such objection exists to Mitylene. There are other islands in the Archipelago which have been pointed out as affording a good naval station. A port on the north coast of Syria such as Alexandretta or Suedia,[1] which would command the terminus of the railway through Mesopotamia, might be of great advantage to England."[2] Layard, then has already dismissed from his own mind

[1] The port of Antioch.
[2] *Layard Papers*, 15 May, Layard to Salisbury. On 31 May, however, he wrote: "I had often thought of Cyprus as a desirable position to be occupied by us, as it commands the east end of the Mediterranean and the way from the Bosphorus to

Cyprus, to which most of the objections raised to other places applied.

The motives which actuated the Turks in these critical negotiations are revealed in a secret telegram sent by Layard to Salisbury on 19 May.[1] The Sultan had asked him that morning "what course England would take, should Russia attempt to occupy Constantinople and the Bosphorus, and if he were to defend them. She might send some ships to hold the Bosphorus in her own interests, but would she make an alliance with Turkey? He was now about to concentrate all his available troops in strong positions around Constantinople, but works were necessary, and the Russians might object to their construction." The Sultan added that "he was in the greatest lack of money", could no longer give meat rations to his troops and might soon be unable to provide bread! He therefore begged for a British Loan of £4,000,000, offering "any security in his power", under a commission. In all this it is quite obvious that Cyprus was simply a sort of *quid pro quo*—to Turkey a pledge committing Britain to practical help, to Britain an insurance against returning from the Congress with empty hands.

On 10 May, then, the Cabinet decided that to expel the Russians from Kars would be either impossible or too costly to be justified, and yet that its retention would "hasten the disintegration of the Turkish Empire in Asia" and "offer strong temptation for fresh aggression". In that event Britain would "have to choose between allowing Russia to dominate over Syria and Mesopotamia, or taking the country for ourselves, and either alternative is formidable. To Turkey however it is a question of existence. Asia is the nursery of her troops: when they cease to obey her, no European compacts can keep her at Constantinople. *The only remedy we can think of is a direct alliance, limited to this purpose.*

"This will be a very different engagement from the Treaty of Paris. It will be limited to ourselves, and therefore not giving any Government the excuse of abstaining from acting on it, on the ground of the refusal of some co-signatory to act. And what is more important, it will be what the Treaty of Paris was not, a direct engagement to Turkey, to defend Turkey, so far as Asia is concerned, by arms, if attacked." But if British public opinion is to be unanimous, the

Suez. . . . But I was under the impression that *the absence of a port* would be an insuperable objection to occupation . . ." (*ibid*. 31 May, Layard to Salisbury).
[1] "Most Secret and Personal."

Porte must give "specific assurances of good government to Asiatic Christians", and "if our defensive alliance is to be worth anything", it must cede a base of operations—and Cyprus is now definitely mentioned. "It has the moral advantage of vicinity both to Asia Minor and Syria: it would enable us without any act of overt hostility and without disturbing the peace of Europe, to accumulate material of war and, if requisite, the troops necessary for operations in Asia Minor or Syria, while it would not excite the jealousy which other Powers would feel at any acquisitions on the mainland."[1] It was this last argument that led to the abandonment of Scanderoon (Alexandretta) as an alternative: and here Salisbury was influenced especially by Lyons's warning that France would resent any interference with Syria.

On 24 May, then, Layard was definitely instructed to propose secretly to the Sultan a defensive alliance to secure his Asiatic dominions. If "Batum, Ardahan, Kars or any of them" should be retained by Russia and any attempt should be made to seize further territories, England would engage to defend them "by force of arms". In return, the Sultan must promise to introduce "the necessary reforms for the protection of his Christian and other subjects", and must assign Cyprus to England, it being impossible for her "to exercise the necessary vigilance over Syria and Asia Minor and to accumulate when required troops and material of war in time to be of use in repelling invasion, unless she possesses a stronghold near the coast".[2] A further telegram bade Layard "press an immediate acceptance . . . with all the energy in your power. Point out that the arrangement makes safe Asiatic Turkey, the field from which the Sultan's army is supplied with men: and that it must be accepted at once if the Sultan wishes to retain the goodwill of England. The opportunity, if neglected, will never recur. We are on the point of an arrangement by which the Russian army will be withdrawn from Constantinople and the autonomous Bulgarian Principality will be limited to north of the Balkans. If the Sultan does not consent to the above arrangement, it will not be in the power of England to pursue negotiations any further, and the capture of Constantinople and partition of Empire will be the immediate result."[3]

---

[1] *Layard Papers*, 16 May, Salisbury to Layard: partially quoted in *Life of Salisbury*, ii. p. 269 [the original is marked 10 May, by mistake for 16].

[2] *Ibid.* 24 May, Salisbury to Layard (Personal and Most Confidential).

[3] *Ibid.* 24 May, Salisbury to Layard, tel. (Personal and Most Secret). The original draft of this telegram (published by Mr. Buckle in *Queen Victoria's Letters*,

Layard lost no time in laying the proposal before the Sultan and his ministers, and already on 27 May he was able to report that a draft agreement had been reached between himself, Ahmed Vefik and Safvet. But at the last moment the situation was greatly complicated by events inside Constantinople itself. On 24 May Ali Suavi Effendi, the scatter-brained Turkish ulema and professor of whom we have already heard as the friend and informant of Butler-Johnstone, made an attempt to seize the Tcheragan Palace and restore the ex-Sultan Murad to the throne. Ali was shot down by the loyal guard, while actually trying to drag away the poor imbecile by main force! Over sixty of his adherents were also killed, but the plot, though probably connived at by Murad's mother and other ladies of the harem, never had any real chance of success and might be dismissed in a word, were it not for its singular effect upon the mind of Abdul Hamid. Heredity and *milieu* alike conspired against him: the abnormal streak so noticeable in his brother Murad, his uncle Abdul Aziz and his grandfather the redoubtable Mahmud, had not passed him over, and in his case a feeble physique and high-strung nerves were accentuated by the constant dangers of his situation. The Ali Suavi plot threw him into a positive panic of suspicion and fear, which is vividly described by Layard in some of his secret dispatches. One night he sent Said Pasha to the Embassy, begging that the British *stationnaire* should be placed opposite the palace, so that the Sultan could take refuge on it in case of need: but no sooner had this been done than a fresh urgent message arrived, requesting that the *Antelope* should at once return to her old moorings. Next morning the Sultan sent for Layard, received him alone in the harem and declared that he was in "the greatest possible peril". The army was now against him, he had lost the affections of his people: after all the horrors of the war, could they do otherwise than hate him? But he had suffered as much as any of his subjects: since his accession he had not enjoyed one night's rest. He was not afraid of death, but could not bear the thought of being immured for the remainder of his

2nd Series, ii. pp. 623-4) contains two further sentences, as follows: "Nothing has saved the Sultan from this extremity, for which not only Russia but other Powers wished, except the friendship of England: but England will desist from all further efforts, unless Sultan agrees to allow her to protect his Asiatic Empire by an alliance on these terms. Make Sultan understand that you must have written engagement as above not later than Sunday evening; and that the most absolute secrecy must be observed."

But in the telegram *as received by Layard* these two additional sentences are missing. *It thus appears that Lord Salisbury desisted from the original intention of bluffing Turkey into acceptance within forty-eight hours.*

life. Would the Ambassador protect his family, if he were killed? While he was speaking thus, he kept starting at the slightest noise: and once when trumpets blew from a neighbouring barracks, he summoned a negro slave and sent him to enquire the cause! He gradually calmed down and spoke of the projected reforms: but next morning Layard received a note from the Sultan's own hand, re-iterating his sense of danger.[1]

Under such circumstances Layard wired that he was ready to take responsibility for immediate signature, in view of the Sultan's health and a possible change of ministers, "which might be accompanied by a complete change of policy":[2] and Salisbury at once replied, bidding him "sign without delay". The final signature of the Convention took place on 4 June, but even then Layard had to spend most of the day at the palace, trying to obtain the Irade with the Sultan's endorse-ment: and during the first fortnight of June there were "almost daily changes of ministers", Sadik Pasha being suddenly replaced as Grand Vizier by Safvet Pasha, Mahmud Damad being ejected from the Ministry of War, and even the faithful Said being dismissed from the Palace. Layard's reaction to all this is highly significant. "*I grieve most sincerely for the poor Sultan, for whom I cannot but feel pity and even affection. If however the safety of the state and our paramount interests require that he should be put aside, he must be sacrificed.*"[3] Layard then is led to consider the possibility of a Regency, during which Abdul Hamid might travel abroad and take a rest: but he doubts either the practicability of this or the capacity of either of the Sultan's brothers as a substitute, and he is mainly concerned with forming "a strong Cabinet, ready to follow what is called the English policy"—in which he would include Sadik, Safvet, Mukhtar, Osman, Reouf and even Midhat.

Salisbury, on his side, views with anxiety a despotic monarch "who appears to be at the mercy of his capital or the treachery of his palace", and he is led to ask, "*Would not the Janissaries or Pretorians be better than this? Would it not suit the Sultan better to have some officer of ability—some western who could be trusted—Baker for instance—attached to his person with a small 'Varangian' Guard?*"[4] Needless to say, nothing came of this, and the Sultan continued, in the words of Layard, to "afford material for a psychological study.

[1] *Layard Papers*, 31 May, Layard to Salisbury.
[2] *Ibid*. tel. 31 May, Layard to Salisbury (Personal and Most Secret).
[3] *Ibid*. 7 June, Layard to Salisbury.
[4] *Ibid*. 30 May, Salisbury to Layard.

He is a strange mixture of common sense, the most excellent intentions and physical weakness."[1]

Events were by now effectually destroying the legend of an amiable
and well-meaning Sultan, so ardently propagated by Layard: but
rarely in history has there been a grimmer sequel than the long
Hamidian despotism that was to follow—resting upon fear, suspicion and espionage, and honeycombing the whole body politic with
corruption.

The Convention was a very brief document, simply embodying the
actual phrases of Layard's original instructions. An annexe was
eventually signed on 1 July, establishing a Moslem religious tribunal
in the island, making special provision for the administration of
Moslem property, pledging England to pay in tribute the surplus of
revenue over expenditure and finally undertaking to evacuate the
island if Russia should restore her Armenian conquests.[2]

Lord Salisbury had insisted very specially upon extreme secrecy
for as long as possible—the explanation which he gave to Layard
being that "we cannot expect that France will receive it without
a wry face. But if she is not prepared to help us in defending the
equilibrium of the Levant, she must let us do it in our own fashion."[3]
But the major explanation lay in the complicated triple parallel
negotiations in which he was engaged, and each of which had to be
concealed from the parties to the other two.

Meanwhile Salisbury made considerable show of the treaty being
so drafted "that it will fall to the ground"[4] if Russia did not
insist on Batum and Kars: but he must of course by this time
have been very well aware that such a renunciation was ruled out
by the European concessions on which he himself was insisting: and
it may well be doubted whether his desire for Cyprus did not now
outweigh his dislike of seeing Russia in Armenia. Mr. Buckle admits
that the attraction of Cyprus may be traced to that Oriental imagination which gave birth to the preposterous Tancred.

This imaginative quality is still further revealed by the phrases in
which he laid the Cyprus project before the Queen: "If this policy be
carried into effect, Your Majesty need fear no coalition of Emperors.
It will weld together Y.M.'s Indian Empire and Great Britain."[5]

---

[1] *Ibid.* 12 June, Layard to Salisbury.
[2] Hertslet, *Map of Europe*, iv. p. 2724.
[3] *Layard Papers*, 30 May, Salisbury to Layard (Private).
[4] *Ibid.* 10 May (cit. *Life*, ii. p. 269).   [5] Buckle, vi. p. 291, 5 May.

430 SALISBURY AT THE FOREIGN OFFICE CHAP. IX

Again, Beaconsfield assured the Queen on 26 May that no commitment was being entered upon regarding Batum and Kars until the Turkish answer about Cyprus was received: and both Mr. Buckle and Lady Gwendolen Cecil treat the convention as "the keystone of the diplomatic structure".[1] This view clearly represents Beaconsfield's inclinations, but it will scarcely hold water as an account of what actually happened. For Salisbury went on negotiating with Russia, and the signature of the Protocol on 30 May was a commitment from which it would no longer have been possible to recede, even if Turkey had rejected the scheme. This we may conclude to have been the main reason why the *Globe* revelation was felt to be so awkward. It presented the Government's policy in a one-sided light, in that it gave no inkling of the *quid pro quo*: and at the same time it made secrecy as to the Turkish negotiations more imperative than before. It was a truly awkward dilemma, and its effect upon the already suspicious Andrássy may easily be imagined!

Salisbury himself was at first disposed to lay the blame for publication upon the Russian secret service, and this was why, against the judgment of several of his colleagues (including Northcote, and indeed the Prime Minister himself), he insisted upon the prosecution of the insignificant Marvin at Bow Street. But not a vestige of proof was ever forthcoming, and no less an authority than Lord Hammond, who could quote a career of fifty years in defence of Foreign Office discretion, declared in the House of Lords that no shadow could rest upon the Russian Embassy.[2] Only acute contemporary distrust could have made such a suggestion: to us it is obvious, even without the Shuvalov correspondence in our hands, that Russia's interest lay very definitely on the side of discretion.

[1] Buckle, vi. pp. 295-7; *Life*, ii. p. 271.   [2] 1 July—Hansard, ccxli. p. 482.

CHAPTER X

THE CONGRESS OF BERLIN

> Every sensible man believes that the Turkish rule was so bad that it could not continue as it was, but the real difficulty has always been to replace it.
>
> LAYARD to Derby, 6 March 1878

> Everything that will make the Treaty of Berlin an epoch in the history of Europe, was due to the sword of Russia, and to that sword alone.
>
> GLADSTONE at West Calder, 27 Nov. 1879

No real history of the Congress of Berlin has as yet been written, and it may well be doubted whether an entirely satisfactory documentary account can ever be put together, for the simple reason that almost all the principals were actually present in person, conducted the most essential bargaining orally and in the *coulisses*, and did not find it necessary to write the full details to their colleagues at home. Lord Beaconsfield, it is true, kept a diary for the special benefit of Queen Victoria; but though it helps to fill many important gaps, it is really above all a series of snapshots and impressions rather than a systematic survey of events or conversations. Andrássy telegraphed to Francis Joseph on all major points requiring decision, but kept most of the details for a verbal statement after his return. The reports of M. Waddington, which, being addressed to one of the few heads of Government who had stayed at home, might be expected to be fuller, are in the main colourless and banal. Prince Gorchakov's reports to the Tsar, if they were available, would doubtless throw light on certain dark corners of the Congress, and notably on his jealousy of Shuvalov, but it may be doubted whether they would add materially to our knowledge: while Bismarck's own account was written long afterwards, rests on an imperfect memory and makes no claim to be more than a sketch.

If, however, the incomplete or inaccessible nature of the sources is an obstacle to a detailed history of the Congress, there is a further reason against adopting a method which might only serve to obscure the essential facts. Just as the Conference of Constantinople was predestined to sterility and its details were therefore quite futile, so by contrast the real work of the Congress of Berlin had already been done before it ever met, and its function, however brilliantly camouflaged,

was in the main one of registration. For the main settlement between Britain and Russia had already been achieved by the secret
Salisbury-Shuvalov Protocol of 30 May—as is abundantly clear from
a point by point comparison of its clauses with the treaty as finally
drafted. In other words, the British plenipotentiaries did not really
go to Berlin as free agents, and the difficulties which they raised and
the menacing attitude which they occasionally assumed had a considerable element of bluff, intended to prevent their Jingo supporters from grasping the true significance of the *Globe* revelations.
Thus *Punch* once more hit the nail on the head—and indeed never
more effectually—when it depicted Beaconsfield, about to enter the
conference chamber, turning with his hand upon the handle of the
door, and addressing Bismarck in a genial confidential whisper: "Oh,
I say, by the bye, what's the French for compromise?"

The Rôle of Bismarck

The Congress of Berlin occupies an intermediate position between
the Congress of Paris, where several statesmen of the front rank were
present, but had to refer decisions to the heads of their Governments
or to their sovereigns, and the Conference of 1919, which inaugurated
new methods of procedure and has left behind it surprisingly detailed
records, even of the most intimate conversations. It may be pointed
out in passing that while the telephone at first seemed likely to reduce
the volume of oral records, this tendency has been more than compensated by the confidential shorthand clerk, the typewriter, the
carbon copy, and even the roneo.

Quite apart, however, from the sudden relative dearth of written
sources after the plethora of 1877–8, a minute account of what
happened during the four weeks of the Congress would only tend
to obscure the general narrative. For the real key to an understanding of the Eastern Question in the seventies lies not in the Congress
itself, but in the critical months of negotiation that preceded it, just
as the clue to the very peculiar internal situation in England is to
be found not in the period of waiting and suspense which the Congress
imposed upon Parliament and public opinion, but in the prolonged
faction fighting in the six months between Plevna and Berlin.

There is another sense in which the Congress of Berlin represents
a transition from the old manner which culminated at Vienna in
1814–15 to the new manner which was inaugurated by the Great War.

At Vienna, though three statesmen of the very front rank were present—Metternich, Castlereagh and Talleyrand—the last word often lay with the sovereigns who glittered in the foreground. At Paris in 1856 the only sovereign was one who with a strange insincere sincerity blended democratic doctrine with autocratic practice. At Berlin in 1878 no sovereigns were present—only a fortnight earlier fate, by the hand of an assassin, had rendered William I. incapable even of receiving his guests—and though the will of the three Emperors was still supreme in the background, it was the ministers who filled the public gaze. Never before had the four Powers mainly concerned—Russia, Austria-Hungary, Britain and Germany—been directly represented by the statesmen in whose hands policy rested: and in the case of Britain never had both Premier and Foreign Secretary been absent simultaneously on such an errand. With Beaconsfield and Salisbury, Gorchakov and Shuvalov, Andrássy and Haymerle, Bismarck and Bülow, Waddington and Corti, all present at Berlin, there was practically no statesman of the first rank absent from the European council chamber, and their decisions would obviously bind Europe in a peculiarly solemn way.

The choice of Berlin was the obvious compromise between the two impossibilities of St. Petersburg and London: and its advantages even over Vienna had been so obvious that Andrássy was the first to withdraw his original proposal and to recommend Berlin. This choice in its turn made the selection of Prince Bismarck as President almost inevitable, though he himself saw only too clearly the numerous pitfalls before him and would gladly enough have evaded the doubtful honour. What finally decided his acceptance—and on this the memoirs of Radowitz lay the utmost possible stress—was the Tsar's special personal request, "As a proof of your attachment to him", and of course, by inference, of Germany's gratitude for 1866 and 1870. But he was under no illusions and frankly faced the possibility of failure and the danger of earning more kicks than halfpence. His loyal helper Bülow told his son (the future Chancellor) that Bismarck genuinely feared lest either Russia or Austria or England might withdraw in dudgeon and saddle him with the responsibility.[1] For this very reason, however, he spared no effort to achieve a settlement, being well aware that his failure would not merely confront Germany with a momentous choice in foreign policy, but would also probably undermine his situation at home. It must be remembered that the

[1] Bülow, *Denkwürdigkeiten*, iv. p. 436.

Congress came at a most critical juncture in the internal situation, when Bismarck's old feud with the Centre had given place to another with the Socialists. He now used Nobiling's attempted assassination of the Emperor to order the dissolution of the Reichstag, holding the Socialists responsible for the crime, splitting the National Liberals and defying the refractory group. His triumph at the Congress was needed to consolidate his internal position as Chancellor, which failure would have correspondingly undermined.[1]

From the very first day, Bismarck, to a far greater degree than Metternich in 1814, dominated the whole assembly by his combination of forcefulness and flexibility, by his alternate charm and brutality. It was his settled policy to prepare the ground carefully before each sitting and then to force the pace and adjourn acrimonious discussion—a method very neatly defined by Beaconsfield in the phrase, "All questions are publicly introduced and then privately settled".[2] Bismarck had to bear the brunt of every conflict, and his tremendous personality was often a decisive factor. Starting from the axiom, "Believe me, work never killed anyone", he put an amazing energy into his task. Behind a bluff and sometimes positively offensive manner was a voice of great charm, and a spirit of infinite adaptability which ranged from calculated indiscretions to real tact and a sense of fitness. A French observer wrote of him that he spoke French slowly but with ease, "affecting here and there to hesitate upon a phrase when judging men and events with a disdainful and sometimes ironic freedom: but if he seemed to be searching for his word, it was in order to launch it all the better, and he always found the phrase that was most just and pointed".[3] He quickly took the measure of each delegate, and varying his treatment from deference and reserve to impatience and severity, tried to set the pace by dire threats of Berlin's summer heat and his own determination to start his cure at Kissingen with a minimum of delay. His subordinates were probably not far wrong in thinking that if his health had given way, the whole Congress would have speedily collapsed. Europe's destinies were in the hands of one statesman whose nerves had become an obsession and of two others who seemed permanently on the verge of collapse.

---

[1] On the news of the crime Bismarck exclaimed, "Now I have them (*i.e.* the Opposition): now we'll dissolve". See H. Oncken, *Rudolf von Bennigsen*, ii. p. 370.

[2] Buckle, vi. p. 322.

[3] Mouy, *Souvenirs,* p. 96.

The British Delegates

Beaconsfield, in attending the Congress himself as first delegate, but taking Salisbury with him, was influenced by a number of complex motives. In the first place, his own health was admittedly precarious; he walked laboriously on a stick or on the faithful Montagu Corry's arm, and only avoided with an effort Gorchakov's fate of being carried upstairs to the council chamber. Even his worst enemies have never accused him of a niggardly or grudging attitude to colleagues or subordinates, and he afterwards laid the fullest possible stress upon Salisbury having "pulled the labouring oar". Indeed he had every reason for leaving the spadework to Salisbury, while deliberately reserving himself for great occasions and decisive encounters behind the scenes: and he was, of course, far too shrewd not to realise that he himself had not the same grasp of details in the questions at issue in Berlin. If, as Münster thought, he did not wish the entire glory to fall to his Foreign Secretary, it is hard to blame him for so human an attitude after all that had passed between them.

Certainly the alliance between the two men was one rather of the head than of the heart, and though events had gradually imposed it upon them, it is quite impossible to suppose that Salisbury really trusted his chief to the uttermost, or, again, that the latter had any illusion as to the very profound differences in their Near Eastern policy. Their bond of union was the maintenance of the Conservative party. Events had produced the situation foreseen and advocated by Gladstone, nothing was left of that policy of Turkish integrity which Disraeli had taken over from Palmerston, and all that could be hoped was to camouflage partition under some other name, and to diminish wherever possible the impression that Russia had achieved her essential aims. The person of Salisbury, combined with the weakness of the Opposition leaders, provided Beaconsfield with the possibility of a strategic retreat, under crossfire from the Jingoes who denounced the Protocol as a betrayal and were ready for war with Russia, and from the Radicals who hoped to see the *coup de grâce* administered to Turkey. If he had gone to Berlin alone, he would have found it difficult to recede from his old attitude of extreme Turcophilism, and a rupture with Russia would have been inevitable. By taking Salisbury with him he was able to repeat his famous manœuvre of "stealing the Whigs' clothes": for Salisbury, who had never believed in Turkey, had always sympathised with her Christian subjects and differed from Gladstone not so much in substance as in form—objecting to his tactics and mentality and political creed, but not challenging his facts—was now able as it were to provide a more suitable and more conservative mould for the liquid lava set in motion by his great Liberal rival. The result was a virtual abandonment of the Turkish cause, the recognition of the more clamant Christian claims at the expense of an unhappy residue, and an arrangement with Russia on the basis "thus far and no farther". In a word, Salisbury provided a certain synthesis between the two extremes of Gladstone and Disraeli.

Meanwhile, it was natural that all eyes should turn upon Beaconsfield, the most romantic and unconventional figure in the whole diplomatic throng, armed with all the authority of the British Government, known to possess the peculiar favour of the Queen, yet never before seen in such a setting—which his letters show him to have felt and enjoyed as a novelty. It was in this sense that Bismarck may have coined the famous phrase, "Der alte Jud', das ist der Mann": it certainly did not mean, as Mr. Buckle seems to think, that Bismarck regarded him as the greatest figure there, but above all as one who could "deliver the goods", and as one whom it was his own special business to cajole and flatter and manœuvre.[1] Mr. Buckle also quotes as decisive the opinion of the Empress Augusta to Queen Victoria, that Beaconsfield "formed the real centre of the Congress and represented the greatest authority there".[2] He evidently does not realise that this verdict was inspired by her implacable enmity to Bismarck, and at the same time that—as Salisbury was quick to notice[3]—she was "a very foolish woman", just clever enough to know what would please the Queen!

On the eve of the Prime Minister's journey Münster sent home to Berlin the following comment: "Your Highness will find it very

[1] An admirable proof that Bismarck did not always mean what he said is provided by his subsequent remark to Goschen (long afterwards quoted by Gladstone to Rendel, and of course perhaps mangled in transmission): "I like the old Jew. He is the man who hustled the Conference through" (*Personal Papers of Lord Rendel*, p. 112). No student of the Congress, whatever his views on other points, will challenge the view that it was pre-eminently Bismarck himself who "hustled it through", and that Beaconsfield—for reasons not at all necessarily open to criticism—delayed the settlement.

[2] Buckle, vi. p. 311.

[3] *Life*, ii. p. 280: "She was very foolish, and Beaconsfield's compliments were a thing to hear!"

difficult to carry on a really serious conversation with him, as he is very vain and also enfeebled by age. It is true that illuminating and brilliant ideas are often produced, but the higher conception, the moral groundwork, is lacking." At the same time Münster quotes the satisfaction expressed by Salisbury at his chief's impending meeting with Bismarck: for "he will then hear truths on the Eastern Question such as were not yet put to him, and Prince Bismarck will easily gain great influence over him, and that I desire".[1] It may well be that the copious flow of "autobiography" which Bismarck inflicted upon both the English statesmen was his own peculiar way of acting upon Münster's hint, while at the same time keeping them at arm's length until he was ready for the final wrestle.

Lord Salisbury's own private view, as confided to his wife a week after the Congress had opened, is sufficiently revealing: "What with deafness, ignorance of French and Bismarck's extraordinary mode of speech, Beaconsfield has the dimmest idea of what is going on, understands everything crossways and imagines a perpetual conspiracy".[2] But at the same time he realised that his chief had the immense merit of shouldering, even welcoming, responsibility at a critical moment and took the outbursts of the Tory press much more calmly than he might otherwise have done, because he felt that "the Jingoes require to be calmed in their own language, and he is the only one among us who speaks it fluently".[3] That Beaconsfield himself accepted this rôle is revealed in one of his letters to Northcote: "I have had a hard time of it, as I am brought forward as the man of war on all occasions and have to speak like Mars".[4] A few weeks earlier he had confessed to the Queen his belief that continental statesmen were afraid of him:[5] and this belief was most probably genuine, though not altogether well grounded.

Much has been made of the famous incident of the opening session, when his staff were on tenterhooks lest he should address the Congress in his *français d'épicier*, and therefore put up the adroit and genial Lord Odo to urge upon him the general desire to hear an address from "the greatest living master of English oratory".[6] As Lord Odo afterwards put it, no one ever knew whether Beaconsfield

---

[1] *G.P.* no. 431, Münster to Bismarck, 10 June.
[2] 23 June—*Life*, ii. p. 287.   [3] *Ibid.* p. 288.
[4] Buckle, vi. p. 324.   [5] *Life*, p. 295, 26 May.
[6] Freeman, with his pen dipped in acid, doubted whether "the Jew's Hebrew was first-rate or whether he knows any tongue beside the dialect of his own novels"— *The M.P. for Russia*, i. p. 503. *Punch* (22 June) wrote of Disraeli's "facility lingual, if not quite linguistic".

took the hint or accepted the compliment. But it appears to be a fact that the secretariat were only informed by Montagu Corry a few minutes before the actual opening, of Beaconsfield's intention to speak in English,[1] and that Bismarck, true to his policy of humouring him to the utmost, accepted without a murmur this first international breach upon the monopoly enjoyed by French on such occasions. The plain fact is that Beaconsfield's own French was altogether impossible, and that he was quite unable to follow what was said in that language,[2] just as Gorchakov was unable to understand speeches in English: and as neither statesman was willing to give himself away, a series of comic misunderstandings ensued, glossed over by common consent.

Radowitz, the able organiser of the Congress machine, has recorded the keen curiosity with which "the 'great' Disraeli" was awaited in Berlin. "Bismarck", he tells us in his memoirs—and no one had better means of judging—"had a strong prejudice against him. With the romantic-oratorical Semite he did not expect to find many personal points of contact: he did not think him sufficiently honourable and reliable, despite his traits of genius and great political resourcefulness. In short, their impending acquaintance was distasteful to him, and according to reliable evidence the same was true of Beaconsfield towards Bismarck."[3] Indeed as late as 21 April he was expressing to the Queen herself his doubt whether Bismarck could "withstand the temptation of embroiling and exhausting both Great Britain and Russia"[4]—as we have seen, an altogether unfounded charge. But direct contact speedily changed all this. "The two statesmen found each other, agreed more than either had expected, and despite the great difference of character, entered into a good personal relation, which finally developed into real friendship." It may be doubted whether Bismarck ever really liked "the old Jew", and on the opening day he characterised the British delegates to Hohenlohe as "impudent and clumsy":[5] but he soon felt a growing respect for Disraeli's wit, his energy, his defiance of physical disabilities, and

[1] Radowitz, *op. cit.* ii. p. 24.

[2] In Bismarck's words to Mittnacht, "Beaconsfield not only speaks no French, but hardly understands it"—Mittnacht, *Erinnerungen an Bismarck*, Neue Folge, p. 12. On 2 July Busch records Beaconsfield's bad humour, due to his inability to follow French—Busch, *Nachlass*, iii. p. 375 (*Deutsche Rundschau*).

[3] Radowitz, *Denkwürdigkeiten*, ii. p. 25.   [4] Buckle, vi. p. 292.

[5] *Unverschämt und ungeschickt.* Hohenlohe superciliously records in his diary two days later, "Beaconsfield displeases me more and more: a loathsome Jew face" (*ein scheussliches Judengesicht*)—Hohenlohe, *Denkwürdigkeiten*, ii. p. 236.

above all he knew that real power lay in his hands, and that to win him over meant success. His own verdict differs in no way from our quotation from Radowitz: "In spite of his fantastic novel-writing, he is a capable statesman, far above Gorchakov. It was easy to transact business with him: in a quarter of an hour you knew exactly how you stood with him, the limits to which he was prepared to go were clearly defined, and a rapid summary soon put a point on matters." He therefore, in Disraeli's own phrase, "loaded him with kindnesses" and took infinite pains to influence or restrain him.

On the whole, Salisbury, for all his dialectic skill and strong principles, made a less favourable impression than his chief, who ignored all details and only emerged from his studied reserve on grand occasions. Count Mouy, the able French adjunct to the secretariat, has written of Salisbury as conveying the impression of "a philosopher and dreamer", but adds sarcastically that his well-known "civilising fervour or sympathies for the oppressed races were always subordinated to British interests", and that "his eagerness to save remote Asiatic tribes from Russian rule fitted ill with his readiness to replace Macedonia and half Bulgaria under the discredited yoke of Turkey".[1] Even Radowitz, whose prejudice against Disraeli slowly melted away, and to whom Odo Russell was the most charming of all Englishmen and "the ideal of a good and useful agent of foreign policy" ("only rivalled by Lord Dufferin", he adds), had his reserves about Salisbury, whom he describes as "difficult and meticulous in routine, not always reliable in recording the agreements arrived at and sometimes even difficult to tie down",[2] and again, as "always making the impression of being ill-pleased at the whole thing".[3] Certainly there was a curious contradictory blend in Salisbury, of high Christian idealism, and of a sardonic, half-mocking humour that was realist enough for any taste. Werner, in painting his "fine apostle's head", compared him to "a Russian priest in mufti".[4]

It was widely suspected in Berlin that the relations between Beaconsfield and Salisbury were not harmonious: Busch even had the impression that "they speak like ministers of different states". There were even many who interpreted the *Globe* revelation as an attempt to compromise Salisbury and correspondingly strengthen his chief. But though this may well have been the motive of those responsible for it, there is no evidence whatever for the suggestion that it was a

---

[1] Mouy, *Souvenirs et causeries*, p. 113.   [2] *Unverbindlich in seinen Formen.*
[3] Radowitz, *op. cit.* ii. p. 26.   [4] Werner, *Erlebnisse und Eindrücke*, p. 230.

deliberate intrigue of Beaconsfield against Salisbury, and we are entitled to claim that such behaviour would not have been in keeping with his known loyalty to friends and colleagues. Salisbury himself showed a dignified and cordial deference to his chief, though never hesitating to speak out or take responsible action of his own, while Beaconsfield had the extreme wisdom—in itself a rare proof of statesmanship—to recognise that Salisbury had a "consummate mastery" of details of which he himself was in the main ignorant, and to concentrate his own efforts upon the supreme issues of policy. To the Turks he once argued that his mission in Berlin was not diplomacy—but presumably, by inference, high politics, and that once he had saved the Balkan line and the Straits for the Turks, he preferred to leave all else to Salisbury.[1]

This reserve was due to a combination of political *flair* and precarious health, which caused the Queen profound and not ungrounded anxiety. But the lengths to which royal solicitude went may best be gathered from the message delivered to the painter of the Congress, Anton von Werner, by Count Seckendorff, on behalf of the Prince of Wales, who had seen the preliminary study for Dizzy's portrait and wondered "whether it would be possible to be a little more flattering—at least the lower lip!"[2]

RIVAL FIGURES AT THE CONGRESS

Next to the British delegates, the main interest of the Congress centred round the Russians, the more so because of the notorious rivalry which had latterly grown up between Gorchakov and Shuvalov. It was generally known that the Tsar, whose confidence the Ambassador in London had not merely retained but still further confirmed, had wished Shuvalov to be the principal delegate and had only reluctantly yielded to the veteran Chancellor's insistence. On the other hand, Shuvalov himself seems to have actually desired Gorchakov's presence as the lesser of two evils: indeed he was quoted as saying that "he would drag Gorchakov alive or dead to Berlin, for since he had made San Stefano, he had better defend it".[3]

Gorchakov, now in his eightieth year, possessed the artificial

[1] Bareilles, *Rapport Secret de Carathéodory Pacha*, p. 107.
[2] *Erlebnisse und Eindrücke*, p. 230.
[3] Reported by Károlyi to Andrássy, 5 June—Wertheimer, iii. p. 118.

graces, the shallow scepticism, the elegant but somewhat discursive style, the passion for *bons mots*, of the eighteenth-century diplomatist. But the dominant note of his character in later life was a deep-seated vanity, and after directing Russian policy for nearly a generation he was anxious to end his diplomatic career with heightened prestige. One of his own chief confidants, Hamburger, put into circulation his sententious phrase, "Je ne veux pas m'éteindre comme une lampe qui file, je veux me coucher comme un astre".[1] The inordinate importance which he attached to form and phrase is shown by an incident reported both by Busch and Mouy: when the minutes of his speech were brought to him for correction, his attention centred itself upon the phrase, "palmes de paix", which after mature reflection he altered to "branches d'olivier".[2] Shuvalov, in his unpublished memoirs, complains that Gorchakov's dispatches and even his telegrams and instructions were full of phrases—"specimens of literature, with rolling periods": and the reader has had more than one opportunity of verifying this statement, though the more verbose portions have often been deleted. In short, he still showed "flashes of dialectic brilliancy, but he was no longer capable of sustained argument or negotiation".

Gorchakov had a threefold objective—to pose as the saviour of Russia, winning more from the Congress than he could hope to secure from England alone, and to saddle his irksome colleague Shuvalov with the odium for such concessions as might prove inevitable, or more correctly, to divide this odium between Shuvalov and Bismarck, and to misrepresent them equally to the Tsar. He was acutely jealous of Bismarck, unable either to undermine or to resign himself to his rival's obvious predominance: and Bismarck on his side, who was both vindictive and distrustful, saw Gorchakov's hand in every intrigue real or imaginary, and therefore grudged bestowing upon him those perfumes of flattery which meant so much to the recipient and would have cost so little to the giver. Shuvalov, on the eve of the Congress, quoted Bismarck as saying, "I won't allow Prince Gorchakov to climb a second time on my shoulders in order to make a pedestal", and this seems to have been an accurate reflection of his feelings. Meanwhile, Gorchakov's speeches to the Congress were not without dignity and force of argument, though Beaconsfield complained of his "lacrymose" style. But he was not above a

---

[1] Radowitz, *op. cit.* ii. p. 24; Bülow, *op. cit.* iv. p. 437.
[2] Busch, *op. cit.* pp. 375, 366.

sprightly banter, and when Salisbury one day assured him that he would no longer dare to return to London and asked for an asylum in Russia, Gorchakov promptly offered him his own post of Chancellor.

It was felt by many present that for widely different reasons Beaconsfield and Gorchakov were the two principal obstacles to rapid progress, and on the other hand that next to Bismarck himself the success of the Congress depended upon Shuvalov. Versatile, insouciant and charming, a *coureur aux dames* whose adventures never interfered with his capacity for hard work and his eagerness to fill every breach, always ready with a witty phrase, but possessed by real earnestness of purpose, he battled unremittingly in the cause of peace and compromise, in the firm conviction that Russia's internal structure could not stand the strain of another war, and that there was no unbridgeable conflict of interest between Russia and Britain. The numerous extracts from his correspondence will have already revealed him as a realist and a man of the world, who none the less differed *toto caelo* in his outlook and methods, both from the platitudinous yet obstinate Gorchakov and the exuberant and ruthless Ignatyev. He had the courage to stake his political reputation and influence with the Tsar upon a peaceful settlement, and it may well be that he would have achieved his ambition to become Russian Chancellor, had not personal vendettas—among them, it is said, that of the Tsar's mistress, Princess Dolgoruki—poisoned the mind of Alexander against him, with highly regrettable results in the sphere of international relations.

The emphasis laid upon the British and Russian delegates must not be interpreted as any diminution of the remarkable figure that represented Austria-Hungary. Count Andrássy was vivacious and charming, a grand seigneur of mildly oriental allures, thanks to the external trappings of Hungarian nobility and the faint reminiscence of gipsy type which the stranger seemed to detect in him. He was constantly misjudged by contemporary statesmen, but though this was in no small degree caused by his own extreme secretiveness, it was above all due to their ignorance of Danubian affairs and to the mediocrity of some of their ambassadors. For Andrássy was not merely a man of strong character and great courage, with a stormy and variegated past—he had been an exile in Turkey, hanged in effigy as a traitor by the common hangman, and then had shared the great Deák's triumph of 1867 and become the first Premier of the restored Hungary—but he possessed that combination of romanticism and legalism which lies at the root of the true Magyar temperament. When asked to write in a lady's album "what he sought in art", he replied, "that which I despise in politics—the ideal": and this may help to explain the peculiar fibre of his mind, composed, as it obviously was, of watertight compartments. Above all else, he knew what he himself wanted, and what was possible and impossible with Francis Joseph. He had the courage of his opinions and could be very outspoken on occasion. But though a champion of constitutional development, he shared the general view of statesmen in that era, that foreign affairs were not a subject for general discussion, and no one went farther than he in the practice of "secret diplomacy". His general outlook was that of a patriotic Magyar magnate, bent upon gradually transferring the political centre of gravity of the Dual Monarchy from Vienna to Budapest, by a constructive policy of foreign alliances and internal assimilation: and this naturally enjoined upon him distrust of Russia and the Slavs on the one hand, friendly reserve towards France and increasingly cordial co-operation with Bismarck on the other.

A sketch of Andrássy from the pen of Blowitz is too good not to be quoted. "His physiognomy is a faithful reflection of the peculiar cast of Andrássy's mind. The sharp deep lines of his head, his bright and restless eye, his vigorous chin, his nervous gait and the vivacity of his expression, all indicate an irresistible will at the service of a fertile and indefatigable imagination. He is at the same time a man of great suppleness and patience, something like one of those Zingari hunters who, not daring to fire a gun for fear of the echo, watch for whole days to throw the lasso round the neck of the wild horse they have determined to capture."[1]

Andrássy's two colleagues at the Congress were Baron Haymerle, a man of more bureaucratic outlook, lacking in magnetism but full of knowledge, who for a brief space of time was to become his successor at the Ballplatz, and Count Alois Károlyi, the Ambassador, a highly efficient diplomatist, but above all a man of brilliant social qualities and leanings. The rôle of such expert officials as Baron Teschenberg and Baron Schwegel deserves a passing mention.

France too sent three representatives. The first, M. Waddington, had but recently succeeded the Duke Decazes as Foreign Minister and was lacking in diplomatic experience. D'Harcourt, the retiring

[1] *The Times*, 26 July, "Austria and the Congress".

French Ambassador in London, had described Waddington to Granville as "an able and moderate man, with great self-confidence"—this may be doubted—"quite ignorant of foreign affairs, and likely to take unexpected steps".[1] English by origin and education, he seemed to fall between the two stools of his double nationality: for though thoroughly honest and sound in his views, he was timorous and seemingly overawed by his more brilliant colleagues at the Congress, and though the French Government had deliberately set him a policy of reserve and effacement, he emphasised the partial eclipse of France in Europe more than was necessary. This was all the more curious because Bismarck paid the most marked attention both to him and to the second delegate, M. de St. Vallier, a diplomat of great charm and ability, who from his first arrival in Berlin had been as *bien vu* as his predecessor Gontaut-Biron had been suspect. St.Vallier, it is true, though a tireless worker and in every way supplementary to his chief, was handicapped by an internal complaint that sapped his energy. The third delegate, Desprez, appears to have been a typical French bureaucrat, *l'homme du protocol par excellence*.

Italy was represented by Count Corti, till recently Ambassador at Constantinople—a man of diminutive and unimpressive exterior, but of great knowledge and common sense, condemned to a negative rôle by Italy's as yet recent admission to the rank of a Great Power and her still somewhat fluid views on Balkan policy. His colleague, Count Launay, was rather a man of social ambitions than of any marked political foresight or ability, but had the advantage of an unusually long acquaintance with Berlin.

The three Turkish delegates came without any written instructions, but the personal order of the new autocrat, Abdul Hamid, to concentrate their efforts on saving Varna, Batum and Armenia, securing the line of the Balkans, ceding a minimum of territory to the two Serb states and avoiding an indemnity. It was highly characteristic of Turkish tactics that, of the three, only the third, Sadullah Pasha, was a real Turk, and a complete mediocrity at that—a palace official whom it was convenient to "kick upstairs" by a decorative appointment—while their leader, Caratheodory Pasha, was a Phanariot Greek, and his colleague Mehmed Ali Pasha a renegade Prussian who had made a career by adopting Islam. Thus, in the more than probable event of their failure to redeem Turkey's situation, no high personage of Islam would be compromised.

[1] *Gladstone Papers*, Granville to Gladstone, 20 Dec. 1877.

Caratheodory was a man of high culture and real intelligence, but equally lacking in authority and backbone, and found himself more than once in an impossible position, notably when he had to defend Turkey against the national claims of Greece. Salisbury's private comment upon him is enlightening—"a poor, weak, frightened creature, and when not frightened, not wholly trustworthy".[1] Moreover, the choice of Mehmed Ali was peculiarly unfortunate: this double apostasy, both national and religious, of young Detroit of Magdeburg, infuriated Bismarck, who called him *un gamin de Berlin* and would hardly speak to him civilly: and though he was a good soldier, he had no tact and disgusted the whole Congress by a speech full of fulsome praises of Turkish progress and enlightenment. "The picture of a regular German landsknecht", such was the impression of the court painter, von Werner. The unhappy Turks soon found themselves completely isolated, excluded from all the secrets of the Congress and constantly confronted by accomplished facts. They complained of the *coups de fouet* by which Bismarck conducted business, for even the mildest protests on their part at once drew down his wrath upon their heads. Their own ineffective character doubtless contributed to the result, but after all the situation was such that they could not hope for a single sincere ally. For that name cannot be applied to Britain, who was less interested in defending Turkey than in checkmating Russia, and had undertaken a series of vital commitments without even consulting the Porte, while both she and Austria-Hungary exacted territorial concessions in return for such limited support as they were ready to give.

Round the principal delegates there hovered a cloud of representatives of the lesser states and races—many, like Bratianu, Kogalniceanu, Ristić, Delyannis, men of high distinction in their own countries, but all treated in a highly cavalier fashion and only occasionally admitted, under closely circumscribed conditions, to state a hurried case and instantly vanish into outer limbo. Behind them again surged the legions of the press, helplessly protesting against the extreme secrecy with which the protocols were guarded, and filling the columns of their journals with more or less intelligent

[1] *Layard Papers*, 12 Aug. 1878, Salisbury to Layard. We may take Caratheodory's measure, *and Layard's*, in a letter of the latter to Salisbury in the following December, when the Phanariot held office at the Porte: "*I have given Caratheodory to understand that if I find him playing false I will leave no stone unturned to break his neck, and as he knows I can do it, it is to his interest to keep well with us*" (*ibid.* 1 Dec. 1878, Layard to Salisbury).

speculation. Foremost among them all, perhaps, was that fantastic adventurer, M. de Blowitz, as he called himself—really a Moravian Jew named Oppert—whose embroidered fictions must be read with all reserve, but who, thanks to Prince Hohenlohe's recommendation, secured from Bismarck a memorable interview that filled his colleagues with envy, and in the end was able to publish the complete text of the treaty in *The Times*, twelve hours before any other London journal. The annoyance and jealousy which his success produced in German circles is well reflected in *Kladderadatsch*, the leading comic journal of the new Empire, which consoled itself for the secretive policy adopted at the Congress by the pointed remark: "Luckily the Chancellor has given full particulars about his policy to the correspondent of *The Times*, so that the German papers can at least learn a little about it at secondhand!"

A SURVEY OF INCIDENTS

(i) *Bulgaria*

The Congress was opened on 13 June, Bismarck being elected President on the motion of Andrássy and declaring as its object "to submit the work of San Stefano to the free discussion of the signatories of the Treaties of 1856 and 1871". Bismarck, whose state of health was scarcely less precarious than that of Gorchakov or Beaconsfield, and who, if he himself is to be believed, had no appetite and had to empty a tumbler of port wine in order to be fit for a few hours' work,[1] at first thought that he would only be able to attend two or three sittings. But his fighting spirit quickly realised the difficulties and rose to the occasion, for he could not allow a fiasco in the capital of the new Empire. Thus from the very outset he dominated the Congress and gave a highly practical lead, by proposing that precedence should be given to the Bulgarian question. He very wisely calculated that success depended upon reaching a compromise in the major European problem which interested the greatest number of Powers; that if once this could be reached, a more favourable atmosphere would have been created for the discussion of all other questions: and that the first energy of the delegates should be expended upon essentials. His wisdom at once became apparent when Beaconsfield adverted to the position of the Russian army outside Constantinople as "abnormal and perilous", and when Shuvalov

[1] Mittnacht, *op. cit.* p. 9.

defended their retention by the argument that they would be followed
in their withdrawal by a large part of the Christian population.
Bismarck side-tracked this dangerous issue by doubting whether it
fell within the competence of the Congress and proposing direct
Russo-British conversations. An interval of four days elapsed before
the second sitting, to allow the delegates to take each other's measure,
intrigue behind the scenes and attend innumerable dinners and
receptions.

It is quite evident that at the outset Beaconsfield set himself the
part of frightening Shuvalov, whom he knew to be sincerely desirous
of peace and handicapped by his vain, obstinate and jealous colleague
Gorchakov. It will never be possible to estimate exactly how much
of his unconciliatory tone towards Russia was bluff, and how much
a necessary concession to Jingo feeling at home, now greatly excited
at the revelations of the *Globe* and inclined to suspect a "climb-
down", or again, how much a bold defiance of what Lord Houghton
rightly described as its "portentous" effect in Europe.[1] The meetings in Congress may have been what Salisbury called them, "perfectly futile": [2] but they ratified step by step the results of a strenuous
fight kept up behind the scenes. According to Beaconsfield's own
report to the Queen, he told Shuvalov that the Russian proposals
about South Bulgaria were "outrageous. To give the Sultan the
line of the Balkans for his frontier and not permit him to fortify
and defend them, is monstrous and a gross insult to England [*sic*].
Lord B. spoke thunder about it. It will be given up by St.
Petersburg." [3] In a further report he assured her that "people here
never mention Batum or questions of that calibre. There is only
one thought—Bulgaria. Article VI. is the real point for which the
Congress is assembled. Upon its treatment depends whether there
shall be a Turkey-in-Europe or not." [4] Here, we may suppose, is
Disraeli's real mind.

At the second session two British proposals were accordingly put
forward—that the Balkan range should form the new northern
frontier of Turkey, and that south of it the Sultan should "exercise
a real political and military power". Russia on her side had favoured
a "longitudinal" division of Bulgaria from north to south, but after
a little skirmishing Shuvalov accepted the Balkan line. The real trial
of strength came over the status of the southern province, and

[1] Hansard, ccxl. p. 1571.   [2] 20 June—*Life of Salisbury*, ii. p. 283.
[3] Buckle, vi. p. 319.   [4] *Ibid.* p. 321.

Shuvalov had to report to the Tsar for further instructions. Bismarck proposed direct Russo-British discussions and went more than half-way towards Andrássy by at once consenting that Austria-Hungary should be associated with them. The Turks in stupefied but helpless fury heard him publicly describe those two Powers as "principally interested in the Bulgarian question", while they themselves were excluded and not even consulted. The triangular talks dragged out interminably: and Beaconsfield described one session to the Queen as "nearly the severest four hours I can well recall". He ended by declaring the two British proposals to be "an ultimatum"—to the Queen he is always painting with his crudest colours and the reality was probably slightly less offensive, and toned down by the long-suffering and pacific Shuvalov. In a private conversation with Gorchakov he took the same stiff line, and at dinner at the Italian Embassy deliberately "took the gloomiest view of affairs" and spoke of his "resolve to break up the Congress", if Russia would not yield, in the calculation that Launay and Corti would spread the story broadcast by breakfast next day. On the 21st he went even further and told Corry to order a special train for the British delegates, knowing that the news would have an immediate effect in expediting affairs.

This time Bismarck was genuinely alarmed, elicited from him during a hurried afternoon call that "ultimatum" was really the right word for his attitude, invited the old man to dinner *en famille* that same evening, and at a *tête-à-tête* conversation afterwards tested his resolve to the uttermost. Unhappily there is no record of what passed between them, save two pregnant lines in Beaconsfield's diary for the Queen—"he (Bismarck) was convinced that the ulti-matum was not a sham, and before I went to bed I had the satisfac-tion of knowing that St. Petersburg had surrendered"[1]—and a mere phrase of Bismarck to Radowitz—"Beaconsfield was at first rather pompous and monosyllabic, then milder and quite sensible", even expressing polite regret for the quandary in which he was placing his "friend" Shuvalov.[2] The high authority of Montagu Corry has been quoted[3] for the assertion that this was no bluff, but deadly earnest, and that it had been his chief's intention to return to London, visit the Queen, and advise a declaration of war upon Russia. It is, however, one thing to affirm that the Prime Minister

---

[1] 21 June—Buckle, vi. p. 324.   [2] Radowitz, *op. cit.* ii. p. 45.
[3] Lord Rowton, as he afterwards became. See A. N. Cummings, "The Secret History of the Treaty of Berlin (Talk with Lord Rowton)"—*Nineteenth Century*, July 1905.

was serious in his warning and that Bismarck took him very seriously, and quite another that he had an irreducible minimum on which he would have risked war.

The essential point is that Bismarck—though not of course Beaconsfield—was by this time aware that the Russian delegates had the Tsar's orders to yield rather than risk war, and that he lost no time in impressing upon them the need for a timely retreat. Next day, then (22 June), Beaconsfield was able to assure the Queen of Russia's surrender: the "Big Bulgaria" of San Stefano was to be abandoned, and with it Bulgaria's access to the Aegean, and the Sultan's authority was to be maintained over the new province of "Eastern Roumelia". Salisbury on his side, after having actually held out for the exclusion of Sofia even from the new and curtailed Bulgaria, now abandoned the longitudinal division of the two provinces, in favour of a line running along the Balkan peaks and so was graciously pleased to include Sofia after all. At the same time he consented to including the port of Varna in Eastern Roumelia. The Turkish delegates were "knocked flat" (*atterrés*)[1] by what was really a double blow—firstly because their secret instructions from the Sultan bade them make a special effort to save Varna, and also because they had fondly clung to the absurd longitudinal division, in the hope that this would spell the exclusion of Bulgaria from the Black Sea coast and Turkey's retention of the quadrilateral! Salisbury's concession was really less generous than might seem at first sight: for it was obvious from a mere glance at the map, that an Eastern Roumelia shut off from the Aegean was simply not "viable" at all, if also deprived of its only possible port on the Black Sea. Caratheodory Pasha timidly protested, but was soon reduced to silence by Bismarck, who in his rudest and most domineering vein warned the Turks that after signing San Stefano they had no right to raise objections, that he could not tolerate any attempt to block the work of the Congress, and that if they persisted, he "would be obliged to give a practical sanction to his remarks".[2] The inference which the unhappy Turks drew from this incident—that Bismarck was determined to exclude them from any share in the real decisions taken outside the Congress and to have them publicly endorsed on the spot, lest there should be any relapse from the approaching

---

[1] Bareilles, *Rapport Secret*, p. 95.
[2] His "violence of language" was very much toned down in the protocol. See Bareilles, *op. cit.* p. 97.

Russo-British agreement—was probably quite accurate. Again and again during the Congress he snubbed and browbeat the Turks, making it abundantly clear that he believed neither in the future of Turkey nor in a programme of reform and had no intention, if he could help it, of allowing their interests to stand in the way of a settlement. At the very outset he had told them quite bluntly, "If you think the Congress has met for Turkey, disabuse yourselves. San Stefano would have remained unaltered, if it had not touched certain European interests. The severity of certain clauses may be toned down, but if you try for more than that, you won't succeed, and further war would only mean the ruin of Turkey."[1] Caratheodory has recorded his view that they might have won Bismarck's support if they had accepted his original proposal for a Turkish evacuation of Varna, as the first stage to a joint Russo-British withdrawal: but being tied by their instructions and by Mehemed Ali's strategic theories, they offended the all-powerful Chancellor, and ended by losing both the fortress and such advantages as its prompt cession would have earned them.

The discussion of the details of Bulgarian administration still dragged on for some days in the triangular Russo-British-Austrian commission, which had been appointed at Bismarck's instance, and Shuvalov maintained the solemn farce of waiting for a message of authorisation from St. Petersburg, while the Tsar's full powers were all the time in his pocket.[2] He too had his internal difficulties, for Gorchakov, by a critical attitude towards the necessary concessions, tried to foist upon Shuvalov the whole responsibility and unpopularity with Russian public opinion. This doubtless explains why Shuvalov put forward proposals for a *third* province of "*Western* Roumelia" which never had the faintest chance of acceptance and were speedily dropped.

At the fourth session, however, the Russo-British agreement on Bulgaria was publicly announced, and it was now safe for Bismarck to pull up even Lord Salisbury when he betrayed all too great a zeal for minute outstanding details. Meanwhile he concealed his relief and sought to guard against second thoughts on the part of Beaconsfield, by such phrases as "There is again a Turkey-in-Europe" and "You have made a present to the Sultan of the richest province in the world: 4000 square miles of the richest soil". This last phrase is solemnly endorsed by Mr. Buckle, who evidently has no inkling of

---

[1] Bareilles, *op. cit.* p. 73.   [2] *Ibid.* pp. 88-9.

its absurdity or of the extreme probability that Bismarck was "pulling Disraeli's leg". Macedonia and the north Aegean coast were of course provinces of potential wealth, but it is only necessary to consider their steady decay under Turkish rule during the previous two generations, and still more the hideous accentuation of that process during the thirty years that were still to elapse between their restoration to the Porte and their final liberation, in order to condemn the phrase as tragically misleading.

(ii) *Bosnia*

After the Bulgarian storm had subsided, there was a certain lull during which "rearguard actions" were fought between Salisbury and Shuvalov regarding the period of occupation by Russian troops and the manner of election of the future Prince, and compliments of a formal but public kind were exchanged between Beaconsfield and Gorchakov, as a proof that the first cyclone had been weathered. The second main phase opened on 28 June, when Lord Salisbury, in a written speech, proposed that the Powers should entrust Austria-Hungary with a mandate for the occupation of Bosnia-Hercegovina. Like a schoolmaster with cane in hand, he assured the Turks that it was greatly to their advantage to surrender territory of no strategic value and involving them in trouble and expense, while he dismissed as objectionable the alternative of a chain of Slav states across the Balkan Peninsula. Andrássy, who had the secret consent of Britain in his pocket ever since the convention of 6 June, had consistently given her his backing throughout the Bulgarian controversy, in view of favours to come. Finding now that the Turks could not be induced to accept the inevitable and make a voluntary offer of the two provinces, he preferred that the initiative should come from London rather than Berlin, lest public opinion at home should accuse him of undue subservience to the victors of Königgrätz. He could have had "annexation" had he desired it, but he preferred "occupation" for opportunist reasons—first, as a concession to public opinion among the dominant Germans and Magyars who disliked the incorporation of fresh Slav populations ; second, to avert the inevitable complications of "State Rights" as between Austria and the Crown of St. Stephen (to say nothing of Croatia); and third, to make it easier for the Turks to yield, by evading the theory that the Sultan can never cede territory unless it has actually been conquered.

Salisbury's motion was promptly endorsed by Bismarck on behalf of Germany, again in a written speech, which proved to the Turks, if proof were necessary, that the whole matter was prearranged. The French, who may have regarded consent as the equivalent for the veto on a discussion of Syria and Egypt, and who hoped to win Andrássy's favour for Greece, immediately followed. The Italians were aghast and taken by surprise, but reduced to silence when Andrássy, turning to Corti pointedly, addressed to him the laconic phrase, "Austria-Hungary, in occupying Bosnia, places herself upon the European standpoint. I have nothing to add." [1] The Russians, being bound by the secret engagements of Reichstadt and Budapest and the confirmatory memoranda of the spring of 1878 in their pockets, could not of course oppose, though Shuvalov—doubtless in order to "save face" towards Moscow opinion—made certain reservations as to the Sandjak of Novipazar. It is characteristic of the relations between the leading Russian delegates, that Gorchakov and Shuvalov each separately assured Andrássy afterwards that he himself had favoured and his colleague opposed the Austrian claim. The solemn farce was completed by a speech of Lord Beaconsfield, insisting that the motive of this decision was to "prevent partition", and covering up the paradox by an abundance of elusive precedents. The unhappy Turks, taken utterly by surprise, and as usual misjudging the situation, begged for adjournment and argued that Turkey was quite able to restore and maintain order in Bosnia—an assertion which Andrássy at once flatly contradicted, and with every reason. This brought down Bismarck with sledge-hammer force upon them. "Turkey", he said, "already had to thank the Congress for the recovery of several lost provinces, and she must now accept the decisions of the Powers as a whole, not pick and choose between them. The agreement of the Powers is irrevocable, and the minutes remain open to receive the adhesion of Turkey." [2] As Count Mouy records, the Congress was left speechless by such blunt language, but Beaconsfield also visited the Turks with his displeasure, warned them "as their old friend and avowed defender" that their refusal would upset the whole scheme of British policy at Berlin, while Salisbury lectured them on the Porte's blindness to its own interests. [3]

How little the Turks had grasped the realities of the situation is shown by their offer to Andrássy, soon after the Congress opened—

[1] Hanotaux, *op. cit.* iv. p. 367. Corti told the Turks that he had been warned that his opposition would have meant war with Austria—Bareilles, *Rapport Secret*, p. 143. This was probably bluff.

[2] *Souvenirs et causeries*, p. 127.   [3] Bareilles, *op. cit.* pp. 139-40.

the occupation of certain districts of Hercegovina nearest to Dalmatia, but none of Bosnia, and even this only in return for a triple pledge that Montenegro should receive nothing to the south or east, that the proposed concessions to Serbia should be cut down, and that there should be no autonomy for the provinces left inside Turkey![1] Andrássy of course would not look at anything so preposterous, and the next stage was to offer the cession of Hercegovina and the occupation of Bosnia, if Andrássy would undertake to defend Turkish integrity in Europe and evacuate within a fixed period.[2] The Phanariot Caratheodory, who had had the effrontery to assure the Congress of the immemorial good relations of Turks and Bulgaria, now took the line that the Bosnian Moslems were clamouring to remain under Turkey and that the Porte was preparing the necessary reforms. Andrássy rightly brushed aside these insincerities, but he might well have quoted the recent report of a high German officer, Colonel von Thommel, who had travelled for three days in Hercegovina without seeing a single human being, dog or cat![3]

In the end the most that they could do was to hold out for some days and to make their consent dependent on a direct preliminary agreement[4] with Austria-Hungary. This latter announcement was made on 4 July, and it soon transpired that what the Turks demanded was a written declaration from Andrássy, admitting the sovereign rights of the Sultan in Bosnia and the provisional nature of the occupation.[5] Andrassy, whose general attitude and appetite was stimulated by the publication of the Cyprus Convention, at first refused to sign any such document, but did eventually comply on 13 July, under the usual form of dire secrecy, and also against the feeling of his two colleagues, Haymerle and Károlyi. On the same day, however, he signed a convention with Gorchakov—acting on the express orders of the Tsar—according to which Russia engaged herself "to raise no objection, if owing to the inconveniences due to the maintenance of Ottoman administration in the Sandjak of Novipazar, Austria-Hungary found it necessary to occupy this territory definitively, like the rest of Bosnia-Hercegovina".[6] Herr von Wertheimer is almost certainly exaggerating when he claims that there was a real danger

---

[1] *Ibid.* pp. 133-4.   [2] *Ibid.* p. 138.
[3] Busch, *op. cit.* p. 372.   [4] "Directement et préalablement."
[5] It is characteristic of the shifty methods of the Turks that they inveigled Salisbury into adding to the Protocol the words "with the assent of the Powers". After a conversation between Radowitz, Currie and Andrássy, these words were again cut out—Radowitz, *op. cit.* ii. p. 52.   [6] Wertheimer, *op. cit.* iii. p. 135.

of the whole Congress breaking down over the Turkish resistance to
Andrássy: for as the Powers were unanimous, they could unquestionably have imposed their will in the Bosnian question. But it is
true that it remained almost to the close of the Congress an element
of uncertainty and discomfort. Waddington, in a sentimental tone
which hardly rings true, reminded Caratheodory that the Congress
was "the Turkish Ferrières" (the scene of the French armistice of
1871), that they "must submit to the law of the strongest", and
that their only hope was to extract *"un profit quelconque"* from
Austria in the form of cash or reservation of rights.[1] In the words of
Count Moüy—whether conscience-struck at the time or only taught
by later experience—"the Congress assigned or refused to the Serbs
and to the Turks this or that territory with an equal and superb
indifference for the remarks and claims of either".[2]

(iii) *Batum*

The third and final crisis of the Congress came over Russia's
Asiatic frontier, and though there were dangerous moments, it was
also not without its comic relief. Shuvalov, who confided to Radowitz
that he still feared *"des cochonneries du côté de Dizzy"*,[3] was greatly
disconcerted to find that Gorchakov insisted on reserving this question for direct discussion between himself and Beaconsfield alone:
and when he complained of this to Salisbury, the latter in his turn
answered with some feeling, "But Lord Beaconsfield can't negotiate:
he has never seen a map of Asia Minor".[4] The Russian General Staff
had prepared a map of the disputed area, with two coloured lines
showing, first the frontier which they desired, and second what they
regarded as the *ne plus ultra* of concession: and this Gorchakov took
with him to his conversation with Beaconsfield. From this point
we have two delightfully divergent accounts, and again, unhappily,
no record of Beaconsfield's second solitary dinner with Bismarck.[5]
According to Shuvalov's memoirs, Bismarck next day asked the
two statesmen to sit side by side at the table, with the various maps
unrolled before them. That produced by Gorchakov only contained
a single line—that of San Stefano, which he declared to have been
accepted by Beaconsfield. The latter denied this and produced a map
with the Russian *ne plus ultra* line—the alleged explanation being

[1] Bareilles, *op. cit.* p. 166.
[2] Moüy, *Souvenirs*, p. 129.
[3] 3 July—Radowitz, *op. cit.* ii. p. 54.
[4] Hanotaux, *op. cit.* iv. p. 357.
[5] Buckle, vi. p. 332.

that Gorchakov had lent the original staff map to Beaconsfield at their talk the night before, and that the British had copied the *ne plus ultra* line from it. Gorchakov got up in great excitement, exclaiming, "There's treason: they have the map of our Staff": but there was now no escape, and it was left to Shuvalov, Salisbury and Hohenlohe between them to hammer out a compromise line.[1]

Salisbury, on the other hand, writing home to Cross, describes how he himself on the Monday had agreed with Shuvalov upon a line, according to which Russia renounced a territory of 80,000 inhabitants, and next day Beaconsfield received the map with this modification from Gorchakov himself, but that when they entered the Congress "Gorchakov produced the map marked with a totally different line, not giving half the population, and swore it was the right one. It was in vain that B. and I swore the contrary. He faced me out, the matter was referred to a committee", which "voted for a sort of compromise, and we were done. The old wretch knew that Beaconsfield was short-sighted and ignorant of detail, and took the opportunity of substituting another line."[2]

Exactly what occurred will perhaps never be known: but Colonel Wellesley's explanation seems the most probable—that the two statesmen inadvertently exchanged their most secret maps![3] It is still open to the reader to accept Mr. Buckle's view, that "as both statesmen were old and both ill . . . it is perhaps most charitable to assume a *bona fide* misunderstanding".[4]

The district whose fate was affected by this solemn farce was that of Ardahan, and had already figured in an absurd incident at a previous meeting of Congress. Salisbury had declared that in the question of Batum England "had the duty to defend a gallant Moslem nation which objects to Russian rule". Shuvalov in honeyed tones asked if the Congress might know the name of this interesting people, on which Lord Salisbury was gravely embarrassed, "because he had mislaid his notes and could not remember whom he meant". After an awkward pause the notes were found for him by Lord Odo Russell,

[1] *Ibid.* p. 358.
[2] "Shuvalov acknowledges we were done, but professes his inability to help"—10 July, *Life*, ii. p. 293.
[3] *With the Russians in Peace and War*, p. 297. Lord Rowton told Mr. Cumming (*Nineteenth Century*, July 1905, p. 90) that he reproached Shuvalov afterwards with the story of the altered map. "What followed was very curious. He looked straight into my eyes for a couple of seconds, patted me gently on the shoulder with his right hand and then turned and walked silently away. Such are the methods of Russian diplomacy."
[4] Buckle, vi. p. 339.

and it transpired that he had meant "the Lazes in Lazistan". Gorchakov having promptly denied the existence of more than 50,000 Lazes and Mehemed Ali having affirmed that there were 150,000 in Batum alone, Bismarck with biting sarcasm suggested that the British and Russian delegates should be left to discuss "*cette intéressante tribu*" between themselves. The incident is recorded with a sarcastic chuckle in the memoirs both of Radowitz and Busch:[1] and the sarcasm is fully confirmed by a perusal of Salisbury's confidential views as expressed to Layard while the controversy was at its height.

"Our negotiations here are going on well," he wrote on 25 June. "The Slav state will be put across the Balkans" [he means, not allowed to extend south of the mountains] "and the territory left to the Sultan south of them will be for all political and military purposes entirely under his control. Against the danger resulting from the capture of Kars and Batum the Convention which you have signed is a sufficient guarantee. It is possible we may compel them to give up Batum, or to convert it into a free and neutralised port. It is very difficult to make any prophecy in that regard. *On both sides Batum is little more than a flag.* It will bring little real advantage to Russia, and without a very large expenditure of money it will not enable her to threaten or injure Turkey. To Turkey the port is of the smallest possible value and can only have the sentimental advantage mentioned to you by Safvet Pasha."[2]

This view, so obviously unpalatable to Layard, fits in entirely with the Prime Minister's message to the Queen[3] and shows the British delegates to be relying upon the Balkan mountain range and the Anglo-Turkish Convention as the two main bulwarks of the new structure in Europe and Asia respectively. It proves their attitude on Batum to have rested, not on principle, but on tactics—as a means of bargaining with the Russians and of demonstrating their own firmness to their Jingo followers.

The compromise converted Batum into a free port and restored Bayazid to Turkey. With this, Beaconsfield regarded his own main function as fulfilled, and withdrew into the background to nurse his gout and other ailments. All that was really left was to clear away the mass of technical details, which, in Radowitz's view, might have overwhelmed the delegates altogether but for Bismarck's energetic interpositions, often of a really drastic kind. But, although the

---

[1] Radowitz, *op. cit.* ii. p. 56; Busch, *op. cit.* p. 377.
[2] *Layard Papers*, 25 June, Salisbury to Layard.　　[3] Quoted *supra*, p. 447.

indemnity question for a time presented serious obstacles, it was by this time pretty obvious that all the major issues were settled, and no one was prepared to risk failure and war.

(iv) *Cyprus*

One question, however, still caused a lively flutter at the Congress. It was already bad enough that the secret Protocol of 30 May, which had never been intended to see the light, should have been published *urbi et orbo* at the initial stages of the Congress: but now the no less secret Anglo-Turkish Convention was slowly leaking out, and a fresh scandal was only narrowly averted, its text being laid before Parliament on the same day as its publication in the *Daily Telegraph*.[1] Most fortunately, Lord Salisbury, just before it was too late, had informed France, the Power most likely to take offence. He notified Waddington by letter that though "very earnestly pressed by advisers of no mean authority" to take Egypt, the British Government had rejected the idea: that in its reluctance to occupy territory on the western Asiatic mainland, it had also rejected Alexandretta and that it had therefore assumed "the *provisional occupation*" of Cyprus. There was, he added, "just ground of hope that the Russians will find in a short time that the territory they have acquired is costly and unproductive: that the chances of making it a stepping-stone to further conquests is cut off, and that they will abandon it as a useless acquisition. *In that case our* raison d'être *at Cyprus will be gone and we shall retire.*"[2] Waddington, though "not concealing his emotion",[3] and even warning Beaconsfield that he might have to leave the Congress, soon yielded to the seductions of that magic word "compensation". Salisbury, seeing that the embarrassed Frenchman was both weak and wavering, warmed to his task, declared it to be impossible to "leave Carthage in the hands of the barbarians", promised a system of dual control in Egypt, disclaimed all desire of prejudicing French interests in Syria, and ended by advising France to occupy Tunis. "Do what you like," he said: "it is not our affair."[4] "If", he wrote in a similar strain to Lord Lyons,

---

[1] It is not certain how the secret leaked out. Layard suspected that the Sultan's Greek physician, Dr. Mavrogeni, had learnt it from Abdul Hamid himself and betrayed it to the Greek Legation, or that Mehmed Rushdi Pasha had told Count Zichy (*Layard Papers*, Layard to Salisbury, 26 June). But obviously it was becoming a *secret de polichinelle*.

[2] Salisbury to Waddington, 6 July—Newton, *Life of Lyons*, p. 383.

[3] "Tres émus"—*D.D.F.* no. 325, Waddington to Dufaure, 8 July.

[4] Hanotaux, *op. cit.* iv. p. 387.

"France occupied Tunis to-morrow, we should not even remonstrate. But to promise that publicly would be a little difficult . . .," and he hoped that Waddington would not put "categorical questions".[1] The sequel was an exchange of letters between London and Paris, which amounted to an endorsement of the *status quo* in Egypt and the pegging out of a French claim to Tunis. But the concrete nature of Waddington's appeal caused Salisbury certain prickings of conscience: "he makes me talk of Tunis and Carthage", so he complained to Lyons, "as if they had been my own personal property".[2]

At the last moment Layard encountered great difficulties in obtaining the firman for the surrender of the island from the Porte:[3] and they were only overcome by the following drastic telegram from Salisbury: "H.M.G. regards Porte's refusal of firman as a flagrant breach of faith and act of ingratitude for the efforts they have made to save Turkey. Firman must be issued. Until it is signed, England will take no further steps here [*i.e.* in Berlin] in favour of the Porte. Bismarck proposed to give Thessaly, Epirus and Crete to Greece, England refused to accede and the proposal has been dropped. But if firman is not issued at once, England will offer no further opposition".[3] Such language, however provoking might be the procrastinating tactics of the Porte, was scarcely calculated to strengthen their belief in a beneficent ally, bent mainly on securing their interests against a common foe.

In this connection a matchless example of pot calling kettle black is to be found in Layard's attitude to Andrássy's Bosnian policy. No wonder the Turks were deeply indignant at it, he told Salisbury—presumably not realising the extent to which his chief was backing Andrássy or the ulterior motives of this support—"no wonder, as history can scarcely furnish a more flagrant example of an unprincipled plot to rob a neighbour of his territory".[4] There was an unexpectedly sardonic vein in Salisbury which may have chuckled over this outburst when it reached him. It does not, however, follow that he would have appreciated the private comments of the Germans: for Radowitz records that Bismarck laughed on hearing the news and treated it as a pledge that Disraeli "now really wanted agreement, as he had made sure of his *pot de vin*".[5] It is well to see ourselves as others see us.

[1] *Life of Lyons*, p. 386.   [2] *Ibid.* p. 389.
[3] *Layard Papers*, 9 July, tel.: Salisbury to Layard.
[4] *Ibid.* 2 July, Layard to Salisbury.
[5] *Denkwürdigkeiten*, ii. p. 60.

As a direct bargain between Britain and Turkey, relating to a matter that lay outside the actual provisions of San Stefano, the Convention was not opposed by any member of the Congress, but it was, of course, made the subject of sarcastic comment on all sides, and completely demolished the theory of British disinterestedness and high-minded principle. Radowitz regarded it as "more a matter of vanity for Disraeli than an act of political importance": which is another way of saying that Disraeli required a bird in the hand to bring home to his Turcophil supporters after releasing so many others in the bushes of the Tiergarten!

On 13 July the Treaty was ready for signature, and the delegates separated amid a chorus of mutual congratulation.

CHAPTER XI

THE TREATY OF BERLIN AND ITS RESULTS

The one fatal blunder in the Treaty of Paris was that it provided no effectual guarantee for better government on the part of the Porte . . . Turkey has been let alone for twenty years, and the result is the disastrous collapse which provoked the war. Our Government would therefore be acting reasonably if it recognised that for the future this *laissez-faire* policy with respect to Turkey must be abandoned. It will not be enough to establish an independent Bulgaria north of the Balkans and a semi-independent Bulgaria south of them, to maintain Turkish communications with the west of the peninsula and to obviate the entire predominance of Russia in Armenia. If nothing else is done, the difficulty will inevitably recur in another twenty years or perhaps in another five or ten. Nothing can solve the Eastern question permanently except some such arrangement as will ensure good government within the Turkish dominions and at the same time . . . confine the advance of Russia within certain definite limits.

The Times, 27 June 1878

A weak and decaying Empire must of necessity sooner or later fall under the influence, if not under the military control, of a strong and adjacent Power. No diplomacy and no treaties can avert the operation of a law of nature of this kind.

The Times, 10 August 1878

A Summary and a Criticism

The settlement reached at Berlin, though comprising sixty-four clauses, falls under nine very clearly defined headings.

(1) The "Big Bulgaria" of San Stefano is partitioned into three—the new autonomous Principality of Bulgaria, with a Christian Government and a national militia (i.), the semi-autonomous province of Eastern Roumelia, with a Christian Governor-General, but "under the direct political and military authority of the Sultan" (xiii.), and those wide Slav and Greek districts in Macedonia and Thrace which are restored to unrestricted Turkish rule. In the first of these, the Prince is to be freely elected and "confirmed by the Porte, with the assent of the Powers"—no member of the reigning dynasties of the Great Powers being eligible: and before, not after, his election an assembly of notables is to meet at Tirnovo, to draft a new "*Règlement Organique*" (iii. and iv.).[1] For the first nine months, but not longer,

---

[1] A word of good omen in the Balkans, originally applied to the first modern constitution of the Roumanians, granted under the Russian occupation of 1828–34.

the provisional administration remains in the hands of a Russian Commissioner, assisted by a Turkish representative and by the consuls of the Powers, acting *ad hoc* (vi., vii.). Meanwhile the Turkish army is to leave Bulgaria and all fortresses are to be razed within a year (xi.).

(2) In Eastern Roumelia, lying between the Balkans and the Rhodope, the Sultan is free to erect fortresses and maintain troops, but may no longer use irregulars "such as Bashibazuks and Circassians" (xv.)—a phrase against the indignity of which Cartheodory had protested in vain—and the Governor may summon more Turkish troops in case of need, though the Porte must then notify the Powers (xvi.). But order is in the hands of a native *gendarmerie* and militia, with officers nominated by the Sultan (xv.). The Governor-General is appointed by the Porte, with the assent of the Powers, for a term of five years (xvii.) and an European Commission is formed to draw up the internal statute of the new province (xviii.) and to manage its finances till that statute can come into force (xix.).

Meanwhile Turkey promises a rigorous application in Crete of the *Règlement Organique* of 1868, and also the introduction of similar schemes in all provinces of European Turkey, not specifically provided for, special commissions being appointed to draw them up (xxiii.). In other words, Thrace, Macedonia, Albania, Thessaly and Epirus, though remaining integral parts of Turkey, were at last to receive the first rudiments of good government. Unhappily this provision was from the first a dead letter, and the Porte never even appointed commissions!

(3) Bosnia-Hercegovina is to be occupied and administered by Austria-Hungary, and though she does not desire to undertake the administration of the Sandjak of Novipazar—the district "stretching between Serbia and Montenegro in a south-easterly direction to beyond Mitrovica"—she reserves the right to garrison it and to control its roads (xxv.).

(4) Montenegro is declared independent and acquires Nikšić on the north, Podgorica on the south-east, and Antivari, with a small strip of coast, on the south-west. But Dulcigno is returned to Turkey, Spizza is assigned to Austria-Hungary, who acquires control of the little state's coastal trade and customs, and with whom she is to agree respecting new roads and railways. She is allowed no warships of her own, and may not receive foreign warships at Antivari (xxvi.-xxix.).

(5) Serbia also becomes independent, and acquires Mali Zvornik on

the Bosnian border, and the districts of Niš, Pirot, Leskovac to the south-east (xxxiv.-xxxvi.).

(6) Roumania becomes independent (xliii.). She restores southern Bessarabia to Russia (xlv.), and in return acquires the Delta of the Danube and the Dobrogea, with the "port" of Mangalia (xlvi.).

In the case of all three states recognition is made dependent upon the introduction of religious equality for all citizens, the absence of religious tests and the freedom of worship (xxvii., xxxv., xliv.).

(7) The international Danubian Commission is maintained, with its seat at Galatz (liii.), and a revision of its statutes is agreed upon (liv.). All the Danubian fortresses below the Iron Gates are to be razed, and the regulation of that danger-point is entrusted to Austria-Hungary (lvii.).

(8) In Asia Turkey cedes Ardahan, Kars and Batum to Russia (lviii.)—the latter as a free port *"essentiellement commerciel"* (lix.)—but recovers Bayazid (lx.). The Porte pledges itself to introduce without delay such reforms as "shall meet the needs of the Armenians and guarantee them against the Circassians and Kurds". The progress of these reforms is to be notified periodically to the Powers, who "shall supervise their application" (lxi.).

(9) Finally, Turkey pledges herself to religious liberty throughout the Empire, and equality for all citizens, both as suitors before the courts (in other words abrogating the engrained Moslem practice of rejecting the evidence of a Christian against a Moslem) and as candidates for office. The monks of Mount Athos acquire a privileged position; special reference is made to religious pilgrims of every nationality and to the diplomatic protection afforded to religious establishments in the Levant: the *status quo* at the Holy Places is to remain undisturbed, and French rights are expressly reserved (lxii.). The Treaties of 1856 and 1871 are still to be regarded as valid, where not abrogated by these new provisions.

It will at once be apparent that the settlement of Berlin corrected the worst flaws in that of San Stefano, but cannot possibly be regarded as having overthrown or abrogated it. On the contrary, its most essential provisions were upheld, even if in a modified form. Bulgaria was denied complete independence and divided into three fragments—a vassal state, an autonomous province and a residue which was only to enjoy the same self-government as other integral parts of European Turkey. But this could not obscure the fact that

the main kernel of Bulgaria was henceforth freed from Turkish
control, and certain to exercise such irresistible attraction upon its
artificial "Roumelian" neighbour that their union was now only a
question of time: while its curtailment to the west was a concession
to the claims of four other Balkan nationalities, and was perhaps
more than outweighed by the prospect, under clause 23, of Macedonia
soon forming a self-governing unit, with equal rights for all Christians. The fact that this latter provision was allowed to remain a dead
letter warped the whole settlement, and eventually led to desperate
trouble of an international character: but the blame for this obviously
falls, not upon the Congress of Berlin, but upon European statesmanship in the years that followed. The provisions for provincial reform
did not greatly differ in the two schemes, and indeed the separate
plan for Armenian reform under the Anglo-Turkish Convention
followed parallel lines.

Meanwhile the treaty recognised that the independence of Roumania, Serbia and Montenegro were accomplished facts which could
not be undone, and that each of the three was entitled to a certain
territorial compensation whose inadequacy it was left to later generations to correct. Again, Russia's right to territorial compensation was
amply recognised, both in Europe and in Asia: in the former case the
Powers meanly found a scapegoat in Roumania, while her main
demands on the Armenian frontier were satisfied, and this was but
thinly camouflaged by the formula of a free port at Batum and by
the evacuation of Bayazid in the interest of an imaginary Persian
trade route. The *status quo* was upheld on the Danube and in the
Straits, but this even San Stefano had been careful to respect. The
idea of an indemnity was dropped, but for this there were precedents
in earlier treaties. In short, it may quite fairly be argued that Berlin
differed from San Stefano only in degree, but not in principle—except,
strangely enough, on one point, namely, the fate of Bosnia: and here
the main reason for the change was not so much the approval of
Britain and the other Powers, as the existence of binding Russian
pledges to Austria-Hungary, which Ignatyev had ignored at San
Stefano, but which the Tsar could not possibly repudiate before
Europe without risking exposure.

The Treaty was an overwhelming blow to Turkey, much more
serious than the settlements of 1739, 1774, 1792, 1812, 1829, 1833 and
1856—in fact, the most disastrous peace since the Treaty of Belgrade
in 1718. The champions of the Turk had strenuously denied that he was

a Sick Man, but they now agreed with his declared enemies to carry out a whole series of amputations upon his shattered frame.

In the words of the Duke of Argyll, it was a long step towards final partition, and put the Sultan under pledge of good government, but it "postponed many questions already ripe for settlement"—postponed them in such a way as to envenom the wound and to render the surgeon's knife again inevitable. And this had been accomplished in such a manner as to "place Britain in opposition to the progress of the Christian East" and to "damage the honour of the British Crown".[1]

Meanwhile the disgust of the uncompromising Turcophils is much more easily understood than the paeans of praise with which the opportunists greeted Disraeli's *apologia*. But for a right understanding of the situation in 1878 it must be realised that in every country there were powerful groups bent upon obscuring the true issues and either minimising or exaggerating the success or failure of their respective Governments, and this had important reactions beyond the frontiers. The most notable example was the extent to which Russian public opinion was inflamed against Germany and the latter's consequent approach to Austria-Hungary, with all its momentous consequences for Europe. In summarising the main facts of this incident, we are of course anticipating the course of events, but we are at the same time enabling the reader to form a clearer estimate of British policy at Berlin, as defended by Beaconsfield himself on his return to England.

RUSSIA AND GERMANY AFTER THE TREATY

In the famous painting of the Congress from the brush of Anton von Werner, the eye is at once attracted by the massive figure of Bismarck, who offers his hand to Shuvalov, while Andrássy stands approvingly at his side. The ineffable Blowitz asked the artist whether he had meant to convey the impression that "the alliance of the three Emperors, of which the Congress is the consequence, unquestionably survives the Treaty". Much more to the point are Werner's verdict upon Shuvalov as "the real father of the Congress", and the blunt opinion of General von Winterfeld that "this painted handshake broke Shuvalov's neck".[2]

At the close of the Congress Bismarck was warmly congratulated

---

[1] Argyll, *The Eastern Question*, ii. p. 214.
[2] *Erlebnisse und Eindrücke*, pp. 228-9.

by his own officials and greeted them with the confident phrase, "Now I'll drive Europe with four horses from the box". Radowitz would seem to have been more acute than his chief, for already in his diary for 23 June he refers to Gorchakov as "trying to unload upon Bismarck the whole odium for the failure of San Stefano".

There is no doubt whatever that Bismarck was much elated and assumed that everyone would be pleased with the result, "in spite of chauvinist outcry". In August he wrote to King Ludwig of Bavaria that the danger of a breach between Austria and Russia had been averted and Germany's relations with both remained unimpaired. In retrospect he constantly upheld the view that he "had done a service to a foreign Power such as a foreign minister rarely has the chance of doing".[1] A good example of his attitude is to be found in a memorandum submitted to the Russian Government in December 1886,[2] in which he claimed to have thrown his "whole personal and political influence in Europe" into the scale on Russia's side: and it is worth noting that the Russian Foreign Minister of the day, M. de Giers, in accepting the memorandum from the German representative, frankly admitted the Chancellor's contention, adding, "I was then acting head of the Foreign Office and know how much Germany did for us".[3] It is this phrase of Bismarck, and not his earlier self-imposed nickname of the honest broker, which provides the true key both to his intentions and to his actual achievement. But that cannot alter the fact that he profoundly miscalculated the reactions of Russian opinion.

Quite a number of causes conspired in the same direction. In the first place, the Moscow chauvinists were in a dangerously disillusioned mood, angry not least of all with the Tsar himself, but still ready to accept suitable scapegoats and choosing for that office Shuvalov as the most western of Russian diplomatists. Aksakov, in a resounding speech at the Moscow Benevolent Society, spoke of "this shameful treachery to the duty and historic mission of Russia", and asked, "which kind of nihilism is worst, the open or the disguised, the coarse anarchists or the refined statesmen?"[4] The Tsar for his part had, under the strain of war and conspiracy, lost to a great extent his former clearness of judgment and critical perceptions, and in his

---

[1] This phrase occurs in his Reichstag speech of 6 Feb. 1888.

[2] *G.P.* v. nos. 1001 and 1003.

[3] "Le Prince," said Giers of his old chief, "nous a fait alors le plus grand mal: il était complètement éteint et ramolli, ses mauvais instincts seuls avaient survécu" (*ibid.*).

[4] 3 July—J. von Eckhardt, *Russia before and after the War,* p. 349.

nerve-racked state listened only too readily to the insinuations of those around him. Gorchakov had fondly hoped to crown his long career by a successful settlement of the Eastern Question: he had joined hands with Shuvalov to prevent the selection of Ignatyev as a delegate to Berlin, and had seemed at first to be playing the game of Shuvalov by going there himself. But despite his failing powers he was astute enough to saddle his colleague with the main responsibility when concessions were necessary, and his reports home effectually poisoned the mind of the Tsar. When the Congress ended, he got back to St. Petersburg well ahead of the all-too confident Shuvalov, who met with a most frigid reception from Alexander II. and found his prospects of the Chancellorship dashed away 'twixt cup and lip. The Tsar's aide-de-camp described to young Bernhard von Bülow, then an attaché at the German Embassy, the crestfallen and bedraggled appearance of Shuvalov after the fatal audience, and his own *cri de cœur*, "I have been vilely calumniated . . . by Gorchakov, that corrupted and malicious old man".[1]

In a word, it suited Gorchakov for motives of revenge and self-preservation, Ignatyev from *Schadenfreude*, and the Tsar and his innermost circle from a combination of nerves, timidity and pique, not to contradict the illusions of the Slavophils and to let them concentrate their fire upon Bismarck and Shuvalov, in uninformed good faith. There was every motive for diverting public attention from the dangerous internal situation and for nursing the injured prestige of the dynasty: and it was found convenient to exploit the Germanophobe feelings of the Heir Apparent and his wife.[2]

Shuvalov again passed through Berlin on his return to London and confided to Radowitz his difficulties with the Tsar, who had actually spoken of "the European coalition against Russia, under the leadership of Prince Bismarck". Shuvalov had defended himself valiantly against the charge of being Bismarck's dupe, and had tried to convince the Tsar that Bismarck had saved the situation for Russia on three vital issues at the Congress—the Bulgarian frontier, the fate of Sofia and the cession of Batum—any one of which might easily have become a *casus belli* but for German help. He had argued with great skill that the only essential difference between San Stefano and Berlin was the curtailment of the "Big Bulgaria"; that the former was incompatible with the survival of the Sultan at Con-

---

[1] "Ce vieillard pourri et méchant"—Bülow, *Denkwürdigkeiten*, iv. p. 452.
[2] Afterwards Alexander III. and Empress Marie (Dagmar of Denmark).

stantinople, and that as Russian policy did not aim at ejecting the Sultan (and here Alexander II. assented), a modification was inevitable.[1] On this occasion he believed himself to have made an impression upon the Tsar personally: but he was helpless to check the unbridled agitation of the Russian press, which distorted in a violently anti-German sense the whole course of events at the Congress.

Unfortunately such arguments as these were unknown to the general public, which was allowed to suppose that the whole of San Stefano could have been realised if only Bismarck had given adequate backing. The cession of Bosnia was especially resented by the Slavophils, who ascribed the initiative to Bismarck, in ignorance of the repeated and explicit pledges given by Russia to Austria-Hungary as the price of neutrality. The fact that Bismarck saved Batum for Russia when Beaconsfield was trying to reverse its cession under the Salisbury-Shuvalov Protocol, was obscured by annoyance at the veto upon fortification.

Bismarck for his part was furious at these reproaches, feeling that he had only involved himself in the Eastern Question at all out of very special consideration for the Tsar. His own attitude was admirably defined by his speech on the Pomeranian musketeer, and in his contemptuous references at the Congress to "the people down there" (*die Leute dort unten*) in the Balkans—a phrase doubtless borrowed from the famous passage in Faust. In defending himself to the Emperor William, he maintained, with some exaggeration, that "the whole Congress was only summoned by us on Russia's proposal and in Russia's interest", and with much more truth, that he sacrificed his own health to conduct it, and that "but for me it would have been shipwrecked every day".[2]

Long afterwards, in his memoirs, Bismarck denounced Gorchakov's charge of German disloyalty at the Congress as "a dishonest fiction", since Germany "had never let Russia expect anything but a benevolent neutrality".[3] History has endorsed this view. Bismarck's diplomatic correspondence proves up to the hilt that he genuinely desired Russia's friendship and fully recognised that Germany, having "nothing to gain by a conflict with Russia, must try to avoid it and not enter, unless forced to do so, upon the path leading to a breach".[4] Most instructive of all, perhaps, Bismarck and Saburov

---

[1] *G.P.* iii. no. 440, Radowitz to Bismarck, 8 Aug. 1878.
[2] *Ibid.* no. 461, Bismarck to William I., 7 Sept. 1879.
[3] *Reflections and Reminiscences*, chap. xxviii.
[4] *G.P.* iii. no. 513, 29 Jan. 1880, Bismarck to Reuss.

agreed in 1880 that the Treaty of Berlin provided a sound basis for an alliance of the Three Emperors![1] Their relations would have caused Disraeli no little astonishment.

For the next year Russo-German relations may be said to have rested on a double basis. Russian public opinion quite unjustly blamed Germany for frustrating the achievement of the full Slav programme, while official Russia in secret was far more resentful at Bismarck's double refusal—when discreetly sounded by Shuvalov in 1877 and again in May 1878—of an offensive and defensive Russo-German alliance. Now, as ever, Bismarck was firmly resolved that only the direst necessity should force him to "opt" between Russia and Austria: and even the celebrated phrase of Shuvalov, "Coalitions are your nightmare", could not shake him. He feared, and not without reason, that by committing himself thus unreservedly to Russia, he would deprive Germany of all restraint upon an aggressive Russia and would simply drive the other Powers into a counter-alliance, the full military weight of which would fall upon Germany.

Bismarck kept a close watch upon the many symptoms of Russian resentment and came gradually to the conclusion that Germany must take precautionary measures. Milyutin, for seventeen years Russian Minister of War, had certainly not desired war in 1877 and had urged the conclusion of peace early in 1878, but he now seemed to be growing more bellicose and certainly more Germanophobe, and Bismarck noted uneasily that the military strength of Russia remained on an increased level after the war, and that an undue proportion of troops was concentrated along the German frontier. Moreover, there was constant friction in the commission for the delimitation of the Bulgarian frontier, and here again the Russians accused Germany of withholding her support—a charge which Bismarck vigorously repelled. Above all, Bismarck noted the lack of directive in Russian policy, the Tsar's irritable despondency and unbalanced pessimism, and the frequent acts of terrorism which seemed to portend a Russian revolution. He felt that there could be no guarantee of a long reign for Alexander II. and still less of continuity of policy under his successor.

Under these circumstances he began cautiously to search for possible substitutes or "reinsurance": what finally roused him to action were two incidents in the summer of 1879. In June of that year Prince Gorchakov gave an interview at Baden-Baden to a French journalist, hinting at the possibility of a Franco-Russian alliance and

[1] *G.P.* iii. nos. 514-16.

explaining Bismarck's hostility towards him by his known desire that France should again be strong and take her proper place among the nations. Nothing whatever came of this feeler; indeed Wadding-ton was quite out of sympathy with Russia and held that a Russian alliance would provoke the very war which it was designed to avert. He saw the interest of France far rather in co-operation with Germany and Britain.

Far more serious, however, was the initiative taken by Tsar Alex-ander at the August manœuvres. In conversation with the German Ambassador, General von Schweinitz, he complained that in the questions still outstanding from the Congress Germany everywhere took the Austrian side against Russia: "if you want the friendship which has linked us for a hundred years to continue, you should alter this". Then referring to the reactions in the Russian press, he added, "that will finish in a very serious way", and said that he intended to write to the Emperor William about it.[1] In the letter which he duly dispatched a week later—known to history as "the box on the ear letter" [2]—these complaints lost nothing in the telling: in the polemics of the Russian and German press he affected to see "the work of our common enemies, the same who could not digest the alliance of the three Emperors. . . . I perfectly understand that you are anxious to maintain your good relations with Austria, but I do not understand the interest of Germany in sacrificing that of Russia. Is it worthy of a real statesman to let a personal quarrel weigh in the balance when it is a question of the interests of two great states, made to live on good terms, and one of whom rendered to the other in 1870 a service which, to use your own expression, you would never forget. I should not have ventured to remind you of this, but circumstances are becoming too grave for me to conceal the fears which preoccupy me and whose consequences might be disastrous for our two countries".[3]

Bismarck expressed to his own master regret that such a letter had ever been written and argued that "such language, between monarchs who are in a position to decide war and peace, is the regular forerunner of the breach, unless this is prevented by treaties".[4] William I. sent a long and cordial reply, refusing to admit that such trifles as frontier delimitation in the Balkans could disturb

[1] *Ibid.* no. 443, Schweinitz to Bismarck, 8 Aug. 1879.
[2] *Der Ohrfeigebrief.*
[3] *G.P.* iii. no. 446, 15 August, Alexander II. to William II.
[4] *Ibid.* nos. 455 (31 Aug.), 458 (5 Sept.), 461 (7 Sept.).

their traditional friendship, and assuring his nephew that Bismarck's attitude towards Russia had been entirely misrepresented. The Tsar demonstrated his nervous and unbalanced state by inviting his uncle to meet him at Alexandrovo, denying the interpretations placed upon his letter, begging that it should be regarded as "not written", and disclaiming all idea of aggressive designs upon Germany.[1] But by this time Bismarck's mind was made up: he presented his master with a series of masterly statements of policy[2] and never rested until by serried argument and scarcely veiled threat of resignation he had won a reluctant assent to discussions with Andrássy for an Austro-German defensive alliance. His arguments culminated in the audacious phrase: "If Tsar Alexander can be brought to threaten war on account of some Bulgarian bagatelles, not only to the official ambassador but in an autograph letter to Your Majesty, he will just as readily, and even more so, wage such a war while continuing his assurances of personal friendship."[3]

For a brief moment, before he stood irrevocably committed to Andrássy, he sounded the British Government as to its attitude in the event of a breach between Germany and Russia: and Beaconsfield, whom Münster visited at Hughenden, went so far as to declare that "the most natural allies for England are Germany and Austria", that he would welcome a German alliance, and that Britain would "keep France quiet, you may depend on us".[4] But this was not enough for Bismarck, who had no intention of breaking with Russia if he could possibly help it, and least of all in order to pull chestnuts out of the fire for Britain in the Eastern Question. The enthusiasm with which Salisbury endorsed his chief's attitude and followed up a private talk with Münster by a public reference to the possibility of alliance as "good tidings of great joy",[5] annoyed rather than encouraged Bismarck, and the overture was not pursued further. Bismarck realised that Britain was bound to be negative and might be too dearly bought, and henceforth concentrated on the negotiations with Vienna.

The details of these negotiations lie altogether outside the scope of this book: but it was important to show that the Dual Alliance was the direct outcome of the Russo-German misunderstanding after

---

[1] In 1886 Giers represented the letter as "merely the expression of a momentary pique"—*G.P.* v. no. 1003.
[2] *G.P.* iii. nos. 455 (31 Aug.), 458 (5 Sept.) and 461 (7 Sept.).
[3] *Ibid.* no. 455.   [4] *Ibid.* v. no. 712, 27 Sept. 1879.
[5] Speech at Manchester, 17 Oct.

the Congress, which in its turn was materially influenced by the manner in which British opinion greeted the settlement as a notable discomfiture of Russia.

Count Shuvalov, the other scapegoat, of whom Bismarck himself had said that he had "known how to stand up to the whole Congress", was allowed to return to his London post, but rapidly fell into disfavour. Recalled in November 1879, he was never given another opportunity of serving the sovereign whom his loyalty and talent had saved from disaster—a victim of the vindictive Chancellor and the fickle Tsar. He afterwards became the *bête noire* of Alexander III., who disliked his easy manners and talkative disposition, and as Giers once said, "the distrust of *ce bon Empereur* is difficult to overcome".[1] Shuvalov died in 1889, deeply wounded at his unmerited ostracism.

AUSTRIA-HUNGARY AND GERMANY

It would obviously have been more logical if Russian opinion had concentrated its anger against Vienna rather than Berlin, for it was specially galling to see Austria-Hungary occupy two Turkish provinces after a comfortable neutrality, while Russia herself was prevented from enjoying the full fruits of her costly victory. It was all the more galling, because it meant placing a million and a half Slavs under a predominantly non-Slavonic rule. The Russian Government, perhaps wisely in its generation, but certainly not wisely for posterity, kept silent as to its extremely concrete commitments in the Bosnian question.

Andrássy's position was distinctly delicate: for though his policy enjoyed the full approval of the Crown—which to the very end retained its control of foreign affairs—he was confronted by a hostile majority in both the Austrian and Hungarian Parliaments and therefore by opposition—somewhat toned down but still really serious—in the two Delegations. This was due to the fact that in Austria the German Liberals, whose predominance in the Reichsrat was as yet rendered absolute by Czech abstention, and in Hungary all the Magyar parties, Liberal and Kossuthist alike (and the other nationalities were at this time unrepresented at Budapest), were almost equally averse to the inclusion of more Slavs inside the Dual Monarchy. Andrássy had considerable difficulty in convincing Koloman Tisza, the Chauvinistic and all-powerful Hungarian Premier,

[1] *G.P.* v. no. 1003, 24 Dec. 1886.

that the sole alternative to Austro-Hungarian occupation was an eventual partition of the two provinces between Serbia and Montenegro, which in its turn would inevitably stimulate the national movement among the Southern Slavs of the Monarchy. The extreme Turcophils in Hungary organised public meetings against the occupation, and in the following November a motion for the impeachment of the Cabinet obtained as many as ninety-five votes. Hence it is not so surprising as it doubtless seemed at the time to foreign opinion, that Andrássy, on his return from Berlin, was greeted not with flags and banners, but with what he himself called "a sort of cats' music".

He thus had good grounds for wishing to avoid military coercion against the Turks, or indeed any action which might savour too strongly of "conquest": yet in the end he found it necessary to mobilise very considerable forces, and two months elapsed before the desperate armed resistance of the Bosnians could be overpowered. The defence of his policy before Hungarian public opinion was not rendered more easy by the army chiefs selecting, against his wishes, two Slav Generals, Filipović and Jovanović, for the command of the invading armies. This in turn greatly excited Croat opinion, which aspired to the union of the two provinces with Croatia-Slavonia, in right of medieval claims upon Bosnia, vested in the Croatian Crown (long since swallowed up in the Hungarian). It was this hostility at home, loudly voiced in the press of Vienna and Budapest and afterwards fanned by the unexpected delays and expenses of the campaign, that explains Andrássy's capital blunder in contenting himself with an ill-defined provisional occupation, instead of proclaiming annexation outright. He might just as well have been hanged for a sheep as for a lamb: the British attitude affords proof that a majority of the Powers would have approved annexation, and it is doubtful whether even Russia would have protested. No doubt one reason which held him back was the fear lest complete annexation might give Russia an unanswerable excuse for taking some similar action farther east.

In any case, Andrássy, to the very end of the international crisis and at the Delegations in the following autumn and spring, adhered resolutely to the assertion that the occupation of Bosnia had never been the aim of his policy, and that he had been reluctantly forced to it by the march of events. This was, to say the least, disingenuous: for though undoubtedly true in the months preceding the Andrássy Note of December 1875, it had certainly ceased to be true ever since

Reichstadt. Throughout the remainder of the crisis his delays had been tactical and directed very reasonably to the aim of acquiring the two provinces by diplomacy, while leaving Russia to wage an exhausting war.

Andrássy's innermost aims are revealed in a private letter to the Duke of Würtemberg, a General in the Austrian service, whose task it was to occupy the Sandjak of Novipazar. Here he explains why he could not allow Serbia and Montenegro to acquire a common frontier. "Bosnia would have become a blind alley instead of a position which should lead to political and material influence in the East. We should have been shut in by hostile neighbours, and our trade paralysed, for every railway and road which should carry our trade to the sea would have been dependent on the goodwill of Serbia and Montenegro. . . . Turkey, cut off from us, could hardly have maintained her position in Albania, most of which would naturally have fallen to Montenegro. . . . Finally, unforeseen events or the natural course of things might lead to a union of the Principalities under one dynasty, and so to the creation of a great Slav state which would be bound to show expansive tendencies towards Bosnia and Dalmatia."[1]

To the German Austrian leader, Ernst von Plener, Andrássy expressed himself privately as follows: "If we get Bosnia, that is quite good, but that is not the final aim of our Eastern policy. . . . The acquisition of Bosnia is a police measure which we require in order to master frontier risings; but our aim is to bring the western half of the Balkan Peninsula—I do not wish to conquer it—permanently under our influence."[2] It is safe to assume that in the question of Salonica he took the same opportunist attitude as in that of Bosnia: he would not precipitate events or try to seize it, but no one else must have it if the Turks could no longer hold it. By garrisoning Novipazar he sought to keep open his line of advance to the Aegean; but a generation later the General Staff reached the conclusion that the only strategic line lay through the heart of Serbia, and for this reason, and to appease Italy, his successor Aehrenthal balanced the annexation of Bosnia by the evacuation of the Sandjak.

Looking back with the perspective of fifty years and the final lessons of the World War, it is easy enough to see that Andrássy's action in 1878 placed the Habsburg Monarchy in conflict with

[1] Wertheimer, *op. cit.* iii. pp. 275-6.
[2] Quoted by Plener in the Herrenhaus, 27 June 1913: see also *Oesterr. Rundschau*, 7 Aug. 1913.

Southern Slav aspirations, and especially with the sentiment of
Serbia after her unsuccessful fight for union with Bosnia. But
Andrássy himself was one of the makers of the settlement between
Hungary and Croatia in 1868, and despite certain grave defects
in this he had good grounds for hoping that Budapest and Zagreb
might combine against both Vienna and Belgrade, and that the
eventual centre of gravity for all the Southern Slavs might be established not merely inside the Dual Monarchy, but within the territory
of the Hungarian Crown.

Above all, however, Andrássy calculated upon bringing Serbia herself within the sphere of the Monarchy, thanks to the more than
maladroit attitude of Russia towards the smaller Balkan Powers.
The disillusioned Ristić had found himself at Berlin between two
fires. He was warned off Bosnia by Austria-Hungary and found that
Russia stood committed in that question and could not help him
even if she wished to do so: while Russia took the side of Bulgaria in
the dispute about Pirot and was for a time even disposed to deprive
Serbia of Niš, though Prince Milan made it clear that he and his
army would resist even the Russians in any attempt to eject them.
Both Gorchakov and Shuvalov advised Ristić to come to terms with
Vienna, and one of the most illogical features of Russian policy
during the eighties was the open resentment shown at St. Petersburg
towards Serbia for taking Russia's proffered advice. Prince Milan,
it is true, lacked all balance or restraint and plunged from his former
Russophilism into the opposite extreme of abject vassalage to
Vienna, concluding a secret treaty of alliance in 1881, based on commercial and railway concessions, and hoping that Austrian expansion
towards Salonica would bring him some access of territory in northern Macedonia. As interpreted by his bosom friend, Vladan Gjorgjević, the aim of Milan and the Austrophil party was to consolidate
Serbia during the interval before the next European complication,
and to win the friendship of Austria-Hungary, in the calculation that
if events should one day force her to evacuate Bosnia, she would
prefer to do so in favour of a faithful friend and ally, whereas if she
should win over the population by tactful administration on national
lines, a natural evolution would lead his dynasty to accept the same
sort of status in the Dual Monarchy as the Wittelsbach enjoyed in
Germany, and thus Jugoslav unity and probably a wider Balkan
federation might be achieved under the auspices of the Habsburgs.
Unfortunately Milan lacked the qualities of a stable ruler, inculcated

his own fatal habits in his only son and heir, and utterly alienated his own subjects without in any way winning the confidence of Vienna. The downfall of his dynasty in 1903 was the direct outcome of the new policy inaugurated in Berlin. Austria-Hungary on her side introduced an ordered administration in the two provinces and did much to promote their material welfare; but she never won the hearts of any section of the population, she failed to solve the land question, she established good secondary schools but utterly neglected primary education, she encouraged the religious cleavage between Orthodox, Moslem and Catholic (on the lines of her ancient motto, 'Divide et Impera') and she delayed the grant of political institutions till it was too late. Thus the desire for national unity continued to smoulder beneath the ashes, alike in Bosnia-Hercegovina, in Serbia and Montenegro and in Croatia-Dalmatia: and when the Turkish Revolution of 1908 brought the Bosnian question once more into the forefront of European politics, the flames shot forth and were not extinguished until they had produced the incident that precipitated the greatest war in history.[1]

Andrássy's policy in the period following the Congress was to hold Russia at arm's length and above all to prevent her from absorbing either Turkey or Bulgaria, while at the same time extending Austrian influence in the western half of the Peninsula and keeping open the road to the Aegean, and to consolidate these aims by a defensive alliance with Germany, as a wheel within the larger wheel of the Three Emperors' League, or if need be, as a substitute for it. *"Now the Monarchy's road to the East is free"*—so Andrássy telegraphed to the Emperor Francis Joseph[2] on the conclusion of the German alliance: and in this phrase he reveals his ulterior motive.

FRENCH POLICY AT BERLIN

The rôle of France had been in keeping with the effaced attitude which she had assumed in Europe ever since 1871, and with the essentially mediocre and cautious outlook of M. Waddington himself. His own definition—*un rôle non pas inactif mais réservé*[3]—exactly defined it: for he was always looking to see what other Powers would

---

[1] See my Raleigh Lecture (British Academy, 1931), *The Rôle of Bosnia in International Politics,* and also a series of my articles in *Le Monde Slave,* entitled "Les Relations de la Serbie et de l'Autriche-Hongrie".

[2] Quoted by Count Aehrenthal in the Crown Council of 14 Sept. 1909—*Öesterreich-Ungarns Aussenpolitik,* ii. no. 1735.

[3] *D.D.F.* no. 317, 18 June, Waddington to Dufaure.

do, before acting himself. He had but little choice, for the internal crisis beginning with the "Seize Mai" and leading up to the fall of Broglie after the October elections, still absorbed French opinion and kept foreign questions in the background.

The net result, however, was by no means unsatisfactory. Though the projected meeting of those strange protagonists, Bismarck and Gambetta, failed to materialise at the last moment, there was now no doubt whatever about Bismarck's desire to conciliate France, and he was distinctly mollified by the substitution of Waddington and St. Vallier for Decazes and Gontaut-Biron, the last of whom he rightly suspected of intrigues with his own enemy, the Empress Augusta. The aggrieved Decazes felt the bitter irony in a situation in which Conservative Europe positively preferred to deal with the French Radicals rather than with him and his Conservatives.[1] Bismarck, already somewhat reassured by the change on the Papal throne and the prospect of liquidating the "Kulturkampf", was most anxious to establish working relations with France, where Gambetta was now the real power since Macmahon's failure. "Our foreign policy", Waddington wrote privately to Gladstone, "delivered from all clerical influence, will be very prudent, quiet and steady: our influence will be exerted everywhere in favour of peace. We are quite aware that in order to contract alliances, we must begin by inspiring confidence by an honest, truthful and disinterested policy." [2]

Paris on its side exploited the situation not unskilfully, to secure the elimination of Egypt, Syria and Tunis as subjects of discussion at the Congress, all the other Powers accepting this with surprising readiness. This veiled veto was faithfully observed to the very end, and France viewed with equanimity the various provisions for the fate of the Near East, Waddington—partly as a Hellenist in private life, famed for his antiquarian and numismatic interests—reserving to himself the rôle of championing the Greeks, all the more so when Salisbury's slackening interest in the Greek cause seemed to offer special opportunities for Codlin as against Short. But the Cyprus Convention stung the French, even the Radical Gambetta, to envy, and greatly whetted their appetite for North Africa. After Salisbury's all too successful attempt to whet it still further, it was only a matter of time for France to aspire to Tunis and thus to console herself for Britain's increasing control over Egypt.

[1] Hanotaux, *Hist. de la France contemp.* iv. p. 316.
[2] *Gladstone Papers*, 3 Jan. 1878.

The Congress, then, ended one phase in French policy—that of nervous effacement after 1870—and ushered in that new phase of active colonial enterprise which was to achieve such remarkable results during the next half-century and which no one was to encourage more strenuously than Bismarck, for obvious reasons of his own.

In passing, it is not without profit for us to note certain French reactions to British policy in the Near East. St. Vallier, whose situation in Berlin continued to be very strong, wrote a letter later to Waddington: "I am far from edified at the latest exuberant manifestations of English policy at Constantinople. I don't like the diplomacy *à la trompette* which Beaconsfield practises. England with the Turk is like a surgeon who, to help someone who has had both legs broken by a wicked neighbour, should break his arms also. 'Count on me, I am coming to your aid: he is threatening you in Armenia, I'll take charge of Syria. He would like to relieve you of your capital, I'll take it from you before him'—that is since the Congress the rôle of British diplomacy in the East." [1]

ITALY AT THE CONGRESS

The Congress marked Italy's first real appearance on equal terms as one of the Great Powers, and she was necessarily still feeling her way, without much active support from any quarter. Her internal policy was still dominated by the question of the Church, and the return visits paid by the Emperors Francis Joseph and William to the King of United Italy had been almost ostentatiously paid at Venice and Milan, not in the Eternal City, while the choice of a General who had helped Garibaldi in arms against the Papal States, as Italian Ambassador to France, evoked attacks from the French Clericals and embarrassed apologies from Decazes—for once in his life on the same side as Gambetta.

In the autumn of 1877 Crispi, the most notable member of the Depretis Cabinet, was sent on a round of visits to test European opinion. From Bismarck he received the blunt, if tentative, advice to look towards Albania rather than Africa. Beaconsfield he failed to see, but from Derby he received the warning that Italy must not

---

[1] 14 Nov. 1879—*F.D.D.* ii. no. 477. Of Layard he writes: "Mauvais esprit, haineux et jaloux, capacité surfaite, le tout dirigé par une vanité sans limites: je le regarde comme un agent dangereux pour toute l'Europe, à commencer par son gouvernement, à qui il se fait une gloire de ne jamais obéir".

hope for compensation in the Eastern question. In Vienna he was introduced to realities by his own very able ambassador, General Robilant, who assured him that "if we want to maintain friendly relations with Austria-Hungary, it is absolutely necessary to make no allusion of any kind to hopes of annexation". Next day the official *Fremdenblatt* wrote that if Austria-Hungary should be forced by the march of events to annex Turkish territory, "that would not be a sufficient motive for yielding to Italy our principal port and Italian Tirol. Italy can give up these ideas for ever." [1]

Italy's position was still further weakened by the death of Victor Emmanuel and Pius IX. within a week of each other, in February 1878. The new King Humbert had to feel his way, both at home and abroad, all the more so that Leo XIII. showed a marked disposition to end the Kulturkampf by a compromise with Bismarck. While the question of a Congress was under discussion, both the King and the Premier Cairoli strongly urged Count Luigi Corti, then Ambassador at the Porte, to become Foreign Minister and represent Italy at Berlin. His reluctance to accept is shown by his first reaction: he would sooner, he said, throw himself into the Tiber than take over the direction of foreign affairs at such a moment. He had disagreed with the policy of the previous two years, which had been leading in the direction of a conflict with Austria-Hungary, and he only took office on the distinct understanding that the anti-Austrian tendency should be renounced, and after expressing the view that there was no danger for Italy in an Austrian occupation of Bosnia.

Corti went to Berlin with instructions to promote peace, to work for occupation—as provisional as possible—rather than annexation, and if the latter could not be prevented, to attempt to secure some compensation.[2] He was received by Bismarck with great reserve and was assured by Andrássy—with an obvious insincerity which contained a veiled menace—that occupation rather than annexation had been resolved upon, "only out of consideration for Italy".[3] His position was increasingly awkward, for public opinion in Italy became extremely excited, the irredentists began to demonstrate, the Cabinet was weak and the King nervous, and both sent messages drawing an altogether futile comparison between Austria's occupation of Bosnia and Russia's occupation of Bulgaria. Corti warned

[1] Chiala, *Dal* 1856 *al* 1892, i. p. 292.
[2] E. Conte Corti, "Bismarck und Italien am Berliner Kongress", *Hist. Viertel. jahrschrift*, xxiii. p. 459.
[3] *Ibid*. p. 463.

Cairoli that "if Italy refused her consent, she might have had to take on herself the responsibility for a European conflict", and assured the War Minister, General Bruzzi—who was only too conscious of Italy's isolation and impotence—that the Powers "would simply have overridden Italy's protest".[1]

The decisions of the Congress accentuated still further the irredentist campaign, and the Cairoli Cabinet did not dare to prohibit the demonstrations, as Corti desired. Bismarck gave vent to his annoyance and officially informed Rome that such incidents "could only shake our confidence in the political development and the future of Italy". But this, and his praise of Corti as "a true statesman and ardent patriot", had the very opposite effect from that intended. The attacks upon Corti redoubled, and on 20 October he resigned office.

The interest of the whole incident lies in two directions. It served to stimulate the current of opinion now setting towards Tunis, and this was during the next few years skilfully exploited by Bismarck to destroy the reviving friendship of Italy and France. But it is also the germ of that policy of Adriatic and Balkan compensation which Italy eventually induced Austria-Hungary to accept as a bribe for her renewal of the Triple Alliance—an even more fatal blunder on the part of Aehrenthal than his parallel policy towards Serbia.

THE BALKAN STATES AND THE CONGRESS

It still remains to summarise the rôle of the Near Eastern states at Berlin. At the Congress of Vienna the Eastern Question had been relegated to the background, and in any case the Christian nationalities were as yet too much under Turkish control to secure an independent hearing from statesmen indifferent to, or immune from, the principle of nationality. Forty years later, at the Congress of Paris, these nationalities were already reborn and forcing themselves upon the attention of Europe, but all decisions were kept exclusively in the hands of the Concert. In 1878 the Balkan nations could no longer be ignored, and though it was not till 1919 that they were admitted on at least nominally equal terms to an international conference, their claims formed a main subject of discussion and their partial admission was under consideration.

---

[1] *Ibid.* p. 466, 30 June and 7 July.

(i) *Greece*

Greece had the best chance of a hearing, not merely because she enjoyed full independence, but above all because the Greeks were regarded in many quarters as a convenient offset to the Slavs. When the Bosnian insurrections first broke out, Greek sentiment had been definitely neutral and opposed to any Balkan adventure: the secret Serbo-Greek alliance of 1867 was known to few and could no longer be regarded as valid. The Salonica murders, however, in May 1876, stirred Athens, and there was a certain agitation for armaments. Greece was refused admittance to the Conference of Constantinople and showed a natural nervousness at the frontiers proposed by Ignatyev for the new Bulgaria. But while Saburov, the Russian Minister at Athens, was engaged in a trial of strength with his British colleague Wyndham, Ignatyev definitely wooed Greece and defended the Greeks of Macedonia. Both he and Salisbury returned home via Athens, in order to study the situation at first hand: and the latter was pointedly asked by the Greek Foreign Minister whether Britain still upheld Turkish integrity and would in case of war prevent the Greeks from recovering their liberty.

The outbreak of war convinced Greece of the need for increased vigilance, if the final settlement was not to be unduly weighted in favour of the Slavs: and the result was the formation of a National Government under the veteran hero Kanaris, with Tricoupis, Koumondouros and Deligeorges all together in the Cabinet. In June this Government asked the advice of the London Cabinet, but Lord Derby refused all support of Greek territorial claims and merely promised to use his influence after the war in favour of "administrative reforms and advantages" for the Greek provinces of Turkey. This led the Greeks to turn more towards Russia and to continue military preparations. The Russian disasters before Plevna deterred them from action, but they also encouraged the Porte to take a high hand at Athens: and on 4 September Britain took the Turkish side and demanded clear assurances that the Greeks would not attack Turkey. Naturally enough, this was regarded by Athens as an unfriendly act, and led to further Russo-Greek negotiations, but these hung fire, because Gorchakov would not commit himself to any concessions beyond Thessaly and Epirus.

As the fortunes of war turned against Turkey, Greek opinion grew more bellicose and strained at the leash, despite the British Minister's

warnings against intervention. King George credited Disraeli with
the resolve to occupy the Piraeus, and Layard's correspondence with
his chiefs and with his colleague Wyndham reveal him as constantly
urging this Palmerstonian method of pressure. The re-entry of Serbia
caused fresh excitement in Athens: and Greece was on the very point
of war when the Sultan sued the Tsar for peace. A fresh *démarche* of
Wyndham against intervention (22 January 1878) brought down
the National Government, and ten days later Greek troops and
irregulars crossed the Thessalian frontier. This led to direct intervention by the Powers, and Greece, entirely isolated, had to withdraw
her troops, in order to avert a naval blockade. She was in obvious
danger of falling between two stools—her friends in Europe were tied
to the maintenance of the Turks in Stamboul and Thrace, while
Turkey's chief enemy was hostile to the "Great Idea" in Byzantium
and was committing herself to a rival "Big Bulgaria".

At this moment Lord Derby made a direct overture to Mr. Gen-
nadius, hinting at a common basis against the Slav danger, and Greece,
acting on British advice, put forward a formal request for admission
to the future Congress, her avowed aim being the emancipation of
the enslaved Hellenes. This application was formally endorsed by
Britain on 9 March and supported by France and Italy: but Germany
and Austria-Hungary objected to the principle of inviting the smaller
Powers to Berlin. Meanwhile the Athens Government, its hands tied
by its friends, saw itself forced to take measures against the irregular
Greek bands in Thessaly, and in return Layard extracted from the
Porte a pledge not to send the Turkish fleet against Greece. It was
becoming abundantly obvious that Britain counted upon Greece as
a useful auxiliary in the event of war with Russia, and was playing
the card of Greek against Slav in the Balkan Peninsula—a card which
the unwarrantable exaggerations of San Stefano fully entitled her to
play.

In respect of Greece the two British parties were at least agreed in
theory: and Gladstone, in a famous article, pointed out—as a leading
factor in the decisions of which he wrote—that in surrendering the
Ionian Islands in 1862 Palmerston, Russell and his colleagues had
been unanimous in desiring "even at that late period, to retrieve
the error committed at the inception of the Hellenic State, by the
deplorable restriction of its territory"—in other words, to assign
Thessaly and Epirus to Greece. Britain had not, however, pressed
this, because it still hoped for Turkish reform: but, he added, "the

position is now wholly different. Turkey has herself trodden under foot those promises, bought from her with such an effusion of western blood and treasure."[1]

The tendency to favour Greek against Slav was accentuated after Salisbury's transfer to the Foreign Office, and there arose a certain competition between Britain and France as the chief champion of the Greek cause. Salisbury quite definitely recommended the Porte to make territorial concessions to Greece, and committed himself to a new frontier following the rivers Kalamas and Peneus—in other words, giving to Greece a considerable portion, but not all, of Thessaly and Epirus. Layard was set the unpromising, and to him most uncongenial, task of effecting a Turco-Greek alliance!—and it is hard to say whether Turkish obstinacy or Greek appetite was the greater obstacle. Greece demanded as a minimum the whole of Epirus and Thessaly, with Crete and Samos.

The following extract from one of Salisbury's dispatches to Layard on the eve of the Congress sums up very lucidly the British stand-point in the Greek question.

"Events have proved that the Greek Kingdom possesses very con-siderable power of exciting to revolt the Greek subjects of the Porte, and that this power is exercised with especial force in the southern part of Thessaly. The King is well disposed, but he has no power of restraining his subjects, until he can show them that a policy of conciliation has been as valuable to them as a policy of provocation. *If Turkey would give Greece something substantial* and Greece would be brought to accept it of her own free will, the settlement would suffice for half a century. If nothing is given, I cannot doubt that Greece will continue agitating when the Congress is over and fleets and armies have retired: and the constitution of Turkey is not suffi-ciently robust to resist many more shocks of this description. It is this consideration which has led me to suggest to you the line of the Kalamas and Peneus. It is undoubtedly asking the Turks to give up a good deal, and I should not urge it if the Greeks were found to be impracticable: but if their consent can be obtained, it is well worth the Turks' while to buy respite from agitation for a long period at this price. I am very much afraid that the Congress will be too im-patient to examine the matter carefully, and that either it will adopt some summary settlement which must be disadvantageous for the Turk, or Germany and Russia will designedly leave the matter open

[1] "The Hellenic Factor in the Eastern Question", *Contemp. Rev.*, Dec. 1876.

to furnish material for a future conflict. It is therefore a matter of some importance that it should be settled outside Congress if possible."[1]

At the Congress, then, Salisbury almost at once proposed the full admission of Greece, arguing that as the Slavs had Russia as their protector, the Hellenes needed the presence of their motherland. To this Gorchakov retorted not unskilfully that Russia drew no distinction between the various Christian populations of the East. As however Germany and Austria-Hungary shared Russia's coolness towards Greece's claim, Salisbury could not press his proposal too far, and Waddington suggested as a half-way house that Greece should be represented whenever the question of the provinces bordering on the Greek Kingdom—a phrase of some obscurity—came under discussion. Bismarck and Gorchakov both accepted the French scheme, which was formally adopted by the Congress. But Greece, in her desire for the whole, missed the part: she delayed appointing her delegates, and Bismarck followed the tactics of not inviting them until he had been formally notified. Thus it was not till 29 June that Delyannis and Rhangabe were able to state their case before the Congress: and they were not invited to appear again. On 5 July the Greek question was discussed without them, and though much goodwill was shown, the results were barren enough. Waddington, in the name of the Powers, invited Turkey to agree with Greece upon a rectification of frontier and openly put forward the Peneus-Kalamas line first indicated by Salisbury: but the Cretan insurrection was ignored, and all that the great Greek island was to receive was a screwing-up of the very inadequate *Règlement Organique* of 1868. Beaconsfield's speech in support of Waddington was a final squib against Russia rather than an effective demonstration in favour of Greece.

These ideas were finally embodied in Articles 23 and 24 of the Treaty, the latter reserving the right of offering mediation between Turkey and Greece. The next three years were to be an impromptu upon this note.

Much as the Greeks of the kingdom were exercised by the general fate of the Hellenes still under Turkish rule, it was natural enough that they should concentrate their efforts upon Thessaly and Epirus, which lay within their more immediate reach, and whose partial redemption was at last achieved by 1881. To the fate of Crete they

[1] *Layard Papers*, Salisbury to Layard, 30 May 1878.

had to resign themselves, in the knowledge that time was on their side. That the fate of Cyprus caused so much less emotion in Greece at the time may be ascribed to the prevalent assumption that that island had long been virtually lost to Hellenism, and that British rule in Corfu and its sister isles offered a seductive precedent and might be terminated one day in the same manner.

(ii) *Serbia*

The situation of Serbia at Berlin was very peculiar. The Tsar, who felt, not altogether without reason, that Serbian nationalism had an uncomfortably revolutionary tinge, had turned noticeably away from Serbia after her failure to hold the Turks at bay, had openly criticised her in his famous Moscow speech, and in the summer of 1877 had treated with blunt disfavour Prince Milan's offer to resume hostilities. When at last Serbia did actually declare war, it was not so much because of Russian encouragement as from a desperate fear of being overlooked at the final apportionment of the spoils. Andrássy's very explicit warnings forced the Serbs to refrain from operations in Bosnia and to concentrate upon Niš, which fell on 10 January. That they were wise to hold a gage in their hands, was soon shown by the inconsiderate attitude of Russia at the negotiations for an armistice and again at San Stefano. Ignatyev even offered Vidin to Roumania as compensation for the loss of Bessarabia,[1] and while Bulgaria was to obtain frontiers far beyond her wildest dreams and Montenegro was to be almost doubled, Serbia was to obtain little more than the merest rectification. The Serbian General Lješanin was sent to the Grand Duke's headquarters, but found next to no support: Bulgaria almost monopolised attention and was now to be the chief instrument of Russian influence in the Peninsula.

There was great bitterness and disillusionment in Belgrade, and Prince Milan turned more and more towards Vienna, recognising that Bosnia was bound to fall to Austria and hoping to secure her backing in the direction of Pirot and even Skoplje, in return for far-reaching economic and railway concessions. It is likely enough, though not certain, that the Serbs were allowed to know how much territory Ignatyev, during his final mission to Vienna, had been prepared to concede to Austria-Hungary at Serbia's expense. In any case, on the eve of the Congress Ristić, in the name of Prince Milan, from whom he brought an autograph letter, made a direct appeal

[1] Austrian Archives, Wrede to Andrássy, 4 and 5 Feb. 1878.

for help to Andrássy at a personal interview in Vienna. Andrássy was bluntly genial, made it clear that public opinion in the Dual Monarchy was hostile to the Serbs, and, though expressing his readiness to help, added that he saw no real reason for it, since Serbia had never followed his advice in the past.[1] He indicated Niš and Pirot, but definitely refused Novipazar, and he left Ristić to discuss commercial matters with the Balkan experts of the Ballplatz, Kállay and Schwegel. The latter proposed a permanent railway commission on administration and tariffs, in which Austria-Hungary would obviously have more to say than the three others—Serbia, Bulgaria and Turkey—combined.[2]

Ristić reached Berlin a few days before the Congress opened, and sounded the various Governments. There never was any chance of Serbia being admitted. He reported England as disapproving, but ready to tolerate Serbia, and not merely the French, but even the Russian delegates as warning him that his sole chance was "to come to terms with Austria-Hungary on all points".[3] This indeed was the attitude equally of Gorchakov and of Shuvalov, and the latter especially was bent upon doing nothing to offend Vienna, to whom Russia had already promised Bosnia. Thus even apart from Bosnia, which could not be discussed at all, the unhappy Ristić found himself between two fires—an Austrian veto upon Novipazar and a Russian claim upon Pirot for Bulgaria. He did his best to convince Shuvalov that a great day of reckoning would come between Russia and Austria, and that at that moment Serbia would be of far more value than Bulgaria.[4] Shuvalov appears to have been convinced that Austria-Hungary would not be able to retain Bosnia for very long, and this of course coincided with the all too optimistic view prevalent among the Serbs. Jomini expressed the view of official Petersburg when he told Ristić, "Your consolation is that in fifteen years at the most the situation will be such that Russia will have to settle accounts with Austria".[5]

Britain's attitude to Serbia throughout the Eastern crisis was frankly hostile and showed no perception of her difficulties, her rights or her future. Disraeli was at one time content that Turkey should reimpose her garrisons, and Salisbury as late as the fall of

---

[1] Ristić, *Diplomatska Istorija Srbije*, ii. p. 165.
[2] *Ibid.* p. 179.   [3] Grujić, *Zapisi*, p. 335.
[4] Slobodan Jovanović, *Vlada Milana, 1868–78*, p. 429.
[5] Vladan Gjorgjević, "La Serbie au Congrès de Berlin," *Revue d'Hist. Diplom.* 1891, p. 522; Ristić, *Diplomatska Istorija Srbije*, ii. p. 251.

Plevna advised the Austrians to "go into Serbia".[1] All the leading British statesmen, save Gladstone, were indifferent to the Southern Slav movement and to Bosnia's affinity to Serbia: and the British Government encouraged Austria-Hungary to occupy the two provinces, with the deliberate motive of permanently embroiling her with Russia. The hostility of British official circles towards Serbia was in some small degree compensated by the rôle of individual Britons, such as Humphrey Sandwith, Arthur Evans, Pauline Irby, Frank Mackenzie of Gairloch, and of course above all others, Gladstone himself, whose name became and has ever since remained a household word, not among the Serbs alone, but throughout the Balkan Peninsula.

For Serbia the net result of the Congress was to force her willy nilly into the orbit of Austria-Hungary, and the secret alliance of 1881 followed quite logically from her frank abandonment by Russia. That Prince Milan was utterly lacking in principles or balance and sank voluntarily to be a mere vassal of the Habsburgs, making offers such as caused grave embarrassment and doubt even to the court of Vienna itself, served greatly to aggravate the situation and to compromise the Austrophil current, which, with a little more statesmanship, might eventually have prevailed.

(iii) *Roumania*

The situation of Roumania differed essentially from that of either Greece or Serbia, owing to her geographical position athwart Russia's line of advance against Turkey. She held warily aloof from Serbia's rash policy of aggression, but as Russian intervention became increasingly probable, she felt it necessary to provide for all eventualities, and during the winter of 1876-7 Ion C. Bratianu went to Livadia in order to discuss with the Tsar and Gorchakov the rôle of Roumania in the event of a Russo-Turkish war. Austria favoured a Roumanian declaration of neutrality, but it rapidly became obvious that the Principality could not hope to keep aloof and would be overrun by the contending armies. Prince Charles therefore signed, on 16 April 1877, a military convention with Russia, guaranteeing a free passage for her armies in return for an engagement to respect Roumania's political rights and integrity.[2] Unhappily Russia showed a minimum of consideration for the Roumanians and seemed anxious to prove that they were either not free agents or an almost negligible

---

[1] *Life of Salisbury*, ii. p. 283, 17 June, to Lady Salisbury.
[2] Text in *Aus dem Leben König Karls*, iii. pp. 120-21.

quantity, with whose aid she could dispense: and thus her armies crossed the Pruth before the Roumanian Chamber had had time to ratify the Convention. The manifesto issued by the Grand Duke to the Roumanian people on this occasion abounded in assurances of friendship, but was none the less felt as an open rebuff by the Government in Bucarest. Prince Charles, however, kept his head: his small but admirable army, already mobilised, was concentrated in Wallachia, to await developments: but in declaring war upon Turkey, the Chamber also declared all ties with its former suzerain to be severed (12 May) and appealed to the Powers for an endorsement of its renewed independence.[1]

Roumania preserved a masterly inactivity until the Russian reverses before Plevna in July, but then sheer need of reinforcements made both the Tsar and the Grand Duke more reasonable and disposed them to grant highly favourable terms for Roumania's active intervention. Thus Prince Charles was given the chief command over the combined Russo-Roumanian forces before Plevna: the Roumanian army was successfully thrown across the Danube, and by its gallantry in storming the redoubts of Grivitsa (11 September) contributed very materially to saving the general situation.

With the fall of Plevna Roumania regarded her military task as completed and resumed her attitude of vigilant reserve. This was all the more necessary because it could no longer be concealed from public opinion, that Russia desired to reannex those southern districts of Bessarabia of which the Treaty of Paris had deprived her; that the Tsar himself had set his heart upon the recovery of territory which his father had lost: and that the Powers, though they might disapprove, were not prepared to raise any active opposition. As early as June 1877 Gorchakov had spoken to Prince Charles in terms which left little doubt as to Russia's intentions: but the Premier Bratianu and his no less able Foreign Minister Kogalniceanu, continued till the last moment to hug the illusion that comradeship in arms could not thus be rewarded. They found themselves in an exactly analogous situation to that of Cavour after Villafranca, but, like most Balkan politicians before and since, they were incapable of acting on the principle of *do ut des*, even though southern Bessarabia was a trifling loss compared with Nice and Savoy. Russia indeed was willing to assign them liberal compensation in the Dobrogea—then, it is true, as barren as four centuries of Turkish

---

[1] See *Corresp. Diplom. Roumaine sous le Roi Charles*, ed. N. Iorga.

neglect could make it: but the inelastic Roumanians still reckoned upon securing both one and the other. On 29 January 1878 Gorchakov warned General Ghika in plain terms: "whatever arguments you may invoke, you cannot modify our resolutions, for they are unchangeable. You are faced by a political necessity." Soon after Ignatyev arrived as the bearer of a personal message from the Tsar, affirming his sentiments of affection and sympathetic interest for Roumania, but at the same time insisting upon "interests and rights on which we cannot negotiate".[1] At this stage Bratianu, instead of yielding with good grace to the inevitable, induced the Chamber to vote the intangibility of Roumanian territory: and there seems little doubt that he acted in a mistaken belief that Britain was about to enter the war against Russia. Even Prince Charles, generally a realist in politics, preferred to listen to the intransigeant Bratianu, rather than to his own father's wise though unpalatable advice. Meanwhile the formal protest against San Stefano was fully justified and was not without its effect on the Powers.[2]

How little reason Roumania had for building upon British support, became apparent when the secret Salisbury-Shuvalov Protocol was made public, and it was found that the London Cabinet, while expressing strong disapproval of Russia's action in Bessarabia, acquiesced on the ground that no Power would oppose it by force. This attitude—never intended to become public—contrasted most unfavourably with Gladstone's open criticism of Russia the moment her intentions were revealed at San Stefano.

Roumania had no better success than Serbia with her claim for admittance to the Congress. Her two delegates, Bratianu and Kogalniceanu, found no support for their view of the Bessarabian question except from France and Italy, and even they allowed themselves to be overruled by the other Powers. Bismarck showed but little sympathy for Roumania, and indeed later on developed a strong animus against her in the Jewish question and in the matter of the railway concessions enjoyed by the German-Jewish contractor Strousberg. Just as the Russians had told Serbia to make terms with Austria-Hungary, so now Bismarck told Roumania to settle quickly with Russia.[3] The two delegates were kept waiting for ten days, and even on 29 June were only allowed to state their case and withdraw. Lord Salisbury, it is true, had suggested that the Congress, having heard

[1] Damé, *Hist. de la Roumanie*, pp. 300-301.
[2] Iorga, *op. cit.* p. 276, circular of 5 April, no. 614.   [3] *Aus dem Leben*, iv. p. 72.

the delegates of a nation which demanded foreign provinces, might in fairness listen to the representatives of a country which demanded provinces that belonged to it."[1] But Beaconsfield merely listened politely to the arguments of Bratianu and Kogalniceanu and remarked that "in politics ingratitude is often the price of the best services": and in the full session he laid far more stress upon the Treaty of Paris and the status of the Danube than upon Roumanian rights.[2] Bismarck, in introducing the two delegates—"nervous and unhappy", records Radowitz, and small wonder—more than hinted that their claims were hardly likely to promote a general accord: and after they had read their memoranda, he was the first to override all the arguments contained in them and to propose that the recognition of her independence should be made dependent upon Roumania accepting the territorial changes and granting full political rights to the Jews. The Dobrogea was assigned to Roumania, but the important fortress of Silistria remained still in doubt and was eventually assigned to Bulgaria by the commission for delimiting the frontier.

It is difficult to say whether Russia or Germany showed greater indifference at the Congress to Roumanian interests: but despite the curious feud which Bismarck kept up for the next two years the final result of the Berlin settlement could not really be in doubt. Russia, by the ineptitude of her policy, had thrust Serbia into the arms of Vienna, and all too soon alienated Bulgarian sympathies: she encouraged Roumania also, under her Hohenzollern Prince, to gravitate towards the Central Powers, and indeed from 1883 till 1914 a treaty whose extreme secrecy was successfully guarded, made of Roumania an annexe to the Triple Alliance. The only great nation which had shed its blood for Balkan liberty lost for a time its legitimate moral primacy, thanks to the stupidity and arrogance of official Russian policy.

[1] *Ibid.* iii. p. 75.
[2] According to Radowitz's contemporary phrase, Beaconsfield protested against Gorchakov's refusal to discuss Bessarabia, "und damit war es fertig"—*Denkwürdigkeiten*, ii. p. 52. The only worthy protest against "the mutilation of Roumania" had come from Gladstone, who at a moment when the Jingoes were denouncing him as a Russian agent, openly expressed the hope that Russia would not "stoop to this petty spoliation from a humble but brave ally"—"The Paths of Honour and of Shame", *XIXth Century*, March 1878. See also his difference of opinion with Madame Novikov on this point.

On 17 October 1878 Lord Salisbury, in a famous speech at Manchester, emphasised still further, and quite gratuitously, the Tory attitude on this question. "When we had satisfied ourselves that no other Power was inclined to take up the cudgels in that matter, and that Roumania was not very much in earnest on the subject, we did not think the matter was of first-rate importance"—*The Times*, 18 Oct.

CHAPTER XII

"PEACE WITH HONOUR": FROM BERLIN TO MIDLOTHIAN

I hope we are opening a gentler period of contemporary politics. . . .
We have rights of interference which never before were acquired by this
country. . . .   LORD SALISBURY at Mansion House, 3 Aug. 1878.

BEACONSFIELD'S WELCOME HOME: THE DISCUSSIONS IN PARLIAMENT

BEACONSFIELD and Salisbury had a positively triumphant reception
on their return to England, and it deserves special emphasis, as
thoroughly characteristic of his loyal and ungrudging character, that
the Prime Minister, in receiving a civic welcome at Dover, pointedly
reminded his audience that they were "equally indebted" to Salisbury for whatever success they might have achieved at Berlin. It
was on his arrival in London that he coined the famous phrase
"Peace with Honour", which has found such wide acceptance among
his admirers: and nothing illustrates better the intensity of feeling
and the gulf which divided the two camps than the ribald contemporary gibe which spoke of "the peace that passeth all understanding
and the honour that is common among thieves".

The Queen was almost lyrical in her delight at the reception of
her favourite, and offered him not merely the Garter, which he
accepted on condition that it was given to Salisbury also, but a
marquisate or dukedom for himself and a barony or viscounty for
his brother and nephew, both of which he respectfully declined,
assuring her that her confidence in him was "more precious than
rubies".[1] His fragile health compelled him to postpone his visit to
Windsor and to husband all his strength for a full statement of
policy in Parliament. It was felt that this would brook no delay,
since for a moment the Government seemed likely to be taken
between the two fires of the Radical stalwarts round Gladstone and
the group of disappointed and uncompromising Turcophils in his
own party. Moreover, the tone of the more sober and central organs
of the press made it abundantly clear that the country, after two
months of self-restraint and parliamentary silence during the supreme

---

[1] Buckle, vi. 347, 17 July.

negotiations, was now impatiently demanding the frankest and fullest possible explanations.

On 18 July, Lord Beaconsfield laid on the table the protocols of the Congress and delivered his great defence.[1] San Stefano, he reminded the House, had been "looked on with much distrust and alarm" by the Government, as "calculated to bring about a state of affairs dangerous to European independence and injurious to the interests of the British Empire": but the changes effected at Berlin had "averted the menace and the injury". The Powers had restored to the Sultan two-thirds of the territory which he had lost, with 30,000 sq. miles and a population of 2½ millions, "one of the wealthiest, most ingenious and most loyal of his subjects".

He then proceeded to deal with a series of objections raised to the Treaty. Firstly, doubt had been thrown upon the impregnability of the new frontier: but "it is by the courage, discipline, patriotism, and devotion of a population that impregnable frontiers can alone be formed"—thereby inferring that the population of Eastern Roumelia answered this description! He thought it necessary to find excuses for leaving Sofia to Bulgaria, its position not being "of a commanding character", and not regarded as of strategic value even by Mehemed Ali Pasha himself, and its population being purely Bulgarian. On the other hand, he excused the surrender of Varna to Bulgaria, as inevitable when once the Balkans were accepted as Turkey's northern line of defence: and in any case "Varna itself is not a place of importance", being "only a roadstead", and Burgas, which Turkey was to retain, was far more important. The name of "Eastern Roumelia" had been deliberately chosen, because if it were called Southern Bulgaria, "there would be constant intriguing to bring about a union between the two provinces"—it being implied that the divergence of names would prevent nationalist agitation! He touched only lightly on the reforms provided for the new province: their "three good points" were a Government for a specific period, public assemblies to levy and administer taxes, and a local militia to maintain order. The details were referred to an Imperial Commission in Constantinople.

Most singular were the grounds on which he justified Austria-Hungary's mandate in Bosnia. "No language can describe adequately the condition of that large portion of the Balkan Peninsula occupied by Roumania, Serbia, Bosnia, Hercegovina and other provinces—

[1] Hansard, ccxli. pp. 1753-74.

political intrigues, constant rivalries, a total absence of all public spirit . . . and hatred of races, animosities of rival religions and absence of any controlling power . . . to keep order. . . . Nothing short of an army of 50,000 of the best troops would produce anything like order in those parts", and the attempt to impose it would have brought Turkey to ruin. This, and the passing admission that Austria had for three years past had 150,000 refugees on her territory, offered a striking contrast to Beaconsfield's original belief that a little baksheesh might have suppressed the rising in a few weeks,[1] and to his obstinate refusal to listen to the warnings of those who knew the provinces at first hand and realised the spontaneous character of the national movement inside them and beyond each of their four frontiers.

He then turned to refute the charge of having partitioned Turkey. His Government had "at all times resisted the partition of Turkey", believing that it "would inevitably lead to a long, sanguinary and often recurring struggle", and Europe had now reached "the unanimous conclusion that the best chance for the tranquillity and order of the world is to retain the Sultan as part of the acknowledged political system of Europe. . . . *A country may have lost provinces, but that is not partition*. France not long ago lost provinces, yet she has a commanding future, Austria lost "more provinces even than Turkey", even England lost provinces as the result of bad government. "Had the principles which now obtain between the metropolis and her dependencies prevailed then, we should not perhaps have lost those provinces, and the power of this Empire would have been proportionally increased. It is perfectly true that the Sultan has lost provinces . . . that his armies have been defeated . . . that his enemy is even now at his gates, but all that has happened to other Powers. But a sovereign who has not yet forfeited his capital, whose capital has not yet been occupied by his enemy, and that capital one of the strongest in the world—who has armies and fleets at his disposal, and who still rules over 20,000,000 inhabitants, cannot be described as a Power whose dominions have been partitioned."

His next concern was to meet the charge of neglecting Greek interests. He reminded the Greeks that the large Slav state of San Stefano would have absorbed a considerable Greek population, and that they had been saved from this. But they had made "a cardinal error" of calculation: *"we were not there to partition, but so far as*

[1] See *supra*, p. 22, and Buckle, vi. p. 13.

possible to re-establish the dominion of the Sultan on a rational basis", and it was therefore impossible to give satisfaction to a state which coveted Constantinople for its capital. He did, however, approve "a rectification of frontier" in favour of Greece, though he took care not to be too precise in the matter.

Summing up his arguments, he pointed out that European Turkey still retained 60,000 square miles, with 6,000,000 inhabitants. "Turkey-in-Europe once more exists", and this satisfactory result had been obtained without war.

Turning to Asia, he reminded the House that the Turks were only losing a population of some 250,000 in the territories of Kars and Batum, that Russia had three times conquered Kars and three times relinquished it, mainly at the instance of England, and that we must have gone to war to prevent this, but "it would not have been a short war". Batum was talked of as if it were a sort of Portsmouth: in reality it was a Cowes, which "would hold three considerable ships —six if packed like the London docks"—and could only be increased by the expenditure of millions. Meanwhile the caravan route to Persia through Bayazid had been preserved for Turkey.

The time had come to prevent the recurrence of war and uncertainty between Russia and Turkey and so termii ate British anxieties concerning India: and as the Tripartite Treaty of 1856 "could not be acted on, from the unwillingness of the parties to it", a direct arrangement between Britain and Turkey had been substituted relating to Asia Minor and Cyprus. "We avoided Egypt, knowing how susceptible France is with regard to Egypt: we avoided Syria, knowing how susceptible France is on the subject of Syria, and we avoided availing ourselves of any part of the *terra firma*, because we would not hurt the feelings or excite the suspicions of France. France knows that for the last two or three years we have listened to no appeal which involved anything like an acquisition of territory, because the territory which might have come to us would have been territory which France would see in our hand with suspicion and dislike." But while anxious to see French influence "fairly and justly maintained" in the Lebanon and Egypt, "we must remember that our connection with the East is not merely an affair of sentiment and tradition" (as France admitted hers to be), "but that we have urgent, substantial, and enormous interests which we must guard and keep". Indeed, in view of "the progress of Russia" and of Turkish disorganisation, "it comes to this—that if we do not interfere in vindication of our own interests, that part of Asia must become the victim of anarchy, and ultimately part of the possessions of Russia". He would not blame Russia for availing herself of the anarchy in Asiatic Turkey, but after the concessions of the treaty it was necessary to say to her, "thus far and no farther". "Asia is large enough for both of us. There is no reason for these constant wars, or fears of wars, between Russia and England."

"In taking Cyprus", he went on, "the movement is not Mediterranean, it is Indian": its aim was "the maintenance of our Empire and its preservation in peace", and it was strengthened by the Sultan's desire "to act with England and Europe in the better administration of his affairs". He closed on a high note. "But it is not on our fleets and armies, however necessary they may be for the maintenance of our material strength, that I alone or mainly depend in that enterprise on which this country is about to enter. It is on what I most highly value—the consciousness that in the Eastern nations there is confidence in this country, and that while they know we can enforce our policy, at the same time they know that our Empire is an Empire of liberty, of truth and of justice".

It will be seen that Beaconsfield here dwelt more fully and frankly than ever before in public with the whole complex of the Eastern question: but there were, naturally enough, many aspects which he still left untouched. It is the aim of the present narrative to summarise the main contemporary arguments of the protagonists on both sides inside and outside Parliament, and then only, to estimate their relative value in the light of actual facts and of subsequent events.

Lord Granville, as leader of the Opposition in the House of Lords, naturally opened the debate that followed.[1] His congratulations were perfunctory, and after an uncomplimentary reference to the treatment of the Greeks, he blamed the Prime Minister for "ingeniously arguing against partition and for partition", and affected great surprise at his assumed satisfaction: "for up to the last moment, as I have understood it, his principle has been the *status quo* and independence of the Turkish Empire. I can hardly conceive that anything but a stern sense of duty could have brought him to agree to the secret memorandum" of Salisbury and Shuvalov, and he must have felt "pain and grief" at the signature, "though he may not like to acknowledge it".

Granville admitted that "the withdrawal of ten million Christian

[1] Hansard, ccxli. pp. 1775-87.

Slavs" from Turkish rule [1] was "a great advantage", though "the simple expedient of calling one of these populations East Roumelian instead of South Bulgarian" could not command confidence, and there was an ominous silence as to Bessarabia. The treaty, he claimed, "gives Russia all she really wished or ever expected to have": and he waxed sarcastic as to the territorial changes. His main criticism centred round the Anglo-Turkish Convention. The promise to return Cyprus to Turkey in certain eventualities was in his view "of a perfectly illusory character". He pointed out that there were "no good harbours, nothing but open roadsteads", and that the island was actually farther from the Dardanelles than Malta. The defence of Suez was "of the greatest importance": but did the acquisition of Cyprus "in the least augment the means of defence"? The promise of Turkish reforms was very vague, and it was not clear how the responsibility of defending Asiatic Turkey was to be implemented. "Nothing would have induced Wellington or Peel or Palmerston or Clarendon to sign a single guarantee of this sort", which might easily prove "both embarrassing and entangling".

Much more forcible and weighty was the speech of Lord Derby,[2] who after admitting that anything was better than the alternative of war, meted out his criticism in more than one unexpected direction. He began by condemning Russia's seizure of Bessarabia, by which she had "turned a devoted and submissive ally into an enemy", though, he added, "Roumania made war as a matter of speculation and has only her own Government to thank". Greece had no right to complain of her disappointments, but the union of Crete ought to have been allowed. Austria's occupation of Bosnia he admitted to be the only possible solution of that question, but at once scored a clever point by arguing that the process by which this and other changes was being effected "I never heard described by any other name than partition".

Still more trenchant was his condemnation of the absurdity of finding different names for north and south Bulgaria. "You may keep a man quiet if you tie both his hands: but if you allow one hand to be free, he will, you may be quite sure, use it to liberate the other." It might therefore be doubted "whether our diplomacy or Turkish forces will keep them apart", and meanwhile Bulgaria would be under Russian influence, whereas if allowed to debouch upon the Aegean, she might have been under British influence. Later in the speech he

[1] Here he obviously classed the Roumanians as "Slavs"!　　[2] *Ibid.* pp. 1788-1803.

refused to "argue with anyone who supposes the Bulgarian arrangement is final": to which Salisbury retorted, "I venture to say it will be far more permanent than any which has been proposed to supersede it". History has long since shown which was the true prophet.[1]

The crowning sensation of the speech was a reference to the circumstances under which he had resigned office in March: his lips had been sealed so long as negotiations continued, but it had now become "really an historical fact" and could do no harm.[2] We reserve for separate treatment the controversy which arose out of this revelation, and concentrate meanwhile upon the debates.

Lord Derby insisted that though the action to which he had objected in March now had the sanction of the Sultan and was not challenged by the Powers, he still remained sceptical, for a number of reasons. It was doubtful whether a new naval station was really required, in addition to Malta: Cyprus was inconveniently situated, it was very unhealthy, it had no harbour, it could never command the Euphrates Valley railway and was a "hopelessly unremunerative undertaking"; it was too far off to be a means of defence either for Suez or Constantinople, and *after a generation it will be a Greek community, not an English one*". The Russians in Batum were "not in any threatening proximity to Egypt". The fact that this last phrase was uttered not sarcastically but in all sincerity, is the measure of the distance between the arguments appealing to that generation and our own.

And the price for this useless acquisition was a guarantee, "absolute and singlehanded", dangerous and indefinite, and not limited by the lapse of years. Under it, "you must either hold yourself in readiness to go into a war utterly repugnant to the feelings and opinions of this country, or you must contemplate the possibility in certain circumstances of being obliged to say you cannot fulfil your bargain". The question "went much deeper than a mere question of military protection and administration": "an alliance for protection must become in fact a virtual annexation of the country"—for "if you protect Turkey from external aggression and do nothing regarding the internal administration beyond giving advice which will not be taken, then you make yourself responsible for the maintenance of a Government which will probably be abominably bad". Could it be good policy to create a second India, by becoming *de facto* masters of Turkey? It might be answered that Russia would keep quiet for

[1] Hansard, ccxli. pp. 1791-1808.   [2] See *infra*, p. 513-15.

twenty years and that we should not interfere much in Turkey. But "if engaged elsewhere, we should have no means of carrying out the pledge. . . . In the event of a Russian war, we should no longer have the choice of the field of operations: we should have virtually a frontier open to invasion". If again the motive for taking Cyprus was the defence of India, "the Russian road to India does not lie through Asia Minor, but *Persia*". He did not believe in permanent hostility to Russia, but if he did, he still could not regard the treaty with exultation. He ended by quoting the verdict of Sir Philip Francis on the Treaty of Amiens—"Though nobody is proud of it, still everybody is glad of it".

This brought Lord Salisbury to his feet.[1] Three years earlier, he contended, "the very elements of the problem were to a great extent unknown: was Turkey still capable of defence, or worn out and effete? After the late war the problem was solved: "the Government was wretched, the governing class corrupt", but there was a vast substratum with high qualities, and it must therefore be our aim "to purify, strengthen and improve the Turkish dominion, using it for the purpose of resisting Russian encroachment". The time of partition had not yet arrived, and Turkey was "an integral member of the European system".

This lukewarm defence of Turkey led him to reproach Derby for underestimating the part played by Austria. Hitherto Russia had known that "if she should shake the fabric of Turkey to pieces, she was the only possible heir to its remains", Greece not being a serious competitor. But the arrival of Austria at Novipazar showed that "if Turkey falls, it will not be Russia that will rule on the Bosphorus". Turkey's cession of Bosnia, then, was "a high act of statesmanship".

After a polemical attack of no small violence upon Derby's revelations, he poured scorn on the latter's criticism of the Cyprus Convention. A hundred years earlier, he said, Lord Derby would have objected to an extension of territory in India. The real question, he added, was whether we should have given a guarantee of Asiatic Turkey. "*If we are to evade responsibility, we ought to renounce Empire. . . .* Are you prepared to see the allegiance of the people of Asia given up to the advancing Power? If so, what chance is there of maintaining the loyalty of the people of India, if they know Russia to be dominant on the Tigris and the Euphrates?" The Crimean War would have been avoided, if the Tsar had known for certain that war would

[1] Hansard, ccxli. pp. 1804-14.

ensue: "we desire, and have succeeded in our desire, to avoid any such danger". After a speech whose tone was perhaps intended to dispel the charges of Russophilism sometimes levelled against him on his own side of politics, he closed by pointing out that there existed in Russia "a statesmanlike party which does not desire this indefinite policy of extension and annexation".

One other speech in this debate deserves attention. Lord Northbrook, Lytton's predecessor as Viceroy, added very damaging criticism of the Convention. He hoped that Indian troops would not be employed again without the question being discussed with the Government of India! He regretted the Government's failure to explain the dangers which the Convention was intended to meet, or how it would add to India's security. In his view the Government and many others "very greatly exaggerated the power of Russia for offence". There were only three possible routes of Russian invasion—over the Himalayas, which was quite impracticable, from Turkestan, which was beyond her resources, and through Persia: and though this latter was more serious, Teheran was fifteen hundred miles from the Indian frontier. The question of the Russian menace had often been considered by Indian statesmen—Lord Canning, Lord Lawrence, Lord Mayo (and he might have added, himself): and a passage in Lawrence's minute of 1869 still held good—"Our strongest security would . . . be found to be in previous absence from entanglements either at Cabul, Candahar, or any similar outpost; in full reliance on a compact, highly equipped and disciplined army . . . ; in the contentment, if not the attachment, of the masses; in the sense of security of title and possession . . . in the native aristocracy; in the construction of material works . . . ; in husbanding our finances and consolidating our resources; in quiet preparation . . . and a trust in the rectitude of our intentions . . . , coupled with the avoidance of all sources of complaint which either invite foreign aggression or stir up restless spirits to domestic revolt."

There were, Northbrook further pointed out, no stipulations for executing the military objects of the Convention, which thus remained a mere paper obligation. It was, moreover, very doubtful whether Cyprus could form a base of military operations, the natural base being Constantinople or Trebizond. The policy had been "prompted by exaggerated apprehensions" with regard to Armenia, and it was not clear how our obligation could be carried out, in view of the dreadful conditions of Asiatic Turkey.

To this Lord Cranbrook gave a vague rejoinder: "We have not undertaken to defend the frontiers of Asiatic Turkey by military operations on that particular point. We merely say that if those frontiers are menaced, we will defend Turkey against the aggressor, but the mode of doing so is a military question to be solved at the time".

A week later further criticism came from Lords Carnarvon and Bath. The former contended that secret engagements were at variance with the traditional policy and feeling of England, and drew a contrast between the Government's Convention with Turkey and Clarendon's reply to the Tsar's secret offer of Crete and Egypt in 1853—"England would be no party to any understanding that was kept secret from the other Powers". Carnarvon sarcastically reminded the House that Turkey had been "not partitioned, but redistributed": Russia had got "nearly all she desired", yet the seeds of illwill had been sown between us. Salisbury denied the betrayal of Greece, but Greece felt herself betrayed, and "while Greece desired Crete, we have taken Cyprus". The speech culminated in alarm at our new commitments in Asia. "Is there a reasonable chance that Turkey will ever reform her institutions herself? The whole history of Turkey is against it." If then we intended to redeem our engagements, we should be "compelled to land on the mainland", to use British agents and British troops; we should not be able to stop in Asia Minor, we should have to govern from Constantinople. "If the Sultan is a strong man, he will resist our dictation; if he is a puppet, the danger will be no less." The precedent of the King of Delhi must occur to all. Here he ended, on a note of "deep regret, disappointment and disapproval". Lord Bath reiterated the argument that "they who objected to partition were parties to partition, which they called redistribution". He was on unassailable ground when he contended that "the defenders of the public law of Europe made separate conventions disregarding the decisions of the Congress", and that we had "committed the very offences imputed to Russia". He could see no finality in the Berlin settlement. "Her Majesty's Government had gained a protectorate it could not enforce, and obtained pledges which it knew beforehand could not and would not be kept. For these ends we had lost our ancient alliances and also the respect of Europe."

Salisbury was at his very worst in the House of Lords: he was at his very best in the covering dispatch which he now published with the official text of the Treaty.

In this he put forward the argument that the policy sanctioned by the Treaty was "generally coincident with that which has been sustained by H.M.G. since the Treaty of San Stefano was published, and which was indicated in the Circular of 1 April": and he expressly denied any abandonment of the views expressed in that circular. Nearly two-thirds of Ignatyev's Bulgaria had now been "replaced under the direct political and military rule of the Sultan", Bulgaria losing half her seaboard and only retaining Varna, which could only be a commercial port. "*The new Slav state is therefore no longer strong*". The worst feature of San Stefano—its territorial severance of Constantinople from the European provinces remaining to Turkey—had now been abandoned, an indemnity had been ruled out, and "the menace to the liberty of the Black Sea" had been obviated by the provisions respecting Burgas and Batum and the land route through Bayezid. In short, the three cardinal objections to San Stefano had been remedied. (1) A large Greek population no longer falls within the Slav state, and Russian influence has been removed to a distance from the shores of the Aegean: (2) Turkish independence is ensured by giving to the Sultan "a defensible frontier, far removed from his capital", by interposing Austria-Hungary between the two Slav states, by restoring "rich and extensive provinces" to Turkish rule, and by "careful provision against future misgovernment". (3) A special arrangement had been reached in Asia.

Specially notable was the final phrase regarding the Asiatic guarantee—"Whether use will be made of *this—probably the last— opportunity which has thus been obtained for Turkey* by the interposition of the Powers of Europe, and of England in particular, or whether it is to be thrown away, will depend upon the sincerity with which Turkish statesmen now address themselves to the duties of good government and the task of reform".

Not the least striking feature of the political situation at this moment was the lead assumed by the House of Lords in the discussion. This was in the first instance due to the accident that the two chief protagonists at Berlin, and their late colleague at the Foreign Office, all belonged to the Upper House: but a no less effectual cause was the divided state of opinion within the ranks of the Opposition, whose satisfaction at one half of the treaty paralysed its attack upon the other. In any case Lord Hartington's motion in the House of Commons was fixed for 29 July, and the Prime Minister in presenting his case, thus had a start of eleven days. This was evidently too

much for his great rival, whose passions and persuasions the Eastern
Question had kindled to a white heat, and who now exploded at a
public meeting in Southwark on the 21st. In this, one of the most
effective, if not necessarily the most balanced, of his many oratorical
efforts during the long crisis, he struck more clearly than ever before
the high note which has made the name of Gladstone a household
word in every Balkan country from that day to this. "We are not
the friends of Turkey, we are not the friends of Russia. . . . *The cause
which we have supported from the first has been, not the cause of Turkey
or of Russia: it has been the cause of the subject populations*." And
turning a full volley upon the Turks, he exclaimed, "we have seen
this degrading despotism bursting out at times into a fury of cruelty,
savagery, lust and every imaginable depravity". He once more
criticised Britain's rejection of the Berlin memorandum as the
beginning of the real trouble: and here he was on weak ground, since
the Liberal leaders had, at the time, endorsed the Government's
attitude to the memorandum. Of the treaty he freely admitted that
it had brought "*some great results for humanity*"—the independence
of Roumania, Serbia and Montenegro, autonomy for Bulgaria, and
the removal of eleven millions from Turkish rule, even though the
phrase "bag and baggage" was not used. Meanwhile Russia secured
Bessarabia—which was again to "fall under her despotic institutions"—Armenia and an indemnity: and Turkey was subjected to
the right of foreign interference in the government of her subjects.
"That is the condition to which Turkey has been brought by the
action of her friends."

His main criticisms were reserved for the Anglo-Turkish Convention, by which we had undertaken to defend Turkey in Asia
"*alone and singlehanded*", and "to be responsible for the good government of perhaps the worst governed country in the world". For this
there was "*but one epithet—an insane convention*": and he was confident that neither Peel, Wellington nor Aberdeen, neither Russell,
Palmerston nor Lansdowne, would ever have put their names to
such an arrangement. The defence of Asia Minor against Russia was
an absurdity, for it "has no imaginable connection with keeping
Russia from her route to India". The country had been kept in hot
water since San Stefano, "because we insisted that no part of it could
be valid without the consent of Europe, and consequently that it
must be brought before the Powers: yet at the same moment we were
framing a secret engagement with Turkey—"*an act of duplicity not*

surpassed and rarely equalled in the history of nations". The Government, he contended, had sold Bessarabian liberty to Russia, had sold "much of what the brave Montenegrins had conquered to Austrian jealousies and selfishness, had sold the Greeks to Turkey and had finally sold Turkey to 'British interests', and by its action in ratifying before submission to Parliament had been guilty of 'unconstitutional and dangerous proceedings'".

KNIGHTSBRIDGE AND THE GUILDHALL

This was hard hitting, but Beaconsfield took the first occasion to pay Gladstone back in his own coin and to add a little by way of interest. A banquet was organised by the High Tories of both Houses in honour of Beaconsfield and Salisbury, and took place on 27 July in the Riding School at Knightsbridge, with the Duke of Buccleuch in the chair: and amid this atmosphere of genial adulation and aristocratic triumph the Prime Minister let himself go. After reminding his hearers that he sat in a House "where our opponents never unsheathe their swords"—a gibe fully deserved by Granville, but certainly not by Argyll—he repelled with some feeling the charge of deserting Greece, to whom he and Salisbury had given the best possible advice. He sought to strengthen his case by emphasising the Sultan's friendliness to Greece: and he then spoke of Abdul Hamid —doubtless on the strength of private letters from Layard[1]—as "apparently a man whose every impulse is good, . . . not a tyrant, not dissolute, not a bigot or corrupt".[2]

Beaconsfield turned to defend the Convention and boldly claimed that by it we had actually "lessened our responsibilities". For in ten or twenty years Russia would again be assailing Turkey and her capital, and "I fear there might then be a want of decision, of firmness" on the part of Her Majesty's Government (presumably if his opponents were then in power). It was therefore "extremely important to take a step *beforehand* which should indicate what the policy of England would be": for indeed neither the Crimean War nor this late war "would have taken place if England had spoken with the necessary firmness". And then with a spring he was at his rival's throat, astonished at the charge of concluding an "insane" convention. Such

---

[1] See *supra*, pp. 45, 406, 428.

[2] We may contrast Gladstone's juster description of Abdul Hamid as "the unhappy heir of bad traditions and of triumphant wrong"—House of Commons, 30 July, Hansard, ccxlii. p. 687.

a charge could only come from "a *sophistical rhetorician, inebriated with the exuberance of his own verbosity*, and gifted with an egotistical imagination that can at all times command an interminable and inconsistent series of arguments to malign an opponent and to glorify himself". For his part he left the decision to the Parliament and people of England.

Salisbury's speech on this occasion was tactfully devoted to a defence of his chief, who, he claimed, had not wished to go to Berlin and had only reluctantly yielded to the argument that his presence there, "with the full mandate of the English people, would produce an effect on the negotiations and action of other Powers such as no other man could have produced". Yet "every calumny, every misconception that malignant ingenuity could invent was paraded forth in order to lessen our influence and hinder our efforts", though what they had tried to do at Berlin was "to pick up the broken thread of England's old Imperial position".

The Times, commenting on these speeches, acutely observed that Beaconsfield possessed some of the rarest qualities of a party chief—generosity to colleagues, patience under defeat and constant readiness of retort, and claimed as one of his special qualities "a certain tact which springs from a knowledge of the world and a command of temper". All the more surprising, then, was his "curious little burst of irritation" against Gladstone—an invective that betrayed an unusual "lack of finish". Clearly, this time the sweet was not intended to conceal the taste of the pill.

The crowning moment of triumph was reached on 3 August, when the two statesmen were presented with an address at the Guildhall and entertained by the Lord Mayor at a City banquet. On this occasion Beaconsfield spoke with greater dignity and restraint, claiming that under the new settlement everyone was benefited and no one humiliated. It was "a great check to the restlessness of the military authority of Russia" and a lesson for the extremists. The wisdom of the Congress had made Russia "relinquish the greater portion and the wealthiest portion of her conquests", and the Sultan "has now in Europe a rich and abounding country which in area is equal to England and Wales, while in the Asiatic portion of his dominions *his anxieties are terminated*". Austria's occupation of Bosnia "permits us to check, I should hope for ever, that Panslavist confederacy and conspiracy which has already proved so disadvantageous to the happiness of the world". France and Italy "have the satisfaction of knowing that the balance of power in the Mediterranean has not been disturbed". *"The great peacemaker Germany"* has attained her object, "the peace of Europe". And with supreme audacity the orator contrasted the Treaty of Paris, which contained "no engagement on the part of the Sultan to Europe", with the Anglo-Turkish Convention, which contained "a distinct engagement on the part of the Sultan to England"—in other words, *"the right and privilege of our interference"*. He had great confidence in the policy of occupying Cyprus: "I believe it will exercise a most beneficial influence over Asia Minor". In conclusion, he had never known a moment when the relations of the Powers were "so essentially friendly"—"I make no exception with regard to Russia"—and he refused to contemplate an estrangement between England and France.

Salisbury, in a much briefer speech, laid the same strong emphasis upon the rights acquired by Britain and the civilising mission thereby assumed: and amid this flow of oratory one phrase deserves to be weighed carefully by posterity. *"We have rights of interference which never before were acquired by this country"*—a phrase which in other times, before and since, would have met with strong repudiation from every section of opinion, and certainly did not correspond with its author's mood and policy in later life, but which after the Congress seems to have pleased the palate of the great majority on both sides.

One other notable phrase deserves immortality: for while it opens and closes with two pious hopes destined to disappointment, its central thesis is profoundly true and provides the excuse for treating a long-dead controversy as a live issue—a warning and a deterrent. "For good or for evil, I hope we have done with the Eastern Question in English politics. *I never remember a question which has so deeply excited the English people, moved their passions so thoroughly and produced such profound divisions and such rancorous animosity. . . .* I hope we are opening a gentler period of contemporary politics".

THE FINAL DEBATE

The full dress debate in the House of Commons extended over four whole evenings from 29 July to 3 August.[1] But while no account of

[1] Hansard, ccxlii. A list of speakers is appended: first night, Lord Hartington, Plunket, Sir C. Dilke, Baillie-Cochrane, Evelyn Ashley, R. E. Plunkett, Grant Duff, Bourke, Hussey Vivian; second night, Lord Sandon, Gladstone, Sidebottom, Osborne Morgan, Birley, Evans, Goldney, Stansfeld, Assheton Cross; third night, Robert Lowe, Lord John Manners, Joseph Chamberlain, Nolan, Sir J. Hay, Holms,

contemporary reactions would be at all complete without it, it is obviously impossible to do more than select a few of the most salient features. The Opposition was torn hopelessly in two directions, unable to pass unqualified condemnation and conscious that the country, for good or for bad, accepted the Berlin settlement as final and conclusive. The half-hearted nature of the attack was once more specially evident in the opening speech of Lord Hartington, who expressed his satisfaction at a settlement without war and the extension of liberty and self-government, but at the same time regretted the failure to meet Greek claims, the extension of Britain's military liabilities under the Turkish convention, "the undefined engagements" respecting Turkish reform, and the taking of so grave a decision without previous knowledge of Parliament. He was on strong ground when he quoted Layard's dispatch treating Russia's demands in June 1877 as "equivalent to the destruction of Turkey" and then showed their singular resemblance to the terms so much vaunted by the Government in July 1878. He was equally effective when he contrasted the Tory protests against the secrecy of San Stefano with the secret agreement soon afterwards concluded with Shuvalov behind the back of Europe. His criticisms, then, avoided the treaty and were concentrated on the convention, which, he held, had extended our liabilities, "to defend Asia Minor, not when we please, but when Russia pleases": and he adopted Gladstone's phrase, "an insane policy", while protesting against the Prime Minister's abusive personalities. But he ended on a very weak note, admitting that from the party point of view it was better to bow the head to the "breeze of popularity" which carried the Government, while preparing a way of honourable "retreat from this false and ill-advised course".

Sir Charles Dilke also was less convincing than usual, arguing very dubiously that the conclusion of the Convention without the sanction of Parliament was "a new departure in foreign policy", that "any direct engagement such as the construction of a railway from Scanderoon to Bagdad would be better than the enormous, because utterly vague, responsibilities we have undertaken".

The most violent speeches on the two sides were those of Robert Lowe and Lord Elcho. The former lamented Greece's blunder in

Hill, Knatchbull-Hugessen, Arthur Balfour, Laing, Lewis, Sir John Lubbock; fourth night, Lord Elcho, W. E. Forster, Hamond, O'Donell, Carpenter-Garnier, O'Brien, Onslow, Shaw-Lefevre, Courtney, Sir W. Harcourt, Butt, O'Clery, Sir Stafford Northcote, Sullivan, Lord Hartington.

choosing the alliance of England, referred to Salisbury's instructions to Odo Russell as "done merely to see how many falsehoods could be put in a dispatch", and accused the Government of doing all in its power "to drag Royalty into collision with its subjects".[1] Lord Elcho explained the late war as due to "a great chronic Slav conspiracy", said that in Russia Christianity was "an apology for a filibustering crusade", and in referring to the St. James's Hall atrocity meeting, praised the appropriate selection as Chairman, of Lord Shaftesbury, "the First Commissioner of Lunacy". Lord John Manners, too, was very trenchant, denouncing Lowe for "his tremendous threat of a revolutionary campaign",[2] and pouring contempt on his argument that England had not been a military power for five centuries. "To listen to him, one would think that Marlborough never existed and that the Duke of Wellington was a Quaker." He claimed that the "secret treaty" had been negotiated in accordance with strict precedent, that the settlement had destroyed Turkey's "strength, vitality and independence", that Greece would have been overrun if she had disregarded British advice, that Cyprus was "well and admirably suited for our purposes in Asia, and that the Convention actually reduced our obligations as compared with those of the Tripartite Treaty of April 1856—which, he too failed to realise, had been regarded as a dead letter almost from the first by the two co-signatories France and Austria.

In many ways the most original speech of the debate was that of Joseph Chamberlain, for point after point in it has been justified by later events. The British protest about Bessarabia was "a comedy rehearsed in private". The abandonment of Greece was all the worse because "England had long owed reparation", owing to our action in imposing the cramped boundaries of 1830: and the failure to liberate Crete would bring its revenge. It was no less certain that Epirus and Thessaly would "in due time" join free Greece, and that Eastern Roumelia would "ultimately" unite with Bulgaria. Above all, it was "inconceivable that the central authority at Constantinople, bankrupt and discredited, torn by internal dissensions, could ever institute the reforms required of it: and if Turkey was not to reform herself, who was to reform her? The Government could not maintain that they were entering on a great work of civilisation and at the same time deny that they were undertaking new responsibilities." The Opposition was taunted with the lack of an alternative

[1] Hansard, ccxlii. pp. 875, 879, 890.　　[2] *Ibid.* pp. 897, 900.

policy: his idea of one would be to "ascertain where the vital interests of England really lay and where her real defence properly began, and to wait till those interests were menaced instead of rushing to meet a danger which possibly had no existence". The Convention had "brought our defence of India up to the very jaws of the Russian fortresses" and had "left to Russia the choice of time, place and circumstances for attacking us".

Once again, however, Gladstone dominated the whole debate, and his speech was full of passion and the fire of battle, though far more open to logical assault. After a preliminary defence of the late Government's policy and of his own attitude towards Disraeli, he declared himself thankful that the Treaty had brought peace: "for many months we have been unable to discern any danger to the existence of the peace which was re-established at San Stefano, excepting in the opinions and the warlike preparations of Her Majesty's Government". It was a great fact that seven million people were entirely removed from Turkish rule, and that the new status of Bulgaria was "very nearly equivalent to total emancipation". It was a little difficult to argue that there had been no partition. We spoke of the first partition of Poland, which reduced that state from 12 to 6 millions: but European Turkey, reduced from 17 millions to 6, had not been partitioned. Greece and Crete had been abandoned; "the Slavs who relied on Russia have in the main obtained what they desired, the Hellenes who relied on England have in the main failed to obtain it". England might have expected her delegates "to lean towards the side of freedom and away from the side of servitude", but precisely the reverse of this occurred, for she had given the Turks the right to send troops to Eastern Roumelia, she had handed over Bosnia to Austria, whose history was "one long series of efforts to resist and repress freedom wherever it arose", she had wished to deprive Serbia of Vranja, she had opposed the French proposal to cede Thessaly and Epirus to Greece, and while publicly condemning Russia's seizure of Bessarabia, she had told the Russians that she would not resist it. Beaconsfield and Salisbury had spoken in the tones of Metternich, not of Canning, Palmerston or Russell.

His main criticism was reserved for the Convention. His desire to see Turkey diminished forced him to describe Cyprus as "a solid residuum": but that "Turkey in Asia is to be managed as an outpost of British power—maintained and reformed", seemed to him "*a mad undertaking*", such as no minister of the last forty years would

have risked. Lord Salisbury had spoken with some contempt of the
philosophical historian, but in his own opinion "the philosophical
historian, when he gets his turn—and he will get his turn—will make
a formidable rejoinder: he will say that it is from the councils of statesmen that on this occasion there has proceeded the most extraordinary
crop of wild and speculative ideas which were ever grown in the
hottest of all the hothouses of politics". The Government posed as
the champions of public law by making Russia submit: but they had
broken public law by sending the fleet through the Straits and by
the Convention with Turkey, with its single-handed right of intervention in Asiatic Turkey. Indeed, they had violated the principle
on which the Crimean War had been fought. "I value our insular
position, but I dread the day when we shall be reduced to a moral
insularity. I desire that sympathy should be cherished with every
country, and I fear the conclusion of this convention will be injurious to the action of that sympathy." Moreover, the Government
had done "great and needless harm to the rights and prerogatives
of Parliament". A year earlier he had said that "if the work of liberation was effected without the approval, nay, rather, under the ban of
England, as a man I should rejoice, but as an Englishman I should
hide my head. That is the result which has actually arrived." The
Government had set up British interests, "not real but imaginary":
it had pursued them "by means of strange and unheard-of schemes",
showing "very deficient regard" for the law of Europe: it had
neglected the rights of Parliament, and it had withheld essential
financial information.

The Times next morning put its finger on the weak spots of the
speech, while admitting that it had "stimulated to the highest
degree" the flagging interest of the debate and was "equal to his
greatest efforts"—a verdict reflecting the contemporary impressions
of that volcanic figure in the House, but not acceptable to a later
generation. Gladstone, it wrote, seemed to be "wrestling with a result
wrought out by an adverse destiny and protesting with the utmost
vehemence of his whole intellectual and moral nature against a policy
which he seems to abhor". Yet it could not admit that "the black
account can correspond to any reality in the actual world of politics":
his prolonged invective proved too much. On the one hand, he seemed
to think that Turkey was "an absolutely inanimate substance", to
be carved and rearranged at pleasure, and that the Congress only had
to consider Russia and the Christian nationalities of Turkey, whereas

resettlement in Europe really affected the whole status of the Turkish Empire, and consequently the interests of the various Great Powers. On the other hand, it was quite inconsistent for him to argue against the need of action in Asia: and indeed "it is difficult to argue with a statesman who after passionately denouncing Turkish rule as irreconcilable, now declares as vehemently that there is no reason to apprehend the spread of anarchy in the Turkish Empire".[1]

Sir Stafford Northcote summed up the debate on the Government side in his usual urbane way. He admitted that the arrangements of 1856 had failed, owing to the weakness of the Turkish Government, the intrigues of "some other Powers" and the "apathy and negligence" of the Concert, not excluding Britain. San Stefano would have "entirely destroyed" 1856, but Berlin had removed this danger, and Turkey, having lost territory, but not independence and integrity, would now be all the stronger. He challenged Gladstone's view that the British Government had always leaned against freedom and excused the restoration of populations to Turkey, who could not be spoken of as "entirely and necessarily antagonistic to freedom". The Convention aimed at keeping Turkey as strong as possible "consistently with the introduction of good government": it did not add to our responsibilities, but merely recognised them. It was necessary in the interest of India, and a precedent could be found in the tripartite treaty concluded with France and Austria before the Congress of Paris and only made public afterwards. The great trouble was "the weakness of the Porte, not its malice or evil-mindedness", and he hoped for support from Turkey herself and for the moral goodwill of other nations.

The debate thus ended on a note of pious hope which had but little relation to the real Turkish situation. On a division the Government had a majority of 143 (195-338)—its normal working majority being 52: and *The Times* was fully justified in its closing comment, that despite its occasional vigour the debate as a whole had been "a half-hearted attack on a position which the assailants felt they could not win, and from which they did not care to dislodge the occupants".[2]

LAYARD'S REACTIONS TO THE TREATY

In these pages we have followed with some closeness the activities of our Ambassador in Constantinople: and the story would not be

[1] *The Times* leader of 31 July.   [2] *Ibid.* 3 Aug.

complete without his reactions to the Treaty, as revealed by his correspondence with his predecessor, Sir Henry Elliot. The two arch-Turcophils were almost equally disgusted at the result.

"I am fairly well informed (not, however, from our own people)[1] of what is going on at Berlin. I fancy you will agree with me in the opinion that no arrangement can be made there in the circumstances in which the Congress has met, which will do more than patch up matters for a few years—Safvet says two. As for settling the Turkish or Eastern Question, it will unsettle everything. We are calling into life new nationalities and dangerous ambitions, and affording fresh motives and fresh facilities for Russia to carry on her intrigues with the object of destroying the Empire and possessing herself of the heritage. There was only one way of settling the question, and we have been unable to avail ourselves of it."[2]

Elliot's answer came from Berlin, whither he had been summoned by Salisbury, and it evidently contained similar strictures, for Layard replied, "I certainly agree with you in your opinion of the Treaty and maybe go even further than you in condemning it. . . . Not having been consulted on any matters connected with it, I have not offered advice. But I reserve to myself the right of criticising it officially. . . . I believe that instead of settling anything it has unsettled everything, and that instead of preserving what remains of Turkey in the East it will lead to its break-up and partition within a very short period".[3] To Lord Lyons he was even more gloomy and violent. "I see in it the elements of future wars and disorders without number, and an upsetting of all the principles of justice and right which have hitherto governed the relations of and intercourse of states. Force and fraud have triumphed, and when Turkey has been completely destroyed and cut up under the new system it will probably be applied with similar successful results to other countries. Russia has gained, with the assistance of Germany, all and more than she wanted, and the interests of England and of other Powers were sacrificed in order to enable Bismarck to recruit his beery stomach by drinking some mineral waters."[4]

These tirades had a very human basis, for the *Globe's* publication

<hr />

[1] The *Layard Papers* provide the clue to this phrase. In vol. 39, 137, containing the original letters received by Layard, there are a number of roughly pencilled notes, summarising Caratheodory Pasha's account of the *coulisses* of the Congress, and communicated to Layard by the Porte.

[2] *Layard Papers* (Add. MSS. 39, 138, vol. ccviii.), 5 July, Layard to Elliot.

[3] *Ibid.* 26 July.   [4] Newton, *Life of Lyons*, p. 390.

of the secret Protocol had had a disastrous effect upon Britain's position in Turkey, or, as he wrote very frankly to Lord Salisbury, "has toppled over at a blow the edifice that it has taken me months of labour to raise": Turkish confidence in Britain had been suddenly replaced by "the most entire distrust", and incidentally the Sultan's hereditary tendency towards persecution mania had been greatly accentuated. "I presume", Layard wrote to Elliot, "it was published to discredit England and to destroy the splendid position and unparalleled influence that she had obtained by her policy. It has had that effect. The consequences here are most serious, and there is not a Turk or Christian who is not now convinced that we have been playing Turkey and Europe false, that while we have been professing to uphold the cause of justice, treaties and international rights and to be the champions of the liberties of Europe and humanity, we have been all along in secret agreement with Russia and Austria, to dismember the Turkish Empire and take our share of the spoils."[1]

Salisbury was too much of a realist to be altogether surprised. "I am afraid", he replied,[2] "you prognosticate aright the effect of the Berlin Treaty on the future position of the Ambassador at Constantinople. It will be one of constant struggle: he will be in the front of the battle for the interest both of England and humanity in the East. But had we any other choice? Battle there must be, for there are rival interests to satisfy, and we had to choose between an immediate appeal to arms or postponing, with the chance of avoiding, that arbitrament, by substituting for it a protracted diplomatic struggle.

"Our greatest difficulty will of course be with the Asiatic reforms. In order to do any good—and indeed in order to satisfy the opinions of the English nation—they must be far-reaching: but they must not withdraw any of the semblance of power from the Sultan, nor too much of the reality." The four heads under which he summarised the idea of reform in Asia were: (1) the choice of better Governors, "more free from interference from Constantinople and less corrupt"; (2) "an adequate *gendarmerie*"; (3) free tribunals; and (4) no extortion in the raising of revenue.

This shows—and it is confirmed by his correspondence for many months to come—that Salisbury was genuinely desirous of making the Asiatic reforms a reality and attached the greatest importance to them. Unfortunately, he soon found himself without sufficient

[1] *Layard Papers*, 5 July, Layard to Elliot.   [2] *Ibid*. 24 July, Salisbury to Layard.

backing either from the Government or from public opinion: and this country, as on other occasions before and since, after throwing its weight into the scales of European decision, withdrew into a no less exaggerated isolation and allowed many matters to go by default to which it had recently attached a capital importance.

LORD DERBY'S REVELATIONS

The speech of Lord Derby at the opening debate of 18 July revived in an acrimonious form the old controversy regarding his final resignation in March, and it is unfortunately impossible to evade the issues thus raised. He now explained that resignation by the Cabinet's dubious decision "to secure a naval station in the eastern Mediterranean, and therefore to seize Cyprus and a point of the Syrian coast", with or without the consent of the Sultan. This, he contended, only self-defence would have justified, and it "would have thrown Turkey into the arms of Russia" and led to a Russian occupation of Constantinople. It was this fear which had led him to declare that the Government were not merely drifting but rushing into war.[1] His lips had been sealed so long as the negotiations continued, but now the incident was "really an historical fact", which it could do no harm to state. He then passed on to those criticisms of the Convention which we have already recorded.

Lord Salisbury replied in perhaps the most violent speech of his whole career,[2] claiming that this was the third instalment of revelations since Derby had left the Cabinet, and comparing such tactics to Titus Oates's "successive fragments of disclosure". This comparison was rendered doubly offensive by recalling Oates's own excuse "that he did not know how much the public would endure". Not merely had Derby broken the Privy Council rule of secrecy, but his account of the Cabinet resolution was "not true—well, not correct". Instantly challenged by both Derby and Granville, he took the curious line that "the language I have used does not necessarily impugn the veracity of the speaker", but at once added that he was relying not on his own memory, but on that of the Prime Minister, the Lord Chancellor, the Chancellor of the Exchequer, the Secretary for India and three other members of the Cabinet! "All kinds of con-

---

[1] See *supra*, p. 388.
[2] He could, however, be "rough-tongued" on occasion. He once, to use Harcourt's phrase (14 Jan. 1879 at Oxford), "compared the most illustrious of his opponents to a pettifogging attorney and afterwards apologised to the attorneys."

tingencies are spoken of, all possible policies discussed, and it is quite possible that my noble Friend may have heard some project discussed by this member of the Cabinet or that": but he appealed "in the interests of parliamentary government, not to give the sanction of his authority to this plan of discussing what has passed in the Cabinet".[1]

By this time the sluggish Derby was thoroughly roused and "distinctly and positively" repeated the statement. "When a man has to consider whether a particular decision will or will not allow him to remain in the Cabinet, he is not likely to be careless or forgetful. . . . I made within two hours of the time a memorandum of what I understood to have passed."[2]

Everyone seems to have been agreed in not pressing home so painful an incident, though a week late Lord Granville could not resist protesting against a comparison between the late Foreign Secretary and "the vilest character in English history". But it had reverberations behind the scenes, which have only reached the public ear in post-war days, through the publication of Mr. Buckle's *Life of Disraeli* and the *Letters of Queen Victoria*. In the former we can now read the note of the Cabinet proceedings on 27 March and the relevant extract from Lord Derby's diary of the same day:[3] and from these, which correspond on all essential points, we learn that Beaconsfield did propose the occupation of Cyprus and Scanderoon by Indian troops, as being "the key of Asia", and in order to "neutralise the effect of the Armenian conquest" by Russia; that Salisbury spoke of Scanderoon as "commanding the route both to the Suez Canal and to the Persian Gulf", both of which "we must be ready to defend"; that Salisbury and Cairns showed their previous knowledge and detailed approval of the plan, and that Derby thereupon dissented and resigned. The two documents, in themselves already conclusive, are confirmed by Lord Sanderson's record of what Lord Derby told him, by what Beaconsfield himself wrote to the Queen, and by a perfectly explicit, if not quite contemporary, memorandum of Northcote.[4] All this constitutes evidence which, as Mr. Buckle points out, far outweighs the conflicting memories of Gathorne Hardy and Assheton Cross, and proves all to have admitted that there was "no audible dissent, save Derby's, from Beaconsfield's proposals". The Cross memorandum treats as conclusive the argument "that as we

---

[1] Hansard, ccxlii. pp. 1808-10.   [2] *Ibid.* p. 1815.
[3] Buckle, vi. pp. 264-6.   [4] Letters of 26 and 27 March, *ibid.*

were at the time contending for the integrity of Turkey, we could never have contemplated dismemberment by the seizure of Cyprus":[1] but this only proves two things—first, the confusion of mind even in so able a minister as Cross, in not seeing that we were searching quite definitely for a place of arms, and that Cyprus and Scanderoon were the two points most favoured; and again, that throughout the period of the Convention and the Congress we were still talking of Turkish integrity, while demanding Cyprus for ourselves and to that extent promoting dismemberment: and secondly, the fact that the real Cabinet decisions on foreign policy were in the hands of an inner ring of two or three.

The Gladstone and Granville Papers provide further convincing proofs in confirmation of Mr. Buckle's view. They show that at least from the beginning of June onwards Lord Derby was in close consultation with Lord Granville and gravitating rapidly towards the Liberal camp. What served as incentive was quite definitely the original *Globe* revelation, which Derby had reason to regard as "substantially accurate", and of which he indignantly wrote: "*A more complete surrender of all that the Cabinet professed to stand out for could not be. I prefer it to a war, and so probably do you: but it is an odd result of six millions spent in preparation for war. There was no moment when Russia would not have made this bargain with us, without pressure or intimidation. In fact, she has got all she wants. I fancy there will be great discontent in the House of Commons among the ultras on both sides.*"[2]

Three days later he wrote again: "*I entirely agree with what you and Lord Grey said about the double embassy [of Beaconsfield and Salisbury to Berlin], but you could not say what is probably the truth, that the two Ambassadors go out to watch one another, on the Japanese principle. . . . I shall have something to add as to the original destination of those Indian troops, which will create a little surprise, but that must be reserved till all is settled.*"[3]

The *Globe's* publication of the full text of the Protocol brought a

---

[1] This passage is reproduced by special permission in the *Life of Gathorne Hardy*, ii. p. 76. The relevant passage from Hardy's own Diary *of* 19 *July, not of* 27 *March* (*ibid.*), runs as follows: "I feel confident that Cyprus was not mentioned when he [Derby] left the Cabinet, nor was any special expedition decided on. . . . The discussion about Alexandretta (*i.e.* Scanderoon) and contemplation of the possibility of taking it by Indian troops was on the day he decided to leave us, but enquiries were to be made, and no action was taken."

[2] *Granville Papers*, Derby to Granville, 2 June.

[3] *Ibid.* Derby to Granville, 5 June.

further letter from Knowsley to Granville, in which Derby declares: "I never heard the idea of a special protectorate of Asia Minor raised by any of the Cabinet, and it is so insane a project, if England alone is to be the protecting Power, that I cannot believe it. May not the whole resolve itself into the occupation of an island for a naval station? That notion has long been in favour in Downing Street. I think the policy of bluster and expenditure has received a severe blow: witness the fury of the P.M., the grumbling of the *Standard* and the coolness of the *Telegraph*."[1]

And again: "How if the suggested protectorate of Asiatic Turkey should resolve itself into the acquisition of Cyprus as a naval station, and some guarantee or other assistance given to the long suspended plan of the Euphrates valley line? So many schemes have been taken up and dropped again, that it is impossible to feel sure what is the one that will in the end be adopted. But I have the best reason for believing that Cyprus is an object with the Cabinet. It is well, at least, that this time there should be no question of getting it otherwise than as the result of negotiation."[2]

Lord Derby came up from Knowsley for the great debate on the Treaty and pronounced himself in the sense already indicated. The rough rejoinders from his former colleagues seem to have taken him altogether by surprise, for on rising next morning he sent the following note to Lord Granville. "Salisbury's denial last night of what I stated leaves me in utter perplexity as to what they mean to acknowledge or to repudiate. The more I think of the matter, the less intelligible it is to me. If you allow me, I will step over to you at 11."[3]

What followed is recorded in a letter of Granville to Gladstone.[4]

"I saw Derby twice to-day. He was very low in the morning, but much relieved in the afternoon, having found his memorandum. This is a detailed account of the conversation in the Cabinet, written in the Cabinet Room. A long report of what Dizzy had said—beginning with a declaration that the moment had come, when action must be taken, and the plan he proposed was a secret expedition of Indian troops to take Cyprus and Alexandretta. Cairns supporting, Salisbury ditto, urging that it would be fairer to the Turks not to ask their leave—Northumberland[5] and others supporting the P.M.—none objecting but Derby himself.

[1] *Ibid*. Derby to Granville, 18 June. [2] *Ibid*. Derby to Granville, 25 June.
[3] *Ibid*. Derby to Granville, 19 July.
[4] *Gladstone Papers*, Granville to Gladstone, 19 July.
[5] Lord Privy Seal since February.

"On the next day he requested Northcote to inform Dizzy that after the decisions in the Cabinet he must resign. This was answered by Dizzy in writing [that] he accepted the resignation. The denial of Salisbury and his colleagues was that it was untrue that there had been *any resolution* to that effect.

"I asked Derby whether it was customary in this Cabinet to decide everything by written minutes. He said he only remembered once, when a resolution was passed, evidently intended to drive Carnarvon and himself to resign.

"He does not like initiating a defence. He says, 'Qui s'excuse, s'accuse'. He seems inclined to lean on my advice."

The internal evidence of this letter shows that Derby's speech must have been based only upon his recollection of what passed in the Cabinet and of his memorandum upon it, but also—and this is the point—that when he laid his hands upon the memorandum next day, it confirmed the accuracy of his memory and left him satisfied. This, and almost certainly the further motive of deference to the Queen's sentiments, would serve to explain the fact that Lord Derby did not defend himself further in Parliament, and that the incident remained in doubt until the publication of Mr. Buckle's volume a whole generation later.[1]

The only question open, then, is whether Derby was justified in revealing what he did: and this seems to be settled in the affirmative by the terms of the Queen's letter to him on retirement, granting her express permission to make "such statement as you, in *your discretion*—in which the Queen has entire confidence—may think fit".[2] After the July incident the Queen, with the Prime Minister's approval, wrote and reproved Derby for "a most unusual and (she cannot but think) hardly constitutional course": but he was able, very respectfully, to silence her by recalling the terms of this permission.[3] He had been subjected to much obloquy owing to the secrecy in which his motives had been shrouded, and when he found the Cabinet persisting in a course which he regarded as highly dangerous, he felt it to be at once his duty and his right to speak out.

Before we leave this incident, we may allude to another aspect of

[1] There is a final phrase to the letter of Granville to Gladstone: "What do you think? Would it be best for him to make a personal explanation on Monday, on the strength of having found his memorandum, which he means to show at once to Northcote, or to wait for an incidental debate, which is sure to occur in the course of the week?" I have not found any indication of Mr. Gladstone's answer.

[2] Buckle, vi. p. 269.   [3] 19 and 21 July—*Letters*, ii. pp. 631-2.

the extreme cult of official secrecy upheld by Lord Salisbury in particular. As Lord Rosebery effectively pointed out in the House of Lords,[1] the British public, "but for the ill-advised conduct of a very subordinate clerk" in the Foreign Office, "would not have the faintest conception of such an agreement, and the keystone of the whole purpose of the Government would be wrapped in obscurity". So far indeed had secret diplomacy been pushed that on 8 June— only a week before the Congress opened—Lord Odo Russell had received instructions to work against the cession of Batum and Kars to Russia, though this very point had been conceded as recently as 30 May under the Shuvalov-Salisbury Protocol. In short, "we had called an European Congress, yet bound ourselves in private to consent to those stipulations which we continued to denounce".

The denials of the Government had proved, to say the least, disingenuous: and the best that could be said for the insistence upon the *Globe* revelations as "unauthentic" was that they omitted the clause establishing the Balkan line as the military frontier of Turkey, and that the Government regarded this as "a cardinal point". Even to ardent apologists at the time this must have rung false.

THE AFTERMATH OF BERLIN

Every great European Congress must, almost inevitably, leave many "ragged edges" to be tidied up afterwards: but this was more than usually the case with that of Berlin, and nearly three years elapsed before the Near East could be reduced to even a semblance of order. Both Bulgaria and Eastern Roumelia remained under provisional Russian occupation, the former under Prince Dondukov Korsakov at Sofia, the latter under General Stolypin at Philippopolis. The international commission, which met at the latter town in October 1878 to draw up an Organic Statute for the southern province, did not complete its task till 24 April 1879, and the result of its labours, framed on truly liberal lines, was only accepted with great reluctance by the inhabitants themselves, as a substitute for union. Meanwhile the first Bulgarian National Assembly met at Tirnovo in February 1879, adopted a new constitution on broader lines than those contemplated by St. Petersburg, and on 29 April elected Prince Alexander of Battenberg, nephew of the Tsar, as its

[1] Hansard, ccxlii. p. 345, 26 July.

Prince. Definitive peace having at last been signed between Russia and Turkey on 11 February, the Russian troops began to evacuate by gradual stages—Adrianople in March, Eastern Roumelia from May to July, and Bulgaria proper not till August.

Bulgarian national consciousness kindled very rapidly, and while the desert freed from the Turkish blight literally began to blossom as a rose garden, this nation of peasants showed a firm resolve to manage its own affairs and not to submit to Russian dictation. Even in Eastern Roumelia Turkish power remained the merest shadow; little more was heard of Turkish garrisons or the much vaunted "line of the Balkans": and when the inevitable movement for union, at first held under tactical control, burst into flames in 1885, it achieved its aim instantly and without bloodshed, triumphantly overcame the craven and miscalculated onslaught of King Milan, frankly defied the Tsar and his Government, and proved to Europe its ability to stand alone.

In the Bulgarian question the treaty had left Turkey virtually no loophole for evasion: in the Greek and Montenegrin questions it was able to play a truly oriental game of procrastination, in the hope of setting its enemies by the ears. In one direction only did it show real initiative: this was in sending Mukhtar Pasha to Crete to negotiate direct with the insurgents. The Haleppa Convention of 23 October 1878 provided for a Christian Governor-General, an Assembly with a Greek majority and the use of Greek as the official language, and peace was thus secured at any rate for a decade, and, more important, the Cretans were temporarily detached from the cause of the Greek Kingdom.

Meanwhile the occupation of Bosnia by Austria-Hungary was strongly resisted, especially by the Moslem population: both Sarajevo and Mostar had to be taken by force of arms, and guerilla warfare was not suppressed till October. In April 1879 Turkey concluded a detailed convention with Vienna, reserving the Sultan's suzerainty and full religious rights, and in the following summer a small Austrian garrison was allowed to occupy the Sandjak of Novipazar.

Far more serious was the trouble evoked by the arbitrary assignment to Montenegro of the two, in themselves insignificant, districts of Gusinje and Plava. The local population, being overwhelmingly Albanian, intensely resented such treatment and rose in insurrection. Mehemed Ali Pasha, the plenipotentiary of Berlin, was sent by the Porte to pacify them, but was besieged in Djakovica and massacred early in September. The "Albanian League", in which Tosk and Gheg, Moslem, Orthodox and Catholic, combined with unwonted fervour, organised wholesale resistance during the winter, and the Porte not unnaturally showed no inclination to enforce the submission of its own recalcitrant subjects, and remained unmoved by a demand of the Powers that it should first occupy, and then hand over, the disputed territory. The Albanian League, now firmly entrenched in Skutari, successfully defied Europe throughout 1879: and the situation was as unsettled as ever when the Liberals came into power in London. It took a joint naval demonstration off the Albanian coast and threats of the occupation of Smyrna as a pledge, before the Porte yielded even to the compromise suggested. Gusinje and Plava remained Turkish, and at last, in November 1880, the so-called "port" of Dulcigno and a strip of land along the Bojana river were handed over to Montenegro. In April 1881 the Albanian League was suppressed by Dervish Pasha with a high hand, and the Albanian movement sank to sleep for another quarter of a century. Outstanding disputes on the Montenegrin frontier were not finally settled till 1884.

Equally troublesome was the question of the Greek frontier, which, for the remainder of Lord Salisbury's tenure of office, kept Greece and Turkey on the very edge of war. The Porte showed no inclination whatever to make the territorial concessions adumbrated at Berlin, and interminable negotiations followed throughout 1879 and the spring of 1880. In July of that year a commission sitting at Berlin drew up proposals for a new frontier, but the Turks absolutely declined to surrender Larissa, Metzovo or Janina, and in the case of the latter they found a convenient ally in Albanian agitation. Lord Granville favoured coercive measures to enforce the treaty, but the other Powers were not disposed to take an active share, and Bismarck showed considerable irritation in his talks with Odo Russell. It was not till May 1881 that the Powers, acting through their Ambassadors at Constantinople, imposed a settlement that gave Greece Larissa, but not Janina, and indeed a territory decidedly smaller than that advocated by her friends, with less than 300,000 inhabitants. The Sultan gave a reluctant consent on 2 July. The Greeks, who had more than once seemed about to plunge into a warlike adventure, submitted with a bad grace and, of course, continued to nurse their dreams of national unity, until the outbreak of another Cretan insurrection beguiled them into war and swift defeat in 1897 and gave fresh occupation to the fleets and diplomacy of the Concert.

In all these disputes the main difficulty proceeded from the deliberate prevarications and bad faith of the Porte. There remained the question of internal reform in Turkey: and to all but the wilfully blind it should have soon been only too obvious that the Sultan's foremost aim was its complete evasion. The proposed reforms fell under two distinct heads—under § 23 of the Treaty for the European provinces, and under § 61 for Armenia. The former automatically applied to Thrace, Macedonia, Albania and Epirus, but was allowed to remain a dead letter, and the failure to enforce it—due to Sultan Abdul Hamid himself—eventually proved the ruin of Turkey, by leading to the Macedonian complications of 1903–8 and the Albanian risings of 1909–11, with all their many repercussions across the Turkish frontiers.

If Lord Beaconsfield, once the treaty was an accomplished fact, was content to rest upon his laurels and showed little interest in Turkish reform, his enfeebled health and his past record of indifference may serve as explanation. Lord Salisbury, on the other hand, was fully alive to the danger and warned Sir Henry Layard that "the Sultan's inclination to come to an agreement, and our power of insisting upon it, will diminish with every succeeding month".[1] He therefore submitted to Layard a scheme for the appointment of Governors in five Asiatic vilayets and European control of the police, the courts and the collection of taxes. He told Layard to direct his attention "to persons rather than to paper institutions", to follow Indian rather than western models, and to look out for good officers, capable of creating "suitable traditions of administration". The Ambassador needed no prompting, for apart from his own ultra-Turcophil views, he had to justify the hopes of the Jingoes at home, rendered highly restive by what they regarded as unwarranted concessions at Berlin. But he at once came up against the desperate financial straits of the Turkish Government, which accentuated tenfold its natural lethargy, corruption and thinly veiled xenophobia: while even Salisbury in London met with a dead weight of resistance from Sir Stafford Northcote, when he appealed to the Treasury to finance the ventures to which we stood committed. Beaconsfield "did not see his way to any immediate help";[2] Northcote felt that at best such a scheme could not run the gauntlet of

1 25 June and 7 Aug.—*Life of Salisbury*, ii. p. 305.   2 23 Sept.—*ibid.* ii. p. 312.

Parliament before February, and the Turkish bondholders opposed a scheme which involved some sort of lien upon Turkish revenues, while the impending financial complications in Egypt and their reaction upon Franco-British relations provided a further excuse for caution.

In September Salisbury expressed to Layard his belief in "a very considerable increase in the authority and influence of Great Britain at Constantinople": but as the Sultan's Fabian tactics grew more obvious, he became increasingly impatient and wrote that "the reluctance of England to enter on a full policy of partition will not bear more than a certain amount of strain—and that reluctance is the solitary support on which the Sultan's Empire now rests".[1] But though he was not long in modifying his favourable view of Abdul Hamid,[2] and had few illusions as to the parlous internal state of Turkey, he stubbornly persevered. Sir Charles Wilson was appointed Consul-General for Anatolia, with four other British officers as consuls under him: and then after a struggle Baker Pasha was given the post of Inspector-General of Reforms. As, however, this did not carry with it any executive authority, he was virtually powerless, while in popular parlance the higher officials appointed acquired the nickname of "Evet Effendis" ("Yes, Sirs"), because they took no action save on instructions from headquarters. Salisbury's letters to Wilson and Trotter reveal a dwindling confidence and a sense of the extremely slow course of reform. The plain fact is that there was from the first not the slightest hope of success, unless Britain imposed her will upon the Porte and made herself responsible for the administration of Asia Minor—in other words, carried the Convention to what Lord Derby and other critics saw to be its only logical conclusion. Here indeed lay its essential weakness from the beginning, that to make it effective we must have repeated our Indian experiment, on a smaller but none the less impossibly large scale. There was no other alternative, so long as Turkey was a despotic and highly centralised Government, in which negation was carried to its highest pitch and rested upon a basis of mutual suspicion, fear and espionage. It is indeed no exaggeration to describe the Hamidian régime as the supreme negation of government, even though we may not endorse Sir William Watson's indictment of its author as "immortally,

---

[1] 17 Oct.—*ibid.* p. 315.
[2] "The character of the Sultan appears likely to be the doom of his race" (6 Nov. 1879)—*ibid.* p. 319.

beyond all mortals, damned". Failure, then, may be said to have been inevitable unless the British Government boldly shouldered the responsibility for the actual administration in Asia Minor, and so perhaps in European Turkey as well, and made obstruction as impossible for Abdul Hamid and his favourites as it did about the same time for the Khedive Ismail and his predatory clique. The initial blunder was Sir Henry Layard's profoundly mistaken estimate of Abdul Hamid, readily endorsed by Beaconsfield and for a time accepted by Salisbury: the second blunder was the refusal of the Chancellor of the Exchequer and of his parliamentary majority to face the logical financial consequences of enforcing our commitments under the Convention.

The apologists of the Beaconsfield Government have argued that the prospects of success were ruined by "the abrupt change in British policy when Gladstone returned to power in 1880",[1] and the subsequent withdrawal of the military consuls: and even Lady Gwendolen Cecil, whose legitimate pride in her father's career never obscures her critical acumen, quotes Lord Salisbury, on his return to office in 1885, as saying of British influence at the Porte under his Liberal rivals, "They have just thrown it away into the sea, without getting anything whatever in exchange".[2]

Neither criticism can be upheld. Failure was inherent in the Turkish situation, which nothing could have redeemed save a resolute British protectorate: for this the Tories were as little inclined as the Liberals, and indeed it would have led us into quite incalculable commitments. As for British influence at the Porte, none knew better than Layard himself that ever since his arrival its mainstay had been the hope of British intervention on the Turkish side, and that from the moment when this proved illusory, the Turks simply regarded us as betraying our friends and were in a mood to welcome the first serious new friend that presented himself. Stated brutally, the provision about Cyprus did not in their eyes differ from the commission extracted by a fraudulent broker from a hard-pressed client! Moreover, a no less essential factor in the decline of our influence was the course of events in Egypt, which were driving us—quite irrespective of party labels—towards occupation. It suited the Porte on the whole to play our game, because it lacked the power to challenge it: but it did not love us any the more for it, and even before the Conservatives fell, there were never wanting candid diplomatic friends at Constantinople

[1] Buckle, vi. p. 368.   [2] *Life of Salisbury*, ii. p. 326.

bent upon poisoning the Sultan's tortuous mind against us. In a word, the widening of the gulf between Turkey and Britain was a perfectly natural evolution, leading to the events of the nineties, when Salisbury in power was no less severe on Turkey than Gladstone in opposition, and not merely admitted publicly that we had "backed the wrong horse" in the Eastern Question, but secretly suggested to Germany that the moment for partition had arrived.

Never was a catchword launched with nicer judgment or more timely effect than "Peace with Honour" to the gathering crowds that welcomed home the two statesmen. The angry consternation of the Jingoes, the moral indignation of the Radicals at the adroit change of attitude, the sarcastic outlook of that solid "middle" opinion whose pulse-beat is reflected in the columns of *Punch*—all was for a moment swallowed up in the nation's intense relief at having escaped from war. Cyprus was the sop to Cerberus which averted any too close or critical inspection of the platter from which it had been flung. In the first days of the Congress Blowitz, with his usual acumen, had said of Beaconsfield that he had British opinion behind him, but only because it was thought that he could win without war.[1] In other words, the nation did not want war, and would have turned very rapidly against him if war had come.

THE ATTITUDE OF MR. PUNCH

Yet again it is worth while stopping for a moment to note some of the more memorable comments of *Punch* upon the Congress, for never was Tenniel's instinct surer. During the opening week we are shown Disraeli with his hand upon the door of the council-chamber, turning to Bismarck and whispering, "Oh, I say! By-the-bye! What's the French for '*Compromise*'?"[2] A week later Disraeli, as showman of a menagerie, announces to the alarmed audience that "the British Lion and the Rooshian Bear will now embrace", but adds the prompt aside, "It's all right, ladies and gentlemen, this effect has been *well rehearsed*".[3] In the third week a new wooden leg is being fitted on

---

[1] Commander Verney Cameron devotes the concluding chapter of *Our Future Highway* to an analysis of ten rival overland routes to India: "We wish the Sultan to be a talented and able man, virtuous, just and honest, and we hug to our hearts the belief that he is what we desire: the awakening will come and no one will be to blame but we ourselves. As a foreign diplomat once said to me, we enjoy being deceived" (ii. p. 329).

[2] "Façon de parler", 22 June.   [3] "A 'Happy Family' at Berlin", 29 June.

the mangled and disgruntled Turk.[1] At the final stage of the Congress
Bismarck and Disraeli are smoking their after-dinner cigars together
and waxing both familiar and confidential. "I fancy our friend the
Turk don't half like it," says Bizzy, to which Dizzy replies, puffing
the white smoke of a sybarite, "Ha, that's another 'Party' that will
have to be EDUCATED!!"[2]

After the first welcome home we are shown how "Dizzy with
Cyprus and All the Queen's Men, hopes to set Humpty Dumpty
(Turkey) up again".[3] For the moment there was "a blaze of triumph"
—depicted by Punch in the shape of Dizzy as Blondel on his tight-
rope, successfully balancing a fat and jovial Turk upon his shoulders.
But the comment is significant.

> But to assist the Russ in the rough work
> Of cutting up the Empire of the Turk,
> Then presto! in a transformation scene
> Change colours, and as Turk's friend pose serene!
> After we've fought for right with boast and brag,
> Cut in the game and sudden pouch the swag!

Everyone knows Tenniel's famous cartoon of the two statesmen
on their return—"The Pas de Deux"—but not so many know the
accompanying commentary—"She did praise my leg being cross-
gartered". Beaconsfield's reminder to Salisbury, "But mind, let's
foot it together", produces an aside from the latter, "Ah yes, that's
his cue. Am I hero or martyr?" and a further aside from his chief,
"Aha, does he wince at the gall of the tether?"[4] There is a scarcely
veiled undercurrent of incredulous suspicion, of suggestion that the
two men did not really see eye to eye, whatever they wished the
outside world to believe.

RIVAL EXTREMES OF COMMENT

Much more significant than the pained comment of the Turcophils
was the attitude of Sir Henry Layard. Already at the height of the
Congress he had expressed himself most unfavourably to his old
enemy Prince Reuss on the weakness of the British ministers in
yielding up Varna, Sofia and Bosnia. The much-boasted Balkan line
seemed to him no equivalent: "He sees the gradual collapse of his

[1] "The New Leg", 6 July.
[2] "The Schoolmaster Abroad", 13 July. A reference to his famous speech at
Edinburgh on 9 November 1867: "I had—if it be not arrogant to use such a phrase—
to educate our party".   [3] 20 July.   [4] *Punch* of 27 July and 3 Aug. 1878.

hope of restoring Turkey, at least seemingly and under exclusive English influence: but he prophesies that under such circumstances the peace will not be of long duration".[1]

In his memoirs he records his considered view that more could have been obtained at Berlin, "had a more decided course been pursued by the British plenipotentiaries". He *"could not understand why Sofia should have been given to Bulgaria"*, or if so, why Varna was not retained as compensation for Turkey.[2] To-day such verdicts border on the grotesque and are the measure of Layard's blindness: but it is only fair to point out that he saw from the first that an autonomous Eastern Roumelia was certain to achieve speedy union with Bulgaria.

Mr. Buckle writes of Layard's "ascendancy at Constantinople",[3] and it was for a time so much of a reality that he virtually overthrew and set up ministers and generals. What Mr. Buckle fails to realise is how fatally that ascendancy was undermined by the Disraelian "Peace with Honour".

So much for the reactions of a foremost exponent of Palmerstonian doctrine. As for the anti-Disraelian opinion, it was once more split into two sections and thus paralysed for the time being. It would perhaps be more correct to say that Liberal opinion was torn in two directions, condemning our unwise commitments in Asia and the loss of our reputation for disinterestedness involved in the "deal" over Cyprus,[4] yet constrained to admit that the treaty contained far more good than bad. This latter view was admirably voiced by Sir William Harcourt, who boldly described the treaty as "beneficial", though insisting that its results would not have been attained without the Russian war.[5] Indeed the more a man might detest the Turk, the greater was bound to be his satisfaction at the many amputations imposed upon Turkey, and even the convention (however objectionable the manner of its conclusion) might on this showing be condoned, as freeing at least one more important island from its ancestral yoke, and opening the way for further use of the surgeon's knife in Asia. This view is reflected in the utterances of Lord Carnarvon and of James Bryce, who argued that "happily the object which the friends

---

[1] Reuss to Bülow, 27 June—*G.P.* ii. no. 432.
[2] *Layard Papers* (add. MSS. 38937, *Memoirs*, vol. vii. p. 209). He quotes the view of Mr. Mackenzie Wallace, then correspondent at St. Petersburg, that Russia could have been forced to abandon Batum.   [3] Buckle, vi. p. 366.
[4] Cf. Mr. Shaw-Lefevre in the House of Commons, 3 Aug. 1878.
[5] *Ibid.* 3 Aug.

of Armenia have sought is now, *by our assumption of the protectorate of Asiatic Turkey*, in large measure attained".[1] Liddon, too, argued with very sound logic, "The real question is whether the good government of Asia can be made a reality. If so, I am content with the Convention, but everything depends on that IF."[2] Or again, Lord Selborne put on record his inability to reconcile this secret bargaining "with any high idea of political morality: but the motives which led me to rejoice in the liberation of other parts of Turkey from misgovernment made it impossible for me to be sorry that Cyprus should partake. . . ."[3]

Viewed from this angle, the shrill attitude adopted by Gladstone was undoubtedly a tactical blunder, which for a time obscured the extent to which the treaty, despite certain deplorable lapses, realised many of his own and Argyll's aspirations. In fact, Gladstone, who had seen so much further than his rival into the essence of the problem, and had on many points shown a really prophetic instinct, now for a time lost self-restraint and due perspective, seemingly under the stress of personal feeling.

Though the Congress kept the Christian states in the anteroom and treated their interests as only secondary, it none the less recognised if not all the facts, at least the hardest of them, and created or accepted a situation equivalent to the restoration of the nations whom the Turkish conquest had submerged. Translated into modern terms, this meant the formation of a chain of buffer states between Turkey and Russia, and the possibility of a gradual evolution in the same direction by those whose claims had not yet obtained recognition.

Mr. Buckle, in his defence of Disraeli, admits that the settlement did not secure peace in the Balkans, but argues that "no arrangement that was possible in the conditions of 1878 could have effected that". The history of the next fifty years, so far from bearing out this contention, proves the direct contrary: for every breach of Balkan peace between the Congress of Berlin and the Great War is directly traceable to some more or less deliberate imperfection or omission in the Treaty. The troubles of 1885–6 followed logically from the artificial separation of North and South Bulgaria, in the teeth of common sense and of popular feeling. The Serbo-Bulgarian War of 1885—for which the blame should lie more upon the de-

---

[1] Letter to *The Times* of 15 July 1878.
[2] 25 July, *Life of Liddon*, p. 225.   [3] *Memorials*, iii. p. 453.

generate King Milan than upon his people, but which was the beginning of the deplorable and quite unnatural feud between the two Slav brethren—would of course never have occurred if union had been ordained in 1878, when Serbia could not have resisted, even if it had occurred to her to do so. The Turco-Greek War of 1897, and the long international crisis that followed, would never have taken place if Crete had been allowed to follow its eager desire to unite with Greece in 1878, and if the Thessalian and Epirote frontiers had been drawn more intelligently. The Armenian massacres of the nineties, and the culminating tragedy of 1915, might have been avoided if Article LXI. of the Treaty had been enforced: while in the same way the insurrection of 1903, the internecine racial quarrels that preceded and followed it and all the European complications which it evoked, might have been avoided if the Powers had held the Porte to its pledges, and if the local government envisaged under Article XXIII. had been enforced. In a word, the Powers brought down all subsequent troubles on their own heads by a series of provisions that sinned against the light: though this must not of course be allowed to obscure the fact that certain of the more ripe problems were finally solved, and though it might plausibly be contended that the worst troubles were due to the non-enforcement of certain clauses which even contemporary critics regarded as a saving grace of the treaty.

BRITAIN'S CONTINENTAL AIMS

In two notable directions only, then, did the Berlin settlement differ from that of San Stefano—in the grant of an European mandate to Austria-Hungary and in the division of "Big Bulgaria" into three sections, the free, the half-free and the once more enslaved. As regards the first of these, Western Europe, though not of course Germany, acted in ignorance of the jealously guarded secret that Russia—not once, but four separate times since the rising began —had acknowledged Austria-Hungary's right to occupy Bosnia-Hercegovina at her own discretion, and that it was therefore impossible for her to raise any active obstacle. In other words—as Bismarck accurately points out in his *Recollections*—Reichstadt and Budapest, not Berlin, were the real foundation of the Austrian mandate, though the secrecy in which the agreements were shrouded prevented London from realising this fact. Meanwhile, on the British side, it was only too obvious that the favour accorded to an Austrian mandate was prompted by the desire to perpetuate the alienation of Austria and Russia. It completely ignored the wishes of the local population and sowed the seeds of future discord between Vienna and Belgrade: but it must be added that at this stage there was still a possibility of winning not merely Bosnia but even Serbia to a Habsburg solution of Southern Slav unity. The chief elements that contributed to frustrate this dream were the persons of Milan and Alexander Obrenović, whose subserviency compromised Austrophilism in the eyes of their subjects, the fatal influence of Magyar racialism upon the general policy of the Dual Monarchy, and the stubborn adherence of Francis Joseph to the Magyar hegemony as against the Slavs at home and abroad.

As regards Bulgaria, it is quite impossible to suppose that either Beaconsfield or Salisbury really believed that so cynical and artificial an arrangement could last very long. It was an attempt to dam back an irresistible current, and it failed as hopelessly as the earlier attempt of Palmerston and Clarendon to prevent the union of Wallachia and Moldavia. As Prince Charles of Roumania assured the new Prince some months after his accession, a greater Bulgaria was a moral certainty, and "the diplomats with all their tricks cannot hold up the course of events".[1] Already at his first official visit to Vienna Prince Alexander used very outspoken language to Count Andrássy, making it clear that he would respect the treaty as long as possible, but that a separation, which was mainly "due to Lord Beaconsfield's inadequate knowledge of Bulgarian character and aims, could not be expected to be permanent".[2] It must, however, be added that Beaconsfield himself, during the Congress, admitted to the German Crown Princess that "without Eastern Roumelia the affair would not hold for more than seven years"[3]—a singularly accurate prophecy which shows that he had no illusions and was merely using the Bulgarians as pawns in the great game. His insistence, in more than one speech, upon the loyalty of the subject populations to the Porte was, to say the least, disingenuous.

[1] 29 July 1879—Corti, *Alexander von Battenberg*, p. 48.

[2] 10 Feb. 1880—*ibid*. p. 64. In this connection it is interesting to read a letter of Sir Charles Dilke to Lord Granville, on 22 September 1885, when the long-due Bulgarian crisis had come: "It may interest you to be reminded that in 1880, shortly after our Government was formed, a secret agent of the Prince of Bulgaria came over. I saw him several times. He said that the union of Bulgaria and E. Roumelia could not be prevented, and that it had better be carried out at once by the Prince himself. We discouraged him" (*Granville Papers*).

[3] See a letter of 2 Oct. 1885 from the Crown Princess to Prince Alexander, quoted *ibid*. p. 46.

Salisbury on his side was not, like his chief, indifferent to the fate of the Balkan Christians, but genuinely feared that the Bulgarians would be helpless instruments in the hands of Russia: and his attitude changed in proportion as he realised, albeit very tardily, how radically mistaken any such assumption was. And so it came about that during his second tenure of the Foreign Office events led him to write: "A Bulgaria friendly to the Porte and jealous of foreign influence would be a far surer bulwark against foreign aggression than two Bulgarias, severed in administration but united in considering the Porte as the only obstacle to the national development".[1] In the words of Sir Spencer Walpole, in 1885 Britain under Salisbury "neither moved a sepoy from India, nor sent a frigate to the Dardanelles" to enforce the principles laid down by him at Berlin in 1878.[2] When Derby ridiculed the artificial rechristening of southern Bulgaria, no one reacted more indignantly than Salisbury: but after seven years the Spirit of Irony assigned to him a foremost rôle in achieving the union which he had prevented.

This criticism of the Bulgarian clauses of the Treaty must, however, be strictly limited to the artificial separation of northern and southern Bulgaria, to the farcical attempt to water down the call of the blood by imposing upon the latter the meaningless name of Eastern Roumelia, and to the amputation of the Dobrogea—inhabited, it is true, by a very scanty and mixed population—as Roumania's compensation for Russia's theft of Bessarabia. In other respects, the curtailment of "Big Bulgaria" was a just and salutary feature of the Treaty: for its extension southwards to the Aegean coast, and westwards to the Shar mountains and into the heart of Albania, would have been to satisfy Bulgaria's uttermost ambitions at the expense of all the other races of the Peninsula—Serb, Greek, Albanian and Vlach alike. In the territory now restored to the Turks —which Shuvalov suggested should be formed into a third autonomous unit known as "*Western* Roumelia", but of which Europe was to hear only too much, under the more comprehensive name of "Macedonia"—these other races, together with the Turks themselves, would have formed an actual majority of the population: and all without exception were strongly opposed to the transaction. There was a further valid reason for revision, in that the frontiers of San Stefano would have made Turkey's position in her remaining European possessions utterly untenable, by cutting all land connection

---

[1] *Turkey No. I.* (1886), p. 424.   [2] *Twenty-five Years*, iv. p. 175.

between them and Constantinople, and by establishing, in equal
defiance of physical geography and political evolution, a narrow
corridor connecting Bosnia with Albania and keeping Serbia and
Montenegro apart. Hence the fault of this section of the treaty lay
not in detaching these territories from Bulgaria, but in not forming
them into further natural units, with an autonomous status of their
own, or—next best thing—in not enforcing there the inadequate
measure of local administration provided under Article XXIII.

There were other provisions of the Treaty also which show how
speedily and drastically Beaconsfield had unlearned his former
professions. In his first fury at San Stefano he had solemnly declared
in the House of Lords that it made "the Black Sea as much a Russian
lake as the Caspian",[1] and much was made of the "strongholds of
Armenia" and "the important harbour" of Batum. But writing home
from Berlin, he airily dismissed "Batum or questions of that calibre"[2]
—the emphasis laid upon it at the Congress being mainly intended
to reassure his Jingoes at home: then on his return he assured an
astonished Parliament that Batum was as unimportant as Cowes.
Again, there had been a time when Beaconsfield stressed the capital
importance attached by Palmerston to Bessarabia, as involving the
freedom of the Danube. But now, after rightly condemning Russia
for resuming possession, he privately indicated to St. Petersburg
that Britain had no intention of resisting the accomplished fact, and
then turned round to describe Bessarabia as "a very small portion
of territory, occupied by 130,000 inhabitants".

Again, following up the Cassandran warnings of Layard about the
military defence of Turkey, Beaconsfield proclaimed "the line of the
Balkans", which was to form the boundary between the two Bulgarias, as one of the most vital features of the whole settlement.
But no sooner was the treaty signed than this contention was
dropped, and—very fortunately for Eastern Roumelia—no attempt
was made to introduce Turkish garrisons, much less to fortify the
frontier, with the result that the Revolution of 1885 could be effected
without bloodshed. Earlier in the year Layard had been anxiously
contending that there was an end of Turkey's military defence if
once she abandoned the fortresses of the Danube and the Quadrilateral. In June he was arguing in all seriousness that "it would
require the constant presence in Bulgaria of at least 100,000 Russian
troops to protect her unwarlike population against the Albanians".

[1] 8 April 1878.   [2] To Northcote—Buckle, vi. p. 321.

It is hard to avoid the conclusion that Layard was altogether at sea in military tactics, and that Beaconsfield was merely using "the line of the Balkans" as a drum on which to thump the Jingo tune and thus divert attention from his own strategic retreat.

In plain fact, this successful retreat from an impossible situation, which Beaconsfield could not have effected alone, was brilliantly achieved, but it broke many windows in Europe and in particular it strengthened the extreme Slavophils in their criticism of the settlement, placed the Tsar in an embarrassing position and helped him to misjudge the general situation, thereby producing that passing estrangement with Germany which had such momentous consequences for the world. Salisbury, as his daughter very pertinently remarks, thus had "a first experience in the evils of trumpeting a diplomatic victory",[1] which may be said to have given an incentive to his habitual reserve, not to say secretiveness, in foreign affairs.

If, then, Disraeli's attitude at Berlin rested very largely upon bluff, it was largely thanks to the blunders of his opponents in more than one country that he contrived to conceal from contemporary Europe the extent to which he had abandoned his original policy. For this, however, in the blunt phrase of Sir William Harcourt, "it was necessary to bring back something, and that something was Cyprus". There were, it is true, critics who pointed out that Cyprus could not fulfil the functions claimed for it, that it had no harbours, that it was equally unsuitable as a naval or as a military base, that it was unhealthy and neglected, and would be a heavy charge upon the British taxpayer. Naval and military opinion from that day to this has been virtually unanimous in this sense, and it ought to have been obvious that if ever we had to shoulder the burden of defending Turkey against Russia, Cyprus would be the last, not the first, base which we should require, since every Turkish port would then stand open to us, and that our transports would be needed on the Bosphorus, in the Black Sea and perhaps on the Persian Gulf, rather than on the coast of Syria. But all save a small section of public opinion felt flattered at the acquisition and were disinclined to be critical, as is best shown by the way in which the House of Lords accepted Beaconsfield's preposterous assurance that "by next year there will be enough ports in Cyprus".[2] Next year there had been no

---

[1] *Life*, ii. p. 327.

[2] 23 July 1878—Hansard, ccxlii. p. 27. On this occasion Lord Granville said: "I do not know a single naval officer of high or low command who has not pronounced

change: but in the interval the *soldiers* had been advising the civilians
on *naval* affairs, and Colonel Hamley "says that Famagusta will turn
out a harbour, which will conveniently receive all Your Majesty's
ironsides". So Beaconsfield gaily wrote to the Queen and drew the
conclusion that "Cyprus will be a marvellous success".[1] Far more
accurate was the estimate of the well-known traveller Sir Samuel
Baker that, "if we are supreme at sea, Cyprus is not wanted, and if
not, it is an encumbrance".[2]

On one point, and on one only, the Turks themselves and the
British Opposition were in agreement—that the pretence of be-
friending Turkey, so often stressed by Beaconsfield, was proved by
the Cyprus Convention to be "a complete sham".[3] After the crisis
was over, Salisbury in cold blood told Drummond Wolff—who
records it with seeming pride in his recollections—that "we acted
for Turkey on principles of pure egotism, and have no right to claim
the credit of a romantic friendship":[4] and it was because the Turks
felt this in the marrow of their bones and distrusted our high professions, that they sought other friendships in the eighties and
nineties.

It is, however, easy to detect an ulterior motive in British policy
at Berlin—namely, to sow discord between Russia and Austria.
This aim, which runs right through Disraeli's action from 1875 to
1880, is clearly avowed in a letter addressed to Drummond Wolff on
4 November 1880: "Next to making a tolerable settlement for the
Porte, our great object was to break up, and permanently prevent,
the alliance of the three Empires".[5] This explains the ostentatious
support given to Austria-Hungary in the Bosnian question, which
was defined in Beaconsfield's crude and indiscreet phrase at the
Mansion House—"the occupation permits us to check, I should hope
for ever, that Panslavist confederacy and conspiracy which has
already proved so disadvantageous to the happiness of the world".[6]
Somewhat more veiled was the reference in Salisbury's covering
dispatch to the text of the Treaty—claiming the interposition of
Austria between the two Slav states, Serbia and Montenegro, as
offering the Sultan "security against renewed aggression on their

against it", and Lord Hammond found it "difficult to understand how an island in
a remote corner of the Mediterranean could serve as a basis of operations against a
Russian invasion of the north-east corner of Asiatic Turkey".
[1] 27 Nov. 1878—Buckle, vi. p. 395.   [2] *Cyprus as I saw it in 1879*, p. 441.
[3] See, *e.g.*, Lord Selborne, *Recollections*, iii. p. 465.
[4] *Rambling Recollections*, i. p. 233.
[5] Buckle, vi. p. 367.   [6] *The Times*, 3 Aug. 1878.

part". But in the House of Lords Salisbury had gone even further when he claimed that Russia had hitherto seemed the only possible heir to the remains of Turkey, but that now the arrival of Austria at Novipazar showed that "if Turkey falls, it will not be Russia that will rule on the Bosphorus".[1] In Lord Selborne's phrase, fear of Panslavism led the British Government to put forward Austria as "candidate for the succession to Constantinople".[2] This exaggerated reliance on Austria in 1878 is all the more curious if we contrast it with Disraeli's absurd underestimate of Andrássy in 1875–6 or with Salisbury's low estimate of Austrian power as revealed in his private correspondence and above all in his first conversation with Bismarck, who—*en pleine connaissance de cause*—endeavoured to disabuse him.[3]

Beaconsfield, in the letter to Wolff already quoted, goes on: "I maintain there never was a general diplomatic result more completely effected" [than the break-up of the Three Emperors' League]. "Of course it does not appear on the protocols, it was realised by personal influence alone, both with Andrássy and Bismarck." This phrase, and Mr. Buckle's emphatic endorsement of it, show both the statesman and his biographer to have been under a misapprehension as to the underlying forces of Eastern Europe, and not least of all, as to Bismarck's fundamental aims. Thanks to the screaming of the Slavophils, Gorchakov's vendetta against Shuvalov and Tsar Alexander's recurrent fits of nerves, the Congress was followed by serious friction between Russia and her Imperial allies, and this, as we saw, resulted in the momentous Austro-German alliance of October 1879. But the League of the Three Emperors remained the ideal of the sovereigns and statesmen of all three capitals, for many reasons entirely unconnected with the Eastern Question: though in abeyance, it was never abandoned, and in 1881, under Alexander III., took on a new lease of life. A year after the Congress Bismarck, even in the midst of his efforts to win his reluctant master for the Austrian alliance, and though eager for closer relations with Britain, was very much on his guard against what he called "an aggressive coalition in favour of the policy of Layard and other hotspurs", and warned his Ambassador at the Porte against the danger of "taking sides in Turkey more for England than for Russia". In a word, before, at and after the

[1] Hansard, ccxxxix. p. 1806.   [2] *Memorials*, iii. p. 468.
[3] Radowitz in his *Denkwürdigkeiten* (i. p. 364), commenting on the Bismarck-Salisbury conversation, notes the latter's "clearly marked underestimate" (*deutlich hervortretende Unterschätzung*) "of Austrian power".

Congress alike, Russia was Bismarck's main preoccupation, and friendship with her was his ardent desire, though he had no intention of being caught unawares by her and would find other friends and give a good account of himself if she became an enemy. The history of Bismarck's dealings with Saburov, who was sent as Russian Ambassador to Berlin in January 1880 for the express purpose of restoring the old relations, shows still more conclusively the extent to which Beaconsfield misjudged the fundamental aims of the Eastern Courts and not least of Bismarck, despite their recent *rapprochement*.

The mutual suspicions and intrigues of Russia and Austria in the Balkans were not permanently allowed to interfere with the ancient tradition, dating back to Catherine and even Peter the Great, of parallel advance in eastern and western spheres of influence. These relations were strained for a time under Kálnoky, but the old cordiality was renewed in the nineties and found fresh expression in the Austro-Russian agreements of 1897 and 1903. In a word, Disraeli had helped to derange temporarily the Concert of three—then for good or for ill the only solid combination in Europe—but he had entirely failed to destroy it, and it may well be doubted whether success would have been in the true interests of the Europe of those days.

One of Bismarck's most prophetic sayings—none the less daring because to-day it has passed into a commonplace—was that "no one can foresee the results of war between the three Empires, but the three monarchs would probably pay the bill".[1] There is nothing to show that Beaconsfield realised the *imponderabilia* of the European situation which such a phrase reveals.

Perhaps the most surprising aspect of British policy during and after the Congress is the openly avowed abandonment of that insularity to which the Conservative party had so long been wedded, in favour of "intervention" on a new and vaster scale. At the Mansion House banquet both Beaconsfield and Salisbury laid the greatest possible stress on the "rights of interference" which the Convention secured to Britain, and contrasted the position with that under the former tripartite treaty of April 1856, under which there was a guarantee on the side of the three Powers, but no corresponding one on the part of Turkey, and which—this was not said in so many words, both because emphasis would have been tactless and because the facts were notorious—had long since been a dead letter so far as

[1] Bülow, *Denkwürdigkeiten*, i. p. 580.

France and Austria were concerned. This doctrine of interference not merely passed almost unchallenged on the Conservative side, but met with some response among those Liberals whose zeal for the elimination of Turkish rule overrode their dislike of new commitments: and indeed there was something illogical in Gladstone condemning in Asia what he had so clamorously commended in Europe.

To sum up, it cannot be denied that despite certain very important changes the Treaty of Berlin did not really differ in essential principles from the Treaty of San Stefano, and that it only ratified the fundamental facts already sanctioned by the secret Salisbury-Shuvalov Protocol of 30 May. This was only dimly perceived at the time, Mr. Punch once more coming probably nearer to the heart of the matter than any other commentator, when he assumed that Disraeli had gone to Berlin resolved to compromise. This does not, however, in any way mean that Britain's insistence upon a Congress was wrong, still less superfluous. Obviously, if she and the other Powers had simply allowed Russia to enforce the Treaty of San Stefano, there would have been an end of the Concert of Europe in the Eastern Question, and Turkey would have become a Russian vassal to a far greater degree even than in the years following Adrianople and Unkiar Skelessi (1828–33). But the emphasis laid upon the settlement as an anti-Russian settlement was a grave tactical blunder, really intended to conceal the extent to which Britain had receded from her original impossible position and accepted with a bad grace so many accomplished facts which she ought to have either forestalled or welcomed with both hands.

THE TORY GOVERNMENT AND DISSOLUTION

IT was widely held at the time, and probably with good reason, that Beaconsfield committed a capital blunder in not dissolving in the autumn following the Congress, and that if he had done so, he would have been returned with an overwhelming majority. The final *dénouement* at Berlin had closed the Conservative ranks, reduced the Turcophil malcontents to silence and filled both the party and the ranks of waverers with a sense of triumph: whereas the Opposition was more divided than ever, its leadership in feeble and ineffective hands, and even the old chief by no means immune from grave errors of tactics. It may be said, then, that the intense relief at the preservation of peace produced a temporary rally in favour of the Sphinx of British politics and a corresponding discouragement among the Liberals.

It is fascinating to speculate what would have been the consequences of such a dissolution. It is safe to assume that Beaconsfield himself could not have retained the leadership much longer, and that Salisbury would have succeeded him in due course, as he did in actual fact. But it may also be plausibly argued that a Liberal defeat in 1878 would have finally ended the political career of Gladstone, that the South African and Egyptian troubles would have followed an entirely different course, above all that the effects of Irish land agitation would have been less catastrophic, that the devolution of Carnarvon rather than the Home Rule of Gladstone would have resulted, that there would have been no such upheaval among the parties as the events of 1885 and 1886 produced—in a word, that the whole course of British and perhaps of world politics would have been different. How short a distance even the greatest of statesmen can see into the future! Pitt and most of his colleagues confidently believed in 1789 that France was out of the picture for decades to come. Now Salisbury in his Guildhall speech expressed the hope that these rancorous controversies would shortly belong to the past and that we were "opening a gentler period of contemporary politics". And in the same way Gladstone, in returning to office in 1880 expected the new Parliament "to act in the main on well-tried and established lines and do much for the people and little to disquiet my growing years".[1]

Was Lord Cranbrook right in his seemingly naïve opinion that Beaconsfield's motive in not going to the country was that he declined to make party capital out of foreign policy?[2] Was Lord Selborne simply lapsing from his usual serenity and breadth of view when he declared Beaconsfield to be "short-sighted as well as vainglorious".[3] The true explanation would seem rather to lie in the fact that the Central Office of the Conservatives in 1878 and 1880 made the same grave miscalculation as the Central Office of the Liberals in 1874,[4] and that the chief was above all guided by the oversanguine advice of Whigs and agents who failed to count the pulsebeats of erratic King Demos. They felt that to dissolve "would be

[1] Morley, *Life of Gladstone*, ii. p. 631.
[2] *Life of Gathorne Hardy*, ii. p. 78.   [3] Selborne, *Memorials*, iii. p. 456.
[4] Cf. letter of Sir Geo. Russell to Lord Cranbrook, 29 March 1880—*Life of Hardy*, ii. p. 132.

like throwing up a rubber at whist, while holding nothing but good cards".[1] After the crash, in the retirement of Hughenden, Beaconsfield assured Lord Ronald Gower: "I am the unluckiest of mortals: six bad harvests in succession, one worse than the former, this has been the cause of my overthrow. Like Napoleon, I have been beaten by the elements. Bismarck and I were perfectly *d'accord*. Had the late Government lasted, we would have kept the democrats of Europe in check."[2]

The Liberals Renew the Attack

During the summer months following the Congress there was a perhaps natural tendency for the Government to rest on its laurels: and the genuine eagerness of Salisbury and Layard to make a reality of reform in Asiatic Turkey was thwarted by the indifference of their colleagues and lack of the necessary funds. The official chiefs of the Liberal party were on their side distinctly relieved at what was not so much a truce as a suspension of arms by common consent: and how little even Gladstone foresaw what the future held in store for him shown by his expression of the hope that "Lord Granville's succession . . . may be within a twelvemonth", coupled with the opinion that an immediate change was not desirable, since "the people want a little more experience of Beaconsfield Toryism".[3] He himself had made it known that he would not again contest his old seat of Greenwich and did not respond to the offer of a safe seat in Edinburgh: and it seems certain that by the close of 1878 he did not as yet contemplate a return to the leadership. On 2 November 1878 he wrote to Lord Granville: "The pot is beginning to boil. I hope it will not boil too fast. My belief has been pretty firm since the Anglo-Turkish Convention that the Tory party is travelling towards a great smash, perhaps a greater and a more enduring smash than ours. And this although it seems to have the support of the Papal party. It is well that the country should know thoroughly before the crisis comes the manner in which they are being governed. Still I should not much wonder at seeing you in their place before a twelve-month: and a pretty bed of thorns it assuredly will be."[4]

Yet in January 1879 there was a very definite change of tactics, and Mr. Gladstone made the memorable decision to challenge

---

[1] Buckle, vi. p. 369.   [2] *Reminiscences*, p. 548.
[3] Morley, *Life of Gladstone*, ii. p. 583.   [4] *Granville Papers*, 2 Nov.

Scottish Toryism in its stronghold of Midlothian, fully conscious that the struggle would be "a tooth and nail affair", and would "gather into itself a great deal of force and heat".[1] Though it was not till the following November that he opened his campaign, Midlothian became almost at once a symbol of contending forces, and Gladstone's challenge was denounced with amazing virulence and defended with almost ecstatic fervour.

Amid the acute controversies of 1879 the Eastern Question naturally held the field, in proportion as it became obvious how many important points of detail remained unsolved. Quite apart from Gladstone himself, Sir William Harcourt—who still by no means saw eye to eye with him—based many trenchant arguments on the fundamental claim that the old traditional policy of Turkish integrity and independence was "a thing neither desirable in itself nor useful as a means of resisting the aggression of Russia"; that the future "naturally and inevitably belonged to the Christian races of Turkey, and that to assume an attitude of hostility to their emancipation was to ally ourselves with a hopeless cause and to leave to Russia all the advantages which we ourselves have secured". With admirable precision he argued from the history of the previous three years that our policy had failed to maintain Turkish independence, but had effectually turned the sympathies of Serbia, Montenegro and Bulgaria towards Russia, and that if we persevered in our errors, the same thing would happen in Roumelia, Macedonia, Epirus, Thessaly and Albania.[2]

SOUTH AFRICA AND AFGHANISTAN

The more confident, or aggressive, mood now assumed by the Liberals was due to the unexpectedly unfavourable turn of events in two continents. Shepstone's annexation of the Transvaal in April 1877 had not merely failed to pacify the Boers, but was soon followed by growing friction with the Zulus. Sir Bartle Frere, the very able and energetic High Commissioner, had scarcely reached his post when he plunged into a forward policy and presented Cetewayo with an ultimatum. It was widely felt that the Zulu War could have been avoided, and the disaster of Isandhlwana led to acrimonious attacks on Frere and Chelmsford, and did considerable damage to the reputation of the Government. The death of the Prince Imperial set a

[1] 11 Jan. 1879—*Granville Papers*, p. 585.
[2] 14 Jan. 1879, to Liberal Association at Oxford.

further stamp of gloom upon the war, which was not ended till the capture of the Zulu king in August 1879.

Events in South Africa lie quite outside the scope of this volume, and only require to be mentioned as contributing materially to the decline of the Conservative Government. But other clouds were obscuring the horizon from a quarter much more closely connected with the Eastern Question. The close of the Russo-Turkish War was followed by renewed Russian activity in Central Asia, and already in July 1878 a Russian agent was sent to Kabul, against the wishes of the Ameer, Shere Ali, and with the obvious aim of embroiling Afghanistan with the Indian Government. Lord Lytton, the brilliant but all too imaginative Viceroy, lost his head and embarked upon a forward policy, which was virtually a reversal of that so effectively pursued by Lawrence and Northbrook. In June 1877 Lytton had told Salisbury that "every bazaar and every native Government in India is now vibrating to a strain of suspended sentiment in a condition of extreme tension". An explosion would be terrible, and all depended "on the course of your Eastern policy and its freedom from all appearance of subserviency to Russia".[1] His nervousness was certainly not diminished by the periodical jeremiads of Layard from Constantinople and his diatribes against Russia.

Baluchistan had already, by the Treaty of Jacobabad (December 1876) been successfully brought within the British sphere, and a garrison established at Quetta. Lytton now came to favour a revision of the North-west Frontier and a British mission to Kabul, to overawe the Ameer and counteract Russian influence. During the first half of 1878 he was assuming initiative and acting ahead of the India Office—first of Lord Salisbury, then of his successor, Gathorne Hardy, now Lord Cranbrook: nor was he deterred by the protests in *The Times* of such men as Lord Lawrence, Sir Henry Havelock and Sir John Adye. Salisbury had long since had his doubts about the Viceroy's discretion, but his chief urged on him "complete and unflinching" support of Lytton. "We wanted a man of ambition, imagination, some vanity and much will—and we have got him."[2]

On 12 September Beaconsfield expressed to Cranbrook his alarm at "the grave error" of Lytton, but already a week later they both swallowed the new policy whole, the former declaring that he was "always opposed to masterly inactivity", yet fully conscious that the Viceroy was disobeying orders and forcing the hands of the home

---

[1] *Letters of First Earl of Lytton*, ii. p. 65.   [2] Buckle, vi. p. 379, 1 April 1877.

Government.[1] In his Guildhall speech he spoke of a haphazard frontier, which ought to be scientific—thereby implying a desire for further annexations—and he declined to receive a deputation led by Lawrence himself. Lytton quite definitely favoured the deposition of Shere Ali and the occupation of Afghanistan, and in due course a British punitive expedition occupied Kandahar, under the brilliant leadership of General Roberts. His success for a time placed the Opposition critics at a disadvantage, and Beaconsfield, encouraged by the Queen's keen approval, was exultant at what he described to her as a complete "check to Russia".[2] During his defence in the House of Lords he very soon assumed the offensive against "that principle of peace at any price which a certain party in this country upholds" and which had "occasioned more wars than the most ruthless conquerors".

For a time he seemed to have carried all before him. Shere Ali fled to Russian territory and very soon died in exile: and his weak son Yakub Khan in May 1879 concluded the Treaty of Gundamak, which acknowledged British control of his foreign policy, accepted a British Resident and ceded certain frontier districts near the Khyber Pass. Beaconsfield, deliberately harking back to his much challenged Guildhall speech, affirmed that the treaty had "secured a scientific and adequate frontier for our Indian Empire". But Salisbury's prophecy, spoken "with great bitterness", that the Viceroy's conduct, "unless curbed, would bring about some terrible disaster",[3] was not very slow of fulfilment. Only four months after the treaty the murder of Cavagnari produced an open rupture with Afghanistan, and Roberts undertook his second expedition, this time to Kabul itself. By this time the policy of Lytton was quite frankly the disintegration of Afghanistan and a territorial advance on the part of Britain, which could only have ended in our acquiring a joint frontier with Russia between the Oxus and the Persian borders and an immense extension of our military and political liabilities in Asia. The dangers involved were kept before the public by the "Afghan Committee", composed of a number of men highly versed in the problems of the East, and hammered in by the more impatient and aggressive leaders of the Opposition. In the winter of 1879 the Afghan complications, the analogy which it was so easy to draw between the Government's handling of it and of the Eastern Question a year earlier, and the fact, by now incontestable and obvious to all, that the Treaty of Berlin had

[1] 12 and 26 Sept. and 26 Oct.—Buckle, vi. 381, 382, 387.
[2] 6 Dec.—*ibid.* p. 398.   [3] Beaconsfield to Queen, 26 Oct.—*ibid.* p. 387.

left many acute problems unsolved, all contributed to that discontent and *malaise* of opinion which the Midlothian campaign kindled into sudden conflagration. But Beaconsfield remained unrepentant, and at his last Guildhall banquet defended Lytton in the phrase, "I have rarely met a man in whom genius and sagacity were more happily allied".

In the whole Afghan affair our strained relations with Russia played a decisive part. Even the pacific Shuvalov admitted quite freely to Salisbury that his Government, learning of the summons of Indian troops to Malta and assuming the two countries to be very near *"les coups de canon"*, had in self-defence attempted "a diversion by way of Afghanistan".[1] The British press had then written in a violent strain about Central Asia and even after the Congress had produced a *détente*, official Russia hesitated to withdraw its mission from Kabul, lest it should be represented—either in London or in Moscow—as a retreat. On the other hand, Russia's renewed activity in Central Asia was the logical result of our challenge to the San Stefano settlement, in exactly the same way as her renewed activity in the Balkans after 1905 resulted from her check in the Far East. Beaconsfield was perfectly courteous to Russia and contrasted her "honourable amends to England" with the shifty conduct of the Ameer.[2] Early in 1879 he even gave practical proof of a more conciliatory attitude, by appointing to the vacant Embassy at St. Petersburg the newly retired Viceroy of Canada, Lord Dufferin, whose party connections were with the Liberals, and whose rôle in the Lebanon dispute of 1860 naturally prepossessed the Russians in his favour. This was duly appreciated by the Tsar and Gorchakov. Moreover the selection of Alexander of Battenberg for the Bulgarian throne proved almost equally acceptable to British and Russian feelings and for a time served as a sedative. On the other hand, Gorchakov's vendetta had effectively poisoned the Tsar's mind against Shuvalov, who instead of acquiring the Chancellor's position (as Salisbury, Bismarck and many others had hoped) was in the autumn of 1879 removed from the London Embassy and for the remainder of his life severely excluded from public affairs. His successor, the moderate Prince Lobanov, was on good terms with Lord Salisbury, but it was not till the return of Lord Granville to the Foreign Office that relations again became cordial.[3]

---

[1] 25 Nov. 1878, Salisbury to Queen—*Letters*, ii. p. 647.   [2] Buckle, vi. p. 400.
[3] See documents published by me in *Slavonic Review*, no. 25 ("Mr. Gladstone, Lord Granville and Russia").

BEACONSFIELD'S SWAN SONG

This brief outline of external events provides the clue to the rising tide of Opposition feeling during 1879. Other very material causes were of course the natural swing of the political pendulum and a long spell of trade depression at home—what *The Times* did not hesitate to describe as "six years of unparalleled distress in commerce, industry and agriculture".[1]

Nothing is perhaps more characteristic of reviving Liberal confidence than the aggressive tone of Sir William Harcourt in opening the campaign by a speech at Southport. Declaring that "the action of an opposition, even in defeat, exercises a salutary and powerful control over the policy even of the strongest Government", he launched into an attack upon the whole Eastern and Afghan policy. In the Near East the Government had tried to settle the question on wrong principles and had totally failed to give effect to them. It had the choice between upholding the traditional policy of 1856, of "integrity and independence", or of abandoning it and taking a leading part in reconstruction: it did neither and preferred "impotent protest and garrulous obstruction". The Treaty of Berlin, "in all essential particulars except one", confirmed the much-abused San Stefano and negatived the Salisbury Circular: and even in that particular, Bulgaria, its provisions had not been effective. "The Pass of Ishtiman on the one side and the port of Burgas on the other were to flank an impregnable frontier. But there is not a Turkish soldier in the Balkans . . . and at this moment it is notorious that the Turkish flag cannot fly and no insignia of Turkish supremacy can be with safety displayed within the limits of Eastern Roumelia." "Under such circumstances the grant of self-government means nothing else than the surrender of dominion." Meanwhile Cyprus had become "the practical joke of the British Empire", and no progress had been made with the regeneration of Asia Minor. The Government's Eastern policy "has broken down everywhere . . ., the impregnable frontier has disappeared, the populations are not pacified and the reforms are not begun".

This volley of unpalatable truths was followed by a frontal attack upon the whole Zulu and Afghan policy: but here criticism was unduly centred in the one case upon Sir Bartle Frere, in the other

[1] *The Times*, 17 Dec.

upon Lord Salisbury, who had "sinned against the light" and shown "a fixed resolve to set aside the experience and judgment of those who have real knowledge of India"—in other words, had got rid of Northbrook, as of Derby, "because common sense and common prudence are qualities which refuse to dwell among them".

These "extravagant accusations"[1] undoubtedly marred the effect of his criticisms on the Eastern Question. But when Lord Salisbury, contrary to his usual habit, addressed a popular audience at Manchester a fortnight later,[2] he was definitely, though effectively, on the defensive. By the Cyprus protectorate he claimed to be "merely following the traditional policy of England for a long time past". The right to occupy Quetta had existed twenty years before we availed ourselves of it. Bessarabia was described as "not a matter of first-rate importance". "Big Bulgaria" was "the head and front of the offending of San Stefano": if it had been upheld, Constantinople could not have been defended, and Russia would have dominated at Adrianople and Salonica. The curious argument was added that "the question of a reformed or unreformed Turkey does not affect the necessity of keeping Russia from Constantinople and from the Aegean": and it was suggested, none too tactfully, that "in the present circumstances of the Russian Empire" Turkey had "no reasonable prospect of having to resist Russian aggression". The danger of "a Slav Principality practically from sea to sea" had been averted: and "if you do not trust the Turk, who is on the rampart of the fortress, at least you must trust the Austrian sentinel who is at the door. . . . If the Turk falls, remember that Austria is now at Novipazar . . . and that no advance of Russia beyond the Balkans and the Danube can now be made unless the resistance of Austria is conquered." In conclusion he greeted as "good tidings of great joy" the report of a defensive alliance between Austria-Hungary and Germany.

This speech was in many ways the weakest that Lord Salisbury ever delivered, and its crude encouragement of Austro-Russian divergences was equally unwelcome to Bismarck and to Andrássy, and played its part in making the former think better of his overtures to England.

A week later (24 Oct.) Hartington answered Salisbury on the same ground of Manchester and claimed that there had been a "transfer of interest from Parliament to the country". The cautious leader has become confident and even aggressive. He admitted that

[1] *Ibid*. leader of 3 Oct.   [2] *Ibid*. 17 Oct.

on the morrow of Berlin there were dissensions in the Liberal party and that not "argument", but "ovations were then the fashion". But now he openly denounced Salisbury's indifference to reformed or unreformed government as "an immoral policy, wanting in political sagacity", and the triumphs of Britain as "all won at the expense of the independent Christian nationalities". He was followed in October by a perfect bombardment of rival speeches, until *The Times* could write of the political world as "generally pugilistic". While the Duke of Argyll joined Hartington in denouncing the Government policy as "both a wicked and stupid doctrine" and declined to "argue with men who refuse to carry into politics the first principles of Christian morals",[1] the failure of all Layard's efforts to enforce reform in Asiatic Turkey was revealed in yet another of the endless Blue Books of the period, and the Government—thanks to what Cranbrook called "our ineffectual attempts to save Turkey from her own idiotic follies during and since her war"[2]—found itself increasingly on the defensive.

The Prime Minister's Guildhall speech was in a sense his political swan-song. Opening with the doubtful prophecy that the revival of trade was not temporary but permanent, it culminated in the famous phrase, "One of the greatest of Romans, when asked what were his politics, replied, *Imperium et Libertas*. That would not make a bad programme for a British Ministry." But the passage which perhaps deserves most emphasis was this.

"If . . . one of the most extensive and wealthiest empires in the world . . . from a perverse interpretation of its insular geographical position, turns an indifferent ear to the feelings and fortunes of continental Europe, such a course would, I believe, only end in its becoming an object of general plunder. *So long as the power and advice of England are felt in the councils of Europe, peace, I believe, will be maintained, and for a long period.* Without their presence war . . . seems to me inevitable."

It may be argued that that there was nothing very new in this statement, and that ever since 1874 he had been pursuing (none too successfully) those interventionist ideas which Britain had temporarily abandoned after Palmerston's death. But in reality this pronouncement goes to the root of our whole policy, and in a few succinct phrases reminds us that despite all we owe to our island position and to those overseas connections which it has brought us,

[1] 14 Nov.   [2] *Life of Gathorne Hardy*, ii. p. 139, 5 April 1880.

we none the less cannot neglect Europe save at our mortal peril. The conception that Britain cannot stand aside from Europe, and must always be mindful of her international responsibilities, lies behind the greatest achievements of three centuries: our repeated failures to carry it to its logical conclusion, our occasional plunges from extreme intervention to exaggerated isolation and even reversal of policy (and the pages of eighteenth- and nineteenth-century history are strown with examples) should serve as a constant warning. It is well that those who to-day still acknowledge Disraeli's leadership should remember that the greatest exponent of Imperialism recognised and insisted upon our fundamental and decisive rôle as a European Power.

THE MIDLOTHIAN CAMPAIGN AND THE PRINCIPLES OF FOREIGN POLICY

No greater contrast can be imagined than that between this last great utterance of Disraeli and the reviving flood of Gladstonian eloquence. What Mr. Ramsay Muir has well described as Gladstone's "thrilling adventure" of the seventies was about to enter upon a new and final phase, in which, no longer content with eloquent denunciation of his rival's policy, he set himself to define the "right principles" on which our foreign policy should be conducted. The Homeric effort of the two Midlothian campaigns, opening with a triumphal progress by rail and road and sustained in each case for a fortnight of thunderous oratory, lies outside our present scope. But the West Calder speech of 27 November 1879 is a real landmark in British policy.[1] Coming from the statesman who had done more than any other for the cause of international arbitration and was about to return to active leadership and power, it is no mere *pium desiderium*, but an intimation of principles to be earnestly pursued.

These principles fall under six heads:

I. "To foster the strength of the Empire . . . and to reserve it for great and worthy occasions." The means of attainment are characteristically defined as "just legislation and economy at home, thereby producing two great elements of national power—namely wealth, which is a physical element, and union and contentment, which are moral elements".

[1] Even after allowing for the absorption of John Morley in the parliamentary exploits of his hero, it is amazing to find that the West Calder speech is not even mentioned in his great three-volume *Life of Gladstone*, much less the issues which it raises discussed!

II. "To preserve to the nations . . . the blessings of peace"—and here occurs the no less characteristic parenthesis, "especially were it but for shame, when we recollect the sacred name we bear as Christians, for the Christian nations".

III. "To cultivate to the utmost the Concert of Europe", because you thus "neutralise and fetter the selfish aims of each", and because common action alone can unite the Great Powers for the common good.

IV. "To avoid needless and entangling engagements", which only reduce the power of the Empire.

V. "To acknowledge the rights of all nations." "You may, you must, sympathise with one nation more than another, and as a rule with those most closely linked by language, blood, religion or other circumstances of the time." "But in point of right all are equal, and you have no right to set up a system under which one is to be placed under moral suspicion or espionage, or made the subject of constant invective. If you do that, and especially if you claim for yourself a pharisaical superiority . . . you may talk about your patriotism as you please, but you are a misjudging friend of your country and are undermining the basis of esteem and respect of others for it."

VI. Finally, foreign policy "should always be inspired by love of freedom"—"a desire to give it scope, founded not on visionary ideas but upon the long experience of many generations within the shores of this happy isle. In freedom you lay the firmest foundation both of loyalty and of order, for the development of individual character and the best protection for the happiness of the nation at large. In the foreign policy of this country the names of Canning, of Russell, of Palmerston, will ever be honoured by those who recollect the erection of the Kingdom of Belgium and the union of the disjointed provinces of Italy. It is that sympathy—not with disorder, but on the contrary founded on the deepest and most profound love of order—which ought in my opinion to be the very atmosphere in which the Foreign Secretary of England ought to live and move."

Lest such axioms might appear too abstract, the speaker was "prepared to apply them" at once to burning issues of the day, and in particular to the relations of Britain and Russia. "You have heard me denounced as a Russian spy, a Russian agent. . . . But when you go to evidence, the worst thing that I have ever seen quoted of mine about Russia is this—I recommend Englishmen to imitate Russia in her good deeds." The Government, on the other hand, he contended, had completely alienated the feelings of this nation of eighty millions, yet had aggrandised Russia in two directions—in Bessarabia, which a Liberal Government had wrested from her in 1856, and in Armenia, which he looked upon with much greater equanimity, because he disbelieved in Russian territorial expansion in Asia Minor. As for Central Asia, he argued most forcefully that Russia had been "led on by causes in some degree analogous, but certainly more stringent and imperative than the causes which have commonly led us to extend our frontier in India".

The good points of the Berlin settlement were the removal of Turkish sovereignty over the vassal states, the erection of the two Bulgarias, and (not least) the promise extracted from Turkey regarding the government of her remaining provinces: but all these points came from San Stefano, and everything that will make the Treaty of Berlin an epoch in the history of Europe was due to the sword of Russia, and to that sword alone". It was not even true, as the Prime Minister had recently affirmed, that we had prevented Russia from taking Constantinople: our fleet could not have prevented her entry, but could only have bombarded the city. The Tsar had given his word and had got his terms without occupation. "All these great gains to Europe have been obtained for Europe against the remonstrances of our screaming Ambassador, and under the muzzles of our silent guns." The new Prince of Bulgaria, in meeting his first Parliament, had spoken of the Tsar Liberator, but had not a word for England.

He closed his speech with a no less weighty indictment of the Government's Afghan policy, showing the folly of neglecting the wisdom of successive Viceroys. The war had amply confirmed Lord Lawrence's claim that "you can overthrow the Government of Afghanistan in a few weeks, but you cannot replace it by any other without imposing the greatest burdens on the people of India and causing most serious financial embarrassments". Russia's new base on the Caspian was about 800 miles from the nearest point of Afghanistan, and the Caspian could not be used as a basis of attack on India except with the help of Persia. He, too, would not allow Russia to possess Afghanistan, but that had nothing to do with the question at issue. Britain had her maritime position in the world, and in India a mountain frontier admirably suited to defence.

There is nothing quite like the Midlothian campaign in our annals. The high sentiment and exultation of the one side, the open scorn and denunciation of the other, all centred upon the figure of an old man of seventy, whose amazing vitality surmounted every obstacle and enabled him to perform feats of oratorical and physical endurance that most men of thirty might envy. Never was the contrast between the two great rivals more fundamental. In his diary, for his own private eye, taking stock of "the seventh decade of my life", Gladstone recorded his belief that he was engaged in "a battle of justice, humanity, freedom, law, all in their first elements from the very root, and all on a gigantic scale". Nay more, a long line of Calvinist ancestors guided his pen as he added, "a great and high election of God". Beaconsfield remained less impressed—indeed, more contemptuous than ever, and wrote to Cranbrook: "It certainly is a relief that this drenching rhetoric has at last ceased: but I have never read a word of it".[1] On one occasion Disraeli caustically remarked, "It is a great impediment to public business that Mr. Gladstone cannot be made to understand a joke": and on the other hand, Gladstone's verbosity and "tortuous method of reasoning"[2] can hardly be denied.

With the further details of the Midlothian campaign, and of its no less astonishing sequel, which began on 16 March 1880—a week before the dissolution of Parliament—and ended with Gladstone's victory at the polls on 5 April, this narrative is only concerned in so far as it rounds off a period of political history. The sweeping Liberal victories at the general election of 1880 followed quite logically from the feeling generated during the "atrocity agitation" of 1876 and the renewed agitation of January and April 1878. The Beaconsfield Government stood or fell by its Eastern policy, and, basing its calculations on opinion in London and the home counties, had expected its endorsement by the country. On all sides it was now assumed that the reversal of that policy would be one of the first results of the Conservative *débâcle*: and when the Queen found that not Granville or Hartington, but the "People's William", was the only possible candidate for the Premiership, it at once became obvious that the aims and objects associated with the name of Layard would no longer be upheld.

In his electoral manifesto Gladstone had not minced words. He claimed that "abroad they (the Government) have strained, if they have not endangered, the prerogative by gross misuse, and have

<hr />

[1] *U.R.B.D.*, 19 February.
[2] Lecky, *Democracy and Liberty*, new edition, pp. xx, xxiii.

weakened the Empire by needless wars, unprofitable extensions and unwise engagements, and have dishonoured it in the eyes of Europe by filching the island of Cyprus from the Porte under a treaty clause distinctly concluded in violation of the Treaty of Paris, which formed part of the international law of Christendom". It might have been supposed that when such violent denunciation was followed by a great victory, he would have hastened to restore Cyprus to the Turks and to repudiate those military obligations in Asia Minor which had been the price of its surrender: and one of the most unanswerable criticisms which can be levelled against Gladstone's foreign policy is the fact that he weakly retained Cyprus, while recalling Layard, and destroying British influence at Constantinople by the support afforded to Greece and by the new forward policy into which events equally unforeseen by both the great parties were soon to force us in Egypt.

There is another passage in the manifesto which deserves our attention. Gladstone attacked Beaconsfield for the lack of any programme of domestic legislation and reproached him for promising in its stead an ascendancy in the councils of Europe. "There is, indeed," he went on, "an ascendancy in European councils to which Great Britain might reasonably aspire, by steadily sustaining the character of a Power no less just than strong; attached to liberty and law, jealous of peace, and therefore opposed to intrigue and aggrandisement, from whatever quarter they may come; jealous of honour, and therefore averse to the clandestine engagements which have marked our two latest years. To attain a moral and envied ascendancy such as this is indeed a noble object for any minister or any empire."[1]

As a pious sentiment this was admirable, but the cynic is entitled to point out that during five years of office Gladstone and Granville failed to fulfil the high hopes which had been set upon their foreign policy. It is true that they proved unequal to the three burning problems which their predecessors bequeathed to them—Afghanistan, South Africa and Egypt—and in 1885 left the two latter not merely unsolved, but gravely complicated; that after all the sound and fury of the Eastern agitation they acquiesced in Abdul Hamid's evasion of his pledges and left the reform clauses of the Treaty unenforced; that the improved relations with Russia which they were able to establish all too soon deteriorated and ended in acute

[1] Morley, *op. cit.* pp. 607-8.

friction in Central Asia; that problems of colonial expansion provoked a coolness between London and Paris, without any counter-
vailing friendship being established between London and Berlin,
while Austria-Hungary did not forget the new Prime Minister's ill-
considered onslaught upon her[1] and regarded with suspicion his
outlook upon Near Eastern questions. In a word, the future historian,
with his calmer perspective, is likely to describe the period of the
early eighties as one of the least successful examples of Liberal
foreign policy, and will be careful to distinguish between exalted
theory and meagre fulfilment, while declining to endorse the unfair
criticism which lays the entire blame upon the shoulders of Mr.
Gladstone himself. But there is much to be said for the verdict of
Mr. Ramsay Muir, who boldly claims for the principles enunciated
at West Calder, and on many other occasions, that they "anticipate
the international scheme embodied in the League of Nations", and
that "Gladstone was the greatest prophet of this ideal". Certainly
it is true to affirm that Gladstone's "doctrine conceives of an ideal
Europe, neither as a group of natural enemies, perpetually suspicious
and on the alert to take advantage of one another, nor as a single vast
super-state dominated by a single cosmopolitan authority, but as a
partnership of free nations working in organised co-operation".[2]

Neither of the great Victorian parties can claim a monopoly of
wisdom in foreign policy, and to-day nothing is more amazing than
the manner in which now one and now the other interpreted the
doctrine of Non-Intervention, until it virtually provided a mandate
for adventurous interference of every kind. Gladstone had endorsed
this doctrine in his Palmerstonian days, and was not immune from
it, even while he attacked Disraeli for giving it an opposite interpretation: while Salisbury on his return from Berlin advocated it more
openly than any statesman before or since. But the idea of international arbitration, by which Gladstone, in the face of an unripe
public opinion, had placed our relations with America on new and
durable foundations and which he was now ready, though more
vaguely, to apply to European problems also, was a leaven destined
to leaven the whole lump. It was something altogether above party
and has become the common heritage of British statesmen.

[1] "There is not a spot upon the whole map where you can lay your finger and
say, 'there Austria did good'."—Morley, *op. cit.* iii. p. 8. See also correspondence
between Mr. Gladstone and Count Károlyi, in May 1880, published in the Appendix
to the *British Documents*, ix. pt. i. p. 773.
[2] In *Prime Ministers of the XIXth Century*, ed. F. J. C. Hearnshaw, p. 251.

A CONFRONTATION: DISRAELI, DERBY, SALISBURY, GLADSTONE

ALL successful diplomacy rests upon the study of psychology, whether of individuals or of nations: and our history of the tortuous diplomacy of the seventies would not be complete without some attempt at a critical estimate of the four men out of whose opinions, conflicts and hesitations the highest common factor of British policy was evolved.

Disraeli, on taking office for the last time, found Britain in a position of splendid isolation more accentuated, though certainly far less dangerous, than at any moment since 1815. Since France's defeat in 1870 the only political structure on the Continent was the Three Emperors' League, which neither collectively nor individually was hostile to Britain, but which showed a natural inclination to settle the affairs of eastern Europe without much regard for the views of the West. Almost from the first, then, Disraeli seems to have aimed at driving a wedge between the three Powers. But of the three, it was Germany upon whom he and his colleagues looked most askance, as the history of the Kulturkampf and the War Scare amply shows: Bismarck was a bugbear to Disraeli, Derby and Salisbury alike, and there is nothing to show that Gladstone differed on this point. Towards Austria-Hungary Disraeli had looked with friendly eyes ever since his youthful admiration for and acquaintance with Metternich, but he curiously misjudged Andrássy and Francis Joseph. Towards Russia he as yet showed no trace of hostility, welcoming the Duke of Edinburgh's marriage with a Russian princess, and Tsar Alexander's visit to England, and actually suggesting to the Queen a Russian alliance.[2] Nor did Russian progress in Central Asia cause him as yet any anxiety, and in appointing Lord Lytton as Viceroy of India, neither he nor his Indian Secretary Lord Salisbury showed any sign of abandoning the long tradition of Lawrence, Mayo and Northbrook. It is true that in 1877 he spoke of Lytton

---

[1] As the Epilogue is full of assertions for which the documentary proof has been adduced earlier in the book, it seemed only fair to the reader to provide page references which will enable him to check the facts for himself. [2] P. 24.

having been *sent out* to prepare a forward policy in Asia, but in reality there can be no doubt that the reversal of previous policy carried out by Lytton was due to the course of events on the north-west frontier in the two years following his arrival.

Disraeli's attitude towards the three Empires was influenced by no stern principle, but by sheer expediency, and by the same considerations of prestige which led him to proclaim the Queen as Empress of India and to assume such mottoes as *Imperium et Libertas*. Thanks to our strong colonial and naval position, nothing could happen outside Europe without us: and Disraeli wished this to be true of Europe also. That he saw no irreconcilable conflict of interest between Britain and Russia is clearly shown by the hitherto unknown overture which he made to Russia in June 1876.[1] That it came to nothing was in large measure due to his essentially negative attitude in the Eastern Question since it had again become acute in 1875.

To Disraeli, in contrast with his great rival, the movements for liberation in Bosnia, Serbia, Montenegro, Roumania, Bulgaria, Greece or Albania were a sealed book, or were to be explained by the preposterous mare's-nest of foreign secret societies.[2] He thought the Turks might have suppressed the Bosnian rising by timely baksheesh;[3] he refused as long as possible to believe in the Bulgarian atrocities and still wrote of them in inverted commas two months after the official report of Baring had been received; he would have liked to see Turkish garrisons reimposed upon Serbia;[4] he was ready to revive Palmerston's method of a naval blockade against Greece:[5] he was indifferent to Roumanian claims except as affecting Danubian commerce.[6]

He not only stubbornly upheld the Palmerstonian doctrine of Turkish independence and integrity, but clung to every favourable verdict upon Turkey and gave his support to Turkey wherever he could. In the early days of the Bosnian rising he intervened in Vienna at the request of the Porte to dissuade Andrássy from any countenance to the insurgents. In the autumn he only associated himself with consular intervention when the Porte specially requested him to do so: and again in January 1876 it was only at the Porte's request that he accepted the Andrássy Note, after a delay of three weeks.[7] In each case London's reserve weakened the prospects of

[1] P. 38.   [2] Pp. 88 and 44.   [3] P. 22.   [4] P. 38.
[5] Pp. 184, 481.   [6] P. 489.   [7] P. 28.

success: in each case London carefully abstained from any constructive proposal. Worse still, it was Disraeli's deliberate abstention that wrecked the Berlin Memorandum when all the other Powers had accepted: and no alternative proposal was put forward. There was at first some excuse for regarding the Turkish Revolution as a real step towards reform, but Argyll was quite entitled to argue that Disraeli's emphatic denial of any connection between the risings and atrocities and the sending of the British fleet was equivalent to advising prompt suppression before the Powers had time to intervene.

Up to the summer of 1876 Disraeli and Derby had acted in full agreement: the first signs of disagreement were due to the atrocity agitation. It is not merely that Derby was extremely susceptible to public opinion, and indeed sometimes laid himself open to the charge of following rather than leading, while Disraeli was for a time disposed to regard the agitation as a product of the silly season. Disraeli, after coining the phrase "coffee-house babble",[1] remained quite unrepentant and sceptical, whereas Derby, like the Queen, was profoundly moved, ordered Elliot to remonstrate stiffly with the Porte and resented his cynical response as to the irrelevancy of massacres to British interests.[2] Derby, Salisbury and Carnarvon—the three Lords, as they came to be called—were drawn together by a common sympathy with the Eastern Christians, while Disraeli made no attempt to conceal his preference for the Turks. The Queen too was horrified and protested for a time,[3] but the Disraelian hypnosis gradually asserted itself, and her Russophobe obsession turned the scale. That the moral indignation of many Conservatives was as deeply stirred as that of the Liberals cannot be doubted: the real difference was that on the one side this indignation found a positively volcanic expression in the lava stream of Gladstone's eloquence. In the autumn of 1876 there was no great difference of opinion between him and the three lords, but a very profound difference of mentality and method.

Here again it is impossible to argue that Disraeli's attitude rested upon any deep-seated principle. In June, in talking to Shuvalov, he had envisaged partition as inevitable and "blood-letting" as necessary, and showed to poor advantage when the Ambassador appealed to him *not* to raise the Eastern Question in too drastic a form.[4] In September he again considered with Derby partition under the auspices of England, and declared that all the Turks might be in the

---

[1] Pp. 55, 88, 96.   [2] P. 63.   [3] P. 61.   [4] P. 41.

Propontis so far as he was concerned.[1] The popular clamour of the autumn and winter merely drove him on to the defensive, but in no way changed his views. Neither the nation nor his own Cabinet would contemplate co-operation with Turkey, and the Russian ultimatum to the Porte could not reasonably be opposed. The Conference proposal came from Derby rather than from his chief, and the choice of Salisbury as chief British delegate was an admirable compromise,[2] accepted by the vast mass of opinion in both parties, as the attitude of Gladstone and Argyll no less than of Northcote and Cross clearly shows. The best proofs of the Premier's utter opportunism at this juncture are Salisbury's letter accepting the mission to Constantinople—"It is essential that your policy should be settled first"[3]—and Disraeli's vague message to Derby on the very same day, as to the necessity of "coming to some understanding with some European Power".

While however Salisbury and Derby were bent on making the Conference succeed, Disraeli did nothing to help. He followed up his Aylesbury speech of September by his menacing pronouncement at the Guildhall in November on the possibility of a second or third campaign in case of need.[4] He sent out his own confidential agents to Constantinople to sound Turkish opinion and to draw up detailed military plans:[5] and he was already considering territorial compensation in the Near or Middle East—a new Gibraltar aimed at Russia and obviously only attainable through war.[6]

During the Conference of Constantinople his attitude stiffened. He was angry at Salisbury's understanding with Ignatyev and at his solicitude for the Balkan Christians; he refused Salisbury's urgent request for the recall of Elliot and thereby confirmed the Turks in the belief that Elliot, not Salisbury, enjoyed the confidence of Premier and Queen.[7] He altogether rejected—and here he carried Derby with him—the idea of the coercion of Turkey, as advocated not merely by Salisbury, but by the representatives of all the other Powers also.[8] The failure of the Conference, like the failure of the Berlin Memorandum, was in the main due to the negative policy of London: and Carnarvon from inside the Cabinet earnestly warned Salisbury that the Prime Minister was bent upon war on behalf of Turkey.[9] Derby, loyal to his chief, but suspicious and slow to move, even though capable of sudden bursts of energy, was essentially

[1] P. 88.   [2] P. 106.   [3] P. 103.   [4] P. 104.   [5] Pp. 129, 136, 325.
[6] P. 99.   [7] Pp. 131-3.   [8] P. 131.   [9] Pp. 134, 131.

pacific, and perhaps not yet fully alive to the true sentiments of Disraeli and the Queen. Hence from January to April 1877 there was a lull in Europe, in which once again London offered no alternative, though by now it was obvious that war was inevitable unless some such alternative could be found. The Tsar and his Government had for over eighteen months shown very great forbearance, had watched the overthrow of one plan of pacification after another, had risked much odium and unpopularity at home by holding back, and now saw no escape from the long-drawn-out unrest and uncertainty, save by reluctantly forcing an issue with the Turks. Disraeli had not even the excuse of ardent conviction, for he greeted Salisbury on his return to England with a prophecy of inevitable partition.[1] It is difficult to escape from the conclusion that Disraeli's persistently negative and blocking policy was one of the main causes of the Russo-Turkish war, and indeed that he was not greatly concerned to avert it and ready to engage Britain on the Turkish side. And lest there should be any doubt as to his essential opportunism, we have at this stage the second overture to Shuvalov—treating Turkey's days as numbered:[2] and this time there is no escape from the dilemma, either that he had no fixed principles in the Turkish question or that he was insincere in his advances and merely laying some trap.

With Salisbury's return from the East, the coalition of the three Lords inside the Cabinet was reaffirmed, and though Salisbury could not carry his idea of Turkish partition and sacrificed it on the altar of party unity,[3] Disraeli on his side had to accept the March Protocol of the five Powers, though he told Salisbury next day that he could not yet quite make head or tail of it.[4] It was his misfortune that while the Russians accepted, the Turks refused and thereby put themselves in the wrong: and though the Queen began to talk of laying down the Crown rather than "kiss Russia's feet", he had no plausible excuse for the occupation of the Dardanelles and could not carry the Cabinet with him.[5]

The Note of 6 May 1877, defining Britain's "conditional neutrality", represents the height of Derby's effort, and affords decisive proof that at times he was capable of active and constructive statesmanship. All the dissensions of the next twelve months could not avail to eject this policy of conditional neutrality from the field: resting upon a clear minimum definition of that much-vaunted but singularly elastic and evasive phrase "British interests", and upon the

[1] P. 139.   [2] P. 159.   [3] P. 157.   [4] P. 166.   [5] P. 171.

assumption that the Tsar would keep his public pledges, it may be said to have eventually checkmated the Jingoes and averted an unnecessary war.[1] Henceforth Derby held on his way with admirable fortitude, and his power of opposing a dead weight of resistance—in other circumstances a grave handicap—now stood the country in good stead. He finds a perhaps unexpected ally in the versatile Shuvalov, and their unconventional alliance is one of the chief factors of peace.

Meanwhile, throughout the summer, the Prime Minister and the Queen are united behind the scenes in their bellicose tendencies: and though she obviously goes too far even for him, he prefers to humour rather than restrain her. He involves the reluctant Derby in overtures to Vienna, which are foredoomed to failure, because of the secret Austro-Russian commitments and of Andrássy's profound distrust of London.[2] Meanwhile he indulges in wild day-dreams of expeditions to the Persian Gulf, Tiflis and the Caspian, and discusses secretly with Layard the strategically much saner but no less fatally warlike project of occupying Gallipoli.[3] At last in August he and the Queen, finding Derby utterly opposed to this and immune to a most royal snub, dispatch Colonel Wellesley on a special mission to the Tsar, behind the back of the Foreign Secretary of whom they cannot get rid, but whom they no longer trust, because their aims are by now divergent.[4]

During the late summer and autumn the Cabinet, having failed to secure an ally, was too riddled with internal dissensions to take any real action, and was fain to wait upon events, hoping against hope that the Turks would hold their own till mid-winter and that it might then prove possible to prevent a second campaign and a decisive end to the war, failing which British intervention would follow.[5] Disraeli may doubtless be excused for the vigour with which he denied all suggestions of a divided Cabinet, but we know now from his own lips and those of his colleagues how utterly false those denials were. "Seven parties in a cabinet of twelve", is the *locus classicus* in a letter to the Queen.[6]

Meanwhile there is no shadow of doubt about Disraeli's own sentiments. His new Guildhall speech was a glorification of Turkey, with marked attentions to the Turkish Ambassador, and the alarm which it caused was hardly offset by Derby's reassuring speech of 28 November, for the disagreement between them was by now known

[1] Pp. 170-4.   [2] Pp. 199-202.   [3] Pp. 218, 209.   [4] P. 228.
[5] P. 233.   [6] P. 236.

to too many.[1] To Lady Bradford he wrote, "Plevna is our only chance", while in his secret correspondence with Layard he discussed the abandonment of neutrality.[2]

The fall of Plevna and the speedy collapse of Turkish resistance meant the failure of the original Disraelian policy of Turkish integrity, unless Britain, or better still, Britain and Austria, took a hand in the game, and it was towards this goal that he now moved. On his own initiative he encouraged Turkey to appeal for mediation, and his language to the Turkish Ambassador led the Sultan to count upon British "armed support".[3] The "grave divergence of opinion" inside the Cabinet, which Layard was quick to perceive, now reached its climax, and the three lords refused to assent to that alliance with the Turks for which their chief was ready.[4] The breach between Disraeli and Derby became irreparable, for the fundamental reason that Derby believed that peace with Russia could still be preserved, whereas Disraeli regarded war as a risk worth taking.[5] There is clear proof of this in the profound alarm of Carnarvon and in the attitude of Disraeli and the Queen towards him after his pacific speech of 3 January, and again in the way in which Disraeli eggs on the Queen instead of checking her extravagances.[6]

During January 1878 Disraeli found himself between two fires. The Russian advance caused frantic alarm among the Jingoes, but their very fury stimulated the Opposition to fresh agitation throughout the country: and the Queen's desire to remove Derby from the Foreign Office was shattered against his colleagues' view that this would involve the break-up not only of the Cabinet but of the Conservative party, at any rate in the north.[7] Layard's theory that the Russo-Turkish war was the result of the earlier atrocities agitation is merely grotesque: [8] but there can be no doubt that this second agitation, continued (not very adroitly, it is true) in Parliament during February and March, checkmated the war party at home and isolated us in Europe. For the extent to which Disraeli misjudged both Bismarck and Andrássy, and the bearing of this upon the final issue, can hardly be exaggerated.[9]

At the opening of Parliament Disraeli used menacing phrases, but Argyll was entitled to rub in the fact that the "integrity of Turkey" had vanished from his vocabulary. Behind the scenes he was writing

[1] Pp. 238, 239.   [2] Pp. 238, 244.   [3] Pp. 243, 245, 292.   [4] P. 246.
[5] P. 249.   [6] Pp. 251-2.   [7] Pp. 293, 301.   [8] P. 207.
[9] Pp. 23, 34, 98, 293.

to the Queen of "inevitable war with Russia"—a phrase which she promptly endorsed.[1] He was encouraging Musurus and Layard, and he certainly would have occupied Gallipoli if only he could have carried the Cabinet with him.[2] He was only too glad to shed the obnoxious Carnarvon, but he had to bear with Derby for party reasons, and this explains the contradictory measures regarding the fleet at the Dardanelles and the reinstatement of Derby after his first resignation. The sending of the fleet in defiance not merely of the wishes of the Sultan and his ministers, but even of the urgent advice of Layard himself, was due to the general disorientation inside the Cabinet—Salisbury finally imposing upon the others the view that only prompt and firm action could save British prestige before Europe.[3] It may be argued that prestige was actually reaffirmed, but it was the merest accident that war was not precipitated.

During the last three critical months of Derby's tenure of the Foreign Office Disraeli falls back upon the more than questionable method of conducting foreign policy through a secret committee of three, behind the back of the Secretary of State.[4] This reaches its height in his discussions with Wellesley, in his instructions to Layard for the purchase of the Turkish fleet, in his project of a Mediterranean League, and above all in his search for a place *d'armes* in the eastern Mediterranean, to hold Russia in check.[5]

Psychologically this is the most interesting moment in the whole crisis: for the time has come when Salisbury must make a momentous choice between allegiance to his chief, a doubtful *fronde* in conjunction with Derby and Carnarvon, or an alliance with a disunited opposition. The third alternative was out of the question, for though his views on the Eastern Question coincided on essentials with those of Gladstone, and though the religious background of the two men might at first sight have seemed a bond of union, this was far outweighed by a fundamental difference of outlook in many spheres of home politics. There remained the choice between Derby and Disraeli, and it was by now obvious that Derby's days were in any case numbered, that Disraeli's fragile health made it impossible for him to assume unrestricted control of foreign policy, and that Salisbury alone possessed the combined energy, prestige and knowledge to fill the vacant post. The close working alliance established between Lord and Lady Derby and the Russian Ambassador was also presumably distasteful to Lord Salisbury,[6] though he must of course

[1] P. 293.   [2] P. 292.   [3] P. 315.   [4] P. 320.   [5] Pp. 321, 326, 324.   [6] P. 249.

have been fully aware of the dangers which it sought to counter. That Derby had judged Shuvalov aright was strikingly vindicated within a very few weeks of the change of minister: for Salisbury, though at first extremely suspicious and *boutonné*, was speedily convinced of Shuvalov's straight dealing and zeal for peace and entered into still closer and more fruitful co-operation with him.[1]

Torn then between his two colleagues, Salisbury chose the Prime Minister, in the belief that Derby's force was spent, that he himself could provide the synthesis between the rival extremes, and that the only real alternative was the triumph of the Liberals, whom he saw to be no less riddled with dissensions than the Tories. It is impossible to blame him under such difficult circumstances, and our foreign policy at one bound recovered both energy and initiative. Henceforward Disraeli was content more and more to leave all details in the hands of Salisbury,[2] and to those who had eyes to see there was soon but little left of the original Palmerstonian and Disraelian policy.

The motives which prompted Derby's final resignation have already been fully considered and need not detain us in this general survey. There can be no doubt that Disraeli was roused by the terms imposed upon Turkey at San Stefano, that he was again ready to risk a conflict with Russia, that the use of Indian troops for the defence of Asia was conceived as a spectacular effect, and that he was once more searching for a Gibraltar in the eastern Mediterranean.[3] But those who believe that he was guided by principle in the Eastern Question must be reminded that he appointed Salisbury with his eyes open, after the frankest possible warnings that he was no believer in the restoration of Turkey.[4] Disraeli had already sadly admitted to the Queen that partition might be inevitable, though it was not for her Government to set the example.[5]

Once again, Lady Gwendolen Cecil does not exaggerate one whit when she speaks of a "supreme concentration of energy" on the part of her father during the spring of 1878, "to wrench the ship round into peaceful channels"—an effort which in the next two years brought him to the verge of a break-down.[6] Here there is no attempt to create any false illusion of continuity of policy.[7]

[1] Pp. 409, 412. [2] P. 407. [3] P. 364. [4] P. 377. [5] Pp. 376-7. [6] Pp. 382, 394.
[7] *Life of Salisbury*, iii. p. 203. Nearly a decade later Salisbury told MacColl that in his view both Beaconsfield and Derby "had acquired an exaggerated view of Turkish vitality and power, and thought that my recommendations sacrificed too much of the Turkish Empire"—*Life of MacColl*, p. 281, 13 Dec. 1887.

Henceforward the danger of war slowly recedes. The Salisbury
Circular of 1 April contains effective criticism of San Stefano, drawing special attention to the over-emphasis laid upon the Slavs and
putting forward the Greeks as counterweight: but it contains nothing
that conflicts with the ideas in which the Conference of Constantinople broke up, or with the definition of British interests in that
landmark of diplomacy, the Derby Note of 6 May 1877 and the
answers of Shuvalov and Gorchakov. London's insistence upon the
right of Europe to submit all clauses of San Stefano to examination
—on the ground that it modified by unilateral action the solemn
international agreements of 1856 and 1871—might be distasteful to
Russian sentiment after a victorious war, but it was quite unexcep-
tionable from the legal standpoint and had the nation behind it.

Disraeli's speech of 8 April in the House of Lords, with its hints
of "a great war" and its exaggerated denunciation of San Stefano—
was in a sense the final gesture of his bellicose period. It provoked
the most vigorous protest that Derby had ever uttered, culminating
in the warning that we were "not drifting but rushing into war":
and this was followed by a whole chorus of Opposition diatribes.[1] But
meanwhile Salisbury had feelers out in Berlin, and by the end of
April was sounding Shuvalov as to an honourable compromise. The
greater part of May was taken up by Shuvalov's visit to St. Petersburg, to acquaint the Tsar with the British point of view: and on his
return a compromise was soon reached between him and Salisbury.
The Protocol of 30 May, which had been intended to remain
indefinitely secret, but which an impish accident almost instantly
betrayed, was a decisive factor in the Russo-British conflict. The
obstacles to the Congress were thus removed, but Britain could no
longer enter it with free hands: "Big Bulgaria" had been drastically
curtailed, but in other respects the essential features of San Stefano
remained. The germ of the final Treaty of Berlin is already clearly
visible in the Protocol, and the successive incidents that fluttered the
dovecots (or falcon nests) of the Congress were but a series of well-
staged demonstrations to conceal the fact that the plenipotentiaries
had virtually ceased to be free agents before ever they reached the
council chamber.[2]

The settlement of Berlin has already been fully criticised in its
international aspect. In its British aspect it was a strategic retreat,
brilliantly concealed by what we should now call the propagandist

---

[1] Pp. 384, 386-7, 391.   [2] Pp. 416-20.

effect of "Peace with Honour" and by the spoils won through the
Cyprus Convention. The reality, however, was the abandonment of
the traditional policy of Turkish integrity, the final acceptance of
the principle of national Balkan states—which already to the clear-
sighted in 1878 was bound to end as we in 1934 see that it has ended
—and a concentration of effort to save what could still be saved of
Turkey in Asia, not so much out of love of Turkey as from fear of
Russia. Salisbury had far fewer illusions than his chief, he was by
no means indifferent to the wider European aspect of the problem,
and he was too big a man to regard Turkey merely as a pawn in
British politics: but even he was swayed by party considerations
when he submitted to the trumpet calls of victory on his return from
Berlin. His Asiatic policy in 1878–9 may be called the highest
common factor between himself, Layard and the Prime Minister:
but as we have already seen, it was doomed to failure, partly owing
to Turkish suspicion and resentment, partly because the Conservatives were content to rest on their laurels and withheld the money
grants which alone could have regenerated Turkey. When, then, the
Liberals took office, it was already too late, and co-operation between
them and the Hamidian despotism was impossible.[1] Salisbury's own
relations with Constantinople during his second and third administra-
tions are an indirect recognition of this fact. The only hope of real
success was to govern Turkey as a second India, and this was far too
big a proposition for either party to entertain, even if Europe had
been willing to tolerate it.

Rarely in our history has there been so complete a contrast between
two notable protagonists as that between Disraeli and Gladstone:
and the international issues raised by the Eastern Question only
served to accentuate it still further. If Disraeli possessed the oriental
imagination and resource of his ancient race, Gladstone had all
the *"perfervidum ingenium Scotorum"* and a certain Celtic vision,
tempered by a viking's fire. The Jew knew how to infect his royal
mistress and his aristocratic followers with enthusiasm for a programme of self-interest seductively decked out in imperial trappings.
The Scot, transplanted to Liverpool and Eton, with his innate
Calvinism transfused by a High Church training, cast a strange

[1] Sobered by the election result of 1880, that most ardent of Disraelians, Lord
Cranbrook, could write of "our ineffectual attempts to save Turkey from her own
idiotic follies during and since her war"—*Life of Gathorne Hardy*, ii. p. 139.

glamour over the nonconformist and middle-class mind by his dialectics and Biblical eloquence. Between these two extremes stand the two typical English patricians, Derby and Salisbury, with those qualities of calm compromise, distrust of resonant logic, and fear of emotionalism, all the greater because of a strong inward dash of sentimentalism in themselves—to which their class has so long owed its relative success in the art of government. To suggest that those who sounded the moral issue most loudly were alone in caring for it would be as unjust and exaggerated as to argue that possible over-emphasis rested upon mere hypocrisy. The straightforward but cautious Derby, the subtly reserved Salisbury, who kept his religious faith while conscious of the futilities and irony of daily life, were as jealous of public and private honour as any man of their time, but their English nature cried out against Disraeli's ornate cynicism and Gladstone's relentless flow of moral precepts.

It must be remembered that in the Eastern Question Gladstone had in some ways a still more Palmerstonian past than Disraeli. Indeed, one of the main motives that prompted his re-emergence on such an issue was a keen sense of his own responsibility—shared by Argyll—as a member of the Crimean Cabinet which made the settlement of 1856, and as head of the later Cabinet which reaffirmed that settlement in a modified form in 1871. The theory that he plunged into the arena for mere party ends will not hold water for a moment. He might indeed, on his own showing—and of this he was frankly conscious—be blamed for the slowness with which he acted. For a whole year after the Bosnian outbreak he remained virtually silent, and though he took part in the atrocity debate of 31 July he did not publish his first pamphlet till the campaign of protest was already in full swing. It was not till four months after the Bulgarian massacres, and until the earlier reports had received official confirmation, that he came unreservedly into the open:[1] and in this he was above all influenced by the indifference of the Government, the cynicism and prevarication of Disraeli, the incorrigible Turcophilism of Elliot. When Derby spoke out and warned Turkey, Gladstone was partially reassured; he welcomed Derby's proposal of a Conference; he was heartily delighted at the selection of Salisbury as our delegate, and he publicly urged the country to strengthen Salisbury's hands and back him to the utmost.[2]

It soon became obvious, however, that Disraeli's Turcophil lean-

---

[1] P. 73. [2] Pp. 102, 111.

ings were in no way affected by what he described as "imaginary" atrocities, that he was indifferent to the cause of reform and only too ready to pick a quarrel with Russia. The menace and misrepresentation of the Aylesbury and Guildhall speeches roused the indignation not only of Gladstone and Argyll, but of Granville and many others: [1] and the movement launched at the St. James's Hall meeting in December was an attempt to organise thoughtful opinion in defence of the Christians of Turkey, and to prevent the country from being rushed into a sudden war of emotion against Russia. [2] Perhaps the greatest of Gladstone's merits in the long controversy was his insistence that the central issue was not between support of Turkey or support of Russia, but between Turkish misrule and Balkan liberty, and that if we ranged ourselves on the Turkish side, all the Christians of the Near East would be automatically driven into the arms of Russia. He saw what Disraeli never saw, that these populations were not seeking alliance with Russia, or indeed with any specific Power, but "to be delivered from an intolerable yoke", and above all, that it was not the decaying Turkish Empire, but the native "populations of those countries that will ultimately possess them". [3]

Gladstone was never an unreserved champion of Russia, [4] he was as fully conscious as any Tory controversialist of the weak spots of Russian Tsarism and of its oppressive attitude towards Poland or Hungary: but he simply brushed away the flimsy argument "that because Russia has sinned against the Poles, Turkey may maltreat *ad libitum* her subject races". But while freely admitting that there existed legitimate grounds for jealousy of Russian policy, he argued —with the voice of the twentieth century—that the safest check upon Russia was the Concert of Europe, and the avoidance or limitation of "separate interests and claims". [5] He saw, then, and had the courage to admit publicly, the fact so obvious to posterity, that Russia was this time on the side of liberty and progress. On one occasion he expressed regret that Balkan liberation should be the work, "not of a state which had achieved its own liberty, but of the state least

---

[1] On 7 Dec. 1876 Granville wrote to Gladstone (*Gladstone Papers*): "I was pleased at the universal reprobation of his attack upon you, and the equally universal approbation of dignified contempt which you showed. I own it would be difficult to speak on the present aspect of the Eastern Question without alluding to his sayings, if not doings, during the autumn. But if you cannot do this by a skilful narrative, without any vituperation or strong language, I shall feel I have miscalculated your powers."

[2] Pp. 110-12.　　　　[3] Pp. 81, 179, 185.　　　　[4] Pp. 77, 184, 349.
[5] "The Peace to come", by W. E. Gladstone, *XIXth Century*, Feb. 1878.

fitted for such a task".[1] Gladstone was at his very greatest when he
dared to affirm before Parliament that if Russia succeeded in this
task which we had refused to share, he as an Englishman would hide
his head, but as a man would rejoice, and when he declared his firm
belief that the knell of Turkish tyranny had sounded, and that the
new liberty would be "a noble boon".[2]

In their earlier days Disraeli and Gladstone had both accepted
the Palmerstonian delusion of the reformability of Turkey, but while
the former still clung obstinately to it, the latter had in the twenty
years following the Treaty of Paris come to realise that Turkey
lacked both the inclination and the capacity for reform, that corruption and maladministration were ineradicable and that the status
of the Christians was intolerable. He had been a member of the
Cabinet which gave Turkey a new lease of life and an international
guarantee, contingent upon pledges of reform which she had not
fulfilled, and he rightly held that by annulling those rights of interference which earlier treaties had assured to Russia, and yet not
enforcing in our turn the reforms intended as a substitute, we had
incurred grave responsibility towards the Christians of Turkey and
rendered their revolt well-nigh inevitable. Again, he had been a
member of the Cabinet which forced Turkey to accept the Lebanon
Commission and to execute a Pasha implicated in the massacres, and
he failed to see why the successful precedent of 1860 should not be
followed in Bosnia and Bulgaria in 1876. He could not therefore
remain indifferent to the Government's failure to insist upon Turkey
punishing Ahmed Aga, Shefvet and other perpetrators of atrocities
in Bulgaria: and his second pamphlet, *Lessons in Massacre*, was an
attempt to revive the public's flagging indignation.[3]

If, however, Disraeli could not control the inner ring of his Cabinet,
still less could Gladstone, since his retirement from the Liberal
leadership, control the inner ring of the Opposition, who were seriously embarrassed by his uncompromising attitude and would fain
have let the Eastern Question rest.[4] They could not restrain him
from bringing forward his famous May Resolutions in Parliament,
but they criticised, not without reason, his indifference to tactics.[5]
But herein lay both his strength and his weakness. For the moment
his failure to rally more than one wing of the Liberals to his views
on foreign policy may have encouraged the Tory Turcophils: but
his continued insistence upon the moral issue was the beginning of a

[1] P. 305.   [2] P. 185.   [3] P. 165.   [4] Pp. 165, 175-7.   [5] P. 182.

process which made his triumphant return to leadership and power in the long run inevitable.

The violence with which he was assailed by a certain section of the Tory press[1] is almost as discreditable, and as groundless, as the attacks upon the Queen and Prince Albert on the eve of the Crimean War. Layard was not alone in the perverse view that the Gladstonian agitation was the direct cause of the Russo-Turkish war:[2] but to-day it is surely obvious that war was sooner or later inevitable unless Turkish reform could at long last be made effective; that it was, above all, London's negative policy that encouraged the Turks to resist effective reform and to court British support against Russia: and finally that Russia, after enduring the uncertainty for twenty months, entered the lists alone, in the cause of her kinsmen and co-religionists. It was not the least cogent argument of Gladstone and his friends that instead of leaving Russia in the position of solitary champion, it should have been our endeavour to tie her down to joint European action in a task which had to be faced before ever there could be peace in the Near East. He saw more clearly than most of his contemporaries that blatant Russophobia, so far from bringing any solution, would only involve fresh conflicts, and that a chain of emancipated Christian states, stretching from the Adriatic to the Aegean and the Euxine, was far more likely to serve as a barrier to Russian aggression than any bolstering up of Turkish rule over a host of disaffected rayah. In striking contrast to Disraeli, Gladstone saw the great possibilities of self-government among the reviving Balkan races: he had a long record of devotion to the Hellenic cause, he and Tennyson had joined in their homage to Montenegrin heroism: he had long before pled the cause of Roumanian unity[3] and now defended Roumanian integrity against Russian appetite, while Salisbury was perverse enough to regret that Roumania had not been swallowed up by Austria. Of Serbia and Bosnia he already knew the essential facts, and Bishop Strossmayer's fervent advocacy of Jugoslav unity was not without effect upon him. Of his appeal on behalf of Bulgaria it is enough to say that it will always remain part of her charter of liberation.

With this profound difference of outlook, it is not surprising that Gladstone's distrust of his rival should have grown month by month, till it flared out in the admission that his main effort was "to counter-

[1] Pp. 177, 280, 351.   [2] Pp. 207, 213, 355.
[3] Seton-Watson, *History of the Roumanians*, pp. 257, 323.

work the purpose of Lord Beaconsfield", whose utterances "form a
perfectly consistent whole", in no way ambiguous or uncertain.[1] At
the back of his mind, unavowed but very real and very well grounded,
was his alarm at the ascendancy of Disraeli over the mind of the
Queen, her unbalanced views on the Eastern crisis and on Russia,
and the constitutional dangers which might so easily result.[2] His fear
of a secret "deal" about Egypt proved unfounded,[3] but there were
even better grounds than he as yet knew for suspecting territorial
ambitions in the Near East.[4] Hence in January 1878 and again in
April, he was the soul of a renewed agitation throughout the country
against active intervention on Turkey's behalf:[5] and it can at least
be affirmed that his criticism of the Jingoes and of the small but
fanatical war party was better grounded than their ignoble attack
upon him as "a Russian agent".[6] The extraordinary bitterness
with which the contending factions vilified each other during the
early months of 1878 is one of the least edifying features of the
long crisis.

Whatever may be said of the exchange of personalities between
the two men—and it has already been pointed out that this was a
case of six and half a dozen—it was unquestionably a true instinct
on Gladstone's part to concentrate his attack upon the Prime
Minister, for as he said, "in the Eastern Question, when you speak
of the Government, you mean Lord Beaconsfield, and there is not
one man in the Government that has a tenth part of his tenacity of
will and patient purpose".[7] The question over which they joined issue
struck at the very root of international relations. To Disraeli's
insistence upon "British interests" as the essential test of policy,[8]
Gladstone boldly retorted by an appeal to "civilisation and
humanity".[9] Even after war had broken out, he contended that the
dispute could still be settled "by the authority of Europe": and he
put forward the unanswerable argument that if British interests
were accepted as "the sole measure of right or wrong" for British
agents throughout the world, the same attitude could be logically
upheld by every other country, and the result would be international
anarchy.[10] On a later occasion he urged "the pursuit of objects which
are European by means which are European, in concert with the
mind of the rest of Europe and supported by its authority".[11] He was

[1] P. 305.   [2] Pp. 293, 301, 344, 402-3.   [3] P. 310.   [4] Pp. 217-18, 243.
[5] Pp. 272-6.   [6] P. 280.   [7] P. 304.   [8] P. 238.   [9] Pp. 178, 184.
[10] P. 185.   [11] P. 349.

not afraid to denounce the sending of the fleet through the Straits as "an act of war, a breach of European law". He was denounced in every note of passion and contempt for his alleged indifference to British interests, but he appealed to a higher tradition "which teaches you to seek the promotion of those interests in obeying the dictates of honour and justice".[1] In his international outlook and in his would-be solution of the Eastern Question he was as far ahead of his time as in the precedent which he and his Government had set by the adoption of the principle of international arbitration.

In all this Gladstone found much more sympathy and comprehension among the lower middle and working classes than in the class to which he himself belonged: and this helps to explain a feature that makes him unique among British statesmen—namely the fact that he became increasingly radical as he grew older, and showed a distressing disregard for social conventions in politics. This deepened still further his antagonism to Disraeli and helped to estrange the Queen from him. In the Eastern Question he left Clubland and Mayfair to the Turcophils, and flatly warned the House of Commons that "the West End of London does not express the true sentiments of England".[2] The best comment on this is the contrast between the rowdies who hooted him in Harley Street and the tumultuous northern crowds who flocked to do him honour. And there was the further strange phenomenon—incomprehensible to the Queen, with her *simpliste* and Erastian Church views—that Gladstone the High Churchman and such kindred spirits as Liddon and Church turned in frank sympathy towards the Nonconformists, whom even Lord Granville did not hesitate to describe as "the backbone of the Liberal party". This forms a chapter by itself into which we cannot enter here. But it is worth noting the excuses put forward by the Bishop of Oxford for the attitude of the Anglican clergy. "It is to be accounted for partly by their feeling that the politicians who chiefly deprecate war are also the abettors of these unscrupulous assailants on themselves and on the Church. I deplore the error which they are committing in suffering themselves to be regarded as in any way advocates for war: I think them wholly and grievously wrong: but I own I cannot altogether be surprised—knowing what human nature is—at their feelings".[3] To-day we may reasonably enter a *caveat* and, remembering Hartington's aversion to the "innumerable parsons"[4]

[1] P. 185. [2] *Gladstone Papers*, 11 Oct. 1877, Granville to Gladstone.
[3] *Ibid.* 8 Jan. 1878. [4] *Supra*, p. 114.

who flocked to support Gladstone at the St. James's Hall, may admit
that the Bishop did much less than justice to his own clergy. Such
hesitation as arose later came from the fear that Liberalism was
identified with Disestablishment.

Perhaps, however, the most striking commentary on this phase of
the question is a letter from Canon Liddon to Dr. Dale, the famous
Midland Nonconformist divine—"I cannot help saying to you how
greatly the history of the Eastern Question has affected my own
feelings towards those who are not members of the Church of
England. I have often and often wished that we, as a body,
could have been as true to what was morally as well as theologically
the cause of Christ in East Europe as were the English Nonconformists." [1]

During the spring of 1878 Gladstone faced much obloquy and even
mob insults, but he helped to turn the scale against war: he was
reassured by the appointment of Lord Salisbury and by the tenour
of his famous Circular—especially its unwonted regard for Greek
interests: and he deliberately refrained from public utterance during
the critical negotiations with Shuvalov and during the Congress
itself. But in all this period nothing is more remarkable than his
sureness of instinct regarding the San Stefano settlement, and
nothing shows better how absurd it was to charge him with subservience to Russia. For he did not hesitate to condemn Russia's
claim to Bessarabia; he condemned the inadequate treatment of
Greek claims, and, eager as he was for Bulgarian liberty, he condemned the exaggerated extension of Bulgaria westwards. His
verdict on the final settlement of Berlin is more open to criticism,
and some of his followers were more logical in refusing to condemn
an attempt to apply in Asia the very reforms which he had advocated
so gallantly in Europe. But he instinctively felt that Britain had
placed herself on a lower plane by her secret bargain for Cyprus
behind the back of Europe, and that she was taking undue risks on
the Armenian frontier and making promises which she might not be
ready or able to implement. This and his acute personal distrust of
Disraeli made him unable to see how many of his own aspirations
were at least partially fulfilled, and led him to do less than justice to
Salisbury's very real desire to make reform a reality.

In this connection it is highly instructive to contrast Gladstone's
outlook to Disraeli and to Salisbury. It is not too much to describe

[1] *Life of Liddon*, p. 284.

him as obsessed by a sense of permanent danger from his great rival. "Disraeli", he once wrote, "is a man who is *never beaten*. Every reverse, every defeat is to him only an admonition to wait and catch his opportunity of retrieving, and more than retrieving, his position." And indeed this was not far removed from the truth: fortitude and persistence were two of Disraeli's foremost qualities.

Salisbury he judged very differently, welcoming his mission to Constantinople and again his appointment to succeed Derby. A year after the Congress, at Gladstone's London house, Hayward—in the presence of Malcolm MacColl, to whom we owe the story[1]—attacked Salisbury for taking office under Beaconsfield after having criticised him so severely. "But Gladstone at once disagreed and said, 'I think it was Salisbury's duty to take office, and I remember saying as much to Lady Salisbury at the time'. Lord Salisbury was not likely to become a Liberal: as an independent member of the House of Lords he would have been powerless, and the only way in which he could serve his country was by taking office in the only possible Conservative ministry. Nobody can dislike Lord Salisbury's present foreign policy more than I do, but I do not despair of him, and I regard his reputation *as part of the heritage of England.*"

MacColl, who was on excellent terms with both men, had the temerity to write this to Lord Salisbury, seemingly in the hope of promoting a new political alliance. Salisbury replied with large-minded modesty, "To be the leader of a large party—still more anything resembling a coalition—requires in a large measure the gifts of pliancy and optimism, and I unfortunately am very poorly endowed in either respect". This letter MacColl in turn showed to Mr. Gladstone, who replied, "I have always believed that he is not governed by personal ambition: and I agree strongly with him as to the unsatisfying character of political life. There is something to which every heart must answer sympathetically in his remarks on his own qualities." "Lord Salisbury", Mr. Gladstone wrote a week later—as Prime Minister on the leader of the Opposition—"is a man who is capable of making sacrifices for the sake of his convictions, and such a man will always be respected in England."[2] This, one of the most creditable incidents in British party politics, is not as well known as it ought to be.

---

[1] 11 Aug. 1877, to MacColl—*Life of MacColl*, p. 248.
[2] Letters of 9, 11 and 13 July 1884, between MacColl and Gladstone—*Life of MacColl*, pp. 94-9.

The conclusions to be drawn from this survey are that Disraeli inherited and upheld the Palmerstonian tradition in the Eastern Question and, like the elder statesman, profoundly misunderstood the forces at work in the Balkan Peninsula, but that the Turks were to him a mere pawn in the great game against Russia; that he leant towards partition or reform according to opportunist grounds of the moment; that he led his country to the very brink of war and was only held back by a combination of ill-health, Cabinet dissensions and popular outcry: that in the end he receded from his original position, utterly abandoned Turkish integrity in Europe and consoled himself with an Asiatic policy which he afterwards lacked the energy to pursue to its logical conclusion. Disraeli was always a supreme master of strategy, and it was only gradually that the nation realised the extent to which he had shifted his ground from first to last. The settlement with which his name is so closely associated in no way represented his aims during the crisis, and its credit is really due to Bismarck, Shuvalov and Salisbury rather than to him.

While, then, Disraeli clung to the very last to his illusions on Turkey and identified British interests with the artificial maintenance of a decadent state, Gladstone saw that the future lay with the nations whom Ottoman tyranny had so long submerged. It is well for Disraeli that there are other fields in which his fame stands sure and unassailable: for his last great incursion into foreign policy was a failure and nearly involved us in a war still more unnecessary than the Crimean. His bugbear, Russian Tsarism, has also gone the way of all flesh, and its memory evokes mixed feelings in the Balkans, even though the statue of the Tsar Liberator stands before the Bulgarian Parliament. But the name of Gladstone is still held in equal honour in Sofia and Belgrade, in Athens and Bucarest, in Cetinje and Zagreb, and wherever the principle of "the Balkans for the Balkan peoples", or indeed the wider principle of self-government for small nations, has any meaning.

STANFORD'S GEOG. ESTAB., LONDON.

GENERAL INDEX

Abdul Aziz, Sultan, 17, 36, 427
Abdul Hamid II., Sultan, 45, 50, 123, 186, 346, 520, 522, 549; relations with Elliot, 50; banishes Midhat, 147; and Layard, 45, 207, 229, 352-4, 406; encouraged by Disraeli's language to Musurus, 245; appeals to Queen, 247, 332; asks for armistice, 263; and San Stefano, 353; receives Grand Duke, 362; Austen's verdict on, 362; secret message to Disraeli, 374; fresh conversations with Layard, 407; Ali Suavi's attack, 427; Disraeli's praise of, 502; evasion of treaty, 520
Abdul Kerim, 49, 95, 211, 220
Abdul Medjid, Sultan, 17
Aberdeen, Lord, 137, 277, 350, 366, 398, 501
Abyssinia, 395
Acre, 324, 325
Adlerberg, Count, 25
Adrianople, 254, 264, 268, 292, 329, 518
Adrianople armistice, 266, 311
Adriatic, 43, 77, 326, 370, 479
Adye, Sir John, 220, 539
Aegean, 371, 380, 418, 449, 473, 495, 500, 529
Aehrenthal, Count, 371, 473, 475, 479
Afghan Committee, 540
Afghanistan, 5, 41, 540-41, 547
Ahmed Aga, 58, 60, 61, 184, 207, 564
Ahmed Vefik Pasha, 352, 354, 427
Aksakov, Ivan, 168, 465
Albania, 46, 326, 334, 371, 461, 473, 477, 518, 519, 529
Albanian League, 519
Albert, Prince, 354, 392, 397-400, 564
Albrecht, Archduke, 141, 294
Aleksinac, 49, 95
Aleppo, 325
Alexander II., Tsar: visits Windsor, 6; and Bismarck, 13; at Ems, 13; and Berlin Memorandum, 32-4: and Russian volunteers, 48-9, 95; and Francis Joseph, 92, 99; speech at Moscow, 104; thanks Andrássy, 145; and Ignatyev mission, 162; and Schweinitz, 169; declares war on Turkey, 170; Gladstone on, 187; peace policy of, 194;

assurances to Vienna, 223; overture for mediation, 228; and Wellesley, 228-9; and Prince Milan, 230; attitude to a second campaign, 240; at Shipka, 263; orders advance on Bosphorus, 265; relies on Ignatyev, 265; offer to Francis Joseph, 270-71; desire for peace, 271; fresh letter to Francis Joseph, 296; orders Grand Duke to occupy Constantinople, 331; alleged demand for Andrássy's dismissal, 331; Shuvalov submits British proposals, 412; and Protocol of 30 May, 417-18; anger at Shuvalov after Congress, 466; Russo-German relations, 467-9
Alexander III., Tsar, 48, 471, 517, 533
Alexander of Battenberg, Prince, 331, 517, 528, 541, 547
Alexander of Hesse, Prince, 369, 372
Alexandretta, 325, 424, 426, 437, 514
Alexandrovo, 470
Alexis, Grand Duke, 40
Ali Pasha, 17
Ali Suavi, 129, 427
Allon, Dr., 111, 118, 351
Alsace-Lorraine, 9
Amiens, Treaty of, 497
Andrássy, Count Julius : on Bismarck, 9; and War Scare, 14; Note of 30 December, 27; and Disraeli, 33, 199, 201; and Reichstadt Convention, 46-8, to Beust, 47; warns Prince Milan, 50; Sumarokov Mission, 92, 94; sends Münch to Berlin, 94; talk with Salisbury, 107; secret negotiations with Russia, 140-45; British overture to, 199-203; reserved attitude, 223-5; conceals negotiations from Bismarck, 224; attitude to Serbia, 231; Layard's criticism, 235; and Tsar's peace terms, 270-71; and Beaconsfield's fresh overtures, 293; distrusts Gorchakov and Tsar, 294-5; resists British alliance, 322; discussions with Novikov and Stolberg, 336; proposes a conference, 336; policy after San Stefano, 338; and Ignatyev Mission, 368-73; on Dalmatia and Bosnia, 371; on Macedonian question, 372; reception of Salisbury

INDEX TO QUOTATIONS FROM
UNPUBLISHED SOURCES

I. *British*

II. *Austrian*

III. *Russian*

THE   END

Compound type	Functional group	Simple example	Name ending
Ester	$\overset{\displaystyle O}{\underset{\displaystyle \parallel}{-C}}-O-C\overset{\diagup}{\underset{\diagdown}{}}$	$CH_3\overset{\displaystyle O}{\overset{\parallel}{C}}-OCH_2CH_3$ Ethyl ethanoate (ethyl acetate)	-oate
Carboxylic acid	$\overset{\displaystyle O}{\overset{\parallel}{-C}}-O-H$	$CH_3CH_2CH_2\overset{\displaystyle O}{\overset{\parallel}{C}}-OH$ Butanoic acid	-oic acid
Carboxylic acid chloride	$\overset{\displaystyle O}{\overset{\parallel}{-C}}-Cl$	$CH_3CH_2\overset{\displaystyle O}{\overset{\parallel}{C}}-Cl$ Propanoyl chloride	-yl chloride
Amide	$\overset{\displaystyle O}{\overset{\parallel}{-C}}-N\overset{\diagup}{\diagdown}$	$CH_3\overset{\displaystyle O}{\overset{\parallel}{C}}-NH_2$ Ethanamide	-amide
Amine	$\overset{\diagup}{\underset{\diagdown}{-C}}-N\overset{\diagup}{\diagdown}$	$CH_3CH_2NH_2$ Ethylamine	-amine
Nitrile	$-C\equiv N$	$CH_3C\equiv N$ Ethanenitrile (acetonitrile)	-nitrile
Nitro	$\overset{\diagdown}{\underset{\diagup}{-C}}-\overset{+}{N}\overset{\diagup O}{\diagdown O^-}$	$CH_3CH_2NO_2$ Nitroethane	None
Organometallic	$\overset{\diagdown}{\underset{\diagup}{-C}}-M$ M = metal	CH_3-Li Methyllithium	None

FUNDAMENTALS OF
Organic Chemistry

FUNDAMENTALS OF
Organic Chemistry

John McMurry
CORNELL UNIVERSITY

Brooks/Cole Publishing Company
Monterey, California

Brooks/Cole Publishing Company
A Division of Wadsworth, Inc.

Printed in the United States of America

10 9 8 7 6 5 4 3 2 1

Library of Congress Cataloging-in-Publication Data
McMurry, John.
  Fundamentals of organic chemistry.

  Includes index.
  1. Chemistry, Organic.   I. Title.
QD251.2.M4   1986   547   85-17098
ISBN 0-534-05280-0

Sponsoring Editor: Sue Ewing
Editorial Assistant: Lorraine McCloud
Production Editor: Phyllis Niklas/Joan Marsh
Manuscript Editor: Phyllis Niklas
Interior Design: Robert Ishi
Cover Design: Jamie Sue Brooks
Interior Illustration: Vantage Art, Inc.
Typesetting: Jonathan Peck Typographers, Ltd.
Cover Printing: Phoenix Color Corp.
Printing and Binding: R. R. Donnelley & Sons Company

On the Cover: A computer model simulating
interaction of DNA with a protein molecule. Green
represents carbon, blue represents nitrogen, and red
represents oxygen. Courtesy of the Computer
Graphics Laboratory, University of California, San
Francisco. Copyright © Regents, University of
California.

Preface

Present textbooks of organic chemistry fall into two broad categories. On the one hand are the 1000+-page books intended for full-year courses, and on the other hand are the 450-page books intended for one-semester courses. The reduction in book size on going from the long to the short course is often not accomplished entirely by a reduction in subject matter. Instead, a substantial portion of the reduction is often accomplished by removing pedagogical devices—shortening explanations, deleting examples, eliminating repetition, and providing fewer problems. Unfortunately, it is just these pedagogical devices that are most needed by students in the short course.

My goal in writing this book has been to cover only those subjects required for a one-semester or two-quarter course in organic chemistry, but to do so without loss of the important pedagogical tools necessary for learning at this level. By comparison with other short-course texts, this book has longer and more lucid explanations of difficult subjects, more illustrations, more examples of individual reactions, and more repetition of important points. The result, I believe, is a book that is less terse, more readable, and easier to learn from.

Organization

The primary organization of this book is by functional group, beginning in Chapter 2 with simple alkanes and going on to more complex compounds. Within this primary organization, heavy emphasis is placed on explaining the fundamental mechanistic similarities of organic reactions. Chapter 11, "Carbonyl Alpha-Substitution and Condensation Reactions," is particularly notable in this respect, showing how all carbonyl compounds undergo similar processes.

Organic molecules and organic reactions are presented as early as possible. After a brief review of structure and bonding in Chapter 1, organic molecules and functional groups are introduced in Chapter 2, followed by an initial discussion of organic reactions in Chapter 3.

The Lead-Off Reaction: Addition of HBr to Alkenes

A simple polar reaction—the addition of HBr to an alkene—is used as the lead-off to illustrate general principles of organic reactions. This choice has the advantage of relative simplicity (prior knowledge of stereochemistry and kinetics is not required, as it is when a nucleophilic substitution reaction is used as lead-off), yet it is also an important polar reaction on a common functional group. Many students attach great importance to a text's lead-off reaction because it is the first reaction encountered and is discussed in such detail. I believe that my choice serves to introduce students to functional group chemistry better than does a lead-off such as free-radical alkane chlorination.

Spectroscopy

Spectroscopy is treated as a tool, not as a specialized field of study. Infrared, ultraviolet, ^{13}C NMR, and ^1H NMR spectroscopies are all covered by showing the kind of information that can be derived from each and how each can be used to answer specific structural questions.

Nomenclature

The IUPAC nomenclature is used throughout. For the most part, this involves the use of systematic names, although a few IUPAC-approved nonsystematic names (such as acetic acid, acetone, ethylene, and phenol) are also employed. Since it's unlikely that these few common names will disappear from everyday use in the near future, it's probably best for students to learn them. An appendix on nomenclature of polyfunctional organic compounds is included at the end of the book.

Coverage

The coverage in this book is up-to-date, reflecting important advances of the past decade. For example, ^{13}C NMR is introduced as a routine spectroscopic tool, equal in importance to ^1H NMR. Similarly, the chemistry of nucleic acids is covered, including a section on DNA sequencing by the Maxam–Gilbert method.

Interludes

Twenty-one brief interludes are included at appropriate points in the text. Meant to serve as short "breathers" between chapters, these interludes show interesting applications of organic chemistry to industrial and biological systems. They can be covered by the instructor or left for individual student reading.

Practice Problems

Each chapter contains carefully worked-out examples that illustrate how problems can be solved. Each practice problem and solution is then followed by a similar problem for the reader to solve. These worked-out examples are valuable because of their appearance in the text, but they are not meant to serve as a replacement for the accompanying *Study Guide and Solutions Manual*.

Pedagogy

In addition to the above features, every effort has been made to make this book as effective, clear, and readable as possible—to make it easy to learn from:

Paragraphs usually start with summary sentences.

Transitions between paragraphs and between topics are smooth.

Extensive use is made of three-dimensional airbrushed art and carefully rendered stereochemical formulas.

Extensive cross-referencing to earlier material is used.

A second color is used to indicate the changes that occur during reactions.

More than 750 problems are included, both within the text and at the end of every chapter. These include both drill and thought problems.

An innovative vertical format is used to explain reaction mechanisms. The mechanisms are printed vertically, while explanations of the changes taking place in each step are printed next to the reaction arrow. This format allows the reader to see easily what is occurring at each step in a reaction without having to jump back and forth between the text and structures.

Study Guide and Solutions Manual

A carefully prepared *Study Guide and Solutions Manual* accompanies this text. Written by Susan McMurry, this companion volume answers all in-text and end-of-chapter problems and explains in detail how answers are obtained. In addition, the following supplemental materials are included: summaries of each chapter, lists of study goals for each chapter, reaction summaries for each chapter, a glossary, a summary of name reactions, a summary of methods for preparing functional groups, a summary of the uses of important reagents, tables of spectroscopic information, and a list of suggested readings.

Acknowledgments

I sincerely thank the many people whose help and suggestions were so valuable in the creation of this book. Foremost is my wife Susan, who read, criticized, and improved all aspects of the text, and who authored the accompanying *Study Guide and Solutions Manual*. Among the reviewers providing thoughtful comments were Harry N. Barnet, Palomar College; Joseph Gettler, New York University; Stan Grenda, University of Nevada; Lawrence Gries, Queens College of CUNY; Lars Hellberg, San Diego State University; G. L. Lange, University of Guelph; Alfred Levinson, Portland State University; Linda Munchausen, Southeastern Louisiana University; Ralph Shaw, Southeastern Louisiana University; Michael Tempesta, University of Missouri; Jack W. Timberlake, University of New Orleans; Alan Wingrove, Towson State University; and James R. Wright, U.S. Air Force Academy.

Special thanks are due Phyllis Niklas, Sue Ewing, Joan Marsh, and others of the Brooks/Cole staff for their usual first-rate work.

A Note for Students

We have the same goals. Yours, as students, is to learn organic chemistry. Mine, as author, is to do everything possible to help you learn. It's going to require work on your part, but the following suggestions should prove useful in your study:

Don't read the text immediately.   As you begin each new chapter, look it over first. Read the introductory paragraphs and find out what topics will be covered. You'll be in a much better position to understand new material if you first have a general idea of where you're heading. Once you've begun a chapter, read it at least twice. First read the chapter rapidly, making checks or comments in the margin next to important or difficult points; then return for an in-depth study.

Keep up with the material.   Who's likely to do a better job—the runner who trains 5 miles per day for weeks before a race, or the one who suddenly trains 20 miles the day before the race? Organic chemistry is a subject that builds on previous knowledge. You have to keep up with the material on a daily basis.

Work the problems.   There are no shortcuts here. Working problems is the only way to master organic chemistry (and the only way to prove to yourself that you've mastered it). The in-text problems are placed at the ends of sections to provide immediate practice on material just covered. The end-of-chapter problems provide both additional drill and real challenges. Full answers and explanations for all problems are given in the accompanying *Study Guide and Solutions Manual*.

Ask questions.   Faculty members and teaching assistants are there to help you. Most of them will turn out to be extremely helpful and genuinely interested in seeing you learn.

Use molecular models.   Organic chemistry is a three-dimensional science. Although this book uses many drawings to help you visualize molecules, there's no substitute for building a molecular model, turning it in your hands, and looking at it from different viewpoints.

Use the study guide.   The *Study Guide and Solutions Manual* that accompanies this text gives complete solutions to all problems and provides a wealth of supplementary material. Included are lists of study goals for each chapter, summaries of each chapter, reaction summaries for each chapter, a large glossary, a summary of name reactions, a summary of methods for preparing functional groups, a summary of the uses of important reagents, tables of spectroscopic information, and a list of suggested readings. Find out ahead of time what's there so that you'll know where to go when you need help.

Good luck. I sincerely hope you enjoy learning organic chemistry and that you come to see the logic and beauty of its structure. I would be glad to receive comments and suggestions from any who have learned from this book.

Brief Contents

Contents

FUNDAMENTALS OF
Organic Chemistry

CHAPTER 1

Structure and Bonding

In the eighteenth century, as chemistry was evolving from an alchemist's art into a modern science, unexplainable differences were noted between compounds derived from living sources and those derived from mineral sources. Compounds from plant and animal sources were often difficult to isolate and purify. Even when pure, these compounds were difficult to work with and were more sensitive to decomposition than compounds from mineral sources. The Swedish chemist Torbern Bergman was the first person to express this difference between "organic" and "inorganic" substances, and the phrase "organic chemistry" soon came to mean the chemistry of compounds from living organisms.

To many chemists at the time, the only explanation for the difference in behavior between organic and inorganic compounds was that organic compounds contained a peculiar and undefinable "vital force" as a result of their derivation from living sources. One consequence of the presence of this vital force, chemists believed, was that organic compounds could not be prepared and manipulated in the laboratory as could inorganic compounds.

Although the vitalistic theory was believed by many influential chemists, its acceptance was by no means universal. As early as 1816, the theory received a heavy blow when Michel Chevreul found that soaps, prepared by the reaction of alkali with animal fat, could be separated into several pure organic compounds, which he termed "fatty acids." Thus, for the first time, one organic compound (animal fat) had been converted into others (fatty acids plus glycerin) without the intervention of an outside vital force.

$$\text{Animal fat} \xrightarrow[\text{H}_2\text{O}]{\text{NaOH}} \text{Soap} + \text{Glycerin}$$

$$\text{Soap} \xrightarrow{\text{H}_3\text{O}^+} \text{``Fatty acids''}$$

A little more than a decade later, the vitalistic theory suffered still further when Friedrich Wöhler discovered in 1828 that it was possible to convert the "inorganic" salt ammonium cyanate into the previously known "organic" substance urea.

$$NH_4^+ \ ^-OCN \xrightarrow{\text{Heat}} H_2N-\overset{\displaystyle O}{\overset{\|}{C}}-NH_2$$

Ammonium cyanate   **Urea**

By the mid-nineteenth century, the weight of evidence was against the vitalistic theory, and it had become clear that the same basic scientific principles were applicable to all compounds. The only unifying characteristic of organic compounds was that all contained the element carbon.

Organic chemistry, then, is the study of the compounds of carbon. But why is carbon special? What is it that sets carbon apart from all other elements in the periodic table? The answers to these questions are complex but have much to do with the unique ability of carbon atoms to bond together, forming long chains and rings. Carbon, alone of all elements, is able to form an immense diversity of compounds, from the simple to the staggeringly complex—from methane, containing one carbon, to DNA, which can contain tens of *billions* of carbons.

All organic compounds are *not* derived from living organisms. Chemists have become highly sophisticated in their ability to synthesize new organic compounds in the laboratory. Medicines, dyes, polymers, plastics, pesticides, and a host of other substances are prepared in the laboratory, and all are organic chemicals. Organic chemistry is a subject that touches the lives of everyone. Its study can be a fascinating undertaking.

1.1   ATOMIC ORBITALS

Throughout the nineteenth century and into the twentieth, chemists and physicists sought to understand the nature of the atom and the nature of the forces holding atoms together in molecules. A major breakthrough occurred in 1926 when Erwin Schrödinger proposed a mathematical expression for describing the electronic structure of atoms. In essence, Schrödinger devised a mathematical equation for predicting the volume of space around a nucleus where different electrons are most likely to be found.

The volume of space around a nucleus where an electron is most likely to be found is called an orbital. It's often helpful to think of an orbital as a kind of time-lapse photograph of an electron's movement around the nucleus. Such a photograph would show the orbital as a blurry cloud indicating where the electron has been. This electron cloud does not have a discrete boundary, but, for practical purposes, we can set the limits of an orbital by saying that it represents the space where an electron spends most (90–95%) of its time.

What do orbitals look like? The exact size and shape of an electron's orbital depends on its energy level. Electrons can be thought of as belonging to different layers, or **shells**, around the nucleus. Each shell contains different numbers and kinds of orbitals. For example, the first shell (the one nearest the nucleus) has only one orbital, called a 1s orbital. The second shell has four orbitals, one 2s and three 2p; the third shell has nine orbitals, one 3s, three 3p, and five 3d; and so on. Relative energy levels of the different kinds of atomic orbitals are shown in Figure 1.1.

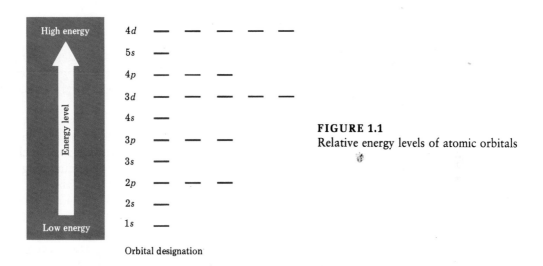

FIGURE 1.1
Relative energy levels of atomic orbitals

The lowest-energy electrons occupy the 1s orbital. The s atomic orbitals are spherical and have the nucleus of the atom at their center, as shown in Figure 1.2. Next in energy after the 1s electrons are the 2s electrons. Because they are higher in energy, 2s electrons are farther from the nucleus on average, and their spherical orbital is somewhat larger than that of 1s electrons.

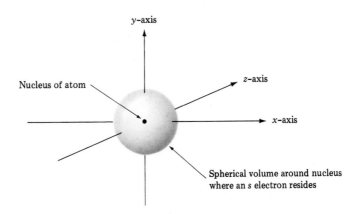

FIGURE 1.2
An s atomic orbital (spherical)

The $2p$ electrons are next higher in energy. As Figure 1.3 indicates, there are three $2p$ orbitals, each of which is roughly dumbbell shaped. The three $2p$ orbitals are of equal energy and are oriented in space such that each is perpendicular to the other two. They are denoted $2p_x$, $2p_y$, and $2p_z$, depending upon which axis they lie.

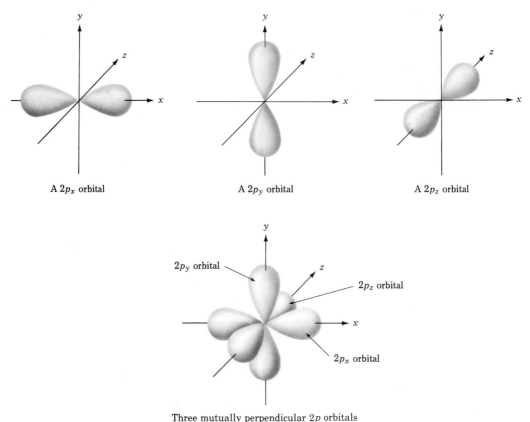

A $2p_x$ orbital   A $2p_y$ orbital   A $2p_z$ orbital

Three mutually perpendicular $2p$ orbitals

FIGURE 1.3
The shapes of the $2p$ orbitals

1.2   ELECTRONIC CONFIGURATION OF ATOMS

The lowest-energy arrangement, or **ground-state electronic configuration**, of any atom is a description of what orbitals the electrons occupy in the atom. Available electrons are assigned to the proper shells and orbitals by following three rules:

1. The orbitals of lowest energy are filled first.
2. Only two electrons can occupy the same orbital, and they must be of opposite spin.[1]

[1]Electrons can be thought of as spinning around an axis in much the same way that the earth spins. This spin can have two equal and opposite orientations, denoted as up ↑ and down ↓.

3. If two or more empty orbitals of equal energy are available, one electron is placed in each until all are half-full.

Let's look at some examples to see how these rules are applied. Hydrogen, the lightest element, has only one electron, which we must assign to the lowest-energy orbital. This gives hydrogen a $1s$ ground-state electronic configuration. Carbon has six electrons, and a ground-state electronic configuration $1s^2 2s^2 2p^2$ is arrived at by applying the three rules.[2] These and other examples are shown in Table 1.1.

TABLE 1.1 Ground-state electronic configurations of some elements

Element	Atomic number	Configuration		Element	Atomic number	Configuration
Hydrogen	1	$1s$ ↑		Lithium	3	$2s$ ↑ $1s$ ↑↓
Carbon	6	$2p$ ↑ ↑ — $2s$ ↑↓ $1s$ ↑↓		Neon	10	$2p$ ↑↓ ↑↓ ↑↓ $2s$ ↑↓ $1s$ ↑↓
Sodium	11	$3s$ ↑ $2p$ ↑↓ ↑↓ ↑↓ $2s$ ↑↓ $1s$ ↑↓		Argon	18	$3p$ ↑↓ ↑↓ ↑↓ $3s$ ↑↓ $2p$ ↑↓ ↑↓ ↑↓ $2s$ ↑↓ $1s$ ↑↓

PRACTICE PROBLEM Give the ground-state electronic configuration of nitrogen.

Solution The periodic table indicates that nitrogen has atomic number 7 and thus has seven electrons. Using Figure 1.1 to find the relative energy levels of orbitals, and using the three rules to assign the seven electrons to orbitals, we find that the first two electrons go into the lowest-energy orbital ($1s^2$), the next two electrons go into the second-lowest-energy orbital ($2s^2$), and the remaining three electrons go into the three third-lowest-energy orbitals ($2p^3$). Thus, the complete configuration of nitrogen is $1s^2 2s^2 2p^3$.

PROBLEM 1.1 Give the ground-state electronic configuration for each of the following elements:

(a) Boron   (b) Phosphorus   (c) Oxygen   (d) Argon

PROBLEM 1.2 How many electrons does each of the following elements have in its outermost electron shell?

(a) Potassium   (b) Krypton   (c) Aluminum

---

[2]A superscript is used here to represent the number of electrons at a particular energy level. For example, $1s^2$ indicates that there are two electrons in the $1s$ orbital. No superscript is used when there is only one electron in an orbital.

1.3   DEVELOPMENT OF CHEMICAL BONDING THEORY

By the mid-nineteenth century, with the vitalistic theory of organic chemistry dead, chemists began to probe the forces holding molecules together. In 1858, August Kekulé and Archibald Couper independently proposed that, in all organic compounds, carbon always has four "affinity units." In other words, carbon is *tetravalent*—it always forms four bonds when it joins other elements to form compounds. Furthermore, said Kekulé, carbon atoms can bond to each other to form extended chains, and chains can double back on themselves to form rings.

Although Kekulé had satisfactorily described the tetravalent nature of carbon, chemistry was still viewed in an essentially two-dimensional way until 1874. In that year Jacobus van't Hoff and Joseph Le Bel added a third dimension to our ideas about molecules. They proposed that the four bonds of carbon are not randomly oriented, but instead have a specific spatial orientation. Van't Hoff went even further and correctly proposed that the four atoms to which carbon is bonded sit at the corners of a tetrahedron, with carbon in the center. A representation of a tetrahedral carbon atom is shown in Figure 1.4. Note the conventions used to show three-dimensionality: Normal lines are assumed to be in the plane of the paper; heavy wedged lines come out of the plane of paper toward the viewer; and dashed lines recede into the plane away from the viewer. These representations will be used frequently in this text.

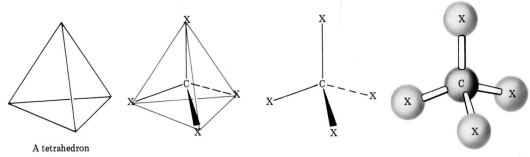

A tetrahedron

FIGURE 1.4
Van't Hoff's tetrahedral carbon atom: The heavy wedged line comes out of the plane of the paper; the normal lines are in the plane of the paper; and the broken line goes back behind the plane.

PROBLEM 1.3   Draw a molecule of chloromethane, CH_3Cl, using wedged, normal, and dashed lines to show its tetrahedral geometry.

1.4   MODERN PICTURE OF CHEMICAL BONDING: IONIC BONDS

What is our modern picture of chemical bonding? Why do atoms bond together, and how can bonding be described in terms of atomic structure? The *why* question is relatively easy to answer. Atoms form bonds because the compound that results is more stable than the alternative arrangement of isolated atoms. Energy is always *released* when chemical bonds are formed. The *how* question is more difficult. To answer it, we need to know more about the properties of atoms.

We know through observation that eight electrons (an electron octet) in the outermost shell imparts a special stability to the inert-gas elements in Group 0: neon (2 + 8), argon (2 + 8 + 8), krypton (2 + 18 + 8). We also know that the chemistry of many elements with nearly inert-gas configurations is dominated by attempts to achieve the stable inert-gas electronic makeup. For example, the alkali metals in Group I have single *s* electrons in their outer shells. By *losing* this electron, they form *positive* ions and achieve an inert-gas configuration. Such elements are called **electropositive**.

Just as the alkali metals at the left of the periodic table have a tendency to form positive ions by losing an electron, the halogens (Group VIIA elements) at the right of the periodic table have a tendency to form *negative* ions by *gaining* an electron. By so doing, the halogens also achieve inert-gas configurations. Such elements are called **electronegative**.

The simplest kind of chemical bonding occurs between an electropositive element and an electronegative element. For example, when sodium metal (electropositive) reacts with chlorine gas (electronegative), sodium donates an electron to chlorine to form positively charged sodium ions and negatively charged chloride ions. The product, sodium chloride, is said to have **ionic bonding**. That is, the ions are held together by purely electrostatic attraction between unlike charges. The structure of the sodium chloride crystal lattice shown in Figure 1.5 illustrates how each positively charged sodium ion is surrounded by negatively charged chloride ions and vice versa.

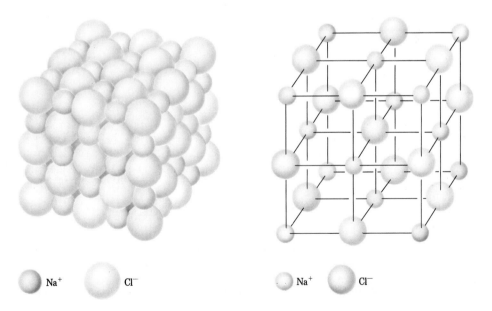

Na^+ Cl^- Na^+ Cl^-

FIGURE 1.5
Ionic bonding in a sodium chloride crystal: Each sodium ion is surrounded by six chloride ions, and each chloride ion is surrounded by six sodium ions.

1.5   MODERN PICTURE OF CHEMICAL BONDING: COVALENT BONDS

Elements form ionic bonds if they can readily attain an inert-gas configuration by gaining or losing an electron. How, though, do the elements in the middle of the periodic table form bonds? Let's look at methane, CH_4, as an example. Certainly the bonding in methane is not ionic since it would be very difficult for carbon ($1s^2 2s^2 2p^2$) to either gain or lose *four* electrons to achieve an inert-gas configuration.[3] In fact, carbon bonds to other atoms, not by donating electrons, but by *sharing* them. Such shared-electron bonds, first proposed in 1916 by G. N. Lewis, are called **covalent bonds**. The covalent bond is the most important bond in organic chemistry.

A simple shorthand way of indicating covalent bonds in molecules is to use what are known as **Lewis structures**. In Lewis structures, an atom's outer-shell electrons are represented by dots. Thus, hydrogen has one dot ($1s$), carbon has four dots ($2s^2 2p^2$), oxygen has six dots ($2s^2 2p^4$), and so on. A stable molecule results whenever the inert-gas configuration has been achieved for all atoms, as in the following examples:

$$4 \cdot \ddot{C} \cdot \; + \; 4\,H \cdot \; \longrightarrow \; H \! : \! \overset{\overset{\displaystyle H}{\ddot{}}}{\underset{\underset{\displaystyle H}{\ddot{}}}{C}} \! : \! H$$

Methane (CH_4)

$$3\,H \cdot \; + \; \cdot \dot{\ddot{N}} \cdot \; \longrightarrow \; H \! : \! \overset{\overset{\displaystyle H}{\cdot}}{\underset{\ddot{}}{N}} \! : \! H$$

Ammonia (NH_3)

$$2\,H \cdot \; + \; \cdot \ddot{O} \! : \; \longrightarrow \; H \! : \! \underset{\underset{\displaystyle H}{}}{\overset{\ddot{}}{O}} \! :$$

Water (H_2O)

$$3H \cdot \; + \; \cdot \dot{C} \cdot \; + \; \cdot \ddot{O} \! : \; + \; H \cdot \; \longrightarrow \; H \! : \! \underset{\underset{\displaystyle H}{}}{\overset{\overset{\displaystyle H}{}}{C}} \! : \! \underset{}{\overset{\ddot{}}{O}} \! :$$

Methanol (CH_3OH)

$$2\,H \cdot \; + \; \cdot \ddot{O} \cdot \; + \; H^+ \; \longrightarrow \; H \! : \! \underset{\underset{\displaystyle H}{}}{\overset{\overset{\displaystyle +}{\ddot{}}}{O}} \! : \! H$$

Hydronium ion (H_3O^+)

Lewis structures are valuable because they make electron "bookkeeping" possible and constantly remind us of the number of outer-shell electrons (**valence electrons**) we are dealing with. Simpler still is the use of **Kekulé structures**, also called **line-bond structures**, where the two electrons in a covalent bond are indicated simply by a line. Pairs of nonbonding valence electrons are often ignored when drawing line-bond structures, but we must still keep mentally aware of their existence. Some examples are shown in Table 1.2.

---

[3] The electronic configuration of carbon can be written either as $1s^2 2s^2 2p^2$ or as $1s^2 2s^2 2p_x 2p_y$. Both notations are correct, but the latter is more informative since it indicates which of the three equivalent p orbitals are half-filled.

TABLE 1.2 Lewis and Kekulé structures of some simple molecules

Name	Lewis structure	Kekulé structure
Water (H_2O)	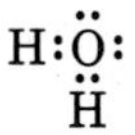 H:Ö: Ḧ	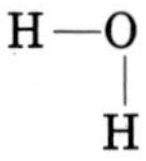 H—O | H
Ammonia (NH_3)	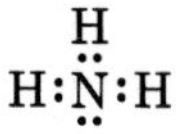 H H:N̈:H	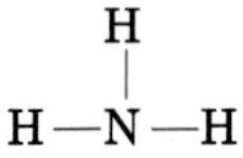 H | H—N—H
Methane (CH_4)	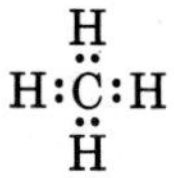 H H:C̈:H Ḧ	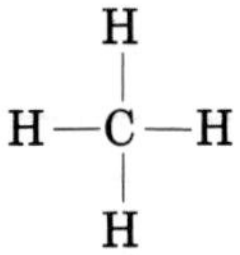 H | H—C—H | H
Methanol (CH_3OH)	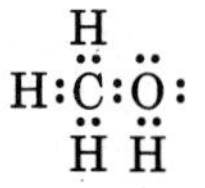 H .. H:C̈:Ö: Ḧ Ḧ	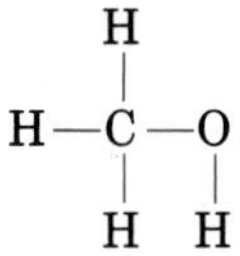 H | H—C—O | | H H

PRACTICE PROBLEM Draw a Lewis structure and a line-bond structure for chloromethane, CH_3Cl.

Solution Hydrogen has one outer-shell electron; carbon has four outer-shell electrons; and chlorine has seven outer-shell electrons. Thus, chloromethane can be represented as

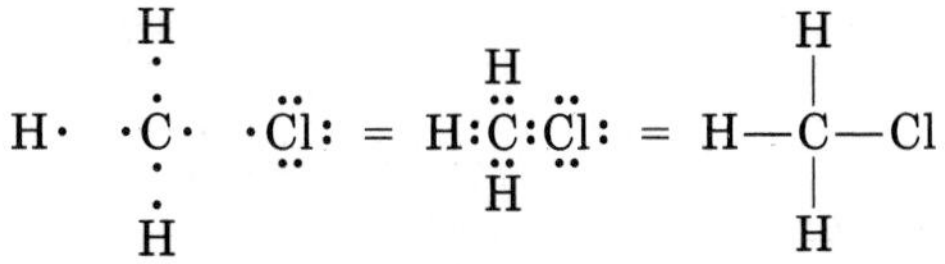

$$
\begin{array}{ccc}
\text{H} & & \text{H} \\
\cdot & \text{H} & | \\
\text{H}\cdot\ \cdot\text{C}\cdot\ \ \cdot\ddot{\text{C}}\ddot{\text{l}}:\ =\ \text{H}:\ddot{\text{C}}:\ddot{\text{C}}\ddot{\text{l}}:\ =\ \text{H}-\text{C}-\text{Cl} \\
\cdot & \ddot{\text{H}} & | \\
\text{H} & & \text{H}
\end{array}
$$

PROBLEM 1.4 Write both Lewis and line-bond structures for these molecules:

(a) $CHCl_3$, chloroform   (b) H_2S, hydrogen sulfide
(c) CH_3NH_2, methylamine   (d) CH_3OCH_3, dimethyl ether

PROBLEM 1.5 Which of these molecules would you expect to have covalent bonds and which ionic bonds?

(a) CH_4 (b) CH_2Cl_2 (c) LiI
(d) KBr   (e) $MgCl_2$ (f) Cl_2

PROBLEM 1.6 Write a line-bond structure for ethane, C_2H_6.

1.6   FORMATION OF COVALENT BONDS

How can we describe the covalent bond in electronic terms? The most generally satisfactory method is to imagine the formation of covalent bonds by an **overlapping** of atomic orbitals. For example, we can describe the hydrogen molecule (H—H) by imagining what might happen if two hydrogen atoms, each with an atomic $1s$ orbital, meet and press together. As the two spherical atomic orbitals approach each other and combine, a new, egg-shaped H—H orbital results. The new orbital is filled by two electrons, one donated from each hydrogen:

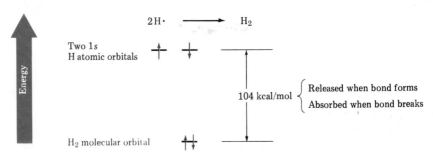

| $1s$ atomic orbital | $1s$ atomic orbital | H_2 orbital |

This new arrangement of electrons in a hydrogen molecule is considerably more stable than the original arrangement of individual atoms.

During the reaction $2\ H\cdot \rightarrow H_2$, 104 kcal/mol of energy is *released*. Since the product H_2 molecule has 104 kcal/mol *less* energy than the starting $2\ H\cdot$, we say that the product is more stable than the starting material, and that the new H—H bond has a **bond strength** of 104 kcal/mol. Expressed another way, we would have to put 104 kcal/mol of energy (heat) *into* the H—H bond in order to break the hydrogen molecule into two hydrogen atoms. Figure 1.6 shows the relative energy levels of the different orbitals.

FIGURE 1.6
Relative energy levels of H· and H_2 orbitals

How close are the two nuclei in the hydrogen atom? If the two positively charged nuclei are too close together, they will repel each other electrostatically. Yet if they are too far apart, they will not be able to share the bonding electrons adequately. Thus, there is an optimum distance between nuclei that leads to maximum bond stability. This optimum distance is called the **bond length**. In the hydrogen molecule, the bond length is 0.74 angstrom (Å) (1 Å $= 10^{-10}$ meter). Every covalent bond has both a characteristic bond strength and bond length.

The orbital formed in the hydrogen molecule has the elongated egg shape that we might get by pressing two spheres together, and a cross section cut by a plane through the middle of the H—H bond reveals a circle. In other words, the H—H bond is *cylindrically symmetrical*, as shown in Figure 1.7.

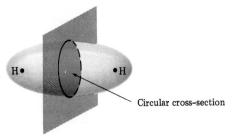

FIGURE 1.7
Cylindrical symmetry of the H—H sigma bond

Bonds that have circular cross-sections and are formed by head-on overlap of two atomic orbitals are called **sigma (σ) bonds**. There are other types of bonds, however. Let's consider the fluorine molecule, F_2. A fluorine atom has seven outer-shell electrons and the electronic configuration $1s^2 2s^2 2p^5$. By covalently bonding together, two fluorine atoms can each achieve stable outer-shell octets:

$$:\ddot{F}\cdot \ + \ \cdot\ddot{F}: \ \longrightarrow \ :\ddot{F}\!:\!\ddot{F}:$$

Unlike the situation in the hydrogen atom, however, the unshared electron in a fluorine atom is in a *p* orbital rather than in an *s* orbital. How can two *p* orbitals come together to form a bond?

There are two geometric possibilities for *p* orbital overlap in the fluorine molecule. One choice is that the *p* orbitals can be oriented in a head-on manner to form a sigma bond. Alternatively, they can overlap in a sideways manner to form what is called a **pi (π) bond**, as shown in Figure 1.8.

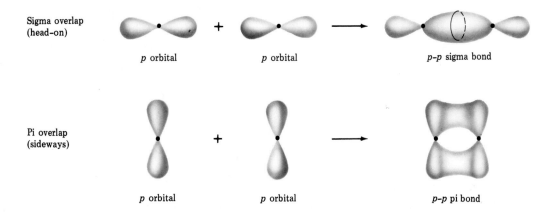

Sigma overlap (head-on)

p orbital   *p* orbital   *p-p* sigma bond

Pi overlap (sideways)

p orbital   *p* orbital   *p-p* pi bond

FIGURE 1.8
The formation of sigma and pi bonds by *p* orbital overlap

It's difficult to predict which kind of bonding, sigma or pi, leads to maximum overlap, but it usually turns out that sigma bonding is more effective. Fluorine therefore forms a sigma molecular bond between two $2p$ orbitals. The F—F bond formed has a bond strength of 38 kcal/mol and a bond length of 1.42 Å. We'll soon see, however, that pi bonding is of great importance when *multiple* bonds form between carbon atoms.

PROBLEM 1.7 We said that sigma bonds, formed by head-on overlap of orbitals, have cylindrical symmetry. Draw a cross section of a pi bond, formed by sideways overlap of p orbitals. How does pi bond symmetry differ from sigma bond symmetry?

1.7 HYBRIDIZATION—THE FORMATION OF sp^3 ORBITALS

The bonding in both the hydrogen molecule and the fluorine molecule is fairly straightforward. The situation becomes more complex, however, when we turn to organic molecules with tetravalent carbon atoms. Let's start with the simplest case and consider methane, CH_4. Carbon has the ground-state electronic configuration $1s^2 2s^2 2p_x 2p_y$. The outer shell has four electrons, two of which are paired in the $2s$ orbital and two of which are unpaired in different $2p$ orbitals:

$$2p \quad \uparrow \; \uparrow \; -$$
$$2s \quad \uparrow\downarrow$$
$$1s \quad \uparrow\downarrow$$

Ground-state electronic configuration of carbon

The first question we face is immediately apparent: How can carbon form *four* bonds if it only has *two* unpaired electrons? Why doesn't carbon bond to two hydrogen atoms to form CH_2? In fact, CH_2 is a known compound, but it is highly unstable and has only fleeting existence. We can see why carbon prefers to form four bonds instead of two by looking at the amount of energy released in forming CH_2 versus forming CH_4. By experimental measurement, we know that a typical C—H bond has a strength of approximately 100 kcal/mol. Thus, the reaction of a carbon atom with two hydrogen atoms to form CH_2 should be energetically favored by about 200 kcal/mol:

$$\cdot \ddot{C} \cdot \; + \; 2\,H\cdot \; \longrightarrow \; H\!:\!\ddot{C}\!:\!H \; + \; 200 \text{ kcal/mol}$$

Alternatively, carbon can adopt an electronic configuration different from the ground-state configuration. By promoting one electron from the $2s$ orbital into the vacant $2p_z$ orbital, carbon can achieve the new configuration $1s^2 2s 2p_x 2p_y 2p_z$. This new electronic arrangement is called an **excited-state configuration**; 96 kcal/mol of energy is required to accomplish the electron promotion from lower-energy ground state to higher-energy excited state.

$$
\begin{array}{lll}
2p & \uparrow\;\;\uparrow\;\;- & \qquad\qquad \uparrow\;\;\uparrow\;\;\uparrow \\[4pt]
2s & \uparrow\!\downarrow & \xrightarrow{\text{96 kcal/mol}} \quad \uparrow \\[4pt]
1s & \uparrow\!\downarrow & \qquad\qquad \uparrow\!\downarrow
\end{array}
$$

Ground-state carbon   **Excited-state carbon**

In the excited state, carbon has four unpaired electrons and can form four bonds to hydrogens. Although 96 kcal/mol is required to promote the $2s$ electron to a $2p$ orbital, this energy loss is more than offset by the formation of four stable C—H bonds. Approximately 300 kcal/mol energy is released in forming CH_4 versus the 200 kcal/mol energy released in forming CH_2. In Lewis structures:

$$
:\!\overset{\displaystyle .}{C}\!\cdot \xrightarrow{\text{96 kcal/mol}} \cdot\overset{\displaystyle .}{\underset{\displaystyle .}{C}}\!\cdot \xrightarrow{\text{4 H}\cdot}
\begin{matrix}
& H & \\
& \overset{\displaystyle ..}{} & \\
H:\!C\!:\!H & & \\
& \underset{\displaystyle ..}{H} &
\end{matrix}
\; + \; 400 \text{ kcal/mol}
$$

Net energy change $=$ (400 $-$ 96) kcal/mol $=$ 304 kcal/mol

How can we describe the four C—H bonds in methane? Since excited-state carbon uses *two* kinds of C—H orbitals for bonding purposes, we might expect methane to have two kinds of C—H bonds. In fact, this is not the case. A large amount of evidence shows that all four C—H bonds in methane are identical. How can we explain this?

The answer was provided by Linus Pauling in 1931. Pauling showed how the mathematical descriptions of an *s* orbital and three *p* orbitals can be combined or **hybridized** to form four equivalent new atomic orbitals that are spatially oriented toward the four corners of a tetrahedron. These new tetrahedral orbitals, shown in Figure 1.9, are called sp^3 **hybrids**,[4] since they arise from mathematical combination of three *p* orbitals and one *s* orbital.

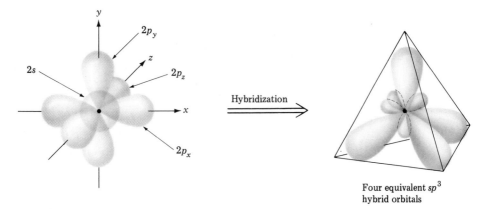

FIGURE 1.9

The formation of sp^3 hybrid orbitals by mathematical combination of three *p* orbitals and one *s* orbital

---

[4]Note that the superscript used to identify an sp^3 hybrid orbital tells how many of each type of atomic orbital combine in the hybrid; it does not tell how many electrons occupy that orbital.

The concept of hybridization explains *how* carbon forms four equivalent tetrahedral bonds, but doesn't answer the question of *why* it does so. Viewing a cross section of an sp^3 hybrid orbital suggests the answer. When an *s* orbital hybridizes with three *p* orbitals, the resultant hybrids are unsymmetrical about the nucleus. One of the two lobes of an sp^3 orbital is much larger than the other, as shown in Figure 1.10. As a result, sp^3 hybrid orbitals form much stronger bonds than do unhybridized *s* or *p* orbitals.

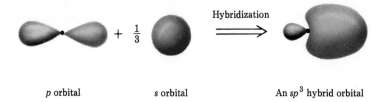

| *p* orbital | *s* orbital | An sp^3 hybrid orbital |

FIGURE 1.10

Formation of an sp^3 hybrid orbital by combination of a *p* orbital with part of an *s* orbital: The sp^3 orbital is strongly oriented in one direction.

1.8 THE STRUCTURE OF METHANE

We have described sp^3 hybrid orbitals of carbon as being strongly *directed*. One consequence of this directed nature is that sp^3 hybrids are capable of forming very strong bonds by overlapping the orbitals of other atoms. For example, overlap of a carbon sp^3 hybrid orbital with a hydrogen 1*s* orbital gives a strong C—H sigma bond (Figure 1.11).

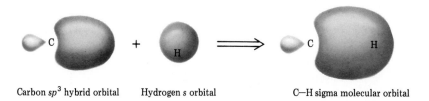

| Carbon sp^3 hybrid orbital | Hydrogen *s* orbital | C—H sigma molecular orbital |

FIGURE 1.11

The formation of a C—H bond by overlap of a carbon sp^3 hybrid orbital with a hydrogen 1*s* orbital

When an sp^3-hybridized carbon atom overlaps with four hydrogen atoms, methane, CH_4, results. A C—H bond of methane has a strength of 104 kcal/mol and a length of 1.10 Å. Since the four bonds have a specific geometry, we can also define a third important physical property, called the **bond angle**. The angle formed by each H-C-H is exactly 109.5°, the tetrahedral angle. Methane therefore has the structure shown in Figure 1.12.

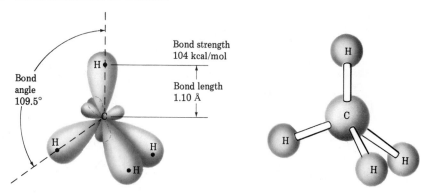

FIGURE 1.12
The structure of methane

1.9   THE STRUCTURE OF ETHANE

A special characteristic of carbon is that it can form stable bonds to other carbon atoms. Exactly the same kind of hybridization that explains the methane structure also explains how one carbon atom can bond to another to form a chain. Ethane, C_2H_6, is the simplest molecule containing a carbon–carbon bond:

$$
\begin{array}{ccc}
\text{H H} & \quad \text{H H} \\
\text{H:\ddot{C}:\ddot{C}:H} & \quad \text{H—C—C—H} & \quad CH_3CH_3 \\
\text{H H} & \quad \text{H H}
\end{array}
$$

Some representations of ethane

We can picture the ethane molecule by assuming that the two carbon atoms bond to each other by sigma overlap of an sp^3 hybrid orbital from each. The remaining three hybrid orbitals on each carbon are then used to form the six C—H bonds, as shown in Figure 1.13 on page 16. The C—H bonds in ethane are similar to those in methane, though a bit weaker (98 kcal/mol for ethane versus 104 kcal/mol for methane). The C—C bond is 1.54 Å long and has a strength of 88 kcal/mol. All the bond angles of ethane are very near the tetrahedral value, 109.5°.

PROBLEM 1.8 Draw all the bonds in propane, $CH_3CH_2CH_3$. Predict the value of each bond angle and indicate the overall shape of the molecule.

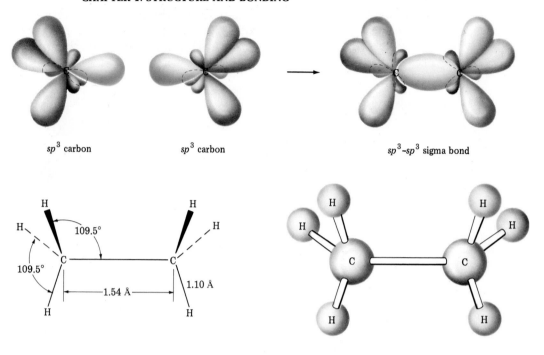

sp³ carbon   *sp³* carbon   *sp³*–*sp³* sigma bond

FIGURE 1.13
The structure of ethane: The central C—C bond is formed by overlap of two *sp³* hybrid orbitals.

1.10   HYBRIDIZATION—*sp²* ORBITALS AND THE STRUCTURE OF ETHYLENE

Although *sp³* hybridization is the most common electronic state of carbon, it is not the only possibility. For example, let's look at ethylene, C_2H_4. It was recognized over 100 years ago that ethylene carbons can be tetravalent only if the two carbon atoms are linked by a *double* bond. How can we explain the formation of the carbon–carbon double bond?

Top view   **Side view**

Ethylene

When we formed *sp³* hybrid orbitals to explain the bonding in methane, we first promoted an electron from the *2s* orbital of ground-state carbon to form excited-state carbon with four unpaired electrons. We then mathematically mixed the four singly occupied atomic orbitals to construct four equivalent *sp³* hybrids. Imagine instead that we mathematically combine the carbon *2s* orbital with only two of the three available *2p* orbitals. Three hybrid orbitals, which we call **sp²** **hybrids**, result, and one unhybridized *2p* orbital remains unchanged. The three *sp²* orbitals lie in a plane at angles of 120° to each other, with the remaining *p* orbital perpendicular to the *sp²* plane, as shown in Figure 1.14.

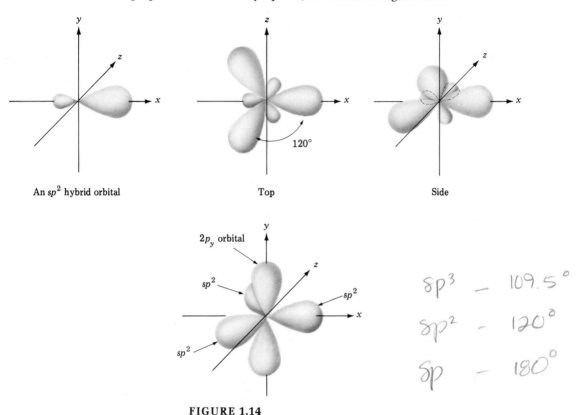

An *sp²* hybrid orbital   Top   Side

$$sp^3 \quad — \quad 109.5°$$

$$sp^2 \quad - \quad 120°$$

$$sp \quad — \quad 180°$$

FIGURE 1.14
An *sp²*-hybridized carbon atom

As with *sp³* hybrid orbitals, *sp²* hybrids are oriented in specific directions and can therefore form strong bonds. If we allow two *sp²*-hybridized carbon atoms to approach each other, they can form a strong sigma bond by *sp²–sp²* overlap. When this occurs, the unhybridized *p* orbitals on each carbon also approach each other with the correct geometry for sideways overlap to form a pi bond. The combination of *sp²–sp²* sigma overlap and *2p–2p* pi overlap results in the net sharing of four electrons and the formation of a carbon–carbon double bond (Figure 1.15, page 18).

To complete the structure of ethylene, we need only allow four hydrogen atoms to sigma bond to the remaining carbon *sp²* orbitals. From this we can predict that ethylene should be a planar (flat) molecule with H-C-H and H-C-C bond angles of approximately 120°. This prediction has been verified by experimental observation. Ethylene is indeed flat, with H-C-H bond angles of 116.6° and H-C-C bond angles of 121.7°. Each C—H bond has a bond length of 1.076 Å and a bond strength of 103 kcal/mol.

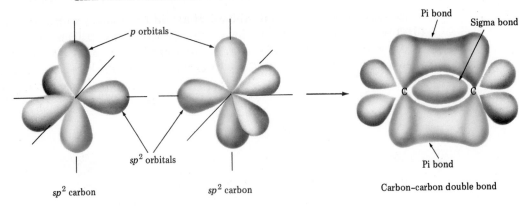

sp² carbon   sp² carbon   Carbon–carbon double bond

FIGURE 1.15
Orbital overlap in the carbon–carbon double bond.

We might also expect the carbon–carbon double bond in ethylene to be both shorter and stronger than the ethane single bond. This prediction has also been verified. Ethylene has a carbon–carbon bond length of 1.33 Å and a bond strength of 152 kcal/mol, whereas ethane has values of 1.54 Å and 88 kcal/mol, respectively. The structure of ethylene is shown in Figure 1.16.

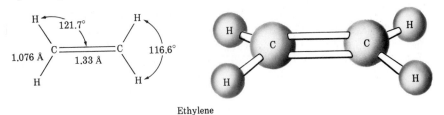

Ethylene

FIGURE 1.16
The structure of ethylene

PROBLEM 1.9 Draw all the bonds in propene, $CH_3CH{=}CH_2$. Indicate the hybridization of each carbon and predict the value of each bond angle.

1.11 HYBRIDIZATION—*sp* ORBITALS AND THE STRUCTURE OF ACETYLENE

In addition to being able to form single and double bonds, carbon can also form a third kind of bond. Acetylene, C_2H_2, can be satisfactorily pictured only if we assume that it contains a carbon–carbon *triple* bond.

$$H{:}C{:}{:}{:}C{:}H \qquad H{-}C{\equiv}C{-}H$$

Acetylene

We must construct yet a third kind of hybrid orbital—an **sp hybrid**—to explain the bonding in acetylene. Imagine that, instead of combining with two or three p orbitals, the carbon 2s orbital hybridizes with only a single p orbital. Two sp hybrid orbitals result, and two p orbitals remain unchanged. The two sp orbitals are linear; that is, they are 180° apart on the x-axis. The remaining two p orbitals are perpendicular on the y-axis and the z-axis, as shown in Figure 1.17.

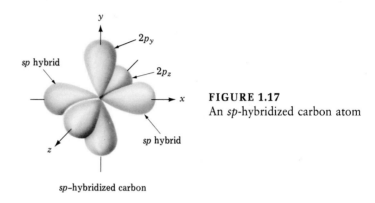

sp-hybridized carbon

FIGURE 1.17
An *sp*-hybridized carbon atom

If we allow two *sp*-hybridized carbon atoms to approach each other, *sp* orbitals from each carbon overlap head-on to form a strong *sp–sp* sigma bond. In addition, the p_z orbitals from each carbon form a p_z–p_z pi bond by sideways overlap, and the two p_y orbitals similarly overlap to form a p_y–p_y pi bond. The net effect is formation of one sigma bond and two pi bonds—a carbon–carbon triple bond. The remaining *sp* hybrid orbitals sigma bond to hydrogen 1s orbitals to complete the acetylene molecule (Figure 1.18).

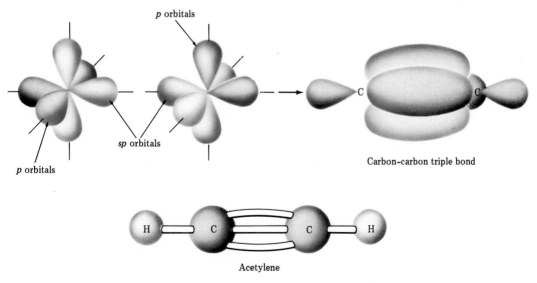

Acetylene

FIGURE 1.18
The carbon–carbon triple bond in acetylene

Because of *sp* hybridization, acetylene is a linear molecule with H-C-C bond angles of 180°. The C—H bond is 1.06 Å in length and has a strength of 125 kcal/mol. The C≡C bond length is 1.20 Å, and its strength is 200 kcal/mol. Table 1.3 provides a comparison of ethane, ethylene, and acetylene.

TABLE 1.3   Comparison of carbon–carbon and carbon–hydrogen bonds in methane, ethane, ethylene, and acetylene

Molecule	Bond	Bond strength (kcal/mol)	Bond length (Å)
Methane, CH_4	C_{sp^3}—H_{1s}	104	1.10
Ethane, CH_3CH_3	C_{sp^3}—C_{sp^3}	88	1.54
	C_{sp^3}—H_{1s}	98	1.10
Ethylene, $H_2C{=}CH_2$	$C_{sp^2}{=}C_{sp^2}$	152	1.33
	C_{sp^2}—H_{1s}	103	1.076
Acetylene, $HC{\equiv}CH$	$C_{sp}{\equiv}C_{sp}$	200	1.20
	C_{sp}—H_{1s}	125	1.06

PROBLEM 1.10   Draw all the bonds in propyne, $CH_3C{\equiv}CH$. Indicate the hybridization of each carbon and predict a value for each bond angle.

PROBLEM 1.11   Carry out an orbital analysis of 1,3-butadiene, $H_2C{=}CH{-}CH{=}CH_2$, similar to the one you carried out in Problem 1.10.

1.12   BOND POLARITY AND ELECTRONEGATIVITY

Thus far, we have viewed chemical bonding in an either/or manner; that is, a given bond is either ionic or covalent. A more accurate view is to look at bonding as a *continuum* of possibilities, from a perfectly covalent bond with a symmetrical electron distribution on the one hand, to a perfectly ionic bond on the other (Figure 1.19). For example, the carbon–carbon bond in ethane is electronically symmetrical and therefore perfectly covalent; the two bonding electrons are equally shared by the two equivalent carbon atoms. The bond in sodium chloride, by contrast, is purely ionic; it is the result of electrostatic attraction between

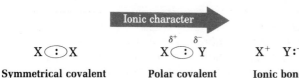

FIGURE 1.19
The bonding continuum from covalent to ionic bonds: The symbol δ (Greek delta) means *partial* charge, either positive (δ^+) or negative (δ^-).

positively charged sodium ions and negatively charged chloride ions. In between these two extremes lie the great majority of chemical bonds, in which the bonding electrons are attracted *somewhat* more strongly by one atom than by the other. We call such bonds **polar covalent bonds**.

Bond polarity is due to **electronegativity**—the intrinsic ability of an atom to attract electrons. As shown in the electronegativity table (Table 1.4), carbon and hydrogen have similar electronegativities. Carbon–hydrogen bonds are therefore relatively nonpolar. Elements on the right side of the periodic table, such as oxygen, nitrogen, and chlorine, are more electronegative than carbon. When carbon bonds to one of these elements, the bond is polarized so that the bonding electrons are drawn more toward the electronegative atom than toward carbon. This unsymmetrical distribution of bonding electrons leaves carbon with a *partial positive charge* (denoted by δ^+; δ is the Greek letter delta) and the electronegative atom with a *partial negative charge* (δ^-). For example, the C—Cl bond in chloromethane is a polar covalent bond:

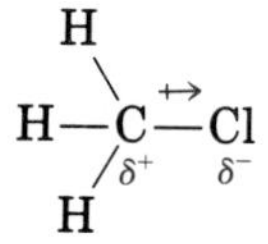

$$
\begin{array}{c}
\text{H} \\
\diagdown \\
\text{H}\!-\!\!\underset{\underset{\delta^+}{\diagup}}{\text{C}}\!\overset{\leftrightarrow}{-}\!\underset{\delta^-}{\text{Cl}} \\
\text{H}
\end{array}
$$

Chloromethane

The arrow $\leftrightarrow$ is used to indicate the direction of polarity. By convention, *electrons move in the direction of the arrow.* The tail of the arrow is electron-poor (δ^+), and the head of the arrow is electron-rich (δ^-).

TABLE 1.4   Electronegativities of some common elements

Element	Electronegativity	Element	Electronegativity
H	2.2	Mg	1.3
Li	1.0	Al	1.6
Be	1.6	Si	1.9
B	2.0	P	2.2
C	2.5	S	2.6
N	3.0	Cl	3.1
O	3.4	Br	3.0
F	4.0	I	2.6
Na	1.0		

The data in this table are on an arbitrary scale, with H = 2.2 and F = 4.0. Carbon has an electronegativity value on this scale of 2.5; any element more electronegative than carbon has a value greater than 2.5, and any element less electronegative than carbon has a value less than 2.5.

Metallic elements on the left side of the periodic table are less electronegative than carbon and attract electrons less strongly. Thus, when carbon bonds to one of these elements, the bond is polarized so that carbon bears a partial negative charge and the other atom bears a partial positive charge. Organometallic compounds such as tetraethyllead, the "lead" in gasoline, provide good examples of this kind of polar bond.

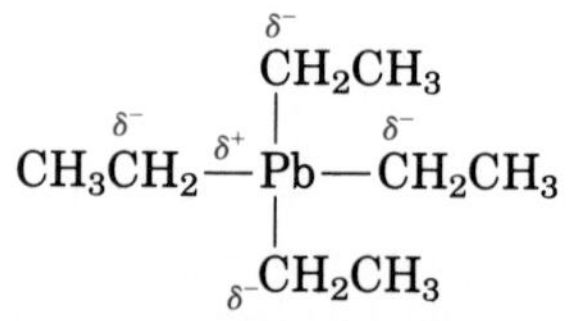

$$\overset{\delta^-}{CH_2CH_3}$$
$$\overset{\delta^-}{CH_3CH_2} \overset{\delta^+}{-Pb} \overset{\delta^-}{-CH_2CH_3}$$
$$\underset{\delta^-}{-CH_2CH_3}$$

Tetraethyllead

When we speak of an atom's ability to polarize a bond, we use the term **inductive effect**. Electropositive elements such as lithium and sodium inductively *donate* electrons, whereas electronegative elements such as oxygen and chlorine inductively *withdraw* electrons. Inductive effects and bond polarity play a major role in chemical reactivity and will be encountered many times throughout this text.

PRACTICE PROBLEM   Predict the direction of polarization of an O—H bond in water.

Solution   Oxygen is more electronegative than hydrogen according to Table 1.4 and will therefore attract electrons more strongly (δ^-):

$$\overset{\delta^+}{H} - \overset{\delta^-}{O} - \overset{\delta^+}{H}$$

PROBLEM 1.12   Which element in each of the following pairs is more electronegative?
(a) Li or H   (b) Be or Br   (c) Cl or I

PROBLEM 1.13   Indicate the direction of expected polarity for each of the bonds shown:
(a) H_3C-Br (b) H_3C-NH_2 (c) H_3C-Li (d) H_2N-H
(e) H_3C-OH (f) $H_3C-MgBr$ (g) H_3C-F

1.13   ACIDS AND BASES: THE BRØNSTED–LOWRY DEFINITION

According to the **Brønsted–Lowry** definition, an acid is a substance that donates a proton (H^+), and a base is a substance that accepts a proton. For example, when HCl gas dissolves in water, an acid–base reaction occurs. Hydrogen chloride acts as an acid to donate a proton; water acts as a base to accept the proton.

The products of the reaction, H_3O^+ and Cl^-, are called the **conjugate acid** and the **conjugate base**, respectively. Other common mineral acids such as sulfuric acid and nitric acid behave similarly, as do organic acids such as acetic acid, CH_3COOH.

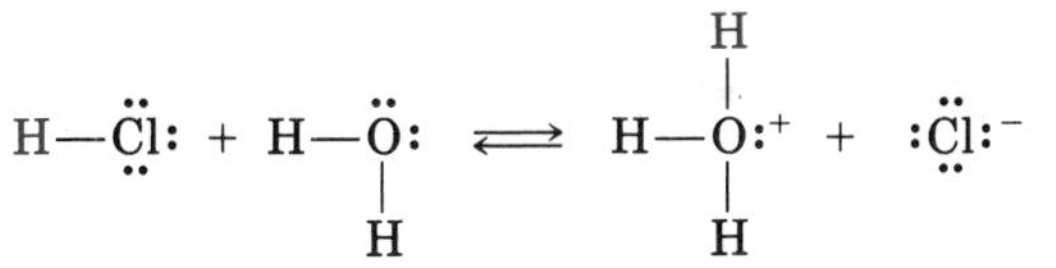

$$H-\ddot{\underset{\cdot\cdot}{C}l}: \;+\; H-\underset{\underset{H}{|}}{\ddot{O}}: \;\rightleftharpoons\; H-\underset{\underset{H}{|}}{\overset{\overset{H}{|}}{O}}:^+ \;+\; :\ddot{\underset{\cdot\cdot}{C}l}:^-$$

| Acid | Base | Conjugate acid | Conjugate base |

Acids differ in their proton-donating ability. Strong acids such as HCl react almost completely with water, whereas weaker acids such as acetic acid react only slightly. Since these acid–base reactions are equilibrium processes, we can describe them using **equilibrium constants, K_{eq}**:

$$HA + H_2O \rightleftharpoons H_3O^+ + A^-$$

$$K_{eq} = \frac{[H_3O^+][A^-]}{[HA][H_2O]}$$

where HA represents any acid.[5]

In the customary dilute acid solution for measuring K_{eq}, the concentration of water, $[H_2O]$, remains nearly unchanged at approximately $55.5M$. We can therefore rewrite the equilibrium expression using a new term called the **acidity constant, K_a**. The acidity constant for any generalized acid, HA, is simply the equilibrium constant multiplied by the molar concentration of water:

$$HA + H_2O \rightleftharpoons H_3O^+ + A^-$$

$$K_a = K_{eq}[H_2O] = \frac{[H_3O^+][A^-]}{[HA]}$$

Strong acids force the equilibrium to the *right* and have large acidity constants. In the case of weaker acids, the equilibrium is toward the *left* and the acidity constants are smaller. We normally express acid strengths by quoting pK_a values, where the pK_a is equal to the negative logarithm of the acidity constant:

$$pK_a = -\log K_a$$

A strong acid (high K_a) has a low pK_a; conversely, a weak acid (low K_a) has a high pK_a. Table 1.5 lists the pK_a's of some common acids in order of strength.

---

[5]Recall that brackets, [ ], refer to the concentration of the enclosed species, expressed in moles per liter.

TABLE 1.5   **Strengths of some common acids and their conjugate bases**

	Acid	Name	pK_a	Conjugate base	Name	
Weak acid	CH_3CH_2OH	Ethanol	16.00	$CH_3CH_2O^-$	Ethoxide ion	Strong base
	H_2O	Water	15.74	HO^-	Hydroxide ion	
	HCN	Hydrocyanic acid	9.2	CN^-	Cyanide ion	
	CH_3COOH	Acetic acid	4.72	CH_3COO^-	Acetate ion	
	HF	Hydrofluoric acid	3.2	F^-	Fluoride ion	
	HNO_3	Nitric acid	-1.3	NO_3^-	Nitrate ion	Weak base
Strong acid	HCl	Hydrochloric acid	-7.0	Cl^-	Chloride ion	

Although we have considered only acids thus far, similar arguments can be used to measure base strength. Thus, the conjugate base of a strong acid must be a weak base, since it has little affinity for protons. Similarly, the conjugate base of a weak acid must be a strong base, since it has a high affinity for protons. For example, chloride ion (the conjugate base of the strong acid, HCl) is a weak base; acetate ion (the conjugate base of the weaker acid CH_3COOH), is a stronger base; and hydroxide ion (the conjugate base of the weak acid, H_2O) is a still stronger base. Table 1.5 also lists the relative strengths of several common conjugate bases.

PRACTICE PROBLEM   Formic acid, HCOOH, has $pK_a = 3.7$, and picric acid, $C_6H_3N_3O_7$, has $pK_a = 0.3$. Which is the stronger acid?

Solution   Since a lower pK_a value means a stronger acid, picric acid is stronger than formic acid.

PROBLEM 1.14   Amide ion ($^-NH_2$) is a much stronger base than hydroxide ion (^-OH). Which would you expect to be a stronger acid, $H-NH_2$ (ammonia) or $H-OH$ (water)?

1.14   ACIDS AND BASES: THE LEWIS DEFINITION

The Brønsted–Lowry concept of acidity is a useful one that can be extended to include all compounds containing hydrogen. But even more useful to the organic chemist is the Lewis definition of acids and bases. A **Lewis acid** is a substance that can accept an electron pair; a **Lewis base** is a substance that can donate an electron pair.

The Lewis definition of acidity is broadly applicable. It includes not only proton donors but many other species as well. A proton (hydrogen ion) is a Lewis acid because it has a vacant s orbital and needs a pair of electrons to fill its empty valence shell. Compounds such as BF_3 and $AlCl_3$ are also Lewis acids, because they too have vacant valence orbitals that can accept electron pairs from Lewis bases, as Figure 1.20 shows.

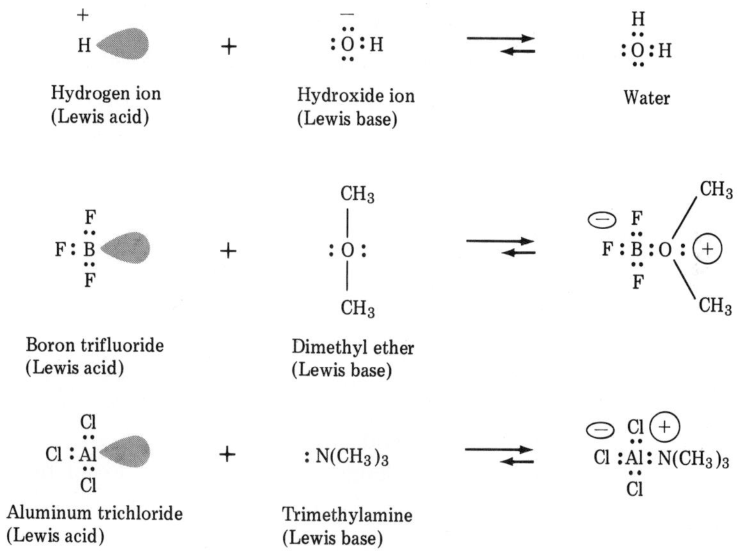

FIGURE 1.20
Some Lewis acids and Lewis bases

The trivalent boron atom in compounds such as BF_3 has only six electrons in its outer shell and can thus accept an electron pair from a Lewis base donor to form a stable acid–base complex. Similarly, $AlCl_3$ has only six electrons in the outer shell of aluminum and is a powerful Lewis acid.

The Lewis definition of basicity is quite similar to the Brønsted–Lowry definition. A Lewis base has a lone pair of electrons that it can donate to a Lewis acid in forming a new bond. Thus, H_2O, with its two lone pairs of nonbonding electrons on oxygen, can serve as a Lewis base by donating an electron pair to a proton in forming the hydronium ion, H_3O^+:

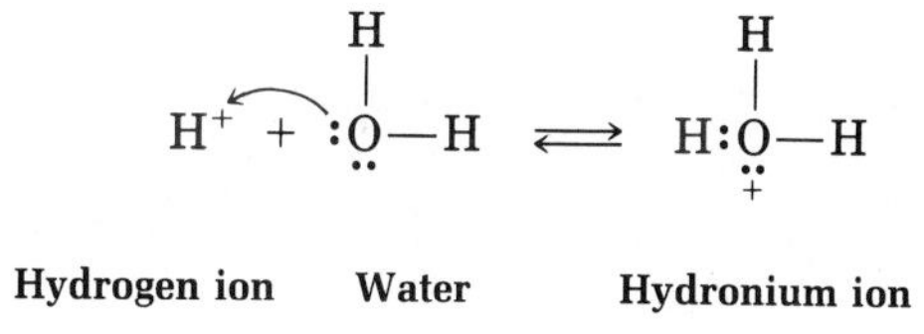

Hydrogen ion   Water   Hydronium ion

In a more general sense, most oxygen- and nitrogen-containing organic compounds are good Lewis bases, since they have lone pairs of available electrons. For example:

$$H_3C-\overset{\cdot\cdot}{\underset{\cdot\cdot}{O}}-CH_3 \qquad H_3C-\overset{\cdot\cdot}{\underset{\cdot\cdot}{O}}-H \qquad H_3C-\overset{\cdot\cdot}{\underset{|}{N}}-H \qquad \overset{:O:}{\overset{\|}{H_3C-C-CH_3}}$$

Dimethyl ether   **Methyl alcohol**   H

Acetone (a ketone)

Methylamine

PROBLEM 1.15   Which of the following are Lewis acids and which are Lewis bases?

(a) $CH_3CH_2-\overset{\cdot\cdot}{\underset{\cdot\cdot}{O}}-H$

(b) $H_3C-\overset{\cdot\cdot}{N}H-CH_3$

(c) $MgBr_2$

(d) $H_3C-\overset{\underset{|}{CH_3}}{B}-CH_3$

(e) $ZnCl_2$

(f) $H_3C-\overset{\cdot\cdot}{\underset{|}{P}}-CH_3$
$\qquad\qquad CH_3$

Working Problems

Learning organic chemistry requires familiarity with a large number of facts. Although careful reading and rereading of this text is important, this alone is not enough. In addition, you must be able to *apply* the information you read and be able to *use* your knowledge in new situations. Problems give you the opportunity to do this. There is no surer way to learn organic chemistry than by working problems.

Each chapter in this book provides many problems of different sorts. The in-chapter problems are placed for immediate reinforcement of ideas just learned. The end-of-chapter problems provide additional practice, but are of two types. Early problems tend to be of the drill type, which provide an opportunity for you to practice your command of the fundamentals. Later problems tend to be more challenging and thought-provoking.

As you study organic chemistry, take the time to work the problems. Work the ones you can, and ask for help on the ones you can't. If you are stumped by a particular exercise, check the accompanying answer book for an explanation that should help clarify the difficulty. Working problems takes effort, but the payoff in knowledge and understanding is immense.

ADDITIONAL PROBLEMS

PROBLEM 1.16   How many outer-shell (valence) electrons does each of the following atoms have?

(a) Oxygen   (b) Beryllium   (c) Magnesium   (d) Fluorine

PROBLEM 1.17   Give the ground-state electronic configuration of these elements (for example, carbon is $1s^2 2s^2 2p^2$):

(a) Lithium   (b) Sodium   (c) Aluminum
(d) Sulfur   (e) Boron   (f) Selenium

PROBLEM 1.18   Write Lewis (electron-dot) structures for these molecules:

   (a) $H-C\equiv C-H$ (b) AlH_3 (c) $CH_3\overset{\cdot\cdot}{\underset{\cdot\cdot}{O}}H$

   (d) $H_2C=CHCl$ (e) $H_2C=CH-CH=CH_2$ (f) $H_2C=\overset{\cdot\cdot}{\underset{\cdot\cdot}{O}}$

PROBLEM 1.19   Write a Lewis (electron-dot) structure for acetonitrile, $CH_3C\equiv N$. How many electrons does the nitrogen atom have in its outer shell? How many are used for bonding and how many are not used for bonding?

PROBLEM 1.20   Fill in any unshared electrons that are missing in the following line-bond structures:

$$\text{(a)} \quad H_3C-O-CH_3 \qquad \text{(b)} \quad H_3C-\overset{\overset{\displaystyle O}{\|}}{C}-CH_3 \qquad \text{(c)} \quad H_3C-\overset{\overset{\displaystyle O}{\|}}{C}-NH_2 \qquad \text{(d)} \quad CH_2ClF$$

PROBLEM 1.21   Convert the following molecular formulas into Kekulé line-bond structures that are consistent with the rules of valency:

   (a) C_3H_8 (b) C_3H_7Br (2 possibilities)
   (c) C_3H_6 (2 possibilities)   (d) C_2H_6O (2 possibilities)

PROBLEM 1.22   There are two different structures corresponding to the formula C_4H_{10}. Draw them.

PROBLEM 1.23   Indicate the kind of hybridization you would expect for each carbon atom in these molecules:

   (a) Butane, $CH_3CH_2CH_2CH_3$ (b) 1-Butene, $CH_3CH_2CH=CH_2$
   (c) Cyclobutene, 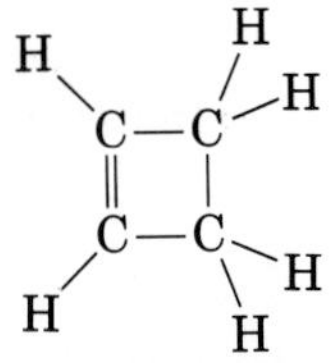   (d) 1-Buten-3-yne, $H_2C=CH-C\equiv CH$

PROBLEM 1.24   What is the hybridization of each carbon atom in benzene? What shape would you expect benzene to have?

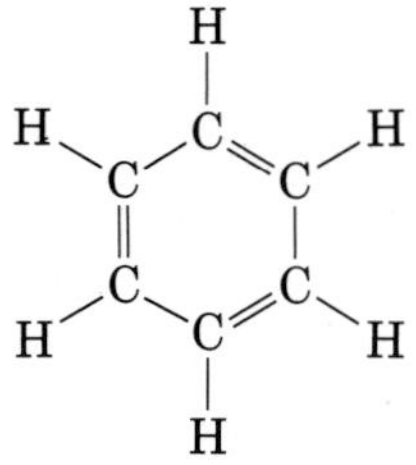

Benzene

PROBLEM 1.25   What is the hybridization of each carbon atom in acetonitrile, $CH_3C\equiv N$?

PROBLEM 1.26   Write Lewis (electron-dot) structures for these molecules:

   (a) $H_3C-Be-CH_3$ (b) $H_3C-\overset{\cdot\cdot}{P}-CH_3$ (c) $TiCl_4$
                                        $\quad\quad\quad\;\; |$
                                        $\quad\quad\quad CH_3$

PROBLEM 1.27   Draw line-bond structures for these covalent molecules:

   (a) Br_2 (b) CH_3Cl (c) HF   (d) CH_3CH_2OH

PROBLEM 1.28   Indicate which of the bonds in the structures you drew for Problem 1.27 are polar. Indicate bond polarity by using the symbols δ^+ and δ^-.

PROBLEM 1.29   Identify all the bonds in these molecules as either ionic or covalent:

(a) NaOH
(b) HOH
(c) CH_3OH
(d) CH_3OCH_3
(e) FF

PROBLEM 1.30   Sodium methoxide, H_3CONa, contains both covalent and ionic bonds. Indicate which is which.

PROBLEM 1.31   Use the electronegativity table (Table 1.4) to predict which bond in each of the following sets is more polar:

(a) $H_3C—Cl$ and $Cl—Cl$
(b) $H_3C—H$ and $H—Cl$
(c) $HO—CH_3$ and $(CH_3)_3Si—CH_3$

PROBLEM 1.32   Indicate the direction of polarity for each bond in Problem 1.31.

PROBLEM 1.33   How can you explain the fact that the $O—H$ hydrogen in acetic acid is more acidic than any of the $C—H$ hydrogens? [*Hint:* Consider bond polarity.]

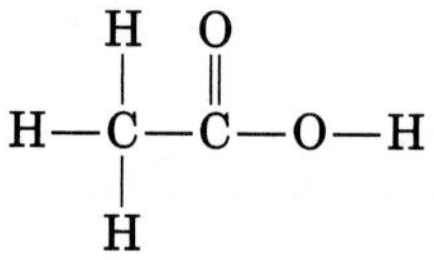

$$\begin{array}{ccc} H & O & \\ | & \| & \\ H—C—C—O—H \\ | & & \\ H & & \end{array}$$

Acetic acid

PROBLEM 1.34   Which atoms in the following structures have unshared valence electrons? Draw in these unshared electrons.

(a) CH_3SH
(b) $(CH_3)_3N$
(c) CH_3CH_2Br

(d) 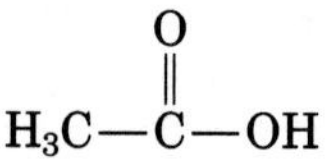 $H_3C—\overset{\displaystyle O}{\overset{\|}{C}}—OH$
(e) 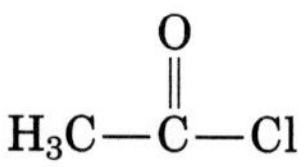 $H_3C—\overset{\displaystyle O}{\overset{\|}{C}}—Cl$

PROBLEM 1.35   Classify the following reagents as either Lewis acids or Lewis bases:

(a) $AlCl_3$
(b) $(CH_3)_3N\!:$
(c) BH_3
(d) HF
(e) $H_3C—\ddot{\underset{..}{S}}—CH_3$
(f) $TiCl_4$

PROBLEM 1.36   Draw a three-dimensional representation of chloroform, $CHCl_3$, using the standard convention of normal, heavy wedged, and dashed lines. Do the same for the oxygen-bearing carbon atom in ethanol, CH_3CH_2OH.

PROBLEM 1.37   The ammonium ion, NH_4^+, has a geometry identical to that of methane, CH_4. What kind of hybridization do you think the nitrogen atom has? Explain.

PROBLEM 1.38   Identify the acids and bases in these reactions:

(a) $CH_3OH + H^+ \longrightarrow CH_3\overset{+}{O}H_2$

(b) $CH_3OH + {}^-NH_2 \longrightarrow CH_3O^- + NH_3$

(c) 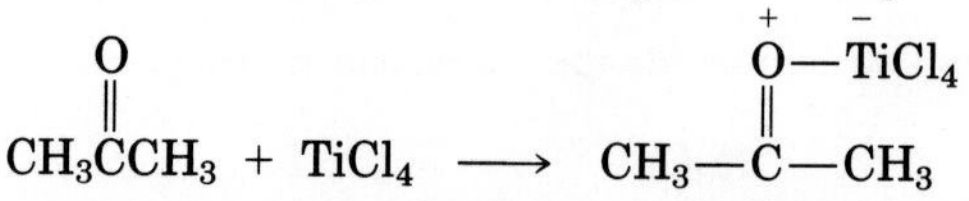 $CH_3\overset{\displaystyle O}{\overset{\|}{C}}CH_3 + TiCl_4 \longrightarrow CH_3—\overset{\displaystyle \overset{+}{O}—\overset{-}{TiCl_4}}{\overset{\|}{C}}—CH_3$

PROBLEM 1.39 Indicate the kind of hybridization you might expect for each carbon atom in these molecules:

(a) Acetic acid,

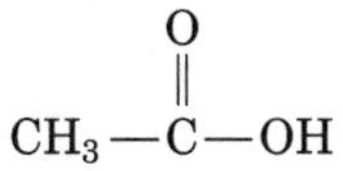

$$CH_3-\overset{\displaystyle O}{\overset{\|}{C}}-OH$$

(b) 3-Buten-2-one,

$$H_2C=CH-\overset{\displaystyle O}{\overset{\|}{C}}-CH_3$$

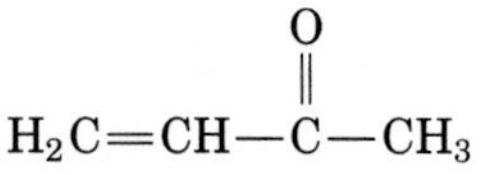

(c) Acrylonitrile,

$$H_2C=CH-C\equiv N$$

(d) Benzoic acid,

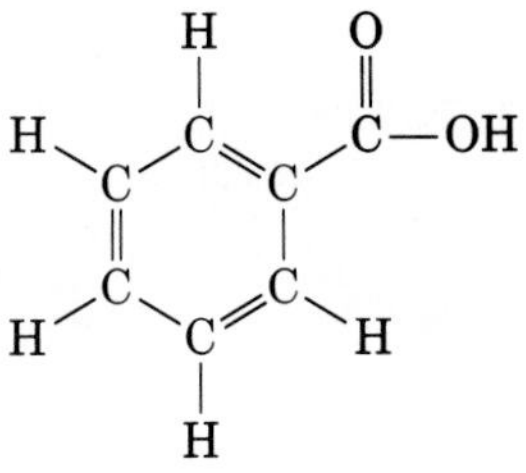

PROBLEM 1.40 Allene is an unusual molecule that has the structure $H_2C=C=CH_2$. Draw an orbital picture of allene and indicate the hybridization of each carbon. What shape would you predict for allene?

PROBLEM 1.41 Although almost all stable organic species have tetravalent carbon atoms, species with trivalent carbon atoms are known to exist. *Carbocations* are one such class of compounds. What hybridization might you expect the carbon atom to have? What geometry would this lead to? What relationship do you see between a carbocation and a trivalent boron compound?

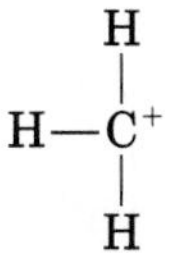

$$H-\overset{\displaystyle H}{\overset{|}{\underset{|}{C^+}}}-H$$

$$\overset{\displaystyle }{\underset{\displaystyle H}{}}$$

A carbocation

CHAPTER 2

The Nature of Organic Compounds: Alkanes

According to *Chemical Abstracts*, the service that abstracts and indexes the chemical literature, there are more than 8 million known organic compounds. Each of these compounds has unique physical properties such as melting point and boiling point, and each has unique chemical reactivity.

Chemists have learned through experience that organic compounds can be classified into groups according to their structural features, and that the chemical reactivity of the members of a given group is often predictable. Instead of 8 million compounds with random reactivity, there are several dozen general classes of organic compounds whose chemistry is roughly predictable.

2.1 FUNCTIONAL GROUPS

The structural features that allow us to class compounds together according to reactivity are called **functional groups**. A functional group is a part of a larger molecule; it is composed of an atom or group of atoms and has characteristic chemical reactivity. Chemically, a given functional group behaves approximately the same in all molecules where it occurs.

For example, one of the simplest functional groups is the carbon–carbon double bond. We saw in Section 1.10 that a carbon–carbon double bond consists of two parts—a sigma bond formed by head-on overlap of an sp^2 orbital from each carbon, and a pi bond formed by sideways overlap of a p orbital from each carbon. Since the electronic structure of a carbon–carbon double bond remains the same in all molecules where it occurs, its chemical reactivity also remains the same. Ethylene, the simplest compound with a double bond, undergoes chemical reactions almost identical to those of cholesterol, a much more complex molecule. Both, for example, react with bromine in the same manner (Figure 2.1).

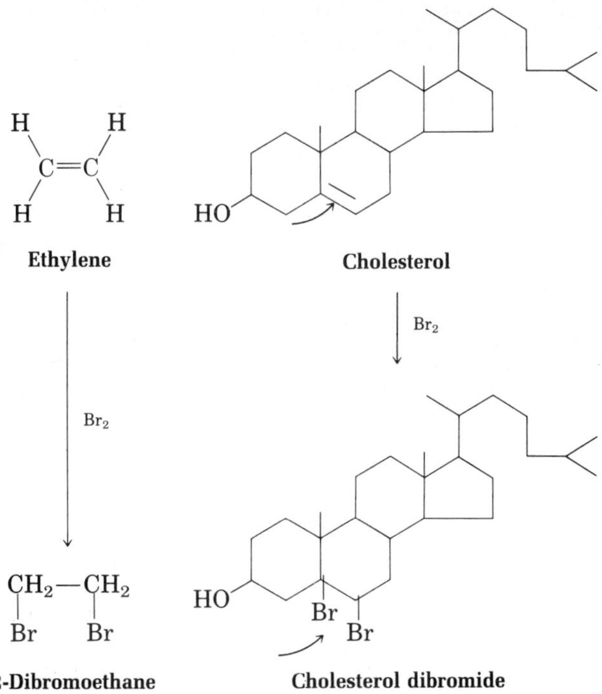

FIGURE 2.1

The reactions of ethylene and cholesterol with bromine: In both cases, bromine adds to the carbon–carbon double bond.

This example is typical. The chemistry of a molecule is determined by the functional groups it contains. Table 2.1 on pages 32 and 33 lists many of the common functional groups found in organic molecules and gives examples of their occurrence. Look carefully to see the wide variety of functional groups found in organic molecules. Some functional groups contain only carbon and hydrogen; others have halogens; and still others include oxygen or nitrogen. Most of the chemistry you will be studying in the remainder of this book is the chemistry of these functional groups.

PROBLEM 2.1   Circle and identify the functional groups present in these molecules:

(a) Acrylic acid,

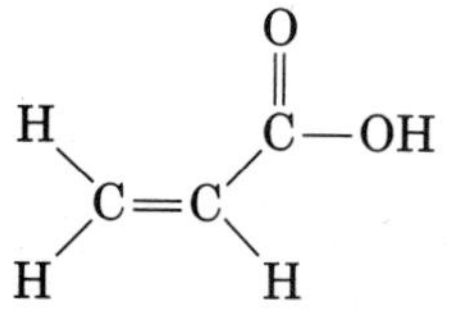

(b) Aspirin,

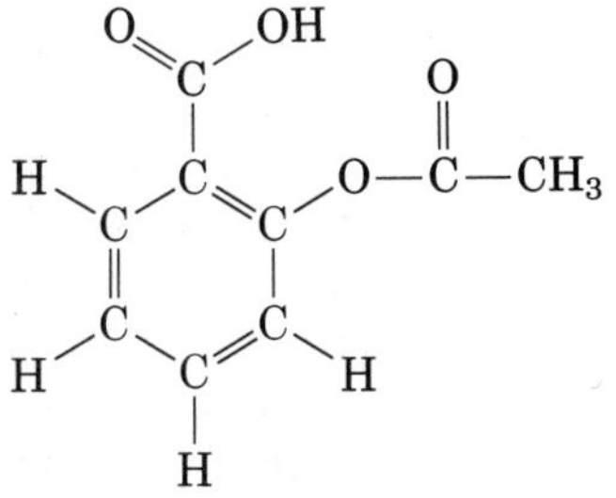

(c) Glucose,

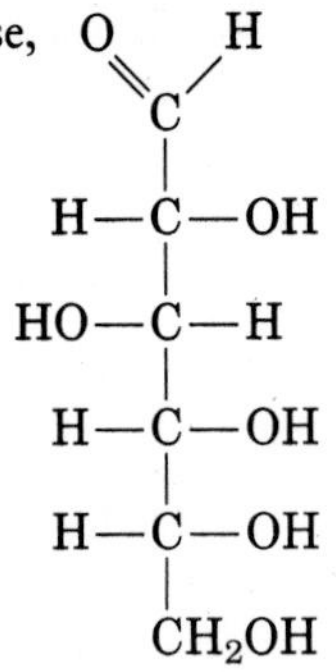

(d) Cocaine,

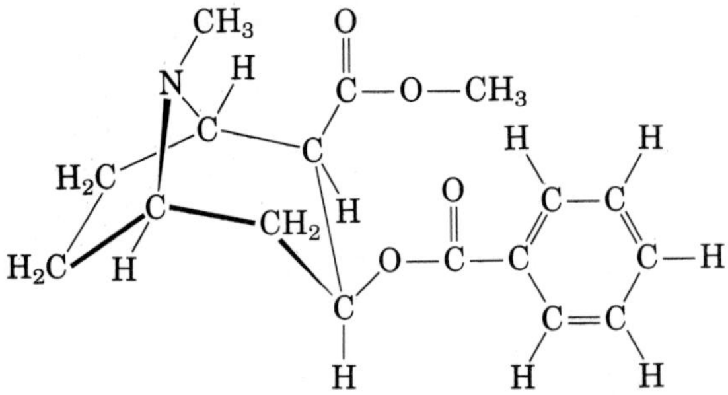

PROBLEM 2.2   Propose structures for simple molecules that contain these functional groups:

(a) Aromatic ring   (b) Alcohol   (c) Amine
(d) Carboxylic acid   (e) Both ketone and alcohol

TABLE 2.1   Some functional groups

Compound type	Functional group	Simple example	Name ending
Alkene (double bond)	$\begin{array}{c}\diagdown\diagup\\ C{=}C\\ \diagup\diagdown\end{array}$	$CH_3CH{=}CH_2$ Propene	-ene
Alkyne (triple bond)	$-C{\equiv}C-$	$CH_3C{\equiv}CH$ Propyne	-yne
Arene (aromatic ring)	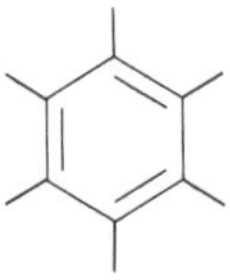	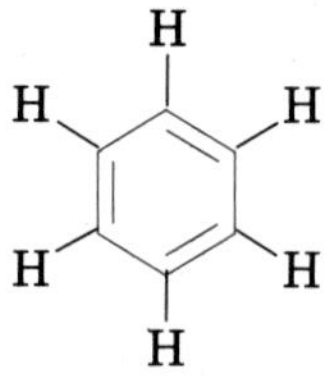 Benzene	None
Halide	$\begin{array}{c}\diagdown\\ {-}C{-}X\\ \diagup\end{array}$ X = F, Cl, Br, I	CH_3CH_2I Iodoethane	None
Alcohol	$\begin{array}{c}\diagdown\\ {-}C{-}O{-}H\\ \diagup\end{array}$	CH_3CH_2OH Ethanol	-ol
Ether	$\begin{array}{c}\diagdown\diagup\\ {-}C{-}O{-}C{-}\\ \diagup\diagdown\end{array}$	$CH_3CH_2OCH_2CH_3$ Ethoxyethane (diethyl ether)	ether
Carbonyl	$\begin{array}{c}\diagdown\\ C{=}O\\ \diagup\end{array}$.		

do not need to know

Compound type	Functional group	Simple example	Name ending
Aldehyde	$\begin{array}{c}H\\ \backslash\\ C{=}O\\ /\\ -C\\ /\end{array}$	$\underset{\text{Ethanal}}{\overset{\overset{\displaystyle O}{\|}}{CH_3- C-H}}$ (acetaldehyde)	-al
Ketone	$\begin{array}{c}-C\\ /\\ C{=}O\\ \backslash\\ -C\\ /\end{array}$	$\underset{\text{2-Propanone}}{\overset{\overset{\displaystyle O}{\|}}{CH_3- C-CH_3}}$ (acetone)	-one
Ester	$\overset{\overset{\displaystyle O}{\|}}{-C-O-C-}$	$\underset{\text{Ethyl ethanoate}}{\overset{\overset{\displaystyle O}{\|}}{CH_3 C-OCH_2CH_3}}$ (ethyl acetate)	-oate
Carboxylic acid	$\overset{\overset{\displaystyle O}{\|}}{-C-O-H}$	$\underset{\text{Butanoic acid}}{\overset{\overset{\displaystyle O}{\|}}{CH_3CH_2CH_2 C-OH}}$	-oic acid
Carboxylic acid chloride	$\overset{\overset{\displaystyle O}{\|}}{-C-Cl}$	$\underset{\text{Propanoyl chloride}}{\overset{\overset{\displaystyle O}{\|}}{CH_3CH_2 C-Cl}}$	-yl chloride
Amide	$\overset{\overset{\displaystyle O}{\|}}{-C-N\big\langle}$	$\underset{\text{Ethanamide}}{\overset{\overset{\displaystyle O}{\|}}{CH_3 C-NH_2}}$	-amide
Amine	$-\overset{\|}{\underset{\|}{C}}-N\big\langle$	$\underset{\text{Ethylamine}}{CH_3 CH_2 NH_2}$	-amine
Nitrile	$-C{\equiv}N$	$\underset{\substack{\text{Ethanenitrile}\\\text{(acetonitrile)}}}{CH_3 C{\equiv}N}$	-nitrile
Nitro	$-\overset{\|}{\underset{\|}{C}}-\overset{+}{N}\big\langle{\overset{O}{\underset{O^-}{}}}$	$\underset{\text{Nitroethane}}{CH_3 CH_2 NO_2}$	None
Organometallic	$-\overset{\|}{\underset{\|}{C}}-M$ M = metal	$\underset{\text{Methyllithium}}{CH_3- Li}$	None

2.2   ALKANES AND ALKYL GROUPS

We've seen earlier (Section 1.9) that carbon–carbon single bonds such as that in ethane result from sigma (head-on) overlap of carbon sp^3 orbitals. If we imagine joining three, four, five, or even more carbon atoms together, we can generate a large number of molecules of *increasing chain length*, as shown in Figure 2.2. The compounds generated are called **straight-chain alkanes** or **normal alkanes**.

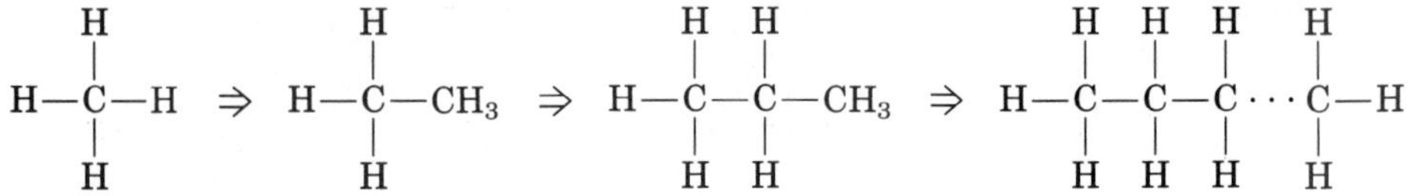

FIGURE 2.2
Increasing chain length in the normal alkanes, C_nH_{2n+2}

Alkanes are compounds that contain only carbon–hydrogen and carbon–carbon *single* bonds. They have the general formula C_nH_{2n+2}, where n is any integer. Alkanes are also occasionally referred to as **aliphatic compounds**, derived from the Greek word *aleiphas*, "fat." (We'll see later that animal fats do indeed contain long carbon chains similar to alkanes.)

A given alkane may be arbitrarily depicted in a great many ways. For example, the straight-chain four-carbon alkane called butane may be represented by any of the structures shown in Figure 2.3. These structures do not imply any particular geometry for butane; they indicate only that butane has a chain of four carbons. In practice, we soon tire of drawing all the bonds in a molecule and usually refer to butane as $CH_3CH_2CH_2CH_3$ or simply as $n\text{-}C_4H_{10}$, where n signifies *normal*, straight-chain butane.

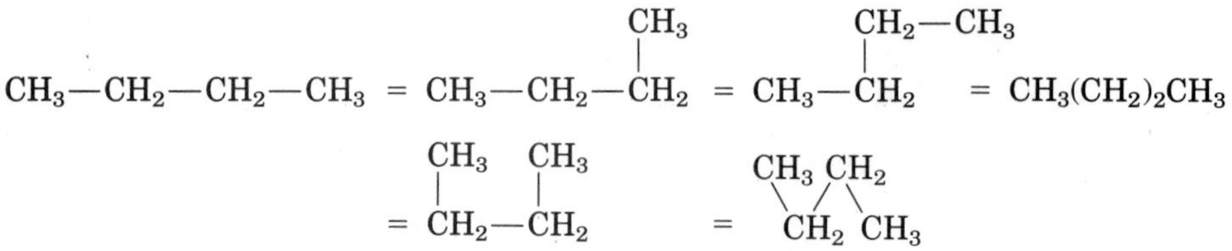

FIGURE 2.3
Some representations of butane, C_4H_{10}: The molecule is the same regardless of how it's drawn.

Alkanes are named according to the number of carbon atoms in the chain, as shown in Table 2.2. With the exception of the first four compounds—methane, ethane, propane, and butane—whose names have historical origins, the alkanes are named from Greek numbers according to the number of carbons present. The suffix *-ane* is added to the end of each name to indicate that the molecule identified is an alkane.

TABLE 2.2   Alkane names

Number of carbons (n)	Name	Formula (C_nH_{2n+2})	Number of carbons (n)	Name	Formula (C_nH_{2n+2})
1	Methane	CH_4	14	Tetradecane	$C_{14}H_{30}$
2	Ethane	C_2H_6	15	Pentadecane	$C_{15}H_{32}$
3	Propane	C_3H_8	20	Eicosane	$C_{20}H_{42}$
4	Butane	C_4H_{10}	21	Heneicosane	$C_{21}H_{44}$
5	Pentane	C_5H_{12}	22	Docosane	$C_{22}H_{46}$
6	Hexane	C_6H_{14}	23	Tricosane	$C_{23}H_{48}$
7	Heptane	C_7H_{16}	30	Triacontane	$C_{30}H_{62}$
8	Octane	C_8H_{18}	31	Hentriacontane	$C_{31}H_{64}$
9	Nonane	C_9H_{20}	32	Dotriacontane	$C_{32}H_{66}$
10	Decane	$C_{10}H_{22}$	40	Tetracontane	$C_{40}H_{82}$
11	Undecane	$C_{11}H_{24}$	50	Pentacontane	$C_{50}H_{102}$
12	Dodecane	$C_{12}H_{26}$	60	Hexacontane	$C_{60}H_{122}$
13	Tridecane	$C_{13}H_{28}$			

If one hydrogen atom is removed from an alkane, the fragment remaining is called an **alkyl group**. Alkyl groups are named by replacing the *-ane* ending of the parent alkane by an *-yl* ending. For example, removal of a hydrogen atom from methane, CH_4, generates a methyl group, H_3C—. Similarly, removal of a terminal hydrogen atom from any of the *n*-alkanes produces the series of *n*-alkyl groups shown in Table 2.3. Combination of an alkyl group with some of the functional groups listed earlier then allows us to generate and name many thousands of compounds.

TABLE 2.3   Some straight-chain alkyl groups

Alkane	Alkyl group	Example
CH_4	CH_3—	CH_3OH
Methane	Methyl	Methyl alcohol
CH_3CH_3	CH_3CH_2—	$CH_3CH_2NH_2$
Ethane	Ethyl	Ethylamine
$CH_3CH_2CH_3$	$CH_3CH_2CH_2$— or $n\text{-}C_3H_7$	$CH_3CH_2CH_2Li$
Propane	Propyl	Propyllithium
$CH_3(CH_2)_8CH_3$	$CH_3(CH_2)_8CH_2$— or $n\text{-}C_{10}H_{21}$	$CH_3(CH_2)_8CH_2NH_2$
Decane	Decyl	Decylamine

Methane and ethane each have only one kind of hydrogen; that is, the four hydrogens in CH_4 are equivalent and the six hydrogens in CH_3CH_3 are equivalent. No matter which hydrogen we remove, only one kind of methyl group and one kind of ethyl group result. The situation is more complex with higher alkanes, however. Propane and butane each have two kinds of hydrogens; pentane and hexane each have three kinds of hydrogens; and so on, as shown in Figure 2.4 on page 36.

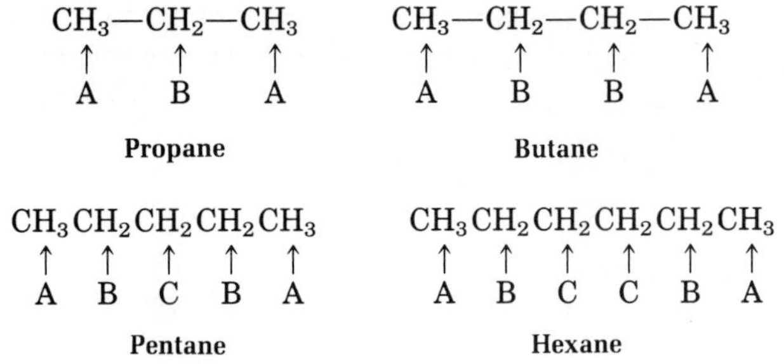

$$CH_3—CH_2—CH_3 \qquad CH_3—CH_2—CH_2—CH_3$$

$$\uparrow \quad \uparrow \quad \uparrow \qquad\qquad \uparrow \quad \uparrow \quad \uparrow \quad \uparrow$$

$$A \quad\; B \quad\; A \qquad\quad\; A \quad\; B \quad\; B \quad\; A$$

Propane   Butane

$$CH_3\,CH_2\,CH_2\,CH_2\,CH_3 \qquad CH_3\,CH_2\,CH_2\,CH_2\,CH_2\,CH_3$$

$$\uparrow \quad \uparrow \quad \uparrow \quad \uparrow \quad \uparrow \qquad\quad \uparrow \quad \uparrow \quad \uparrow \quad \uparrow \quad \uparrow \quad \uparrow$$

$$A \quad B \quad C \quad B \quad A \qquad\quad A \quad B \quad C \quad C \quad B \quad A$$

Pentane   Hexane

FIGURE 2.4
Kinds of hydrogen atoms in propane and higher alkanes:
The letters denote the different kinds of hydrogens in each
molecule.

We generated the homologous series of straight-chain alkanes in Table 2.2 by successively replacing a terminal hydrogen of a lower alkane with a methyl group. It is equally possible to imagine replacing *internal* hydrogens with alkyl groups and to generate thereby a vast number of **branched-chain alkanes.**

Beginning with propane, for example, either we can replace a terminal hydrogen by a methyl group to generate butane or we can replace an internal hydrogen by a methyl group to generate the branched four-carbon alkane, 2-methylpropane or *isobutane*. Although butane and isobutane have the same formula, C_4H_{10}, they have clearly different structures.

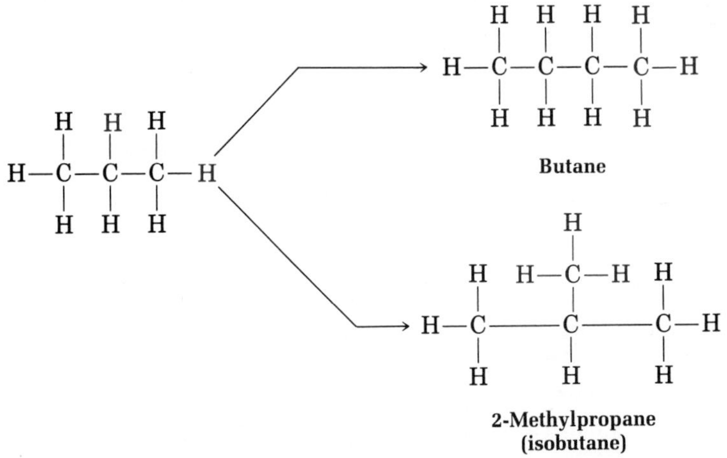

Butane

2-Methylpropane
(isobutane)

Compounds that have the same molecular formula but different structures are called **isomers** (from the Greek *isos* + *meros*, meaning "made of the same parts"). Isomers are indeed made of the same parts; they have the same numbers and kinds of atoms, but their atoms are connected differently. To be more specific, compounds such as butane and isobutane, which differ in their connections between atoms, are called **constitutional isomers**. We will soon see that other kinds of isomerism are sometimes possible, even among compounds whose atoms are connected in the same order.

There is a vast number of possibilities for chain branching in the alkane series. Although there is only one methane, one ethane, and one propane, there are two butane isomers, three pentane isomers, five hexane isomers, and so on. As Table 2.4 shows, there are more than 62 trillion possible isomers of $C_{40}H_{82}$! Fortunately, not all have been made.

TABLE 2.4 Possible alkane isomers

Formula	Isomers
C_1H_4	CH_4
C_2H_6	CH_3CH_3
C_3H_8	$CH_3CH_2CH_3$
C_4H_{10}	$CH_3CH_2CH_2CH_3$ CH_3CHCH_3 (CH_3) 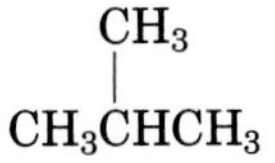
C_5H_{12}	$CH_3CH_2CH_2CH_2CH_3$ $CH_3CHCH_2CH_3$ (CH_3) CH_3-C-CH_3 (CH_3, CH_3) 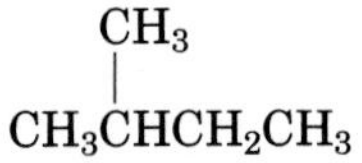 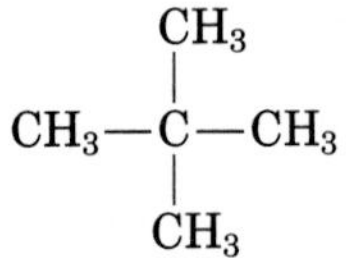

Formula	Number of isomers	Formula	Number of isomers
C_6H_{14}	5	$C_{12}H_{26}$	355
C_7H_{16}	9	$C_{15}H_{32}$	4,347
C_8H_{18}	18	$C_{20}H_{42}$	366,319
C_9H_{20}	35	$C_{30}H_{62}$	4,111,846,763
$C_{10}H_{22}$	75	$C_{40}H_{82}$	62,491,178,805,831
$C_{11}H_{24}$	159		

PRACTICE PROBLEM Propose structures for two isomers of formula C_2H_6O.

Solution We know that carbon forms four bonds, oxygen forms two, and hydrogen forms one. Putting the pieces together yields two isomeric structures:

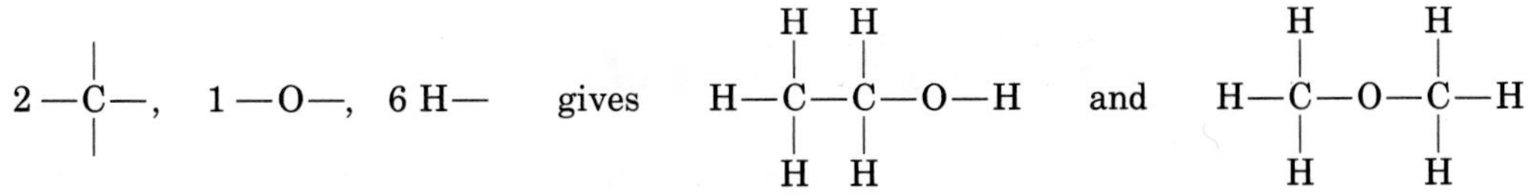

$2-C-$, $1-O-$, $6 H-$ gives H—C—C—O—H and H—C—O—C—H

PROBLEM 2.3 Draw the structures of the five isomers of C_6H_{14}.

PROBLEM 2.4 Draw structures that meet the following descriptions:

(a) Three isomers with the formula C_8H_{18}
(b) Two isomeric esters with the formula $C_4H_8O_2$
(c) Two isomeric nitriles with the formula C_4H_7N

PROBLEM 2.5 How many isomeric alcohols are there with the formula C_3H_8O? Draw them.

2.3 NOMENCLATURE OF ALKANES

In earlier times when relatively few pure organic chemicals were known, new compounds were named at the whim of their discoverer. Thus, urea (CH_4N_2O) is a crystalline substance isolated from urine, and barbituric acid is a tranquilizing agent named by its discoverer in honor of his friend Barbara. As the science of organic chemistry grew in the nineteenth century, however, so too did the need for a rational and systematic method of naming organic compounds. The system of **nomenclature** most often used by organic chemists is that devised by the International Union of Pure and Applied Chemistry (IUPAC, usually spoken as eye′-you-pac). IUPAC rules allow the unambiguous naming of all but the most complex structures.

In the IUPAC system, a chemical name has three parts: prefix, parent, and suffix. The parent name specifies the overall size of the molecule by identifying how many carbon atoms are present in the main chain; the suffix identifies the functional groups present in the molecule; and the prefix specifies the location of the functional groups and other substituents on the main chain:

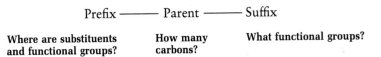

| Prefix —— Parent —— Suffix |
| Where are substituents and functional groups? | How many carbons? | What functional groups? |

As we cover new functional groups in later chapters, the applicable rules of nomenclature will be given. For the present, let's see how to name branched-chain alkanes.

All but the most complex branched-chain alkanes can be named by following four steps:

Step 1 Find the parent hydrocarbon.

a. Find the *longest continuous carbon chain* present in the molecule and use the name of that chain as the parent name. The longest chain may not always be apparent from the manner of writing; you may have to "turn corners."

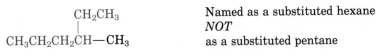

Named as a substituted hexane
NOT
as a substituted pentane

b. If two different chains of equal length are present, select the one with the larger number of branch points as the parent:

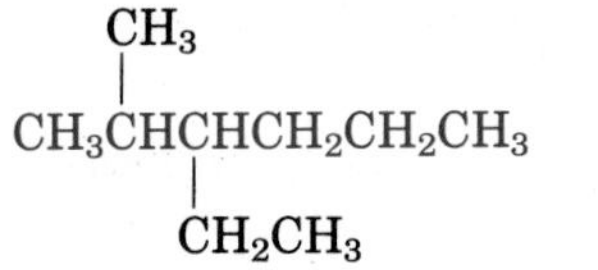

$$CH_3$$
$$|$$
$$CH_3CHCHCH_2CH_2CH_3$$
$$|$$
$$CH_2CH_3$$

Named as a hexane with *two* substituents

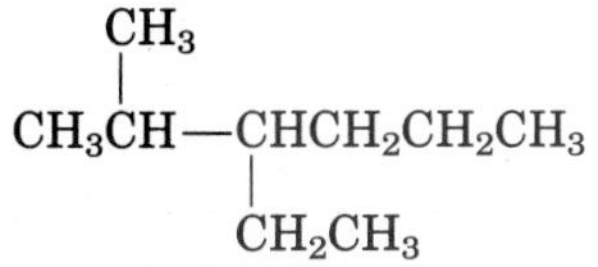

$$CH_3$$
$$|$$
$$CH_3CH—CHCH_2CH_2CH_3$$
$$|$$
$$CH_2CH_3$$

NOT

as a hexane with *one* substituent

Step 2 Number the atoms in the main chain.

a. Beginning at the end *nearer the first branch point*, number each carbon atom in the parent chain:

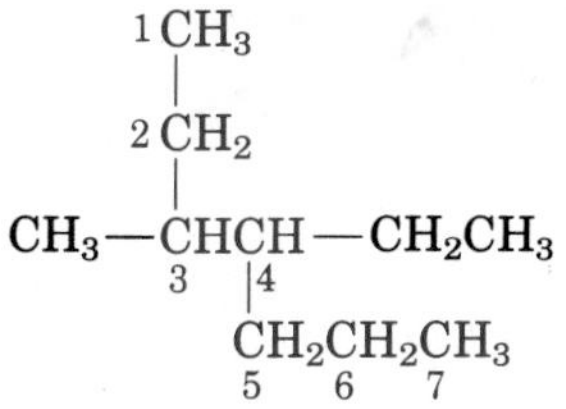

$$1\ CH_3$$
$$|$$
$$2\ CH_2$$
$$|$$
$$CH_3—CHCH—CH_2CH_3$$
$$3\ \ \ |4$$
$$CH_2CH_2CH_3$$
$$5\ \ \ 6\ \ \ 7$$

NOT

$$7\ CH_3$$
$$|$$
$$6\ CH_2$$
$$|$$
$$CH_3—CHCH—CH_2CH_3$$
$$5\ \ \ |4$$
$$CH_2CH_2CH_3$$
$$3\ \ \ 2\ \ \ 1$$

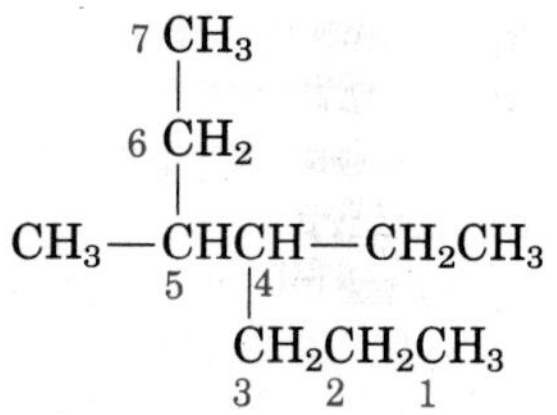

The first branch occurs at C3 in the proper numbering system, but at C4 in the improper system.

b. If there is branching an equal distance away from both ends of the parent chain, begin numbering at the end nearer the *second* branch point:

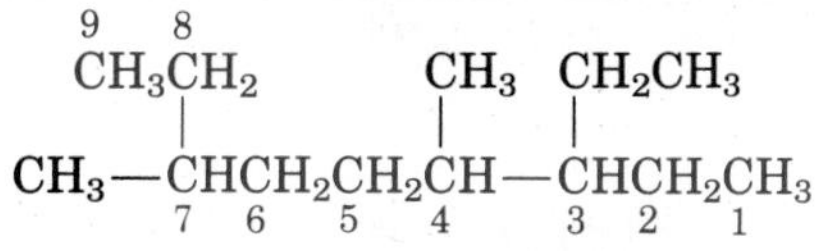

$$9\ \ \ 8$$
$$CH_3CH_2 \quad\quad CH_3\ \ CH_2CH_3$$
$$|\quad\quad\quad\quad |\ \ \ |$$
$$CH_3—CHCH_2CH_2CH—CHCH_2CH_3$$
$$7\ \ 6\ \ \ 5\ \ \ 4\ \ \ \ 3\ \ 2\ \ \ 1$$

NOT

$$1\ \ \ 2$$
$$CH_3CH_2 \quad\quad CH_3\ \ CH_2CH_3$$
$$|\quad\quad\quad\quad |\ \ \ |$$
$$CH_3—CHCH_2CH_2CH—CHCH_2CH_3$$
$$3\ \ 4\ \ \ 5\ \ \ 6\ \ \ \ 7\ \ 8\ \ \ 9$$

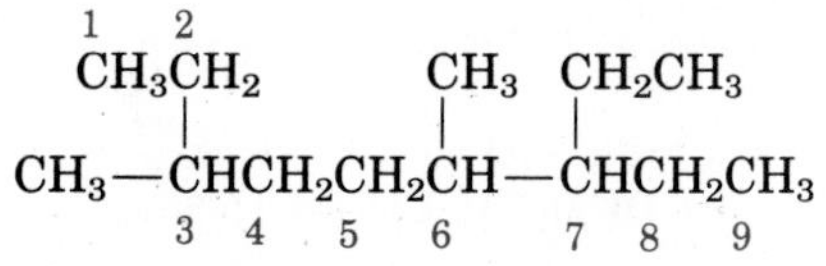

The first branch from either end is at C3, but the *second* branch is at C4 in the correct system and at C6 in the incorrect system.

Step 3 Identify and number the substituents.

a. Assign a number to each substituent according to its point of attachment on the parent chain:

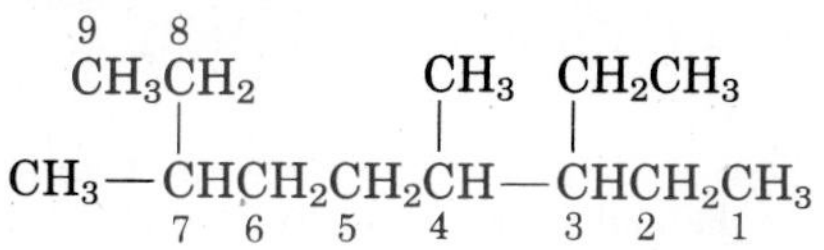

$$9\ \ \ 8$$
$$CH_3CH_2 \quad\quad CH_3\ \ CH_2CH_3$$
$$|\quad\quad\quad\quad |\ \ \ |$$
$$CH_3—CHCH_2CH_2CH—CHCH_2CH_3$$
$$7\ \ 6\ \ \ 5\ \ \ 4\ \ \ \ 3\ \ 2\ \ \ 1$$

Named as a nonane

Substituents:
On C3, CH_2CH_3 (3-ethyl)
On C4, CH_3 (4-methyl)
On C7, CH_3 (7-methyl)

b. If there are two substituents on the same carbon, assign them both the same number. There must always be as many numbers in the name as there are substituents.

$$\underset{6}{CH_3}\underset{5}{CH_2}-\underset{4}{\overset{\overset{\displaystyle CH_3}{|}}{\underset{\underset{\displaystyle CH_3}{|}}{\underset{\displaystyle CH_2}{C}}}}-\underset{3}{CH_2}\underset{2}{CH}\underset{1}{CH_3}$$

Named as a hexane

Substituents:
On C2, CH_3 (2-methyl)
On C4, CH_3 (4-methyl)
On C4, CH_2CH_3 (4-ethyl)

Step 4 Write the name as a single word, using hyphens to separate the different prefixes and commas to separate numbers. If two or more *different* side chains are present, cite them in alphabetical order. If two or more *identical* side chains are present, use one of the prefixes *di-, tri-, tetra-,* and so forth. Do not use these prefixes for alphabetizing purposes, however:

$$\underset{6}{CH_3}\underset{5}{CH_2}\underset{4}{CH_2}\underset{3}{\overset{\overset{\displaystyle \underset{2}{CH_2}\underset{1}{CH_3}}{|}}{CH}}-CH_3$$

3-Methylhexane

$$\underset{1}{CH_3}\underset{2}{\overset{\overset{\displaystyle CH_3}{|}}{CH}}\underset{3}{\overset{\overset{\displaystyle}{}}{CH}}\underset{4}{CH_2}\underset{5}{CH_2}\underset{6}{CH_3}$$
$$\underset{}{\underset{CH_2CH_3}{|}}$$

3-Ethyl-2-methylhexane

$$\underset{9}{CH_3}\underset{8}{CH_2}\qquad CH_3 \quad CH_2CH_3$$
$$\underset{7}{CH_3}-\underset{6}{CH}\underset{5}{CH_2}\underset{4}{CH_2}\underset{}{CH}-\underset{2}{CH}\underset{1}{CH_2}CH_3$$

3-Ethyl-4,7-dimethylnonane

$$\underset{1}{CH_3}-\underset{3}{\overset{\overset{\displaystyle \underset{2}{CH_2}}{|}}{CH}}\underset{4}{CH}-\underset{5}{CH_2}\underset{6}{CH_2}\underset{7}{CH_3}$$

4-Ethyl-3-methylheptane

$$\underset{6}{CH_3}\underset{5}{CH_2}-\underset{4}{\overset{\overset{\displaystyle CH_3}{|}}{\underset{\underset{\displaystyle CH_3}{|}}{\underset{\displaystyle CH_2}{C}}}}-\underset{3}{CH_2}\underset{2}{CH}\underset{1}{CH_3}$$

4-Ethyl-2,4-dimethylhexane

PRACTICE PROBLEM What is the IUPAC name of the following alkane?

$$CH_3\overset{\overset{\displaystyle CH_2CH_3}{|}}{CH}CH_2CH_2CH_2\overset{\overset{\displaystyle CH_3}{|}}{CH}CH_3$$

Solution The molecule has a chain of eight carbons (octane) with two methyl substituents. Numbering from the end nearer the first methyl substituent indicates that the methyls are at C2 and C6, giving the name 2,6-dimethyloctane.

PROBLEM 2.6 Provide proper IUPAC names for these alkanes:

(a) The three isomers of C_5H_{12}

(b)
$$\underset{\underset{CH_2CH_3}{|}}{CH_3CH_2CHCHCH_3}\overset{\overset{CH_3}{|}}{}$$

3, 4 dimethyl heptane

(c) $(CH_3)_2CHCH_2\overset{\overset{CH_3}{|}}{C}HCH_3$

2 methyl hexane

(d) $(CH_3)_3CCH_2CH_2\overset{\overset{CH_3}{|}}{C}H\underset{CH_2CH_3}{}$

3 methyl nonane

PROBLEM 2.7 Draw structures corresponding to these IUPAC names:

(a) 3,4-Dimethylnonane
(b) 3-Ethyl-4,4-dimethylheptane
(c) 2,2-Dimethyl-4-propyloctane
(d) 2,2,4-Trimethylpentane

2.4 NOMENCLATURE OF ALKYL GROUPS

Earlier in this chapter, we saw that straight-chain alkyl groups can be formed by the removal of terminal hydrogen atoms from straight-chain alkanes. It is equally possible to generate an enormous number of *branched* alkyl groups by removing *internal* hydrogen atoms. For example, there are two possible three-carbon alkyl groups and four possible four-carbon alkyl groups (Figure 2.5).

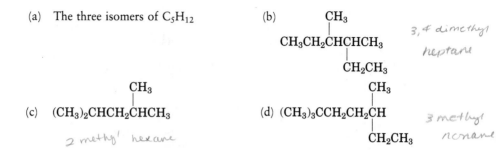

FIGURE 2.5
Generation of branched-chain alkyl groups from *n*-alkanes

Branched-chain alkyl groups can be named by carefully following the four steps already discussed. Note that, as shown in Figure 2.5, these groups are always numbered so that the branch point is C1. The longest continuous chain *beginning from the branch point* is taken as the parent.

For historical reasons, some of the simpler branched alkyl groups have retained nonsystematic or *trivial* names:

1. Three-carbon alkyl group:

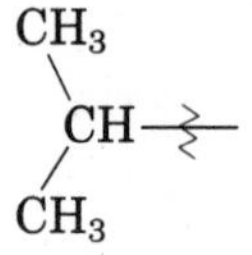

$$CH_3 \\ \diagdown \\ CH \!\!-\!\!\xi\!\!- \\ \diagup \\ CH_3$$

Isopropyl

2. Four-carbon alkyl groups:

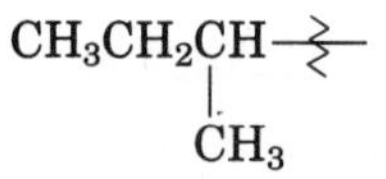

$$CH_3CH_2CH\!\!-\!\!\xi\!\!- \\ | \\ CH_3$$

sec-Butyl (for secondary)

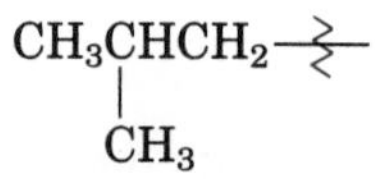

$$CH_3CHCH_2\!\!-\!\!\xi\!\!- \\ | \\ CH_3$$

Isobutyl

$$CH_3 \\ | \\ CH_3\!\!-\!\!C\!\!-\!\!\xi\!\!- \\ | \\ CH_3$$

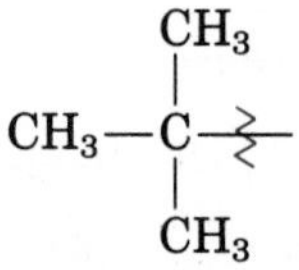

tert-Butyl or t-butyl (for tertiary)

These nonsystematic names are so well entrenched in common usage that the IUPAC rules make allowance for them. Thus,

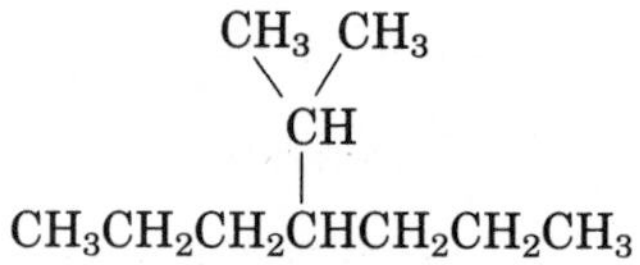

$$CH_3\ CH_3 \\ \diagdown\ \diagup \\ CH \\ | \\ CH_3CH_2CH_2CHCH_2CH_2CH_3$$

4-(1-Methylethyl)heptane

may properly be named *either* 4-isopropylheptane or 4-(1-methylethyl)heptane.

One further word of explanation: The prefixes *sec-* (for secondary) and *tert-* (for tertiary) refer to the *degree of alkyl substitution* at the carbon atom in question. There are four possible substitution patterns for carbon:

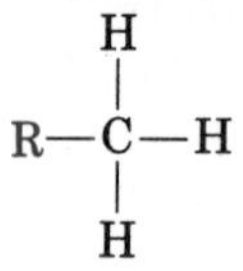

$$H \\ | \\ R\!\!-\!\!C\!\!-\!\!H \\ | \\ H$$
Primary carbon (1°); one alkyl substituent on carbon

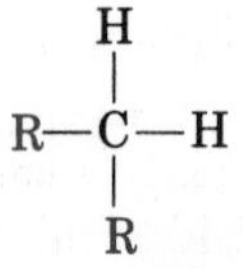

$$H \\ | \\ R\!\!-\!\!C\!\!-\!\!H \\ | \\ R$$
Secondary carbon (2°); two alkyl substituents on carbon

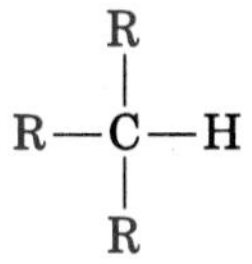

$$
\begin{array}{c}
R \\
| \\
R-C-H \\
| \\
R
\end{array}
$$

Tertiary carbon (3°); three alkyl substituents on carbon

$$
\begin{array}{c}
R \\
| \\
R-C-R \\
| \\
R
\end{array}
$$

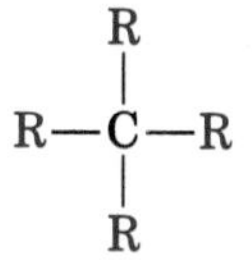

Quaternary carbon (4°); four alkyl substituents on carbon

The symbol R is used here and throughout this text to represent a *generalized* alkyl group. The group R may stand for methyl, ethyl, or any of a multitude of other alkyl groups; when more than one type of alkyl group is present, we will use R', R", etc., to differentiate among the groups.

PROBLEM 2.8   Draw and name the eight possible five-carbon alkyl groups (pentyl isomers).

PROBLEM 2.9   Draw and name alkanes that meet these descriptions:

   (a)   An alkane with two tertiary carbons
   (b)   An alkane that contains an isopropyl group
   (c)   An alkane that has one quaternary and one secondary carbon

PROBLEM 2.10   Identify the carbon atoms in these molecules as primary, secondary, tertiary, or quaternary:

   (a) $(CH_3)_2CHCH_2CH_3$ (b) $CH_3CH_2CH(CH_3)C(CH_3)_3$ (c) $C(CH_3)_4$

2.5 PROPERTIES OF ALKANES

Alkanes are often referred to as **paraffins**, a word derived from the Latin *parum affinis* meaning "slight affinity." This term for alkanes aptly describes their behavior, since they show little chemical affinity for other molecules and are chemically inert to most laboratory reagents. Alkanes do, however, react with oxygen and with chlorine under appropriate conditions.

Reaction of alkanes with oxygen occurs during combustion in an engine or furnace when the alkane is used as a fuel. Carbon dioxide and water are formed as products, and a large amount of heat is released. For example, methane (natural gas) reacts with oxygen according to the equation

$$
CH_4 + 2\,O_2 \longrightarrow CO_2 + 2\,H_2O + 213\ \text{kcal/mol}
$$

Reaction of alkanes with chlorine occurs when a mixture of the two reagents is irradiated with ultraviolet light. Depending on the relative amounts of the two starting materials and on the time of reaction, a sequential substitution of the alkane hydrogen atoms by chlorine occurs, leading to chlorinated products. For example, methane reacts with chlorine to yield a mixture of chloromethane

(CH$_3$Cl), dichloromethane (CH$_2$Cl$_2$), trichloromethane (CHCl$_3$), and tetrachloromethane (CCl$_4$):

$$\text{CH}_4 + \text{Cl}_2 \xrightarrow{\text{light (h}\nu)} \text{CH}_3\text{Cl} + \text{CH}_2\text{Cl}_2 + \text{CHCl}_3 + \text{CCl}_4 + \text{HCl}$$

We will see how this chlorination reaction occurs when we take up the chemistry of alkyl halides in Chapter 7.

Alkanes show regular increases in both boiling point and melting point as molecular weight increases (Table 2.5). This regularity is also reflected in other properties. Average carbon–carbon bond parameters are nearly the same in all alkanes, with bond lengths of 1.54 ± 0.01 Å and bond strengths of 85 ± 3 kcal/mol. Carbon–hydrogen bond parameters are also nearly constant at 1.09 ± 0.01 Å and 95 ± 3 kcal/mol.

TABLE 2.5   Physical properties of some alkanes

Number of carbons	Alkane	Melting point (°C)	Boiling point (°C)	Density (g/mL)
1	Methane	−182.5	−164.0	0.5547
2	Ethane	−183.3	−88.6	0.509
3	Propane	−189.7	−42.1	0.5005
4	Butane	−138.3	−0.5	0.5788
5	Pentane	−129.7	36.1	0.6262
6	Hexane	−95.0	68.9	0.6603
7	Heptane	−90.6	98.4	0.6837
8	Octane	−56.8	125.7	0.7025
9	Nonane	−51.0	150.8	0.7176
10	Decane	−29.7	174.1	0.7300
20	Eicosane	36.8	343.0	0.7886
30	Triacontane	65.8	450.0	0.8097
4	2-Methylpropane	−159.4	−11.7	0.579
5	2-Methylbutane	−159.9	27.85	0.6201
5	2,2-Dimethylpropane	−16.5	9.5	0.6135
8	Isooctane	−107.4	99.3	0.6919

Table 2.5 shows that increased chain branching in alkanes lowers the boiling point. Thus, pentane boils at 36.1°C, 2-methylbutane (one branch) boils at 27.85°C, and 2,2-dimethylpropane (two branches) boils at 9.5°C.

2.6   MOLECULAR MODELS

One very simple technique that simplifies the learning of organic chemistry is to use molecular models. Organic chemistry is a three-dimensional science, and molecular shape often plays a critical role in determining the chemistry a compound undergoes. With practice, you can learn to see many spatial relationships even when viewing two-dimensional drawings, but there is no substitute for building a molecular model and turning it in your hands to get different perspectives.

There are many kinds of models available at modest cost. Research chemists generally prefer either **space-filling** or **skeletal models**, but simple ball-and-stick models are best to begin with. Figure 2.6 shows some models of acetic acid, CH_3COOH.

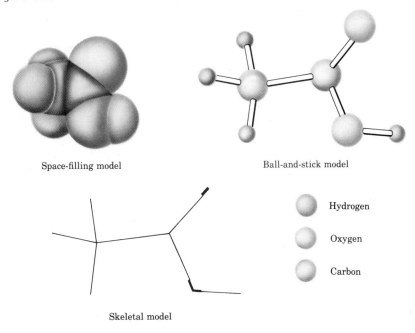

Space-filling model

Ball-and-stick model

Hydrogen

Oxygen

Carbon

Skeletal model

FIGURE 2.6
Molecular models of acetic acid, CH_3COOH

PROBLEM 2.11   Build a molecular model of ethane, CH_3CH_3, and look at the relationships between hydrogens on the different carbons.

2.7 CONFORMATIONS OF ETHANE

We saw earlier that methane has a tetrahedral structure and that carbon–carbon bonds in alkanes result from sigma overlap of two tetrahedral carbon sp^3 orbitals. Let's now look into the three-dimensional consequences of such bonding. What are the spatial relationships between the hydrogens on one carbon and the hydrogens on the other?

We know that sigma bonds result from the head-on overlap of two atomic orbitals and that they are cylindrically symmetrical. In other words, a cross section of a sigma bond is circular. As a consequence of this sigma bond symmetry, *rotation* is possible around the carbon–carbon single bond. Bond overlap is exactly the same for all geometric arrangements of the hydrogens (Figure 2.7, page 46).

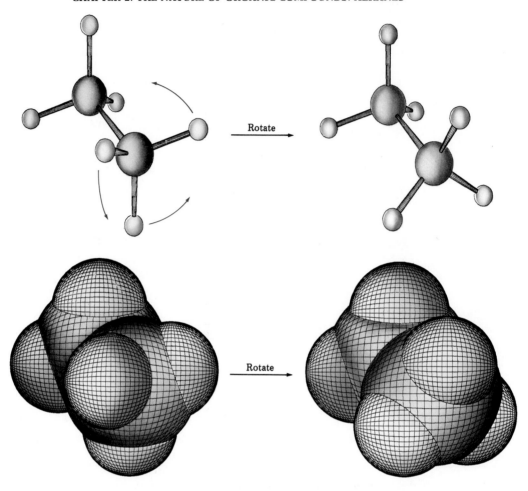

FIGURE 2.7
Some conformations of ethane: Rotation around the carbon–carbon single bond
interconverts the different forms. The drawings are computer-generated.

The different arrangements of atoms caused by rotation around a single bond
are called **conformations**, and a specific structure is called a **conformer** (**conformational isomer**). Unlike constitutional isomers (Section 2.2), different con-
formers cannot be isolated, since they interconvert too rapidly.

Chemists have adopted two ways of representing conformational isomers.
Sawhorse representations view the carbon–carbon bond from an oblique angle
and indicate spatial relationships by showing all the C—H bonds. **Newman
projections** view the carbon–carbon bond directly end-on and represent the two
carbon atoms by a circle. Bonds to the front carbon are represented by lines to the
center of the circle, whereas bonds to the rear carbon are represented by lines to
the edge of the circle (Figure 2.8).

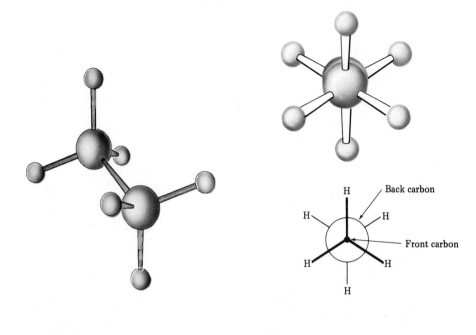

Sawhorse representation   Newman projection

FIGURE 2.8
A sawhorse representation and a Newman projection of ethane

Perhaps surprisingly in view of sigma bond symmetry, we do not observe perfectly free rotation in ethane. Experiments show that there is a slight (2.9 kcal/mol) barrier to rotation and that some conformations are more stable than others. The lowest-energy, most stable, conformation is the one in which all six carbon–hydrogen bonds are as far away from each other as possible (**staggered** when viewed end-on in a Newman projection). The highest-energy, least stable, conformation is the one in which the six carbon–hydrogen bonds are as close as possible (**eclipsed** in a Newman projection). Any conformation partway between staggered and eclipsed is referred to as a **skew** conformation.

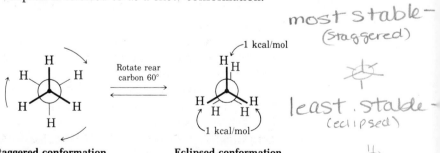

**Staggered conformation
of ethane**

Rotate rear
carbon 60°

**Eclipsed conformation
of ethane
(C—H bonds on front and
back carbon atoms are parallel)**

We call the 2.9 kcal/mol of strain energy present in the eclipsed conformation of ethane **torsional strain.** Since this strain is caused by three equal hydrogen–hydrogen eclipsing interactions, we can assign a value of approximately 1 kcal/mol to each single interaction.

The barrier to rotation that results from torsional strain can be represented on a graph of potential energy versus degree of rotation. Energy minima occur at staggered conformations; energy maxima occur at eclipsed conformations, as shown in Figure 2.9.

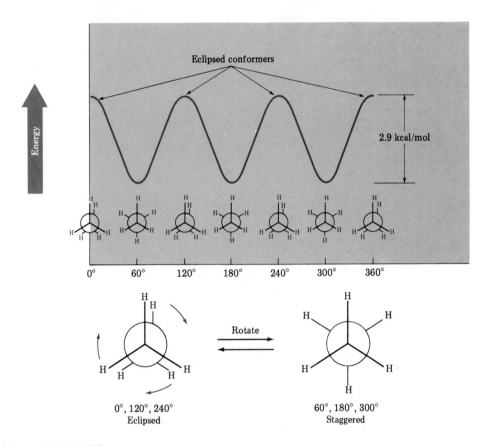

FIGURE 2.9
A graph of energy versus bond rotation in ethane: The staggered conformer is 2.9 kcal/mol lower in energy than the eclipsed conformer.

To what is torsional strain due? Most chemists believe that the strain is due to the slight repulsion between electron clouds in the carbon–hydrogen bonds as they pass by each other at close quarters in the eclipsed conformation. The distance between hydrogens is 2.55 Å in the staggered conformation, but decreases to 2.29 Å in the eclipsed conformation.

2.8 CONFORMATIONS OF PROPANE

Propane is the next higher member in the alkane series, and we again find a torsional barrier that results in a slightly hindered rotation about the carbon–carbon bonds. In the eclipsed conformer, there are two ethane-type hydrogen–hydrogen interactions (1.0 kcal/mol each) and one additional interaction between a hydrogen and a neighboring methyl group. This new interaction introduces about 1.4 kcal/mol of strain into the molecule, giving the eclipsed conformer of propane a total strain energy of 3.4 kcal/mol (Figure 2.10).

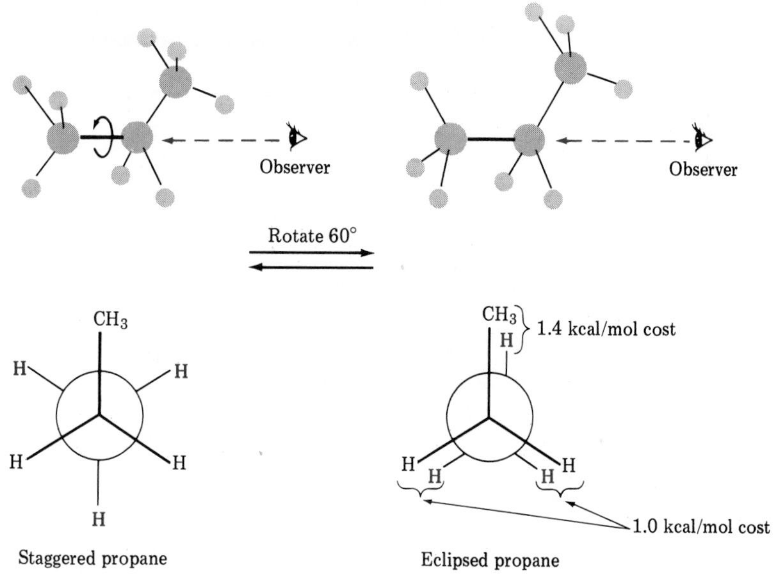

FIGURE 2.10
Newman projections of propane showing staggered and eclipsed conformations: The staggered form is lower in energy by 3.4 kcal/mol.

The same principles just developed for ethane and propane apply to butane, pentane, and to all higher alkanes. The most favored conformation for any alkane is the one in which all carbon–carbon bonds have staggered arrangements.

PROBLEM 2.12 Construct a graph of energy versus angle of bond rotation for propane. Assign quantitative values to the energy maxima (H—H interaction = 1.0 kcal/mol; H—CH$_3$ interaction = 1.4 kcal/mol).

PROBLEM 2.13 Consider 2-methylpropane. Sighting along the C1–C2 bond:

(a) Draw a Newman projection of the most stable conformation.
(b) Draw a Newman projection of the least stable conformation.
(c) Construct a qualitative graph of energy versus angle of rotation around the C1–C2 bond.

PROBLEM 2.14 Make a molecular model of butane. Looking along the C2–C3 bond, what conformation looks like the most stable?

2.9 DRAWING CHEMICAL STRUCTURES

In the structures we have been using, a line between atoms represents the two electrons in a bond. Most chemists find themselves drawing many structures each day, however, and it would soon become awkward if every bond and every atom had to be indicated. Chemists have therefore devised a shorthand way of drawing **line structures** that greatly simplifies matters. Such structures are particularly useful for representing cyclic compounds.

The rules for drawing line structures are simple:

1. Carbon atoms are not shown. Instead, a carbon atom is assumed to be at each intersection of two lines (bonds) and at the end of each line. Occasionally, carbon atoms may be indicated for emphasis or for clarity.

2. Neither hydrogen atoms nor carbon–hydrogen bonds are shown. Since carbon always has a valence of four, we mentally supply the correct number of hydrogen atoms to fill the valence of each carbon.

3. All atoms other than carbon and hydrogen are indicated.

Table 2.6 indicates how these rules are applied in some specific cases.

TABLE 2.6   Line structures for several organic compounds

Compound	Kekulé structure	Shorthand structure
Butane, C_4H_{10}	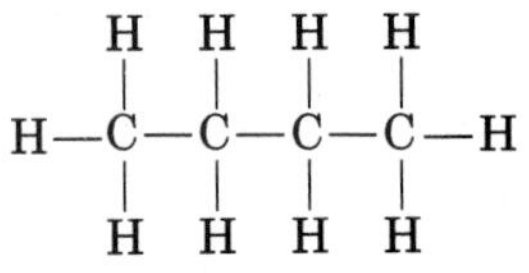	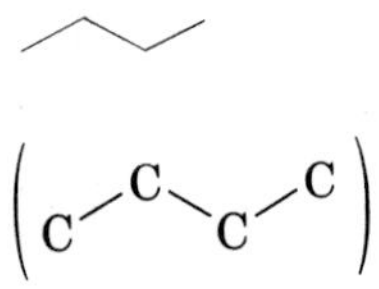
2-Methyl-1,3-butadiene (isoprene), C_5H_8	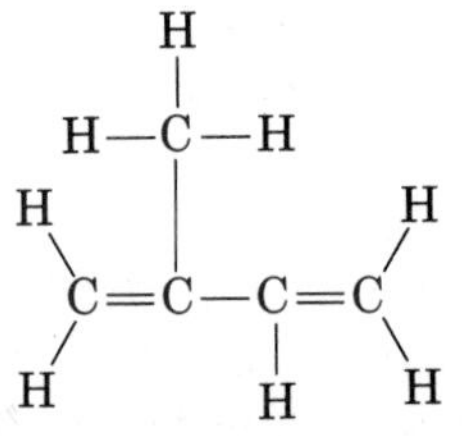	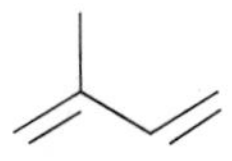
Cyclohexane, $C_6H_{12}{}^a$	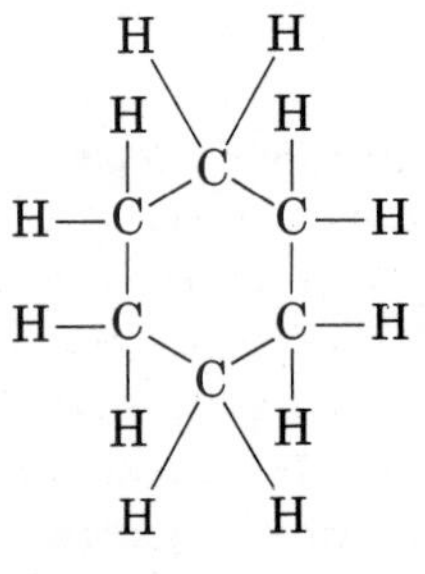	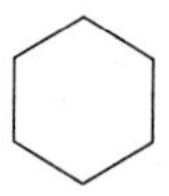

[a]Note that cyclohexane has a *ring* of carbon atoms.

PROBLEM 2.15 Convert these line structures into molecular formulas:

(a)

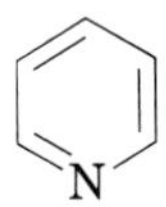

Pyridine

(b)

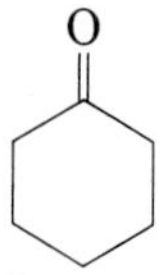

Cyclohexanone

(c)

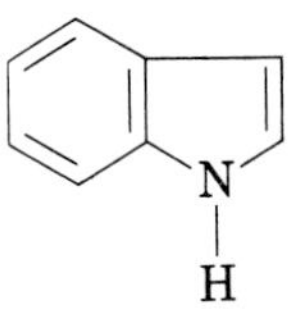

Indole

PROBLEM 2.16 Propose line structures that are consistent with these molecular formulas:

(a) C_4H_8 (b) C_3H_6O (c) C_4H_9Cl

2.10 CYCLOALKANES: CIS–TRANS ISOMERISM

Although we have only discussed open-chain alkanes up to now, compounds that contain *rings* of carbon atoms are also well known. Such compounds are called **cycloalkanes** or **alicyclic compounds** (aliphatic cyclic). Since cycloalkanes consist of rings of $-CH_2-$ units (methylene units), they have the general formula $(CH_2)_n$ or C_nH_{2n}. Physical data for some simple cycloalkanes are given in Table 2.7.

TABLE 2.7 Physical properties of some cycloalkanes

Name	Formula	Melting point (°C)	Boiling point (°C)	Density (g/mL)
Cyclopropane	C_3H_6	−127.6	−32.7	
Cyclobutane	C_4H_8	−50.0	12.0	0.720
Cyclopentane	C_5H_{10}	−93.9	49.3	0.7457
Cyclohexane	C_6H_{12}	6.6	80.7	0.7786
Cycloheptane	C_7H_{14}	−12.0	118.5	0.8098
Cyclooctane	C_8H_{16}	14.3	148.5	0.8349

In many respects, the chemistry of cycloalkanes mimics that of open-chain (acyclic) alkanes. Both classes of compounds are relatively nonpolar and are chemically inert to most reagents. There are, however, some differences between cyclic and acyclic alkanes.

One difference is that cycloalkanes have less conformational mobility than their open-chain counterparts. Although open-chain alkanes have nearly free rotation around carbon–carbon single bonds and are thus able to adopt a large number of conformations, the same is not true of cycloalkanes. Cycloalkanes have less freedom of rotation around bonds and are therefore restrained to fewer conformations. For example, cyclopropane must be a flat, planar molecule with a rigid structure. No bond rotation about carbon–carbon bonds in cyclopropane is possible without breaking open the ring.

As a consequence of their cyclic structure, cycloalkanes have two distinct sides, a "top" side and a "bottom" side. Isomerism is therefore possible in substituted cycloalkanes. For example, there are two different 1,2-dibromocyclopropane isomers. One isomer has the two bromines on the same side of the ring, and the other isomer has them on opposite sides. Both isomers are stable, isolable compounds; they can't be interconverted without breaking chemical bonds.

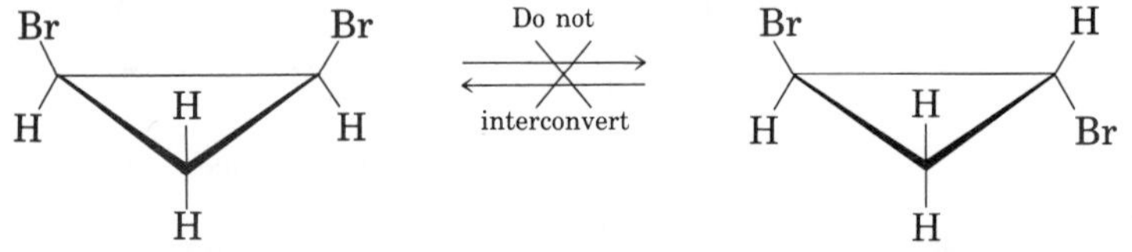

cis-1,2-Dibromocyclopropane
(bromines on same side of ring)

trans-1,2-Dibromocyclopropane
(bromines on opposite sides of ring)

Unlike the constitutional isomers butane and isobutane (Section 2.2), which have a different order of connection of their atoms, the two 1,2-dibromocyclopropanes have the same order of connection. They differ, however, in the spatial orientation of their atoms. Compounds that have their atoms connected in the same order but that differ in three-dimensional orientation are called **stereoisomers**.

The 1,2-dibromocyclopropanes are special kinds of stereoisomers called **cis–trans isomers**; the prefixes *cis-* (Latin, "on the same side") and *trans-* (Latin, "across") are used to distinguish between them. Cis–trans isomerism is often possible with substituted cycloalkanes.

2.11   NOMENCLATURE OF CYCLOALKANES

The systematic naming of substituted cycloalkanes follows directly from the rules for open-chain alkanes. For most cases, there are only two rules:

1. Use the cycloalkane name as the parent. Compounds should be named as alkyl-substituted cycloalkanes rather than as cycloalkyl-substituted alkanes.

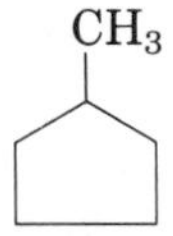

Methylcyclopentane
(*NOT* cyclopentylmethane)

2. Number substituents on the ring so as to arrive at the lowest sum. If two or more different substituents are present, number them in order of alphabetical priority.

NOT

1,3-Dimethylcyclohexane   **1,5-Dimethylcyclohexane**

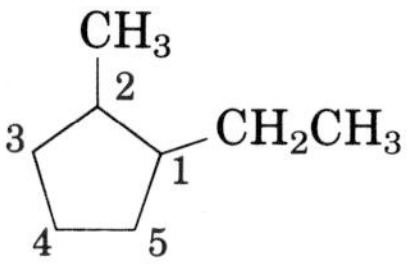

CH₃

$$\underset{4 \quad 5}{\overset{CH_3}{\underset{3}{\triangle}}} \quad -CH_2CH_3$$

1-Ethyl-2-methylcyclopentane

NOT

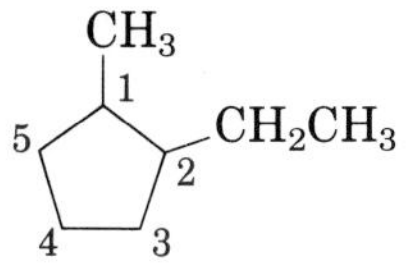

2-Ethyl-1-methylcyclopentane

PROBLEM 2.17 Give IUPAC names for the following cycloalkanes:

(a) CH₃

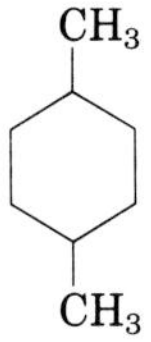

(b) CH₂CH₂CH₃

CH₃

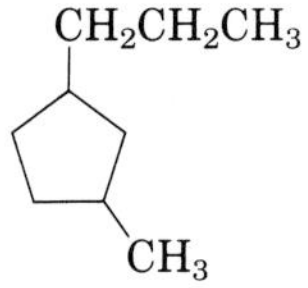

(c)

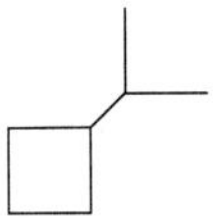

PROBLEM 2.18 Draw a line structure for *cis*-1-chloro-3-methylcyclopentane.

2.12 STABILITY OF CYCLOAKLANES: CYCLOPROPANE

By the late 1800s, chemists had accepted the idea that cyclic molecules exist, but the limitations on feasible ring sizes were unclear. Numerous compounds containing five-membered and six-membered rings were known, but smaller ring sizes had not been prepared.

A theoretical interpretation of this observation was proposed in 1885 by Adolf von Baeyer. Baeyer suggested that, if carbon prefers to have tetrahedral geometry with bond angles of 109°, ring sizes smaller than five may be too strained to exist. This hypothesis was based on the simple geometric notion that a three-membered ring (cyclopropane) must be an equilateral triangle with bond angles of 60° and that a four-membered ring (cyclobutane) must be a square with bond angles of 90°. According to this analysis, cyclopropane, with a bond angle compression of 109° − 60° = 49°, must have a large amount of **angle strain**. Cyclobutane (109° − 90° = 19° bond compression) should be similarly strained.

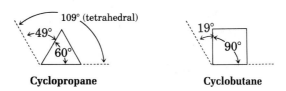

Cyclopropane **Cyclobutane**

Although there is some truth to Baeyer's assertions about angle strain in small rings, he was incorrect in his belief that cyclopropane and cyclobutane must be too strained to exist. Cyclopropane is a colorless gas (bp = −33°C) that was first prepared by reaction of sodium metal with 1,3-dibromopropane:

$$\text{BrH}_2\text{C} \overset{\displaystyle \text{CH}_2}{\diagup \diagdown} \text{CH}_2\text{Br} \xrightarrow{\text{2 Na}} \text{H}_2\text{C} \overset{\displaystyle \text{CH}_2}{\diagup \diagdown} \text{CH}_2 + 2\ \text{NaBr}$$

1,3-Dibromopropane   **Cyclopropane**

Although cyclopropane must be a flat, symmetrical molecule with C-C-C bond angles of 60° as indicated in Figure 2.11, it is nevertheless reasonably stable. How can we account for the great distortion of the bonds from their normal 109° tetrahedral values?

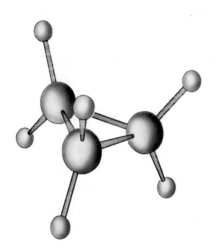

FIGURE 2.11
A ball-and-stick model of cyclopropane

Cyclopropane is best thought of as having *bent bonds* (Figure 2.12). In an unstrained alkane, maximum bonding efficiency is achieved when two atoms are located so that their overlapping orbitals point directly toward each other. In cyclopropane, however, the orbitals cannot point directly toward each other; instead, they must overlap at a slight angle. The result of this poor overlap is that cyclopropane carbon–carbon bonds are weaker and more reactive than normal alkane bonds.

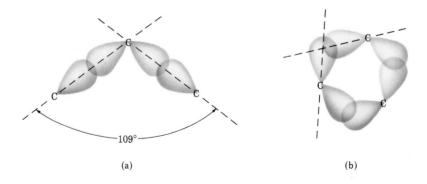

(a)   (b)

FIGURE 2.12
An orbital view of cyclopropane: (a) Normal C—C bonds have good overlap of orbitals; (b) cyclopropane bent bonds have poor overlap of orbitals.

2.13 CONFORMATIONS OF CYCLOHEXANE

Cyclohexane compounds are the most important of all cycloalkanes because of their wide occurrence in nature. A large number of compounds, including steroids and many other important pharmaceutical agents, have cyclohexane rings.

Although early chemists, including Baeyer, assumed that cyclohexane must be a flat hexagonal molecule, we now know that this is not the case. Cyclohexane rings are not flat; they are puckered into a strain-free, three-dimensional conformation called the **chair conformation**. In this conformation the C-C-C bond angles of cyclohexane have the strain-free 109° tetrahedral value, as shown in Figure 2.13. In addition to being free of angle strain, we also find that chair cyclohexane has no eclipsing strain. All neighboring C—H bonds are perfectly staggered, as indicated by the Newman projection of cyclohexane shown in Figure 2.13.

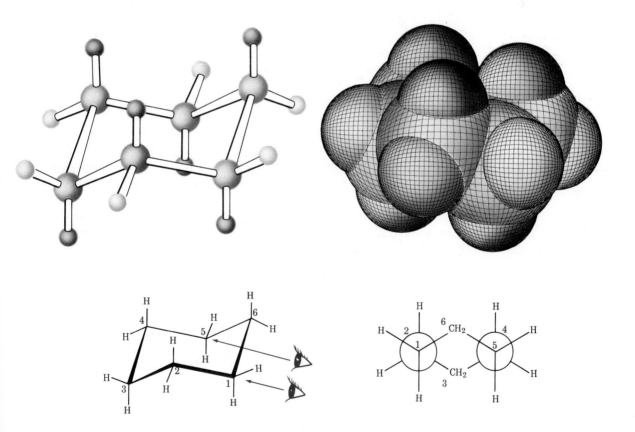

FIGURE 2.13
The chair conformation of cyclohexane: This conformation has no eclipsing strain and no angle strain. All bond angles are 109°.

The simplest way to see this strain-free conformation of cyclohexane is to build and examine molecular models. Two-dimensional drawings such as Figure 2.13 are useful, but there is no substitute for holding, twisting, and turning a three-dimensional molecular model in your hands.

Chair conformations are easily drawn by following three steps:

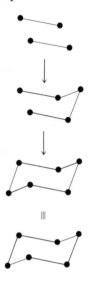

1. Draw two parallel lines, slanted downward and slightly offset from each other. These lines show that four of the cyclohexane carbon atoms lie in a plane.

2. Locate the topmost carbon atom above and to the right of the plane of the other four and connect the bonds.

3. Locate the bottommost carbon atom below and to the left of the plane of the middle four and connect the bonds. Note that the bonds to the bottommost carbon atom are parallel to the bonds to the topmost carbon.

It is important to remember when viewing cyclohexane that the lower bond is considered to be in front, while the upper bond is in back. If this convention is not defined, an optical illusion can make it appear that the reverse is true.

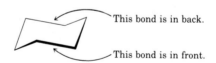

This bond is in back.

This bond is in front.

2.14   AXIAL AND EQUATORIAL BONDS IN CYCLOHEXANE

There are many consequences of the chair conformation of cyclohexane. For example, some of the chemical behavior of substituted cyclohexanes is affected by conformation. Another consequence of the chair cyclohexane conformation is that there are two kinds of hydrogen atoms on the ring—**axial hydrogens** and **equatorial hydrogens** (Figure 2.14).

As indicated in Figure 2.14, cyclohexane has six axial hydrogens that are perpendicular to the ring (parallel to the ring *axis*) and six equatorial hydrogens that are more or less in the rough plane of the ring (around the ring *equator*).

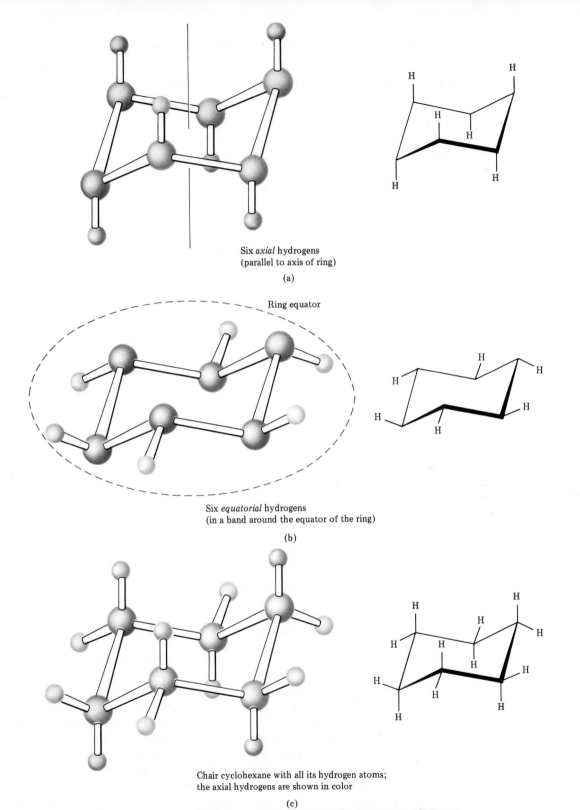

Six *axial* hydrogens
(parallel to axis of ring)

(a)

Ring equator

Six *equatorial* hydrogens
(in a band around the equator of the ring)

(b)

Chair cyclohexane with all its hydrogen atoms;
the axial hydrogens are shown in color

(c)

FIGURE 2.14
Axial and equatorial hydrogen atoms in cyclohexane

Each carbon atom has one axial hydrogen and one equatorial hydrogen. Axial and equatorial bonds can be drawn in the following way (illustrated in Figure 2.15):

1. **Axial bonds:** All six axial bonds (one on each carbon) are parallel. As you proceed around the ring, the axial bonds alternate between top and bottom faces.

2. **Equatorial bonds:** The six equatorial bonds (one on each carbon) come in three sets of parallel lines. Each set is also parallel to two ring bonds, as shown in Figure 2.15. In proceeding around the ring, equatorial bonds alternate between top and bottom faces.

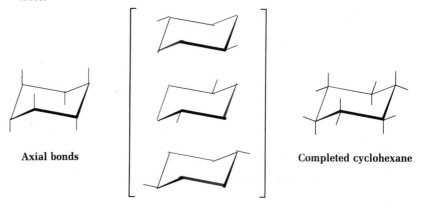

Axial bonds   **Completed cyclohexane**

Equatorial bonds

FIGURE 2.15
Drawing axial and equatorial bonds in chair cyclohexane

PROBLEM 2.19   Make a molecular model of cyclohexane and identify both axial and equatorial bonds.

2.15   CONFORMATIONAL MOBILITY OF CYCLOHEXANE

In light of the fact that chair cyclohexane has two kinds of positions, axial and equatorial, we might expect a monosubstituted cyclohexane to exist in two isomeric forms. In fact, this expectation is wrong; there is only one methyl-cyclohexane, one bromocyclohexane, and so forth.

The explanation for this paradox is that cyclohexane is conformationally mobile. Different chair cyclohexanes can readily interconvert, with the result that axial and equatorial positions become interchanged. This interconversion of chair conformations, usually referred to as a **ring-flip**, is shown in Figure 2.16. Molecular models show the process more clearly, and you should practice with models while studying this material.

We can mentally ring-flip a chair cyclohexane by holding the middle four carbon atoms in place while folding the two ends in opposite directions. The net result of carrying out a ring-flip is the interconversion of axial and equatorial

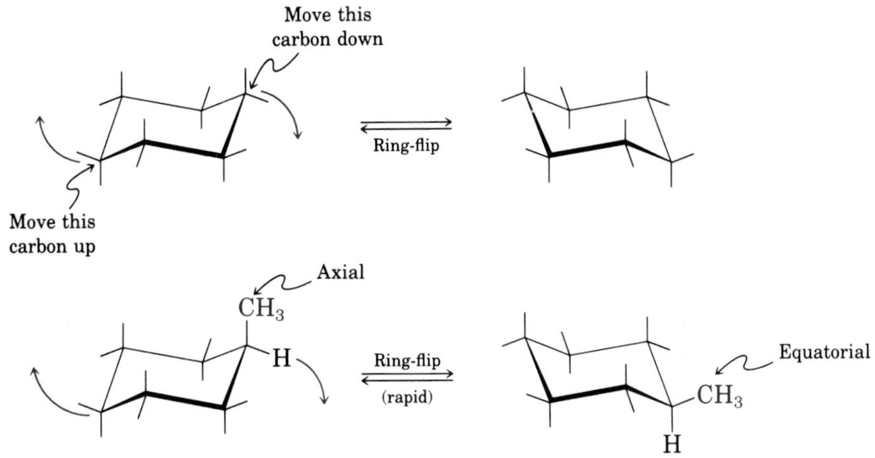

Move this
carbon down

Ring-flip

Move this
carbon up

Axial
CH_3

H

Ring-flip
(rapid)

Equatorial
CH_3

H

FIGURE 2.16
Cyclohexane ring-flips interconvert axial and equatorial positions

positions. An axial position in one chair form becomes an equatorial position in the ring-flipped chair form, and vice versa. For example, axial methylcyclohexane becomes equatorial methylcyclohexane after a ring-flip (Figure 2.16). Since this interconversion occurs rapidly at room temperature, we can isolate only a single structure rather than distinct axial and equatorial isomers.

Even though axial and equatorial methylcyclohexanes interconvert rapidly, they are not equally stable. At any given instant, approximately 95% of methyl-cyclohexane molecules have an equatorial methyl group and only 5% have an axial methyl group. Equatorial methylcyclohexane is unstrained, but axial methylcyclohexane has an unfavorable interaction between the methyl group on C1 and axial hydrogen atoms on C3 and C5 (Figure 2.17). This **1,3-diaxial**

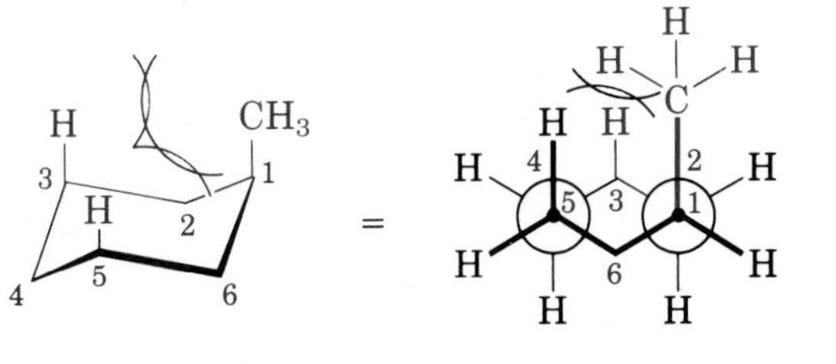

Axial methylcyclohexane
(1.8 kcal/mol steric strain)

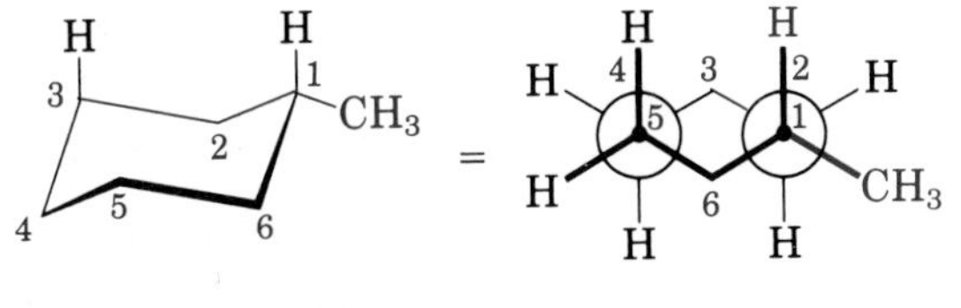

FIGURE 2.17
1,3-Diaxial steric interactions in axial methylcyclohexane

Equatorial methylcyclohexane
(no steric strain)

interaction introduces 1.8 kcal/mol of **steric** (spatial) **strain** into the molecule, and is due to the fact that the axial methyl group and the nearby axial hydrogens are too close together and are trying to occupy the same space.

What is true for methylcyclohexane is also true for all other monosubstituted cyclohexanes: *A substituent is always more stable in an equatorial position than in an axial position.* As might be expected, the amount of steric strain increases as the size of the substituent group increases.

PRACTICE PROBLEM   Draw 1,1-dimethylcyclohexane, indicating whether each methyl group is axial or equatorial.

Solution   First draw a chair cyclohexane ring and then put two methyl groups on the same carbon. The methyl group in the rough plane of the ring must be equatorial and the other (above or below the ring) must be axial.

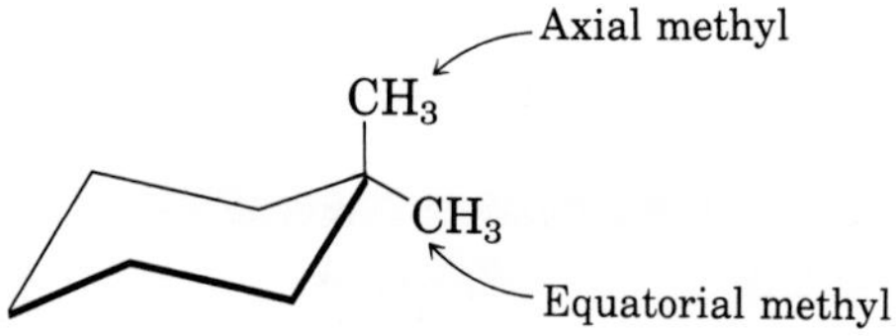

PROBLEM 2.20   Draw two different chair conformations of bromocyclohexane showing all hydrogen atoms. Label all positions as axial or equatorial. Which of the two conformations do you think is more stable?

PROBLEM 2.21   Explain why a *cis*-1,2-disubstituted cyclohexane such as *cis*-1,2-dichlorocyclohexane must have one group axial and one equatorial.

PROBLEM 2.22   Explain why a *trans*-1,2-disubstituted cyclohexane must either have both groups axial or both equatorial.

ADDITIONAL PROBLEMS

PROBLEM 2.23   Locate and identify the functional groups present in these molecules:

(a)

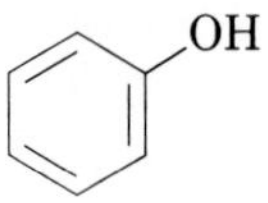

Phenol

(b)

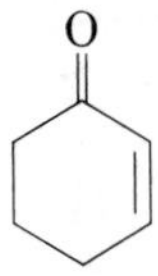

2-Cyclohexenone

(c)

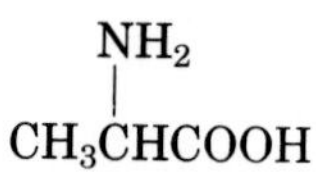

$$CH_3CHCOOH$$

with NH_2 above

Alanine

(d)

NHCOCH$_3$

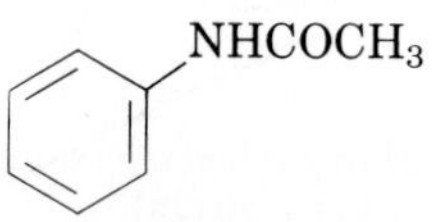

Acetanilide

(e)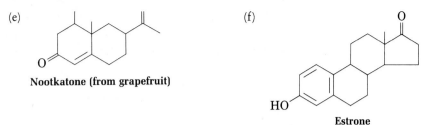

Nootkatone (from grapefruit)

(f)

Estrone

PROBLEM 2.24 Propose structures that fit these descriptions:

(a) An alkene with six carbons
(c) A ketone with five carbons
(e) A five-carbon ester

(b) A cycloalkene with five carbons
(d) An amide with four carbons
(f) An aromatic alcohol

PROBLEM 2.25 Propose suitable structures for the following:

(a) An alkene, C_7H_{14}
(c) A ketone, C_4H_8O
(e) A dialkene, C_5H_8

(b) A cycloalkene, C_3H_4
(d) A nitrile, C_5H_9N
(f) A dialdehyde, $C_4H_6O_2$

PROBLEM 2.26 How many compounds can you write that fit these descriptions?

(a) Alcohols with formula $C_4H_{10}O$
(c) Ketones with formula $C_5H_{10}O$
(e) Ethers with formula $C_4H_{10}O$

(b) Amines with formula $C_5H_{13}N$
(d) Aldehydes with formula $C_5H_{10}O$
(f) Esters with formula $C_4H_8O_2$

PROBLEM 2.27 Draw all monobromo derivatives of *n*-pentane, $C_5H_{11}Br$.

PROBLEM 2.28 Draw all monochloro derivatives of 2,5-dimethylhexane.

PROBLEM 2.29 Propose structures for compounds that contain the following:

(a) A quaternary carbon
(c) An isopropyl group
(e) An amino group ($-NH_2$) bonded to a secondary carbon

(b) Four methyl groups
(d) Two tertiary carbons

PROBLEM 2.30 What hybridization would you expect for the carbon atom in these functional groups?

(a) Ketone   (b) Nitrile   (c) Ether   (d) Alcohol

PROBLEM 2.31 Which of the following structures represent the same compound, and which represent different compounds?

(a)

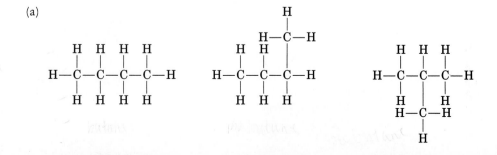

(b)

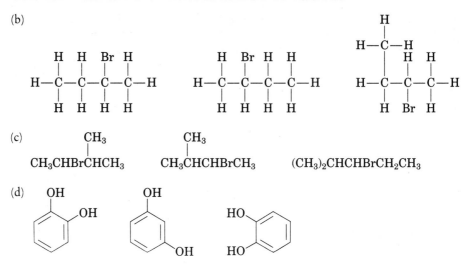

(c)

CH₃CHBrCHCH₃ with CH₃ above

CH₃CHCHBrCH₃ with CH₃ above

(CH₃)₂CHCHBrCH₂CH₃

(d)

[three phenol/catechol ring structures with OH groups]

PROBLEM 2.32 Draw structural formulas for the following:

(a) 2-Methylheptane
(c) 4-Ethyl-3,4-dimethyloctane
(e) 1,1-Dimethylcyclopentane

(b) 4-Ethyl-2-methylhexane
(d) 2,4,4-Trimethylheptane
(f) 4-Isopropyl-3-methylheptane

PROBLEM 2.33 Give IUPAC names for the following alkanes:

(a) 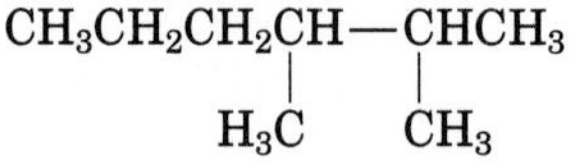 CH₃CH₂CH₂CH—CHCH₃
             | |
            H₃C CH₃

(b) 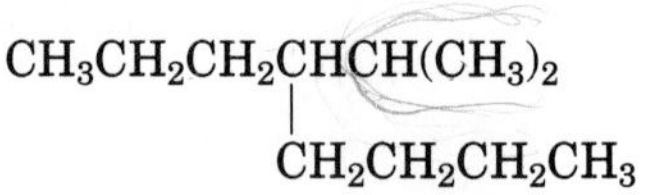 CH₃CH₂CH₂CHCH(CH₃)₂
                  |
             CH₂CH₂CH₂CH₃

(c) 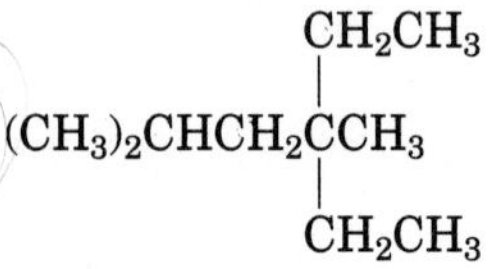 (CH₃)₂CHCH₂CCH₃
           CH₂CH₃ (above)
           CH₂CH₃ (below)

(d) C(CH₂CH₃)₄

PROBLEM 2.34 For each of the following compounds, draw an isomer having the same functional groups:

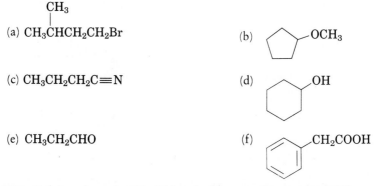

(a) CH₃CHCH₂CH₂Br with CH₃ above

(b) [cyclopentane]—OCH₃

(c) CH₃CH₂CH₂C≡N

(d) [cyclohexane]—OH

(e) CH₃CH₂CHO

(f) [benzene ring]—CH₂COOH

PROBLEM 2.35 Sighting along the C2–C3 bond of butane, there are two different staggered conformations possible. Draw them both in Newman projection. Which of the two do you think is lower in energy?

PROBLEM 2.36   Sighting along the C2–C3 bond of butane (Problem 2.35), there are also two differ-ent eclipsed conformations possible. Draw them both in Newman projection. Which of the two do you think is lower in energy?

PROBLEM 2.37   *cis*-1-*tert*-Butyl-4-methylcyclohexane exists almost exclusively in the conformation shown. What does this tell you about the relative sizes of a *tert*-butyl substituent and a methyl substituent?

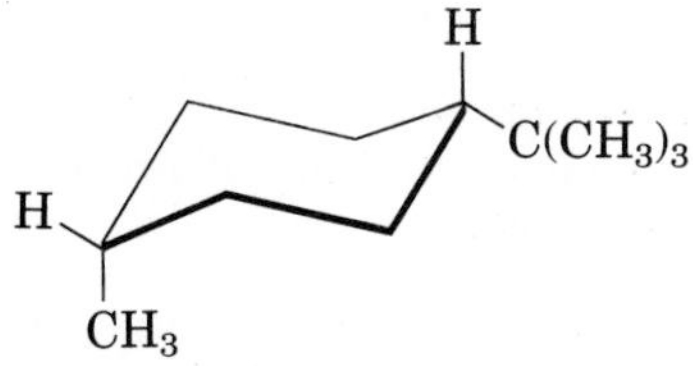

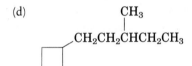

cis-1-*tert*-Butyl-4-methylcyclohexane

PROBLEM 2.38   Supply proper IUPAC names for the following:

(a) 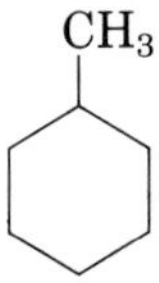   CH₃

(b) 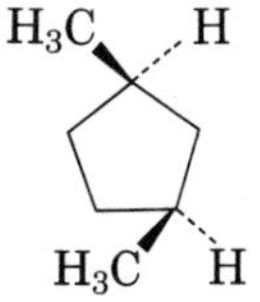   H₃C.   ..H

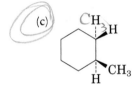

(c)

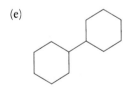

(d)   CH₃
                                                              |
                                        CH₂CH₂CHCH₂CH₃

(e)

PROBLEM 2.39   Provide IUPAC names for the five isomers of C_6H_{14}.

PROBLEM 2.40   Draw structures for the nine isomers of C_7H_{16}.

PROBLEM 2.41   Propose structures and give correct IUPAC names for the following:

(a)   A dimethyloctane   (b)   A diethyldimethylhexane
(c)   A cycloalkane with three methyl groups

PROBLEM 2.42   Consider 2-methylbutane. Sighting along the C2–C3 bond:

(a)   Draw a Newman projection of the most stable conformation.
(b)   Draw a Newman projection of the least stable conformation.

PROBLEM 2.43   The barrier to rotation about the C—C bond in bromoethane is 3.6 kcal/mol.

(a)   What energy value can you assign to an H—Br eclipsing interaction?
(b)   Construct a quantitative diagram of energy versus angle of rotation.

PROBLEM 2.44 Malic acid, $C_4H_6O_5$, has been isolated from apples. Since malic acid reacts with 2 equiv of base, it can be formulated as a dicarboxylic acid.

(a) Draw at least five possible structures for malic acid.
(b) If malic acid is also a secondary alcohol (has an —OH group attached to a secondary carbon), what is its structure?

PROBLEM 2.45 Cyclopropane was first prepared by reaction of 1,3-dibromopropane with sodium.

(a) Formulate the reaction.
(b) What product might the following reaction give? What geometry would you expect for the product?

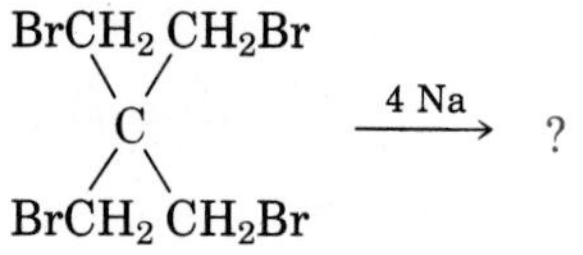

$$\begin{array}{c} BrCH_2\ CH_2Br \\ \diagdown\ \diagup \\ C \\ \diagup\ \diagdown \\ BrCH_2\ CH_2Br \end{array} \xrightarrow{\ 4\ Na\ } \ ?$$

PROBLEM 2.46 Draw *trans*-1,2-dimethylcyclohexane in its most stable chair conformation. Are the methyl groups axial or equatorial?

PROBLEM 2.47 Draw *cis*-1,2-dimethylcyclohexane in its most stable chair conformation. Are the methyl groups axial or equatorial. Which do you think is more stable, *cis*-1,2-dimethylcyclohexane or *trans*-1,2-dimethylcyclohexane (Problem 2.46)?

PROBLEM 2.48 *N*-Methylpiperidine is known to have the conformation shown. What does this tell you about the relative steric requirements of a methyl group versus an electron lone pair?

N-Methylpiperidine

PROBLEM 2.49 Glucose contains a six-membered ring in which all the substituents are equatorial. Draw glucose in its more stable chair conformation.

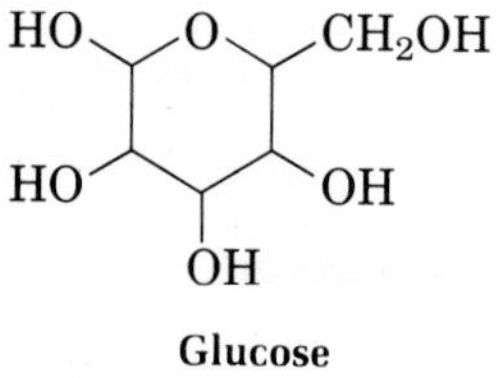

Glucose

Occurrence and Uses of Alkanes. Petroleum

Many alkanes occur naturally in the plant and animal world. For example, the waxy coating on cabbage leaves contains nonacosane, $C_{29}H_{60}$, and the wood oil of the Jeffrey pine common to the Sierra Nevada mountains contains heptane, C_7H_{16}. But by far the major sources of alkanes are the world's natural gas and petroleum deposits. Laid down eons ago, these natural deposits are derived from the decomposition of organic matter, primarily of marine origin.

Natural gas consists chiefly of methane, but ethane, propane, and butane are also present. **Petroleum** is a highly complex mixture of hydrocarbons that must be *refined* into different *fractions* before it can be used. Refining begins by fractional distillation of crude petroleum into three principal cuts: straight-run gasoline (bp 30–200°C), kerosene (bp 175–300°C), and gas oil (bp 275–400°C). Finally, distillation under reduced pressure gives lubricating oils and waxes, and leaves an undistillable tarry residue of asphalt (Figure A.1).

Petroleum
- Asphalt
- Lubricating oil
- Waxes
- Gas oil (bp 275–400°C) C_{14}–C_{25} hydrocarbons
- Kerosene (bp 175–300°C) C_{11}–C_{14} hydrocarbons
- Straight-run gasoline (bp 30–200°C) C_5–C_{11} hydrocarbons
- Natural gas C_1–C_4 hydrocarbons

FIGURE A.1
The products of petroleum refining

It turns out that straight-run gasoline is a rather poor fuel because of the phenomenon of engine knock. Thus, the simple distillation of petroleum into fractions is just the beginning of the process by which automobile fuel is made. In the normal automobile engine, a piston draws a mixture of fuel and air into the cylinder on its downward stroke, and compresses the mixture on its upward stroke. Just before the end of the compression, a spark plug ignites the fuel and smooth combustion occurs. Not all fuels burn equally well, however. When poor fuels are used, combustion can be initiated in an uncontrolled manner by a hot surface in the cylinder before the spark plug fires. This *preignition*, detected as an engine knock, can destroy the engine in short order by putting irregular forces on the crankshaft.

The fuel **octane number** is the measure by which antiknock properties of a fuel are judged. It has long been known that straight-chain alkanes are far more prone to induce engine knock than are branched-chain compounds. Heptane, a particularly bad fuel, is assigned a base value of 0 octane number; 2,2,4-trimethyl-pentane (trivially known as isooctane) is given a rating of 100.

$$CH_3CH_2CH_2CH_2CH_2CH_2CH_3$$

$$CH_3\overset{\overset{\displaystyle CH_3}{|}}{C}CH_2\overset{\overset{\displaystyle CH_3}{|}}{C}HCH_3$$
$$\underset{|}{}$$
$$CH_3$$

Heptane

Octane number = 0

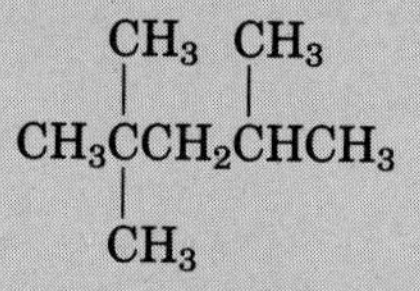

2,2,4-Trimethylpentane
(isooctane)

Octane number = 100

Since straight-run gasoline has a high percentage of unbranched alkanes, it is a poor fuel. Thus, petroleum chemists have devised sophisticated methods for producing better fuels. One of these methods, **catalytic cracking**, involves taking the kerosene cut (C_{11}–C_{14}) and "cracking" it into smaller molecules at high temperature on a silica–alumina catalyst. The major products of cracking are light hydrocarbons in the C_3–C_5 range. These small hydrocarbons are then catalytically recombined to yield C_7–C_{10} branched-chain molecules that are perfectly suited for use as high-octane fuels.

CHAPTER 3

Alkenes: The Nature of Organic Reactions

Alkenes are hydrocarbons that contain a carbon–carbon double-bond functional group. Because of the double bond, alkenes have fewer hydrogens than related alkanes and are therefore referred to as **unsaturated**. Alkanes, by contrast, have the maximum number of hydrogens and are thus **saturated**. For example, the alkene ethylene has the formula C_2H_4, but ethane has the formula C_2H_6.

Alkenes occur abundantly in nature, and many have important biological roles. For example, ethylene is a plant hormone that induces ripening in fruit, and α-pinene is the major constituent of turpentine.

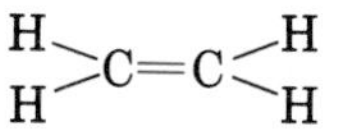

Ethylene   **α-Pinene**

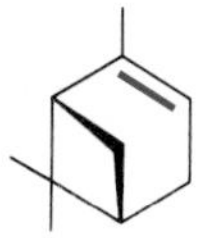

3.1 NOMENCLATURE OF ALKENES

Alkenes are named systematically by following a series of rules similar to those developed for alkanes, with the suffix *-ene* used in place of *-ane*. Three basic steps are used:

Step 1 Name the parent hydrocarbon. Find the longest carbon chain containing the double bond, and name the compound accordingly, using the suffix *-ene*:

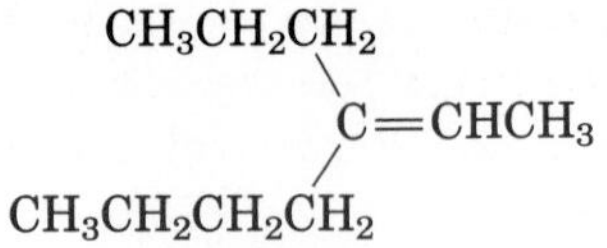

$$CH_3CH_2CH_2$$
$$CH_3CH_2CH_2CH_2$$
C=CHCH₃   Named as a heptene

NOT

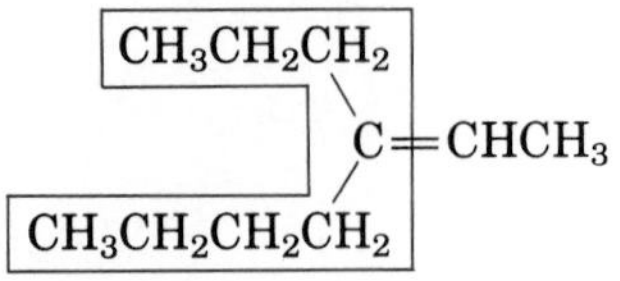

$CH_3CH_2CH_2$
$CH_3CH_2CH_2CH_2$
C=CHCH₃   as an octene, since the double bond is not contained in the eight-carbon chain

Step 2 Number the carbon atoms in the chain. Beginning at the end nearer the double bond, assign numbers to the carbon atoms in the chain. If the double bond is equidistant from the two ends, begin numbering at the end nearer the first branch point:

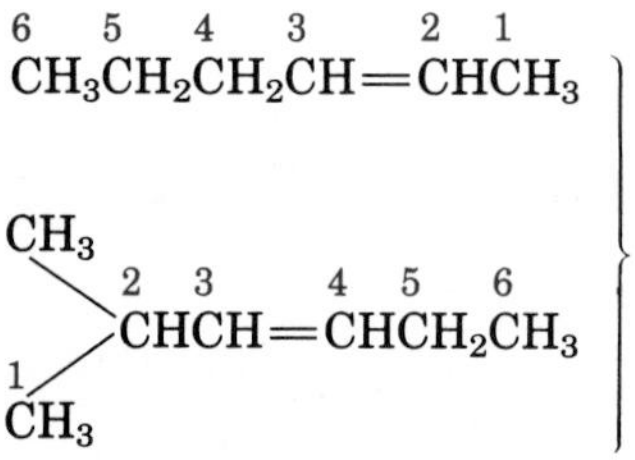

$$\overset{6}{C}H_3\overset{5}{C}H_2\overset{4}{C}H_2\overset{3}{C}H=\overset{2}{C}H\overset{1}{C}H_3$$

CH_3
$\overset{2}{C}H\overset{3}{C}H=\overset{4}{C}H\overset{5}{C}H_2\overset{6}{C}H_3$
$\overset{1}{C}H_3$

Correct numbering

Step 3 Write out the full name. Number the substituents according to their position in the chain and list them alphabetically. Indicate the position of the double bond by giving the number of the *first* alkene carbon. If more than one double bond is present, indicate the position of each and use one of the suffixes *-diene*, *-triene*, and so on.

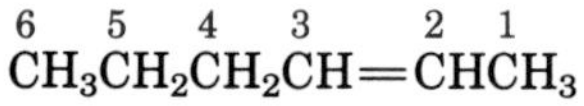

$$\overset{6}{C}H_3\overset{5}{C}H_2\overset{4}{C}H_2\overset{3}{C}H=\overset{2}{C}H\overset{1}{C}H_3$$

2-Hexene

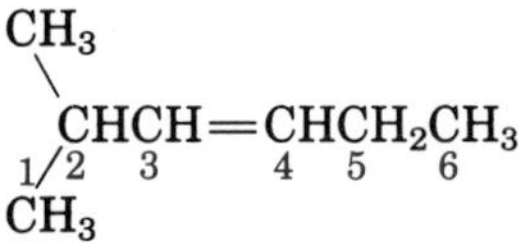

CH_3
$\underset{1/2}{C}H\overset{3}{C}H=\overset{4}{C}H\overset{5}{C}H_2\overset{6}{C}H_3$
CH_3

2-Methyl-3-hexene

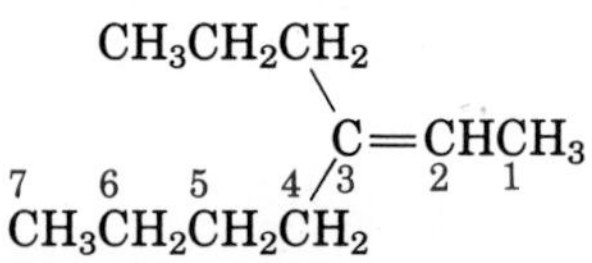

$CH_3CH_2CH_2$
$CH_3CH_2CH_2CH_2$
$\underset{7\ \ 6\ \ 5\ \ 4/3}{}$ C=$\overset{2}{C}$H$\overset{1}{C}$H₃

3-Propyl-2-heptene

CH_3
$H_2\overset{1}{C}=\overset{2}{C}-\overset{3}{C}H=\overset{4}{C}H_2$

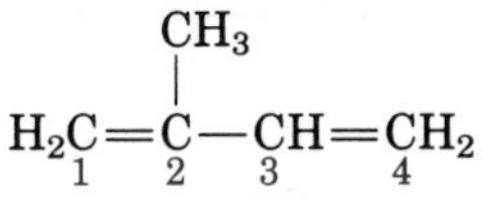

2-Methyl-1,3-butadiene

Cycloalkenes are named in a similar way, but since there is no chain end to begin from, we number the cycloalkene so that the double bond is between C1 and C2 and the first substituent has as low a value as possible:

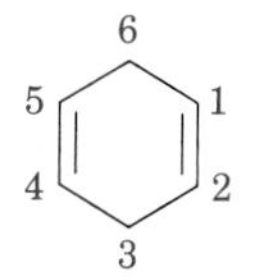

1,4-Cyclohexadiene 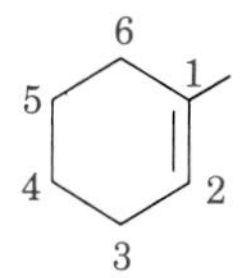   **1-Methylcyclohexene**

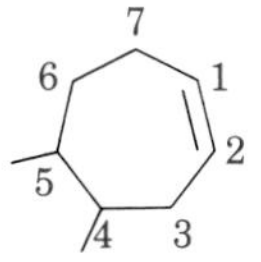

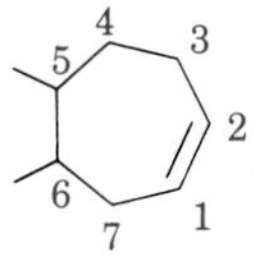

4,5-Dimethylcycloheptene *NOT* **5,6-Dimethylcycloheptene**

There are a small number of alkenes whose names, though firmly entrenched in common usage, do not conform to strict rules of nomenclature. For example, the alkene corresponding to ethane should properly be called ethene. The name ethylene has been used so long, however, that it is accepted by IUPAC. Table 3.1 lists some other trivial names that are recognized by IUPAC.

TABLE 3.1   Trivial names of some common alkenes[a]

Compound	Systematic name	Trivial name
$H_2C{=}CH_2$	Ethene	Ethylene
$CH_3CH{=}CH_2$	Propene	Propylene
$\begin{matrix} CH_3 \\ \diagdown \\ C{=}CH_2 \\ \diagup \\ CH_3 \end{matrix}$	2-Methylpropene	Isobutylene
$H_2C{=}\overset{\overset{\textstyle CH_3}{\vert}}{C}{-}CH{=}CH_2$	2-Methyl-1,3-butadiene	Isoprene
$CH_3CH{=}CHCH{=}CH_2$	1,3-Pentadiene	Piperylene
$H_2C{=}CH{\lessgtr}$	Ethenyl	Vinyl (an alkenyl group)
$H_2C{=}CH{-}CH_2{\lessgtr}$	2-Propenyl	Allyl
$H_2C{\lessgtr}$	Methylene	
$CH_3CH{\lessgtr}$	Ethylidene	

[a]Both trivial and systematic names are recognized by IUPAC.

PROBLEM 3.1   Give proper IUPAC names for these compounds:

(a) $H_2C\!=\!CHCH_2CH(CH_3)_2$ (b) $CH_3CH_2CH\!=\!CHCH_2CH_2CH_3$
(c) $H_2C\!=\!CHCH_2CH_2CH\!=\!CHCH_3$ (d) $CH_3CH_2CH\!=\!CHCH(CH_3)_2$

PROBLEM 3.2   Draw structures corresponding to these IUPAC names:

(a) 2-Methyl-1-hexene   (b) 4,4-Dimethyl-2-pentene
(c) 2-Methyl-1,5-hexadiene   (d) 3-Ethyl-2,2-dimethyl-3-heptene

3.2 ELECTRONIC STRUCTURE OF ALKENES

As we saw earlier in Section 1.10, the carbon atoms in a double bond are sp^2 hybridized and have three equivalent orbitals directed to the corners of an equilateral triangle. The fourth carbon orbital is an unhybridized p orbital, which is perpendicular to the sp^2 plane. When two such carbon atoms approach each other, they form two kinds of bonds—a sigma bond formed by head-on overlap of sp^2 orbitals and a pi bond formed by sideways overlap of p orbitals. The doubly bonded carbons and the four atoms attached to them therefore lie in a plane. The bond angles are approximately 120° (Figure 3.1). As we might expect,

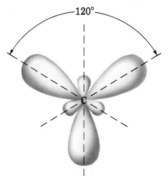

sp^2 hybrid orbitals
(top view)

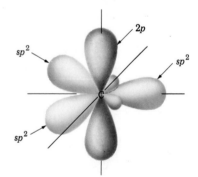

sp^2-hybridized carbon

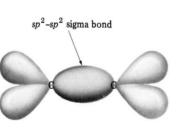

Carbon–carbon double bond;
sigma bonds only

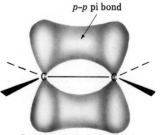

Carbon–carbon double bond;
pi bond only

FIGURE 3.1
An orbital picture of the carbon–carbon double bond

a carbon–carbon double bond is both stronger (152 kcal/mol versus 88 kcal/mol) and shorter (1.33 Å versus 1.54 Å) than a carbon–carbon single bond.

The presence of the double bond in alkenes has numerous consequences. One consequence is the phenomenon of **restricted rotation.** We know from Section 2.7 that relatively free rotation is possible around single bonds and that open-chain alkanes such as propane therefore have many rapidly interconverting conformations. The same is not true for double bonds. Carbon–carbon double bonds do not have circular cross-sections, and therefore, rotation cannot occur freely (Figure 3.2).

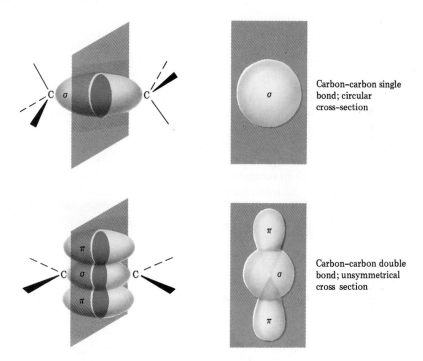

Carbon–carbon single bond; circular cross-section

Carbon–carbon double bond; unsymmetrical cross section

FIGURE 3.2
Cross sections of carbon–carbon single and double bonds: Free rotation is possible around a single bond, but not around a double bond.

If we were to *force* rotation to occur, we would need to break the pi bond temporarily (Figure 3.3, page 72). Thus, the energy barrier to rotation must be at least as great as the strength of the pi bond.

Breaking a chemical bond normally requires a large amount of energy. We can make a rough estimate of how much energy is required to break the pi bond of an alkene by subtracting the value for the strength of an average carbon–carbon single bond from the total bond strength value for ethylene:

Ethylene C=C bond strength (sigma + pi)	152 kcal/mol
− Ethane C—C bond strength (sigma only)	− 88 kcal/mol
Difference (pi bond only)	64 kcal/mol

We predict an approximate bond strength of 64 kcal/mol for the ethylene pi bond, and it is therefore clear why rotation cannot occur (recall that the barrier to rotation for ethane is only 2.9 kcal/mol).

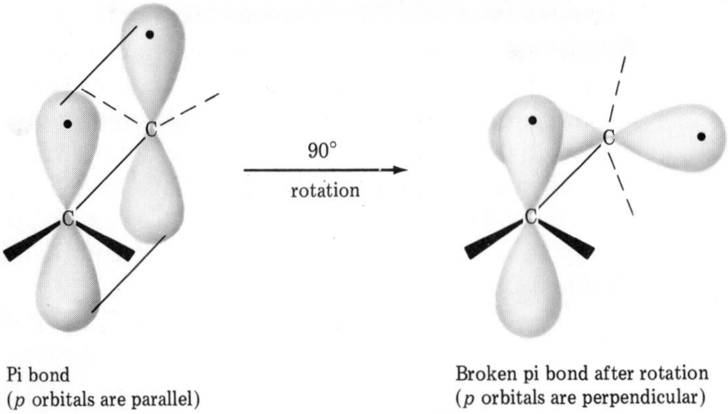

Pi bond
(*p* orbitals are parallel)

Broken pi bond after rotation
(*p* orbitals are perpendicular)

FIGURE 3.3
Breaking the pi bond to bring about rotation

3.3 CIS–TRANS ISOMERS

The lack of rotation around the carbon–carbon double bond is of more than just theoretical interest; it also has chemical consequences. Imagine the situation for a disubstituted alkene such as 2-butene. (*Disubstituted* means two substituents other than hydrogen are bonded to the double-bond carbons.) In 2-butene, the two methyl groups can be either on the *same* side of the double bond or on *opposite* sides (Figure 3.4), a situation that is reminiscent of substituted cyclo-alkanes (Section 2.10).

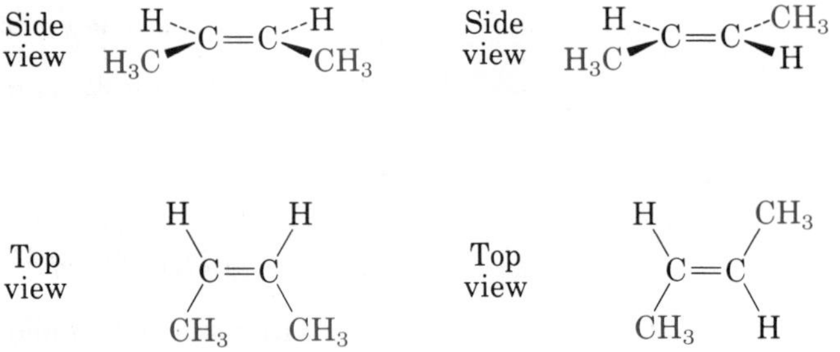

cis-2-Butene

trans-2-Butene

FIGURE 3.4
Cis and trans isomers of 2-butene

Since bond rotation cannot occur, the two 2-butenes do not spontaneously interconvert; they are distinct, isolable compounds. As in Section 2.10, we call such compounds **cis–trans isomers**, because they have the same formula and overall skeleton but differ in the spatial arrangement of atoms. The compound with substituents on the same side is referred to as *cis*-2-butene, and the isomer with substituents on opposite sides is *trans*-2-butene.

Cis–trans isomerism is a common feature of alkene chemistry and is not limited to disubstituted alkenes. Isomerism can occur whenever each of the double-bond carbons is attached to two different groups. If one of the double-bond carbons is attached to two identical groups, however, then cis–trans isomerism is not possible (Figure 3.5).

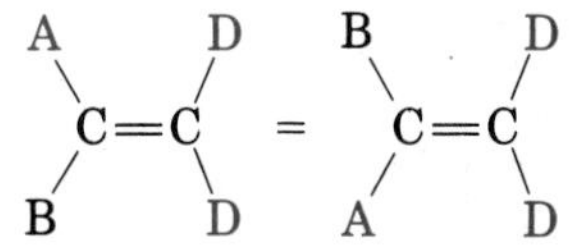

$$
\begin{array}{ccc}
\underset{B}{\overset{A}{}}C=\underset{D}{\overset{D}{}}C & = & \underset{A}{\overset{B}{}}C=\underset{D}{\overset{D}{}}C
\end{array}
$$

These two compounds are identical; they are not cis–trans isomers.

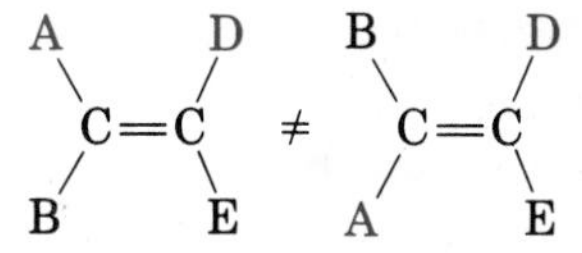

$$
\begin{array}{ccc}
\underset{B}{\overset{A}{}}C=\underset{E}{\overset{D}{}}C & \neq & \underset{A}{\overset{B}{}}C=\underset{E}{\overset{D}{}}C
\end{array}
$$

These two compounds are not identical; they are cis–trans isomers.

FIGURE 3.5
The requirement for cis–trans isomerism in alkenes

PRACTICE PROBLEM Draw the two cis–trans isomers of 2-chloro-2-pentene.

Solution 2-Chloro-2-pentene is $CH_3CH_2CH=C(Cl)CH_3$. The ethyl and methyl groups are on the same side of the double bond in one isomer and on opposite sides in the other isomer.

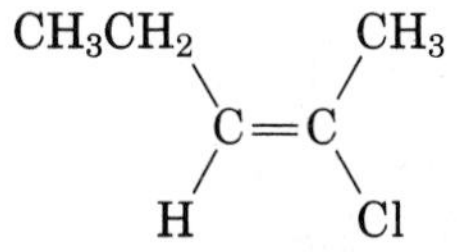

$$
\underset{H}{\overset{CH_3CH_2}{}}C=\underset{Cl}{\overset{CH_3}{}}C \quad \text{and} \quad \underset{H}{\overset{CH_3CH_2}{}}C=\underset{CH_3}{\overset{Cl}{}}C
$$

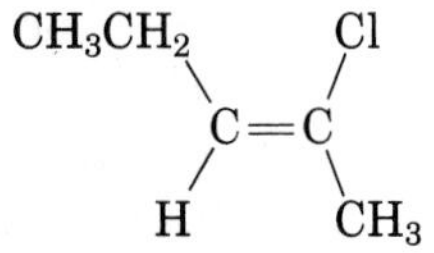

PROBLEM 3.3 Which of the following compounds can exist as pairs of cis–trans isomers? Draw each cis–trans pair.

(a) $CH_3CH=CH_2$ (b) $(CH_3)_2C=CHCH_3$ (c) $ClCH=CHCl$
(d) $CH_3CH_2CH=CHCH_3$
(e) $CH_3CH_2CH=CBrCH_3$
(f) 3-Methyl-3-heptene

PROBLEM 3.4 How can you account for the observation that cyclohexene does not show cis–trans isomerism, whereas cyclodecene can exist in both cis and trans forms? Making molecular models should be helpful.

3.4   SEQUENCE RULES: THE *E,Z* DESIGNATION

In the previous discussion of isomerism in the 2-butenes, we used the terms *cis* and *trans* to denote alkenes whose two substituents were on the same side and opposite sides of a double bond, respectively. This cis–trans nomenclature is unambiguous and quite acceptable for all disubstituted alkenes. But how do we denote the geometry of *tri*substituted (three substituents other than hydrogen) and *tetra*substituted (four substituents other than hydrogen) double bonds?

The answer is provided by the **E,Z system** of nomenclature, which uses a system of **sequence rules** to assign priorities to the groups on the double-bond carbons. Considering each of the double-bond carbons separately, we use the sequence rules to decide which of the two groups on each carbon is higher in priority. If the higher-priority groups on each carbon are on the same side of the double bond, the alkene is designated Z (for the German word *zusammen*, "together"). If the higher-priority groups are on opposite sides, the alkene is designated E (for the German word *entgegen*, "opposite"). The easiest way to remember which is which is to think with a German accent: Z = groups on *ze* zame zide (E = the other one). These assignments are shown in Figure 3.6.

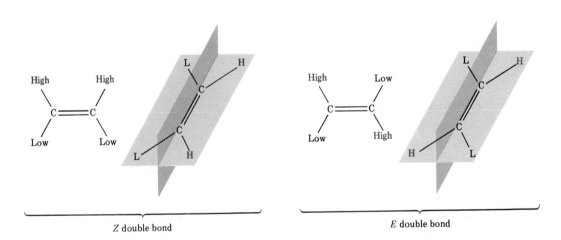

Z double bond   *E* double bond

FIGURE 3.6
The *E,Z* system of nomenclature

The sequence rules used in assigning priorities are as follows:

Sequence rule 1   Look at the atoms directly attached to each carbon and rank them in order of decreasing atomic weight. That is, a high-atomic-weight atom receives higher priority than a low-atomic-weight atom. Thus, the common atoms that we might find attached to a double bond would be assigned the priority sequence Br > Cl > O > C > H. For example:

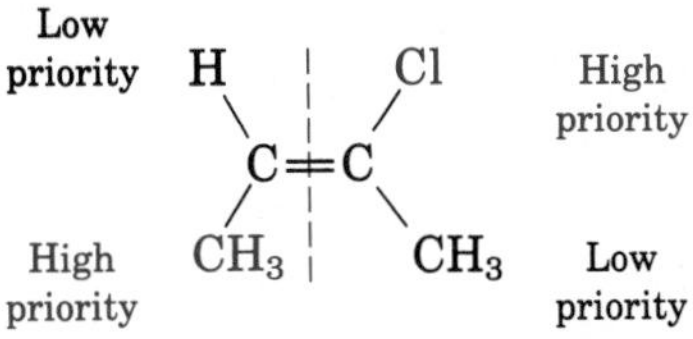

Low
priority H   Cl   High
priority

C=C

High CH₃   CH₃ Low
priority   priority

(E)-2-Chloro-2-butene

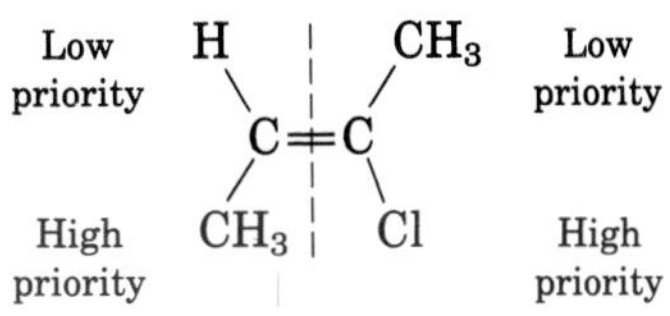

Low H   CH₃ Low
priority   priority

C=C

High CH₃   Cl High
priority   priority

(Z)-2-Chloro-2-butene

Since chlorine has a higher atomic number than carbon, it receives higher priority than a methyl ($-CH_3$) group. Methyl receives higher priority than hydrogen, however, and the left-hand isomer is therefore assigned E geometry (high-priority groups on opposite sides of the double bond). The right-hand isomer has Z geometry (high-priority groups on *ze zame zide* of the double bond).

Sequence rule 2 If a decision cannot be reached by considering the first atoms in the substituent (rule 1), look at the second, third, or fourth atoms away from the double-bond carbons until a difference is found. Thus, an ethyl substituent, $-CH_2CH_3$, and a methyl substituent, $-CH_3$, are equivalent by rule 1 (since both have carbon as the first atom), but by rule 2, ethyl receives higher priority than methyl since the *second* atoms are one carbon and two hydrogens rather than three hydrogens. Look at the following examples to see how this rule is applied:

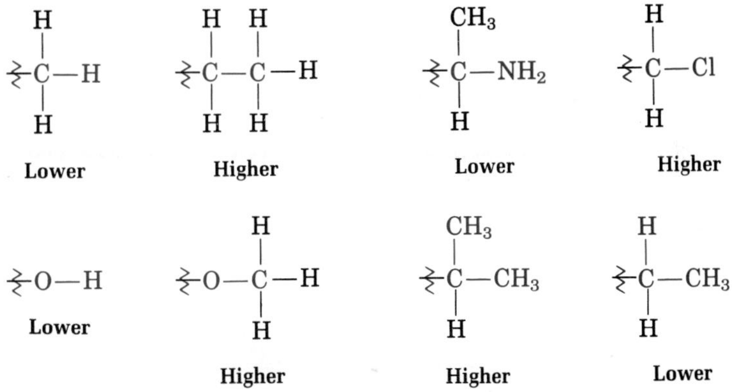

$-C-H$ with H above and H below	$-C-C-H$ with H H above and H H below	$-C-NH_2$ with CH_3 above and H below	$-C-Cl$ with H above and H below
Lower	**Higher**	**Lower**	**Higher**

$-O-H$	$-O-C-H$ with H above and H below	$-C-CH_3$ with CH_3 above and H below	$-C-CH_3$ with H above and H below
Lower	**Higher**	**Higher**	**Lower**

Sequence rule 3 Multiple-bonded atoms are considered to be equivalent to the same number of singly bonded atoms. For example, an aldehyde substituent ($-CH=O$), which has a carbon atom *doubly* bound to *one* oxygen, is considered equivalent to a substituent having a carbon atom *singly* bound to *two* oxygens:

$-C=O$ is equivalent to $-C-O$ (with H above, O and C below)

This carbon is doubly bound to one oxygen   This oxygen is doubly bound to one carbon   This carbon is singly bound to two oxygens   This oxygen is singly bound to two carbons

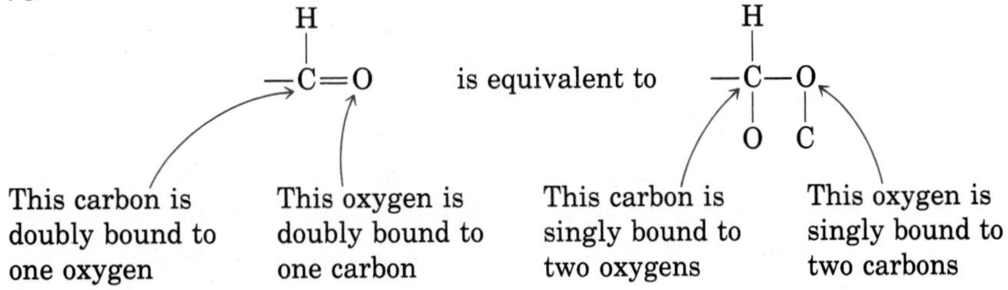

As some further examples, the following pairs are equivalent:

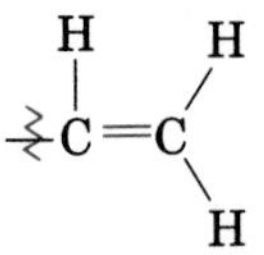

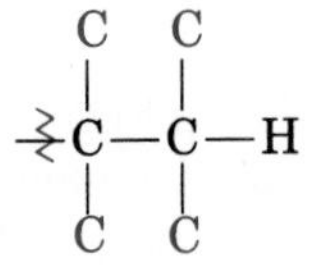

PRACTICE PROBLEM   Assign *E* or *Z* configuration to the double bond in this compound:

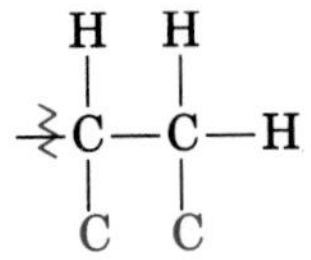

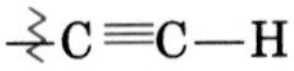

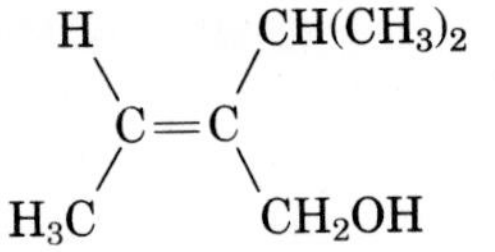

Solution   Look at the two double-bond carbons individually. The left-hand carbon has two substituents, —H and —CH_3, of which —CH_3 receives higher priority by rule 1. The right-hand carbon also has two substituents, —$CH(CH_3)_2$ and —CH_2OH, but rule 1 does not allow a priority assignment to be made since both groups have carbon as their first atom. By rule 2, however, —CH_2OH receives higher priority than —$CH(CH_3)_2$, since —CH_2OH has an *oxygen* and two hydrogens as its second atoms, whereas —$CH(CH_3)_2$ has two *carbons* and one hydrogen as its second atoms. Thus, the two high-priority groups are on the same side of the double bond, and we assign *Z* configuration.

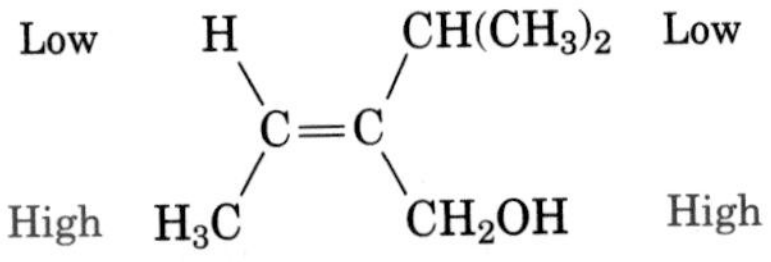

Z configuration

PROBLEM 3.5   Which member in each set is higher in priority?

(a)   —H   or   —Br   (b)   —Cl   or   —Br

(c)   —CH_3 or   —CH_2CH_3 (d)   —NH_2 or   —OH

(e)   —CH_2OH or   —CH_3 (f)   —CH_2OH or   —CH=O

PROBLEM 3.6   Which is higher in priority, $-\overset{\overset{\textstyle O}{\|}}{C}-OH$ or $-\overset{\overset{\textstyle O}{\|}}{C}-OCH_3$? Explain.

PROBLEM 3.7   Which is higher in priority, isopropyl or *n*-octyl? Explain.

PROBLEM 3.8 Assign *E* or *Z* configuration to these alkenes:

(a)

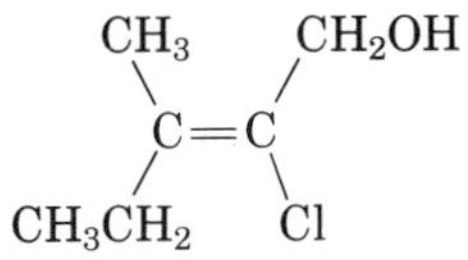

$$CH_3 \quad CH_2OH$$
$$C=C$$
$$CH_3CH_2 \quad Cl$$

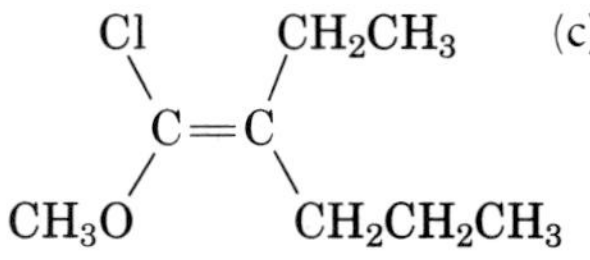

(b)

$$Cl \quad CH_2CH_3$$
$$C=C$$
$$CH_3O \quad CH_2CH_2CH_3$$

(c)

$$H$$
$$H \quad C=CH_2$$
$$C=C$$
$$CH_3 \quad CH_3$$

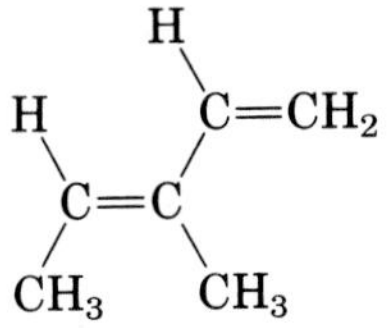

3.5 ALKENE STABILITY

Although the cis–trans interconversion of alkene isomers does not occur spontaneously, it can be made to happen under appropriate experimental conditions (for example, on treatment of the alkene with a strong acid catalyst). If we were to interconvert *cis*-2-butene with *trans*-2-butene and allow them to reach equilibrium, we would find that they are not of equal stability. At equilibrium, the ratio of isomers is 76% trans to 24% cis.

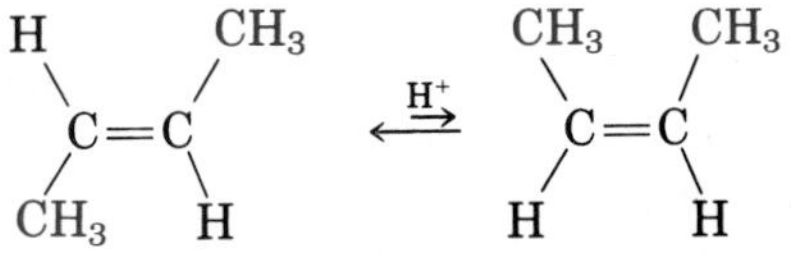

$$H \quad CH_3$$
$$C=C$$
$$CH_3 \quad H$$

$$\overset{H^+}{\rightleftharpoons}$$

$$CH_3 \quad CH_3$$
$$C=C$$
$$H \quad H$$

Trans (76%)   **Cis (24%)**

It turns out to be a general phenomenon that cis alkenes are less stable than their trans isomers because of spatial interference (steric strain) between the bulky substituents on the same side of the double bond. This is the same kind of steric strain that we saw previously in axial methylcyclohexane (Section 2.15).

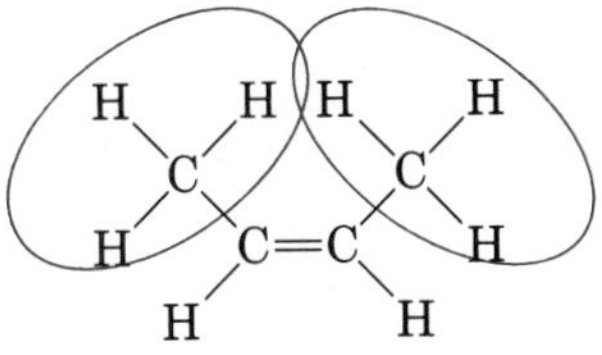

Steric strain in
***cis*-2-butene**

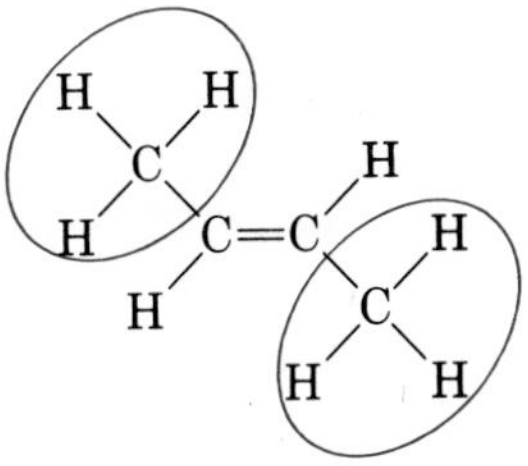

No steric strain in
***trans*-2-butene**

It also turns out to be generally true that alkenes become more stable with increasing alkyl substitution. Thus, alkenes follow the stability order:

Tetrasubstituted > Trisubstituted >   Disubstituted   > Monosubstituted

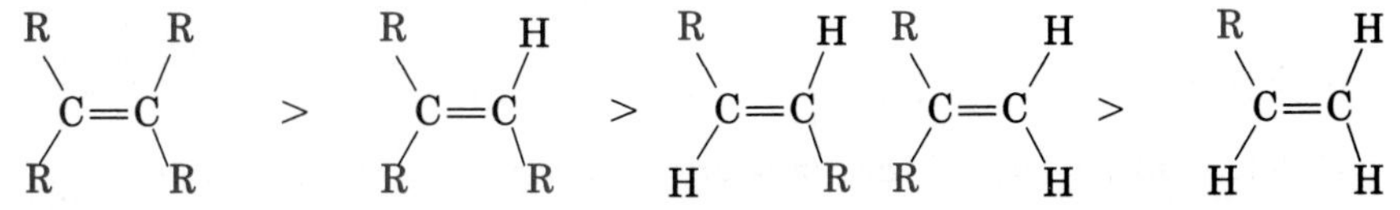

$$R \quad R$$
$$C=C$$
$$R \quad R$$
>
$$R \quad H$$
$$C=C$$
$$R \quad R$$
>
$$R \quad H \quad R \quad H$$
$$C=C \quad C=C$$
$$H \quad R \quad R \quad H$$
>
$$R \quad H$$
$$C=C$$
$$H \quad H$$

PROBLEM 3.9   Which alkene in each of the following sets is more stable?

    (a) 1-Butene or 2-butene   (b) (Z)-2-Hexene or (E)-2-hexene

    (c) 1-Methylcyclohexene or 3-methylcyclohexene

3.6   ORGANIC REACTIONS

When first approached, organic chemistry can seem like a bewildering collection of isolated facts—a collection of millions of compounds, dozens of functional groups, and a seemingly endless number of reactions. With study, however, it soon becomes evident that there are only a few fundamental concepts that underlie *all* organic reactions. Far from being a collection of isolated facts, organic chemistry is a beautifully logical subject that is unified by a few broad themes. When these themes are understood, learning organic chemistry becomes much easier and rote memorization can be avoided. The aim of this book is to point out the patterns and to clarify the themes that unify organic chemistry. Let's begin by seeing what fundamental kinds of organic reactions take place and how they can be described.

All chemical reactions involve bond breaking and bond making. When two starting materials come together, react, and yield products, specific chemical bonds in the starting materials are broken, and new bonds in the products are formed.

Fundamentally, there are only two ways in which a covalent two-electron bond can break. A bond can break in an electronically *symmetrical* way such that one electron remains with each product fragment, or a bond can break in an electronically *unsymmetrical* way such that both bonding electrons remain with one product fragment, leaving the other fragment with an empty orbital. The symmetrical cleavage is called a **homolytic** process, and the unsymmetrical cleavage is called a **heterolytic** process.

$$A\!:\!B \longrightarrow A\!\cdot\; +\; \cdot B \qquad \text{Radical bond breaking (homolytic)}$$

$$A\!:\!B \longrightarrow A^+\; +\; :\!B^- \qquad \text{Polar bond breaking (heterolytic)}$$

Conversely, there are only two ways in which a covalent two-electron bond can form. A bond can form in an electronically symmetrical (**homogenic**) way when one electron is donated to the new bond by each reactant, or a bond can form in an electronically unsymmetrical (**heterogenic**) way when both bonding electrons are donated to the new bond by one reactant.

$$A\!\cdot\; +\; \cdot B \longrightarrow A\!:\!B \qquad \text{Radical bond making (homogenic)}$$

$$A^+\; +\; :\!B^- \longrightarrow A\!:\!B \qquad \text{Polar bond making (heterogenic)}$$

Those processes that involve symmetrical bond breaking and making are called **radical reactions**. A radical is a species that contains an *odd* number of valence electrons and thus has an orbital that contains only one electron. Those processes that involve unsymmetrical bond breaking and making are called **polar reactions**. Polar reactions always involve species that contain an *even* number of valence electrons. Polar processes are the more commonly encountered reaction type in organic chemistry, and a large part of this book is devoted to their description.

3.7 POLAR REACTIONS

In order to see how polar reactions occur, we need to recall our previous discussion of polar covalent bonds and to look further into the effects of bond polarity on organic molecules. We saw in Section 1.12 that specific bonds within a molecule, particularly the bonds in functional groups, often have an unsymmetrical distribution of electrons and are therefore polar. When carbon bonds to an electronegative atom such as chlorine or oxygen, the bond is polarized such that carbon bears a partial positive charge (δ^+) and the electronegative atom bears a partial negative charge (δ^-). Conversely, when carbon bonds to an atom that is less electronegative than itself, polarity in the opposite sense results. Such is the case with most carbon–metal (**organometallic**) bonds:

$$\overset{\delta^+}{C}-\overset{\delta^-}{X} \qquad\qquad \overset{\delta^-}{C}-\overset{\delta^+}{M}$$

$$X = O, N, F, Cl, Br, I \qquad M = \text{a metal such as Mg or Li}$$

The polarity patterns of some common functional groups are shown in Table 3.2 on page 80.

What does functional group polarity mean with respect to chemical reactions? *Since unlike charges attract, the fundamental characteristic of all polar reactions is that the electron-rich sites in the functional groups of one molecule react with electron-poor sites in the functional groups of another molecule.* Bonds are made in a polar reaction when the electron-rich reagent donates a *pair* of electrons to the electron-poor reagent; conversely, bonds are broken in polar reactions when one of the two product fragments leaves with the electron *pair*.

Chemists normally indicate the electron movement that occurs during a polar reaction by using curved arrows. By convention, a curved arrow means that, during the reaction, an electron pair has moved from the tail to the head of the arrow. In referring to this fundamental process, chemists have coined the words **nucleophile** and **electrophile**. A nucleophile is a reagent that is "nucleus-loving"; nucleophiles have electron-rich sites and can form a bond by *donating* an electron pair to an electron-poor site. An electrophile, by contrast, is "electron-loving"; electrophiles have electron-poor sites and can form a bond by *accepting* an electron pair from a nucleophile.

TABLE 3.2　Polarity patterns in some functional groups

Compound type	Functional group structure	Compound type	Functional group structure
Alcohol	$\overset{\displaystyle\diagdown}{\underset{\diagup}{\text{C}}}\!\!\overset{\delta^+}{-}\!\!\overset{\delta^-}{\text{OH}}$	Carbonyl	$\overset{\displaystyle\diagdown}{\underset{\diagup}{\text{C}}}\!\!\overset{\delta^+}{=}\!\!\overset{\delta^-}{\text{O}}$
Alkene	$\overset{\diagdown}{\underset{\diagup}{\text{C}}}=\overset{\diagup}{\underset{\diagdown}{\text{C}}}$ Symmetrical, nonpolar	Carboxylic acid	$\overset{\delta^+}{-}\text{C} \overset{\text{O}\ \delta^-}{\underset{\text{OH}\ \delta^-}{\diagup\diagdown}}$
Alkyl halide	$\overset{\displaystyle\diagdown}{\underset{\diagup}{\text{C}}}\!\!\overset{\delta^+}{-}\!\!\overset{\delta^-}{\text{X}}$	Carboxylic acid chloride	$\overset{\delta^+}{-}\text{C} \overset{\text{O}\ \delta^-}{\underset{\text{Cl}\ \delta^-}{\diagup\diagdown}}$
Amine	$\overset{\displaystyle\diagdown}{\underset{\diagup}{\text{C}}}\!\!\overset{\delta^+}{-}\!\!\overset{\delta^-}{\text{NH}_2}$	Aldehyde	$\overset{\delta^+}{-}\text{C} \overset{\text{O}\ \delta^-}{\underset{\text{H}}{\diagup\diagdown}}$
Ether	$\overset{\displaystyle\diagdown}{\underset{\diagup}{\text{C}}}\!\!\overset{\delta^+}{-}\!\!\overset{\delta^-}{\text{O}}\!\!\overset{\delta^+}{-}\text{C}$		
Nitrile	$\overset{\delta^+}{-}\text{C}\overset{\delta^-}{\equiv}\text{N}$	Ester	$\overset{\delta^+}{-}\text{C} \overset{\text{O}\ \delta^-}{\underset{\text{O—C}\ \delta^-}{\diagup\diagdown}}$
Grignard reagent	$\overset{\displaystyle\diagdown}{\underset{\diagup}{\text{C}}}\!\!\overset{\delta^-}{-}\!\!\overset{\delta^+}{\text{MgBr}}$		
Alkyllithium	$\overset{\displaystyle\diagdown}{\underset{\diagup}{\text{C}}}\!\!\overset{\delta^-}{-}\!\!\overset{\delta^+}{\text{Li}}$	Ketone	$\overset{\delta^+}{-}\text{C} \overset{\text{O}\ \delta^-}{\underset{\text{C}}{\diagup\diagdown}}$

The curved arrow shows that
electrons are moving from :B⁻ to A⁺

$$\text{A}^+ \quad + \quad :\text{B}^- \longrightarrow \text{A}:\text{B}$$

Electrophile　　**Nucleophile**
(electron-poor)　　(electron-rich)

The definitions of electrophile and nucleophile are similar to those given in Section 1.14 for Lewis acid and Lewis base, and there is indeed a correlation. Lewis bases are electron donors and usually behave as nucleophiles, whereas Lewis acids are electron acceptors and usually behave as electrophiles. The major difference, however, is that the terms *electrophile* and *nucleophile* are used specifically when talking about bonds to *carbon*.

PROBLEM 3.10　What is the direction of bond polarity in these functional groups?

(a)　Ketone　　　　　(b)　Alkyl chloride　　　(c)　Alcohol
(d)　Alkyllithium

PROBLEM 3.11   Identify the functional groups present in these molecules and show the direction of bond polarity in each:

(a)   Acetone, $CH_3\overset{\overset{\displaystyle O}{\|}}{C}CH_3$

(b)   Chloroethane, CH_3CH_2Cl

(c)   Methylamine, CH_3NH_2

(d)   Tetraethyllead (the "lead" in gasoline), $(CH_3CH_2)_4Pb$

PROBLEM 3.12   Which of the following would you expect to behave as electrophiles, and which as nucleophiles?

(a) H^+

(b) $H\ddot{O}:^-$

(c) Br^+

(d) $:NH_3$

(e) $H-C\equiv C-H$

(f) CO_2

3.8   AN EXAMPLE OF A POLAR REACTION: ADDITION OF HBr TO ETHYLENE

Let's look in detail at a typical polar reaction, the reaction of ethylene with HBr. When ethylene is treated with hydrogen bromide at room temperature, bromoethane is produced. Overall, the reaction can be formulated as follows:

| Ethylene | Hydrogen bromide | Bromoethane |
| (nucleophile) | (electrophile) | |

This reaction, an example of a general polar reaction type known as an **electrophilic addition,** can be understood in terms of the general concepts just discussed. We'll begin by looking at the nature of the two reactants.

What do we know about ethylene? We know from Sections 1.10 and 3.2 that a carbon–carbon double bond results from orbital overlap of two sp^2-hybridized carbon atoms. The sigma part of the double bond results from sp^2–sp^2 overlap, and the pi part results from p–p overlap.

What kind of chemical reactivity might we expect of carbon–carbon double bonds? First, we know that alkanes, such as ethane, are rather inert, since all outer-shell electrons are tied up in strong, relatively nonpolar, carbon–carbon and carbon–hydrogen bonds. Furthermore, alkane bonding electrons are inaccessible to external reagents since they are localized in sigma orbitals between nuclei. The situation for ethylene and other alkenes is quite different, however. Double bonds have greater electron density than single bonds—four electrons in a double bond versus only two electrons in a single bond. Equally important is the fact that the electrons in the pi bond are accessible to external reagents because they are located above and below the plane of the double bond, rather than between the nuclei (Figure 3.7, page 82).

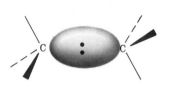

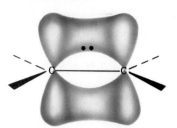

Carbon–carbon sigma bond:
strong; inaccessible bonding electrons

Carbon–carbon pi bond:
weak; accessible electrons

FIGURE 3.7

A comparison of carbon–carbon single and double bonds: A double
bond is both more electron-rich and more accessible than a single bond.

Both electron richness and electron accessibility lead us to predict high reactivity for carbon–carbon double bonds. In the terminology of polar reactions used earlier, we might predict that carbon–carbon double bonds should behave as *nucleophiles*. That is, the chemistry of alkenes should be dominated by reaction of the electron-rich double bond with electron-poor reagents. This is exactly what we find: The most important reaction of alkenes is their reaction with electrophiles.

What about HBr? As a strong mineral acid, HBr is a powerful proton (H^+) donor. Since a proton is positively charged and electron-poor, it is a good electrophile. Thus, the reaction between H^+ and ethylene is a typical electrophile–nucleophile combination, characteristic of all polar reactions.

3.9 THE MECHANISM OF AN ORGANIC REACTION: ADDITION OF HBr TO ETHYLENE

An overall description of how a specific reaction occurs is called a **reaction mechanism**. A mechanism describes in detail exactly what takes place at each stage of a chemical transformation. It describes which bonds are broken and in what order, which bonds are formed and in what order, how many steps are involved, and what the geometric position of each atom is at each moment. A complete mechanism must also account for all reactants used, all products formed, and the amounts of each. When we delve into mechanisms, we are discovering the intimate details by which chemistry takes place.

We can view the electrophilic addition reaction between ethylene and HBr as proceeding by the mechanism shown in Figure 3.8. As indicated, the overall reaction takes place in two distinct steps. The reaction begins with an attack on the electrophile, H^+, by the electron pair from the nucleophilic ethylene pi bond. Two electrons from the pi bond form a new sigma bond between the entering hydrogen and one of the ethylene carbons, as shown by tracing the path of the curved arrow in Figure 3.8. [*Remember:* A curved arrow is used to indicate how electrons move in a polar reaction. In this case, the electrons move away from the carbon–carbon pi bond to form a new bond with the incoming H^+.] The other ethylene carbon atom, having lost its share of the pi electrons, is now trivalent and is left with a vacant *p* orbital. Since the double-bond pi electrons were used in formation of the new C—H bond, the trivalent carbon center remaining has only six electrons in its outer shell and carries a positive charge. This positively charged species, a carbon cation or **carbocation**, is itself an electrophile that can accept an electron pair from nucleophilic bromide anion to form a C—Br bond, yielding the neutral addition product.

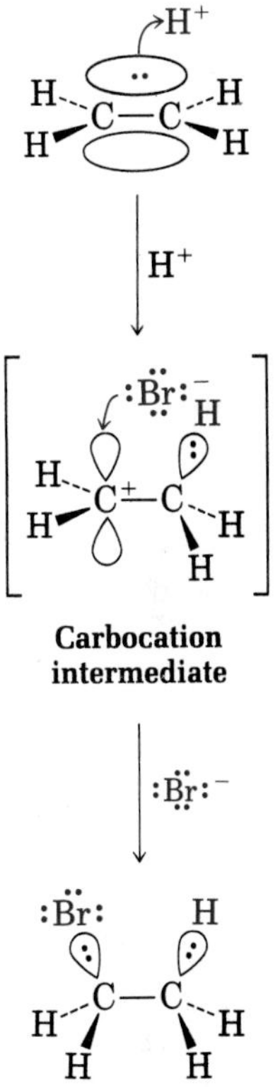

The electrophile, H^+, is attacked by the pi electrons of the alkene, and a new C—H sigma bond is formed. This leaves the other carbon atom with a ⊕ charge and a vacant p orbital.

Carbocation intermediate

Br:⁻ donates an electron pair to the positively charged carbon atom, forming a C—Br bond and yielding a neutral addition product.

FIGURE 3.8
The mechanism of the electrophilic addition of HBr to ethylene: The reaction takes place in two steps and involves an intermediate carbocation.

PRACTICE PROBLEM   What product would you expect from reaction of HBr with cyclohexene?

Solution   HBr should add to the double-bond functional group in cyclohexene in exactly the same way it adds to ethylene, to yield an addition product.

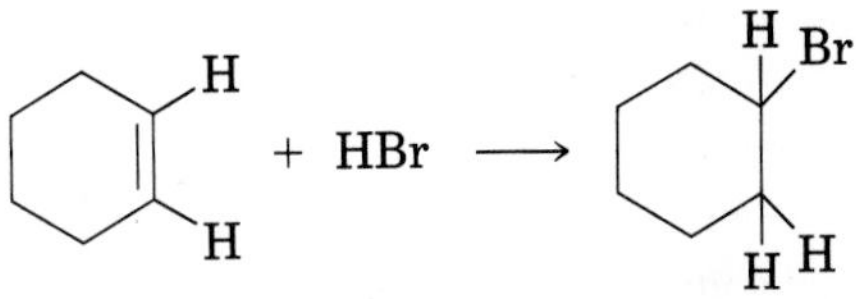

+ HBr ⟶

Bromocyclohexane

PROBLEM 3.13   Reaction of HBr with 2-methylpropene yields 2-bromo-2-methylpropane. Formulate the mechanism of the reaction. What is the structure of the carbocation formed during the reaction?

$$(CH_3)_2C=CH_2 + HBr \longrightarrow (CH_3)_3C—Br$$

PROBLEM 3.14   Reaction of HBr with 2-pentene yields a mixture of two addition products. Write out the reaction and show the two products.

3.10   DESCRIBING A REACTION: RATES AND EQUILIBRIA

In principle, all chemical reactions can be written as equilibrium processes; starting materials react to give products, and products can revert back to starting materials. We usually express a chemical equilibrium by an equation in which K_{eq}, the equilibrium constant (Section 1.13), is equal to the concentration of products divided by the concentration of starting materials. For the reaction,

$$A + B \rightleftharpoons C + D$$

we have

$$K_{eq} = \frac{[\text{Products}]}{[\text{Reactants}]} = \frac{[C][D]}{[A][B]}$$

This equation tells us the position of the equilibrium—that is, which side of the reaction arrow is energetically more favored. If K_{eq} is large, then the product concentrations $[C][D]$ are larger than the reactant concentrations $[A][B]$, and the reaction proceeds as written from left to right. Conversely, if K_{eq} is small, the reaction does not take place as written.

What the equilibrium equation does not tell us is the *rate* of the reaction—How fast is the equilibrium established? Some reactions are extremely slow even though they have highly favorable equilibrium constants. For example, gasoline is stable indefinitely in storage because the rate of its reaction with oxygen is slow under normal circumstances. However, under the proper reaction conditions—contact with a lighted match, for example—gasoline reacts rapidly with oxygen and undergoes complete conversion to the equilibrium products, water and carbon dioxide. Rate (*how fast* a reaction occurs) and equilibrium (*how much* a reaction occurs) are two entirely different characteristics.

What determines whether a reaction will take place? In order for a reaction to have a favorable equilibrium constant, the energy level of the products must be lower than the energy level of the reactants. In other words, energy (heat) must be given off. Such reactions are said to be **exothermic** (from the Greek words *exo*, "outside," and *therme*, "heat"). Heat is produced during exothermic reactions. Some reactions take place even though the energy level of the products is *higher* than the energy level of the reactants, but heat must be *added* for this to happen. Such reactions are said to be **endothermic** (Greek *endon*, "within").

The exact amount of energy either released in an exothermic reaction or absorbed in an endothermic reaction is called the **heat of reaction, ΔH** (spoken as delta-H). By convention, ΔH has a *negative* value in an exothermic reaction since heat is *released*, and a *positive* value in an endothermic reaction since heat is *absorbed*. The heat of reaction is a direct measure of the difference in energy between products and starting materials. As such, the size of ΔH determines the size of the equilibrium constant K_{eq}. Favorable reactions with large K_{eq}'s are highly exothermic and have large negative heats of reaction, whereas unfavorable

[handwritten margin notes:]

FAVORS THIS / RXN

exo. – rxn gives off heat

ΔH = neg. then
$K_{eq} = \dfrac{big}{small} = big$

ΔH = pos.   then
$K_{eq} = \dfrac{small}{big} = small$

reactions with small K_{eq}'s are endothermic and have small positive heats of reaction.

Exothermic if $K_{eq} > 1$; negative value of ΔH

$$A + B \rightleftharpoons C + D$$

Endothermic if $K_{eq} < 1$; positive value of ΔH

PRACTICE PROBLEM Which reaction is more favorable, one with $\Delta H = -15$ kcal/mol or one with $\Delta H = +15$ kcal/mol?

Solution According to convention, reactions with negative ΔH are exothermic and thus favorable, whereas reactions with positive ΔH are endothermic and unfavorable. Therefore, the reaction with $\Delta H = -15$ kcal/mol is more favorable.

PROBLEM 3.15 Which reaction is more exothermic, one with $\Delta H = -10$ kcal/mol or one with $\Delta H = +10$ kcal/mol?

PROBLEM 3.16 Which reaction is more exothermic, one with $K_{eq} = 100$ or one with $K_{eq} = 0.001$?

3.11 DESCRIBING A REACTION: REACTION ENERGY DIAGRAMS AND TRANSITION STATES

In order for a reaction to take place, reactant molecules must collide and reorganization of atoms and bonds must occur. As an example, let's look again at the addition reaction between ethylene and HBr:

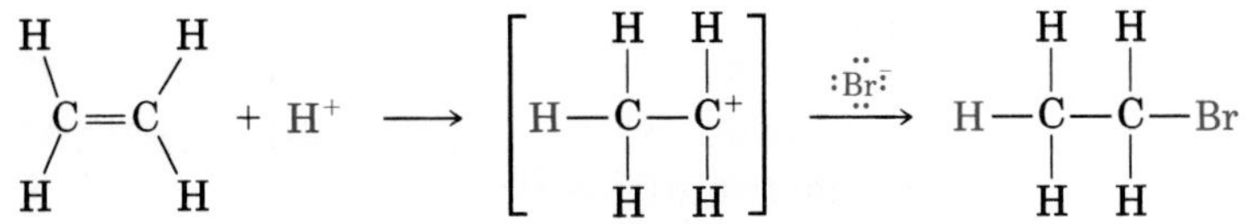

Carbocation

As the reaction proceeds, ethylene and HBr must approach each other, the pi bond must break, a new carbon–hydrogen bond must form in the first step, and a new carbon–bromine bond must form in the second step. Over the years, chemists have developed a method for graphically depicting the energy changes that occur during a reaction using **reaction energy diagrams** of the sort shown in Figure 3.9 on page 86. The vertical axis of the diagram represents the total energy of all reactants, while the horizontal axis represents the progress of the reaction from beginning (left) to end (right). Let's take a careful look at the reaction, one step at a time, and see how the addition of HBr to ethylene can be described on a reaction energy diagram.

At the beginning of the reaction, ethylene and HBr have the total amount of energy indicated by the reactant level on the far left side of the diagram. As the

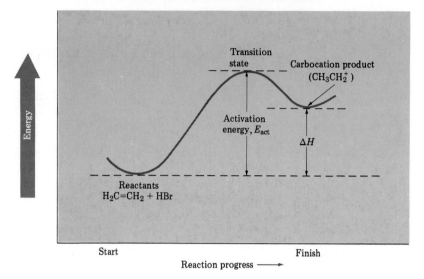

FIGURE 3.9

A reaction energy diagram for the first step in the reaction of ethylene with HBr: The energy difference between reactants and transition state, E_{act}, controls the reaction rate. The energy difference between reactants and carbocation product, ΔH, controls the position of the equilibrium.

two molecules approach each other and reaction commences, a *repulsive* interaction occurs and the energy level therefore rises. This repulsive interaction is due to the spatial (steric) strain introduced by crowding the reactants too closely together. (Recall the similar steric strain encountered in cis alkenes, Section 3.5.) In electronic terms, the electron clouds of the two reactants approach and repel each other. If the collision has occurred with sufficient force and proper orientation, however, the reactants continue to approach each other until the new carbon–hydrogen bond starts to form. At some point, a structure of maximum energy is reached, a structure we call the **transition state** and denote by ‡.

Since the transition state represents the *highest*-energy structure involved in the step, it is unstable and cannot be isolated. We can get no direct information about the exact nature of the transition-state structure, but we can imagine it to be a kind of activated complex of the two reactants in which the carbon–carbon pi bond is partially broken and the new carbon–hydrogen bond is partially formed (Figure 3.10).

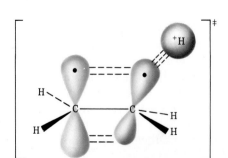

FIGURE 3.10

A hypothetical transition-state structure for the first step of the reaction of ethylene with HBr: The C—C pi bond is just beginning to break, and the C—H bond is just beginning to form.

The energy difference between reactants and transition state, called the **activation energy**, E_{act}, measures how rapidly the reaction occurs. A large activation energy, corresponding to a large energy difference between reactants and transition state, results in a slow reaction because few reacting molecules collide with enough energy to climb the high barrier. A small activation energy results in a rapid reaction since almost all reacting molecules are energetic enough to climb to the transition state. The situation of reactants needing enough energy to climb the barrier from starting material to transition state may be likened to the situation of hikers who need enough energy to climb over a mountain pass. If the pass is a high one, the hikers need a lot of energy and surmount the barrier very slowly. If the pass is low, the hikers need less energy and reach the top quickly.

[handwritten margin notes: large Eact — slow run. small Eact — fast run]

Most organic reactions have activation energies in the range of 10–35 kcal/mol. Reactions with activation energies less than 20 kcal/mol take place spontaneously at room temperature or below, whereas reactions with higher activation energies normally require heating. Heat provides the energy necessary for the reactants to climb the activation barrier.

Once the high-energy transition state has been reached, the reaction continues on to give the carbocation product. Energy is released as the new C—H bond forms fully, and the curve on the reaction energy diagram therefore turns downward until it reaches a minimum. This minimum point represents the energy level of the carbocation product of the first step. The energy change, ΔH, between starting materials and carbocation product is simply the difference between the two levels on the diagram.[1] Since the carbocation is less stable than the starting alkene, the first step is endothermic, and energy is absorbed.

PROBLEM 3.17 Which reaction is faster, one with $E_{act} = 15$ kcal/mol or one with $E_{act} = 20$ kcal/mol? Is it possible to predict which of the two has the larger K_{eq}?

3.12 DESCRIBING A REACTION: INTERMEDIATES

How can we describe the carbocation structure formed in the first step of the reaction of ethylene with HBr? The carbocation is clearly different from the starting materials, yet it is not a transition state and it is not a final product.

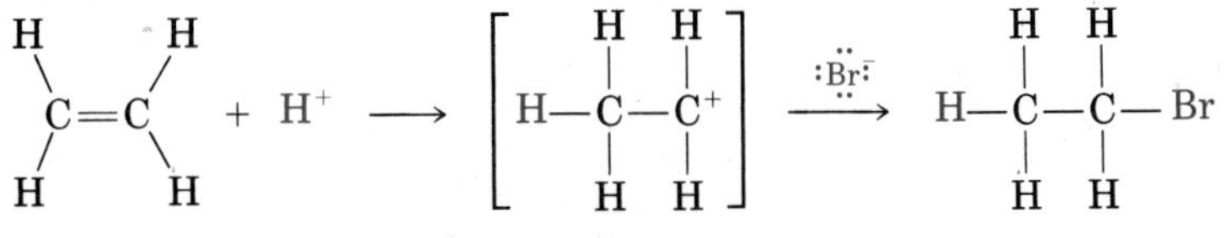

Reaction intermediate

---

[1]Strictly speaking, it is not accurate to say that the energy difference between starting materials and products is due entirely to the heat of the reaction, ΔH. The energy difference is actually defined as the **Gibbs free energy, ΔG**, which is equal to the heat of reaction, ΔH, minus an **entropy contribution, ΔS** ($\Delta G = \Delta H - T\Delta S$, where T is temperature). Normally, however, the entropy contribution is small, and we make the simplifying assumption that ΔG and ΔH are approximately equal.

We call the carbocation, which is formed briefly during the course of the multistep reaction, a **reaction intermediate**. As soon as the intermediate is formed in the first step by reaction of ethylene with H^+, it reacts further with Br^- in a second step to give the final product, bromoethane. This second step has its own activation energy, E_{act}, its own transition state, and its own energy change, ΔH. We can view the second transition state as an activated complex between the electrophilic carbocation intermediate and the nucleophilic bromide anion, in which the new C—Br bond is just starting to form.

A complete energy diagram for the overall reaction of ethylene with HBr can be constructed as shown in Figure 3.11. In essence, we draw diagrams for each of the individual steps and then join them in the middle so that the *product* of step 1 (the carbocation) serves as the *starting material* for step 2. As indicated in Figure 3.11, the reaction intermediate lies at an energy minimum between steps 1 and 2. Since the energy level of this intermediate is considerably higher than the level of either starting material (ethylene + HBr) or product (bromoethane), the intermediate is highly reactive and cannot be isolated. It is, however, more stable than either of the two transition states that surround it.

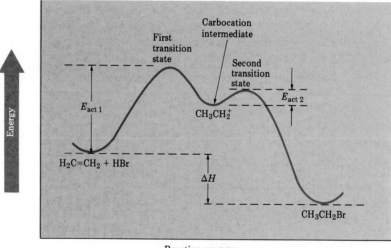

FIGURE 3.11
Overall reaction energy diagram for the reaction of ethylene with HBr: Two separate steps are involved, each with its own transition state. The energy minimum between the two steps represents the reaction intermediate.

Each individual step in a multistep process can be considered separately. Each step has its own E_{act} (rate) and its own ΔH (energy change). The *overall* ΔH of the reaction is the energy difference between initial reactants (far left) and final products (far right). This is always true regardless of the shape of the reaction energy curve. Note, for example, that the energy diagram for the reaction of HBr with ethylene (Figure 3.11) shows the energy level for the final product lower than the energy level for the starting material. Thus, the overall reaction is exothermic.

PROBLEM 3.18   Sketch reaction energy diagrams to represent the following situations. In each case, label the parts of the diagram corresponding to starting material, product, transition state, intermediate (if any), activation energy, and ΔH.

(a)   An exothermic reaction that takes place in one step
(b)   An endothermic reaction that takes place in one step

PROBLEM 3.19   Draw a reaction energy diagram for a two-step reaction with an endothermic first step and an exothermic second step. Label the intermediate.

ADDITIONAL PROBLEMS

PROBLEM 3.20   Provide IUPAC names for these alkenes:

$$CH_3$$
(a) $CH_3CH{=}CHCHCH_2CH_3$

$$CH_2CH_2CH_3$$
(b) $CH_3CH{=}CHCHCH_2CH_2CH_3$

(c) $H_2C{=}C(CH_2CH_3)_2$

(d) $H_2C{=}C{=}CHCH_3$

PROBLEM 3.21   Draw structures corresponding to these IUPAC names:

(a)   3-Propyl-2-heptene
(b)   2,4-Dimethyl-2-hexene
(c)   1,5-Octadiene
(d)   4-Methyl-1,3-pentadiene

PROBLEM 3.22   Neglecting cis–trans isomers, there are five possible isomers of formula C_4H_8. Draw and name them.

PROBLEM 3.23   Draw four possible structures for each of these formulas:

(a) C_6H_{10}
(b) C_8H_8O
(c) $C_7H_{10}Cl_2$

PROBLEM 3.24   Rank the following sets of substituents in order of priority according to the sequence rules:

(a) $-CH_3$, $-Br$, $-H$, $-I$
(b) $-OH$, $-OCH_3$, $-H$, $-COOH$
(c) $-CH_3$, $-COOH$, $-CH_2OH$, $-CHO$
(d) $-CH_3$, $-CH{=}CH_2$, $-CH_2CH_3$, $-CH(CH_3)_2$

PROBLEM 3.25   Assign E or Z configuration to the following alkenes:

(a) $HOCH_2$ \quad CH_3
$$C{=}C$$
CH_3 \quad H

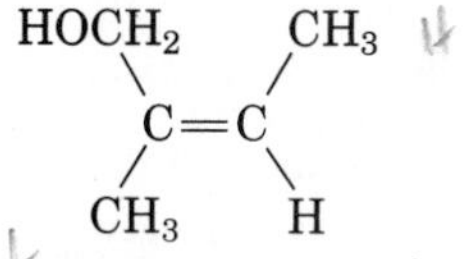

(b) $HOOC$ \quad H
$$C{=}C$$
Cl \quad OCH_3

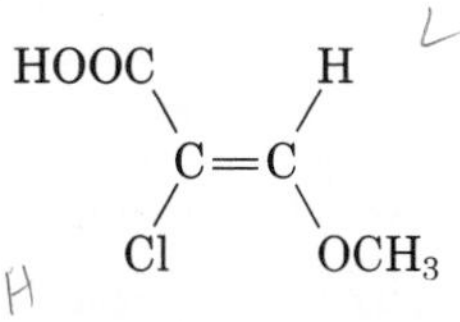

PROBLEM 3.26   Draw and name the five possible C_5H_{10} alkene isomers. Ignore cis–trans isomers.

PROBLEM 3.27   Menthene, a hydrocarbon found in mint plants, has the IUPAC name 1-isopropyl-4-methylcyclohexene. What is the structure of menthene?

PROBLEM 3.28 Name these cycloalkenes according to IUPAC rules:

(a) 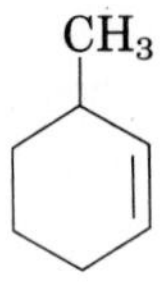 CH₃   (b) 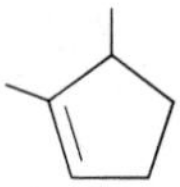   (c) 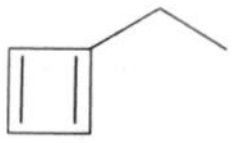   (d)

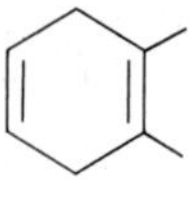

PROBLEM 3.29 Identify the functional groups present in these molecules:

(a) $CH_3C\equiv N$ (b) 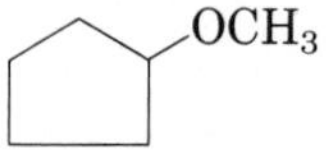   OCH₃

$$\overset{O}{\underset{\parallel}{}}\quad\overset{O}{\underset{\parallel}{}}$$

(c) $CH_3CCH_2COCH_3$ (d)   O

                                                          O

PROBLEM 3.30 Predict the direction of polarization of each of the functional groups you identified in Problem 3.29.

PROBLEM 3.31 Classify the following reagents as either electrophiles or nucleophiles:

$$:O:$$
$$\parallel$$

(a) Zn^{2+} (b) $CH_3\ddot{N}H_2$ (c) $CH_3\overset{..}{C}-\overset{..}{O}:^-$ (d) $H\ddot{S}:^-$

Acetate ion

PROBLEM 3.32 α-Farnesene is a constituent of the natural waxy coating found on apples. What is its IUPAC name?

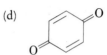

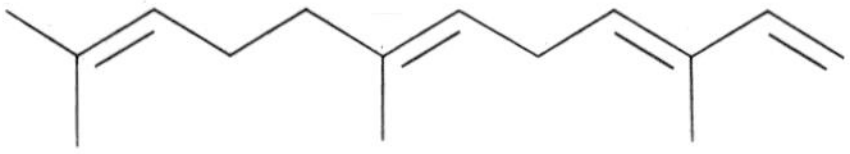

α-Farnesene

PROBLEM 3.33 Indicate E or Z configuration for each of the double bonds in α-farnesene (Problem 3.32).

PROBLEM 3.34 Define the following terms:

(a) Polar reaction   (b) Radical reaction
(c) Functional group   (d) Reaction intermediate

PROBLEM 3.35 Give an example of each of the following:

(a) An electrophile   (b) A nucleophile
(c) An oxygen-containing functional group
(d) A molecule that contains two different functional groups.

PROBLEM 3.36 If a reaction has K_{eq} = 0.001, is it likely to be exothermic or endothermic? Explain.

PROBLEM 3.37 Draw a reaction energy diagram for a two-step exothermic reaction whose first step is faster than its second step. Label the parts of the diagram corresponding to reactants, products, transition state, activation energies, and overall ΔH.

PROBLEM 3.38   Draw a reaction energy diagram for a two-step reaction whose second step is faster than its first step.

PROBLEM 3.39   Draw a reaction energy diagram for a reaction with $K_{eq} = 1$.

PROBLEM 3.40   Describe the difference between a transition state and a reaction intermediate.

PROBLEM 3.41   Consider the reaction energy diagram shown here and answer the following questions:

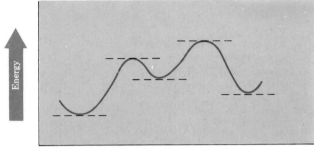

Reaction progress ⟶

(a)   Indicate the overall ΔH for the reaction. Is it positive or negative?
(b)   How many steps are involved in the reaction?
(c)   Which step is faster (has the lower activation energy)?
(d)   How many transition states are there? Label them.

Folk medicine has long held that eating carrots improves night vision. Although this holding is probably not true for healthy adults on a proper diet, there is no question that the chemistry of carrots and the chemistry of vision are related. Alkenes play a role in each.

Carrots are rich in β-carotene, a purple-orange polyene that serves as an excellent dietary source of vitamin A. β-Carotene is converted in the liver, first into vitamin A, and then into 11-*cis*-retinal, the light-sensitive pigment on which the visual systems of all living things are based.

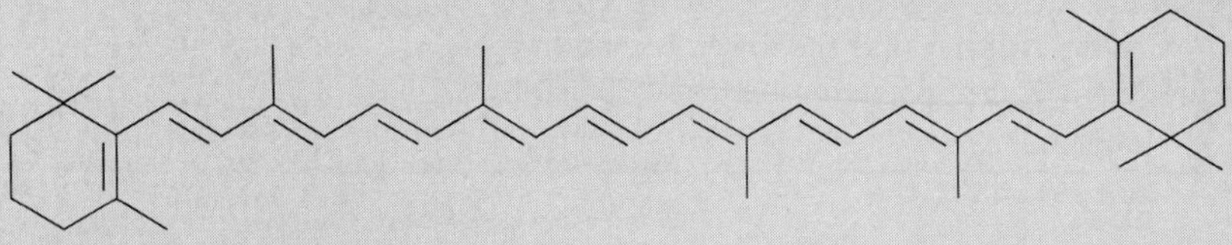

β-Carotene

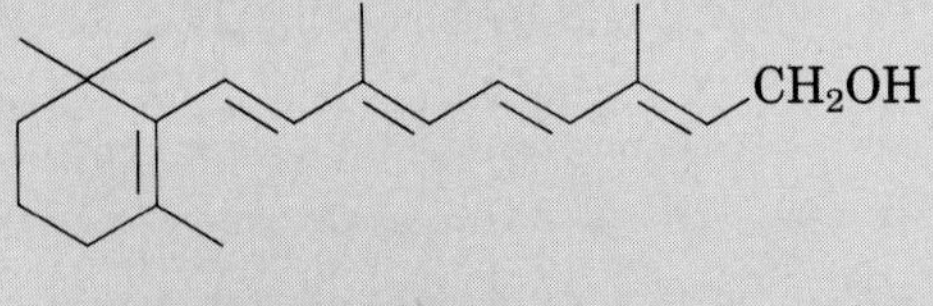

Vitamin A

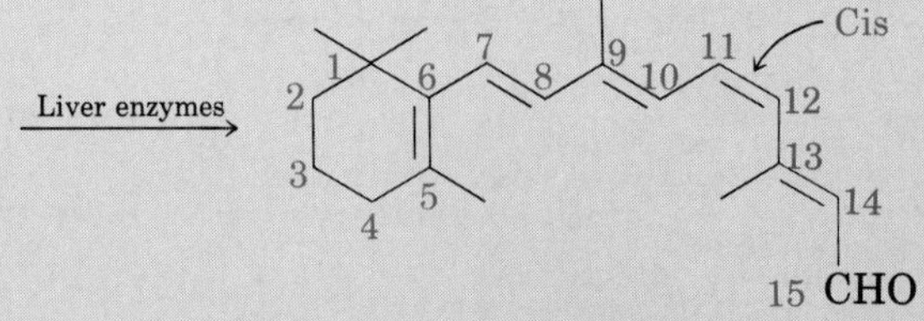

Liver enzymes

11-*cis*-Retinal

There are two types of light-sensitive receptor cells in the eye, *rod* cells and *cone* cells. Rod cells are primarily responsible for seeing in dim light, whereas cone cells are responsible for seeing in bright light and for the perception of bright colors. In the rod cells of the eye, 11-*cis*-retinal is converted into *rhodopsin*, a light-sensitive substance formed from the protein *opsin* and 11-*cis*-retinal. When light strikes the rod cell, isomerization of the C11-C12 double bond occurs and *trans*-rhodopsin, called metarhodopsin II, is produced. This cis–trans isomerization of rhodopsin is accompanied by a change in molecular geometry, which in turn causes a nerve impulse to be sent to the brain where it is perceived as vision.

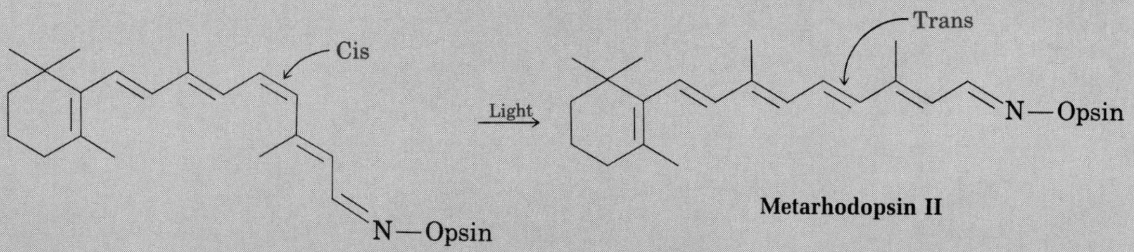

Rhodopsin **Metarhodopsin II**

Metarhodopsin II is then recycled back into rhodopsin by a multiple-step sequence involving cleavage into all *trans*-retinal, conversion to vitamin A, cis–trans isomerization to 11-*cis*-vitamin A, and conversion back to 11-*cis*-retinal (Figure B.1).

β-Carotene
↓
Vitamin A → 11-*cis*-Vitamin A ⟶ 11-*cis*-Retinal
↑ ↓
Retinal ← Metarhodopsin II + Nerve impulse ←(Light)— Rhodopsin

FIGURE B.1
The visual cycle: The actual series of events is more complicated than the diagram indicates, involving several intermediate steps in the light-induced conversion of rhodopsin into metarhodopsin II.

CHAPTER **4**

Alkenes and Alkynes

4.1 REACTIONS OF ALKENES: ADDITION OF HX

We saw in Section 3.9 that alkenes react with HBr to yield addition products. For example, 2-methylpropene reacts with HBr to yield 2-bromo-2-methylpropane. The reaction takes place in two steps and involves a carbocation intermediate.

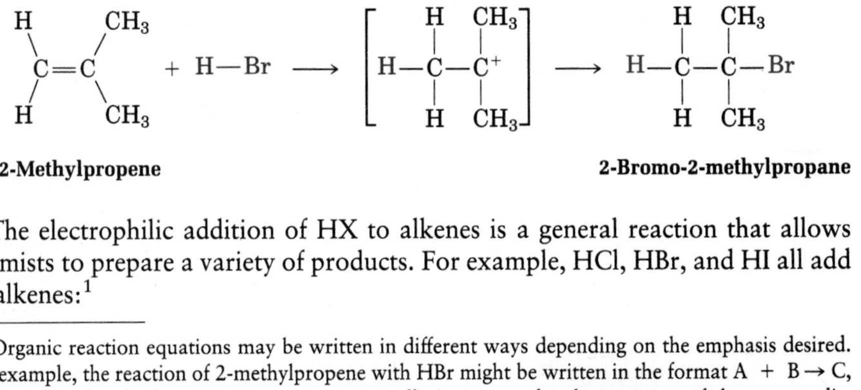

2-Methylpropene   **2-Bromo-2-methylpropane**

The electrophilic addition of HX to alkenes is a general reaction that allows chemists to prepare a variety of products. For example, HCl, HBr, and HI all add to alkenes:[1]

---

[1]Organic reaction equations may be written in different ways depending on the emphasis desired. For example, the reaction of 2-methylpropene with HBr might be written in the format A + B → C, emphasizing that *both* reaction partners are equally important for the purposes of the present discussion. The reaction solvent and notes about other reaction conditions such as temperature can then be noted either above or below the reaction arrow. For example:

$$(CH_3)_2C{=}CH_2 + HBr \xrightarrow{\text{Ether}} (CH)_3CBr$$

Alternatively, we might choose to write the same reaction in the format

$$A \xrightarrow{B} C$$

emphasizing that reagent A is the starting material whose chemistry is of greater interest. Reagent B is then placed above the reaction arrow, together with notes about solvent and reaction conditions. For example:

$$(CH_3)_2C{=}CH_2 \xrightarrow[\text{Ether, 25°C}]{\text{HCl}} (CH_3)_3CCl$$

Reagent

Solvent

Both reaction formats are used in this book, and it is important that the different roles of chemicals shown next to the reaction arrow be understood.

94

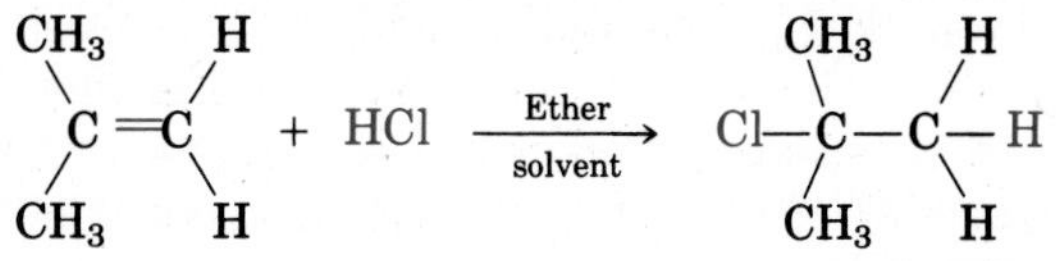

2-Methylpropene

**2-Chloro-2-methylpropane
(94%)**

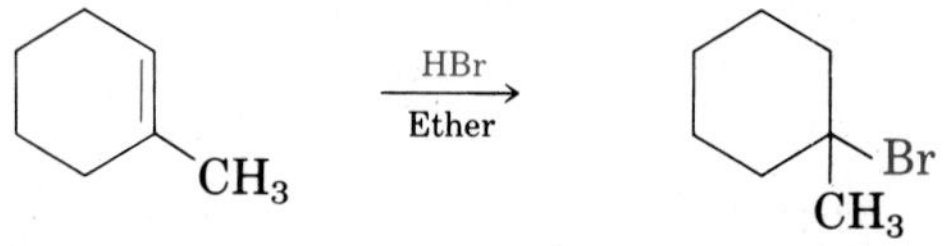

1-Methylcyclohexene

**1-Bromo-1-methylcyclohexane
(91%)**

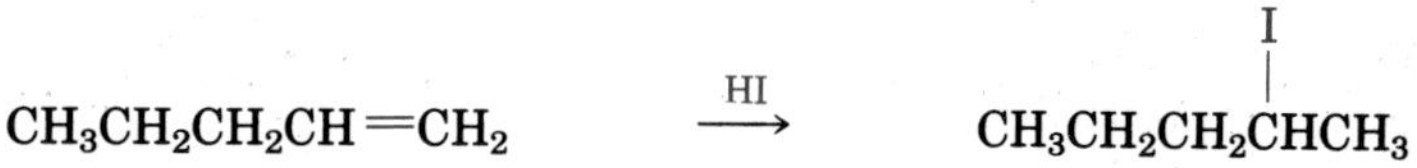

$$CH_3CH_2CH_2CH=CH_2 \xrightarrow{\text{HI}} CH_3CH_2CH_2\overset{\overset{\displaystyle I}{|}}{C}HCH_3$$

1-Pentene

2-Iodopentane

4.2   ORIENTATION OF ELECTROPHILIC ADDITION: MARKOVNIKOV'S RULE

In all the examples just shown, an unsymmetrically substituted alkene has given a *single* addition product, rather than the mixture that might have been expected. For example, 2-methylpropene might have given 1-chloro-2-methylpropane, but it did not. We say that such reactions are **regiospecific** (ree'-jee-oh-specific) when only one of the two possible directions of addition is observed.

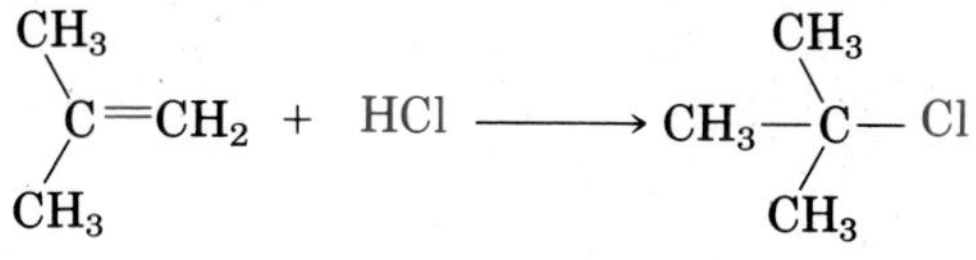

2-Methylpropene

**2-Chloro-2-methylpropane
(sole product; a regiospecific reaction)**

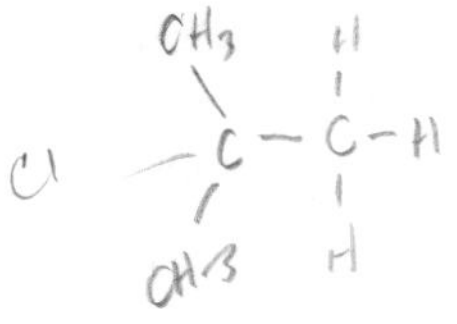

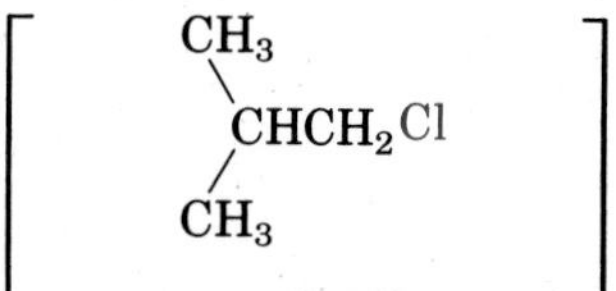

**1-Chloro-2-methylpropane
(*not formed*)**

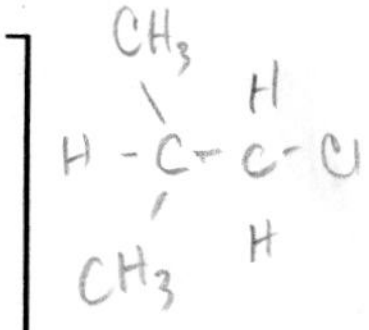

From an examination of many such reactions, the Russian chemist Vladimir Markovnikov proposed in 1869 what has come to be known as **Markovnikov's rule:** *In the addition of HX to an alkene, the H becomes attached to the carbon with fewer alkyl substituents, and the X becomes attached to the carbon with more alkyl substituents.*

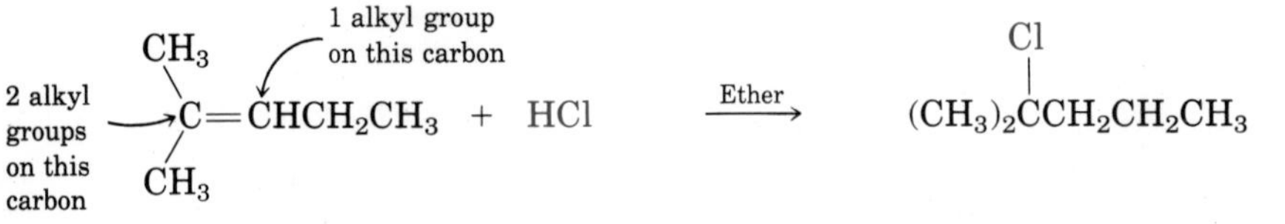

CH₃ handwritten: CH_3 H
$-C-C-H$
CH_3 CH_2CH_3

$(CH_3)_2 C-CH_2CH_2CH_3$
Cl

$$\underset{\text{2-Methyl-2-pentene}}{\underset{\substack{\text{2 alkyl} \\ \text{groups} \\ \text{on this} \\ \text{carbon}}}{}\ \overset{\text{CH}_3}{\underset{\text{CH}_3}{C}}=\overset{\overset{\substack{\text{1 alkyl group} \\ \text{on this carbon}}}{}}{\text{CHCH}_2\text{CH}_3} + \text{HCl}} \xrightarrow{\text{Ether}} \underset{\text{2-Chloro-2-methylpentane}}{(\text{CH}_3)_2\overset{\text{Cl}}{\text{C}}\text{CH}_2\text{CH}_2\text{CH}_3}$$

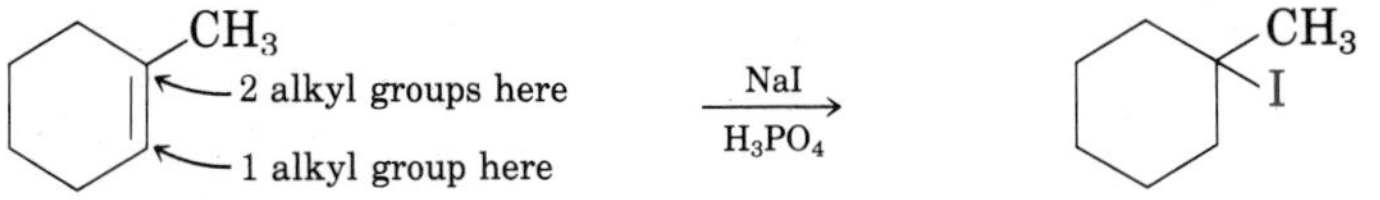

1-Methylcyclohexene
- 2 alkyl groups here
- 1 alkyl group here

$\xrightarrow[\text{H}_3\text{PO}_4]{\text{NaI}}$

1-Iodo-1-methylcyclohexane

When both ends of the double bond have the same degree of substitution, however, a mixture of addition products results:

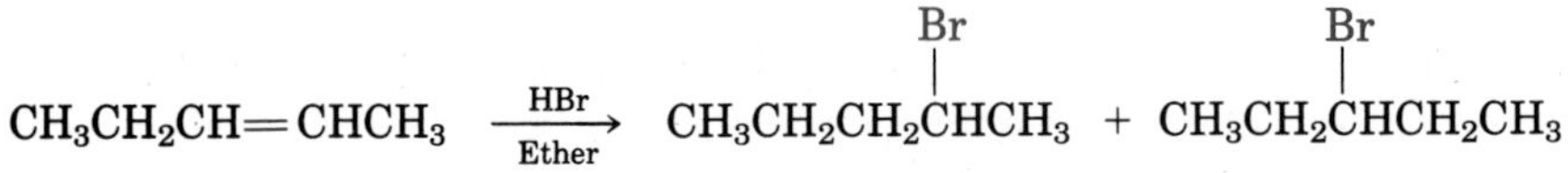

$$\underset{\text{2-Pentene}}{\text{CH}_3\text{CH}_2\text{CH}=\text{CHCH}_3} \xrightarrow[\text{Ether}]{\text{HBr}} \underset{\text{2-Bromopentane}}{\text{CH}_3\text{CH}_2\text{CH}_2\overset{\text{Br}}{\text{CHCH}_3}} + \underset{\text{3-Bromopentane}}{\text{CH}_3\text{CH}_2\overset{\text{Br}}{\text{CHCH}_2\text{CH}_3}}$$

handwritten:
H H H H
$H-C-C-C\#C-H$
H H Br CH_3
or
H H H H
$H-C-C-C\#C-Br$
H H H C
H_3

Since carbocations are involved as intermediates in these reactions, another way to express Markovnikov's rule is to say that, in the addition of HX to alkenes, the more highly substituted carbocation intermediate is formed in preference to the less highly substituted one. For example, addition of H⁺ to 2-methylpropene yields the intermediate *tertiary* carbocation rather than the primary carbocation. Why should this be so?

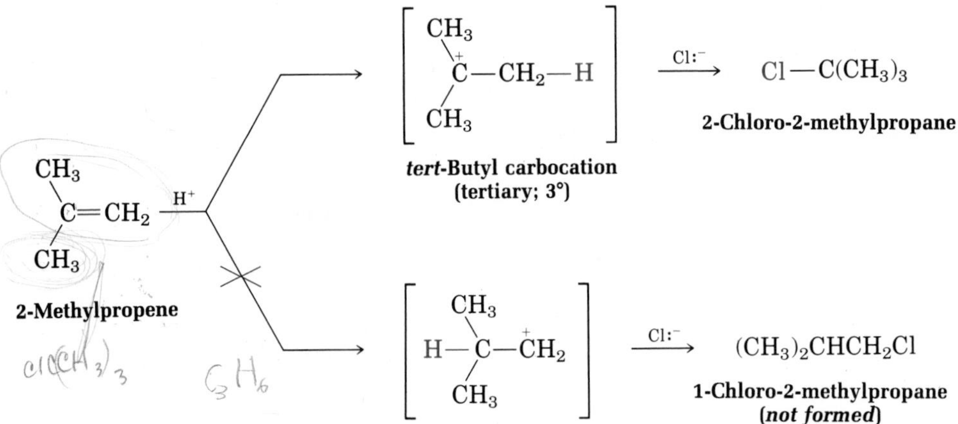

$$\left[\begin{array}{c}\text{CH}_3 \\ \overset{+}{\text{C}}-\text{CH}_2-\text{H} \\ \text{CH}_3\end{array}\right] \xrightarrow{\text{Cl:}^-} \underset{\text{2-Chloro-2-methylpropane}}{\text{Cl}-\text{C}(\text{CH}_3)_3}$$

tert-Butyl carbocation (tertiary; 3°)

$$\underset{\text{2-Methylpropene}}{\overset{\text{CH}_3}{\underset{\text{CH}_3}{C}}=\text{CH}_2} \xrightarrow{\text{H}^+}$$

handwritten: $Cl(CH_3)_3$ C_3H_6

$$\left[\begin{array}{c}\text{CH}_3 \\ \text{H}-\text{C}-\overset{+}{\text{CH}}_2 \\ \text{CH}_3\end{array}\right] \xrightarrow{\text{Cl:}^-} \underset{\substack{\text{1-Chloro-2-methylpropane} \\ (\textit{not formed})}}{(\text{CH}_3)_2\text{CHCH}_2\text{Cl}}$$

Isobutyl carbocation (primary; 1°) (*not formed*)

handwritten:
CH_3
$Cl -C \# CH_2$
CH_3 H

PRACTICE PROBLEM What product would you expect from reaction of HBr with 1-methylcyclo-hexene?

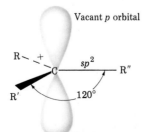

Solution Markovnikov's rule predicts that the hydrogen will add to the double-bond carbon having one alkyl group present (C2 on the ring), and the bromine will add to the double-bond carbon having two alkyl groups (C1 on the ring). The expected product is 1-bromo-1-methylcyclohexane.

PROBLEM 4.1 Predict the products of these reactions:

(a) $CH_3CH_2CH{=}CH_2$ + HCl →   (b) $(CH_3)_2C{=}CHCH_2CH_3$ + HI →

(c) Cyclohexene + HCl ⟶

PROBLEM 4.2 What alkenes would you start with to prepare these alkyl halides?

(a) Bromocyclopentane   (b) $CH_3CH_2CHBrCH_2CH_2CH_3$

(c) 1-Iodo-1-methylcyclohexane

4.3 CARBOCATION STRUCTURE AND STABILITY

To understand the reasons for the Markovnikov orientation of electrophilic addition reactions, we need to learn more about the structure and stability of substituted carbocations. First, a great deal of evidence points to the conclusion that carbocations are *planar*: The carbon atom is sp^2 hybridized, and the three substituents are oriented to the corners of an equilateral triangle (Figure 4.1). Since there are only six electrons in the carbon outer shell, and since all six are used in the three sigma bonds, the p orbital extending above and below the plane is unoccupied.

Vacant p orbital

FIGURE 4.1
Carbocation structure: The carbon is sp^2 hybridized and has a vacant p orbital.

The second point we need to explore involves carbocation stability. In principle, 2-methylpropene can react with HBr to form a carbocation having either *three* alkyl substituents (a tertiary cation, 3°) or *one* alkyl substituent (a primary cation, 1°). Since the tertiary bromide, 2-bromo-2-methylpropane, is the only product observed, formation of the tertiary cation is evidently favored over formation of the primary cation.

$$H_2C=\underset{\underset{CH_3}{|}}{\overset{\overset{CH_3}{|}}{C}} \;+\; H^+ \;\longrightarrow\; H_3C-\underset{\underset{CH_3}{|}}{\overset{\overset{CH_3}{|}}{\overset{+}{C}} } \qquad \text{or} \qquad H_2\overset{+}{C}-\underset{\underset{CH_3}{|}}{\overset{\overset{CH_3}{|}}{C}}-H$$

A tertiary cation (3°)   **A primary cation (1°)**

Thermodynamic measurements show that, indeed, the stability of carbocations increases with increasing alkyl substitution: More highly substituted carbocations are more stable than less highly substituted ones. The stability order of carbocations is:

Tertiary (3°) > Secondary (2°) > Primary (1°) > Methyl

$(CH_3)_3C^+ \quad > \quad (CH_3)_2CH^+ \quad > \quad CH_3CH_2^+ \quad > \quad {}^+CH_3$

4.4 ADDITION OF HALOGENS TO ALKENES

Many reagents besides HX add to alkenes. Bromine and chlorine are particularly effective electrophilic addition reagents, and their reaction with alkenes provides a general method of synthesis of 1,2-dihaloalkanes. For example, more than 5 million tons of 1,2-dichloroethane (ethylene dichloride) are synthesized each year in the chemical industry by addition of Cl_2 to ethylene. The product is used both as a solvent and as starting material for the synthesis of poly(vinyl chloride), PVC.

$$H_2C=CH_2 \quad \xrightarrow{Cl_2} \quad \underset{\overset{|}{H_2C}}{\overset{\overset{Cl}{|}}{}}-\underset{\overset{|}{CH_2}}{\overset{\overset{Cl}{|}}{}}$$

Ethylene   **1,2-Dichloroethane**
                        (ethylene dichloride)

Addition of bromine also serves as a simple and rapid laboratory test for the presence of a carbon–carbon double bond in a molecule of unknown structure. A sample of unknown structure is dissolved in tetrachloromethane, CCl_4, and several drops of bromine are then added. Immediate disappearance of the reddish bromine color signals a positive test and indicates that the sample is an alkene.

$$\text{Cyclopentene} \quad \xrightarrow{Br_2 \text{ in } CCl_4} \quad \text{1,2-Dibromocyclopentane (95\%)}$$

Cyclopentene   **1,2-Dibromocyclopentane (95%)**

INFO—

Fluorine tends to be too reactive and difficult to control for most laboratory applications, and iodine does not react with alkenes.

Bromine and chlorine react with alkenes by the electrophilic addition pathway shown in Figure 4.2. Although bromine is nonpolar, it nevertheless reacts with alkenes as if it were polarized Br^+Br^-. The pi electron pair of the alkene attacks the Br^+ end of the Br_2 molecule, displacing Br^-. The net result is that electrophilic Br^+ adds to the alkene, yielding an intermediate carbocation that immediately reacts further with Br^- to give the dibromo addition product.

The electron *pair* from the alkene bond attacks the positively polarized bromine, forming a C—Br bond and causing the Br—Br bond to break. Bromide ion departs with *both* Br—Br bond electrons.

Bromide ion then uses an electron pair to attack the carbocation intermediate, forming a C—Br bond and yielding a neutral addition product.

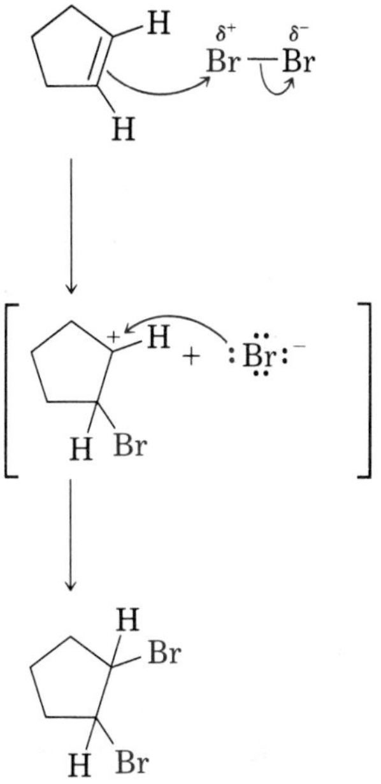

FIGURE 4.2
Electrophilic addition of bromine to cyclopentene

The mechanism of halogen addition to alkenes shown in Figure 4.2 is similar to the mechanism of HX addition that we developed earlier and is consistent with what we have learned thus far. Further examination, however, shows that it is not completely consistent with known data. In particular, the mechanism proposed does not explain the *stereochemistry* of halogen addition. Let's look more closely at the addition of bromine to cyclopentene to see what is meant by "stereochemistry of addition."

Let's assume that Br^+ adds to cyclopentene from the bottom face to form the carbocation intermediate shown in Figure 4.3, page 100. (The addition could equally well occur from the top face, but we will consider only one possibility for simplicity.) Since this carbocation intermediate is planar and sp^2 hybridized, it could be attacked by bromide ion in the second step of the reaction from either the top side or the bottom side. Thus, a mixture of products might result, in which the two bromine atoms are either on the same side of the ring (cis) or on opposite sides (trans). We observe, however, that only *trans*-1,2-dibromocyclopentane is produced. The two bromine atoms add to opposite faces of the double bond, a result we describe by saying that the reaction occurs with **anti stereochemistry**. (If

adds onto
opp. sides

adds on to same sides

the two bromines had added to the same face, the reaction would have **syn stereochemistry**.) The word "anti" means that the two bromines that have added are 180° apart. The word "stereochemistry" refers to which possible stereo-isomers (Section 2.10) are formed in the reaction.

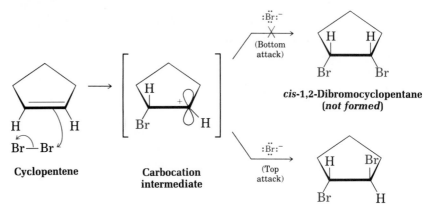

cis-1,2-Dibromocyclopentane
(*not formed*)

trans-1,2-Dibromocyclopentane

FIGURE 4.3
Stereochemistry of the addition of bromine to cyclopentene: Only the trans product is formed.

The observation of anti addition of bromine is best explained by postulating that the true reaction intermediate is not a carbocation, but is instead a **bromonium ion**. A bromonium ion is a species containing a positively charged, divalent bromine, R_2Br^+. (Similarly, a **chloronium ion** has the structure R_2Cl^+.) In the case of bromine addition to an alkene, the bromonium ion is in a three-membered ring and is formed by the overlap of a bromine lone pair of electrons with the neighboring vacant carbocation p orbital (Figure 4.4). Although Figure 4.4 depicts three-membered-ring bromonium ion formation as stepwise, this is done only for the sake of clarity. It's likely that the bromonium ion is formed directly by the interaction of Br^+ with the alkene double-bond electrons.

If a bromonium ion is indeed formed as an intermediate in electrophilic addition reactions, the bromine atom ought to "shield" one face of the alkene. Further reaction with bromide ion in the second step could then occur only from the opposite, more accessible face to give the anti product.

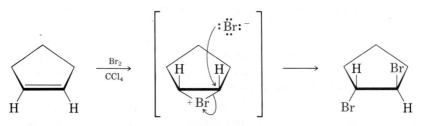

Cyclopentene   Bromonium ion intermediate   *trans*-1,2-Dibromocyclopentane
                      (bottom side is blocked so
                      reaction with bromide occurs
                      from the top side)

Alkene pi electrons attack bromine, pushing out bromide ion and leaving a bromo carbocation.

The neighboring bromo substituent stabilizes the positive charge by using two of its electrons to overlap the vacant carbon p orbital, giving a three-membered-ring bromonium ion.

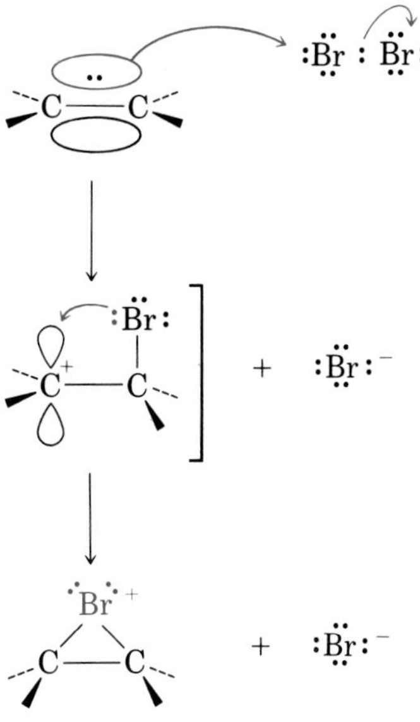

A bromonium ion

FIGURE 4.4
Formation of a bromonium ion intermediate by electrophilic addition of Br^+ to an alkene

PROBLEM 4.3 What product would you expect to obtain from addition of Cl_2 to 1,2-dimethylcyclo-hexene? Show the stereochemistry of the product.

PROBLEM 4.4 Show the structure of the intermediate chloronium ion formed in Problem 4.3.

4.5 HYDRATION OF ALKENES

Water can be added to simple alkenes such as ethylene and 2-methylpropene to yield alcohol products. This **hydration** reaction takes place on treatment of the alkene with aqueous acid by a mechanism similar to that of HX addition. Thus, reaction of the alkene double bond with H^+ yields a carbocation intermediate that then reacts with water as nucleophile to yield a protonated alcohol (ROH_2^+) product. Loss of H^+ from the protonated alcohol gives the neutral alcohol and regenerates the acid catalyst (Figure 4.5, page 102). Note that addition of water to an alkene follows Markovnikov's rule just as addition of HX does, and that the more highly substituted alcohol is therefore produced in the hydration reaction of an unsymmetrical alkene.

Unfortunately, the reaction conditions required for hydration are so severe that molecules with sensitive functional groups are sometimes destroyed by the high temperatures and strongly acidic conditions. For example, the hydration of ethylene to produce ethanol requires a sulfuric acid catalyst and reaction temperatures of up to 250°C.

The alkene double bond reacts with H^+ to yield a carbocation intermediate.

$$\begin{array}{c} H \\ \diagdown \\ C \end{array} = \begin{array}{c} CH_3 \\ \diagup \\ C \\ \diagdown \end{array} \begin{array}{c} \\ \\ CH_3 \end{array}$$

Nucleophilic water then donates a lone pair of electrons from oxygen to carbon to form a carbon–oxygen bond and produce a protonated alcohol.

Loss of H^+ from the protonated alcohol then gives the neutral alcohol product.

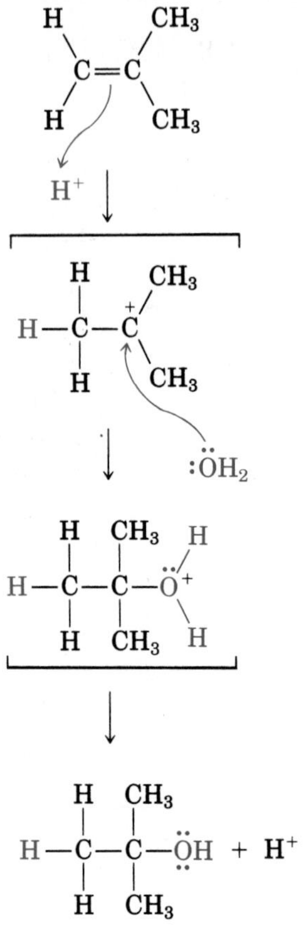

FIGURE 4.5
Mechanism of the acid-catalyzed hydration of an alkene

PROBLEM 4.5 What product would you expect to obtain from addition of water to these alkenes?

(a) $CH_3CH_2C(CH_3)=CHCH_2CH_3$ (b) 1-Methylcyclopentene

(c) 2,5-Dimethyl-2-heptene

PROBLEM 4.6 What alkene do you suppose the following alcohols were prepared from?

(a) $CH_3CH_2CH(OH)CH_3$

(b) $CH_3CH_2-\overset{\displaystyle OH}{\underset{\displaystyle CH_3}{\overset{|}{\underset{|}{C}}}}-CH_2CH_3$

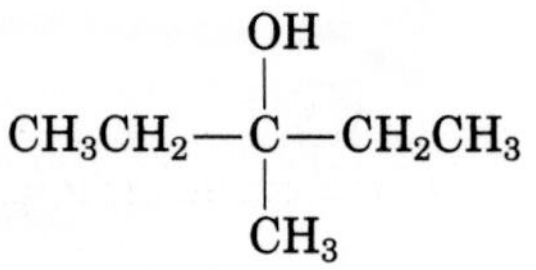

(c)

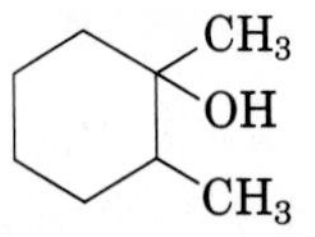

sTReSsEd OuT
CHiLL OuT!

DANCE

with ASU

〈Asian Student Union〉

The Place: COCO PALMS
The Date: October 16
The Time: 8:00 'til ?
21 & over
only-

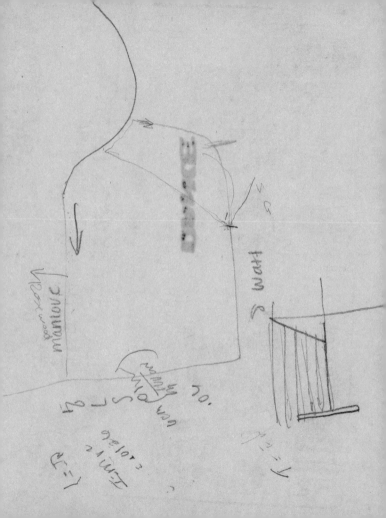

4.6 HYDROGENATION OF ALKENES

When alkenes are exposed to an atmosphere of hydrogen gas in the presence of an appropriate catalyst, addition of hydrogen to the double bond occurs. We describe the result by saying that the double bond has been **hydrogenated** or **reduced.** For most alkene hydrogenations, either platinum or palladium is used as the catalyst. Palladium is normally used in a very finely divided state "supported" on an inert material such as charcoal to maximize surface area (abbreviated as Pd/C); platinum is normally used as PtO_2.

Catalytic hydrogenation of alkenes is unlike most other organic reactions in that it is a *heterogeneous* process, rather than a homogeneous one. That is, the hydrogenation reaction occurs on the surface of solid catalyst particles rather than in solution. The reaction occurs with syn stereochemistry, both hydrogens adding to the double bond from the same side.

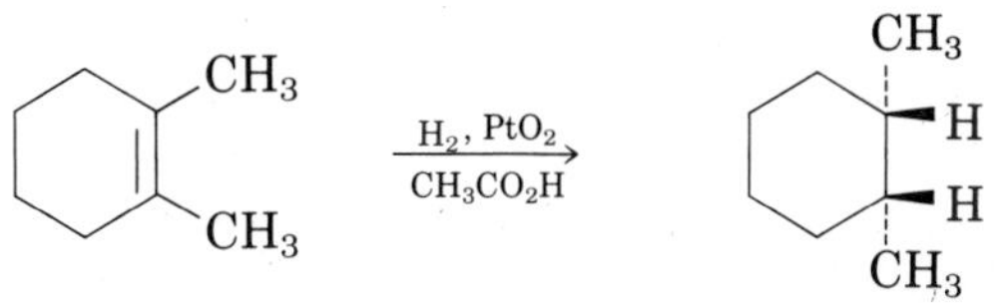

1,2-Dimethylcyclohexene   *cis*-1,2-Dimethylcyclohexane
(82%)

Alkenes are much more reactive toward catalytic hydrogenation than are most other functional groups. Functional groups such as ketones and esters survive normal alkene hydrogenation conditions unchanged, although reaction with these groups does occur under more vigorous conditions.

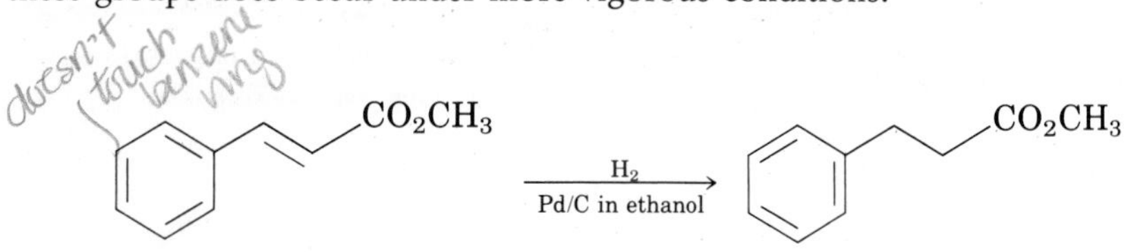

Methyl 3-phenylpropenoate   Methyl 3-phenylpropanoate

Benzene ring, ester not reduced

Note that in the hydrogenation of methyl 3-phenylpropenoate the benzene ring functional group is not affected even though the ring contains three double bonds. We will account for this remarkable stability of benzene rings in Chapter 5.

In addition to its usefulness in the laboratory, alkene hydrogenation is also a reaction of great commercial value. In the food industry, unsaturated vegetable oils, which usually contain numerous double bonds, are catalytically hydrogenated on a vast scale to produce the saturated fats used in margarine.

PROBLEM 4.7 What product would you expect to obtain from catalytic hydrogenation of these alkenes?

(a) $(CH_3)_2C{=}CHCH_2CH_3$

(b) 3,3-Dimethylcyclopentene

4.7 OXIDATION OF ALKENES

Hydroxylation of an alkene—the addition of a hydroxyl group to each of the alkene carbons—can be carried out by treatment of the alkene with potassium permanganate, $KMnO_4$, in basic solution. Since oxygen is added to the alkene during the reaction, we call this an **oxidation**. The reaction occurs with syn stereochemistry and yields a *cis*-1,2-dialcohol (**diol**) product. For example, cyclohexene gives *cis*-1,2-cyclohexanediol in 37% yield.

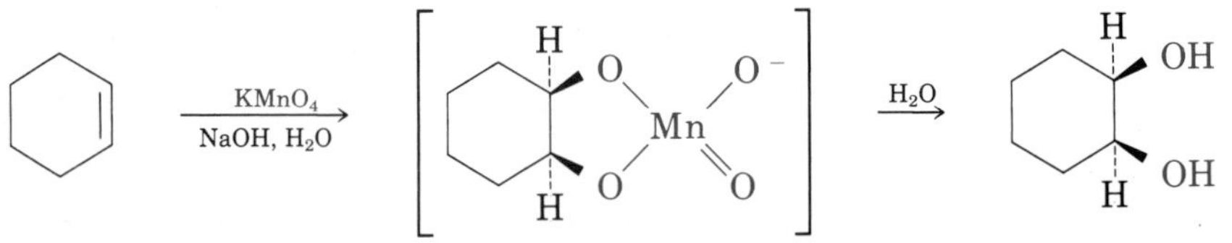

Cyclohexene   A cyclic manganate   *cis*-1,2-Cyclohexanediol
                                  intermediate   (37%)

If the reaction of the alkene with $KMnO_4$ is carried out in either neutral or acidic solution, *cleavage* of the double bond occurs, giving carbonyl-containing products in moderate yield. If the double bond is tetrasubstituted, the two carbonyl-containing products are ketones; if a hydrogen is present on the double bond, one of the carbonyl-containing products is a carboxylic acid; and if two hydrogens are present on one carbon, CO_2 is formed:

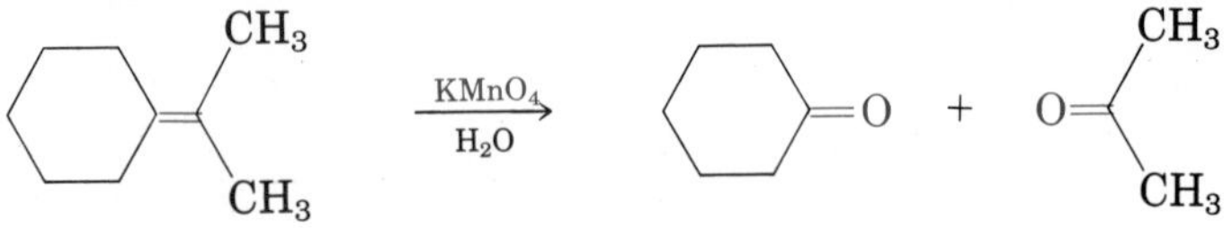

Isopropylidenecyclohexane   Cyclohexanone   Acetone
                                       Two ketones

$$(CH_3)_2CHCH_2CH_2CH_2\overset{\underset{\textstyle |}{CH_3}}{C}HCH{=}CH_2 \xrightarrow{\ KMnO_4\ }{H_2O}$$

3,7-Dimethyl-1-octene

$$(CH_3)_2CHCH_2CH_2CH_2\overset{\underset{\textstyle |}{CH_3}}{C}HCOOH + CO_2$$

2,6-Dimethylheptanoic acid (45%)

An alternative method for oxidatively cleaving carbon–carbon double bonds is to treat an alkene with ozone, O_3. Ozone, which is conveniently prepared in the laboratory by passing a stream of oxygen through a high-voltage electrical discharge, adds rapidly to alkenes at low temperature to yield **ozonides**.

$$3\ O_2 \xrightarrow[\text{discharge}]{\text{Electric}} 2\ O_3$$

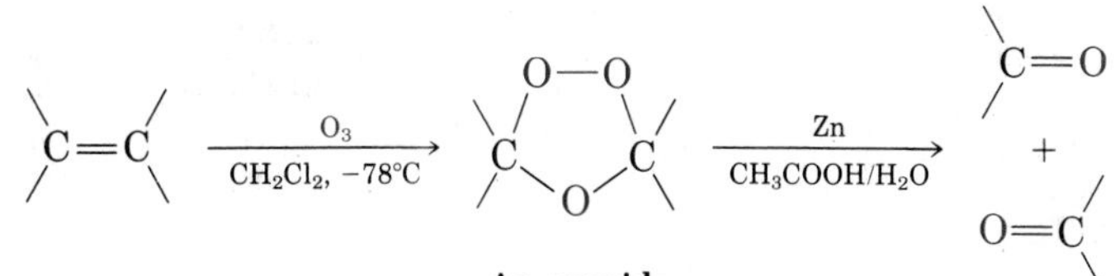

An ozonide

Because they are highly explosive, low-molecular-weight ozonides are not isolated. Instead, ozonides are further treated with a reducing agent such as zinc metal in acetic acid to convert them to carbonyl compounds. The net result of the ozonolysis/zinc reduction sequence is that the carbon–carbon double bond is cleaved, and oxygen becomes doubly bonded to each of the original alkene carbons. If a tetrasubstituted double bond is ozonized, two ketones result; if a trisubstituted double bond is ozonized, one ketone and one aldehyde result; and so on.

$$CH_3(CH_2)_7CH = CH(CH_2)_7COOCH_3 \xrightarrow[\text{2. Zn, H}_3O^+]{\text{1. O}_3} CH_3(CH_2)_7CH = O$$

**Methyl 9-octadecenoate
(disubstituted)**

Nonanal

+

$$O = CH(CH_2)_7COOCH_3$$

Methyl 9-oxononanoate

78%; two aldehydes

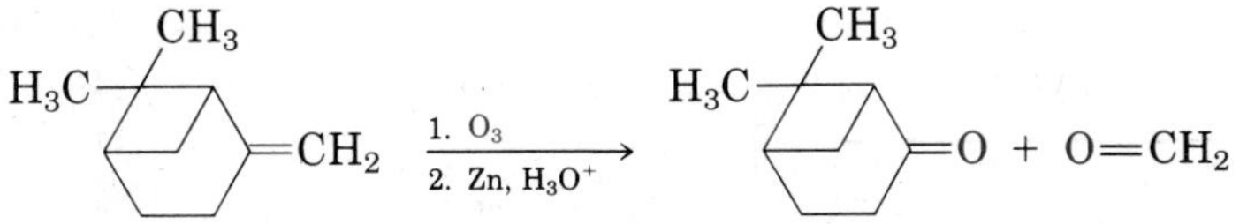

**β-Pinene
(disubstituted)**

Nopinone   **Formaldehyde**

75%; one ketone, one aldehyde

PROBLEM 4.8   Predict the product of the reaction of 1,2-dimethylcyclohexene with:

(a)   Aqueous acidic $KMnO_4$ (b)   Ozone, followed by zinc

PROBLEM 4.9   Propose structures for alkenes that yield the following products on ozonolysis/reduction:

(a) $(CH_3)_2C = O\ +\ CH_2 = O$ (b)   2 equiv $CH_3CH_2CH = O$
(c)   Cyclohexanone $+\ CH_3CH = O$

4.8   PREPARATION OF ALKENES: ELIMINATION REACTIONS

Just as the reactions of alkenes are dominated by electrophilic additions, the preparation of alkenes is dominated by **elimination reactions**. Additions and eliminations are, in many respects, two sides of the same coin:

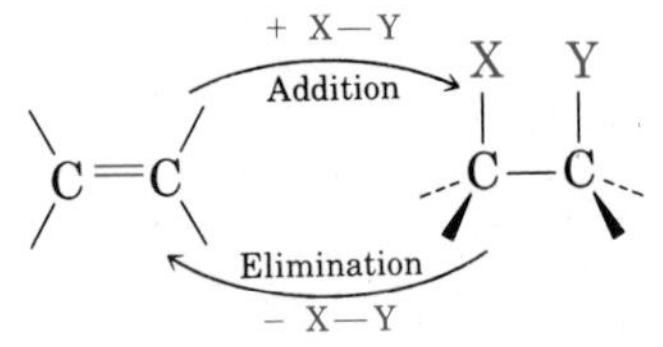

Let's look briefly at two elimination reactions—the **dehydrohalogenation** of an alkyl halide (elimination of HX) and the **dehydration** of an alcohol (elimination of water). We'll return for a closer look at how these reactions take place in Chapter 7.

Elimination of HX from Alkyl Halides: Dehydrohalogenation

Alkyl halides can be synthesized by addition of HX to alkenes. Conversely, alkenes can be synthesized by elimination of HX from alkyl halides. Elimination is usually effected by treating the alkyl halide with a strong base. Thus, bromo-cyclohexane yields cyclohexene when treated with potassium hydroxide in alcohol solution:

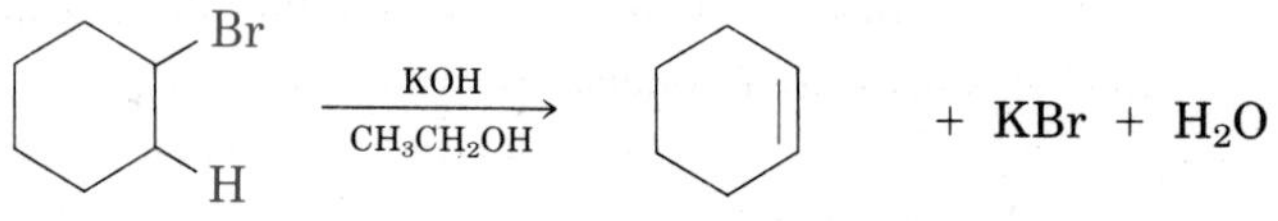

Bromocyclohexane   **Cyclohexene (81%)**

Elimination reactions are somewhat more complex than addition reactions. There is, for example, the problem of direction (regiochemistry) of elimination—What products result from dehydrohalogenation of *unsymmetrical* halides? In fact, elimination reactions almost always give mixtures of alkene products. The best we can usually do is to predict which product will be major.

According to a rule formulated by the Russian chemist Alexander Zaitsev,[2] base-induced elimination reactions generally give the more highly substituted alkene product. For example, if 2-bromobutane is treated with sodium ethoxide in ethanol, Zaitsev's rule predicts that 2-butene (disubstituted; two alkyl group substituents on the double-bond carbons) should predominate over 1-butene (monosubstituted; one alkyl group substituent on the double-bond carbons). This is exactly what is found.

[2]Also spelled Saytzeff, according to the German pronunciation.

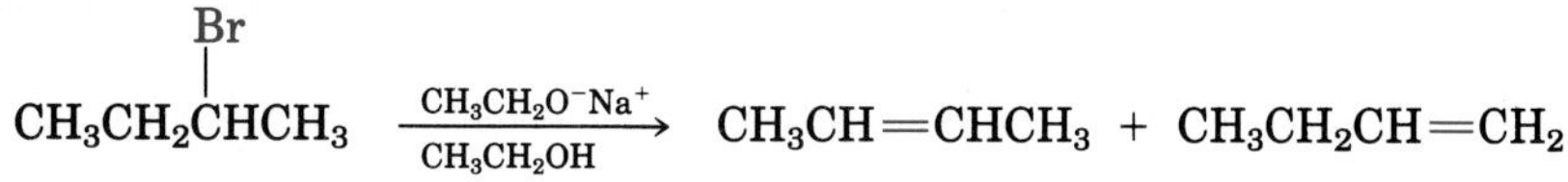
Br
$CH_3CH_2CHCH_3$
$CH_3CH_2O^-Na^+$
CH_3CH_2OH
$CH_3CH{=}CHCH_3$ + $CH_3CH_2CH{=}CH_2$

2-Bromobutane **2-Butene (81%)** **1-Butene (19%)**

PROBLEM 4.10 What products would you expect from the reaction of 2-bromo-2-methylbutane with sodium ethoxide? Which will be major?

Elimination of H_2O from Alcohols: Dehydration

The dehydration of alcohols is one of the most useful methods of alkene synthesis, and many alternative ways of carrying out the reaction have been devised. A method that works particularly well for tertiary alcohols is **acid-catalyzed dehydration.** For example, when 1-methylcyclohexanol is treated with aqueous sulfuric acid, dehydration occurs to yield 1-methylcyclohexene.

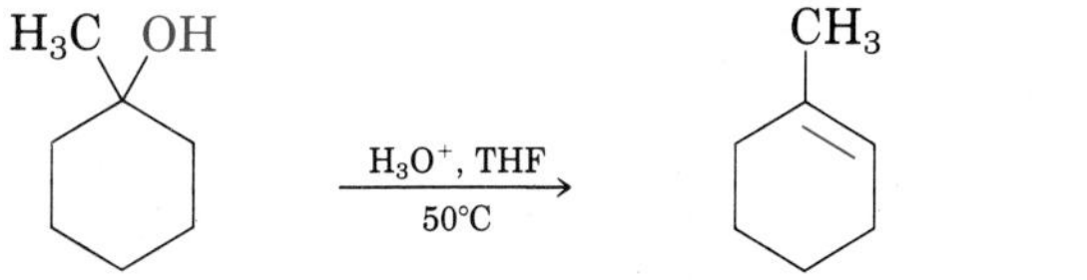
H_3C OH
H_3O^+, THF
50°C
CH_3

1-Methylcyclohexanol **1-Methylcyclohexene (91%)**

Acid-catalyzed dehydrations normally follow Zaitsev's rule and yield the more highly substituted alkene as major product. Thus, 2-methyl-2-butanol gives primarily 2-methyl-2-butene (trisubstituted) rather than 2-methyl-1-butene (disubstituted):

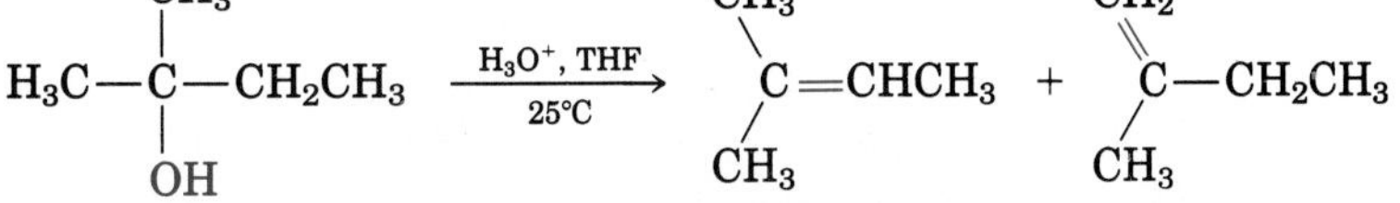
CH_3
$H_3C—C—CH_2CH_3$
OH
H_3O^+, THF
25°C
CH_3
$C{=}CHCH_3$
CH_3
+
CH_2
$C—CH_2CH_3$
CH_3

2-Methyl-2-butanol **2-Methyl-2-butene (trisubstituted)** **2-Methyl-1-butene (disubstituted)**

Major product **Minor product**

The reactivity order for acid-catalyzed dehydrations is:

$$R_3COH\ (3°) > R_2CHOH\ (2°) > RCH_2OH\ (1°)$$

Tertiary alcohols dehydrate easily, but secondary alcohols react only under severe experimental conditions (75% H_2SO_4, 100°C). Primary alcohols are sometimes unreactive. The mechanisms of these dehydrations will be discussed in Chapter 7.

PRACTICE PROBLEM   Predict the major product of the following reaction:

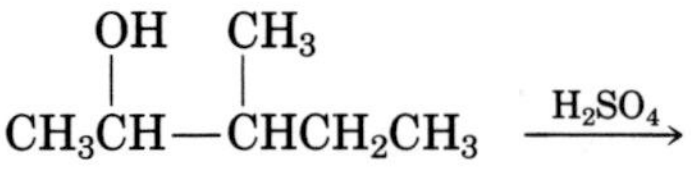

$$\underset{CH_3CH-CHCH_2CH_3}{\overset{\overset{\displaystyle OH \quad\ \ CH_3}{|\qquad\quad |}}{}} \xrightarrow{\ H_2SO_4\ }$$

Solution   Treatment of an alcohol with acid leads to dehydration and formation of the more highly substituted alkene product (Zaitsev's rule). Thus, dehydration of 3-methyl-2-pentanol should yield 3-methyl-2-pentene rather than 3-methyl-1-pentene as the major product.

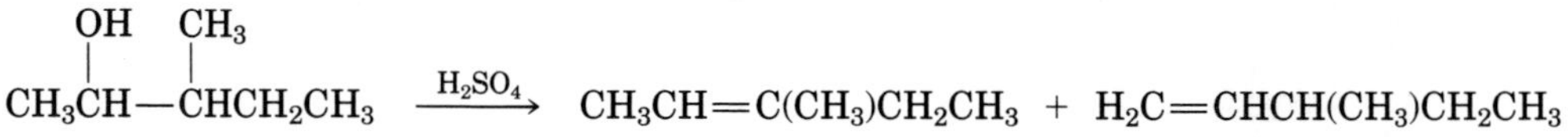

$$\underset{\textbf{3-Methyl-2-pentanol}}{\overset{\overset{\displaystyle OH \quad\ \ CH_3}{|\qquad\quad |}}{CH_3CH-CHCH_2CH_3}} \xrightarrow{\ H_2SO_4\ } \underset{\substack{\textbf{3-Methyl-2-pentene}\\ \textbf{(major)}}}{CH_3CH=C(CH_3)CH_2CH_3} + \underset{\substack{\textbf{3-Methyl-1-pentene}\\ \textbf{(minor)}}}{H_2C=CHCH(CH_3)CH_2CH_3}$$

PROBLEM 4.11   Predict the products you would expect from these reactions. Indicate the major product in each case.

(a)   Reaction of 2-bromo-2-methylpentane with KOH in ethanol

(b) 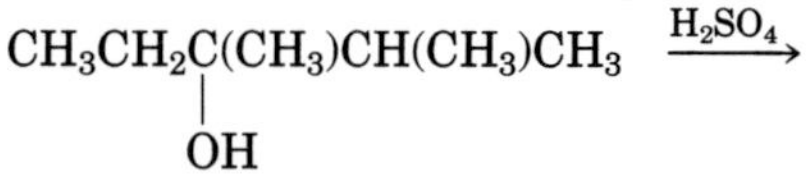 $\underset{\overset{|}{OH}}{CH_3CH_2C(CH_3)CH(CH_3)CH_3} \xrightarrow{\ H_2SO_4\ }$

4.9   CONJUGATED DIENES

Double bonds that alternate with single bonds are said to be **conjugated**. Thus, 1,3-butadiene is a **conjugated diene**, whereas 1,4-pentadiene is a nonconjugated diene with *isolated* double bonds.

$$\underset{\substack{\textbf{1,3-Butadiene}\\ \textbf{(conjugated; alternating}\\ \textbf{double and single bonds)}}}{H_2C=CH-CH=CH_2} \qquad \underset{\substack{\textbf{1,4-Pentadiene}\\ \textbf{(nonconjugated; nonalternating}\\ \textbf{double and single bonds)}}}{H_2C=CH-CH_2-CH=CH_2}$$

There are other types of conjugated systems in addition to dienes (Figure 4.6), and many play an important role in nature. For example, many of the pigments responsible for the brilliant reds and yellows of fruits and flowers are conjugated **polyenes** (*poly* = "many"); lycopene is one such molecule. Conjugated **enones** (alkene + ketone) are common structural features of such important molecules as progesterone, the "pregnancy hormone." Conjugated cyclic molecules such as benzene are a major field of study in themselves and will be considered in detail in the next chapter.

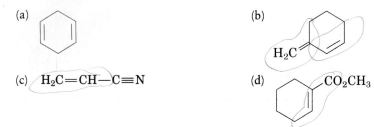

(a)

CH₃
|
C=O

H₃C

H₃C

O

(b)   (c)

FIGURE 4.6
(a) Lycopene, a conjugated polyene from tomatoes; (b) progesterone, a conjugated enone; and (c) benzene, a conjugated cyclic molecule

---

PROBLEM 4.12   Circle the conjugated parts of these molecules:

(a)   (b)

H_2C

(c) $H_2C=CH-C\equiv N$ (d) CO_2CH_3

4.10   STRUCTURE OF 1,3-BUTADIENE

Comparison of bond lengths shows that the carbon–carbon single bond of 1,3-butadiene is shorter than the single bond of ethane by 0.06 Å (Table 4.1). The C2–C3 single bond in 1,3-butadiene has a length of 1.48 Å whereas that of ethane is 1.54 Å.

TABLE 4.1   Some carbon–carbon bond lengths

Bond	Bond length (Å)	Bond hybridization
CH_3-CH_3	1.54	$C_{sp^3}-C_{sp^3}$
$H_2C=CH_2$	1.33	$C_{sp^2}-C_{sp^2}$
$H_2C=CH-CH=CH_2$	1.48	$C_{sp^2}-C_{sp^2}$
$H_2C=CHCH=CH_2$	1.34	$C_{sp^2}-C_{sp^2}$

Why should the C2–C3 single bond in 1,3-butadiene be so short? The orbital view of 1,3-butadiene shown in Figure 4.7 provides a clue to the answer: *There is an electronic interaction between the two conjugated double bonds.* Pi orbital overlap across the C2–C3 single bond results in *partial* double-bond character and consequent bond shortening to a value midway between a pure single bond (1.54 Å) and a pure double bond (1.33 Å). The partial double-bond character of the C2–C3 bond is sufficient to give the molecule an extra amount of stability, but not to prevent bond rotation from occurring.

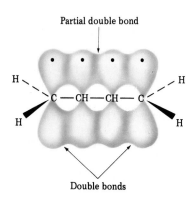

FIGURE 4.7
An orbital view of 1,3-butadiene,
$H_2C{=}CH{-}CH{=}CH_2$: The C2–C3 bond has
partial double-bond character.

4.11 ELECTROPHILIC ADDITIONS TO CONJUGATED DIENES: ALLYLIC CARBOCATIONS

Much of the chemistry of conjugated dienes and isolated alkenes is similar. One striking difference, however, is in their addition reactions with electrophiles. As we've seen, isolated carbon–carbon double bonds react with a wide variety of electrophiles to yield addition products. Markovnikov regiochemistry is observed for these reactions because the more highly substituted carbocation is involved as an intermediate. Thus, addition of HCl to 2-methylpropene yields 2-chloro-2-methylpropane rather than 1-chloro-2-methylpropane. Similarly, addition of 2 mole equivalents of HCl to the nonconjugated diene 1,4-pentadiene yields 2,4-dichloropentane.

$$(CH_3)_2C{=}CH_2 \xrightarrow[\text{Ether}]{\text{HCl}} \left[(CH_3)_3C^+\right]$$

$$\longrightarrow (CH_3)_3C{-}Cl$$

$$\xrightarrow{\quad\times\quad} (CH_3)_2CHCH_2Cl$$

2-Methylpropene   **Tertiary carbocation intermediate**

2-Chloro-2-methylpropane

1-Chloro-2-methylpropane (*not formed*)

$$H_2C=CHCH_2CH=CH_2 \xrightarrow[\text{Ether}]{2\,HCl} CH_3\overset{\overset{\displaystyle Cl}{|}}{C}HCH_2\overset{\overset{\displaystyle Cl}{|}}{C}HCH_3$$

1,4-Pentadiene
(a nonconjugated diene)   **2,4-Dichloropentane**

Conjugated dienes also undergo electrophilic addition reactions readily, but mixtures of products are invariably obtained. For example, addition of HBr to 1,3-butadiene yields a mixture of two products:

$$H_2C=CHCH=CH_2 \xrightarrow[0°C]{HBr} H_2C=CH\overset{\overset{\displaystyle Br\;H}{|\;\;|}}{C}HCH_2 + CH_2CH=CHCH_2$$

1,3-Butadiene   **3-Bromo-1-butene**   **1-Bromo-2-butene**
                           (71%; 1,2 addition)   **(29%; 1,4 addition)**

3-Bromo-1-butene (a secondary bromide) is the normal product of Markovnikov addition, but 1-bromo-2-butene (a primary bromide) appears unusual. The double bond in this product has moved to a position between C2 and C3, and H—Br has added to C1 and C4. How can we account for the formation of this **1,4-addition** product?

The answer is that an **allylic carbocation** is involved as an intermediate in the reaction (*allylic* = "next to a double bond"). When H^+ adds to an electron-rich pi bond of 1,3-butadiene, two carbocation intermediates are possible—a primary nonallylic carbocation, and a secondary allylic carbocation. Allylic carbocations are highly stable and therefore form in preference to less stable, nonallylic carbocations.

$$H_2C=CH-CH=CH_2$$

1,3-Butadiene

$$\xrightarrow{H^+} \left[H_2C=CH-CH_2-\overset{+}{C}H_2 \right]$$

Primary carbocation
(*not formed*)

$$\xrightarrow{H^+} \left[H_2C=CH-\overset{+}{C}H-CH_3 \right]$$

Secondary, allylic carbocation

4.12 STABILITY OF ALLYLIC CARBOCATIONS: RESONANCE

Why are allylic carbocations stable? To get an idea of the reason, look at the orbital picture of an allylic carbocation in Figure 4.8 on page 112. The positively charged carbon atom has a vacant p orbital that can overlap the p orbitals of the neighboring double bond.

From an orbital point of view, an allylic carbocation is symmetrical: All three carbon atoms are sp^2 hybridized, and each has a p orbital. Thus, the p orbital on the central carbon can overlap equally well with *either* of the two neighboring carbons. The two electrons are free to move about and spread out over the entire three-orbital array, as indicated in Figure 4.8.

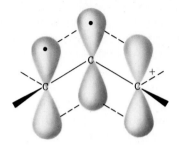

FIGURE 4.8
An orbital picture of an allylic carbocation:
The vacant p orbital on the positively charged
carbon can overlap the double-bond p orbitals.

One consequence of this orbital picture of the allylic carbocation is that there
are *two* ways in which we can draw it. We can draw it with the vacant orbital on
the left and the double bond on the right, or we can draw it with the vacant
orbital on the right and the double bond on the left. *Neither structure is correct by
itself; the true structure of an allylic carbocation is somewhere in between the
two.*

Two resonance forms of an allylic carbocation

The two individual structures are called **resonance forms,** and their relationship is indicated by the double-headed arrow between them. The only difference
between resonance forms is the position of the bonding electrons. The nuclei do
not move; they occupy exactly the same places in both resonance forms.

Resonance is an extremely useful concept in organic chemistry and is one we
will turn to on numerous occasions in the remainder of this book. Resonance is
also a very simple concept if we keep in mind that a species like the allylic
carbocation is no different from any other organic substance. An allylic carbocation does not jump back and forth between two resonance forms, spending
part of its time looking like one and the rest of its time looking like the other.
Rather, an allylic carbocation has a single unchanging structure that we call a
resonance hybrid.

The real difficulty in visualizing the resonance concept is that we cannot draw
an accurate single picture of a resonance hybrid using the familiar line-bond
representations of structure that serve so well for depicting other organic molecules. The difficulty lies in the *representation,* however, not in the structure itself.

We might try to represent an allylic carbocation by using a dotted line to indicate that the two C—C bonds are equivalent, that each is approximately 1.5 bonds, and that the positive charge is shared equally by the two end carbons. Such a drawing is imprecise, however, and raises more questions than it answers. (How many electrons should a dotted line represent?)

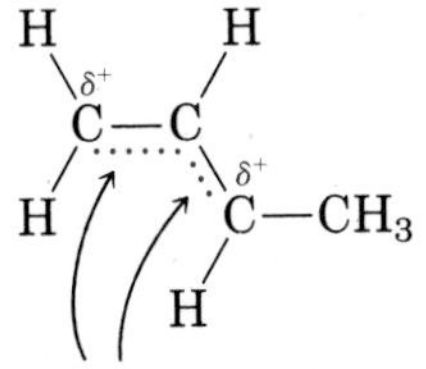

$$
\begin{array}{c}
\overset{H}{\underset{H}{\diagdown}} \overset{\delta^+}{\underset{}{C}} {\cdots} C \overset{H}{\diagup} \\
\end{array}
$$

1.5 bonds average

One of the most important postulates of resonance theory is that the more possible resonance forms there are for a substance, the greater the stability of the substance. For example, an allylic carbocation is a resonance hybrid of two line-bond structures and is therefore more stable than an alkyl carbocation, which has only one line-bond representation. This stability is due to the fact that the pi electrons can be spread out (*delocalized*) over an extended p orbital network, rather than centered on only one site.

In addition to affecting stability, the resonance picture of an allylic carbocation also has chemical consequences: When the allylic carbocation produced by protonation of 1,3-butadiene reacts with bromide ion to complete the electrophilic addition reaction, attack can occur at either C1 or C3, since both share the positive charge. The result is a mixture of 1,2- and 1,4-addition products.

$$\overset{+}{C}H_2-CH=CHCH_3 \longleftrightarrow CH_2=CH-\overset{+}{C}HCH_3$$

$$\downarrow :\overset{..}{\underset{..}{Br}}:^-$$

$$BrCH_2-CH=CHCH_3 \quad + \quad H_2C=CH-\overset{\overset{\displaystyle Br}{|}}{C}HCH_3$$

1,4 addition (29%)   **1,2 addition (71%)**

Many other electrophiles besides HBr add to conjugated dienes. For example, Br_2 adds to 1,3-butadiene to give the mixture of products shown.

$$H_2C=CH-CH=CH_2 \xrightarrow[25°C]{Br_2} BrCH_2-CH=CH-CH_2Br \quad \text{1,4 addition}$$

1,3-Butadiene   **1,4-Dibromo-2-butene (45%)**

$$+$$

$$BrCH_2-\overset{\overset{\displaystyle Br}{|}}{C}H-CH=CH_2 \quad \text{1,2 addition}$$

3,4-Dibromo-1-butene (55%)

PRACTICE PROBLEM   Show how ozone, O_3, is stabilized by resonance.

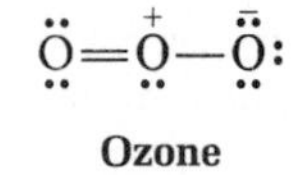

$$\ddot{O}=\overset{+}{\underset{}{\ddot{O}}}-\ddot{\ddot{O}}:$$

Ozone

Solution   Ozone is a resonance hybrid of two individual resonance forms. The two resonance forms can be drawn by showing the double bond either on the left or on the right. Only the positions of the electrons are different in the two structures.

$$\ddot{O}=\overset{+}{\underset{}{\ddot{O}}}-\ddot{\ddot{O}}: \longleftrightarrow :\ddot{\ddot{O}}-\overset{+}{\underset{}{\ddot{O}}}=\ddot{O}$$

PROBLEM 4.13   Give the structure of all possible monoaddition products of HCl and 1,3-pentadiene.

PROBLEM 4.14   Look at the possible carbocation intermediates produced during addition of HCl to 1,3-pentadiene (Problem 4.13). Predict which 1,2-addition product will predominate and which 1,4-addition product will predominate.

PROBLEM 4.15   Draw as many resonance structures as you can for these species:

(a)   Formate ion, $H-\overset{\overset{\textstyle :O:}{\|}}{C}-\ddot{\ddot{O}}\overline{:}$ (the oxygens are equivalent)

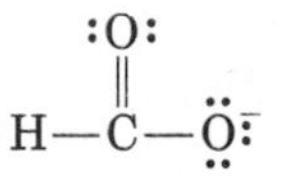

(b)   Carbonate ion, $\ddot{\ddot{O}}=\overset{\overset{\textstyle :\ddot{O}\overline{:}}{|}}{C}-\ddot{\ddot{O}}\overline{:}$ (all three oxygens are equivalent)

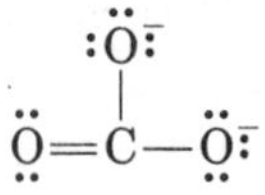

4.13   ALKYNES

Alkynes are hydrocarbons that contain a carbon–carbon triple bond. Since two pairs of hydrogens must be removed from an alkane, C_nH_{2n+2}, to generate a triple bond, the general formula for an alkyne is C_nH_{2n-2}. As we saw in Section 1.11, a carbon–carbon triple bond results from the overlap of two sp-hybridized carbon atoms. The two sp hybrid orbitals of carbon adopt a linear geometry. They lie at an angle of 180° to each other along an axis that is perpendicular to the axes of the two unhybridized $2p_y$ and $2p_z$ orbitals. When two such sp-hybridized carbons approach each other for bonding, the geometry is perfect for formation of one $sp–sp$ sigma bond and two $p–p$ pi bonds—a net *triple* bond (Figure 4.9).

The two remaining sp orbitals form bonds to other atoms at an angle of 180° from the carbon–carbon sigma bond. For example, acetylene, $H-C\equiv C-H$, is a linear molecule; the H-C-C bond angles are 180°. The bond strength of a carbon–carbon triple bond is approximately 200 kcal/mol, making it the strongest known carbon–carbon bond; the bond length is 1.20 Å.

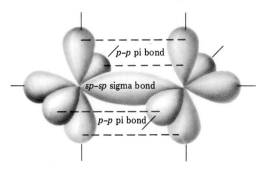

p–p pi bond

sp–sp sigma bond

p–p pi bond

The carbon–carbon triple bond

FIGURE 4.9
The electronic structure of a carbon–carbon triple bond

4.14 NOMENCLATURE OF ALKYNES

Alkynes follow closely the general rules of hydrocarbon nomenclature already discussed for alkanes (Section 2.3) and alkenes (Section 3.1). The suffix *-yne* is used in the base hydrocarbon name to denote an alkyne, and the position of the triple bond is indicated by its number in the chain. Numbering always begins at the chain end nearer the triple bond so that the triple bond receives as low a number a possible. For example:

$$\overset{8}{C}H_3\overset{7}{C}H_2\overset{6}{C}H\overset{5}{C}H_2\overset{4}{C}\equiv\overset{3\ \ 2}{C}\overset{1}{C}H_2CH_3$$
$$|$$
$$CH_3$$

Begin numbering at the end nearer the triple bond

6-Methyl-3-octyne

Compounds with more than one triple bond are called *diynes*, *triynes*, and so forth; compounds containing both double and triple bonds are called *enynes* (not *ynenes*). Numbering of the hydrocarbon chain should always start from the end nearer the first multiple bond. When there is a choice in numbering, however, double bonds receive lower numbers than triple bonds. For example:

$$\overset{1}{C}H_3\overset{2}{C}H=\overset{3}{C}H\overset{4}{C}H_2\overset{5}{C}H_2\overset{6}{C}\equiv\overset{7\ 8}{C}CH_3$$

2-Octen-6-yne (*NOT* 6-octen-2-yne)

As was the case with hydrocarbon substituents derived from alkanes and alkenes, *alkynyl* groups are also possible:

$$CH_3CH_2CH_2CH_2\overset{\xi}{-}$$

Butyl
(an alkyl group)

$$CH_3CH_2CH=CH\overset{\xi}{-}$$

1-Butenyl
(a vinylic group)

$$CH_3CH_2C\equiv C\overset{\xi}{-}$$

1-Butynyl
(an alkynyl group)

PROBLEM 4.16 Provide correct IUPAC names for the following compounds:

(a) $CH_3CH_2C \equiv CCH_2CH(CH_3)_2$ (b) $HC \equiv CC(CH_3)_3$
(c) $CH_3CH(CH_3)CH_2C \equiv CCH_3$ (d) $CH_3CH = CHCH_2C \equiv CCH_3$

4.15 REACTIONS OF ALKYNES: ADDITION OF HX AND X_2

Based on their structural similarity, we might predict that alkynes and alkenes should also show chemical similarities. In other words, the pi bond of an alkyne might be expected to react similarly to the pi bonds of alkenes. As a general rule, this prediction is true: Alkynes react with electrophilic reagents in much the same way that alkenes do.

Alkynes give the expected addition products with HCl, HBr, and HI. Although the reactions can usually be stopped after addition of 1 mol equiv of HX to yield a haloalkene, an excess of reagent leads to formation of the dihalide product. As the following examples indicate, the regiochemistry of addition to monosubstituted alkynes follows Markovnikov's rule. The H atom adds to the terminal triple-bond carbon and the X atom adds to the internal, more highly substituted carbon. Trans stereochemistry of H and X is normally found in the product.

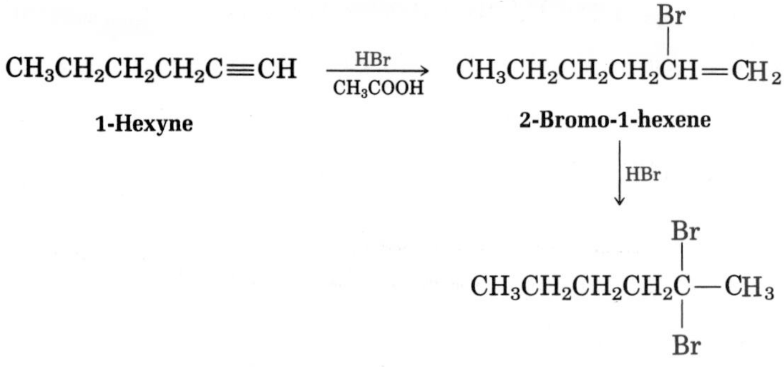

$$CH_3CH_2CH_2CH_2C \equiv CH \xrightarrow[CH_3COOH]{HBr} CH_3CH_2CH_2CH_2\overset{\overset{\displaystyle Br}{|}}{C}H = CH_2$$

1-Hexyne   **2-Bromo-1-hexene**

$$\bigg\downarrow HBr$$

$$CH_3CH_2CH_2CH_2\overset{\overset{\displaystyle Br}{|}}{\underset{\underset{\displaystyle Br}{|}}{C}}-CH_3$$

2,2-Dibromohexane

$$CH_3CH_2C \equiv CCH_2CH_3 \xrightarrow[CH_3COOH]{HCl,\ NH_4Cl} \begin{array}{c} Cl \qquad\quad CH_2CH_3 \\ \diagdown \qquad\quad \diagup \\ C = C \\ \diagup \qquad\quad \diagdown \\ CH_3CH_2 \qquad H \end{array}$$

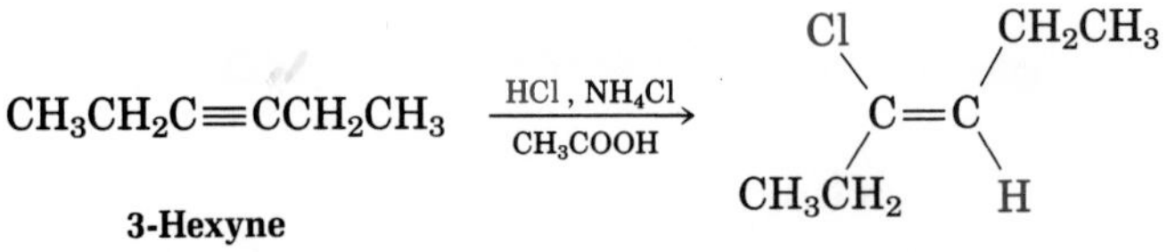

3-Hexyne   **(Z)-3-Chloro-3-hexene (95%)**

Bromine and chlorine also add to alkynes to give addition products, and trans stereochemistry again results:

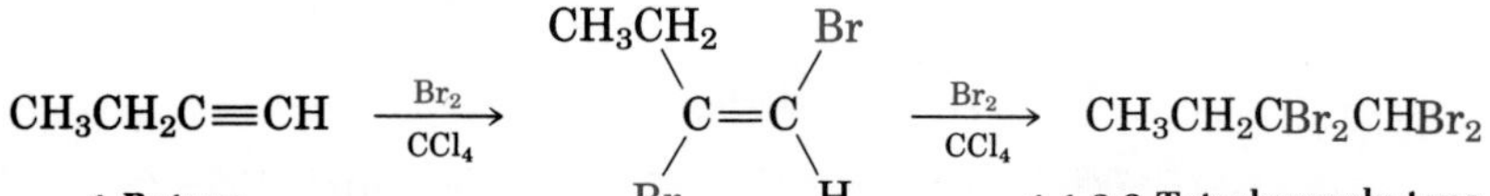

$$CH_3CH_2C \equiv CH \xrightarrow[CCl_4]{Br_2} \begin{array}{c} CH_3CH_2 \qquad Br \\ \diagdown \qquad\quad \diagup \\ C = C \\ \diagup \qquad\quad \diagdown \\ Br \qquad\quad H \end{array} \xrightarrow[CCl_4]{Br_2} CH_3CH_2CBr_2CHBr_2$$

1-Butyne   **1,1,2,2-Tetrabromobutane**

(E)-1,2-Dibromo-1-butene

The mechanisms of these alkyne electrophilic addition reactions are similar to those of the corresponding alkene reactions. An initial reaction of the alkyne triple bond with an electrophile (either H^+ or Br^+) leads to formation of an intermediate carbocation that then reacts further with halide ion. Note, however, that the carbocation intermediate is a *vinylic* cation rather than an alkyl cation (*vinylic* = "on a double bond").

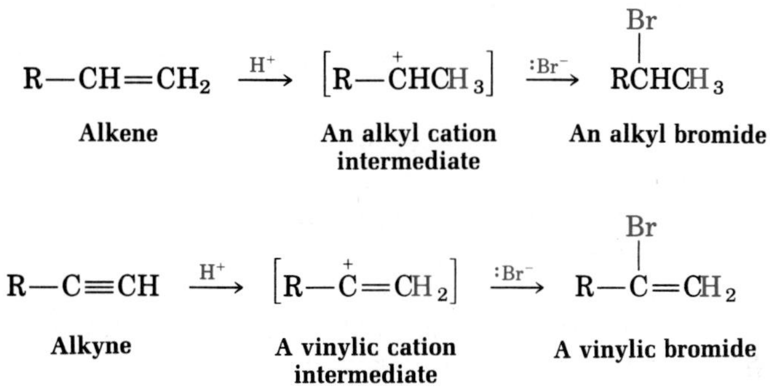

$$R-CH=CH_2 \xrightarrow{H^+} \left[R-\overset{+}{CHCH_3}\right] \xrightarrow{:Br^-} R\overset{\overset{\textstyle Br}{|}}{CHCH_3}$$

Alkene   An alkyl cation   An alkyl bromide
             intermediate

$$R-C\equiv CH \xrightarrow{H^+} \left[R-\overset{+}{C}=CH_2\right] \xrightarrow{:Br^-} R-\overset{\overset{\textstyle Br}{|}}{C}=CH_2$$

Alkyne   A vinylic cation   A vinylic bromide
             intermediate

PROBLEM 4.17   What products would you expect from the following reactions?

(a) $CH_3CH_2CH_2C\equiv CH$ + 1 equiv Cl_2

(b) $CH_3CH_2CH_2C\equiv CCH_2CH_3$ + 1 equiv HBr

4.16   HYDRATION OF ALKYNES

Addition of water to alkynes (hydration) takes place when the alkyne is treated with aqueous sulfuric acid in the presence of mercuric sulfate catalyst:

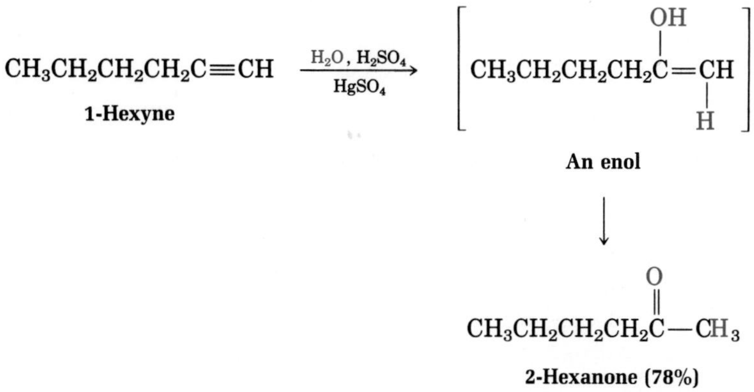

$$CH_3CH_2CH_2CH_2C\equiv CH \xrightarrow[\text{HgSO}_4]{\text{H}_2\text{O, H}_2\text{SO}_4} \left[CH_3CH_2CH_2CH_2\overset{\overset{\textstyle OH}{|}}{C}=\underset{\underset{\textstyle H}{|}}{CH} \right]$$

1-Hexyne   **An enol**

$$\downarrow$$

$$CH_3CH_2CH_2CH_2\overset{\overset{\textstyle O}{||}}{C}-CH_3$$

2-Hexanone (78%)

Markovnikov regiochemistry is observed for the hydration reaction, with the H attaching to the less substituted carbon and the OH attaching to the more substituted carbon. Interestingly, however, the expected alkenyl alcohol or **enol** (alkene; alcohol) is not isolated. Instead, this intermediate enol rearranges to a more stable isomer, a ketone ($R_2C=O$). It turns out that enols and ketones rapidly interconvert—a process called **tautomerism.** Tautomers, which are special kinds of isomers that are readily interconvertible through a rapid equilibration, will be studied in more detail in Section 11.1. With few exceptions, the tautomeric equilibrium heavily favors the ketone; enols are almost never isolated.

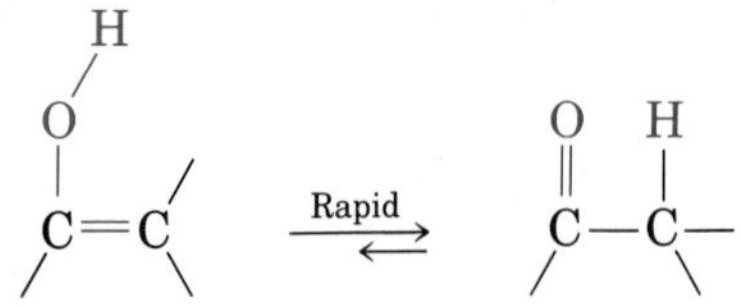

$$C=C \xrightarrow[\text{Rapid}]{} C-C$$

Enol tautomer   **Keto tautomer**
(less favored)   **(more favored)**

A mixture of both possible ketones results when an *internal* alkyne ($R—C\equiv C—R'$) is hydrated, but only a single product is formed from reaction of a *terminal* alkyne ($R—C\equiv CH$).

$$R—C\equiv C—R' \xrightarrow[\text{HgSO}_4]{\text{H}_3\text{O}^+} R—\overset{O}{\overset{\|}{C}}—CH_2—R' + R—CH_2—\overset{O}{\overset{\|}{C}}—R'$$

An internal alkyne   **A mixture**

$$R—C\equiv C—H \xrightarrow[\text{HgSO}_4]{\text{H}_3\text{O}^+} R—\overset{O}{\overset{\|}{C}}—CH_3$$

A terminal alkyne   **A methyl ketone**

PROBLEM 4.18   What alkynes would you start with to prepare the following ketones by a hydration reaction?

(a) $CH_3CH_2CH_2\overset{O}{\overset{\|}{C}}CH_3$

(b) $CH_3CH_2\overset{O}{\overset{\|}{C}}CH_2CH_2CH_3$

4.17 HYDROGENATION OF ALKYNES

Alkynes are easily converted into alkanes by reduction with 2 mol equiv of hydrogen over a palladium catalyst:

$$CH_3(CH_2)_3C\equiv C(CH_2)_3CH_3 \xrightarrow[\text{Pd catalyst}]{2\ \text{H}_2} CH_3(CH_2)_8CH_3$$

5-Decyne   **Decane (96%)**

The catalytic hydrogenation of an alkyne to yield an alkane must proceed through an intermediate alkene, and it has been found that reaction can be stopped at the alkene stage if the proper catalyst is used. The catalyst most often used for this purpose is the *Lindlar catalyst*, a finely divided form of palladium metal that has been precipitated onto a calcium carbonate support and then slightly deactivated by treatment with lead acetate. Since hydrogenation occurs with syn stereochemistry, alkynes are catalytically reduced to give cis alkenes. For example:

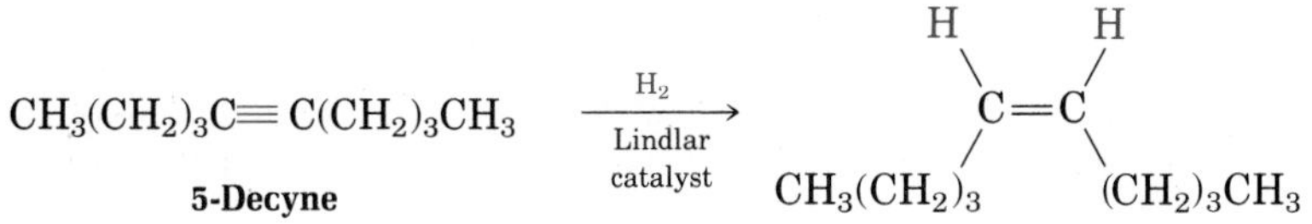

$$CH_3(CH_2)_3C \equiv C(CH_2)_3CH_3 \xrightarrow[\text{Lindlar catalyst}]{H_2}$$

5-Decyne

cis-5-Decene (96%)

Another method for the reduction of alkynes to alkenes employs lithium metal in liquid ammonia solvent. Remarkably, lithium metal dissolves in pure liquid ammonia at −33°C to produce a deep blue solution. When an alkyne is added to this blue solution, reduction of the triple bond occurs. This method is complementary to the Lindlar reduction, since it yields trans alkenes rather than cis alkenes.

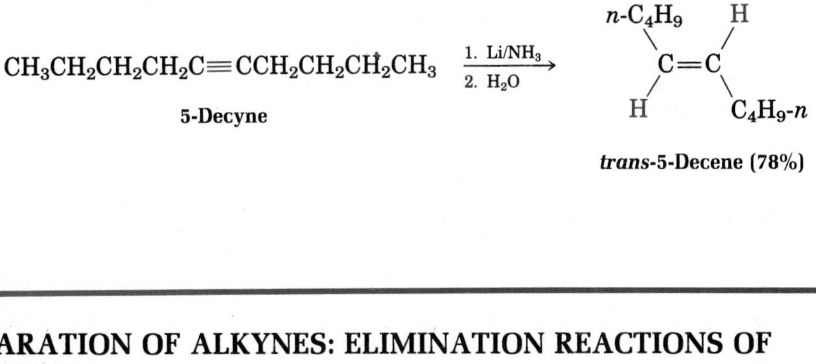

$$CH_3CH_2CH_2CH_2C \equiv CCH_2CH_2CH_2CH_3 \xrightarrow[\text{2. H}_2\text{O}]{\text{1. Li/NH}_3}$$

5-Decyne

trans-5-Decene (78%)

4.18 PREPARATION OF ALKYNES: ELIMINATION REACTIONS OF DIHALIDES

Alkynes can be prepared in much the same manner as alkenes by dehydrohalogenation of alkyl halides. Since an alkyne is *doubly* unsaturated, however, we must eliminate *two* molecules of HX.

Treatment of a 1,2-dihalide (a *vicinal* dihalide) with strong base leads to the twofold elimination of HX, producing an alkyne. The method is particularly useful because vicinal dihalides are readily available by addition of bromine or chlorine to alkenes. Thus, the overall halogenation/dehydrohalogenation sequence provides an excellent method of converting an alkene to an alkyne. For example:

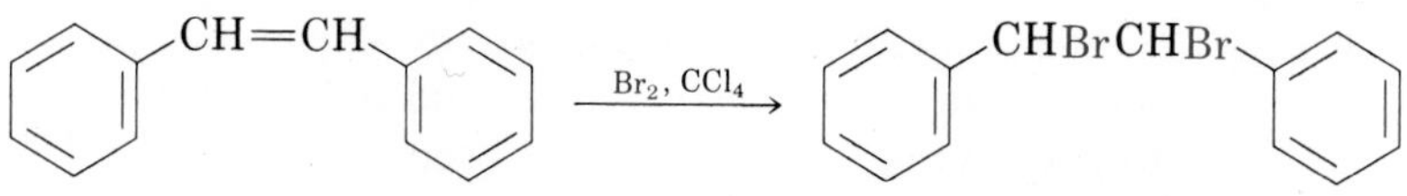

1,2-Diphenylethylene
(stilbene)

1,2-Dibromo-1,2-diphenylethane
(a vicinal dibromide)

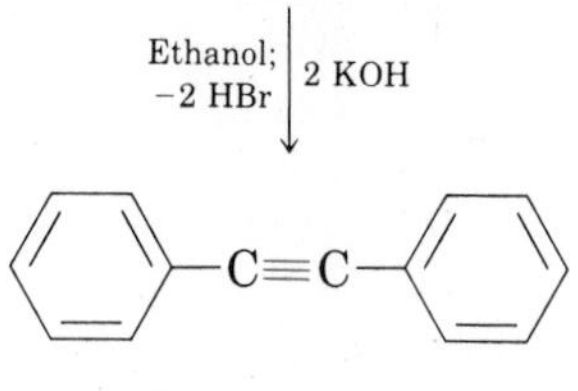

Diphenylacetylene (85%)

PROBLEM 4.19 If the twofold elimination of HX from a vicinal dihalide takes place in two steps, what intermediate would you expect to be formed? What product would you expect to obtain by treatment of a vinylic halide such as 2-chloro-2-pentene with strong base?

$$CH_3C\!\!=\!\!CHCH_2CH_3 \quad \xrightarrow{\text{KOH, }\Delta} \quad ?$$
$$| $$
$$Cl$$

ADDITIONAL PROBLEMS

PROBLEM 4.20 Provide IUPAC names for these compounds:

               CH_3

(a) $CH_3CH\!\!=\!\!CHC\!\!=\!\!CHCH_3$

(b) $CH_3CH\!\!=\!\!CHCHCH_2C\!\!\equiv\!\!CH$ [with $CH_2CH_2CH_3$ substituent]

(c) $H_2C\!\!=\!\!C\!\!=\!\!C(CH_3)_2$

(d) $HC\!\!\equiv\!\!CCH_2C\!\!\equiv\!\!CCH(CH_3)_2$

PROBLEM 4.21 Draw structures corresponding to these IUPAC names:

(a)   3-Ethyl-1-heptyne

(b)   3,5-Dimethyl-4-hexen-1-yne

(c)   1,5-Heptadiyne

(d)   1-Methyl-1,3-cyclopentadiene

PROBLEM 4.22 Draw three possible structures for each of these formulas:

(a) C_6H_8

(b) C_6H_8O

PROBLEM 4.23 Name the following alkynes according to IUPAC rules:

(a) $CH_3CH_2C\!\!\equiv\!\!CCH_2CH_2CH_3$

(b) $CH_3CH_2C\!\!\equiv\!\!CC(CH_3)_3$

(c) $CH_3C\!\!\equiv\!\!CCH_2C\!\!\equiv\!\!CCH_2CH_3$

(d) $H_2C\!\!=\!\!CHCH\!\!=\!\!CHC\!\!\equiv\!\!CH$

PROBLEM 4.24 Draw structures corresponding to these IUPAC names:

(a) 3-Heptyne   (b) 3,3-Dimethyl-4-octyne
(c) 3,4-Dimethylcyclodecyne   (d) 2,2,5,5-Tetramethyl-3-hexyne

PROBLEM 4.25 Draw and name all the possible pentyne isomers, C_5H_8.

PROBLEM 4.26 Draw and name the six possible diene isomers of formula C_5H_8. Which of the six are conjugated dienes?

PROBLEM 4.27 Predict the products of the following reactions. Indicate regiochemistry where relevant. (The benzene ring is inert to all of the indicated reagents.)

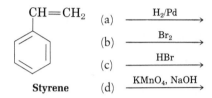

(a) $\xrightarrow{\text{H}_2/\text{Pd}}$

(b) $\xrightarrow{\text{Br}_2}$

(c) $\xrightarrow{\text{HBr}}$

(d) $\xrightarrow{\text{KMnO}_4,\ \text{NaOH}}$

Styrene

PROBLEM 4.28 Using an oxidative cleavage reaction, explain how you would distinguish between the following two isomeric cyclohexadienes:

and

PROBLEM 4.29 What products would you expect to obtain from reaction of 1,3-cyclohexadiene with each of the following?

(a) 1 mol Br_2 in CCl_4 (b) O_3, followed by Zn
(c) 1 mol HCl   (d) 1 mol DCl (D = deuterium)
(e) H_2 over a Pd catalyst

PROBLEM 4.30 Draw the structure of a hydrocarbon that reacts with only 1 mol equiv of hydrogen on catalytic hydrogenation and that gives only pentanal, $n\text{-}C_4H_9CHO$, on treatment with ozone. Write out the reactions involved.

PROBLEM 4.31 What alkenes would you start with in order to obtain the following alcohols?

(a) $CH_3CH_2\overset{\overset{\displaystyle OH}{|}}{C}HCH_3$

(b) Cyclohexanol,

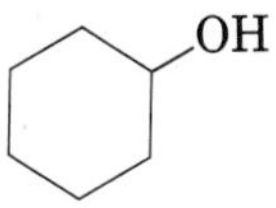

PROBLEM 4.32 Draw the structure of a hydrocarbon that reacts with 2 mol equiv of hydrogen on catalytic hydrogenation and that gives only butanedial, $OHCCH_2CH_2CHO$, on reaction with ozone.

PROBLEM 4.33 Predict the products of the following reactions:

$CH_3CH_2CH_2CH_2C\equiv CH$

1-Hexyne

(a) $\xrightarrow{\text{1 equiv HBr}}$

(b) $\xrightarrow{\text{1 equiv Cl}_2}$

(c) $\xrightarrow{\text{H}_2,\ \text{Lindlar catalyst}}$

PROBLEM 4.34   Predict the products of the following reactions:

(a) $\xrightarrow{\text{H}_2, \text{ Lindlar catalyst}}$

$CH_3CH_2CH_2CH_2C\equiv CCH_2CH_2CH_2CH_3$ (b) $\xrightarrow{\text{Li, NH}_3}$

5-Decyne   (c) $\xrightarrow{\text{2 equiv Br}_2}$

(d) $\xrightarrow{\text{H}_2\text{O, H}_2\text{SO}_4, \text{HgSO}_4}$

PROBLEM 4.35   Acrylonitrile, $H_2C\!=\!CHC\equiv N$, contains a carbon–carbon double bond and a carbon–nitrogen triple bond. Sketch the orbitals involved in the bonding in acrylonitrile and indicate the hybridization of the carbons. Is acrylonitrile conjugated?

PROBLEM 4.36   Using 1-butyne as the only organic starting material, along with any inorganic reagents needed, how would you synthesize the following compounds? More than one step may be needed.

(a)   Butane   (b)   1,1,2,2-Tetrachlorobutane
(c)   2-Bromobutane   (d)   2-Butanone, $CH_3CH_2COCH_3$

PROBLEM 4.37   Give the structure of an alkene that provides only acetone, $(CH_3)_2C\!=\!O$, on reaction with ozone.

PROBLEM 4.38   Compound A has the formula C_8H_8. It reacts rapidly with acidic $KMnO_4$, but reacts with only 1 equiv of H_2 on catalytic hydrogenation over a palladium catalyst. On hydrogenation under conditions that reduce aromatic rings, A reacts with 4 equiv of H_2, and hydrocarbon B, C_8H_{16}, is produced. The reaction of A with $KMnO_4$ gives CO_2 and a carboxylic acid C, $C_7H_6O_2$. What are the structures of A, B, and C? Write out all the reactions.

PROBLEM 4.39   Draw a reaction energy diagram for the addition of HBr to 1-pentene. Let one curve on your diagram show the formation of 1-bromopentane product and another curve on the same diagram show the formation of 2-bromopentane product. Label the positions of all reactants, intermediates, and products.

PROBLEM 4.40   Make sketches of what you imagine the transition-state structures to look like in the reaction of HBr with 1-pentene (Problem 4.39).

PROBLEM 4.41   Ethylidenecyclohexane, on treatment with strong acid, isomerizes to yield 1-ethylcyclohexene:

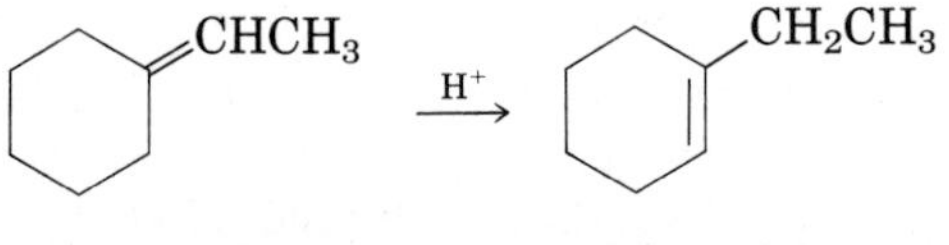

Ethylidenecyclohexane   **1-Ethylcyclohexene**

Propose a mechanism by which this reaction might occur.

Alkene Polymers

No other group of synthetic organic compounds has had as great an impact on our day-to-day living as the synthetic polymers. As plastics, adhesives, and paints, synthetic polymers have a multitude of uses, from the foam coffee cup to the life-saving artificial heart valve.

A **polymer** is a large molecule built up by repetitive bonding together of many smaller units called **monomers**. As we'll see in later chapters, nature makes wide use of biological polymers. For example, cellulose is a carbohydrate polymer built of repeating sugar units; proteins are polymers built of repeating amino acid units; and nucleic acids are immense polymers built of repeating nucleotide units. Synthetic polymers are chemically much simpler than biopolymers, since the repeating monomer units tend to be small, simple, and inexpensive molecules. There is, however, an immense diversity to the structure and properties of synthetic polymers, depending on the nature of the monomer and on the reaction conditions used for polymerization.

Radical Polymerization of Alkenes

Many low-molecular-weight alkenes undergo rapid polymerization when treated with catalytic amounts of a radical initiator. For example, ethylene yields polyethylene on polymerization. Ethylene polymerization is usually carried out at high pressure (1000–3000 atm) and high temperature (100–250°C) with a radical catalyst such as benzoyl peroxide. The resultant polymer may have anywhere from a few hundred to a few thousand monomer units incorporated into the chain.

Radical polymerizations of alkenes involve three kinds of steps: initiation, propagation, and termination. **Initiation** occurs when small amounts of radicals are generated by the catalyst (step 1). For example, when benzoyl peroxide is used as initiator, the oxygen–oxygen bond is broken by heating to yield benzoyloxy radicals. One of these radicals reacts with the double bond of an ethylene molecule to generate a new carbon radical (step 2), and the polymerization is off and running. Note that this radical addition step results in formation of a bond between the initiator and the ethylene molecule in which one electron has been contributed by each partner. The remaining electron from the ethylene pi bond remains on carbon as the new radical site.

Step 1

$$C_6H_5-\overset{\overset{O}{\|}}{C}-O-O-\overset{\overset{O}{\|}}{C}-C_6H_5 \xrightarrow{\Delta} 2\ C_6H_5\overset{\overset{O}{\|}}{C}-O\cdot$$

Benzoyl peroxide   **Initiator, In·**
Benzoyloxy radical

Step 2 $In \cdot \ + \ CH_2 = CH_2 \ \longrightarrow \ In - CH_2 - CH_2 \cdot$

Propagation of the reaction occurs when the carbon radical adds to another ethylene molecule (step 3). Repetition of step 3 for hundreds or thousands of times builds the polymer chain.

Step 3 $In - CH_2 - CH_2 \cdot \ + \ CH_2 = CH_2$

$$\longrightarrow \ In - CH_2 - CH_2 - CH_2 - CH_2 \cdot$$

$$\xrightarrow[\text{many times}]{\text{Repeat}} \ In - (CH_2 - CH_2)_n CH_2 - CH_2 \cdot$$

Eventually, the polymer chain is **terminated** by reactions that consume the radical. For example, combination of two chains by chance meeting (step 4) is a possible chain-terminating reaction.

Step 4 $2 \, In - (CH_2 - CH_2)_n - CH_2 CH_2 \cdot$

$$\longrightarrow \ In \, (CH_2 CH_2)_n CH_2 CH_2 - CH_2 CH_2 (CH_2 CH_2)_n In$$

Polymerization of Substituted Ethylenes

Many substituted ethylenes (**vinyl monomers**) undergo radical-initiated polymerization to yield polymers with substituent groups (denoted by a circled S) regularly spaced along the polymer backbone.

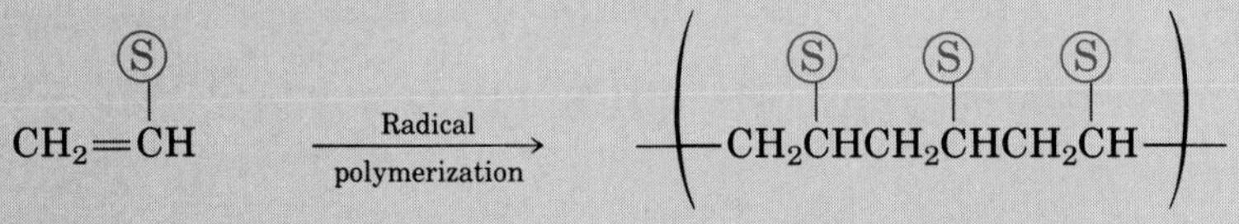

Monomer   **Polymer**

Table C.1 shows some of the more important vinyl monomers and lists the industrial uses of the different polymers that result.

TABLE C.1   Some alkene polymers and their uses

Monomer name	Formula	Trade or common names of polymer	Uses
Ethylene	$H_2C\!=\!CH_2$	Polyethylene	Packaging, bottles, cable insulation, films and sheets
Propene (propylene)	$H_2C\!=\!CHCH_3$	Polypropylene	Automotive moldings, rope, carpet fibers
Chloroethylene (vinyl chloride)	$H_2C\!=\!CHCl$	Poly(vinyl chloride), Tedlar	Insulation, films, pipes
Styrene	$H_2C\!=\!CHC_6H_5$	Polystyrene, Styron	Foam and molded articles
Tetrafluoroethylene	$F_2C\!=\!CF_2$	Teflon	Valves and gaskets, coatings
Acrylonitrile	$H_2C\!=\!CHCN$	Orlon, Acrilan	Fibers
Methyl methacrylate	$\overset{\displaystyle CH_3}{\underset{\displaystyle \vert}{H_2C\!=\!C}}CO_2CH_3$	Plexiglas, Lucite	Molded articles, paints
Vinyl acetate	$H_2C\!=\!CHOCOCH_3$	Poly(vinyl acetate)	Paints, adhesives
Vinyl alcohol	"$H_2C\!=\!CHOH$"	Poly(vinyl alcohol)	Fibers, adhesives

CHAPTER 5

Aromatic Compounds

In the early days of organic chemistry, the word *aromatic* was used to describe fragrant substances such as benzaldehyde (from cherries, peaches, and almonds), toluene (from tolu balsam), and benzene (from coal distillate). It was soon realized, however, that these aromatic substances behave in a chemically different manner from most other organic compounds.

Today, we use the term **aromatic** to refer to the class of compounds composed of benzene and its structural relatives. We will see in this chapter that aromatic substances show chemical behavior quite different from that of the alkanes, alkenes, and alkynes we have studied up to this point. Thus, chemists of the early nineteenth century were correct when they realized that a chemical difference exists between aromatic compounds and other types, but the association of aromaticity with fragrance has long been lost.

Many important compounds are aromatic in part. In addition to benzene, benzaldehyde, and toluene, compounds such as the steroidal hormone estrone and the tranquilizer diazepam (Valium) have aromatic rings.

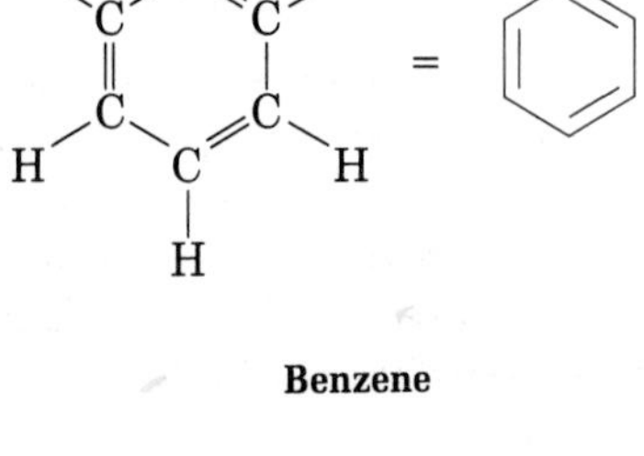

Benzene 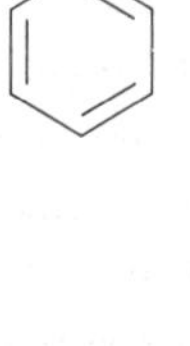   Benzaldehyde    Toluene

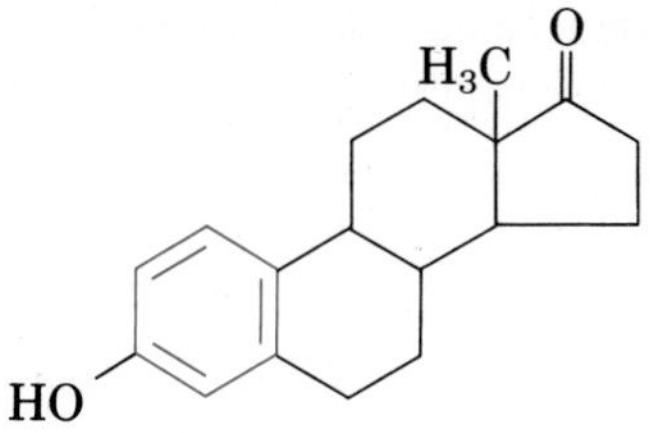

Estrone

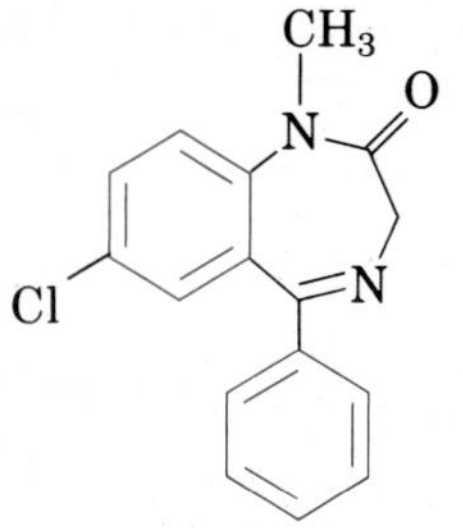

Diazepam
(Valium, a tranquilizer)

PROBLEM 5.1 Circle the aromatic portions of these molecules:

(a) CH(OH)CH₂NHCH₃

OH
OH

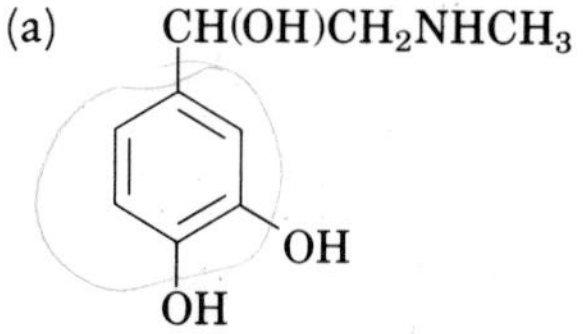

Adrenaline (epinephrine)

(b)

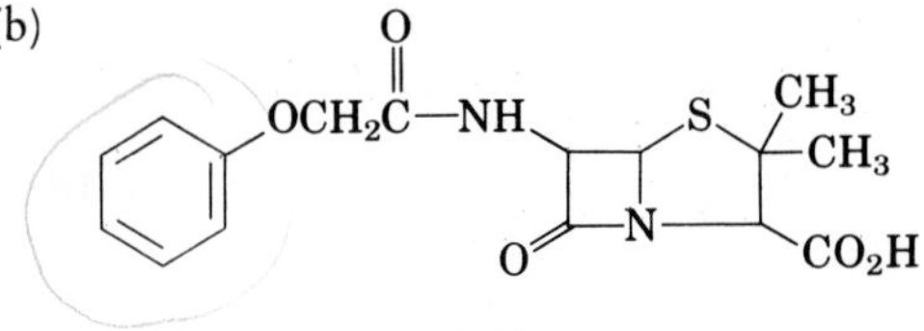

Penicillin V

5.1 NOMENCLATURE OF AROMATIC COMPOUNDS

Aromatic substances, more than any other class of organic compounds, have acquired a large number of trivial, nonsystematic names. Although the use of such names is discouraged, IUPAC rules allow for some of the more common ones shown in Table 5.1 (page 128) to be retained. Thus, methylbenzene is known familiarly as toluene, hydroxybenzene as phenol, aminobenzene as aniline, and so on.

Monosubstituted benzene derivatives are systematically named in the same manner as other hydrocarbons, with *-benzene* used as the parent name. Thus, C_6H_5Br is bromobenzene, $C_6H_5CH_2CH_3$ is ethylbenzene, and $C_6H_5NO_2$ is nitrobenzene.

Bromobenzene   **Ethylbenzene**   **Nitrobenzene**

Alkyl-substituted benzenes, sometimes referred to as **arenes**, are named in two ways depending on the size of the alkyl group. If the alkyl group has six or fewer carbons, the arene is named as an alkyl-substituted benzene. If the alkyl substituent has more than six carbons, the compound is named as a phenyl-substituted alkane. The name **phenyl** (fen′-nil) is used for the C_6H_5 unit when the benzene ring is considered a substituent group.

TABLE 5.1   Trivial names of some common aromatic compounds

Formula	Name	Formula	Name
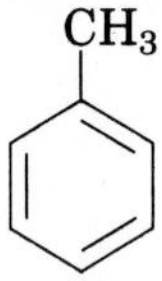 CH_3 (benzene ring)	Toluene (bp 110°C)	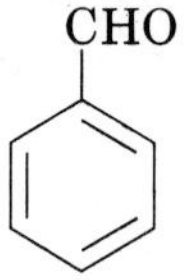 CHO (benzene ring)	Benzaldehyde (bp 178°C)
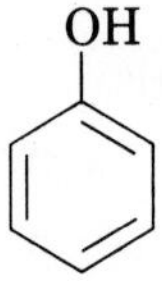 OH (benzene ring)	Phenol (mp 43°C)	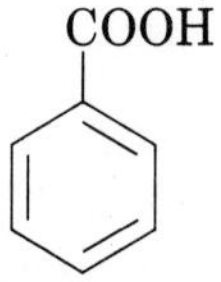 COOH (benzene ring)	Benzoic acid (mp 122°C)
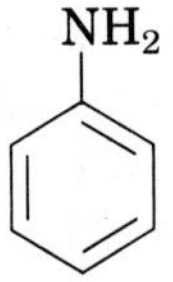 NH_2 (benzene ring)	Aniline (bp 184°C)	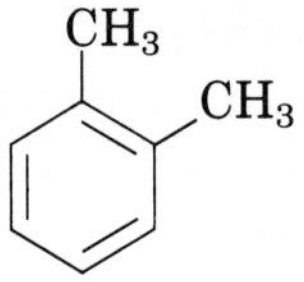 CH_3, CH_3 (benzene ring)	*ortho*-Xylene (bp 144°C)
 CH_3, CH_3 (benzene ring)	*para*-Xylene (bp 138°C)	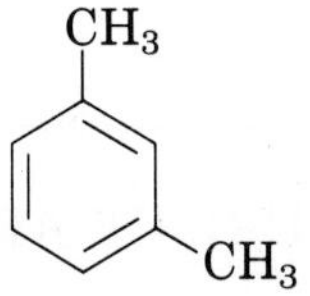 CH_3, CH_3 (benzene ring)	*meta*-Xylene (bp 139°C)

$$\overset{1}{C}H_3\overset{2}{C}H_2 \qquad \overset{4}{C}H_2\overset{5}{C}H_2\overset{6}{C}H_2\overset{7}{C}H_2\overset{8}{C}H_3$$
$$\overset{3}{C}H$$

A phenyl group 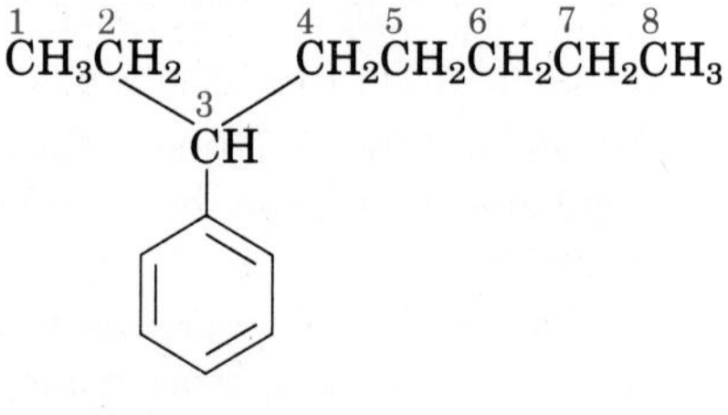   3-Phenyloctane

Disubstituted benzenes are named by using one of the prefixes *ortho-*, *meta-*, or *para-*. An *ortho-* or *o*-disubstituted benzene has its two substituents in a 1,2 relationship on the ring; a *meta-* or *m*-disubstituted benzene has its two substituents in a 1,3 relationship; and a *para-* or *p*-disubstituted benzene has its substituents in a 1,4 relationship.

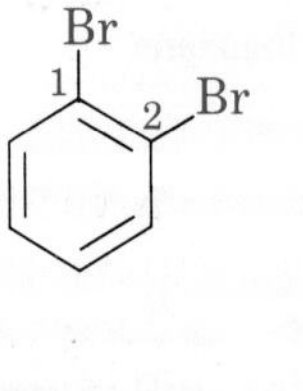

***ortho*-Dibromobenzene,   *meta*-Dimethylbenzene   *para*-Bromochlorobenzene,**
1,2 disubstituted   (*m*-xylene)   1,4 disubstituted
                                1,3 disubstituted

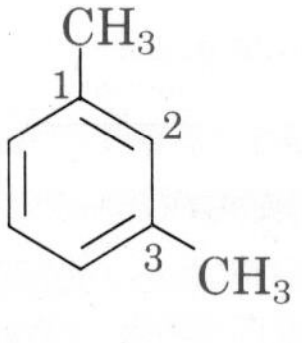

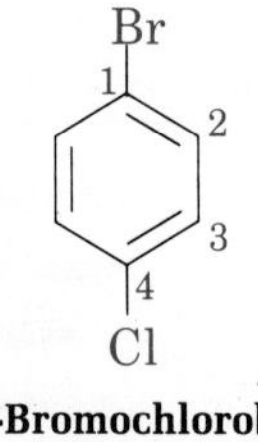

The ortho, meta, para system of nomenclature is also valuable when discussing reactions. For example, we might describe the reaction of bromine with toluene by saying, "Reaction occurs at the para position." In other words, reaction occurs at the position para to the methyl group already present on the ring.

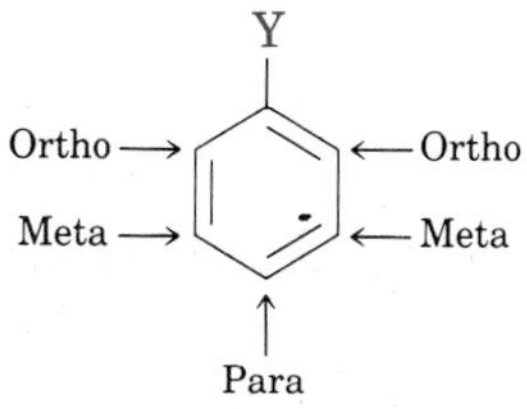

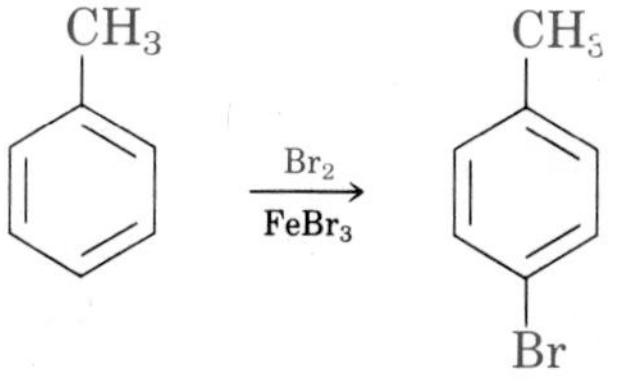

Toluene   **p-Bromotoluene**

Benzenes with more than two substituents must be named by numbering the position of each substituent on the ring. The numbering should be carried out in such a way that the lowest possible numbers are used. The substituents are listed alphabetically when writing the name.

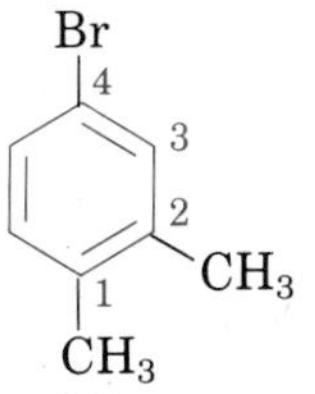

4-Bromo-1,2-dimethylbenzene 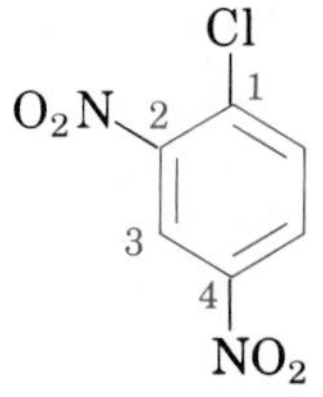   **1-Chloro-2,4-dinitrobenzene** 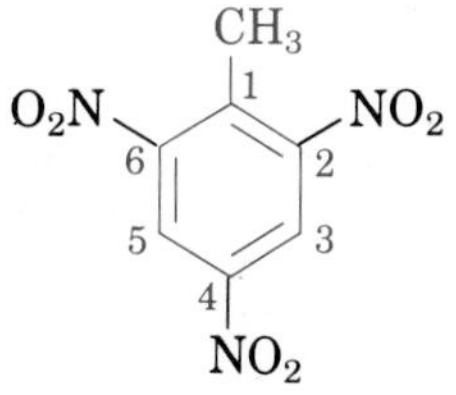   **2,4,6-Trinitrotoluene (TNT)**

In the third example shown, note that *-toluene* is used as the parent name, rather than *-benzene*. Any of the monosubstituted aromatic compounds shown in Table 5.1 can serve as a parent name. In such cases, the principal substituent ($-CH_3$ in toluene, for example) is assumed to be on C1. The following two examples further illustrate this rule:

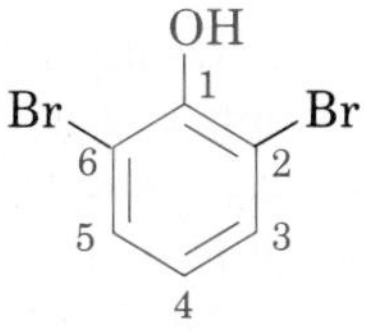

2,6-Dibromophenol   ***m*-Chlorobenzoic acid**

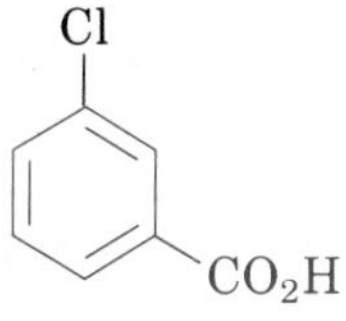

PROBLEM 5.2   Provide correct IUPAC names for these compounds:

(a)

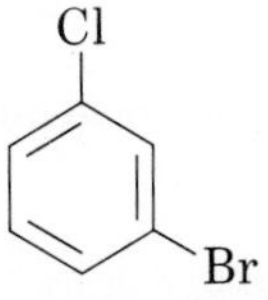

(b) $CH_2CH_2CH(CH_3)_2$

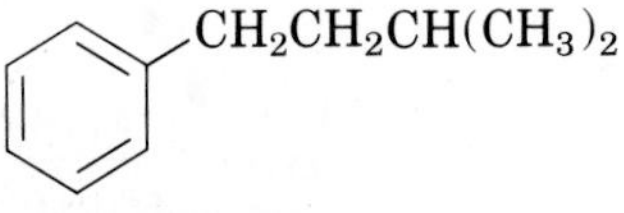

(c) 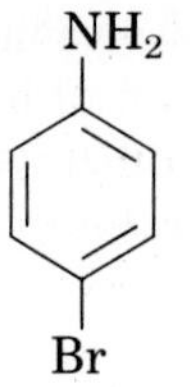   NH$_2$

Br

(d) 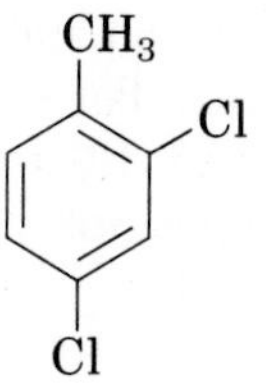   CH$_3$

Cl

Cl

PROBLEM 5.3   Draw structures corresponding to these IUPAC names:

(a)   1-Bromo-2-chlorobenzene
(c)   *m*-Chloroaniline

(b)   *p*-Bromotoluene
(d)   1-Chloro-3,5-dimethylbenzene

5.2   STRUCTURE OF BENZENE: THE KEKULÉ PROPOSAL

By the mid-1800s, benzene was known to have the molecular formula C_6H_6, and its chemistry was being actively explored. For example, it was known that, although benzene was relatively unreactive toward most reagents that attack alkenes, it would react with bromine in the presence of iron to give the *substitution* product, C_6H_5Br, rather than the possible *addition* product $C_6H_6Br_2$. Furthermore, only one monobromo substitution product was known; no isomers had been prepared.

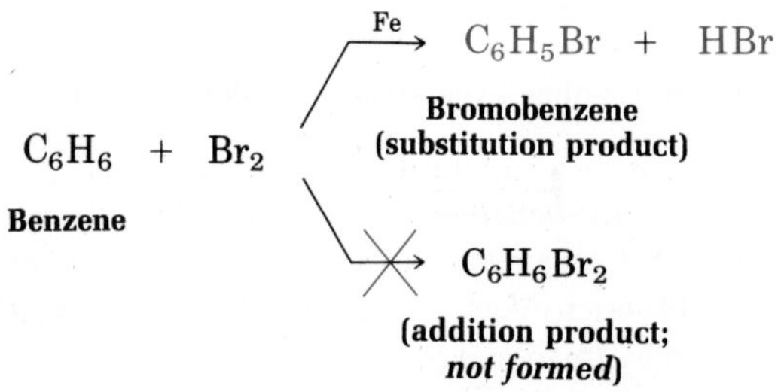

$$C_6H_6 \ + \ Br_2$$

Benzene

$\xrightarrow{Fe}$ $C_6H_5Br \ + \ HBr$

Bromobenzene
(substitution product)

$\rightarrow$ $C_6H_6Br_2$

(addition product;
***not formed*)**

On the basis of these and other results, Kekulé proposed in 1865 that benzene consists of a *ring* of carbon atoms and may be formulated as cyclohexatriene. Kekulé reasoned that this structure would readily account for the isolation of only a single monobromo substitution product, since all six carbon atoms and all six hydrogens in cyclohexatriene are equivalent.

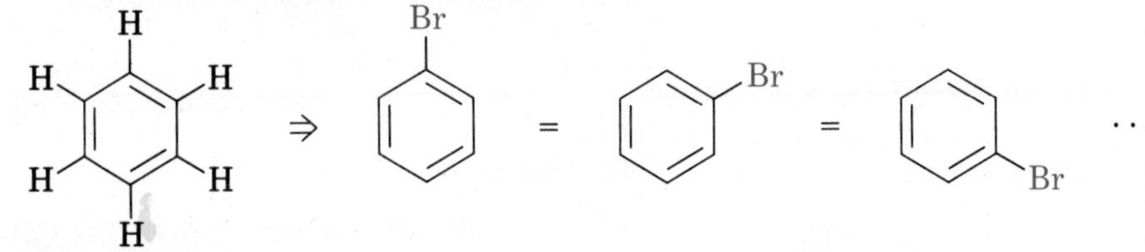

All six hydrogens of cyclohexatriene are equivalent

Only one possible monobromo product

Kekulé's proposal was widely criticized by other chemists of the day. Although it satisfactorily accounts for the correct number of monosubstituted benzene isomers, the proposal does not answer the critical questions of why benzene is unreactive compared to other alkenes, and why benzene gives a substitution product rather than an alkene-type addition product on reaction with bromine.

PROBLEM 5.4   How many dibromobenzene derivatives are possible according to Kekulé's theory? Draw and name them.

5.3   STABILITY OF BENZENE

The unusual chemical stability of benzene was a great puzzle to early chemists. Although its formula, C_6H_6, indicates that several double bonds must be present, benzene shows none of the behavior characteristic of alkenes. For example, alkenes react readily with $KMnO_4$ to give 1,2-diols; with aqueous acid to give alcohols; and with gaseous HCl to give saturated chloroalkanes. Benzene does none of these things. *Benzene does not undergo electrophilic addition reactions* (Figure 5.1).

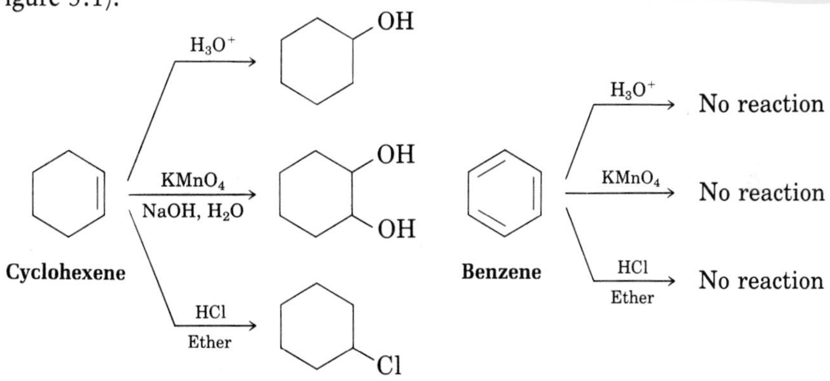

FIGURE 5.1
A comparison of the reactivity of cyclohexene and benzene

Further evidence for the unusual nature of benzene comes from studies indicating that all carbon–carbon bonds in benzene have the same length, intermediate between a normal single bond and a normal double bond. Most carbon–carbon single bonds have lengths near 1.54 Å, and most carbon–carbon double bonds are about 1.33 Å long. All carbon–carbon bonds in benzene, however, are 1.39 Å long.

All C-C-C bond angles = 120°
All C—C bond lengths = 1.39Å

Benzene

5.4   STRUCTURE OF BENZENE: THE RESONANCE PROPOSAL

How can we account for benzene's properties, and how can its structure best be represented? To answer this question, we need to review the concept of **resonance**. We saw in Section 4.12 that an allylic carbocation is best described as a resonance hybrid of two contributing resonance forms. Neither form is correct by itself—the true structure of an allylic carbocation cannot be drawn using a single line-bond structure, but must be considered as intermediate between the two resonance forms:

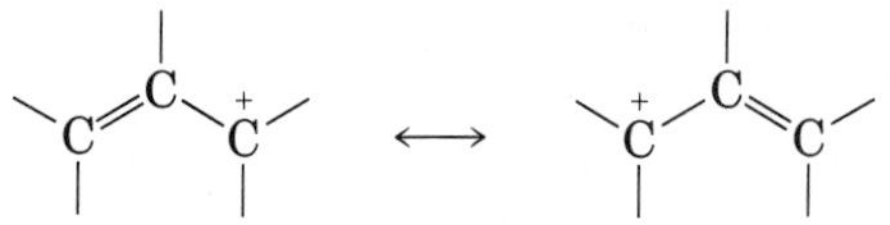

By the same token, resonance theory says that benzene cannot be satisfactorily described by a single line-bond structure. Instead, benzene can best be described as a resonance hybrid of two equivalent structures. Benzene does *not* oscillate back and forth between two extremes; its true structure is somewhere in between the two extremes but is impossible to draw with our usual conventions (Figure 5.2).

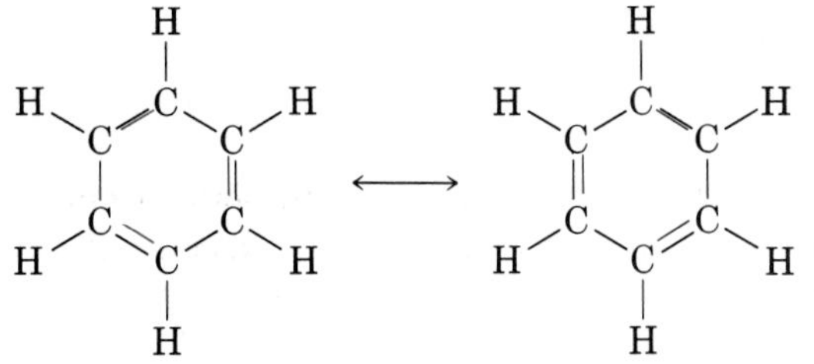

FIGURE 5.2
Two equivalent resonance structures of benzene: Each carbon–carbon connection averages out to be 1.5 bonds—midway between single and double bonds.

An orbital view of benzene (Figure 5.3) shows the situation more clearly, emphasizing the *cyclic conjugation* of the benzene molecule and the equivalence of the six carbon–carbon bonds. Benzene is a flat, symmetrical molecule in the

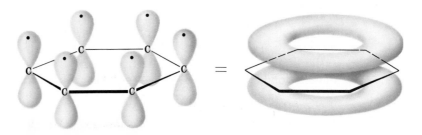

FIGURE 5.3
An orbital picture of benzene

shape of a regular hexagon. All C-C-C bond angles are 120°; each carbon atom is sp^2 hybridized; and each carbon has a p orbital perpendicular to the plane of the six-membered ring. Since all six p orbitals are equivalent, it is impossible to define three localized alkene pi bonds in which a given p orbital overlaps only *one* neighboring p orbital. Rather, each p orbital can overlap equally well with *both* neighboring p orbitals, leading to a picture of benzene in which the pi electrons are completely delocalized around the ring in two doughnut-shaped clouds (Figure 5.3).

To complete the resonance description of benzene, we can now see why benzene is unusually stable. According to resonance theory, the more stable resonance forms a substance has, the more stable it is. Benzene, with two resonance forms of equal energy, is thus highly stabilized.

Resonance theory also explains why there is only one *ortho*-dibromobenzene, rather than the two that Kekulé's proposal might suggest. The two possible 1,2-dibromobenzene "isomers" are in fact just different resonance forms of a single compound whose true structure is intermediate between the two (Figure 5.4).

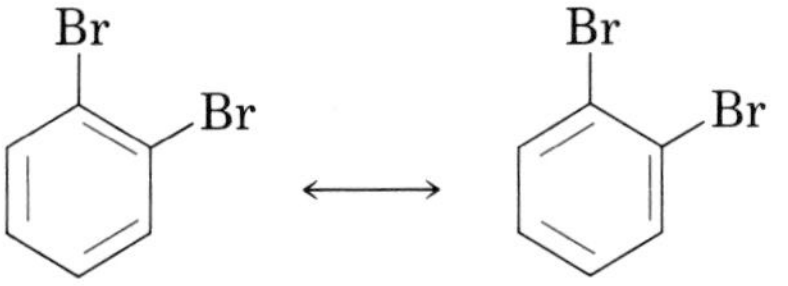

FIGURE 5.4
Two equivalent resonance forms of *ortho*-dibromobenzene

5.5 CHEMISTRY OF BENZENE: ELECTROPHILIC AROMATIC SUBSTITUTION

The most important reaction of aromatic compounds is **electrophilic aromatic substitution.** That is, an electron-poor reagent (an electrophile) reacts with an aromatic ring and substitutes for one of the ring hydrogens (Figure 5.5).

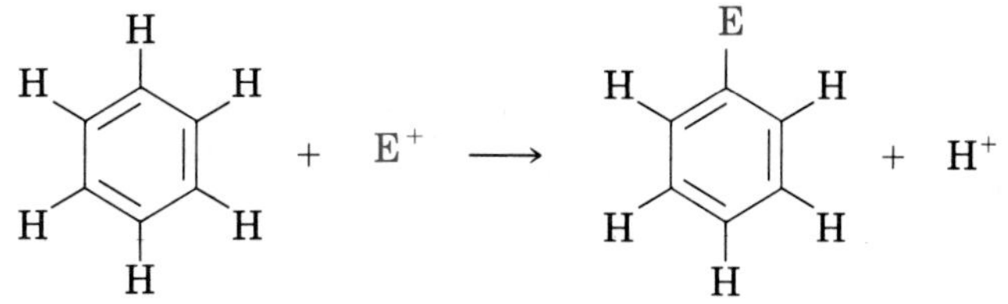

FIGURE 5.5
An electrophilic aromatic substitution reaction (E^+ represents an electrophile)

Many different substituents may be introduced onto the aromatic ring using electrophilic substitution reactions. By choosing the proper conditions and reagents, we can **halogenate** (substitute a halogen: —F, —Cl, —Br, or —I), **nitrate** (substitute a nitro group: —NO_2), **sulfonate** (substitute a sulfonic acid group: —SO_3H), or **alkylate** (substitute an alkyl group: —R) the aromatic ring. Starting from only a few simple materials, we can prepare many thousands of substituted aromatic compounds. Table 5.2 (page 134) shows some of these possibilities.

TABLE 5.2   Some electrophilic aromatic substitution reactions

Name	Example		
Bromination	Ar—H + Br$_2$	$\xrightarrow{\text{FeBr}_3}$	Ar—Br (an aryl bromide)
Chlorination	Ar—H + Cl$_2$	$\xrightarrow{\text{FeCl}_3}$	Ar—Cl (an aryl chloride)
Nitration	Ar—H + HNO$_3$	$\xrightarrow{\text{H}_2\text{SO}_4}$	Ar—NO$_2$ (a nitro aromatic compound)
Sulfonation	Ar—H + SO$_3$	$\xrightarrow{\text{H}_2\text{SO}_4}$	Ar—SO$_3$H (an aromatic sulfonic acid)
Friedel–Crafts alkylation	Ar—H + R—Cl	$\xrightarrow{\text{AlCl}_3}$	Ar—R (an arene)
Friedel–Crafts acylation	Ar—H + R—$\overset{\displaystyle O}{\overset{\|}{C}}$Cl	$\xrightarrow{\text{AlCl}_3}$	Ar—$\overset{\displaystyle O}{\overset{\|}{C}}$—R (an aryl ketone)

All these reactions (and many more as well) take place by a similar mechanism. Let's begin a study of this reaction by looking at one reaction in detail—the bromination of benzene.

5.6   BROMINATION OF BENZENE

Benzene reacts with bromine in the presence of FeBr$_3$ as catalyst to yield the substitution product bromobenzene:

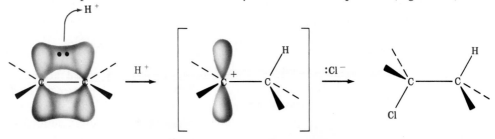

Benzene   **Bromobenzene (80%)**

Before seeing how this electrophilic *substitution* reaction occurs, let's briefly recall what we have learned about electrophilic *additions* to alkenes. When an electrophile such as H$^+$ adds to an alkene, it approaches perpendicular to the plane of the double bond and forms a bond to one carbon, leaving a positive charge at the other carbon. This carbocation intermediate is then attacked by a nucleophile such as chloride ion to yield the addition product (Figure 5.6).

Alkene   **Carbocation intermediate**   **Addition product**

FIGURE 5.6
The mechanism of an electrophilic addition to an alkene

An electrophilic aromatic substitution reaction begins in a similar way, but there are a number of differences. One difference is noticeable immediately—aromatic rings are much less reactive than alkenes toward electrophiles. For example, bromine in CCl_4 solution reacts instantly with most alkenes, but does not react with benzene. For bromination of benzene to take place, a catalyst such as $FeBr_3$ is needed. The catalyst exerts its effect by reacting with bromine to form $FeBr_4^-$ and Br^+, a highly reactive electrophile.

$$FeBr_3 + Br_2 \longrightarrow FeBr_4^- + Br^+$$

The electrophilic Br^+ then reacts with the pi electrons of the electron-rich (nucleophilic) benzene ring in a slow step to yield a nonaromatic carbocation intermediate. This carbocation is doubly allylic (recall the allyl cation, discussed in Section 4.12) and can be drawn in three resonance forms:

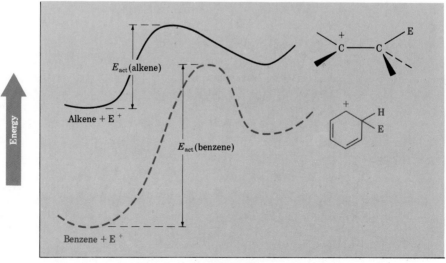

Although stable by comparison with most other carbocations, the intermediate in electrophilic aromatic substitution is nevertheless much less stable than the starting benzene ring itself. Thus, reaction of an electrophile with a benzene ring is highly endothermic, has a high activation energy, and is therefore rather slow. Figure 5.7 gives reaction energy diagrams for the reaction of an electrophile, E^+, with an alkene and with benzene. The benzene reaction is slower (that is, has a higher E_{act}) because the starting material is so stable.

FIGURE 5.7

A comparison of the reactions of an electrophile with an alkene and with benzene: E_{act} (alkene) $\ll E_{act}$ (benzene).

A second major difference between alkene addition and aromatic substitution reactions occurs after the electrophile has added to the benzene ring to give the carbocation intermediate. Although it would presumably be possible for a nucleophile such as bromide ion to attack the carbocation intermediate to yield the addition product, dibromocyclohexadiene, this is not observed. Instead, the bromide ion abstracts the hydrogen from the bromine-bearing carbon to yield the neutral, aromatic substitution product plus HBr. The net effect of reaction of Br_2 with benzene is substitution of H^+ by Br^+. The overall mechanism is shown in Figure 5.8.

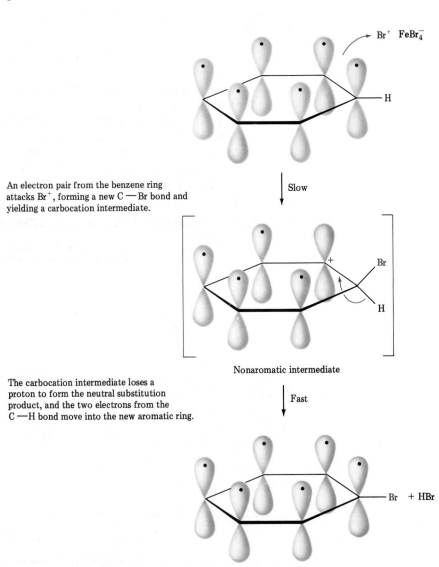

FIGURE 5.8

The mechanism of the electrophilic bromination of benzene

Why does the reaction of bromine with benzene take a different course than its reaction with an alkene? The answer is quite simple: If addition to benzene occurred, the great stability of the aromatic ring would be lost and the reaction would be endothermic. By losing a proton, the carbocation intermediate reverts to an aromatic ring structure and regains aromatic stabilization. The reaction energy diagram for the overall process is shown in Figure 5.9.

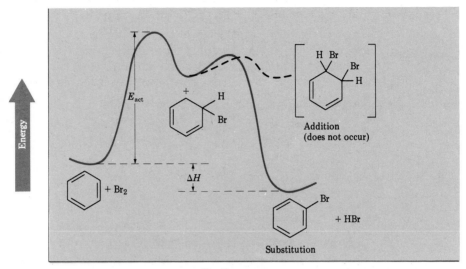

FIGURE 5.9
A reaction energy diagram for the electrophilic bromination of benzene

5.7 OTHER ELECTROPHILIC AROMATIC SUBSTITUTION REACTIONS

There are many other electrophilic aromatic substitutions besides bromination, and all are thought to occur by the same general mechanism. Let's briefly see what some of these other reactions are.

Chlorine and iodine can be introduced onto aromatic rings under the proper conditions. As with bromination, a catalyst such as $FeCl_3$ is required for chlorination.

$$[\,Cl_2 + FeCl_3 \longrightarrow Cl^+ + FeCl_4^-\,]$$

Benzene + Cl_2 $\xrightarrow{FeCl_3 \text{ (catalyst)}}$ Chlorobenzene (86%) + HCl

Iodinations are best carried out by treatment of the aromatic compound with iodine and a mild oxidizing agent such as $CuCl_2$. The $CuCl_2$ is thought to work by oxidizing I_2 to the more powerful electrophile, I^+, which then reacts with the aromatic ring.

$$[I_2 + 2\,Cu^{2+} \longrightarrow 2\,I^+ + 2\,Cu^+]$$

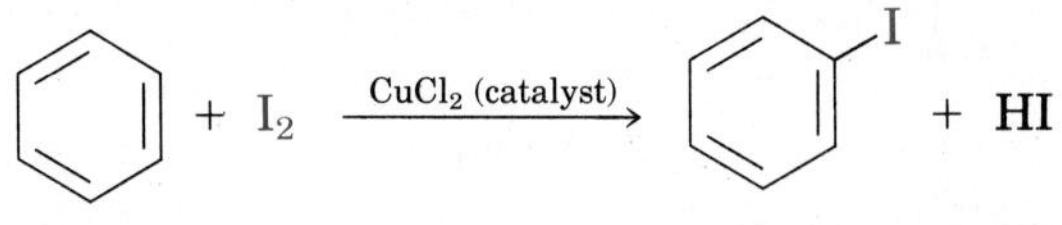

Benzene   Iodobenzene (65%)

Aromatic rings can be nitrated by reaction with a mixture of concentrated nitric and sulfuric acids. The electrophile in this reaction is thought to be the nitronium ion, NO_2^+. The nitronium ion then reacts with benzene to yield a carbocation intermediate in much the same way that we discussed for Br^+. Loss of a proton from this intermediate gives the neutral substitution product, nitrobenzene.

$$[HO\!-\!NO_2 + H_2SO_4 \longrightarrow NO_2^+ + H_2O + HSO_4^-]$$

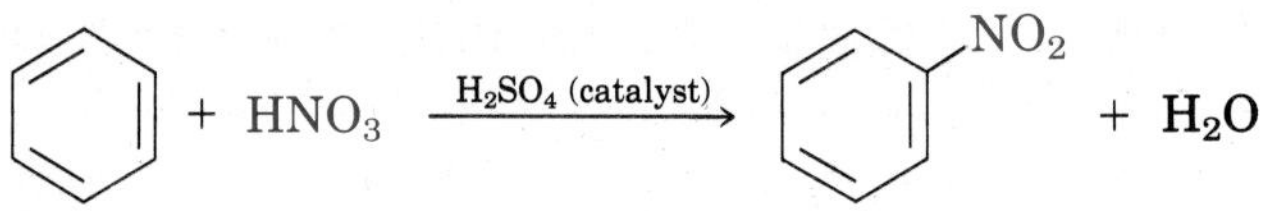

Benzene   Nitrobenzene (85%)

Aromatic rings can be sulfonated by reaction with fuming sulfuric acid, a mixture of SO_3 + H_2SO_4. The reactive electrophile under these conditions is HSO_3^+, and substitution occurs by the same two-step mechanism we've seen previously for bromination and nitration.

$$[SO_3 + H_2SO_4 \longrightarrow {}^+SO_3H + HSO_4^-]$$

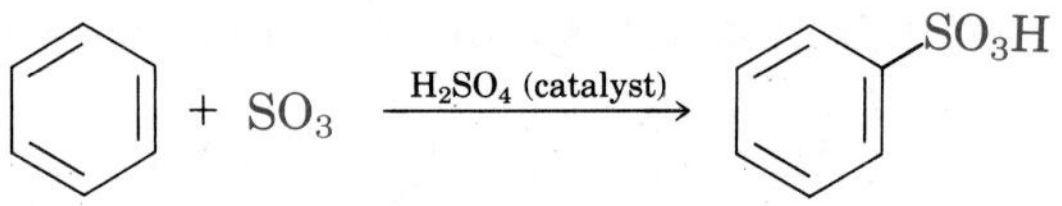

Benzene   Benzenesulfonic acid (95%)

Aromatic sulfonic acids are valuable because of the further chemistry they undergo. For example, treatment of an arenesulfonic acid with NaOH at 300°C in the absence of solvent yields a phenol—a net replacement of the sulfonic acid group by hydroxyl.

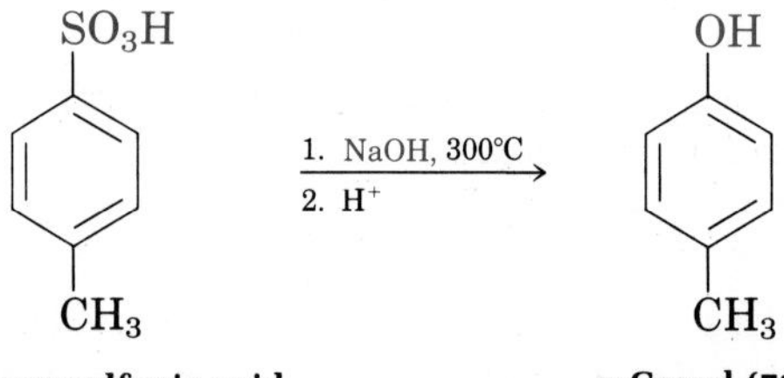

p-Toluenesulfonic acid   p-Cresol (72%)
                                    (a phenol)

PROBLEM 5.5   Show all steps in the mechanism of the reaction of benzene with nitric acid and sulfuric acid to yield nitrobenzene.

PROBLEM 5.6   How can you account for the fact that deuterium slowly replaces hydrogen in the aromatic ring when benzene is treated with D_2SO_4?

5.8   THE FRIEDEL–CRAFTS ALKYLATION REACTION

Charles Friedel and James Crafts reported in 1877 that benzene rings can be alkylated by reaction with an alkyl chloride in the presence of aluminum chloride catalyst. That is, an alkyl group can be introduced onto an aromatic ring. For example, benzene reacts with 2-chloropropane in the presence of $AlCl_3$ to yield isopropylbenzene (also called cumene).

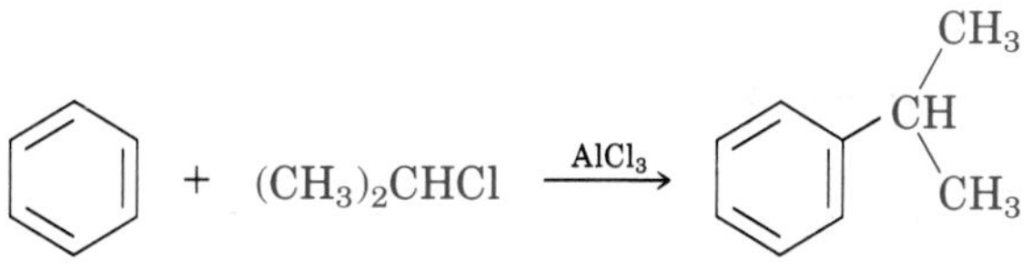

| Benzene | 2-Chloropropane | Cumene (85%) (isopropylbenzene) |

The **Friedel–Crafts alkylation reaction** is an electrophilic aromatic substitution in which the aromatic ring attacks a carbocation. Loss of a proton from the intermediate then yields the alkylated aromatic ring. The carbocation is normally generated by reaction of an alkyl chloride with a Lewis acid catalyst such as aluminum chloride. It is thought that the $AlCl_3$ catalyst acts by helping the alkyl chloride to ionize, in much the same way that $FeCl_3$ catalyzes aromatic ring chlorinations by helping Cl_2 to ionize. The overall Friedel–Crafts mechanism for the synthesis of isopropylbenzene is shown in Figure 5.10 on page 140.

PROBLEM 5.7   What products would you expect to obtain from reaction of the following compounds with chloroethane and $AlCl_3$?

(a)   Benzene   (b)   p-Dimethylbenzene

PROBLEM 5.8   If o-dimethylbenzene is treated with chloromethane and $AlCl_3$, a mixture of *two* trimethylbenzene products is obtained. Explain.

$$(CH_3)_2CHCl + AlCl_3 \longrightarrow (CH_3)_2CH^+ \; AlCl_4^-$$

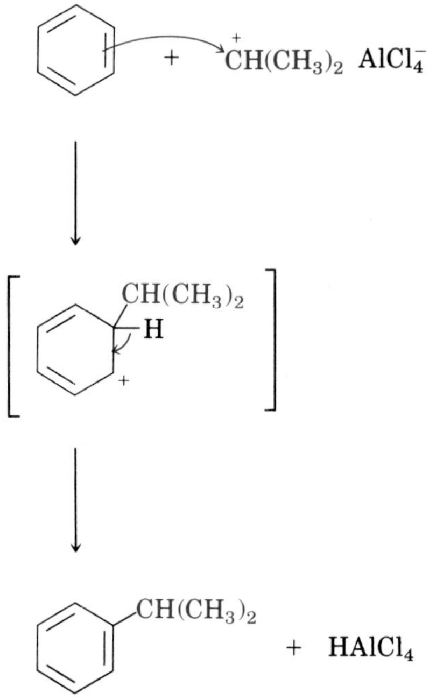

An electron pair from the aromatic
ring attacks the carbocation, forming
a C—C bond and yielding a new
carbocation intermediate.

Loss of a proton then gives the
neutral arene product.

FIGURE 5.10
Mechanism of the Friedel–Crafts alkylation reaction in the synthesis of
isopropylbenzene

5.9   LIMITATIONS OF THE FRIEDEL–CRAFTS REACTION

The Alkyl Halide

Friedel–Crafts alkylations are limited to *alkyl* halides. Alkyl fluorides, chlorides,
bromides, and iodides react well, but aromatic (*aryl*) halides and alkenyl (*vinylic*)
halides do not react. Aryl and vinylic carbocations are too unstable to form under
Friedel–Crafts reaction conditions.

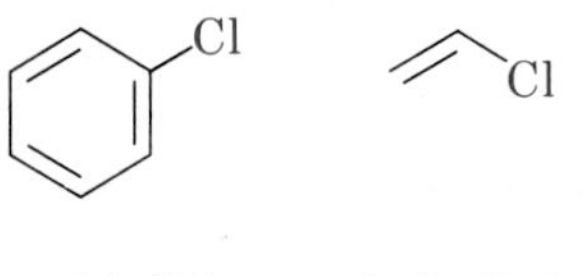

An aryl halide   **A vinylic halide**
Not reactive

The Aromatic Reactant

Friedel–Crafts reactions do not succeed on aromatic rings that are already substituted by groups such as —NO_2, —C≡N, —SO_3H, or —COR (Figure 5.11).

Such aromatic rings are much less reactive than benzene for reasons to be discussed in Section 5.11.

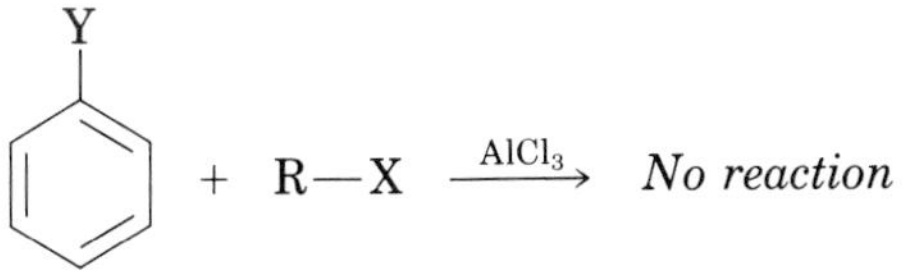

where Y = $-\overset{+}{N}R_3$, $-NO_2$, $-CN$, $-SO_3H$, $-CHO$,

$-COCH_3$, $-COOH$, $-COOCH_3$

FIGURE 5.11
Limitations on the aromatic partner in Friedel–Crafts reactions

Structural Rearrangements During Friedel–Crafts Reactions

A final limitation to the Friedel–Crafts alkylation is that structural *rearrangements* of the alkyl group can occur during reaction. For example, when benzene reacts with 1-chloropropane in the presence of AlCl$_3$, isopropylbenzene is isolated as the major product instead of *n*-propylbenzene.

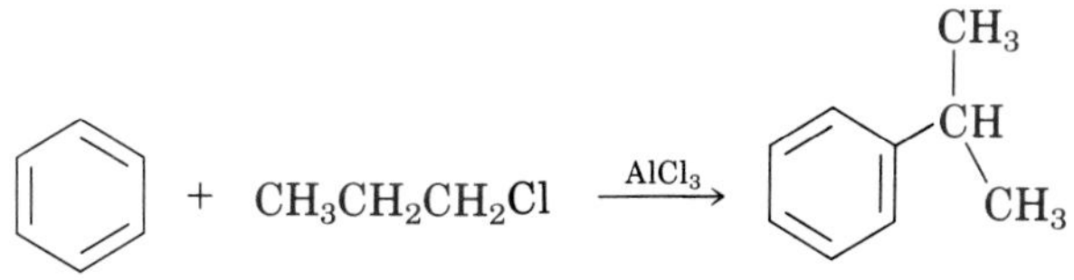

Benzene   1-Chloropropane   Cumene
(isopropylbenzene)

Rearrangement of the alkyl group structure is a common occurrence in Friedel–Crafts reactions, particularly when primary alkyl halides, R—CH$_2$—Cl, are used. Pioneering studies carried out in the 1930s by F. C. Whitmore and others indicated that these rearrangements occur by **hydride shifts**, which isomerize a less stable carbocation into a more stable one. (Recall the order of carbocation stability from Section 4.3: tertiary > secondary > primary.) For example, the relatively unstable primary propyl carbocation can rearrange to a more stable secondary carbocation by the shift of a hydrogen atom and its electron pair (a **hydride ion, H:$^-$**) from C2 to C1.

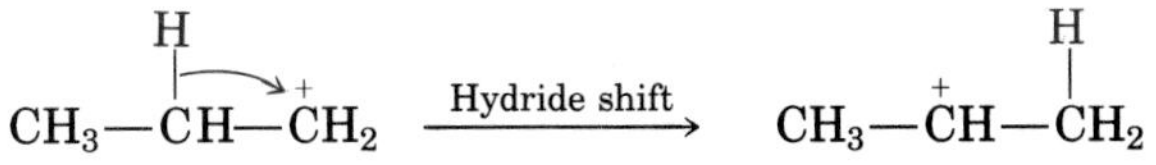

1° cation (less stable)   2° cation (more stable)

PRACTICE PROBLEM   What is the major product you would expect to obtain from the reaction of benzene and 1-chloro-2-methylpropane in the presence of AlCl$_3$?

Solution   Rearrangements in Friedel–Crafts reactions occur by conversion of a less stable carbocation into a more stable carbocation. In the present instance, 1-chloro-2-methylpropane would react with AlCl$_3$ to yield the primary 2-methylpropyl carbocation, which could undergo a hydride shift to yield the more stable *tert*-butyl carbocation:

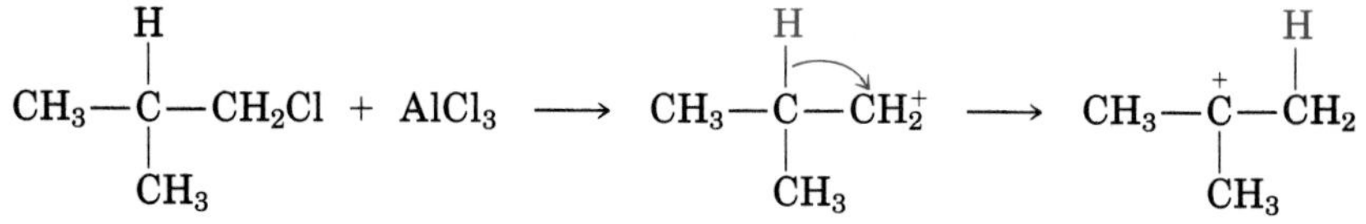

$$\text{CH}_3-\overset{\overset{\displaystyle H}{|}}{\underset{\underset{\displaystyle CH_3}{|}}{C}}-\text{CH}_2\text{Cl} + \text{AlCl}_3 \longrightarrow \text{CH}_3-\overset{\overset{\displaystyle H}{|}}{\underset{\underset{\displaystyle CH_3}{|}}{C}}-\text{CH}_2^+ \longrightarrow \text{CH}_3-\overset{\overset{\displaystyle H}{|}}{\underset{\underset{\displaystyle CH_3}{|}}{\overset{+}{C}}}-\text{CH}_2$$

Reaction of the *tert*-butyl carbocation with benzene would then yield *tert*-butylbenzene.

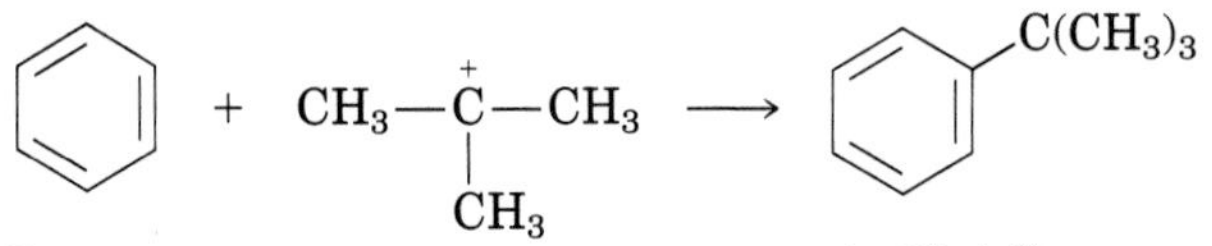

Benzene   + $\text{CH}_3-\overset{+}{\underset{\underset{\displaystyle CH_3}{|}}{C}}-\text{CH}_3$ $\longrightarrow$ *tert*-Butylbenzene

PROBLEM 5.9   What product would you expect to obtain from reaction of benzene with 1-chloro-butane in the presence of AlCl$_3$?

5.10   THE FRIEDEL–CRAFTS ACYLATION REACTION

Closely related to the Friedel–Crafts alkylation reaction, is the **Friedel–Crafts acylation** (pronounced a'-sil-a-tion). When an aromatic compound is allowed to react with a carboxylic acid chloride in the presence of AlCl$_3$, an **acyl group,** —COR, is introduced onto the ring. For example, reaction of benzene with acetyl chloride yields the ketone, acetophenone.

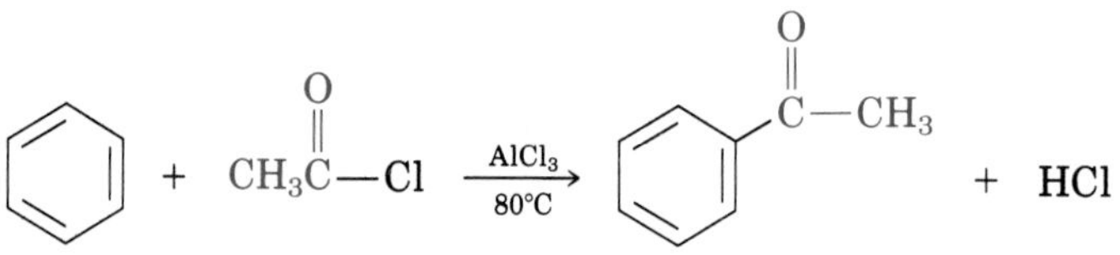

Benzene   Acetyl chloride   Acetophenone (95%)

The way in which the Friedel–Crafts acylation occurs is analogous to other electrophilic aromatic substitutions. The reactive electrophile is the **acylium ion,** R—$\overset{+}{C}$=O, generated by reaction of the acid chloride with AlCl$_3$. Once formed, the acylium ion does not rearrange; rather, it reacts with an aromatic ring to give a normal substitution product (Figure 5.12).

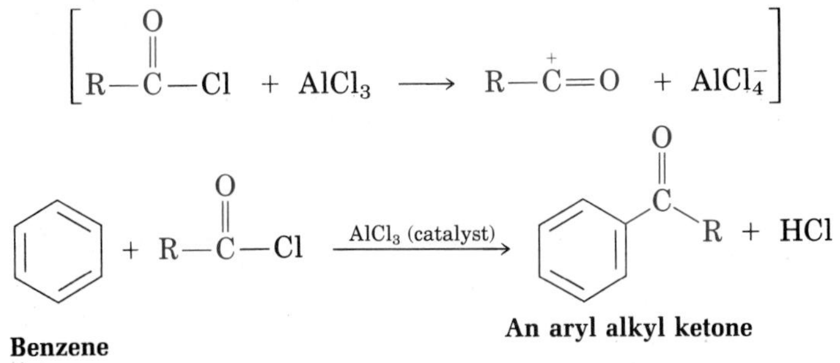

$$\left[R-\overset{\displaystyle O}{\overset{\|}{C}}-Cl \ + \ AlCl_3 \ \longrightarrow \ R-\overset{+}{C}=O \ + \ AlCl_4^- \right]$$

Benzene + R—C—Cl $\xrightarrow{\text{AlCl}_3 \text{ (catalyst)}}$ An aryl alkyl ketone + HCl

FIGURE 5.12
The Friedel–Crafts acylation reaction

One of the most important uses of the Friedel–Crafts acylation reaction is that the acylbenzene product can be converted into an alkylbenzene, ArCOR → ArCH$_2$R, where Ar = any aromatic ring. This reaction can be carried out in many ways, but catalytic hydrogenation over a palladium catalyst is one of the simplest and best. For example, propiophenone, prepared by reaction of benzene with propanoyl chloride, is reduced to propylbenzene in 100% yield by catalytic hydrogenation. Thus, the net effect of Friedel–Crafts acylation followed by catalytic hydrogenation is the preparation of a primary alkylbenzene. This sequence of reactions allows us to circumvent the carbocation rearrangement problems associated with direct Friedel–Crafts alkylation using primary alkyl halides (Figure 5.13). Note that this removal of the ketone group by catalytic reduction is limited to ketones next to an aromatic ring. Normal dialkyl ketones do not undergo this reaction.

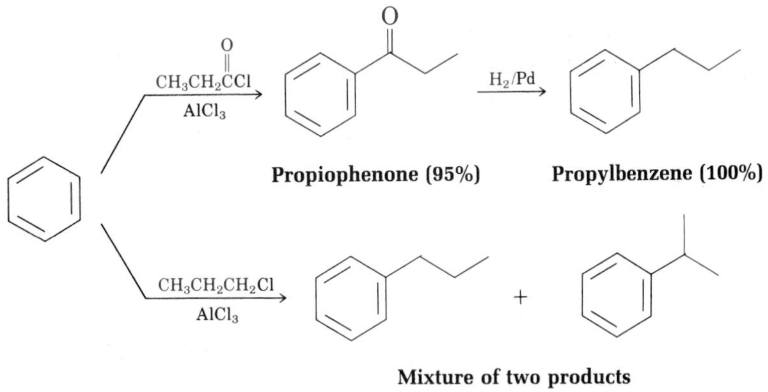

$\xrightarrow[\text{AlCl}_3]{\text{CH}_3\text{CH}_2\text{CCl}}$ Propiophenone (95%) $\xrightarrow{\text{H}_2/\text{Pd}}$ Propylbenzene (100%)

$\xrightarrow[\text{AlCl}_3]{\text{CH}_3\text{CH}_2\text{CH}_2\text{Cl}}$ + Mixture of two products

FIGURE 5.13
Use of the Friedel–Crafts acylation reaction to prepare propylbenzene by reduction of propiophenone

5.11   REACTIVITY AND ORIENTATION IN ELECTROPHILIC AROMATIC SUBSTITUTION

Only one monosubstitution product can result when electrophilic substitution occurs on benzene. But what would happen if we were to carry out an electrophilic substitution reaction on an already substituted ring? Substituents on an aromatic ring have two effects:

1. Substituents affect the *reactivity* of the aromatic ring. Some substituents make the ring more reactive than benzene, and some make it less reactive.

2. Substituents affect the *orientation* of the reaction. Three possible disubstituted products can result: ortho, meta, and para. These three products are not formed in random amounts; the nature of the substituent already present on the benzene ring usually determines the position of the second substitution.

Let's look at these two effects more closely.

Classification of Substituents

Substituents can be classified into two groups: those that *activate* the aromatic ring toward further electrophilic substitution and those that *deactivate* it. Rings that contain an activating substituent are more reactive than benzene, whereas those that contain a deactivating substituent are less reactive than benzene. Table 5.3 lists some groups in both categories.

TABLE 5.3   Activating and deactivating substituents for electrophilic aromatic substitution

Activating groups è donor	Deactivating groups è acceptors
Strongly activating —NH$_2$	**Strongly deactivating** —N(CH$_3$)$_3^+$
—ÖH	—NO$_2$
—ÖCH$_3$	—CN
—NHCCH$_3$ (O above C)	—CCH$_3$ (O above C)
—CH$_3$ (alkyl)	—COH (O above C)
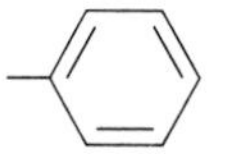 **Weakly activating** — (phenyl)	—COCH$_3$ (O above C)
	—CH (O above C)
	—I
	—Br
	—Cl
	Weakly deactivating —F

The common feature of all substituents within a category is that all activating groups are electron donors and all deactivating groups are electron acceptors. An aromatic ring with an electron-donating substituent is more electron-rich (more nucleophilic) than benzene and therefore more reactive toward electrophiles. An aromatic ring with an electron-withdrawing substituent is less electron-rich (less nucleophilic) than benzene and therefore less reactive toward electrophiles.

Y is an electron donor; ring is electron-rich and very reactive

Y is an electron acceptor; ring is electron-poor and less reactive

Resonance and Inductive Effects

A substituent can donate or withdraw electrons from the aromatic ring in two ways—by **inductive effects** and by **resonance effects**. Inductive effects are due to the intrinsic electronegativity of atoms and thus to the bond polarity in functional groups. These effects operate by donating or withdrawing electrons through sigma bonds. For example, halogens, carbonyl groups, cyano groups, and nitro groups deactivate an aromatic ring by inductively withdrawing electrons from the ring through the sigma bond linking the substituent to the ring.

$$X = F, Cl, Br, or I;$$ inductively electron-withdrawing because of electronegativity

Carbonyl, cyano, nitro; inductively electron-withdrawing because of functional group polarity

Alkyl groups are inductively electron-donating, and they therefore activate the ring. The reasons for this are not fully understood, but probably involve the same factors that cause alkyl substituents to stabilize alkenes. (Recall that more highly substituted alkenes are more stable.)

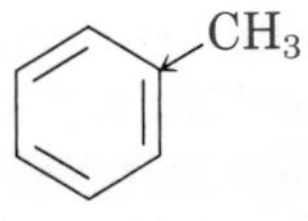

Alkyl group; inductively electron-donating

Resonance effects operate by donating or withdrawing electrons by p orbital overlap with the aromatic ring pi electrons. Substituents such as nitro, carbonyl, and cyano are bonded to the ring through atoms that have p orbitals. Aromatic ring pi electrons can therefore be withdrawn by these substituents. For example, we can draw resonance structures of nitrobenzene and benzaldehyde in which aromatic ring pi electrons move out onto the substituents, leaving a positive charge in the ring, thereby deactivating the ring toward reaction with an electrophile.

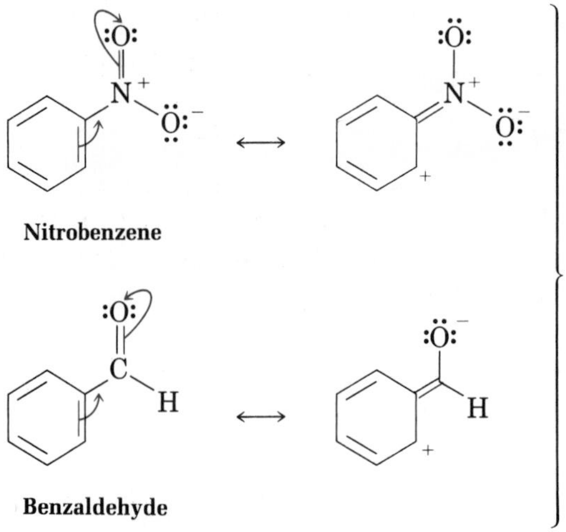

Nitrobenzene

Benzaldehyde

Carbonyl, nitro, and similar substituents deactivate the aromatic ring by resonance withdrawal of pi electrons from the ring

Conversely, substituents such as hydroxyl, methoxyl, and amino activate the aromatic ring by resonance effects that donate pi electrons from the substituents to the ring. As the resonance structures indicate, this electron donation places a negative charge in the ring, making the ring more reactive toward electrophiles.

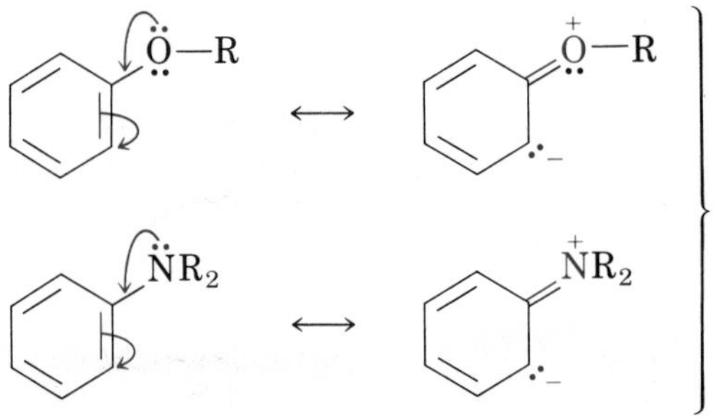

Hydroxyl, methoxyl, and amino substituents activate the ring by resonance donation of pi electrons

It probably comes as a surprise to learn that hydroxyl, methoxyl, and amino groups activate the ring. Since oxygen and nitrogen are both highly electronegative, we expect them to deactivate the ring inductively. We find, however, that the resonance electron-donation effect far outweighs the inductive electron-withdrawal effect for these substituents. Thus, there is a net activating influence.

PROBLEM 5.10 Using the information in Table 5.3, rank the compounds in each of the following groups in order of their reactivity to electrophilic substitution:

(a) Nitrobenzene, phenol (hydroxybenzene), toluene
(b) Phenol, benzene, chlorobenzene, benzoic acid
(c) Benzene, bromobenzene, benzaldehyde, aniline (aminobenzene)

5.12 ORIENTATION OF REACTIONS ON SUBSTITUTED AROMATIC RINGS

The second effect a substituent can have is to direct the position of electrophilic substitution. For example, a methyl substituent shows a strong ortho- and para-directing effect. Nitration of toluene thus yields predominately *o*-nitrotoluene (63%) and *p*-nitrotoluene (34%), along with only 3% of the meta isomer.

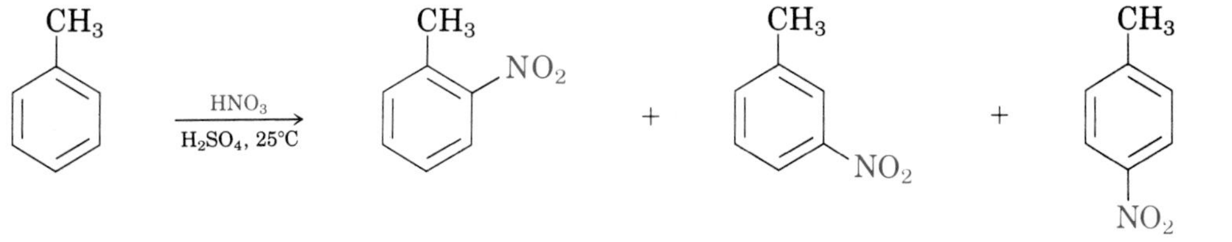

| Toluene | *o*-Nitrotoluene (63%) | *m*-Nitrotoluene (3%) | *p*-Nitrotoluene (34%) |

On the other hand, a cyano substituent shows a strong meta-directing effect. Nitration of benzonitrile (cyanobenzene) yields 81% *m*-nitrobenzonitrile, along with only 17% of the ortho isomer and 2% of the para isomer.

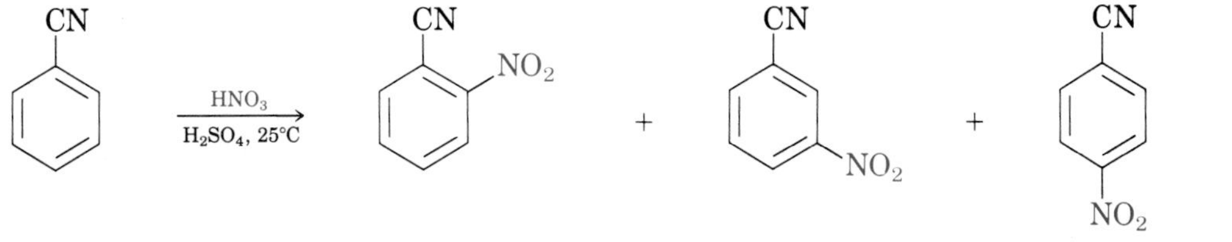

| Benzonitrile | *o*-Nitrobenzonitrile (17%) | *m*-Nitrobenzonitrile (81%) | *p*-Nitrobenzonitrile (2%) |

Substituents can be classified into three groups: ortho- and para-directing activators; ortho- and para-directing deactivators; and meta-directing deactivators. No meta-directing activators are known. Table 5.4 lists some of the groups in each category.

TABLE 5.4   Classification of directing effects for some common substituents

Ortho- and para-directing activators	Ortho- and para-directing deactivators	Meta-directing deactivators
—ṄH₂	—Ï:	—N̟(CH₃)₃⁺
—ÖH	—B̈r:	—NO₂
—ÖCH₃	—C̈l:	—CN
—ṄHCOCH₃	—F̈:	O‖—CCH₃
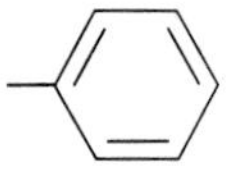		O‖—COCH₃
—CH₃		O‖—COH
		O‖—CH

In order to understand how substituents exert their directing influence, let's look further into the consequences of electron-donating and electron-withdrawing effects.

PROBLEM 5.11   Using the information in Table 5.4, predict the major monosubstitution products of these reactions:

(a)   Nitration of bromobenzene
(b)   Bromination of nitrobenzene
(c)   Chlorination of phenol
(d)   Bromination of aniline

Ortho- and Para-Directing Activators

When groups are classified as activators, it's important to realize that they activate *all* positions on the aromatic ring. These substituents are ortho- and para-directing only because they activate the ortho and para positions more than they activate the meta positions. *In activated benzenes, substitution occurs where activation is felt most.* For example, let's look at what happens in the nitration of toluene.

In the first step of the reaction between toluene and the nitronium ion electrophile (NO_2^+), attack can occur either ortho, meta, or para to the methyl group, giving the carbocation intermediates shown in Figure 5.14. All three carbocations are resonance-stabilized, but the ortho and para products are more stable than the meta product. For both ortho and para (but not meta) attack, a resonance form places the positive charge directly on the methyl-substituted carbon, where it can best be stabilized by the methyl group's electron-donating inductive effect. These two intermediates are therefore lower in energy than the meta intermediate, and are formed faster.

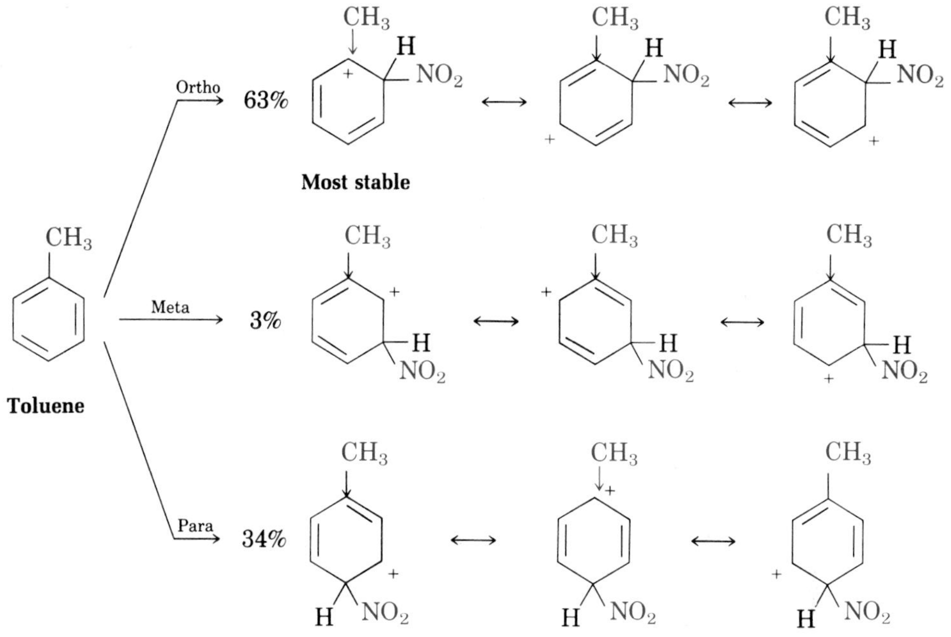

FIGURE 5.14
Carbocation intermediates in the nitration of toluene: Ortho and para intermediates are more stable than the meta intermediate.

A similar line of reasoning explains why hydroxyl and amino groups (and their derivatives) are also ortho- and para-directing. These groups exert their electron-donating, activating influence through a strong resonance effect, which is most pronounced at the ortho and para positions. For example, when phenol is nitrated, the three carbocation intermediates shown in Figure 5.15 (page 150) are possible. All three are stabilized, but the intermediates from ortho and para attack are stabilized most, because only in these intermediates can the positive charge be stabilized by an electron pair from oxygen.

Meta-Directing Deactivators

When groups are classified as deactivators, it's important to remember that these groups deactivate *all* positions on the ring. Meta directors exert their influence

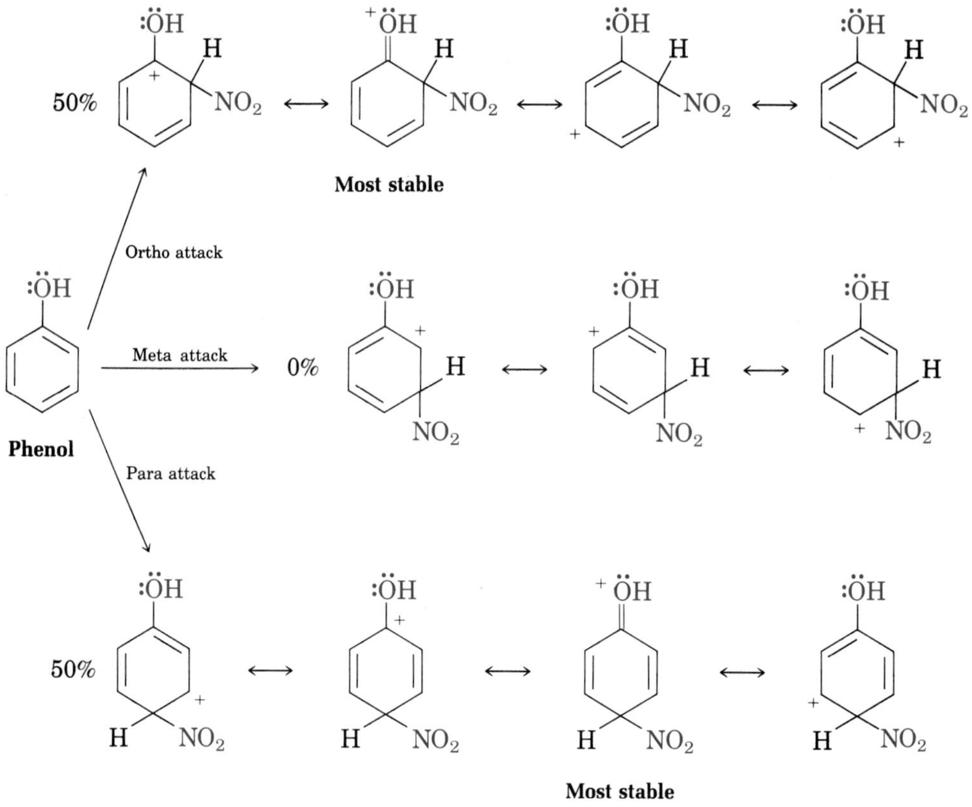

FIGURE 5.15
Intermediates in the nitration of phenol: The ortho and para intermediates are more stable than the meta intermediate because of resonance electron donation from lone-pair electrons on oxygen.

only because they deactivate the meta positions less than they deactivate the ortho and para positions. *In deactivated benzenes, substitution occurs where deactivation is felt least.*

We can explain the influence of meta-directing deactivators by using the same kinds of arguments we used for ortho- and para-directing activators. For example, let's look at the chlorination of benzaldehyde, shown in Figure 5.16. Of the three possible intermediates, the carbocations produced by reaction at ortho and para positions are least stable. In both ortho and para intermediates, the unfavorable resonance forms indicated in Figure 5.16 place the positive charge directly on the carbon bearing the deactivating group. A severe repulsive interaction between the positive charge and the positive end of the dipole of the carbonyl functional group strongly disfavors these intermediates. Hence, the meta intermediate is most favored.

Ortho- and Para-Directing Deactivators: Halogens

Halogen substituents occupy a unique position since they are deactivating, yet are ortho- and para-directing. Why should this be?

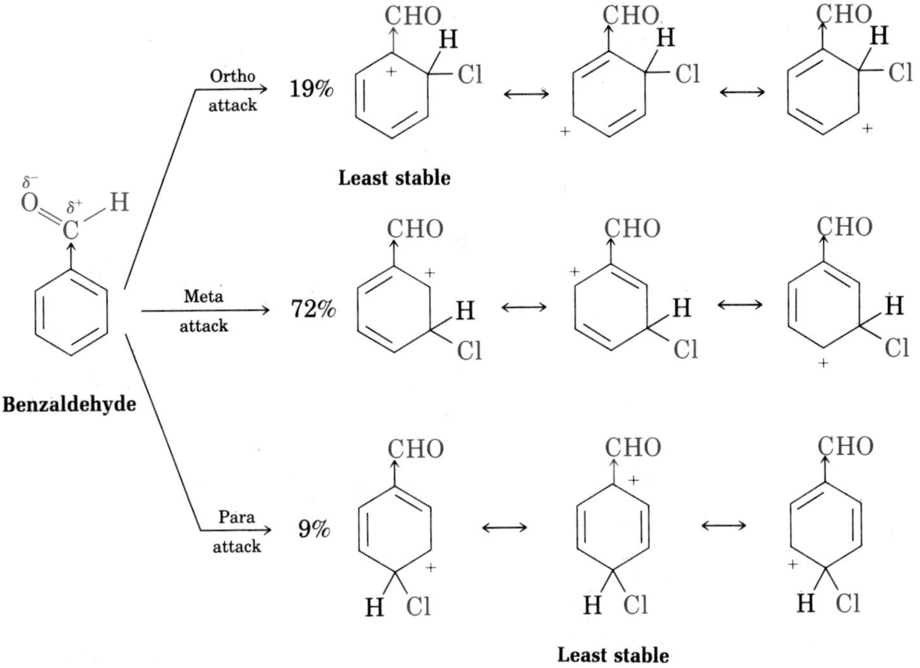

FIGURE 5.16
Intermediates in the chlorination of benzaldehyde: The ortho and para intermediates are less stable than the meta intermediate.

As we saw in Section 5.11, halogens are deactivating because of their strongly electron-withdrawing inductive effect. Unlike other deactivating groups, however, halogens deactivate the ortho and para positions less than they deactivate the meta positions. The reasons for this behavior can be seen by looking at the possible intermediates formed on nitration of chlorobenzene (Figure 5.17, page 152). Although the halogens have an electron-*withdrawing* inductive effect, they have an electron-*donating* resonance effect because of their lone-pair electrons. Thus, the carbocation intermediates from ortho and para attack have their positive charges resonance-stabilized by the halogen substituents, whereas the meta intermediate has no such stabilization.

In general, any substituent that has a lone pair of electrons on the atom bound to the aromatic ring will have an electron-donating resonance effect and will thus be an ortho and para director:

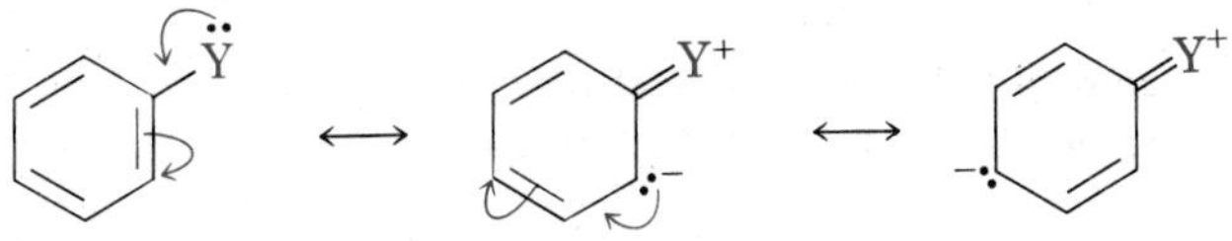

Whether the substituent will be activating or deactivating depends on the strength of its inductive effect. For example, halogens, hydroxyl groups, and amino groups have electron-donating resonance effects and are therefore ortho–para directors.

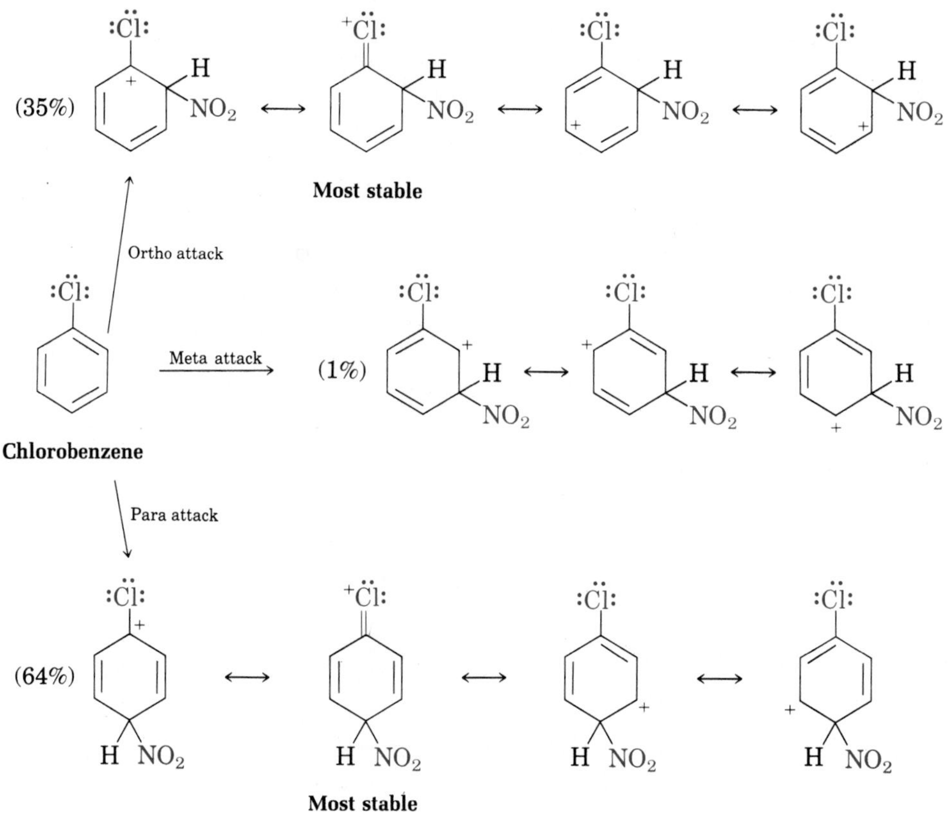

FIGURE 5.17
Carbocation intermediates from nitration of chlorobenzene: The ortho and para intermediates are more stable and form faster than the meta intermediate.

The magnitudes of their inductive effects, however, are different. Halogens have a strong electron-withdrawing inductive effect but a weak electron-donating resonance effect and are thus deactivators. Hydroxyl and amino groups have weak electron-withdrawing inductive effects but have strong electron-donating resonance effects and are thus activators.

A Summary of Substituent Effects

We have seen that both reactivity and orientation in electrophilic aromatic substitution are controlled by the interplay of two factors: resonance effects and inductive effects. Different substituents behave differently depending on the direction and strength of the two effects. Table 5.5 summarizes the situation.

PROBLEM 5.12   Draw the products you would expect to obtain from mononitration of these compounds:

(a) Nitrobenzene   (b) Bromobenzene   (c) Toluene
(d) Benzoic acid   (e) *p*-Xylene

PROBLEM 5.13 Which would you expect to be more reactive toward electrophilic substitution, toluene or (trifluoromethyl)benzene? Explain your answer.

$$\text{CF}_3$$

(Trifluoromethyl)benzene

PROBLEM 5.14 The nitroso group, $-\ddot{\text{N}}=\text{NO}$, is one of the few nonhalogen substituents that is an ortho- and para-directing deactivating group. Draw resonance structures of the three possible intermediates from electrophilic attack on nitrosobenzene, and explain why the ortho and para intermediates are favored over meta.

$$\ddot{\text{N}}=\text{O}$$

Nitrosobenzene

TABLE 5.5 A summary of substituent effects in electrophilic aromatic substitution

Substituent	Reactivity	Orientation	Inductive effect	Resonance effect
—CH₃	Activating	Ortho, para	Weak; electron-donating	None
—ÖH	Activating	Ortho, para	Weak; electron-withdrawing	Strong; electron-donating
—N̈H₂				
—F̈:, —C̈l:	Deactivating	Ortho, para	Strong; electron-withdrawing	Weak; electron-donating
—B̈r:, —Ï:				
—N̟(CH₃)₃⁺	Deactivating	Meta	Strong; electron-withdrawing	None
—NO₂, —CN	Deactivating	Meta	Strong; electron-withdrawing	Strong; electron-withdrawing
—CHO, —CO₂CH₃				
—COCH₃				

5.13 TRISUBSTITUTED BENZENES: ADDITIVITY OF EFFECTS

Further electrophilic substitution of a disubstituted benzene is governed by the same orientation effects just discussed. The only difference is that now we must consider the *additive* effects of two directing groups. Three rules are usually sufficient to predict the results of a reaction:

1. If the directing effects of the two groups *reinforce* each other, there is no problem. For example, in *p*-nitrotoluene, both the methyl group and the nitro group direct further substitution to the same position (ortho to the methyl = meta to the nitro); a single product is thus formed on electrophilic substitution.

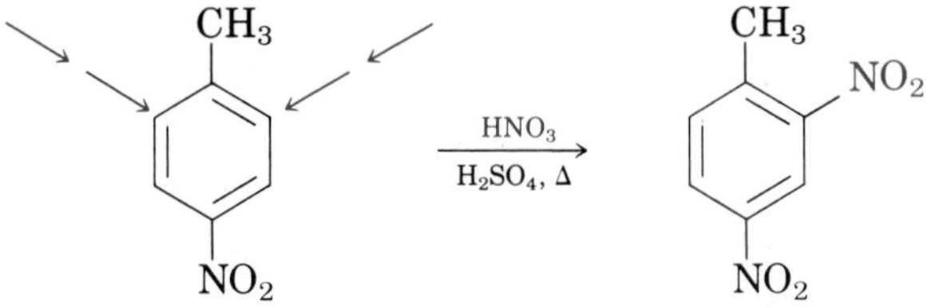

p-Nitrotoluene

2,4-Dinitrotoluene
(sole product)

2. If the directing effects of the two groups *oppose* each other, the more powerful activating group has the dominant influence. For example, bromination of p-methylphenol yields largely 2-bromo-4-methylphenol, since hydroxyl is a more powerful activator than methyl.

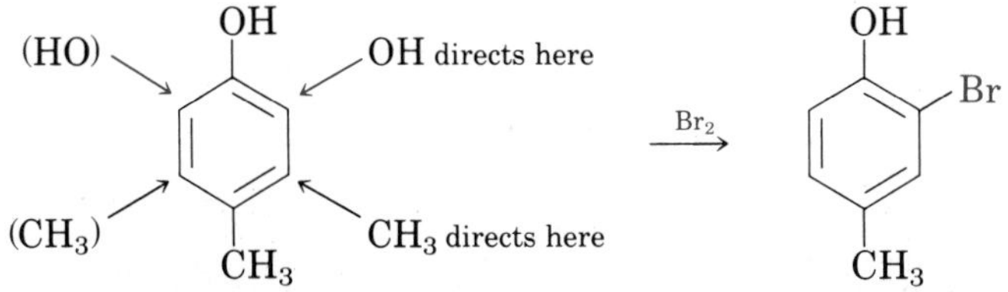

p-Methylphenol
(p-cresol)

2-Bromo-4-methylphenol
(major product)

3. Further substitution rarely occurs between the two groups in a meta disubstituted compound, because this site is too crowded for reaction to occur easily.

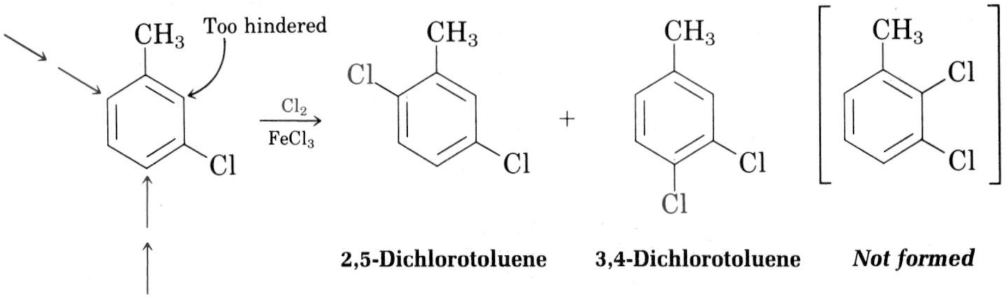

2,5-Dichlorotoluene   **3,4-Dichlorotoluene**   *Not formed*

m-Chlorotoluene

PRACTICE PROBLEM   What product would you expect from bromination of p-methylbenzoic acid?

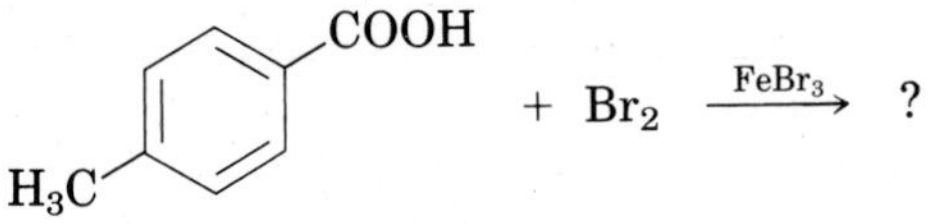

$$+ \ Br_2 \ \xrightarrow{FeBr_3} \ ?$$

Solution   The carboxyl group (—COOH) is a meta director, and the methyl group is an ortho–para director. Both groups therefore direct bromination to the position next to the methyl group, yielding 3-bromo-4-methylbenzoic acid.

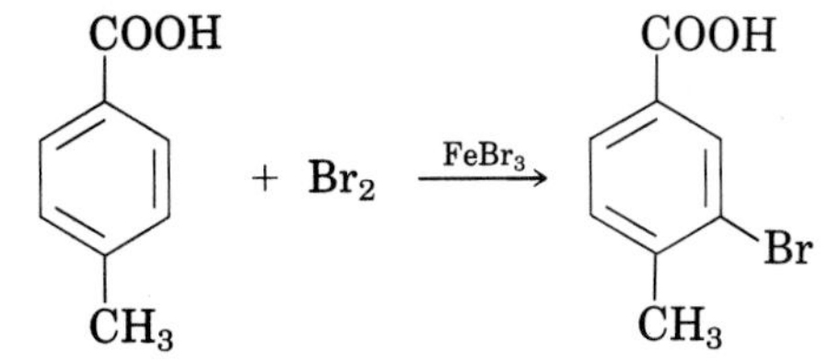

$$\text{COOH} \quad + \text{Br}_2 \quad \xrightarrow{\text{FeBr}_3} \quad \text{COOH, Br, CH}_3$$

p-Methylbenzoic acid   **3-Bromo-4-methylbenzoic acid**

PROBLEM 5.15   Where would you expect electrophilic substitution to occur in these substances?

(a) OCH$_3$, Br   (b) NH$_2$, Br   (c) NO$_2$, H$_3$C

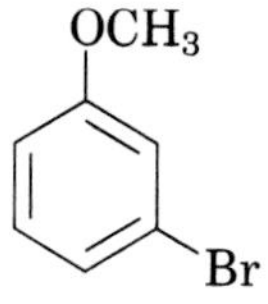

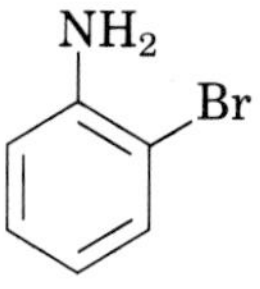

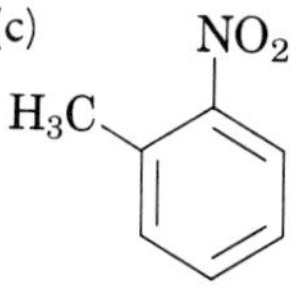

5.14   OXIDATION AND REDUCTION OF AROMATIC COMPOUNDS

The benzene ring, despite its unsaturation, is normally inert to strong oxidizing agents such as potassium permanganate. (Recall that this reagent will cleave alkene carbon–carbon double bonds; see Section 4.7.) Alkyl side chains, however, are readily attacked by these reagents and are converted into carboxyl groups (—COOH). For example, butylbenzene is oxidized by KMnO$_4$ in high yield to give benzoic acid.

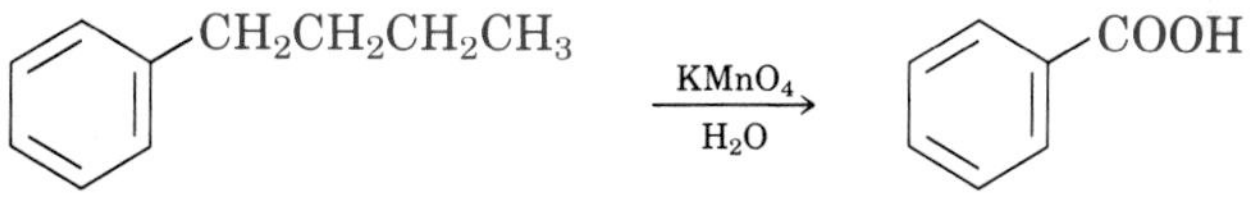

$$\text{—CH}_2\text{CH}_2\text{CH}_2\text{CH}_3 \quad \xrightarrow[\text{H}_2\text{O}]{\text{KMnO}_4} \quad \text{—COOH}$$

Butylbenzene   **Benzoic acid (85%)**

The exact mechanism of this side-chain oxidation reaction is not fully understood, but probably involves attack on the side-chain C—H bonds at the position next to the aromatic ring (the **benzylic** position). *tert*-Butylbenzene has no benzylic hydrogens, however, and is therefore inert.

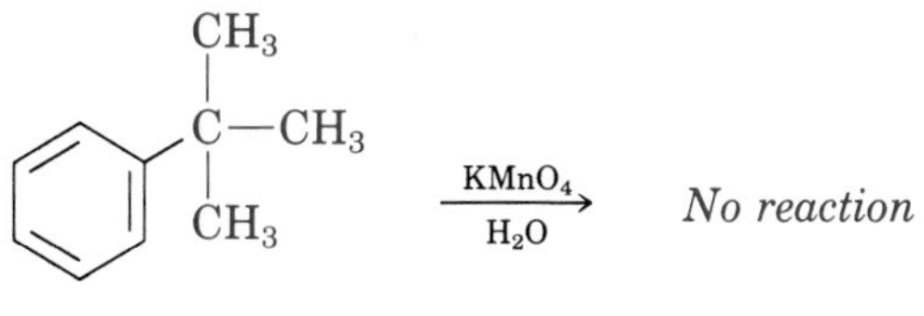

$$\begin{array}{c} \text{CH}_3 \\ | \\ \text{C—CH}_3 \\ | \\ \text{CH}_3 \end{array} \quad \xrightarrow[\text{H}_2\text{O}]{\text{KMnO}_4} \quad \textit{No reaction}$$

t-Butylbenzene

As well as being inert to oxidation, aromatic rings are inert to reduction under standard alkene hydrogenation conditions using a palladium catalyst. With a more powerful platinum or rhodium catalyst, however, reduction of aromatic rings to cyclohexanes occurs. For example, *o*-dimethylbenzene gives 1,2-dimethylcyclohexane in 100% yield.

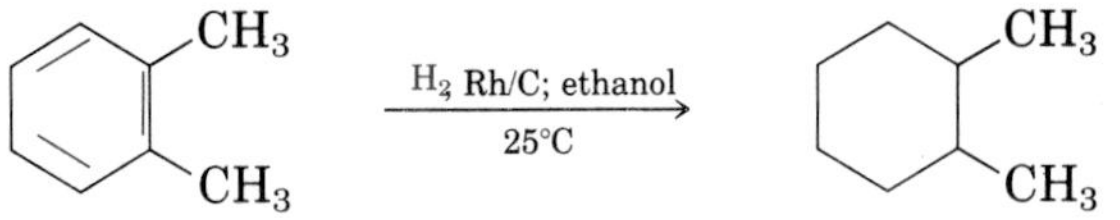

$$\text{CH}_3 \qquad \xrightarrow[\text{25°C}]{\text{H}_2\ \text{Rh/C; ethanol}} \qquad \text{CH}_3$$

o-Xylene
(o-dimethylbenzene)

1,2-Dimethylcyclohexane (100%)

PROBLEM 5.16   What aromatic products would you expect to obtain from the KMnO₄ oxidation of these substances?

(a) *m*-Chloroethylbenzene

(b) Tetralin,

5.15 NAPHTHALENE, A POLYCYCLIC AROMATIC HYDROCARBON

Aromaticity is a concept that can be extended beyond simple monocyclic compounds to include **polycyclic aromatic compounds**. Naphthalene, with two benzene-like rings fused together, and anthracene, with three fused rings, are two of the simplest polycyclic aromatic molecules.

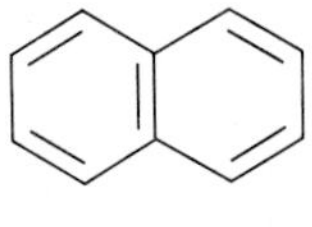

Naphthalene 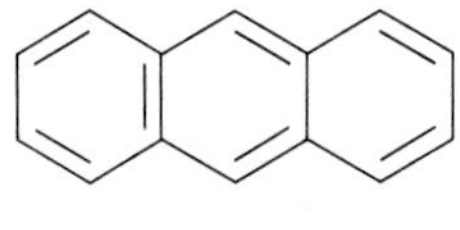   **Anthracene**

Naphthalene and other polycyclic aromatic hydrocarbons show many of the chemical properties we associate with aromaticity. For example, naphthalene reacts with electrophilic reagents such as bromine to give substitution products, rather than double-bond addition products.

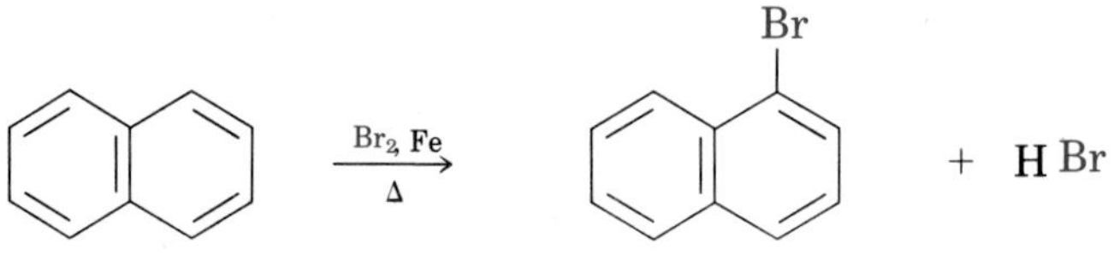

$$\xrightarrow[\Delta]{\text{Br}_2,\ \text{Fe}}$$

+ H Br

Naphthalene   **1-Bromonaphthalene (75%)**

PROBLEM 5.17 There are three different resonance structures of naphthalene, of which only one is shown here. Draw the other two.

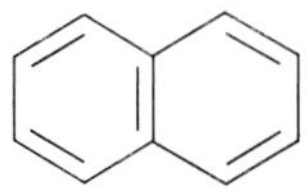

Naphthalene

5.16 ORGANIC SYNTHESIS

The laboratory synthesis of organic molecules from simple precursors is carried out for many reasons. In the pharmaceutical industry, new organic molecules are designed and synthesized for evaluation as medicines. In the chemical industry, syntheses are often undertaken to devise more economical routes to known compounds. In this book, too, we will sometimes devise syntheses of complex molecules from simpler precursors, but our purpose is different. Our purpose is to learn organic chemistry.

Planning workable synthetic sequences demands knowledge of a wide variety of organic reactions. Furthermore, it requires the ability to fit together a sequence of steps such that each reaction does only what is desired. It makes us approach chemical problems in a logical way, drawing on our knowledge and organizing that knowledge into a workable plan. Doing synthesis problems is an excellent way to learn organic chemistry.

There are no secrets to learning how to plan an organic synthesis—it takes a lot of work and practice. But one hint will be helpful: *Work backwards.* Look at the final product and ask yourself, "What was the *immediate* precursor of that product?" Having found an immediate precursor, proceed backwards again, one step at a time, until a suitable starting material is found. Let's try some examples.

PRACTICE PROBLEM Synthesize *m*-chloronitrobenzene starting from benzene.

Solution Ask, "What is an immediate precursor of *m*-chloronitrobenzene?"

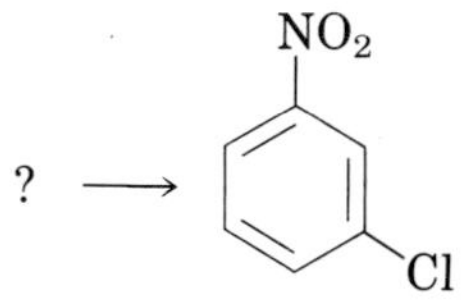

$$? \longrightarrow$$

m-**Chloronitrobenzene**

There are only two substituents on the ring, a chloro group, which is ortho–para-directing, and a nitro group, which is meta-directing. We cannot nitrate chlorobenzene, since the wrong isomers (*o*- and *p*-chloronitrobenzenes) would result, but chlorination of nitrobenzene should give us the desired product.

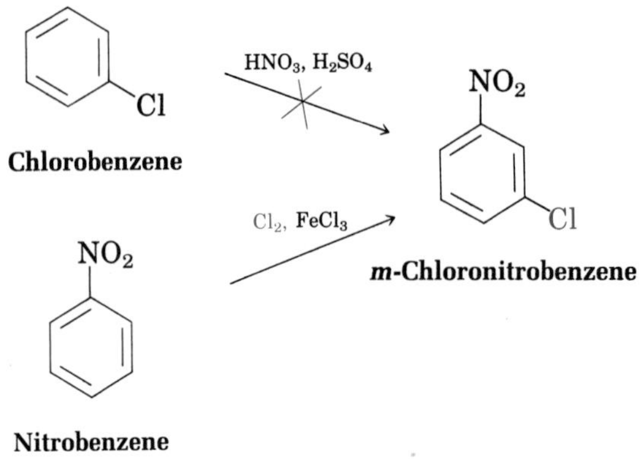

Chlorobenzene

Nitrobenzene

m-Chloronitrobenzene

Now, "What is an immediate precursor of nitrobenzene?" Benzene, which can be nitrated. Thus, in two steps, we have solved the problem.

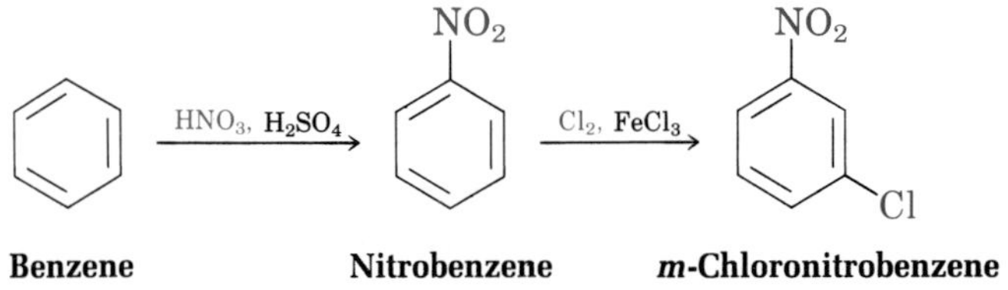

Benzene   **Nitrobenzene**   **m-Chloronitrobenzene**

PRACTICE PROBLEM   Synthesize *p*-bromobenzoic acid starting from benzene.

Solution   Ask, "What is an immediate precursor of *p*-bromobenzoic acid?"

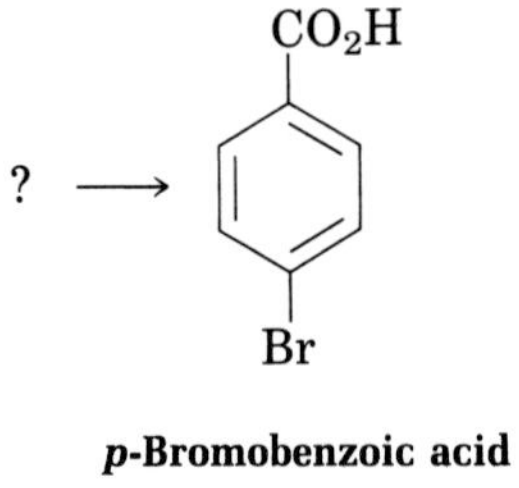

$$? \longrightarrow$$

p-Bromobenzoic acid

There are only two substituents on the ring, a carboxyl group (—COOH), which is meta-directing, and a bromine, which is ortho–para-directing. We cannot brominate benzoic acid, since the wrong isomer (*m*-bromobenzoic acid) would be produced. We know, however, that oxidation of alkylbenzene side chains yields benzoic acids. An immediate precursor of our target molecule might therefore be *p*-bromotoluene.

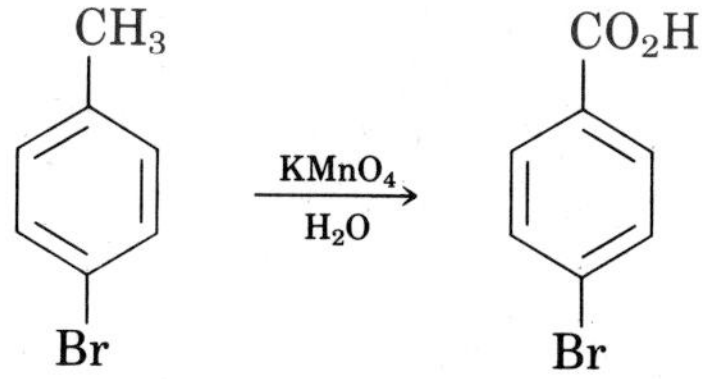

p-Bromotoluene   **p-Bromobenzoic acid**

"What is an immediate precursor of p-bromotoluene?" Perhaps toluene is an immediate precursor, since the methyl group would direct bromination to the ortho and para positions, and we could then separate isomers. Alternatively, bromobenzene might be an immediate precursor, since we could carry out a Friedel–Crafts methylation and obtain para product. Both answers are satisfactory (Figure 5.18).

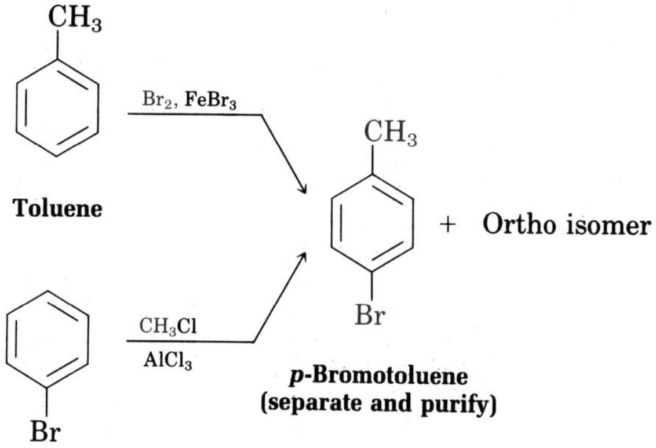

FIGURE 5.18
Two routes for the synthesis of p-bromotoluene

"What is an immediate precursor of toluene?" Benzene, which can be methylated in a Friedel–Crafts reaction.

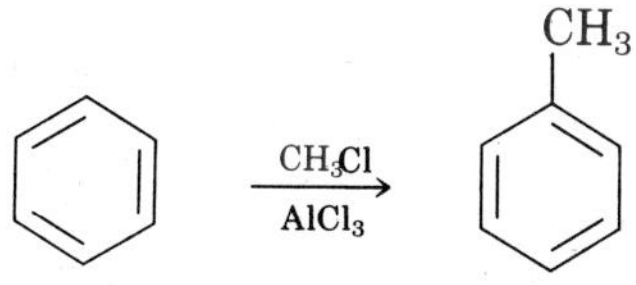

Benzene   **Toluene**

Alternatively, "What is an immediate precursor of bromobenzene?" Benzene, which can be brominated.

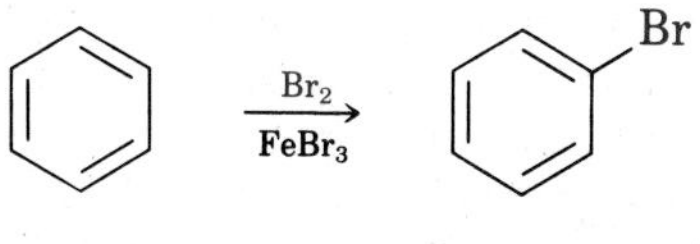

Benzene   **Bromobenzene**

Our backwards synthetic (*retrosynthetic*) analysis has provided two valid routes from benzene to *p*-bromobenzoic acid (Figure 5.19).

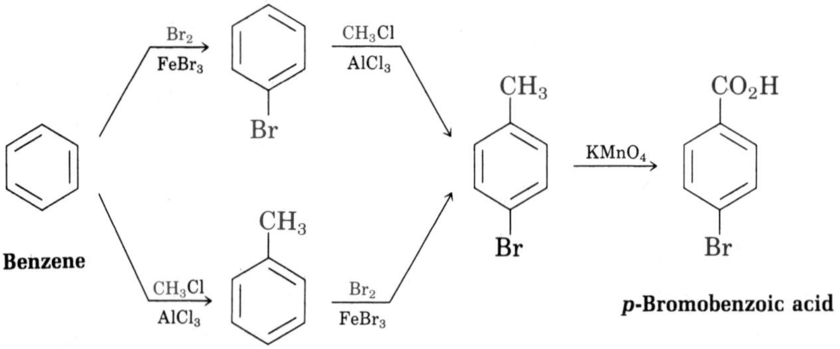

FIGURE 5.19
Two routes for the synthesis of *p*-bromobenzoic acid from benzene

PROBLEM 5.18   Propose a synthesis of each of the following substances, starting from benzene:

(a)   *p*-Methylacetophenone
(c)   *m*-Bromobenzoic acid

(b)   *p*-Chloronitrobenzene
(d)   2-Bromo-1,4-dimethylbenzene

PROBLEM 5.19   How would you prepare *p*-chloropropylbenzene from benzene? More than two steps will be required. How would you prepare *m*-chloropropylbenzene?

ADDITIONAL PROBLEMS

PROBLEM 5.20   Provide IUPAC names for these compounds:

(a)

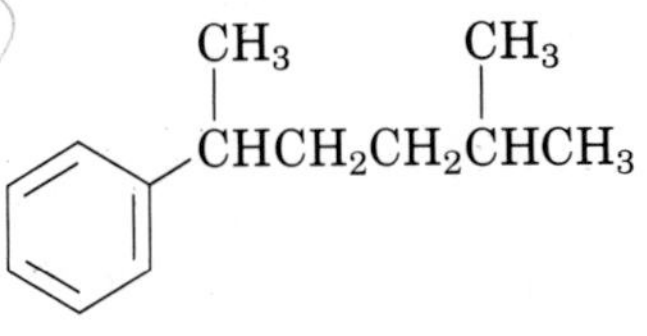

(b)

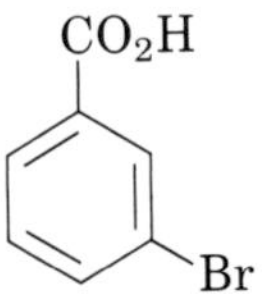

(c)

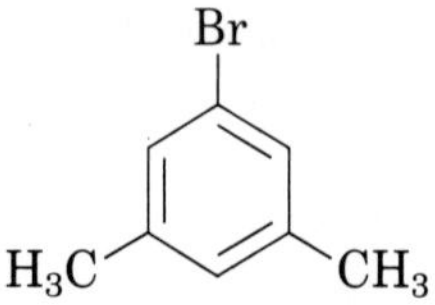

(d)

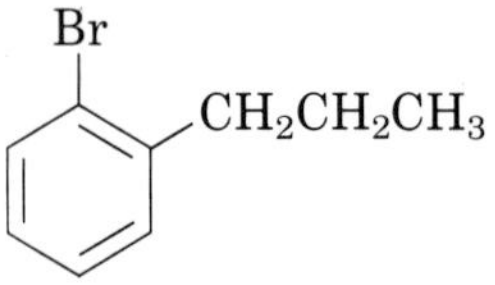

PROBLEM 5.21   Draw structures corresponding to these names:

(a)   *m*-Bromophenol
(c)   *p*-Iodonitrobenzene
(e)   *o*-Aminobenzoic acid

(b)   1,3,5-Benzenetriol
(d)   2,4,6-Trinitrotoluene (TNT)
(f)   3-Methyl-2-phenylhexane

PROBLEM 5.22 Draw and name all aromatic compounds with the formula C_7H_7Cl.

PROBLEM 5.23 Draw and name all isomeric:

(a) Dinitrobenzenes   (b) Bromodimethylbenzenes

PROBLEM 5.24 Propose structures for aromatic hydrocarbons meeting these descriptions:

(a) C_9H_{12}; can give only one product on aromatic bromination
(b) C_8H_{10}; can give three products on aromatic chlorination
(c) $C_{10}H_{14}$; can give two products on aromatic nitration

PROBLEM 5.25 Show how *tert*-butylbenzene is produced from the reaction of benzene with 2-chloro-2-methylpropane in the presence of aluminum chloride catalyst.

PROBLEM 5.26 Predict the major product(s) of mononitration of these substances. Which react faster than benzene, and which slower?

(a) Bromobenzene   (b) Benzonitrile (cyanobenzene)
(c) Benzoic acid   (d) Nitrobenzene
(e) Phenol   (f) Benzaldehyde

PROBLEM 5.27 Rank the compounds in each group according to their reactivity toward electrophilic substitution.

(a) Chlorobenzene, *o*-dichlorobenzene, benzene
(b) *p*-Bromonitrobenzene, nitrobenzene, phenol
(c) Fluorobenzene, benzaldehyde, *o*-dimethylbenzene

PROBLEM 5.28 Show in detail all the steps involved in the Friedel–Crafts reaction of benzene with CH_3Cl.

PROBLEM 5.29 Name and draw the structure of the major product(s) of electrophilic chlorination of these substances:

(a) *m*-Nitrophenol   (b) *o*-Dimethylbenzene
(c) *p*-Nitrobenzoic acid   (d) 2,4-Dibromophenol

PROBLEM 5.30 Predict the major product(s) you would expect to obtain from sulfonation of the following substances:

(a) Bromobenzene   (b) *m*-Bromophenol
(c) 2,4-Dichloronitrobenzene   (d) 2,4-Dichlorophenol
(e) 2,5-Dibromotoluene

PROBLEM 5.31 What is the structure of the compound C_8H_9Br that gives *p*-bromobenzoic acid on oxidation with $KMnO_4$?

PROBLEM 5.32 Draw the five resonance structures of phenanthrene.

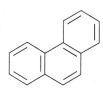

Phenanthrene

PROBLEM 5.33 Suggest a reason for the observation that bromination of biphenyl occurs at ortho and para positions, rather than at meta. Use resonance structures of the carbocation intermediates to explain your answer.

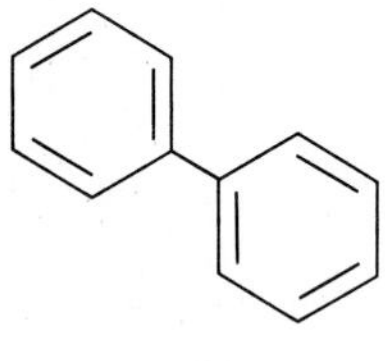

Biphenyl

PROBLEM 5.34 In light of your answer to Problem 5.33, at what position and on what ring would you expect nitration of 4-bromobiphenyl to occur?

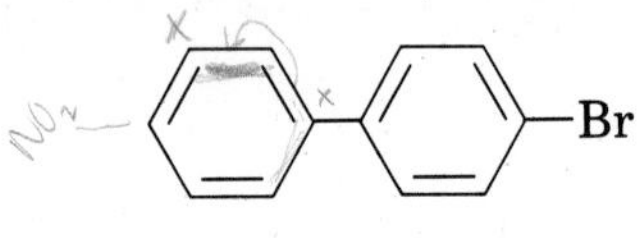

4-Bromobiphenyl

PROBLEM 5.35 At what position and on what ring would you expect bromination of benzanilide to occur? Explain your answer by drawing resonance structures of the potential carbocation intermediates.

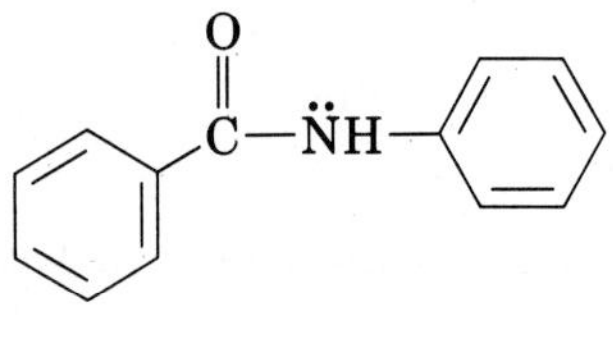

Benzanilide

PROBLEM 5.36 Starting with benzene, how would you synthesize these substances? Assume that you can separate ortho and para isomers if necessary.

(a) *m*-Bromobenzenesulfonic acid
(c) *p*-Chlorophenol

(b) *o*-Chlorobenzenesulfonic acid
(d) *p*-Methylphenol

PROBLEM 5.37 Starting with either benzene or toluene, how would you synthesize these substances. Ortho and para isomers can be separated if necessary.

(a) 2-Bromo-4-nitrotoluene
(c) 2,4,6-Trinitrobenzoic acid

(b) 1,3,5-Trinitrobenzene
(d) *p-tert*-Butylbenzoic acid

PROBLEM 5.38 Phenylboronic acid reacts with HNO_3 to give 15% ortho substitution product and 85% meta product. Account for the meta-directing effect of the $-B(OH)_2$ group.

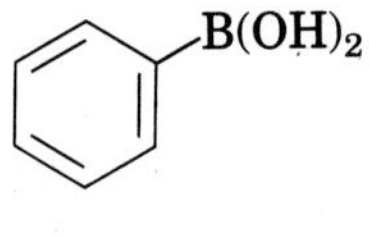

Phenylboronic acid

PROBLEM 5.39 Draw resonance structures of the intermediate carbocations and account for the fact that naphthalene undergoes electrophilic aromatic substitution at C1 rather than C2.

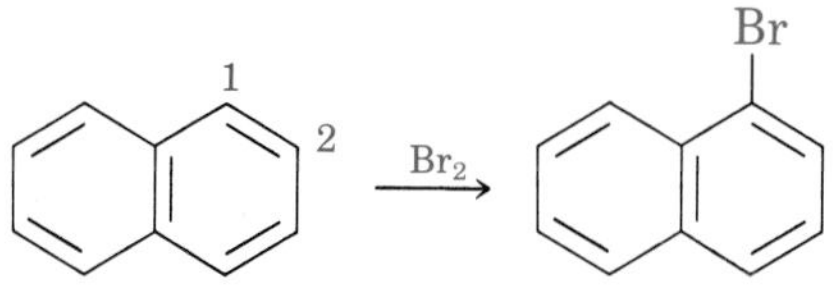

PROBLEM 5.40 We said in Section 4.12 that an allylic carbocation is stabilized by resonance. Draw resonance structures to account for a similar stabilization of *benzylic* carbocations.

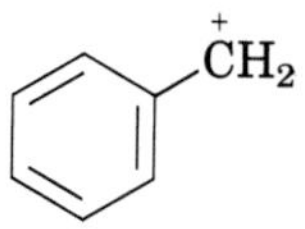

A benzylic carbocation

PROBLEM 5.41 In light of your answer to Problem 5.40, which of the two possible addition products would you expect from reaction of HBr with the following substance?

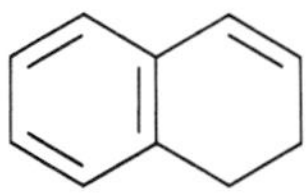

PROBLEM 5.42 Starting from benzene, how would you synthesize the following?

(a) *m*-Bromopentylbenzene   (b) 2,4-Dinitrobenzoic acid
(c) 3,5-Dinitrobenzoic acid   (d) *m*-Chlorophenol

PROBLEM 5.43 Pyridine is a cyclic nitrogen-containing organic compound that shows many of the properties associated with aromaticity. For example, pyridine undergoes electrophilic substitution reactions. Draw an orbital picture of pyridine and account for its aromatic properties.

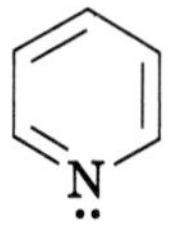

Pyridine

PROBLEM 5.44 Would you expect the trimethylammonium group to be an activating or deactivating substituent? Explain your answer.

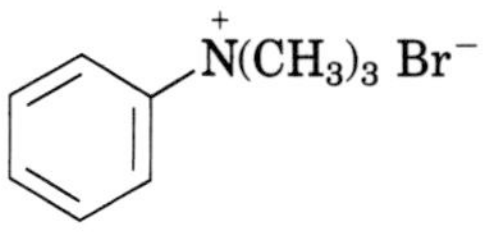

Phenyltrimethylammonium bromide

PROBLEM 5.45   Starting from toluene, how would you synthesize the three nitrobenzoic acids?

PROBLEM 5.46   Carbocations generated by reaction of an alkene with a strong acid catalyst can react with aromatic rings in a Friedel–Crafts reaction. Propose a mechanism to account for the industrial synthesis of the food preservative BHT from *p*-cresol and 2-methylpropene.

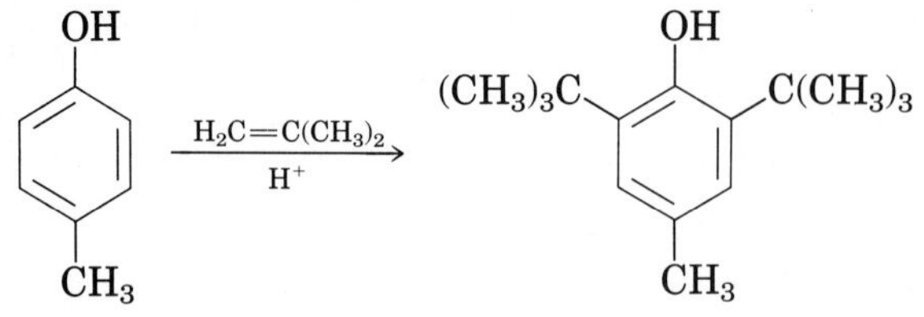

p-Cresol   BHT

PROBLEM 5.47   One method of formylating an aromatic ring (substituting a formyl group, —CHO, onto it) is to treat an aromatic substance with formyl fluoride, FCHO, in the presence of BF_3 as Lewis acid catalyst. Propose a mechanism for this reaction.

Polycyclic Aromatic Hydrocarbons and Cancer

In addition to naphthalene, which contains two benzene rings fused together, there are many more complex polycyclic aromatic hydrocarbons (Figure D.1). Coronene, for example, contains six benzene rings joined together to form a large ring; 1,2-benzpyrene contains five benzene rings compacted together; and ordinary graphite (the "lead" in pencils) consists of essentially infinite, two-dimensional sheets of benzene rings.

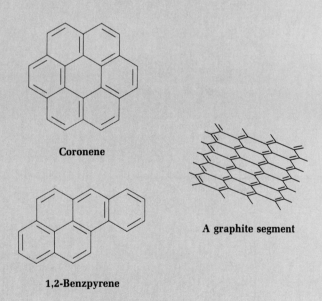

Coronene

A graphite segment

1,2-Benzpyrene

FIGURE D.1
Some polycyclic aromatic hydrocarbons

1,2-Benzypyrene is of particular interest because it is one of the cancer-causing substances found in chimney soot and cigarette smoke. Though harmless itself, once absorbed into the body, 1,2-benzpyrene is oxidized by certain enzymes to convert it into an oxygenated metabolite. This metabolite is able to bind to cellular DNA, thus causing mutations and interfering with the normal flow of genetic information.

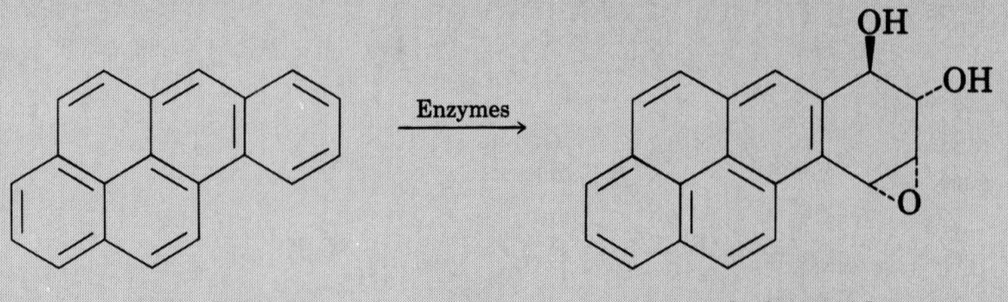

1,2-Benzpyrene   A diol epoxide

We'll look at the mechanism by which the diol epoxide reacts with DNA in Section 8.11.

CHAPTER 6

Stereochemistry

Up to this point, we have been concerned primarily with the general nature of chemical reactions and with the specific chemistry of hydrocarbon functional groups. Although we considered constitutional isomers of alkanes in Section 2.2 and cis–trans stereoisomers of cycloalkanes in Section 2.10, we've given little thought to the chemical consequences that arise as a result of specific spatial arrangements of atoms in molecules. It's now time to look more deeply into these consequences. **Stereochemistry** is the branch of chemistry concerned with the three-dimensional nature of molecules.

6.1 STEREOCHEMISTRY AND THE TETRAHEDRAL CARBON

Are you right-handed or left-handed? Though most of us don't often think about it, handedness plays a surprisingly large role in our daily activities—many musical instruments, such as oboes and clarinets, have a handedness to them; the last available softball glove always fits the wrong hand; left-handed people write in a "funny" way. The fundamental reason for these difficulties, of course, is that our hands are not identical—they are **mirror images**. When you hold a *right* hand up to a mirror, the image that you see looks like a *left* hand. Try it.

Handedness also plays a large role in organic chemistry. To see why this might be so, look at the molecules shown in Figure 6.1 on page 168. On the left of Figure 6.1 are three molecules, and on the right are their images reflected in a mirror. The CH_3X and CH_2XY molecules are *identical* to their mirror images and thus are not handed. If you were to make molecular models of each molecule and of its mirror image, you would find that you could superimpose one on top of the other. Get out your molecular model set and try it.

The CHXYZ molecule, however, is *not* identical to its mirror image. No matter how hard you try, you can't superimpose a model of the original molecule on top of a model of its mirror image, for the same reason that you can't superimpose a

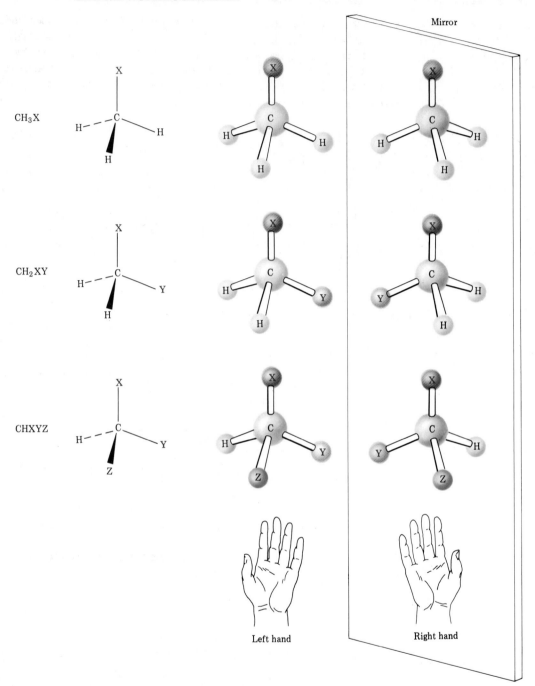

FIGURE 6.1
Three tetrahedral carbons and their mirror images: Molecules of the type CH_3X and CH_2XY are superimposable on their mirror images, but a molecule of the type CHXYZ is *not* superimposable on its mirror image for the same reason that a left hand is not superimposable on a right hand.

left hand on a right hand. You might superimpose *two* of the substituents, X and Y for example, but H and Z would be reversed. If the H and Z substituents were superimposed, X and Y would be reversed.

Molecules that are nonsuperimposable mirror images of each other are special kinds of stereoisomers called **enantiomers** (e-nan'-tee-o-mer; Greek *enantio*, "opposite"). Enantiomers are related to each other in the same way as a right hand is related to a left hand.

In a general sense, handedness (enantiomerism) can result whenever a tetrahedral carbon is bonded to four different substituents (one need not be H). For example, lactic acid (2-hydroxypropanoic acid) can exist in either right- or left-handed form because there are four different groups (—H, —OH, —CH$_3$, —COOH) attached to the central carbon atom:

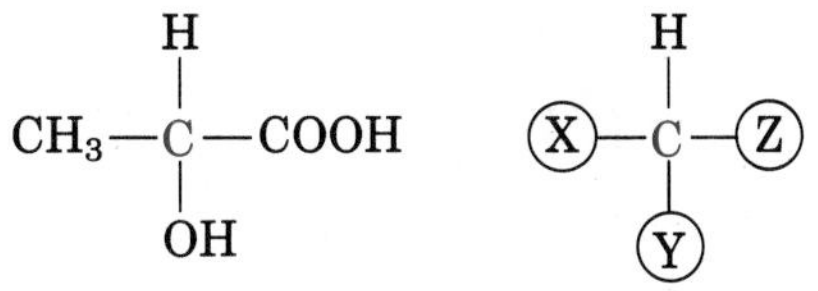

$$CH_3 - \underset{\underset{OH}{|}}{\overset{\overset{H}{|}}{C}} - COOH \qquad \underset{\underset{\text{Y}}{|}}{\overset{\overset{H}{|}}{X - C - Z}}$$

Lactic acid; a molecule of general formula CHXYZ

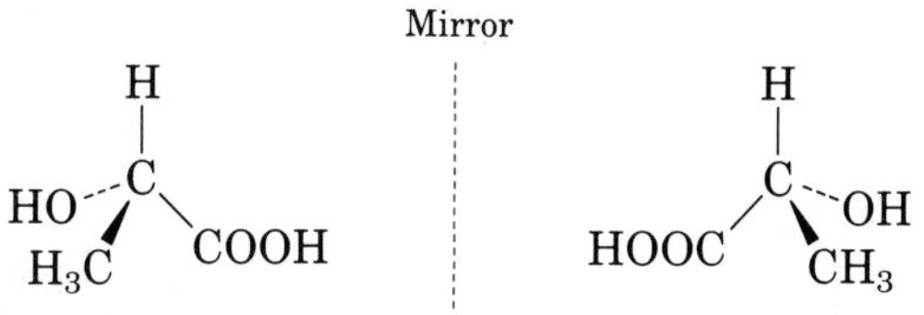

Mirror

You can't superimpose a molecule of "right-handed" lactic acid on top of a molecule of "left-handed" lactic acid; the two molecules are simply not identical, as shown in Figure 6.2 on page 170.

6.2 CHIRALITY

Compounds that are not superimposable on their mirror images, and thus exist as a pair of enantiomers, are said to be **chiral** (pronounced ky'-ral, from the Greek *cheir*, "hand"). We cannot take a chiral molecule and its mirror image (enantiomer) and place one on top of the other so that all atoms coincide.

How can we predict whether a certain compound is or is not chiral? *A compound cannot be chiral if it contains a plane of symmetry.* A **plane of symmetry** is an imaginary plane that bisects an object (or molecule) so that one half of the object is an exact mirror image of the other half. For example, a coffee cup has a plane of symmetry. If we were to cut the cup in half, one half would be an exact mirror image of the second half. A hand, however, does not have a plane of symmetry. One half of a hand is not a mirror image of the other half (Figure 6.3, page 171).

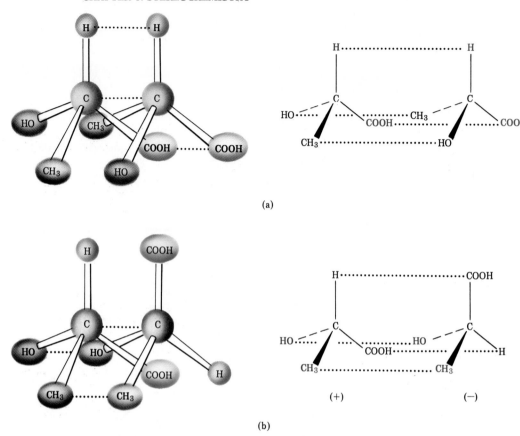

(a)

(b)

FIGURE 6.2
Attempts at superimposing the two mirror-image forms of lactic acid: (a) When the
—H and —COOH substituents match up, the —OH and —CH$_3$ substituents do
not. (b) When —OH and —CH$_3$ match up, —H and —COOH do not. Regardless
of how the molecules are turned or oriented, they are not identical. (Note that, for
clarity, the —OH, —CH$_3$, and —COOH substituent groups are shown as single
ovals. The individual atoms are not shown.)

Molecules that have planes of symmetry *must* be superimposable on their
mirror images and hence must be nonchiral or **achiral** (a-ky′-ral). Thus, hydroxyacetic acid, HOCH$_2$COOH, contains a plane of symmetry and is achiral, whereas
lactic acid CH$_3$CH(OH)COOH has no plane of symmetry and is chiral (Figure
6.4).

The most common (although not the only) cause of chirality in organic molecules is the presence of a carbon atom bonded to four different groups. Such
carbons are referred to as **chiral centers,** and we have seen an example in lactic
acid. Detecting chiral centers in a complex molecule can be difficult, because it's
not always immediately apparent that four different groups are bonded to a given
carbon. The differences don't necessarily appear right next to the chiral center.
For example, 5-bromodecane is a chiral molecule because four different groups
are bonded to C5, the chiral center (marked by an asterisk), as shown on the
facing page.

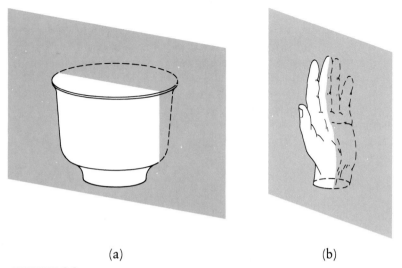

(a)   (b)

FIGURE 6.3
The meaning of symmetry planes: (a) An object like a coffee cup has a
plane of symmetry passing through it, making the right and left halves
mirror images. (b) An object like a hand does not have a symmetry plane.
The right half of a hand is not a mirror image of the left half.

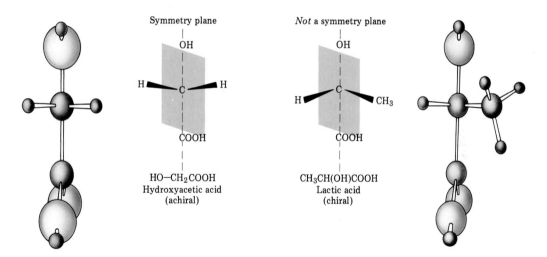

Symmetry plane

OH

H —— C —— H

COOH

HO—CH₂COOH
Hydroxyacetic acid
(achiral)

Not a symmetry plane

OH

H —— C —— CH₃

COOH

CH₃CH(OH)COOH
Lactic acid
(chiral)

FIGURE 6.4
The achiral hydroxyacetic acid molecule and the chiral lactic acid molecule:
Hydroxyacetic acid has a plane of symmetry making one side of the molecule a
mirror image of the other side. Lactic acid, however, has no such symmetry plane.

$$CH_3CH_2CH_2CH_2CH_2 - C^* - CH_2CH_2CH_2CH_3$$

Br

H

5-Bromodecane (chiral)

Substituents on carbon 5

—H

—Br

—$CH_2CH_2CH_2CH_3$ (butyl)

—$CH_2CH_2CH_2CH_2CH_3$ (pentyl)

A butyl substituent is similar to a pentyl substituent, but is not identical. The difference is not apparent until four carbons away from the chiral center, but there is still a difference.

As other examples, look at methylcyclohexane and 2-methylcyclohexanone. Are either of these molecules chiral?

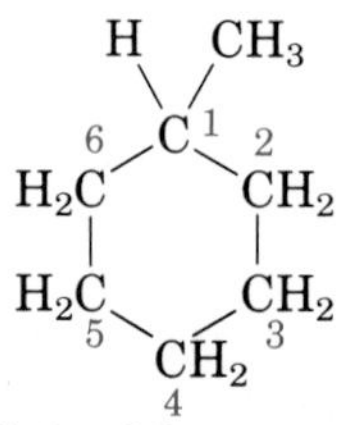

Methylcyclohexane (achiral) 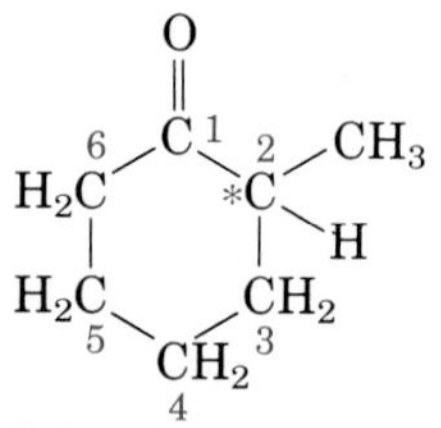   2-Methylcyclohexanone (chiral)

Methylcyclohexane is achiral because no carbon atom is bonded to four different groups. We can immediately eliminate all $-CH_2-$ carbons and the $-CH_3$ carbon, but what about C1 on the ring? The C1 carbon is bonded to a $-CH_3$ group, to an $-H$ atom, and to C2 and C6 of the ring. Carbons 2 and 6 are equivalent, however, as are C3 and C5. Thus, the C6–C5–C4 "substituent" is equivalent to the C2–C3–C4 "substituent," and methylcyclohexane is achiral. An alternative way of arriving at the same conclusion is to realize that methylcyclohexane has a symmetry plane, which passes through the methyl group and through ring carbons C1 and C4. 2-Methylcyclohexanone, on the other hand, has no plane of symmetry. It is chiral because C2 is bonded to four different groups: a $-CH_3$ group, an $-H$ atom, a $-COCH_2-$ ring bond (C1), and a $-CH_2CH_2-$ ring bond (C3).

Two more examples of chiral molecules appear in Figure 6.5. Check for yourself that the labeled centers are indeed chiral. [*Remember:* $-CH_2-$, $-CH_3$, and $C=C$ carbons cannot be chiral, since they have at least two identical bonds.]

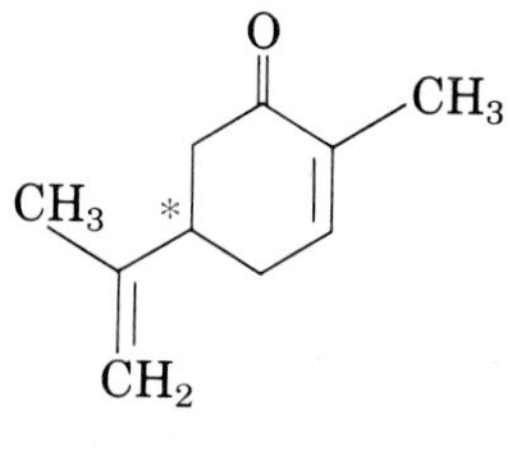

Carvone (spearmint oil) 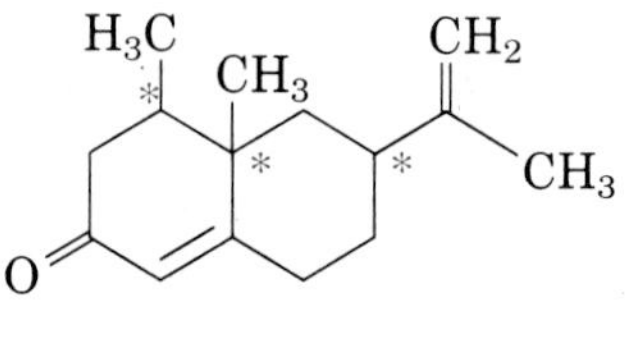   Nootkatone (grapefruit oil)

FIGURE 6.5
Two chiral molecules with their chiral centers marked by asterisks: Note that nootkatone has three chiral centers.

PROBLEM 6.1   Which of the following objects are chiral (handed)?

(a) Bean stalk   (b) Screwdriver   (c) Screw   (d) Shoe

PROBLEM 6.2 Which of these molecules are chiral? Identify the chiral centers in each and build molecular models if you need help in seeing spatial relationships.

(a) CH₃

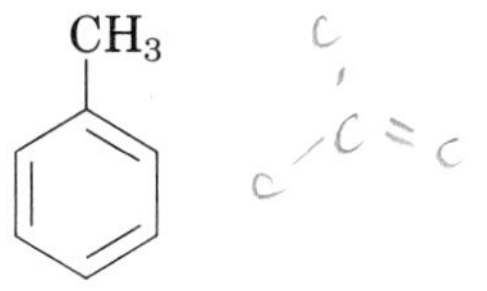

Toluene

(b) H

CH₂CH₂CH₃

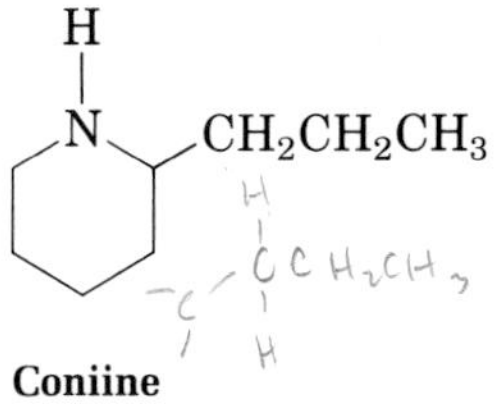

Coniine

(c)

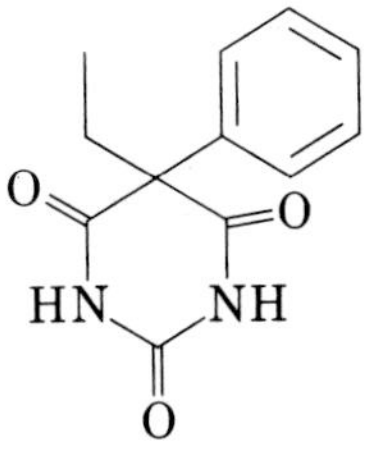

Phenobarbital

PROBLEM 6.3 Place asterisks at all the chiral centers in these molecules.

(a) Nicotine

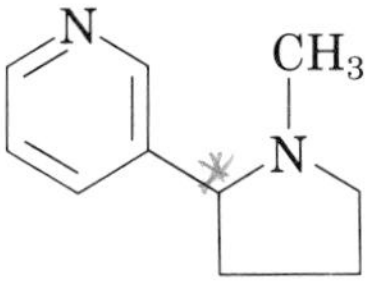

(b) Muscone (musk oil)

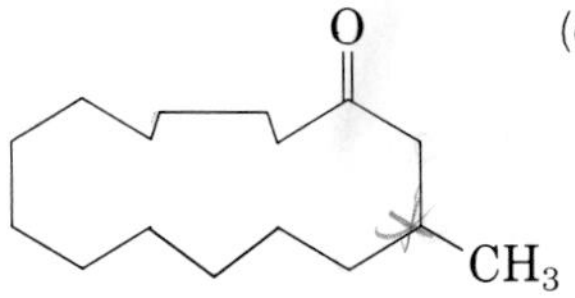

(c) Camphor

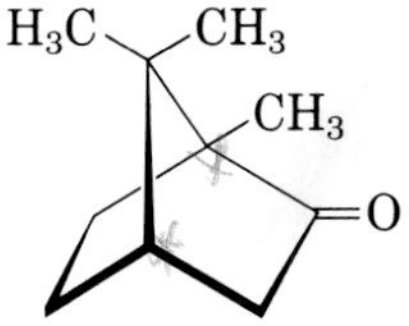

PROBLEM 6.4 Alanine, an amino acid found in proteins, is a chiral molecule. Use the standard convention of wedged, normal, and dashed lines to draw the two enantiomers of alanine.

$$CH_3CH(NH_2)COOH$$

Alanine

6.3 OPTICAL ACTIVITY

The study of stereochemistry has its origins in the work of Jean Baptiste Biot in the early nineteenth century. Biot, a French physicist, was investigating the nature of **plane-polarized light**. A beam of ordinary light consists of electromagnetic waves that oscillate at right angles to the direction of light travel. Since ordinary light is unpolarized, this oscillation takes place in an infinite number of planes. When a beam of ordinary light is passed through a device called a **polarizer**, only the light waves oscillating in a *single* plane pass through. Light waves in all other planes are blocked out. The light that passes through the polarizer has its electromagnetic waves vibrating in a well-defined plane, hence the name plane-polarized light. The polarization process is represented in Figure 6.6 (page 174).

Biot made the remarkable observation that when a beam of plane-polarized light is passed through solutions of certain organic molecules, such as sugar or camphor, the plane of polarization is *rotated.* Not all organic molecules exhibit this property, but those that do rotate plane-polarized light are said to be **optically active.**

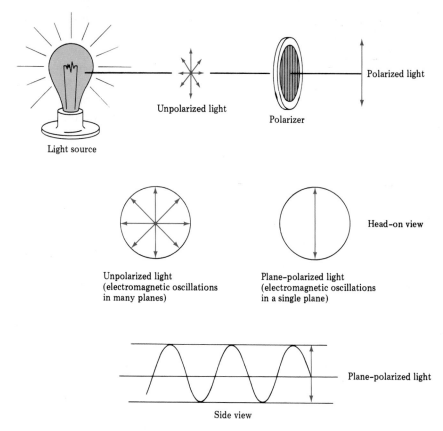

FIGURE 6.6
Plane-polarized light

The amount of rotation can be measured with an instrument called a **polar-imeter,** represented schematically in Figure 6.7. Optically active organic mole-cules are first placed in a sample tube; plane-polarized light is passed through the tube; and rotation of the plane occurs. The light then goes through a second polarizer known as an **analyzer.** By rotating the analyzer until light passes through it, we can find the new plane of polarization and can tell to what extent

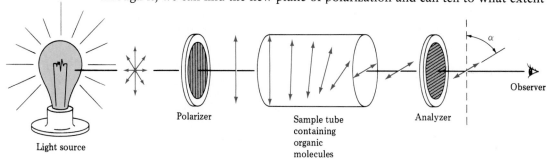

FIGURE 6.7
Schematic representation of a polarimeter

rotation has occurred. The amount of rotation observed is denoted by α (Greek alpha) and is expressed in degrees.

In addition to determining the extent of rotation, we can also find out its direction. Some optically active molecules rotate plane-polarized light to the left (counterclockwise) and are said to be **levorotatory**. Other molecules rotate light to the right (clockwise) and are said to be **dextrorotatory**. By convention, rotation to the left is denoted by a minus sign $(-)$ and rotation to the right is given a plus sign $(+)$. For example, $(-)$-morphine is levorotatory and $(+)$-sucrose is dextrorotatory.

6.4 SPECIFIC ROTATION

Since the rotation of plane-polarized light is an intrinsic property of optically active organic molecules, it follows that the amount of rotation depends on the number of molecules encountered by the light beam. The more molecules encountered by the light, the greater the observed rotation will be. Thus, the amount of rotation observed is dependent both on sample concentration and on sample path length. If we double the concentration of sample in a tube, the observed rotation is doubled. Similarly, if we keep concentration constant but double the length of the sample tube, the observed rotation is doubled.

To express optical rotation data in a meaningful way, we must choose standard conditions. By convention, the **specific rotation, $[\alpha]_D$,** of a compound is defined as the observed rotation when light of 5896 Å wavelength (the yellow sodium D line) is used with a sample path length of 1 decimeter (1 dm; 10 cm) and a sample concentration of 1 g/mL. Specific rotation:

$$[\alpha]_D = \frac{\text{Observed rotation, } \alpha}{\text{Path length, } l \text{ (dm)} \times \text{Concentration of sample, } C \text{ (g/mL)}}$$

$$[\alpha]_D = \frac{\alpha}{l \times C}$$

When optical rotation data are expressed in this standard way, the specific rotation, $[\alpha]_D$, is a physical constant that is characteristic of each optically active compound. Some examples are listed in Table 6.1.

TABLE 6.1 Specific rotations of some organic molecules

Compound	$[\alpha]_D$ (degrees)	Compound	$[\alpha]_D$ (degrees)
Camphor	+ 44.26	Penicillin V	+223
Morphine	−132	Monosodium glutamate	+ 25.5
Sucrose	+ 66.47	Benzene	0
Cholesterol	− 31.5	Acetic acid	0

PRACTICE PROBLEM   A 1.2 g sample of cocaine, $[\alpha]_D = -16°$, was dissolved in 7.5 mL chloroform and placed in a sample tube having a 5 cm path length. What was the observed rotation?

Solution   Rearranging the formula for $[\alpha]_D$, we find that observed rotation, α, is equal to specific rotation, $[\alpha]_D$, times sample concentration, C, times path length, l:

$$\alpha = [\alpha]_D \times C \times l$$

We have $[\alpha]_D = -16°$, $l = 5$ cm $= 0.5$ dm, and C $= 1.2$ g/7.5 mL $= 0.16$ g/mL. Thus,

$$\alpha = -16° \times 0.16 \times 0.5 = -1.28°$$

PROBLEM 6.5   A 1.5 g sample of coniine, the toxic extract of poison hemlock, was dissolved in 10 mL ethanol and placed in a sample tube with a 5 cm path length. The observed rotation at the sodium D line was $+1.2°$. Calculate the specific rotation, $[\alpha]_D$, for coniine.

6.5   PASTEUR'S DISCOVERY OF ENANTIOMERS

After Biot's discovery of optical activity in 1815, little was done until Louis Pasteur entered the picture in 1848. Pasteur was working on crystalline salts of tartaric acid derived from wine and was repeating some measurements published a few years earlier when he made a surprising observation. When he recrystallized a concentrated solution of sodium ammonium tartrate below 28°C, two distinct kinds of crystals precipitated. Furthermore, the two kinds of crystals were *mirror images* of each other. That is, they were not symmetrical, but were related to each other in exactly the same way that a right hand is related to a left hand.

Working carefully with a pair of tweezers, Pasteur was able to separate the crystals into two piles, one of "right-handed" crystals and one of "left-handed" crystals like those shown in Figure 6.8. Although the original sample (a 50:50 mixture of right and left) was optically inactive, *solutions of the crystals in each of the individual piles were optically active*, and their specific rotations were equal in amount but opposite in sign.

Pasteur was far ahead of his time. Although the structural theory of Kekulé had not yet been proposed, in explaining his results Pasteur spoke of the *molecules themselves*, saying, "It cannot be a subject of doubt that [in the *dextro* tartaric acid] there exists an asymmetric arrangement having a nonsuperimposable image. It is not less certain that the atoms of the *levo* acid possess precisely the inverse asymmetric arrangement." Pasteur's vision was extraordinary, for it was not until 25 years later that his theories regarding the asymmetric carbon atom were confirmed.

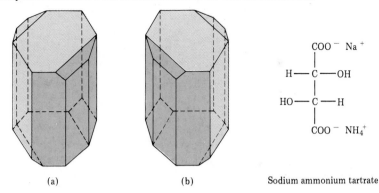

(a)　　　　　　　(b)　　　　Sodium ammonium tartrate

FIGURE 6.8
Crystals of sodium ammonium tartrate: One of the crystals is
dextrorotatory, "right-handed," and the other crystal is levorotatory,
"left-handed." The drawings are taken from Pasteur's original
sketches.

Today, we would describe Pasteur's work by saying that he had discovered the
phenomenon of enantiomerism or **optical isomerism**. Enantiomers (also called
optical isomers) have identical physical properties, such as melting point and
boiling point, but differ in the direction in which they rotate plane-polarized light.

6.6 SEQUENCE RULES FOR SPECIFICATION OF CONFIGURATION

Although drawings can provide a pictorial representation of stereochemistry, they
are difficult to translate into words. Thus, a verbal method of specifying the exact
three-dimensional arrangement (**configuration**) at a chiral center is also necessary.
The method used employs the same **sequence rules** that we used in connection
with the specification of alkene stereochemistry (Z versus E) in Section 3.4. Let's
briefly review these sequence rules and see how they can be used to specify the
configuration of a chiral center. For a more thorough explanation, however, you
should refer back to Section 3.4.

1. Look at the four atoms directly attached to the chiral center and assign priorities in
   order of decreasing atomic number. The atom with highest atomic number is ranked
   first; the atom with lowest atomic number is ranked fourth.

2. If a decision about priority cannot be reached by applying rule 1, compare atomic
   numbers of the second atoms in each substituent, continuing on as necessary
   through the third or fourth atoms outward until the first point of difference is
   reached.

3. Multiple-bonded atoms are considered as if they were an equivalent number of
   single-bonded atoms. For example, a $-CH=O$ substituent is equivalent to
   $-CH-O-C$.
   $\quad\quad\;\;|$
   $\quad\quad\;\;O$

Following these sequence rules, we can assign priorities to the four substituent groups attached to a chiral carbon. To describe the stereochemical configuration around that carbon, we mentally orient the molecule so that the group of lowest priority (fourth) is pointing directly back away from us. We then look at the three remaining substituents, which now appear to radiate toward us from the chiral center like the spokes on a steering wheel. If a curved arrow drawn from highest to second-highest to third-highest substituent (1 → 2 → 3) is *clockwise*, we say that the chiral center has the R configuration (Latin *rectus*, "right"). If a curved arrow from 1 → 2 → 3 is *counterclockwise*, the chiral center has the S configuration (Latin *sinister*, "left"). To remember these assignments, think of a car's steering wheel when making a right (clockwise) turn or a left (counterclockwise) turn.

For example, let's look at (+)-lactic acid:

Priorities

H—C

OH

CH₃

COOH

(+)-Lactic acid

4 —H   (low)

3 —CH₃

2 —$\overset{\text{O}}{\overset{\|}{\text{C}}}$—OH

1 —OH   (high)

Our first step is to assign priorities to the four substituents. Sequence rule 1 tells us that —OH is first priority and —H is fourth priority, but this rule does not allow us to distinguish between —CH₃ and —COOH, since both groups have carbon as their first atom. Sequence rule 2 tells us that —COOH is higher in priority than —CH₃, since oxygen outranks hydrogen (the second atom in each group).

We next orient the molecule so that the fourth-priority group (—H) is toward the rear, away from the observer. Since the direction of travel from 1 → 2 → 3 (—OH → —COOH → —CH₃) is counterclockwise (left turn of the steering wheel), we assign the S configuration to (+)-lactic acid (Figure 6.9). Applying the same procedure to (−)-lactic acid should (and does) lead to the opposite assignment. Try it for yourself.

A further example is provided by the naturally occurring compound (−)-glyceraldehyde, which has the S configuration shown in Figure 6.10. Note that the sign of optical rotation is not related to the R,S designation. (S)-Lactic acid *happens* to be dextrorotatory (+), and (S)-glyceraldehyde *happens* to be levorotatory (−). There is no correlation between the direction of rotation and R,S configuration.

One further point bears mentioning—the matter of **absolute configuration**. How do we know for certain that our assignments of R,S configurations are correct in an absolute sense? Since we can't see the molecules themselves, how do we know for certain that it is the dextrorotatory enantiomer of lactic acid that has the R configuration? This difficult question was not solved until 1951 when J. M. Bijvoet reported an X-ray spectroscopic method for determining the absolute spatial arrangement of atoms in molecules. On the basis of his results, we can say with certainty that our conventions are correct.

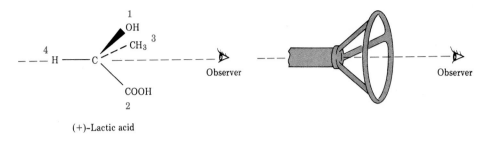

(+)-Lactic acid

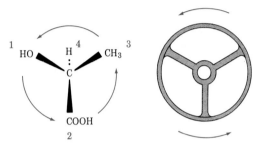

S configuration (left turn of steering wheel)

FIGURE 6.9
Assignment of configuration to (S)-(+)-lactic acid

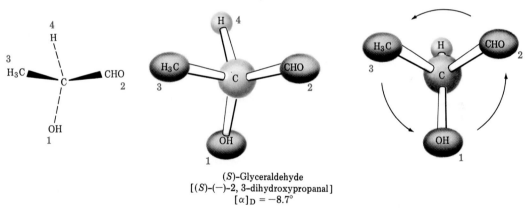

(S)-Glyceraldehyde
[(S)-(−)-2, 3-dihydroxypropanal]
[α]$_D$ = −8.7°

FIGURE 6.10
Configuration of (−)-glyceraldehyde

PRACTICE PROBLEM   Draw a tetrahedral representation of (R)-2-chlorobutane.

Solution   The four substituents bound to the chiral carbon of (R)-2-chlorobutane can be assigned the following priorities: (1) —Cl, (2) —CH$_2$CH$_3$, (3) —CH$_3$, (4) —H. To draw a tetrahedral representation of the molecule, first orient the low-priority —H group toward the rear and imagine that the other three groups are coming out of the page toward you. Place the remaining three substituents so that the direction of travel from 1 → 2 → 3 is clockwise (right turn), and then tilt the molecule slightly to bring the rear hydrogen into view and end up with a standard tetrahedral representation:

$$Cl \underset{\overset{|}{CH_3}}{\overset{H}{\underset{C}{}}} CH_2CH_3 \quad = \quad \underset{H_3C}{\overset{Cl}{\underset{CH_2CH_3}{\overset{|}{C}}} H}$$

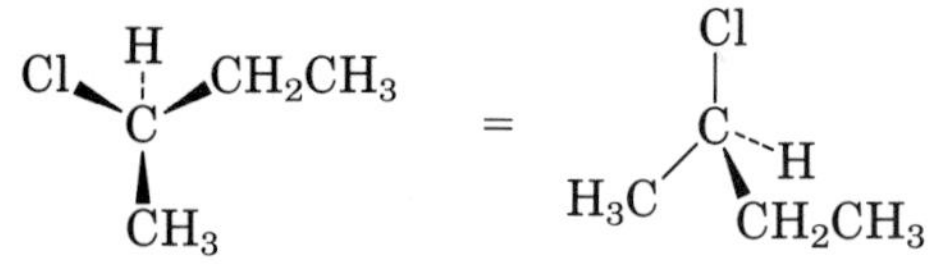

Using molecular models is a great help in working problems of this sort.

PROBLEM 6.6   Assign priorities to these sets of substituents:

(a) —H, —Br, —CH$_2$CH$_3$, —CH$_2$CH$_2$OH
(b) —COOH, —COOCH$_3$, —CH$_2$OH, —OH
(c) —Br, —CH$_2$Br, —Cl, —CH$_2$Cl
(d) —CN, —H, —NH$_2$, —CH$_2$NH$_2$

PROBLEM 6.7   Assign R,S configurations to these molecules:

(a) 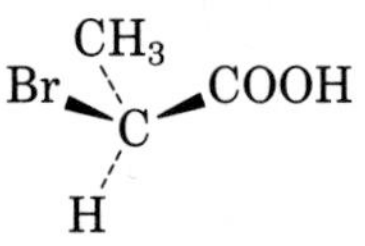
$$Br \underset{\overset{\vdots}{H}}{\overset{CH_3}{\underset{C}{}}} COOH$$

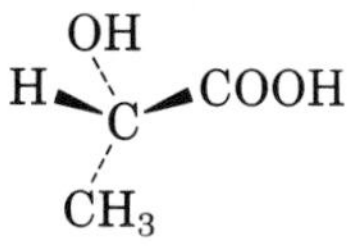

(b)
$$H \underset{\overset{\vdots}{CH_3}}{\overset{OH}{\underset{C}{}}} COOH$$

(c)
$$H \underset{\overset{\vdots}{CN}}{\overset{NH_2}{\underset{C}{}}} CH_3$$

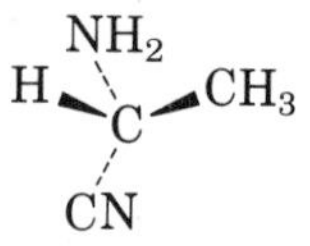

PROBLEM 6.8   Draw a tetrahedral representation of (S)-2-hydroxypentane (2-pentanol).

6.7 DIASTEREOMERS

Molecules such as lactic acid, alanine, and glyceraldehyde are relatively simple to deal with since each has only one chiral center and only two enantiomeric forms. The situation becomes more complex, however, for molecules that have more than one chiral center.

Let's take the essential amino acid threonine (2-amino-3-hydroxybutanoic acid) as an example. Since threonine has *two* chiral centers (C2 and C3), there are *four* possible stereoisomers, as shown in Figure 6.11. (Check for yourself that the R,S configurations are correct as shown.)

A careful look at the four threonine stereoisomers shows that they can be classified into two mirror-image pairs of enantiomers. The 2R,3R stereoisomer is the mirror image of 2S,3S, and the 2R,3S stereoisomer is the mirror image of 2S,3R. But what is the relationship between any two configurations that are not mirror images? What, for example, is the relationship between the 2R,3R compound and the 2R,3S compound? These two compounds are stereoisomers, yet they are not superimposable and they are not enantiomers.

To describe such a relationship, we need a new term. **Diastereomers** are stereoisomers that are not mirror images of each other. Since we used the right-hand/left-hand analogy to describe the relationship between two enantiomers, we might extend the analogy by saying that diastereomers have a hand–foot relationship. Hands and feet look very *similar*, but they are not identical and are not

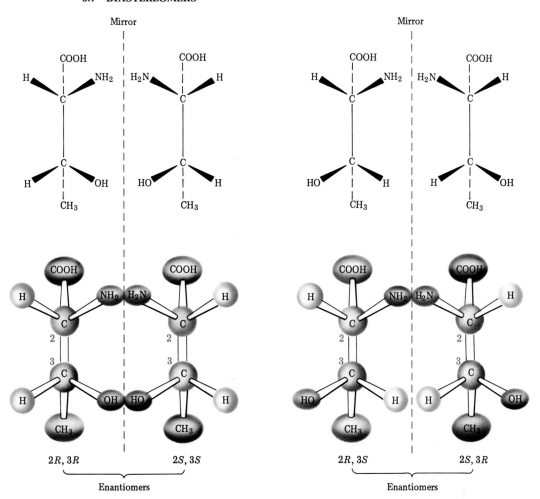

FIGURE 6.11
Four stereoisomers of threonine (2-amino-3-hydroxybutanoic acid): Note that the —OH, —COOH, —CH₃, and —NH₂ substituent groups on the two chiral carbon atoms are depicted as single ovals for clarity. The individual atoms in these substituent groups are not indicated.

mirror images. The same is true of diastereomers. They are similar but not identical and not mirror images.

A full description of the four threonine stereoisomers is given in Table 6.2 (page 182). Enantiomers must have opposite (mirror-image) configurations around *all* chiral centers; diastereomers have the same configuration at at least one chiral center, but opposite configurations at the others.

Of the four possible stereoisomers of threonine, only the 2S,3R isomer, $[\alpha]_D = -28.3°$, occurs naturally in plants and animals and is an essential human nutrient. Most biologically important molecules are chiral, and usually only a single stereoisomer is found in nature.

TABLE 6.2   **Relationships between the four stereoisomeric threonines**

Stereoisomer	Enantiomeric with	Diastereomeric with
2R,3R	2S,3S	2R,3S, 2S,3R
2S,3S	2R,3R	2R,3S, 2S,3R
2R,3S	2S,3R	2R,3R, 2S,3S
2S,3R	2R,3S	2R,3R, 2S,3S

PROBLEM 6.9   Assign R,S configurations to each chiral center in these molecules. Which are enantiomers and which are diastereomers?

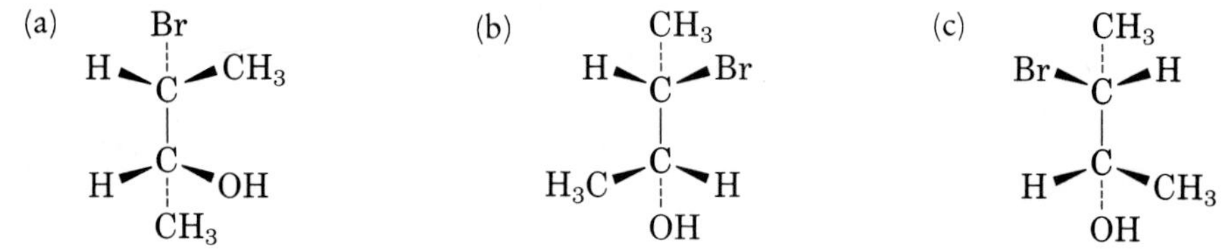

(a)

$$Br$$
$$H \diagdown \underset{C}{} \diagup CH_3$$
$$H \diagup \underset{C}{} \diagdown OH$$
$$CH_3$$

(b)

$$CH_3$$
$$H \diagdown \underset{C}{} \diagup Br$$
$$H_3C \diagup \underset{C}{} \diagdown H$$
$$OH$$

(c)

$$CH_3$$
$$Br \diagdown \underset{C}{} \diagup H$$
$$H \diagup \underset{C}{} \diagdown CH_3$$
$$OH$$

PROBLEM 6.10   Chloramphenicol is a powerful antibiotic isolated from the *Streptomyces venezuelae* bacterium. It is active against a broad spectrum of bacterial infections and is particularly valuable against typhoid fever. Assign R,S configurations to the chiral centers in chloramphenicol.

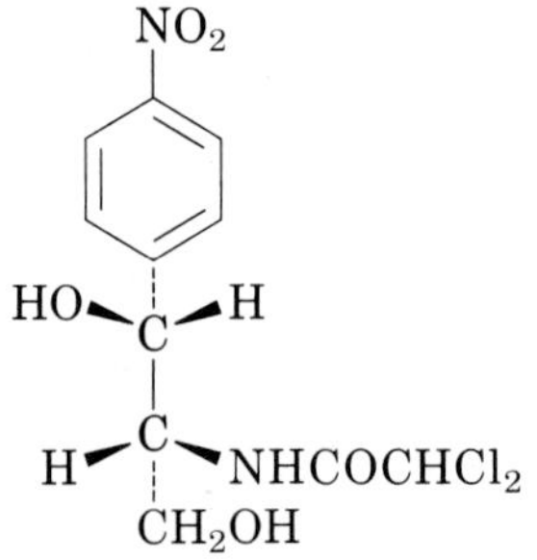

$$NO_2$$

$$HO \diagdown \underset{C}{} \diagup H$$
$$H \diagup \underset{C}{} \diagdown NHCOCHCl_2$$
$$CH_2OH$$

Chloramphenicol, $[\alpha]_D = +18.6°$

6.8   MESO COMPOUNDS

Let's look at one more example of a compound with two chiral centers—tartaric acid. We're already acquainted with tartaric acid for its role in Pasteur's discovery of optical activity, and we can now draw the four stereoisomers:

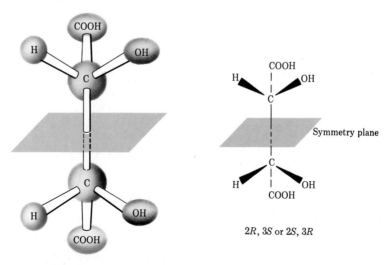

Mirror

₁COOH
H—C₂—OH
HO—C₃—H
₄COOH

2R,3R

Mirror

₁COOH
HO—C₂—H
H—C₃—OH
₄COOH

2S,3S

₁COOH
H—C₂—OH
H—C₃—OH
₄COOH

2R,3S

₁COOH
HO—C₂—H
HO—C₃—H
₄COOH

2S,3R

The mirror-image 2R,3R and 2S,3S structures are nonsuperimposable and there-fore represent an enantiomeric pair. A close look, however, reveals that the 2R,3S and 2S,3R structures are *identical*. We can see this readily by rotating one struc-ture 180°:

₁COOH
H—C₂—OH
H—C₃—OH
₄COOH

2R,3S

Rotate 180° →

₁COOH
HO—C₂—H
HO—C₃—H
₄COOH

2S,3R

Identical

The identity of the 2R,3S and 2S,3R structures is a consequence of the fact that the molecule has a plane of symmetry. The symmetry plane cuts through the C2–C3 bond, making one half of the molecule a mirror image of the other half (Figure 6.12).

FIGURE 6.12
A symmetry plane through the C2–C3 bond of *meso*-tartaric acid

184   CHAPTER 6: STEREOCHEMISTRY

Because of the plane of symmetry, the tartaric acid stereoisomer shown in Figure 6.12 must be achiral, despite the fact that it has two chiral centers. Compounds that are achiral by virtue of a symmetry plane, yet contain chiral centers, are called **meso compounds** (me'-zo). Thus, tartaric acid exists in only three stereoisomeric configurations: two enantiomers and one meso form.

PRACTICE PROBLEM Does *cis*-1,2-dimethylcyclobutane have any chiral centers? Is it a chiral molecule?

Solution Draw the structure of *cis*-1,2-dimethylcyclobutane and make a molecular model. Examination shows that both of the methyl-bearing ring carbons (C1 and C2) are chiral. Overall, however, the compound is achiral because there is a symmetry plane bisecting the ring between C1 and C2. Thus, the molecule is a meso compound.

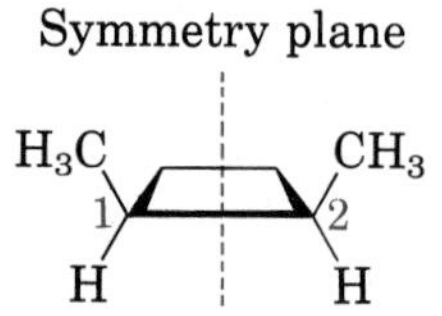

Symmetry plane

H_3C 1 2 CH_3

H   H

PROBLEM 6.11   Which of these substance can exist in a meso form?

(a) 2,3-Dibromobutane   (b) 2,3-Dibromopentane   (c) 2,4-Dibromopentane

PROBLEM 6.12   Which of these structures represent meso compounds?

(a) H, OH / OH / H

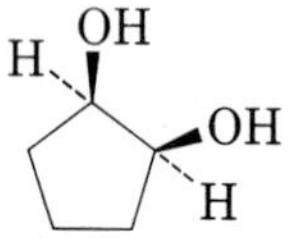

(b) H, OH / OH / H

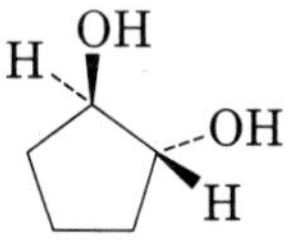

(c) H Br—C—CH$_3$ H$_3$C—C—H Br

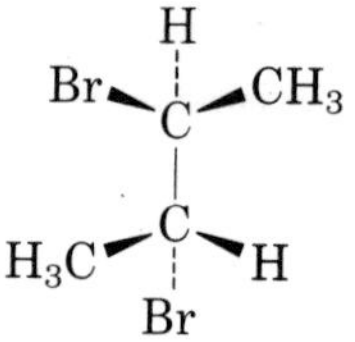

6.9   MOLECULES WITH MORE THAN TWO CHIRAL CENTERS

We have seen how a single chiral center gives rise to two stereoisomers (one pair of enantiomers), and how two chiral centers in a molecule give rise to a *maximum* of four stereoisomers (two pairs of enantiomers). In general, a molecule with n chiral centers gives rise to a maximum of 2^n stereoisomers (2^{n-1} pairs of enantiomers). For example, cholesterol has eight chiral centers. Thus, $2^8 = 256$ stereoisomers, or 128 pairs of enantiomers, are possible in principle, though many would be too strained to exist. Only *one*, however, is produced in nature.

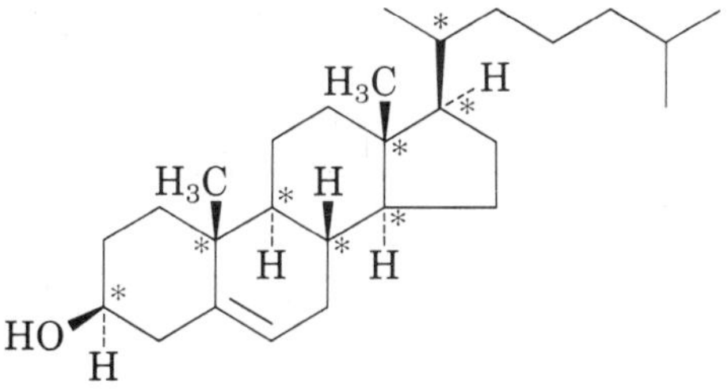

Cholesterol (eight chiral centers)

6.10 RACEMIC MIXTURES

To conclude our discussion of stereoisomerism, let's return for a last look at Pasteur's pioneering work. Pasteur took an optically inactive form of a tartaric acid salt and found that he could crystallize two optically active forms from it. The two optically active forms were the 2R,3R and 2S,3S configurations, but what was the optically inactive form he started with? It could not have been *meso*-tartaric acid, since *meso*-tartaric acid is a different chemical compound and cannot interconvert with the two chiral enantiomers without breaking and re-forming chemical bonds.

As we noted in Section 6.5, the answer is that Pasteur started with a 50:50 mixture of the two chiral tartaric acid enantiomers. Such a mixture is called a **racemic** (ray-see'-mic) **mixture** or **racemate**. Racemic mixtures, often denoted by the symbol (±), must show zero optical rotation because equal amounts of (+) and (−) forms are present. The (+) rotation from one enantiomer exactly cancels the (−) rotation from the other enantiomer.

Through good fortune, Pasteur was able to separate or **resolve** (±)-tartaric acid into its (+) and (−) enantiomers. Unfortunately, the physical technique of fractional crystallization he used does not work for most racemic mixtures, and other methods are required. We will see the most often used method in Section 12.4.

6.11 PHYSICAL PROPERTIES OF STEREOISOMERS

We have seen how seemingly simple compounds such as tartaric acid can exist in different stereoisomeric configurations. The question therefore arises whether the different stereoisomers have different physical properties. The answer is yes, they do.

Some physical properties of the three different stereoisomers of tartaric acid and of the racemic mixture are shown in Table 6.3 (page 186). As indicated, the (+) and (−) enantiomers have identical melting points, solubilities, and densities. They differ only in the sign of their rotation of plane-polarized light. The meso isomer, by contrast, is diastereomeric with the (+) and (−) forms. As such, it is a different compound altogether and has different physical properties.

The racemic mixture is different still. For reasons beyond our present scope, racemates act as though they were pure compounds, different from either enantiomer. Thus, the physical properties of racemic tartaric acid differ from those of the two enantiomers and from those of the meso form.

TABLE 6.3   Some properties of the stereoisomers of tartaric acid

Stereoisomer	Melting point (°C)	$[\alpha]_D$ (degrees)	Density (g/cm³)	Solubility at 20°C (g/100 mL H₂O)
(+)	168–170	+12	1.7598	139.0
(−)	168–170	−12	1.7598	139.0
meso	146–148	0	1.6660	125.0
(±)	206	0	1.7880	20.6

6.12 STEREOCHEMISTRY OF REACTIONS: ADDITION OF HBr TO ALKENES

Many organic reactions, including some that we have studied, yield products with chiral centers. For example, addition of HBr to 1-butene yields 2-bromobutane, a chiral molecule. What predictions can we make about the stereochemistry of this chiral product? The answer is that 2-bromobutane is produced as a racemic mixture of R and S enantiomers.

$$CH_3CH_2CH{=}CH_2 \xrightarrow[\text{Ether}]{\text{HBr}} CH_3CH_2\overset{*}{C}HCH_3$$
$$\overset{|}{Br}$$

1-Butene
(achiral)

(±)-2-Bromobutane
(chiral)

To understand why a racemic product results, let's consider what happens during the reaction. 1-Butene is first protonated to yield an intermediate secondary (2°) carbocation. This ion is sp^2 hybridized; it therefore has a plane of symmetry and is achiral. As a result, it can be attacked by bromide ion (also achiral) equally well from either the top or the bottom (Figure 6.13). Attack from the top leads to (S)-2-bromobutane, and attack from the bottom leads to (R)-2-bromobutane. Since both modes of attack occur with equal probability, a racemic product mixture results.

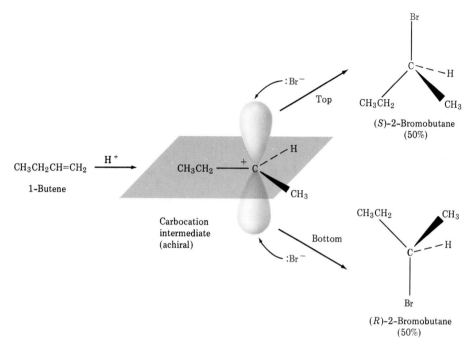

FIGURE 6.13
Stereochemistry of the addition of HBr to 1-butene: The intermediate carbocation is attacked equally well from both top and bottom sides, giving rise to a racemic mixture of products: 50% *R* and 50% *S*.

6.13 STEREOCHEMISTRY OF REACTIONS: ADDITION OF Br₂ TO ALKENES

Addition of Br_2 to 2-butene leads to the formation of 2,3-dibromobutane and the generation of two chiral centers. What stereochemistry would we predict for such a reaction? If we begin with planar, achiral *cis*-2-butene, we would expect bromine to add to the double bond equally well from either the top or bottom face to generate two intermediate bromonium ions. For the sake of simplicity, let's consider only the result of attack from the top, while keeping in mind that every structure we consider also has a mirror image (Figure 6.14, page 188).

The bromonium ion formed by reaction from the top of *cis*-2-butene can be attacked by bromide ion from either the right or left side. Attack from the left (path a) leads to (2*S*,3*S*)-dibromobutane; attack from the right (path b) leads to (2*R*,3*R*)-dibromobutane. Since both modes of attack on the symmetrical bromonium ion are equally likely, a 50:50 (racemic) mixture of the two enantiomeric products is formed.

What about bromination of *trans*-2-butene? Is a racemic product mixture formed here also? Perhaps surprisingly at first glance, the answer is no.

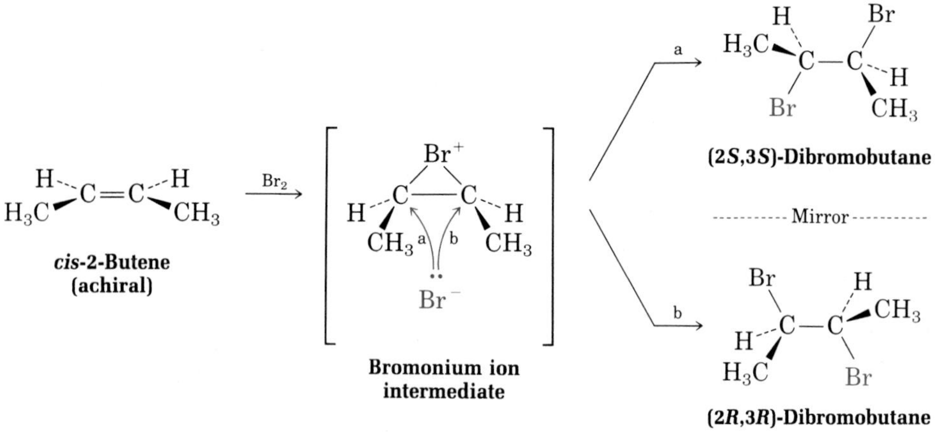

FIGURE 6.14
Stereochemistry of the addition of Br$_2$ to *cis*-2-butene: A racemic mixture of 2S,3S and 2R,3R products is formed.

trans-2-Butene reacts with bromine in the normal manner to form an intermediate bromonium ion. Once again, we will consider only attack from the top for simplicity (Figure 6.15). Attack of bromide ion on the bromonium ion intermediate leads to formation of 2R,3S and 2S,3R products in equal amounts. These two structures, however, are *identical*—both structures represent *meso*-2,3-dibromobutane.

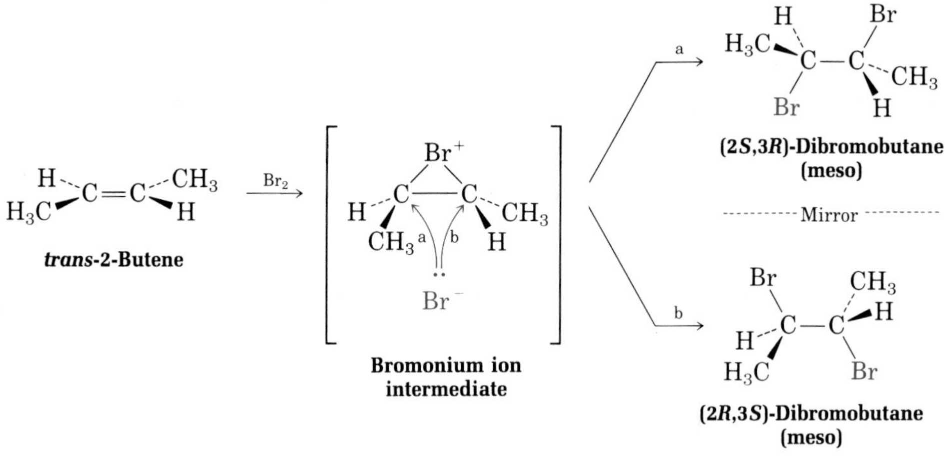

FIGURE 6.15
Stereochemistry of the addition of Br$_2$ to *trans*-2-butene: A meso product is formed.

The key conclusion in all three of the alkene addition reactions just discussed is that optically inactive product has been formed. This is a general rule: *Any reaction between two achiral partners always leads to optically inactive products—either racemic or meso.* Optically active products cannot be produced from optically inactive starting materials.

PROBLEM 6.13 Addition of Br_2 to cyclohexene yields *trans*-1,2-dibromocyclohexane. Is this product optically active? Is it chiral or is it a meso compound? [*Hint:* Remember that the double bond in cyclohexene must be cis, like the double bond in *cis*-2-butene.]

ADDITIONAL PROBLEMS

PROBLEM 6.14 Cholic acid, the major steroid found in bile, was observed to have a specific rotation of +2.22° when a 3.0 g sample was dissolved in 5.0 mL alcohol in a sample tube with a 1 cm path length. Calculate $[\alpha]_D$ for cholic acid.

PROBLEM 6.15 Polarimeters are quite sensitive and can measure rotations to the thousandth of a degree. This can be important when only small amounts of sample are available. For example, when 7.0 mg of ecdysone, an insect hormone that controls molting in the silkworm moth, was dissolved in 1.0 mL chloroform in a cell with a 2 cm path length, an observed rotation of +0.087° was found. Calculate $[\alpha]_D$ for ecdysone.

PROBLEM 6.16 Define these terms in your own words:
(a) Chirality   (b) Chiral center   (c) Diastereomer
(d) Racemate   (e) Meso compound   (f) Enantiomer

PROBLEM 6.17 Which of these objects are chiral?

(a) A basketball   (b) A wine glass   (c) An ear
(d) A snowflake   (e) A coin   (f) A pair of scissors

PROBLEM 6.18 Place asterisks by the chiral carbons in these molecules:

(a)

(b) $HOCH_2CH(OH)CHO$

Glyceraldehyde

(c)

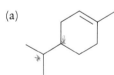

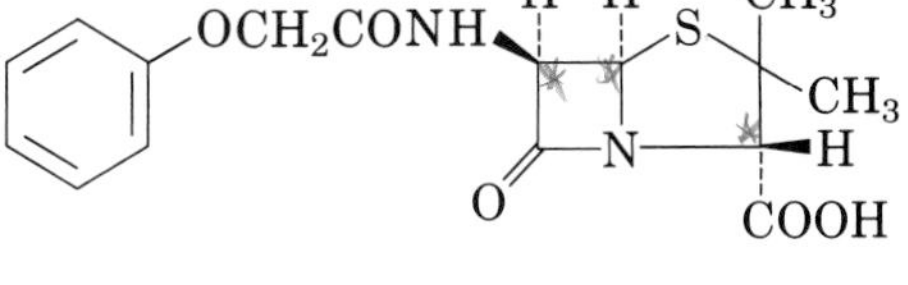

Penicillin V (antibiotic)

(d)

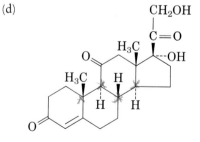

Cortisone (anti-inflammatory)

PROBLEM 6.19 Draw chiral molecules that meet these descriptions:

(a) A chloroalkane, $C_5H_{11}Cl$ (b) An alcohol, $C_6H_{14}O$
(c) An alkene, C_6H_{12} (d) An alkane, C_8H_{18}

PROBLEM 6.20   Which of these compounds are chiral? Label all chiral centers.

      (a) $CH_3CH_2C(CH_3)_2\overset{*}{C}H(CH_3)CH_2CH_3$ (b) 3-Methylcyclopentanone
      (c) 4-Methylcyclohexanone   (d) 1,2-Dibromo-2,3-diphenylbutane
      (e) Aspirin   (f) *cis*-1,4-Dimethylcyclohexane

PROBLEM 6.21   There are eight alcohols with the formula $C_5H_{12}O$. Draw them and tell which are chiral.

PROBLEM 6.22   Propose structures for compounds that meet these descriptions:

      (a) A chiral alcohol with four carbons
      (b) A chiral carboxylic acid
      (c) A compound with two chiral centers

PROBLEM 6.23   What is the relationship between the specific rotations of (2R,3R)-dihydroxypentane and (2S,3S)-dihydroxypentane? Between (2R,3S)-dihydroxypentane and (2R,3R)-dihydroxypentane?

PROBLEM 6.24   What is the stereochemical configuration of the enantiomer of (2S,4R)-dibromooctane?

PROBLEM 6.25   What are the stereochemical configurations of the two diastereomers of (2S,4R)-dibromooctane?

PROBLEM 6.26   Draw examples of the following:
      (a) A meso compound with the formula C_8H_{18}
      (b) A compound with two chiral centers, one R and the other S

PROBLEM 6.27   Draw a tetrahedral representation of (S)-2-butanol, $CH_3CH_2CH(OH)CH_3$.

PROBLEM 6.28   Draw a Newman projection of *meso*-tartaric acid.

PROBLEM 6.29   Draw Newman projections of (2R,3R)- and (2S,3S)-tartaric acid and compare them to the projection you drew in Problem 6.28 for the meso form.

PROBLEM 6.30   The simple sugar glucose has four chiral centers. How many stereoisomers of glucose are possible?

PROBLEM 6.31   Draw a tetrahedral representation of (R)-3-chloro-1-pentene.

PROBLEM 6.32   Assign priorities to these sets of substituents:
      (a) —H, —OH, —OCH$_3$, —CH$_3$
      (b) —Br, —CH$_3$, —CH$_2$Br, —Cl
      (c) —CH$=$CH$_2$, —CH(CH$_3$)$_2$, —C(CH$_3$)$_3$, —CH$_2$CH$_3$
      (d) —COOCH$_3$, —COCH$_3$, —CH$_2$OCH$_3$, —OCH$_3$

PROBLEM 6.33   Draw all the stereoisomers of 1,2-dimethylcyclopentane. Assign R,S configurations to the chiral centers in all isomers, and indicate which stereoisomers are chiral and which, if any, are meso.

PROBLEM 6.34 Assign *R* or *S* configuration to each chiral center in these molecules:

(a)

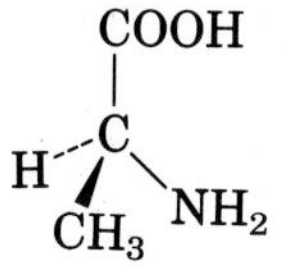

```
      COOH
       |
   H   C
    \ / \
     CH₃  NH₂
```

(b)

```
        (phenyl ring)
         |
  HO     C     H
      \  |  /
  H₂N    C    CH₃
         |
         H
```

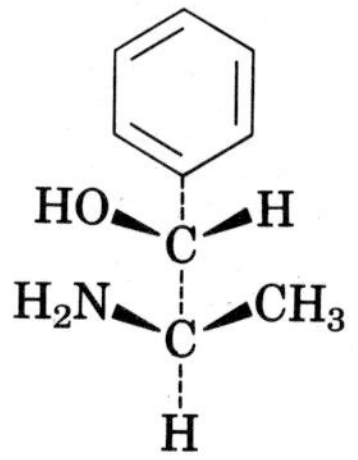

PROBLEM 6.35 Hydroxylation of *cis*-2-butene with $KMnO_4$ yields 2,3-butanediol. What is the stereochemistry of the product? (Review Section 4.7.)

PROBLEM 6.36 Answer Problem 6.35 for *trans*-2-butene.

PROBLEM 6.37 How many stereoisomers of 2,4-dibromo-3-chloropentane are there? Draw them and indicate which are optically active.

PROBLEM 6.38 Alkenes undergo reaction with peroxycarboxylic acids, RCO_3H, to give three-membered-ring ethers called *epoxides*. For example, 4-octene reacts with peroxycarboxylic acids to yield 4,5-epoxyoctane:

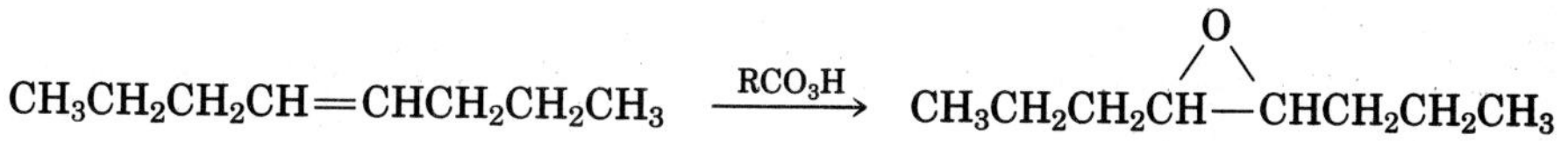

$$CH_3CH_2CH_2CH=CHCH_2CH_2CH_3 \xrightarrow{RCO_3H} CH_3CH_2CH_2CH\overset{\displaystyle O}{\overset{\diagup\diagdown}{\text{—}}}CHCH_2CH_2CH_3$$

4-Octene   **4,5-Epoxyoctane**

Assuming that the reaction occurs with syn stereochemistry, show the stereochemistry of the product. Is the epoxide chiral? How many chiral centers does it have? How would you describe the product stereochemically?

PROBLEM 6.39 Answer Problem 6.38 assuming that the epoxidation was carried out on *trans*-4-octene.

PROBLEM 6.40 Ribose, an essential part of ribonucleic acid (RNA), has the following structure:

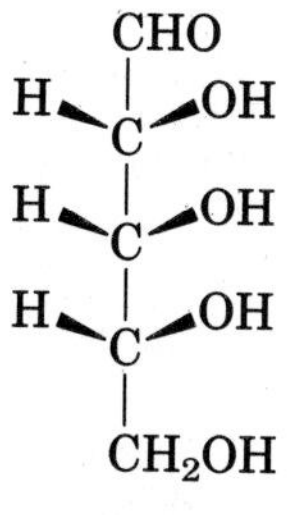

```
        CHO
         |
   H     C    OH
         |
   H     C    OH
         |
   H     C    OH
         |
       CH₂OH
```

Ribose

How many chiral centers does ribose have? Identify them with asterisks. How many stereoisomers of ribose are there?

PROBLEM 6.41 Draw the structure of the enantiomer (mirror image) of ribose (Problem 6.40).

PROBLEM 6.42 Draw the structure of a diastereomer of ribose (Problem 6.40).

PROBLEM 6.43   On catalytic hydrogenation over a platinum catalyst, ribose (Problem 6.40) is converted into ribitol. Is ribitol optically active or inactive? Explain.

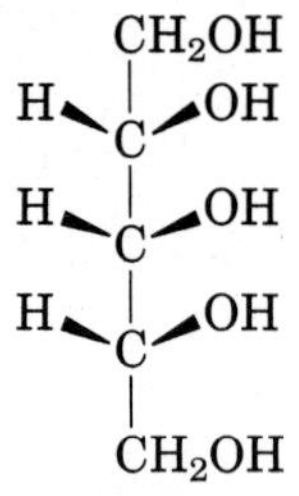

$$CH_2OH$$

H——C——OH

H——C——OH

H——C——OH

$$CH_2OH$$

Ribitol

PROBLEM 6.44   Draw the two enantiomers of the amino acid cysteine, $HSCH_2CH(NH_2)COOH$, and identify each as *R* or *S*.

PROBLEM 6.45   Draw the structure of (*R*)-2-methylcyclohexanone.

PROBLEM 6.46   Compound A, C_7H_{12}, was found to be optically active. On catalytic reduction over a palladium catalyst, 2 equiv of hydrogen were absorbed, yielding compound B, C_7H_{16}. On cleavage of compound A with ozone, two fragments were obtained. One fragment was identified as acetic acid, CH_3COOH, and the other fragment, C, was found to be an optically active carboxylic acid. Formulate the reactions and propose structures for compounds A, B, and C.

PROBLEM 6.47   *Allenes* are compounds with adjacent carbon–carbon double bonds. Even though they do not contain chiral carbon atoms, many allenes are chiral. For example, mycomycin, an antibiotic isolated from the bacterium *Nocardia acidophilus*, is chiral and has $[\alpha]_D = -130°$. Can you explain why mycomycin is chiral? Making a molecular model should be helpful.

$$HC{\equiv}C-C{\equiv}C-CH{=}C{=}CH-CH{=}CH-CH{=}CH-CH_2COOH$$

Mycomycin (an allene)

We saw in Section 6.11 that the different stereoisomeric forms of tartaric acid have different physical properties. It's usually the case that stereoisomers have different chemical and biological properties as well. For example, (+)-lactic acid is rapidly converted into pyruvic acid by the enzyme lactic acid dehydrogenase. (−)-Lactic acid, however, is not affected by the enzyme.

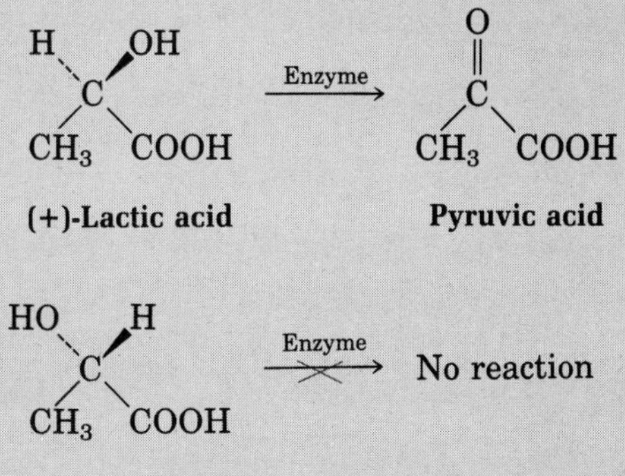

$$\underset{\textbf{(+)-Lactic acid}}{\overset{\displaystyle H \quad OH}{\underset{CH_3 \quad COOH}{C}}} \xrightarrow{\text{Enzyme}} \underset{\textbf{Pyruvic acid}}{\overset{\displaystyle O}{\underset{CH_3 \quad COOH}{C}}}$$

$$\underset{\textbf{(−)-Lactic acid}}{\overset{\displaystyle HO \quad H}{\underset{CH_3 \quad COOH}{C}}} \xrightarrow{\text{Enzyme}} \text{No reaction}$$

One particularly dramatic example of how a simple change in chirality can affect the biological properties of a molecule is found in the amino acid, dopa, more properly named 2-amino-3-(3,4-dihydroxyphenyl)propanoic acid. Dopa has a single chiral center and can thus exist in two stereoisomeric forms. Although the dextrorotatory enantiomer, (+)-dopa, has no physiological effect on humans, the levorotatory enantiomer, (−)-dopa, is widely used for its potent activity against Parkinsonism, a chronic disease of the central nervous system.

(+)-Dopa (no biological effect)   **(−)-Dopa (anti-Parkinsonism agent)**

Why do different stereoisomers have such widely different biological properties? In order to exert its biological action, a chiral molecule must fit into a chiral receptor at the target site, much as a hand fits into a glove. Just as a right hand can only fit into a right glove, so a particular stereoisomer can only fit into a receptor with the proper complementary shape. Any other stereoisomer will be a misfit, like a right hand in a left glove. For example, we might imagine that (−)-dopa fits perfectly into a receptor site but that its (+)-enantiomer is unable to fit (Figure E.1).

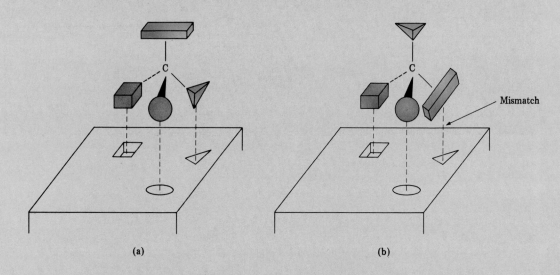

(a)   (b)

FIGURE E.1
(a) (−)-Dopa fits easily into a receptor site to exert its biological effect, but
(b) (+)-dopa can't fit into the same receptor and is thus without effect.

CHAPTER 7

Alkyl Halides

It would be difficult to study organic chemistry for long without becoming aware of the importance of halo-substituted alkanes. For example, alkyl halides are common industrial chemicals—tetrachloromethane, trichloromethane, and 1,1,1-trichloroethane are widely used as solvents (although all cause liver damage on chronic exposure). Alkyl halides also occur widely in nature, mostly in marine rather than terrestrial organisms. For example, simple halomethanes such as $CHCl_3$, CCl_4, CH_3I, and CH_3Cl are constituents of the Hawaiian alga *Asparagopsis taxiformis*.

Before discussing the chemistry of alkyl halides, it should be pointed out that we will be referring only to compounds having halogen atoms bonded to saturated, sp^3-hybridized carbon. Other classes, such as aromatic (*aryl*) and alkenyl (*vinylic*) halides also exist, but much of their chemistry is different.

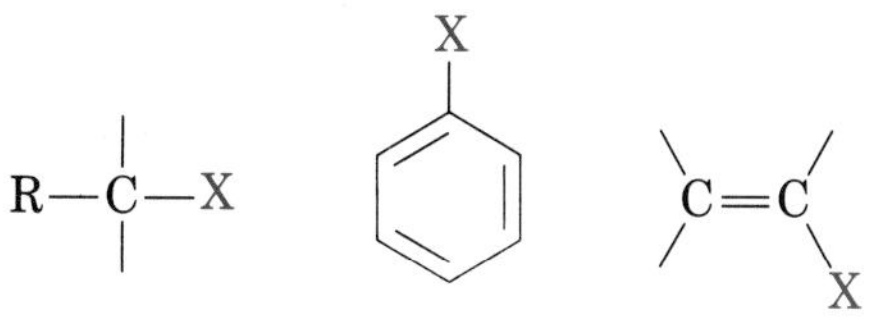

Alkyl halide   **Aryl halide**   **Vinylic halide**

7.1 NOMENCLATURE OF ALKYL HALIDES

Alkyl halides are named by an extension of the rules of alkane nomenclature (Section 2.3). According to IUPAC rules, halogens are considered as substituents on the parent alkane chain in the same sense that alkyl groups are substituents. Three rules suffice for naming alkyl halides:

1. Find and name the parent chain. As in naming alkanes, select the longest chain as the parent. (If a multiple bond is present, however, the parent chain must contain it.)

2. Number the chain beginning at the end nearer the first substituent, regardless of whether it is alkyl or halo. For example:

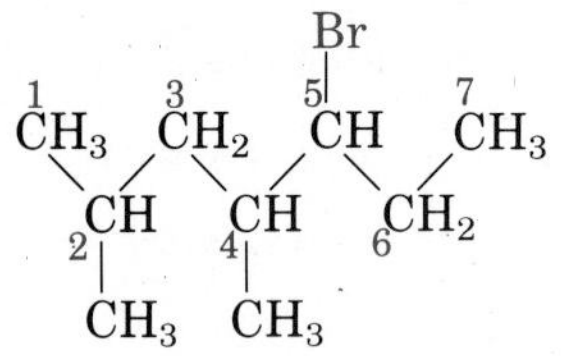

$$\overset{\scriptsize\text{Br}}{\underset{5}{\text{CH}}}$$

5-Bromo-2,4-dimethylheptane 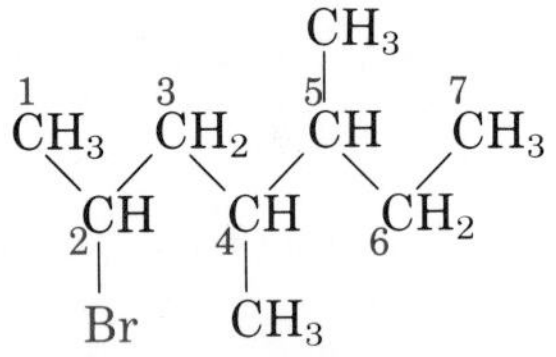   2-Bromo-4,5-dimethylheptane

a. If more than one of the same kind of halogen is present, number each and use one of the prefixes di-, tri-, tetra-, and so on. For example:

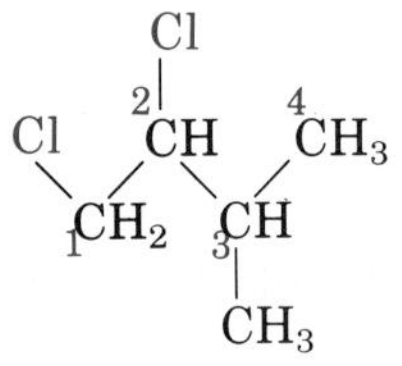

1,2-Dichloro-3-methylbutane

b. If different halogens are present, number each according to its position on the chain, but list all substituents in alphabetical order when writing the name. For example:

$$\text{BrCH}_2\text{CH}_2\text{CH(Cl)CH(CH}_3)\text{CH}_2\text{CH}_3$$

1-Bromo-3-chloro-4-methylhexane

3. If the chain can be properly numbered from either end by rule 2, begin at the end nearer the substituent (either alkyl or halo) that has alphabetical precedence. For example:

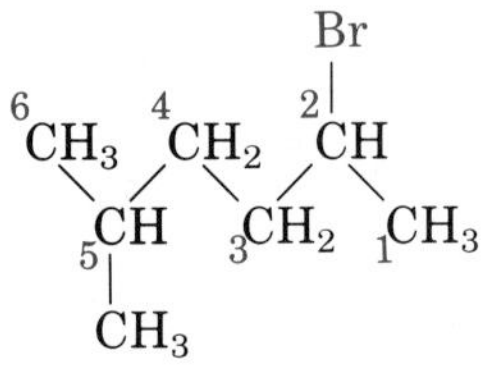

2-Bromo-5-methylhexane
(*NOT* 5-bromo-2-methylhexane)

In addition to their systematic names, a small number of simple alkyl halides have alternative names that are well entrenched in common usage. Table 7.1 lists some of these common names, but they will not be used in this book.

TABLE 7.1 Alternative names of some common alkyl halides

Structure	Systematic name	Alternative name
CH_3I	Iodomethane	Methyl iodide
CH_3CH_2Br	Bromoethane	Ethyl bromide
$CH_3CHClCH_3$	2-Chloropropane	Isopropyl chloride
$CH_3CHBrCH_2CH_3$	2-Bromobutane	sec-Butyl bromide
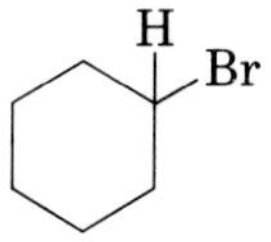	Bromocyclohexane	Cyclohexyl bromide

---

PROBLEM 7.1 Give the IUPAC names of these alkyl halides:

(a) $CH_3CH_2CHBrCH_3$ (b) $CH_3CH_2CHClCH(CH_3)_2$
(c) $(CH_3)_2CHCH_2CH_2Cl$ (d) $(CH_3)_2CClCH_2CH_2Cl$
(e) $BrCH_2CH_2CH_2CH_2Cl$ (f) $CH_3CHBrCH_2CH_2CH_2Cl$

PROBLEM 7.2 Draw structures corresponding to these names:

(a) 2-Chloro-3,3-dimethylhexane   (b) 3,3-Dichloro-2-methylhexane
(c) 3-Bromo-3-ethylpentane   (d) 2-Bromo-5-chloro-3-methylhexane

---

7.2 STRUCTURE OF ALKYL HALIDES

The carbon-halogen bond in alkyl halides results from overlap of a carbon sp^3 orbital with a halogen orbital. Thus, alkyl halide carbons have approximately tetrahedral geometry with H-C-X bond angles near 109°. Halogens increase in size going down the periodic table, an increase that is reflected in the bond lengths of the halomethane series (Table 7.2). Table 7.2 also indicates that C—X bond strengths decrease going down the periodic table.

TABLE 7.2 Parameters for the C—X bond in halomethanes

Halomethane	Bond length (Å)	Bond dissociation energy (kcal/mol)
CH_3—F	1.39	109
CH_3—Cl	1.78	84
CH_3—Br	1.93	70
CH_3—I	2.14	56

In an earlier discussion of bond polarity in functional groups (Section 3.7), we noted that halogens are electronegative with respect to carbon. Thus, a C—X bond is polar, with the carbon bearing a slight positive charge (δ^+) and the halogen a slight negative charge (δ^-):

$$\overset{\delta^+}{C}-\overset{\delta^-}{X} \qquad \text{where } X = F, Cl, Br, I$$

Since the carbon atom of alkyl halides is positively polarized, alkyl halides are good electrophiles (Section 3.7). We will soon see that much of their chemistry is dominated by this electrophilic behavior.

7.3 PREPARATION OF ALKYL HALIDES: RADICAL CHLORINATION OF ALKANES

We have already seen several methods of alkyl halide preparation. For example, both HX and X_2 react with alkenes in electrophilic addition reactions to yield haloalkanes (Sections 4.1 and 4.4).

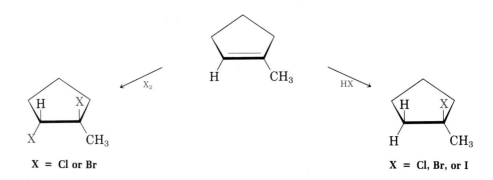

X = Cl or Br   X = Cl, Br, or I

Another method of alkyl halide synthesis is the reaction of alkanes with chlorine or bromine. Although inert to most reagents, alkanes react readily with chlorine to give chlorinated alkane products. For example, methane reacts with chlorine gas in the presence of light to yield chloromethane.

$$CH_4 + Cl_2 \xrightarrow{\text{Light } (h\nu)} CH_3Cl + HCl$$

Methane   **Chloromethane**

The chlorination of methane is a typical **radical substitution reaction**, rather than a polar reaction of the sort we have been studying until now. Recall from Section 3.6 that *radical* reactions involve reagents that have an odd number of valence electrons. Bonds are formed in radical reactions when each partner donates *one* electron to the new bond, and bonds are broken when each fragment leaves with *one* electron.

$$A \cdot + \cdot B \longrightarrow A{:}B \qquad \text{Radical bond-making}$$

$$A{:}B \longrightarrow A \cdot + \cdot B \qquad \text{Radical bond-breaking}$$

Radical substitution reactions normally require three kinds of steps: **initiation,** **propagation,** and **termination.** As its name implies, the initiation step starts the reaction by producing reactive radicals. In the example above, the relatively weak chlorine–chlorine bond is homolytically broken by irradiation with ultraviolet light. Two chlorine radicals are produced, and further chemistry ensues (Figure 7.1).

Once chlorine radicals have been produced in small amounts, reaction of Cl_2 with methane occurs by a series of repeating propagation steps. When a chlorine radical collides with a methane molecule, it abstracts a hydrogen atom to produce HCl and a methyl radical, $\cdot CH_3$, in the first propagation step. This methyl radical then abstracts a chlorine atom from Cl_2 in a second propagation step to yield chloromethane and a new chlorine radical. Since this new chlorine radical can cycle back into the first propagation step, the overall process is a **radical chain** **reaction.** Once the reaction has been initiated, it becomes a self-sustaining cycle of endlessly repeating propagation steps 1 and 2.

Occasionally, two radicals might collide and combine to form a stable product. When this happens, the reaction cycle is terminated and the chain is ended. Such termination steps occur infrequently, however, because the concentration of radicals in the reaction at any given moment is very small, Thus, the likelihood that two radicals will collide is also small. The overall mechanism for radical chlorination of methane is shown in Figure 7.1.

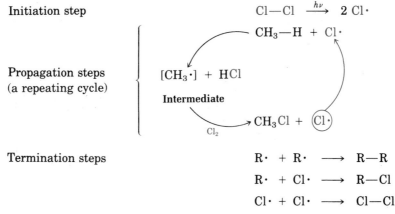

FIGURE 7.1
Mechanism of the radical chlorination of methane

Though interesting from a mechanistic point of view, alkane chlorination is not a generally useful method of alkyl halide synthesis because mixtures of products invariably result. For example, chlorination of methane doesn't stop cleanly at the monochlorinated stage, but continues, giving a mixture of dichloro-, trichloro-, and even tetrachloro- products that must be separated by distillation:

$$CH_4 + Cl_2 \xrightarrow{h\nu} CH_3Cl + CH_2Cl_2 + CHCl_3 + CCl_4 \,(+ HCl)$$

The situation is even worse for chlorination of alkanes having more than one kind of hydrogen. For example, chlorination of butane gives two monochlorinated products as well as several dichlorobutanes, trichlorobutanes, and so on. Of the monochloro products, 30% is 1-chlorobutane, and 70% is 2-chlorobutane:

$$CH_3CH_2CH_2CH_3 + Cl_2 \xrightarrow{h\nu} CH_3CH_2CH_2CH_2Cl + CH_3CH_2\overset{\displaystyle Cl}{\underset{\displaystyle |}{C}}HCH_3 +$$

Butane   1-Chlorobutane   2-Chlorobutane

Dichloro-, trichloro-, tetrachloro-, and so on

30:70

PROBLEM 7.3 Draw and name all monochloro products you would expect to obtain from radical chlorination of 2-methylpentane. Which, if any, are chiral?

PROBLEM 7.4 Radical chlorination of pentane is a poor way to prepare 1-chloropentane, but radical chlorination of neopentane [2,2-dimethylpropane, $(CH_3)_4C$] is a good way to prepare 1-chloro-2,2-dimethylpropane. Explain.

7.4 ALKYL HALIDES FROM ALCOHOLS

The most valuable method for the preparation of alkyl halides is their synthesis from alcohols. Because of the importance of the reaction, many different reagents have been developed for carrying out the transformation.

The simplest method for converting an alcohol to an alkyl halide involves treating the alcohol with HX:

$$R\text{—}OH \xrightarrow{\text{HX}} R\text{—}X + H_2O \qquad \text{where } X = Cl, Br, I$$

3° c w/ HX

For reasons to be discussed later in this chapter (Sections 7.8 and 7.9), the reaction works best when applied to tertiary alcohols. Primary and secondary alcohols react at considerably lower rates.

Reactivity order: Tertiary > Secondary > Primary

$$R_3COH > R_2CHOH > RCH_2OH$$

info

The reaction of HX with a tertiary alcohol is so rapid that it is often carried out simply by bubbling the pure HX gas into a cold ether solution of the alcohol.

$1° \lesssim 2° C$

$w/$

$SOCl_2$

or

PBr_3

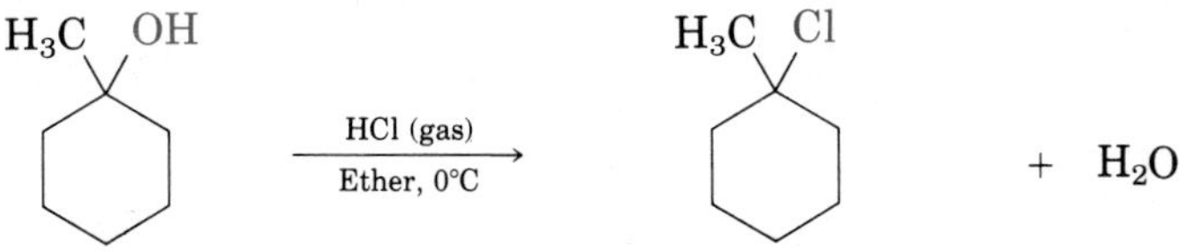

1-Methylcyclohexanol

1-Chloro-1-methylcyclohexane
(90%)

$+ H_2O$

Primary and secondary alcohols are usually converted into alkyl halides by treatment with either thionyl chloride ($SOCl_2$) or phosphorus tribromide (PBr_3). These reactions normally take place under fairly mild conditions, and yields are usually high.

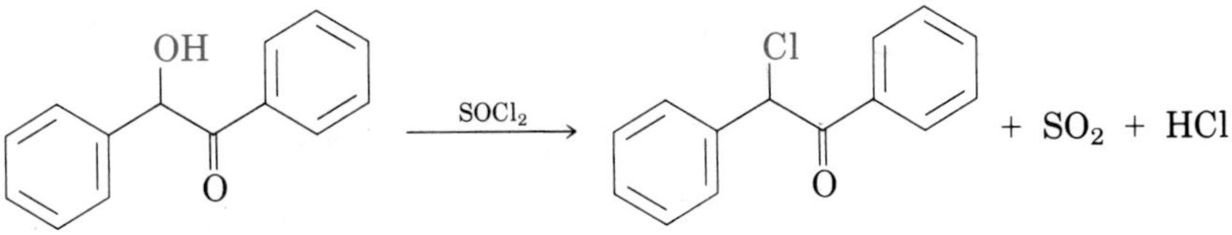

Benzoin

Desyl chloride (86%)

$+ SO_2 + HCl$

$3 \ CH_3CH_2CHCH_3 \xrightarrow[\text{Ether, 35°C}]{PBr_3} 3 \ CH_3CH_2CHCH_3 + P(OH)_3$

2-Butanol

2-Bromobutane (86%)

PROBLEM 7.5   How would you prepare these alkyl halides from the appropriate alcohols?

(a)   2-Chloro-2-methylpropane
(b)   2-Bromo-4-methylpentane
(c) $BrCH_2CH_2CH_2CH_2CH(CH_3)_2$
(d) $CH_3CH_2CH(CH_3)CH_2CCl(CH_3)_2$

7.5   REACTIONS OF ALKYL HALIDES: FORMATION OF ORGANOMETALLIC REAGENTS

Organic halides of varying structure—alkyl, aryl, and vinylic—react with magnesium metal in ether solvent to yield organomagnesium halides. These compounds, named **Grignard reagents** after their discoverer, Victor Grignard, are examples of **organometallic compounds**, since they contain a carbon-to-metal bond.

$$R — X + Mg \xrightarrow{\text{Ether}} R — Mg — X$$

where R = 1°, 2°, or 3° alkyl, aryl, or vinylic; and X = Cl, Br, or I.

For example,

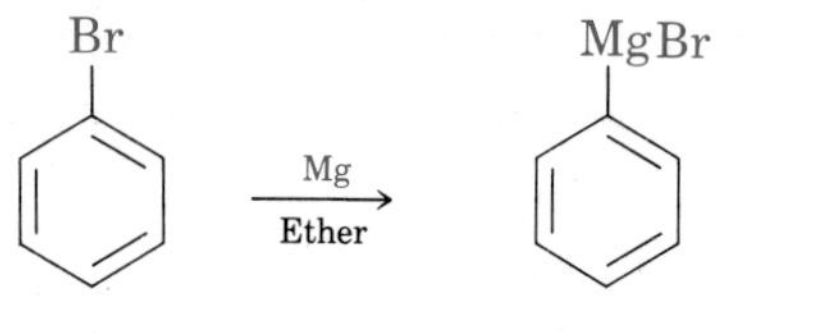

Phenylmagnesium bromide

$$(CH_3)_3CCl \xrightarrow[\text{Ether}]{\text{Mg}} (CH_3)_3C\text{—}MgCl$$

***t*-Butylmagnesium chloride**

Grignard reagents are extraordinarily useful and versatile. As we might expect from our previous discussion of electronegativities and bond polarities (Section 3.7), a carbon–magnesium bond is strongly polarized,

$$\overset{\delta^-}{C}\text{—}\overset{\delta^+}{Mg}$$

making the organic part both nucleophilic and basic. In a formal sense, a Grignard reagent can be considered a carbon anion or carbanion—the magnesium salt of a hydrocarbon acid. It's more accurate, however, to view Grignard reagents as containing a highly polar covalent C—Mg bond, rather than an ionic bond between C^- and ^+MgBr.

Because of their nucleophilic, basic character, Grignard reagents react with a wide variety of electrophiles. For example, they react with protic acids such as HCl or H_2O to yield hydrocarbons. The overall sequence, $R\text{—}X \rightarrow R\text{—}MgX \rightarrow R\text{—}H$, is a useful method for *reducing* organic halides to yield alkanes:

$$R\text{—}X \xrightarrow{\text{Mg}} R\text{—}Mg\text{—}X \xrightarrow{H_2O} R\text{—}H + HOMgX$$

Alkyl   Grignard   Alkane
halide   reagent

For example,

$$CH_3(CH_2)_8CH_2Br \xrightarrow[\text{2. } H_2O]{\text{1. Mg}} CH_3(CH_2)_8CH_3$$

1-Bromodecane   Decane (85%)

PROBLEM 7.6   An advantage of preparing alkanes by reduction of Grignard reagents is that deuterium (D, the isotope of hydrogen with atomic weight 2) can be introduced into a specific site in a molecule. How might you convert 2-bromobutane into 2-deuteriobutane?

$$\overset{\text{Br}}{\underset{|}{CH_3CHCH_2CH_3}} \xrightarrow{?} \overset{\text{D}}{\underset{|}{CH_3CHCH_2CH_3}}$$

PROBLEM 7.7   By using several reactions in sequence, transformations are possible that cannot be done in a single step. For example, how would you prepare the alkane 1-methylcyclohexane from the alcohol 1-methylcyclohexanol?

7.6 NUCLEOPHILIC SUBSTITUTION REACTIONS: THE DISCOVERY OF WALDEN INVERSIONS

In 1896, the German chemist Paul Walden reported a remarkable discovery. He found that the pure enantiomeric (+)- and (−)-malic acids could be *inter-converted* by a series of simple reactions. When Walden treated (−)-malic acid with PCl₅, he isolated (+)-chlorosuccinic acid. This, on reaction with wet silver oxide, gave (+)-malic acid. Similarly, reaction of (+)-malic acid with PCl₅ gave (−)-chlorosuccinic acid, which was converted into (−)-malic acid when treated with wet silver oxide. The full cycle of reactions reported by Walden is shown in Figure 7.2.

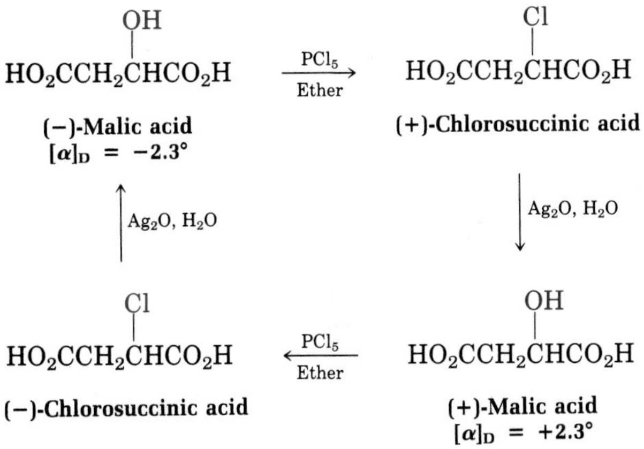

OH
|
HO₂CCH₂CHCO₂H $\xrightarrow[\text{Ether}]{\text{PCl}_5}$ HO₂CCH₂CHCO₂H
                                                          |
                                                          Cl

(−)-Malic acid   (+)-Chlorosuccinic acid
$[\alpha]_D = -2.3°$

↑ Ag₂O, H₂O   ↓ Ag₂O, H₂O

FIGURE 7.2
Walden's cycle of reactions interconverting (+)- and (−)-malic acids

Cl
|
HO₂CCH₂CHCO₂H $\xleftarrow[\text{Ether}]{\text{PCl}_5}$ HO₂CCH₂CHCO₂H
                                                          |
                                                          OH

(−)-Chlorosuccinic acid   (+)-Malic acid
                                                  $[\alpha]_D = +2.3°$

At the time, the results were astonishing. The eminent chemist Emil Fischer called Walden's discovery "the most remarkable observation made in the field of optical activity since the fundamental observations of Pasteur." Since (−)-malic acid was being converted into (+)-malic acid, some reactions in the cycle must have occurred with a change in the configuration of the chiral center. But which ones? (Recall that the sign of rotation and the configuration are not related. We can't tell by looking at the sign of rotation whether a change in chirality has occurred during a reaction.)

Today we would refer to the transformations taking place in Walden's cycle as **nucleophilic substitution reactions**, since each step involves the substitution of one nucleophile (chloride ion, :Cl:⁻, or hydroxide ion, HÖ:⁻) for another. Nucleophilic substitution reactions are one of the most important types of reactions of alkyl halides, and indeed are one of the most important general reaction types in organic chemistry.

7.7 KINDS OF NUCLEOPHILIC SUBSTITUTION REACTIONS

Following the work of Walden, a series of investigations was undertaken during the 1920s and 1930s to clarify the mechanism of nucleophilic substitution reactions and to find out how inversions of configuration occur. We now know that there are two major ways by which nucleophilic substitutions can occur; they are named the S_N1 mechanism and the S_N2 mechanism. In both cases, the "S_N" part of the name stands for "substitution, nucleophilic." What the 1 and the 2 stand for will become clear soon.

Regardless of mechanism, the overall change occurring during all nucleophilic substitution reactions is the same. In all cases, a nucleophile (Nu:) reacts with a substrate R—X and substitutes for X: to generate the product R—Nu. The X: species that is displaced during the reaction is called the **leaving group**, and it may be any of a number of different groups, although it is most commonly one of the halides $:\ddot{C}l:^-$, $:\ddot{B}r:^-$, or $:\ddot{I}:^-$. The nucleophile may be either neutral (Nu:) or negatively charged (Nu:$^-$). If it is neutral, then the product is positively charged; if it is negatively charged, the product is neutral.

$$\text{Nu:} + \text{R—X} \longrightarrow \text{R—}\overset{+}{\text{N}}\text{u} + \text{X:}^-$$

$$\text{Nu:}^- + \text{R—X} \longrightarrow \text{R—Nu} + \text{X:}^-$$

Because of the wide scope of nucleophilic substitution reactions, a great many product types can be prepared from alkyl halides. For example, Table 7.3 lists some products resulting from nucleophilic substitutions on bromomethane.

TABLE 7.3   Some nucleophilic substitution reactions on bromomethane:

$$\text{Nu:}^- + \text{CH}_3\text{Br} \longrightarrow \text{Nu—CH}_3 + :\ddot{\text{B}}\text{r:}^-$$

Attacking nucleophile		Product	
Formula	*Name*	*Formula*	*Name*
H:$^-$	Hydride	CH_4	Methane
$CH_3\ddot{S}:^-$	Methanethiolate	$CH_3S—CH_3$	Dimethyl sulfide
$H\ddot{S}:^-$	Hydrosulfide	$HS—CH_3$	Methane thiol
$:N\equiv C:^-$	Cyanide	$N\equiv C—CH_3$	Acetonitrile
$:\ddot{I}:^-$	Iodide	$I—CH_3$	Iodomethane
$H\ddot{O}:^-$	Hydroxide	$HO—CH_3$	Methanol
$CH_3\ddot{O}:^-$	Methoxide	$CH_3O—CH_3$	Dimethyl ether
$:\ddot{N}=N=\ddot{N}:^-$	Azide	$N_3—CH_3$	Azidomethane
$:\ddot{C}l:^-$	Chloride	$Cl—CH_3$	Chloromethane
$CH_3CO_2:^-$	Acetate	$CH_3CO_2—CH_3$	Methyl acetate
$H_3N:$	Ammonia	$H_3\overset{+}{N}—CH_3\ Br^-$	Methylammonium bromide
$(CH_3)_3N:$	Trimethylamine	$(CH_3)_3\overset{+}{N}—CH_3\ Br^-$	Tetramethylammonium bromide

PROBLEM 7.8   What products would you expect to obtain from these reactions?

(a) $CH_3CH_2CHBrCH_3 + LiI \rightarrow ?$ (b) $(CH_3)_2CHCH_2Cl + H\ddot{S}:^- \rightarrow ?$

7.8   CHARACTERISTICS OF THE S$_N$2 REACTION

The essential features of the S$_N$2 reaction are shown in Figure 7.3. As indicated, the reaction takes place in a single step without intermediates when the entering nucleophile attacks the substrate from a direction 180° away from the leaving group. As the nucleophile comes in on one side of the molecule, the leaving group departs from the other.

We can picture the reaction as occurring when an electron pair on the nucleophile, Nu:⁻, forces out the leaving group, X:⁻, with the electron pair from the C—X bond. This can occur through a transition state in which the new Nu—C bond is partially forming at the same time that the old C—X bond is partially breaking, and in which the negative charge is shared by the incoming nucleophile and the outgoing leaving group.

The nucleophile Nu:⁻ uses its lone-pair electrons to attack the alkyl halide 180° away from the halogen. This leads to a transition state with a partially formed C—Nu bond and a partially broken C—X bond.

The stereochemistry at carbon is inverted as the C—Nu bond forms fully and the halide departs with the electron pair from the original C—X bond.

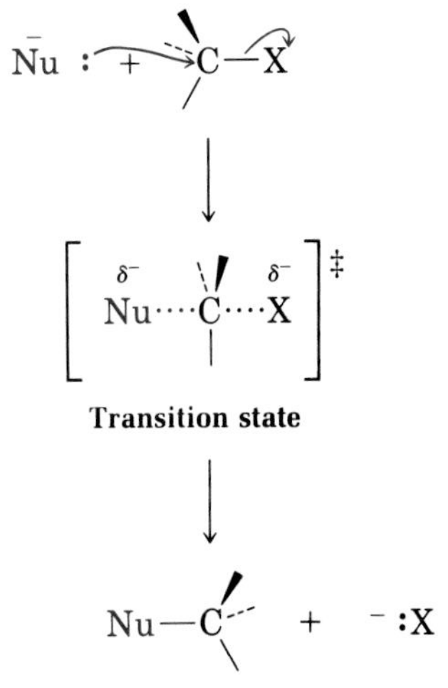

Transition state

FIGURE 7.3
The mechanism of the S$_N$2 reaction

Let's see what evidence there is for this mechanism and what chemical consequences arise as a result.

Stereochemistry of S$_N$2 Reactions

Look carefully at the mechanism of the S$_N$2 reaction shown in Figure 7.3. This mechanism shows that, as the incoming nucleophile attacks the substrate and begins pushing out the leaving group on the opposite side, the stereochemistry of the molecule becomes *inverted*, much like an umbrella turning inside out in the wind. The transition state for this inversion must have the three remaining bonds to carbon in a planar arrangement, as shown in Figure 7.4 on page 206.

Evidence for the occurrence of stereochemical inversion during S$_N$2 reactions comes not only from Walden's early research, but also from much later work. For

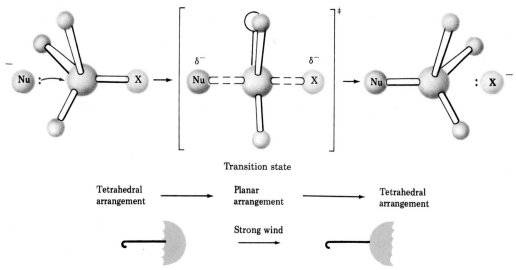

Transition state

| Tetrahedral arrangement | → | Planar arrangement | → | Tetrahedral arrangement |

Strong wind

FIGURE 7.4
The stereochemistry of an S_N2 reaction: The inversion of configuration that occurs may be likened to the inversion of an umbrella in a strong wind.

example, nucleophilic substitution reaction of the following chiral molecule with acetate ion converts S starting material into R product:

S configuration   *R* configuration + $^-:\ddot{O}$—Tos

where O—Tos = $-O-\overset{\displaystyle O}{\underset{\displaystyle O}{\overset{\|}{\underset{\|}{S}}}}$—⟨⟩—CH$_3$

Note that this reaction occurs on a *p*-toluenesulfonate ester or **tosylate**, rather than on an alkyl halide. Tosylates, abbreviated Tos, are readily prepared from alcohols by reaction with *p*-toluenesulfonyl chloride, and undergo rapid substitution reactions in the same way that alkyl halides do.

PRACTICE PROBLEM   What product would you expect to obtain from reaction of (*R*)-2-iodooctane with sodium cyanide, Na$^+$ $^-$:CN?

Solution Table 7.3 shows that cyanide ion is a good nucleophile in the S$_N$2 reaction. We would therefore expect it to displace iodide ion from (R)-2-iodooctane, with inversion of configuration to yield (S)-2-methyloctanenitrile.

(R)-2-Iodooctane   **(S)-2-Methyloctanenitrile**

PROBLEM 7.9 What product would you expect to obtain from reaction of (S)-2-bromohexane with sodium acetate, Na$^+$ $^-$:OOCCH$_3$? Show the stereochemistry of both starting material and product.

PROBLEM 7.10 How can you explain the fact that treatment of (R)-2-bromohexane with sodium bromide, NaBr, yields *racemic* 2-bromohexane as product?

Rates of S$_N$2 Reactions

Chemists often speak in qualitative terms about a reaction being fast or slow. The exact speed at which a starting material reacts to give product is called the **reaction rate** and is a quantity that can often be measured. The determination of reaction rates and the dependence of reaction rates on reagent concentrations can be a powerful tool for probing reaction mechanisms. Let's see what can be learned about the S$_N$2 reaction by a study of reaction rates.

For all chemical reactions, there is a definite relationship between the reaction rate and the concentrations of the reagents. For example, let's look at the effect of reagent concentrations on the rate of a simple S$_N$2 reaction, the reaction of hydroxide ion nucleophile with bromomethane to yield methanol:

$$HO\colon^- + CH_3 - Br \longrightarrow HO - CH_3 + \colon\!\ddot{Br}\colon^-$$

Our picture of the S$_N$2 reaction is one in which two reagents—alkyl halide and nucleophile—collide and react in a single step. At a given concentration of reagents, the reaction takes place at a certain rate. If we double the concentration of hydroxide ion, the frequency of encounter between the two reagents is also doubled, and we might therefore expect that the reaction rate will double. Similarly, if we double the concentration of bromomethane, we might expect that the reaction rate will double. *This is exactly what is found.* Measurements of reaction rates are in perfect agreement with our understanding of the S$_N$2 mechanism.

We call a reaction in which the rate is linearly dependent on the concentrations of two reagents a **second-order reaction**. Thus, the derivation of the "2" in S$_N$2; two molecules—alkyl halide and nucleophile—are involved in the step whose rate is measured.

PROBLEM 7.11   What effects would the following changes have on the rate of reaction between iodomethane and sodium acetate?

(a)   The CH_3I concentration is tripled.
(b)   Both CH_3I and $Na^+ \ ^-OOCCH_3$ concentrations are doubled.

Steric Effects in S_N2 Reactions

We have said that an attacking nucleophile must approach the substrate closely to expel the leaving group in an S_N2 reaction. It therefore seems reasonable that the ease of approach should depend on the steric (spatial) nature of the substrate. Sterically bulky substrates, in which the carbon atom is shielded from attack by the rest of the molecule, should react slower than substrates in which the carbon is more sterically accessible (Figure 7.5).

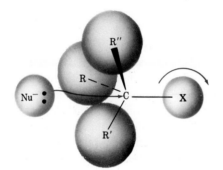

FIGURE 7.5
Steric hindrance to the S_N2 reaction: When R, R', and R" = H, a fast reaction occurs. When R, R', and R" = alkyl, a slow reaction occurs.

Careful measurements on numerous S_N2 reactions have shown that the rates do indeed depend on the steric nature of the substrates; a listing of relative reactivities is shown in Table 7.4.

TABLE 7.4   Relative rates of S_N2 reactions on alkyl halides

Alkyl halide	Type	Relative rate of reaction
CH_3—X	Methyl	3,000,000
CH_3CH_2—X	1°	100,000
$CH_3CH_2CH_2$—X	1°	40,000
$(CH_3)_2CH$—X	2°	2,500
$(CH_3)_3CCH_2$—X	1°—neopentyl	1
$(CH_3)_3C$—X	3°	~0

As indicated in Table 7.4, methyl halides are by far the most reactive substrates in S$_N$2 reactions, followed by primary alkyl halides such as ethyl and propyl. Alkyl branching next to the leaving group, as in secondary halides, slows the reaction greatly; further branching, as in tertiary halides, effectively halts the reaction. Even branching one carbon removed from the leaving group, as in 2,2-dimethylpropyl (neopentyl) halides, greatly slows nucleophilic displacement. Thus, the reactivity order of substrates in S$_N$2 reactions is

$$CH_3 > 1° > 2° \gg Neopentyl > 3°$$

Although not shown in Table 7.4, *vinylic* halides (R$_2$C=CRX) and *aryl* halides (Ar—X) are completely unreactive toward S$_N$2 displacements. This lack of reactivity is probably due to steric hindrance, since the incoming nucleophile would have to approach in the plane of the carbon–carbon double bond or ring in order to carry out a back-side displacement.

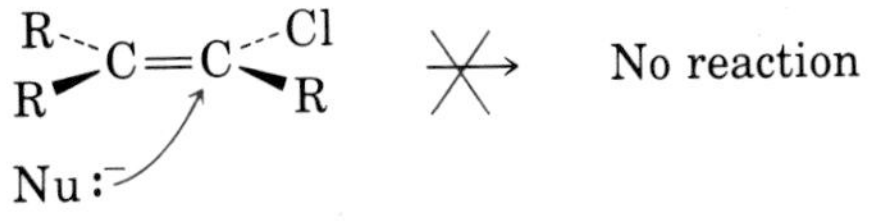

Vinylic halide
(back-side approach of attacking
nucleophile is hindered,
and S$_N$2 reaction cannot occur)

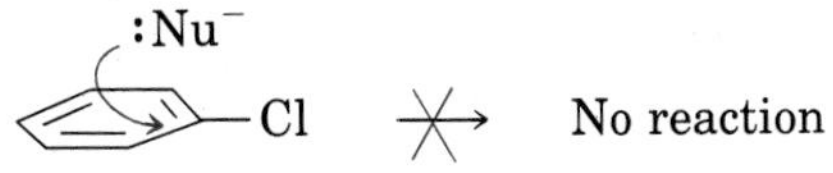

PROBLEM 7.12 Which of the following reactions would you expect to go faster?

(a) Reaction of ⁻:CN (cyanide ion) with CH$_3$CHBrCH$_3$ or with CH$_3$CH$_2$CH$_2$Br?

(b) Reaction of :Ï:⁻ with (CH$_3$)$_2$CH$_2$CH$_2$Cl or with H$_2$C=CHCl?

The Leaving Group in S$_N$2 Reactions

Another variable that can strongly affect the S$_N$2 reaction is the nature of the species expelled by the attacking nucleophile—the leaving group. In most S$_N$2 reactions, the leaving group is expelled with a negative charge, and we might therefore expect the best leaving groups to be those that best stabilize the negative charge. Furthermore, since anion stability is related to basicity, we can also say that the best leaving groups should be the weakest bases. The reason is that, in the transition state for S$_N$2 reactions, the charge is distributed over both the attacking and the leaving groups. The greater the extent of charge stabilization by the leaving group, the more stable the transition state and the faster the reaction.

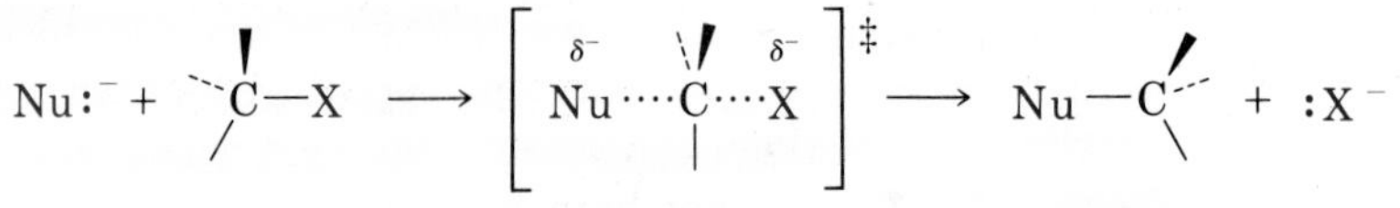

$$Nu:^- + \overset{\displaystyle /}{\underset{\displaystyle /}{C}}-X \longrightarrow \left[\overset{\delta^-}{Nu} \cdots \underset{|}{\overset{\displaystyle /}{C}} \cdots \overset{\delta^-}{X} \right]^{\ddagger} \longrightarrow Nu-\overset{\displaystyle /}{\underset{\displaystyle \backslash}{C}} + :X^-$$

Transition state

In fact, this prediction is borne out reasonably well. Table 7.5 lists a variety of leaving groups in order of reactivity and shows the correlation with basicity. The weakest bases (anions derived from the strongest acids) are the most reactive as leaving groups.

TABLE 7.5   The correlation of leaving-group ability with basicity: the anions of strong acids make good leaving groups in S_N2 reactions

Leaving group	pK_a of conjugate acid	Relative reactivity
$CH_3-\!\!\bigcirc\!\!-\overset{O}{\underset{O}{\overset{\|}{\underset{\|}{S}}}}-\ddot{\text{O}}:^-$		
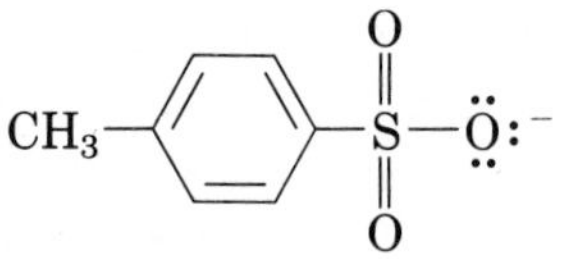 Tosylate	−6.5	60,000
:Ï:⁻	−9.5	30,000
:Br:⁻	−9	10,000
:Cl:⁻	−7	200
:F:⁻	3.2	1
CH_3CO_2:⁻	4.8	~0
HÖ:⁻	15.7	~0
$CH_3CH_2\ddot{\text{O}}$:⁻	16	~0
$H_2\ddot{\text{N}}$:⁻	35	~0

Decreasing reactivity ↓

It is just as important to know which leaving groups are *unreactive* as to know which are reactive. Table 7.5 clearly shows that fluoride, acetate, hydroxide, alkoxide (RO^-), and amide ($^-NH_2$) ions cannot be displaced.

PROBLEM 7.13   Rank the following compounds in order of their expected S_N2 reactivity: CH_3I, CH_3OH, CH_3Br, CH_3OTos (where Tos = tosylate)

7.9 CHARACTERISTICS OF THE S$_N$1 REACTION

We have seen that the S$_N$2 reaction is sensitive to steric hindrance in the substrate. Primary alkyl halides react well with a variety of nucleophiles, but secondary halides are sometimes sluggish, and tertiary halides are inert to back-side attack. Remarkably, however, a completely different picture of reactivity emerges when special reaction conditions are used. When alkyl halides are treated with nonbasic nucleophiles in hydroxylic solvents such as water or acetic acid, tertiary halides react much faster than primary or secondary halides. For example, Table 7.6 gives the relative rates for reaction of some alkyl halides with water, a neutral nucleophile. The tertiary halide 2-bromo-2-methylpropane is more than *1 million times* as reactive as bromoethane.

TABLE 7.6 **Relative rates of reaction of some alkyl halides with water:**

$$R-Br + H_2O: \longrightarrow R-OH + HBr$$

Alkyl halide	Type	Product	Relative rate of reaction
CH_3Br	Methyl	CH_3OH	1.0
CH_3CH_2Br	1°	CH_3CH_2OH	1.0
$(CH_3)_2CHBr$	2°	$(CH_3)_2CHOH$	12
$(CH_3)_3CBr$	3°	$(CH_3)_3COH$	1,200,000

What are the reasons for this reversal of reactivity? These reactions are clearly not taking place by an S$_N$2 mechanism, and we must therefore conclude that *an alternative substitution mechanism is operating*. This alternative mechanism is called the **S$_N$1 reaction**. The mechanism of the S$_N$1 reaction of 2-bromo-2-methylpropane with acetate ion is shown in Figure 7.6 (page 212).

We can picture the S$_N$1 reaction as taking place by the *spontaneous dissociation* of an alkyl halide into a carbocation plus halide anion. The intermediate carbocation then reacts with added nucleophile in a second step to yield the substitution product.

Let's see what evidence is available to support this S$_N$1 mechanism.

Rates of S$_N$1 Reactions

Since the reaction of acetate ion in acetic acid with 2-bromo-2-methylpropane appears similar to the reaction of hydroxide ion with bromomethane, we might expect to observe a similar dependence of rate on reagent concentrations. In fact, we do not. We find instead that the reaction rate is dependent only on the alkyl halide concentration, but is *independent of acetate ion concentration*. Only *one* species is involved in the step whose rate is measured, and we therefore call the reaction a **first-order process**—thus the meaning of the "1" in S$_N$1.

$$CH_3-\overset{\overset{\displaystyle CH_3}{|}}{\underset{\underset{\displaystyle CH_3}{|}}{C}}-Br$$

Spontaneous dissociation of the alkyl bromide occurs in a slow, rate-limiting step to generate a carbocation intermediate plus bromide ion.

Slow (rate-limiting) step

$$CH_3-\overset{\overset{\displaystyle CH_3}{|}}{\underset{\underset{\displaystyle CH_3}{|}}{C}}{}^+ \quad + \quad :\ddot{B}r:^-$$

Intermediate

The carbocation intermediate reacts with added nucleophile (acetate ion) in a fast step to yield neutral product.

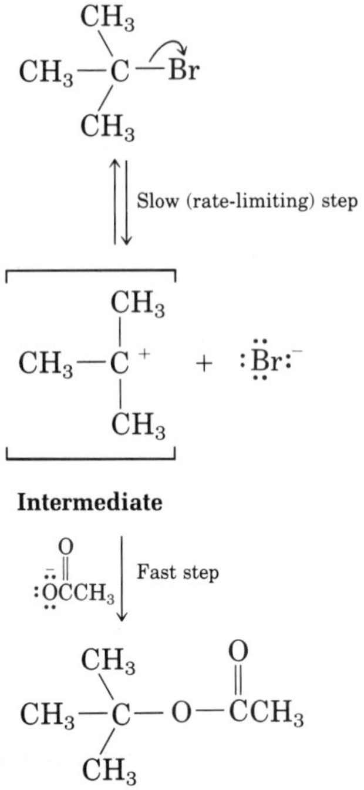

$$:\ddot{O}\overset{\displaystyle O}{\overset{\|}{C}}CH_3 \quad \text{Fast step}$$

$$CH_3-\overset{\overset{\displaystyle CH_3}{\backslash}}{\underset{\underset{\displaystyle CH_3}{/}}{C}}-O-\overset{\displaystyle O}{\overset{\|}{C}}CH_3$$

FIGURE 7.6
The mechanism of the S_N1 reaction: The first of the two steps is slower than the second.

How can we explain the observation that S_N1 reaction rates depend only on the alkyl halide concentration, and that nucleophile concentration does not affect the rate? To answer this question, we must first learn more about reaction rate measurements.

Many organic reactions are rather complex and occur in successive steps. One of the steps is usually slower than the others, and we call this the **rate-limiting step**. No reaction can proceed faster than its rate-limiting step, which acts as a kind of bottleneck to the reaction. When we measure the rate of a reaction, it is this slow, rate-limiting step we are measuring.

The observation that the S_N1 reaction of 2-bromo-2-methylpropane with acetate ion is a first-order process indicates that the alkyl halide is somehow involved all by itself in the slow, rate-limiting step. In other words, the tertiary alkyl halide must undergo some manner of spontaneous reaction without assistance from the nucleophile. This is exactly what the mechanism shown in Figure 7.6 accounts for. If the alkyl halide dissociates to a stable carbocation in a slow, rate-limiting step, and if this carbocation intermediate is immediately trapped by nucleophile in a fast step, then the overall rate will be first-order because acetate ion plays no role in the slow step whose rate is measured. A reaction energy diagram for the process is shown in Figure 7.7.

Stereochemistry of S_N1 Reactions

If the mechanism of the S_N1 reaction involves formation of a carbocation intermediate as shown in Figure 7.6, there should be clear stereochemical consequences. Carbocations are planar, sp^2-hybridized species and are therefore

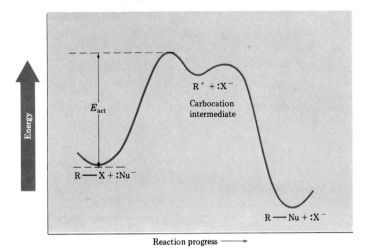

FIGURE 7.7
A reaction energy diagram for an S$_N$1 reaction: The first step—
spontaneous dissociation of the alkyl halide—is rate limiting.

achiral. Thus, if we carry out an S$_N$1 reaction on a *chiral* starting material and go
through an *achiral* carbocation intermediate, our product must be optically inactive. Another way of looking at this is to say that the symmetrical intermediate
carbocation can be attacked by a nucleophile equally well from either side,
leading to a racemic mixture of enantiomers (Figure 7.8).

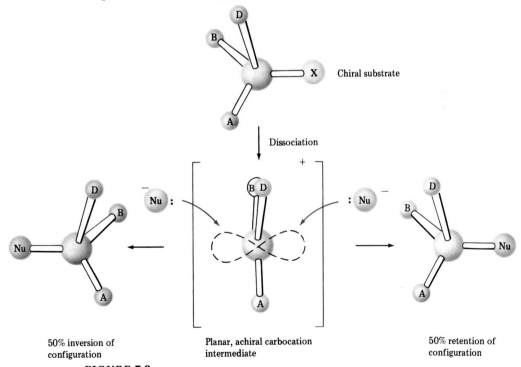

50% inversion of configuration

Planar, achiral carbocation intermediate

50% retention of configuration

FIGURE 7.8
An S$_N$1 reaction on a chiral substrate: An optically active starting material must give
a racemic product.

The prediction that S$_N$1 reactions on chiral substrates should lead to racemic products has been amply borne out by experiment. For example, reaction of optically active (R)-1-chloro-1-phenylbutane with water leads to a racemic alcohol product:

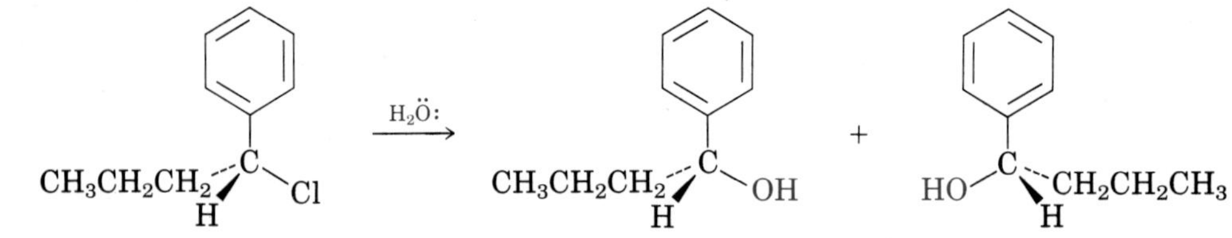

CH$_3$CH$_2$CH$_2$—C—Cl H	CH$_3$CH$_2$CH$_2$—C—OH H	HO—C—CH$_2$CH$_2$CH$_3$ H
(R)-1-Chloro-1-phenylbutane	**50% R (retention)**	**50% S (inversion)**

PROBLEM 7.14   What product would you expect to obtain from S$_N$1 reaction of (S)-3-chloro-3-methyloctane with sodium acetate in acetic acid? Show the stereochemistry of both starting material and product.

The Leaving Group in S$_N$1 Reactions

In the discussion of S$_N$2 reactivity, we reasoned that the best leaving groups should be those that are most stable. For the usual case of negatively charged leaving groups, the most stable anions are those corresponding to the strongest acids. The same reactivity order is found for S$_N$1 reactions, since the leaving group is intimately involved in the rate-limiting step. Thus, we find an S$_N$1 reactivity order:

$$\text{Tosylate} > \text{:I:}^- > \text{:Br:}^- > \text{:Cl:}^- > H_2\text{Ö:}$$

Note that in the S$_N$1 reaction, which is often carried out under acidic conditions, neutral water can act as a leaving group. For example, this can occur when a tertiary alcohol reacts with HX to yield an alkyl halide (Section 7.4). As shown in Figure 7.9, treatment of 2-methyl-2-propanol with HCl yields 2-chloro-2-methylpropane by a sequence involving: (1) protonation of the alcohol hydroxyl group; (2) S$_N$1 dissociation of the protonated alcohol to yield water and a tertiary carbocation; and (3) subsequent trapping of the carbocation by chloride ion.

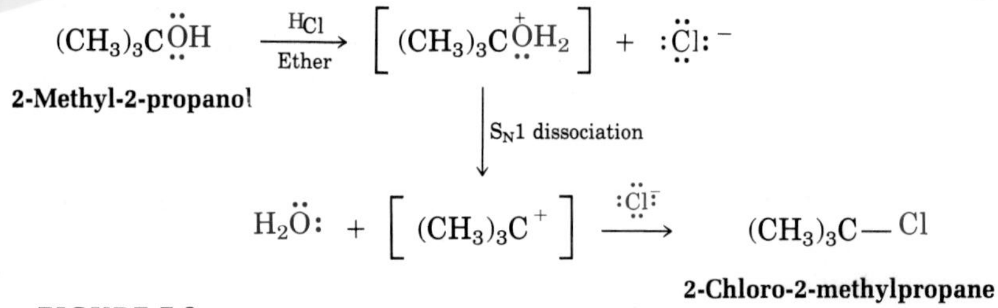

$$(CH_3)_3C\ddot{O}H \xrightarrow[\text{Ether}]{\text{HCl}} \left[(CH_3)_3C\overset{+}{\ddot{O}}H_2 \right] + :\ddot{C}l:^-$$

2-Methyl-2-propanol

$$\downarrow \text{S}_N\text{1 dissociation}$$

$$H_2\ddot{O}: + \left[(CH_3)_3C^+ \right] \xrightarrow{:\ddot{C}l:^-} (CH_3)_3C—Cl$$

2-Chloro-2-methylpropane

FIGURE 7.9

The S$_N$1 reaction of a tertiary alcohol with HCl to yield an alkyl chloride: Neutral water is the leaving group in this reaction.

PROBLEM 7.15   Which of these reactions would you expect to occur faster?

    (a)   Reaction of $(CH_3)_3C$—Cl or $(CH_3)_3C$—OTos with Na^+ $^-OOCCH_3$ in CH_3COOH
    (b)   Reaction of CH_3Br or $(CH_3)_3CBr$ with water in an S_N1 reaction
    (c)   Reaction of CH_3Cl or $(CH_3)_3CCl$ with $CH_3\ddot{S}:^-$ in ether in an S_N2 reaction

PROBLEM 7.16   How do you account for the fact that 1-chloro-1,2-diphenylethane reacts with the nucleophiles fluoride ion and triethylamine at the same rate?

7.10   ELIMINATION REACTIONS OF ALKYL HALIDES: THE E2 REACTION

When a nucleophile/Lewis base attacks an alkyl halide, two kinds of reactions are possible. Often, as we have seen, the nucleophile will substitute for the halide ion in either an S_N1 or an S_N2 reaction. Alternatively, however, an **elimination reaction** may occur, leading to formation of an alkene:

Substitution: CH_3— Br + $^-:\ddot{O}H$ $\longrightarrow$ CH_3—$\ddot{O}H$ + $:\ddot{Br}:^-$

Elimination:

$$H_3C-\underset{\underset{CH_3}{|}}{\overset{\overset{Br}{|}}{C}}-\overset{\overset{H}{|}}{CH_2} \;+\; ^-:\ddot{O}H \;\longrightarrow\; H_3C-\underset{\underset{CH_3}{|}}{C}=CH_2 \;+\; :\ddot{Br}:^- \;+\; HOH$$

We have seen (Section 4.8) that the elimination of HX from alkyl halides is an extremely useful reaction for preparing alkenes. The subject is a complex one, however, and there is good evidence that elimination reactions can take place through several different mechanistic pathways.

The **E2 reaction** (for elimination, second-order), which occurs when an alkyl halide is treated with a strong base such as hydroxide ion or alkoxide ion, RO^-, is the most widely studied and commonly occurring pathway for elimination. It is closely analogous to the S_N2 reaction in many respects, and may be formulated as shown in Figure 7.10 (page 216).

The essential feature of the E2 reaction is that it is a one-step process without intermediates. As the attacking base begins to abstract a proton from a carbon atom *next to* the leaving group, the C—H bond begins to break at the same time that the C=C double bond begins to form and the C—X bond begins to break. When the leaving group departs, it takes with it the two electrons from the former C—X bond.

One of the most important pieces of evidence supporting this mechanism comes from reaction rate measurements. Since both base and alkyl halide enter into the single step, E2 reactions show the same second-order behavior that S_N2 reactions do.

A second and more compelling piece of evidence involves the stereochemistry of E2 reactions. Elimination always occurs from a well-defined **periplanar geometry**, meaning that all five reacting atoms must lie in the same plane. There are two

Base (B:) attacks a neighboring C—H bond and begins to remove the H at the same time as the alkene double bond starts to form and the X group starts to leave.

Neutral alkene is produced when the C—H bond is fully broken and the X group has departed with the C—X bond electron pair.

FIGURE 7.10

The mechanism of the E2 reaction of alkyl halides: The reaction takes place in a single step, without intermediates. (Dotted lines indicate partial bonding in the transition state.)

such geometries possible: **syn periplanar,** in which the H and X depart from the *same* side of the molecule; and **anti periplanar,** in which the H and X depart from *opposite* sides of the molecule:

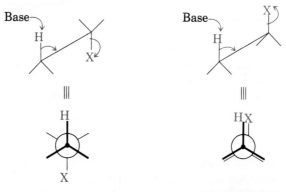

**Anti periplanar geometry
Staggered (lower energy)**

**Syn periplanar geometry
Eclipsed (higher energy)**

Of the two choices, anti periplanar and syn periplanar, anti periplanar geometry is much preferred. This is because the anti geometry allows substituents on the two carbon atoms to adopt a staggered relationship. Syn geometry requires a higher-energy eclipsed conformation.

What's so special about periplanar geometry? Since the original C—H and C—X sp^3 sigma orbitals in the starting material must overlap and become *p* orbitals in the alkene product, *there must also be partial overlap in the transition state.* This necessary overlap in the transition state can only occur if the two orbitals are in the same plane (are periplanar) to begin with (Figure 7.11).

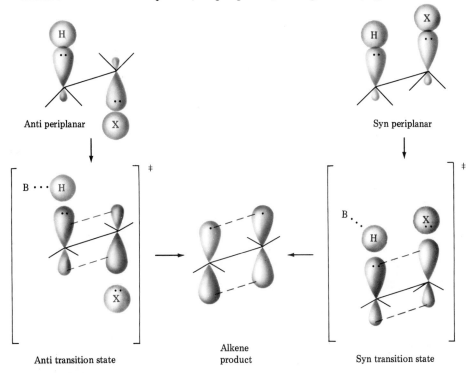

FIGURE 7.11
Transition state for the E2 reaction: Partial overlap of developing *p* orbitals in the transition state requires periplanar geometry.

Anti periplanar geometry for E2 reactions has definite stereochemical consequences that provide strong evidence for the proposed mechanism. To cite just one example, *meso*-1,2-dibromo-1,2-diphenylethane undergoes E2 elimination on treatment with base to give the pure *E* alkene, rather than a mixture of *E* and *Z* alkenes.

meso-**1,2-Dibromo-1,2-diphenylethane**   **(E)-1-Bromo-1,2-diphenylethylene**

PRACTICE PROBLEM   What stereochemistry would you expect for the alkene obtained by E2 elimination of (1S,2S)-1,2-dibromo-1,2-diphenylethane?

Solution   First we have to draw (1S,2S)-1,2-dibromo-1,2-diphenylethane so that we can see its stereochemistry and so that the —H and —Br groups to be eliminated are anti periplanar (molecular models are extremely helpful here). Keeping all substituents in approximately their same positions, we then eliminate HBr and see what alkene results. The product is (Z)-1-bromo-1,2-diphenylethylene.

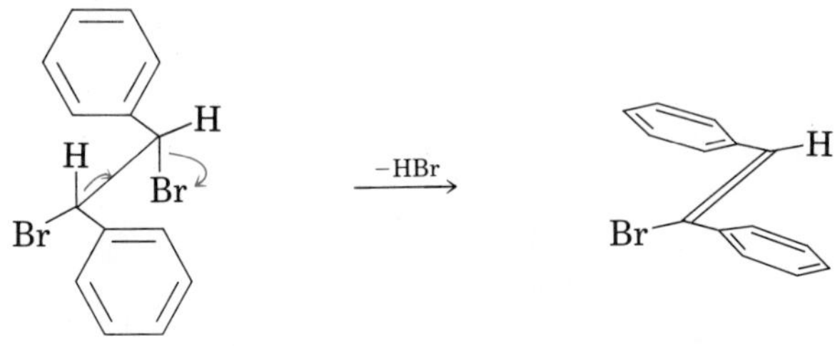

(1S,2S)-1,2-Dibromo-1,2-diphenylethane   **(Z)-1-Bromo-1,2-diphenylethylene**

PROBLEM 7.17   What stereochemistry would you expect for the alkene obtained by E2 elimination of (1R,2R)-1,2-dibromo-1,2-diphenylethane? Draw a Newman projection of the reacting conformation.

7.11   ELIMINATION REACTIONS OF ALKYL HALIDES: THE E1 REACTION

Just as the S_N2 reaction is analogous to the E2 reaction, the S_N1 reaction also has a close analog—the **E1 reaction** (elimination, first-order). The mechanism of the E1 reaction can be formulated as shown in Figure 7.12 for 2-chloro-2-methylpropane.

The E1 reactions occur by spontaneous dissociation of an alkyl halide and subsequent loss of a proton from the intermediate carbocation. As expected, E1 reactions are first-order processes, consistent with a spontaneous dissociation pathway.

The E1 mechanism normally takes place when the substrate is simply heated in a hydroxylic solvent in the absence of an added base. Thus, the best substrates are those that are also subject to S_N1 reaction. In practice, we often find that E1 reactions occur in *competition* with S_N1 reactions; mixtures of substitution and elimination products are almost always obtained. For example, warming 2-chloro-2-methylpropane to 65°C in 80% aqueous ethanol yields a 64:36 mixture of 2-methyl-2-propanol (via S_N1 reaction) and 2-methylpropene (via E1 reaction).

$$CH_3-\overset{\overset{\displaystyle CH_3}{|}}{\underset{\underset{\displaystyle CH_3}{|}}{C}}-Cl$$

Spontaneous dissociation of the tertiary chloride yields an intermediate carbocation in a slow, rate-limiting step.

Slow, rate-limiting

$$\left[CH_3-\overset{\overset{\displaystyle CH_3}{|}}{\underset{\underset{\displaystyle CH_2-H}{|}}{C}}{}^+ \quad + \quad :\overset{..}{\underset{..}{Cl}}{}^- \right]$$

Intermediate

Loss of a neighboring H$^+$ in a fast step yields neutral alkene product. The C—H bond electron pair goes to form the alkene pi bond.

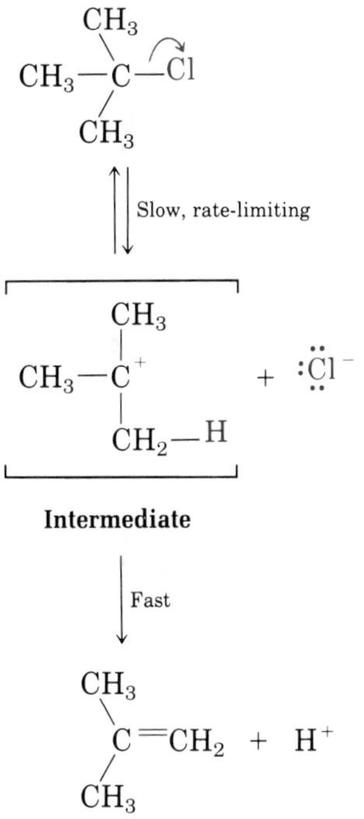

Fast

$$\overset{\displaystyle CH_3}{\underset{\displaystyle CH_3}{}}\!\!\diagdown\!\!C{=}CH_2 \quad + \quad H^+$$

FIGURE 7.12
Mechanism of the E1 reaction: Two steps are involved, of which the first is rate limiting.

$$(CH_3)_3CCl \xrightarrow[\text{65°C}]{H_2O, \ CH_3CH_2OH} (CH_3)_3COH \ + \ (CH_3)_2C{=}CH_2$$

2-Chloro-2-methylpropane   **2-Methyl-2-propanol**   **2-Methylpropene**
                                                 (64%)   **(36%)**

PROBLEM 7.18   Considering what is known about the S$_N$1 reaction, what effect would you expect a change of leaving group from bromide ion to chloride ion to have on the rate of an E1 reaction?

7.12   A SUMMARY OF REACTIVITY: S$_N$1, S$_N$2, E1, E2

We've looked at four possible modes of reaction between an alkyl halide and a nucleophile/base, and you may well wonder how to predict what will take place in any given case. Will substitution or elimination occur? Will the reaction be first-order or second-order? Can we *choose* the desired pathway by adjusting reaction conditions?

There are no absolute answers to these questions, but we can make some broad generalizations:

1. **Primary alkyl halides** react by either S_N2 or E2 mechanisms because they are relatively unhindered and because their dissociation would give unstable primary carbocations. If a nucleophile such as $:\ddot{I}:^-$, $:\ddot{B}r:^-$, $R\ddot{S}:^-$, $H_3N:$, or $:CN^-$ is used, only S_N2 substitution occurs. If a strong base such as alkoxide ion, $R\ddot{O}:$, is used, a small amount of competitive E2 elimination also occurs.

2. **Secondary alkyl halides** can react by any of the four possible mechanisms, and we can often make a specific pathway predominate by choosing appropriate experimental conditions. If a weak base such as iodide ion is used, S_N2 substitution occurs. If a strong base such as hydroxide ion is used, however, E2 elimination occurs. Secondary alkyl halides can also be made to undergo S_N1 and E1 reactions, but mixtures of products are usually obtained.

3. **Tertiary alkyl halides** can react by three pathways: S_N1, E1, and E2. One of the three can often be made to predominate by proper choice of reaction conditions. Strong bases cause E2 elimination to occur, but heating in hydroxylic solvents leads to a mixture of S_N1 and E1 products.

These generalizations are summarized in Table 7.7.

TABLE 7.7   Correlation of structure and reactivity for substitution and elimination reactions

Halide type	S_N1	S_N2	E1	E2
Primary halide	Does not occur	Highly favored under most conditions	Does not occur	Favored when strong, hindered bases are used
Secondary halide	Can occur under solvolysis conditions in polar solvents	Favored by good nucleophiles in polar aprotic solvents	Can occur under solvolysis conditions in polar solvents	Favored when strong bases are used
Tertiary halide	Favored by nonbasic nucleophiles in polar solvents	Does not occur	Occurs under solvolysis conditions	Highly favored when bases are used

PROBLEM 7.19   Identify these reactions as to type (S_N1, S_N2, E1, or E2):

(a)   1-Bromobutane + NaN_3 $\longrightarrow$ 1-Azidobutane
(b)   Bromocyclohexane + NaOH $\longrightarrow$ Cyclohexene
(c)   Iodoethane + $Na^+ \ ^-:C{\equiv}CH$ $\longrightarrow$ 1-Butyne
(d)   Chlorodiphenylmethane $\xrightarrow{\text{HCOOH}}$ Diphenylmethyl formate

ADDITIONAL PROBLEMS

PROBLEM 7.20 Name these alkyl halides according to IUPAC rules:

(a) $(CH_3)_2CHCHBrCHBrCH_2CH(CH_3)_2$ (b) $CH_3CH=CHCH_2CHICH_3$
(c) $(CH_3)_2CBrCH_2CH_2CHClCH(CH_3)_2$ (d) $CH_3CH_2CH(CH_2Br)CH_2CH_2CH_3$

PROBLEM 7.21 Draw structures corresponding to these IUPAC names:

(a) 2,3-Dichloro-4-methylhexane   (b) 4-Bromo-4-ethyl-2-methylhexane
(c) 3-Iodo-2,2,4,4-tetramethylpentane

PROBLEM 7.22 The C—H bonds in the methyl group of propene are 11 kcal/mol weaker than the
C—H bonds in ethane. In other words, the $H_2C=CHCH_2\cdot$ radical is 11 kcal/mol more
stable than the $CH_3CH_2\cdot$ radical. Draw resonance structures of the 1-propenyl (*allyl*)
radical to account for its stability.

PROBLEM 7.23 How would you prepare the following compounds, starting with cyclopentene and
any other reagents needed?

(a) Chlorocyclopentane   (b) Cyclopentanol
(c) Cyclopentylmagnesium chloride

PROBLEM 7.24 Predict the product(s) of these reactions:

(a) 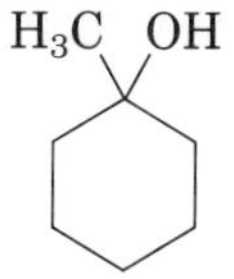 H$_3$C OH
$\xrightarrow[\text{Ether}]{\text{HBr}}$?

(b) $CH_3CH_2CH_2CH_2OH$ $\xrightarrow{\text{SOCl}_2}$?

(c) 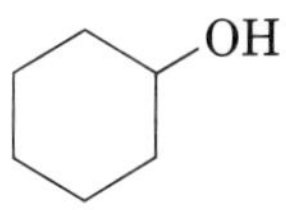
OH $\xrightarrow[\text{Ether}]{\text{PBr}_3}$?

(d) $CH_3CH_2CHBrCH_3$ $\xrightarrow[\text{Ether}]{\text{Mg}}$ A $\xrightarrow{\text{H}_2\text{O}}$ B

PROBLEM 7.25 Which reagent in each pair will react faster in an S$_N$2 reaction with hydroxide ion?

(a) CH_3Br or CH_3I (b) CH_3Cl or $(CH_3)_3CCl$
(c) $H_2C=CHBr$ or $H_2C=CHCH_2Br$

PROBLEM 7.26 How might you prepare each of the following molecules using a nucleophilic substitution reaction at some step?

(a) CH_3CH_2Br (b) $CH_3CH_2CH_2CH_2CN$
(c) $CH_3OC(CH_3)_3$ (d) $CH_3CH_2CH_2-\overset{+}{N}=N=\overset{-}{N}$

(e) CH_3CH_2SH (f) $H_3C-O-\overset{\overset{\displaystyle O}{\|}}{C}-CH_3$

PROBLEM 7.27 What products would you expect from reaction of 1-bromopropane with these
reagents?

(a) NaI   (b) NaCN   (c) NaOH
(d) Mg, then H$_2$O   (e) NaOCH$_3$

PROBLEM 7.28   Order each set of compounds with respect to S_N1 reactivity.

(a) $(CH_3)_3C-Cl$, $\text{C}_6\text{H}_5-C(CH_3)_2Cl$, $CH_3CH_2\overset{\overset{\displaystyle NH_2}{|}}{C}HCH_3$

(b) $(CH_3)_3C-F$, $(CH_3)_3C-Br$, $(CH_3)_3C-OH$

PROBLEM 7.29   Order each set of compounds with respect to S_N2 reactivity.

(a) $(CH_3)_3CCl$, $CH_3CH_2CH_2Cl$, $CH_3CH_2CHClCH_3$
(b) $(CH_3)_2CHCHBrCH_3$, $(CH_3)_2CHCH_2Br$, $(CH_3)_3CCH_2Br$
(c) $CH_3CH_2CH_2OCH_3$, $CH_3CH_2CH_2OTos$, $CH_3CH_2CH_2Br$

PROBLEM 7.30   Predict the product and give the stereochemistry of reaction of the following nucleophiles with (R)-2-bromooctane:

(a) $^-{:}CN$ (b) $CH_3CO\ddot{O}{:}^-$ (c) $:\!\ddot{B}r\!:^-$

PROBLEM 7.31   Ethers can be prepared by S_N2 reaction of alkoxide ions with alkyl halides:

$$R-O^- + R'-Br \longrightarrow R-O-R' + Br^-$$

Suppose you wanted to prepare cyclohexyl methyl ether. Which route would be better, reaction of methoxide ion, CH_3O^-, with bromocyclohexane, or reaction of cyclohexoxide with bromomethane? Explain.

PROBLEM 7.32   The S_N2 reaction can also occur *intramolecularly* (within the same molecule). What product would you expect from treatment of 4-bromo-1-butanol with base?

$$BrCH_2CH_2CH_2CH_2OH \xrightarrow{\text{Na}^+ \ ^-OCH_3} CH_3OH + [BrCH_2CH_2CH_2CH_2O^- \ Na^+] \longrightarrow \ ?$$

PROBLEM 7.33   In light of your answer to Problem 7.32, can you propose a synthesis of 1,4-dioxane starting from 1,2-dibromoethane?

1,4-Dioxane

PROBLEM 7.34   Propose a structure for an alkyl halide that can give a mixture of three alkenes on E2 reaction.

PROBLEM 7.35   Propose a structure for an alkyl halide that gives (Z)-2,3-diphenylbutane on E2 reaction.

PROBLEM 7.36   Describe the effects of the following variables on S_N2 and S_N1 reactions.

(a)   Leaving group   (b)   Substrate structure

PROBLEM 7.37 Predict the major alkene product from each of these eliminations:

(a)

$\xrightarrow{\text{CH}_3\text{O}^-\ \text{Na}^+}$

(b)

$$(\text{CH}_3)_2\text{CH}-\overset{\overset{\displaystyle \text{CH}_3}{|}}{\underset{\underset{\displaystyle \text{CH}_2\text{CH}_3}{|}}{\text{C}}}-\text{Br} \quad \xrightarrow[\text{Heat}]{\text{CH}_3\text{COOH}}$$

PROBLEM 7.38 (2R,3S)-2-Bromo-3-phenylbutane undergoes E2 reaction on treatment with sodium ethoxide to yield (Z)-2-phenyl-2-butene.

$$\text{CH}_3\text{CHCHCH}_3 \quad \xrightarrow{\text{CH}_3\text{CH}_2\text{O}^-\ \text{Na}^+} \quad \text{CH}_3\text{C}=\text{CHCH}_3$$
$$\underset{\displaystyle \text{Br}}{|}$$

Formulate the reaction, showing the proper stereochemistry. Explain the observed result using Newman projections.

PROBLEM 7.39 In light of your answer to Problem 7.38, which alkene, E or Z, would you expect from the E2 reaction of (2R,3R)-2-bromo-3-phenylbutane?

PROBLEM 7.40 It has been observed that optically active 2-butanol slowly becomes racemic upon standing in dilute sulfuric acid. Propose a mechanism to account for this racemization.

PROBLEM 7.41 Account for the fact that the rate of the S_N2 reaction of 1-chlorooctane with acetate ion to yield octyl acetate is increased by the presence of a small quantity of iodide ion.

PROBLEM 7.42 There are eight possible diastereomers of 1,2,3,4,5,6-hexachlorocyclohexane. Draw them. One isomer loses HCl in an E2 reaction nearly 1000 times more slowly than the others. Which isomer reacts so slowly, and why?

PROBLEM 7.43 Compound A is optically inactive and has the formula $C_{16}H_{16}Br_2$. On treatment with strong base, A gives hydrocarbon B, $C_{16}H_{14}$, which absorbs 2 equiv of hydrogen when reduced over a palladium catalyst and reacts with ozone to give two carbonyl-containing products. One product, C, is an aldehyde with the formula C_7H_6O. The other product can be identified as glyoxal, OHCCHO. Formulate the reactions involved and suggest structures for A, B, and C. What is the stereochemistry of A?

PROBLEM 7.44 Consider the following cleavage reaction of a methyl ester:

$$\text{CH}_3\text{CH}_2\text{CH}_2\overset{\overset{\displaystyle O}{\|}}{\text{C}}-\text{O}-\text{CH}_3 \quad \xrightarrow{\text{LiI}} \quad \text{CH}_3\text{CH}_2\text{CH}_2\overset{\overset{\displaystyle O}{\|}}{\text{C}}-\text{O}^-\ \text{Li}^+ \ + \ \text{CH}_3\text{I}$$

The following evidence is available: (1) The rate of this reaction depends both on ester concentration and on iodide ion concentration. (2) The corresponding ethyl ester cleaves approximately 10 times more slowly than the methyl ester. Using this evidence, propose a mechanism for the reaction.

Substitution Reactions in Biological Systems

Many biological processes occur by reaction pathways analogous to those carried out in the laboratory. Thus, a number of reactions occurring in living organisms are known to take place by nucleophilic substitution reactions.

Perhaps the most common of all biological substitution reactions is **methylation**—the transfer of a methyl group from an electrophilic donor to a nucleophile.

$$\text{\textschwa}Y\text{—}CH_3 + \ddot{N}u^- \longrightarrow CH_3\text{—}Nu + \text{\textschwa}Y{:}^-$$

Methyl donor   **Methylated nucleophile**

Although a laboratory chemist might choose iodomethane for such a reaction, living organisms operate in a more subtle way. The large and complex molecule *S*-adenosylmethionine is the biological methyl group donor. Since the sulfur atom of *S*-adenosylmethionine has a positive charge (a *sulfonium ion*), it is an excellent leaving group for S_N2 displacements on the methyl carbon.

One example of the action of *S*-adenosylmethionine in biological methylations takes place in the adrenal medulla during the formation of adrenaline from norepinephrine, as shown in Figure F.1.

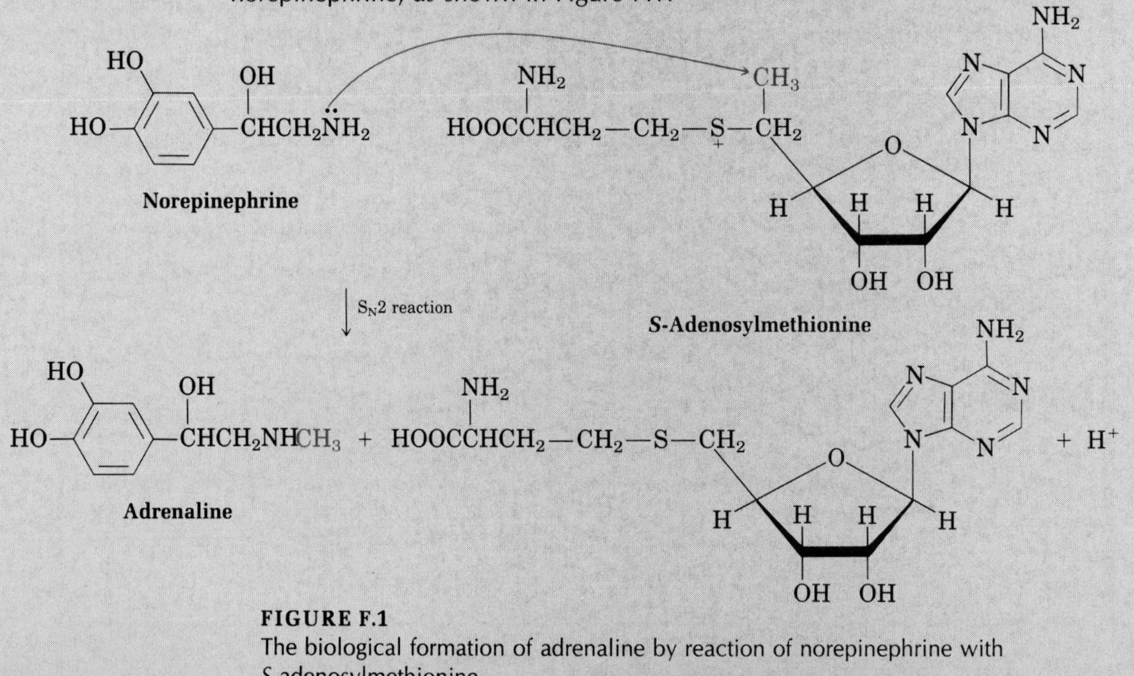

FIGURE F.1
The biological formation of adrenaline by reaction of norepinephrine with *S*-adenosylmethionine

After becoming used to dealing with simple alkyl halides such as iodomethane used for laboratory alkylations, it is a real shock to encounter molecules as complex as *S*-adenosylmethionine. The shock is only psychological, however. From the chemical standpoint, iodomethane and *S*-adenosylmethionine are doing exactly the same thing—transferring a methyl group in an S_N2 reaction. The same chemical principles apply in both cases.

Alkyl Halides and the Ozone Layer

The lowly aerosol can is a fixture of modern life—something we take for granted to spray our deodorants, hairsprays, and insect repellents. In the early 1970s, however, it became apparent that the proliferation of aerosol sprays was leading to a serious environmental problem.

The volatile propellents used in aerosols at the time were various alkyl halides called *Freons*. The Freons are **chlorofluorocarbons**—simple alkanes in which all the hydrogens have been replaced by either chlorine or fluorine. Fluorotrichloromethane (CCl_3F, Freon 11) and dichlorodifluoromethane (CCl_2F_2, Freon 12) are two of the most common Freons, although other somewhat more complex chlorofluorocarbons are still used as refrigerants. The advantage of using Freons as aerosol propellents is that they are chemically inert and nonflammable. Thus, they don't react with the contents of the can, they leave no residue, they have no odor, and they are safe. They do escape into the atmosphere, however, and ultimately they find their way into the stratosphere.

The **ozone layer** is an atmospheric band extending from about 20 to 40 km above the earth's surface. Although toxic if breathed in high concentrations, ozone (O_3) is critically important in the upper atmosphere because it acts to shield the earth from intense solar radiation. If the ozone layer is depleted or destroyed, this solar radiation will reach the earth, where it can cause skin cancers and eye cataracts. Unfortunately, destruction of the ozone layer is exactly what chlorofluorocarbons do. Estimates of the extent of ozone destruction differ, but a recent report predicted a 5–9% depletion over the next 50–100 years.

The mechanism of ozone destruction by chlorofluorocarbons involves radical reactions of the same sort we saw in the radical chlorination of methane (Section 7.3). Ultraviolet light ($h\nu$) striking a Freon molecule causes breakage of a carbon–chlorine bond, producing a chlorine radical. This radical then reacts with ozone to yield oxygen and ClO:

$$CCl_2F_2 \xrightarrow{h\nu} \cdot CClF_2 + Cl\cdot$$

$$Cl\cdot + O_3 \longrightarrow O_2 + ClO$$

Recognition of the problem led the U.S. government in 1980 to ban the use of Freon aerosol propellents. They have been replaced by simple alkanes, primarily 2-methylpropane and propane.

CHAPTER 8

Alcohols, Ethers, and Phenols

Alcohols are compounds that have hydroxyl groups bonded to saturated, sp^3-hybridized carbon atoms; **phenols** have hydroxyl groups bonded to an aromatic ring; and **ethers** have an oxygen atom bonded to two organic groups. Compounds in all three classes can therefore be thought of as organic derivatives of water in which one or both of the water hydrogens are replaced by an organic substituent (R—O—H, Ar—O—H, and R—O—R′ versus H—O—H).

$$CH_3CH_2OH$$

OH

$$CH_3CH_2—O—CH_2CH_3$$

Ethanol

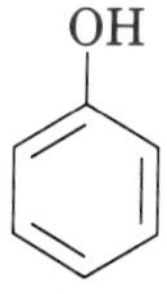

Phenol
(also known as carbolic acid)

Diethyl ether

Alcohols, phenols, and ethers all occur widely in nature and have a variety of valuable industrial and pharmaceutical applications. For example, ethanol is used as a fuel additive, an industrial solvent, and a beverage; menthol, an alcohol isolated from peppermint oil, is used as a flavoring agent; BHT (butylated hydroxytoluene) is widely used as a food additive to prolong shelf life and protect against oxidation; diethyl ether, the familiar "ether" of medicinal use, was once popular as an anesthetic agent but is now mainly used as an industrial solvent; and tetrahydrofuran (THF), a cyclic ether, is also widely used as a solvent.

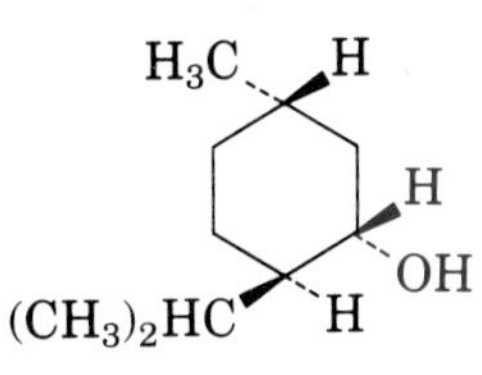

H₃C   H

H

OH

$(CH_3)_2HC$ H

$(CH_3)_3C$ OH $C(CH_3)_3$

CH₃

O

Menthol

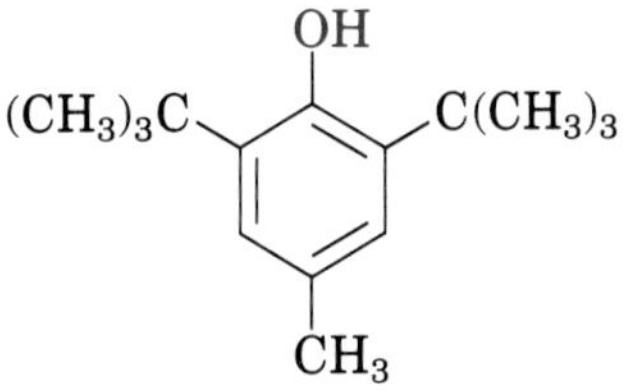

Tetrahydrofuran (THF)   **227**

8.1   NOMENCLATURE OF ALCOHOLS, PHENOLS, AND ETHERS

Alcohols

Alcohols are classified as either primary (1°), secondary (2°), or tertiary (3°), depending on the number of carbon substituents bonded to the hydroxyl-bearing carbon.

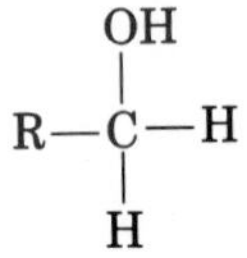

A primary alcohol 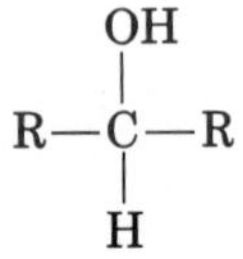   A secondary alcohol 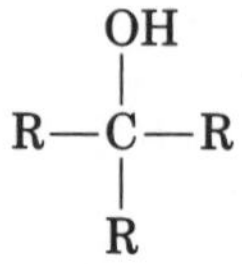   A tertiary alcohol

Simple alcohols are named in the IUPAC system as derivatives of the parent alkane:

1. Select the longest carbon chain *containing the hydroxyl group*, and derive the parent name by replacing the *-e* ending of the corresponding alkane with *-ol*.

2. Number the alkane chain beginning at the end nearer the hydroxyl group.

3. Number all substituents according to their position on the chain and write the name, listing the substituents in alphabetical order.

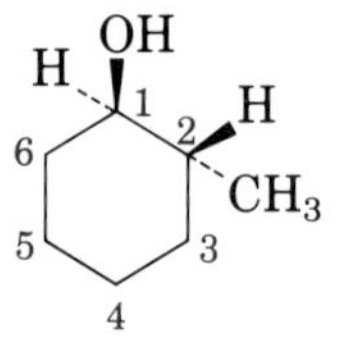

trans-2-Methylcyclohexanol 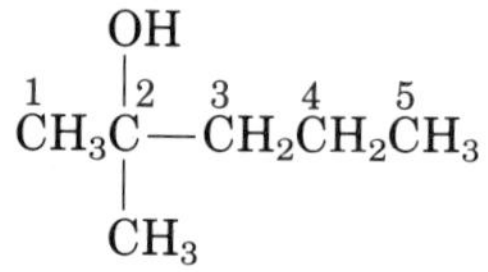   2-Methyl-2-pentanol 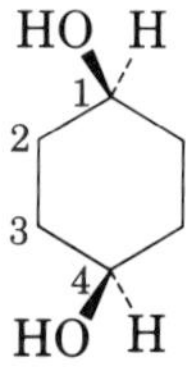   *cis*-1,4-Cyclohexanediol

Certain commonly occurring alcohols have trivial names that are accepted by IUPAC. For example:

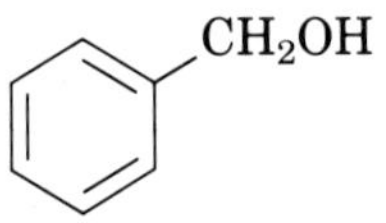

Benzyl alcohol
(phenylmethanol)

Allyl alcohol
(2-propen-1-ol)

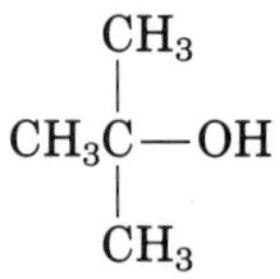

tert-Butyl alcohol
(2-methyl-2-propanol)

$HO-CH_2CH_2-OH$ $HO-CH_2CHCH_2-OH$
                                          |
                                          OH

Ethylene glycol
(1,2-ethanediol)

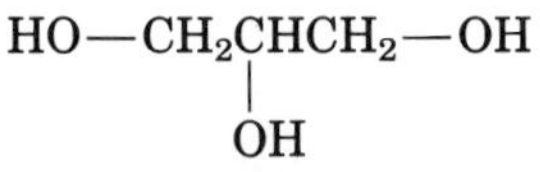

Glycerol
(1,2,3-propanetriol)

Phenols

Phenols are named as substituted aromatic compounds according to the rules discussed in Section 5.1. Note, however, that *-phenol* is used as the parent name, rather than *-benzene*. For example:

p-Methylphenol 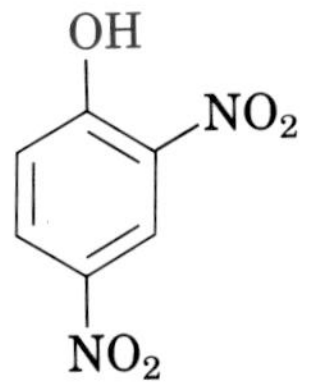   **2,4-Dinitrophenol**

Ethers

Two different systems of ether nomenclature are allowed by IUPAC rules. Relatively simple ethers are best named by identifying the two organic residues and adding the word *ether*. For example:

$CH_3OC(CH_3)_3$ $CH_3CH_2-O-CH=CH_2$

tert-Butyl methyl ether   **Ethyl vinyl ether**   **Cyclopropyl phenyl ether**

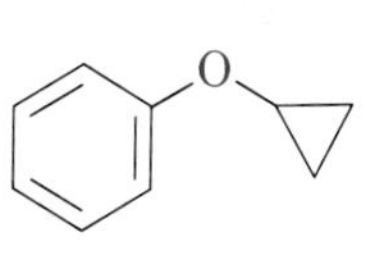

If more than one ether linkage is present in the molecule, or if other functional groups are present, the ether group is considered as an *alkoxy* substituent on the parent compound. For example:

p-Dimethoxybenzene   **4-tert-Butoxy-1-cyclohexene**

PROBLEM 8.1   Provide IUPAC names for these alcohols:

(a)   OH   OH
         | |
   $CH_3CHCH_2CHCH(CH_3)_2$

(b)   OH
                                      |
          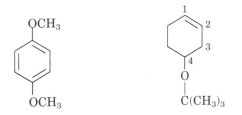$CH_2CH_2C(CH_3)_2$

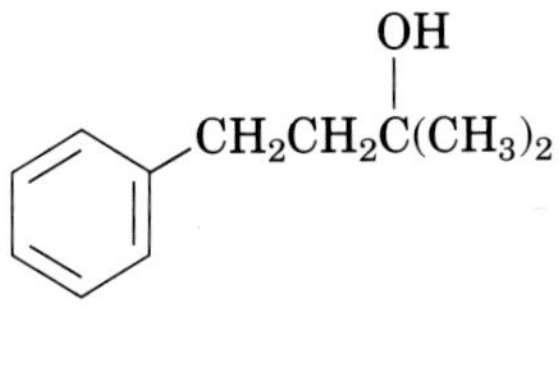

(c) 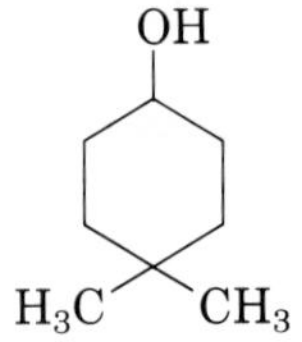   OH

H₃C   CH₃

(d) 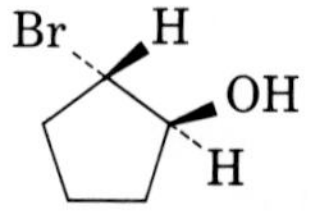   Br   H
                OH
             H

PROBLEM 8.2   Draw structures corresponding to these IUPAC names:

(a)   2-Methyl-2-hexanol
(c)   2-Ethyl-2-buten-1-ol
(e)   o-Bromophenol

(b)   1,5-Hexanediol
(d)   3-Cyclohexen-1-ol
(f)   2,4,6-Trinitrophenol

PROBLEM 8.3   Name these ethers according to IUPAC rules:

(a) $(CH_3)_2CH-O-CH(CH_3)_2$

(b) 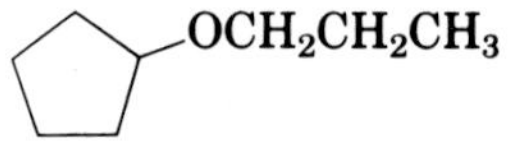   ⬠—OCH₂CH₂CH₃

(c) 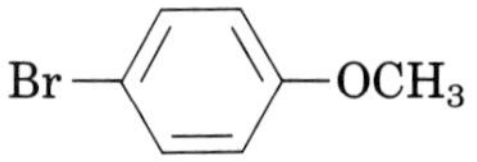   Br—⬡—OCH₃

(d) $(CH_3)_2CHCH_2OCH_2CH_3$

8.2 PROPERTIES OF ALCOHOLS, PHENOLS, AND ETHERS: HYDROGEN BONDING

As mentioned earlier, alcohols, phenols, and ethers can be thought of as organic derivatives of water in which one or both of the hydrogens have been replaced by organic residues. As such, all three classes of compounds have nearly the same geometry as water. The R—O—H or R—O—R′ bonds have an approximately tetrahedral bond angle (112° in dimethyl ether, for example), and the oxygen atom is sp^3 hybridized:

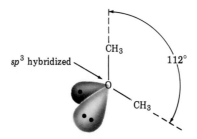

Alcohols and phenols are quite different from the hydrocarbons and alkyl halides we have studied thus far. Not only is their chemistry much richer, but their physical properties are also different. Table 8.1, which provides a comparison of the boiling points of some simple alcohols, alkanes, and chloroalkanes, indicates that alcohols have much higher boiling points. For example, 1-propanol (mol wt = 60), butane (mol wt = 58), and chloroethane (mol wt = 65) are close in weight, yet 1-propanol boils at 97°C, compared to −0.5°C for the alkane and 12.5°C for the chloroalkane.

TABLE 8.1 Boiling points of some alkanes, chloroalkanes, and alcohols (°C)

Alkyl group, R	Alkane, R—H	Chloroalkane, R—Cl	Alcohol, R—OH
CH_3-	−162	−24	64.5
CH_3CH_2-	−88.5	12.5	78.3
$CH_3CH_2CH_2-$	−42	46.6	97
$(CH_3)_2CH-$	−42	36.5	82.5
$CH_3CH_2CH_2CH_2-$	−0.5	83.5	117
$(CH_3)_3C-$	−12	51	83

Similarly, phenols have higher boiling points than arenes. Phenol itself, for example, boils at 182°C, whereas toluene boils at 110.6°C.

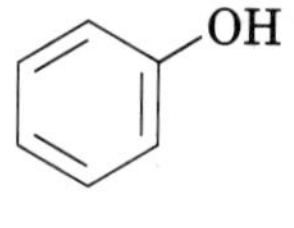

Phenol (b.p. = 182°C) 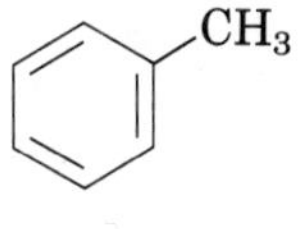   **Toluene (b.p. = 110.6°C)**

The reason for their unusually high boiling points is that alcohols and phenols, like water, are highly associated in solution owing to the formation of hydrogen bonds. The positively polarized hydroxyl hydrogen atom from one molecule forms a weak hydrogen bond to the negatively polarized oxygen atom of another molecule (Figure 8.1). Although hydrogen bonds have a strength of only about 5 kcal/mol (versus 103 kcal/mol for a typical O—H bond), the presence of a great many such hydrogen bonds in solution means that extra energy is required to break them during the boiling process.

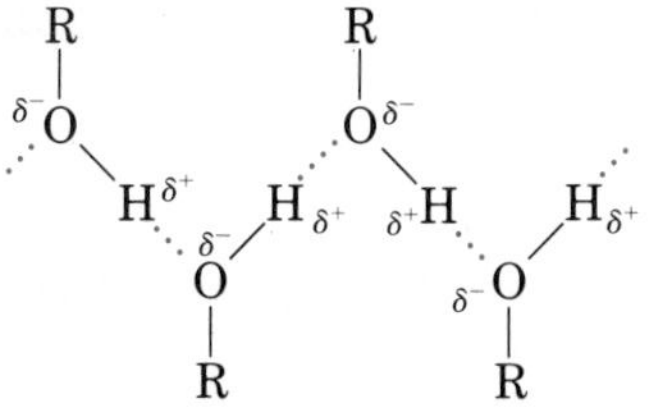

FIGURE 8.1
Hydrogen bonding in alcohols and phenols

Ethers, because they lack hydroxyl groups, cannot form hydrogen bonds and therefore have relatively lower boiling points (Table 8.2).

TABLE 8.2 Comparison of boiling points of ethers and hydrocarbons

Compound	Boiling point (°C)	
CH_3OCH_3 (versus $CH_3CH_2CH_3$)	−25	(−45)
$CH_3CH_2OCH_2CH_3$ (versus $CH_3CH_2CH_2CH_2CH_3$)	34.6	(36)
	65	(49)
 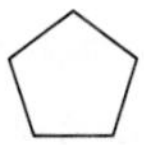 Tetrahydrofuran (THF) (versus cyclopentane)		

8.3 PROPERTIES OF ALCOHOLS AND PHENOLS: ACIDITY

Like water, alcohols and phenols are weakly acidic. In dilute aqueous solution, alcohols and phenols dissociate to a slight extent by donating a proton to water:

$$R-\ddot{O}-H + H_2\ddot{O}: \; \rightleftharpoons \; R-\ddot{O}:^- + H_3O:^+$$

In our earlier discussion of acidity (Section 1.13), we said that the acidity of any acid HA (such as H—OR or H—OAr) can be defined by the expressions

$$K_a = \frac{[A^-][H_3O^+]}{[HA]} \qquad pK_a = -\log K_a$$

where K_a is the acidity constant. Compounds with a small K_a (or high pK_a) are weakly acidic, whereas compounds with a larger K_a (or smaller pK_a) are more strongly acidic. Table 8.3 gives the pK_a values of some common alcohols and phenols in comparison with water and with HCl.

TABLE 8.3 Acidity constants of some alcohols and phenols

Alcohol or phenol	pK_a	
		Weaker acid
$(CH_3)_3COH$	18.00	
CH_3CH_2OH	16.00	
HOH (water)[a]	(15.74)	
CH_3OH	15.54	
p-Methylphenol	10.26	
Phenol	10.00	
p-Bromophenol	9.35	
p-Nitrophenol	7.16	Stronger acid
HCl (hydrochloric acid)[a]	(−7.00)	

[a]Values for water and hydrochloric acid are shown for reference.

The data in Table 8.3 show that alcohols are about as acidic as water, whereas phenols are considerably more acidic. Structural effects, however, play a significant role in determining the exact acidity of a compound. For example, methanol and ethanol are similar in acidity to water, whereas *tert*-butyl alcohol is slightly less acidic. The effect of alkyl substitution on acidity is thought to be due to solvation. Water is able to surround the sterically accessible oxygen atom of unhindered alcohols such as ethanol and to stabilize the alkoxide ion by solvation, thus favoring its formation. Hindered alkoxides such as *tert*-butoxide, however, prevent solvation by their bulk and are therefore less stabilized.

Alcohols are generally much weaker acids than carboxylic acids or mineral acids, and they do not react with weak bases such as bicarbonate ion. Alcohols do, however, react with alkali metals such as sodium and potassium, and with strong bases such as sodium amide ($NaNH_2$) and sodium hydride (NaH). The metal salts of alcohols are strong bases that are used frequently as reagents in organic chemistry.

$$2 \ CH_3OH + 2 \ Na \ (or \ Na^+ \ H^-) \longrightarrow 2 \ CH_3O^- \ Na^+ + H_2$$

Sodium methoxide

$$2 \ (CH_3)_3COH + 2 \ K \longrightarrow 2 \ (CH_3)_3CO^- \ K^+ + H_2$$

Potassium *tert*-butoxide

Phenols are much more acidic than alcohols, as Table 8.3 shows. Indeed, some phenols, such as the nitro-substituted ones, approach or surpass the acidity of carboxylic acids. One practical consequence of this acidity is that phenols are soluble in dilute aqueous sodium hydroxide.

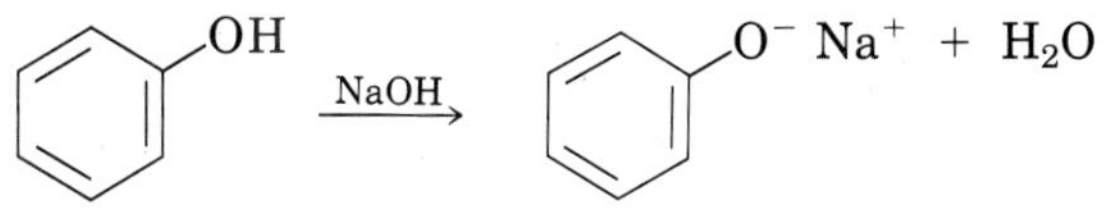

Phenol   Sodium phenoxide

Phenols are more acidic than alcohols because the phenoxide anion is resonance-stabilized by the aromatic ring. Sharing of the negative charge results in increased stability of the phenoxide anion and consequently in increased acidity of the corresponding phenol.

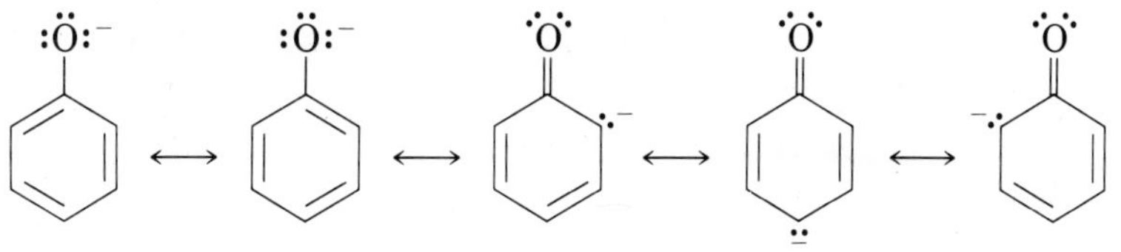

Substituted phenols can be either more acidic or less acidic than phenol itself, depending on their structure. As a general rule, phenols that are substituted by an electron-withdrawing substituent are more acidic. Electron-withdrawing substituents *stabilize* the corresponding phenoxide ion by delocalizing the negative charge, thus favoring ionization. Phenols with an electron-donating substituent, however, are less acidic. Electron-donating substituents *destabilize* the phenoxide by concentrating the charge, thus disfavoring ionization.

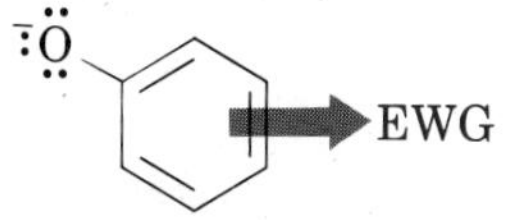

Electron-withdrawing groups (EWG) stabilize phenoxide anion, resulting in increased phenol acidity

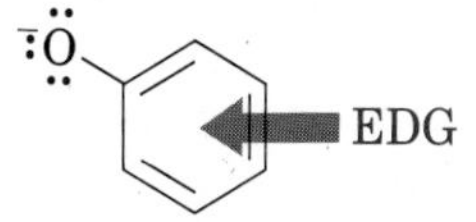

Electron-donating groups (EDG) destabilize phenoxide anion, resulting in decreased phenol acidity

PRACTICE PROBLEM   Which would you expect to be more acidic, *p*-methylphenol or *p*-cyanophenol?

Solution   We know from their effects on aromatic substitution (Section 5.11) that methyl is an activating group (electron donor), whereas cyano is a deactivating group (electron acceptor). Thus, *p*-cyanophenol is more acidic.

PROBLEM 8.4   Rank the compounds in each group in order of increasing acidity.

    (a)   Methanol, phenol, *p*-nitrophenol, *p*-methylphenol
    (b)   Benzyl alcohol, *p*-bromophenol, 2,4-dibromophenol, *p*-methoxyphenol

PROBLEM 8.5   Which do you think would be more acidic, *p*-methylphenol or *p*-(trifluoromethyl)-phenol? Explain your answer.

8.4   PREPARATION OF ALCOHOLS AND PHENOLS

Alcohols

In many ways, alcohols occupy a central position in organic chemistry. They can be prepared from a variety of functional group classes (alkenes, alkyl halides, ketones, aldehydes, and esters, among others), and they can be transformed into an equally wide assortment of compound classes. Let's review briefly some of the methods of alcohol preparation we have already seen.

Alcohols can be prepared by hydration of alkenes. Treatment of the alkene with sulfuric acid and water leads to the Markovnikov (more highly substituted) product. This reaction is directly analogous to the Markovnikov addition of HBr to an alkene (Section 4.4).

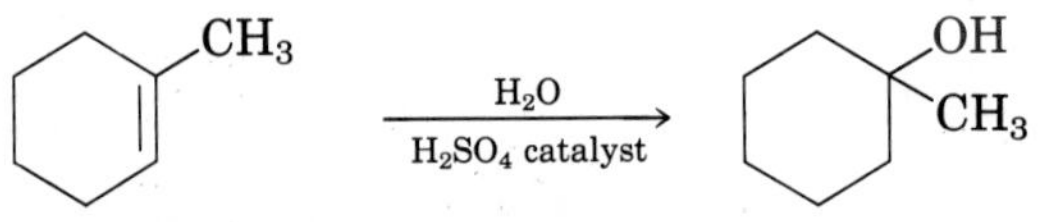

      1-Methylcyclohexene   **1-Methylcyclohexanol**

1,2-Diols can be prepared by direct hydroxylation of an alkene with basic potassium permanganate (Section 4.7). The reaction takes place with syn stereochemistry.

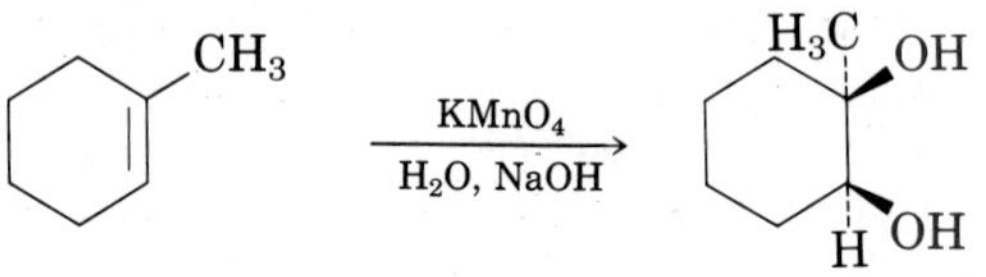

      1-Methylcyclohexene   **1-Methyl-**
                                              cis-1,2-cyclohexanediol

In addition to being able to prepare alcohols from alkenes, we will soon see that alcohols can also be prepared from all types of carbonyl-containing compounds.

Phenols

We saw in Section 5.7 that phenols can be prepared from aromatic starting materials by a two-step sequence. The starting compound is first sulfonated by treatment with SO_3/H_2SO_4, and the arenesulfonic acid thus produced is converted into a phenol by high-temperature reaction with NaOH.

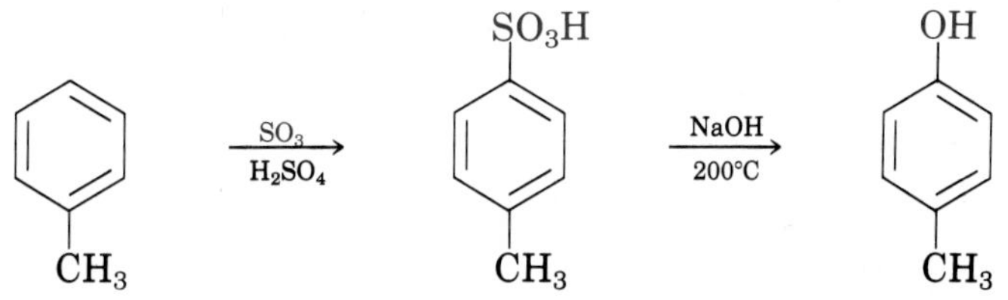

Toluene   p-Toluenesulfonic acid   p-Methylphenol (72%)

PROBLEM 8.6   p-Cresol (p-methylphenol) is used industrially both as an antiseptic and as a starting material to prepare the food additive BHT. How could you synthesize p-cresol from benzene?

8.5 ALCOHOLS FROM REDUCTION OF CARBONYL COMPOUNDS

The most valuable method for preparing alcohols is by **reduction** of carbonyl compounds:

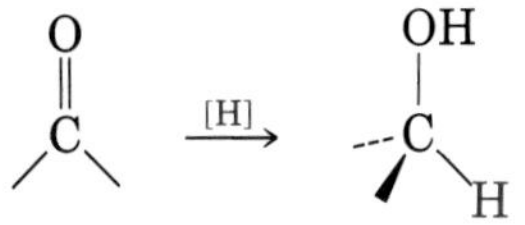

where [H] is a reducing agent

In inorganic chemistry, reduction is defined as the gain of electrons by an atom, and oxidation is defined as the loss of electrons by an atom. In organic chemistry, however, it is often difficult to decide whether an atom gains or loses electrons during a reaction. Thus, the terms "oxidation" and "reduction" have less precise meanings. For organic chemists, a *reduction* is a reaction that either *increases* the hydrogen content or *decreases* the oxygen, halogen, or nitrogen content of a molecule. Conversely, an organic *oxidation* is a reaction that either *decreases* the hydrogen content or *increases* the oxygen, halogen, or nitrogen content of a molecule.

For example, catalytic hydrogenation of an alkene is clearly a reduction, since two hydrogens are added to the starting material. Conversely, hydroxylation of an alkene with $KMnO_4$ is an oxidation since oxygen is added. Hydration of an alkene is neither an oxidation nor a reduction, however, since *both* oxygen and hydrogen are added to the alkene in the same step.

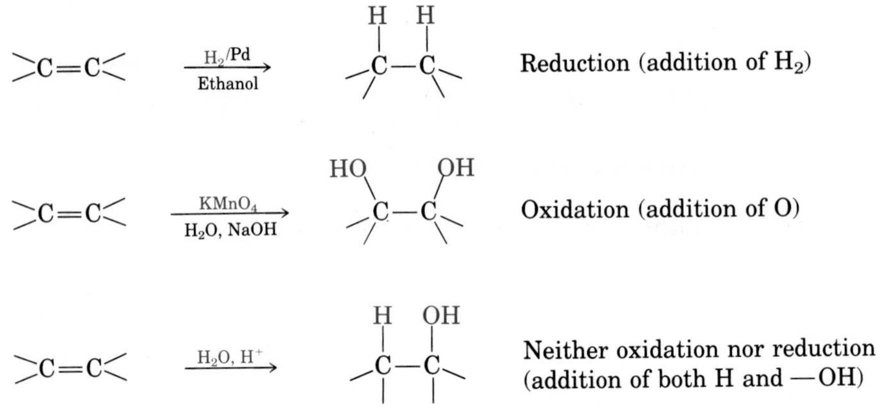

$$>C=C< \xrightarrow[\text{Ethanol}]{H_2/Pd} \quad \overset{\overset{\text{H}}{|}}{C}-\overset{\overset{\text{H}}{|}}{C} \qquad \text{Reduction (addition of } H_2)$$

$$>C=C< \xrightarrow[\text{H}_2\text{O, NaOH}]{KMnO_4} \quad \overset{\overset{\text{HO}}{}}{C}-\overset{\overset{\text{OH}}{}}{C} \qquad \text{Oxidation (addition of O)}$$

$$>C=C< \xrightarrow{H_2\text{O, H}^+} \quad \overset{\overset{\text{H}}{|}}{C}-\overset{\overset{\text{OH}}{|}}{C} \qquad \begin{array}{l}\text{Neither oxidation nor reduction}\\ \text{(addition of both H and } -\text{OH)}\end{array}$$

A list of functional group classes of increasing oxidation state is shown in Figure 8.2. Any reaction that converts a functional group from a lower state to a higher state is an oxidation; any reaction that converts a functional group from a higher state to a lower state is a reduction; and any reaction that does not change the state is neither an oxidation nor a reduction.

	$H_2C=CH_2$	$HC\equiv CH$		
CH_3CH_3	CH_3CH_2OH	$CH_3CH=O$	CH_3CO_2H	CO_2
	$CH_3CH_2NH_2$	$CH_3CH=NH$	$CH_3C\equiv N$	
	CH_3CH_2Cl	CH_3CHCl_2	CH_3CCl_3	CCl_4

Low oxidation state ⟶ High oxidation state

FIGURE 8.2
Oxidation states for some functional groups

PRACTICE PROBLEM We saw in Section 4.8 that tertiary alcohols can be dehydrated on treatment with acid to yield alkenes. Is this reaction an oxidation, a reduction, or neither?

Solution Since oxygen and hydrogen are both removed from the alcohol at the same time, a dehydration reaction is neither an oxidation nor a reduction.

PROBLEM 8.7 Rank the following series of compounds in order of increasing oxidation state:

(a)

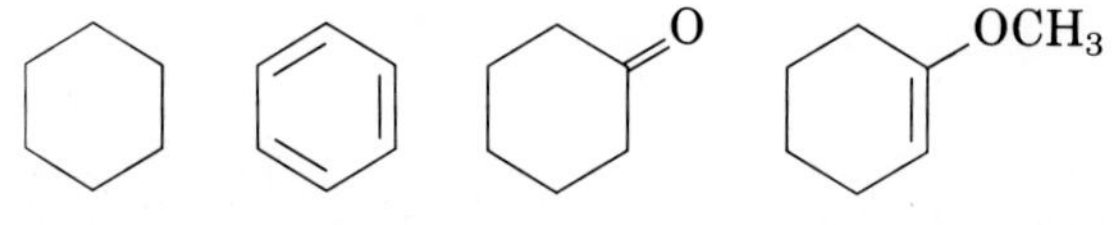

(b) CH_3CN, $CH_3CH_2NH_2$, $NH_2CH_2CH_2NH_2$

PROBLEM 8.8 Are these reactions oxidations, reductions, or neither?

(a) 3-Bromocyclohexene + Base $\longrightarrow$
(b) Benzene + $Cl_2/FeCl_3$ $\longrightarrow$
(c) 1-Bromobutane + Mg, then H^+ $\longrightarrow$
(d) Benzene + $CH_3Cl/AlCl_3$ $\longrightarrow$

Reduction of Aldehydes and Ketones

Aldehydes and ketones are easily reduced to yield alcohols:

$$R-CHO \xrightarrow{[H]} R-CH_2OH \qquad R_2C=O \xrightarrow{[H]} R_2CH-OH$$

An aldehyde   **A primary alcohol**   **A ketone**   **A secondary alcohol**

Although many reagents are available, sodium borohydride, NaBH₄, is usually chosen for ketone/aldehyde reductions because of its safety and ease of handling. Aldehydes are reduced by NaBH₄ to give primary alcohols, and ketones are reduced to give secondary alcohols. High yields are usually obtained, as the following examples indicate:

Butanal   **1-Butanol (85%)**

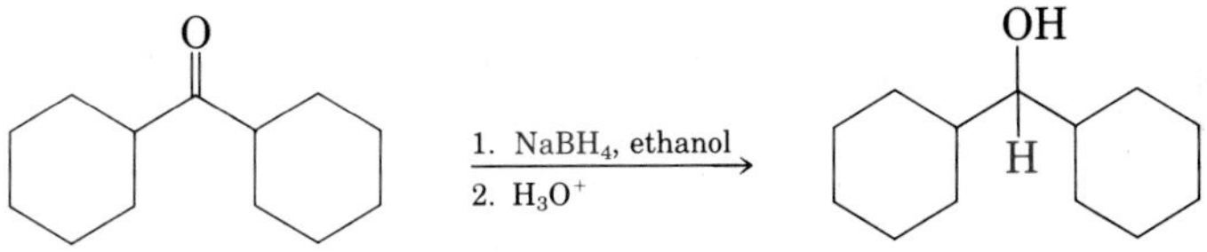

Dicyclohexyl ketone   **Dicyclohexylmethanol (88%)**

Lithium aluminum hydride, LiAlH₄, is another reducing agent that is sometimes used. Although far more powerful and reactive than NaBH₄, LiAlH₄ is also far more dangerous. It reacts violently with water and ethanol, decomposes explosively when heated above 120°C, and should be handled only by skilled persons.

Reduction of Esters and Carboxylic Acids

Esters and carboxylic acids are reduced to give primary alcohols:

$$R-CO_2CH_3 \quad \text{or} \quad R-CO_2H \xrightarrow{[H]} R-\overset{\displaystyle H}{\underset{\displaystyle H}{C}}-OH$$

Ester   **Carboxylic acid**

Since these reactions are more difficult than the corresponding reductions of ketones and aldehydes, $LiAlH_4$ rather than $NaBH_4$ is used. For example, $NaBH_4$ only slowly reduces esters and does not reduce carboxylic acids at all, but $LiAlH_4$ reduces all kinds of carbonyl groups rapidly and in high yield. Note that only *one* hydrogen is added to the carbonyl carbon atom during reductions of ketones and aldehydes, but that *two* hydrogens become bonded to the carbonyl carbon during ester and carboxylic acid reductions.

Aldehyde:

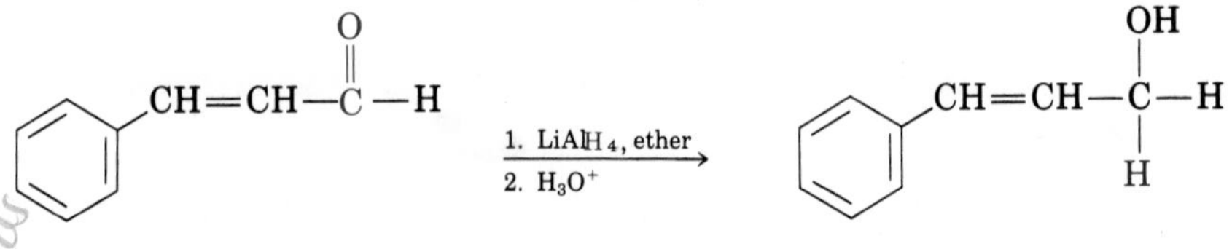

3-Phenylpropenal

$$\xrightarrow[\text{2. } H_3O^+]{\text{1. } LiAlH_4, \text{ ether}}$$

3-Phenyl-2-propen-1-ol (90%)

Ester:

$$CH_3CH_2CH\!=\!CHCOCH_2CH_3$$

Ethyl 2-pentenoate

$$\xrightarrow[\text{2. } H_3O^+]{\text{1. } LiAlH_4, \text{ ether}}$$

$$CH_3CH_2CH\!=\!CH\!-\!\overset{\displaystyle H}{\underset{\displaystyle H}{C}}\!-\!OH$$

2-Penten-1-ol (91%)

Acid:

$$CH_3(CH_2)_7CH\!=\!CH(CH_2)_7CO_2H$$

Oleic acid

$$\xrightarrow[\text{2. } H_3O^+]{\text{1. } LiAlH_4, \text{ THF}}$$

$$CH_3(CH_2)_7CH\!=\!CH(CH_2)_7\overset{\displaystyle H}{\underset{\displaystyle H}{C}}\!-\!OH$$

9-Octadecen-1-ol (87%)

PRACTICE PROBLEM   Predict the product of the following reaction:

$$CH_3CH_2CH_2\overset{\displaystyle O}{\overset{\displaystyle \|}{C}}CH_2CH_3 \xrightarrow{NaBH_4} \text{?}$$

Solution   We know that ketones are reduced by treatment with $NaBH_4$ to yield secondary alcohols. Thus, reduction of 3-hexanone should yield 3-hexanol.

$$CH_3CH_2CH_2\overset{\displaystyle O}{\overset{\displaystyle \|}{C}}CH_2CH_3 \xrightarrow{NaBH_4} CH_3CH_2CH_2\overset{\displaystyle OH}{\overset{\displaystyle |}{C}H}CH_2CH_3$$

3-Hexanone   **3-Hexanol**

NaBH₄ – for ketones & aldehydes

LiAlH₄ – for ketones, aldehydes, esters & carboxylic acids

PROBLEM 8.9   What reagent would you use to accomplish these reductions?

(a)

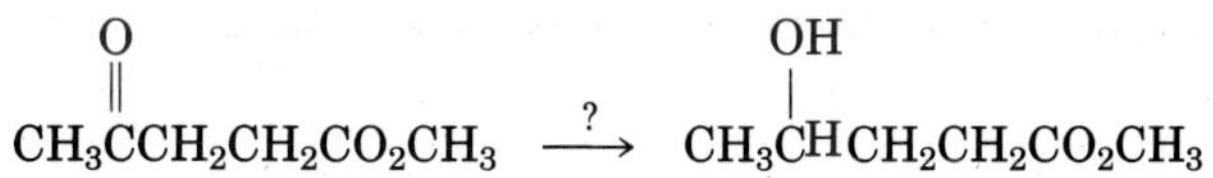

$$CH_3CCH_2CH_2CO_2CH_3 \xrightarrow{?} CH_3CHCH_2CH_2CO_2CH_3$$

(with O double bond on first carbon, OH on product)

(b)

$$CH_3CCH_2CH_2CO_2CH_3 \xrightarrow{?} CH_3CHCH_2CH_2CH_2OH$$

(with O double bond on first carbon, OH on product)

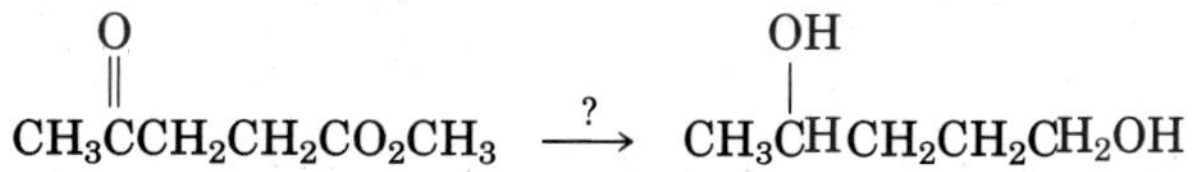

(c)

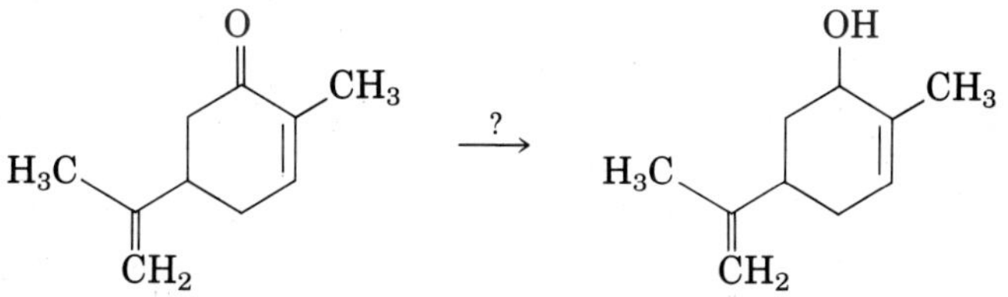

Carvone
(from spearmint oil)

PROBLEM 8.10   What carbonyl compounds give the following alcohols on reduction with LiAlH$_4$? Show all possibilities.

(a)

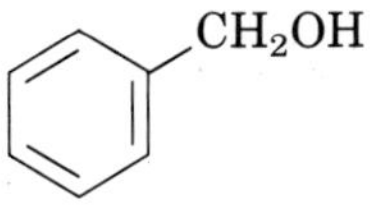

(b)

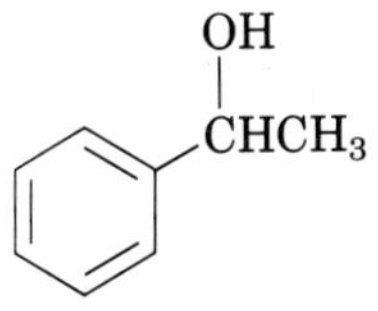

(c)

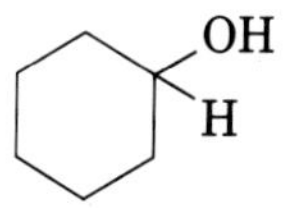

$C-O-C$

8.6   ETHERS FROM ALCOHOLS: THE WILLIAMSON ETHER SYNTHESIS

Metal alkoxides react with alkyl halides to yield ethers, a reaction known as the **Williamson ether synthesis**. Though discovered more than 100 years ago, the Williamson synthesis remains the best method for the preparation of both symmetrical and unsymmetrical ethers.

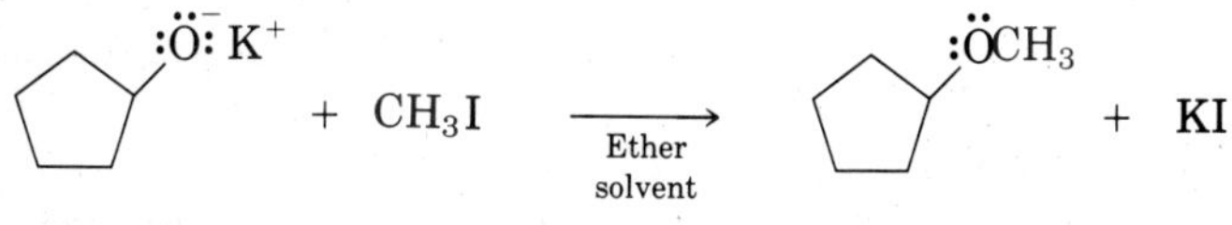

Potassium   **Iodomethane**   **Cyclopentyl methyl ether**
cyclopentoxide   **(74%)**

The alkoxide ion needed in the reaction is normally prepared by reaction of an alcohol with a strong base such as sodium hydride (Section 8.3):

$$R-\ddot{O}-H + NaH \longrightarrow R-\ddot{O}:^- Na^+ + H_2$$

Mechanistically, the Williamson synthesis occurs by S_N2 displacement of halide ion by the alkoxide ion nucleophile. The Williamson synthesis is subject to all the normal limitations of the S_N2 reaction discussed in Section 7.8. Thus, primary alkyl halides work best, since competitive E2 elimination of HX can occur with more hindered substrates. For this reason, unsymmetrical ethers should be prepared by reaction of the more hindered alkoxide partner with the less hindered halide partner, rather than vice versa. For example, tert-butyl methyl ether is best synthesized by reaction of tert-butoxide ion with iodomethane, rather than by reaction of methoxide ion with 2-chloro-2-methylpropane.

S_N2 reaction

tert-Butoxide ion   Iodomethane   tert-Butyl methyl ether

E2 reaction

Methoxide ion   2-Chloro-2-methylpropane   2-Methylpropene

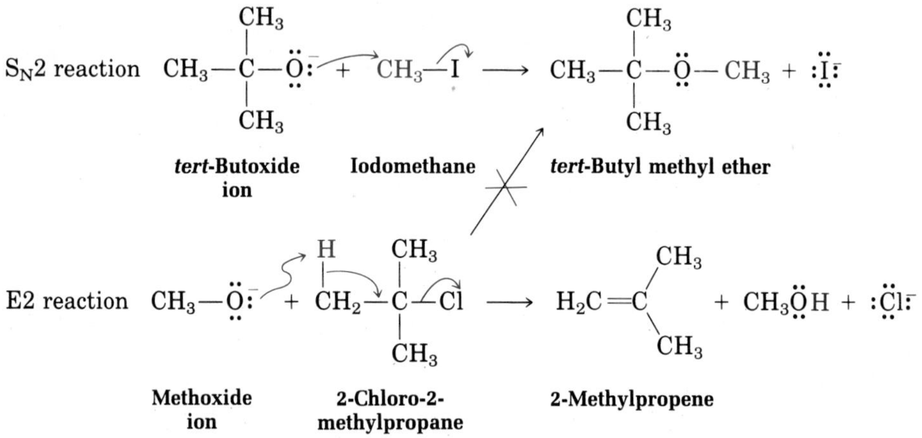

PROBLEM 8.11   Treatment of cyclohexanol with NaH gives an alkoxide ion that undergoes reaction with iodoethane to yield cyclohexyl ethyl ether. Write out the reaction showing all the steps.

PROBLEM 8.12   How would you prepare the following ethers?

(a) Methyl propyl ether   (b) Anisole (methyl phenyl ether)
(c) Benzyl isopropyl ether

PROBLEM 8.13   Rank the following compounds in order of their expected reactivity toward alkoxide ion nucleophiles in the Williamson ether synthesis: bromoethane, 2-bromopropane, chloroethane, 2-chloro-2-methylpropane.

8.7   REACTIONS OF ALCOHOLS

Dehydration

Alcohols can be dehydrated to give alkenes (Section 4.8). Tertiary alcohols lose water when treated with mineral acid under fairly mild conditions, but primary and secondary alcohols require higher temperature. The mechanism of this dehydration is simply an E1 reaction (Section 7.11), as shown in Figure 8.3. Strong acid protonates the alcohol oxygen, and the protonated intermediate spontaneously loses water via an E1 mechanism to generate a carbocation. Loss of a proton from a neighboring carbon atom then yields the alkene product.

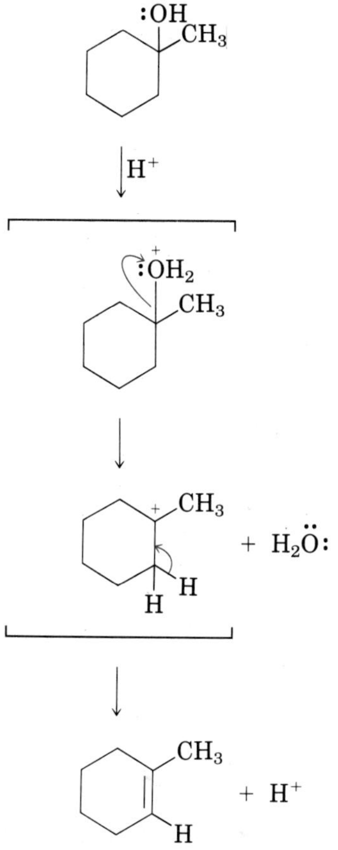

H$^+$ protonates the alcohol oxygen atom in an acid–base reaction.

Loss of water by an E1 mechanism yields a carbocation intermediate.

Loss of a proton from the carbocation gives the alkene product.

FIGURE 8.3
Mechanism of the acid-catalyzed dehydration of alcohols

Once the acid-catalyzed dehydration is recognized to be an E1 reaction, the reason why tertiary alcohols react fastest becomes clear. Tertiary substrates always react fastest in E1 reactions because they lead to highly stable tertiary carbocation intermediates.

Conversion into Alkyl Halides and Ethers

Alcohols can be converted into alkyl halides, as we saw earlier in Section 7.4, and into ethers, as we saw in Section 8.6. Tertiary alcohols are readily transformed into alkyl halides by an S$_N$1 mechanism on treatment with either HCl or HBr at 0°C. Primary and secondary alcohols are much more resistant to reaction with halogen acids, however, and are best converted into halides by treatment with either SOCl$_2$ or PBr$_3$.

Oxidation of Alcohols

The most important reaction of alcohols is their oxidation to yield carbonyl compounds. Primary alcohols yield aldehydes or carboxylic acids; secondary alcohols yield ketones; and tertiary alcohols do not react with most oxidizing agents except under the most vigorous conditions.

$$1° \quad R-CH_2OH \xrightarrow{[O]} R-CHO \xrightarrow{[O]} R-CO_2H$$

$$\text{An aldehyde} \qquad \text{A carboxylic acid}$$

$$2° \quad R-\underset{\underset{OH}{|}}{CH}-R' \xrightarrow{[O]} R-\underset{\underset{O}{\|}}{C}-R'$$

$$\text{A ketone}$$

$$3° \quad R-\underset{\underset{R'}{|}}{\overset{\overset{OH}{|}}{C}}-R'' \xrightarrow{[O]} \text{No reaction under most conditions}$$

Oxidation of primary and secondary alcohols can be accomplished by a large number of reagents, including $KMnO_4$, CrO_3, $Na_2Cr_2O_7$, and HNO_3. Which reagent is used in a specific case depends on such factors as cost, convenience, reaction yield, and alcohol sensitivity. For example, a large-scale oxidation of a simple alcohol such as cyclohexanol would probably best be done with a cheap oxidant such as nitric acid or potassium permanganate. On the other hand, a small-scale oxidation of a delicate and expensive polyfunctional alcohol would best be done with a mild and high-yielding reagent, regardless of cost.

Primary alcohols are oxidized either to aldehydes or to carboxylic acids, depending on the reagents chosen and on the conditions used. Probably the best method for preparing aldehydes from primary alcohols on a laboratory scale (as opposed to an industrial scale) is by use of pyridinium chlorochromate (PCC), $C_5H_6NCrO_3Cl$, in dichloromethane solvent.

$$CH_3(CH_2)_5\,CH_2OH \xrightarrow[CH_2Cl_2]{PCC} CH_3(CH_2)_5\,CHO$$

$$\textbf{1-Heptanol} \qquad\qquad \textbf{Heptanal (78\%)}$$

Most other oxidizing agents, such as chromium trioxide (CrO_3) in aqueous sulfuric acid (Jones' reagent), oxidize primary alcohols to carboxylic acids. Although aldehydes are involved as intermediates in these oxidations, they cannot usually be isolated because they are further oxidized too readily.

$$CH_3(CH_2)_8\,CH_2OH \xrightarrow[\text{Acetone}]{\text{Jones' reagent } (CrO_3,\ H_2SO_4,\ H_2O)} CH_3(CH_2)_8\,CO_2H$$

$$\textbf{1-Decanol} \qquad\qquad\qquad \textbf{Decanoic acid (93\%)}$$

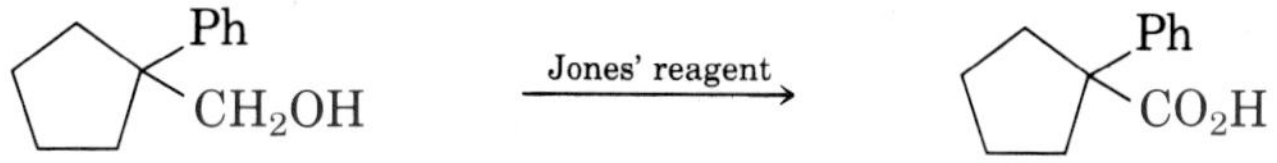

(1-Phenylcyclopentyl)methanol

1-Phenylcyclopentanecarboxylic acid
(85%)

Secondary alcohols are oxidized easily and in high yields to produce ketones. For large-scale oxidations, an inexpensive reagent such as sodium dichromate in aqueous acetic acid might be used:

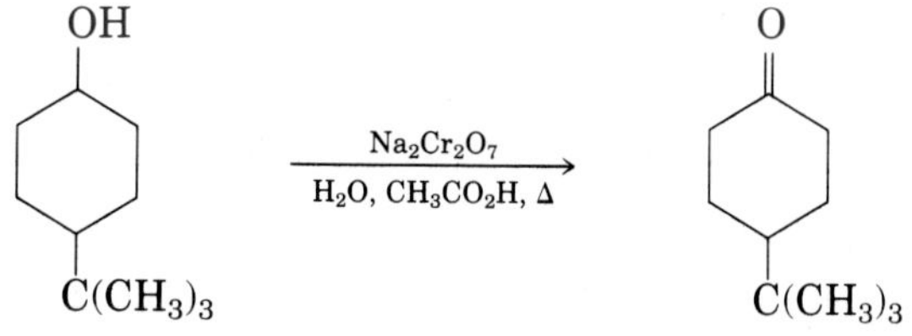

4-*tert*-Butylcyclohexanol

4-*tert*-Butylcyclohexanone
(91%)

For more sensitive alcohols, however, pyridinium chlorochromate is often used, since the reaction is milder and occurs at lower temperatures.

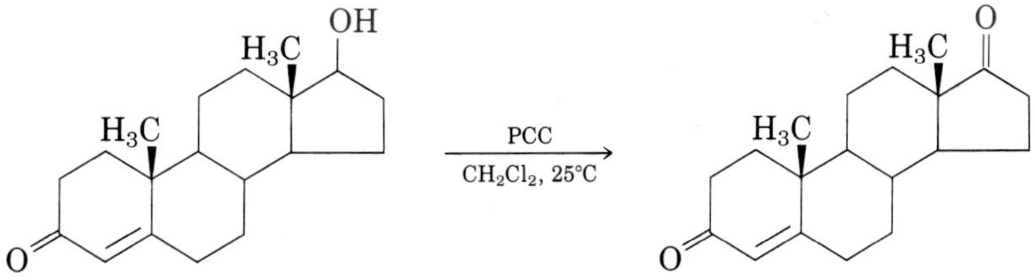

Testosterone
(steroid; male sex hormone)

4-Androstene-3,17-dione (82%)

PRACTICE PROBLEM What product would you expect from reaction of benzyl alcohol with Jones' reagent?

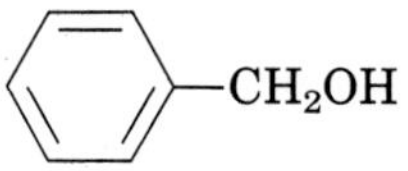

Benzyl alcohol

Solution We know that treatment of primary alcohols with Jones' reagent yields carboxylic acids. Thus, oxidation of benzyl alcohol should yield benzoic acid.

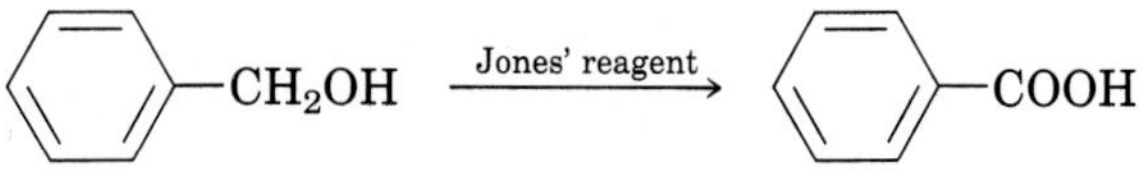

Benzyl alcohol

Benzoic acid

PROBLEM 8.14   What alcohols would give these products on oxidation?

(a)

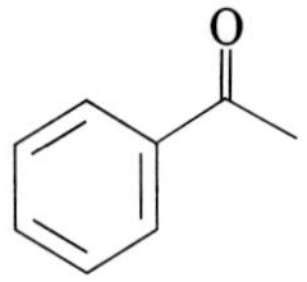

(b)

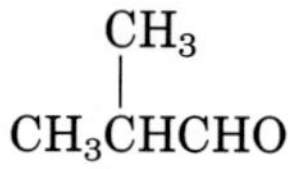

$$CH_3CHCHO$$
(with CH_3 substituent on the second carbon)

(c)

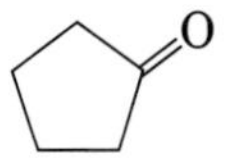

PROBLEM 8.15   What products would you expect to obtain from oxidation of these alcohols with Jones' reagent?

(a)   Cyclohexanol   (b)   1-Hexanol   (c)   2-Hexanol

PROBLEM 8.16   What products would you expect to obtain from oxidation of the alcohols shown in Problem 8.15 with pyridinium chlorochromate (PCC)?

8.8   REACTIONS OF PHENOLS

Alcohol-Like Reactions

Considerable differences exist between the chemistry of phenols and that of alcohols. Thus, phenols cannot be dehydrated by treatment with acid and cannot be converted into alkyl halides by treatment with HX. Phenols can, however, be converted into ethers by reaction with alkyl halides in the presence of base. Williamson ether synthesis with phenols occurs under relatively mild conditions since phenols are so much more acidic than alcohols and are therefore more easily converted into their anions.

Ether formation

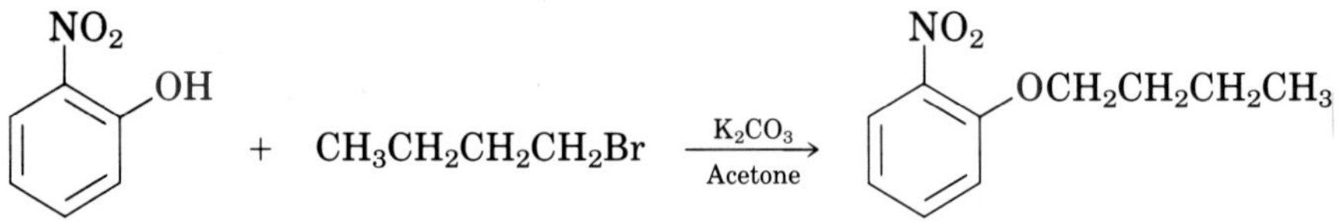

o-Nitrophenol   1-Bromobutane   Butyl *o*-nitrophenyl ether (80%)

Electrophilic Aromatic Substitution Reactions

The hydroxyl group is a strongly activating, ortho- and para-directing substituent in electrophilic aromatic substitution reactions (see Sections 5.11 and 5.12). As a result, phenols are highly reactive substrates for electrophilic halogenation, nitration, and sulfonation.

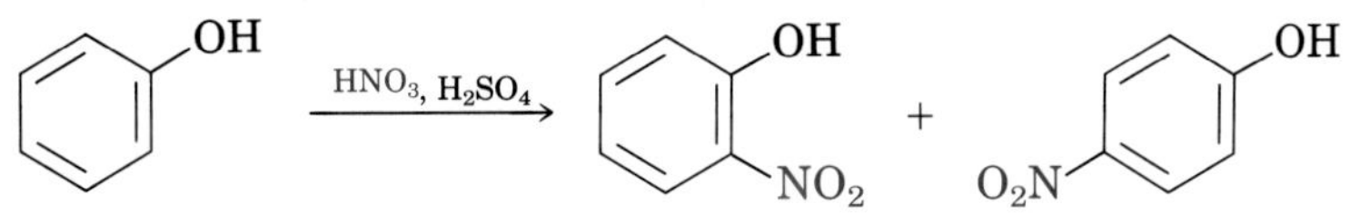

Phenol   o-Nitrophenol (50%)   p-Nitrophenol (50%)

Oxidation of Phenols: Quinones

Treatment of a phenol with a strong oxidizing agent yields a **quinone**—a cyclo-hexadienedione. Older procedures employed sodium dichromate as oxidant, but potassium nitrosodisulfonate [Fremy's salt, $(KSO_3)_2NO$] is now preferred. The reaction takes place under mild conditions through a radical mechanism to give good yield of the quinone product.

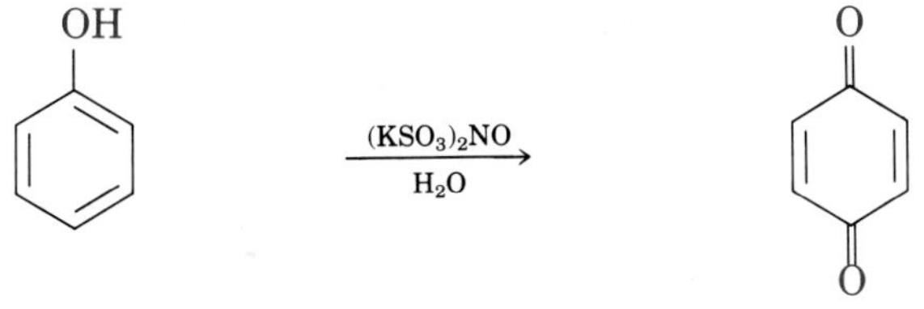

Phenol   Benzoquinone (79%)

Quinones are an interesting and valuable class of compounds because of their oxidation–reduction properties. They can easily be reduced to **hydroquinones** (*p*-dihydroxybenzenes) by $NaBH_4$ or $SnCl_2$, and hydroquinones can be easily oxidized back to quinones by Fremy's salt.

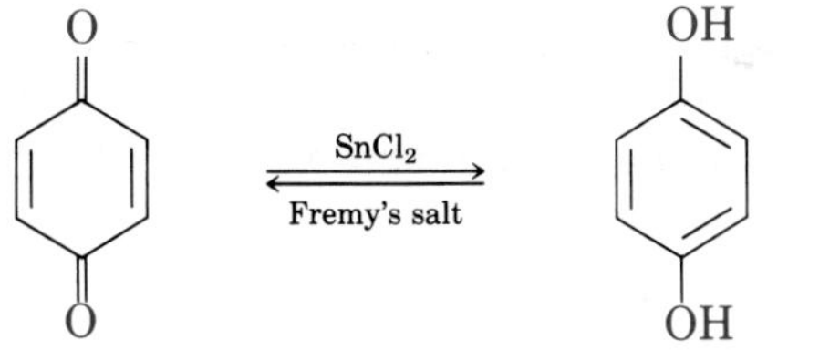

Benzoquinone   Hydroquinone

8.9 REACTIONS OF ETHERS: ACIDIC CLEAVAGE

Ethers are unusually stable to most reagents used in organic chemistry, a property that accounts for their wide use as inert reaction solvents. Halogens, mild acids, bases, and nucleophiles have no effect on most ethers. In fact, ethers undergo only one reaction of general use—cleavage by strong acids. Aqueous HI is the preferred reagent for cleaving ethers, although aqueous HBr can also be used. Hydrochloric acid does not react readily.

$$\text{CH}_3\text{CH}_2\text{OCH(CH}_3)_2 \xrightarrow[\text{Reflux}]{\text{HI, H}_2\text{O}} \text{CH}_3\text{CH}_2\text{I} + \text{(CH}_3)_2\text{CHOH}$$

Ethyl isopropyl ether   **Iodoethane**   **Isopropyl alcohol**

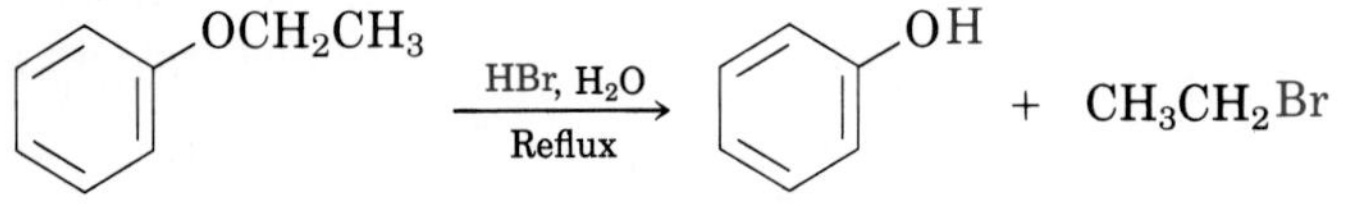

Ethyl phenyl ether   **Phenol**   **Bromoethane**

Acidic ether cleavages are typical nucleophilic substitution reactions. They take place through either S_N1 or S_N2 pathways, depending on the structure of the ether. Primary and secondary alkyl ethers react by an S_N2 pathway, in which nucleophilic iodide ion or bromide ion attacks the protonated ether at the less highly substituted site. This usually results in a selective cleavage into a single alcohol and a single alkyl halide, rather than a mixture of products. The ether oxygen atom stays with the more hindered alkyl group, and the halide attacks the less hindered group. For example, butyl isopropyl ether yields exclusively iso-propyl alcohol and 1-iodobutane on cleavage by HI, since nucleophilic attack by iodide ion occurs at the less hindered primary site rather than at the more hindered secondary site.

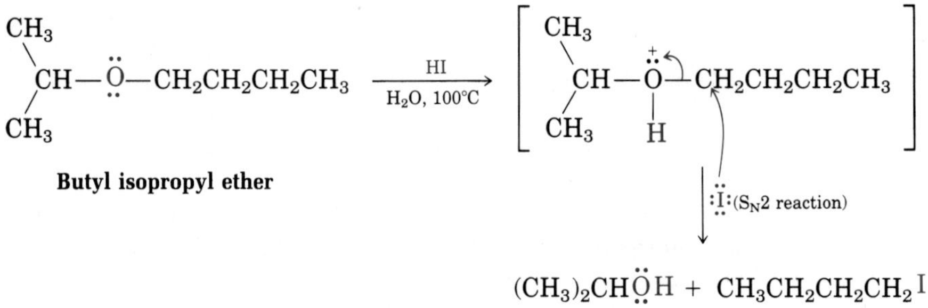

Butyl isopropyl ether

$$\text{(CH}_3)_2\text{CH}\ddot{\text{O}}\text{H} + \text{CH}_3\text{CH}_2\text{CH}_2\text{CH}_2\text{I}$$

Isopropyl alcohol   **1-Iodobutane**

Tertiary ethers tend to cleave by an S_N1 or E1 mechanism, since they can produce such stable intermediate carbocations. These reactions are often fast and take place at room temperature or below. Trifluoroacetic acid seems to be best for these reactions, as in the following example:

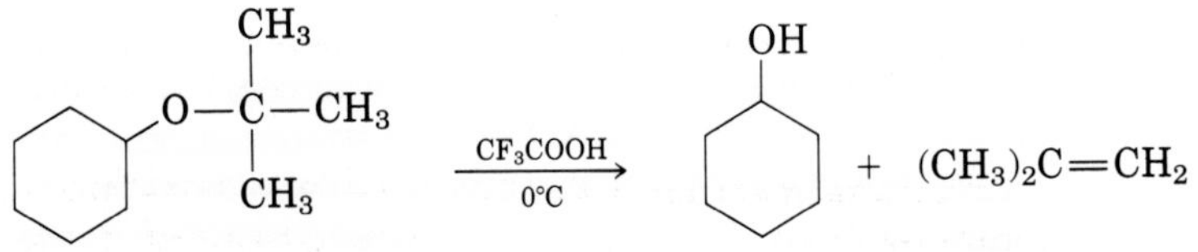

***tert*-Butyl cyclohexyl ether**   **Cyclohexanol**   **2-Methylpropene**
                                              (90%)

PROBLEM 8.17 What products would you expect from reaction of the following ethers with HI?

(a) $CH_3CH_2OCH_2CH_3$ (b) Cyclohexyl ethyl ether   (c) $(CH_3)_3COCH_2CH_3$

PROBLEM 8.18 Write out the detailed mechanism for the trifluoroacetic acid-catalyzed cleavage of *tert*-butyl cyclohexyl ether to yield cyclohexanol and 2-methylpropene. What kind of reaction is occurring?

PROBLEM 8.19 Which would you expect to be faster, reaction of HI with diethyl ether or with dimethyl ether? Explain.

8.10 CYCLIC ETHERS: EPOXIDES

For the most part, cyclic ethers behave like acyclic ethers. The chemistry of the ether functional group is the same, whether it is in an open chain or in a ring. For example, common cyclic ethers such as tetrahydrofuran and dioxane are often used as solvents because of their inertness, yet they can be cleaved by strong acids.

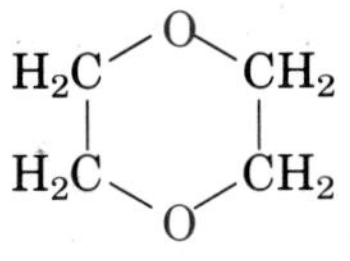

1,4-Dioxane 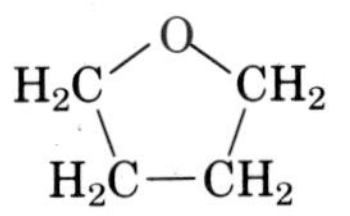   **Tetrahydrofuran**

The one group of cyclic ethers that behaves differently are the **three-membered-ring compounds called epoxides or oxiranes**. The strain of the three-membered ether ring makes epoxides highly reactive (recall the reactivity of cyclopropane, Section 2.12).

Epoxides are normally prepared by treatment of an alkene with a peroxyacid, RCO_3H. *m*-Chloroperoxybenzoic acid is the preferred reagent, since it is more stable and more easily handled than other peroxyacids.

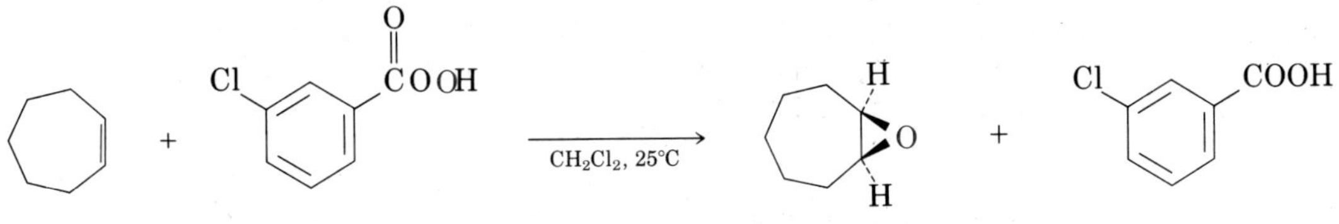

Cycloheptene   **m-Chloroperoxybenzoic acid**   **1,2-Epoxycycloheptane (78%)**
(cycloheptene epoxide)

Another method for the synthesis of epoxides is through the use of **halohydrins**, compounds that have a halogen and a hydroxyl group on neighboring carbon atoms. When a halohydrin is treated with base, HX is eliminated and an epoxide is produced. Note that this reaction is actually an *intramolecular* Williamson ether synthesis (*intramolecular* means within the same molecule). The nucleophilic alkoxide ion and the electrophilic alkyl halide are within the *same* molecule, rather than in different molecules.

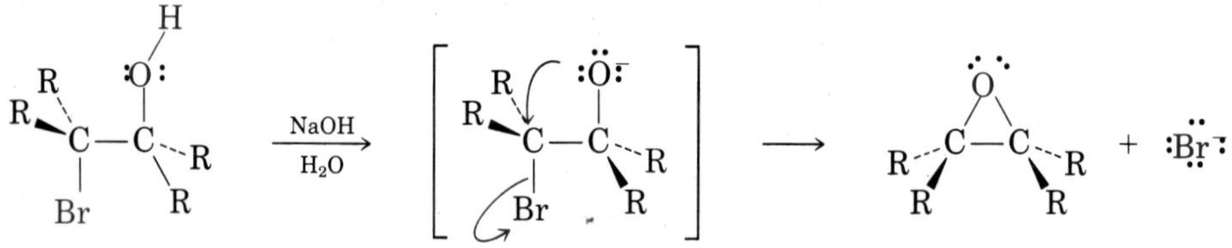

A bromohydrin   Intramolecular substitution   Epoxide
                   (within the same molecule)

Recall the following:

$$CH_3\ddot{\underset{..}{O}}: \;\; + \;\; CH_3\!-\!\overset{..}{\underset{..}{Br}} \;\longrightarrow\; CH_3\ddot{\underset{..}{O}}\!-\!CH_3 \;+\; :\overset{..}{\underset{..}{Br}}:^-$$

Intermolecular substitution (between different molecules)

The halohydrins necessary for this epoxide synthesis are prepared by electrophilic addition of HO—Br or HO—Cl to alkenes. Treatment of an alkene with Cl_2 or Br_2 in water solvent generates a cationic intermediate that reacts with water to produce a halohydrin.

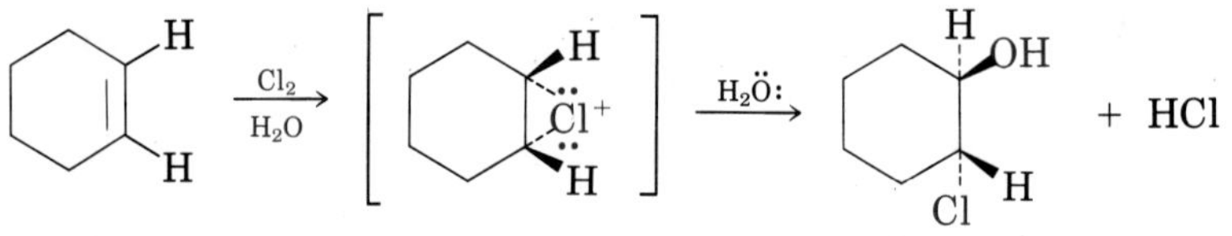

Cyclohexene   2-Chlorocyclohexanol

PRACTICE PROBLEM What product would you expect to obtain if 2,3-dimethyl-2-butene were treated first with Br_2 in water and then with NaOH?

Solution Reaction of 2,3-dimethyl-2-butene with bromine and water should yield a bromohydrin that will be converted into 2,3-dimethyl-2,3-epoxybutane on subsequent base treatment:

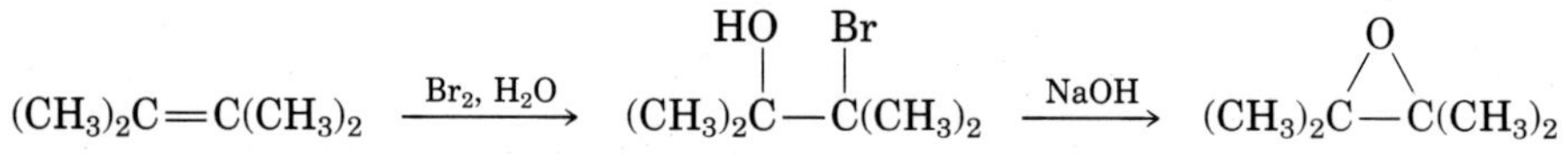

PROBLEM 8.20 What product would you expect from reaction of *cis*-2-butene with *m*-chloroperoxybenzoic acid? Be sure to indicate stereochemistry.

PROBLEM 8.21 Reaction of *trans*-2-butene with *m*-chloroperoxybenzoic acid yields an epoxide different from that obtained from reaction of the cis isomer (Problem 8.20). How can you account for this?

8.11 RING-OPENING REACTIONS OF EPOXIDES

Epoxide rings can be opened by treatment with acid in much the same way that other ethers are cleaved. The major difference is that epoxides react under much milder conditions because of ring strain. Dilute aqueous mineral acid at room temperature is sufficient to cause the hydrolysis of epoxides to 1,2-diols (also called *vicinal glycols*). Two million tons of ethylene glycol, most of it used as automobile antifreeze, are produced each year by acid-catalyzed hydration of ethylene oxide.

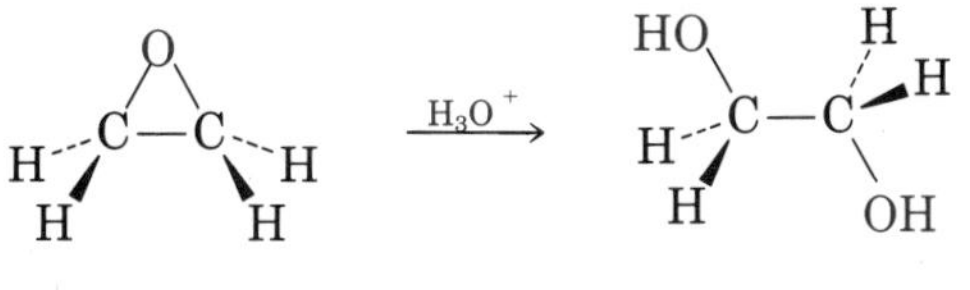

Ethylene oxide   **Ethylene glycol**
                            (1,2-ethanediol)

Acid-induced epoxide ring opening takes place by S$_N$2 attack of a nucleophile on the protonated epoxide, in a manner analogous to the final step of alkene bromination, where a three-membered-ring bromonium ion is opened by nucleophilic attack (Section 4.4). When a cycloalkane epoxide is opened by aqueous acid, a *trans*-1,2-diol results (just as a *trans*-1,2-dibromide results from alkene bromination).

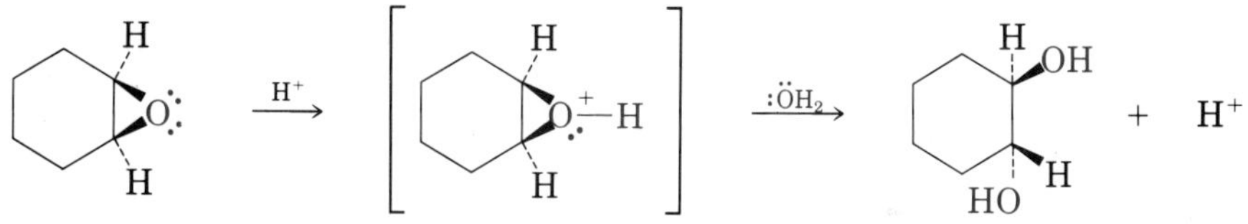

1,2-Epoxycyclohexane   ***trans*-1,2-Cyclohexanediol**
                                            (86%)

Recall the following reaction:

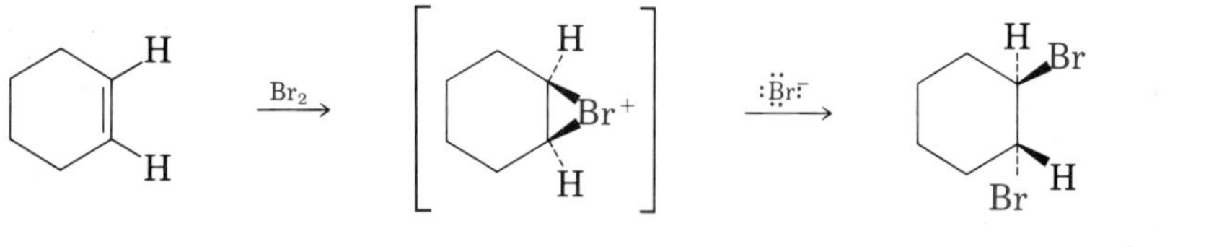

Cyclohexene   ***trans*-1,2-Dibromocyclohexane**

Epoxides can also be opened by halogen acids, HX, in the same way that other ethers can be cleaved (Section 8.9). The product is a trans halohydrin:

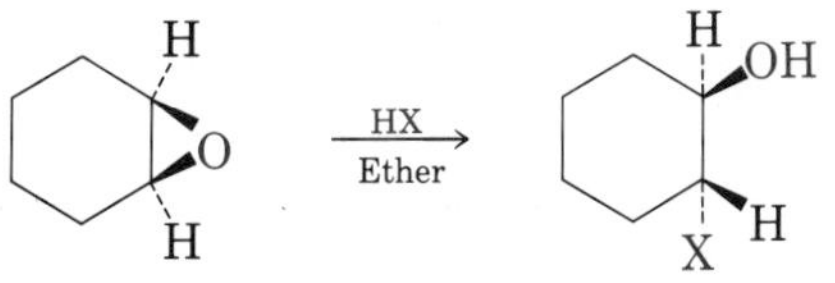

A trans 2-halocyclohexanol

where X = F, Br, Cl, or I.

Unlike other ethers, epoxides can also be cleaved by good nucleophiles. Although an ether oxygen is normally a very poor leaving group in an S_N2 reaction (Section 7.8), the reactivity of the three-membered ring is sufficient to allow epoxides to react with hydroxide ion and with alkoxide ions.

S$_N$2 reaction

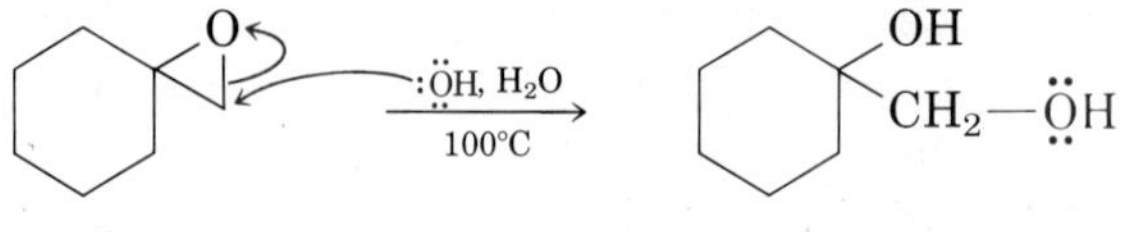

Methylenecyclohexane oxide   **1-Hydroxymethylcyclohexanol (70%)**

Nucleophilic epoxide opening is also involved in the cancer-causing effects of polycyclic aromatic hydrocarbons (PAH's) present in chimney soot and cigarette smoke. As we saw in Interlude D, benzpyrene, one of the best studied PAH's, is converted by metabolic oxidation into a diol epoxide. In the body, the epoxide ring reacts by an S_N2 type ring opening with an amino group in cellular DNA to give an altered DNA that is covalently bound to the PAH. With its DNA thus altered, the cell is unable to reproduce normally.

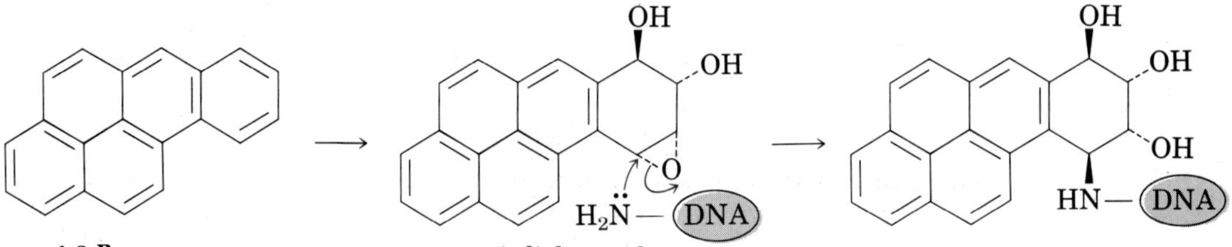

1,2-Benzpyrene   **A diol epoxide**

Even as simple a molecule as benzene itself is thought to cause certain types of cancer, presumably by a mechanism similar to that of benzpyrene.

PROBLEM 8.22 Show all the steps involved in the acidic hydrolysis of *cis*-2,3-epoxybutane to yield 2,3-butanediol. What is the stereochemistry of the product if the ring opening takes place by normal backside S_N2 attack?

PROBLEM 8.23 Answer Problem 8.22 for the acidic hydrolysis of *trans*-2,3-epoxybutane. Is the same product formed?

PROBLEM 8.24 Studies have indicated that base-induced ring opening of epoxides usually occurs by attack at the less hindered epoxide carbon atom. What product would you expect to obtain from reaction of methoxide ion with 1,2-epoxypropane? Explain why this result can be taken as evidence that the ring-opening reaction occurs by an S_N2 mechanism.

8.12 THIOLS

Sulfur is the element just below oxygen in the periodic table, and many oxygen-containing organic compounds have sulfur analogs. For example, **thiols, R—SH,** are sulfur analogs of alcohols. They are named in the same way as alcohols, with the suffix *-thiol* used in place of *-ol*. The —SH group itself is referred to as a **mercapto** group.

$$CH_3CH_2SH$$

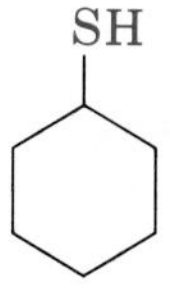

SH

COOH

SH

Ethanethiol   **Cyclohexanethiol** 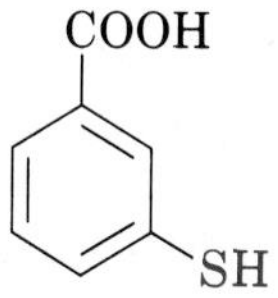   ***m*-Mercaptobenzoic acid**

The outstanding characteristic of thiols is their appalling odor. For example, skunk scent is caused primarily by the simple thiols 3-methyl-1-butanethiol and 2-butene-1-thiol.

Thiols are usually prepared from the corresponding alkyl halide by S_N2 displacement with a sulfur nucleophile such as hydrosulfide anion, $HS:^-$.

$$CH_3(CH_2)_6CH_2Br + Na^+:\ddot{S}H^- \longrightarrow CH_3(CH_2)_6CH_2—\ddot{S}H + NaBr$$

1-Bromooctane **Sodium hydrosulfide**   **1-Octanethiol**

Thiols can be oxidized by mild reagents such as bromine to yield disulfides, R—S—S—R. The reaction is easily reversed, and disulfides can be reduced back to thiols by treatment with zinc metal and acetic acid.

$$2\,R—SH \underset{Zn,\ H^+}{\overset{Br_2}{\rightleftharpoons}} R—S—S—R + 2\,HBr$$

A thiol   **A disulfide**

We will see in Section 15.5 that the thiol–disulfide interconversion is extremely important in biochemistry, where disulfide bridges form the cross-links between protein chains that help stabilize the three-dimensional conformations of proteins.

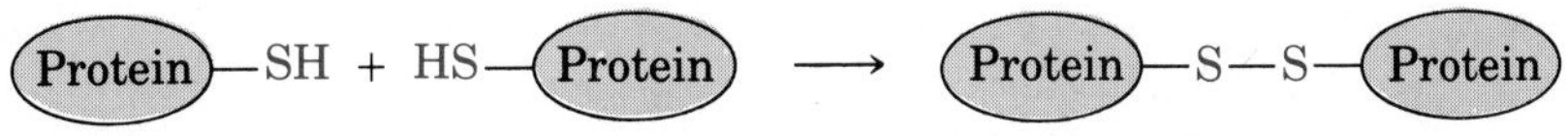

$$\boxed{Protein}—SH + HS—\boxed{Protein} \longrightarrow \boxed{Protein}—S—S—\boxed{Protein}$$

A cross-linked protein

PROBLEM 8.25 Name the following thiols by IUPAC rules:

(a) $CH_3CH_2CH(SH)CH_3$ (b) $(CH_3)_3CCH_2CH(SH)CH_2CH(CH_3)_2$

(c)

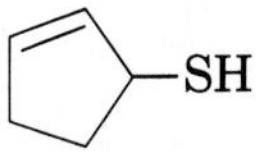

⬠—SH

PROBLEM 8.26 2-Butene-1-thiol is one component of skunk spray. How would you synthesize this substance from 2-buten-1-ol? From methyl 2-butenoate, $CH_3CH=CHCOOCH_3$? More than one step will be required in each instance.

8.13 SULFIDES

Sulfides, R—S—R, are sulfur analogs of ethers in the same sense that thiols are sulfur analogs of alcohols. Sulfides are named in the same way as ethers, with *sulfide* used in place of *ether* for simple compounds, and with *alkylthio* used in place of *alkoxy* for more complex substances.

$$CH_3—S—CH_3$$

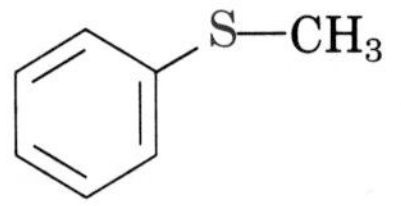

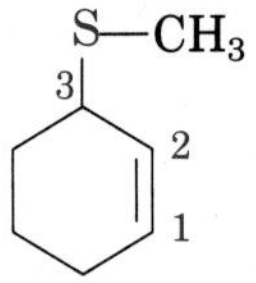

Dimethyl sulfide   **Methyl phenyl sulfide**   **3-(Methylthio)cyclohexene**

Sulfides are best prepared by treatment of a primary or secondary alkyl halide with a thiolate ion, RS^-. Reaction occurs by an S_N2 mechanism, analogous to the Williamson ether synthesis (Section 8.6). Thiolate anions are among the best nucleophiles known, and product yields are usually high in these sulfide-forming reactions.

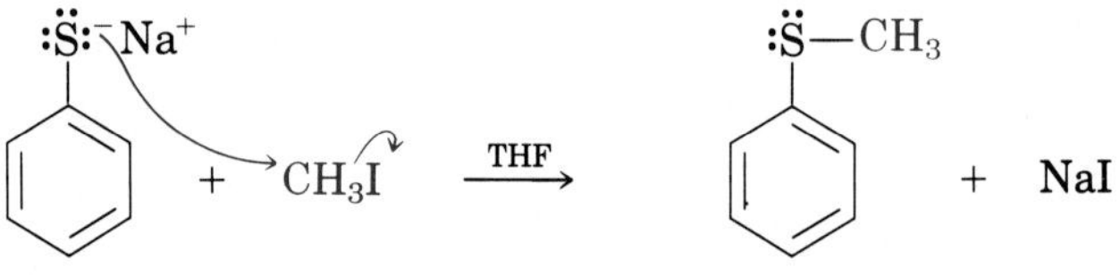

Sodium benzenethiolate   **Methyl phenyl sulfide (96%)**

Although sulfides and ethers are similar in many respects, sulfides are generally more reactive. For example, unlike dialkyl ethers, dialkyl sulfides are good nucleophiles that react rapidly with primary alkyl halides by an S_N2 mechanism. The products of such reactions are **trialkylsulfonium salts, R_3S^+.**

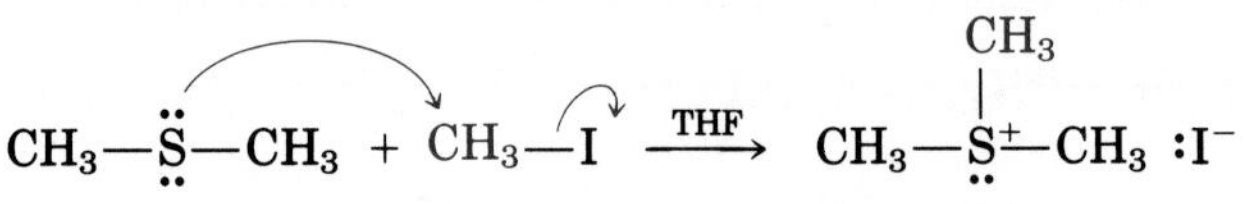

$$CH_3—\overset{..}{\underset{..}{S}}—CH_3 + CH_3—I \xrightarrow{THF} CH_3—\overset{CH_3}{\underset{..}{\overset{|}{S^+}}}—CH_3 \ :I^-$$

Dimethyl sulfide   Iodomethane   Trimethylsulfonium iodide

As we saw in Interlude F, nature makes extensive use of the trialkylsulfonium salt *S*-adenosylmethionine as a biological methylating agent.

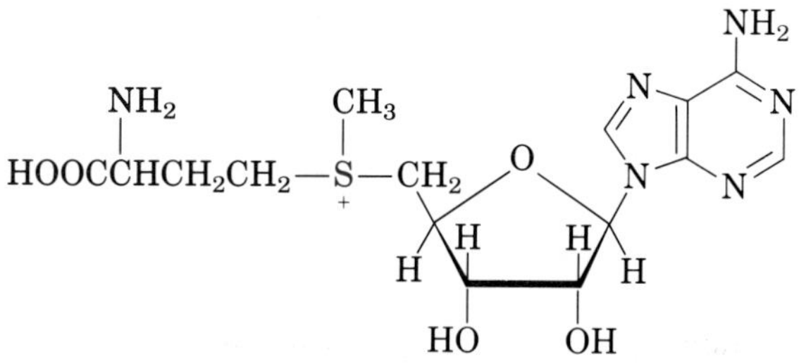

S-Adenosylmethionine (a sulfonium salt)

PROBLEM 8.27 Name the following compounds by IUPAC rules:

(a) $CH_3CH_2SCH_3$

(b) $(CH_3)_3CSCH_2CH_3$

(c)

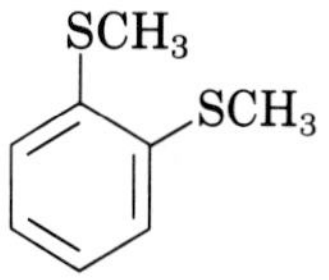

ADDITIONAL PROBLEMS

PROBLEM 8.28 Draw structures corresponding to these IUPAC names:

(a) Ethyl isopropyl ether
(b) 3,4-Dimethoxybenzoic acid
(c) 2-Methyl-2,5-heptanediol
(d) *trans*-3-Ethylcyclohexanol
(e) 4-(2-Propenyl)-2-methoxyphenol (Eugenol, from oil of cloves)

PROBLEM 8.29 Name the following compounds according to IUPAC rules:

(a)

$HOCH_2CH_2CHCH_2OH$ (with CH_3 group)

(b) $CH_3CH(OH)CHCH_2CH_3$ (with $CH_2CH_2CH_3$ group)

(c)

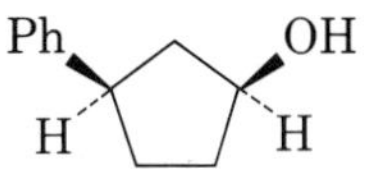

(d) $(CH_3)_2CHCCH_2CH_2CH_3$ (with SH and CH_3 groups)

PROBLEM 8.30 Draw and name the eight isomeric alcohols having the formula $C_5H_{12}O$.

PROBLEM 8.31 Which of the eight alcohols you identified in Problem 8.30 would react with aqueous CrO_3? Show the products you would expect from each reaction.

PROBLEM 8.32 Predict the likely products of these cleavage reactions:

(a) $CH_3CH_2OCH_2CH_3 \xrightarrow{HI, H_2O}$

(b) $(CH_3)_3CCH_2OCH_3 \xrightarrow{HI, H_2O}$

PROBLEM 8.33   How would you prepare the following compounds from 2-phenylethanol?

(a)   Benzoic acid   (b)   Ethylbenzene
(c)   2-Bromo-1-phenylethane   (d)   Phenylacetic acid, $C_6H_5CH_2COOH$
(e)   Phenylacetaldehyde, $C_6H_5CH_2CHO$

PROBLEM 8.34   When 4-chloro-1-butanol is treated with a strong base such as sodium hydride, NaH, tetrahydrofuran is produced. Suggest a mechanism for this reaction.

$$ClCH_2CH_2CH_2CH_2OH \quad \xrightarrow[\text{Ether}]{\text{NaH}} \quad \text{\Large{\llap{$\bigcirc$}O}} \quad + \quad H_2 \quad + \quad NaCl$$

PROBLEM 8.35   Starting from benzene, how could you prepare benzyl phenyl ether, $C_6H_5OCH_2C_6H_5$? More than one step will be required.

PROBLEM 8.36   Which do you think would undergo electrophilic aromatic substitution more readily, phenol or phenoxide ion? Explain.

PROBLEM 8.37   Since all hamsters look pretty much alike, pairing and mating is governed by chemical means of communication. Investigations have shown that dimethyl disulfide, CH_3SSCH_3, is secreted by female hamsters as a sex attractant for males. How would you synthesize dimethyl disulfide in the laboratory if you wanted to trick your hamster?

PROBLEM 8.38 p-Nitrophenol (pK_a = 7.15) is much more acidic than phenol (pK_a = 9.89). Draw as many resonance structures as you can for the p-nitrophenoxide anion and account for the observed increase in acidity.

PROBLEM 8.39   When 2-methyl-2,5-pentanediol is treated with sulfuric acid, dehydration occurs to yield 2,2-dimethyltetrahydrofuran. Suggest a mechanism for this reaction.

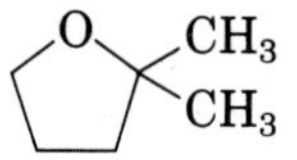

2,2-Dimethyltetrahydrofuran

PROBLEM 8.40   The herbicide 2,4,5-T (2,4,5-trichlorophenoxyacetic acid) can be prepared by heating a mixture of 2,4,5-trichlorophenol and $ClCH_2COOH$ with NaOH. Show the structure of 2,4,5-T and explain how it is formed.

PROBLEM 8.41   Starting from benzene, how would you prepare the 2,4,5-trichlorophenol needed for manufacture of 2,4,5-T (Problem 8.40)?

PROBLEM 8.42   Give the structures of the major products you would expect to obtain from reaction of phenol with these reagents:

(a) Br_2 (1 mol)   (b) Br_2 (3 mol)
(c)   NaOH, then CH_3I (d) $(KSO_3)_2NO$

PROBLEM 8.43   What products would you expect to obtain from reaction of 1-butanol with these reagents?

(a) PBr_3 (b) CrO_3, H_2O, H_2SO_4 (c)   Na
(d)   Pyridinium chlorochromate

PROBLEM 8.44 What products would you expect to obtain from reaction of 1-methylcyclohexanol with these reagents?

(a) HBr
(b) H_2SO_4
(c) CrO_3
(d) NaH
(e) product of (d), then CH_3I

PROBLEM 8.45 *tert*-Butyl ethers can be prepared by the reaction of an alcohol with 2-methylpropene in the presence of an acid catalyst. Propose a mechanism for this reaction.

PROBLEM 8.46 How would you prepare these ethers?

(a)

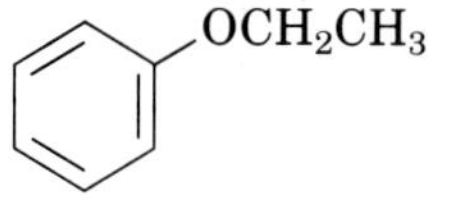

(b)

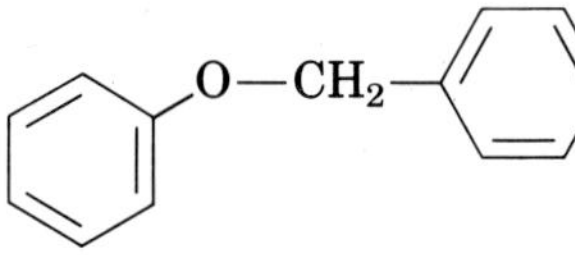

(c) 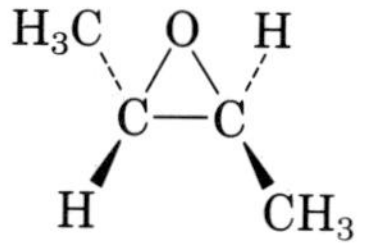 H₃C O H

PROBLEM 8.47 What product would you expect from reaction of tetrahydrofuran (THF) with hot aqueous HI?

Tetrahydrofuran

PROBLEM 8.48 Lithium aluminum hydride, $LiAlH_4$, reacts with epoxides to yield alcohols. Propose a mechanism for this reaction.

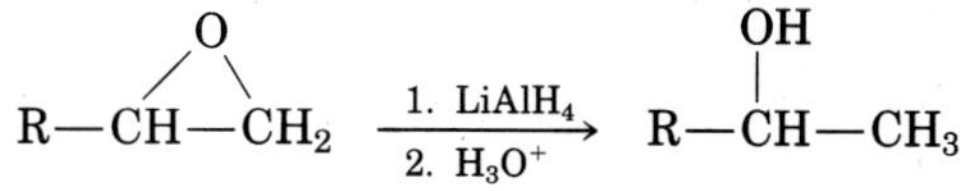

PROBLEM 8.49 What reagents would you use to carry out the following transformations?

(a)

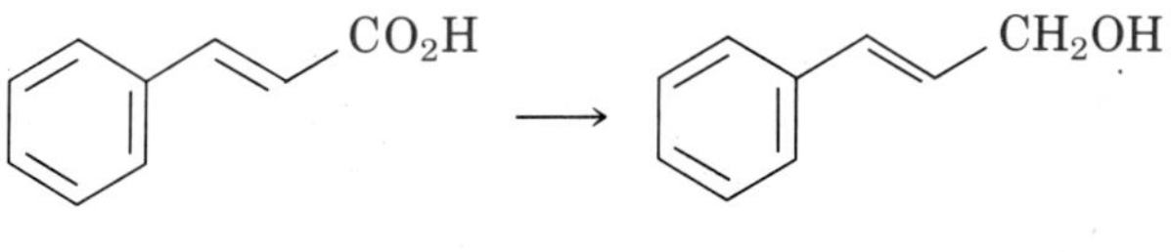

(b)

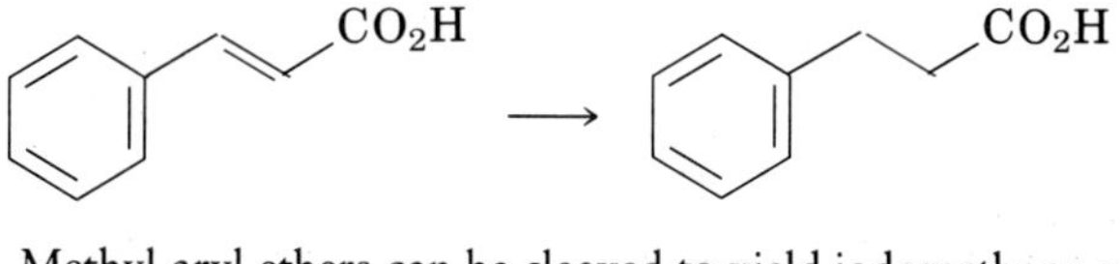

PROBLEM 8.50 Methyl aryl ethers can be cleaved to yield iodomethane and lithium phenoxide upon heating with LiI. Propose a mechanism for this reaction.

PROBLEM 8.51 The **Zeisel method**, a procedure for determining the number of methoxyl groups (CH_3O—) in a compound, involves heating a weighed amount of compound with HI. Ether cleavage occurs, and the iodomethane formed is distilled off and passed into a solution of $AgNO_3$. The silver iodide that precipitates is then weighed and the percentage of methoxy groups in the sample is thereby determined. For example, 1.06 g of vanillin, the material responsible for the characteristic odor of vanilla, yields 1.60 g AgI. If vanillin has a molecular weight of 152, how many methoxyls does it contain?

Industrial Uses of Simple Alcohols and Phenols

Methanol and ethanol are two of the most important of all industrial organic chemicals; both are manufactured on a vast scale for a variety of uses. Prior to the development of the modern chemical industry, methanol was prepared by heating wood in the absence of air and thus came to be called *wood alcohol*. Now, however, approximately 1.2 billion gallons of methanol are manufactured each year in the United States by catalytic reduction of carbon monoxide with hydrogen gas:

$$CO + 2 H_2 \xrightarrow[\text{Zinc oxide/chromia}]{400°C} CH_3OH$$

Methanol is toxic to humans, causing blindness in low doses and death in larger amounts. Industrially, it is used both as a solvent and as a starting material for conversion into formaldehyde, CH_2O, and acetic acid, CH_3COOH.

Ethanol is one of the oldest known pure organic chemicals, its production by fermentation of grains and sugars going back at least as far as the ancient Greeks. Fermentation is carried out by adding yeast to an aqueous sugar solution, where enzymes break down carbohydrates into ethanol and CO_2:

$$C_6H_{12}O_6 \xrightarrow{\text{Yeast}} 2 CH_3CH_2OH + 2 CO_2$$

A carbohydrate

Nearly 300 million gallons of ethanol are produced each year in the United States for use as a solvent or starting material. Only about 5% of this industrial ethanol currently comes from fermentation, however; most is obtained by high-temperature, acid-catalyzed hydration of ethylene:

$$H_2C=CH_2 + H_2O \xrightarrow{H_2SO_4} CH_3CH_2OH$$

Ethylene

Phenol and several of its substituted analogs are also used industrially. Historically, the outbreak of World War I provided the stimulus for industrial preparation of large amounts of phenol, which was needed as starting material for synthesis of picric acid (2,4,6-trinitrophenol), an explosive. Today, approximately 1.5 million tons of phenol per year are manufactured for use in such products as Bakelite resin and adhesives for binding plywood.

In addition to its use in resins and adhesives, phenol serves as starting material for the synthesis of chlorinated phenols and of the food preservative BHT (butylated hydroxytoluene). Thus, pentachlorophenol (Penta), a widely used wood preservative, is prepared by reaction of phenol with excess chlorine. Similarly, 2,4-dichlorophenol is used to prepare the herbicide 2,4-dichlorophenoxyacetic acid (2,4-D), and 2,4,5-trichlorophenol is used to prepare the antiseptic agent hexachlorophene.

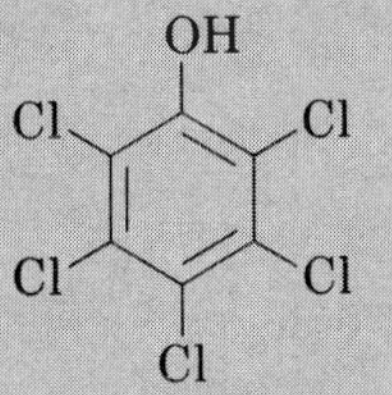

**Pentachlorophenol
(wood preservative)** 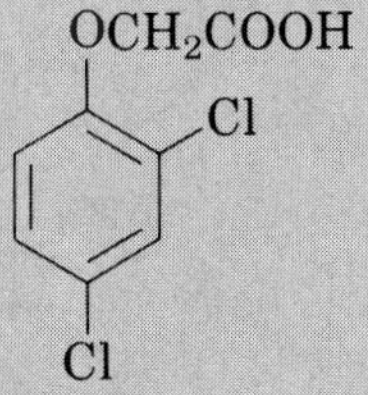   **2,4-Dichlorophenoxyacetic acid,
2,4-D (herbicide)** 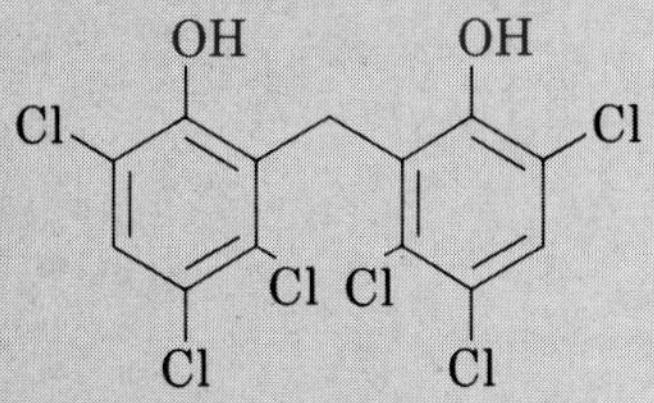   **Hexachlorophene
(antiseptic)**

Ubiquinones: Naturally Occurring Oxidants

Oxidations are usually carried out in the laboratory with powerful but unselective reagents such as sodium dichromate and potassium permanganate. Oxidations are also carried out in the cells of living organisms, but with far more delicacy and by far more selective "reagents." Among the most important biochemical oxidants are a series of compounds called **ubiquinones**, which mediate the electron-transfer processes involved in energy production. Ubiquinones, also called *coenzymes Q*, are components of the cells of all aerobic organisms, from the simplest bacterium to human. They are so named because of their ubiquitous occurrence in nature.

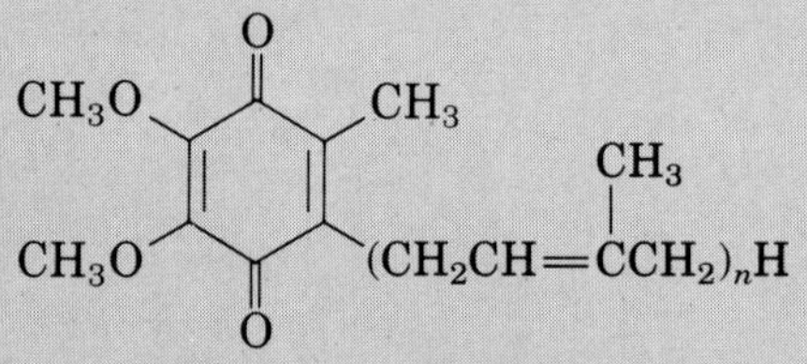

Ubiquinones ($n = 1-10$)

Ubiquinones are able to act as cellular oxidants because they readily accept electrons from mild reducing agents to yield hydroquinones, and hydroquinones in turn react with oxidants to regenerate quinones.

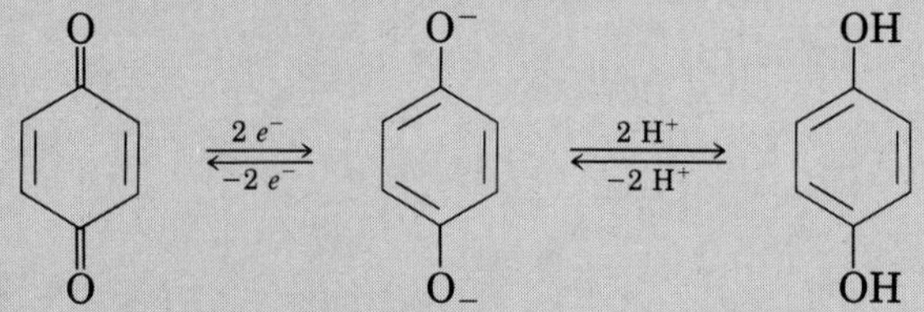

A quinone   **A dianion**   **A hydroquinone**

Ubiquinones function within the mitochondria of cells as mobile electron carriers (oxidizing agents) to mediate the respiration process whereby electrons are transported from the biological reducing agent NADH (reduced form of nicotinamide adenine dinucleotide, NAD) to molecular oxygen. Although a complex series of steps is involved in the overall process, the ultimate result is a cycle whereby NADH is oxidized to NAD, oxygen is reduced to water, and energy is produced. Ubiquinone acts only as an intermediary and is itself unchanged.

Step 1:

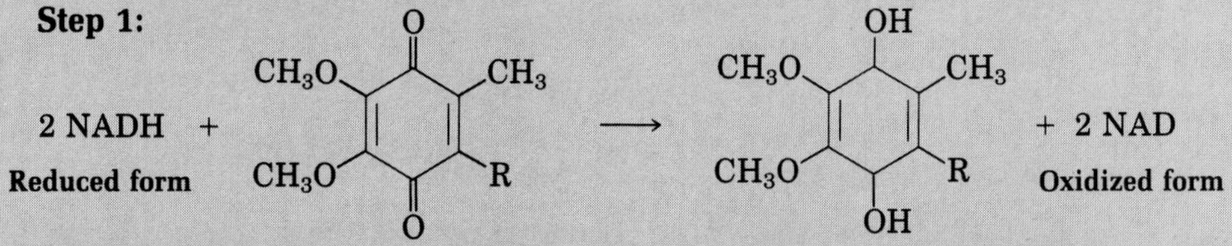

2 NADH +

Reduced form

⟶

+ 2 NAD

Oxidized form

Step 2:

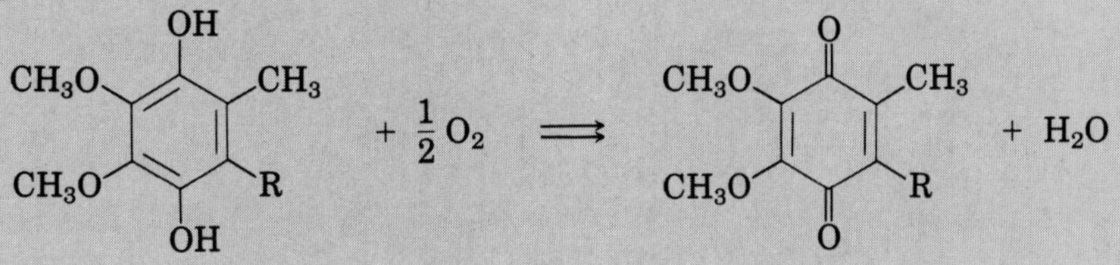

+ $\frac{1}{2}$ O_2 ⟹ + H_2O

Net change:

$$2\ NADH + \frac{1}{2}\ O_2 \longrightarrow 2\ NAD + H_2O$$

CHAPTER 9

Aldehydes and Ketones: Nucleophilic Addition Reactions

In this and the next two chapters, we will discuss the most important functional group in organic chemistry—the **carbonyl group, C=O** (pronounced car-bo-neel').

Carbonyl compounds occur everywhere in nature. Most biologically important molecules contain carbonyl groups, as do many pharmaceutical agents and many of the synthetic chemicals that touch our everyday lives. For example, acetic acid, the chief component of vinegar; phenacetin, an over-the-counter headache remedy; and Dacron, the polyester material used in clothing, all contain different kinds of carbonyl groups.

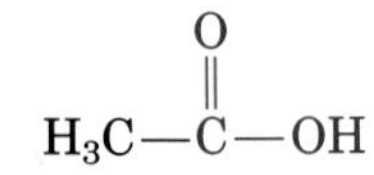

$$H_3C-\overset{\overset{\displaystyle O}{\|}}{C}-OH \qquad\qquad CH_3CH_2O-\!\!\left\langle\bigcirc\right\rangle\!\!-NH-\overset{\overset{\displaystyle O}{\|}}{C}-CH_3$$

Acetic acid
(a carboxylic acid)

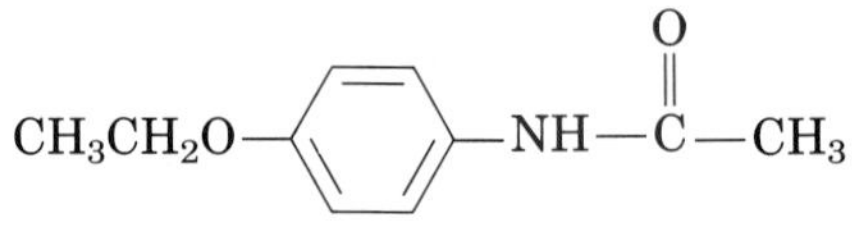

Phenacetin (an amide)

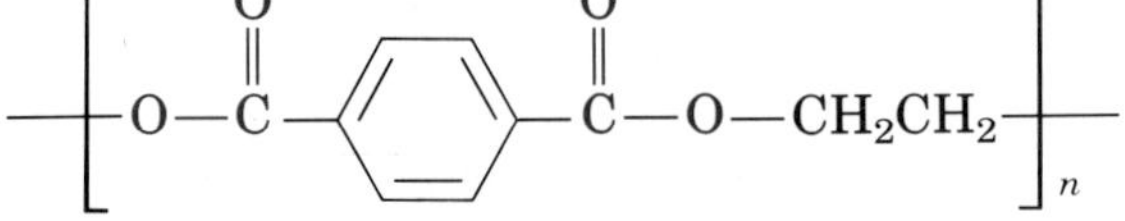

$$\left[\!-O-\overset{\overset{\displaystyle O}{\|}}{C}-\!\!\left\langle\bigcirc\right\rangle\!\!-\overset{\overset{\displaystyle O}{\|}}{C}-O-CH_2CH_2-\!\right]_n$$

Dacron (a polyester)

9.1 KINDS OF CARBONYL COMPOUNDS

There are many different kinds of carbonyl compounds, depending on what groups are bonded to the C=O unit. The chemistry of carbonyl groups is quite similar, however, regardless of their exact structure.

Table 9.1 shows some of the many different kinds of carbonyl compounds. All

contain an **acyl fragment,** $-\overset{\overset{\displaystyle O}{\|}}{C}-R,$ bonded to another residue. The R group of the acyl fragment may be alkyl, aryl, alkenyl, or alkynyl; the other residue to which the acyl group is bonded may be a carbon, hydrogen, oxygen, halogen, sulfur, or other substituent.

TABLE 9.1 Some types of carbonyl compounds

Name	General formula	Name ending
Aldehyde	$R-\overset{\overset{\displaystyle O}{\|}}{C}-H$	*-al*
Ketone	$R-\overset{\overset{\displaystyle O}{\|}}{C}-R'$	*-one*
Carboxylic acid	$R-\overset{\overset{\displaystyle O}{\|}}{C}-O-H$	*-oic acid*
Acid chloride	$R-\overset{\overset{\displaystyle O}{\|}}{C}-Cl$	*-yl* or *-oyl chloride*
Acid anhydride	$R-\overset{\overset{\displaystyle O}{\|}}{C}-O-\overset{\overset{\displaystyle O}{\|}}{C}-R'$	*-oic anhydride*
Ester	$R-\overset{\overset{\displaystyle O}{\|}}{C}-O-R'$	*-oate*
Lactone (cyclic ester)	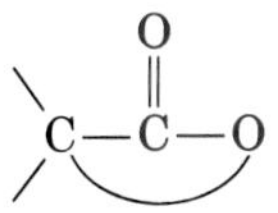	None
Amide	$R-\overset{\overset{\displaystyle O}{\|}}{C}-N\diagup^{\diagdown}$	*-amide*
Lactam (cyclic amide)	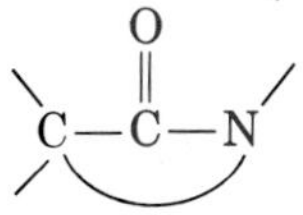	None

It turns out to be very useful to classify carbonyl compounds into two general categories, based on the kinds of chemistry they undergo:

Aldehydes, RCHO Ketones, $R_2C=O$	The acyl units in these two functional groups are bonded to substituents (H and R, respectively) that *cannot stabilize a negative charge and therefore cannot serve as leaving groups. Aldehydes and ketones behave similarly and undergo many of the same reactions.*

Carboxylic acids,
    RCOOH
Esters,
    RCOOR'
Acid chlorides,
    RCOCl
Acid anhydrides,
    RCOOCOR'
Amides,
    RCONH$_2$

The acyl units in carboxylic acids and their derivatives are bonded to substituents (oxygen, halogen, nitrogen) that *can stabilize a negative charge and can therefore serve as leaving groups in substitution reactions.* The chemistry of these compounds is similar.

PROBLEM 9.1   Propose structures for molecules that meet these descriptions:

(a) A ketone,   C$_5$H$_{10}$O
(c) A keto aldehyde,   C$_6$H$_{10}$O$_2$

(b) An aldehyde,   C$_6$H$_{10}$O
(d) A cyclic ketone,   C$_5$H$_8$O

9.2   STRUCTURE AND PROPERTIES OF THE CARBONYL GROUP

The carbon–oxygen double bond of carbonyl groups is similar in many respects to the carbon–carbon double bond of alkenes (Figure 9.1). The carbonyl carbon atom is *sp²* hybridized and forms three sigma bonds. The fourth valence electron remains in a carbon *p* orbital and forms a pi bond to oxygen by overlap with an oxygen *p* orbital. The oxygen also has two nonbonding pairs of electrons, which occupy its remaining two orbitals. (The oxygen atom is probably *sp²* hybridized, although there is some disagreement about this point.)

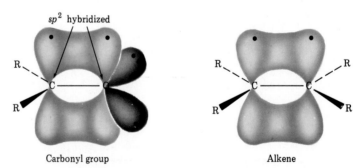

Carbonyl group   Alkene

FIGURE 9.1
Electronic structure of the carbonyl group

Like alkenes, carbonyl compounds are planar about the double bond and have bond angles of approximately 120°. Table 9.2 shows the structure of acetaldehyde and gives the experimentally determined bond lengths and angles. As we would expect, the carbon–oxygen double bond is both shorter and stronger than the normal carbon–oxygen single bond (1.22 Å versus 1.43 Å; 175 kcal/mol versus 92 kcal/mol).

TABLE 9.2 Structure of acetaldehyde

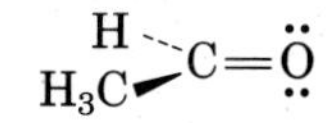

$$\begin{array}{c} H \\ H_3C \end{array} C = \ddot{O}$$

Bond angle (degrees)		Bond length (Å)	
H—C—C	118	C=O	1.22
C—C—O	121	C—C	1.50
H—C—O	121	OC—H	1.09

Carbon–oxygen double bonds are polarized because of the high electro-negativity of oxygen relative to carbon. Since the carbonyl carbon is positively polarized, it is an electrophilic (Lewis acidic) site and is attacked by nucleophiles. Conversely, the carbonyl oxygen is negatively polarized and is a nucleophilic (Lewis basic) site. We will see in this and the next two chapters that most carbonyl group reactions can be understood in terms of simple bond-polarization arguments.

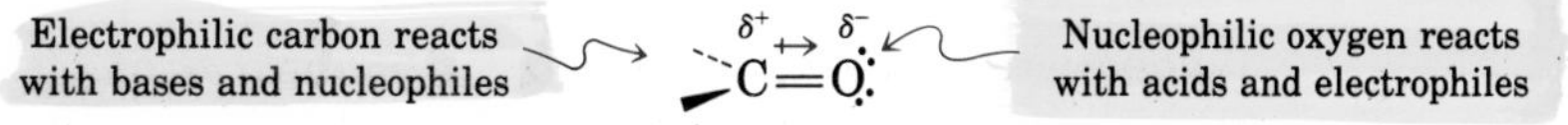

Electrophilic carbon reacts with bases and nucleophiles $\quad C = \ddot{O}: \quad$ Nucleophilic oxygen reacts with acids and electrophiles

9.3 NOMENCLATURE OF ALDEHYDES AND KETONES

Systematic names for aldehydes are derived by replacing the terminal -e of the corresponding alkane name with -al. The longest chain selected to be the base name must contain the —CHO group, and the CHO carbon is always numbered as carbon 1. For example:

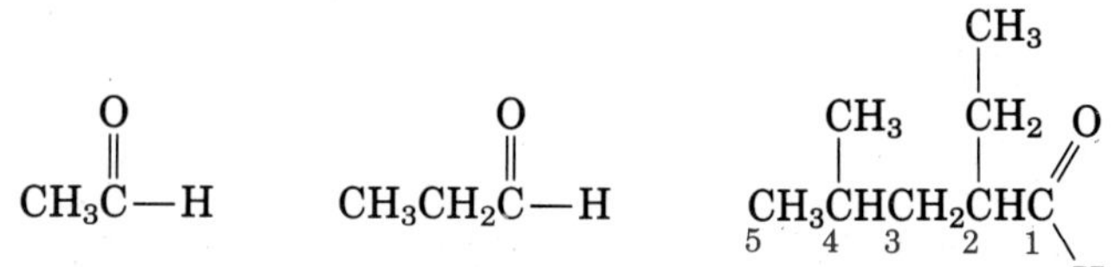

$$CH_3\overset{\displaystyle O}{\overset{\|}{C}}{-}H \qquad CH_3CH_2\overset{\displaystyle O}{\overset{\|}{C}}{-}H \qquad \underset{5}{CH_3}\underset{4}{CH}\underset{3}{CH_2}\underset{2}{CH}\underset{1}{CHC}$$

Ethanal   **Propanal**
(acetaldehyde)   (propionaldehyde)

2-Ethyl-4-methylpentanal

Note that the longest chain in 2-ethyl-4-methylpentanal is a hexane, but this chain does not include the —CHO group.

For more complex aldehydes in which the —CHO group is attached to a ring, the suffix -carbaldehyde is used:

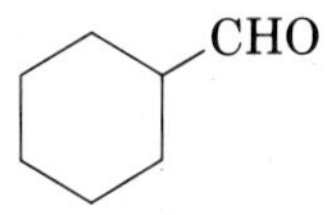

Cyclohexanecarbaldehyde 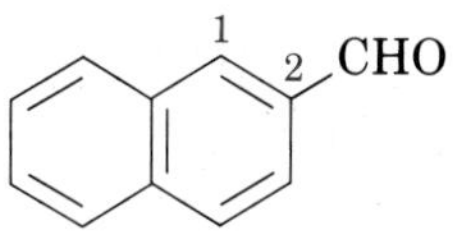   **2-Naphthalenecarbaldehyde**

Certain simple and well-known aldehydes also have trivial names that are recognized by IUPAC. Some of these names are given in Table 9.3.

TABLE 9.3   Trivial names of some simple aldehydes

Formula	Trivial name	Systematic name
HCHO	Formaldehyde	Methanal
CH_3CHO	Acetaldehyde	Ethanal
CH_3CH_2CHO	Propionaldehyde	Propanal
$CH_3CH_2CH_2CHO$	Butyraldehyde	Butanal
$CH_3CH_2CH_2CH_2CHO$	Valeraldehyde	Pentanal
$H_2C{=}CHCHO$	Acrolein	2-Propenal
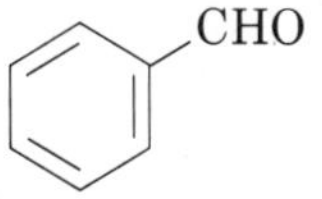 ⬡—CHO	Benzaldehyde	Benzenecarbaldehyde

Ketones are named by replacing the terminal *-e* of the corresponding alkane name with *-one* (pronounced own). The chain selected for the base name is the longest one that contains the ketone group, and the numbering begins at the end nearer the carbonyl carbon. For example:

$$H_3C-\overset{\overset{\displaystyle O}{\|}}{C}-CH_3$$

**Propanone
(acetone)**

$$\underset{1}{C}H_3\underset{2}{C}H_2\overset{\overset{\displaystyle O}{\|}}{\underset{3}{C}}\underset{4}{C}H_2\underset{5}{C}H_2\underset{6}{C}H_3$$

3-Hexanone

$$\underset{6}{C}H_3\underset{5}{C}H{=}\underset{4}{C}H\underset{3}{C}H_2\overset{\overset{\displaystyle O}{\|}}{\underset{2}{C}}\underset{1}{C}H_3$$

4-Hexen-2-one

A few ketones also retain their trivial names:

$$CH_3\overset{\overset{\displaystyle O}{\|}}{C}CH_3$$

Acetone

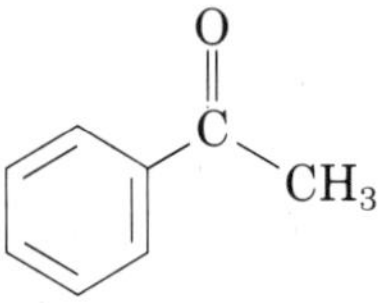

Acetophenone

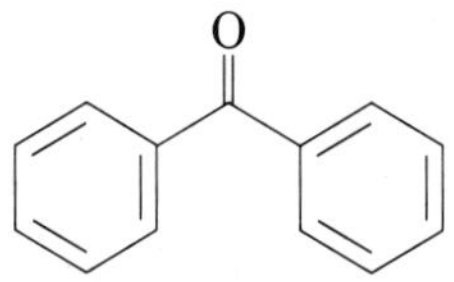

Benzophenone

When it becomes necessary to refer to the —COR group as a substituent, the term *acyl* (a'-sil) is used. Similarly, —CHO is called a *formyl* group, and —COAr is referred to as an *aroyl* group.

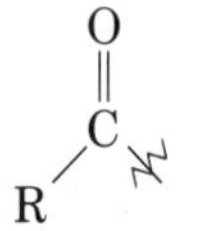

**Acyl
(R = alkyl, alkenyl, or alkynyl)**

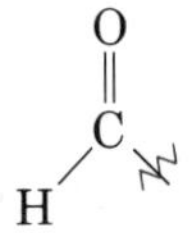

Formyl

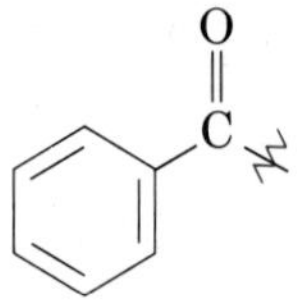

Aroyl

If other functional groups are present and the doubly bonded oxygen must be considered a substituent, the prefix *oxo*- is used. For example:

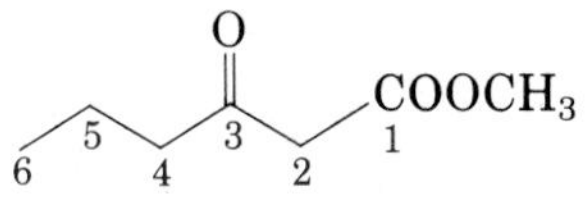

Methyl 3-oxohexanoate

PROBLEM 9.2 Name these aldehydes and ketones according to IUPAC rules:

(a)
$$\underset{\text{CH}_3\text{CH}_2\overset{\displaystyle \|}{\text{C}}\text{CH(CH}_3)_2}{}$$

(b)

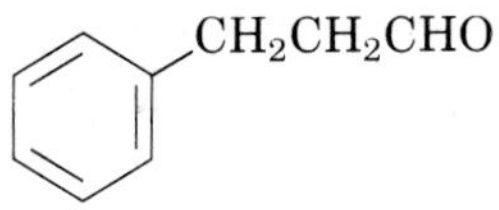

(c)
$$\text{CH}_3\overset{\text{O}}{\overset{\|}{\text{C}}}\text{CH}_2\text{CH}_2\text{CH}_2\overset{\text{O}}{\overset{\|}{\text{C}}}\text{CH}_2\text{CH}_3$$

(d)

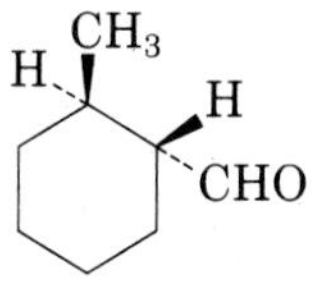

(e) OHCCH$_2$CH$_2$CH$_2$CHO

(f)

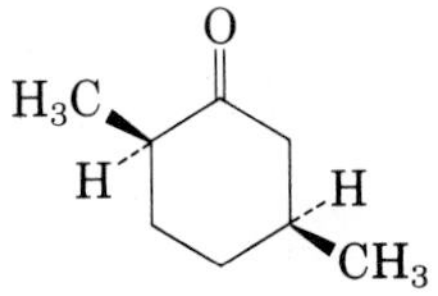

PROBLEM 9.3 Draw structures corresponding to these IUPAC names:

(a) 3-Methylbutanal
(b) 3-Methyl-3-butenal
(c) 4-Chloro-2-pentanone
(d) Phenylacetaldehyde
(e) 2,2-Dimethylcyclohexanecarbaldehyde
(f) 1,3-Cyclohexanedione

9.4 PREPARATION OF ALDEHYDES

We have already discussed two good methods of aldehyde synthesis—oxidation of primary alcohols and cleavage of alkenes. Let's review briefly:

1. Primary alcohols can be oxidized to give aldehydes (Section 8.7). The reaction is often carried out using pyridinium chlorochromate (PCC) in dichloromethane solution. High yields are usually obtained.

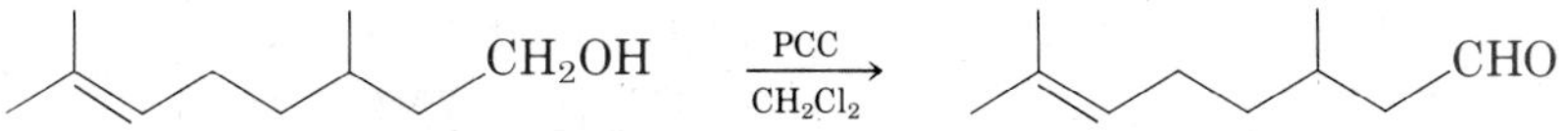

Citronellol   **Citronellal (82%)**

2. Alkenes that have at least one vinylic proton (*remember:* vinylic = on the double-bond carbon) undergo oxidative cleavage when treated with ozone to yield aldehydes (Section 4.7). If the cleavage reaction is carried out on a *cyclic* alkene, a dicarbonyl compound results.

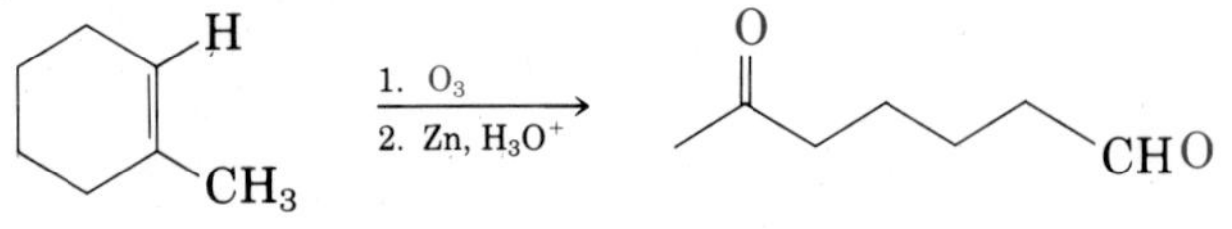

1-Methylcyclohexene   **6-Oxoheptanal (86%)**

PROBLEM 9.4   Show how you might prepare pentanal from the following starting materials:

(a)   1-Pentanol   (b)   1-Hexene   (c)   5-Decene

9.5 PREPARATION OF KETONES

For the most part, methods of ketone synthesis are analogous to those for aldehydes:

1. We have already seen that secondary alcohols can be oxidized to give ketones (Section 8.7). Pyridinium chlorochromate (PCC), CrO_3, $KMnO_4$, and $Na_2Cr_2O_7$ are all effective; the specific choice of reagent depends on such factors as reaction scale, reagent cost, and sensitivity of the alcohol.

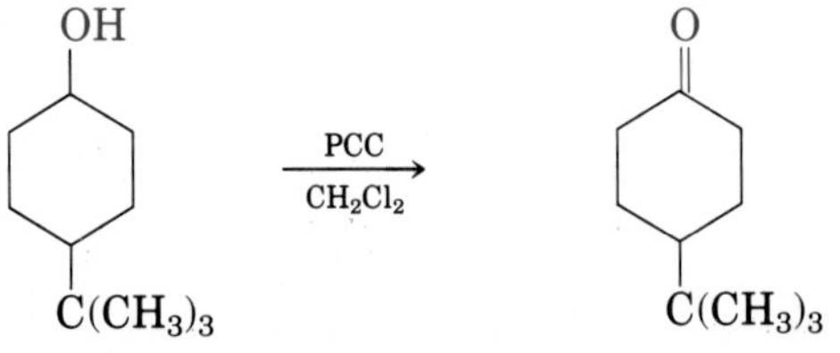

4-*tert*-Butylcyclohexanol   **4-*tert*-Butylcyclohexanone (90%)**

2. We have also seen that alkene ozonolysis yields ketones if one of the double-bond carbon atoms is disubstituted (Section 4.7).

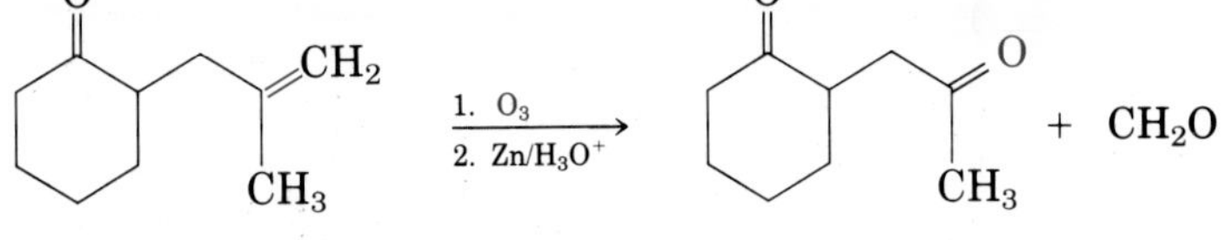

70%

3. Aryl ketones can be prepared by Friedel–Crafts acylation of an aromatic ring with an acid chloride (Section 5.10).

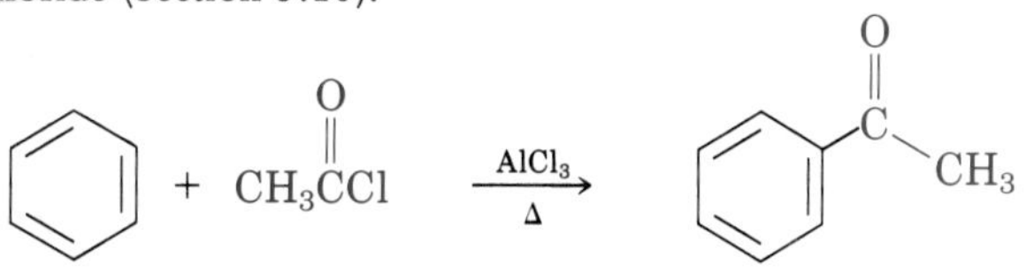

| Benzene | Acetyl chloride | | Acetophenone (95%) |

PROBLEM 9.5 How would you carry out the following reactions? More than one step may be required.

(a) 2-Hexanol → 2-Hexanone
(c) Benzene → 1-Phenylethanol

(b) 3-Hexene → 3-Hexanone

9.6 OXIDATION OF ALDEHYDES

Aldehydes are readily oxidized to yield carboxylic acids, RCHO → RCOOH. Ketones, however, are unreactive toward oxidation except under the most vigorous conditions. This difference in behavior is a consequence of the structural differences between the two functional groups: Aldehydes have a —CHO proton that can be abstracted during oxidation, but ketones do not.

Aldehyde oxidations can be carried out with many reagents, such as hot nitric acid, potassium permanganate, sodium dichromate, or chromium trioxide.

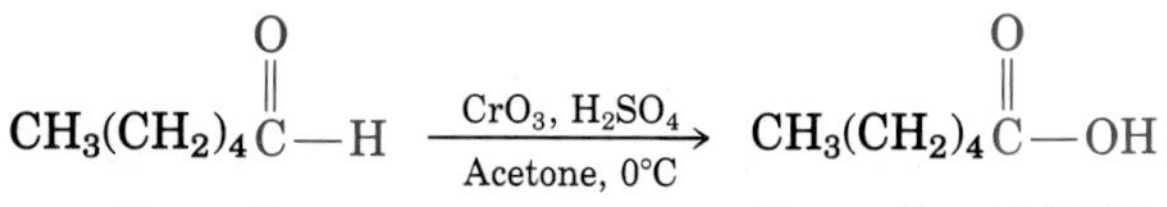

$$CH_3(CH_2)_4 \overset{\overset{\displaystyle O}{\|}}{C}-H \xrightarrow[\text{Acetone, 0°C}]{CrO_3,\ H_2SO_4} CH_3(CH_2)_4 \overset{\overset{\displaystyle O}{\|}}{C}-OH$$

Hexanal   Hexanoic acid (85%)

When a particularly valuable or sensitive aldehyde is being oxidized, a mild reagent such as silver oxide, Ag_2O, in dilute aqueous ammonia (the **Tollens reagent**) is often used.

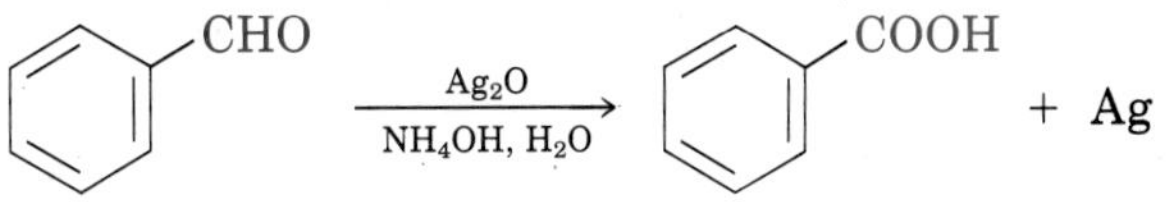

Benzaldehyde   Benzoic acid

A shiny mirror of metallic silver is deposited on the walls of the flask during a Tollens oxidation. Observation of such a mirror forms the basis of a qualitative test for the presence of an aldehyde functional group in a sample of unknown structure: A small amount of the unknown is dissolved in ethanol in a test tube, and a few drops of Tollens' reagent are added. If the test tube becomes silvery, the unknown is presumed to be an aldehyde.

PROBLEM 9.6   Predict the products of the reaction of the following substances with the Tollens reagent:

(a)   Pentanal   (b)   2,2-Dimethylhexanal   (c)   Cyclohexanone

---

9.7   REACTIONS OF ALDEHYDES AND KETONES: NUCLEOPHILIC ADDITIONS

The most important reaction of ketones and aldehydes is the **nucleophilic addition** reaction. As the name indicates, a nucleophilic addition involves the addition of a nucleophile ($^-:Nu$) to an electrophilic acceptor. The electrophile is the carbonyl-group carbon of the ketone or aldehyde, and the nucleophile may be any of a great number of reagents. Hydroxide ion ($H\ddot{O}:^-$), hydride ion ($H:^-$), carbon anions (**carbanions**, $R_3C:^-$), water ($H_2\ddot{O}:$), ammonia ($H_3N:$), and alcohols (ROH) are several of many possibilities.

The general mechanism of nucleophilic addition is shown in Figure 9.2. As indicated, the nucleophile forms a new bond to the carbonyl-group carbon, the carbon–oxygen double bond breaks, and a proton bonds to the oxygen.

PRACTICE PROBLEM   What product would you expect from addition of the nucleophile hydroxide ion, $H\ddot{O}:^-$, to acetaldehyde?

Solution   Hydroxide ion should bond to the carbonyl-carbon atom, giving an alkoxide-ion intermediate, which can be protonated to yield a 1,1-dialcohol.

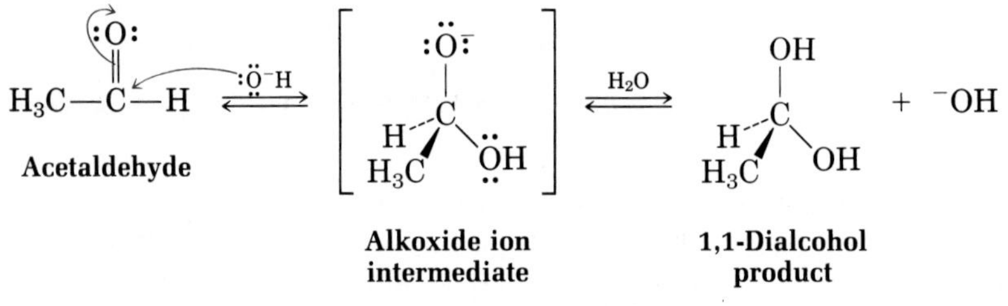

| Acetaldehyde | Alkoxide ion intermediate | 1,1-Dialcohol product |

PROBLEM 9.7   What product would you expect if the nucleophile cyanide ion, $:CN^-$, were to add to acetone, and the intermediate were to be protonated?

PROBLEM 9.8   The reduction of a ketone to a secondary alcohol on treatment with $NaBH_4$ (Section 8.5) is a nucleophilic addition reaction in which the nucleophile hydride ion, $H:^-$, adds to the carbonyl group. Show the mechanism of this reduction.

An electron pair from the nucleophile attacks the electrophilic carbonyl carbon, pushing an electron pair from the C=O bond out onto oxygen. The carbonyl carbon rehybridizes from sp^2 to sp^3.

Aldehyde or ketone

Tetrahedrally hybridized intermediate

Protonation of the anion resulting from nucleophilic attack yields the neutral alcohol addition product.

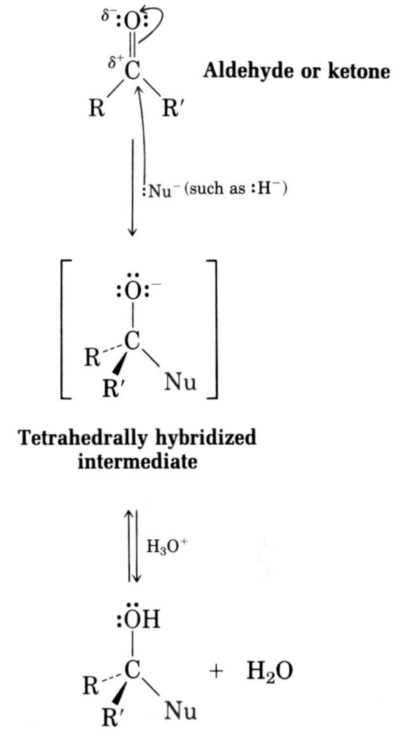

Example:

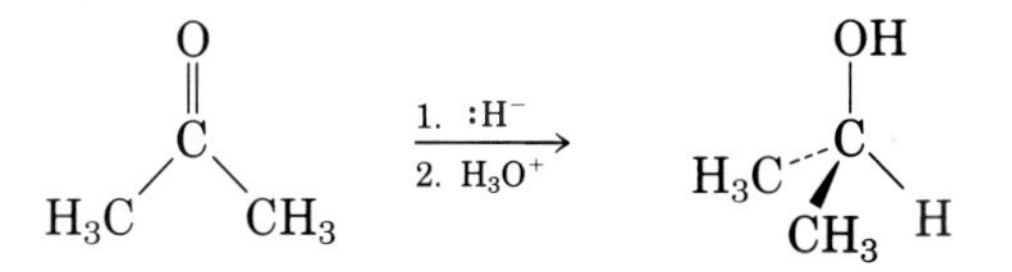

FIGURE 9.2
General mechanism of a nucleophilic addition reaction

9.8 RELATIVE REACTIVITY OF KETONES AND ALDEHYDES

Aldehydes are generally more reactive than ketones in nucleophilic addition reactions for both steric and electronic reasons. Sterically, the presence of two relatively large substituents in ketones versus only one large substituent in aldehydes means that attacking nucleophiles are able to approach aldehydes more readily and that the transition state leading to the tetrahedral intermediate is less crowded for aldehydes than for ketones (Figure 9.3, page 270).

Electronically, aldehydes are more reactive than ketones because of the somewhat greater degree of polarity of the aldehyde carbonyl group. The easiest way to see this polarity difference is to recall the stability order of carbocations (Section 4.3). Primary carbocations are less stable than secondary ones because there is only one alkyl group to stabilize the positive charge, rather than two. For similar reasons, aldehydes are less stable (and therefore more reactive) than

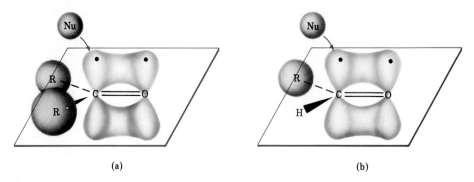

(a)   (b)

FIGURE 9.3
(a) Nucleophilic attack on a ketone is sterically hindered because of the two relatively large substituents. (b) An aldehyde has only one large substituent and is less hindered.

ketones because there is only one alkyl group to stabilize the partial positive charge on the carbonyl carbon, rather than two.

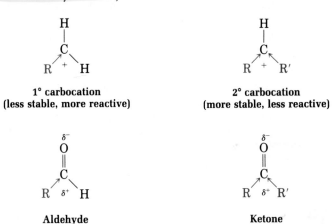

1° carbocation	2° carbocation
(less stable, more reactive)	(more stable, less reactive)

Aldehyde	Ketone
(less stabilization of δ^+, more reactive)	(more stabilization of δ^+, less reactive)

PRACTICE PROBLEM   Which would you expect to be more reactive toward nucleophilic additions, benzaldehyde or *p*-nitrobenzaldehyde?

Solution   We saw in Section 5.11 that a nitro group is a strongly electron-withdrawing (deactivating) substituent. Thus, it should withdraw electrons from the aldehyde carbon, making *p*-nitrobenzaldehyde more highly polarized and more reactive than benzaldehyde.

PROBLEM 9.9   Which would you expect to be more reactive toward nucleophilic additions, *p*-methoxybenzaldehyde or benzaldehyde? Explain.

PROBLEM 9.10   Which would you expect to be more reactive toward nucleophilic additions, propanal or 2,2-dimethylpropanal? Explain.

9.9   NUCLEOPHILIC ADDITION OF H₂O: HYDRATION

Aldehydes and ketones undergo reaction with water to yield 1,1-diols or **geminal (gem) diols:**

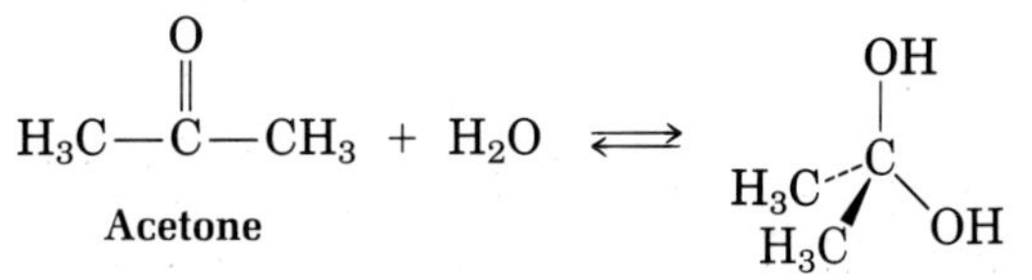

$$H_3C-\overset{\overset{\textstyle O}{\|}}{C}-CH_3 \; + \; H_2O \; \rightleftharpoons$$

Acetone

$$\underset{H_3C}{\overset{H_3C}{>}}\overset{\overset{\textstyle OH}{|}}{C}\overset{}{\diagdown}OH$$

**Acetone hydrate
(a gem diol)**

The hydration reaction is reversible, and gem diols can eliminate water to re-generate ketones or aldehydes. The exact position of the equilibrium between gem diols and ketones/aldehydes depends on the structure of the carbonyl compound. Although the equilibrium strongly favors the carbonyl compound in the great majority of cases, the gem diol is favored for a few simple aldehydes. For exam-ple, an aqueous solution of acetone consists of about 0.1% gem diol and 99.9% ketone, whereas an aqueous solution of formaldehyde consists of 99.9% gem diol and 0.1% aldehyde.

The nucleophilic addition of water to ketones and aldehydes is rather slow in pure water, but is catalyzed by both acid and base. Although these catalysts do not change the *position* of the equilibrium, they strongly affect the speed with which the hydration reaction occurs. The base-catalyzed reaction takes place in several steps, as shown in Figure 9.4. The attacking nucleophile is the negatively charged hydroxide ion.

Hydroxide ion nucleophile adds to the ketone or aldehyde carbonyl group to yield an alkoxide ion intermediate.

The basic alkoxide ion intermediate abstracts a proton (H⁺) from water to yield gem diol product and regenerate hydroxide ion catalyst.

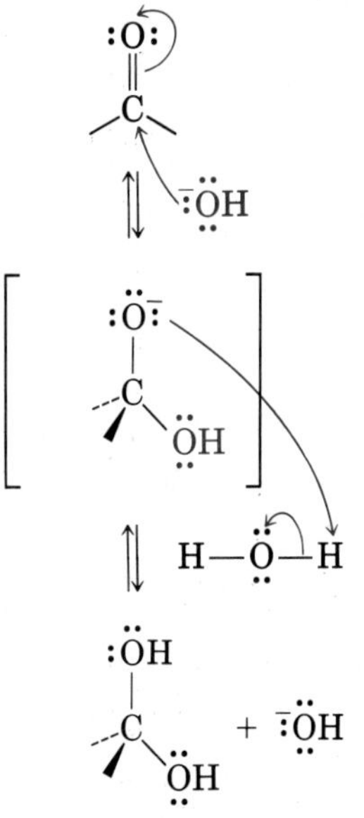

FIGURE 9.4
Mechanism of the base-catalyzed hydration reaction

The acid-catalyzed reaction also takes place in several steps. The acid catalyst first protonates the oxygen atom (Lewis base) of the carbonyl group, and subsequent nucleophilic addition of water occurs to yield a protonated gem diol. Loss of a proton then gives the neutral gem diol product (Figure 9.5).

Acid catalyst protonates the basic carbonyl oxygen atom, making the ketone or aldehyde a much better acceptor of nucleophiles.

Nucleophilic addition of neutral water yields a protonated gem diol.

Loss of a proton regenerates the acid catalyst and gives neutral gem diol product.

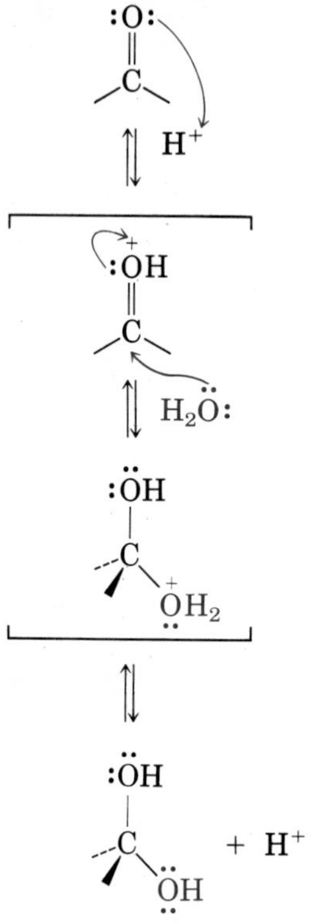

FIGURE 9.5
Mechanism of the acid-catalyzed hydration reaction

Note the important differences between the acid-catalyzed and base-catalyzed processes. The *base*-catalyzed reaction takes place rapidly because water is converted into hydroxide ion, a much better nucleophilic *donor*. The *acid*-catalyzed reaction takes place rapidly because the carbonyl compound is converted by protonation into a much better electrophilic *acceptor*.

PROBLEM 9.11   When dissolved in water, trichloroacetaldehyde (chloral, CCl_3CHO) exists primarily as the gem diol, chloral hydrate, $CCl_3CH(OH)_2$ (better known by the non-IUPAC name of "knock-out drops"). Show the structure of chloral hydrate.

PROBLEM 9.12   The oxygen in water is primarily (99.8%) ^{16}O, but water enriched with the heavy isotope ^{18}O is also available. When a ketone or aldehyde is dissolved in $H_2{}^{18}O$, the isotopic label becomes incorporated into the carbonyl group:

$$R_2C{=}O + H_2O^* \longrightarrow R_2C{=}O^* + H_2O \qquad \text{where } O^* = {}^{18}O$$

Explain.

PROBLEM 9.13 How can you explain the observation that S_N2 reaction of (dibromomethyl)benzene, $C_6H_5CHBr_2$, with NaOH yields benzaldehyde rather than (dihydroxymethyl)benzene, $C_6H_5CH(OH)_2$?

9.10 NUCLEOPHILIC ADDITION OF GRIGNARD REAGENTS: ALCOHOL FORMATION

Grignard reagents, RMgX, react with ketones and aldehydes by a nucleophilic addition pathway to yield alcohols.

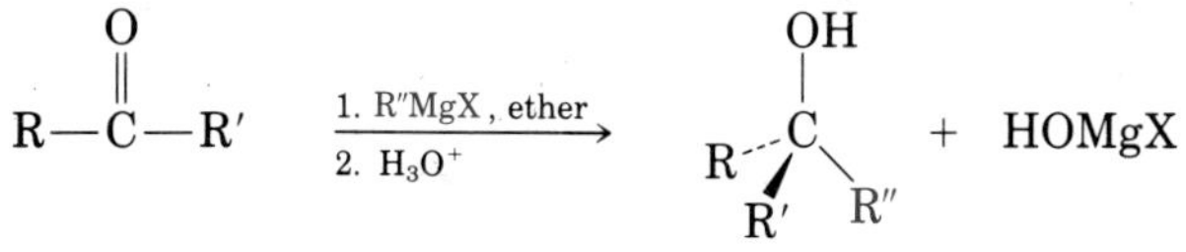

As we saw in Section 7.5, alkyl, aryl, and vinylic halides react with magnesium in ether to generate Grignard reagents:

$$R-X + Mg \longrightarrow \overset{\delta^-}{R}-\overset{\delta^+}{MgX}$$

A Grignard reagent

where R = 1°, 2°, or 3° alkyl, aryl, or vinylic; and X = Cl, Br, or I.

The carbon–magnesium bond of Grignard reagents is strongly polarized, making the carbon atom both nucleophilic and basic. Grignard reagents therefore react as if they were carbanions, $R:^-$, and they undergo nucleophilic addition to ketones and aldehydes just as hydride ion (Section 8.5) and water (Section 9.9) do. Nucleophilic addition first produces a tetrahedrally hybridized, magnesium alkoxide intermediate, which is then protonated to yield the neutral alcohol upon treatment with aqueous acid.

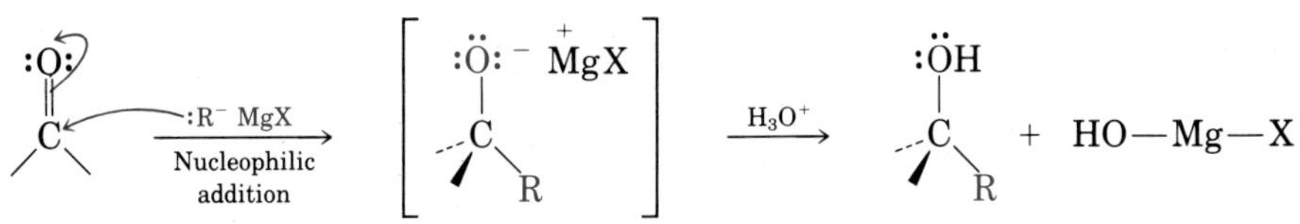

Carbonyl   Tetrahedral   Alcohol
                            intermediate

A large number of alcohol products can be obtained from Grignard reactions, depending on the reagents used. For example, formaldehyde, CH_2O, reacts with Grignard reagents to give primary alcohols, RCH_2OH.

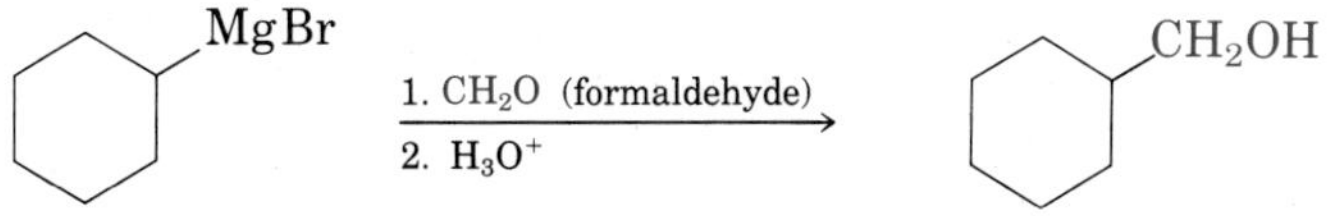

Cyclohexylmagnesium   Cyclohexylmethanol (65%)
bromide   (a primary alcohol)

Aldehydes react with Grignard reagents to give secondary alcohols, and ketones react similarly to yield tertiary alcohols:

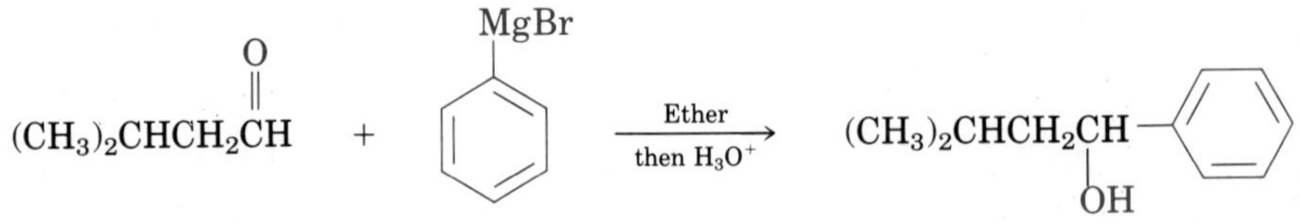

3-Methylbutanal   **Phenylmagnesium bromide**   **3-Methyl-1-phenyl-1-butanol (73%)** (a 2° alcohol)

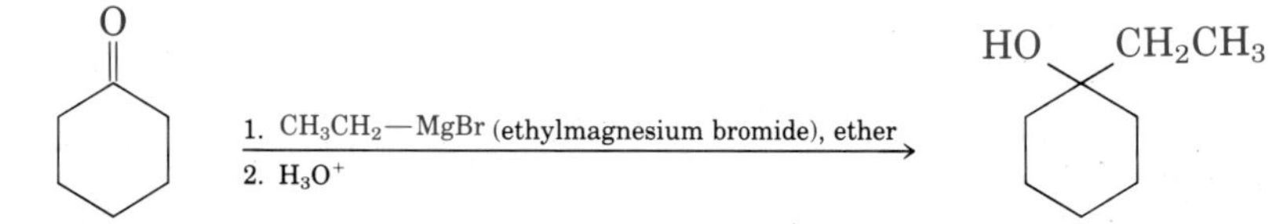

Cyclohexanone   **1-Ethylcyclohexanol (89%)** (a 3° alcohol)

Although broad in scope, the Grignard reaction also has severe limitations: Grignard reagents cannot be prepared from organohalides if there are other reactive functional groups in the same molecule. For example, a compound that is both an alkyl halide and a ketone will not form a Grignard reagent—instead, it reacts with itself. Similarly, a compound that is both an alkyl halide and a carboxylic acid, alcohol, or amine cannot form a Grignard reagent because the acidic RCOOH, ROH, or RNH_2 protons present in the same molecule simply react with the basic Grignard reagent as it is formed.

In general, Grignard reagents *cannot* be prepared from compounds that have these functional groups in the molecule:

$$Br-(Molecule)-FG$$

where FG = —OH, —NH_2, —SH, —COOH, —NO_2, —CHO, —COR, —CN, or —$CONH_2$.

PRACTICE PROBLEM How could you use the addition of a Grignard reagent to a ketone to synthesize 2-phenyl-2-propanol?

Solution First draw the structure of the product and identify the groups bonded to the alcohol carbon atom. In the present instance, there are two methyl groups (—CH_3) and one phenyl (—C_6H_5). One of the three will have come from a Grignard reagent, and the remaining two will have come from a ketone. Thus, the possibilities are addition of methylmagnesium bromide to acetophenone and addition of phenylmagnesium bromide to acetone:

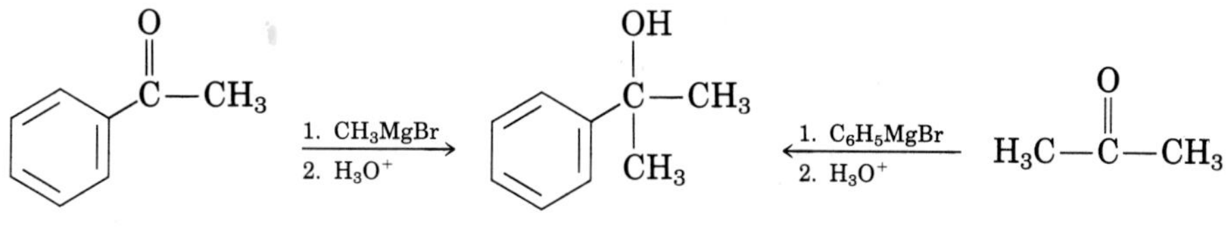

Acetophenone   2-Phenyl-2-propanol   Acetone

PROBLEM 9.14 Show the products obtained from addition of methylmagnesium bromide to these compounds:

(a) Cyclopentanone   (b) Benzophenone (diphenyl ketone)   (c) 3-Hexanone

PROBLEM 9.15 How could you use a Grignard addition reaction to prepare these alcohols?

(a) 2-Methyl-2-propanol   (b) 1-Methylcyclohexanol   (c) 3-Methyl-3-pentanol
(d) 2-Phenyl-2-butanol   (e) Benzyl alcohol

PROBLEM 9.16 How can you explain the observation that treatment of 4-hydroxycyclohexanone with 1 equiv of methylmagnesium bromide yields none of the expected addition product, whereas treatment with an excess of Grignard reagent leads to a good yield of 1-methyl-1,4-cyclohexanediol?

9.11 NUCLEOPHILIC ADDITION OF AMINES: IMINE FORMATION

Ammonia and primary amines, RNH_2, add to aldehydes and ketones to yield **imines, $R_2C{=}NR'$**. Imines are formed by nucleophilic addition to the carbonyl group by the nucleophilic amine, followed by loss of water from the amino alcohol addition product.

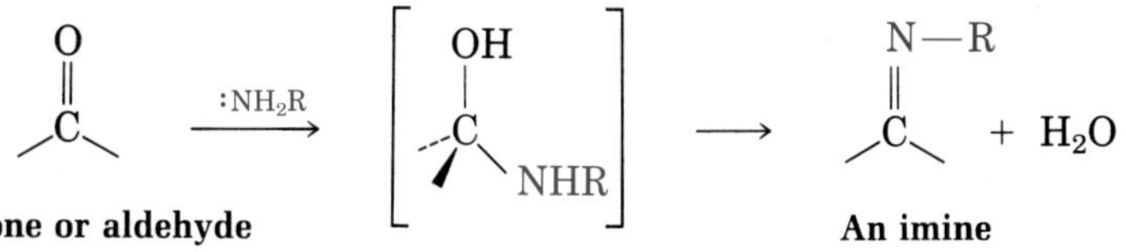

A ketone or aldehyde   Amino alcohol intermediate   An imine

Imine derivatives, such as oximes and 2,4-dinitrophenylhydrazones (2,4-DNP's), are also easily prepared by reaction of a ketone or aldehyde with the appropriate $H_2N{-}Y$ compound. These imine derivatives, which are usually crystalline, easy-to-handle materials, are often prepared as a means of characterizing liquid ketones or aldehydes.

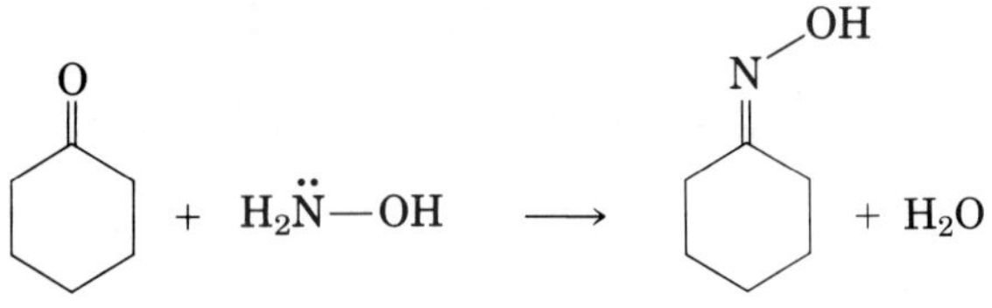

$$\text{Hydroxylamine} \qquad \begin{array}{c}\text{Cyclohexanone oxime}\\ \text{(mp 90°C)}\end{array}$$

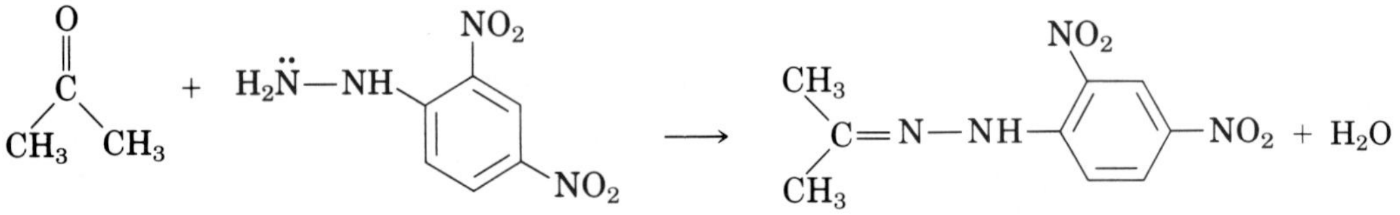

2,4-Dinitrophenylhydrazine   **Acetone 2,4-dinitrophenylhydrazone**
(mp 126°C)

An important variant of imine formation involves the treatment of a ketone or aldehyde with hydrazine, $H_2N\text{—}NH_2$, in the presence of strong base. This process, called the **Wolff–Kishner reaction** after its codiscoverers, is an extremely useful method for converting ketones or aldehydes into alkanes, $R_2C{=}O \rightarrow R_2CH_2$.

The Wolff–Kishner reaction involves initial formation of an imine intermediate called a *hydrazone*, followed by loss of nitrogen and formation of the alkane product. The reaction is very general, and can be used for most aldehydes and ketones.

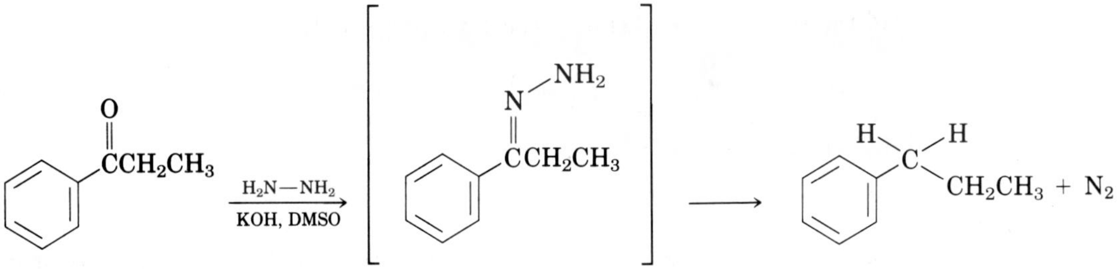

Propiophenone   **A hydrazone**   **Propylbenzene (82%)**

PROBLEM 9.17   Write the products you would expect to obtain from treatment of cyclohexanone with the following reagents:

(a) H_2NOH (b) 2,4-Dinitrophenylhydrazine
(c) N_2H_4, KOH   (d) $NaBH_4$

9.12 NUCLEOPHILIC ADDITION OF ALCOHOLS: ACETAL FORMATION

Ketones and aldehydes react with alcohols in the presence of an acid catalyst to yield **acetals, R$_2$C(OR')$_2$.**

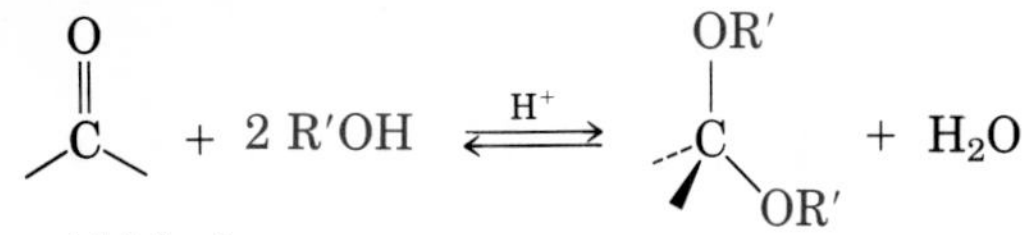

$$\underset{\text{Ketone/aldehyde}}{\overset{\displaystyle O}{\underset{\displaystyle }{\overset{\|}{C}}}} + 2\ R'OH \overset{H^+}{\rightleftharpoons} \underset{\text{An acetal}}{\overset{\displaystyle OR'}{\underset{\displaystyle OR'}{C}}} + H_2O$$

Acetal formation is fundamentally similar to the hydration reaction previously studied (Section 9.9); it involves the acid-catalyzed nucleophilic addition of an alcohol to the carbonyl group. As indicated in Figure 9.6, this initial nucleophilic addition yields a hydroxy ether called a **hemiacetal**. Further reaction of this intermediate with a second equivalent of alcohol then yields the acetal plus water.

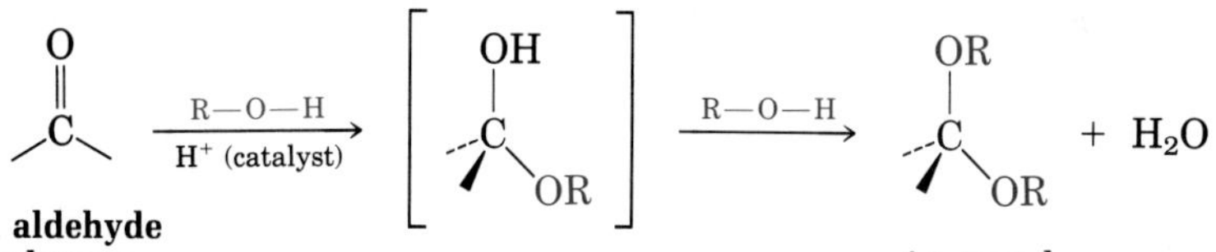

$$\underset{\substack{\text{An aldehyde}\\\text{or ketone}}}{\overset{\displaystyle O}{\overset{\|}{C}}} \xrightarrow[\text{H}^+\ (\text{catalyst})]{\text{R}-\text{O}-\text{H}} \left[\underset{\substack{\text{A hemiacetal}\\\text{intermediate}}}{\overset{\displaystyle OH}{\underset{\displaystyle OR}{C}}} \right] \xrightarrow{\text{R}-\text{O}-\text{H}} \underset{\text{An acetal}}{\overset{\displaystyle OR}{\underset{\displaystyle OR}{C}}} + H_2O$$

FIGURE 9.6
Formation of an acetal by nucleophilic addition of an alcohol to a ketone

All the steps during acetal formation are reversible. Thus, the reaction can be made to go either forward (from carbonyl compound to acetal) or backward (from acetal to carbonyl compound), depending on the reaction conditions. The forward reaction is accomplished by choosing conditions that remove water from the medium and thus drive the reaction to the right. The backward reaction is accomplished by treating the acetal with mineral acid in the presence of a large excess of water.

Acetals are valuable to organic chemists because they can serve as **protecting groups** for ketones and aldehydes. To see what this means, imagine that we are faced with the necessity of reducing the keto ester ethyl 4-oxopentanoate to obtain the keto alcohol 5-hydroxy-2-pentanone. This reaction cannot be done in a single step because of the presence of the ketone carbonyl group in the molecule. If we were to treat ethyl 4-oxopentanoate with LiAlH$_4$, both ketone and ester groups would be reduced.

$$\underset{\text{Ethyl 4-oxopentanoate}}{CH_3\overset{\displaystyle O}{\overset{\|}{C}}CH_2CH_2\overset{\displaystyle O}{\overset{\|}{C}}OCH_2CH_3} \xrightarrow{?} \underset{\text{5-Hydroxy-2-pentanone}}{CH_3\overset{\displaystyle O}{\overset{\|}{C}}CH_2CH_2CH_2OH}$$

This situation is not unusual. It often happens in dealing with complex molecules that one functional group may interfere with intended chemistry on a different functional group elsewhere in the molecule. In such situations, we can often circumvent the problem by first *protecting* the interfering functional group to render it unreactive, then carrying out the desired reaction, and then removing the protecting group.

Ketones and aldehydes can often be protected by converting them into acetals. Like other ethers, acetals are stable to bases, reducing agents, and Grignard reagents, but they are sensitive to acids. Thus, we can accomplish the selective reduction of the ester group in ethyl 4-oxopentanoate by first converting the keto group into an acetal, then treating with $LiAlH_4$ in ether, and then removing the acetal by treatment with aqueous acid. In practice, it is convenient to use ethylene glycol as the alcohol and to form a cyclic acetal. The mechanism of cyclic acetal formation using 1 equiv of ethylene glycol is exactly the same as that using 2 equiv of methanol.

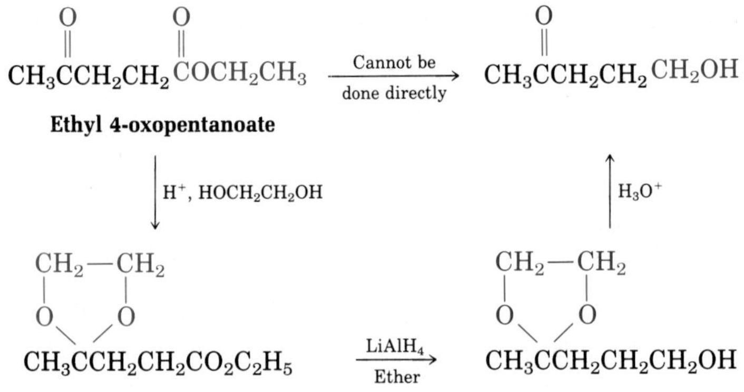

$$CH_3CCH_2CH_2COCH_2CH_3 \xrightarrow[\text{done directly}]{\text{Cannot be}} CH_3CCH_2CH_2CH_2OH$$

Ethyl 4-oxopentanoate

$$\downarrow H^+, HOCH_2CH_2OH \qquad\qquad \uparrow H_3O^+$$

$$CH_3CCH_2CH_2CO_2C_2H_5 \xrightarrow[\text{Ether}]{LiAlH_4} CH_3CCH_2CH_2CH_2OH$$

PROBLEM 9.18　What product would you expect from the acid-catalyzed reaction of cyclohexanone and ethylene glycol?

PROBLEM 9.19　Show the mechanism of the acid-catalyzed formation of a cyclic acetal from ethylene glycol and acetone.

PROBLEM 9.20　Show how you might carry out the following transformation:

$$CH_3COCH_2CH_2CHO \longrightarrow CH_3CH(OH)CH_2CH_2CHO$$

9.13　NUCLEOPHILIC ADDITION OF PHOSPHORUS YLIDES: THE WITTIG REACTION

Ketones and aldehydes can be converted into alkenes by means of the **Wittig reaction**. In this process, a phosphorus **ylide**, $R_2\bar{C}-\overset{+}{P}(C_6H_5)_3$, adds to the ketone or aldehyde to yield an intermediate that reacts further to yield an alkene. The overall result is replacement of the carbonyl oxygen atom by the organic fragment originally bonded to phosphorus (Figure 9.7).

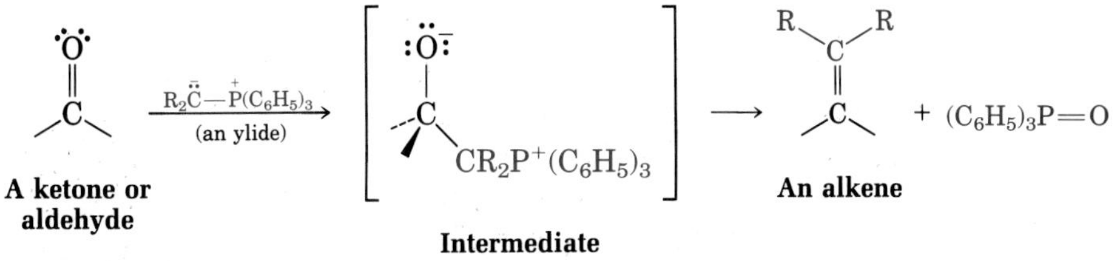

FIGURE 9.7
Formation of an alkene by reaction of a ketone or aldehyde with a phosphorus ylide in the Wittig reaction

The phosphorus ylides necessary for Wittig reaction are easily prepared by S_N2 reaction of primary (but not secondary or tertiary) alkyl halides with triphenylphosphine, $(C_6H_5)_3P:$, followed by treatment with base. Since triorganophosphines are generally excellent nucleophiles in S_N2 reactions, high yields of stable, crystalline tetraorganophosphonium salts are usually obtained. The proton on the carbon atom next to the positively charged phosphorus is acidic and can be removed by a strong base such as sodium hydride or butyllithium (BuLi) to generate the ylide. For example:

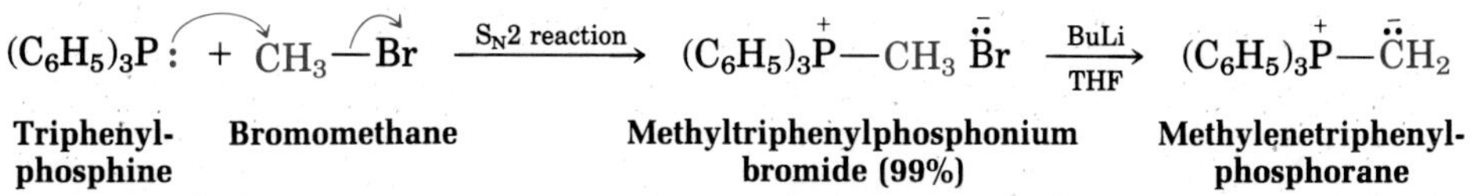

A great many mono-, di-, and trisubstituted alkenes can be prepared from the appropriate combination of phosphorane and ketone or aldehyde. Tetrasubstituted alkenes cannot be prepared, however.

The great value of the Wittig reaction is that pure alkenes of known structure are prepared. The alkene double bond is always exactly where the carbonyl group was in the precursor, and no product mixtures (other than E,Z isomers) are formed. For example, reaction of cyclohexanone with methylenetriphenylphosphorane yields the single pure alkene product, methylenecyclohexane, whereas the alternative synthesis by addition of methylmagnesium bromide to cyclohexanone followed by acid-catalyzed dehydration leads to a mixture of two alkenes.

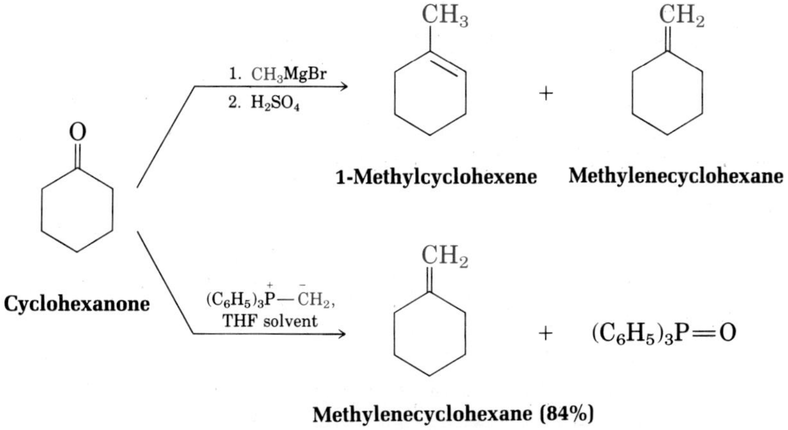

PRACTICE PROBLEM Show the product resulting from reaction of acetophenone with the Wittig reagent prepared from bromoethane.

Solution The Wittig reagent from bromoethane is ethylidenetriphenylphosphorane:

$$CH_3CH_2Br + :P(C_6H_5)_3 \longrightarrow CH_3CH_2\overset{+}{-}P(C_6H_5)_3 \ Br^- \xrightarrow{\text{Base}} CH_3\overset{..}{C}H\overset{+}{-}P(C_6H_5)_3$$

Reaction of a Wittig reagent with a ketone will yield an alkene in which the ketone oxygen atom has been replaced by the group bonded to phosphorus.

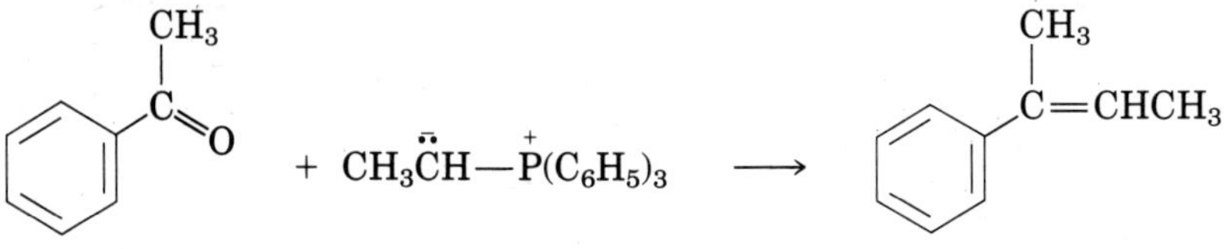

Acetophenone		**2-Phenyl-2-butene**

PROBLEM 9.21 What carbonyl compounds and what phosphorus ylides might you use to prepare the following compounds?

(a) 2-Methyl-2-hexene   (b) $C_6H_5CH{=}C(CH_3)_2$ (c) 1,2-Diphenylethylene

PROBLEM 9.22 Why do you suppose tri*phenyl*phosphine is used in the Wittig reaction rather than, say, tri*methyl*phosphine? What problems might you run into if trimethylphosphine were used?

ADDITIONAL PROBLEMS

PROBLEM 9.23 Identify the different types of carbonyl groups in these molecules:

(a)

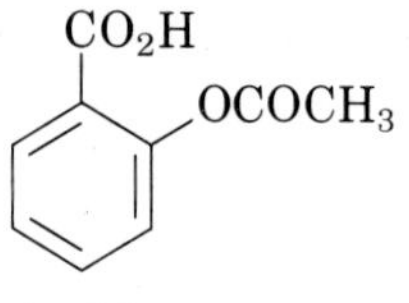

Aspirin

(b)

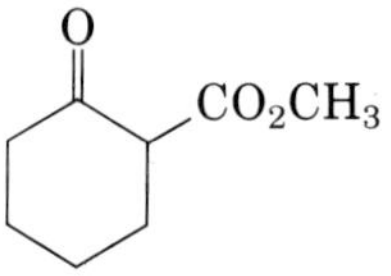

(c)

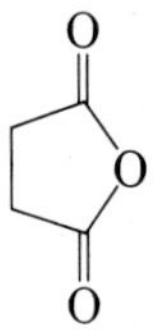

(d)

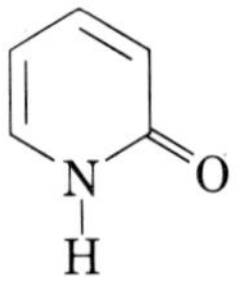

(e)

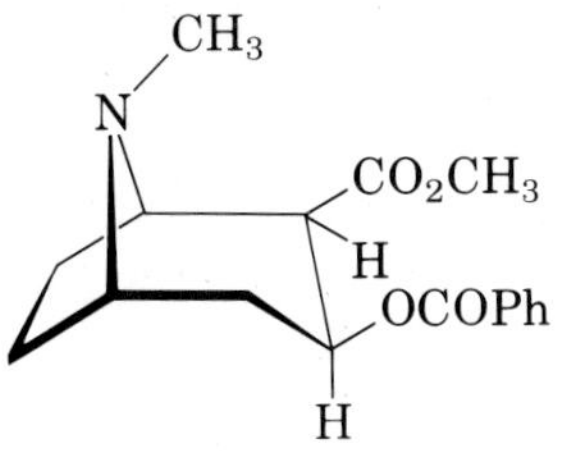

Cocaine

(f)

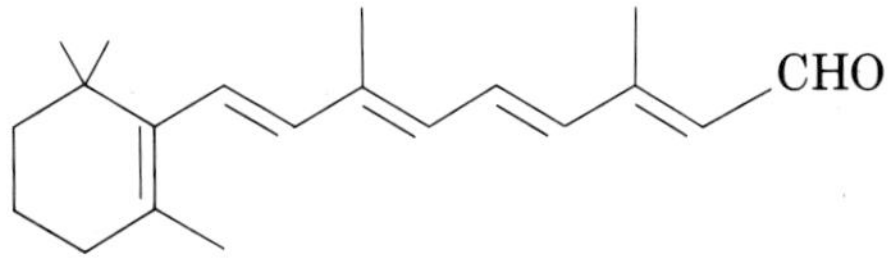

Retinal

(g)

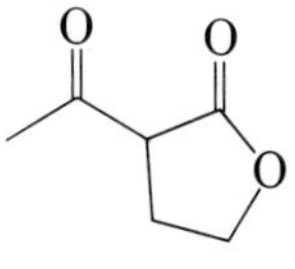

(h) 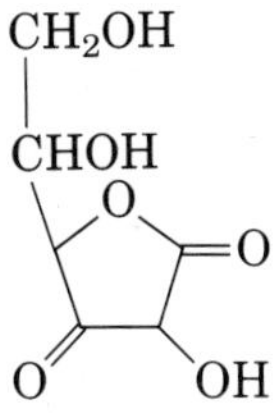 CH_2OH

$CHOH$

Ascorbic acid (vitamin C)

PROBLEM 9.24 Draw structures corresponding to these names:

(a) Bromoacetone
(b) 3-Methyl-2-butanone
(c) 3,5-Dinitrobenzaldehyde
(d) 3,5-Dimethylcyclohexanone
(e) 2,2,4,4-Tetramethyl-3-pentanone
(f) Butanedial
(g) (S)-2-Hydroxypropanal
(h) 3-Phenyl-2-propenal

PROBLEM 9.25 Draw and name the seven ketones and aldehydes with the formula $C_5H_{10}O$.

PROBLEM 9.26 Draw structures of molecules that meet these descriptions:

(a) A cyclic ketone, C_6H_8O
(b) A four-carbon diketone
(c) An aryl ketone, C_9H_{10}
(d) A 2-bromoaldehyde, C_5H_9BrO

PROBLEM 9.27 Provide IUPAC names for these structures:

(a)

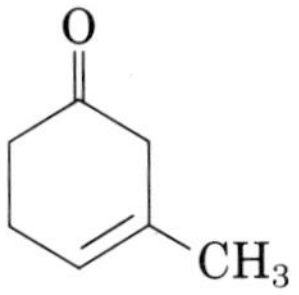

(b)

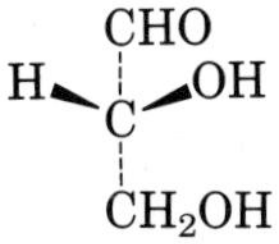

CHO

$H\diagdown\underset{C}{\,}\diagup OH$

CH_2OH

(c)

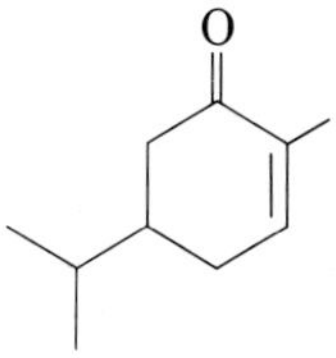

(d) $CH_3CH(CH_3)COCH_2CH_3$

(f)

CHO

CHO

(e) $CH_3CH(OH)CH_2CHO$

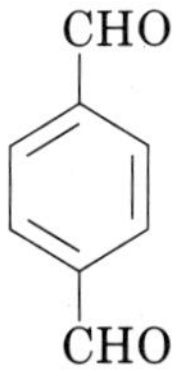

PROBLEM 9.28 Predict the products of the reaction of phenylacetaldehyde, $C_6H_5CH_2CHO$, with these reagents:

(a) $NaBH_4$, then H_3O^+

(b) Tollens' reagent

(c) NH_2OH

(d) CH_3MgBr, then H_3O^+

(e) CH_3OH, H^+ catalyst

(f) H_2NNH_2, KOH

(g) $(C_6H_5)_3\overset{+}{P}\!-\!\overset{-}{C}H_2$

PROBLEM 9.29 Answer Problem 9.28 for reaction of acetophenone, $C_6H_5COCH_3$.

PROBLEM 9.30 Reaction of 2-butanone with $NaBH_4$ yields an alcohol product having a new chiral center. What stereochemistry would you expect the product to have? [*Hint:* Review Sections 6.12 and 6.13.]

PROBLEM 9.31 Starting from 2-cyclohexenone, how would you prepare these substances? More than one step may be required.

(a) Cyclohexene

(b) 1-Methylcyclohexanol

(c) Cyclohexanol

(d) 1-Phenyl-2-cyclohexen-1-ol

PROBLEM 9.32 Show how the Wittig reaction might be used to prepare these alkenes. Identify the alkyl halide and the carbonyl components that would be used.

(a) $C_6H_5CH{=}CH\!-\!CH{=}CHC_6H_5$

(b)

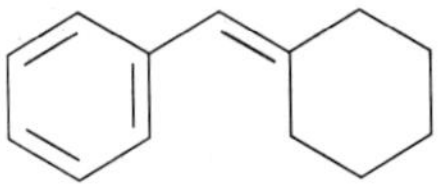

(c)

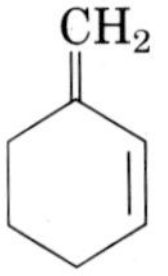

(d)

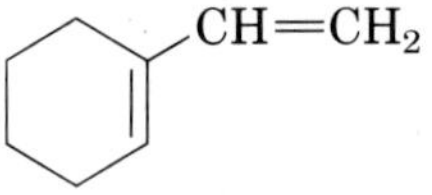

PROBLEM 9.33 β-Carotene, the pigment responsible for the orange color of carrots and a dietary source of vitamin A, can be prepared by a double Wittig reaction between 2 equiv of β-ionylideneacetaldehyde and a *diylide*. What is the structure of the diylide?

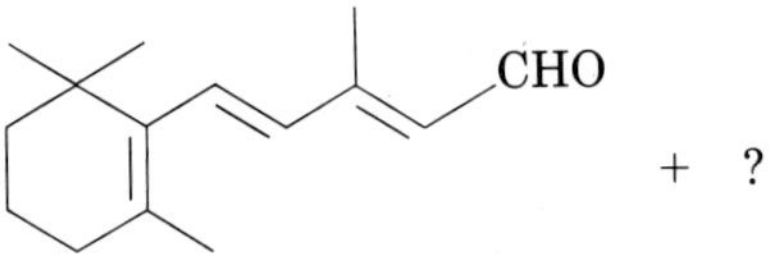

+ ?

β-Ionylideneacetaldehyde

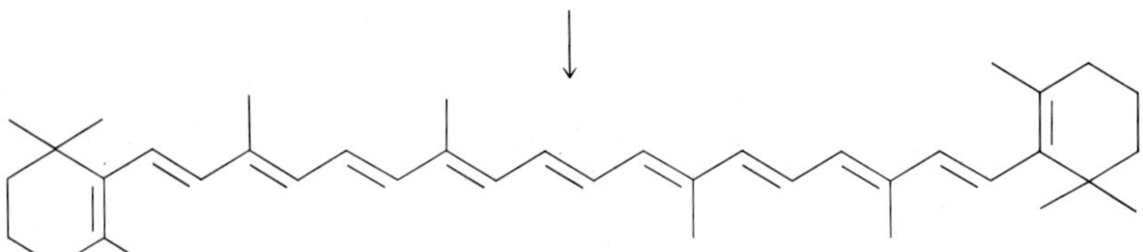

β-Carotene

PROBLEM 9.34 Use a Grignard reaction on a ketone or aldehyde to synthesize these compounds:

(a) 2-Pentanol

(b) 1-Butanol

(c) 1-Ethylcyclohexanol

(d) Diphenylmethanol

PROBLEM 9.35   Carvone is the major constituent of spearmint oil. What products would you expect from reaction of carvone with the following reagents?

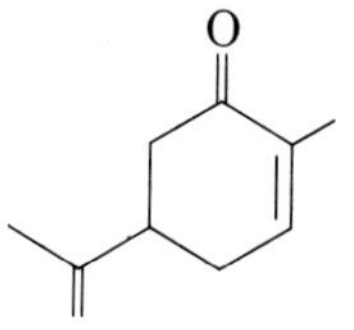

Carvone

(a) LiAlH$_4$, then H$_3$O$^+$ (b) C$_6$H$_5$MgBr, then H$_3$O$^+$ (c) H$_2$, Pd catalyst

(d) HOCH$_2$CH$_2$OH, H$^+$ (e) (C$_6$H$_5$)$_3$$\overset{-}{P}$—$\overset{+}{C}H_2$

PROBLEM 9.36   When 4-hydroxybutanal is treated with methanol in the presence of an acid catalyst, 2-methoxytetrahydrofuran is obtained. Propose a mechanism to account for this result.

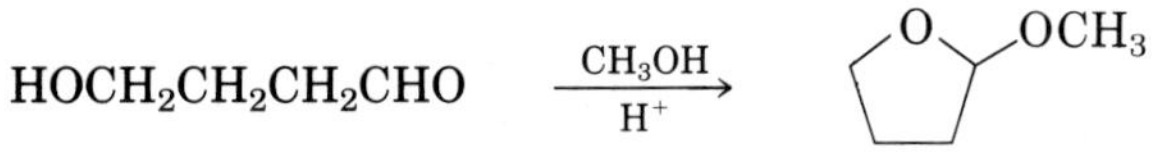

HOCH$_2$CH$_2$CH$_2$CHO $\xrightarrow[\text{H}^+]{\text{CH}_3\text{OH}}$

PROBLEM 9.37   Grignard reagents react with ethylene oxide to yield primary alcohols. Review the chemistry of epoxides in Section 8.11 and propose a mechanism for this ring-opening reaction.

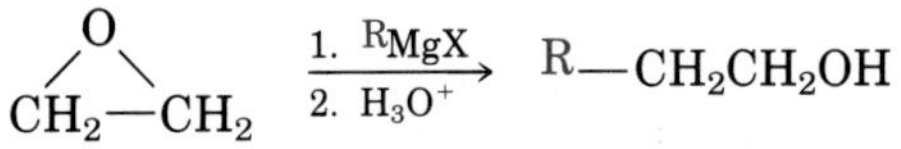

CH$_2$—CH$_2$ $\xrightarrow[\text{2. H}_3\text{O}^+]{\text{1. RMgX}}$ R—CH$_2$CH$_2$OH

Ethylene oxide

PROBLEM 9.38   Grignard reagents also react with oxetane to yield primary alcohols, but the reaction is much slower than with ethylene oxide (Problem 9.37). Can you suggest a reason for the difference in reactivity between oxetane and ethylene oxide?

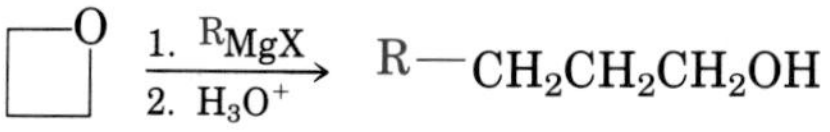

$\xrightarrow[\text{2. H}_3\text{O}^+]{\text{1. RMgX}}$ R—CH$_2$CH$_2$CH$_2$OH

Oxetane

PROBLEM 9.39   Using your knowledge of the reactivity differences between aldehydes and ketones, show how the following two selective reductions might be carried out. One of the schemes requires a protection step.

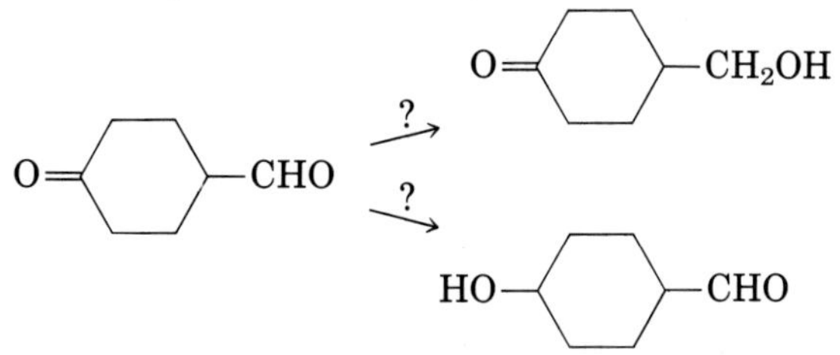

PROBLEM 9.40   Treatment of a ketone or aldehyde with a thiol in the presence of an acid catalyst yields a *thioacetal*, R$_2$C(SR′)$_2$. To what other reaction that we have studied is this thioacetal formation analogous?

PROBLEM 9.41   When crystals of pure α-glucose are dissolved in water, isomerization slowly occurs to produce β-glucose. How does this isomerization occur?

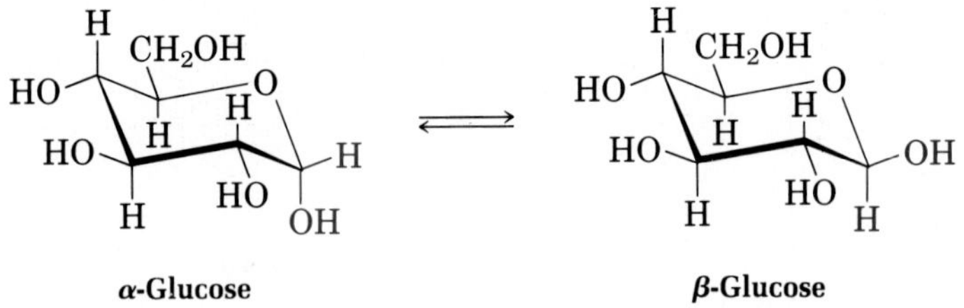

α-Glucose   β-Glucose

PROBLEM 9.42   The Wittig reaction can be used to prepare aldehydes as well as alkenes. This is done by using (methoxymethylene)triphenylphosphorane as the Wittig reagent and treating the product with aqueous acid:

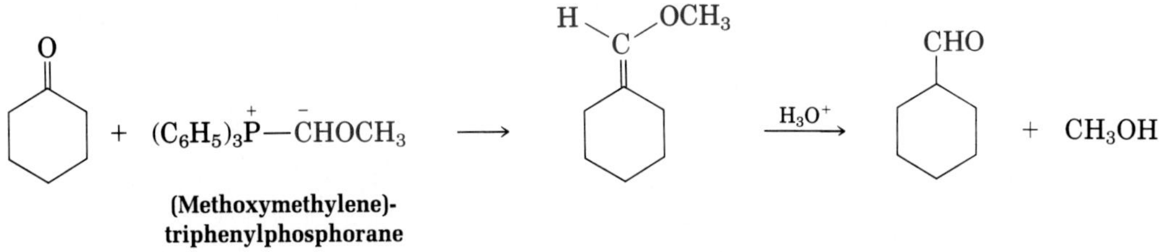

(Methoxymethylene)-
triphenylphosphorane

How would you prepare the necessary ylide?

PROBLEM 9.43   Ketones react with dimethylsulfonium methylide to yield epoxides. Suggest a mechanism for this reaction.

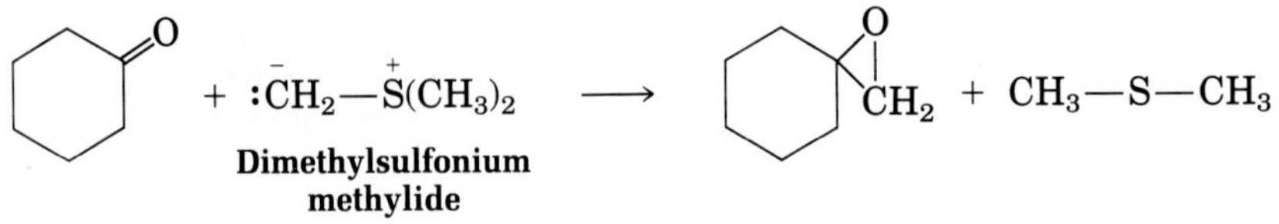

Dimethylsulfonium
methylide

Chemical Warfare in Nature

Among the many known nucleophilic additions is the reaction of ketones and aldehydes with HCN (hydrogen cyanide) to yield cyano alcohols or **cyanohydrins, RCH(OH)CN.**

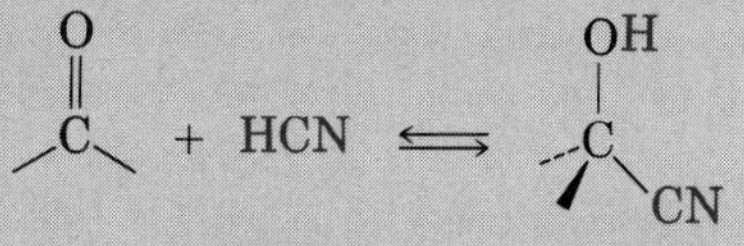

A ketone or aldehyde   **A cyanohydrin**

The reaction of HCN with ketones and aldehydes to yield cyanohydrins is of more than just chemical interest—cyanohydrins also play an interesting role in the chemical defense mechanisms used by certain plants and insects against predators. For example, when the millipede *Apheloria corrugata* is attacked by ants, it secretes mandelonitrile and an enzyme that catalyzes the decomposition of mandelonitrile into benzaldehyde and HCN. The millipede actually protects itself by discharging poisonous HCN at would-be attackers!

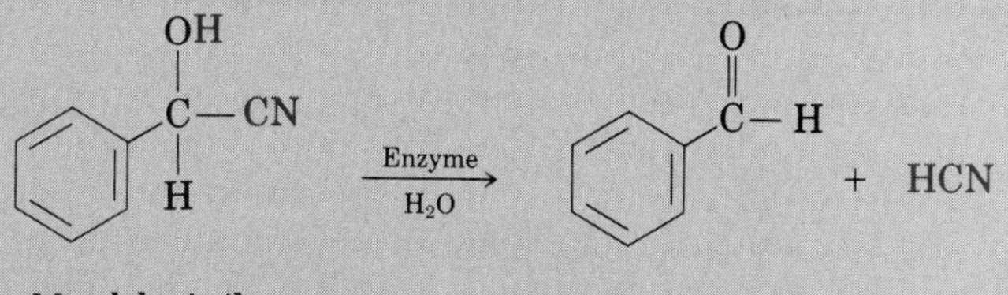

Mandelonitrile
(from *Apheloria corrugata*)

In a similar vein, apricots and peaches contain in their pits a group of substances called *cyanogenic glycosides*. These compounds, of which amygdalin (Laetrile) is the most notorious because of its claimed anticancer activity, consist of benzaldehyde cyanohydrin bonded to simple sugars such as glucose. When eaten, the sugar unit is cleaved off and HCN is released. Predators soon learn to avoid these plants.

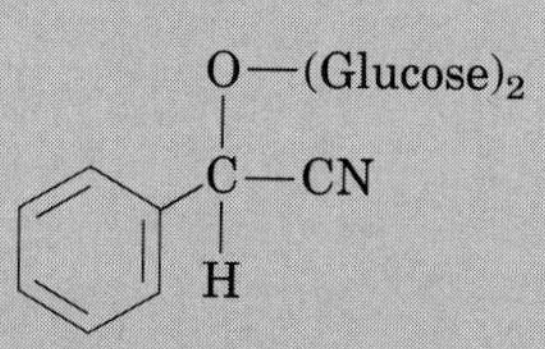

Amygdalin (Laetrile)

Some Biological Nucleophilic Addition Reactions

Nature synthesizes the molecules of life using many of the same reactions that chemists use in the laboratory. This is particularly true of carbonyl-group reactions, where nucleophilic addition steps are an important part of the biosynthesis of many vital molecules.

For example, one of the pathways by which amino acids are made involves a nucleophilic addition reaction of α-keto acids. To choose a specific case, the bacterium *Bacillus subtilis* synthesizes alanine from pyruvic acid and ammonia:

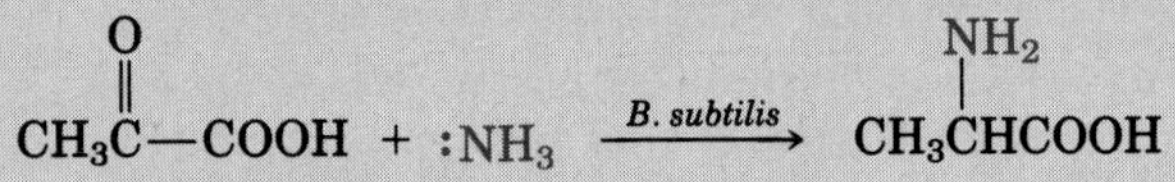

$$\underset{\substack{\textbf{Pyruvic acid} \\ \textbf{(an } \alpha\textbf{-keto acid)}}}{CH_3\overset{\overset{\textstyle O}{\|}}{C}-COOH} + :NH_3 \xrightarrow{\textit{B. subtilis}} \underset{\substack{\textbf{Alanine} \\ \textbf{(an amino acid)}}}{CH_3\overset{\overset{\textstyle NH_2}{|}}{C}HCOOH}$$

The key step in this biological transformation is the nucleophilic addition of ammonia to the ketone carbonyl group of pyruvic acid to give an imine that is further reduced by enzymes.

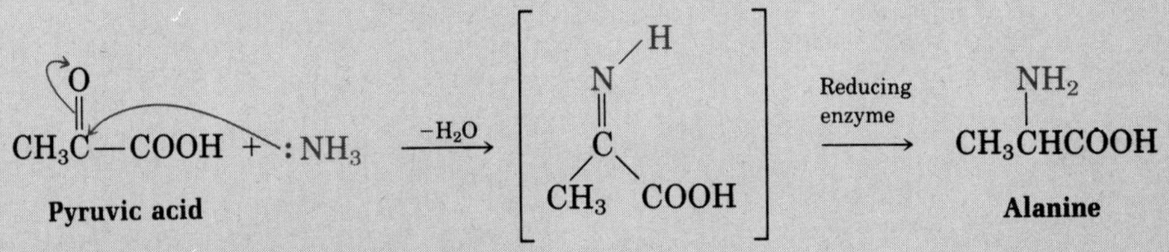

$$\underset{\textbf{Pyruvic acid}}{CH_3\overset{\overset{\textstyle O}{\|}}{C}-COOH} +:NH_3 \xrightarrow{-H_2O} \left[\underset{\substack{\textbf{} \\ \textbf{Imine}}}{\overset{\overset{\textstyle N-H}{\|}}{\underset{CH_3 \quad COOH}{C}}} \right] \xrightarrow[\text{enzyme}]{\text{Reducing}} \underset{\textbf{Alanine}}{CH_3\overset{\overset{\textstyle NH_2}{|}}{C}HCOOH}$$

Other examples of nucleophilic carbonyl addition occur frequently in carbohydrate chemistry. For example, the six-carbon sugar, glucose, acts in some respects as if it were an aldehyde. Thus, glucose can be oxidized to yield a carboxylic acid. Spectroscopic examination of glucose, however, reveals that no aldehyde group is present, but that glucose exists as a *cyclic hemiacetal*. The hydroxyl group at C5 adds to the aldehyde at C1 in an internal nucleophilic addition step.

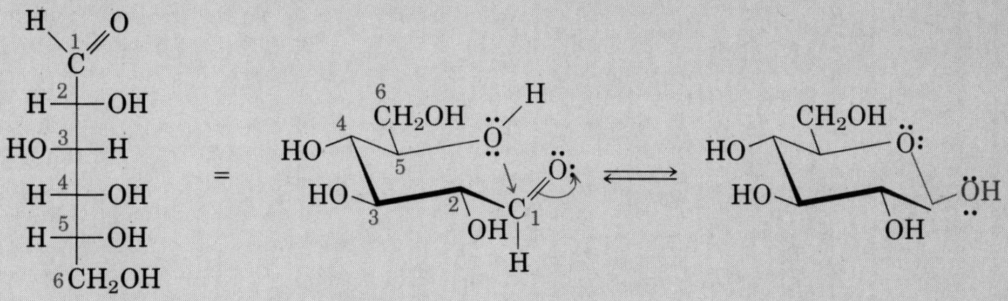

Glucose
(open form)

Glucose
(hemiacetal form)

Further reaction between molecules of glucose leads to the carbohydrate polymer cellulose. Cellulose, which constitutes the major building block of plant cell walls, consists simply of glucose units joined by acetal linkages between C1 of one glucose with the hydroxyl group at C4 of another glucose.

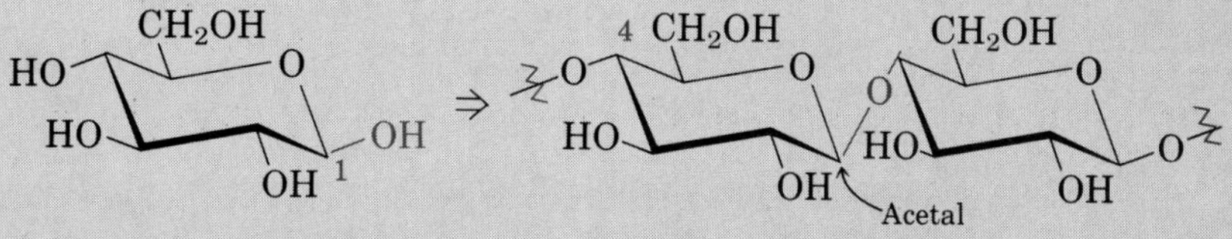

Glucose

Cellulose

We will study this and other reactions of carbohydrates in more detail in Chapter 14.

CHAPTER 10

Carboxylic Acids and Derivatives

Carboxylic acids and their derivatives are carbonyl compounds, $R-\overset{\overset{\displaystyle O}{\|}}{C}-Y$, where the acyl group is bonded to a substituent Y that may be oxygen, halogen, nitrogen, or sulfur. Numerous acyl derivatives are possible, but we will be concerned only with four of the more common ones in addition to carboxylic acids themselves: **acid halides, acid anhydrides, esters,** and **amides.** In contrast to aldehydes and ketones, all these derivatives contain an acyl group, RCO—, bonded to an electronegative atom that can serve as a leaving group in substitution reactions. Also in this chapter, we'll discuss **nitriles,** a class of compounds closely related to carboxylic acids.

$$R-\overset{\overset{\displaystyle O}{\|}}{C}-OH \qquad R-\overset{\overset{\displaystyle O}{\|}}{C}-X \qquad R-\overset{\overset{\displaystyle O}{\|}}{C}-O-\overset{\overset{\displaystyle O}{\|}}{C}-R'$$

Carboxylic acid   **Acid halide (X = F, Cl, Br, I)**   **Acid anhydride**

$$R-\overset{\overset{\displaystyle O}{\|}}{C}-OR' \qquad R-\overset{\overset{\displaystyle O}{\|}}{C}-NH_2 \qquad R-C\equiv N$$

Ester   **Amide**   **Nitrile**

The chemistry of these acyl derivatives is similar and is dominated by a single general reaction type—the **nucleophilic acyl substitution reaction:**

$$R-\overset{\overset{\displaystyle O}{\|}}{C}-Y \ + \ :Nu^- \ \longrightarrow \ R-\overset{\overset{\displaystyle O}{\|}}{C}-Nu \ + \ :Y^-$$

Let's first learn more about carboxylic acids and their derivatives and then explore the chemistry of acyl substitution reactions.

10.1   NOMENCLATURE OF CARBOXYLIC ACIDS AND DERIVATIVES

Carboxylic Acids: RCOOH

The IUPAC rules allow for different systems of acid nomenclature, depending on the structure and complexity of the molecule. Carboxylic acids that are derived from alkanes by replacing a methyl group with a carboxyl group (COOH) are systematically named by replacing the terminal -*e* of the alkane name with -*oic acid*. The carboxyl carbon atom is always numbered C1.

$$CH_3CH_2CH_2CH_2CH_2COOH$$
$$\;\;6\quad\;5\quad\;\;4\quad\;\;3\quad\;\;2\quad\;\;1$$

Hexanoic acid
(caproic acid)

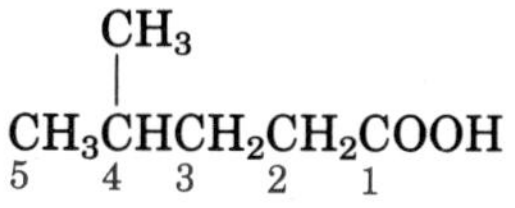

$$CH_3$$
$$|$$
$$CH_3CHCH_2CH_2COOH$$
$$5\quad\;4\quad\;3\quad\;2\quad\;\;1$$

4-Methylpentanoic acid

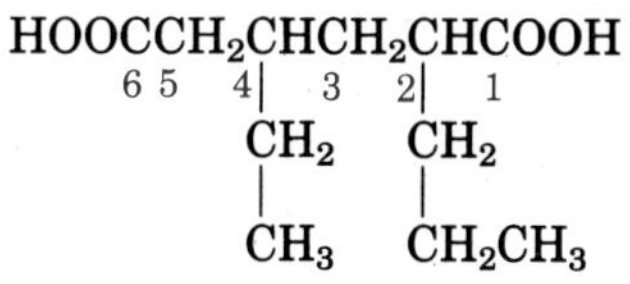

$$HOOCCH_2CHCH_2CHCOOH$$
$$6\;5\quad\;\;4|\quad\;\,3\quad\;2|\quad\;1$$
$$\qquad\qquad CH_2\quad\;\;CH_2$$
$$\qquad\qquad |\qquad\quad\;\,|$$
$$\qquad\qquad CH_3\quad\;\;CH_2CH_3$$

4-Ethyl-2-propylhexanedioic acid

Alternatively, compounds that have a —COOH group bonded to a ring are named using the suffix -*carboxylic acid*. In this alternative system, the carboxylic acid carbon is *attached to* C1, but is not itself numbered.

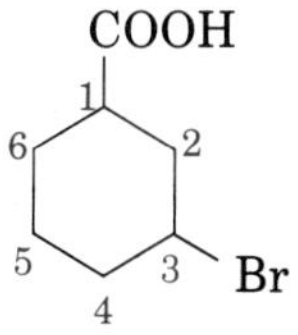

COOH

3-Bromocyclohexanecarboxylic acid 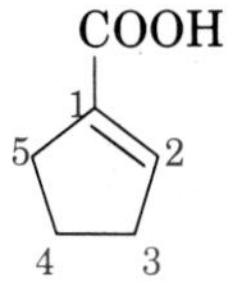   **1-Cyclopentenecarboxylic acid**

For historical reasons having to do with the fact that many carboxylic acids were among the first organic compounds to be isolated and purified, IUPAC rules make allowance for a large number of well-entrenched nonsystematic names. Some of these names are given in Table 10.1 (page 290), together with the names of the corresponding acyl groups. We will use systematic names in this book, with the exception of formic (methanoic) acid, HCOOH, and acetic (ethanoic) acid, CH_3COOH, whose names are so well known that it makes little sense to refer to them in any other way.

TABLE 10.1   Some trivial names of common carboxylic acids and acyl groups

Carboxylic acid		Acyl group	
Structure	Name	Name	Structure
HCOOH	Formic	Formyl	HCO—
CH_3COOH	Acetic	Acetyl	CH_3CO—
CH_3CH_2COOH	Propionic	Propionyl	CH_3CH_2CO—
$CH_3CH_2CH_2COOH$	Butyric	Butyryl	$CH_3(CH_2)_2CO$—
HOOCCOOH	Oxalic	Oxalyl	—OCCO—
$HOOCCH_2COOH$	Malonic	Malonyl	—$OCCH_2CO$—
$HOOCCH_2CH_2COOH$	Succinic	Succinyl	—$OC(CH_2)_2CO$—
$H_2C{=}CHCOOH$	Acrylic	Acryloyl	$H_2C{=}CHCO$—

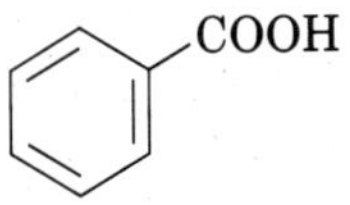

(benzoic acid structure) COOH — Benzoic — Benzoyl — (benzoyl structure with C=O)

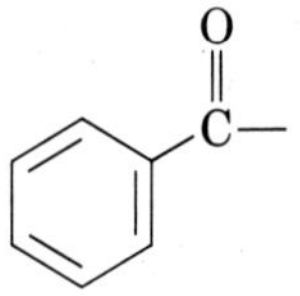

PROBLEM 10.1   Provide IUPAC names for these compounds:

   (a) $(CH_3)_2CHCH_2COOH$

   (b) $CH_3CHBrCH_2CH_2COOH$

   (c) $CH_3CH{=}CHCH_2CH_2COOH$

   (d) $CH_3CH_2\overset{\displaystyle COOH}{\overset{|}{C}}HCH_2CH_2CH_3$

   (e)

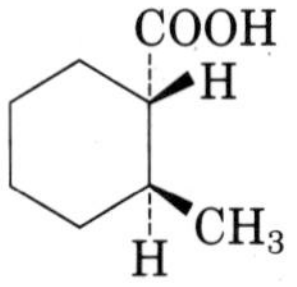

PROBLEM 10.2   Draw structures corresponding to these IUPAC names:

   (a)   2,3-Dimethylhexanoic acid   (b)   4-Methylpentanoic acid
   (c)   o-Hydroxybenzoic acid   (d)   *trans*-1,2-Cyclobutanedicarboxylic acid

Acid Halides: RCOCl

Carboxylic acid halides are named by identifying the acyl group and then citing the halide. The acyl group name is derived from the acid name by replacing the *-ic acid* ending with *-yl*, or the *-carboxylic acid* ending with *-carbonyl*. For example:

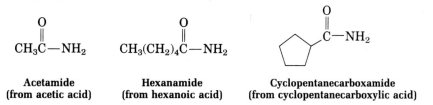

$$CH_3\overset{\displaystyle O}{\overset{\|}{C}}-Cl$$		
Acetyl chloride	**Benzoyl bromide**	**Cyclohexanecarbonyl chloride**
(from acetic acid)	(from benzoic acid)	(from cyclohexanecarboxylic acid)

Acid Anhydrides: RCO_2COR

Symmetrical anhydrides of straight-chain monocarboxylic acids and cyclic anhydrides of dicarboxylic acids are named by replacing the word *acid* with *anhydride*:

$$CH_3\overset{\displaystyle O}{\overset{\|}{C}}-O-\overset{\displaystyle O}{\overset{\|}{C}}CH_3 \qquad CH_3(CH_2)_5\overset{\displaystyle O}{\overset{\|}{C}}-O-\overset{\displaystyle O}{\overset{\|}{C}}(CH_2)_5CH_3$$

        Acetic anhydride   **Heptanoic anhydride**

Amides: $RCONH_2$

Amides with an unsubstituted —NH_2 group are named by replacing the *-oic acid* or *-ic acid* ending with *-amide*, or by replacing the *-carboxylic acid* ending with *-carboxamide*:

$$CH_3\overset{\displaystyle O}{\overset{\|}{C}}-NH_2 \qquad CH_3(CH_2)_4\overset{\displaystyle O}{\overset{\|}{C}}-NH_2$$

Acetamide	**Hexanamide**	**Cyclopentanecarboxamide**
(from acetic acid)	(from hexanoic acid)	(from cyclopentanecarboxylic acid)

If the nitrogen atom is further substituted, the compound is named by first identifying the substituent group and then citing the parent name. The substituents are preceded by the letter N to identify them as being directly attached to nitrogen.

$$CH_3CH_2\overset{\displaystyle O}{\overset{\|}{C}}-NHCH_3$$

        N-Methylpropanamide   **N,N-Diethylcyclobutanecarboxamide**

Esters: RCO_2R'

Systematic names for esters are derived by first citing the name of the alkyl group attached to oxygen and then identifying the carboxylic acid. In so doing, the *-ic acid* ending is replaced by *-ate*:

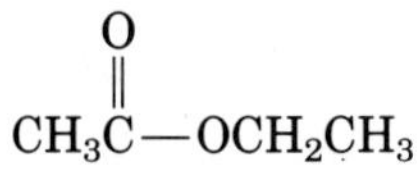

$$CH_3\overset{\displaystyle O}{\overset{\|}{C}}-OCH_2CH_3$$

$$H_2C\begin{matrix} \overset{\displaystyle O}{\overset{\|}{C}}-OCH_3 \\ \\ \underset{\displaystyle O}{\underset{\|}{C}}-OCH_3 \end{matrix}$$

$$\overset{\displaystyle O}{\overset{\|}{C}}-O-C(CH_3)_3$$

Ethyl acetate
(the ethyl ester of
acetic acid)

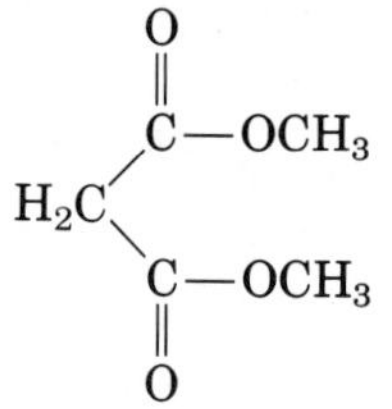

Dimethyl malonate
(the dimethyl ester of
malonic acid)

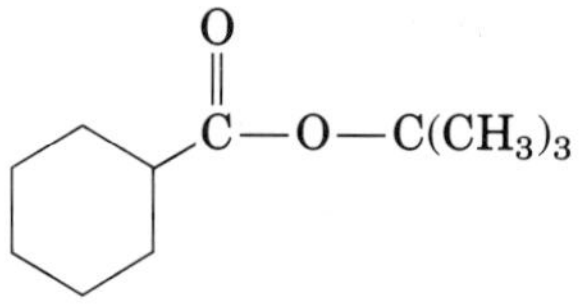

tert-Butyl cyclohexanecarboxylate
(the *tert*-butyl ester of
cyclohexanecarboxylic acid)

Nitriles: R—C≡N

Compounds containing the —C≡N functional group are known as **nitriles**. Simple acyclic nitriles are named by adding *-nitrile* as a suffix to the alkane name, with the nitrile carbon itself being considered as C1.

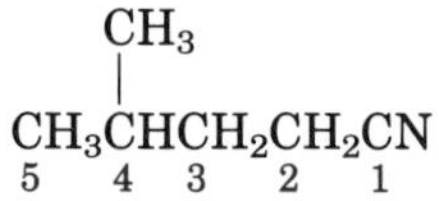

$$\underset{5}{CH_3}\underset{4}{\overset{\displaystyle CH_3}{\overset{\displaystyle |}{CH}}}\underset{3}{CH_2}\underset{2}{CH_2}\underset{1}{CN}$$

4-Methylpentanenitrile

More complex nitriles are named as derivatives of carboxylic acids by replacing the *-ic acid* or *-oic acid* ending with *-onitrile*, or by replacing the *-carboxylic acid* ending with *-carbonitrile*. In this system, the nitrile carbon atom is attached to C1, but is not itself numbered:

$$CH_3-C\equiv N$$

Acetonitrile
(from acetic acid)

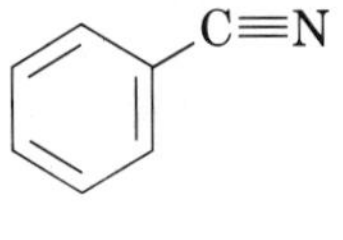

Benzonitrile
(from benzoic acid)

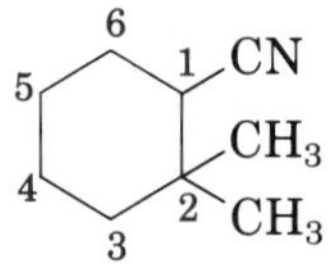

2,2-Dimethylcyclohexanecarbonitrile
(from 2,2-dimethylcyclohexanecarboxylic acid)

PROBLEM 10.3 Give IUPAC names for these structures:

(a) $(CH_3)_2CHCH_2CH_2COCl$

(b) $CH_3CH_2CH(CH_3)CN$

(c) $H_2C=CHCH_2CH_2CONH_2$

(d) $(CH_3CH_2)_2CHCN$

(e) 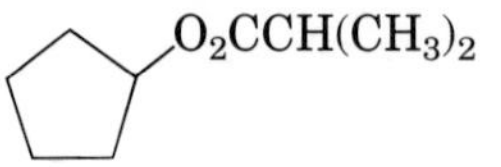 $O_2CCH(CH_3)_2$

(f) 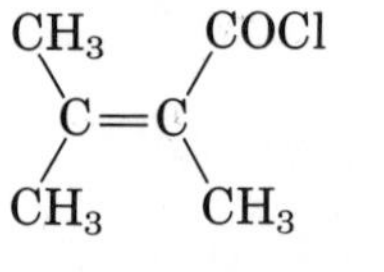 $\underset{CH_3}{\overset{CH_3}{C}}=\underset{CH_3}{\overset{COCl}{C}}$

(g) 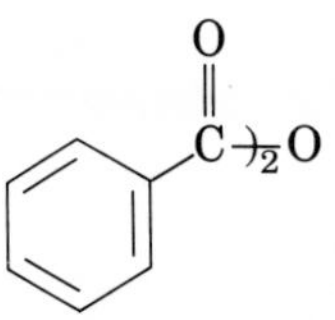 $\overset{\displaystyle O}{\overset{\|}{C}}_{\!\!2}O$

(h) $CO_2CH(CH_3)_2$

PROBLEM 10.4 Draw structures corresponding to these IUPAC names:

(a) 2,2-Dimethylpropanoyl chloride

(b) N-Methylbenzamide

(c) 5,5-Dimethylhexanenitrile

(d) tert-Butyl butanoate

(e) trans-2-Methylcyclohexanecarboxamide

(f) p-Methylbenzoic anhydride

(g) cis-3-Methylcyclohexanecarbonyl bromide

(h) p-Bromobenzonitrile

10.2 OCCURRENCE, STRUCTURE, AND PROPERTIES OF CARBOXYLIC ACIDS

Carboxylic acids occupy a central place among acyl derivatives, both in nature and the laboratory. For example, cholic acid is a major component of human bile, and long-chain aliphatic acids such as oleic acid are biological precursors of fats and other substances.

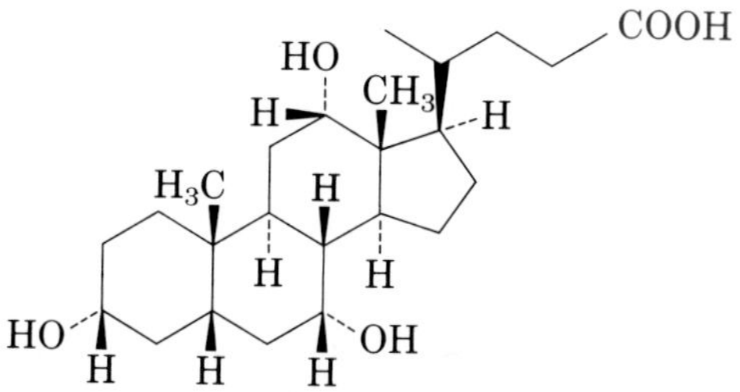

Cholic acid

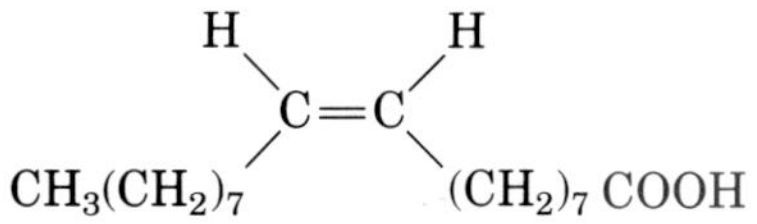

Oleic acid

Many of the simpler saturated carboxylic acids are also found in nature. For example, vinegar, produced by spoilage of wine, is simply a dilute solution of acetic acid, CH_3COOH; butanoic acid, $CH_3CH_2CH_2COOH$, is responsible for the rancid odor of sour butter; and hexanoic acid (caproic acid), $CH_3(CH_2)_4COOH$, is partially responsible for the unmistakable aroma of goats (Latin *caper*, "goat").

Since the carboxylic acid functional group, —COOH, is structurally related to both ketones and alcohols, we might expect to see some familiar properties. Like ketones, the carboxyl carbon is sp^2 hybridized. Carboxylic acid groups are therefore planar, with C—C—O and O—C—O bond angles of approximately 120°. The structural parameters of acetic acid are given in Table 10.2.

TABLE 10.2 Structure of acetic acid

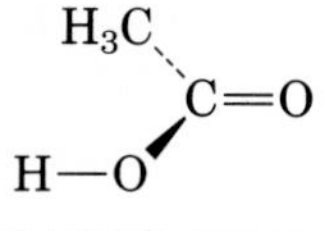

Bond angle (degrees)		Bond length (Å)	
C—C=O	119	C—C	1.52
C—C—OH	119	C=O	1.25
O=C—OH	122	C—OH	1.31

Like alcohols, carboxylic acids are strongly associated because of intermolecular hydrogen bonding. Studies have shown that most carboxylic acids exist as dimers held together by two hydrogen bonds:

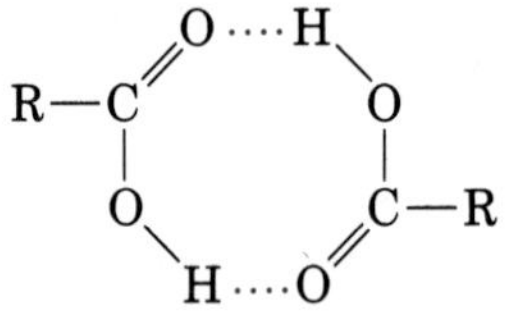

A carboxylic acid dimer

This strong hydrogen bonding has a noticeable effect on boiling points. Carboxylic acids normally boil at much higher temperatures than alkanes or alkyl halides of similar molecular weight. Table 10.3 lists the observed properties of some common acids.

TABLE 10.3   Physical constants of some carboxylic acids

Structure	Name	Melting point (°C)	Boiling point (°C)
HCOOH	Formic	8.4	100.5
CH_3COOH	Acetic	16.6	118
CH_3CH_2COOH	Propanoic	-22	141
$CH_3CH_2CH_2COOH$	Butanoic	-4.2	163
$(CH_3)_3CCOOH$	2,2-Dimethylpropanoic	35.3	164
$H_2C{=}CHCOOH$	Propenoic	13	141
C_6H_5COOH	Benzoic	122.4	249
HOOCCOOH	Oxalic	189.5	Decomposes
$HOOCCH_2COOH$	Malonic	135	Decomposes

10.3   ACIDITY OF CARBOXYLIC ACIDS

As their name implies, carboxylic acids are *acidic*. They therefore react with strong bases such as sodium hydroxide to give metal carboxylate salts. Although carboxylic acids with more than six carbon atoms are only slightly soluble in water, alkali metal salts of carboxylic acids are generally quite water-soluble because of their ionic nature.

Like other Brønsted–Lowry acids discussed in Section 1.13, carboxylic acids dissociate slightly in dilute aqueous solution to give H_3O^+ and carboxylate anion, $RCOO^-$:

$$RCOOH + H_2O \rightleftharpoons RCOO^- + H_3O^+$$

For this reaction, we have

$$K_a = \frac{[RCOO^-][H_3O^+]}{[RCOOH]} \qquad pK_a = -\log K_a$$

For most carboxylic acids, the acidity constant K_a is on the order of 10^{-5}. Acetic acid, for example, has $K_a = 1.8 \times 10^{-5}$, which corresponds to a pK_a of 4.72. In practical terms, K_a values near 10^{-5} mean that only about 1% of the molecules in a $0.1M$ solution are dissociated, as opposed to the 100% dissociation observed for strong mineral acids such as HCl and H_2SO_4.

Although much weaker than mineral acids, carboxylic acids are nevertheless much stronger acids than alcohols are. For example, K_a for ethanol is approximately 10^{-16}, making ethanol a weaker acid than acetic acid by a factor of 10^{11}.

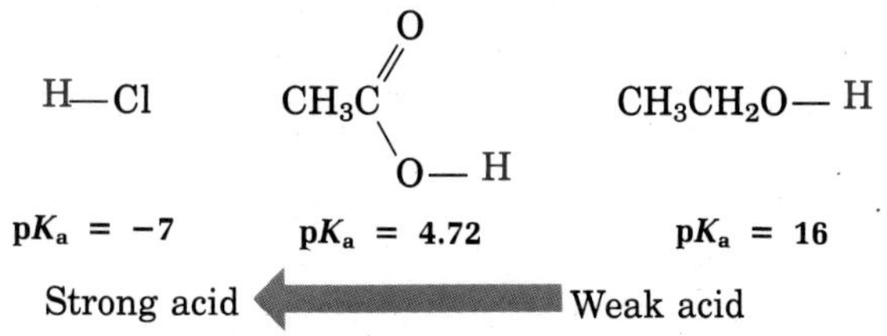

H—Cl

$$CH_3C{\overset{O}{\underset{O-H}{}}}$$

$CH_3CH_2O—H$

$pK_a = -7$ $pK_a = 4.72$ $pK_a = 16$

Strong acid ◀━━━━━━━ Weak acid

Why are carboxylic acids so much more acidic than alcohols even though both contain O—H groups? The easiest way to answer this question is to look at the relative stability of carboxylate anions versus alkoxide anions. Alkoxides are oxygen anions in which the negative charge is localized on the single oxygen atom:

$$CH_3CH_2\ddot{O}—H \rightleftharpoons CH_3CH_2—\ddot{O}:^- + H^+$$

Alcohol   Unstabilized alkoxide ion

Carboxylates are also oxygen anions, but their negative charge can be delocalized or spread out over *both* oxygen atoms, resulting in greater stability of the ion. In resonance terms (Section 4.12), a carboxylate anion is a stabilized resonance hybrid of two equivalent line-bond structures:

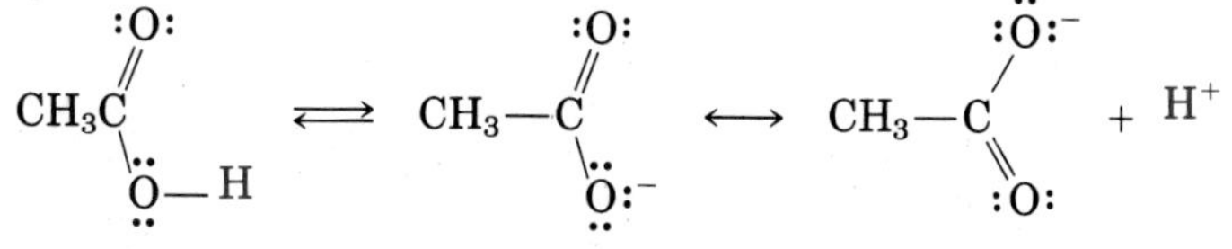

Carboxylic acid   Resonance-stabilized carboxylate ion
(two equivalent resonance forms)

Since a carboxylate ion is more stable than an alkoxide ion, it is lower in energy and is formed more readily. In other words, carboxylic acids are more acidic than alcohols, because resonance stabilization of carboxylate anions favors dissociation.

In the same way that we can't draw an accurate representation of an allylic cation (Section 4.12) or a benzene ring (Section 5.4) using line-bond structures, we can't really draw an accurate representation of the carboxylate resonance hybrid, although we might show one-half negative charge on each oxygen and use dashed lines between carbon and oxygen to indicate one-and-one-half bonds:

$$CH_3-C{\overset{\displaystyle O^{\frac{1}{2}-}}{\underset{\displaystyle O^{\frac{1}{2}-}}{}}}$$

Carboxylate resonance hybrid

An orbital picture of a carboxylate ion is more helpful in making it clear that the carbon–oxygen bonds are equivalent and that each is intermediate between single and double bonds (Figure 10.1). The p orbital on the carbon atom overlaps equally well with p orbitals from both oxygens, and the four p electrons are delocalized throughout the three-atom pi electron system.

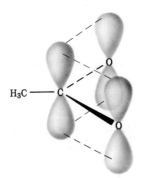

FIGURE 10.1
Orbital picture of acetate ion showing equivalence of the oxygen atoms

Physical evidence for the equivalence of the two carboxylate oxygens has been provided by X-ray studies on sodium formate. Both carbon–oxygen bonds are 1.27 Å in length, midway between the C=O double bond (1.20 Å) and C—O single bond (1.34 Å) of formic acid.

$$\overset{1.27Å}{H-C}\overset{O}{\underset{O}{}}\ ^-\quad Na^+\qquad\qquad H-C\overset{O\ \ 1.20Å}{\underset{O-H}{1.34Å}}$$

Sodium formate   **Formic acid**

PROBLEM 10.5   Draw structures for the products of these reactions:

(a)   Benzoic acid + sodium methoxide $\longrightarrow$
(b) $(CH_3)_3CCOOH$ + KOH $\longrightarrow$

PROBLEM 10.6   Review Section 8.3 and then rank the following compounds in order of increasing acidity: sulfuric acid, methanol, phenol, *p*-nitrophenol, acetic acid.

PROBLEM 10.7   The K_a for bromoacetic acid is approximately 1×10^{-3}. What percentage of the acid is dissociated in a $0.1M$ aqueous solution?

10.4   SUBSTITUENT EFFECTS ON ACIDITY

There is a considerable range in the strengths of different carboxylic acids, as indicated by the K_a values listed in Table 10.4. For example, trichloroacetic acid ($K_a = 0.23$) is more than 12,000 times as strong as acetic acid ($K_a = 1.8 \times 10^{-5}$). How can we account for such differences?

TABLE 10.4   Acid strengths of some carboxylic acids

Structure	K_a	pK_a	
(H—Cl, hydrochloric acid)[a]	(10^7)	(-7)	Strong acid
Cl_3CCOOH	0.23	0.64	
$Cl_2CHCOOH$	5.5×10^{-2}	1.26	
$ClCH_2COOH$	1.4×10^{-3}	2.85	
HCOOH	1.77×10^{-4}	3.75	
$ClCH_2CH_2COOH$	1.04×10^{-4}	3.98	
C_6H_5COOH	6.46×10^{-5}	4.19	
$H_2C{=}CHCOOH$	5.6×10^{-5}	4.25	
CH_3COOH	1.8×10^{-5}	4.72	
$(CH_3CH_2O{-}H$, ethanol)[a]	(10^{-16})	(16)	Weak acid

[a]Values for hydrochloric acid and ethanol are shown for reference.

Since the dissociation of a carboxylic acid is an equilibrium reaction, any factor that stabilizes the carboxylate anion product should favor increased dissociation and result in increased acidity. Conversely, any factor that destabilizes the carboxylate anion should make the equilibrium less favorable and result in decreased acidity. For example, an electron-*withdrawing* group attached to the carboxyl should withdraw electrons, thus helping to stabilize negatively charged carboxylate anion and to increase acidity. An electron-*donating* group, however, should have exactly the opposite effect by destabilizing the carboxylate anion and decreasing acidity.

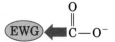

Electron-withdrawing group   Electron-donating group
stabilizes carboxylate   destabilizes carboxylate
and strengthens acid   and weakens acid

The pK_a data in Table 10.4 show exactly this expected effect. Highly electronegative substituents such as the halogens tend to make the carboxylate anion more stable by withdrawing electrons. Thus, chloroacetic acid is stronger than acetic acid by a factor of 75. Introduction of two electronegative substituents makes dichloroacetic acid some 3000 times as strong as acetic acid, and introduction of three substituents makes trichloroacetic acid more than 12,000 times as strong (Figure 10.2).

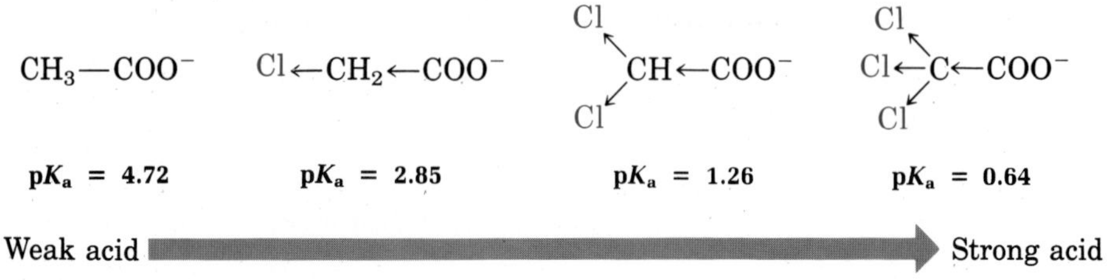

$$CH_3-COO^- \qquad Cl\leftarrow CH_2\leftarrow COO^- \qquad \begin{matrix}Cl\searrow\\Cl\nearrow\end{matrix}CH\leftarrow COO^- \qquad \begin{matrix}Cl\searrow\\Cl\leftarrow C\leftarrow COO^-\\Cl\nearrow\end{matrix}$$

$pK_a = 4.72$ $\qquad\qquad pK_a = 2.85$ $\qquad\qquad pK_a = 1.26$ $\qquad\qquad pK_a = 0.64$

Weak acid ⟶ Strong acid

FIGURE 10.2
Relative strengths of chlorosubstituted acetic acids

PRACTICE PROBLEM Which would you expect to be the stronger acid, benzoic acid or *p*-nitrobenzoic acid?

Solution We know from its effect on aromatic substitution (Section 5.11) that nitro is a deactivating, electron-withdrawing group that can stabilize a negative charge. Thus, *p*-nitrobenzoic acid is stronger than benzoic acid.

PROBLEM 10.8 Rank the following compounds in order of increasing acidity:

(a) CH_3CH_2COOH, $BrCH_2COOH$, $BrCH_2CH_2COOH$
(b) Benzoic acid, ethanol, *p*-methylbenzoic acid

PROBLEM 10.9 Dicarboxylic acids have two ionization constants: one for the initial dissociation into a mono anion and one for the second dissociation into a dianion. For oxalic acid, $HOOC-COOH$, the first ionization constant is $pK_a = 1.2$, and the second ionization constant is $pK_a = 4.2$. Why does the second carboxyl group dissociate less readily than the first?

10.5 PREPARATION OF CARBOXYLIC ACIDS

We have already seen most of the common methods for preparing carboxylic acids, but let's review them briefly:

1. Oxidation of substituted alkylbenzenes with potassium permanganate or sodium dichromate gives substituted benzoic acids (Section 5.14). Either primary or secondary alkyl groups can be oxidized in this manner.

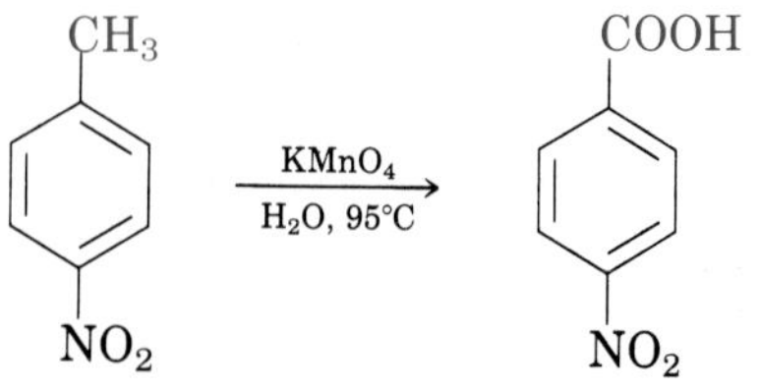

p-Nitrotoluene

p-Nitrobenzoic acid
(88%)

2. Oxidation of primary alcohols and aldehydes yields carboxylic acids (Sections 8.7 and 9.6). Primary alcohols are often oxidized with chromium trioxide or sodium dichromate; aldehydes are oxidized with chromium trioxide or Tollens' reagent ($AgNO_3$ in NH_4OH). All these oxidations take place rapidly and in high yield.

$$CH_3(CH_2)_8 CH_2OH \xrightarrow[\text{H}_2\text{O, H}_2\text{SO}_4]{\text{CrO}_3} CH_3(CH_2)_8 COOH$$

1-Decanol   Decanoic acid (93%)

$$CH_3(CH_2)_4 CHO \xrightarrow[\text{NH}_4\text{OH}]{\text{AgNO}_3} CH_3(CH_2)_4 COOH$$

Hexanal   Hexanoic acid (85%)

Hydrolysis of Nitriles

Carboxylic acids can be prepared from nitriles, $R—C\equiv N$, by a hydrolysis reaction with strong aqueous acid or base. Since nitriles themselves are most often prepared by S_N2 reaction between an alkyl halide and cyanide ion, CN^-, the two-step sequence of cyanide ion displacement followed by nitrile hydrolysis is an excellent method for converting an alkyl halide into a carboxylic acid ($RBr \rightarrow RC\equiv N \rightarrow RCOOH$). A good example of the reaction occurs in the commercial synthesis of the antiarthritis drug, Fenoprofen.

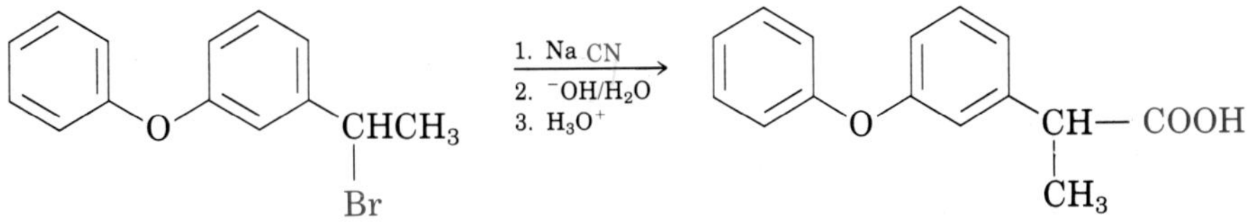

Fenoprofen
(an antiarthritic agent)

The method works best with primary alkyl halides, since an E2 elimination reaction can occur when a secondary or tertiary alkyl halide is used (Section 7.10).

Carboxylation of Grignard Reagents

Yet a further method of preparing carboxylic acids is by reaction of Grignard reagents, RMgX, with carbon dioxide. This **carboxylation** reaction is carried out either by pouring a solution of the Grignard reagent over dry ice (solid CO_2), or by bubbling a stream of dry CO_2 through the Grignard reagent solution.

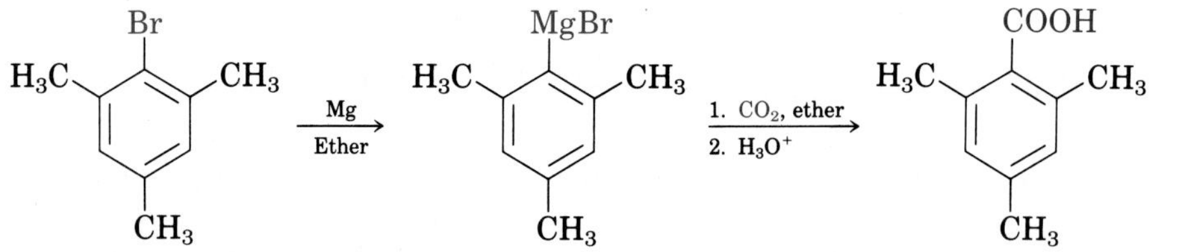

1-Bromo-2,4,6-trimethyl-benzene

2,4,6-Trimethylbenzoic acid (87%)

The mechanism of this carboxylation reaction is similar to that of other Grignard reactions (Section 9.10). The nucleophilic organomagnesium halide adds to one of the $C=O$ bonds of carbon dioxide, yielding a carboxylate salt that is subsequently protonated to give the free carboxylic acid:

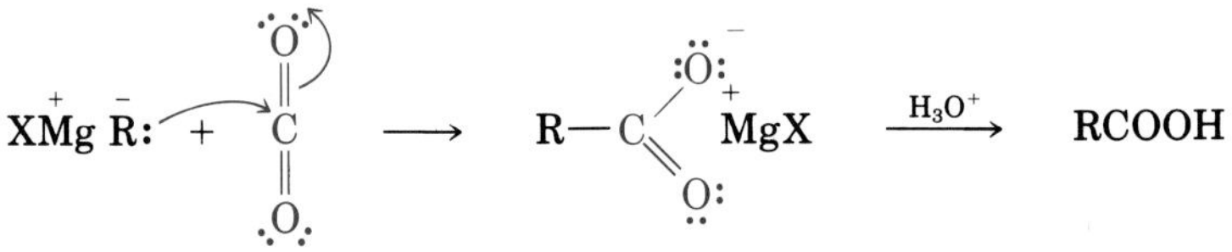

Recall:

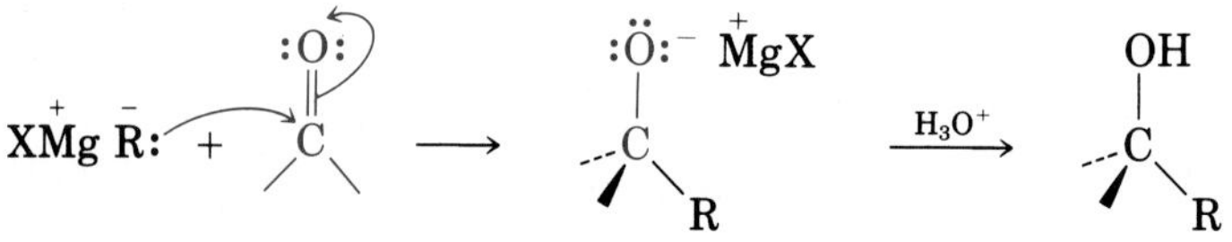

PRACTICE PROBLEM   How could you convert 2-chloro-2-methylpropane into 2,2-dimethylpropanoic acid?

Solution   Since 2-chloro-2-methylpropane, $(CH_3)_3CCl$, is a tertiary alkyl halide, it will not undergo S_N2 substitution with cyanide ion. Thus, the only way we could carry out the desired reaction is to convert the alkyl halide into a Grignard reagent, and then add CO_2.

$$(CH_3)_3C-Cl + Mg \longrightarrow (CH_3)_3C-MgCl \xrightarrow[\text{2. } H_3O^+]{\text{1. } CO_2} (CH_3)_3C-COOH$$

PROBLEM 10.10   Formulate all the steps in the conversion of iodomethane to acetic acid via the nitrile hydrolysis route. Do you think this route would also work for the conversion of iodobenzene to benzoic acid? Explain.

PROBLEM 10.11   Formulate all the steps in the conversion of iodobenzene to benzoic acid via the Grignard carboxylation route. Do you think this route would also work for the conversion of iodomethane to acetic acid?

10.6 NUCLEOPHILIC ACYL SUBSTITUTION REACTIONS

We saw in Chapter 9 that the addition of nucleophiles to the polar C=O bond is a general feature of the chemistry of carbonyl groups. When a ketone or aldehyde reacts with a nucleophile, a tetrahedrally hybridized adduct is formed (Figure 10.3).

Carboxylic acids and their derivatives also react with nucleophiles, but the initially formed tetrahedral intermediate follows a different reaction course, also shown in Figure 10.3. The tetrahedral intermediate expels the Y substituent originally bound to the carbonyl carbon, leading to a net **nucleophilic acyl substitution reaction**.

Ketone or aldehyde
(nucleophilic addition):

Carboxylic acid
(nucleophilic acyl substitution):

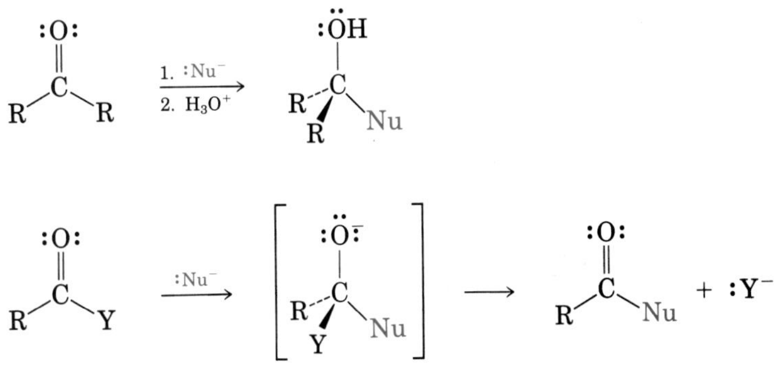

FIGURE 10.3
General reactions of carbonyl groups with nucleophiles: Ketones and aldehydes undergo nucleophilic *addition* reactions, whereas carboxylic acids and their derivatives undergo nucleophilic acyl *substitution* reactions.

What is the reason for the different behavior of ketones/aldehydes and carboxylic acid derivatives? The difference is simply a consequence of structure. Carboxylic acid derivatives have an acyl function bonded to a potential leaving group, Y, which can leave as a stable anion. As soon as the tetrahedral intermediate is formed, the negative charge on oxygen can readily expel this leaving group to generate a new carbonyl compound. Ketones and aldehydes have no such leaving group, and they therefore do not undergo elimination.

Notice that the net effect of the two-step addition/elimination sequence is a *substitution* of the nucleophile for the Y group. Thus, the overall reaction is superficially similar to the kind of nucleophilic substitution that occurs in S_N2 reactions (Section 7.8). The *mechanisms* of the two reactions are quite different, however: S_N2 reactions occur in a single step by back-side displacement of the leaving group, whereas nucleophilic acyl substitutions take place in two steps and involve a tetrahedral intermediate.

10.7 RELATIVE REACTIVITY OF CARBOXYLIC ACID DERIVATIVES

Nucleophilic acyl substitution reactions take place in two steps: (1) addition of the nucleophile and (2) elimination of the leaving group. Both steps can affect the overall rate of the reaction, but it is usually the first step that is rate-limiting. Thus, any factor that makes the carbonyl group more easily attacked by nucleophiles favors the reaction.

Steric and electronic factors are both important in determining reactivity. Sterically, we find that more hindered carbonyl groups are attacked less readily than sterically accessible carbonyls. For example, if we were to compare the reactivity of 2,2-dimethylpropanoyl chloride, $(CH_3)_3COCl$, with that of acetyl chloride, CH_3COCl, we would find that the less hindered acetyl chloride is much more reactive:

$$
\underset{\text{reactive}}{\text{Less}} \qquad
\underset{O}{R_3\overset{\overset{\displaystyle \parallel}{}}{C}C-} \; < \;
\underset{O}{R_2\overset{\overset{\displaystyle \parallel}{}}{C}HC-} \; < \;
\underset{O}{RCH_2\overset{\overset{\displaystyle \parallel}{}}{C}-} \; < \;
\underset{O}{CH_3\overset{\overset{\displaystyle \parallel}{}}{C}-} \qquad
\underset{\text{reactive}}{\text{More}}
$$

Electronically, we find that more highly polar acid derivatives are attacked more readily than less polar derivatives. Thus, acid chlorides are the most reactive compounds because the electronegative chlorine atom strongly polarizes the carbonyl group, whereas amides are the least reactive compounds:

More reactive, less stable   More stable, less reactive

$$
\underset{\text{Acid chloride}}{R-\overset{\overset{\displaystyle O}{\parallel}}{C}-Cl} \; > \;
\underset{\text{Acid anhydride}}{R-\overset{\overset{\displaystyle O}{\parallel}}{C}-O-\overset{\overset{\displaystyle O}{\parallel}}{C}-R} \; > \;
\underset{\text{Ester}}{R-\overset{\overset{\displaystyle O}{\parallel}}{C}-O-R'} \; > \;
\underset{\text{Amide}}{R-\overset{\overset{\displaystyle O}{\parallel}}{C}-NH_2}
$$

An important consequence of these observed reactivity differences is that *it is usually possible to convert a more reactive acid derivative into a less reactive one* (for example, an acid chloride into an amide), but it is not usually possible to convert a less reactive derivative into a more reactive one. Remembering the correct reactivity order is therefore a useful way to keep track of a large number of reactions.

PROBLEM 10.12 Which of the following compounds would you expect to be more reactive in nucleophilic acyl substitution reactions?

(a) CH_3COCl or CH_3COOCH_3 (b) $(CH_3)_2CHCONH_2$ or $CH_3CH_2CONH_2$
(c) CH_3COOCH_3 or $CH_3COOCOCH_3$ (d) CH_3COOCH_3 or CH_3CHO

PROBLEM 10.13   How can you account for the fact that methyl trifluoroacetate, CF_3COOCH_3, is more reactive than methyl acetate, CH_3COOCH_3, in nucleophilic acyl substitution reactions?

10.8   REACTIONS OF CARBOXYLIC ACIDS

Reduction: Conversion of Acids into Alcohols

As we saw in Section 8.5, carboxylic acids are reduced by lithium aluminum hydride (but not by $NaBH_4$) to yield primary alcohols. The reaction is sometimes difficult, and often requires heating to go to completion.

$$CH_3(CH_2)_7CH{=}CH(CH_2)_7COOH \xrightarrow[\text{2. } H_3O^+]{\text{1. LiAlH}_4\text{, THF, } \Delta} CH_3(CH_2)_7CH{=}CH(CH_2)_7CH_2OH$$

Oleic acid   *cis*-9-Octadecen-1-ol (87%)

Conversion of Acids into Acid Chlorides

The most important reactions of carboxylic acids are those that convert the carboxyl group into other acid derivatives by nucleophilic acyl substitution, $RCO{-}OH \rightarrow RCO{-}Y$. Acid chlorides, anhydrides, esters, and amides can all be prepared from carboxylic acids in this manner.

Acid chlorides are prepared by treatment of carboxylic acids with either thionyl chloride, $SOCl_2$, or phosphorus trichloride, PCl_3. For example:

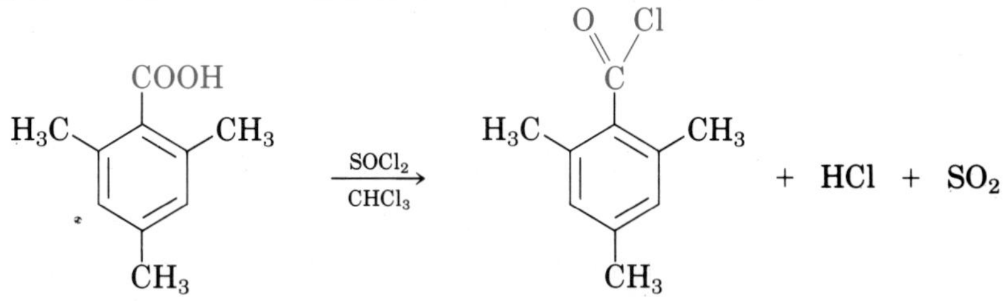

2,4,6-Trimethylbenzoic acid   2,4,6-Trimethylbenzoyl chloride
(90%)

The net effect is substitution of the acid $-OH$ group by $-Cl$.

Conversion of Acids into Acid Anhydrides

Acid anhydrides, which have the general structure $\overset{\text{O}}{\overset{\|}{R}C}{-}O{-}\overset{\text{O}}{\overset{\|}{C}}R$, are derived from two molecules of carboxylic acid by removing one molecule of water. Acyclic anhydrides are rather difficult to prepare directly from the corresponding acids, and only acetic anhydride, $CH_3COOCOCH_3$, is available commercially.

Cyclic anhydrides of ring size five or six can be obtained from diacids by high-temperature dehydration.

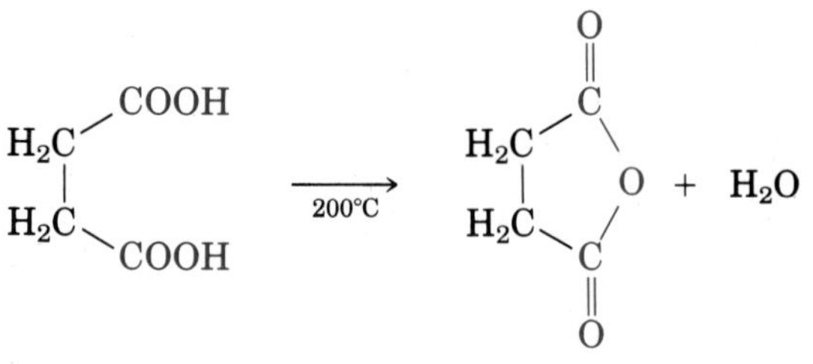

Succinic acid   Succinic anhydride

Conversion of Acids into Esters

One of the most important reactions of carboxylic acids is their conversion into esters, R—COOR. There are many excellent methods for accomplishing this transformation, one of which we have already studied—the S_N2 reaction between a carboxylate anion nucleophile and a primary alkyl halide (Section 7.8):

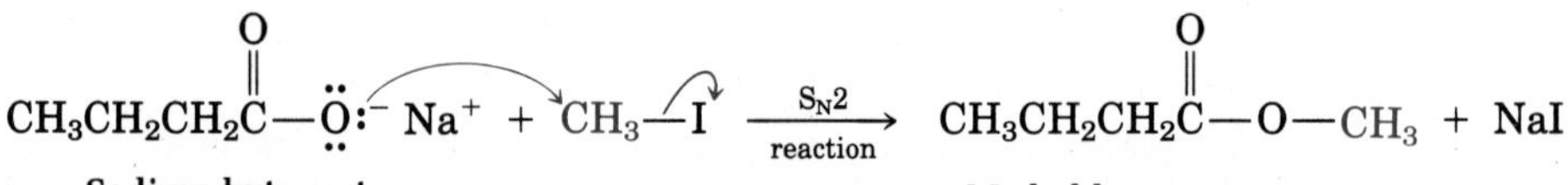

Sodium butanoate   Methyl butanoate, an ester
                                         (97%)

Alternatively, esters can be synthesized by a nucleophilic acyl substitution reaction of a carboxylic acid with an alcohol. Called the **Fischer esterification reaction,** this method involves heating the carboxylic acid with a small amount of mineral acid catalyst in an alcohol solvent.

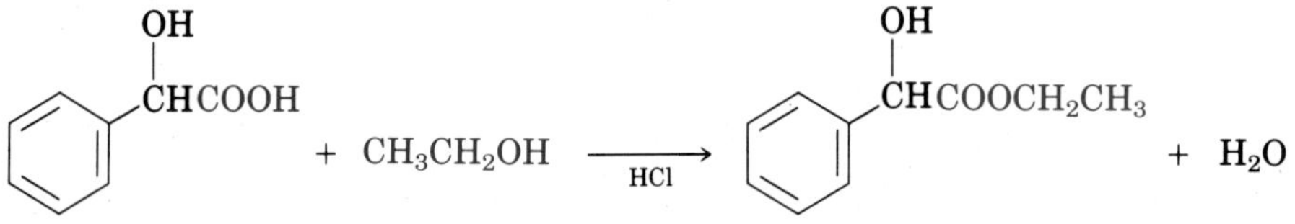

Mandelic acid   Ethyl mandelate (86%)

The Fischer esterification reaction, whose mechanism is shown in Figure 10.4, is a nucleophilic acyl substitution process. Although free carboxylic acids are not reactive enough to be attacked by most nucleophiles, they can be made much more reactive in the presence of a mineral acid such as HCl or H_2SO_4. The mineral acid first protonates an oxygen atom of the —COOH group, which gives the carboxylic acid a full positive charge and renders it much more reactive toward nucleophiles. An alcohol molecule then adds to the protonated carboxylic acid, and subsequent loss of water yields the ester product.

All steps in the Fischer esterification reaction are reversible, and the position of the equilibrium can be driven to either side, depending on the reaction conditions. Ester formation is favored when alcohol is used as solvent, but carboxylic acid is favored when water is used as solvent.

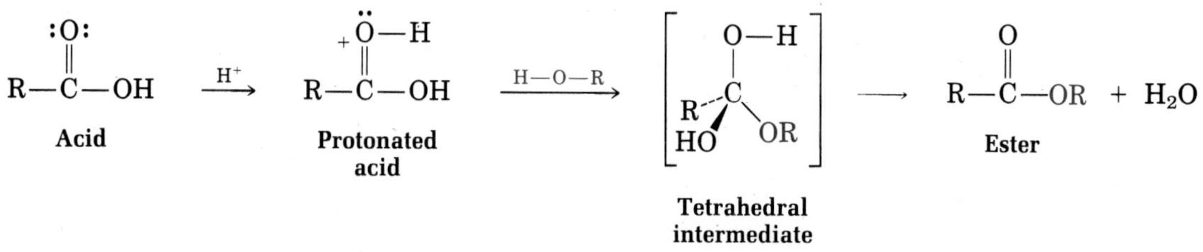

FIGURE 10.4

The Fischer esterification reaction of a carboxylic acid to yield an ester

PRACTICE PROBLEM How would you prepare the following ester using a Fischer esterification reaction?

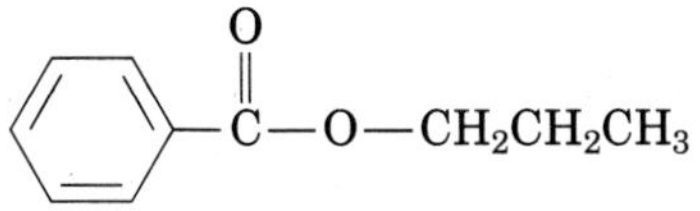

Solution The trick is to identify the two parts of the ester. The target molecule is propyl benzoate, indicating that it can be prepared by treating benzoic acid with 1-propanol.

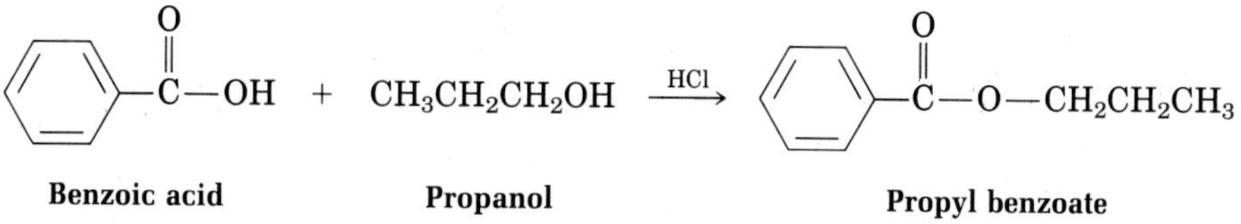

| Benzoic acid | Propanol | Propyl benzoate |

PROBLEM 10.14 Show how you would prepare the following esters:

(a) Butyl acetate

(b) Methyl butanoate

PROBLEM 10.15 If 5-hydroxypentanoic acid is treated with an acid catalyst, an intramolecular esterification reaction occurs. What is the structure of the product? (*Intramolecular* means within the same molecule.)

Conversion of Acids into Amides

Amides are carboxylic acid derivatives in which the acid hydroxyl group has been replaced by a nitrogen substituent, $-NH_2$ (or $-NHR$, or $-NR_2$). Amides are very difficult to prepare directly from acids, and high reaction temperatures are required. The reason for this lack of reactivity is that amines are bases (as we will see in Chapter 12), which convert acidic carboxyl groups into their carboxylate anions. Since the carboxylate anion has a negative charge, it is no longer electrophilic and no longer undergoes attack by nucleophiles.

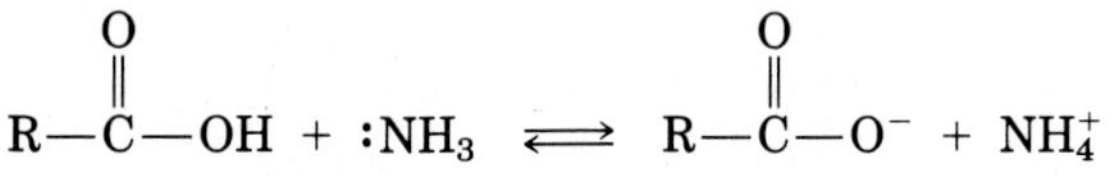

$$R-\overset{\overset{\text{O}}{\|}}{C}-OH + :NH_3 \rightleftharpoons R-\overset{\overset{\text{O}}{\|}}{C}-O^- + NH_4^+$$

10.9   CHEMISTRY OF ACID HALIDES

Preparation of Acid Halides

Acid chlorides are prepared from carboxylic acids by reaction with thionyl chloride, $SOCl_2$, or phosphorus trichloride, PCl_3, as we saw in the previous section. Reaction of an acid with phosphorus tribromide, PBr_3, yields an acid bromide.

$$ R-\overset{\overset{\displaystyle O}{\|}}{C}-OH \xrightarrow{\text{SOCl}_2 \text{ or PCl}_3} R-\overset{\overset{\displaystyle O}{\|}}{C}-Cl $$

$$ R-\overset{\overset{\displaystyle O}{\|}}{C}-OH \xrightarrow[\text{Ether}]{\text{PBr}_3} R-\overset{\overset{\displaystyle O}{\|}}{C}-Br + HOPBr_2 $$

Reactions of Acid Halides

Acid halides are among the most reactive carboxylic acid derivatives and can therefore be converted into a variety of other compound types. For example, we have already seen the value of acid chlorides for preparing ketones in the Friedel–Crafts acylation reaction (Section 5.10).

[handwritten margin note: Halide ion replaced by
OH – acid
OR – ester
NH₂ – amide]

$$ Ar-H + R-\overset{\overset{\displaystyle O}{\|}}{C}-Cl \xrightarrow{\text{AlCl}_3} Ar-\overset{\overset{\displaystyle O}{\|}}{C}-R + HCl $$

Most acid halide reactions occur by nucleophilic acyl substitution mechanisms. As illustrated in Figure 10.5, the halide ion can be replaced by —OH to yield an acid, by —OR to yield an ester, or by —NH$_2$ to yield an amide. In addition, reduction of acid halides yields primary alcohols, and reaction with Grignard reagents yields tertiary alcohols. Although Figure 10.5 illustrates these reactions only for acid chlorides, they also take place with other acid halides.

[handwritten margin note: Reducing acid halides gives 1° alcohols
Rxn w/ MgBr gives 3° alcohols]

Hydrolysis: Conversion of acid halides into acids   Acid chlorides react with water to yield carboxylic acids. This hydrolysis reaction is a typical nucleophilic acyl substitution process, which is initiated by attack of the nucleophile, water, on the acid chloride carbonyl group. The initially formed tetrahedral intermediate undergoes loss of HCl to yield the product.

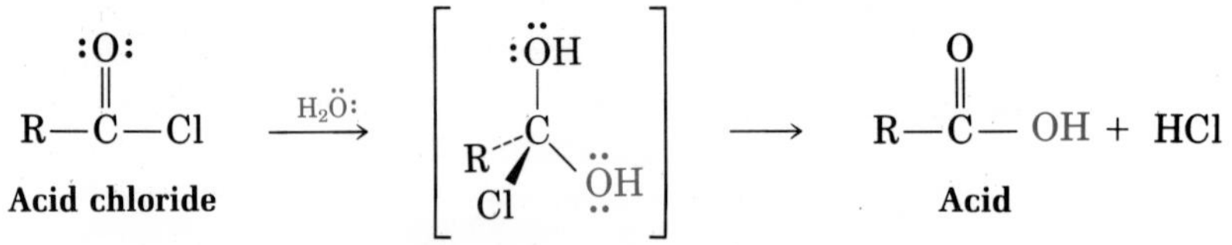

$$ R-\overset{\overset{\displaystyle :O:}{\|}}{C}-Cl \xrightarrow{H_2\ddot{O}:} \left[\underset{\underset{\displaystyle Cl}{}}{R} \overset{\overset{\displaystyle :\ddot{O}H}{|}}{\underset{\displaystyle \ddot{O}H}{C}} \right] \longrightarrow R-\overset{\overset{\displaystyle O}{\|}}{C}-OH + HCl $$

Acid chloride   **Acid**

Tetrahedral intermediate

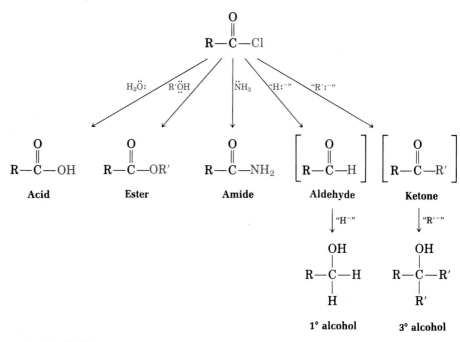

FIGURE 10.5
Some nucleophilic acyl substitution reactions of acid chlorides

Alcoholysis: Conversion of acid halides into esters Acid chlorides react with alcohols to yield esters in a reaction analogous to their reaction with water to yield acids.

$$\underset{\text{Acetyl chloride}}{CH_3\overset{O}{\overset{\|}{C}}{-}Cl} + \underset{\text{1-Butanol}}{CH_3CH_2CH_2CH_2OH} \xrightarrow{\text{Pyridine}} \underset{\text{Butyl acetate (90\%)}}{CH_3\overset{O}{\overset{\|}{C}}{-}O{-}CH_2CH_2CH_2CH_3}$$

Since HCl is generated as a byproduct of alcoholysis, the reaction is usually carried out in the presence of a base to react with the HCl as it is formed and prevent it from causing side reactions. If this were not done, the HCl might react with the alcohol to form an alkyl chloride, or it might add to a carbon–carbon double bond if one were present elsewhere in the molecule. The organic amine base pyridine is often used.

PROBLEM 10.16 How could you prepare these esters using the reaction of an acid chloride with an alcohol?

(a) $CH_3CH_2COOCH_3$
(b) $CH_3COOCH_2CH_3$
(c) Ethyl benzoate
(d) Cyclohexyl acetate

Aminolysis: Conversion of acid chlorides into amides Acid chlorides react rapidly with ammonia and with amines to give amides. Both mono- and disubstituted amines can be used.

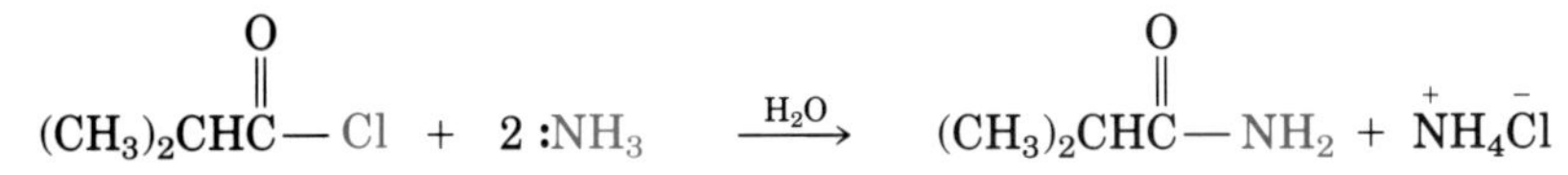

$$(CH_3)_2CHC \overset{O}{\underset{\|}{}} {-} Cl \ + \ 2 \ :NH_3 \quad \xrightarrow{\ H_2O\ } \quad (CH_3)_2CHC \overset{O}{\underset{\|}{}} {-} NH_2 \ + \ \overset{+}{N}H_4\overset{-}{Cl}$$

2-Methylpropanoyl chloride   **2-Methylpropanamide**
                                                  (83%)

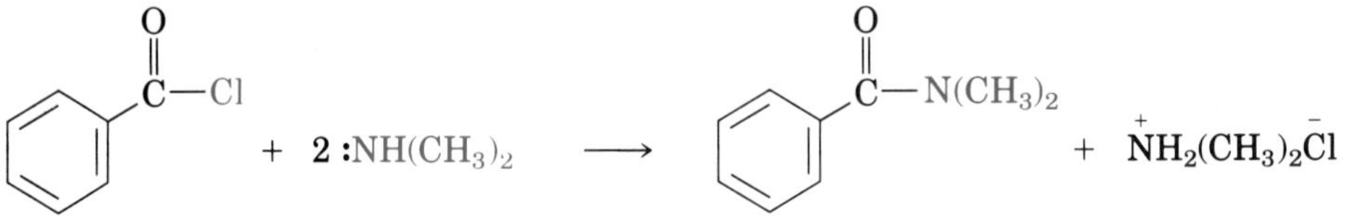

Benzoyl chloride   **N,N-Dimethylbenzamide**
                                               (92%)

Since HCl is formed during the reaction, 2 equiv of the amine must be used; 1 equiv reacts with the acid chloride, and 1 equiv reacts with HCl to form an ammonium chloride salt. If, however, the amine component is too valuable to waste half, amide synthesis can be carried out using 1 equiv of the amine plus 1 equiv of an inexpensive base such as NaOH. For example, the sedative Trimetozine is prepared commercially by reaction of 3,4,5-trimethoxybenzoyl chloride with the amine, morpholine, in the presence of 1 equiv NaOH.

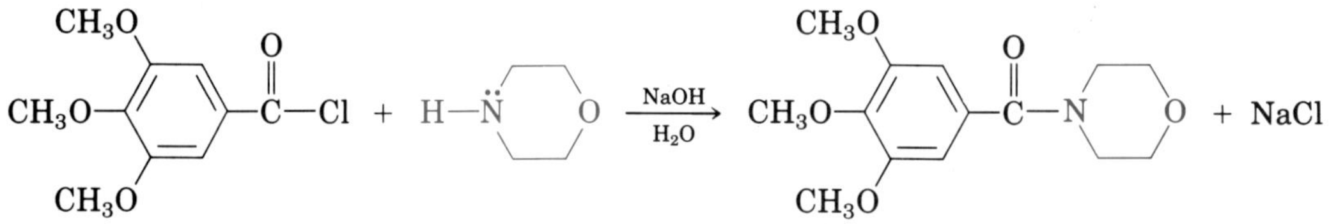

3,4,5-Trimethoxybenzoyl chloride   **Morpholine**   **Trimetozine (an amide)**

PROBLEM 10.17 Write the steps in the mechanism of the reaction between morpholine and 3,4,5-trimethoxybenzoyl chloride to yield Trimetozine.

PROBLEM 10.18 What amines would react with what acid chlorides to give the following amide products?

(a) $CH_3CH_2CONH_2$ (b) $(CH_3)_2CHCH_2CONHCH_3$
(c) N,N-Dimethylpropanamide   (d) N,N-Diethylbenzamide

Reduction: Conversion of acid chlorides into alcohols Acid chlorides are reduced by lithium aluminum hydride to yield primary alcohols. The reaction is of little practical value, however, since the parent carboxylic acids are generally more readily available and are themselves reduced by $LiAlH_4$ to yield alcohols.

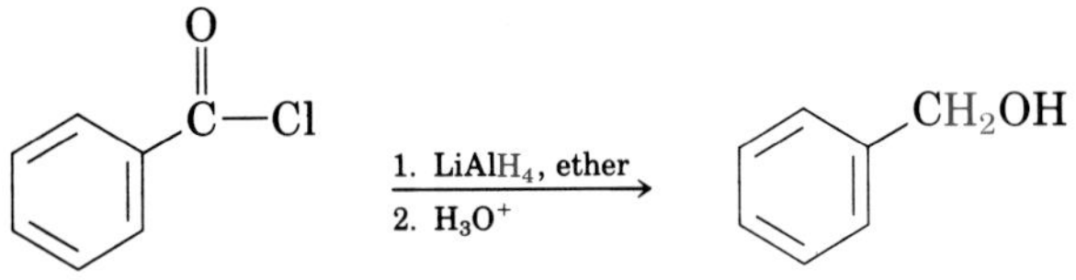

Benzoyl chloride   Benzyl alcohol (96%)

Reaction of acid chlorides with Grignard reagents Grignard reagents react with acid chlorides to yield tertiary alcohols in which two of the substituents are identical:

$$RMgX \ + \ R'-\overset{\overset{\displaystyle O}{\|}}{C}-Cl \ \longrightarrow \ R'-\overset{\overset{\displaystyle OH}{|}}{\underset{\underset{\displaystyle R}{|}}{C}}-R \ + \ MgXCl$$

The mechanism for this reaction is a typical nucleophilic acyl substitution process in which the first equivalent of Grignard reagent adds to the carbonyl group, and elimination of chloride ion then gives a ketone intermediate. Since ketones themselves react rapidly with Grignard reagents (Section 9.10), however, they are not isolated. Instead, the ketone intermediate reacts with a second equivalent of Grignard reagent to yield a tertiary alcohol.

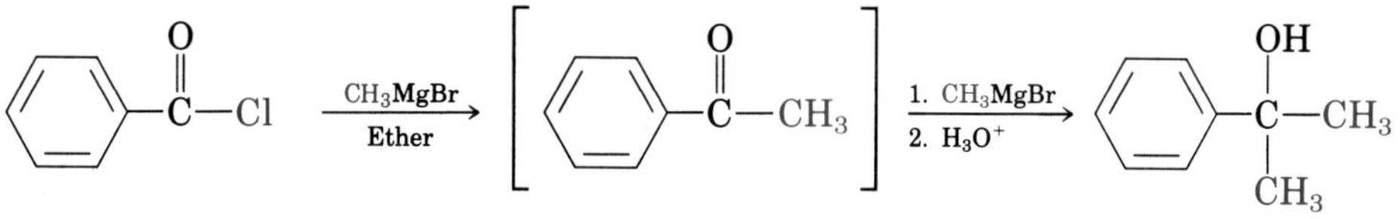

Acid chloride   Ketone   3° alcohol
                          (not isolated)

PROBLEM 10.19 Show the product of the reaction of phenylmagnesium bromide with propanoyl chloride.

10.10 CHEMISTRY OF ACID ANHYDRIDES

Preparation of Acid Anhydrides

The most general method of preparing acid anhydrides is by a nucleophilic acyl substitution reaction of an acid chloride with a carboxylic acid anion. Both symmetrical and unsymmetrical acid anhydrides can be prepared in this way.

$$H-\overset{\overset{\displaystyle O}{\|}}{C}-O^- \ Na^+ \ + \ CH_3\overset{\overset{\displaystyle O}{\|}}{C}-Cl \ \xrightarrow[25°C]{Ether} \ HC-O-\overset{\overset{\displaystyle O}{\|}}{C}CH_3 \ + \ NaCl$$

Sodium formate   Acetyl chloride   Acetic formic
                                                  anhydride (64%)

Reactions of Acid Anhydrides

The chemistry of acid anhydrides is similar to that of acid chlorides. Although anhydrides react more slowly than acid chlorides, the kinds of reactions the two functional groups undergo are the same. Thus, acid anhydrides react with water to form acids, with alcohols to form esters, with amines to form amides, and with $LiAlH_4$ to form primary alcohols (Figure 10.6).

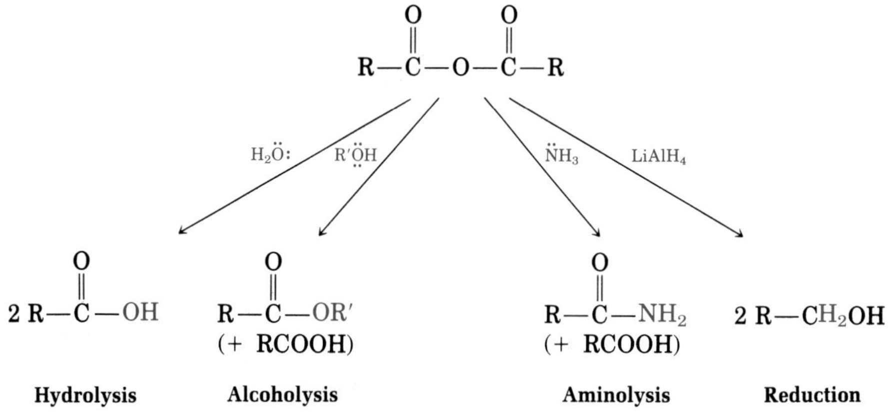

FIGURE 10.6
Some reactions of acid anhydrides

Acetic anhydride is often used to prepare acetate esters of complex alcohols and to prepare substituted acetamides from amines. For example, phenacetin, a drug found in headache remedies, is prepared commercially by reaction of p-ethoxyaniline with acetic anhydride. Aspirin (acetylsalicylic acid) is prepared similarly by reaction of o-hydroxybenzoic acid (salicylic acid) with acetic anhydride.

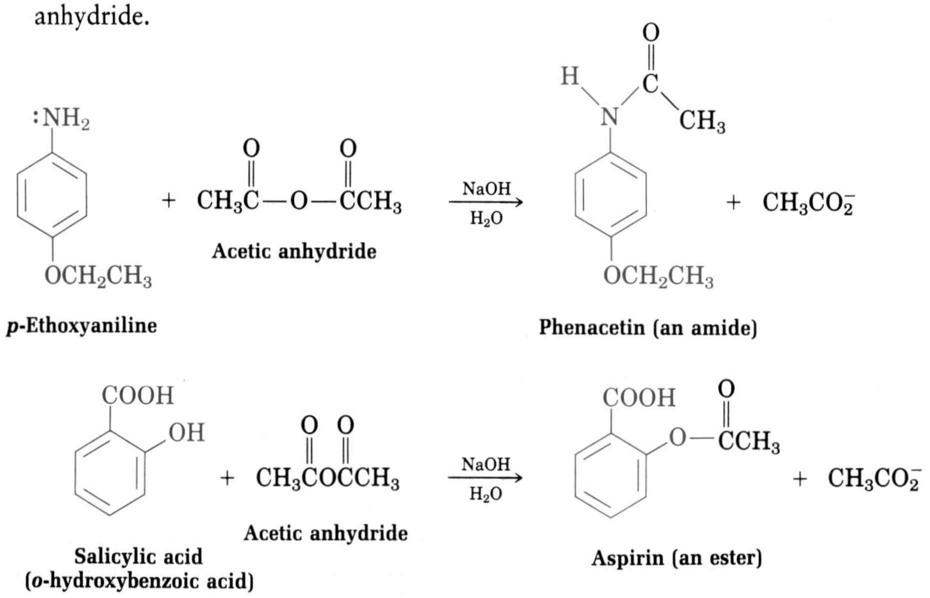

Notice in these two reactions that only "half" of the acetic anhydride molecule is used. The other "half" acts as the leaving group during the nucleophilic acyl substitution step and produces carboxylate ion as by-product. Thus, anhydrides are inefficient to use, and acid chlorides are normally preferred for introducing acyl substituents other than acetyl.

PROBLEM 10.20 Write the steps involved in the mechanism of the reaction between *p*-ethoxyaniline and acetic anhydride to prepare phenacetin.

PROBLEM 10.21 What product would you expect to obtain from reaction of one equivalent of methanol with a cyclic anhydride such as phthalic anhydride? What is the fate of the second "half" of the anhydride in this case?

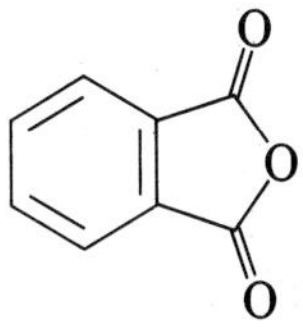

Phthalic anhydride

10.11 CHEMISTRY OF ESTERS

Esters are among the most important and widespread of naturally occurring compounds. Many simple low-molecular-weight esters are pleasant-smelling liquids that are responsible for the fragrant odors of fruits and flowers. For example, methyl butanoate has been isolated from pineapple oil, and isopentyl acetate has been found in banana oil. The ester linkage is also present in animal fats and other biologically important molecules.

$$CH_3CH_2CH_2\overset{\displaystyle O}{\overset{\displaystyle \|}{C}}-OCH_3 \qquad CH_3\overset{\displaystyle O}{\overset{\displaystyle \|}{C}}-OCH_2CH_2CH(CH_3)_2 \qquad \begin{array}{l} CH_2-OCOR \\ | \\ CH-OCOR' \\ | \\ CH_2-OCOR'' \end{array}$$

| Methyl butanoate (from pineapples) | Isopentyl acetate (from bananas) | A fat (R, R', R'' = C_{12-18} chains) |

Preparation of Esters

Esters are usually prepared either from acids or from acid chlorides by the methods already discussed. Thus, carboxylic acids can be converted directly into esters either by S_N2 reaction of a carboxylate salt with a primary alkyl halide or by reaction of the acid with an alcohol in the presence of mineral acid catalyst (Section 10.8). Acid chlorides can be converted into esters by reaction with an alcohol in the presence of base (Section 10.9).

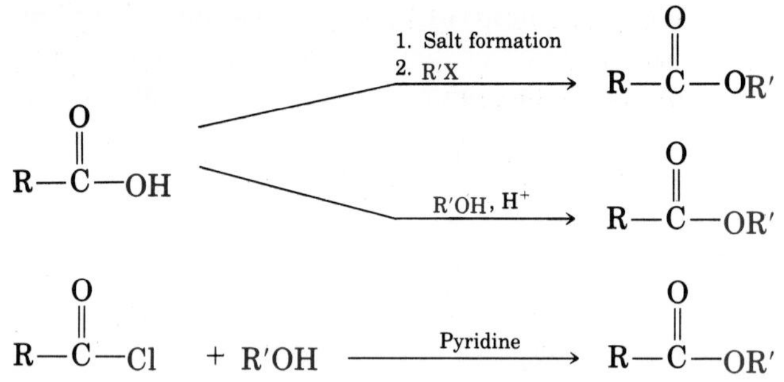

$$R-\overset{\overset{\displaystyle O}{\|}}{C}-OH \quad \xrightarrow[\text{2. R'X}]{\text{1. Salt formation}} \quad R-\overset{\overset{\displaystyle O}{\|}}{C}-OR'$$

$$\xrightarrow{\text{R'OH, H}^+} \quad R-\overset{\overset{\displaystyle O}{\|}}{C}-OR'$$

$$R-\overset{\overset{\displaystyle O}{\|}}{C}-Cl \; + \; R'OH \quad \xrightarrow{\text{Pyridine}} \quad R-\overset{\overset{\displaystyle O}{\|}}{C}-OR'$$

Reactions of Esters

Esters exhibit the same kinds of chemistry that we have seen for other acyl derivatives, but they are less reactive toward nucleophiles than acid chlorides or anhydrides. Figure 10.7 shows some general reactions of esters.

$$R-\overset{\overset{\displaystyle O}{\|}}{C}-OR'$$

An ester

$H_2\ddot{O}:$ $\ddot{N}H_3$ $H:^-$ $:R''MgX$

| Hydrolysis | Aminolysis | Reduction | Grignard reaction |

$$R-\overset{\overset{\displaystyle O}{\|}}{C}-OH + R'OH \quad R-\overset{\overset{\displaystyle O}{\|}}{C}-NH_2 + R'OH \quad RCH_2OH + R'OH \quad R-\overset{\overset{\displaystyle OH}{|}}{\underset{\underset{\displaystyle R''}{|}}{C}}-R'' + R'OH$$

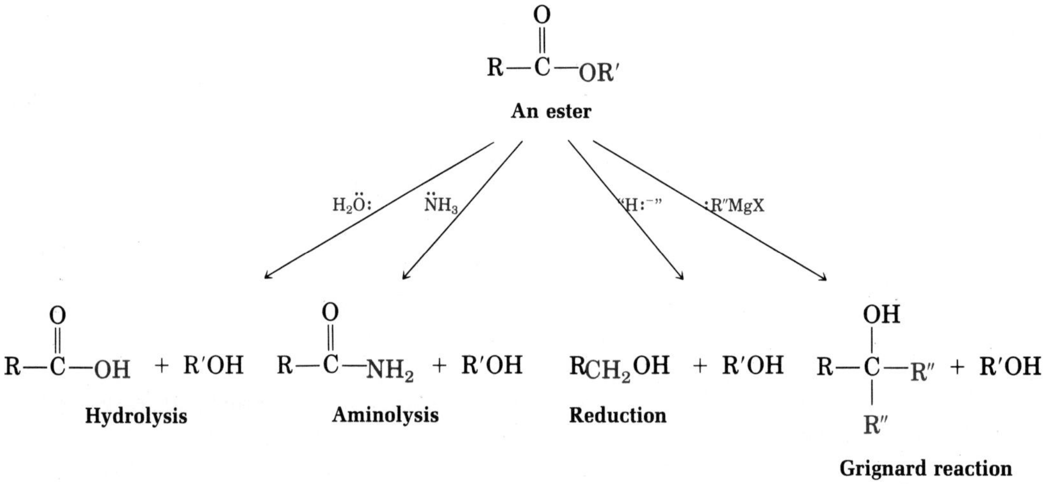

FIGURE 10.7
Some general reactions of esters

Hydrolysis: Conversion of esters into acids   Esters are hydrolyzed either by aqueous base or by aqueous acid to yield carboxylic acid plus alcohol:

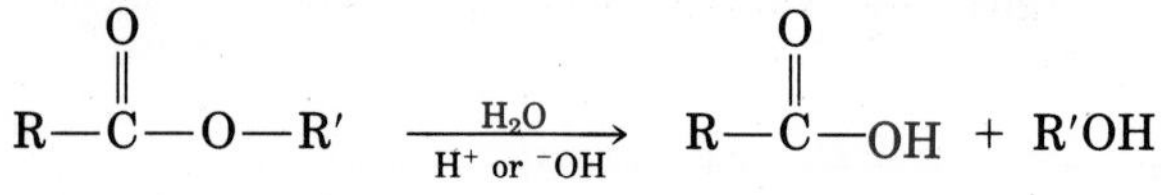

$$R-\overset{\overset{\displaystyle O}{\|}}{C}-O-R' \quad \xrightarrow[\text{H}^+ \text{ or } ^-\text{OH}]{\text{H}_2\text{O}} \quad R-\overset{\overset{\displaystyle O}{\|}}{C}-OH + R'OH$$

Hydrolysis in basic solution is often called **saponification,** after the Latin *sapo,* "soap." As we will see in Section 16.3, the boiling of wood ash extract with animal fat to make soap is indeed a saponification, since wood ash contains alkali and fats have ester linkages. Ester hydrolysis occurs through a typical nucleophilic acyl substitution pathway in which hydroxide ion nucleophile adds to the ester carbonyl group, yielding a tetrahedral intermediate. Loss of alkoxide ion then gives a carboxylic acid, which is deprotonated by a second equivalent of base to give the acid salt:

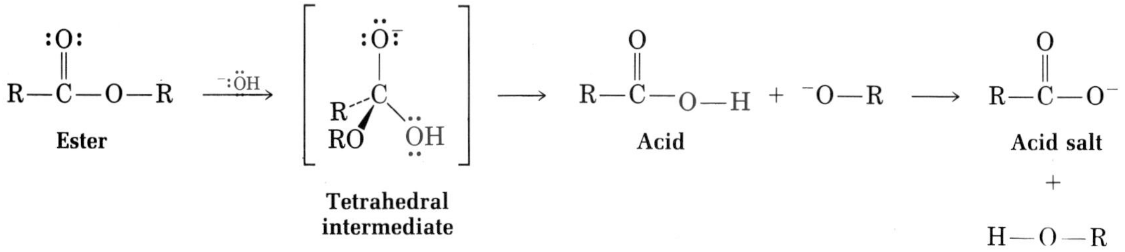

PROBLEM 10.22 Why do you suppose saponification of esters is an irreversible process? In other words, why doesn't treatment of a carboxylic acid with alkoxide ion lead to ester product?

Aminolysis: Conversion of esters into amides Esters react with ammonia and amines to yield amides. The reaction is not often used, however, since higher yields are usually obtained starting from the acid chloride rather than from the ester.

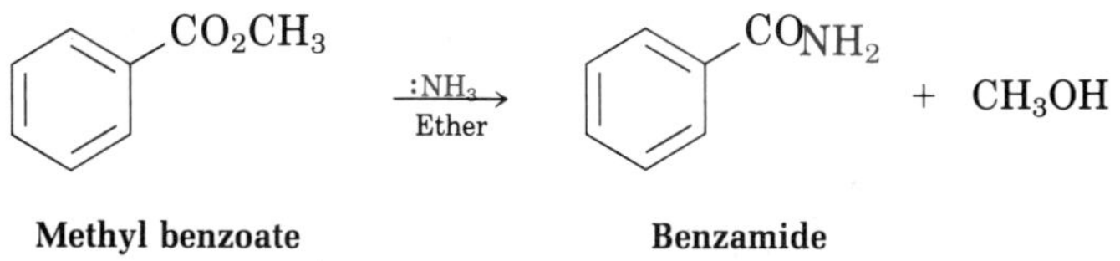

Reduction: Conversion of esters into alcohols Esters are easily reduced by treatment with lithium aluminum hydride to yield primary alcohols (Section 8.5).

$$CH_3CH_2CH=CHCOCH_2CH_3 \xrightarrow[\text{2. } H_3O^+]{\text{1. LiAlH}_4 \text{, ether}} CH_3CH_2CH=CHCH_2OH + CH_3CH_2OH$$

Ethyl 2-pentenoate   **2-Penten-1-ol (91%)**

Hydride ion first adds to the carbonyl group, followed by elimination of alkoxide ion to yield an aldehyde intermediate. Further reduction of the aldehyde gives the primary alcohol.

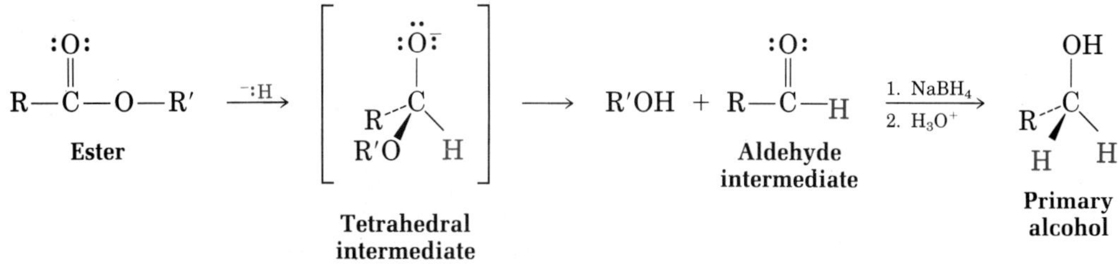

PRACTICE PROBLEM What products would you obtain on reduction of propyl benzoate with LiAlH$_4$?

Solution Reduction of esters with LiAlH$_4$ yields 2 mol of alcohol product, one from the acyl portion of the ester and one from the alkoxy portion. Thus, reduction of propyl benzoate yields benzyl alcohol (from the acyl group) and 1-propanol (from the alkoxyl group).

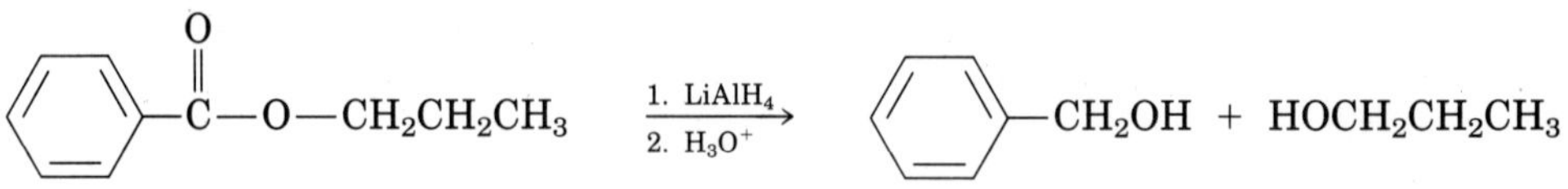

Propyl benzoate   **Benzyl alcohol**   **1-Propanol**

PROBLEM 10.23 Show the products you would obtain by reduction of these esters with LiAlH$_4$.

(a) CH$_3$CH$_2$CH$_2$CH(CH$_3$)COOCH$_3$ (b) Phenyl benzoate

PROBLEM 10.24 What product would you expect from the reaction of a cyclic ester such as butyrolactone with LiAlH$_4$?

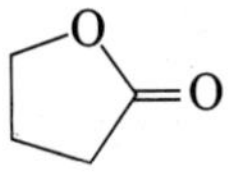

Butyrolactone

Reaction of esters with Grignard reagents Grignard reagents react with esters to yield tertiary alcohols in which two of the substituents are identical. The reaction occurs readily and gives high yields of products by the usual nucleophilic addition mechanism. For example:

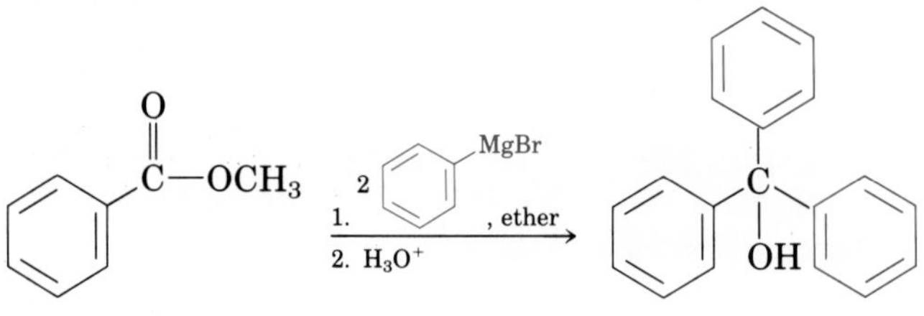

Methyl benzoate   **Triphenylmethanol (96%)**

PRACTICE PROBLEM How could you use the reaction of a Grignard reagent with an ester to prepare 1,1-diphenyl-1-propanol?

Solution The product of reaction between a Grignard reagent and an ester is a tertiary alcohol in which the alcohol carbon and one of the attached groups have come from the ester, and in which the remaining two groups bonded to the alcohol carbon have come from the Grignard reagent. Since 1,1-diphenyl-1-propanol has two phenyl groups and one ethyl group bonded to the alcohol carbon, it may be prepared from reaction of a phenylmagnesium halide and an ester of propanoic acid.

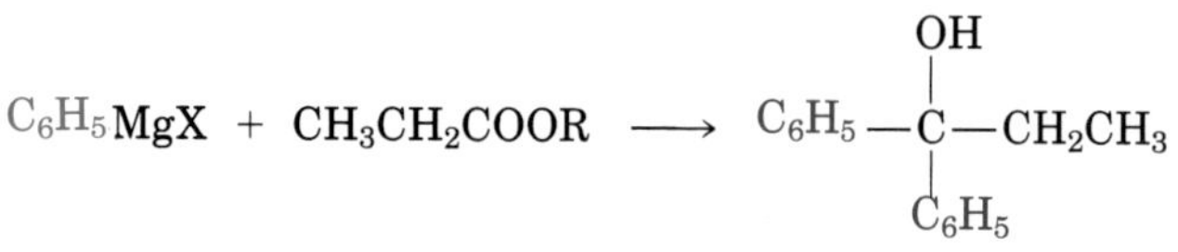

$$C_6H_5MgX + CH_3CH_2COOR \longrightarrow \begin{matrix} & OH \\ & | \\ C_6H_5 - & C - CH_2CH_3 \\ & | \\ & C_6H_5 \end{matrix}$$

1,1-Diphenyl-1-propanol

PROBLEM 10.25 What ester and what Grignard reagent might you start with to prepare these alcohols?

(a) 2-Phenyl-2-propanol   (b) 1,1-Diphenylethanol   (c) 3-Ethyl-3-heptanol

10.12   CHEMISTRY OF AMIDES

Preparation of Amides

As we saw earlier in Section 10.9, amides are usually prepared by reaction of an acid chloride with an amine. Ammonia, monosubstituted amines, and disubstituted amines all undergo this reaction.

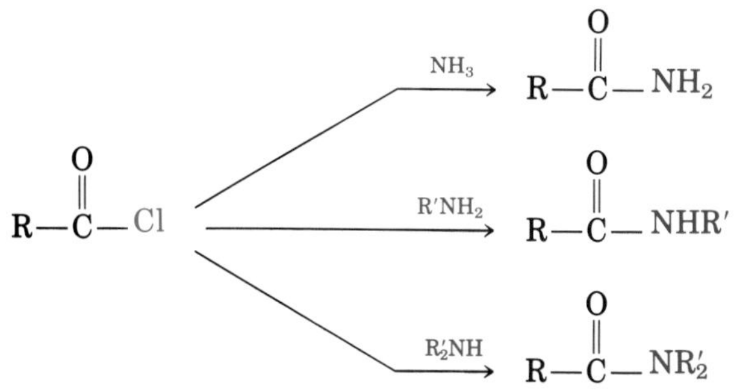

Reactions of Amides

Amides are much less reactive than acid chlorides, acid anhydrides, and esters. Thus, the amide linkage is stable enough to serve as the basic unit from which all proteins are made (Chapter 15).

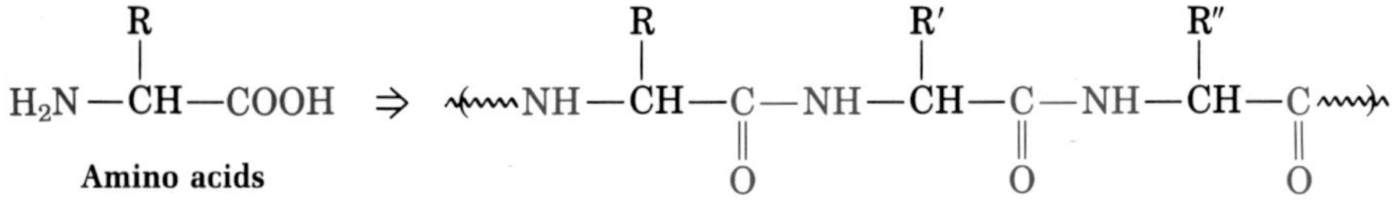

$$\underset{\text{Amino acids}}{H_2N-\overset{\overset{\displaystyle R}{|}}{C}H-COOH} \;\Rightarrow\; \text{wwNH}-\overset{\overset{\displaystyle R}{|}}{C}H-\overset{\overset{\displaystyle \|}{O}}{C}-NH-\overset{\overset{\displaystyle R'}{|}}{C}H-\overset{\overset{\displaystyle \|}{O}}{C}-NH-\overset{\overset{\displaystyle R''}{|}}{C}H-\overset{\overset{\displaystyle \|}{O}}{C}\text{ww}$$

A protein (a polyamide)

Amides undergo a hydrolysis reaction to yield carboxylic acids plus amine upon heating in either aqueous acid or base. Although the experimental conditions necessary for amide hydrolysis are severe, requiring prolonged heating, the overall transformation is a typical nucleophilic acyl substitution of —OH for —NH$_2$.

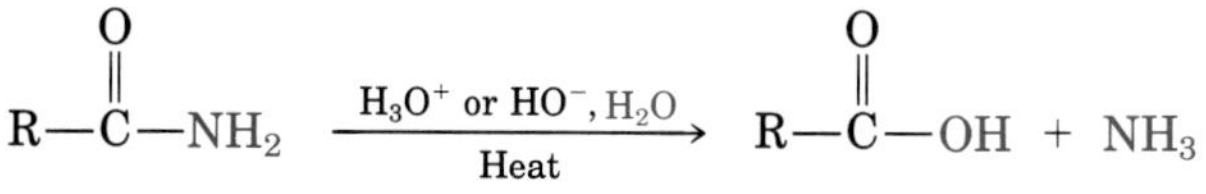

$$\underset{}{R-\overset{\overset{\displaystyle O}{\|}}{C}-NH_2} \quad \xrightarrow[\text{Heat}]{H_3O^+ \text{ or } HO^-, H_2O} \quad R-\overset{\overset{\displaystyle O}{\|}}{C}-OH \;+\; NH_3$$

Like other carboxylic acid derivatives, amides can be reduced by lithium aluminum hydride. The product of this reduction, however, is an amine rather than an alcohol.

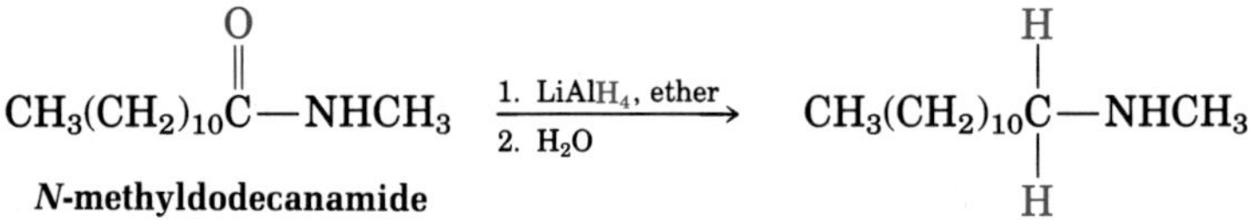

$$\underset{\textbf{\textit{N}-methyldodecanamide}}{CH_3(CH_2)_{10}\overset{\overset{\displaystyle O}{\|}}{C}-NHCH_3} \quad \xrightarrow[\text{2. }H_2O]{\text{1. LiAlH}_4,\text{ ether}} \quad \underset{\overset{\displaystyle |}{H}}{CH_3(CH_2)_{10}\overset{\overset{\displaystyle H}{|}}{C}-NHCH_3}$$

Dodecylmethylamine
(95%)

The effect of amide reduction is to convert the amide carbonyl group into a methylene group, C=O → CH$_2$. This kind of reaction is specific for amides and does not occur with other carboxylic acid derivatives.

PROBLEM 10.26   How would you convert *N*-ethylbenzamide into these products?

(a) Benzoic acid   (b) Benzyl alcohol
(c) *N*-Ethylbenzylamine,   C$_6$H$_5$CH$_2$NHCH$_2$CH$_3$

PROBLEM 10.27   The lithium aluminum hydride reduction of amides to yield amines is equally effective with both acyclic and cyclic amides (**lactams**). What product would you expect to obtain from reduction of 5,5-dimethyl-2-pyrrolidone with LiAlH$_4$?

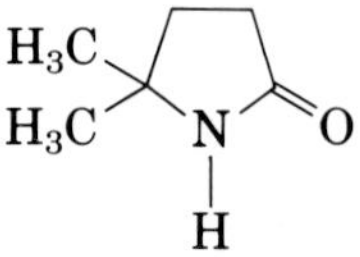

5,5-Dimethyl-2-pyrrolidone (a lactam)

10.13   CHEMISTRY OF NITRILES

Nitriles, $R—C\equiv N$, are not related to carboxylic acids in the same sense that acyl derivatives are. Nevertheless, the chemistry of nitriles and carboxylic acids is so entwined that the two classes of compounds should be considered together.

Preparation of Nitriles

The simplest and best method of preparing nitriles is by the S_N2 displacement reaction of cyanide ion on a primary alkyl halide (Section 7.8).

$$R—CH_2—Br + Na^+CN^- \xrightarrow[\text{reaction}]{S_N2} R—CH_2—CN + NaBr$$

Reactions of Nitriles

The chemistry of nitriles is similar in many respects to the chemistry of carbonyl compounds, as indicated in Figure 10.8. Like carbonyl groups, nitriles are strongly polarized. Thus, the carbon atom in the nitrile group is electrophilic and undergoes ready attack by nucleophiles to yield an sp^2-hybridized intermediate imine anion that is analogous to the sp^3-hybridized intermediate alkoxide anion formed by addition of a nucleophile to a carbonyl group. Once formed, the intermediate imine anion can then go on to yield further products, depending on the exact reaction taking place.

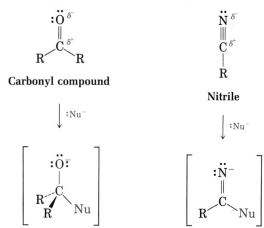

FIGURE 10.8
The similar reactions of carbonyl compounds and nitriles with nucleophiles

Hydrolysis: Conversion of nitriles into carboxylic acids   Nitriles are hydrolyzed in either acidic or basic solution to yield carboxylic acids and ammonia (or an amine).

$$R—C\equiv N \xrightarrow{H_3O^+ \text{ or } ^-:OH} RCOOH + NH_3$$

Reduction: Conversion of nitriles into amines   Treatment of nitriles with lithium aluminum hydride gives primary amines in high yield:

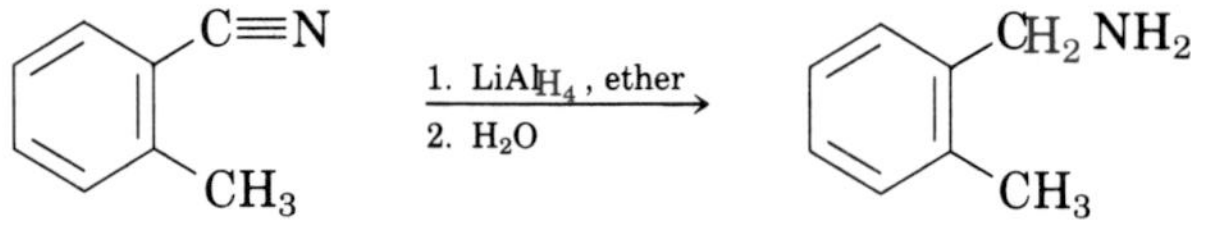

o-Methylbenzonitrile

o-Methylbenzylamine
(88%)

The reaction occurs by nucleophilic addition of hydride ion to the polar C≡N bond, yielding an imine anion. This intermediate undergoes further addition of a second equivalent of hydride ion, giving the final product.

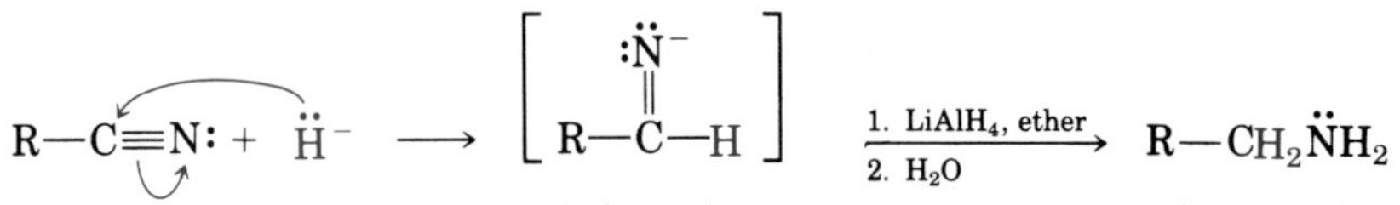

Nitrile

Imine anion

Primary amine

Reaction of nitriles with Grignard reagents   Grignard reagents, RMgX, add to nitriles to give intermediate imine anions that can be hydrolyzed to yield ketones:

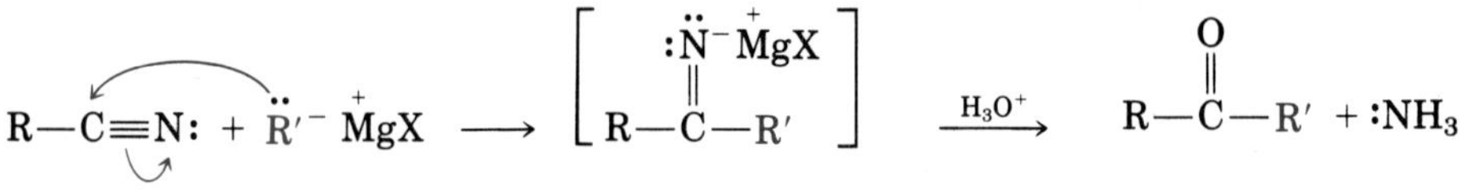

Nitrile

Imine anion

Ketone

For example, benzonitrile reacts with ethylmagnesium bromide to give propiophenone in high yield:

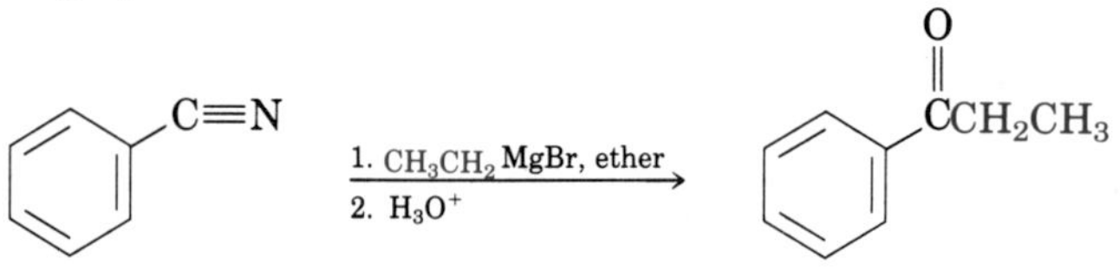

Benzonitrile

Propiophenone (89%)

PROBLEM 10.28   What nitrile would you react with what Grignard reagent to prepare these ketones?

(a) $CH_3CH_2COCH_2CH_3$

(b) $CH_3CH_2COCH(CH_3)_2$

(c) Acetophenone (methyl phenyl ketone)

(d)

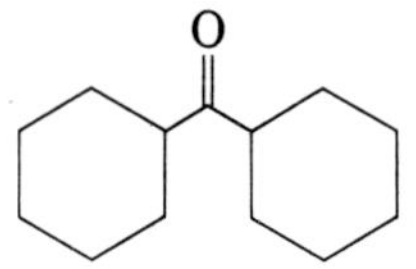

PROBLEM 10.29 By putting the proper reactions together in the appropriate sequence, we can prepare complex molecules from simple starting materials. How would you prepare the following molecules from the indicated starting materials? More than one step is required in each case.

(a) $(CH_3)_2CHCH_2CH_2NH_2$ from $(CH_3)_2CHCH_2I$
(b) 1-Phenyl-2-butanone from benzyl bromide, $C_6H_5CH_2Br$

ADDITIONAL PROBLEMS

PROBLEM 10.30 Provide IUPAC names for these carboxylic acids:

(a)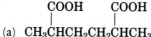

(b) $(CH_3)_3CCOOH$

(c) 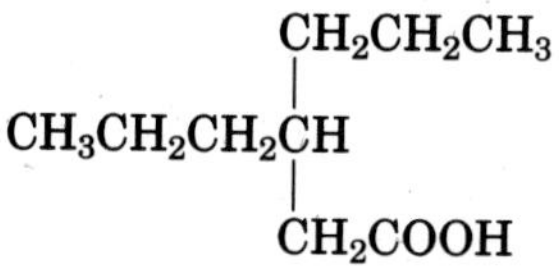
$$CH_3CH_2CH_2\overset{\displaystyle CH_2CH_2CH_3}{\underset{\displaystyle CH_2COOH}{CH}}$$

(d)

COOH

NO₂

(e)

COOH

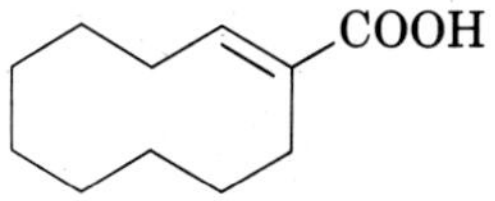

(f) $BrCH_2CHBrCH_2CH_2COOH$

PROBLEM 10.31 Provide IUPAC names for these carboxylic acid derivatives:

(a)

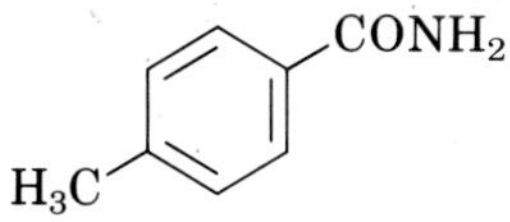

CONH₂

H₃C

(b) $(CH_3CH_2)_2CHCH=CHCN$

(c) $CH_3O_2CCH_2CH_2CO_2CH_3$

(d)

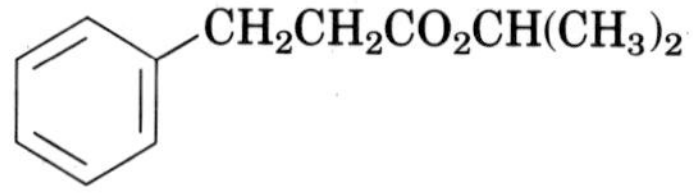

CH₂CH₂CO₂CH(CH₃)₂

(e)

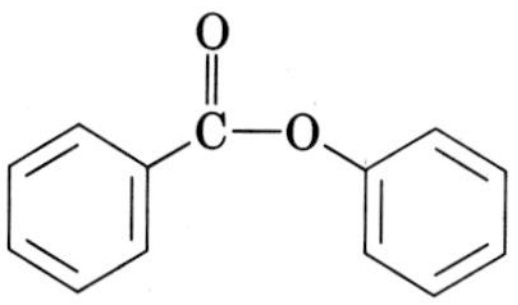

C—O

(f) $CH_3CHBrCH_2CONHCH_3$

(g)

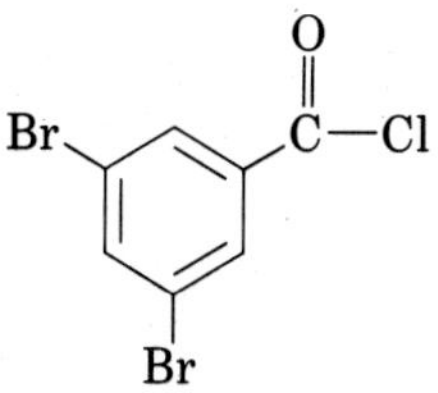

Br

C—Cl

Br

(h)

CN

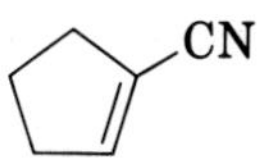

PROBLEM 10.32   Draw structures corresponding to these IUPAC names:

(a) 4,5-Dimethylheptanoic acid   (b) *cis*-1,2-Cyclohexanedicarboxylic acid
(c) Heptanedioic acid   (d) Triphenylacetic acid
(e) 2,2-Dimethylhexanamide   (f) Phenylacetamide
(g) 2-Cyclobutenecarbonitrile   (h) Ethyl cyclohexanecarboxylate

PROBLEM 10.33   Acetic acid boils at 118°C, but its ethyl esters boil at 77°C. Why is the boiling point of the acid so much higher, even though it has the lower molecular weight?

PROBLEM 10.34   Draw and name the eight carboxylic acid isomers with formula $C_6H_{12}O_2$.

PROBLEM 10.35   Draw and name compounds meeting these descriptions:

(a) Three different acid chlorides, C_6H_9ClO (b) Three different amides, $C_7H_{11}NO$
(c) Three different nitriles, C_5H_7N

PROBLEM 10.36   The following reactivity order has been found for the saponification of alkyl acetates by hydroxide ion:

$$CH_3COOCH_3 > CH_3COOCH_2CH_3 > CH_3COOCH(CH_3)_2 > CH_3COOC(CH_3)_3$$

How can you explain this reactivity order?

PROBLEM 10.37   Order the compounds in each set with respect to increasing acidity:

(a) Acetic acid, formic acid, benzoic acid
(b) *p*-Methylbenzoic acid, *p*-bromobenzoic acid, *p*-nitrobenzoic acid
(c) Fluoroacetic acid, 3-fluoropropanoic acid, acetic acid

PROBLEM 10.38   How can you explain the fact that 2-chlorobutanoic acid has $pK_a = 2.86$, 3-chlorobutanoic acid has $pK_a = 4.05$, 4-chlorobutanoic acid has $pK_a = 4.82$, and butanoic acid itself has $pK_a = 4.82$?

PROBLEM 10.39   How could you prepare acetophenone (methyl phenyl ketone) from these starting materials? More than one step may be required.

(a) Benzonitrile   (b) Bromobenzene   (c) Methyl benzoate   (d) Benzene

PROBLEM 10.40   How might you prepare the following products starting with butanoic acid? More than one step may be required.

(a) 1-Butanol   (b) Butanal   (c) 1-Bromobutane   (d) Pentanenitrile
(e) 1-Butene   (f) Butylamine, $CH_3CH_2CH_2CH_2NH_2$

PROBLEM 10.41   Predict the product of the reaction of *p*-methylbenzoic acid with each of the following reagents:

(a) $LiAlH_4$ (b) CH_3OH, HCl   (c) $SOCl_2$ (d) NaOH, then CH_3I
(e) CH_3MgBr

PROBLEM 10.42   We saw earlier that 1 equiv of a base such as sodium hydroxide is required for the reaction of an amine and an acid chloride to go to completion. Also, 1 equiv of a base is required in the reaction of an amine with an acid anhydride. Explain.

PROBLEM 10.43   A chemist in need of 2,2-dimethylpentanoic acid decided to synthesize some by reaction of 2-chloro-2-methylpentane with NaCN, followed by hydrolysis of the product. After carrying out the reaction sequence, however, none of the desired product could be found. What do you suppose went wrong?

PROBLEM 10.44   Which method of carboxylic acid synthesis—Grignard carboxylation or nitrile hydrolysis—would you use for each of the following reactions? Explain the reasons for each choice.

(a)

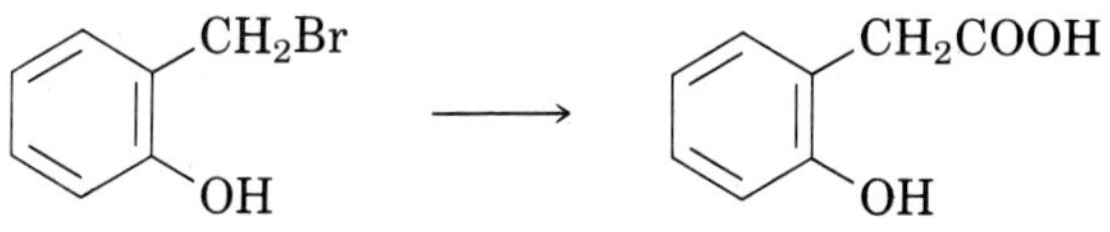

CH_2Br / OH → CH_2COOH / OH

(b) $CH_3CH_2CHBrCH_3$ → $CH_3CH_2CHCOOH$ (with CH_3 group)

(c) $CH_3CCH_2CH_2CH_2I$ (with C=O)   → $CH_3CCH_2CH_2CH_2COOH$ (with C=O)

(d) $HOCH_2CH_2CH_2Br$ → $HOCH_2CH_2CH_2COOH$

PROBLEM 10.45   How can you explain the observation that attempted Fischer esterification of 2,4,6-trimethylbenzoic acid with methanol/HCl is unsuccessful? No ester is obtained, and the starting acid is recovered unchanged.

PROBLEM 10.46   When dimethyl carbonate, $CH_3OCOOCH_3$, is treated with phenylmagnesium bromide, triphenylmethanol is formed. Explain how this occurs.

PROBLEM 10.47   Predict the product, if any, of reaction between propanoyl chloride and the following reagents:

(a)   Excess CH_3MgBr in ether   (b)   NaOH in H_2O (c)   Methylamine
(d)   LiAlH$_4$ (e)   Cyclohexanol   (f)   Sodium acetate

PROBLEM 10.48   Answer Problem 10.47 for reaction between methyl propanoate and the listed reagents.

PROBLEM 10.49   When methyl acetate is heated in pure ethanol containing a small amount of HCl catalyst, ethyl acetate results. Propose a mechanism for this reaction.

PROBLEM 10.50   *tert*-Butoxycarbonyl azide is an important reagent used in protein synthesis. It is prepared by treating *tert*-butoxycarbonyl chloride with sodium azide. Propose a mechanism for this reaction.

$$(CH_3)_3COCOCl + NaN_3 \longrightarrow (CH_3)_3COCON_3 + NaCl$$

PROBLEM 10.51   Tranexamic acid, a drug useful for aiding blood clotting, is prepared commercially from *p*-methylbenzonitrile. Formulate the steps that are likely to be used in the synthesis. [*Note:* The cis and trans isomers of tranexamic acid are thermally interconvertible at 300°C, and the trans isomer is more stable.]

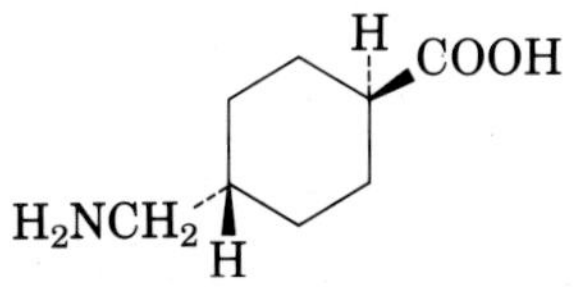

H_2NCH_2 / H / H / COOH

Tranexamic acid

PROBLEM 10.52 What product would you expect to obtain upon treatment of the cyclic ester, butyrolactone, with excess phenylmagnesium bromide?

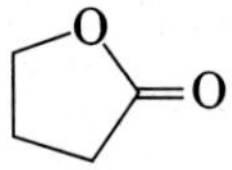

Butyrolactone

PROBLEM 10.53 N,N-Diethyl-*m*-toluamide (DEET) is the active ingredient in many insect-repellent preparations. How might you synthesize this substance starting from *m*-bromotoluene?

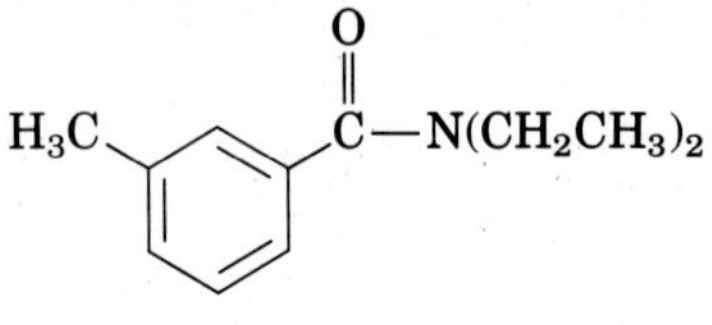

$$H_3C \quad \overset{\overset{\displaystyle O}{\|}}{C} - N(CH_2CH_3)_2$$

N,N-Diethyl-*m*-toluamide

PROBLEM 10.54 In the iodoform reaction, a triiodomethyl ketone reacts with aqueous base to yield a carboxylate ion and iodoform (triiodomethane). Propose a mechanism for this reaction.

$$R - \overset{\overset{\displaystyle O}{\|}}{C} - CI_3 \xrightarrow{\text{NaOH, H}_2\text{O}} R - \overset{\overset{\displaystyle O}{\|}}{C} - O^- + CHI_3$$

Thiol Esters: Biological Carboxylic Acid Derivatives

Nucleophilic acyl substitution reactions take place in living organisms just as they take place in the chemical laboratory; the same principles apply in both cases. Nature, however, uses **thiol esters, RCOSR'**, as the reactive acylating agents, rather than acid chlorides or acid anhydrides. The pK_a of a typical alkanethiol, RSH, is about 10, placing thiols midway between carboxylic acids ($pK_a \approx 5$) and alcohols ($pK_a \approx 16$) in acid strength. As a result, thiolate anions (RS^-) can serve as leaving groups in nucleophilic acyl substitution reactions, and thiol esters are intermediate in reactivity between acid anhydrides and esters. They are not so reactive that they hydrolyze rapidly like anhydrides, yet they are more reactive than normal esters.

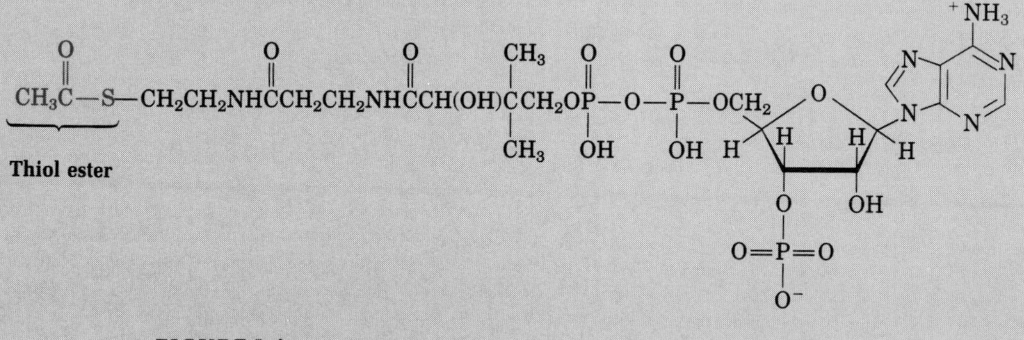

FIGURE L.1
The structure of acetyl coenzyme A (acetyl CoA, $CH_3COSCoA$)

Acetyl coenzyme A (usually abbreviated as acetyl CoA), whose structure is shown in Figure L.1, is the most common thiol ester found in nature. Acetyl CoA is an enormously complex molecule by comparison with acetyl chloride or acetic anhydride, yet it serves exactly the same purpose as either of these simpler reagents. Nature uses acetyl CoA as a reactive acetylating agent in nucleophilic acyl substitution reactions (an *acetylating* agent is one that introduces an acetyl group, CH_3CO):

$$CH_3\overset{O}{\underset{\|}{C}}\!-\!S\!-\!CoA + \ddot{N}u^- \longrightarrow CH_3\!-\!\overset{O}{\underset{\|}{C}}\!-\!Nu + {}^-\!\!:S\!-\!CoA$$

For example, *N*-acetylglucosamine, an important constituent of cell-surface membranes in mammals, is synthesized in nature (**biosynthesized**) by an aminolysis reaction between glucosamine and acetyl CoA:

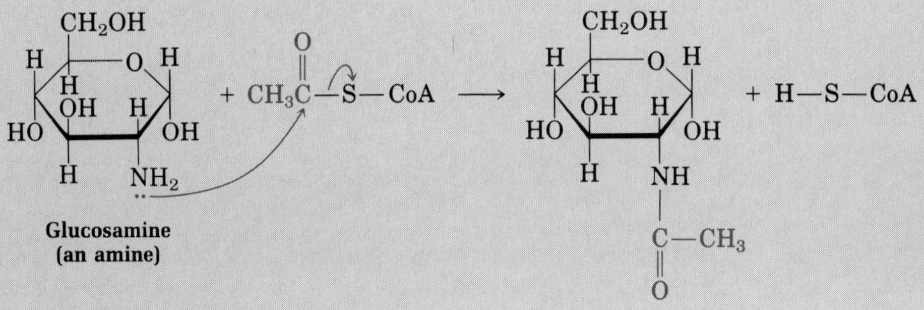

Glucosamine
(an amine)

N-**Acetylglucosamine**
(an amide)

INTERLUDE M
Step-Growth Polymers

We saw earlier in Interlude C that polymers such as polyethylene and polystyrene (**chain-growth polymers**) are prepared by chain reaction processes in which an initiator first adds to the double bond of an alkene monomer to produce a reactive intermediate. This intermediate adds to a second alkene monomer unit, and the polymer chain lengthens as more monomer units add successively to the end of the growing chain.

Step-growth polymers are a second broad class of polymers produced by polymerization reactions between two difunctional molecules. Each new bond is formed in a discrete step, independent of all other bonds in the polymer; chain reactions are not involved. The key bond-forming step is often a carbonyl nucleophilic acyl substitution.

A large number of different step-growth polymers have been made; some of the commercially more important polymers are shown in Table M.1.

TABLE M.1   Some important step-growth polymers and their uses

Monomer name	Formula	Trade or common name of polymer	Uses
Adipic acid Hexamethylene diamine	$HOOC(CH_2)_4COOH$ $H_2N(CH_2)_6NH_2$	Nylon 66	Fibers, clothing, tire cord, bearings
Ethylene glycol Dimethyl terephthalate	$HOCH_2CH_2OH$ (see structure)	Dacron, Terylene, Mylar	Fibers, clothing, tire cord, film
Caprolactam	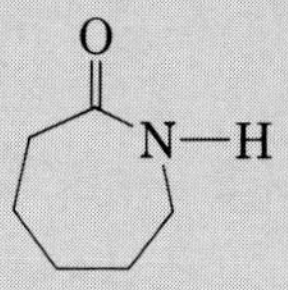 (see structure)	Nylon 6, Perlon	Fibers, large cast articles

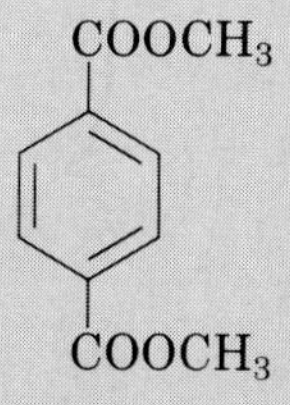

Nylon

The nylons, first synthesized by Wallace Carothers at the Du Pont Company, are the best-known step-growth polymers. Nylons are simply **polyamides**; they are prepared by carbonyl condensation reaction between diamines and diacids. For example, nylon 66 is prepared by heating the six-carbon adipic acid (hexanedioic acid) with the six-carbon hexamethylenediamine (1,6-hexanediamine) at 280°C.

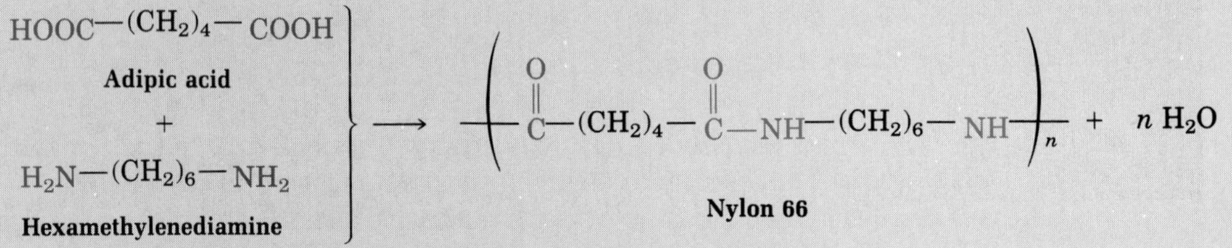

$$HOOC-(CH_2)_4-COOH$$

Adipic acid

+

$$H_2N-(CH_2)_6-NH_2$$

Hexamethylenediamine

$$\longrightarrow \ \ -\left(\!\!\begin{array}{c} \overset{O}{\overset{\|}{C}}-(CH_2)_4-\overset{O}{\overset{\|}{C}}-NH-(CH_2)_6-NH \end{array}\!\!\right)_n + \ n\,H_2O$$

Nylon 66

Nylons are used both in engineering applications and in making fibers. A combination of high impact strength and abrasion resistance makes nylon an excellent metal substitute for bearings and gears. As fibers, nylon is used in a wide variety of applications, from clothing, to Aramid tire cord, to carpets, to Perlon mountaineering ropes.

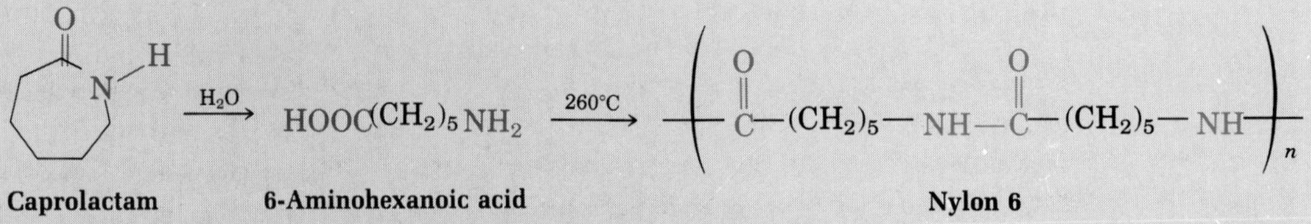

$$\xrightarrow{H_2O} \quad HOOC(CH_2)_5NH_2 \quad \xrightarrow{260°C} \quad -\left(\!\!\begin{array}{c} \overset{O}{\overset{\|}{C}}-(CH_2)_5-NH-\overset{O}{\overset{\|}{C}}-(CH_2)_5-NH \end{array}\!\!\right)_n$$

Caprolactam   **6-Aminohexanoic acid**   **Nylon 6**

Polyesters

Just as polyamides (nylons) can be made by reaction between diacids and diamines, **polyesters** can be made by reaction between diacids and dialcohols. The most generally useful polyester is made by a nucleophilic acyl substitution reaction between dimethyl terephthalate (dimethyl 1,4-benzenedicarboxylate) and ethylene glycol. The product is widely used under the trade name Dacron to make clothing fiber and tire cord, and is used under the name Mylar to make plastic film and recording tape. The tensile strength of polyester film is nearly equal to that of steel.

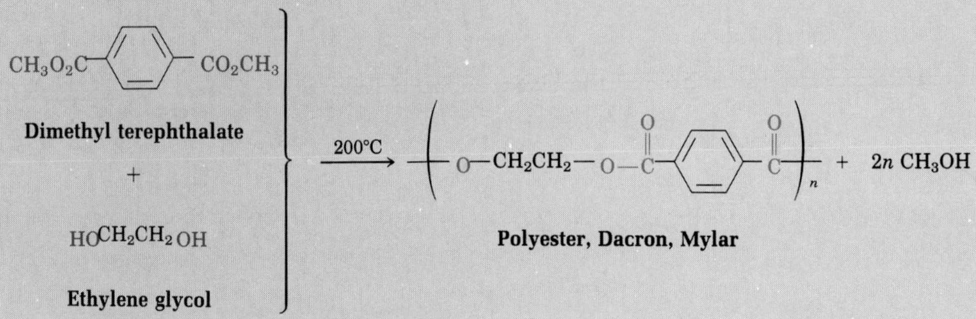

Dimethyl terephthalate

+

$$HOCH_2CH_2OH$$

Ethylene glycol

$$\xrightarrow{200°C} \quad -\left(\!\!\begin{array}{c} O-CH_2CH_2-O-\overset{O}{\overset{\|}{C}}-\!\!\bigcirc\!\!-\overset{O}{\overset{\|}{C}} \end{array}\!\!\right)_n + \ 2n\,CH_3OH$$

Polyester, Dacron, Mylar

CHAPTER **11**

Carbonyl Alpha-Substitution and Condensation Reactions

Much of the chemistry of carbonyl compounds can be explained in terms of just four fundamental reactions. We have already looked in detail at the chemistry of nucleophilic addition reactions (Chapter 9) and nucleophilic acyl substitution reactions (Chapter 10). In this chapter, we will look at the chemistry of the two remaining major reactions of carbonyl groups: the **alpha-substitution reaction** and the **carbonyl condensation reaction**.

Alpha-substitution reactions occur at the position *next to* the carbonyl group, the **alpha (α) position**. They involve the substitution of an alpha hydrogen atom by some other group:

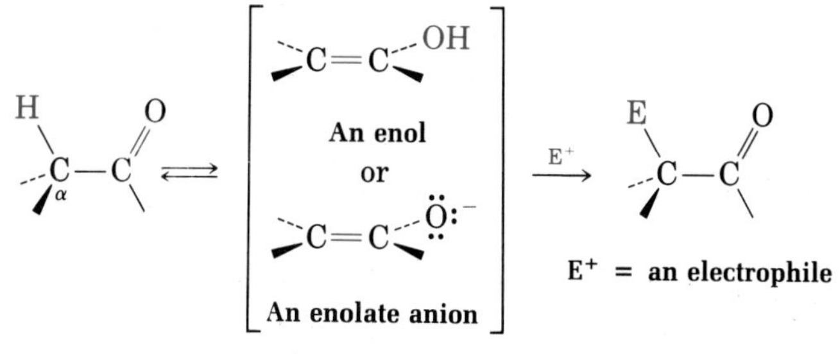

Alpha substitution

E^+ = an electrophile

Carbonyl condensation reactions take place when two carbonyl compounds react with each other in such a way that the alpha carbon of one partner becomes bonded to the carbonyl carbon of the second partner:

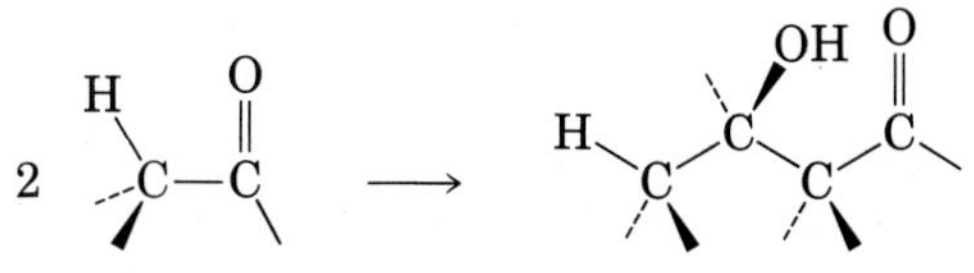

Carbonyl condensation

The key feature of both alpha-substitution reactions and carbonyl condensation reactions is that they take place through the formation of either **enol** or **enolate ion** intermediates. Let's begin our study by learning more about these two species.

11.1 KETO–ENOL TAUTOMERISM

Carbonyl compounds that have hydrogen atoms on their alpha carbons are rapidly interconvertible with their corresponding **enol** (ene + ol, unsaturated alcohol) isomers. This rapid interconversion between **keto** and **enol** forms is a special kind of isomerism called **tautomerism** (taw-tom'-er-ism; from the Greek *tauto*, "the same," and *meros*, "part"). The individual isomers are called **tautomers** (taw'-toe-mers).

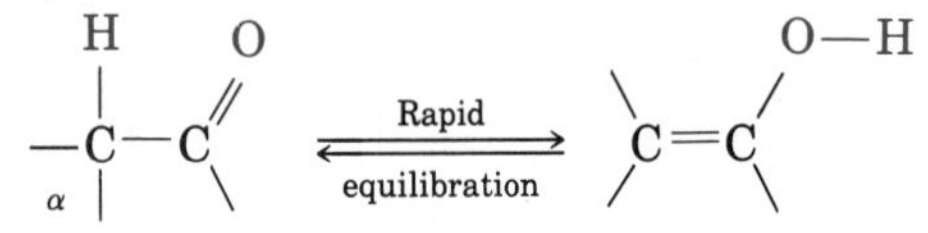

| Keto tautomer | Enol tautomer |

Note that tautomerism requires the two isomers to be *rapidly* interconvertible. Thus, keto and enol isomers of carbonyl compounds are tautomers, but two alkene isomers such as 1-butene and 2-butene are not, since they do not interconvert rapidly.

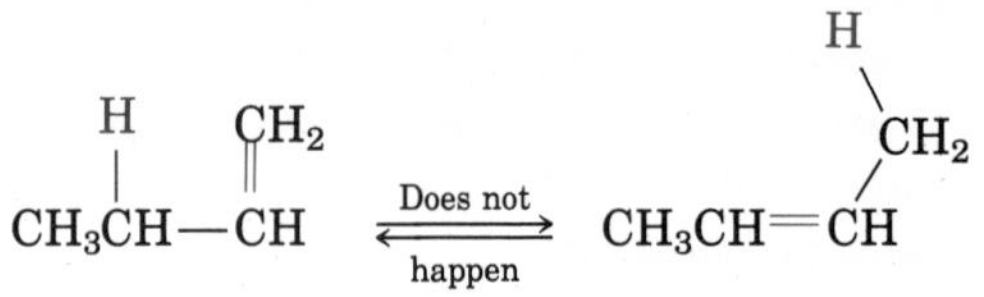

At equilibrium, most carbonyl compounds exist almost exclusively in the keto form, and it is difficult to isolate the pure enol form. For example, cyclohexanone contains only about 0.001% of its enol tautomer at room temperature, and acetone contains about 0.0001% enol. The percentage of enol tautomer is even less for carboxylic acids, esters, and amides. Even though enols are difficult to isolate and are present to only a small extent at equilibrium, they are nevertheless extremely important intermediates in much of the chemistry of carbonyl compounds.

Cyclohexanone

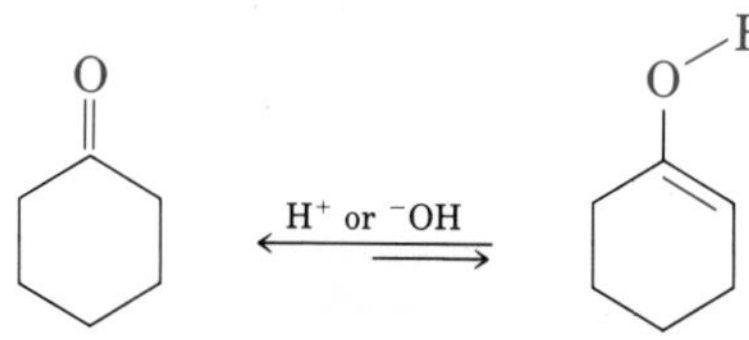

99.999%   0.001%

Acetone CH_3CCH_3

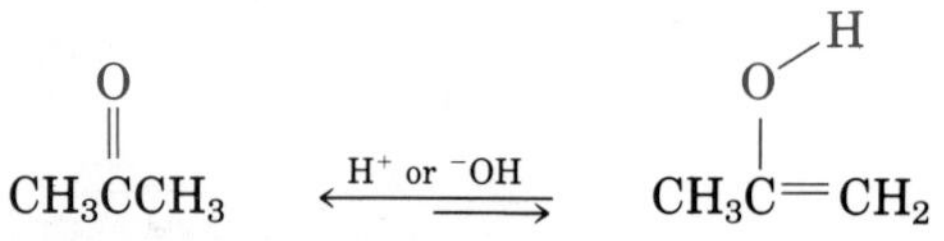

99.9999%   0.0001%

Keto–enol tautomerism of carbonyl compounds is catalyzed by both acids and bases. Acid catalysis involves protonation of the carbonyl oxygen atom (a Lewis base) to give an intermediate cation that can lose a proton from the alpha carbon to yield enol (Figure 11.1). This proton loss from the positively charged intermediate is analogous to what occurs during an E1 reaction when a carbocation loses a proton from the neighboring carbon to form an alkene (Section 7.11).

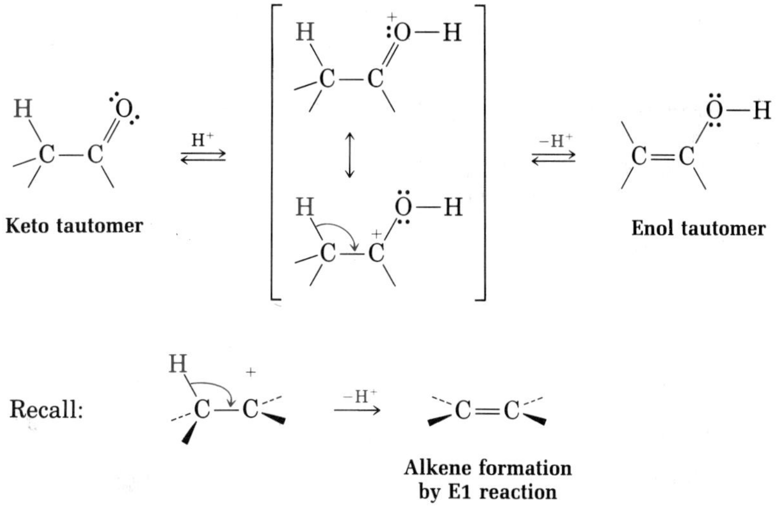

FIGURE 11.1
Mechanism of acid-catalyzed enol formation

Base-catalyzed enol formation occurs by an acid–base reaction between the carbonyl compound and the base catalyst. It turns out that the presence of a carbonyl group makes the hydrogens on the alpha carbon slightly *acidic*. Thus, a carbonyl compound can act as a weak protic acid and donate one of its alpha hydrogens to the base. The resultant resonance-stabilized anion—an **enolate ion**—is then reprotonated to yield a neutral compound. If protonation of the enolate ion takes place on the alpha carbon, the keto tautomer is simply regenerated and no net change takes place. If, however, protonation takes place on the oxygen atom, an enol tautomer is formed (Figure 11.2).

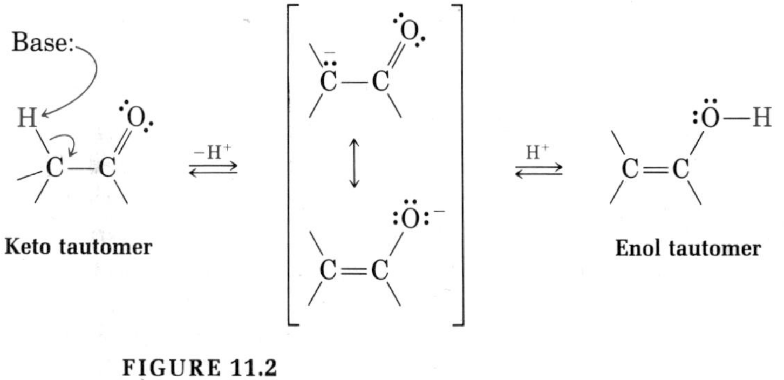

FIGURE 11.2
The mechanism of base-catalyzed enol formation

Note that only the protons on the alpha position of carbonyl compounds are acidic. The protons at beta, gamma, delta, and so on are not acidic because the resulting anions cannot be resonance-stabilized by the carbonyl group.

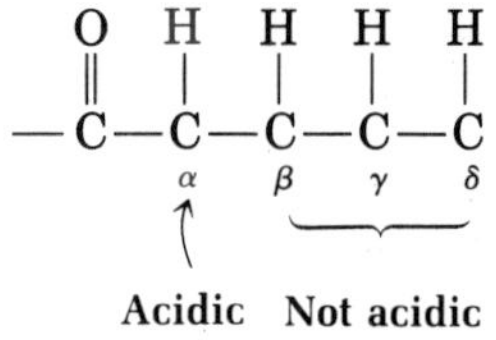

$$-\overset{\overset{\displaystyle O}{\|}}{C}-\overset{\overset{\displaystyle H}{|}}{\underset{\alpha}{C}}-\overset{\overset{\displaystyle H}{|}}{\underset{\beta}{C}}-\overset{\overset{\displaystyle H}{|}}{\underset{\gamma}{C}}-\overset{\overset{\displaystyle H}{|}}{\underset{\delta}{C}}$$

Acidic   Not acidic

PRACTICE PROBLEM   Show the structure of the enol tautomer of propanal.

Solution   Enols are formed by removing a hydrogen from the carbon next to the carbonyl carbon, forming a double bond between the two carbons, and replacing the hydrogen on the carbonyl oxygen:

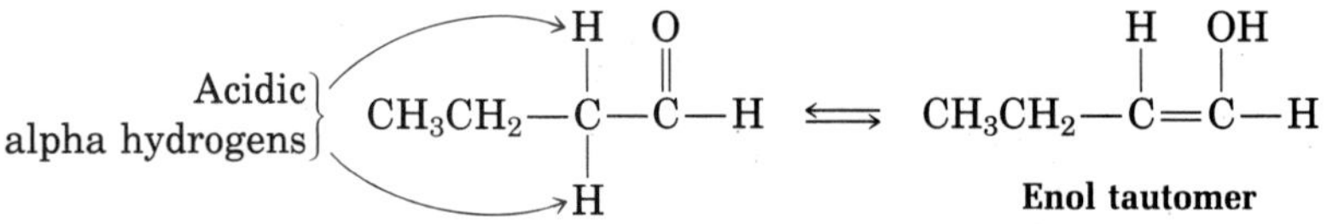

Acidic alpha hydrogens: $CH_3CH_2-\overset{\overset{\displaystyle H}{|}}{\underset{\underset{\displaystyle H}{|}}{C}}-\overset{\overset{\displaystyle O}{\|}}{C}-H \iff CH_3CH_2-\overset{\overset{\displaystyle H}{|}}{C}=\overset{\overset{\displaystyle OH}{|}}{C}-H$

Enol tautomer

PROBLEM 11.1   Draw structures for the enol tautomers of these compounds:

(a) Cyclopentanone   (b) Acetyl chloride   (c) Ethyl acetate
(d) Acetic acid   (e) Acetophenone (methyl phenyl ketone)

PROBLEM 11.2   How many acidic hydrogens does each of the molecules listed in Problem 11.1 have? Identify them.

PROBLEM 11.3   Account for the fact that 2-methylcyclohexanone can form two different enol tautomers. Show the structures of both.

11.2   REACTIVITY OF ENOLS: THE MECHANISM OF ALPHA-SUBSTITUTION REACTIONS

What kind of chemistry should we expect of enols? Since their double bonds are electron-rich, enols behave as nucleophiles and react with electrophiles in much the same way that alkenes do (Section 4.1). Because of electron donation from the oxygen lone-pair electrons, enols are more reactive than alkenes.

When an alkene reacts with an electrophile such as bromine, addition of Br^+ occurs to give an intermediate cation, which reacts with Br^- to give a 1,2-dibromide. When an enol reacts with an electrophile, however, the intermediate cation can lose the hydroxyl proton to regenerate a carbonyl compound. The net result of the reaction is alpha substitution (Figure 11.3).

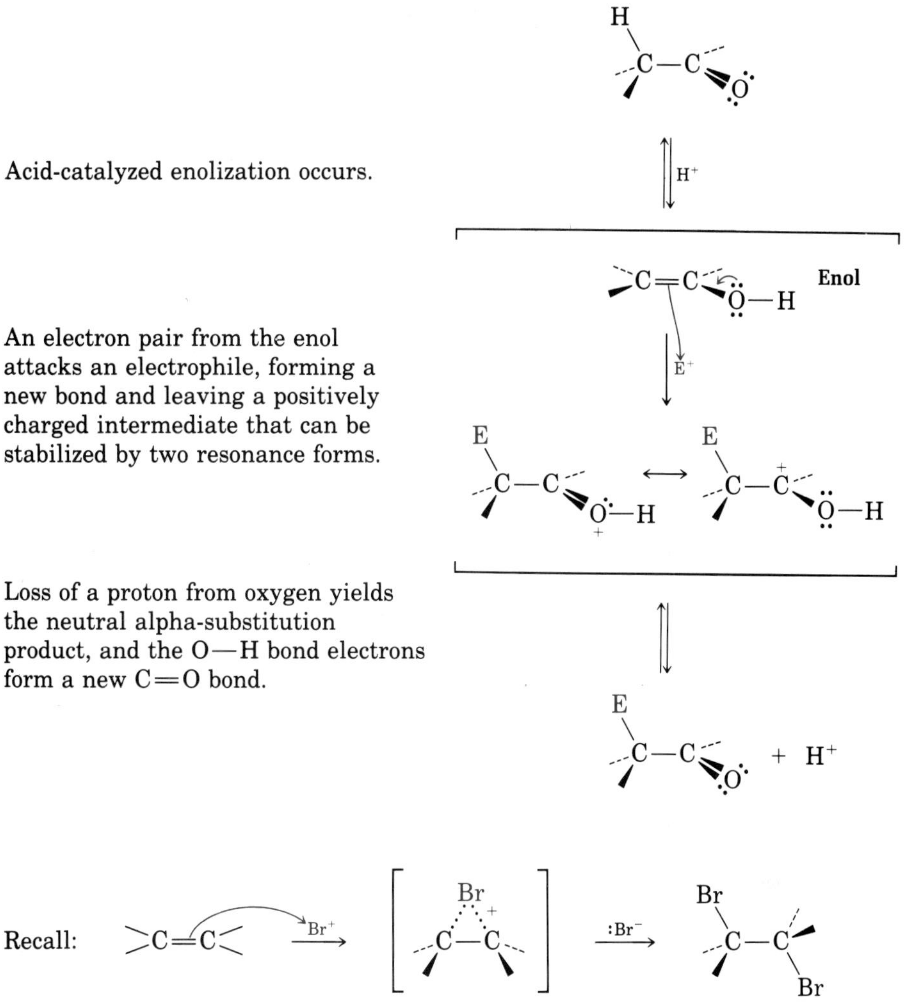

Acid-catalyzed enolization occurs.

An electron pair from the enol
attacks an electrophile, forming a
new bond and leaving a positively
charged intermediate that can be
stabilized by two resonance forms.

Loss of a proton from oxygen yields
the neutral alpha-substitution
product, and the O—H bond electrons
form a new C=O bond.

Recall:

FIGURE 11.3
The general mechanism of a carbonyl alpha-substitution reaction

11.3   ALPHA HALOGENATION OF KETONES AND ALDEHYDES

Alpha halogenation provides one of the best examples of enol reactivity. Ketones
and aldehydes can be halogenated at their alpha positions by reaction with
chlorine, bromine, or iodine in acidic solution. Bromine is most often used, and
acetic acid is often employed as solvent. The reaction is a typical alpha-
substitution process that proceeds through an enol intermediate.

α-Bromo ketones are useful in organic synthesis because they can be dehydro-
brominated by base treatment to yield α,β-*unsaturated* ketones. For example,

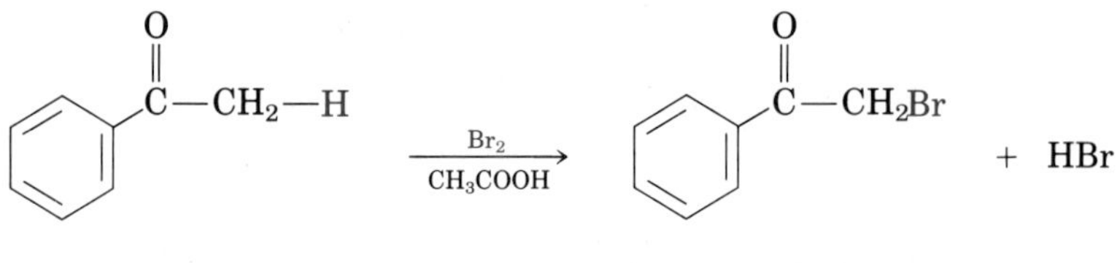

Acetophenone → Phenacyl bromide (72%) + HBr

$$\text{Acetophenone} \xrightarrow[\text{CH}_3\text{COOH}]{\text{Br}_2} \text{Phenacyl bromide (72\%)} + \text{HBr}$$

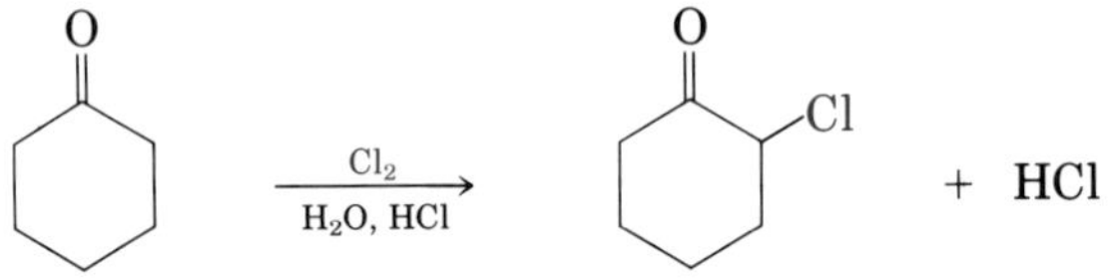

Cyclohexanone → 2-Chlorocyclohexanone (66%) + HCl

$$\text{Cyclohexanone} \xrightarrow[\text{H}_2\text{O, HCl}]{\text{Cl}_2} \text{2-Chlorocyclohexanone (66\%)} + \text{HCl}$$

2-bromo-2-methylcyclohexanone gives 2-methyl-2-cyclohexenone in 62% yield when heated in pyridine. The reaction, which takes place by the normal E2 elimination pathway (Section 7.10), is an excellent way of introducing carbon–carbon double bonds into molecules.

E2 reaction

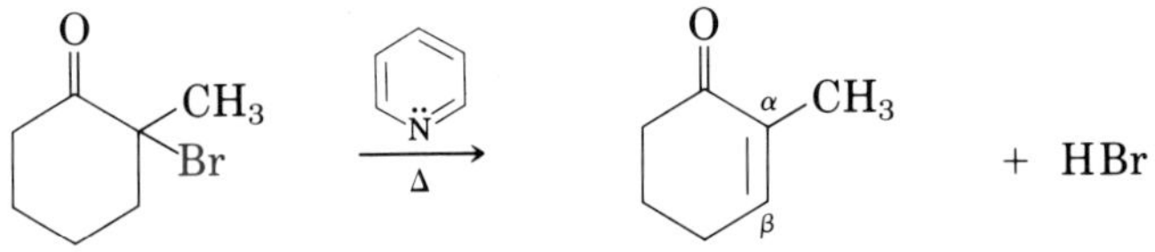

2-Bromo-2-methylcyclohexanone   **2-Methyl-2-cyclohexenone (62%)** + HBr
(an α,β-unsaturated ketone)

PROBLEM 11.4 Show in detail how you would prepare 1-penten-3-one from 3-pentanone:

$$\text{CH}_3\text{CH}_2\overset{\displaystyle O}{\overset{\displaystyle \|}{\text{C}}}\text{CH}_2\text{CH}_3 \longrightarrow \text{CH}_3\text{CH}_2\overset{\displaystyle O}{\overset{\displaystyle \|}{\text{C}}}\text{CH}=\text{CH}_2$$

PROBLEM 11.5 When a ketone such as acetone is treated with acid in deuterated water, D_2O, deuterium becomes incorporated into the molecule. Propose a mechanism to account for this reaction.

$$\text{CH}_3\text{COCH}_3 \xrightarrow{\text{D}_3\text{O}^+} \text{CH}_3\text{COCH}_2\text{D}$$

PROBLEM 11.6 When optically active (R)-3-phenyl-2-butanone is exposed to aqueous acid, a loss of optical activity occurs and racemic 3-phenyl-2-butanone is produced. Explain how this loss of optical activity takes place. [*Hint:* Review Section 6.12.]

11.4   ACIDITY OF ALPHA-HYDROGEN ATOMS: ENOLATE ION FORMATION

During the discussion of base-catalyzed enol formation in Section 11.1, we said that carbonyl compounds act as weak acids. Strong bases can abstract acidic alpha protons from carbonyl compounds to form resonance-stabilized enolate ions.

An enolate ion

Why are carbonyl compounds slightly acidic? If we compare acetone, $pK_a \approx 20$, with ethane, $pK_a \approx 50$, we find that the presence of the neighboring carbonyl group increases the acidity of a neighboring C—H by a factor of 10^{30}.

$$CH_3CH_2 \overset{H}{\underset{|}{}} \qquad \text{versus} \qquad CH_3-\overset{O}{\overset{||}{C}}-\overset{H}{\underset{|}{C}H_2}$$

Ethane, $pK_a \approx 50$ **Acetone, $pK_a \approx 20$**

The reason for this increased acidity is best seen by viewing an orbital picture of the enolate ion (Figure 11.4). Proton abstraction from a carbonyl compound occurs when the alpha C—H sigma bond is oriented in the plane of the p orbitals of the carbonyl group. The alpha carbon of the enolate ion product is sp^2 hybridized and has a p orbital that overlaps the carbonyl p orbitals. Thus, the negative charge can be shared by the electronegative oxygen atom, and the enolate ion is stabilized by resonance between two forms.

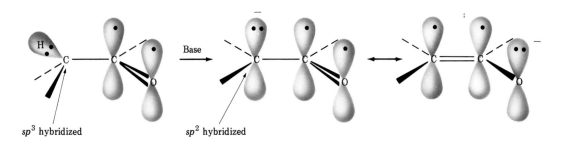

sp^3 hybridized sp^2 hybridized

FIGURE 11.4
Mechanism of enolate ion formation

Carbonyl compounds are more acidic than alkanes for the same reason that carboxylic acids are more acidic than alcohols (Section 10.3). In both cases, the anions are stabilized by resonance. But enolate ions differ from carboxylate ions in that their two resonance forms are not equivalent—the resonance form with the negative charge on the enolate oxygen atom is undoubtedly of lower energy than the form with the charge on carbon. The principle behind resonance stabilization is the same in both cases, however.

$$CH_3CH_2-H \quad \text{versus} \quad CH_3\overset{\overset{\displaystyle :O:}{\|}}{C}-CH_2-H \;\rightleftharpoons\; CH_3\overset{\overset{\displaystyle :O:}{\|}}{C}-\ddot{C}H_2 \longleftrightarrow CH_3\overset{\overset{\displaystyle :\ddot{O}:^-}{|}}{C}=CH_2 + H^+$$

pK$_a$ ≥ 50   pK$_a$ ≈ 20   Nonequivalent resonance forms
                                             of ketone enolate ion

Recall the following:

$$CH_3O-H \quad \text{versus} \quad CH_3\overset{\overset{\displaystyle :O:}{\|}}{C}-\ddot{O}-H \;\rightleftharpoons\; CH_3\overset{\overset{\displaystyle :O:}{\|}}{C}-\ddot{O}:^- \longleftrightarrow CH_3\overset{\overset{\displaystyle :\ddot{O}:^-}{|}}{C}=\ddot{O} + H^+$$

pK$_a$ ≈ 16   pK$_a$ ≈ 5   Equivalent resonance forms
                                             of carboxylate ion

Since alpha-hydrogen atoms of carbonyl compounds are only weakly acidic when compared with mineral acids or with carboxylic acids, strong bases must be used to effect enolate ion formation. If an alkoxide ion base such as sodium ethoxide is used, ionization of acetone takes place only to the extent of about 0.01% since ethanol (pK$_a$ = 16) is a stronger acid than acetone. If, however, a very powerful base such as sodium hydride (NaH, the sodium salt of H_2) or sodium amide (NaNH$_2$, the sodium salt of ammonia) is used, then a carbonyl compound can be completely converted into its enolate ion.

Cyclohexanone   Cyclohexanone enolate (100%)

All types of carbonyl compounds, including aldehydes, ketones, esters, acid chlorides, and amides, have greatly enhanced alpha-hydrogen acidity compared to alkanes. Table 11.1 lists the approximate pK$_a$ values of different kinds of carbonyl compounds and shows how these values compare with other acidic substances we have seen.

When a C—H bond is flanked by two carbonyl groups, acidity is enhanced even more. Thus, Table 11.1 indicates that compounds such as 1,3-diketones (known as *β-diketones*), 1,3-keto esters (*β-keto esters*), and 1,3-diesters are much more acidic than water. This is so because the enolate ions derived from these *β*-dicarbonyl compounds are highly stabilized by delocalization of the negative charge onto both of the neighboring carbonyl oxygens.

TABLE 11.1 Acidity constants for some organic compounds

Compound type	Compound	pK_a	
Carboxylic acid	$CH_3COO{-}H$	5	Stronger acid
1,3-Diketone	$CH_2(COCH_3)_2$	9	
1,3-Keto ester	$CH_3COCH_2CO_2C_2H_5$	11	
1,3-Diester	$CH_2(CO_2C_2H_5)_2$	13	
Water	HOH	16	
Primary alcohol	CH_3CH_2OH	16	
Acid chloride	CH_3COCl	16	
Aldehyde	CH_3CHO	17	
Ketone	CH_3COCH_3	20	
Ester	$CH_3CO_2C_2H_5$	25	
Nitrile	CH_3CN	25	
Dialkylamide	$CH_3CON(CH_3)_2$	30	
Ammonia	NH_3	35	Weaker acid

For example, we can draw three resonance forms for the enolate ion from 2,4-pentanedione:

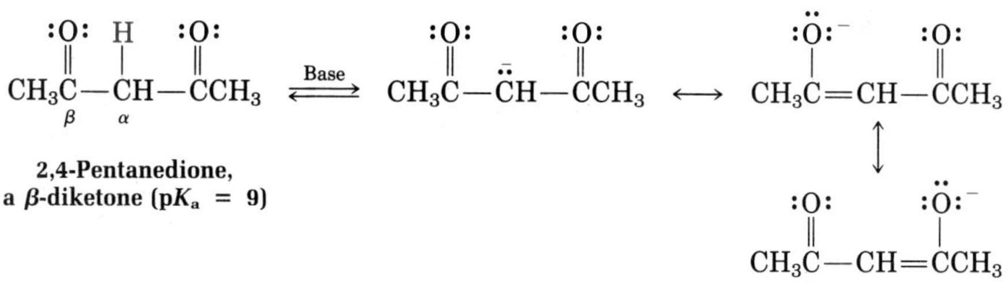

2,4-Pentanedione,
a β-diketone (pK_a = 9)

PROBLEM 11.7 Identify the most acidic hydrogens in these molecules:

(a) CH_3CH_2CHO (b) $(CH_3)_3CCOCH_3$ (c) CH_3COOH
(d) $CH_3CH_2CH_2C{\equiv}N$ (e) 1,3-Cyclohexanedione

PROBLEM 11.8 When optically active (R)-2-methylcyclohexanone is treated with aqueous NaOH, racemic 2-methylcyclohexanone is produced. Propose a mechanism to explain this observation.

PROBLEM 11.9 When optically active (R)-3-methylcyclohexanone is treated with aqueous NaOH, no racemization occurs. Instead, the optically active ketone is recovered unchanged. How can you reconcile this observation with your answer to Problem 11.8?

11.5   REACTIVITY OF ENOLATE IONS

Enolate ions are more useful than enols for two reasons. The first is that pure enols cannot normally be isolated—they are usually generated only as fleeting intermediates in small concentration. By contrast, solutions of pure enolate ions are easily prepared from most carbonyl compounds by treatment with a strong base.

The second reason for their importance is that enolate ions are much more reactive than enols. Whereas enols are neutral, enolate ions carry a full negative charge, making them much better nucleophiles. Thus, the alpha position of enolate ions is highly reactive toward electrophiles.

Enol: neutral, moderately reactive, very difficult to isolate   **Enolate: negatively charged, very reactive, easily prepared**

Since enolate ions are hybrids of two nonequivalent resonance forms, they can be considered either as α-keto carbanions ($^-$C—C=O) or as vinylic alkoxides (C=C—O$^-$). Thus, enolates can react with electrophiles either on oxygen or on carbon. Reaction on oxygen yields an enol derivative, whereas reaction on carbon yields an alpha-substituted carbonyl compound (Figure 11.5). Both kinds of reactivity are known, but reaction on carbon is the more commonly observed pathway.

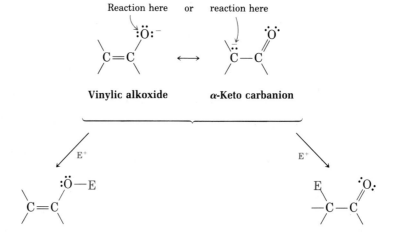

Vinylic alkoxide   **α-Keto carbanion**

An enol derivative (E$^+$ = an electrophile)   **An alpha-substituted carbonyl compound**

FIGURE 11.5
Two modes of enolate ion reactivity: Reaction on carbon to yield an alpha-substituted carbonyl product is the more commonly followed path

11.6   ALKYLATION OF ENOLATE IONS

One of the most important reactions of enolate ions is their **alkylation** by treatment with an alkyl halide. The alkylation reaction is extremely useful for synthesis purposes because it allows the formation of a new carbon–carbon bond, thereby joining two small pieces into one larger molecule. Alkylation occurs when the nucleophilic enolate ion reacts with the electrophilic alkyl halide in an S_N2 reaction, displacing the halide ion by back-side attack.

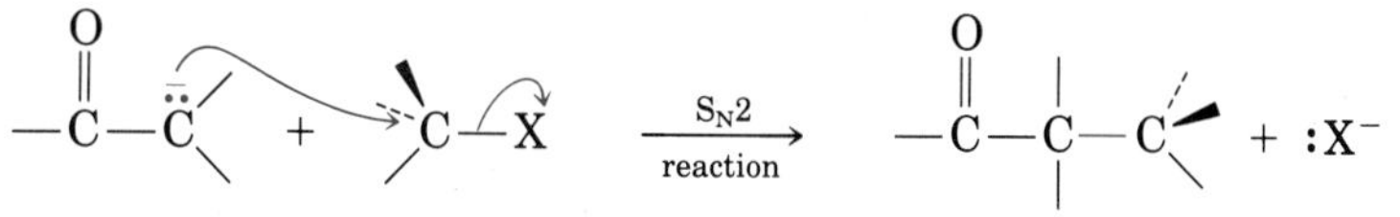

Enolate ion   **Alkyl halide**

Alkylation reactions are subject to the same constraints that affect all S_N2 reactions (Section 7.8). Thus, the leaving group, X, in the alkylating agent can be chloride, bromide, iodide, or tosylate. The alkyl group, R, must be primary or methyl, since competing E2 elimination occurs when secondary or tertiary halides are used.

Let's look at some specific examples of alkylation reactions.

The Malonic Ester Synthesis

The **malonic ester synthesis,** one of the oldest and best known carbonyl alkylation reactions, is an excellent method for preparing substituted acetic acids from alkyl halides:

$$R-X \xrightarrow[\text{ester synthesis}]{\text{Via malonic}} R-CH_2CO_2H$$

Alkyl halide   **Alpha-substituted acetic acid**

Diethyl propanedioate, commonly called diethyl malonate or *malonic ester,* is more acidic than many other carbonyl compounds (pK_a = 13) because its alpha-hydrogen atoms are flanked by two carbonyl groups. Thus, malonic ester is easily converted into its enolate ion by reaction with sodium ethoxide in ethanol. The enolate ion, in turn, is readily alkylated by treatment with an alkyl halide, yielding an alpha-substituted malonic ester.

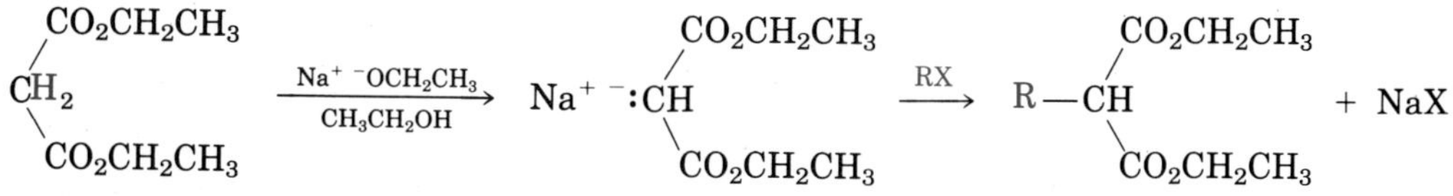

Malonic ester   **Sodio malonic ester**   **An alkylated malonic ester**

The product of a malonic ester alkylation has one acidic alpha hydrogen left, and the alkylation process can therefore be repeated a second time to yield a dialkylated malonic ester:

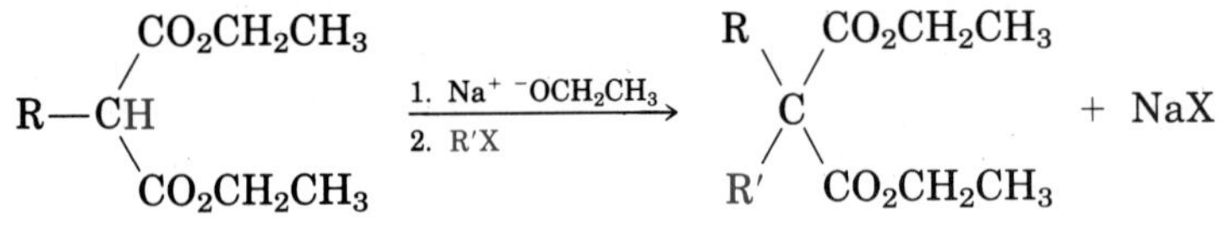

$$R-\overset{\displaystyle CO_2CH_2CH_3}{\underset{\displaystyle CO_2CH_2CH_3}{CH}} \xrightarrow[\text{2. R'X}]{\text{1. Na}^+ \; ^-\text{OCH}_2\text{CH}_3} \quad \overset{\displaystyle R}{\underset{\displaystyle R'}{\overset{|}{\underset{|}{C}}}} \overset{\displaystyle CO_2CH_2CH_3}{\underset{\displaystyle CO_2CH_2CH_3}{}} \quad + \; NaX$$

A dialkylated malonic ester

Once formed, alkylated malonic esters can be hydrolyzed and decarboxylated (**decarboxylation** = loss of carbon dioxide, CO_2) when heated with aqueous HCl. The product is a substituted monoacid. Note that decarboxylation is a unique feature of substituted malonic acids. It is not a general reaction for all carboxylic acids.

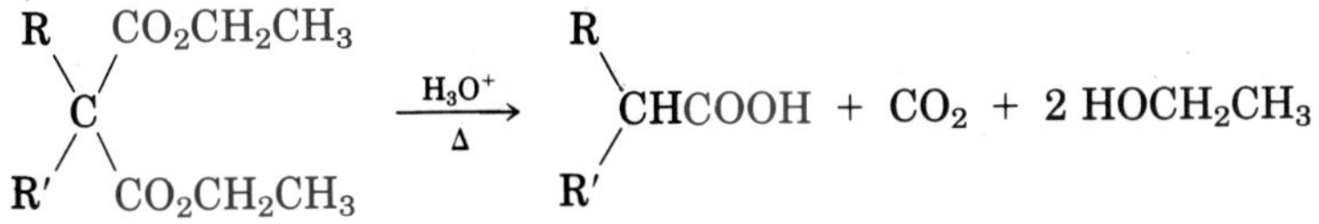

$$\overset{\displaystyle R}{\underset{\displaystyle R'}{\overset{|}{\underset{|}{C}}}} \overset{\displaystyle CO_2CH_2CH_3}{\underset{\displaystyle CO_2CH_2CH_3}{}} \xrightarrow[\Delta]{H_3O^+} \quad \overset{\displaystyle R}{\underset{\displaystyle R'}{}} CHCOOH \; + \; CO_2 \; + \; 2 \; HOCH_2CH_3$$

The malonic ester synthesis is an excellent method for converting alkyl halides into carboxylic acids while lengthening the carbon chain by two atoms. For example:

$$CH_3(CH_2)_2CH_2Br \; + \; Na^+ \; ^-:CH(COOCH_3)_2 \longrightarrow CH_3(CH_2)_2CH_2CH(COOCH_3)_2$$

1-Bromobutane

$$\Big\downarrow H_3O^+, \Delta$$

$$CH_3(CH_2)_2CH_2CH_2COOH \; + \; CO_2 \; + \; CH_3OH$$

Hexanoic acid (75%)

PRACTICE PROBLEM   How would you prepare heptanoic acid via a malonic ester synthesis?

Solution   The malonic ester synthesis converts an alkyl halide into a carboxylic acid having two or more carbons in its chain. Thus, a seven-carbon acid chain must be derived from a five-carbon alkyl halide such as 1-bromopentane.

$$CH_3CH_2CH_2CH_2CH_2Br \; + \; CH_2(COOCH_2CH_3)_2 \xrightarrow[\text{2. } H_3O^+, \Delta]{\text{1. Na}^+ \; ^-\text{OCH}_2\text{CH}_3} CH_3CH_2CH_2CH_2CH_2CH_2COOH$$

PROBLEM 11.10 What alkyl halide would you use to prepare these compounds via a malonic ester synthesis?

(a) Butanoic acid   (b) 3-Phenylpropanoic acid   (c) 5-Methylhexanoic acid

PROBLEM 11.11 How could you use a malonic ester synthesis to prepare these compounds? Show all the steps you would use.

(a) 4-Methylpentanoic acid   (b) 2-Methylpentanoic acid

PROBLEM 11.12 Monoalkylated acetic acids, RCH_2COOH, and dialkylated acetic acids, $R_2CHCOOH$, can be prepared by malonic ester synthesis, but trialkylated acetic acids, R_3CCOOH, cannot be prepared. Explain.

The Acetoacetic Ester Synthesis

The **acetoacetic ester synthesis** provides a method for preparing alpha-substituted acetone derivatives from alkyl halides in the same way that the malonic ester synthesis provides a method for preparing alpha-substituted acetic acids.

$$R-X \xrightarrow[\text{ester synthesis}]{\text{Via acetoacetic}} \overset{\displaystyle O}{\overset{\|}{R-CH_2CCH_3}}$$

Alpha-substituted acetone

Ethyl 3-oxobutanoate, commonly called ethyl acetoacetate or *acetoacetic ester*, is much like malonic ester in that its alpha hydrogens are flanked by two carbonyl groups. It is therefore readily converted into an enolate ion, which can be alkylated by reaction with an alkyl halide. A second alkylation can also be carried out, if desired, since acetoacetic ester has two acidic alpha protons that can be replaced.

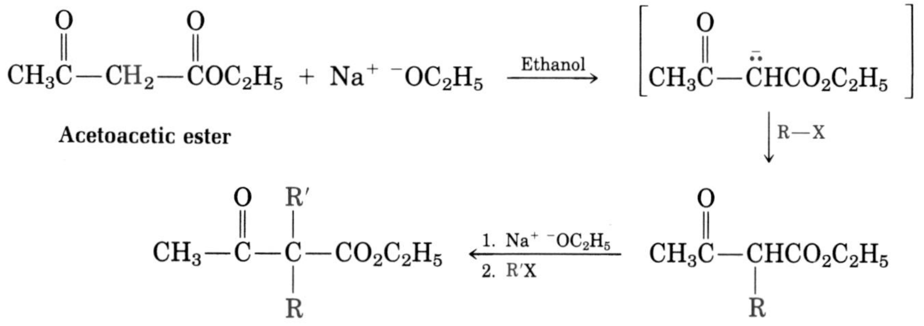

$$CH_3\overset{O}{\overset{\|}{C}}-CH_2-\overset{O}{\overset{\|}{C}}OC_2H_5 + Na^+ \ ^-OC_2H_5 \xrightarrow{\text{Ethanol}} \left[CH_3\overset{O}{\overset{\|}{C}}-\overset{..}{C}HCO_2C_2H_5 \right]$$

Acetoacetic ester

$$CH_3-\overset{O}{\overset{\|}{C}}-\overset{R'}{\underset{R}{\overset{|}{C}}}-CO_2C_2H_5 \xleftarrow[\text{2. R'X}]{\text{1. Na}^+ \ ^-OC_2H_5} CH_3\overset{O}{\overset{\|}{C}}-\underset{R}{\overset{|}{C}}HCO_2C_2H_5$$

Upon heating with aqueous HCl, the alkylated acetoacetic ester is hydrolyzed and decarboxylated to yield an alpha-substituted acetone product. If a mono-alkylated acetoacetic ester is heated with HCl, an alpha-monosubstituted acetone is formed; if a dialkylated acetoacetic ester is heated with HCl, an α,α-dialkylated acetone is formed.

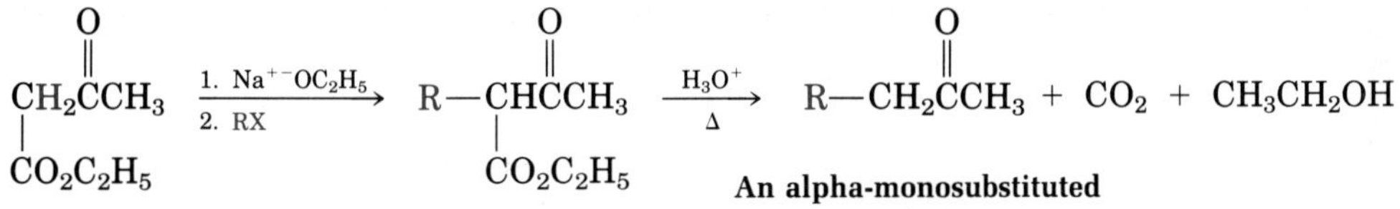

$$CH_3CCH_2 \quad \underset{\underset{2.\ RX}{1.\ Na^+\ ^-OC_2H_5}}{\longrightarrow} \quad R-CHCCH_3 \quad \underset{\Delta}{\overset{H_3O^+}{\longrightarrow}} \quad R-CH_2CCH_3 + CO_2 + CH_3CH_2OH$$

Acetoacetic ester

An alpha-monosubstituted acetone

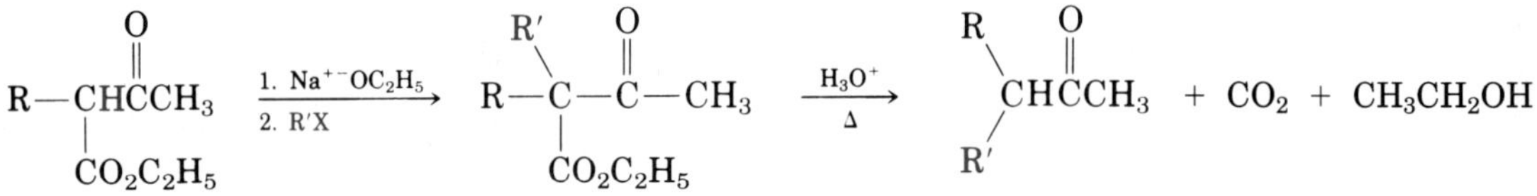

$$R-CHCCH_3 \quad \underset{\underset{2.\ R'X}{1.\ Na^+\ ^-OC_2H_5}}{\longrightarrow} \quad R-C-C-CH_3 \quad \underset{\Delta}{\overset{H_3O^+}{\longrightarrow}} \quad CHCCH_3 + CO_2 + CH_3CH_2OH$$

An α,α-dialkylated acetone

For example,

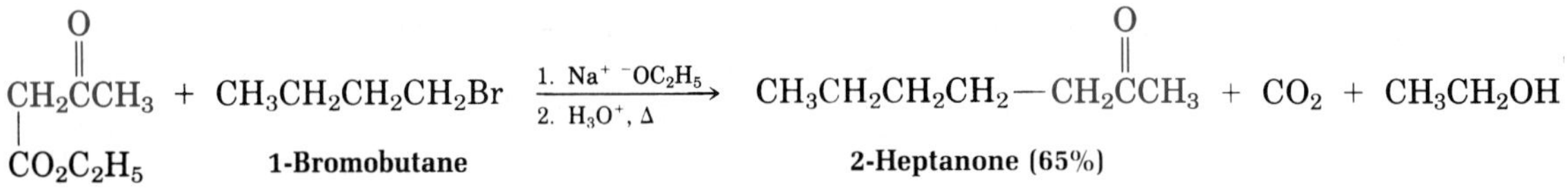

$$CH_3CCH_3 + CH_3CH_2CH_2CH_2Br \quad \underset{\underset{2.\ H_3O^+,\ \Delta}{1.\ Na^+\ ^-OC_2H_5}}{\longrightarrow} \quad CH_3CH_2CH_2CH_2-CH_2CCH_3 + CO_2 + CH_3CH_2OH$$

Acetoacetic ester   1-Bromobutane   2-Heptanone (65%)

PRACTICE PROBLEM How would you prepare 2-pentanone via an acetoacetic ester synthesis?

Solution The acetoacetic ester synthesis yields a ketone product by adding three carbons to an alkyl halide:

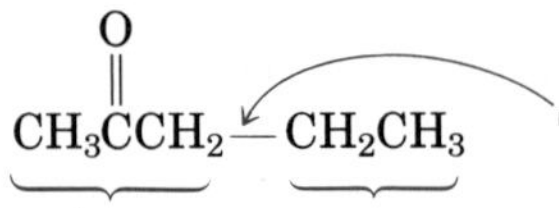

$$CH_3CCH_2 - CH_2CH_3 \quad \text{This bond formed}$$

These three carbons from acetoacetic ester   These carbons from alkyl halide

Thus, the acetoacetic ester synthesis of 2-pentanone would involve reaction with bromoethane:

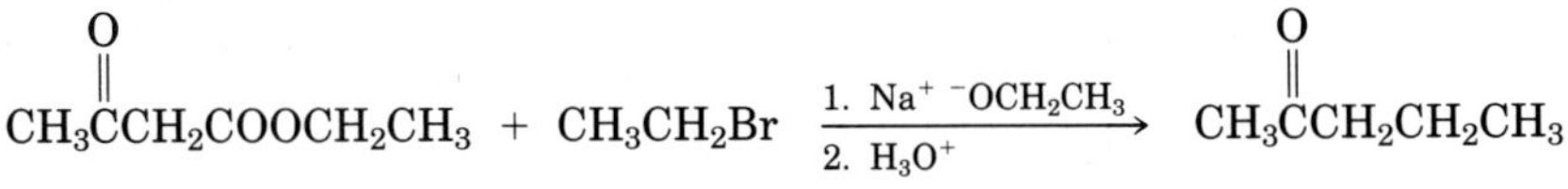

$$CH_3CCH_2COOCH_2CH_3 + CH_3CH_2Br \quad \underset{\underset{2.\ H_3O^+}{1.\ Na^+\ ^-OCH_2CH_3}}{\longrightarrow} \quad CH_3CCH_2CH_2CH_3$$

PROBLEM 11.13   How would you prepare these compounds using an acetoacetic ester synthesis?

(a) 4-Phenyl-2-butanone   (b) 5-Methyl-2-hexanone   (c) 3-Methyl-2-hexanone

PROBLEM 11.14   Which of the following compounds cannot be prepared by an acetoacetic ester synthesis? Explain.

(a) 2-Butanone   (b) Phenylacetone
(c) Acetophenone   (d) 3,3-Dimethyl-2-butanone

11.7   CARBONYL CONDENSATION REACTIONS

We have seen thus far that carbonyl compounds can behave either as electrophiles or as nucleophiles. In nucleophilic addition reactions and nucleophilic acyl substitution reactions, the carbonyl group behaves as an electrophile by accepting electrons from an attacking nucleophile. In alpha-substitution reactions, however, the carbonyl compound behaves as a nucleophile when it is converted into its enolate ion or enol tautomer.

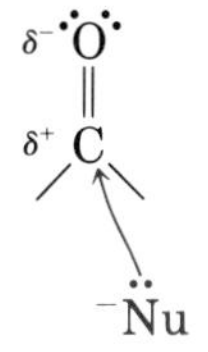

Electrophilic carbonyl is attacked by nucleophiles (:Nu⁻)

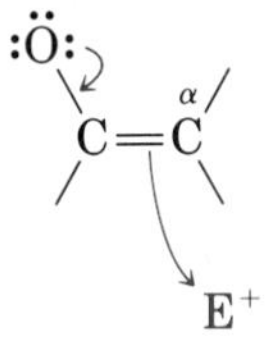

Nucleophilic alpha position of enolates attacks electrophiles (E⁺)

Carbonyl condensation reactions involve *both* of these types of reactivity. These reactions take place between two carbonyl components and involve a *combination* of nucleophilic addition and alpha-substitution steps. One component acts as an electron donor and undergoes an alpha-substitution process, while the other component acts as an electron acceptor and undergoes a nucleophilic addition process. The general mechanism of a carbonyl condensation reaction is shown in Figure 11.6 (page 342).

There are numerous variations of carbonyl condensation reactions, depending on the exact structure of the two carbonyl components, but the general mechanism remains the same in all cases.

One carbonyl component with an alpha-hydrogen atom is converted by base into its enolate anion.

This enolate ion acts as a nucleophilic donor and adds to the electrophilic carbonyl group of the acceptor component.

Protonation of the tetrahedral alkoxide ion intermediate gives the neutral condensation product.

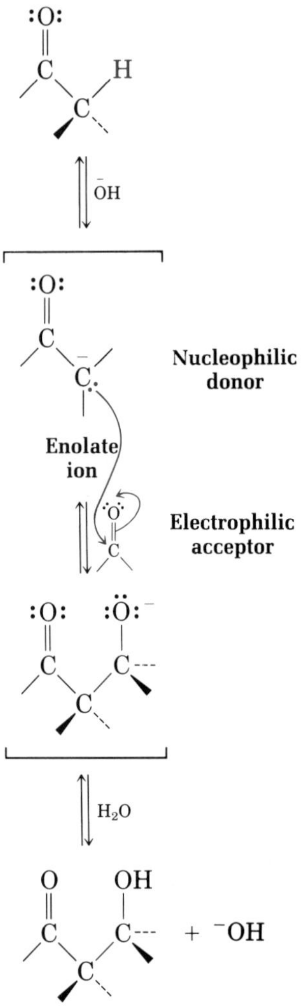

FIGURE 11.6
The general mechanism of a carbonyl condensation reaction

11.8 CONDENSATION OF ALDEHYDES AND KETONES: THE ALDOL REACTION

When acetaldehyde is treated in an alcoholic solvent with a basic catalyst such as sodium hydroxide or sodium ethoxide, a rapid and reversible condensation reaction occurs. The product is the β-hydroxy aldehyde product known trivially as **aldol** (**ald**ehyde + alcoh**ol**).

$$2 \ CH_3CHO \quad \underset{\text{Ethanol}}{\overset{Na^+OC_2H_5}{\rightleftharpoons}} \quad \overset{\overset{\displaystyle OH}{\underset{\displaystyle |}{}}}{\underset{\underset{\displaystyle H}{\displaystyle |}}{CH_3\overset{\beta}{C}}}\overset{\alpha}{-CH_2CHO}$$

Acetaldehyde

Aldol (a β-hydroxy aldehyde)

Known as the **aldol reaction**, this base-catalyzed dimerization is a general reaction for all ketones and aldehydes having alpha-hydrogen atoms. If the ketone or aldehyde does not have an alpha-hydrogen atom, aldol condensation cannot occur. The exact position of the aldol equilibrium is strongly dependent both on reaction conditions and on substrate structure. As the following examples indicate, the aldol equilibrium generally favors condensation product in the case of monosubstituted acetaldehydes, RCH_2CHO, but favors starting material for disubstituted acetaldehydes, R_2CHCHO, and for most ketones.

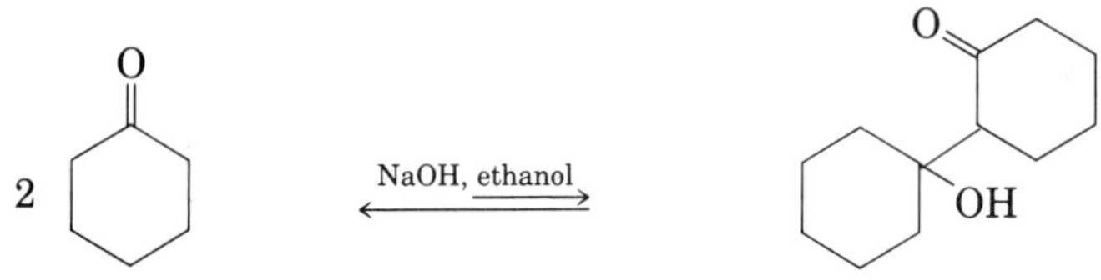

2 Cyclohexanone   → NaOH, ethanol   22%

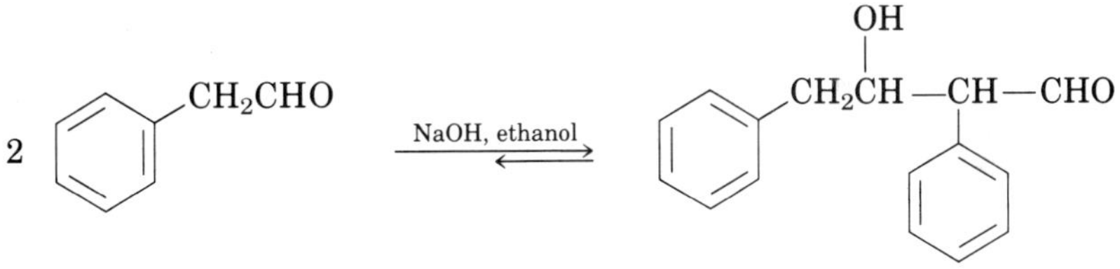

2 Phenylacetaldehyde   → NaOH, ethanol   90%

PRACTICE PROBLEM What is the structure of the aldol product derived from propanal?

Solution An aldol reaction combines two molecules of starting material, forming a bond between the alpha carbon of one partner and the carbonyl carbon of the second partner:

Bond formed here

$$CH_3CH_2-\overset{\overset{\displaystyle O}{\|}}{C}-H \ + \ \underset{\underset{\displaystyle CH_3}{|}}{CH_2}-\overset{\overset{\displaystyle O}{\|}}{C}-H \quad \xrightarrow{NaOH} \quad CH_3CH_2-\underset{\underset{\displaystyle H}{|}}{\overset{\overset{\displaystyle OH}{|}}{C}}-\underset{\underset{\displaystyle CH_3}{|}}{CH}-\overset{\overset{\displaystyle O}{\|}}{C}-H$$

PROBLEM 11.15 Which of the following compounds could undergo the aldol reaction, and which could not?

(a) Cyclohexanone
(b) Benzaldehyde
(c) 2,2,6,6-Tetramethylcyclohexanone
(d) Formaldehyde

PROBLEM 11.16 Show the product of the aldol reaction of these compounds:

(a) Butanal
(b) Cyclopentanone
(c) Acetophenone

PROBLEM 11.17 When 2-butanone is treated with base, a mixture of two aldol condensation products is formed. What are their structures?

11.9 DEHYDRATION OF ALDOL PRODUCTS: SYNTHESIS OF ENONES

The β-hydroxy ketones and β-hydroxy aldehydes formed in aldol reactions can be readily dehydrated to yield conjugated **enones** (**ene** + **one**). In fact, it is this loss of water that gives the aldol *condensation* its name, since water condenses out of the reaction.

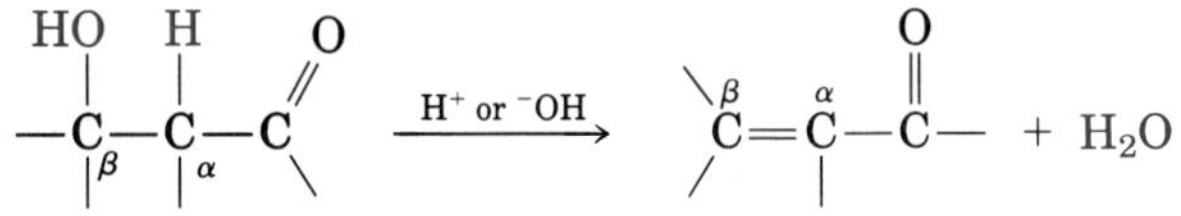

A β-hydroxy aldehyde/ketone **A conjugated enone**

Most alcohols are resistant to dehydration by dilute acid or base (Section 8.7). Hydroxyl groups that are beta to a carbonyl group, however, are special—they are easily eliminated. Under *basic* conditions, an acidic alpha hydrogen is abstracted, and the resultant enolate ion expels hydroxide ion. Under *acidic* conditions, the hydroxyl group is protonated and then expelled by the neighboring enol.

Basic elimination

Enolate

Acidic elimination

Enol

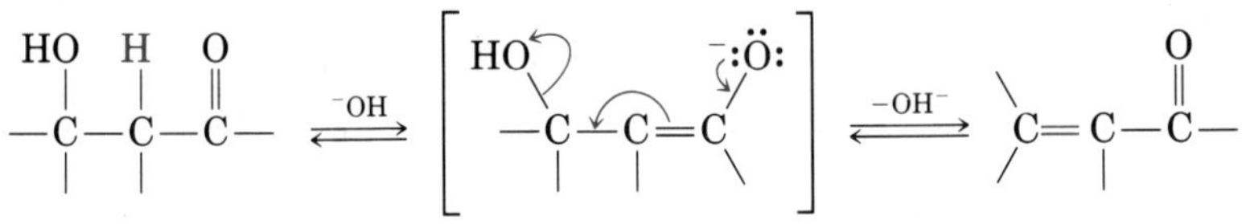

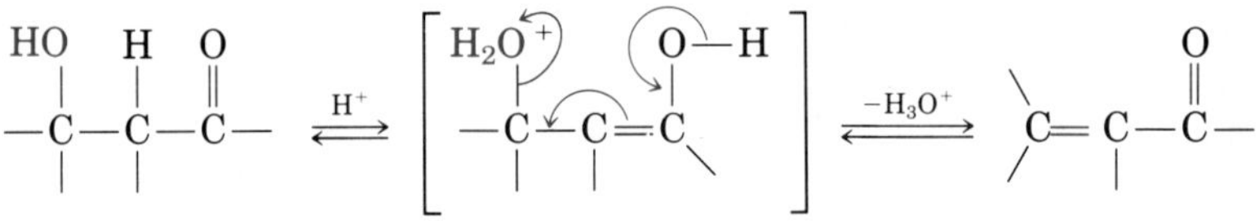

The conditions required to effect aldol dehydration are often only a bit more vigorous (slightly higher temperature, for example) than the conditions required for the aldol dimerization itself. As a result, conjugated enones are often obtained directly from aldol reactions; the intermediate β-hydroxy carbonyl compounds are often not even isolated.

Conjugated enones are more stable than nonconjugated enones for the same reasons that conjugated dienes are more stable than nonconjugated dienes (Section 4.9). Interaction between the pi electrons of the carbon–carbon double bond and the pi electrons of the carbonyl group leads to a description of conjugated enones that shows a delocalization of the pi electrons over all four atomic centers.

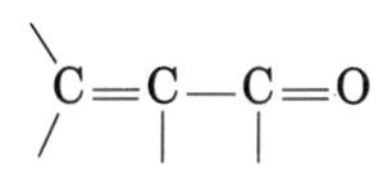

$$\underset{\substack{\text{Conjugated enone}\\\text{(more stable)}}}{\text{C=C—C=O}} \qquad \underset{\substack{\text{Nonconjugated enone}\\\text{(less stable)}}}{\text{C=C—C—C=O}}$$

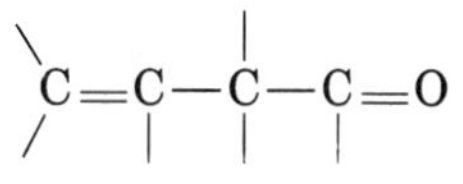

Recall the following:

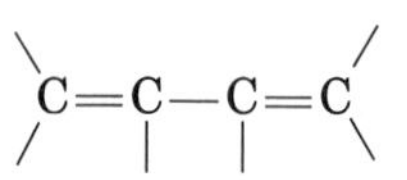

$$\underset{\substack{\text{Conjugated diene}\\\text{(more stable)}}}{\text{C=C—C=C}} \qquad \underset{\substack{\text{Nonconjugated diene}\\\text{(less stable)}}}{\text{C=C—C—C=C}}$$

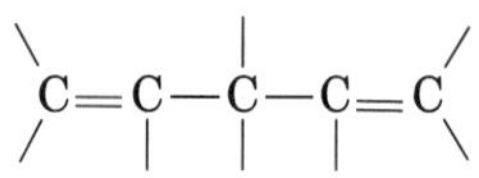

PRACTICE PROBLEM What is the structure of the enone obtained from aldol condensation of acetaldehyde?

Solution In the aldol reaction, H_2O is eliminated by removing two hydrogens from the acidic alpha position of one partner and the oxygen from the second partner:

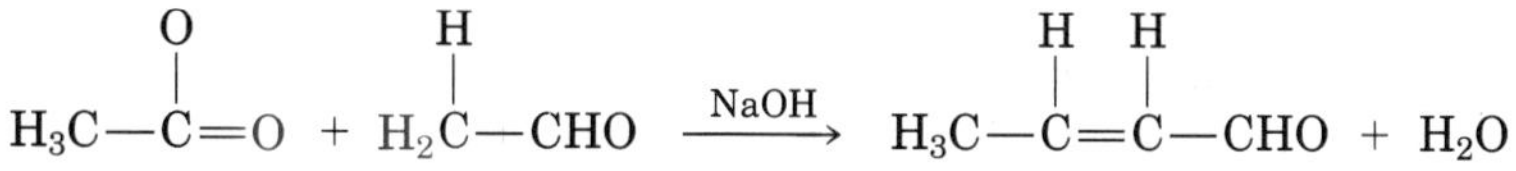

$$H_3C\overset{O}{\underset{}{-}}C{=}O \;+\; H_2\overset{H}{\underset{}{C}}{-}CHO \;\xrightarrow{\text{NaOH}}\; H_3C{-}\overset{H}{\underset{}{C}}{=}\overset{H}{\underset{}{C}}{-}CHO \;+\; H_2O$$

2-Butenal

PROBLEM 11.18 Write the structures of the enone products you would expect to obtain from aldol condensation of these compounds:

(a) Acetone   (b) Cyclopentanone   (c) Acetophenone   (d) Propanal

PROBLEM 11.19 Aldol condensation of 2-butanone leads to a mixture of two enones (ignoring double-bond stereochemistry). Draw the two enones.

11.10 CONDENSATION OF ESTERS: THE CLAISEN CONDENSATION REACTION

Esters, like aldehydes and ketones, are weakly acidic. When an ester having an alpha hydrogen is treated with 1 equiv of a base such as sodium methoxide, a reversible condensation reaction occurs to yield a β-keto ester product. For example, ethyl acetate yields ethyl acetoacetate on base treatment. This reaction between two ester components is known as the **Claisen condensation reaction.**

$$2\ CH_3\overset{O}{\overset{\|}{C}}OCH_2CH_3 \xrightarrow[\text{2. H}_3O^+]{\text{1. Na}^+\ ^-OCH_2CH_3,\ \text{ethanol}} CH_3\overset{O}{\overset{\|}{C}}\underset{\beta}{-}CH_2\underset{\alpha}{-}\overset{O}{\overset{\|}{C}}-OCH_2CH_3\ +\ CH_3CH_2OH$$

Ethyl acetate

Ethyl acetoacetate,
a β-keto ester (75%)

The mechanism of the Claisen reaction is similar to that of the aldol reaction, involving the nucleophilic addition of an ester enolate ion donor to the carbonyl group of a second ester molecule. We can view the Claisen mechanism as shown in Figure 11.7. From the point of view of the donor component, the Claisen condensation is simply an alpha-substitution reaction. From the point of view of the acceptor component, the Claisen condensation is a nucleophilic acyl substitution reaction.

Methoxide ion base abstracts an acidic alpha-hydrogen atom from an ester molecule, yielding an ester enolate ion.

$$CH_3\overset{:\ddot{O}:}{\overset{\|}{C}}OCH_3$$

$$\Updownarrow\ ^-OCH_3$$

$$\left[\ ^-:CH_2\overset{:\ddot{O}:}{\overset{\|}{C}}OCH_3\right]\ +\ HOCH_3$$

The enolate ion adds to a second ester molecule by nucleophilic addition, yielding a tetrahedral intermediate.

$$CH_3\overset{:\ddot{O}:}{\overset{\|}{C}}OCH_3 \quad \Updownarrow$$

$$\left[CH_3\overset{:\ddot{O}:^-}{\overset{|}{C}}-CH_2\overset{:O:}{\overset{\|}{C}}OCH_3\right]$$
$$OCH_3$$

Loss of methoxide ion from the tetrahedral intermediate yields methyl acetoacetate and regenerates the basic catalyst.

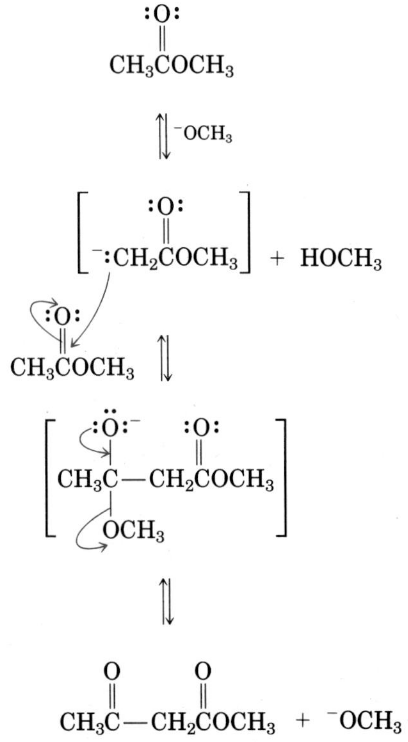

$$\Updownarrow$$

$$CH_3\overset{O}{\overset{\|}{C}}-CH_2\overset{O}{\overset{\|}{C}}OCH_3\ +\ ^-OCH_3$$

FIGURE 11.7
The mechanism of the Claisen condensation reaction

The only difference between an aldol condensation and a Claisen condensation involves the fate of the initially formed tetrahedral intermediate. The tetrahedral intermediate in the aldol reaction is protonated to give a stable alcohol product—exactly the same behavior previously seen for ketones (Section 9.8). The tetrahedral intermediate in the Claisen reaction, however, expels an alkoxide leaving group to yield an acyl substitution product—exactly the same behavior previously seen for esters (Section 10.6).

PRACTICE PROBLEM What product would you obtain from Claisen condensation of methyl propanoate?

Solution The Claisen condensation of an ester results in the loss of 1 mol of alcohol and formation of a product in which an acyl group of one molecule of reactant bonds to the alpha carbon of a second molecule of the reactant:

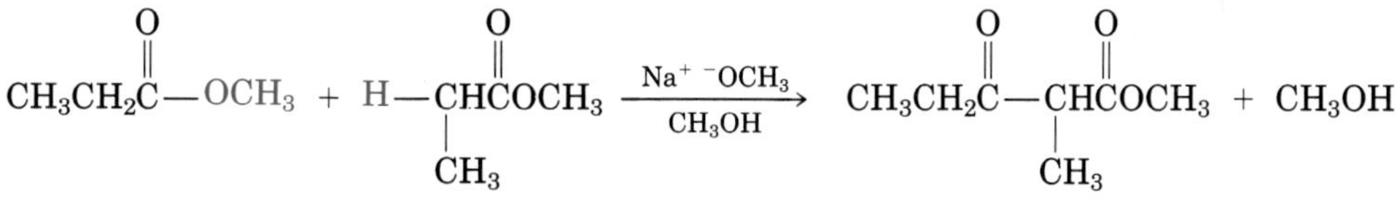

$$CH_3CH_2\overset{\overset{\displaystyle O}{\|}}{C}-OCH_3 \; + \; H-\underset{\underset{\displaystyle CH_3}{|}}{CH}\overset{\overset{\displaystyle O}{\|}}{C}OCH_3 \; \xrightarrow[\text{CH}_3\text{OH}]{\text{Na}^+ \; {}^-\text{OCH}_3} \; CH_3CH_2\overset{\overset{\displaystyle O}{\|}}{C}-\underset{\underset{\displaystyle CH_3}{|}}{CH}\overset{\overset{\displaystyle O}{\|}}{C}OCH_3 \; + \; CH_3OH$$

Methyl propanoate (2 mol)   **Methyl-2-methyl-3-oxopentanoate**

PROBLEM 11.20 Show the products you would expect to obtain by Claisen condensation of these esters:

(a) $(CH_3)_2CHCH_2COOCH_3$ (b) Methyl phenylacetate
(c) Methyl cyclohexylacetate

PROBLEM 11.21 As indicated in Figure 11.7, the Claisen condensation is reversible. That is, a β-keto ester can be cleaved by base into two fragments. Show the mechanism by which the following cleavage occurs:

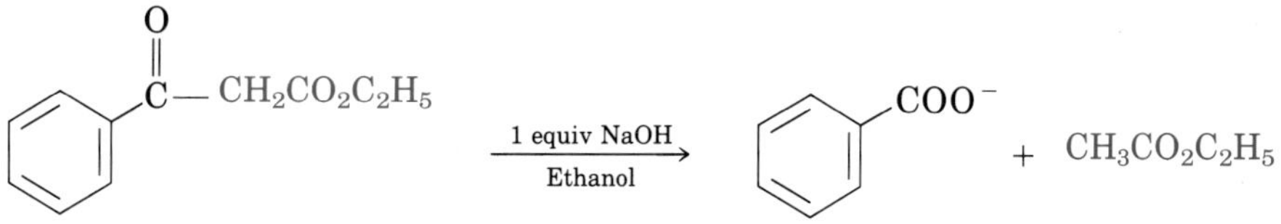

$$\xrightarrow[\text{Ethanol}]{1 \text{ equiv NaOH}}$$

$+ \; CH_3CO_2C_2H_5$

ADDITIONAL PROBLEMS

PROBLEM 11.22 Suggest an explanation for the observation that acetone is enolized only to the extent of about 0.0001% at equilibrium, whereas 2,4-pentanedione is 76% enolized.

PROBLEM 11.23   Write resonance structures for these anions:

(a) $CH_3\overset{O}{\overset{\|}{C}}-\overset{..}{C}H\overset{O}{\overset{\|}{C}}CH_3$

(b) $:CH_2C\equiv N^-$

(c) $CH_3CH=CH-\overset{..}{C}H\overset{O}{\overset{\|}{C}}CH_3$

(d) $N\equiv C-\overset{..}{C}HCO_2C_2H_5$

PROBLEM 11.24   Indicate the acidic hydrogen atoms in these molecules:

(a) $HOCH_2\overset{O}{\overset{\|}{C}}CH_3$

(b) $HOCH_2CH_2\overset{O}{\overset{\|}{C}}C(CH_3)_3$

(c) 1,3-Cyclopentanedione

(d) $CH_3CH=CHCHO$

PROBLEM 11.25   Draw structures for the possible monoenol tautomers of 1,3-cyclohexanedione. How many enol forms are possible? Which would you expect to be most stable? Explain your answer.

PROBLEM 11.26   Rank the following compounds in order of increasing acidity: CH_3CH_2COOH, CH_3COCH_3, CH_3CH_2OH, $CH_3COCH_2COCH_3$.

PROBLEM 11.27   Which of the following compounds would you expect to undergo aldol condensation? Draw the product in each case.

(a)   2,2-Dimethylpropanal
(c)   Benzophenone (diphenyl ketone)
(b)   Cyclobutanone
(d)   Decanal

PROBLEM 11.28   Which of the following esters can be prepared by a malonic ester synthesis? Show what reagents you would use.

(a)   Ethyl pentanoate
(c)   Ethyl 2-methylbutanoate
(b)   Ethyl 3-methylbutanoate
(d)   Ethyl 2,2-dimethylpropanoate

PROBLEM 11.29   Nonconjugated β,γ-unsaturated ketones such as 3-cyclohexenone are in an acid-catalyzed equilibrium with their conjugated α,β-unsaturated isomers. Propose a mechanism for the acid-catalyzed interconversion of the two isomers.

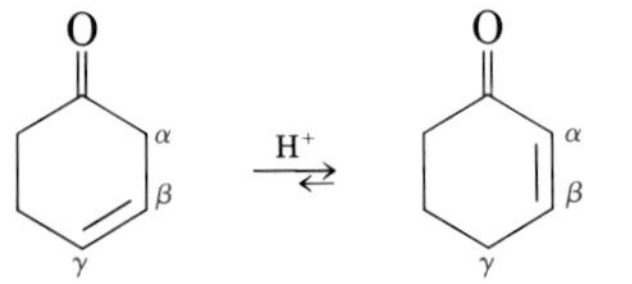

PROBLEM 11.30   The α,β-to-β,γ interconversion of unsaturated ketones (Problem 11.29) is also catalyzed by base. Propose a mechanism by which this occurs.

PROBLEM 11.31   One consequence of the base-catalyzed α,β-to-β,γ isomerization of unsaturated ketones (Problem 11.30) is that C5-substituted 2-cyclopentenones can be interconverted with C2-substituted 2-cyclopentenones. Propose a mechanism to account for this isomerization.

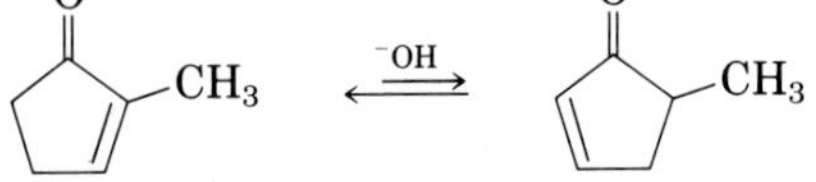

PROBLEM 11.32   If a 1:1 mixture of ethyl acetate and ethyl propanoate is treated with base under Claisen condensation conditions, a mixture of four β-keto ester products is obtained. Show their structures.

PROBLEM 11.33   If a mixture of ethyl acetate and ethyl benzoate is treated with base, a mixture of two Claisen condensation products is obtained. Explain.

PROBLEM 11.34   Cinnamaldehyde, the aromatic constituent of cinnamon oil, can be synthesized by a mixed aldol reaction between benzaldehyde and acetaldehyde. Formulate the reaction. What other product would you expect to obtain?

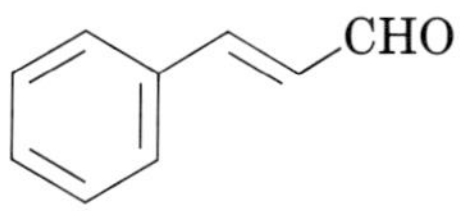

Cinnamaldehyde

PROBLEM 11.35   How might you prepare the following compounds using aldol condensation reactions?

(a) $C_6H_5C(CH_3)\!=\!CHCOC_6H_5$ (b)   4-Methyl-3-penten-2-one

PROBLEM 11.36   1-Butanol is synthesized commercially starting from acetaldehyde by a three-step route that involves an aldol reaction. How might you carry out this transformation?

$$CH_3CHO \xrightarrow{\text{3 steps}} CH_3CH_2CH_2CH_2OH$$

PROBLEM 11.37   How would you prepare these compounds, using either an acetoacetic ester synthesis or a malonic ester synthesis?

(a) $(CH_3)_2C(COOCH_3)_2$ (b) $(CH_3)_2CHCOCH_3$

PROBLEM 11.38   By starting with a dihalide, cyclic compounds can be prepared using the malonic ester synthesis. What product would you expect to obtain from reaction between diethyl malonate, 1,4-dibromobutane, and 2 equiv of base?

PROBLEM 11.39   In light of your answer to Problem 11.38, how might you use the acetoacetic ester synthesis to prepare cyclopentyl methyl ketone?

PROBLEM 11.40   The aldol reaction can sometimes take place *internally* if a dicarbonyl compound is treated with base. What product would you expect to obtain from aldol cyclization of hexanedial, $OHCCH_2CH_2CH_2CH_2CHO$?

PROBLEM 11.41   How can you account for the fact that *cis*- and *trans*-4-*tert*-butyl-2-methylcyclohexanone are interconverted by base treatment? Which of the two isomers do you think is more stable, and why? [*Hint:* See Section 2.15.]

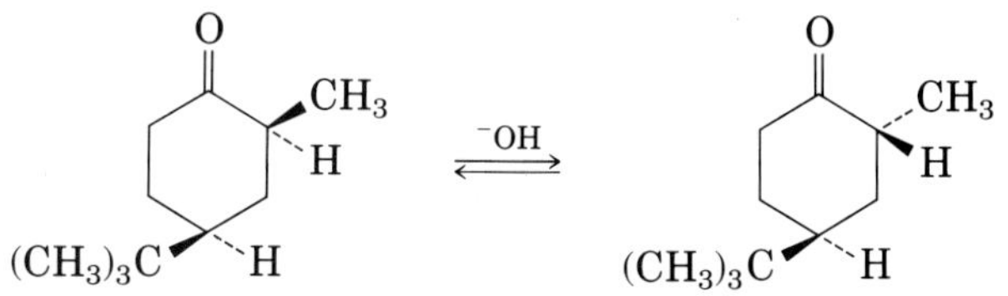

PROBLEM 11.42   Show how you might convert geraniol, the chief constituent of rose oil, into either ethyl geranylacetate or geranylacetone.

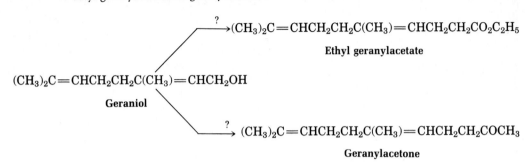

$\overset{?}{\longrightarrow}$ (CH$_3$)$_2$C=CHCH$_2$CH$_2$C(CH$_3$)=CHCH$_2$CH$_2$CO$_2$C$_2$H$_5$

Ethyl geranylacetate

(CH$_3$)$_2$C=CHCH$_2$CH$_2$C(CH$_3$)=CHCH$_2$OH

Geraniol

$\overset{?}{\longrightarrow}$ (CH$_3$)$_2$C=CHCH$_2$CH$_2$C(CH$_3$)=CHCH$_2$CH$_2$COCH$_3$

Geranylacetone

INTERLUDE N
Biological Carbonyl Condensation Reactions

Carbonyl condensation reactions are used in nature for the biological synthesis of a variety of different molecules. Fats, amino acids, steroid hormones, and many other kinds of compounds are biosynthesized by plants and animals using carbonyl condensation reactions as the key step.

The two-carbon acetate fragment of acetyl coenzyme A is the major building block for synthesis. We saw in Interlude L that acetyl CoA can serve as an electrophilic *acceptor* for attack of nucleophiles at the acyl carbon. In addition, it can serve as a nucleophilic *donor* by loss of its acidic alpha proton to generate an enolate ion. The enolate ion of acetyl CoA can then add to another carbonyl group in a condensation reaction. For example, citric acid is biosynthesized by addition of acetyl CoA to the ketone carbonyl group of oxaloacetic acid (2-oxo-butanedioic acid) in a type of aldol reaction.

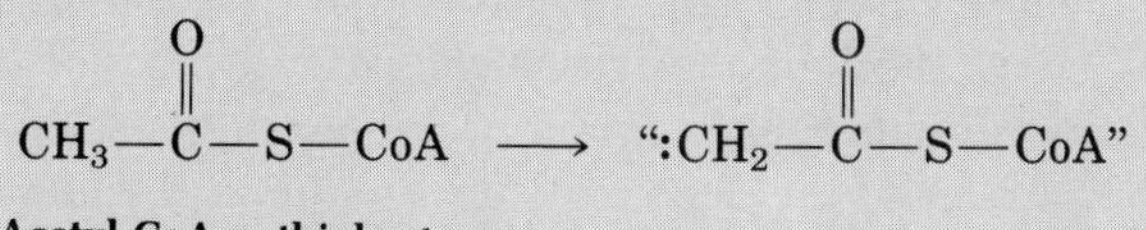

$$CH_3-\overset{\overset{\displaystyle O}{\|}}{C}-S-CoA \longrightarrow \text{":}CH_2-\overset{\overset{\displaystyle O}{\|}}{C}-S-CoA\text{"}$$

Acetyl CoA, a thiol ester

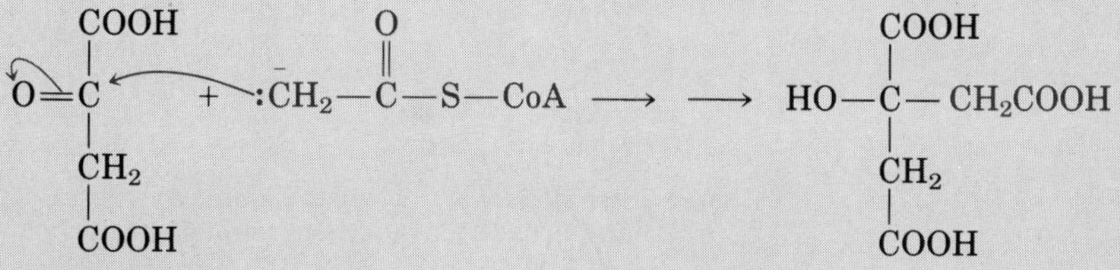

$$\underset{\underset{\displaystyle \text{COOH}}{\overset{\displaystyle |}{\underset{|}{\overset{\displaystyle CH_2}{}}}}}{\overset{\overset{\displaystyle COOH}{|}}{O=C}} + \text{:}CH_2-\overset{\overset{\displaystyle O}{\|}}{C}-S-CoA \longrightarrow \longrightarrow \underset{\underset{\displaystyle \text{COOH}}{\overset{\displaystyle |}{\underset{|}{\overset{\displaystyle CH_2}{}}}}}{\overset{\overset{\displaystyle COOH}{|}}{HO-C-CH_2COOH}}$$

Oxaloacetic acid   **Citric acid**

Acetyl CoA is also involved in the biosynthesis of steroids, fats, and other lipids. The key step in these biosyntheses is a Claisen-like condensation of acetyl CoA to yield acetoacetyl CoA.

CHAPTER 12

Amines

Amines are organic derivatives of ammonia in the same way that alcohols and ethers are organic derivatives of water. Amines are classified either as **primary, RNH_2; secondary, R_2NH;** or **tertiary, R_3N;** depending on the number of organic substituents attached to nitrogen. For example, methylamine, CH_3NH_2, is a primary amine and trimethylamine, $(CH_3)_3N$, is a tertiary amine. Note that this usage of the terms primary, secondary, and tertiary is different from our previous usage. When we speak of a tertiary alcohol or alkyl halide, we refer to the degree of substitution at the alkyl carbon atom; when we speak of a tertiary amine, however, we refer to the degree of substitution at the nitrogen atom.

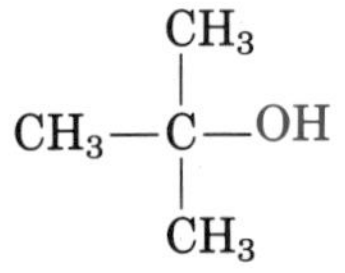

$$CH_3-\underset{\underset{CH_3}{|}}{\overset{\overset{CH_3}{|}}{C}}-OH \qquad CH_3-\underset{\underset{CH_3}{|}}{\overset{\overset{CH_3}{|}}{N}} \qquad CH_3-\underset{\underset{CH_3}{|}}{\overset{\overset{CH_3}{|}}{C}}-NH_2$$

tert-Butyl alcohol	Trimethylamine	*tert*-Butylamine
(a tertiary alcohol)	(a tertiary amine)	(a primary amine)

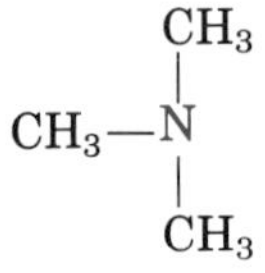

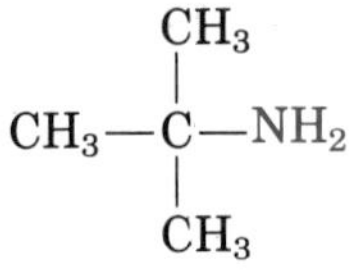

Compounds with four groups attached to nitrogen are also possible, but the nitrogen atom must carry a positive charge. Such compounds are called **quaternary ammonium salts.**

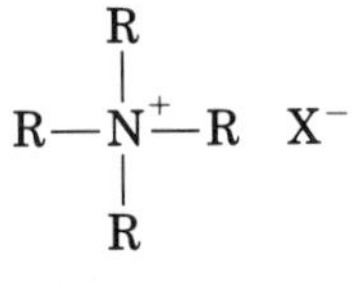

$$R-\underset{\underset{R}{|}}{\overset{\overset{R}{|}}{\overset{+}{N}}}-R \quad X^-$$

A quaternary ammonium salt

Amines can be either alkyl-substituted or aryl-substituted. Much of the chemistry of the two classes is similar, but we will soon see that important differences also exist.

$$CH_3CH_2\ddot{N}H_2$$

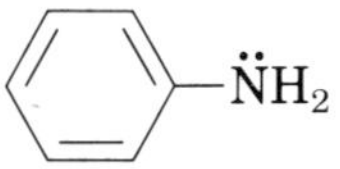

—$\ddot{N}H_2$

Ethylamine
(an aliphatic amine)

Aniline
(an arylamine)

PROBLEM 12.1 Classify the following compounds as either primary, secondary, or tertiary amines, or as quaternary ammonium salts:

(a) $(CH_3)_2CHNH_2$

(b) $(CH_3CH_2)_2NH$

(c)

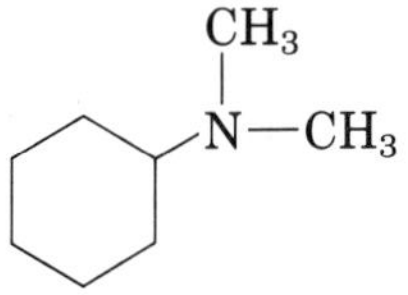

(d)

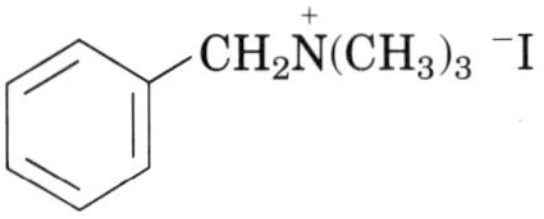

PROBLEM 12.2 Draw structures of compounds that meet these criteria:

(a) A secondary amine with one isopropyl group
(b) A tertiary amine with one phenyl group and one ethyl group
(c) A quaternary ammonium salt with four different groups bound to nitrogen

12.1 NOMENCLATURE OF AMINES

Primary amines, RNH_2, are named in the IUPAC system in either of two ways. For simple amines, the suffix *-amine* is added to the name of the organic substituent.

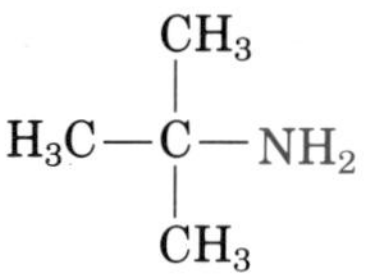

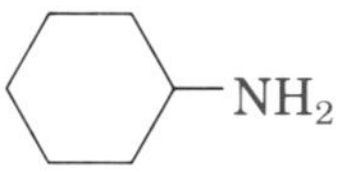

tert-Butylamine   **Cyclohexylamine**   **1,4-Butanediamine**

Amines having more than one functional group are named by considering the —NH_2 as an *amino* substituent on the parent molecule.

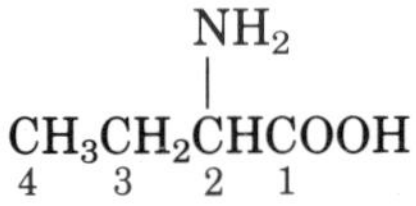

$$\underset{4321}{CH_3CH_2\underset{\overset{\displaystyle |}{NH_2}}{C}HCOOH}$$

$$H_2N-CH_2CH_2\overset{\displaystyle O}{\overset{\displaystyle ||}{C}}CH_3$$
$$4321$$

2-Aminobutanoic acid 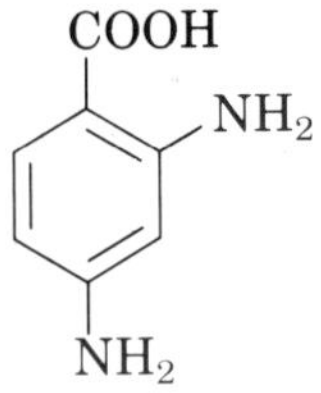   **2,4-Diaminobenzoic acid** 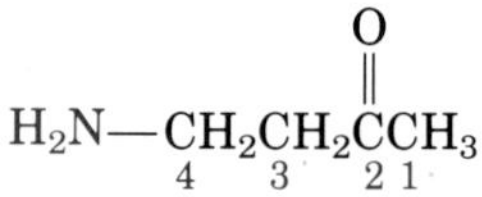   **4-Amino-2-butanone**

Symmetrical secondary and tertiary amines are named by adding the prefix *di-* or *tri-* to the alkyl group.

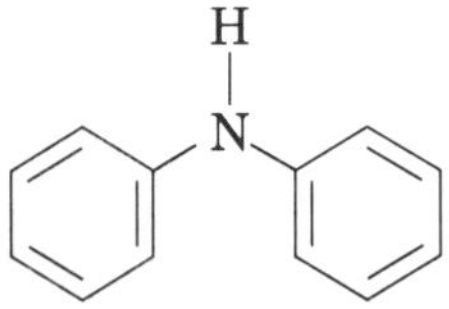

$$CH_3CH_2-\underset{\overset{\displaystyle |}{CH_2CH_3}}{N}-CH_2CH_3$$

Diphenylamine 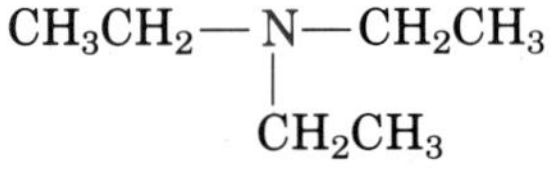   **Triethylamine**

Unsymmetrically substituted secondary and tertiary amines are named as *N*-substituted primary amines. The largest organic group is chosen as the parent, and the other groups are considered as *N*-substituents on the parent (*N* since they are attached to nitrogen).

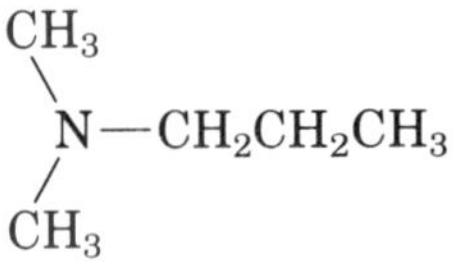

$$\underset{\underset{\displaystyle CH_3}{\diagup}}{\overset{\overset{\displaystyle CH_3}{\diagdown}}{N}}-CH_2CH_2CH_3$$

N,N-Dimethylpropylamine
(propylamine is the parent name; the two
methyl groups are substituents on nitrogen)

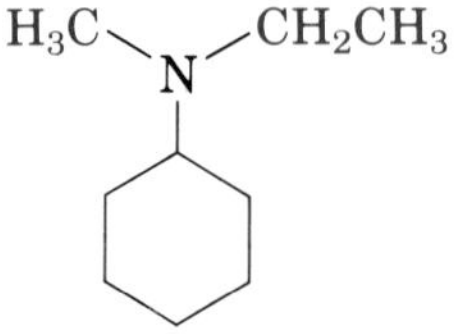

N-Ethyl-N-methylcyclohexylamine
(cyclohexylamine is the parent name;
methyl and ethyl are *N*-substituents)

There are relatively few trivial names for simple amines, but IUPAC rules do recognize the names *aniline* and *toluidine* for phenylamine and (methyl-phenyl)amine, respectively.

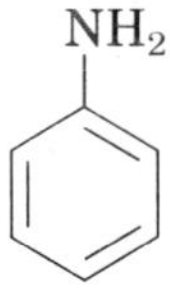

Aniline 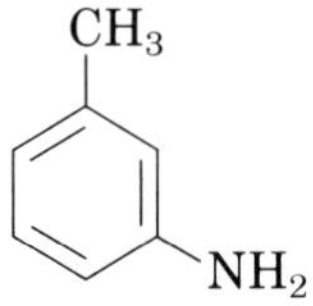   ***m*-Toluidine**

Heterocyclic amines are compounds in which the nitrogen atom occurs as part of a ring. These amines are common, and each different heterocyclic ring system is given its own parent name. In all cases, the nitrogen atom is numbered as position 1.

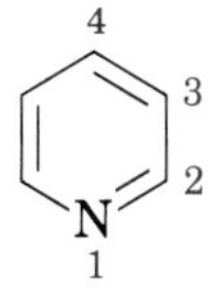

Pyridine 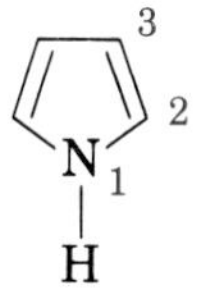   Pyrrole 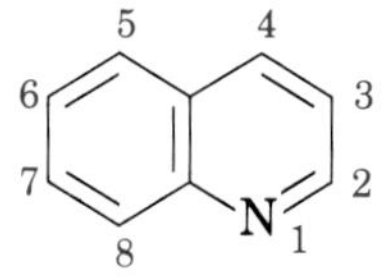   Quinoline

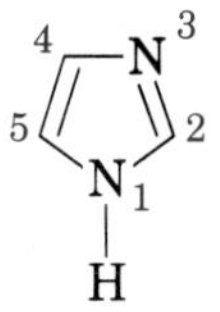

Imidazole 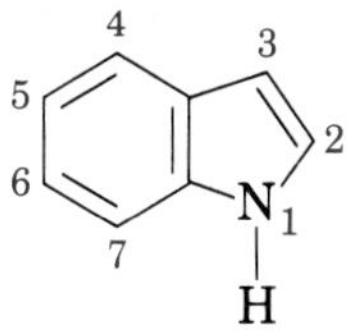   Indole 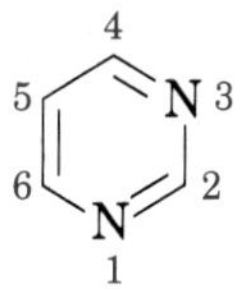   Pyrimidine

---

PROBLEM 12.3   Name the following compounds by IUPAC rules:

(a) $CH_3NHCH_2CH_3$

(b)

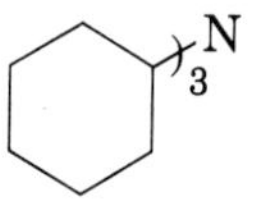

(c) 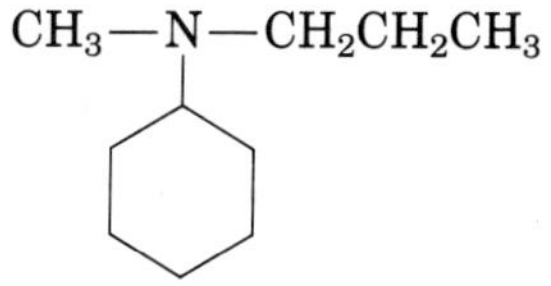 $CH_3-N-CH_2CH_2CH_3$

(d)

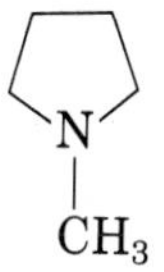

(e) $[(CH_3)_2CH]_2NH$

(f) $H_2NCH_2CH_2\overset{\overset{\textstyle CH_3}{\textstyle |}}{C}HNH_2$

PROBLEM 12.4   Draw structures corresponding to these IUPAC names.

(a)   Triethylamine   (b)   N-Methylaniline
(c)   Tetraethylammonium bromide   (d)   p-Bromoaniline
(e)   N-Ethyl-N-methylcyclopentylamine

12.2   STRUCTURE AND PROPERTIES OF AMINES

Bonding in amines is similar to bonding in ammonia. The nitrogen atom is sp^3 hybridized, with the three substituents occupying three corners of a tetrahedron. The nitrogen's nonbonding lone pair of electrons occupies the fourth corner. As expected, the C-N-C bond angles are very close to the 109° tetrahedral value. For trimethylamine, the C-N-C angle is 108°, and the C—N bond length is 1.47 Å.

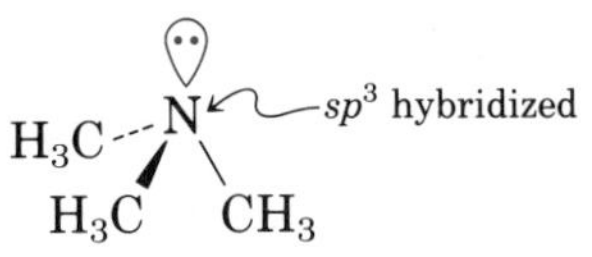

Trimethylamine

← 5 carbons are H_2O soluble

Amines are highly polar and therefore have higher boiling points than alkanes of equivalent molecular weight. Like alcohols, amines with fewer than five carbon atoms are generally water-soluble. Also like alcohols, primary and secondary amines form strong hydrogen bonds and are highly associated in the liquid state.

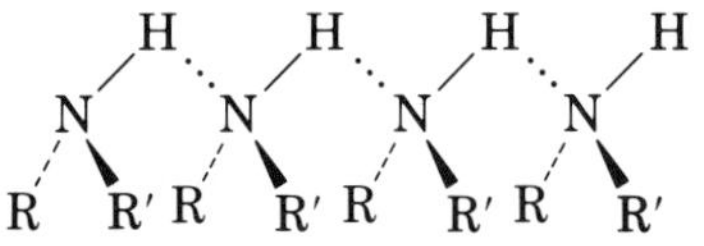

One other characteristic property of amines is odor. Low-molecular-weight amines have a characteristic fishlike aroma. Diamines such as putrescine (1,4-butanediamine) have names that are self-explanatory.

12.3   AMINE BASICITY

The chemistry of amines is dominated by the presence of the nitrogen lone pair of electrons. Because of the lone pair, amines are both basic and nucleophilic. Amines react with Lewis acids to form acid–base salts, and they react with electrophiles in many of the polar reactions seen in past chapters.

An amine   **An acid**   **A salt**
(a Lewis base)

Amines are much more basic than alcohols, ethers, or water. When an amine is dissolved in water, an equilibrium is established in which water acts as a protic acid and donates a proton to the amine.

$$R-\ddot{N}H_2 + H_2\ddot{O}: \rightleftharpoons R-\overset{+}{N}H_3 + :\ddot{O}H$$

Not all amines are equal in base strength, however. Some amines are stronger, and some are weaker. We can measure the ability of an amine to accept a proton from water by determining the position of the equilibrium constant for the reaction, and we can establish a relative ordering of base strengths by expressing the results in terms of **basicity constants, K_b.**

$$K_b = \frac{[R-\overset{+}{N}H_3][\overset{-}{O}H]}{[RNH_2]} \qquad pK_b = -\log K_b$$

If the amine is a stronger base, the equilibrium is shifted toward the right. The constant K_b is therefore larger, and pK_b is smaller. Conversely, if the amine is a weaker base, K_b is smaller and pK_b is larger. Table 12.1 lists the measured pK_b's of some common amines. The values listed indicate that there is relatively little effect of substitution on alkylamine basicity. Most simple alkylamines have pK_b's in the narrow range 3–4.

TABLE 12.1   Base strengths of some common amines

Name	Structure	pK_b
Ammonia	$:NH_3$	4.74
Primary amine		
Methylamine	$CH_3\ddot{N}H_2$	3.36
Ethylamine	$CH_3CH_2\ddot{N}H_2$	3.25
Aniline	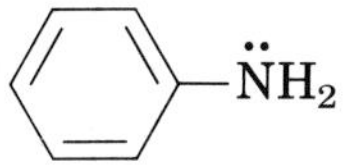 $-\ddot{N}H_2$	9.37
Secondary amine		
Dimethylamine	$(CH_3)_2\ddot{N}H$	3.27
Diethylamine	$(CH_3CH_2)_2\ddot{N}H$	3.06
Tertiary amine		
Trimethylamine	$(CH_3)_3N:$	4.21
Triethylamine	$(CH_3CH_2)_3N:$	3.25

Table 12.1 indicates that arylamines, such as aniline, are much weaker bases than alkylamines. The reason for the lower base strength of arylamines is that the nitrogen lone-pair electrons are delocalized by orbital overlap with the pi orbitals of the aromatic ring; thus, they are less available for bonding to an acid. In resonance terms, arylamines are more stable and less reactive than alkylamines because of the five contributing resonance structures:

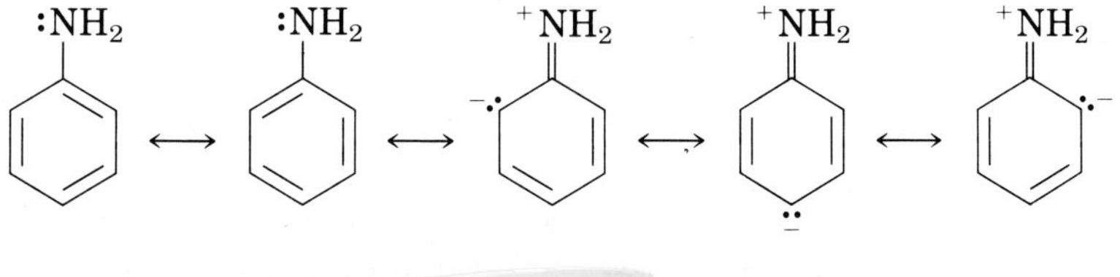

In contrast to amines, **amides, $RCONH_2$,** are completely nonbasic. Amides do not form salts when treated with acids, and their aqueous solutions are neutral. As with arylamines, the major reason for the decreased basicity of amides is that the nitrogen lone-pair electrons are delocalized by orbital overlap with the neighboring carbonyl-group pi orbital. The electrons are therefore much less available for bonding to an acid. In resonance terms, amides are more stable and less reactive than amines because they are hybrids of two contributing resonance forms:

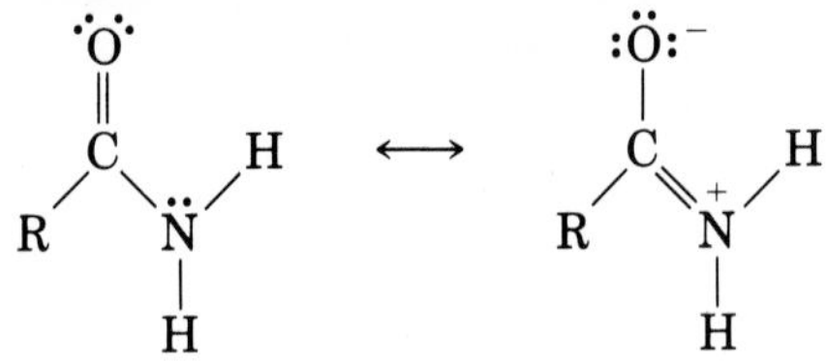

PROBLEM 12.5   Which compound in each of the following pairs is more basic?

(a) $CH_3CH_2NH_2$ or $CH_3CH_2CONH_2$ (b) NaOH   or $C_6H_5NH_2$
(c) CH_3NHCH_3 or $CH_3NHC_6H_5$ (d) CH_3OCH_3 or $(CH_3)_3N$

12.4   RESOLUTION OF ENANTIOMERS VIA AMINE SALTS

We can take advantage of amine basicity to carry out the separation (**resolution**) of a racemic carboxylic acid mixture into its two pure enantiomers. Recall from Section 6.10 that a racemic mixture is a 50:50 mixture of (+) and (−) enantiomers.

$$50\% \ (+) : 50\% \ (-) \xrightarrow{\text{Resolve}} \text{Pure } (+) \ + \ \text{Pure } (-)$$

Racemic mixture of   **Pure separate enantiomers**
enantiomers

Historically, Louis Pasteur was the first person to resolve a racemic mixture when he was able to crystallize a salt of (±)-tartaric acid and to separate two different kinds of crystals by hand (Section 6.5). Pasteur's method is not generally applicable, however, since few racemic mixtures crystallize into separate mirror-image forms. The most commonly used method of resolution makes use of an acid–base reaction between a racemic mixture of carboxylic acids and a chiral amine.

To understand how this method of resolution works, let's see what happens when a racemic mixture of chiral acids such as (+)- and (−)-lactic acid reacts with an achiral amine base such as methylamine (Figure 12.1). Stereochemically, this situation is analogous to what happens when left and right hands (chiral) pick up a ball (achiral). Both left and right hands pick up the ball equally well, and the products—ball in right hand versus ball in left hand—are mirror images. In the same way, both (+)- and (−)-lactic acid react with methylamine equally well. The product is a mixture of two salts: methylammonium (+)-lactate and methyl-ammonium (−)-lactate. Just as with the chiral hands and achiral ball, the two salts are mirror images and we still have a racemic mixture.

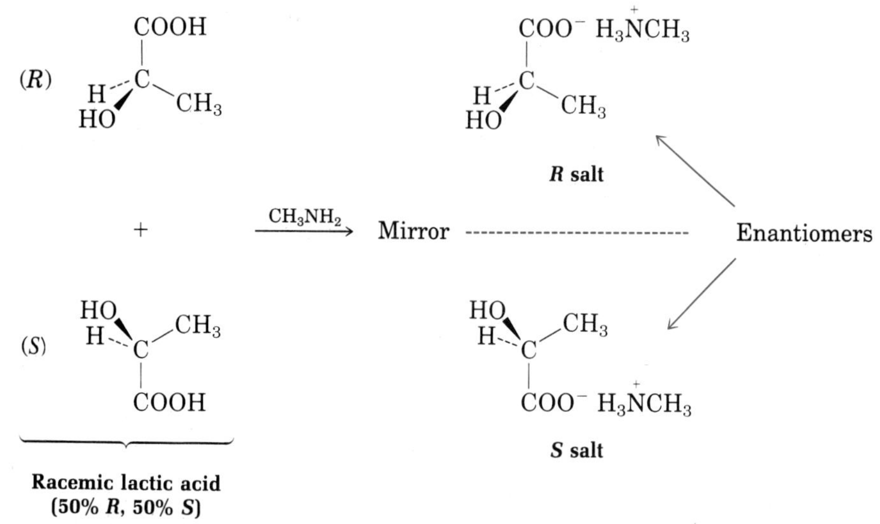

FIGURE 12.1
Reaction of racemic lactic acid with achiral methylamine leads to a racemic mixture of salts.

Now let's see what happens when the racemic mixture of (+)- and (−)-lactic acid reacts with a single enantiomer of a chiral amine base such as (R)-1-phenylethylamine (Figure 12.2). Stereochemically, this situation is analogous to what happens when a hand (a chiral reagent) puts on a right-handed glove (*also a chiral reagent*). *Left and right hands do not put on the same glove in the same way.* The products—right hand in right glove versus left hand in right glove—are not mirror images; they are altogether different.

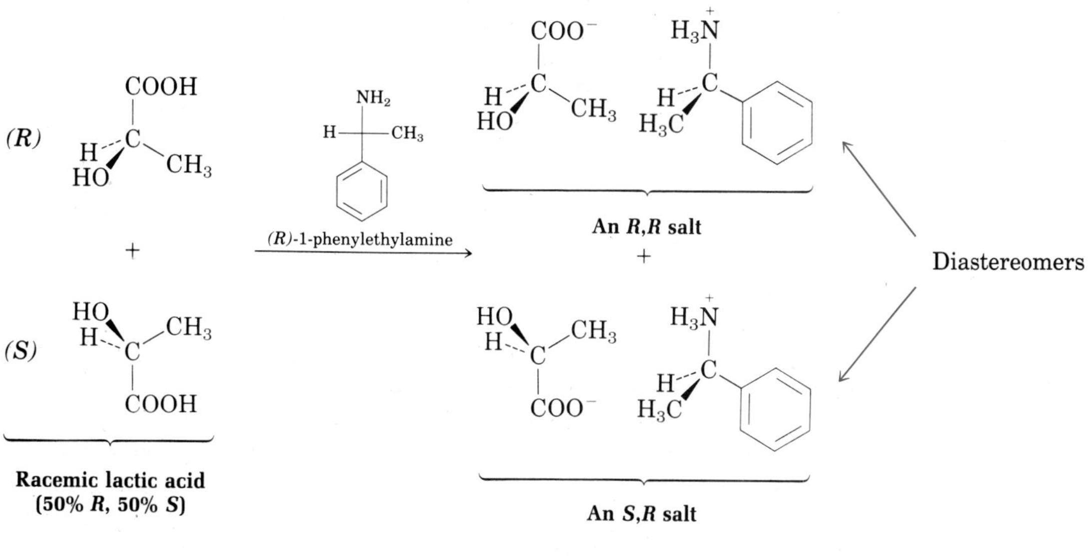

FIGURE 12.2
Reaction of racemic lactic acid with optically pure (R)-1-phenylethylamine leads to a mixture of diastereomeric salts.

In the same way, (+)- and (−)-lactic acid react with (R)-1-phenylethylamine to give different products. (R)-Lactic acid reacts with (R)-1-phenylethylamine to give the R,R salt, whereas (S)-lactic acid reacts with the same R amine to give the S,R salt. *These two salts are diastereomers* (Section 6.7). They are different compounds and have different chemical and physical properties. It may therefore prove possible to separate them by fractional crystallization or by some other laboratory technique. Once separated, acidification of the two diastereomeric salts with mineral acid then allows us to recover and isolate the two pure enantiomers of lactic acid.

PROBLEM 12.6 Suppose that racemic lactic acid reacts with methanol to form the ester, methyl lactate. What stereochemistry would you expect the product(s) to have? What is the relationship of one product to another?

PROBLEM 12.7 Suppose that racemic lactic acid reacts with (S)-2-butanol to form an ester. What stereochemistry would you expect the product(s) to have? What is the relationship of one product to another? How might you use this reaction to resolve (±)-lactic acid?

12.5 SYNTHESIS OF AMINES

S_N2 Reactions of Alkyl Halides

Ammonia and simple alkylamines are excellent nucleophiles in S_N2 reactions (Section 7.7). As a result, the simplest method of amine synthesis is by S_N2 reaction of ammonia or an alkylamine with an alkyl halide. If ammonia is used, a primary amine results; if a primary amine is used, a secondary amine results; and so on. Even tertiary amines react rapidly with alkyl halides to yield quaternary ammonium salts, $R_4N^+ X^-$.

Ammonia	$\ddot{N}H_3 + R{-}X \longrightarrow RNH_3^+ \ddot{X}^-$	$\xrightarrow{NaOH}$ RNH_2	Primary
Primary	$R\ddot{N}H_2 + R{-}X \longrightarrow R_2NH_2^+ \ddot{X}^-$	$\xrightarrow{NaOH}$ R_2NH	Secondary
Secondary	$R_2\ddot{N}H + R{-}X \longrightarrow R_3NH^+ \ddot{X}^-$	$\xrightarrow{NaOH}$ R_3N	Tertiary
Tertiary	$R_3\ddot{N} + R{-}X \longrightarrow R_4N^+ \ddot{X}^-$	Quaternary ammonium salt	

S_N2 reaction

Unfortunately, these reactions do not stop cleanly after a single alkylation has occurred. Since primary, secondary, and tertiary amines are all of similar reactivity, the initially formed monoalkylated product can undergo further reaction to yield a mixture of products. For example, treatment of 1-bromooctane with a twofold excess of ammonia leads to a mixture containing only 45% yield of the desired octylamine. A nearly equal amount of dioctylamine is produced by over-alkylation, along with smaller amounts of trioctylamine and tetraoctylammonium bromide.

$$CH_3(CH_2)_6CH_2Br + :NH_3 \longrightarrow CH_3(CH_2)_6CH_2\ddot{N}H_2 + [CH_3(CH_2)_6CH_2]_2\ddot{N}H$$

1-Bromooctane   Octylamine (45%)   Dioctylamine (43%)

$$+ [CH_3(CH_2)_6CH_2]_3\ddot{N}: + [CH_3(CH_2)_6CH_2]_4\overset{+}{N}\overset{-}{Br}$$

Trace   Trace

PROBLEM 12.8 Show how you might prepare these amines starting from ammonia:

(a) Dimethylamine   (b) N,N-Dimethylethylamine
(c) Tetramethylammonium bromide

Reduction of Nitriles and Amides

We have already seen how amines can be prepared by reduction of nitriles (Section 10.13) and amides (Section 10.12) with LiAlH$_4$. Both reactions usually take place in high yield.

The two-step sequence of reactions involving initial S$_N$2 reaction of an alkyl halide with cyanide ion, followed by reduction, provides an excellent method for converting an alkyl halide into a primary amine having one more carbon atom. Amide reduction provides an excellent method for converting carboxylic acids into amines.

$$R-X \xrightarrow{\text{NaCN}} R-CN \xrightarrow[\text{2. H}_2\text{O}]{\text{1. LiAlH}_4\text{, ether}} R-CH_2NH_2$$

Alkyl halide   1° amine

$$R-COOH \xrightarrow[\text{2. NH}_3]{\text{1. SOCl}_2} R-\overset{\overset{\text{O}}{\|}}{C}-NH_2 \xrightarrow[\text{2. H}_2\text{O}]{\text{1. LiAlH}_4\text{, ether}} R-CH_2NH_2$$

Carboxylic acid   1° amine

PRACTICE PROBLEM What amide would you start with to prepare N-ethylcyclohexylamine?

Solution Reduction of an amide with LiAlH$_4$ yields an amine in which the amide carbonyl group has been replaced by a methylene ($-CH_2-$) unit: RCONR$_2$ → RCH$_2$NR$_2$. Working backwards, we can see that N-ethylcyclohexylamine has only one $-CH_2-$ carbon (in the ethyl group) attached to its nitrogen, while the cyclohexyl group is attached to nitrogen through a $-CH-$ carbon. Thus, the product would have to come from reduction of N-cyclohexylacetamide.

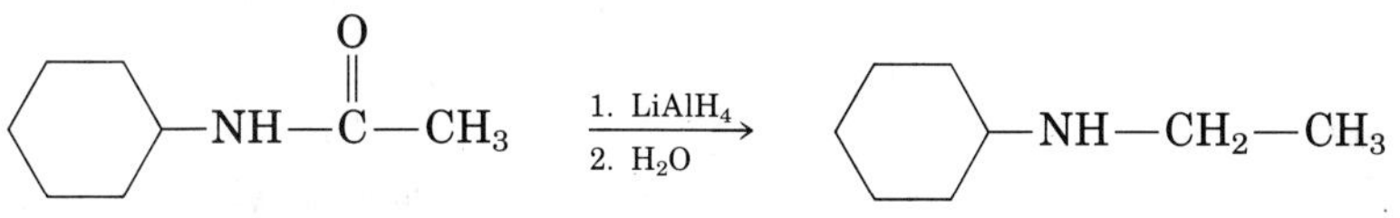

N-Cyclohexylacetamide   N-Ethylcyclohexylamine

PROBLEM 12.9 Propose a structure of either a nitrile or an amide that might be a potential precursor of each of the amines shown:

(a) Propylamine

(b) Dipropylamine

(c) Benzylamine, $C_6H_5CH_2NH_2$

(d) N-Ethylaniline

Reduction of Nitroarenes

Arylamines are almost always prepared by nitration of an aromatic starting material, followed by reduction of the nitro group. No other method of synthesis approaches this nitration–reduction step in its generality and versatility.

The reduction step can be carried out in many different ways, depending on the circumstances. Catalytic hydrogenation over platinum gives high yields, but is often not compatible with the presence elsewhere in the molecule of other reducible groups such as carbon–carbon double bonds and carbonyl groups. Iron, zinc, tin metal, and stannous chloride ($SnCl_2$) are also effective when used in aqueous acid.

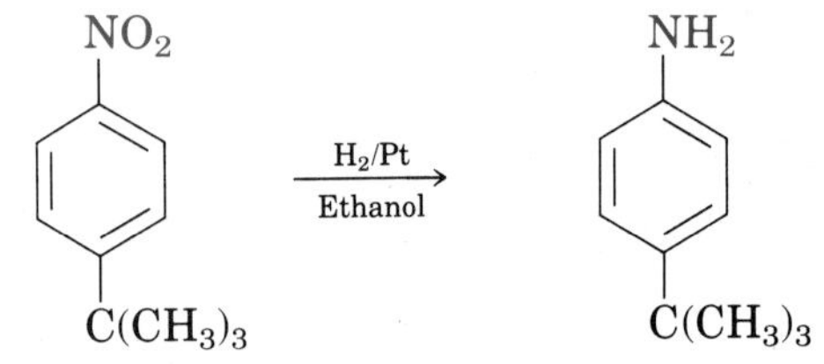

*p-tert-*Butylnitrobenzene   *p-tert-*Butylaniline (100%)

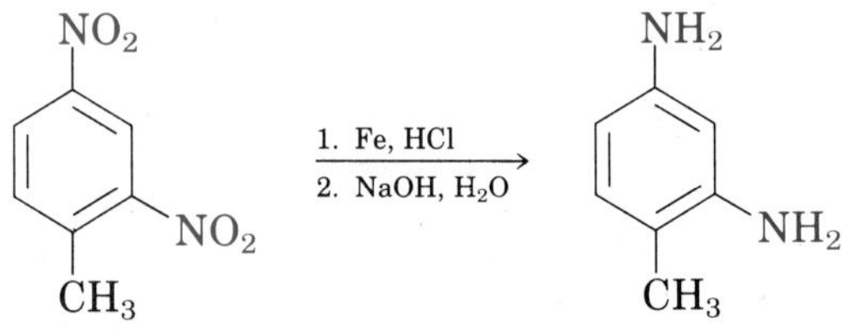

2,4-Dinitrotoluene   Toluene-2,4-diamine (74%)

PROBLEM 12.10 How would you synthesize these amines, starting from benzene? More than one step is required in each case.

(a) *p*-Methylaniline   (b) *m*-Aminobenzoic acid   (c) 2,4,6-Tribromoaniline

12.6 REACTIONS OF AMINES

We have already studied the two most important reactions of alkylamines—alkylation and acylation. As we saw in the previous section, primary, secondary, and tertiary amines can all be alkylated by reaction with alkyl halides. Primary and secondary (but not tertiary) amines can also be acylated by nucleophilic acyl substitution reactions with acid chlorides or acid anhydrides (Section 10.9). The products are amides.

$$NH_3 \xrightarrow[\text{Pyridine}]{\text{RCOCl}} \overset{\displaystyle O}{\overset{\|}{R-C}}NH_2 + HCl$$

$$R'NH_2 \xrightarrow[\text{Pyridine}]{\text{RCOCl}} \overset{\displaystyle O}{\overset{\|}{R-C}}NHR' + HCl$$

$$R'_2NH \xrightarrow[\text{Pyridine}]{\text{RCOCl}} \overset{\displaystyle O}{\overset{\|}{R-C}}NR'_2 + HCl$$

Hofmann Elimination of Amines to Yield Alkenes

Just as alcohols can be dehydrated to yield alkenes (Section 8.7), amines can also be converted into alkenes under suitable conditions. In the **Hofmann elimination reaction**, an amine is first methylated by treatment with excess iodomethane to produce a quaternary ammonium iodide, which then undergoes an elimination reaction on heating with silver oxide. For example, 1-hexene is formed from hexylamine in 60% yield.

$$CH_3CH_2CH_2CH_2CH_2CH_2\overset{..}{N}H_2 \xrightarrow[\text{(excess)}]{CH_3I} CH_3(CH_2)_3CH_2CH_2\overset{+}{N}(CH_3)_3 \; I^-$$

Hexylamine   **Hexyltrimethylammonium iodide**

$$\Big\downarrow \begin{array}{l} Ag_2O \\ H_2O, \Delta \end{array}$$

$$CH_3CH_2CH_2CH_2CH=CH_2 + N(CH_3)_3$$

1-Hexene (60%)

The actual elimination step is an E2 reaction similar to those we saw in Section 7.10 for the elimination of HX from alkyl halides. Hydroxide ion removes a proton, and the positively charged nitrogen atom acts as the leaving group (Figure 12.3, page 364).

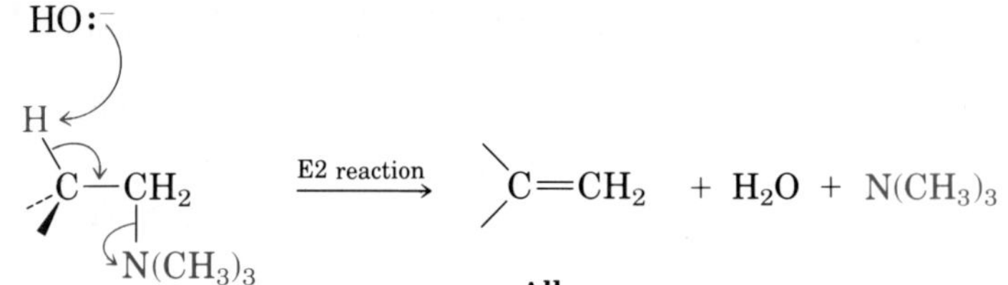

HO:⁻

$$\begin{array}{c} \overset{H}{\underset{|}{\underset{C}{\diagup}}} \text{—CH}_2 \quad \xrightarrow{\text{E2 reaction}} \quad \diagdown \text{C}=\text{CH}_2 \quad + \text{ H}_2\text{O} \; + \; \text{N(CH}_3)_3 \\ \overset{|}{\underset{+}{\text{N(CH}_3)_3}} \end{array}$$

Alkene

FIGURE 12.3
Mechanism of the Hofmann elimination reaction

An interesting feature of the Hofmann elimination is that it gives products different from those of most other E2 reactions. The less highly substituted alkene normally predominates in Hofmann eliminations, as opposed to the more highly substituted product formed from base-induced elimination reactions of alkyl halides (Zaitsev's rule; Section 4.8). The reasons for this selectivity are probably steric. Owing to the large size of the leaving trialkylamine group, hydroxide ion must abstract a hydrogen from the most accessible, least hindered position. For example, (1-methylbutyl)trimethylammonium hydroxide yields 1-pentene and 2-pentene in a 94:6 ratio.

$$\underset{\substack{\textbf{(1-Methylbutyl)trimethylammonium} \\ \textbf{hydroxide}}}{\overset{\overset{+\text{N(CH}_3)_3}{\underset{|}{}}\; ^-\text{OH}}{\text{CH}_3\text{CH}_2\text{CH}_2\text{CHCH}_3}} \quad \xrightarrow{\Delta} \quad \underset{\text{1-Pentene}}{\text{CH}_3\text{CH}_2\text{CH}_2\text{CH}=\text{CH}_2} \; + \; \underset{\text{2-Pentene}}{\text{CH}_3\text{CH}_2\text{CH}=\text{CHCH}_3}$$

94:6 ratio

PROBLEM 12.11   What products would you expect to obtain from Hofmann elimination of these amines? If more than one product is formed, indicate which is major.

(a) $CH_3CH_2CH_2CH(NH_2)CH_2CH_2CH_2CH_3$ (b)   Cyclohexylamine
(c) $CH_3CH_2CH_2CH(NH_2)CH_2CH_2CH_3$ (d)   N-Ethylcyclohexylamine

PROBLEM 12.12   What product would you expect from Hofmann elimination of a cyclic amine such as piperidine? Formulate all the steps involved.

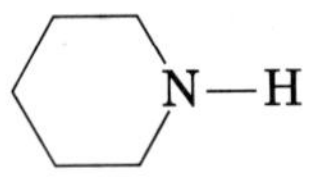

N—H

Piperidine

Diazonium Salts: The Sandmeyer Reaction

Primary amines react with nitrous acid, HNO_2, to yield diazonium salts, $R-\overset{+}{N}\equiv N\ X^-$. Although alkanediazonium salts are too reactive to be isolated, arenediazonium salts, $Ar-\overset{+}{N}\equiv N\ X^-$, are stable. This **diazotization** reaction is versatile and compatible with the presence of a great many substituents on the aromatic ring.

$$ArNH_2 + HNO_2 + H_2SO_4 \longrightarrow Ar-\overset{+}{N}\equiv N\ HSO_4^- + 2\ H_2O$$

Arenediazonium salts are extremely useful compounds since the **diazonio group**, N_2^+, can be replaced by nucleophiles

$$Ar-N_2^+ + :Nu^- \longrightarrow Ar-Nu + N_2$$

Many different nucleophiles react with arenediazonium salts, and many different substituted benzenes can be prepared with this reaction. The overall sequence of (1) nitration, (2) reduction, (3) diazotization, and (4) nucleophilic replacement is probably the single most versatile method for preparing substituted aromatic rings (Figure 12.4).

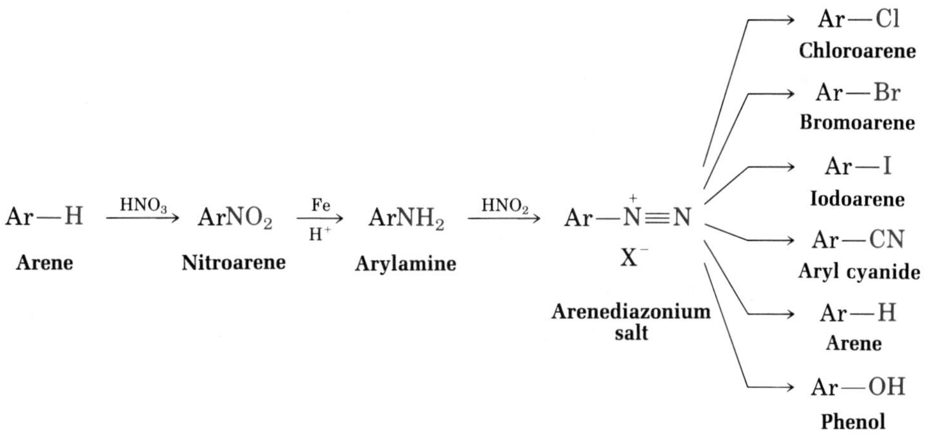

FIGURE 12.4
Preparation of substituted aromatic compounds by diazonio replacement reactions

Aryl chlorides and bromides are prepared by reaction of an arenediazonium salt with the corresponding cuprous halide, CuX, a process called the **Sandmeyer reaction**. Aryl iodides can be prepared by reaction with sodium iodide.

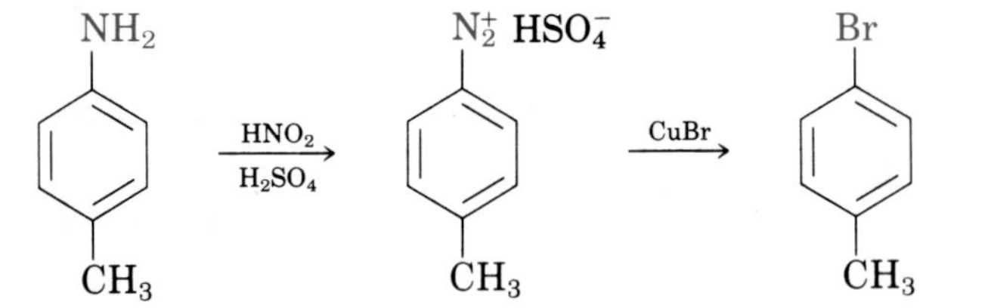

p-Toluidine

$\xrightarrow[\text{H}_2\text{SO}_4]{\text{HNO}_2}$

$\xrightarrow{\text{CuBr}}$

p-Bromotoluene
(73%)

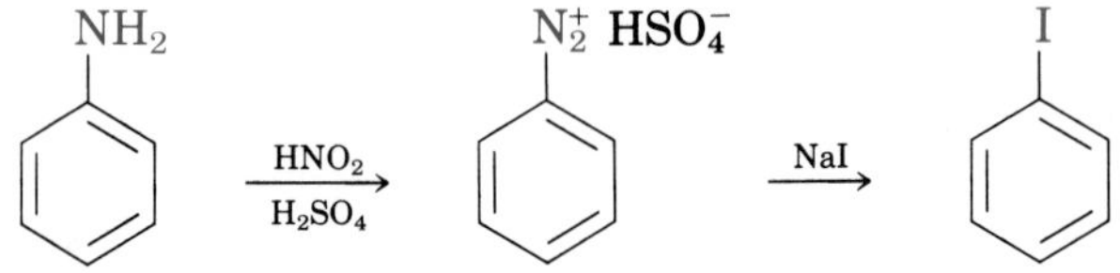

Aniline

$\xrightarrow[\text{H}_2\text{SO}_4]{\text{HNO}_2}$

$\xrightarrow{\text{NaI}}$

Iodobenzene
(67%)

Similar treatment of an arenediazonium salt with cuprous cyanide, CuCN, yields the arenenitrile, ArCN. This reaction is particularly useful, since it allows the replacement of a nitrogen substituent by a carbon substituent. The nitrile can then be elaborated into other functional groups such as carboxyl, —COOH. For example, hydrolysis of o-methylbenzonitrile, produced by Sandmeyer reaction of o-methylbenzenediazonium bisulfate with cuprous cyanide, yields o-methyl-benzoic acid.

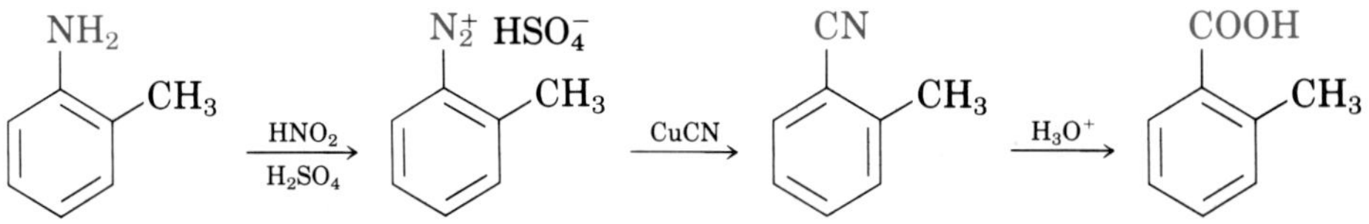

o-Toluidine

$\xrightarrow[\text{H}_2\text{SO}_4]{\text{HNO}_2}$

o-Methylbenzene-
diazonium bisulfate

$\xrightarrow{\text{CuCN}}$

o-Methylbenzonitrile
(70%)

$\xrightarrow{\text{H}_3\text{O}^+}$

o-Methylbenzoic
acid

The diazonio group can also be replaced by —OH to yield phenols and by —H to yield arenes. Phenols are prepared by addition of the arenediazonium salt to hot aqueous acid. For example:

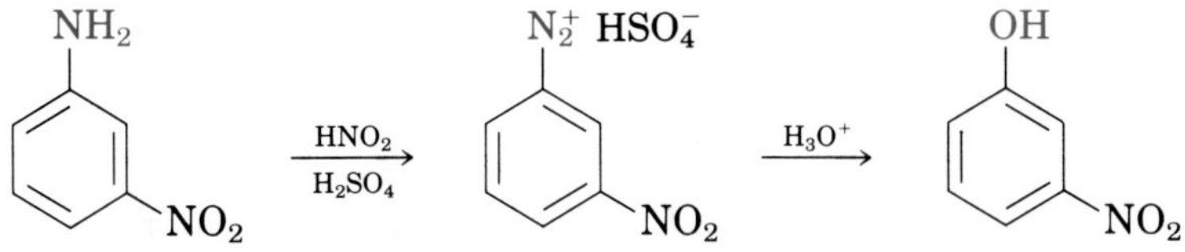

m-Nitroaniline

$\xrightarrow[\text{H}_2\text{SO}_4]{\text{HNO}_2}$

$\xrightarrow{\text{H}_3\text{O}^+}$

m-Nitrophenol (86%)

Arenes are produced by reduction of the diazonium salt with hypophosphorous acid, H_3PO_2. For example, p-toluidine can be converted into 3,5-dibromotoluene by a sequence involving bromination, diazotization, and reduction.

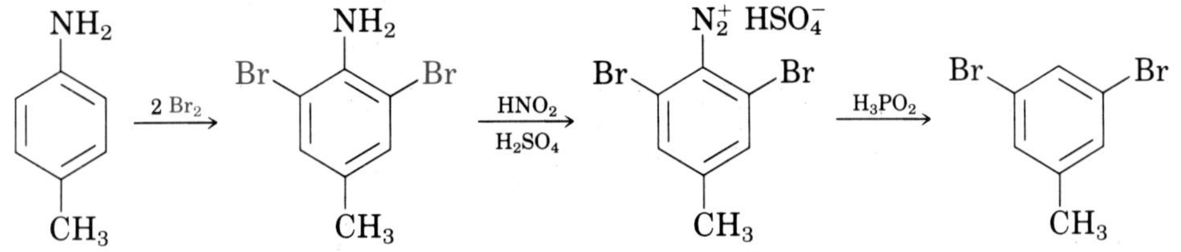

p-Toluidine   **3,5-Dibromotoluene**

PRACTICE PROBLEM How would you prepare *p*-methylphenol from benzene, using a diazonio replacement reaction?

Solution Working backwards, the immediate precursor of the target molecule might be *p*-methyldiazonium ion, which could be prepared from *p*-nitrotoluene. *p*-Nitrotoluene, in turn, could be prepared by nitration of toluene, which could be prepared by Friedel–Crafts methylation of benzene.

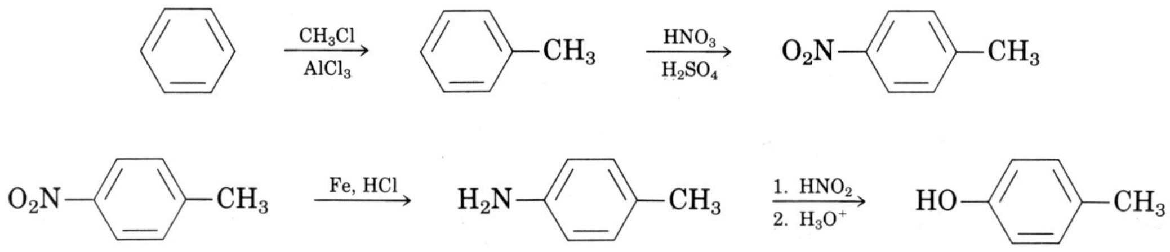

PROBLEM 12.13 How would you prepare these compounds from benzene, using a diazonio replacement reaction at some point in the synthesis?

(a) *p*-Bromobenzonitrile   (b) *m*-Bromobenzoic acid
(c) *m*-Bromochlorobenzene

12.7 HETEROCYCLIC AMINES

Cyclic organic compounds may be classified either as **carbocycles** or as **heterocycles**. Carbocyclic rings contain only carbon atoms, but heterocyclic rings contain one or more different atoms in addition to carbon.

Heterocyclic amines are quite common in organic chemistry, and many have important biological properties. For example, the antiulcer agent cimetidine and the sedative phenobarbital are heterocycles.

NCN
‖
CH₃NHCNHCH₂CH₂SCH₂

N
N CH₃
N
H

Cimetidine (an antiulcer agent)

H
N
O O
N
H N CH₂CH₃
C₆H₅
O

**Phenobarbital
(a sedative)**

For the most part, heterocyclic amines have the same chemistry as their open-chain counterparts. In certain cases, however, particularly when the ring is unsaturated, heterocycles have unique and interesting properties. Let's look at several examples.

Pyrrole, a Five-Membered Aromatic Heterocycle

Pyrrole, the simplest five-membered unsaturated heterocyclic amine, has two double bonds and one nitrogen. Though both an amine and a conjugated diene, the chemistry of pyrrole is not fully consistent with either of these structural features. Unlike most other amines, pyrrole is not basic; unlike most other conjugated dienes, pyrrole does not undergo electrophilic addition reactions. How can we explain these observations?

3
2
N
| 1
H

Pyrrole

In fact, pyrrole is *aromatic*. Even though pyrrole is a five-membered ring, it has six pi electrons in a cyclic conjugated pi orbital system just as benzene does (Section 5.4). Each of the four carbon atoms contributes one pi electron, and the sp^2-hybridized nitrogen atom contributes two more (its lone pair). The six pi electrons occupy p orbitals with lobes above and below the plane of the flat ring, as shown in Figure 12.5.

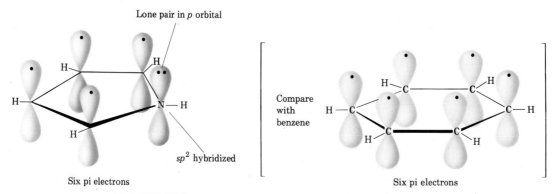

Lone pair in p orbital

sp^2 hybridized

Six pi electrons

Compare with benzene

Six pi electrons

FIGURE 12.5
Pi orbitals in pyrrole, an aromatic heterocycle

Like benzene, pyrrole undergoes substitution of a ring hydrogen atom on reaction with electrophiles. Substitution normally occurs at the position next to nitrogen as the following nitration indicates:

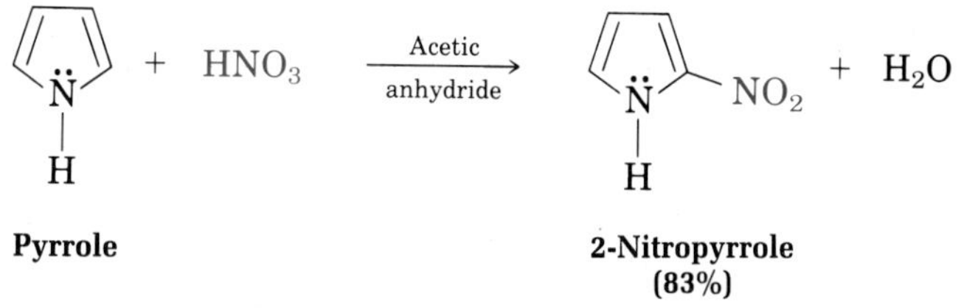

Pyrrole   **2-Nitropyrrole**
                                        (83%)

Highly substituted pyrrole rings also form the basic building blocks from which a number of important plant and animal pigments are constructed. Among these is *heme*, an iron-containing tetrapyrrole present in blood.

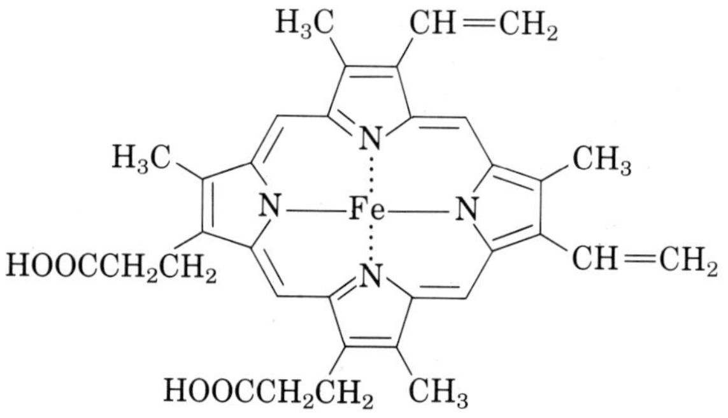

Heme

PROBLEM 12.14 Pyrrole undergoes other typical electrophilic substitution reactions in addition to nitration. In light of your knowledge of benzene chemistry, what products would you expect to obtain from reaction of pyrrole with these reagents?

(a) Br_2 (b) CH_3Cl, $AlCl_3$ (c) CH_3COCl, $AlCl_3$

PROBLEM 12.15 Review the mechanism of the bromination of benzene (Section 5.6) and then propose a mechanism for the nitration of pyrrole.

Pyridine, a Six-Membered Aromatic Heterocycle

Pyridine is the nitrogen-containing heterocyclic analog of benzene. Like benzene, pyridine is aromatic. It is a flat molecule with bond angles of 120° and with carbon–carbon bond lengths of 1.39 Å, intermediate between normal single and double bonds. Each of the five carbon atoms contributes one pi electron, and the sp^2-hybridized nitrogen atom also contributes one pi electron to the cyclic conjugated pi orbitals of the ring. Unlike the situation in pyrrole, the lone pair of electrons on the pyridine nitrogen atom is not part of the pi orbital system, but occupies an sp^2 orbital in the plane of the ring (Figure 12.6, page 370).

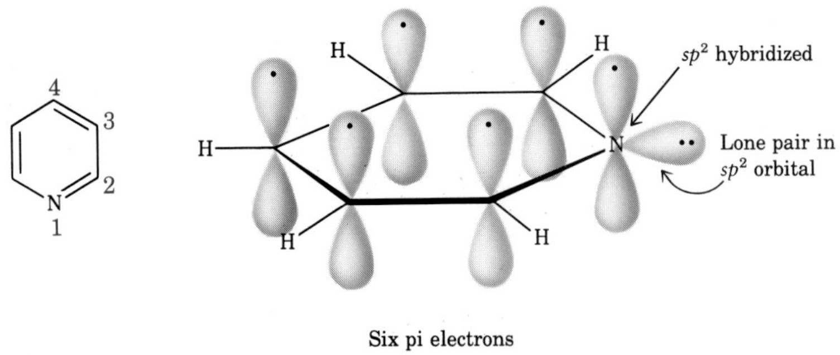

Six pi electrons

FIGURE 12.6
Electronic structure of pyridine

A number of substituted pyridines are important biologically. For example, pyridoxal and pyridoxine are B_6 complex vitamins. Present in many foodstuffs such as yeast, liver, and cereals, the B_6 vitamins play an important role in the synthesis of certain amino acids.

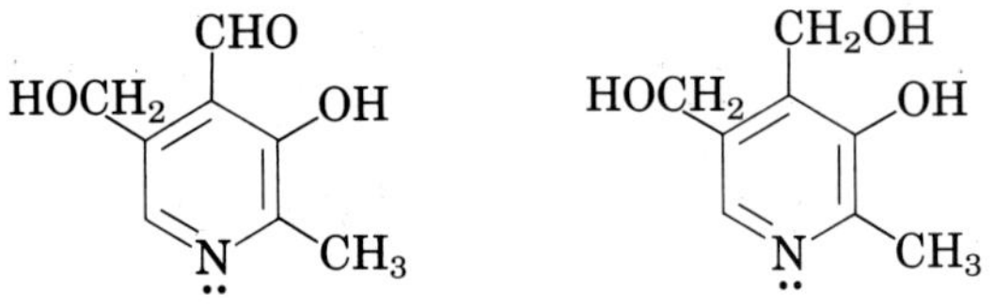

Pyridoxal   Pyridoxine

PROBLEM 12.16   Imidazole, a five-membered heterocycle containing two nitrogen atoms, has $pK_b = 7.05$. Draw an orbital picture of imidazole and indicate in which orbital each nitrogen has its lone-pair electrons.

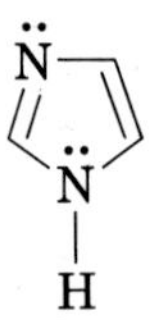

Imidazole

Fused-Ring Aromatic Heterocycles

Quinoline, isoquinoline, and indole are **fused-ring heterocycles** that contain both a benzene ring and a heterocyclic aromatic ring. All three ring systems occur widely in nature, and many members of the class have pronounced biological activity. Thus, quinine, a quinoline derivative found in the bark of the South American *Cinchona* tree, is widely used as an antimalarial drug. Lysergic acid, an indole derivative found in the ergot fungus that grows on decaying grain, is the parent acid from which the psychoactive drug LSD (lysergic acid diethylamide) is derived.

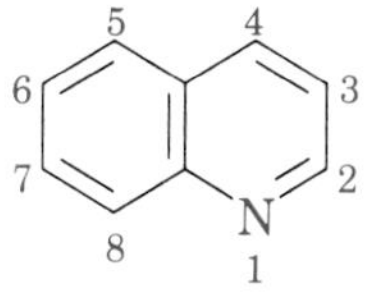

Quinoline 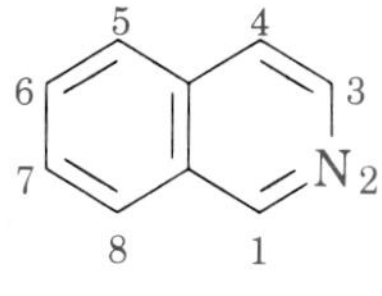   Isoquinoline 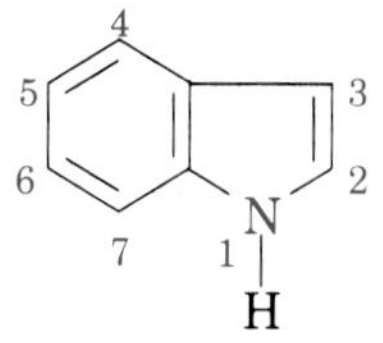   Indole

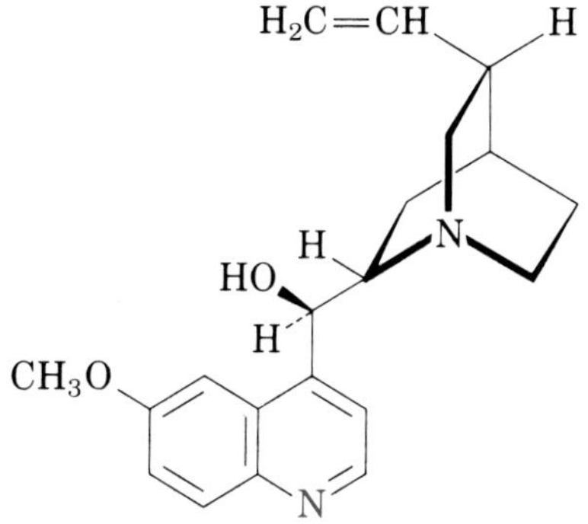

Quinine, an antimalarial drug
(a quinoline alkaloid)

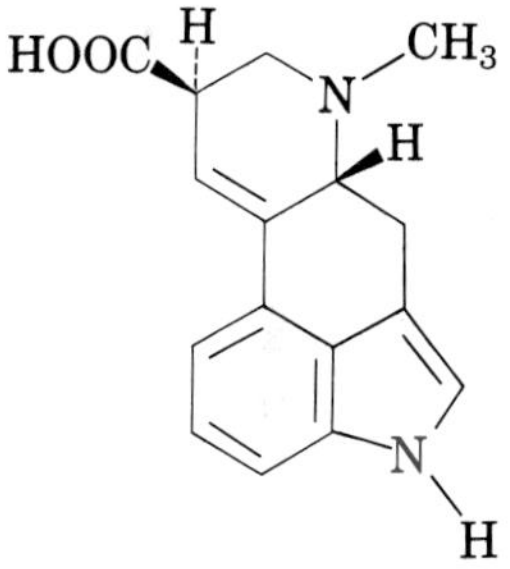

Lysergic acid

ADDITIONAL PROBLEMS

PROBLEM 12.17   Classify each of the amine nitrogen atoms in the following substances as either primary, secondary, or tertiary:

(a)

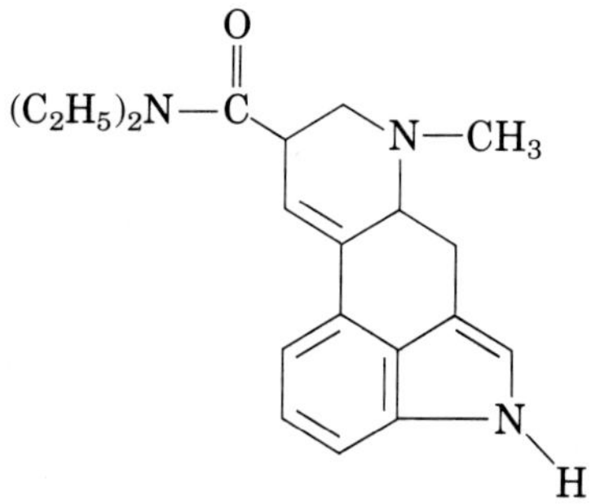

(b)

Caffeine

Lysergic acid diethylamide

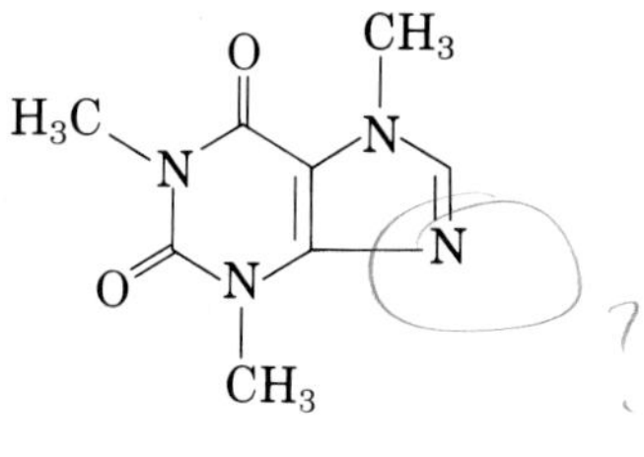

PROBLEM 12.18   Draw structures corresponding to these IUPAC names:

(a) N,N-Dimethylaniline
(b) N-Methylcyclohexylamine
(c) (Cyclohexylmethyl)amine
(d) (2-Methylcyclohexyl)amine
(e) 3-(N,N-Dimethylamino)propanoic acid

PROBLEM 12.19   Name the following compounds according to IUPAC rules:

(a)

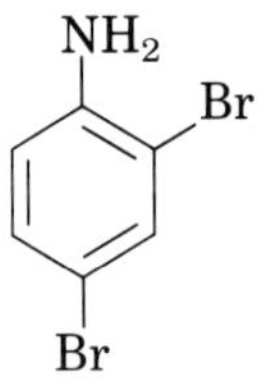

NH$_2$
Br

Br

(b) 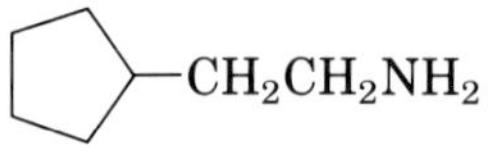   —CH$_2$CH$_2$NH$_2$

(c) 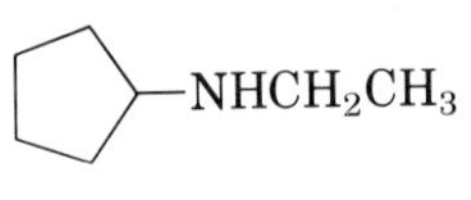   —NHCH$_2$CH$_3$

(d)

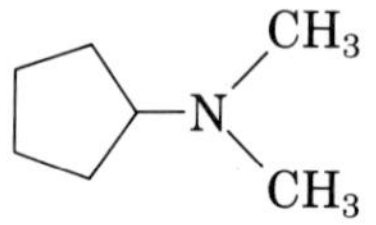

CH$_3$
—N
CH$_3$

(e) 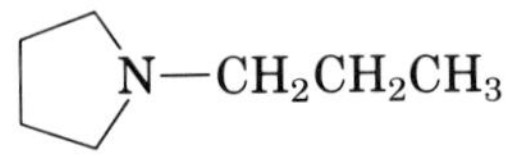   N—CH$_2$CH$_2$CH$_3$

(f)   H$_2$NCH$_2$CH$_2$CH$_2$CN

PROBLEM 12.20   How can you explain the fact that trimethylamine (bp 3°C) boils lower than di-methylamine (bp 7°C)?

PROBLEM 12.21   Propose structures for amines that fit these descriptions:

(a)   A secondary arylamine
(b)   A 1,3,5-trisubstituted arylamine
(c)   An achiral quaternary ammonium salt
(d)   A five-membered heterocyclic amine

PROBLEM 12.22   How might you prepare each of the following amines from 1-bromobutane?

(a)   Butylamine   (b)   Dibutylamine   (c)   Pentylamine

PROBLEM 12.23   How might you prepare each of the amines listed in Problem 12.22 from 1-butanol?

PROBLEM 12.24   How would you prepare benzylamine, C$_6$H$_5$CH$_2$NH$_2$, from each of these starting materials?

(a)   Benzene   (b)   Benzoic acid   (c)   Chlorobenzene   (d)   Toluene

PROBLEM 12.25   Show how you would prepare benzoic acid from aniline. A diazonio replacement reaction will be needed.

PROBLEM 12.26   How might you prepare pentylamine from these starting materials?

(a)   Pentanamide   (b)   Pentanenitrile   (c)   Pentanoic acid

PROBLEM 12.27   1,6-Hexanediamine, one of the starting materials used for the manufacture of nylon 66, can be synthesized by a route that begins with the addition of chlorine to 1,3-butadiene (Section 4.11). How would you carry out the complete synthesis?

PROBLEM 12.28   Coniine, C$_8$H$_{17}$N, is the toxic ingredient in poison hemlock, the drink used by Socrates to commit suicide. When subjected to Hofmann elimination, coniine yields 5-(N,N-dimethylamino)-1-octene. If coniine is a secondary amine, what is its structure?

PROBLEM 12.29   What is the major product you would expect from Hofmann elimination of these amines?

(a)   N-Methylcyclopentylamine   (b)   (CH$_3$)$_2$CHCH(NH$_2$)CH$_2$CH$_2$CH$_3$

PROBLEM 12.30 Cyclooctatetraene was first synthesized in 1911 by Richard Willstätter using a route that involved the following transformation:

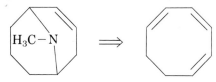

How might you use the Hofmann elimination reaction to accomplish this transformation?

PROBLEM 12.31 Give the structures of the major organic products you would expect to obtain from reaction of *m*-methylaniline with these reagents:

(a) Br_2 (1 mol)   (b) CH_3I (excess)   (c) CH_3COCl

PROBLEM 12.32 How would you synthesize 1,3,5-tribromobenzene from benzene? A diazonio replacement reaction will be needed.

PROBLEM 12.33 Tyramine is an alkaloid found, among other places, in mistletoe and ripe cheese. How would you prepare tyramine from toluene?

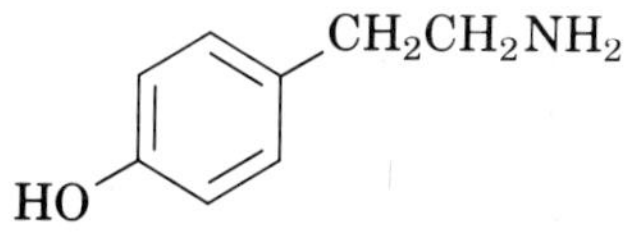

Tyramine

PROBLEM 12.34 Atropine, $C_{17}H_{23}NO_3$, is a poisonous alkaloid isolated from the leaves and roots of *Atropa belladonna*, known as the deadly nightshade. In low doses, atropine acts as a muscle relaxant: 0.5 ng (nanogram, 10^{-9} g) is sufficient to cause pupil dilation. On reaction with aqueous NaOH, atropine yields tropic acid, $C_6H_5CH(CH_2OH)COOH$, and tropine, $C_8H_{15}NO$. Tropine, an optically inactive alcohol, yields tropidene on dehydration. Propose a suitable structure for atropine.

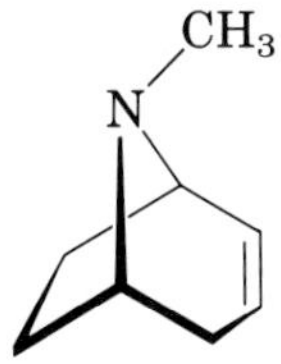

Tropidene

Organic Dyes and the Chemical Industry

The founding of the modern organic chemical industry can be traced to the need for a single organic compound—aniline—and to the activities of one person—Sir William Henry Perkin. Perkin, a student at the Royal College of Chemistry in London, worked during the day on problems assigned him but spent his free time working on his own ideas in an improvised home laboratory. He decided during Easter vacation in 1856 to examine the oxidation of aniline with potassium dichromate. The reaction appeared unpromising at first, yielding a tarry black product. But Perkin was able, by careful extraction with methanol, to isolate a few percent yield of a beautiful purple pigment that had the properties of a dye.

Since the only dyes known at the time were the naturally occurring vegetable dyes such as indigo, Perkin's synthetic purple dye, which he named *mauve*, created a sensation. Realizing the possibilities, Perkin resigned his post at the Royal College and, at the age of 18, formed a company to exploit his remarkable discovery. Since there had never before been a need for synthetic chemicals, no chemical industry existed at the time. Large-scale chemical manufacture was unknown, and Perkin therefore had to devise a procedure for preparing the needed quantities of aniline by nitration of benzene.

Subsequent work showed that Perkin's original mauve was in fact not derived from aniline at all but from a small amount of methylaniline impurity in his starting material. Pure aniline yields a similar dye, however, which came to be marketed under the name *pseudomauveine*.

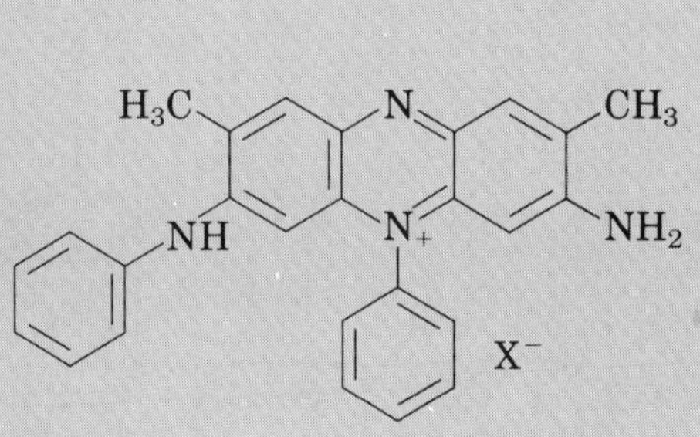

Perkin's mauve
(pseudomauveine has no methyl groups)

Today, dyestuff manufacture is a thriving and important part of the chemical industry, and many commonly used pigments such as *p*-(dimethylamino)-azobenzene, at one time used as a yellow food-coloring agent in margarine under the name "butter yellow," are derived from aniline.

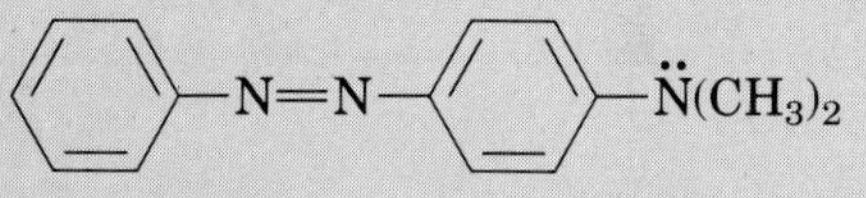

p-**(Dimethylamino)azobenzene (yellow crystals, mp 127°C)**

Naturally Occurring Amines: Morphine Alkaloids

Amines were among the first organic compounds to be isolated in pure form, and a great variety of amines are distributed in plants and animals. For example, morphine is a powerful pain-killer isolated from the opium poppy. Once known as "vegetable alkali" since their water solutions are basic, naturally occurring amines are now referred to as **alkaloids**.

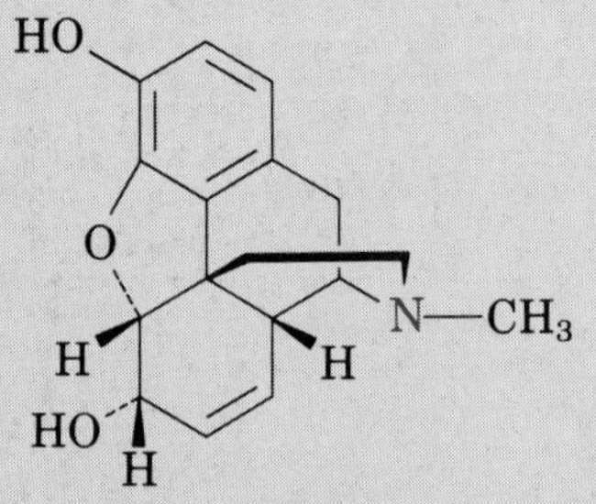

Morphine (analgesic)

The medical uses of the morphine family of alkaloids have been known at least since the seventeenth century, when crude extracts of the opium poppy, *Papaver somniferum*, were used for the relief of pain. Morphine was the first pure alkaloid to be isolated from the poppy, but its close relative, codeine, also occurs naturally. Codeine, which is simply the methyl ether of morphine, is used in prescription cough medicines. Heroin, another close relative of morphine, does not occur naturally but is synthesized by diacetylation of morphine.

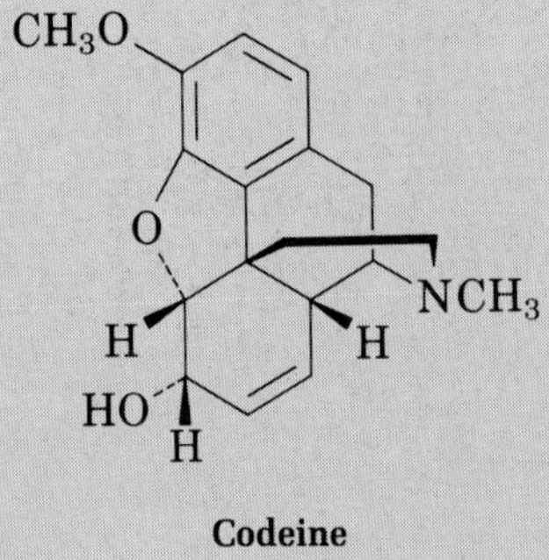

Codeine

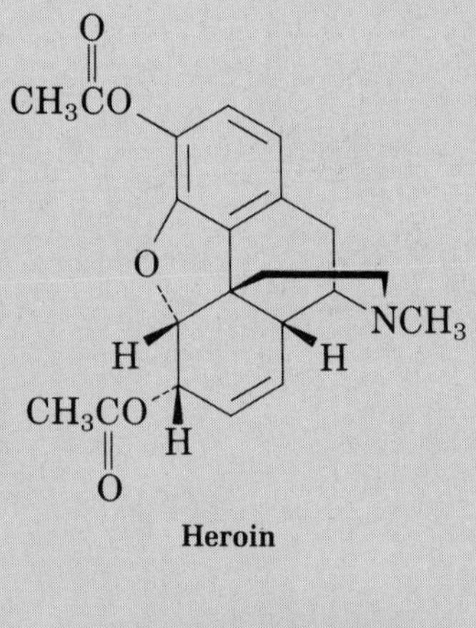

Heroin

Morphine and its relatives constitute a class of extremely useful pharmaceutical agents, yet they also pose a social problem of great proportion because of their addictive properties. Much effort has therefore gone into a search to understand the mode of action of morphine and to develop modified morphine analogs that retain the desired analgesic (pain-killing) activity but do not cause addiction.

A large number of morphine-like molecules have been synthesized and tested for their analgesic properties. Studies have shown that not all of the complex tetracyclic framework of morphine is necessary for biological activity. According to the "morphine rule," biological activity requires (1) an aromatic ring attached to (2) a quaternary carbon atom and (3) a tertiary amine situated (4) two carbon atoms farther away. For example, meperidine (Demerol) is widely used as an effective pain-killer, and methadone has been used as an antagonist in the treatment of heroin addiction to reverse the undesirable side effects of morphine.

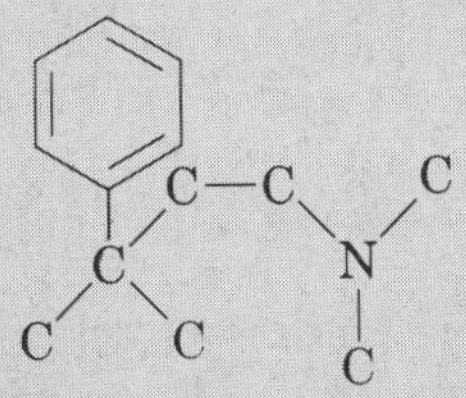

The morphine rule: an aromatic ring,
a quaternary carbon, two carbons, a tertiary amine

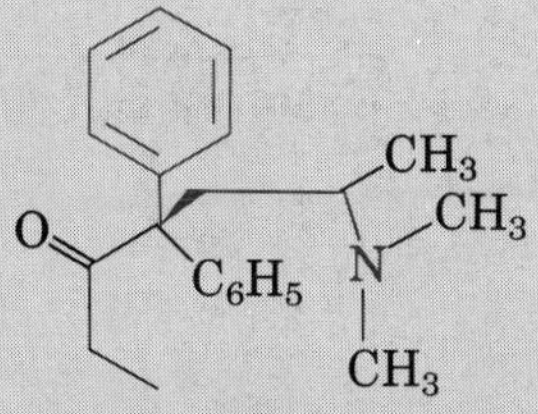

Methadone 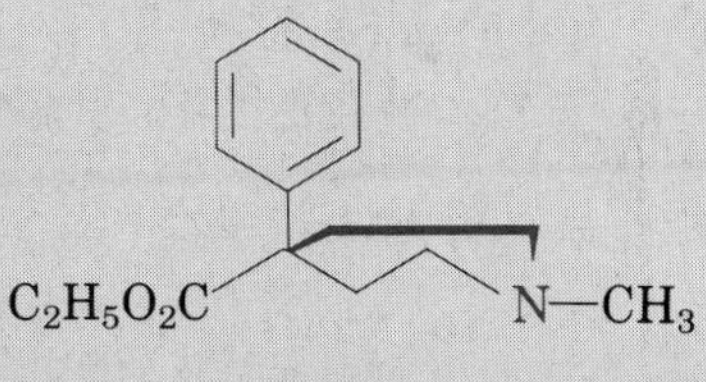   Meperidine

CHAPTER 13

Structure Determination

Structure determination is central to organic chemistry. Every time a reaction is run, the chemist must isolate, purify, and identify the products obtained. In the nineteenth and early twentieth centuries, determining the structures of organic molecules was a time-consuming process requiring great skill and patience. In the past few decades, however, extraordinary advances have been made in chemical instrumentation. Sophisticated instruments are now available that greatly simplify the problem of structure determination. Use of these instruments does not guarantee good results—skill and patience are still required—but it does ease the task.

What are these instruments that allow chemists to determine structures, and how can we use them? Let's answer these questions by looking at three of the most useful methods of structure determination: infrared spectroscopy, ultraviolet spectroscopy, and nuclear magnetic resonance spectroscopy. Each of the three methods yields a different kind of structural information.

1. **Infrared spectroscopy**—What functional groups are present?

2. **Ultraviolet spectroscopy**—Is a conjugated pi electron system present?

3. **Nuclear magnetic resonance spectroscopy**—What carbon–hydrogen framework is present?

13.1 INFRARED SPECTROSCOPY AND THE ELECTROMAGNETIC SPECTRUM

Infrared spectroscopy involves the interaction of molecules with infrared radiant energy. Before beginning a study of infrared spectroscopy, we need to look into the nature of radiant energy and the electromagnetic spectrum.

Visible light, X rays, microwaves, radio waves, and so forth, are all different kinds of **electromagnetic radiation**. Collectively, they make up the **electromagnetic spectrum** shown in Figure 13.1.

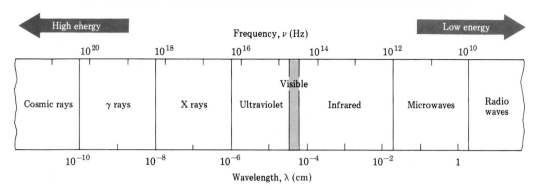

FIGURE 13.1
The electromagnetic spectrum

Electromagnetic radiation can be thought of as having dual behavior. In some respects it has the properties of a particle (called a **photon**), yet in other respects it behaves as a wave traveling at the speed of light. Electromagnetic waves can be described by their wavelength (λ, Greek lambda) and frequency (ν, Greek nu). The wavelength is simply the length of one complete wave cycle from trough to trough; the frequency is the number of wave cycles that travel past a fixed point in a certain unit of time (usually given in cycles per second, cps, or **hertz, Hz**).

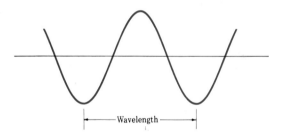

Wavelength and frequency are inversely related by the equation

$$\lambda = \frac{c}{\nu}$$

where

λ = Wavelength in centimeters
c = Speed of light (3×10^{10} cm/sec)
ν = Frequency in hertz

As Figure 13.1 indicates, the electromagnetic spectrum is arbitrarily divided into regions, with the familiar visible region accounting for only a small portion of the overall spectrum (from 3.8×10^{-5} cm to 7.8×10^{-5} cm in wavelength).

Electromagnetic energy is transmitted only in discrete energy packets called **quanta**. The amount of energy corresponding to 1 quantum of energy (or 1 photon) of a given frequency is expressed by the equation

$$\varepsilon = h\nu = \frac{hc}{\lambda}$$

where

$$\varepsilon = \text{The energy of 1 photon (1 quantum)}$$
$$h = \text{Planck's constant } (6.62 \times 10^{-27} \text{ erg sec})$$
$$\nu = \text{Frequency in hertz}$$
$$\lambda = \text{Wavelength in centimeters}$$
$$c = \text{Speed of light } (3 \times 10^{10} \text{ cm/sec})$$

Thus, the energy of a photon varies *directly* with its frequency, but *inversely* with its wavelength. High frequencies and short wavelengths correspond to high-energy radiation such as gamma rays; low frequencies and long wavelengths correspond to low-energy radiation such as radio waves.

When a sample of an organic compound is exposed to electromagnetic radiation, energy of certain wavelengths is absorbed by the sample, and energy of other wavelengths passes through. Whether a given wavelength is absorbed or not depends both on the structure of the sample molecules and on the energy level of the radiation. If we irradiate an organic compound with energy of many different wavelengths and determine which are absorbed, we can determine the **absorption spectrum** of the compound. The results are displayed on a graph that plots wavelength versus amount of radiation transmitted through the sample. For example, the infrared (abbreviated IR) spectrum of ethanol is shown in Figure 13.2. The horizontal axis (explained in the next section) records the wavelength, while the vertical axis records the intensity of various energy absorptions as they occur. The baseline corresponding to 0% absorption (or 100% transmittance) runs along the top of the chart. A downward spike in the chart means that energy absorption has occurred at that wavelength.

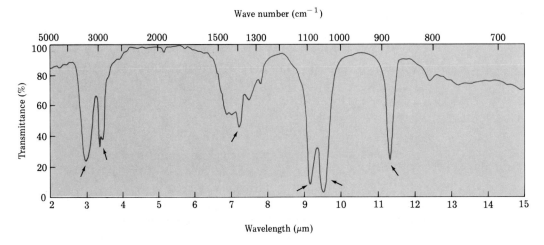

FIGURE 13.2
Infrared spectrum of ethanol: A transmittance of 100% on the spectrum means that all the energy is passing through the sample. A lower transmittance means that some energy is being absorbed. Thus, each downward spike (marked by an arrow) corresponds to an energy absorption.

PROBLEM 13.1   The energy of electromagnetic radiation expressed in units of kilocalories per mole can be determined by the formula

$$E = \frac{2.85 \times 10^{-3} \text{ kcal/mol}}{\lambda \text{ cm}}$$

What is the energy of infrared radiation of wavelength 10^{-4} cm?

PROBLEM 13.2   How does the energy of infrared radiation compare with that of an X ray with $\lambda = 3 \times 10^{-7}$ cm?

13.2   INFRARED SPECTROSCOPY OF ORGANIC MOLECULES

The infrared region of the electromagnetic spectrum covers the range from just above the visible (7.8×10^{-5} cm) to approximately 10^{-2} cm, but only the middle of the region is used by organic chemists (Figure 13.3). This midportion extends from 2.5×10^{-3} to 2.5×10^{-4} cm, and specific wavelengths are usually referred to in micrometers (1 μm $= 10^{-4}$ cm). Specific frequencies are usually given in **wave numbers** or **reciprocal centimeters**, rather than in hertz. The wave number, $\tilde{\nu}$, is the reciprocal of the wavelength in centimeters and is expressed in units of cm^{-1}.

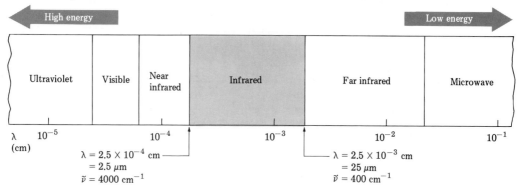

FIGURE 13.3
The infrared region of the electromagnetic spectrum

What causes a molecule to absorb certain wavelengths of infrared light but not absorb others? All molecules contain energy—energy that causes bonds to stretch and bend, atoms to wag and rock, and other molecular vibrations to occur. The *amount* of energy a molecule contains is not continuously variable but is *quantized*. That is, a molecule can stretch, bend, or vibrate only at certain frequencies corresponding to certain energy levels. When a molecule is irradiated with infrared light, the wavelengths absorbed correspond to those quantized stretching and bending energy levels in the molecule.

Since each infrared absorption corresponds to a specific molecular motion, we can see what kinds of motions a molecule has by observing its infrared spectrum. By then working backward and interpreting the infrared spectrum, we can find out what kinds of functional groups are present in the molecule.

The full interpretation of an IR spectrum is not easy. Most organic molecules are so large that there are dozens or hundreds of different possible bond stretchings, rotations, and bendings. Thus, an IR spectrum often contains dozens or hundreds of absorptions. In one sense this complexity is valuable, since an IR spectrum serves as a unique fingerprint of a specific compound. (In fact, the complex region of the IR spectrum below 1500 cm^{-1} is called the **fingerprint region**. If two samples have identical IR spectra in their fingerprint regions, the compounds are almost certainly identical.) For structural purposes, however, the multitude of absorptions present in an IR spectrum makes full interpretation difficult.

Fortunately, we don't need to interpret an IR spectrum fully to get useful information from it. *Most functional groups give rise to characteristic infrared absorptions that change little in going from one compound to another.* For example, the C=O absorption of ketones is almost always in the range 1690–1750 cm^{-1}; the O—H absorption of alcohols is almost always in the range 3200–3600 cm^{-1}; and the C=C absorption of alkenes is almost always in the range 1650–1670 cm^{-1}. By learning to recognize where characteristic functional group absorptions occur, we can gain valuable structural information from IR spectra.

For example, Figure 13.4 shows the IR spectra of 1-hexene, 1-hexanol, and 2-hexanone. Although all three spectra contain many peaks, there are characteristic absorptions of the three different functional groups that allow the three compounds to be distinguished. Thus, 1-hexene shows a characteristic alkene C=C peak at 1660 cm^{-1} and a vinylic =C—H peak at 3100 cm^{-1}; 1-hexanol shows a characteristic alcohol O—H absorption at 3300 cm^{-1} and C—O absorption at 1060 cm^{-1}; and 2-hexanone shows a peak at 1710 cm^{-1}, characteristic of saturated ketones.

One other point about infrared spectroscopy is that we can also derive much structural information from an IR spectrum by noticing which absorptions are *not* present. For example, if the spectrum of an unknown has *no* absorption near 3400 cm^{-1}, the unknown is not an alcohol; if the spectrum has *no* absorption near 1710 cm^{-1}, the unknown is not a ketone; and so on.

As indicated in Figure 13.5 (page 384), the infrared region from 4000 to 200 cm^{-1} can be roughly divided into four regions. Functional groups absorb in the first three regions (4000–1500 cm^{-1}), while the fourth is the fingerprint region mentioned earlier. The region from 4000 to 2500 cm^{-1} corresponds to N—H, C—H, and O—H bond stretching and contracting motions. Both N—H and O—H bonds absorb in the 3200–3600 cm^{-1} range, whereas C—H bond stretching occurs near 3000 cm^{-1}. Since almost all organic compounds have C—H bonds, almost all IR spectra have an intense absorption in this region.

The region from 2500 to 2000 cm^{-1} is where triple-bond stretching occurs; both nitriles (RC≡N) and alkynes show peaks here. The region from 2000 to 1500 cm^{-1} contains double-bond absorptions; C=O, C=N, and C=C bonds all absorb here. Carbonyl groups generally absorb from 1670 to 1780 cm^{-1}, whereas alkene stretching normally occurs in the narrow range from 1650 to

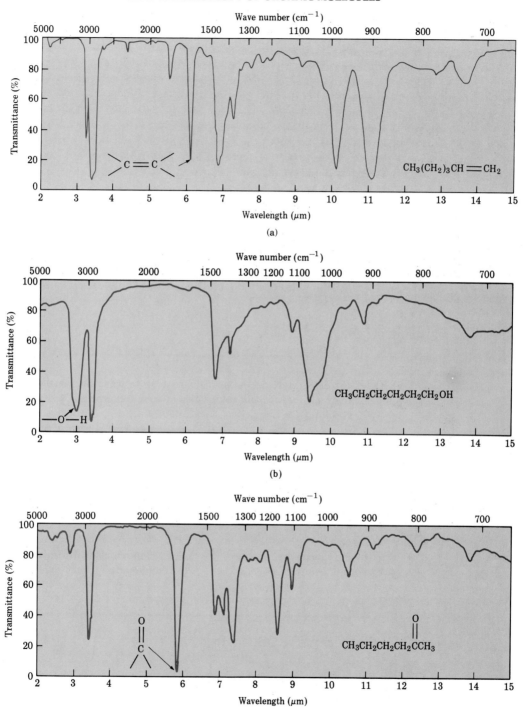

FIGURE 13.4
Infrared spectra of (a) 1-hexene, (b) 1-hexanol, and (c) 2-hexanone: Spectra such as these are easily obtained on 1–2 mg samples in just a few minutes, using routine, commercially available instruments.

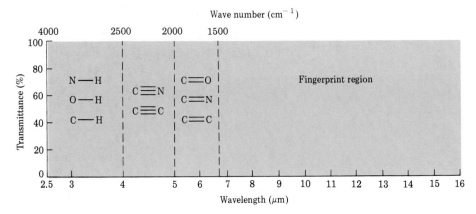

FIGURE 13.5
Regions in the infrared spectrum

1670 cm^{-1}. The exact position of the C=O absorption is often diagnostic of the exact kind of carbonyl group in the molecule. For example, esters usually absorb at 1735 cm^{-1}, aldehydes at 1725 cm^{-1}, and acyclic ketones at 1715 cm^{-1}. Table 13.1 lists the characteristic absorption frequencies of some of the most common functional groups.

PROBLEM 13.3   Refer to Table 13.1 and make educated guesses as to what functional groups molecules might contain if they show IR absorptions at these frequencies:

(a)   1715 cm^{-1} (b)   1540 cm^{-1} (c)   2210 cm^{-1}
(d)   1720 and 2500–3100 cm^{-1} (e)   3500 and 1735 cm^{-1}

PROBLEM 13.4   If C—O single-bond stretching occurs at 1000 cm^{-1} and C=O double-bond stretching occurs at 1700 cm^{-1}, which of the two requires more energy? How does your answer correlate with the known relative strengths of single and double bonds?

PROBLEM 13.5   How might you use IR spectroscopy to help you distinguish between these pairs of isomers?

(a)   Ethanol and dimethyl ether   (b)   Cyclohexane and 1-hexene
(c)   Acetone and 2-propen-1-ol   (d)   Propanoic acid and 3-hydroxypropanal

---

13.3   ULTRAVIOLET SPECTROSCOPY

The **ultraviolet (UV)** region of the electromagnetic spectrum extends from the low-wavelength end of the visible region (4×10^{-5} cm) down to 10^{-6} cm. The portion of greatest interest to organic chemists, however, is the narrow range from 2×10^{-5} cm to 4×10^{-5} cm. Absorptions in this region are usually measured in **nanometers** (1 nm = 10^{-9} m = 10^{-7} cm). Thus, the ultraviolet range of interest is from 200 to 400 nm (Figure 13.6, page 386).

We have seen that when an organic molecule is irradiated with electromagnetic

TABLE 13.1   Characteristic infrared absorptions of some functional groups

Functional group class	Band position (cm^{-1})	Intensity of absorption
Alkanes, alkyl groups		
C—H	2850–2960	Medium to strong
Alkenes		
=C—H	3020–3100	Medium
C=C	1650–1670	Medium
Alkynes		
≡C—H	3300	Strong
—C≡C—	2100–2260	Medium
Alkyl halides		
C—Cl	600–800	Strong
C—Br	500–600	Strong
C—I	500	Strong
Alcohols		
O—H	3200–3600	Strong, broad
C—O	1050–1150	Strong
Aromatics		
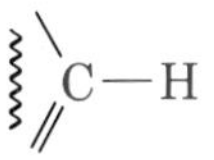 C—H	3030	Medium
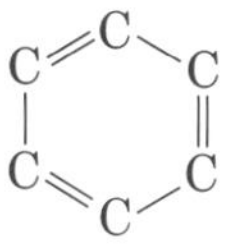	1600, 1500	Strong
Amines		
N—H	3310–3500	Medium
C—N	1030, 1230	Medium
Carbonyl compounds[a]		
C=O	1670–1780	Strong
Carboxylic acids		
O—H	2500–3100	Strong, very broad
Nitriles		
C≡N	2210–2260	Medium
Nitro compounds		
NO_2	1540	Strong

[a]Acids, esters, aldehydes, and ketones.

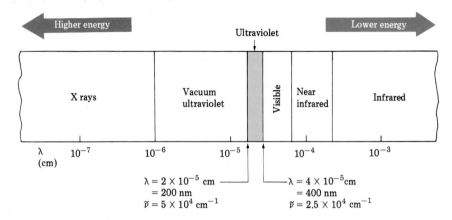

FIGURE 13.6
The ultraviolet region of the electromagnetic spectrum

energy, the radiation is either absorbed by the compound or passes through it, depending on the exact energy level of the waves. With infrared radiation, we saw that the energies absorbed correspond to the amounts necessary to increase molecular motions—stretchings, bendings, and twistings—of functional groups. With ultraviolet irradiation, however, the energies absorbed correspond to the amounts necessary to cause **electronic excitations**. The pi electrons in conjugated molecules are excited to higher energy levels on absorption of ultraviolet light.

Ultraviolet spectra are recorded by irradiating a sample with UV light of continuously changing wavelength. When the wavelength of light corresponds to the energy level required to excite an electron to a higher level, energy is absorbed. The absorption is detected and displayed on a chart that plots wavelength versus percent radiation absorbed.

A typical UV spectrum is shown in Figure 13.7. Unlike IR spectra, which usually show many sharp lines, UV spectra are usually quite simple; often only a single broad peak is produced. We identify the position of the peak by noting the wavelength (λ) at the very top (λ_{max}). For the UV spectrum of 1,3-butadiene shown in Figure 13.7, $\lambda_{max} = 217$ nm.

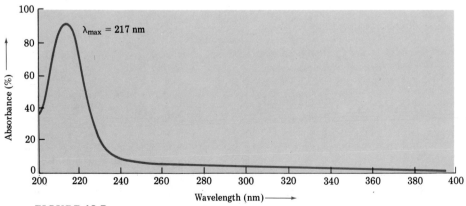

FIGURE 13.7
Ultraviolet spectrum of 1,3-butadiene

PROBLEM 13.6   Using the formula given in Problem 13.1, calculate the energy required to effect the electronic excitation of 1,3-butadiene (λ_{max} = 217 nm).

13.4   INTERPRETING ULTRAVIOLET SPECTRA: THE EFFECT OF CONJUGATION

The exact wavelength of radiation necessary to effect an electronic transition in a conjugated molecule depends on the nature of the conjugated system. Thus, by measuring the UV spectrum of an unknown, we can derive structural information about the nature of any conjugated pi electron system present.

One of the most important factors affecting the wavelength of UV absorption is the extent of conjugation. It turns out that the energy required for an electronic transition decreases as the extent of conjugation increases. Thus, 1,3-butadiene shows an absorption at λ_{max} = 217 nm, whereas 1,3,5-hexatriene absorbs at λ_{max} = 258 nm, and 1,3,5,7-octatetraene has λ_{max} = 290 nm. [*Remember: Longer wavelength means lower energy.*]

Other kinds of conjugated pi electron systems besides dienes and polyenes also show UV absorptions. For example, conjugated enones such as 3-buten-2-one, and aromatic molecules such as benzene, show characteristic UV absorptions that aid in structure determination. The UV absorption maxima of some representative conjugated molecules are given in Table 13.2.

TABLE 13.2   Ultraviolet absorption maxima of some conjugated molecules

Name	Structure	λ_{max} (nm)
Ethylene	$H_2C=CH_2$	171
2-Methyl-1,3-butadiene	$\overset{\displaystyle CH_3}{\overset{\displaystyle \vert}{H_2C=C}}-CH=CH_2$	220
1,3-Cyclohexadiene		256
1,3,5-Hexatriene	$H_2C=CH-CH=CH-CH=CH_2$	258
3-Buten-2-one	$H_2C=CH-\overset{\displaystyle CH_3}{\overset{\displaystyle \vert}{C}}=O$	219
Benzene		254

PROBLEM 13.7   Which of the following compounds would you expect to show UV absorptions in the range 200–400 nm?

(a)   1,3-Cyclohexadiene   (b)   1,4-Cyclohexadiene
(c)   Methyl propenoate   (d)   *p*-Bromotoluene
(e)   2-Methylcyclohexanone   (f)   2-Methyl-2-cyclohexenone

13.5   NUCLEAR MAGNETIC RESONANCE SPECTROSCOPY

Of all techniques available for determining structures, **nuclear magnetic resonance (NMR) spectroscopy** is perhaps the most valuable. It's the method to which most chemists turn first for information.

We've seen in earlier sections of this chapter that infrared spectroscopy provides information about the functional groups a molecule contains and that ultraviolet spectroscopy provides information about the conjugated pi electron system in a molecule. Nuclear magnetic resonance spectroscopy doesn't replace or duplicate any of these techniques; rather, it complements them. NMR spectroscopy provides a "map" of the carbon–hydrogen framework of an organic molecule. Taken together, IR, UV, and NMR often allow us to obtain solutions for the structures of extremely complex unknowns.

13.6   THEORY OF NMR

Many kinds of nuclei, including both ^{1}H and ^{13}C, behave as if they were spinning about an axis. Since they are positively charged, these spinning nuclei act like tiny magnets and can therefore interact with an external magnetic field (denoted H_0).

In the absence of a strong external magnetic field, the nuclear spins of magnetic nuclei are oriented randomly. When these nuclei are placed between the poles of a strong magnet, however, they adopt specific orientations, much as a compass needle orients itself in the earth's magnetic field. A spinning ^{1}H or ^{13}C nucleus can be oriented so that its own tiny magnetic field is aligned either with (*parallel to*) or against (*antiparallel to*) the external field. These two possible orientations do not have equal energy and are therefore not present in equal amounts. The parallel orientation is slightly lower in energy and therefore slightly favored over the antiparallel orientation (Figure 13.8).

If the oriented nuclei are irradiated with electromagnetic radiation of the proper frequency, energy absorption occurs, and the lower-energy state "spin-flips" to the higher-energy state. When this spin-flip occurs, the nucleus is said to be in resonance with the applied radiation—hence the name, nuclear magnetic resonance.

The exact amount of radio-frequency (rf) energy necessary for resonance depends both on the strength of the external magnetic field and on the nucleus being irradiated. If a very strong magnetic field is applied, the energy separation be-

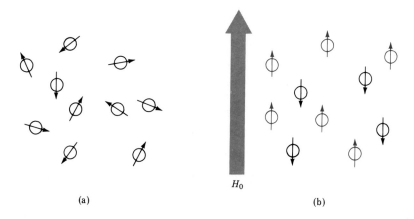

H_0

(a) (b)

FIGURE 13.8
Orientation of nuclear spins: (a) random orientation in the absence of an external magnetic field; (b) specific orientation in the presence of an external magnetic field, H_0. Some of the spins (color) are aligned parallel to the external field, and others are antiparallel. The parallel spin state is lower in energy.

tween the two spin states is large, and higher-energy (higher-frequency) radiation is required. If a weaker magnetic field is applied, less energy is required to effect the transition between nuclear spin states.

In practice, superconducting magnets producing enormously powerful fields up to 140,000 gauss (G) are sometimes used, but a field strength of 14,100 G is more common. At this magnetic field strength, radio-frequency energy in the 60 MHz range (1 MHz = 1 megahertz = 1 million cycles per second) is required to bring a ^{1}H nucleus into resonance, and radio-frequency energy of 15 MHz is required to bring a ^{13}C nucleus into resonance.

PROBLEM 13.8 Using the equation given in Problem 13.1 and the relationship $\lambda = c/\nu$, where $c = 3 \times 10^{10}$ cm/sec (the speed of light), calculate the amount of energy required to spin-flip a proton in a spectrometer operating at 100 MHz. Does increasing the spectrometer frequency from 60 MHz to 100 MHz increase or decrease the amount of energy necessary for resonance?

13.7 THE NATURE OF NMR ABSORPTIONS

From the description given so far, you might expect all protons in a molecule to absorb radio frequency energy at the same frequency and all ^{13}C nuclei to absorb at the same frequency. If this were true, we would observe a single NMR absorption peak in the ^{1}H or ^{13}C spectrum of a molecule, a situation that would be of little use for structure determination. In fact, the absorption frequency is not the same for all nuclei.

All nuclei in molecules are surrounded by electron clouds. When a uniform external magnetic field is applied to a sample molecule, the circulating electron clouds set up tiny local magnetic fields of their own. These local fields act in opposition to the applied field, so that the *effective field* actually experienced by the nucleus is a bit smaller than the applied field.

$$H_{\text{effective}} = H_{\text{applied}} - H_{\text{local}}$$

In describing this effect of local fields, we say that the nuclei are *shielded* from the applied field by the circulating electron clouds. Since each kind of nucleus in a molecule is in a slightly different electronic environment, each nucleus is shielded to a slightly different extent. Thus, the effective magnetic field actually felt is not the same for each nucleus. At a given value of the applied field, every non-equivalent nucleus in a molecule feels a slightly different magnetic field. If our NMR instrument is sensitive enough, the tiny differences in effective magnetic fields experienced by different nuclei can be observed, and we can see different NMR signals for each nucleus.

Each unique kind of proton and each unique kind of ^{13}C in a molecule gives rise to a unique NMR signal. Thus, the NMR spectrum of an organic compound provides us with a map of the carbon–hydrogen framework. With practice, we can learn to read the map and thereby derive structural information about an unknown molecule.

Figure 13.9 shows both the ^1H and the ^{13}C NMR spectra of methyl acetate, CH_3COOCH_3. The horizontal axis shows the difference in effective field strength felt by the nuclei, and the vertical axis indicates intensity of absorption of radio frequency energy. Each peak in the NMR spectrum corresponds to a certain kind of hydrogen or carbon in a molecule. Note, however, that ^1H and ^{13}C spectra cannot be observed at the same time on the same spectrometer, since different amounts of energy are required to spin-flip the different kinds of nuclei. Each of the two kinds of spectra must be recorded separately.

The ^{13}C spectrum of methyl acetate (Figure 13.9) shows three peaks, one for each of the three different carbon atoms present. The ^1H spectrum shows only *two* peaks, however, even though methyl acetate has six protons. One peak is due to the CH_3CO protons, and the other is due to the OCH_3 protons. Since the three protons of each methyl group have the same chemical (and magnetic) environment, they are shielded to the same extent and show a single absorption.

PRACTICE PROBLEM   How many signals would you expect *p*-dimethylbenzene to show in its ^1H and ^{13}C NMR spectra?

Solution   Because of the molecule's symmetry, the two methyl groups in *p*-dimethylbenzene are equivalent, and all four ring hydrogens are equivalent. Thus, there should be two absorptions in the ^1H NMR spectrum. Also because of symmetry, there should be only three absorptions in the ^{13}C NMR spectrum—one for the two equivalent methyl-group carbons, one for the four equivalent $=CH-$ ring carbons, and one for the two equivalent ring carbons bonded to the methyl groups:

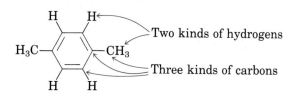

p-Dimethylbenzene

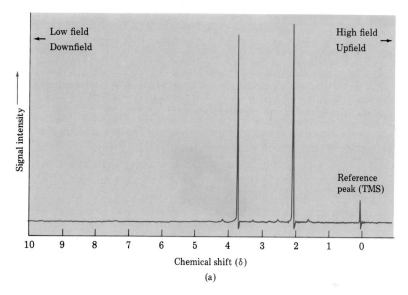

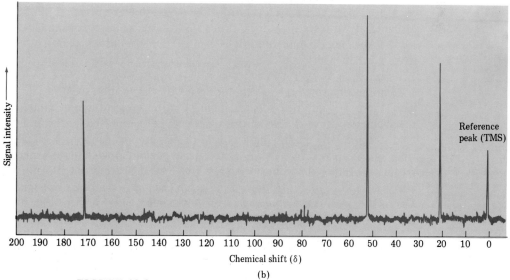

FIGURE 13.9
(a) The ^1H NMR spectrum and (b) the ^{13}C NMR spectrum of methyl acetate, CH_3COOCH_3: The two spectra are recorded separately.

PROBLEM 13.9   How many signals would you expect each of these compounds to show in their ^1H and ^{13}C NMR spectra?

(a) Methane   (b) Ethane   (c) Propane
(d) Cyclohexane   (e) Dimethyl ether   (f) Benzene
(g) $(CH_3)_3COH$ (h) Chloroethane   (i) $(CH_3)_2C{=}C(CH_3)_2$

13.8   CHEMICAL SHIFTS

NMR spectra are displayed on charts that show the applied field strength increasing from left to right, as shown in Figure 13.9. Thus, the left side of the chart is the low-field (or *downfield*) side, while the right side is the high-field (or *upfield*) side. In order to define the position of absorptions, the NMR chart is calibrated and a reference point is used. In practice, a small amount of tetramethylsilane [TMS, $(CH_3)_4Si$] is added to the sample so that an internal, standard reference absorption line is produced when the spectrum is run. Tetramethylsilane is used as a reference for both ^1H and ^{13}C spectra, since it gives rise to a single peak that occurs at a higher field (farther right on the chart) than other absorptions normally found in organic molecules.

The exact place on the chart where a nucleus absorbs is called its **chemical shift**. By convention, the chemical shift of TMS is set at zero, and other peaks normally occur at lower fields (to the left on the chart). For historical reasons, NMR charts are calibrated in units of frequency using the **delta scale**. One delta unit (δ) is equal to 1 part per million (ppm) of the spectrometer operating frequency. For example, if we were measuring the ^1H NMR spectrum of a sample using a 60 MHz instrument, 1 δ (1 ppm of 60×10^6 Hz) would equal 60 Hz. Similarly, if we were measuring the spectrum using a 100 MHz instrument, then 1 δ = 100 Hz.

Although this method of calibrating NMR charts may seem needlessly complex, there is a good reason for it. In practice, many different kinds of NMR spectrometers are available, operating at many different frequencies and magnetic field strengths. By employing a system of measurement in which NMR absorptions are expressed in relative terms (parts per million relative to spectrometer frequency) rather than absolute terms (Hz), we can avoid much confusion. *The chemical shift of an NMR absorption given in ppm or δ units is constant, regardless of the operating frequency of the instrument.* A ^1H nucleus that absorbs at 2.0 δ on a 60 MHz instrument (2 ppm × 60 MHz = 120 Hz to the left of TMS) also absorbs at 2.0 δ on a 300 MHz instrument (2.0 ppm × 300 MHz = 600 Hz to the left of TMS).

PRACTICE PROBLEM   Cyclohexane shows an absorption at 1.43 δ in its ^1H NMR spectrum. How many hertz away from TMS is this on a spectrometer operating at 60 MHz? On a spectrometer operating at 220 MHz?

Solution   On a 60 MHz spectrometer, $1\ \delta = 60$ Hz. Thus, $1.43\ \delta = 86$ Hz away from the TMS reference peak. On a 220 MHz spectrometer, $1\ \delta = 220$ Hz and $1.43\ \delta = 315$ Hz.

PROBLEM 13.10   When the ¹H NMR spectrum of acetone is recorded on a 60 MHz instrument, a single sharp resonance line at 2.1 δ is observed.

(a)   How far away from TMS (in hertz) does the acetone absorption occur?
(b)   What would be the position of the acetone absorption in δ units if it were obtained on a 100 MHz instrument?
(c)   How many hertz away from TMS does the absorption in the 100 MHz spectrum correspond to?

PROBLEM 13.11   The following ¹H NMR resonances were recorded on a spectrometer operating at 60 MHz. Convert each into δ units.

(a) $CHCl_3$,   436 Hz
(c) CH_3OH,   208 Hz

(b) CH_3Cl,   183 Hz
(d) CH_2Cl_2,   318 Hz

13.9   CHEMICAL SHIFTS IN ¹H NMR SPECTRA

Our discussion of NMR has been rather general up to this point—much of what we have said applies to both ¹H and ¹³C spectra. Let's now focus only on ¹H NMR spectra to see what information can be obtained.

The great majority of ¹H NMR absorptions occur in the range from 0 to 8 δ. The precise spot within this range is highly characteristic of the environment of a given proton. As Figure 13.10 indicates, it's convenient to divide the range of proton absorptions into five regions. Once these regions are memorized, you can often tell from a quick glance at the NMR spectrum what kinds of protons a molecule contains. Table 13.3 (page 394) shows the correlation of ¹H chemical shift with environment in more detail. In general, protons bound to saturated, sp^3 carbons absorb upfield, whereas protons bound to sp^2 carbons absorb at lower fields. Protons on carbons bound to electronegative atoms such as N, O, or halogen also absorb at lower fields.

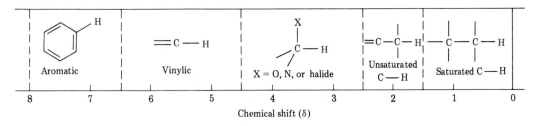

FIGURE 13.10
Chemical shifts of different kinds of protons

TABLE 13.3   Correlation of ^1H chemical shift with environment

Type of proton	Formula	Chemical shift (δ)
Reference peak	$(CH_3)_4Si$	0
Saturated primary	$-CH_3$	0.7–1.3
Saturated secondary	$-CH_2-$	1.2–1.4
Saturated tertiary	$\underset{/}{\overset{\backslash}{-}}C-H$	1.4–1.7
Allylic primary	$\underset{/}{\overset{\backslash}{C}}=\underset{|}{C}-CH_3$	1.6–1.9
Methyl ketones	$-\overset{\overset{\textstyle O}{\|}}{C}-CH_3$	2.1–2.4
Aromatic methyl	$Ar-CH_3$	2.5–2.7
Alkyl chloride	$Cl-\underset{/}{\overset{\backslash}{C}}-H$	3.0–4.0
Alkyl bromide	$Br-\underset{/}{\overset{\backslash}{C}}-H$	2.5–4.0
Alkyl iodide	$I-\underset{/}{\overset{\backslash}{C}}-H$	2.0–4.0
Alcohol, ether	$-O-\underset{/}{\overset{\backslash}{C}}-H$	3.3–4.0
Alkynyl	$-C\equiv C-H$	2.5–2.7
Vinylic	$\underset{/}{\overset{\backslash}{C}}=\underset{|}{C}-H$	5.0–6.5
Aromatic	$Ar-H$	6.5–8.0
Aldehyde	$-\overset{\overset{\textstyle O}{\|}}{C}-H$	9.7–10.0
Carboxylic acid	$-\overset{\overset{\textstyle O}{\|}}{C}-O-H$	11.0–12.0
Alcohol	$-\underset{/}{\overset{\backslash}{C}}-O-H$	Extremely variable (2.5–5.0)

PROBLEM 13.12 Each of the following compounds exhibits a single ¹H NMR peak. Approximately where would you expect each compound to absorb?

(a) Ethane   (b) Acetone   (c) Benzene   (d) Trimethylamine

13.10 INTEGRATION OF ¹H NMR SPECTRA: PROTON COUNTING

Look at the ¹H NMR spectrum of chloropropanone, CH_3COCH_2Cl, shown in Figure 13.11. As expected, there are two peaks, corresponding to the two kinds of protons present. These peaks are not the same size, however. The peak at 2.2 δ due to the CH_3— protons is larger than the peak at 4.1 δ due to the —CH_2Cl protons.

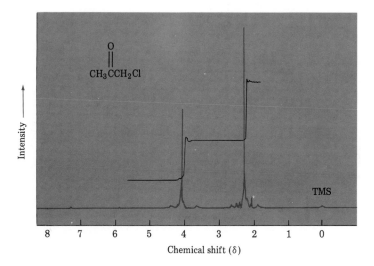

FIGURE 13.11
The ¹H NMR spectrum of chloropropanone, CH_3COCH_2Cl:
Integrating the peaks in a "stair-step" manner shows that they have a 2:3 ratio, corresponding to the number of protons responsible for each peak.

It turns out that the area under each peak is proportional to the number of protons causing that peak. Thus, by electronically measuring (**integrating**) the area under each peak, we can measure the number of each different kind of proton in a molecule. Integrated peak areas are presented on the chart in a "stair-step" manner, with the height of each step proportional to the number of protons under the peak. For example, the two peaks in chloropropanone are found to have a 2:3 ratio when integrated.

PROBLEM 13.13   How many peaks would you expect to see in the ^{1}H NMR spectrum of 1,4-dimethylbenzene (*p*-xylene)? What ratio of peak areas would you expect to find on integration of the spectrum? Refer to Table 13.3 for approximate chemical shift values, and sketch what the spectrum might look like.

13.11   SPIN–SPIN SPLITTING IN ^{1}H NMR SPECTRA

In the ^{1}H NMR spectra seen thus far, each different kind of proton in a molecule has given rise to a single peak. It often happens, however, that the absorption of a proton splits into *multiple* peaks. For example, the ^{1}H NMR spectrum of chloroethane shown in Figure 13.12 indicates that the $Cl—CH_2—$ protons appear as four peaks (a **quartet**) at 3.59 δ, while the $CH_3—$ protons appear as a **triplet** at 1.49 δ.

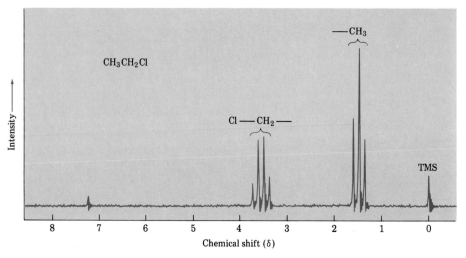

FIGURE 13.12
The ^{1}H NMR spectrum of chloroethane, CH_3CH_2Cl

The phenomenon of multiple absorptions, known as **spin–spin splitting**, is due to the fact that the nuclear spin of one atom can interact with (**couple** with) the nuclear spin of another nearby atom. The tiny magnetic field of one nucleus affects the magnetic field felt by a neighboring nucleus.

To understand the reasons for spin–spin splitting, let's look at the $CH_3—$ protons in chloroethane. The three equivalent $CH_3—$ protons are neighbored by two magnetic nuclei—the $ClCH_2—$ protons. Each of the $—CH_2—$ protons has its own nuclear spin that can align either with or against the applied magnetic field, producing tiny effects that are felt by the neighboring $CH_3—$ protons. There are three ways in which the $—CH_2—$ protons can align: (1) If both protons align *with* the applied magnetic field, the total effective field felt by the neighboring

—CH_3 protons is slightly larger than it would otherwise be. In consequence, the applied field necessary to cause resonance is slightly reduced. (2) If one —CH_2— proton aligns *with* and one aligns *against* the applied field (two possible ways), there is no effect on the neighboring CH_3— protons. (3) If both —CH_2— protons align *against* the applied field, the effective field felt by the CH_3— protons is slightly smaller than it would otherwise be, and the applied field needed for resonance must be slightly increased. These three possible alignments of —CH_2— spins cause the neighboring CH_3— protons to appear as three peaks with a 1:2:1 ratio in the NMR spectrum. Figure 13.13 shows schematically how spin–spin splitting arises.

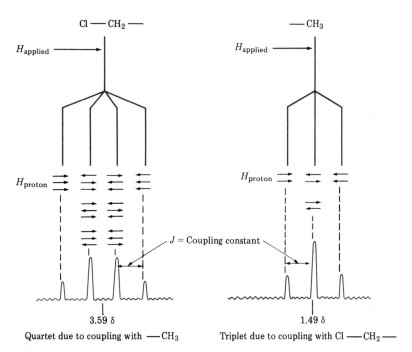

FIGURE 13.13
The origin of spin–spin splitting in chloroethane: The nuclear spins of neighboring protons (indicated by horizontal arrows) can align either with or against the applied field, causing splitting of absorptions into multiplets.

In the same way that the CH_3— protons of chloroethane are split into a triplet in the NMR spectrum, the —CH_2— protons are split into a quartet. The three spins of the neighboring CH_3— protons can align in four combinations: all three with the applied field; two with and one against (three possibilities); one with and two against (three possibilities); or all three against. Thus, four peaks are produced in a 1:3:3:1 ratio.

As a general rule, protons that have *n* neighboring protons show *n* + 1 peaks in their NMR spectrum. For example, the —CHBr— proton in 2-bromopropane ($CH_3CHBrCH_3$) appears as a seven-line multiplet (a *septet*) in the NMR spectrum (Figure 13.14), since its signal is split by the six neighboring protons

$(n + 1 = 7$ when $n = 6)$. Similarly, the CH_3— protons of 2-bromopropane appear as a doublet, since their signal is split only by the single neighboring —CHBr— proton.

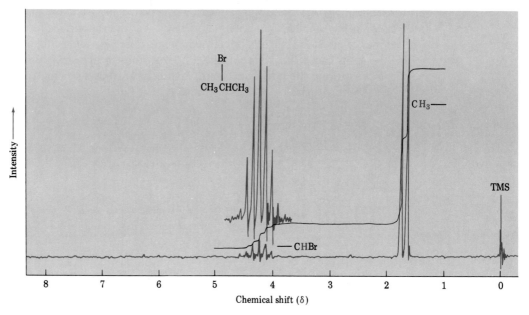

FIGURE 13.14
The ^1H NMR spectra of 2-bromopropane

The distance between individual peaks in the multiplets is called the **coupling constant**. It is denoted J and is measured in hertz. Coupling constants generally fall in the range 0–18 Hz, although their exact value depends on several factors, such as the geometry of the molecule. A typical value for an open-chain alkyl system is 6–8 Hz. Note that the same coupling constant must be shared by both groups of hydrogens whose spins are coupled. In chloroethane, for example, the $ClCH_2$— protons are coupled to the CH_3— protons with coupling constant $J = 7$ Hz. The CH_3— protons are similarly coupled to the $ClCH_2$— protons with the same $J = 7$ Hz coupling constant.

We can summarize three important rules about spin–spin splitting that are illustrated by the spectra of chloroethane in Figure 13.12 and 2-bromopropane in Figure 13.14:

1. Chemically equivalent protons do not exhibit spin-spin splitting. The equivalent protons may be on the same carbon or on different carbons, but their signals still appear as singlets and do not split.

$$Cl-\overset{\displaystyle H}{\underset{\displaystyle H}{C}}-H$$

**Three C—H protons are
chemically equivalent;
no coupling occurs**

$$Cl-\overset{\displaystyle H}{\underset{\displaystyle H}{C}}-\overset{\displaystyle H}{\underset{\displaystyle H}{C}}-Cl$$

**Four C—H protons are
chemically equivalent;
no coupling occurs**

2. A proton that has *n* equivalent neighboring protons gives a signal that is split into a multiplet of *n* + 1 peaks with coupling constant *J*. Protons that are farther than two carbon atoms apart usually do not split each other.

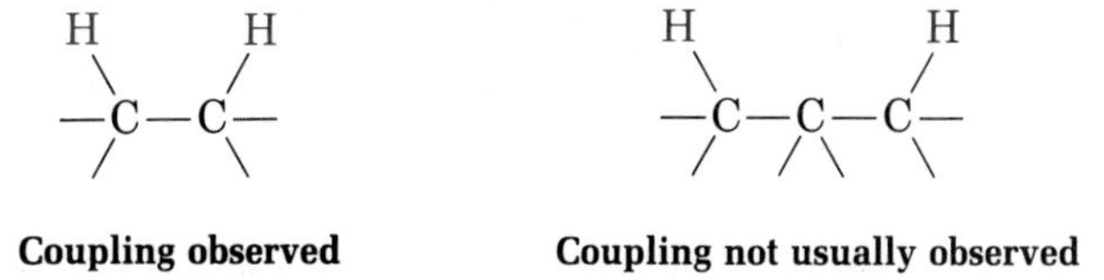

   Coupling observed   **Coupling not usually observed**

3. Two groups of protons coupled with each other must have the same coupling constant *J*.

PRACTICE PROBLEM   Predict the splitting pattern for each kind of hydrogen in isopropyl propanoate, $CH_3CH_2COOCH(CH_3)_2$.

Solution   First find how many different kinds of protons are present (there are four). Then find out how many neighboring protons each of the different kinds has and apply the *n* + 1 rule to determine the splitting patterns:

This —CH_3 has two neighbors and is a triplet

These two —CH_3 groups have one neighbor and are a doublet

This —CH_2— has three neighbors and is a quartet

This —CH has six neighbors and is a septet

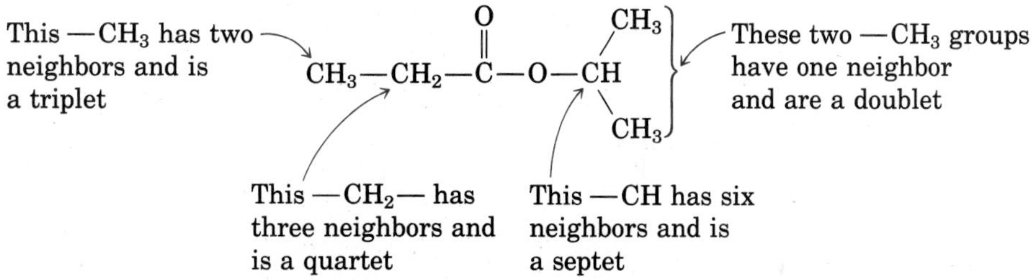

PROBLEM 13.14   Predict the splitting patterns you would expect for each proton in these molecules:

(a) $(CH_3)_3CH$ (b) CH_3CHBr_2 (c) $CH_3OCH_2CH_2Br$
(d) $CH_3CH_2COOCH_3$ (e) $ClCH_2CH_2CH_2Cl$ (f) $(CH_3)_2CHCOOCH_3$

PROBLEM 13.15   Propose structures for compounds that show these ¹H NMR spectra:

(a) C_2H_6O,   one singlet   (b) $C_3H_6O_2$,   two singlets
(c) C_3H_7Cl,   one doublet and one septet

13.12   USE OF ¹H NMR SPECTRA

We can use ¹H NMR to help identify the product of nearly every reaction run in the laboratory. For example, we said in Section 4.2 that addition of HCl to alkenes occurs with Markovnikov orientation; that is, the more highly substituted chloroalkane is formed. With the help of ¹H NMR, we can now prove this statement.

Does addition of HCl to 1-methylcyclohexene yield 1-chloro-1-methylcyclohexane or 1-chloro-2-methylcyclohexane?

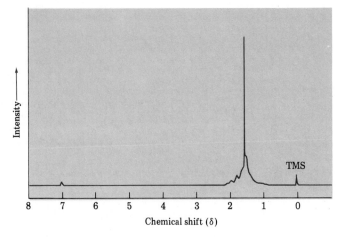

1-Methylcyclohexene   1-Chloro-1-methylcyclohexane   1-Chloro-2-methylcyclohexane
                  (Markovnikov)   (non-Markovnikov)

The ^1H NMR spectrum of the reaction product is shown in Figure 13.15. Although many of the ring protons overlap into a broad, poorly defined multiplet centered around 1.6 δ, the spectrum also shows a large singlet absorption in the saturated methyl region at 1.5 δ, indicating that the product has a methyl group bound to a quaternary carbon (R_3C—CH_3). Furthermore, the spectrum shows *no* absorptions in the range 4–5 δ, where we would expect the signal of a R_2CHCl proton to occur. Thus, it is clear that the reaction product is 1-chloro-1-methylcyclohexane.

FIGURE 13.15
The ^1H NMR spectrum of the reaction product from HCl and 1-methylcyclohexene

13.13 ^{13}C NMR SPECTROSCOPY

At first glance, it appears surprising that carbon NMR is even possible since ^{12}C, the most abundant carbon isotope, has no nuclear spin and is not observable by NMR. The only naturally occurring carbon isotope with a magnetic moment is ^{13}C, but its natural abundance is only 1.1%. Thus, only about 1 of every 100 carbon atoms in organic molecules is observable by NMR. This low natural abundance means that ^{13}C instrumentation must be far more sensitive than that required for ^{1}H NMR. Fortunately, though, the technical problems have been overcome through the use of improved electronics and computer techniques, and ^{13}C NMR has now become a routine structural tool.

At its simplest, ^{13}C NMR allows us to count the number of carbon atoms in a molecule. In addition, we can get information about the environment of each carbon by observing its chemical shift. As illustrated by the ^{13}C NMR spectrum of methyl acetate shown in Section 13.7 (Figure 13.9), we normally observe a single, sharp resonance line for each unique kind of carbon atom present in a molecule. Thus, methyl acetate has three nonequivalent carbon atoms and three peaks in its ^{13}C NMR spectrum. (Coupling between adjacent carbon atoms is not seen because the low natural abundance of ^{13}C makes it unlikely that two such nuclei would be next to each other in a molecule.)

Most ^{13}C resonances are between 0 and 250 δ, with the exact chemical shift dependent on a carbon's environment within the molecule. Figure 13.16 shows how environment and chemical shift may be correlated.

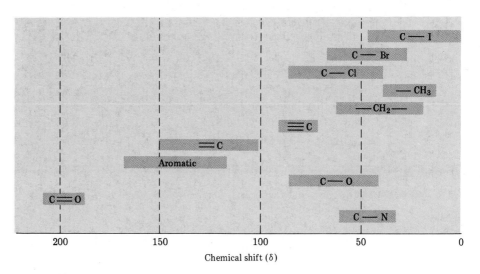

FIGURE 13.16
Chemical shift correlations for ^{13}C NMR

As a general rule, sp^{3}-hybridized carbons absorb in the range 0–100 δ, and sp^{2} carbons absorb in the range 100–200 δ. Carbonyl-group carbons are particularly distinct in the ^{13}C NMR spectrum and are easily observed at the extreme low-field (left) side of the chart in the range 170–210 δ. For example, the ^{13}C NMR spectrum of acetophenone (methyl phenyl ketone) in Figure 13.17 (page 402) shows the carbonyl carbon at 197 δ. In addition, the —CH$_3$ carbon absorbs at 26 δ, while the six carbons in the aromatic ring occur as four peaks in the range 128–137 δ. One of the ring carbons absorbs at 137 δ and one at 133 δ. The remaining four ring carbon atoms are accounted for by the two closely spaced peaks at 128.3 and 128.6 δ.

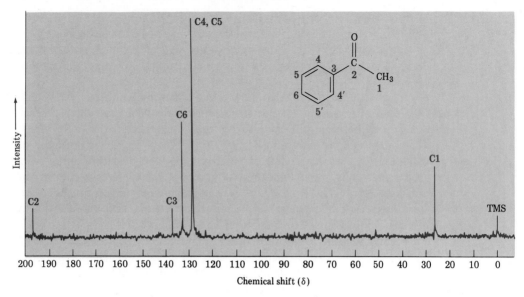

FIGURE 13.17
The ^{13}C NMR spectrum of acetophenone, $C_6H_5COCH_3$

The ^{13}C NMR spectrum of acetophenone is interesting because only six carbon absorptions are observed even though the molecule has eight carbons. This is because the molecule has a symmetry plane that makes ring carbons 4 and 4′ equivalent, and ring carbons 5 and 5′ equivalent. The presence of such symmetry planes in a molecule is easily detected by ^{13}C NMR.

PROBLEM 13.16   How many resonance lines would you expect to observe in the ^{13}C NMR spectra of these compounds?

(a) Cyclopentane   (b) Methylcyclopentane   (c) 1,3-Dimethylbenzene
(d) 1,2-Dimethylbenzene   (e) 1-Methylcyclohexene

PROBLEM 13.17   Propose structures for compounds whose ^{13}C NMR spectra fit these descriptions:

(a) A hydrocarbon with seven peaks in its spectrum
(b) A six-carbon compound with only five peaks in its spectrum
(c) A four-carbon compound with three peaks in its spectrum

ADDITIONAL PROBLEMS

PROBLEM 13.18   What kinds of functional groups might compounds contain if they show the following IR absorptions?

(a) 1670 cm^{-1} (b) 1735 cm^{-1} (c) 1540 cm^{-1}
(d) 1710 cm^{-1} and 2500–3100 cm^{-1} (broad)

PROBLEM 13.19 At what approximate positions might the following compounds show IR absorptions?

(a) Benzoic acid   (b) Methyl benzoate   (c) *p*-Hydroxybenzonitrile
(d) 3-Cyclohexenone   (e) Methyl 4-oxopentanoate

PROBLEM 13.20 The following ^1H NMR absorptions, determined on a spectrometer operating at 60 MHz, are given in hertz downfield from the TMS standard. Convert the absorptions to δ units.

(a) 131 Hz   (b) 287 Hz   (c) 451 Hz

PROBLEM 13.21 At what positions in hertz downfield from TMS standard would the NMR absorptions given in Problem 13.20 appear on a spectrometer operating at 100 MHz?

PROBLEM 13.22 These NMR absorptions, given in δ units, were obtained on a spectrometer operating at 80 MHz. Convert the chemical shifts from δ units into hertz downfield from TMS.

(a) 2.10 δ (b) 3.45 δ (c) 6.30 δ

PROBLEM 13.23 What is meant by each of these terms?

(a) Chemical shift   (b) Coupling constant
(c) λ_{max} (d) Spin–spin splitting
(e) Wave number   (f) Applied magnetic field (NMR)

PROBLEM 13.24 When measured on a spectrometer operating at 60 MHz, chloroform ($CHCl_3$) shows a single sharp absorption at 7.3 δ.

(a) How many parts per million downfield from TMS does chloroform absorb?
(b) How many hertz downfield from TMS would chloroform absorb if the measurement were carried out on a spectrometer operating at 360 MHz?
(c) What would the position of the chloroform absorption be in δ units if it were measured on a 360 MHz spectrometer?

PROBLEM 13.25 How many absorptions would you expect in the ^{13}C NMR spectra of these compounds?

(a) 1,1-Dimethylcyclohexane   (b) Ethyl methyl ether
(c) Cyclohexanone   (d) 2-Methyl-2-butene
(e) *cis*-2-Pentene   (f) *trans*-2-Pentene

PROBLEM 13.26 How many types of nonequivalent protons are there in each of the molecules listed in Problem 13.25?

PROBLEM 13.27 Describe the ^1H NMR spectra you would expect for these compounds:

(a) CH_3CHCl_2 (b) $CH_3COOCH_2CH_3$ (c) $(CH_3)_3CCH_2CH_3$

PROBLEM 13.28 Propose structures for compounds that meet these descriptions:

(a) C_5H_8, with IR absorptions at 3300 and 2150 cm^{-1}
(b) C_4H_8O, with a strong IR absorption at 3400 cm^{-1}
(c) C_4H_8O, with a strong IR absorption at 1715 cm^{-1}
(d) C_8H_{10}, with IR absorptions at 1600 and 1500 cm^{-1}

PROBLEM 13.29 How would you use infrared spectroscopy to distinguish between these pairs of isomers?

(a) $(CH_3)_3N$ and $CH_3CH_2NHCH_3$ (b) CH_3COCH_3 and $CH_2{=}CHCH_2OH$

(c) CH_3COCH_3 and CH_3CH_2CHO

PROBLEM 13.30 Assume that you are carrying out the dehydration of 1-methylcyclohexanol to yield 1-methylcyclohexene. How could you use IR spectroscopy to determine when the reaction was complete? What characteristic absorptions would you expect for both starting material and product?

PROBLEM 13.31 Dehydration of 1-methylcyclohexanol might lead to either of two isomeric alkenes, 1-methylcyclohexene or methylenecyclohexane. How could you use NMR spectroscopy (both ^1H and ^{13}C) to determine the structure of the product?

Methylenecyclohexane

PROBLEM 13.32 3,4-Dibromohexane can undergo base-induced double dehydrobromination to yield either 3-hexyne or 2,4-hexadiene. How could you use UV spectroscopy to help you identify the product? How could you use ^1H NMR spectroscopy?

PROBLEM 13.33 How would you use ^1H NMR spectroscopy to distinguish between the isomer pairs shown in Problem 13.29? List the most distinctive features you would expect in the NMR of each compound.

PROBLEM 13.34 Describe the ^1H and ^{13}C NMR spectra you would expect for these compounds:

(a) $ClCH_2CH_2CH_2Cl$ (b) $CH_3COCH_2CH_2Cl$

PROBLEM 13.35 Propose structures for compounds with the following formulas that show only one peak in their ^1H NMR spectra:

(a) C_5H_{12} (b) C_5H_{10} (c) $C_4H_8O_2$

PROBLEM 13.36 Propose structures for compounds that fit these ^1H NMR data:

(a) $C_5H_{10}O$
6 H doublet at 0.95 δ, J = 7 Hz
3 H singlet at 2.10 δ
1 H multiplet at 2.43 δ

(b) C_3H_5Br
3 H singlet at 2.32 δ
1 H singlet at 5.25 δ
1 H singlet at 5.54 δ

PROBLEM 13.37 We have seen four different spectroscopic techniques for structure determination— UV, IR, ^1H NMR, and ^{13}C NMR. How could you use each of the four to help you distinguish between the following pair of isomers?

3-Methyl-2-cyclohexenone   **4-Cyclopentenyl methyl ketone**

PROBLEM 13.38   The ^{1}H NMR spectrum of compound A, $C_3H_6Br_2$, is shown. Propose a plausible structure for A and explain how the peaks in the spectrum fit your structure.

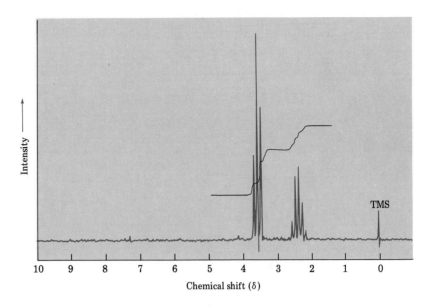

PROBLEM 13.39   The compound whose ^{1}H NMR spectrum is shown has the formula $C_4H_7O_2Cl$ and has an IR absorption peak at 1740 cm^{-1}. Propose a plausible structure.

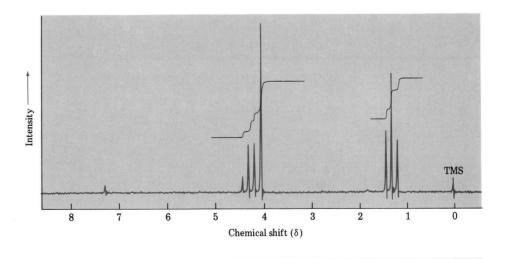

INTERLUDE Q
Colored Organic Compounds

Why are some organic compounds colored but others not? Why is β-carotene (from carrots) orange but benzene colorless? The answers to these questions involve both the structures of colored molecules and the way we perceive light.

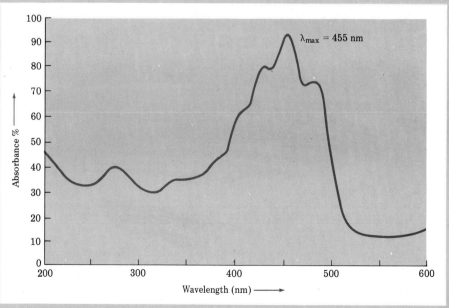

β-Carotene (orange pigment from carrots)

The visible region of the electromagnetic spectrum extends from approximately 400 to 800 nm. Colored compounds such as β-carotene have such extended systems of conjugation that their "UV" absorptions actually extend out into the visible region. β-Carotene's absorption, for example, occurs at $\lambda_{max} = 455$ nm (Figure Q.1).

FIGURE Q.1
Ultraviolet spectrum of β-carotene

Ordinary "white" light, from the sun or from a lamp, consists of all wavelengths in the visible region. When white light strikes β-carotene, the wavelengths from 400 to 500 nm (blue) are absorbed, while all other wavelengths reach our eyes. We therefore see the white light with the blue subtracted out, and we perceive a yellow-orange color for β-carotene. (The yellow-orange coloration accounts for the use of β-carotene as a coloring agent in margarine.)

What is true for β-carotene is true for all other colored organic compounds: All have an extended system of pi electron conjugation that gives rise to an absorption in the visible region of the electromagnetic spectrum.

CHAPTER 14

Biomolecules: Carbohydrates

Carbohydrates are everywhere in nature. They occur in every living organism and are essential to life. The sugar and starch in food, and the cellulose in wood, paper, and cotton are nearly pure carbohydrates. Modified carbohydrates form part of the coating around living cells; others are found in the DNA that carries genetic information; and still others, such as gentamicin, are invaluable as medicines.

The word **carbohydrate** derives historically from the fact that glucose, the first simple carbohydrate to be purified, has the molecular formula $C_6H_{12}O_6$ and was originally thought to be a "hydrate of carbon"—$C_6(H_2O)_6$. This view was soon abandoned, but the name persisted. Today, the term carbohydrate is used to refer loosely to the broad class of polyhydroxylated aldehydes and ketones commonly called *sugars*.

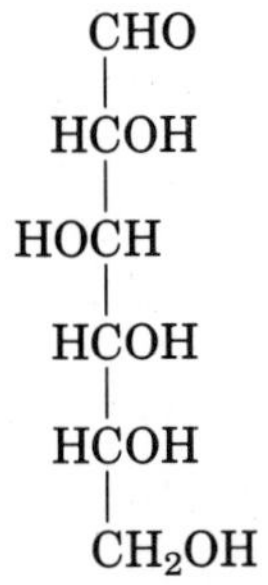

$$
\begin{array}{c}
\text{CHO} \\
| \\
\text{HCOH} \\
| \\
\text{HOCH} \\
| \\
\text{HCOH} \\
| \\
\text{HCOH} \\
| \\
\text{CH}_2\text{OH}
\end{array}
$$

Glucose (also called dextrose)
a pentahydroxyhexanal

Carbohydrates are synthesized by green plants during photosynthesis. They provide the major source of energy required by living organisms after they are eaten and then broken down by metabolic processes in the cells. Thus, carbohydrates act as the chemical intermediaries by which solar energy is stored and used to support life.

Photosynthesis is a complex process during which carbon dioxide is converted into glucose. Many molecules of glucose are then chemically linked for storage by the plant in the form of either cellulose or starch. It has been estimated that more than 50% of the dry weight of the earth's biomass—all plants and animals—consists of glucose polymers.

$$6 \ CO_2 \ + \ 6 \ H_2O \ \xrightarrow{\text{Sunlight}} \ 6 \ O_2 \ + \ \underset{\textbf{Glucose}}{C_6H_{12}O_6} \ \longrightarrow \ \text{Cellulose, starch}$$

When eaten, glucose can be metabolized in the body to provide energy, or it can be stored by the body in the form of glycogen for use at a later time. Since humans lack the enzymes needed for digestion of cellulose, they require starch as their dietary source of carbohydrates. Grazing animals such as cows, however, contain in their rumen microorganisms that are able to digest cellulose. The energy stored in cellulose can thus be moved up the biological food chain when these animals are used for food.

14.1 CLASSIFICATION OF CARBOHYDRATES

Carbohydrates are generally classed into two groups: simple and complex. **Simple sugars** or **monosaccharides** are carbohydrates that cannot be hydrolyzed into smaller molecules. Glucose and fructose are examples. **Complex carbohydrates** or **polysaccharides** are compounds that are made of two or more simple sugars linked together. On hydrolysis, complex carbohydrates can be cleaved to yield simple sugars. For example, sucrose (table sugar) is a disaccharide made up of one glucose molecule linked to one fructose molecule; cellulose is a polysaccharide made up of several thousand glucose molecules linked together.

$$1 \ \text{Sucrose} \ \xrightarrow{H_3O^+} \ 1 \ \text{Glucose} \ + \ 1 \ \text{Fructose}$$
$$\text{Cellulose} \ \xrightarrow{H_3O^+} \ {\sim}3000 \ \text{Glucose}$$

Monosaccharides can be further classified as either **aldoses** or **ketoses**. The *-ose* suffix is used to designate a carbohydrate, and the *ald-* and *ket-* prefixes designate the nature of the carbonyl group (aldehyde or ketone). The number of carbon atoms in the monosaccharide is given by using *tri-*, *tetr-*, *pent-*, *hex-*, and so forth as the parent name. By combining prefix, parent, and suffix, a simple sugar is fully classified. For example, glucose is an aldohexose, a six-carbon aldehydic sugar; fructose is a ketohexose, a six-carbon keto sugar; and ribose is an aldopentose, a five-carbon aldehydic sugar. Most of the commonly occurring sugars are either aldopentoses or aldohexoses.

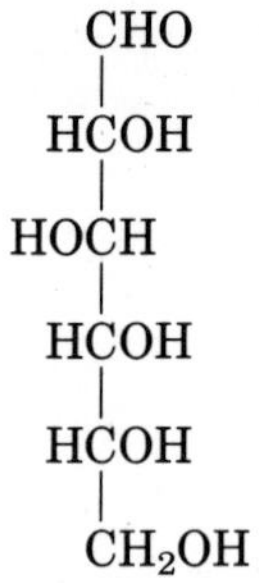

CHO   CH₂OH   CHO

$$
\begin{array}{ccc}
\text{CHO} & \text{CH}_2\text{OH} & \text{CHO}\\
\text{HCOH} & \text{C=O} & \text{HCOH}\\
\text{HOCH} & \text{HOCH} & \text{HCOH}\\
\text{HCOH} & \text{HCOH} & \text{HCOH}\\
\text{HCOH} & \text{HCOH} & \text{CH}_2\text{OH}\\
\text{CH}_2\text{OH} & \text{CH}_2\text{OH} &
\end{array}
$$

Glucose
(an aldohexose) 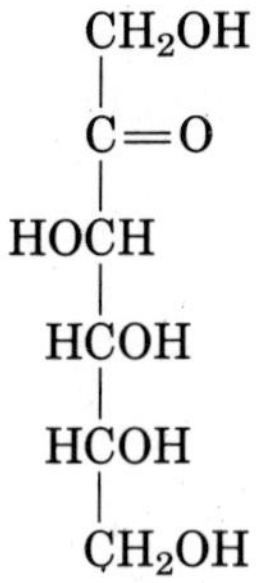   **Fructose**
(a ketohexose) 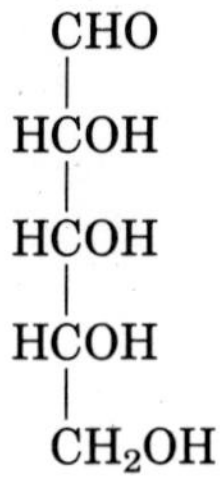   **Ribose**
(an aldopentose)

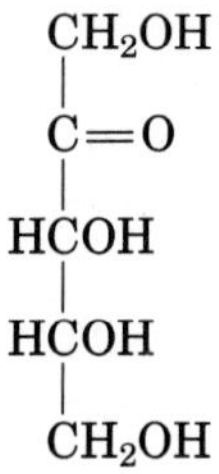

PROBLEM 14.1   Classify each of the following monosaccharides:

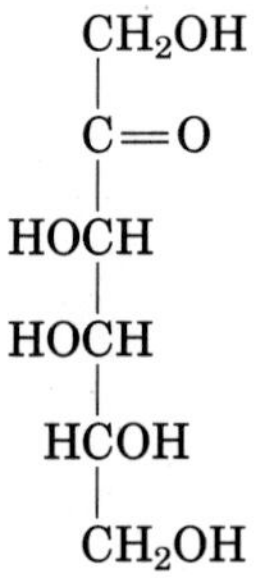

(a)
$$
\begin{array}{c}
\text{CHO}\\
\text{HOCH}\\
\text{HCOH}\\
\text{CH}_2\text{OH}
\end{array}
$$

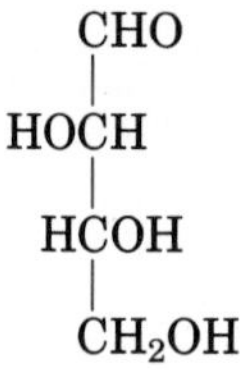

(b)
$$
\begin{array}{c}
\text{CH}_2\text{OH}\\
\text{C=O}\\
\text{HCOH}\\
\text{HCOH}\\
\text{CH}_2\text{OH}
\end{array}
$$

(c)
$$
\begin{array}{c}
\text{CH}_2\text{OH}\\
\text{C=O}\\
\text{HOCH}\\
\text{HOCH}\\
\text{HCOH}\\
\text{CH}_2\text{OH}
\end{array}
$$

(d) 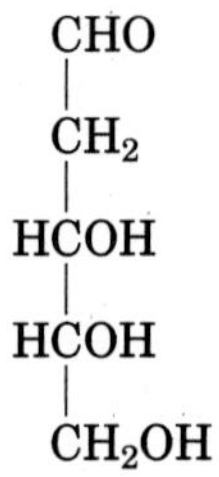
$$
\begin{array}{c}
\text{CHO}\\
\text{CH}_2\\
\text{HCOH}\\
\text{HCOH}\\
\text{CH}_2\text{OH}
\end{array}
$$

Threose   **Ribulose**   **Tagatose**   **2-Deoxyribose**

14.2   CONFIGURATION OF MONOSACCHARIDES: FISCHER PROJECTIONS

Since all carbohydrates have chiral carbon atoms, it was recognized long ago that a standard method of representation was needed to designate carbohydrate stereochemistry. In 1891, Emil Fischer suggested a convention based on the projection of a tetrahedral carbon atom onto a flat surface. These **Fischer projections** were soon adopted and are now a standard means of depicting stereochemistry at chiral centers.

A tetrahedral carbon atom in a Fischer projection is represented by two perpendicular lines. The horizontal lines represent bonds coming out of the page, while the vertical lines represent bonds going into the page. By convention, the carbonyl carbon is placed at or near the top in Fischer projections. Thus, (R)-glyceraldehyde, the simplest monosaccharide, can be represented in the following way:

$$\begin{array}{ccc}
\text{CHO} & {}^{1}\text{CHO} & \text{CHO} \\
\text{H}\!-\!\overset{}{\text{C}}\!-\!\text{OH} \equiv & \overset{2}{\text{H}}\!-\!\text{C}\!-\!\text{OH} \equiv & \text{H}\!-\!\!-\!\text{OH} \\
\text{CH}_2\text{OH} & {}^{3}\text{CH}_2\text{OH} & \text{CH}_2\text{OH}
\end{array}$$

Fischer projection

Carbohydrates with more than one chiral center are depicted simply by "stacking" the atoms, one on top of the other. Again, however, we must obey the convention that the carbonyl carbon is at or near the top of the Fischer projection. Molecular models are particularly helpful in visualizing these structures.

$$\begin{array}{cccc}
\text{CHO} & \text{CHO} & \text{CH}_2\text{OH} & \text{CH}_2\text{OH} \\
\text{H}\!-\!\text{C}\!-\!\text{OH} & \text{H}\!-\!\text{OH} & \text{C}\!=\!\text{O} & =\text{O} \\
\text{HO}\!-\!\text{C}\!-\!\text{H} & \text{HO}\!-\!\text{H} & \text{HO}\!-\!\text{C}\!-\!\text{H} & \text{HO}\!-\!\text{H} \\
\text{H}\!-\!\text{C}\!-\!\text{OH} & \text{H}\!-\!\text{OH} & \text{H}\!-\!\text{C}\!-\!\text{OH} & \text{H}\!-\!\text{OH} \\
\text{H}\!-\!\text{C}\!-\!\text{OH} & \text{H}\!-\!\text{OH} & \text{H}\!-\!\text{C}\!-\!\text{OH} & \text{H}\!-\!\text{OH} \\
\text{CH}_2\text{OH} & \text{CH}_2\text{OH} & \text{CH}_2\text{OH} & \text{CH}_2\text{OH}
\end{array}$$

Glucose (carbonyl group at top)   **Fructose (carbonyl group near top)**

14.3 D,L SUGARS

Glyceraldehyde has one chiral carbon atom and therefore has two enantiomeric (mirror-image) forms, but most naturally occurring glyceraldehyde is dextrorotatory (Section 6.3). A sample of naturally occurring glyceraldehyde placed in a polarimeter will rotate plane-polarized light in a clockwise direction, which we denote (+). Since (+)-glyceraldehyde is known to have the R configuration at C_2, we can represent it as shown in Figure 14.1 on page 412.

For historical reasons dating back long before the adoption of the R,S system, (R)-(+)-glyceraldehyde is also referred to as D-glyceraldehyde (D from dextrorotatory). The (S)-(−)-glyceraldehyde enantiomer is known as L-glyceraldehyde (L from levorotatory). It turns out that glucose, fructose, ribose, and most other naturally occurring monosaccharides have the same stereochemical configuration as D-glyceraldehyde at the chiral carbon atom farthest from the carbonyl group. In Fischer projections, therefore, most naturally occurring sugars have the hydroxyl group at the lowest chiral carbon atom pointing to the *right* (Figure 14.1).

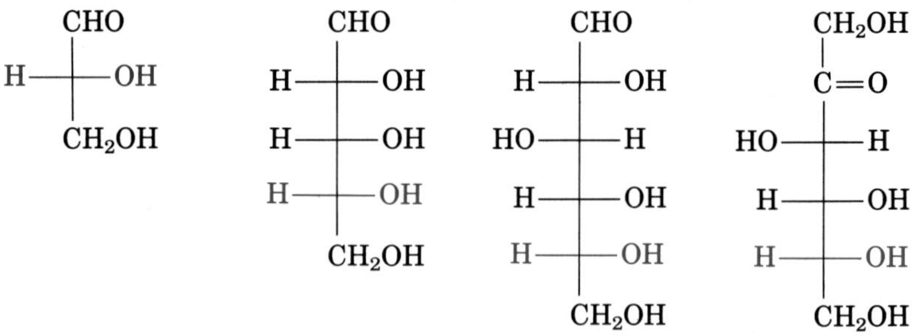

$$
\begin{array}{cccc}
\text{CHO} & \text{CHO} & \text{CHO} & \text{CH}_2\text{OH} \\
\text{H}-\!\!\!-\text{OH} & \text{H}-\!\!\!-\text{OH} & \text{H}-\!\!\!-\text{OH} & \text{C}=\!\!\text{O} \\
\text{CH}_2\text{OH} & \text{H}-\!\!\!-\text{OH} & \text{HO}-\!\!\!-\text{H} & \text{HO}-\!\!\!-\text{H} \\
 & \text{H}-\!\!\!-\text{OH} & \text{H}-\!\!\!-\text{OH} & \text{H}-\!\!\!-\text{OH} \\
 & \text{CH}_2\text{OH} & \text{H}-\!\!\!-\text{OH} & \text{H}-\!\!\!-\text{OH} \\
 & & \text{CH}_2\text{OH} & \text{CH}_2\text{OH}
\end{array}
$$

D-Glyceraldehyde,   D-Ribose   D-Glucose   D-Fructose
(R)-(+)-glyceraldehyde

FIGURE 14.1
Some naturally occurring D sugars: The hydroxyl at the lowest chiral center is on the right in Fischer projections.

Those sugars that have the same configuration as D-glyceraldehyde at their chiral centers farthest from the carbonyl group are called D **sugars**. In contrast to the D sugars, all L **sugars** have the hydroxyl group at the chiral center farthest from the carbonyl group on the *left* in Fischer projections. Thus, L sugars are mirror images (enantiomers) of D sugars. The D,L system of carbohydrate nomenclature is of limited use, since it describes the configuration at only one chiral center and says nothing about other chiral centers that may be present.

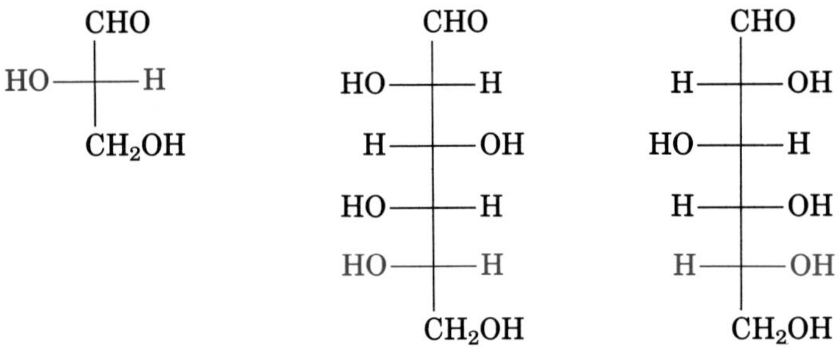

$$
\begin{array}{ccc}
\text{CHO} & \text{CHO} & \text{CHO} \\
\text{HO}-\!\!\!-\text{H} & \text{HO}-\!\!\!-\text{H} & \text{H}-\!\!\!-\text{OH} \\
\text{CH}_2\text{OH} & \text{H}-\!\!\!-\text{OH} & \text{HO}-\!\!\!-\text{H} \\
 & \text{HO}-\!\!\!-\text{H} & \text{H}-\!\!\!-\text{OH} \\
 & \text{HO}-\!\!\!-\text{H} & \text{H}-\!\!\!-\text{OH} \\
 & \text{CH}_2\text{OH} & \text{CH}_2\text{OH}
\end{array}
$$

L-Glyceraldehyde,   L-Glucose   D-Glucose
(S)-(+)-glyceraldehyde   (not naturally occurring)

PRACTICE PROBLEM   Draw a Fischer projection of L-fructose.

Solution   Since L-fructose is the enantiomer (mirror image) of D-fructose, we simply look at the structure of D-fructose and then reverse the configuration at each chiral center.

Mirror
CH2OH
=O
HO—H
H—OH
H—OH
CH2OH
CH2OH
=O
H—OH
HO—H
HO—OH
CH2OH

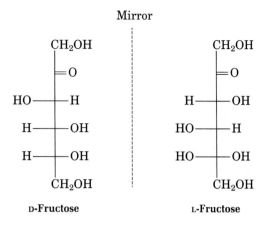

D-Fructose L-Fructose

PROBLEM 14.2 Tell which of the following are L sugars and which are D sugars.

(a)

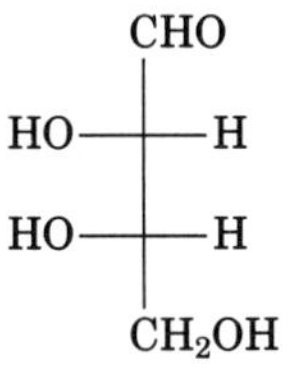

CHO
HO—H
HO—H
CH2OH

(b)

CHO
H—OH
HO—H
H—OH
CH2OH

(c)

CH2OH
C=O
HO—H
H—OH
CH2OH

PROBLEM 14.3 Draw the enantiomers (mirror images) of the carbohydrates shown in Problem 14.2 and identify each as D or L.

14.4 CONFIGURATIONS OF ALDOSES

Aldotetroses are four-carbon sugars with two chiral centers. Thus, there are $2^2 = 4$ possible stereoisomeric aldotetroses, or two D,L pairs of enantiomers. These enantiomeric pairs are called *erythrose* and *threose*.

Aldopentoses have three chiral centers, leading to a total of $2^3 = 8$ stereoisomers, or four D,L pairs of enantiomers. These four pairs are called *ribose*, *arabinose*, *xylose*, and *lyxose*. All except for lyxose occur widely in nature. D-Ribose is an important part of RNA (ribonucleic acid); L-arabinose is found in many plants; and D-xylose is found in wood.

Aldohexoses have four chiral centers, for a total of $2^4 = 16$ stereoisomers, or eight D,L pairs of enantiomers. The names of these eight are *allose*, *altrose*, *glucose*, *mannose*, *gulose*, *idose*, *galactose*, and *talose*. Of the eight, only D-glucose, from starch and cellulose, and D-galactose, from gums and fruit pectins, are found widely distributed in nature. D-Mannose and D-talose also occur naturally, but in lesser abundance.

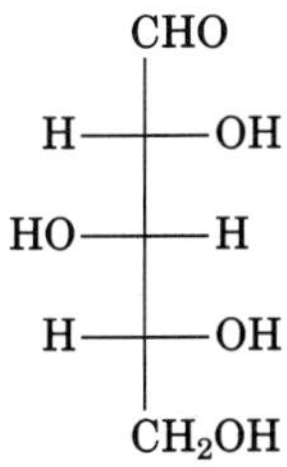

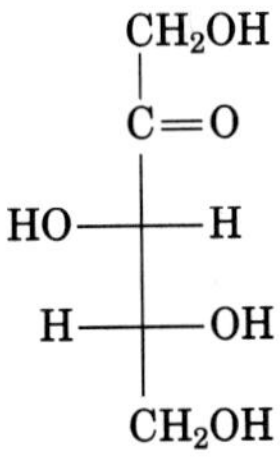

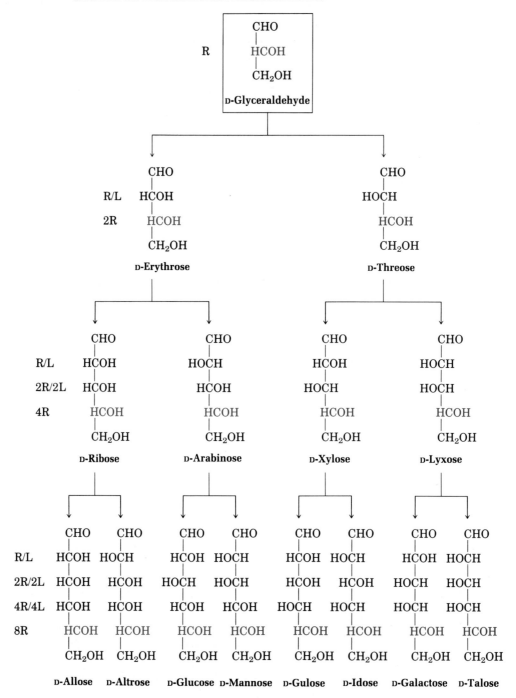

FIGURE 14.2

Configurations of D-aldoses: The structures are arranged in order from left to right so that the hydroxyl groups on C2 alternate right/left (R/L) in going across a series; the hydroxyl groups at C3 alternate two right/two left (2R/2L); the hydroxyl groups at C4 alternate four right/four left (4R/4L); and the hydroxyl groups at C5 are to the right in all eight (8R).

Fischer projections of the four-, five-, and six-carbon aldoses can be constructed as shown in Figure 14.2 for the D series. Starting from D-glyceraldehyde, we can construct the two D-aldotetroses by inserting a new chiral carbon atom just below the aldehyde carbon. Each of the two D-aldotetroses can then lead to two D-aldopentoses (four total), and each of the four D-aldopentoses can lead to two D-aldohexoses (eight total).

PROBLEM 14.4   Only the D sugars are shown in Figure 14.2 Write Fischer projections for the following L sugars. Remember that an L sugar is the mirror image of the corresponding D sugar.

(a)   L-Ribose   (b)   L-Threose   (c)   L-Galactose

PROBLEM 14.5   How many aldoheptoses are possible? How many of them are D sugars and how many are L sugars?

PROBLEM 14.6   Draw Fischer projections for the two D-aldoheptoses (Problem 14.5) whose stereochemistry at C3, C4, C5, and C6 is the same as that of glucose at C2, C3, C4, and C5.

14.5   CYCLIC STRUCTURES OF MONOSACCHARIDES: HEMIACETAL FORMATION

We said during our discussion of carbonyl-group chemistry (Section 9.12) that alcohols undergo a rapid and reversible nucleophilic addition reaction with ketones and aldehydes to form hemiacetals:

$$R{-}O{-}H + R'{-}\overset{\displaystyle O}{\overset{\displaystyle \|}{C}}{-}H \;\underset{}{\overset{H^+}{\rightleftharpoons}}\; RO{-}\overset{\displaystyle OH}{\underset{\underset{R'\quad H}{}}{C}}$$

A hemiacetal

If both the hydroxyl and the carbonyl group are in the same molecule, an *intramolecular* nucleophilic addition can take place, leading to the formation of a *cyclic* hemiacetal. Five- and six-membered cyclic hemiacetals form particularly easily, and many carbohydrates therefore exist in an equilibrium between open-chain and cyclic forms. For example, glucose exists in aqueous solution primarily as the six-membered **pyranose** ring formed by intramolecular nucleophilic addition of the hydroxyl group at C5 to the C1 aldehyde group. Fructose, on the other hand, exists to the extent of about 20% as the five-membered ring **furanose** formed by addition of the hydroxyl group at C5 to the C2 ketone. The words *pyranose*, for a six-membered ring, and *furanose*, for a five-membered ring, are derived from the names of the simple cyclic ethers pyran and furan. The cyclic forms of glucose and fructose are shown in Figure 14.3 on page 416.

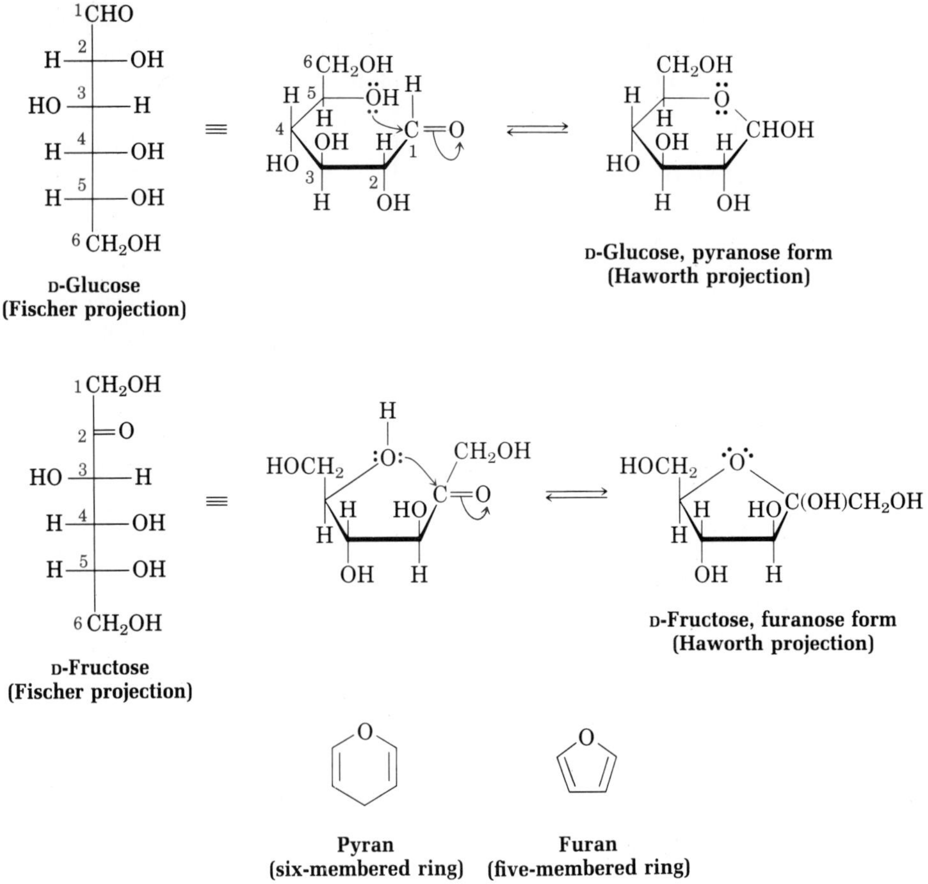

D-Glucose
(Fischer projection)

D-Glucose, pyranose form
(Haworth projection)

D-Fructose
(Fischer projection)

D-Fructose, furanose form
(Haworth projection)

Pyran
(six-membered ring)

Furan
(five-membered ring)

FIGURE 14.3
Glucose and fructose in their cyclic pyranose and furanose forms

Carbohydrate chemists often represent pyranose and furanose forms by using **Haworth projections,** as shown in Figure 14.3, rather than Fischer projections. In a Haworth projection, the hemiacetal ring is drawn as if it were flat and is viewed edge-on, with the oxygen atom at the upper right. This view is not really accurate, since pyranose rings are actually chair-shaped like cyclohexane (Section 2.13), rather than flat. Nevertheless, Haworth projections are widely used because they allow us to see at a glance the cis–trans relationships among hydroxyl groups on the ring.

When converting from one kind of projection to the other, remember that a hydroxyl on the *right* in a Fischer projection is *down* in a Haworth projection. Conversely, a hydroxyl on the *left* in a Fischer projection is *up* in a Haworth projection. For D sugars, the terminal CH_2OH group is always up, whereas for L sugars, the CH_2OH group is down. Figure 14.4 illustrates the conversion for glucose.

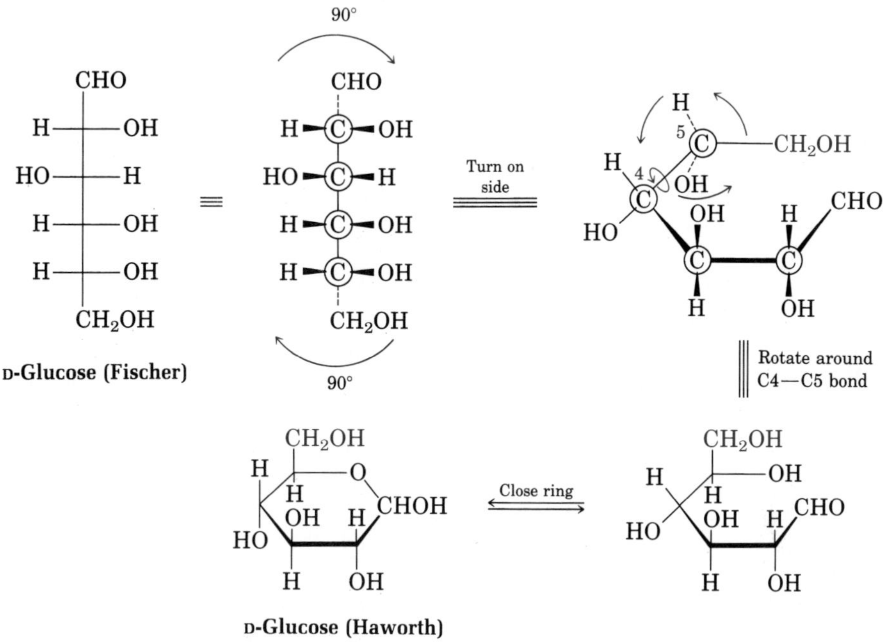

FIGURE 14.4
Interconversion of Fischer and Haworth projections of D-glucose

---

PRACTICE PROBLEM D-Mannose differs from D-glucose in its stereochemistry at C2. Draw a Haworth projection of D-mannose in its pyranose form.

Solution First draw a Fischer projection of D-mannose. Then lay it on its side, and curl it around so that the aldehyde group (C1) is toward the front and the CH₂OH (C6) is toward the rear. Now connect the hydroxyl at C5 to the C1 carbonyl group to form a pyranose ring.

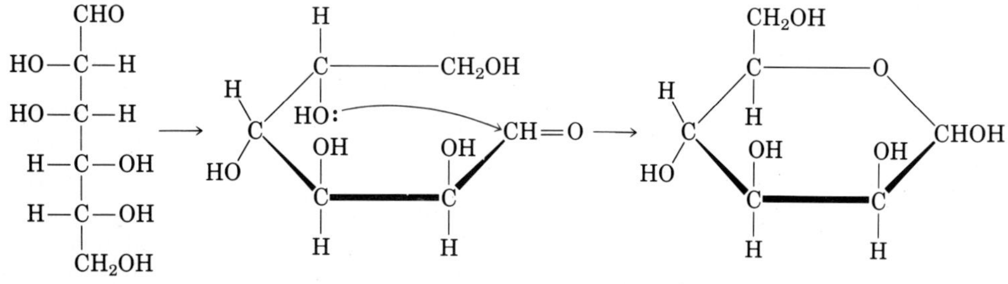

PROBLEM 14.7 D-Galactose differs from D-glucose in its stereochemistry at C4. Draw a Haworth projection of D-galactose in its pyranose form.

PROBLEM 14.8   Ribose exists largely in a furanose form produced by nucleophilic addition of the C4 hydroxyl group to the C1 aldehyde. Draw a Haworth projection of D-ribose in its furanose form.

14.6   MONOSACCHARIDE ANOMERS: MUTAROTATION

When an open-chain monosaccharide cyclizes to a furanose or pyranose form, a new chiral center is formed at what used to be the carbonyl carbon. Two diastereomers, called **anomers** are produced; the hemiacetal carbon is referred to as the **anomeric center**. For example, glucose cyclizes reversibly in aqueous solution to yield a 36:64 mixture of two anomers. The minor anomer, with the C1 hydroxyl group trans to the CH$_2$OH substituent at C5 (and therefore down in a Haworth projection), is called the **alpha anomer**; its complete name is α-D-glucopyranose. The major anomer, with the C1 hydroxyl cis to the CH$_2$OH substituent at C5 (and therefore up in a Haworth projection), is called the **beta anomer**; its complete name is β-D-glucopyranose.

D-Glucose

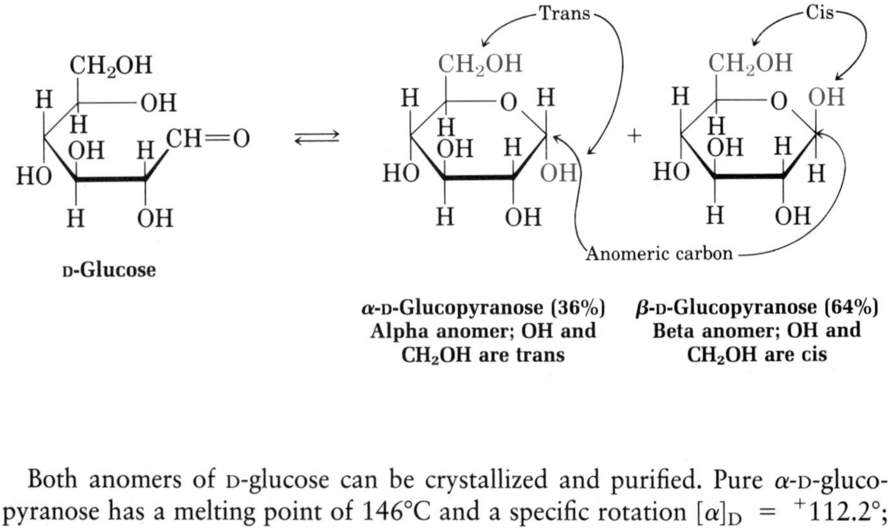

α-D-Glucopyranose (36%)
Alpha anomer; OH and
CH$_2$OH are trans

β-D-Glucopyranose (64%)
Beta anomer; OH and
CH$_2$OH are cis

Both anomers of D-glucose can be crystallized and purified. Pure α-D-glucopyranose has a melting point of 146°C and a specific rotation $[\alpha]_D$ = $^+$112.2°; pure β-D-glucopyranose has a melting point of 148–155°C and a specific rotation of +18.7°. When a sample of either pure alpha anomer or pure beta anomer is dissolved in water, however, the optical rotations slowly change and ultimately converge to a constant value of +52.6°. The specific rotation of the alpha anomer solution decreases from +112.2° to +52.6°, and the specific rotation of the beta anomer solution increases from +18.7° to +52.6°. This phenomenon, known as **mutarotation**, is due to the slow conversion of the pure alpha and beta enantiomers into the 36:64 equilibrium mixture. The equilibration occurs by a reversible ring opening of each anomer to the open-chain aldehyde, followed by reclosure. Although equilibration is slow at neutral pH, it is catalyzed by either acid or base.

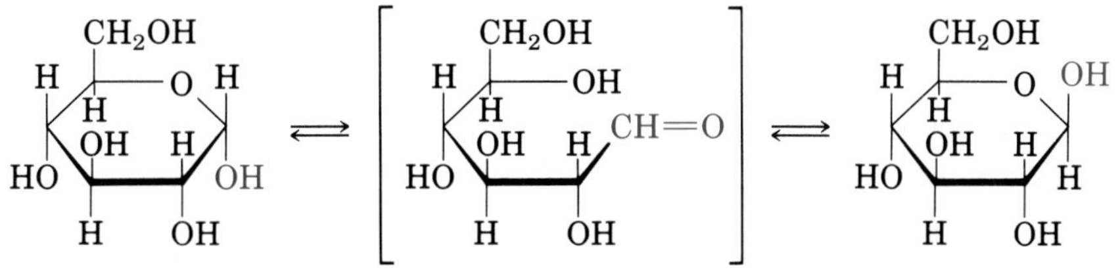

α-D-Glucopyranose (36%)
$[\alpha]_D = +112.2°$

β-D-Glucopyranose (64%)
$[\alpha]_D = +18.7°$

PROBLEM 14.9 If the specific rotation of pure α-D-glucopyranose is $+112.2°$ and the specific rotation of pure β-D-glucopyranose is $+18.7°$, show how the equilibrium percentages of alpha and beta anomers can be calculated from the equilibrium specific rotation of $+52.6°$.

PROBLEM 14.10 Many other sugars besides glucose exhibit mutarotation. For example, α-D-galactopyranose has $[\alpha]_D = +150.7°$ and β-D-galactopyranose has $[\alpha]_D = +52.8°$. If either anomer is dissolved in water and allowed to reach equilibrium, the specific rotation of the solution is $+80.2°$. What are the percentages of each anomer at equilibrium?

14.7 CONFORMATIONS OF MONOSACCHARIDES

Although Haworth projections are relatively easy to draw, they do not give an accurate three-dimensional picture of molecular conformation. Pyranose rings, like cyclohexane rings (Section 2.13), have a chairlike geometry with axial and equatorial substituents. Any substituent that is up in a Haworth projection is also up in a chair conformation, and any substituent that is down in a Haworth projection is also down in the chair formulation. Haworth projections can be converted into chair representations by following three steps:

1. Draw the Haworth projection with the ring oxygen atom at the upper right.
2. Raise the leftmost carbon atom (C4) *above* the ring plane.
3. Lower the anomeric carbon atom (C1) *below* the ring plane.

Figure 14.5 (page 420) shows how this is done for α-D-glucopyranose and β-D-glucopyranose. You should make molecular models to see the process more clearly.

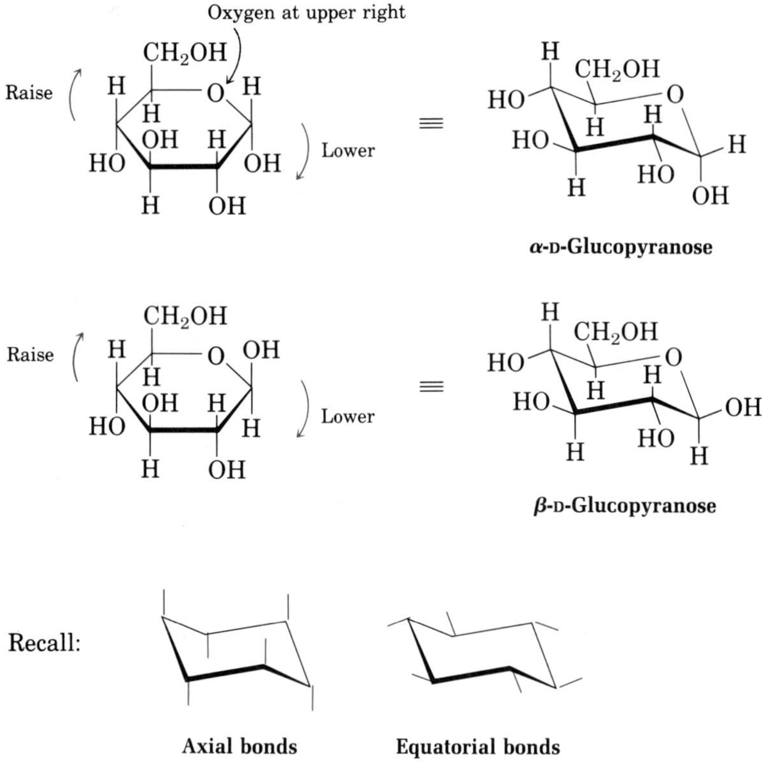

α-D-Glucopyranose

β-D-Glucopyranose

Recall:

Axial bonds   **Equatorial bonds**

FIGURE 14.5
Chair representations of α-D-glucopyranose and β-D-glucopyranose

Note that in β-D-glucopyranose, all the substituents on the ring are equatorial. Thus, β-D-glucopyranose is the least sterically crowded, most stable of the eight D-aldohexoses.

PROBLEM 14.11 Draw β-D-galactopyranose in its chair conformation. Label all the ring substituents as either axial or equatorial.

PROBLEM 14.12 Draw β-D-mannopyranose in its chair conformation and label all substituents as either axial or equatorial. Which would you expect to be more stable, mannose or galactose (Problem 14.11)?

14.8 REACTIONS OF MONOSACCHARIDES

Monosaccharides contain only two kinds of functional groups—aldehyde carbonyls and hydroxyls. Not surprisingly, therefore, most of the chemistry of monosaccharides is the familiar chemistry of these two groups.

Ester and Ether Formation

Monosaccharides behave as simple alcohols in much of their chemistry. For example, carbohydrate hydroxyl groups can be converted into esters and ethers.

Esterification is normally carried out by treating the carbohydrate with an acid chloride or acid anhydride in the presence of a base. *All* the hydroxyl groups react, including the anomeric one. For example, β-D-glucopyranose is converted into its pentaacetate by treatment with acetic anhydride in pyridine solution.

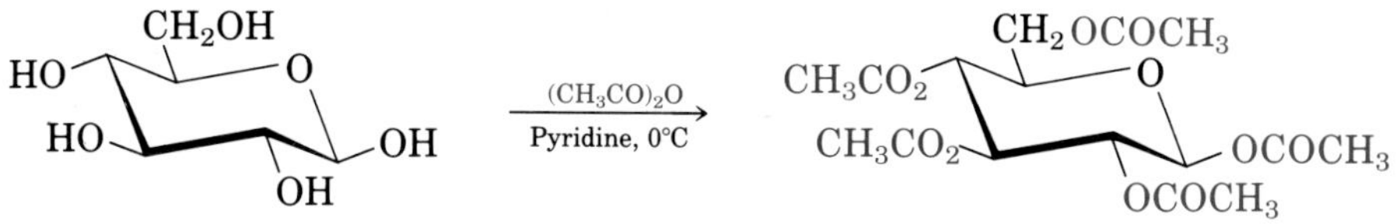

β-D-Glucopyranose $\xrightarrow[\text{Pyridine, 0°C}]{(CH_3CO)_2O}$ **Penta-*O*-acetyl-β-D-glucopyranose (91%)**

Carbohydrates can be converted into ethers by treatment with an alkyl halide in the presence of base—the Williamson ether synthesis (Section 8.6). Silver oxide is a particularly mild and useful base for this reaction, since hydroxide and alkoxide bases tend to degrade the sensitive sugar molecules. For example, α-D-glucopyranose is converted into its pentamethyl ether in 85% yield on reaction with iodomethane and silver oxide.

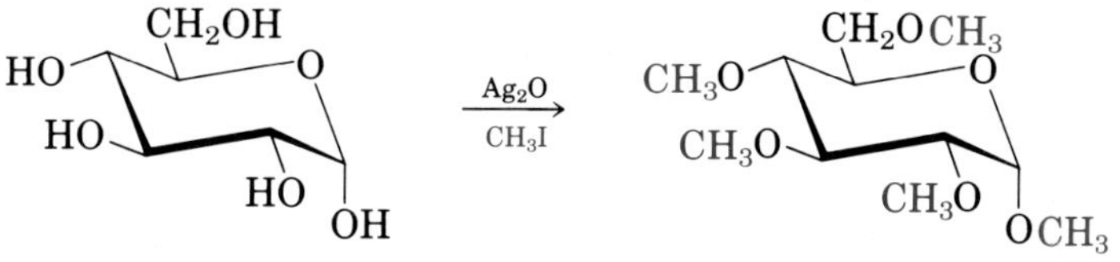

α-D-Glucopyranose $\xrightarrow[\text{CH}_3\text{I}]{\text{Ag}_2\text{O}}$ **α-D-Glucopyranose pentamethyl ether (85%)**

Ester and ether derivatives of carbohydrates are often prepared because they are easier to work with than the free sugars. Because of their many hydroxyl groups, monosaccharides are usually soluble in water but insoluble in organic solvents such as ether. Monosaccharides are also quite difficult to crystallize, since they have a tendency to form syrups when water is removed. Ester and ether derivatives, however, behave like most other organic compounds in that they are soluble in organic solvents and are easily crystallized.

Glycoside Formation

We saw in Section 9.12 that treatment of a hemiacetal with an alcohol and an acid catalyst yields an acetal:

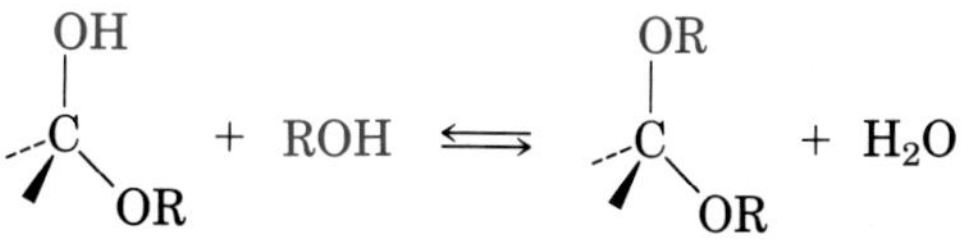

A hemiacetal   + ROH ⇌   **An acetal**   + H_2O

In the same way, treatment of a monosaccharide hemiacetal with an alcohol and an acid catalyst yields an acetal in which the anomeric hydroxyl group has been replaced by an alkoxy group. For example, reaction of glucose with methanol gives methyl β-D-glucopyranoside:

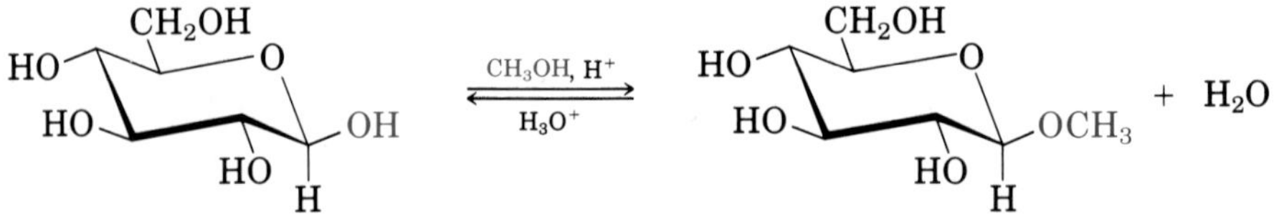

β-D-Glucopyranose
(a hemiacetal)

Methyl β-D-Glucopyranoside
(an acetal)

These carbohydrate acetals are called **glycosides**. They are named by first citing the alkyl group and then adding the -*oside* suffix to the name of the specific sugar. Note that glycosides, like all acetals, are stable to water. They are not in equilibrium with an open-chain form and they do not show mutarotation. They can, however, be converted back to the free monosaccharide by hydrolysis with aqueous acid.

Glycosides are widespread in nature, and a great many biologically active molecules contain glycosidic linkages. For example, digitoxin, the active component of the digitalis preparations used for treatment of heart disease, is a glycoside consisting of a complex steroid alcohol linked to a trisaccharide (Figure 14.6). Note that the three sugars are also linked to each other by glycoside bonds.

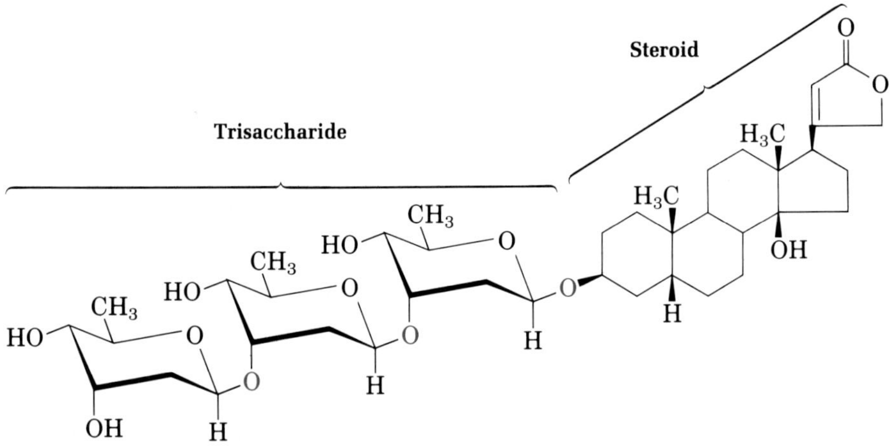

FIGURE 14.6
The structure of digitoxin, a complex glycoside

PROBLEM 14.13   Draw the product you would expect to obtain from acid-catalyzed reaction of β-D-galactopyranose with ethanol.

Reduction of Monosaccharides

The carbonyl groups of monosaccharides undergo many reactions characteristic of simpler aldehydes and ketones. For example, treatment of an aldose or ketose with sodium borohydride reduces it to a polyalcohol called an **alditol**. The reaction occurs by interception of the open-chain form present in the aldehyde $\rightleftarrows$ hemiacetal equilibrium.

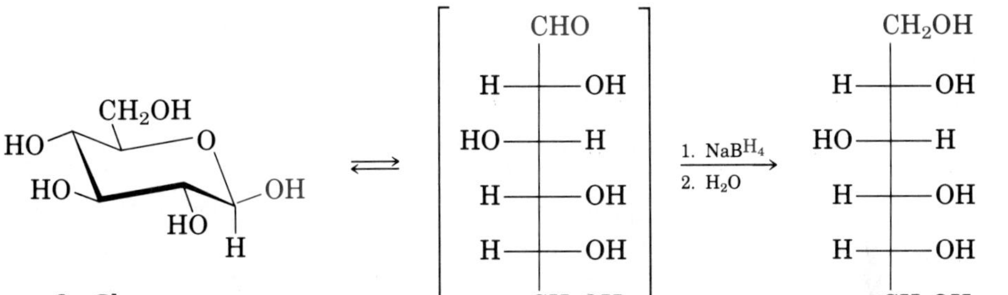

β-D-Glucopyranose   D-Glucose   D-Glucitol (D-sorbitol), an alditol

D-Glucitol, the alditol produced on reduction of D-glucose, is itself a natural product that has been isolated from many fruits and berries. It is used under the name D-sorbitol as a sweetener and sugar substitute in many foods.

PRACTICE PROBLEM Show the structure of the alditol you would obtain from reduction of D-galactose.

Solution First draw D-galactose in its open-chain form and then convert the —CHO group at C1 into a —CH$_2$OH group.

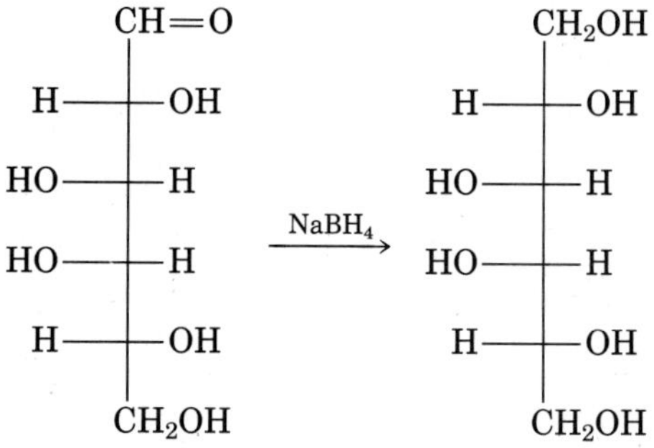

D-Galactose   Galactitol

PROBLEM 14.14   How can you account for the fact that reduction of D-glucose leads to an optically active alditol (D-glucitol), whereas reduction of D-galactose leads to an optically inactive alditol?

PROBLEM 14.15   Reduction of L-gulose with NaBH₄ leads to the same alditol (D-glucitol) as reduction of D-glucose. Explain this result.

Oxidation of Monosaccharides

Like other aldehydes, aldoses are easily oxidized to yield carboxylic acids. Aldoses react with Tollens' reagent (Ag^+ in aqueous ammonia), Fehling's reagent (Cu^{2+} with aqueous sodium tartrate), and Benedict's reagent (Cu^{2+} with aqueous sodium citrate) to yield the oxidized sugar and the reduced metallic species. All three reactions serve as simple chemical tests for what are called **reducing sugars** (*reducing* because the sugar reduces the oxidizing agent).

If Tollens' reagent is used, metallic silver is produced as a shiny mirror on the walls of the reaction flask or test tube. If Fehling's or Benedict's reagent is used, a reddish precipitate of cuprous oxide signals a positive result. The diabetes self-test kits sold in drugstores for home use employ the Benedict's test. As little as 0.1% glucose in urine gives a positive test.

All aldoses are reducing sugars since they contain aldehyde carbonyl groups, but glycosides are nonreducing. Glycosides do not react with Tollens' or Fehling's reagents because the acetal group cannot open to an aldehyde under basic conditions.

For preparative purposes, it has been found that a buffered solution of aqueous bromine oxidizes aldoses in the highest yields. The monocarboxylic acid products are called **aldonic acids**.

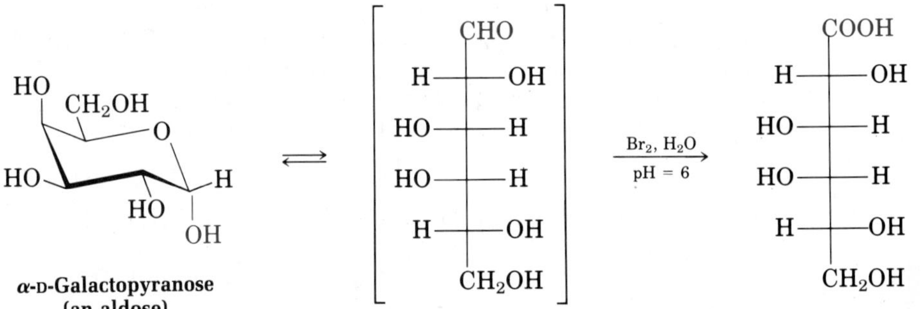

α-D-Galactopyranose (an aldose) ⇌ [CHO, H—OH, HO—H, HO—H, H—OH, CH₂OH] →(Br₂, H₂O, pH = 6)→ COOH, H—OH, HO—H, HO—H, H—OH, CH₂OH D-Galactonic acid (an aldonic acid)

If a more powerful oxidizing agent such as warm dilute nitric acid is used, aldoses are oxidized to dicarboxylic acids, called **aldaric acids**. Both the aldehyde carbonyl and the terminal —CH₂OH group are oxidized in this reaction.

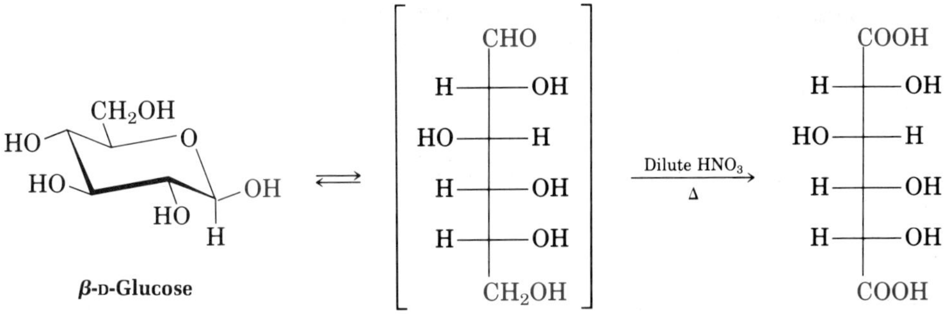

β-D-Glucose   D-Glucaric acid (an aldaric acid)

PROBLEM 14.16   D-Glucose yields an optically active aldaric acid on treatment with nitric acid, but D-allose yields an optically inactive aldaric acid. Explain this result.

PROBLEM 14.17   Which of the other six D-aldohexoses yield optically active aldaric acids, and which yield optically inactive aldaric acids? (See Problem 14.16.)

14.9 DISACCHARIDES

We saw in the previous section that reaction of a monosaccharide hemiacetal yields a glycoside in which the anomeric hydroxyl group is replaced by an alkoxyl substituent. If the alcohol is another sugar, however, the glycoside product is a **disaccharide**.

Cellobiose and Maltose

Disaccharides can contain a glycosidic acetal bond between C1 of one sugar and a hydroxyl group at *any* position on the other sugar. A glycosidic link between C1 of the first sugar and C4 of the second sugar is particularly common but is by no means required. Such a bond is called a **1,4′ link** (read as "one, four-prime"). (The prime superscript indicates that the 4′ position is on a different sugar than the nonprime 1 position.)

A glycosidic bond to the anomeric carbon can be either alpha or beta (recall from Section 14.6 that alpha anomers have the C1 —OH group trans to the —CH$_2$OH group, whereas beta anomers have the C1 —OH group cis to the —CH$_2$OH). For example, cellobiose, the disaccharide obtained by partial hydrolysis of cellulose, consists of two D-glucopyranoses joined by a 1,4′-β-glycoside bond. Maltose, the disaccharide obtained by partial hydrolysis of starch, consists of two D-glucopyranoses joined by a 1,4′-α-glycoside bond.

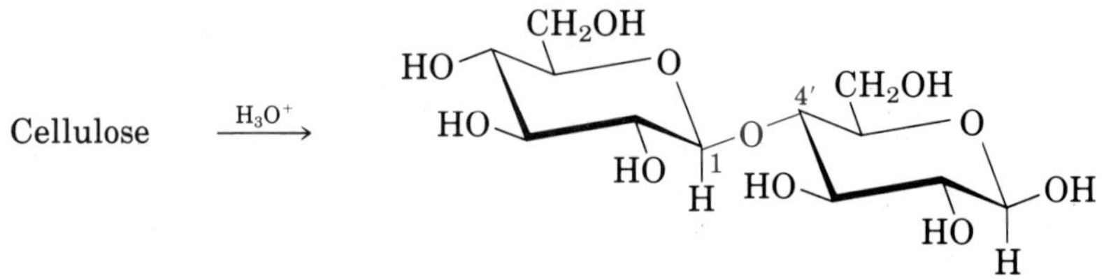

Cellulose $\xrightarrow{H_3O^+}$

Cellobiose, a 1,4'-β-glycoside
[4-*O*-(β-D-glucopyranosyl)-β-D-glucopyranose]

Starch $\xrightarrow{\text{Enzyme}}$

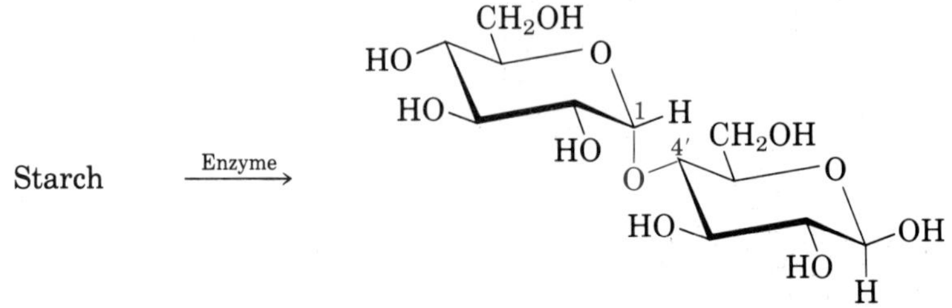

Maltose, a 1,4'-α-glycoside
[4-*O*-(α-D-glucopyranosyl)-β-D-glucopyranose]

Both maltose and cellobiose are reducing sugars because the right-hand portions of the molecules are hemiacetals. Both are therefore in equilibrium with aldehyde forms, which can reduce Tollens' or Fehling's reagent. For a similar reason, both maltose and cellobiose exhibit mutarotation of the alpha and beta anomers of the glucopyranose portion on the right (Figure 14.7).

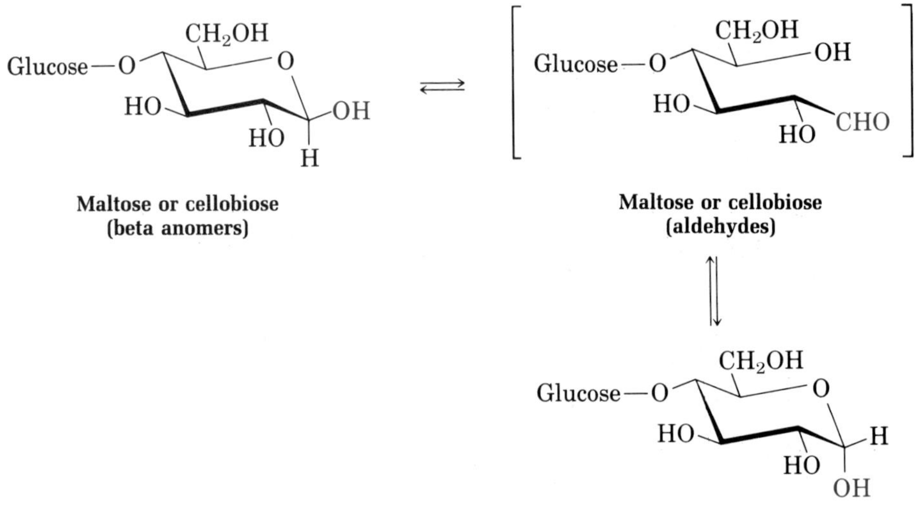

Maltose or cellobiose
(beta anomers)

$\rightleftharpoons$

Maltose or cellobiose
(aldehydes)

Maltose or cellobiose
(alpha anomers)

FIGURE 14.7
Mutarotation of maltose and cellobiose

Despite the similarities of their structures, maltose and cellobiose are dramatically different biologically. Cellobiose cannot be digested by humans and cannot be fermented by yeast. Maltose, however, is digested without difficulty and is readily fermented.

PROBLEM 14.18 Draw the structure of the product obtained from reaction of cellobiose with each of these reagents:

(a) $NaBH_4$ (b) Br_2, H_2O

Sucrose

Sucrose—ordinary table sugar—is probably the single most abundant pure organic chemical in the world. Whether from sugar cane (20% by weight) or from sugar beets (15% by weight), and whether raw or refined, common sugar is still sucrose.

Sucrose is a disaccharide that yields 1 equiv of glucose and 1 equiv of fructose on hydrolysis. This 1:1 mixture of glucose and fructose is often referred to as **invert sugar**, since the sign of optical rotation changes (inverts) during the hydrolysis from sucrose, $[\alpha]_D = +66.5°$, to a glucose/fructose mixture, $[\alpha]_D = -22°$. Certain insects, such as honeybees, have enzymes called **invertases** that catalyze the hydrolysis of sucrose to glucose + fructose. Honey, in fact, is primarily a mixture of glucose, fructose, and sucrose.

Unlike most other disaccharides, sucrose is not a reducing sugar and does not exhibit mutarotation. These facts imply that sucrose has no hemiacetal groups and that the glucose and fructose units must both be glycosides. This can happen only if the two sugars are joined by a glycoside link between C1 of glucose and C2 of fructose.

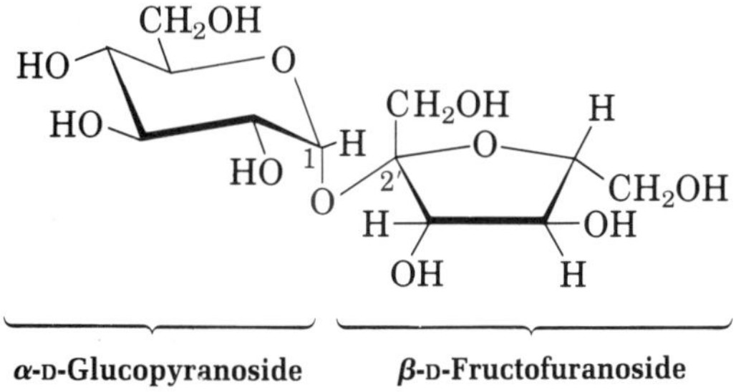

Sucrose, a 1,2'-glycoside
[2-*O*-(α-D-glucopyranosyl)-β-D-fructofuranoside]

α-D-Glucopyranoside   β-D-Fructofuranoside

14.10 POLYSACCHARIDES

Polysaccharides are carbohydrates in which tens, hundreds, or even thousands of simple sugars are linked together through glycoside bonds. Since these compounds have no free anomeric hydroxyls (except for one at the end of the chain), polysaccharides are not reducing sugars and do not show mutarotation. Cellulose and starch are the two most widely occurring polysaccharides.

Cellulose

Cellulose consists simply of D-glucose units linked by the 1,4'-β-glycoside bonds we saw in cellobiose. Several thousand glucose units are linked to form one large molecule, and different molecules can then interact to form a large aggregate structure held together by hydrogen bonds.

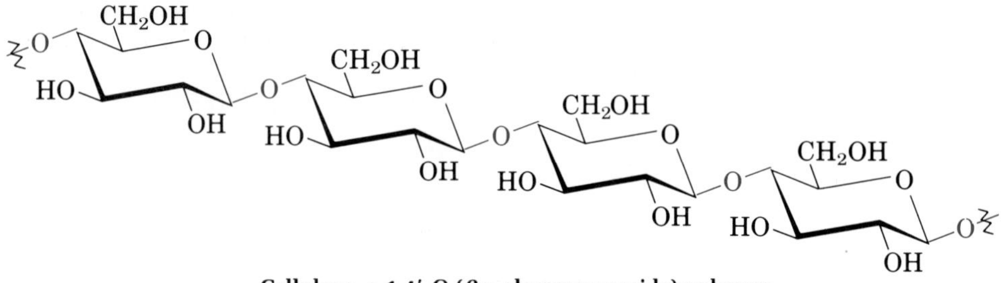

Cellulose, a 1,4'-*O*-(β-D-glucopyranoside) polymer

Nature uses cellulose primarily as a structural material to impart strength and rigidity to plants. Wood, leaves, grasses, and cotton are primarily cellulose. Cellulose also serves as raw material for the manufacture of cellulose acetate, known commercially as **rayon.**

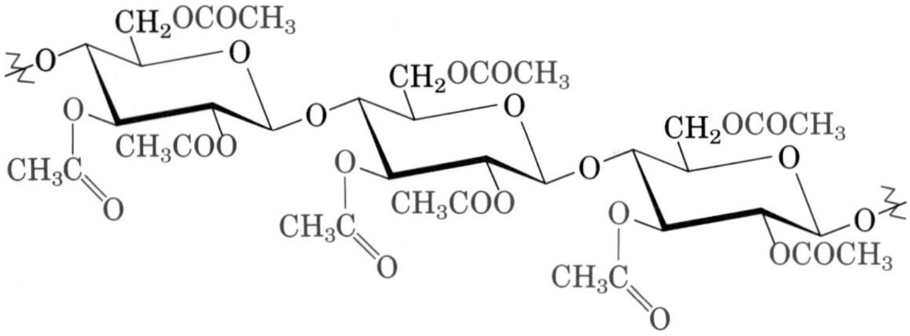

A segment of cellulose acetate (rayon)

Starch

Starch is also a polymer of glucose, but the monosaccharide units are linked by the 1,4'-α-glycoside bonds we saw in maltose. Starch can be separated into two fractions called *amylopectin* and *amylose*. Amylose, which accounts for about

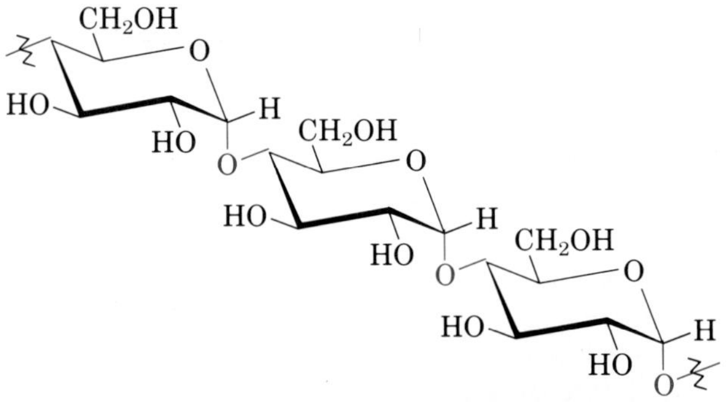

Amylose, a 1,4'-*O*-(α-D-glucopyranoside) polymer

20% by weight of starch, consists of several hundred glucose molecules linked by 1,4'-α-glycoside bonds.

Amylopectin, which accounts for the remaining 80% of starch, is more complex in structure than amylose. Unlike cellulose or amylose, which are linear polymers, amylopectin contains 1,6'-α-glycoside branches approximately every 25 glucose units. As a result, amylopectin has an exceedingly complex three-dimensional structure (Figure 14.8). Nature uses starch as the means by which plants store energy for later use. Potatoes, corn, and cereal grains contain large amounts of starch.

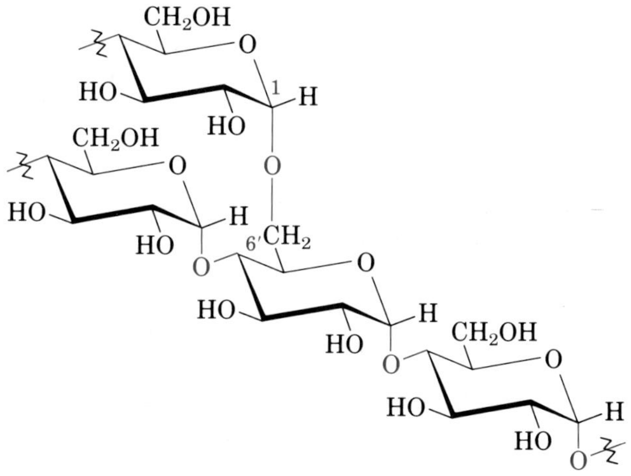

FIGURE 14.8
A 1,6'-α-glycoside branch in amylopectin

ADDITIONAL PROBLEMS

PROBLEM 14.19 Classify the following sugars by type (for example, glucose is an aldohexose):

(a)
$$CH_2OH$$
$$|$$
$$C=O$$
$$|$$
$$CH_2OH$$

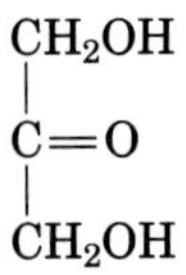

(b)
$$CH_2OH$$
H——OH
$$C=O$$
H——OH
$$CH_2OH$$

(c)
$$CHO$$
H——OH
HO——H
H——OH
HO——H
H——OH
$$CH_2OH$$

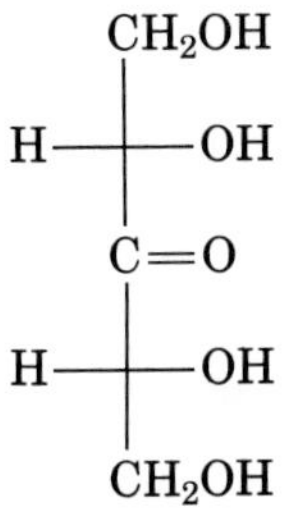

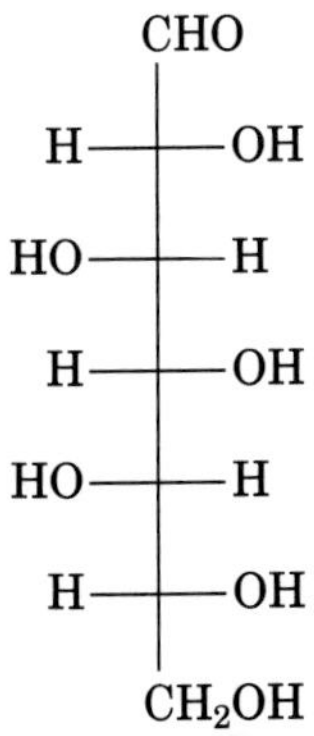

PROBLEM 14.20   The structure of ascorbic acid (vitamin C) is shown here. Does ascorbic acid have a D or L configuration?

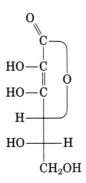

Ascorbic acid

PROBLEM 14.21   Draw a Haworth projection of ascorbic acid (Problem 14.20).

PROBLEM 14.22   Define the following terms, and give an example of each:

(a) Monosaccharide   (b) Anomeric center   (c) Haworth projection
(d) Fischer projection   (e) Glycoside   (f) Reducing sugar
(g) Pyranose form   (h) 1,4′ Link   (i) D Sugar

PROBLEM 14.23   Draw the structure of β-D-talopyranose. Identify the ring substituents as axial or equatorial.

PROBLEM 14.24   Draw structures for the products you would expect to obtain from reaction of β-D-talopyranose (Problem 14.23) with each of the following reagents:

(a) $NaBH_4$ (b) Warm dilute HNO_3 (c) Br_2, H_2O
(d) CH_3CH_2OH, H^+ (e) CH_3I, Ag_2O (f) $(CH_3CO)_2O$, pyridine

PROBLEM 14.25   How many D-2-ketohexoses are possible? Draw them.

PROBLEM 14.26   One of the D-2-ketohexoses (Problem 14.25) is called *sorbose*. On treatment with $NaBH_4$, sorbose yields a mixture of gulitol and iditol. What is the structure of D-sorbose? (Gulitol and iditol are the alditols obtained by reduction of gulose and idose.)

PROBLEM 14.27   Another D-2-ketohexose, *psicose*, yields a mixture of allitol and altritol when reduced with $NaBH_4$. What is the structure of psicose?

PROBLEM 14.28   Fructose exists at equilibrium as an approximately 2:1 mixture of β-D-fructopyranose and β-D-fructofuranose. Draw both forms in Haworth projection.

PROBLEM 14.29   Which of the four D-aldopentoses yield optically inactive (meso) alditols on reduction with $NaBH_4$?

PROBLEM 14.30   What other D-aldohexose would give the same alditol as D-talose?

PROBLEM 14.31   Which of the eight D-aldohexoses give the same aldaric acids as their L enantiomers?

PROBLEM 14.32   Which of the other three D-aldopentoses gives the same aldaric acid as D-lyxose?

PROBLEM 14.33 The *Ruff degradation* is a method used to shorten an aldose chain by one carbon atom. The original C1 carbon atom is cleaved off, and the original C2 carbon atom becomes the aldehyde of the chain-shortened aldose. For example, D-glucose, an aldohexose, is converted by Ruff degradation into D-arabinose, an aldopentose. What other D-aldohexose would also yield D-arabinose on Ruff degradation?

PROBLEM 14.34 D-Galactose and D-talose yield the same aldopentose on Ruff degradation (Problem 14.33). What does this tell you about the stereochemistries of galactose and talose? Which D-aldopentose is obtained?

PROBLEM 14.35 The aldaric acid obtained by nitric acid oxidation of D-erythrose, one of the D-aldotetroses, is optically inactive. The aldaric acid obtained from oxidation of the other D-aldotetrose, D-threose, is optically active. How does this information allow you to assign structures to the two D-aldotetroses?

PROBLEM 14.36 Gentiobiose is a rare disaccharide found in saffron and gentian. It is a reducing sugar and forms only glucose on hydrolysis with aqueous acid. If gentiobiose contains a 1,6'-β-glycoside link, what is its structure?

PROBLEM 14.37 The position of the glycosidic link between sugars in disaccharides can be determined by taking advantage of the known chemistry of acetal groups. For example, reaction of cellobiose with iodomethane and silver oxide yields an octamethyl ether derivative. Hydrolysis of the glycoside bonds in this derivative yields a tri-O-methylglucopyranose and a tetra-O-methylglucopyranose. Look up the structure of cellobiose and formulate the reactions by drawing structures for the octamethyl, tetramethyl, and trimethyl ethers.

PROBLEM 14.38 Trehalose is a nonreducing disaccharide found in the blood of insects. Reaction with iodomethane and silver oxide, followed by acidic hydrolysis, yields 2 equiv of 2,3,4,6-tetra-O-methylglucose (see Problem 14.37). How many possible structures are there for trehalose? If trehalose is cleaved by glycosidase enzymes that hydrolyze α-glycosides but not by enzymes that hydrolyze β-glycosides, which structure is correct?

PROBLEM 14.39 Isotrehalose and neotrehalose are chemically similar to trehalose (Problem 14.38) except that neotrehalose is hydrolyzed only by β-glycosidases whereas isotrehalose is hydrolyzed by both α- and β-glycosidases. What are the structures of isotrehalose and neotrehalose?

PROBLEM 14.40 The cyclitols are a group of carbocyclic sugar derivatives having the general formula 1,2,3,4,5,6-cyclohexanehexaol—a cyclohexane ring with one hydroxyl on each carbon. Draw the structures of the nine stereoisomeric cyclitols in Haworth projection.

INTERLUDE R
Cell-Surface Carbohydrates

For many years, carbohydrates were thought to be rather dull compounds whose only biological purposes were as structural materials and as energy sources. Although carbohydrates do indeed fill these two roles, recent research has shown that they perform many other important biochemical functions as well. For example, polysaccharides are known to be centrally involved in the critical process by which one cell type recognizes another. Small polysaccharide chains, covalently bound by glycoside links to hydroxyl groups on proteins (**glycoproteins**), act as biochemical labels on cell surfaces; this is beautifully illustrated by the human blood-group antigens.

It has been known for over 80 years that human blood can be classified into four blood-group types, A, B, AB, and O, and that blood from a donor of one type cannot be transfused into a recipient with another type unless the two types are compatible. For example, blood from a type B donor is compatible with blood of either a type B or a type AB recipient, but is incompatible with blood of a type A or type O recipient. Should an incompatible mix be made, the red blood cells clump together, or *agglutinate*.

This agglutination of incompatible red blood cells, which indicates that the recipient's immune system has recognized the presence of foreign cells in the body and has formed antibodies to them, results from the presence of polysaccharide markers on the surface of the cells. Type A, B, and O red blood cells each have characteristic markers (**antigenic determinants**); type AB cells have both type A and type B markers. The structures of all three blood-group determinants have been elucidated and are shown in Figure R.1. All three contain N-acetylamino sugars as well as the unusual monosaccharide L-fucose.

The antigenic determinant of blood group O is a trisaccharide, whereas the determinants of blood groups A and B are tetrasaccharides. Type A and B determinants differ only in the substitution of an acetylamino group ($-NHCOCH_3$) for a hydroxyl in the terminal galactose residue.

Elucidation of the role of carbohydrates in cell recognition is an exciting area of current research that offers hope of breakthroughs in the understanding of a wide range of diseases from bacterial infections to cancer.

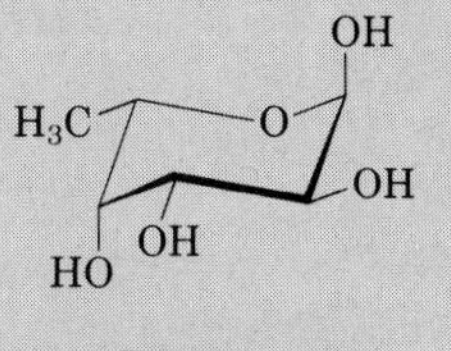

α-L-Fucopyranose
(L-6-deoxygalactose)

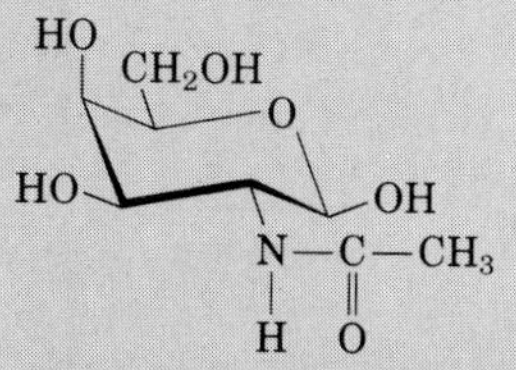

β-D-N-Acetylgalactosamine
(D-2-acetamino-2-deoxygalactose)

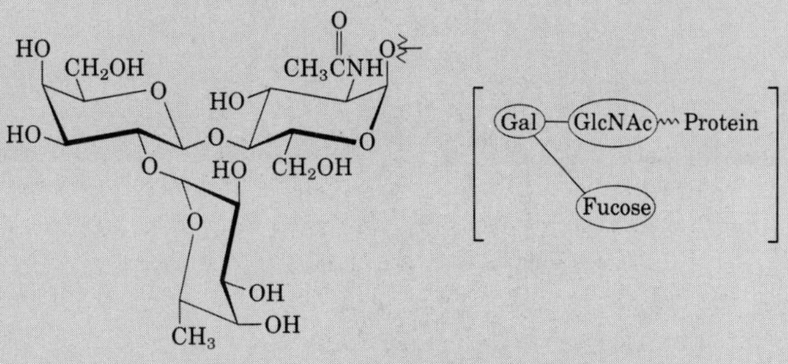

Blood group O

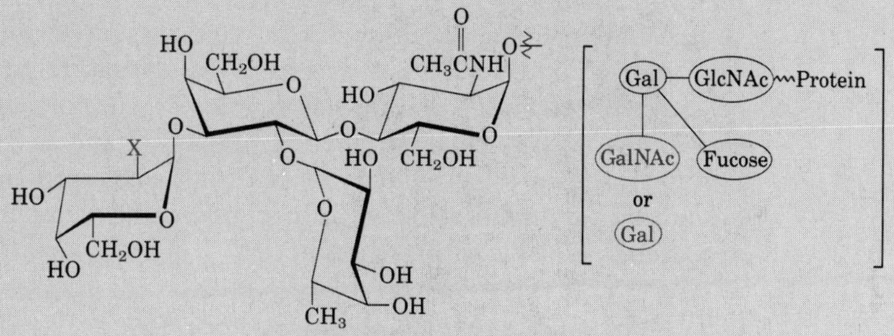

Blood group A, X = NHCOCH₃
Blood group B, X = OH

FIGURE R.1

Structures of the A, B, and O blood-group antigenic determinants
(Gal = D-galactose; GlcNAc = N-acetylglucosamine;
Gal-NAc = N-acetylgalactosamine)

CHAPTER 15

Biomolecules: Amino Acids, Peptides, and Proteins

Proteins are large biomolecules that occur in every living organism. They are of many different types, and they serve many different biological roles. The keratin of skin and fingernails, the insulin that regulates glucose metabolism in the body, and the DNA polymerase that serves as a biological catalyst to synthesize DNA in cells, are all proteins. Regardless of their appearance or function, all proteins are chemically similar—they are made up of many **amino acid** units linked together.

Amino acids are the building blocks from which proteins are made. As their name implies, amino acids are difunctional—they contain both a basic amino group and an acidic carboxyl group.

$$H_2N—CH_2—COOH$$

Glycine, an amino acid

Their value as biological building blocks derives from the fact that amino acids can link together by forming amide or **peptide** bonds. A **dipeptide** results when an amide bond is formed between the —NH$_2$ of one amino acid and the —COOH of a second amino acid; a **tripeptide** results from linkage of three amino acids via

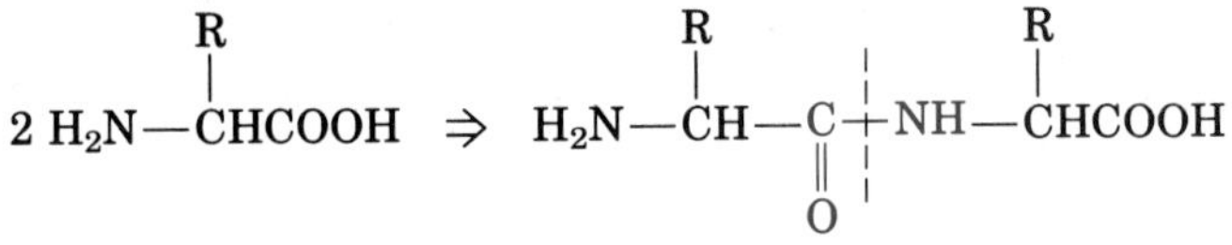

$$2 \; H_2N—\overset{\overset{\displaystyle R}{|}}{C}HCOOH \;\; \Rightarrow \;\; H_2N—\overset{\overset{\displaystyle R}{|}}{C}H—\overset{\overset{}{\underset{\underset{\displaystyle O}{\|}}{C}}}{}+NH—\overset{\overset{\displaystyle R}{|}}{C}HCOOH$$

A dipeptide (one amide bond)

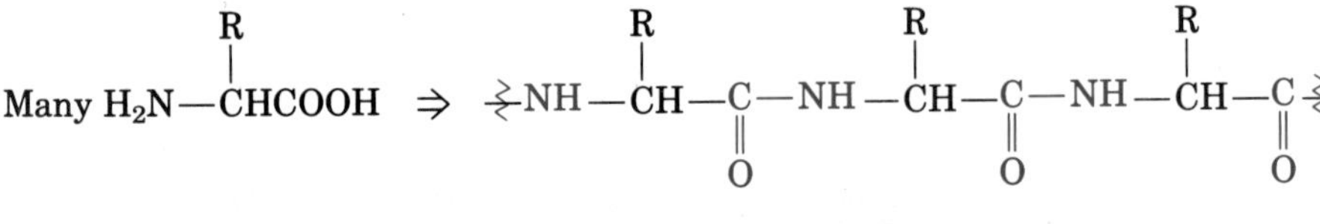

$$Many \; H_2N—\overset{\overset{\displaystyle R}{|}}{C}HCOOH \;\; \Rightarrow \;\; \{NH—\overset{\overset{\displaystyle R}{|}}{C}H—\overset{\overset{}{\underset{\underset{\displaystyle O}{\|}}{C}}}{}—NH—\overset{\overset{\displaystyle R}{|}}{C}H—\overset{\overset{}{\underset{\underset{\displaystyle O}{\|}}{C}}}{}—NH—\overset{\overset{\displaystyle R}{|}}{C}H—\overset{\overset{}{\underset{\underset{\displaystyle O}{\|}}{C}}}{}\}$$

A polypeptide (many amide bonds)

434

two amide bonds; and so on. Any number of amino acids can link together to form large chains. For classification purposes, chains with fewer than 50 amino acids are called **polypeptides**, and the term *protein* is reserved for larger chains.

15.1 STRUCTURES OF AMINO ACIDS

The structures of the 20 amino acids commonly found in proteins are shown in Table 15.1, pages 436–437. All 20 are α-amino acids; that is, the amino group in each is a substituent on the carbon atom alpha to (next to) the carbonyl group. The amino acid structures differ only in the nature of their side chains. Note that 19 of the 20 are primary amines, RNH_2, but that proline is a secondary amine whose nitrogen and alpha-carbon atom are part of a pyrrolidine ring. Proline can still form amide bonds in the same manner as the other 19 α-amino acids, however.

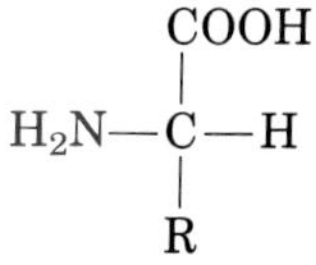

Primary α-amino acids
(R = a side chain)

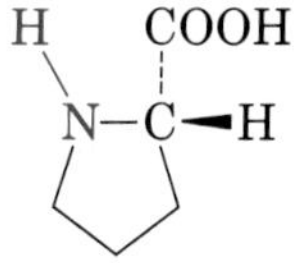

Proline, a secondary
α-amino acid

Note also that each of the amino acids in Table 15.1 can be referred to by a mnemonic three-letter shorthand code: Ala for alanine, Gly for glycine, and so on. In addition, a new one-letter code is gaining in popularity among biochemists; this is shown in parentheses in the table.

With the exception of glycine, H_2NCH_2COOH, the alpha carbons of the amino acids are chiral. Two different enantiomeric forms of each amino acid are therefore possible, but nature uses only a single enantiomer to construct proteins. In Fischer projections, naturally occurring amino acids are represented by placing the carboxyl group at the top as if drawing a carbohydrate (Section 14.2) and then placing the amino group on the left. Because of their stereochemical similarity to L sugars (Section 14.3), the naturally occurring α-amino acids are often referred to as L-amino acids.

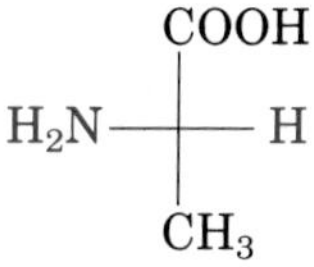

(S)-Alanine
(L-alanine)

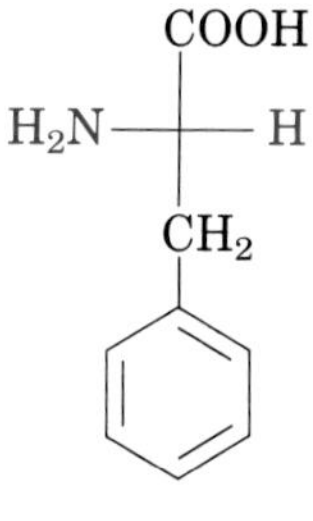

(S)-Phenylalanine
(L-phenylalanine)

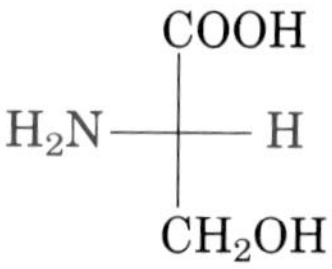

(S)-Serine
(L-serine)

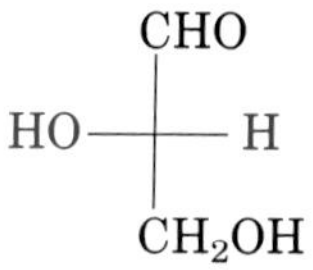

Stereochemically
similar to
L-glyceraldehyde

TABLE 15.1   **Structures of the 20 common amino acids found in proteins: Those amino acids essential to the human diet are shown in color.**

Name	Abbreviations	Molecular weight	Structure	Isoelectric point
Neutral amino acids				
Alanine	Ala (A)	89	$CH_3CHCOOH$ $\mid$ NH_2	6.0
Asparagine	Asn (N)	132	$\overset{\displaystyle O}{\overset{\displaystyle \|}{H_2N-C}}CH_2CHCOOH$ $\mid$ NH_2	5.4
Cysteine	Cys (C)	121	$HSCH_2CHCOOH$ $\mid$ NH_2	5.0
Glutamine	Gln (Q)	146	$\overset{\displaystyle O}{\overset{\displaystyle \|}{H_2N-C}}-CH_2CH_2CHCOOH$ $\mid$ NH_2	5.7
Glycine	Gly (G)	75	CH_2COOH $\mid$ NH_2	6.0
Isoleucine	Ile (I)	131	$CH_3CH_2CH(CH_3)CHCOOH$ $\mid$ NH_2	6.0
Leucine	Leu (L)	131	$(CH_3)_2CHCH_2CHCOOH$ $\mid$ NH_2	6.0
Methionine	Met (M)	149	$CH_3SCH_2CH_2CHCOOH$ $\mid$ NH_2	5.7
Phenylalanine	Phe (F)	165	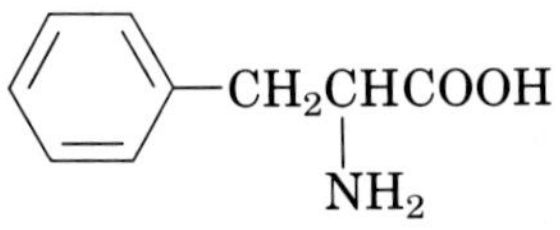 $\langle\bigcirc\rangle-CH_2CHCOOH$ $\mid$ NH_2	5.5
Proline	Pro (P)	115	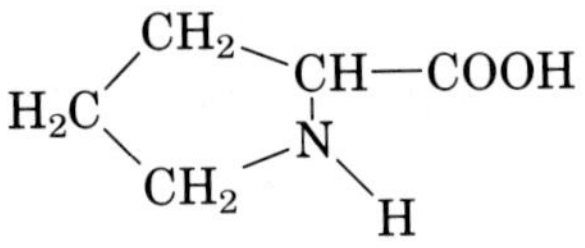 $\underset{CH_2}{\overset{CH_2}{H_2C}}\diagdown\underset{N}{CH}-COOH$ $\mid$ H	6.3
Serine	Ser (S)	105	$HOCH_2CHCOOH$ $\mid$ NH_2	5.7
Threonine	Thr (T)	119	$CH_3CH(OH)CHCOOH$ $\mid$ NH_2	5.6

Name	Abbreviations	Molecular weight	Structure	Isoelectric point
Tryptophan	Trp (W)	204	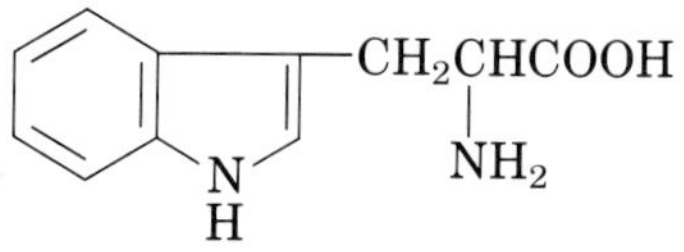 $CH_2CHCOOH$ / NH_2 indole ring with N-H	5.9
Tyrosine	Tyr (Y)	181	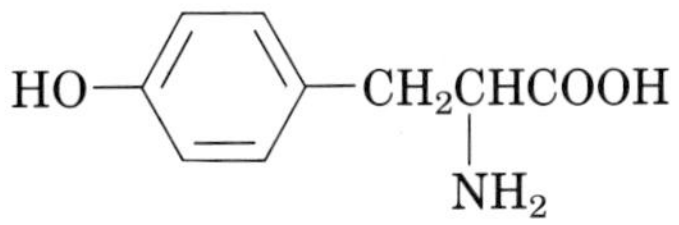 HO— benzene ring —$CH_2CHCOOH$ / NH_2	5.7
Valine	Val (V)	117	$(CH_3)_2CHCHCOOH$ / NH_2	6.0
Acidic amino acids				
Aspartic acid	Asp (D)	133	$HOOCCH_2CHCOOH$ / NH_2	3.0
Glutamic acid	Glu (E)	147	$HOOCCH_2CH_2CHCOOH$ / NH_2	3.2
Basic amino acids				
Arginine	Arg (R)	174	$H_2N-C-NHCH_2CH_2CH_2CHCOOH$ / NH / NH_2	10.8
Histidine	His (H)	155	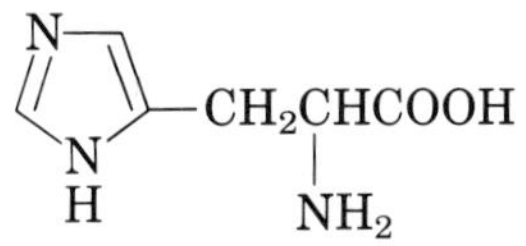 imidazole ring —$CH_2CHCOOH$ / NH_2	7.6
Lysine	Lys (K)	146	$H_2NCH_2CH_2CH_2CH_2CHCOOH$ / NH_2	9.7

The 20 common amino acids can be further classified as either neutral, basic, or acidic, depending on the nature of their specific side chains. Fifteen of the twenty have neutral side chains, but two (aspartic acid and glutamic acid) have an extra carboxylic acid function in their side chains, and three (lysine, arginine, and histidine) have basic amino groups in their side chains.

All 20 of the amino acids are necessary for protein synthesis, but humans are thought to be able to synthesize only 10 of the 20 (the exact number is not known with certainty). The remaining 10 are called **essential amino acids**, since they must be obtained from dietary sources. Failure to include an adequate dietary supply of these essential amino acids can lead to severe deficiency diseases.

PROBLEM 15.1   Look carefully at the 20 amino acids shown in Table 15.1. How many contain aromatic rings? How many contain sulfur? How many are alcohols? How many have hydrocarbon side chains?

PROBLEM 15.2   Eighteen of the nineteen L-amino acids have the S configuration at the alpha carbon. Cysteine is the only L-amino acid that has an R configuration. Explain.

PROBLEM 15.3   The amino acid threonine, $(2S,3R)$-2-amino-3-hydroxybutanoic acid, has two chiral centers whose stereochemistry is similar to that of the four-carbon sugar D-threose. Draw a Fischer projection of threonine.

PROBLEM 15.4   Draw the Fischer projection of a diastereomer of threonine (Problem 15.3).

15.2   DIPOLAR STRUCTURE OF AMINO ACIDS

Amino acids contain both acidic and basic groups in the same molecule. For this reason, they undergo an intramolecular acid–base reaction and exist primarily in the form of a dipolar ion or **zwitterion** (German *zwitter*, "hybrid").

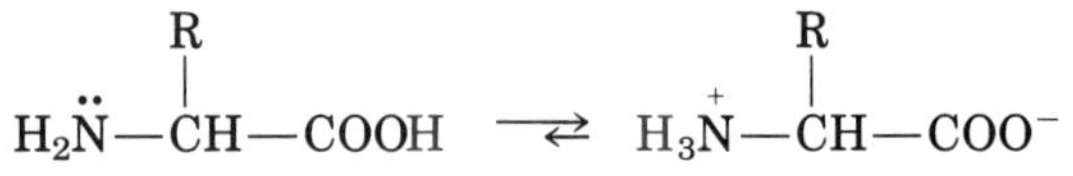

$$\underset{}{H_2\overset{\cdot\cdot}{N}}-\underset{\underset{R}{|}}{CH}-COOH \;\rightleftharpoons\; \underset{}{H_3\overset{+}{N}}-\underset{\underset{R}{|}}{CH}-COO^-$$

A zwitterion

Amino acid zwitterions are a kind of internal salt and therefore have many of the physical properties we associate with salts. Thus, amino acids are crystalline substances with high melting points. They are soluble in water but insoluble in hydrocarbons. In addition, amino acids are **amphoteric**: They can react either as acids or as bases, depending on the circumstances. In aqueous acid solution, an amino acid zwitterion can *accept* a proton to yield a cation; in aqueous basic solution, the zwitterion can *lose* a proton to form an anion.

In acid solution
$$H_3\overset{+}{N}-\underset{\underset{R}{|}}{CH}-CO_2^- + H^+ \;\rightleftharpoons\; H_3\overset{+}{N}-\underset{\underset{R}{|}}{CH}-COOH$$

In base solution
$$H_3\overset{+}{N}-\underset{\underset{R}{|}}{CH}-CO_2^- + {}^-OH \;\rightleftharpoons\; H_2N-\underset{\underset{R}{|}}{CH}-CO_2^- + H_2O$$

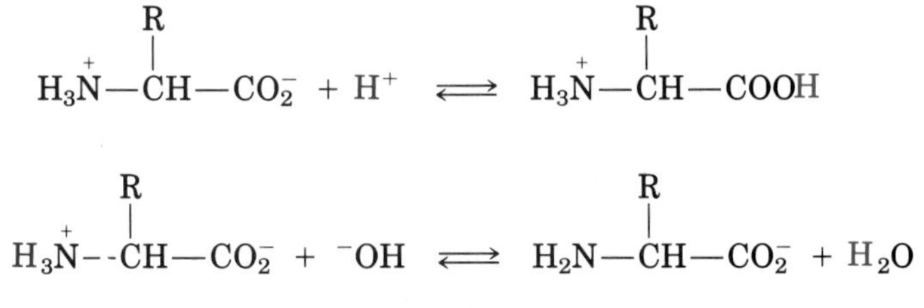

Note that it is the carboxylate anion, $-COO^-$, that acts as the basic site in the zwitterion and accepts the proton in acid solution. Similarly, it is the ammonium cation that acts as the acidic site and donates a proton in basic solution. This behavior is simply another consequence of the zwitterionic structure of amino acids.

PROBLEM 15.5   Draw phenylalanine in its zwitterionic form.

15.3 ISOELECTRIC POINTS

In acid solution (low pH), an amino acid is protonated and exists primarily as a cation; in basic solution (high pH), an amino acid is deprotonated and exists primarily as an anion. Thus, at some intermediate pH, the amino acid must be exactly balanced between anionic and cationic forms and exist primarily as the neutral, dipolar zwitterion. This pH is called the **isoelectric point**.

$$\underset{\text{Low pH} \atop \text{(protonated)}}{\overset{\text{R}}{\underset{|}{H_3\overset{+}{N}-CHCOOH}}} \underset{}{\overset{H^+}{\rightleftharpoons}} \underset{\text{Isoelectric point} \atop \text{(neutral zwitterion)}}{\overset{\text{R}}{\underset{|}{H_3\overset{+}{N}-CHCOO^-}}} \overset{-H^+}{\rightleftharpoons} \underset{\text{High pH} \atop \text{(deprotonated)}}{\overset{\text{R}}{\underset{|}{H_2N-CHCOO^-}}}$$

The isoelectric point of a given amino acid depends on its structure; values for the 20 common amino acids are given in Table 15.1. The 15 amino acids with neutral side chains have isoelectric points near neutrality, in the pH range 5.0–6.5. (These values are not exactly at neutral pH = 7 because carboxyl groups are stronger acids in aqueous solution than amino groups are bases.) The two amino acids with acidic side chains have isoelectric points at lower (more acidic) pH to suppress dissociation of the extra —COOH function, and the three amino acids with basic side chains have isoelectric points at higher (more basic) pH to suppress protonation of the extra amino function. For example, aspartic acid has its isoelectric point at pH = 3.0, and lysine has its isoelectric point at pH = 9.7.

We can take advantage of the differences in isoelectric points to separate a mixture of amino acids (or a mixture of proteins) into its pure constituents. In the technique known as **electrophoresis**, a solution of different amino acids is placed near the center of a strip of paper or gel. The paper or gel is moistened with an aqueous buffer of a given pH, and electrodes are connected to the ends of the strip. When an electric field is applied, those amino acids with negative charges (those that are deprotonated because their isoelectric points are below the pH of the buffer) migrate slowly toward the positive electrode. Similarly, those amino acids with positive charges (those that are protonated because their isoelectric points are above the pH of the buffer) migrate toward the negative electrode.

Different amino acids migrate at different rates, depending both on their isoelectric points and on the pH of the buffer. Thus, the different amino acids can be separated. Figure 15.1 illustrates this separation for a mixture of lysine (basic), glycine (neutral), and aspartic acid (acidic).

Paper strip

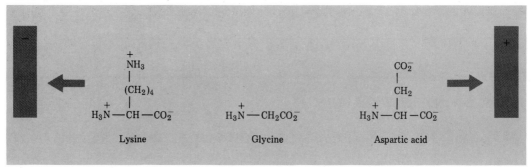

FIGURE 15.1
Separation of an amino acid mixture by electrophoresis: At pH 6.0, glycine molecules are primarily neutral and do not migrate; lysine molecules are largely protonated and migrate toward the negative electrode; aspartic acid molecules are largely deprotonated and migrate toward the positive electrode. (Lysine has its isoelectric point at 9.7, glycine at 6.0, and aspartic acid at 3.0.)

PRACTICE PROBLEM   Draw structures of the predominant forms of glycine at pH $=$ 4.0, pH $=$ 6.0, and pH $=$ 8.0.

Solution   According to Table 15.1, the isoelectric point of glycine is 6.0. At any pH lower than 6.0, glycine will be protonated; at pH $=$ 6.0, glycine will be zwitterionic; and at any pH higher than 6.0, glycine will be deprotonated.

$$\overset{+}{H_3N}-CH_2-COOH \qquad \overset{+}{H_3N}-CH_2-COO^- \qquad H_2N-CH_2-COO^-$$

$$\textbf{At pH = 4.0} \qquad\qquad \textbf{At pH = 6.0} \qquad\qquad \textbf{At pH = 8.0}$$

PROBLEM 15.6   Draw the structures of the predominant forms of these amino acids:

(a) Lysine at pH $=$ 1.0   (b) Aspartic acid at pH $=$ 6.0
(c) Lysine at pH $=$ 12.0

PROBLEM 15.7   For the mixtures of amino acids indicated, predict the direction of migration of each component (toward the positive or negative electrode).

(a) Valine, glutamic acid, and histidine at pH $=$ 7.6
(b) Glycine, phenylalanine, and serine at pH $=$ 5.7
(c) Glycine, phenylalanine, and serine at pH $=$ 6.0

15.4 PEPTIDES

Peptides are amino acid polymers in which the individual amino acid units, called **residues**, are linked together by amide bonds. An amino group from one residue forms an amide bond with the carboxyl of a second residue; the amino group of the second forms an amide bond with the carboxyl of a third; and so on. For example, alanylserine is the dipeptide formed when an amide bond is formed between the alanine carboxyl and the serine amino group:

$$H_2N-\underset{\underset{CH_3}{|}}{CH}-\underset{\underset{O}{\|}}{C}OH \ + \ H_2N-\underset{\underset{CH_2OH}{|}}{CH}-\underset{\underset{O}{\|}}{C}OH \ \Rightarrow \ H_2N-\underset{\underset{CH_3}{|}}{CH}-\underset{\underset{O}{\|}}{C}-NH-\underset{\underset{CH_2OH}{|}}{CH}\underset{\underset{O}{\|}}{C}-OH$$

Alanine (Ala)   **Serine (Ser)**   **Alanylserine (H-Ala-Ser-OH)**

Note that two different peptides can result from reaction between alanine and serine, depending on which carboxyl group reacts with which amino group. If the alanine amino group reacts with the serine carboxyl, serylalanine results:

$$H_2N-\underset{\underset{CH_2OH}{|}}{CH}\underset{\underset{O}{\|}}{C}OH \ + \ H_2N-\underset{\underset{CH_3}{|}}{CH}\underset{\underset{O}{\|}}{C}OH \ \Rightarrow \ H_2N-\underset{\underset{CH_2OH}{|}}{CH}\underset{\underset{O}{\|}}{C}-NH\underset{\underset{CH_3}{|}}{CH}\underset{\underset{O}{\|}}{C}OH$$

Serine (Ser)   **Alanine (Ala)**   **Serylalanine (H-Ser-Ala-OH)**

By convention, peptides are always written with the **N-terminal amino acid** (the one with the free $-NH_2$ group) on the left, and the **C-terminal amino acid** (the one with the free $-COOH$ group) on the right. The name of the peptide is usually indicated by using the three-letter abbreviations listed in Table 15.1 for each amino acid. An H- is often appended to the abbreviation of the leftmost amino acid to underscore its position as the N-terminal group, and an -OH is often appended to the abbreviation of the rightmost amino acid (C-terminal group). Thus, serylalanine is abbreviated H-Ser-Ala-OH, and alanylserine is abbreviated H-Ala-Ser-OH.

The number of possible isomeric peptides increases rapidly as the number of amino acid units increases. Thus, there are six ways in which three amino acids can be joined, and more than 40,000 ways in which the eight amino acids present in the hormone angiotensin II can be joined (Figure 15.2, page 442).

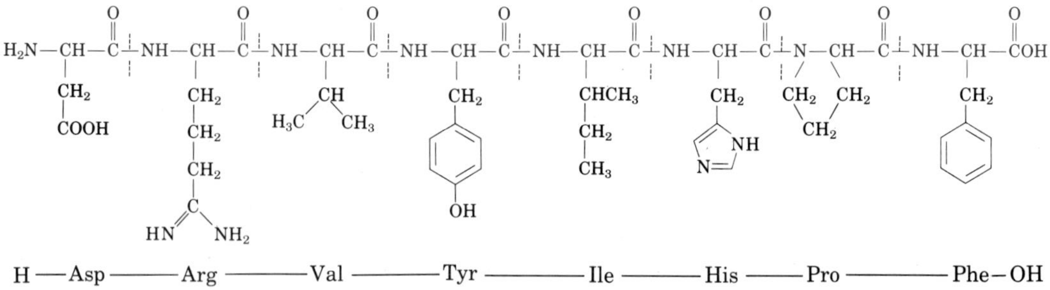

FIGURE 15.2
The structure of angiotensin II, a blood-pressure-regulating hormone present in blood plasma

---

PRACTICE PROBLEM   Draw the full structure of H-Ala-Val-OH.

Solution   By convention, the N-terminal amino acid is written on the left and the C-terminal amino acid on the right. Thus, alanine is N-terminal, valine is C-terminal, and the amide bond is formed between the alanine —COOH and the valine —NH$_2$.

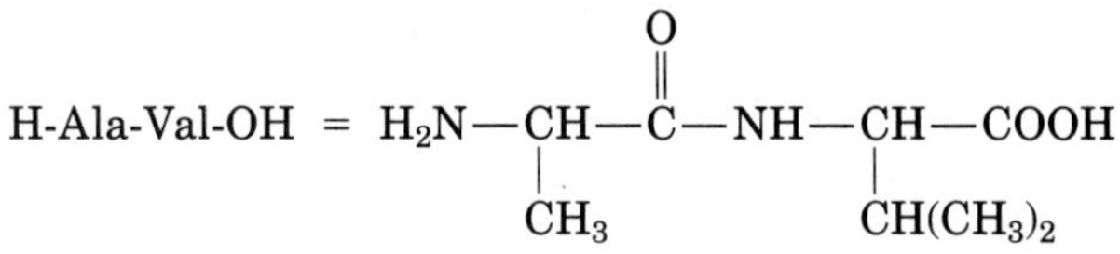

PROBLEM 15.8   Using the three-letter shorthand notations for each amino acid, name the six possible isomeric tripeptides that contain valine, tyrosine, and glycine.

PROBLEM 15.9   Draw the full structure of H-Met-Pro-Val-Gly-OH, and indicate where the amide bonds are.

15.5   COVALENT BONDING IN PEPTIDES

The amide bond linking amino acid residues together is the most important kind of covalent bond in peptides, but a second kind of covalent bonding occurs when a **disulfide linkage, RS—SR**, is formed between two cysteine residues. As we have seen earlier (Section 8.12), disulfide bonds are easily formed by mild oxidation of thiols, RSH, and are converted back to thiols by mild reduction.

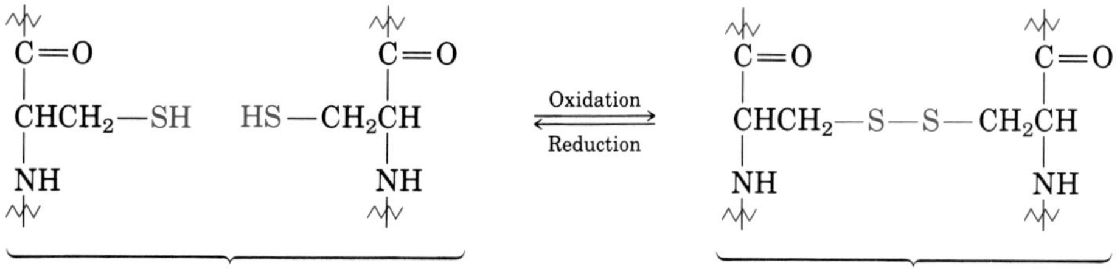

Two cysteines (thiols)   Disulfide

Disulfide bonds between cysteine residues in two different peptide chains can link the otherwise separate chains together. Alternatively, a disulfide bond between two cysteine residues within the same chain can cause a loop in the chain. Such is the case with the nonapeptide vasopressin, an antidiuretic hormone involved in controlling water balance in the body. Note also that the C-terminal end of vasopressin occurs as the primary amide, $-CONH_2$, rather than as the free acid.

Disulfide bridge

H-CyS-Tyr-Phe-Glu-Asn-CyS-Pro-Arg-Gly-NH$_2$

Vasopressin

15.6 PEPTIDE STRUCTURE DETERMINATION: AMINO ACID ANALYSIS

Determining the structure of a peptide is a challenging task that requires finding the answers to three questions: What amino acids are present? How much of each is present? Where does each occur in the peptide chain? The answers to the first two of these questions are provided by a remarkable instrument, the amino acid analyzer.

The amino acid analyzer is an automated instrument based on techniques worked out in the 1950s by W. Stein and S. Moore. The first step is to break the peptide down into its constituent amino acids by reducing all disulfide bonds and then hydrolyzing all amide bonds with $6N$ HCl. The resultant amino acid mixture is then separated by placing it at the top of a glass column filled with a special adsorbent material and pumping a series of aqueous buffers through the column. Different amino acids migrate down the column at different rates, depending on their structures, and are thus separated as they come out (**elute** from) the column end.

As each different amino acid elutes from the end of the glass column, it is allowed to mix with a solution of *ninhydrin*, a reagent that forms a purple color when it reacts with α-amino acids. The intensity of purple color is then measured by a spectrometer and displayed as a function of time.

$$2 \quad \text{(Ninhydrin)} \;+\; \text{H}_2\text{N—CHCOOH} \xrightarrow{\;^-\text{OH}\;} \text{(Purple color)}$$

Ninhydrin   An α-amino acid   Purple color

$$+$$

$$\text{RCHO} + \text{CO}_2$$

Since the amount of time required for a given amino acid to elute from a standard column is reproducible, the identity of all amino acids present in a peptide of unknown composition can be determined by simply noting the various elution times. The amount of each amino acid in the sample can be determined by measuring the intensity of the purple color resulting from its reaction with ninhydrin. Thus, the identity and percentage composition of each amino acid in a peptide can be easily found. Figure 15.3 shows the results of amino acid analysis of a standard equimolar mixture of 17 α-amino acids.

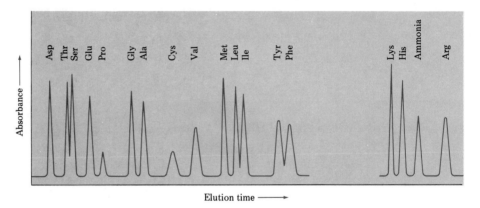

FIGURE 15.3
Amino acid analysis of an equimolar amino acid mixture

PROBLEM 15.10   Give the structures of the products obtained on reaction of valine with ninhydrin.

15.7   PEPTIDE SEQUENCING: THE EDMAN DEGRADATION

With the identity and amount of each amino acid known, the final task of structure determination is to **sequence** the peptide; that is, to find out in what order the amino acids are linked together. The general idea of peptide sequencing is to cleave one amino acid residue at a time from the end of the peptide chain (either C terminus or N terminus). That terminal amino acid is then separated and identified, and the cleavage reaction is repeated on the chain-shortened peptide until the entire peptide sequence is known.

Most peptide sequencing is now done by **Edman degradation,** an efficient method of N-terminal analysis. Automated Edman *protein sequenators* are available that allow a series of 20 or more repetitive sequencing steps to be carried out automatically.

Edman degradation involves treatment of a peptide with phenyl isothiocyanate, C_6H_5—N=C=S, followed by mild acid hydrolysis, as shown in Figure 15.4. The first step attaches a marker to the —NH_2 group of the N-terminal amino acid, and the second step splits the N-terminal residue from the chain, yielding a *phenylthiohydantoin* derivative plus the chain-shortened peptide. The phenylthiohydantoin is then identified by comparison with known derivatives of the common amino acids.

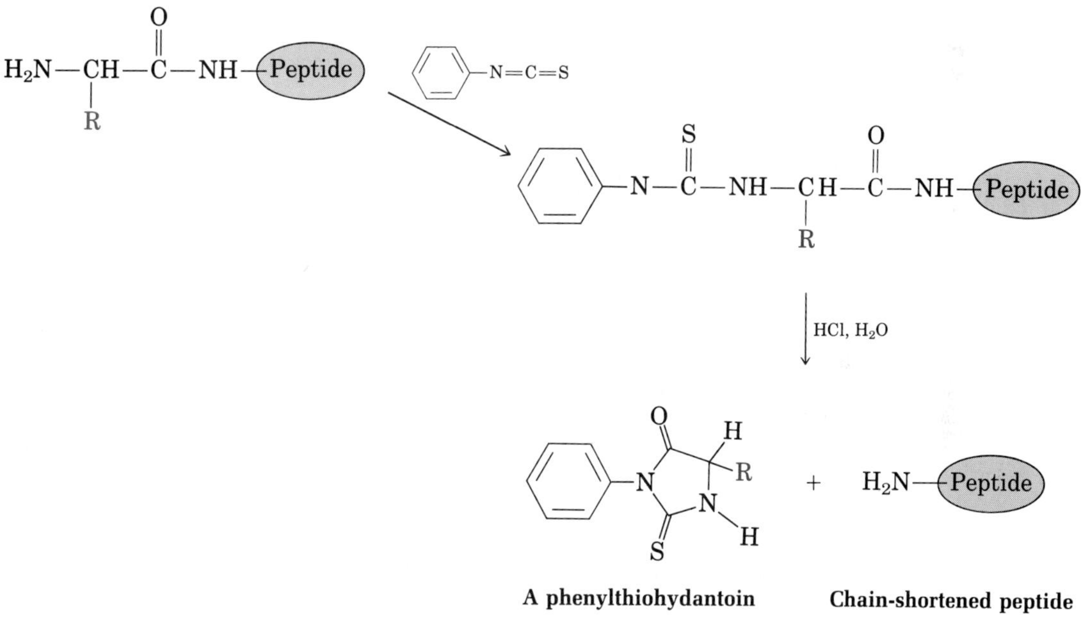

FIGURE 15.4
Edman degradation of a peptide chain

Complete sequencing of large peptides and proteins by Edman degradation is impractical since the method is limited by buildup of unwanted by-products to about 20 cycles. Instead, the large peptide chain is first cleaved by partial hydrolysis into a number of smaller fragments. The sequence of each fragment is then determined, and the individual pieces are fitted together like a jigsaw puzzle.

Partial hydrolysis of a peptide can be carried out either chemically with aqueous acid or enzymatically with enzymes such as trypsin and chymotrypsin. Acid hydrolysis is unselective and leads to a more or less random mixture of small fragments. On the other hand, enzymic hydrolysis is quite specific. For example, trypsin catalyzes hydrolysis only at the carboxyl side of the basic amino acids arginine and lysine; and chymotrypsin cleaves only at the carboxyl side of the aryl-substituted amino acids phenylalanine, tyrosine, and tryptophan.

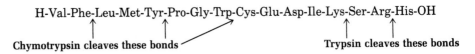

H-Val-Phe-Leu-Met-Tyr-Pro-Gly-Trp-Cys-Glu-Asp-Ile-Lys-Ser-Arg-His-OH

Chymotrypsin cleaves these bonds   Trypsin cleaves these bonds

To take an example of peptide sequencing, let's look at a hypothetical structure determination of angiotensin II, a hormonal octapeptide involved in controlling hypertension by regulating the sodium–potassium salt balance in the body (see Figure 15.2).

1. Amino acid analysis of angiotensin II would show the composition: Arg, Asp, His, Ile, Phe, Pro, Tyr, Val.

2. An N-terminal analysis by the Edman degradation method would show that angiotensin II has an aspartic acid residue at the N terminus.

3. Partial hydrolysis of angiotensin II with dilute HCl might yield the following fragments, whose sequences could be determined by Edman degradation:

   a. H-Asp-Arg-Val-OH
   b. H-Ile-His-Pro-OH
   c. H-Arg-Val-Tyr-OH
   d. H-Pro-Phe-OH
   e. H-Val-Tyr-Ile-OH

4. Matching of overlapping fragment regions provides the full sequence of angiotensin II:

   a. H-Asp-Arg-Val-OH
   c.   H-Arg-Val-Tyr-OH
   e.   H-Val-Tyr-Ile-OH
   b.   H-Ile-His-Pro-OH
   d.   H-Pro-Phe-OH
         H-Asp-Arg-Val-Tyr-Ile-His-Pro-Phe-OH

Angiotensin II

The structure of angiotensin II is relatively simple, and the entire sequence could easily be determined by a protein sequenator instrument. But the methods and logic just used to solve this simple structure are the same as those used to solve more complex structures. Indeed, single protein chains with more than 400 amino acids have been sequenced by these methods.

PROBLEM 15.11 What fragments would result if angiotensin II were cleaved with trypsin? With chymotrypsin?

PROBLEM 15.12 Give the amino acid sequence of a hexapeptide that produces the following fragments on partial acid hydrolysis: H-Pro-Leu-Gly-OH, H-Arg-Pro-OH, H-Gly-Ile-Val-OH.

15.8 PEPTIDE SEQUENCING: C-TERMINAL RESIDUE DETERMINATION

The Edman degradation is an excellent method of analysis for the N-terminal residue, but a complementary method of C-terminal residue analysis is also valuable. The best method currently available makes use of the enzyme *carboxypeptidase* to cleave the C-terminal amide bond in a peptide chain.

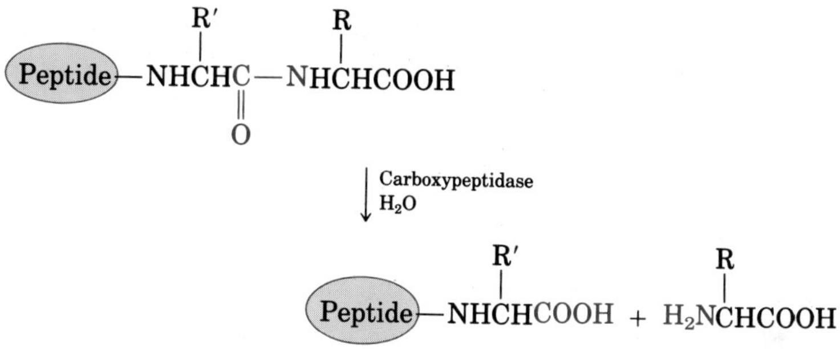

$$\underset{\text{Peptide}}{\boxed{\text{Peptide}}}-\underset{\underset{O}{\parallel}}{\text{NHCHC}}-\underset{R}{\text{NHCHCOOH}}$$

Carboxypeptidase
H_2O

$$\boxed{\text{Peptide}}-\underset{R'}{\text{NHCHCOOH}} + H_2\underset{R}{\text{NCHCOOH}}$$

The analysis is carried out by incubating the polypeptide with carboxypeptidase and watching for the appearance of the first free amino acid produced. Of course, further degradation also occurs, since a new C terminus is produced when the first amino acid residue is cleaved off. Ultimately, the entire peptide is hydrolyzed.

PROBLEM 15.13 A hexapeptide with the composition Arg, Gly, Leu, Pro$_3$ is found to have proline at both C-terminal and N-terminal positions. Partial hydrolysis gives the following fragments:

H-Gly-Pro-Arg-OH   H-Arg-Pro-OH   H-Pro-Leu-Gly-OH

What is the structure of the hexapeptide?

PROBLEM 15.14 Propose two structures for a tripeptide that gives Leu, Ala, and Phe on hydrolysis but does not react with carboxypeptidase and does not react with phenyl isothiocyanate.

15.9 PEPTIDE SYNTHESIS

Once the structure of a peptide has been determined, synthesis is often the next goal. This might be done either as a final proof of structure or as a means of obtaining larger amounts of a valuable peptide for biological evaluation.

Ordinary amide bonds are usually formed by reaction between amines and acylating agents such as acid chlorides (Section 10.9):

$$R'-\overset{\overset{\displaystyle O}{\|}}{C}-X \;+\; H_2N-R \;\longrightarrow\; R'-\overset{\overset{\displaystyle O}{\|}}{C}-NH-R \;+\; HX$$

An amide

Peptide synthesis is much more complex than simple amide synthesis, however, because of the requirement for specificity. Many different amide links must be formed, and they must be formed in a specific order, rather than at random. We can't expect to simply place a mixture of amino acids in a flask and obtain a single polypeptide product.

The solution to the specificity problem is *protection*. We can force a reaction to take only the desired course by protecting all the amine and acid functional groups except for those we want to react. For example, if we want to couple alanine with leucine to synthesize H-Leu-Ala-OH, we can protect the amino group of leucine and the carboxyl group of alanine to render them unreactive. With only the leucine carboxyl and the alanine amine now available, we can form the desired amide bond and then remove the protecting groups.

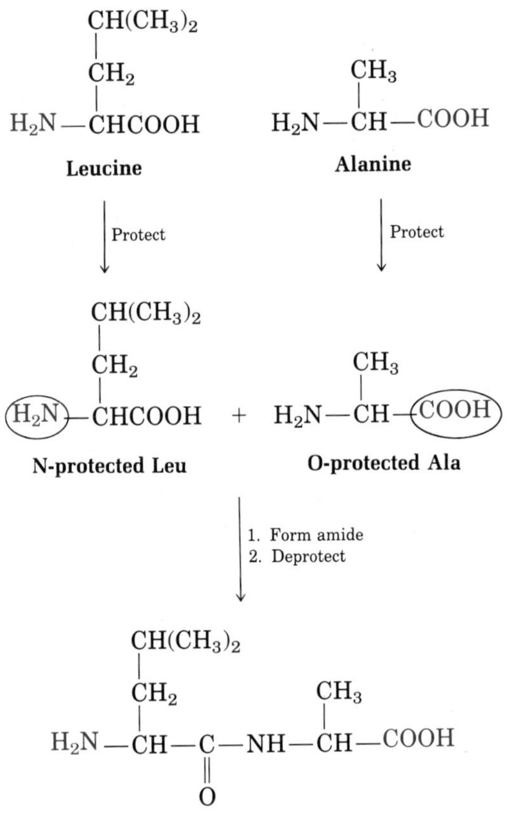

$$
\begin{array}{cc}
\begin{array}{c}
CH(CH_3)_2 \\
| \\
CH_2 \\
| \\
H_2N-CHCOOH
\end{array}
&
\begin{array}{c}
CH_3 \\
| \\
H_2N-CH-COOH
\end{array}
\\[2mm]
\textbf{Leucine} & \textbf{Alanine}
\end{array}
$$

↓ Protect   ↓ Protect

$$
\begin{array}{cc}
\begin{array}{c}
CH(CH_3)_2 \\
| \\
CH_2 \\
| \\
\boxed{H_2N}-CHCOOH
\end{array}
& + \;
\begin{array}{c}
CH_3 \\
| \\
H_2N-CH-\boxed{COOH}
\end{array}
\\[2mm]
\textbf{N-protected Leu} & \textbf{O-protected Ala}
\end{array}
$$

↓ 1. Form amide
2. Deprotect

$$
\begin{array}{c}
CH(CH_3)_2 \\
| \\
CH_2 \qquad\qquad CH_3 \\
| \qquad\qquad\quad | \\
H_2N-CH-\overset{\overset{\displaystyle }{}}{C}-NH-CH-COOH \\
\underset{\displaystyle O}{\|}
\end{array}
$$

H-Leu-Ala-OH

Carboxyl groups are often protected simply by converting them into methyl esters. Ester groups are easily made from carboxylic acids and are easily hydrolyzed by mild treatment with aqueous sodium hydroxide.

$$\underset{\text{Alanine}}{\overset{\overset{\displaystyle CH_3}{|}}{H_2NCHCOOH}} \xrightarrow{CH_3OH,\ HCl} \underset{\text{Alanine methyl ester}}{\overset{\overset{\displaystyle CH_3}{|}}{H_2NCHCOOCH_3}} \xrightarrow[\text{2. H}_3O^+]{\text{1. NaOH, H}_2O} \underset{\text{Alanine}}{\overset{\overset{\displaystyle CH_3}{|}}{H_2NCHCOOH}}$$

Amino groups are often protected as their *tert*-butoxycarbonyl amide (BOC) derivatives. The BOC protecting group is easily introduced by reaction of the amino acid with di-*tert*-butyl dicarbonate and is removed by brief treatment with a strong acid such as trifluoroacetic acid, CF_3COOH.

$$\underset{\text{Leucine}}{\overset{\overset{\displaystyle CH(CH_3)_2}{\overset{|}{\overset{\displaystyle CH_2}{|}}}}{H_2N-CHCOOH}} + \underset{\text{Di-}tert\text{-butyl dicarbonate}}{(CH_3-\overset{\overset{\displaystyle CH_3}{|}}{\underset{\underset{\displaystyle CH_3}{|}}{C}}-O-\overset{\overset{\displaystyle O}{\|}}{C})_2O} \xrightarrow{(CH_3CH_2)_3N} \underset{\text{BOC-Leu}}{CH_3-\overset{\overset{\displaystyle CH_3}{|}}{\underset{\underset{\displaystyle CH_3}{|}}{C}}-O-\overset{\overset{\displaystyle O}{\|}}{C}-NH-\overset{\overset{\displaystyle CH_2}{|}\atop\overset{\displaystyle CH(CH_3)_2}{}}{CH}-COOH}$$

The formation of the peptide bond is usually accomplished by treating a mixture of the protected acid and amine components with dicyclohexylcarbodiimide (DCC). Though its mechanism of action is complex, DCC functions by first converting the acid into a reactive acylating agent that then undergoes further nucleophilic acyl substitution reaction with the amine. Amide bonds are formed in high yield.

$$\underset{\text{Acid}}{R-\overset{\overset{\displaystyle O}{\|}}{C}-OH} + \underset{\text{Amine}}{H_2N-R'} \xrightarrow[\text{DCC}]{\langle\rangle-N=C=N-\langle\rangle} \underset{\text{Amide}}{R-\overset{\overset{\displaystyle O}{\|}}{C}-NHR'} + \underset{\text{Dicyclohexylurea}}{\overset{\overset{\displaystyle H}{\diagdown}\quad\overset{\displaystyle O}{\|}\quad\overset{\displaystyle H}{\diagup}}{N-C-N}}$$

The five separate steps required to synthesize H-Leu-Ala-OH are summarized below:

1. Protect the amino group of leucine as the BOC derivative:

$$\text{H-Leu-OH} + (t\text{-BuO}-\overset{\overset{\displaystyle O}{\|}}{C})_2O \longrightarrow \text{BOC-Leu-OH}$$

2. Protect the carboxyl group of alanine as the methyl ester:

$$\text{H-Ala-OH} + CH_3OH \xrightarrow{H^+} \text{H-Ala-OCH}_3$$

3. Couple the two protected amino acids using DCC:

$$\text{BOC-Leu-OH} + \text{H-Ala-OCH}_3 \xrightarrow{\text{DCC}} \text{BOC-Leu-Ala-OCH}_3$$

4. Remove the BOC protecting group by acid treatment:

$$\text{BOC-Leu-Ala-OCH}_3 \xrightarrow{\text{CF}_3\text{COOH}} \text{H-Leu-Ala-OCH}_3$$

5. Remove the methyl ester by basic hydrolysis:

$$\text{H-Leu-Ala-OCH}_3 \xrightarrow[\text{2. H}_3\text{O}^+]{\text{1. }^-\text{OH}} \text{H-Leu-Ala-OH}$$

These steps can be repeated to add one amino acid at a time to the growing chain or to link two peptide chains together. Many remarkable achievements in peptide synthesis have been reported, including a complete synthesis of human insulin. Insulin, whose structure is shown in Figure 15.5, is composed of two chains totaling 51 amino acids and linked by disulfide bridges. Its structure was determined by Frederick Sanger, who received the 1958 Nobel prize for his work.

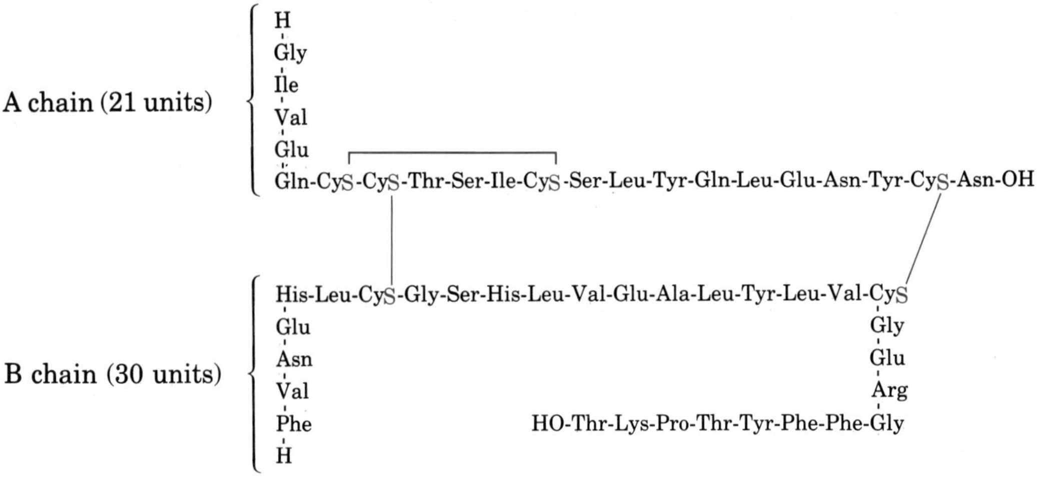

FIGURE 15.5
Structure of human insulin

PROBLEM 15.15   Write the chemical structures of the intermediates in the five-step synthesis of H-Leu-Ala-OH from alanine and leucine.

PROBLEM 15.16   Show all the steps involved in the synthesis of the tripeptide H-Val-Phe-Gly-OH.

15.10   CLASSIFICATION OF PROTEINS

Proteins may be classified into two major types according to their composition. **Simple proteins**, such as blood serum albumin, are those that yield only amino acids and no other compounds on hydrolysis. **Conjugated proteins**, such as are found in cell membranes, yield other compounds in addition to amino acids on hydrolysis. Conjugated proteins, which are far more common than simple proteins, may be further classified according to the chemical nature of the non-amino acid portion. Thus, **glycoproteins** contain a carbohydrate part, **lipoproteins** contain a fatty part, and **nucleoproteins** contain a nucleic acid part. Glycoproteins are particularly widespread in nature, making up a large part of the membrane coating around living cells.

Proteins may also be classified as either **fibrous** or **globular**, according to their three-dimensional shape. Fibrous proteins, such as collagen and α-keratin, consist of polypeptide chains arranged side by side in long threads. Because these proteins are tough and insoluble in water, they are used in nature for structural materials such as tendons, hooves, horns, and fingernails.

Globular proteins, by contrast, are usually coiled into compact, nearly spherical shapes. These proteins are generally soluble in water and are mobile within cells. Most of the 2000 or so known enzymes, as well as hormonal and transport proteins, are globular. Table 15.2 lists some common examples of both fibrous and globular proteins.

TABLE 15.2 Conformational classes of proteins

Protein	Description
Fibrous proteins (insoluble)	
Collagen	Connective tissue, tendons
α-Keratin	Hair, horn, skin, nails
Elastin	Elastic connective tissue
Globular proteins (soluble)	
Insulin	Hormone controlling glucose metabolism
Lysozyme	Hydrolytic enzyme
Ribonuclease	Enzyme controlling RNA synthesis
Albumins	Proteins coagulated by heat
Immunoglobulins	Proteins involved in immune response
Myoglobin	Protein involved in oxygen transport

15.11 PROTEIN STRUCTURE

Proteins are so large in comparison to simple organic molecules that the word *structure* takes on a broader meaning when applied to these immense macromolecules. At its simplest, protein structure is the sequence in which amino acid residues are bound together. Called the **primary structure** of a protein, this is the most fundamental structural level.

There is much more to protein structure, however, than just amino acid sequence. The chemical properties of a protein are also dependent on higher levels of structure—on exactly how the peptide backbone is folded to give the molecule a specific three-dimensional shape. Thus, the term **secondary structure** refers to the way in which segments of the peptide backbone are oriented into a regular pattern; **tertiary structure** refers to the way in which the entire protein molecule is coiled into an overall three-dimensional shape; and **quaternary structure** refers to the way in which several protein molecules come together to yield large aggregate structures.

Let's look at three examples—α-keratin (fibrous), fibroin (fibrous), and myoglobin (globular)—to see how higher levels of structure affect protein properties.

α-Keratin

α-Keratin is the fibrous structural protein found in wool, hair, nails, and feathers. Studies indicate that α-keratin is coiled into a right-handed helical secondary structure, as shown in Figure 15.6. This **α helix** is stabilized by hydrogen bonding between amide N—H groups and other amide carbonyl groups four residues

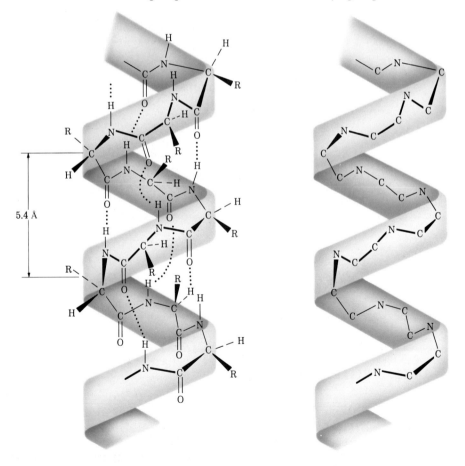

FIGURE 15.6
The helical secondary structure of α-keratin

away. Although the strength of a single hydrogen bond (about 5 kcal/mol) is only about 5% the strength of a C—C or C—H covalent bond, the large number of hydrogen bonds made possible by helical winding imparts a great deal of stability to the α-helical structure. Each coil of the helix—the repeat distance—contains 3.6 amino acid residues; the distance between coils is 5.4 Å.

Further evidence suggests that the α-keratins of wool and hair also have a definite quaternary structure. The individual helical strands are themselves coiled about one another in stiff bundles to form a *superhelix* that accounts for the threadlike properties and strength of these proteins.

Although α-keratin is the best example of an almost entirely helical protein, a great many globular proteins contain α-helical segments. Both hemoglobin and myoglobin, for example, contain many short helical sections in their chains.

Fibroin

Fibroin, the fibrous protein found in silk, has a secondary structure known as a **β pleated sheet**. In this pleated-sheet structure, polypeptide chains line up in a parallel arrangement held together by hydrogen bonds between chains (Figure 15.7). Although not as common as the α helix, small β-pleated-sheet regions are often found in proteins where sections of peptide chains double back on themselves.

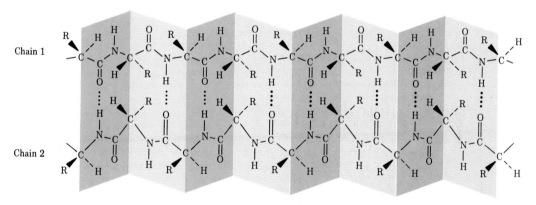

FIGURE 15.7
The β-pleated-sheet structure in silk fibroin

Myoglobin

Myoglobin is a rather small globular protein containing 153 amino acid residues in a single chain. A relative of hemoglobin, myoglobin is found in the skeletal muscles of sea mammals, where it stores oxygen needed to sustain the animals during long dives. X-ray evidence has shown that myoglobin consists of eight straight segments, each of which adopts an α-helical secondary structure. These helical sections are connected by bends to form a compact, nearly spherical, tertiary structure (Figure 15.8, page 454). Although the bends appear to be irregular and the three-dimensional structure appears to be random, this is not the case. All myoglobin molecules adopt this same shape because it has a lower energy level than any other possible shape.

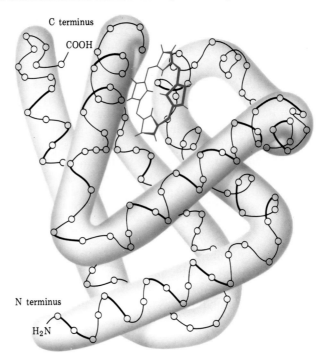

FIGURE 15.8
Secondary and tertiary structure of myoglobin

ADDITIONAL PROBLEMS

PROBLEM 15.17   Although only *S* amino acids occur in proteins, several *R* amino acids are found elsewhere in nature. For example, (*R*)-serine is found in earthworms and (*R*)-alanine is found in insect larvae. Draw Fischer projections of (*R*)-serine and (*R*)-alanine.

PROBLEM 15.18   Draw a Fischer projection of (*S*)-proline.

PROBLEM 15.19   Define these terms:

    (a)   Amphoteric   (b)   Isoelectric point   (c)   Peptide
    (d)   N terminus   (e)   C terminus   (f)   Zwitterion

PROBLEM 15.20   Using the three-letter code names for the amino acids, write the structures of all possible peptides containing the following amino acids:

    (a)   Val, Leu, Ser   (b)   Ser, Leu$_2$, Pro

PROBLEM 15.21   At what pH would you carry out an electrophoresis experiment if you wanted to separate a mixture of histidine, serine, and glutamic acid? Explain.

PROBLEM 15.22   Predict the product of the reaction of valine with these reagents:

    (a) CH_3CH_2OH, H^+ (b)   NaOH, H_2O (c)   Di-*tert*-butyl dicarbonate

PROBLEM 15.37   Oxytocin, a nonapeptide hormone secreted by the pituitary gland, stimulates uterine contraction and lactation during childbirth. Its sequence was determined from the following evidence:

1. Oxytocin is a cyclic peptide containing a disulfide bridge between two cysteine residues.

2. When the disulfide bridge is reduced, oxytocin has the constitution Asn, Cys_2, Gln, Gly, Ile, Leu, Pro, Tyr.

3. Partial hydrolysis of reduced oxytocin yields seven fragments:

H-Asp-Cys-OH	H-Ile-Glu-OH	H-Cys-Tyr-OH
H-Leu-Gly-OH	H-Tyr-Ile-Glu-OH	H-Glu-Asp-Cys-OH
H-Cys-Pro-Leu-OH		

4. Gly is the C-terminal group.

5. Both Glu and Asp are present as their side-chain amides (Gln and Asn) rather than as free side-chain acids.

On the basis of this evidence, what is the amino acid sequence of reduced oxytocin? What is the structure of oxytocin?

INTERLUDE S
Automated Peptide Synthesis

The synthesis of large peptide chains by sequential addition of one amino acid at a time is a long and arduous task. An immense simplification is possible, however, using the **solid-phase method** developed by R. Bruce Merrifield, who received the 1984 Nobel prize in chemistry for his work. In this method, peptide synthesis is carried out on solid polymer beads of polystyrene, prepared so that one of every 100 or so benzene rings bears a chloromethyl (—CH_2Cl) group.

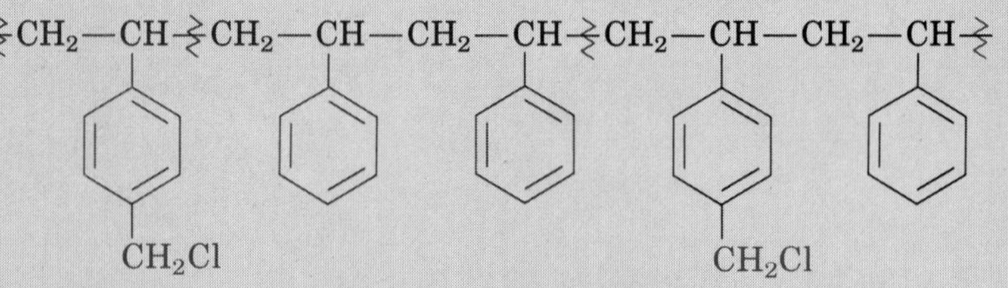

Chloromethylated polystyrene

In the standard, solution-phase method discussed in Section 15.9, a methyl ester was used to protect the carboxyl group during formation of the amide bond. In the solid-phase method, however, the solid polymer serves as the ester-protecting group. Four steps are required in solid-phase peptide synthesis:

Step 1 The ester linkage is formed by S_N2 reaction of a BOC-protected amino acid with the chloromethyl groups on the polystyrene.

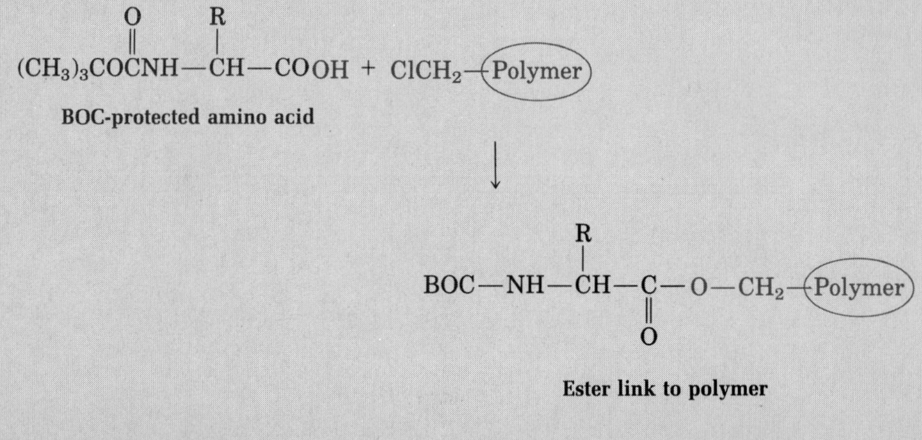

Step 2 After formation of the ester linkage is complete, the polymer-bound amino acid is washed free of excess reagents and treated with trifluoroacetic acid to remove the BOC group and expose the free amine for coupling to the next amino acid.

$$\text{BOC}-\text{NH}-\underset{\underset{\text{O}}{\|}}{\overset{\overset{\text{R}}{|}}{\text{CHC}}}-\text{O}-\text{CH}_2\!-\!\boxed{\text{Polymer}} \quad\xrightarrow[\text{2. CF}_3\text{COOH}]{\text{1. Wash}}\quad \text{H}_2\text{N}-\underset{\underset{\text{O}}{\|}}{\overset{\overset{\text{R}}{|}}{\text{CHC}}}-\text{O}-\text{CH}_2\!-\!\boxed{\text{Polymer}}$$

Polymer-bonded amino acid

Step 3 A second BOC-protected amino acid is added, along with the coupling reagent DCC. Peptide bond formation occurs, and excess reagents are then removed by washing the insoluble polymer.

$$\text{BOC}-\text{NH}-\underset{\underset{\text{O}}{\|}}{\overset{\overset{\text{R}'}{|}}{\text{CHC}}}-\text{OH} \;+\; \text{H}_2\text{N}-\underset{\underset{\text{O}}{\|}}{\overset{\overset{\text{R}}{|}}{\text{CHC}}}-\text{O}-\text{CH}_2\!-\!\boxed{\text{Polymer}}$$

$$\Big\downarrow \begin{array}{l}\text{1. DCC}\\ \text{2. Wash}\end{array}$$

$$\text{BOC}-\text{NH}-\overset{\overset{\text{R}'}{|}}{\text{CH}}-\underset{\underset{\text{O}}{\|}}{\text{C}}-\text{NH}\overset{\overset{\text{R}}{|}}{\text{CHC}}-\underset{\underset{\text{O}}{\|}}{}\text{OCH}_2\!-\!\boxed{\text{Polymer}}$$

Polymer-bonded dipeptide

Step 2 is repeated to again remove a BOC group, and step 3 is repeated to add a third amino acid unit to the chain. In this way, dozens or even a hundred amino acid units can be efficiently and specifically linked to synthesize the desired polymer-bound peptide.

Step 4 At the end of the synthesis, when the proper number of coupling reactions have been done and the desired peptide has been made, treatment with anhydrous hydrogen fluoride cleaves the ester bond to the polymer, yielding free peptide.

$$\text{H}_2\text{N}-\overset{\overset{\text{R}''}{|}}{\text{CH}}-\underset{\underset{\text{O}}{\|}}{\text{C}}-(\text{NH}-\underset{\underset{\text{O}}{\|}}{\overset{\overset{\text{R}'}{|}}{\text{CHC}}})_{\overline{n}}\text{NH}-\overset{\overset{\text{R}}{|}}{\text{CH}}-\underset{\underset{\text{O}}{\|}}{\text{C}}-\text{O}-\text{CH}_2\!-\!\boxed{\text{Polymer}}$$

$$\Big\downarrow \text{HF}$$

$$\text{H}_2\text{N}-\overset{\overset{\text{R}''}{|}}{\text{CH}}-\underset{\underset{\text{O}}{\|}}{\text{C}}-(\text{NH}-\underset{\underset{\text{O}}{\|}}{\overset{\overset{\text{R}'}{|}}{\text{CHC}}})_{\overline{n}}\text{NHCHCOH} \;+\; \text{HO}-\text{CH}_2\!-\!\boxed{\text{Polymer}}$$

Polypeptide

The solid-phase technique has now been automated. Peptide-growing machines are available for automatically repeating steps 2 and 3 with different amino acids as many times as desired. Each step occurs in extremely high yield, and mechanical losses are minimized since the peptide intermediates are never removed from the insoluble polymer until the final step. Among the many remarkable achievements recorded is the synthesis of bovine pancreatic ribonuclease, a protein containing 124 amino acid units. The entire synthesis required only 6 weeks and took place in 17% overall yield.

CHAPTER **16**

Biomolecules: Lipids and Nucleic Acids

In the previous two chapters, we have discussed the organic chemistry of carbohydrates and proteins, two of the four major classes of biomolecules. Let's now look at the two remaining classes, lipids and nucleic acids. Though chemically quite different from one another, all four classes are essential for life.

16.1 LIPIDS

Lipids are naturally occurring organic molecules isolated from cells and tissues by extraction with nonpolar organic solvents. Since they usually have large hydrocarbon portions in their structures, lipids are insoluble in water but soluble in organic solvents. Note that lipids are defined by *physical property* (solubility) rather than by chemical structure as with carbohydrates, proteins, and nucleic acids.

Lipids can be further classified into two general types. **Complex lipids**, such as fats and waxes, contain ester linkages that can be hydrolyzed to yield smaller molecules. **Simple lipids**, such as cholesterol and other steroids, cannot be hydrolyzed.

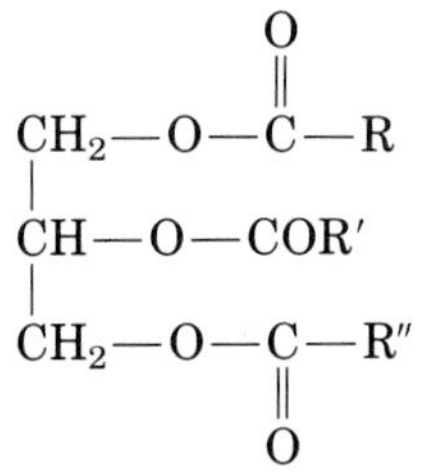

Fat, a complex lipid
(R, R′, R″ = C$_{11}$–C$_{19}$ chains)

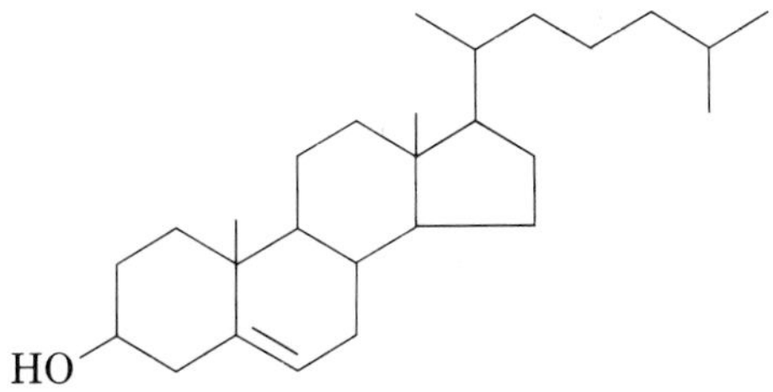

Cholesterol, a simple lipid

16.2 FATS AND OILS

Animal fats and vegetable oils are the most widely occurring lipids. Although they appear different—animal fats such as butter and lard are solids, whereas vegetable oils such as corn and peanut oil are liquids—their structures are closely related. Chemically, fats and oil are **triacylglycerols**, that is, triesters of glycerol with three long-chain carboxylic acids. Thus, hydrolysis of a fat or oil with aqueous sodium hydroxide yields glycerol and three **fatty acids**:

$$
\begin{array}{l}
CH_2O-\overset{\displaystyle O}{\overset{\|}{C}}-R \\[2mm]
CHO-\overset{\displaystyle O}{\overset{\|}{C}}-R' \\[2mm]
CH_2O-\overset{\displaystyle O}{\overset{\|}{C}}-R''
\end{array}
\quad \xrightarrow[\text{2. } H^+]{\text{1. } ^-OH} \quad
\begin{array}{ll}
CH_2OH & RCOOH \\
CHOH & + \ R'COOH \\
CH_2OH & R''COOH \\
\textbf{Glycerol} & \textbf{Fatty acids}
\end{array}
$$

A fat

The fatty acids obtained by hydrolysis of triacylglycerols are generally unbranched and contain an even number of carbon atoms between 12 and 20. If double bonds are present, they usually have Z (cis) geometry. The three fatty acids of a specific molecule are not necessarily the same, and a fat or oil from a given source is likely to be a complex mixture of many different triacylglycerols. Table 16.1 lists some of the commonly occurring fatty acids; Table 16.2 lists the approximate composition of fats and oils from different sources.

The melting points lised in Table 16.1 show that unsaturated fatty acids generally have lower melting points than their saturated counterparts, a trend that also holds true for triacylglycerols. Since vegetable oils generally have a higher

TABLE 16.1   Structures of some common fatty acids

Name	Carbons	Structure	Melting point (°)
Saturated			
Lauric	12	$CH_3(CH_2)_{10}COOH$	44
Myristic	14	$CH_3(CH_2)_{12}COOH$	58
Palmitic	16	$CH_3(CH_2)_{14}COOH$	63
Stearic	18	$CH_3(CH_2)_{16}COOH$	70
Arachidic	20	$CH_3(CH_2)_{18}COOH$	75
Unsaturated			
Palmitoleic	16	$CH_3(CH_2)_5CH{=}CH(CH_2)_7COOH$ (cis)	32
Oleic	18	$CH_3(CH_2)_7CH{=}CH(CH_2)_7COOH$ (cis)	4
Ricinoleic	18	$CH_3(CH_2)_5CH(OH)CH_2CH{=}CH(CH_2)_7COOH$ (cis)	5
Linoleic	18	$CH_3(CH_2)_4CH{=}CHCH_2CH{=}CH(CH_2)_7COOH$ (cis,cis)	−5
Arachidonic	20	$CH_3(CH_2)_4(CH{=}CHCH_2)_4CH_2CH_2COOH$ (all cis)	−50

TABLE 16.2 **Approximate fatty acid composition of some common fats and oils**

| | Saturated fatty acids (%) | | | | Unsaturated fatty acids (%) | | |
Source	C_{12} Lauric	C_{14} Myristic	C_{16} Palmitic	C_{18} Stearic	C_{18} Oleic	C_{18} Ricinoleic	C_{18} Linoleic
Animal fat							
Lard	—	1	25	15	50	—	6
Butter	2	10	25	10	25	—	5
Human fat	1	3	25	8	46	—	10
Whale blubber	—	8	12	3	35	—	10
Vegetable oil							
Coconut	50	18	8	2	6	—	1
Corn	—	1	10	4	35	—	45
Olive	—	1	5	5	80	—	7
Peanut	—	—	7	5	60	—	20
Linseed	—	—	5	3	20	—	20
Castor bean	—	—	—	1	8	85	4

proportion of unsaturated to saturated fatty acids than animal fats (Table 16.2), they are lower melting. This behavior is due to the fact that saturated fats have a uniform shape that allows them to pack together easily in a crystal lattice. Carbon–carbon double bonds in unsaturated vegetable oils, however, introduce bends and kinks into the hydrocarbon chains, making crystal formation difficult. The more double bonds there are, the harder it is for the molecule to crystallize, and the lower-melting the oil. Figure 16.1 illustrates this effect with space-filling molecular models.

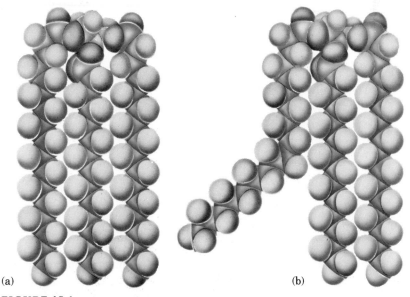

(a)   (b)

FIGURE 16.1
Space-filling molecular models of (a) saturated and (b) unsaturated triacylglycerols: There is one unsaturated acyl group in (b), which prevents the molecule from adopting a regular shape and crystallizing easily.

The carbon–carbon double bonds present in vegetable oils can be reduced by catalytic hydrogenation (Section 4.6) to produce saturated solid or semisolid fats. For example, margarine and solid cooking fats such as Crisco are produced by hydrogenating soybean, peanut, or cottonseed oil until the proper consistency is obtained.

PROBLEM 16.1   Draw structures of these molecules. Which would you expect to be higher melting?

(a) Glyceryl tripalmitate   (b) Glyceryl trioleate

PROBLEM 16.2   Fats and oils may be either optically active or optically inactive, depending on their structure. Draw the structure of an optically active fat that gives 2 equiv palmitic acid and 1 equiv stearic acid on hydrolysis. Draw the structure of an optically inactive fat that gives the same products on hydrolysis.

16.3 SOAPS

Soap has been known since at least 600 BC, when the Phoenicians reportedly prepared a curdy material by boiling goat fat with extracts of wood ash. The cleansing properties of soap were not generally recognized, however, and the use of soap did not become widespread until the eighteenth century.

Chemically, **soap** is a mixture of the sodium or potassium salts of long-chain fatty acids produced by hydrolysis (**saponification**) of animal fat with alkali.

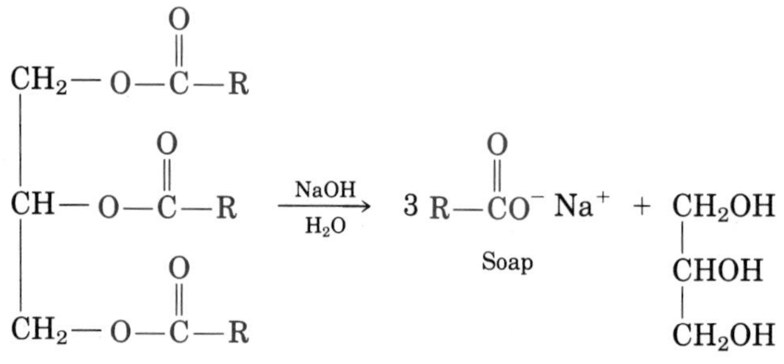

A fat
(R = C_{15}–C_{17} aliphatic chains)

Glycerol

Crude soap curds, which contain glycerol and excess alkali as well as soap, are purified by boiling with water and adding NaCl to precipitate the pure sodium carboxylate salts. The smooth soap that precipitates is dried, perfumed, and pressed into bars for household use. Dyes are added if a colored soap is desired; antiseptics are added for medicated soaps; pumice is added for scouring soaps; and air is blown in for a soap that floats. Regardless of these extra treatments and regardless of price, however, all soaps are fundamentally the same.

Soaps exert their cleansing action because the two ends of a soap molecule are so different. The sodium salt end of the long-chain molecule is ionic; it is therefore **hydrophilic** (water-loving) and tries to dissolve in water. The long aliphatic chain portion of the molecule, however, is **lipophilic** (fat-loving); it tries to dissolve in grease. The net effect of these two opposing tendencies is that soaps are attracted to both grease and water.

When soaps are dispersed in water, the long hydrocarbon tails cluster together in a lipophilic ball, while the ionic heads on the surface of the cluster stick out into the water layer. These spherical clusters, called **micelles**, are shown schematically in Figure 16.2. Grease and oil droplets are made soluble in water when they are coated by the nonpolar tails of soap molecules in the center of micelles. Once solubilized, the grease and dirt can be washed away.

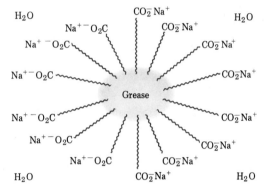

FIGURE 16.2
A soap micelle solubilizing a grease particle in water

PROBLEM 16.3   In hard water, which contains magnesium and calcium ions, soap tends to leave a scummy residue. Draw the structure of magnesium oleate, one of the components of bathtub scum.

16.4   PHOSPHOLIPIDS

Phospholipids are esters of phosphoric acid, H_3PO_4. Most phospholipids are closely related to fats, containing a glycerol backbone linked by ester bonds to two fatty acids and one phosphoric acid. Although the fatty acids in these **phosphoglycerides** may be any of the C_{12}–C_{20} units normally present in fats, the acyl group at C1 is usually saturated and that at C2 is usually unsaturated. The phosphate group at C3 is also bound by a separate ester link to an amino alcohol such as choline, $HOCH_2CH_2\overset{+}{N}(CH_3)_3$, or ethanolamine, $HOCH_2CH_2NH_2$. The most important phosphoglycerides are the *lecithins* and the *cephalins*, which are shown on page 466 (R is saturated and R′ is unsaturated). Note that these compounds are chiral and that they have the L (or R) configuration at C2.

L configuration

$$CH_2O-\overset{\overset{\displaystyle O}{\|}}{C}-R$$

$$R'-\overset{\overset{\displaystyle O}{\|}}{C}-O-\overset{\displaystyle}{\underset{\displaystyle}{C}}-H$$

$$CH_2O-\overset{\displaystyle}{\underset{\overset{\displaystyle}{\underset{\displaystyle O^-}{|}}}{P}}-O-CH_2CH_2\overset{+}{N}(CH_3)_3$$

Phosphatidylcholine, a lecithin

$$CH_2O\overset{\overset{\displaystyle O}{\|}}{C}-R$$

$$R'-\overset{\overset{\displaystyle O}{\|}}{C}-O-CH$$

$$CH_2O-\overset{\displaystyle}{\underset{\overset{\displaystyle}{\underset{\displaystyle O^-}{|}}}{P}}-O-CH_2CH_2\overset{+}{N}H_3$$

Phosphatidylethanolamine, a cephalin

Found widely in both plant and animal tissues, phosphoglycerides are the major lipid component of cell membranes (approximately 40%). Like soaps, phosphoglycerides have a long, nonpolar hydrocarbon tail bound to a polar ionic head (the phosphate group). Cell membranes are composed in large part of phosphoglycerides oriented into a bilayer about 50 Å thick. As shown in Figure 16.3, the lipophilic tails aggregate in the center of the bilayer in much the same way that soap tails aggregate into the center of a micelle (Figure 16.2); the hydrophilic heads lie together on the outside of the bilayer. This bilayer serves as an effective barrier to the passage of water and other components into and out of the cell.

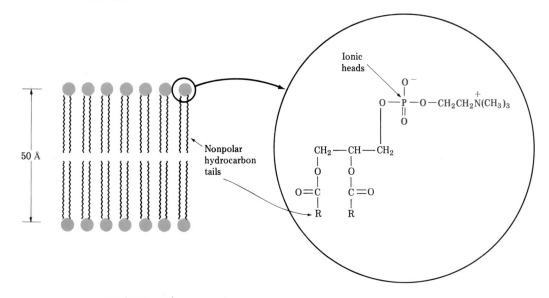

FIGURE 16.3
Aggregation of phosphoglycerides into the lipid bilayer that composes cell membranes

Sphingolipids are the second major group of phospholipids. These complex lipids, which have *sphingosine* or a related dihydroxyamine as their backbones, are constituents of plant and animal cell membranes. They are particularly abundant in brain and nerve tissue, where *sphingomyelins* are a major constituent of the coating around nerve fibers.

$$\begin{array}{l} CH_2OH \\ | \\ CHNH_2 \\ | \\ CHOH \\ | \\ CH{=}CH(CH_2)_{12}CH_3 \end{array}$$

Sphingosine

$$\begin{array}{l} CH_2{-}O{-}\overset{\displaystyle O}{\overset{\displaystyle \|}{P}}{-}O{-}CH_2CH_2\overset{+}{N}(CH_3)_3 \\ | \qquad\qquad | \\ \qquad\qquad O^- \\ CH{-}NHCO(CH_2)_{16-24}{-}CH_3 \\ | \\ CHOH \\ | \\ CH{=}CH(CH_2)_{12}CH_3 \end{array}$$

Sphingomyelin, a sphingolipid

16.5 STEROIDS

In addition to fats and phospholipids, lipid extracts of plants and animals contain **steroids**. A steroid is an organic molecule whose structure is based on the tetracyclic ring system shown in Figure 16.4. The four rings are designated A, B, C, and D, beginning at the lower left, and the carbon atoms are numbered beginning in ring A. Common examples are cholesterol, an animal steroid (and principal component of gallstones), and β-sitosterol, a plant steroid.

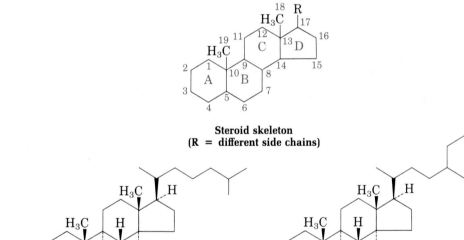

Steroid skeleton
(R = different side chains)

Cholesterol (animal sources)　　　　　**β-Sitosterol (plant sources)**

FIGURE 16.4
Structures of some representative steroids

Steroids are widespread in both plant and animal kingdoms, and many have interesting biological activity. For example, digitoxigenin, a plant steroid found in *Digitalis purpurea* (purple foxglove), is widely used in medicine as a heart stimulant; estradiol is a steroid sex hormone; and cortisone is a steroid hormone useful in the treatment of inflammation (such as skin rashes caused by poison oak and poison ivy).

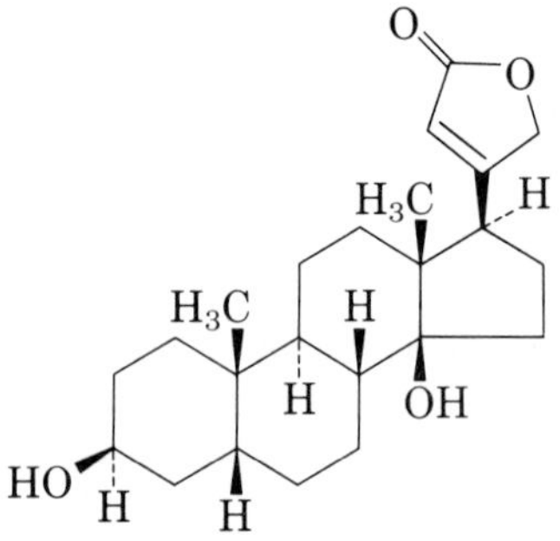

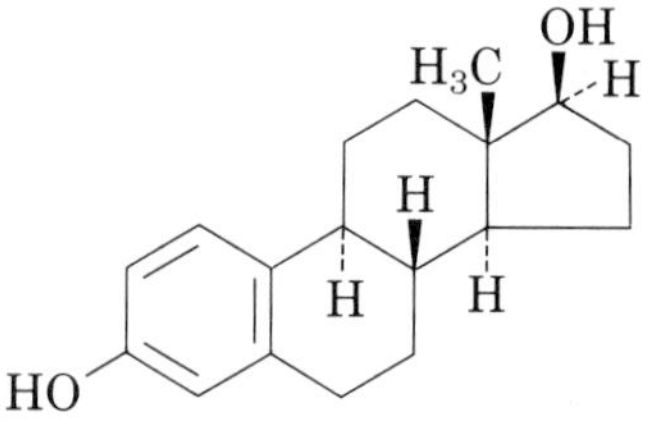

Digitoxigenin (heart stimulant)

Estradiol (female sex hormone)

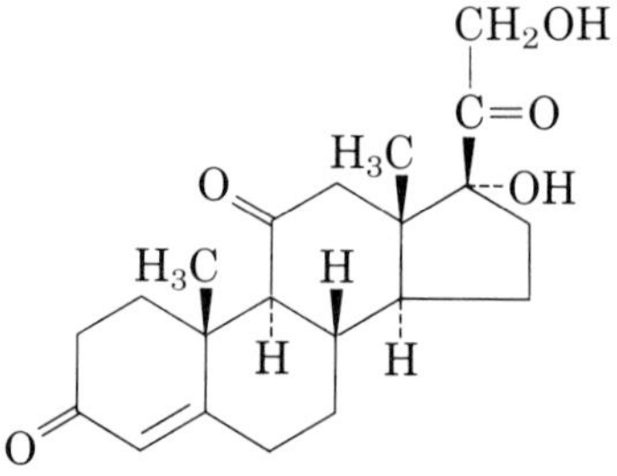

Cortisone (anti-inflammatory drug)

Many other steroids are produced in the laboratory by pharmaceutical companies. Even such synthetic steroids as methandrostenolone (an anabolic, or tissue-building steroid) and norethindrone (Norlutin, an oral contraceptive agent) have potent physiological effects.

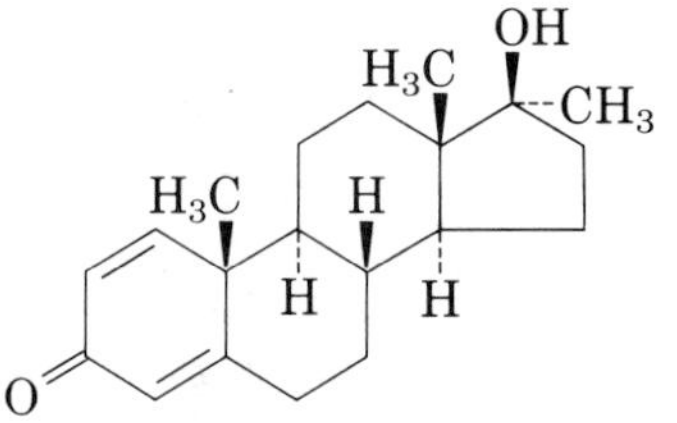

Methandrostenolone (anabolic)

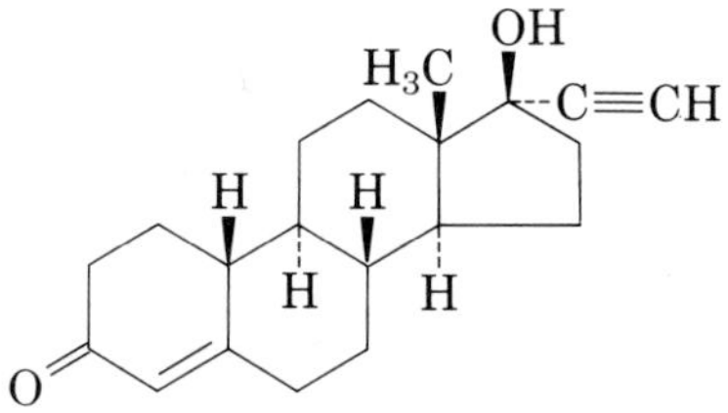

Norethindrone (oral contraceptive)

The steroid carbon skeleton has four rings fused together with a specific stereo-chemistry. All three of the six-membered rings (rings A, B, and C) can adopt strain-free chair conformations, as indicated in Figure 16.5 for cholesterol. But unlike simple cyclohexane rings, which can undergo chair–chair interconversions (Section 2.15), steroids are constrained by their rigid conformation and cannot undergo ring-flips.

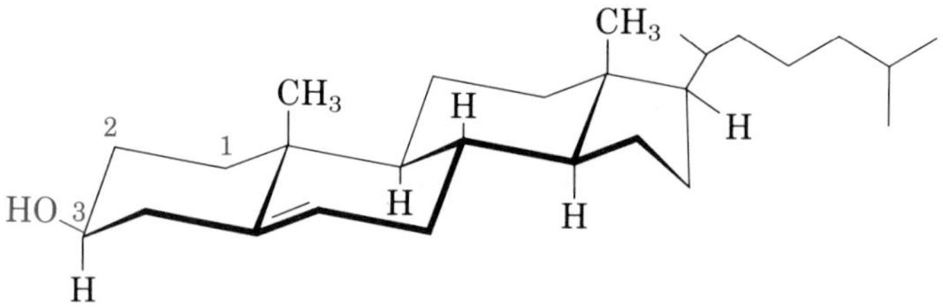

Cholesterol

FIGURE 16.5
Conformation of cholesterol showing the chair conformations

PROBLEM 16.4 Look at the structure of cholesterol shown in Figure 16.5 and tell whether the hydroxyl group is axial or equatorial.

PROBLEM 16.5 Look at the structure of cholesterol in Figure 16.5 to see how chair cyclohexane rings can be joined, and then draw *trans*-decalin in its most stable conformation.

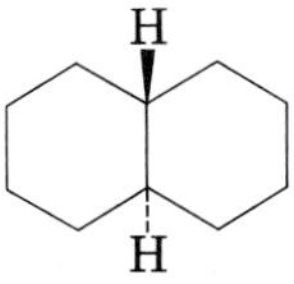

H

H

trans-Decalin

16.6 NUCLEIC ACIDS

The nucleic acids, **deoxyribonucleic acid (DNA)** and **ribonucleic acid (RNA)**, are the chemical carriers of a cell's genetic information. Coded in a cell's DNA is all the information that determines the nature of the cell, controls cell growth and division, and directs biosynthesis of the enzymes and other proteins required for all cellular functions.

Like proteins, nucleic acids are polymers. Mild enzyme-catalyzed hydrolysis cleaves a nucleic acid into its monomeric building blocks called **nucleotides**. Each nucleotide can be further cleaved by enzyme-catalyzed hydrolysis to give a **nucleoside** plus phosphoric acid, H_3PO_4, and each nucleoside can be hydrolyzed to yield a simple aldopentose sugar plus a heterocyclic amine base.

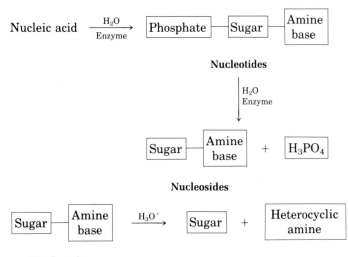

The sugar component in RNA is ribose, whereas the sugar in DNA is 2-deoxy-ribose ("2-deoxy" indicates that oxygen is missing from C2 of ribose).

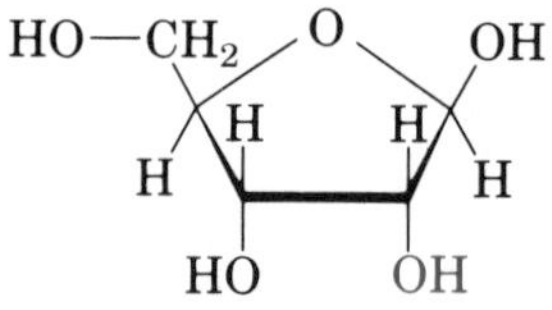

Ribose 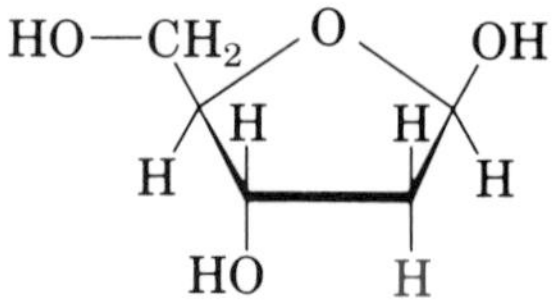   **2-Deoxyribose**

Four different heterocyclic amine bases (Section 12.7) are found in DNA: two are substituted purines (**adenine** and **guanine**), and two are substituted pyrimidines (**cytosine** and **thymine**). Adenine, guanine, and cytosine also occur in RNA, but thymine is replaced in RNA by a different pyrimidine base called **uracil**.

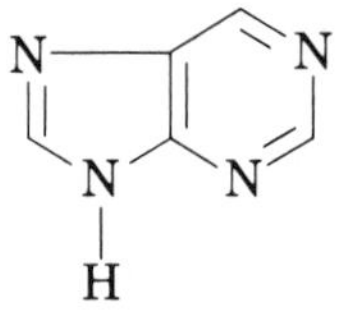

Purine 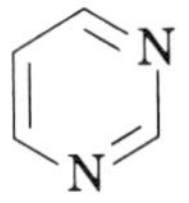   **Pyrimidine**

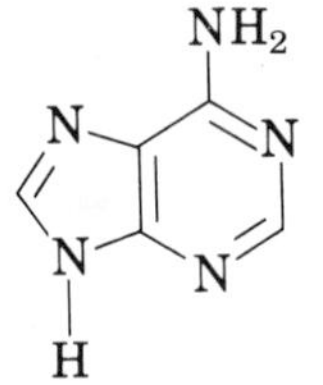

Adenine 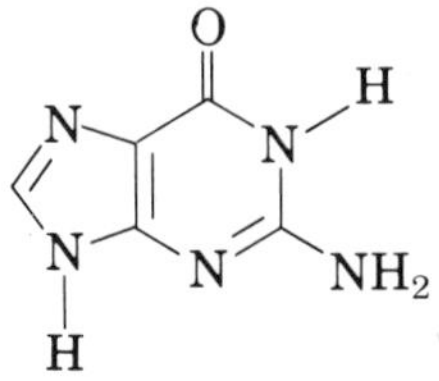   **Guanine**   Purines

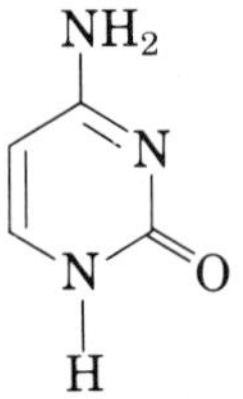

Cytosine 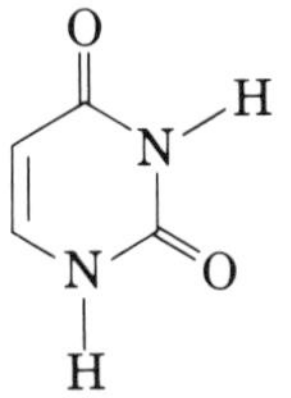   **Uracil (RNA)** 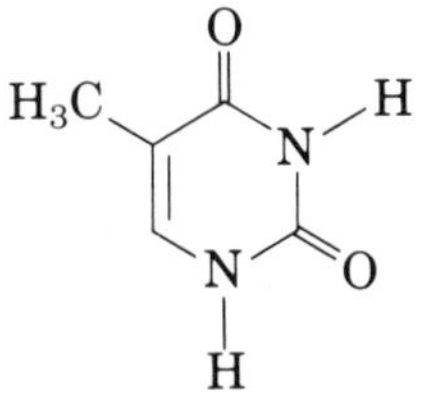   **Thymine (DNA)**   Pyrimidines

In both DNA and RNA, the heterocyclic amine base is bound to C1' of the sugar, while the phosphoric acid is bound by a phosphate ester linkage to the C5' sugar position. Thus, nucleosides and nucleotides have the general structures shown in Figure 16.6. (In discussing RNA and DNA, numbers with a prime superscript refer to positions on the sugar component of a nucleotide; numbers without a prime refer to positions on the heterocyclic amine base.) The complete structures of all four deoxyribonucleotides and all four ribonucleotides are shown in Figure 16.7 on page 472.

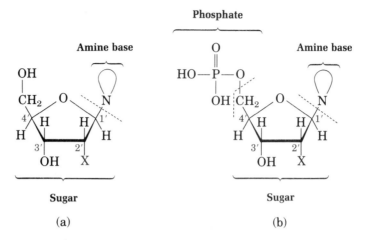

FIGURE 16.6
General structures of (a) a nucleoside and (b) a nucleotide:
When X = H, the sugar is deoxyribose; when X = OH, the sugar is ribose.

Though chemically similar, DNA and RNA are different in size and have different roles within the cell. Molecules of DNA are enormous. They have molecular weights of up to 1 trillion and are found mostly in the nucleus of the cell. Molecules of RNA, by contrast, are much smaller (as low as 35,000 mol wt) and are found mostly outside the cell nucleus. Let's consider the two kinds of nucleic acids separately, beginning with DNA.

16.7   STRUCTURE OF DNA

Nucleic acids consist of nucleotide units joined by a bond between the 5′-phosphate component of one nucleotide and the 3′-hydroxyl on the sugar component of another nucleotide (Figure 16.8, page 473). One end of the nucleic acid polymer has a free hydroxyl at C3′ (called the **3′ end**), and the other end has a phosphoric acid residue at C5′ (the **5′ end**).

Just as the precise structure of a protein depends on the sequence in which individual amino acids are arranged, the precise structure of a nucleic acid depends on the sequence in which individual nucleotides are arranged. To carry the analogy further, just as a protein has a polyamide backbone with different side chains attached to it, a nucleic acid has an alternating sugar–phosphate backbone with different amine base side chains attached to it.

Samples of DNA isolated from different tissues of the same species have the same proportions of heterocyclic bases, but samples from different species can have greatly different proportions of bases. For example, human DNA contains about 30% each of adenine and thymine, and about 20% each of guanine and cytosine. The bacterium *Clostridium perfringens*, however, contains about 37% each of adenine and thymine, and only 13% each of guanine and cytosine. Note that in both of these examples, the bases occur in pairs. Adenine and thymine are usually present in equal amounts, as are cytosine and guanine. The reasons for this pairing of bases has much to do with the secondary structure of DNA.

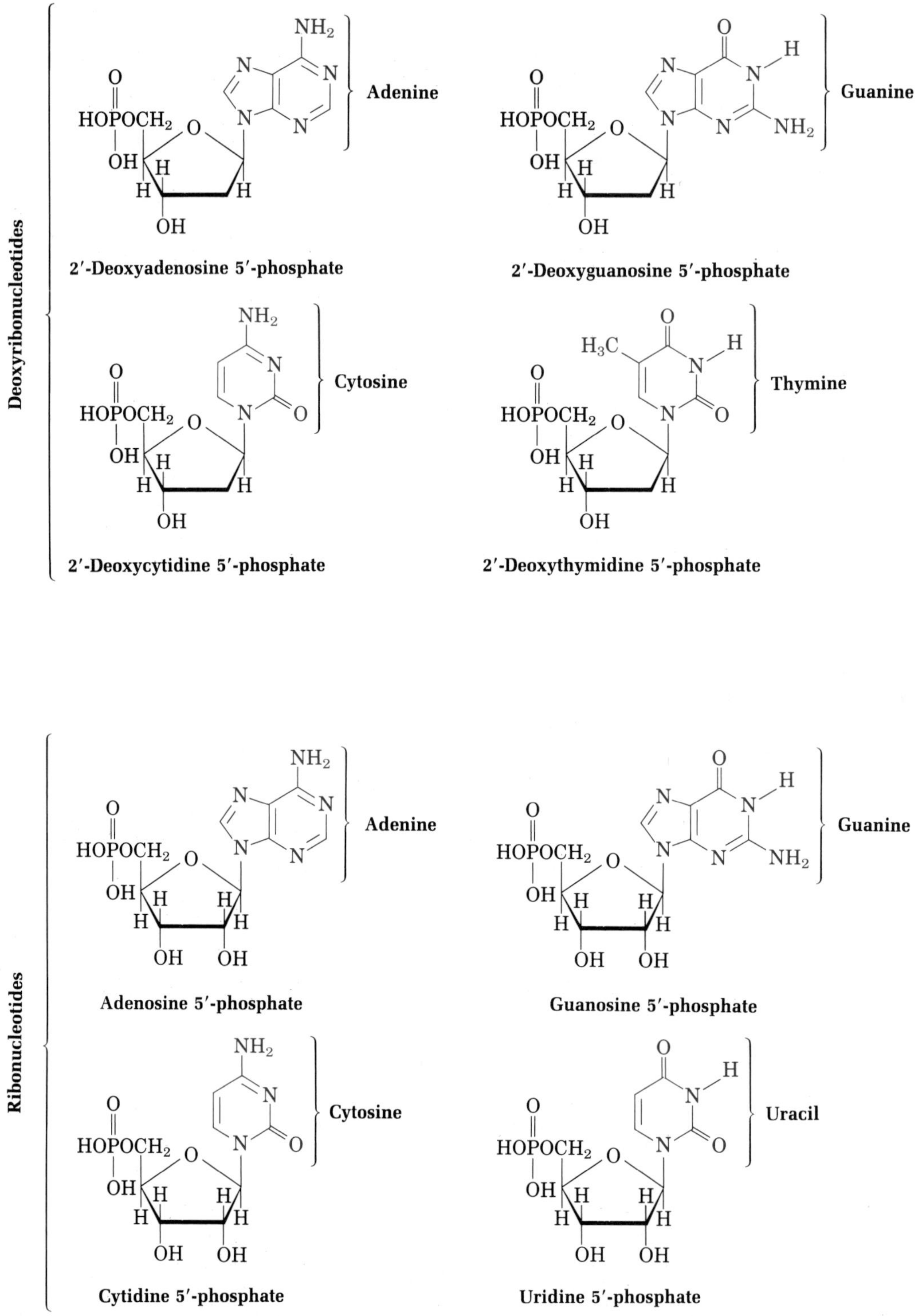

FIGURE 16.7
Structures of the four deoxyribonucleotides and the four ribonucleotides

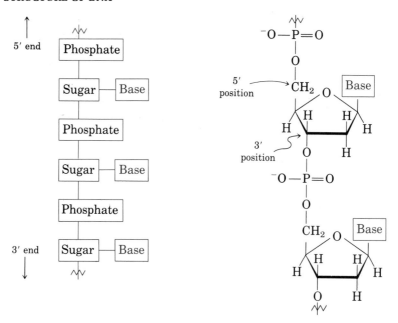

FIGURE 16.8
Generalized structure of DNA

In 1953, James Watson and Francis Crick made their now-classic proposal for the secondary structure of DNA. According to the Watson–Crick model, DNA consists of two polynucleotide strands coiled around each other in a **double helix**. The two strands run in opposite directions and are held together by hydrogen bonds between bases. Adenine (A) and thymine (T) form strong hydrogen bonds to each other but not to other bases; guanine (G) and cytosine (C) form strong hydrogen bonds to each other but not to other bases.

(Adenine) A : : : : : : T (Thymine)

(Guanine) G : : : : : : C (Cytosine)

The two strands of the DNA double helix are not identical; rather, they are complementary. Whenever a C base occurs in one strand, a G base occurs opposite it in the other strand. When an A base occurs in one strand, a T base appears in the other strand. This complementary pairing of bases explains why A and T, and C and G, are always found in equal amounts. Figure 16.9 illustrates this base pairing, showing how the two complementary strands coil into the double helix. X-ray measurements show that the DNA double helix is 20 Å wide, that there are exactly 10 base pairs in each full turn, and that each turn is 34 Å in height.

A helpful mnemonic device to remember the pairing of the four DNA bases is the simple phrase "Pure silver taxi."

Pure	Silver	Taxi
Pur	Ag	TC

The purine bases,   A and G,   hydrogen bond to T and C.

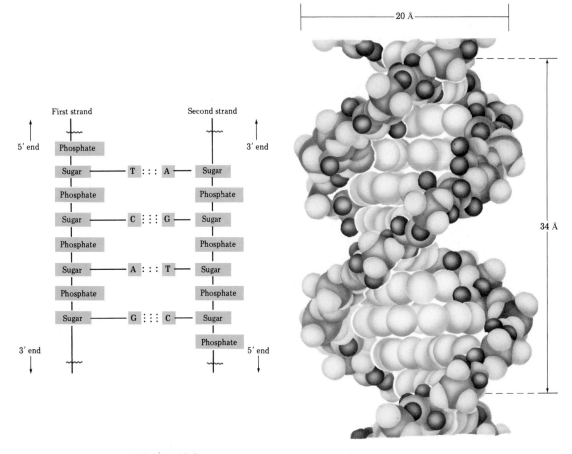

FIGURE 16.9

Complementarity of base pairing in the DNA double helix: The sugar–phosphate backbone of DNA is shown in gray; the atoms of the amine bases are shown in color and lie inside the helix; the small black atoms are hydrogen.

PRACTICE PROBLEM What sequence of bases on one strand of DNA would be complementary to the sequence T-A-T-G-C-A-T on another strand?

Solution Remembering that A and G (silver) bond to T and C (taxi), we go through the given sequence replacing A by T, G by C, T by A, and C by G.

Original:　　T-A-T-G-C-A-T

Complement:　A-T-A-C-G-T-A

PROBLEM 16.6 What sequence of bases on one strand of DNA would be complementary to the following sequence on another strand?

G-G-C-T-A-A-T-C-C-G-T

16.8 NUCLEIC ACIDS AND HEREDITY

A DNA molecule is the chemical repository of an organism's genetic information, which is stored as a sequence of deoxyribonucleotides strung together in a chain. For this information to be preserved, mechanisms must exist for the DNA molecule to be copied and passed on to succeeding generations. For this information to be used, mechanisms must exist for reading the DNA message, for decoding the instructions contained therein, and for implementing those instructions to carry out the myriad biochemical processes necessary to sustain life.

What Crick has termed the *central dogma of molecular genetics* says that three major processes take place:

1. **Replication** is the process by which identical copies of DNA are made, forming daughter molecules and preserving genetic information.
2. **Transcription** is the process by which information in the DNA is read by RNA and carried from the nucleus to the ribosomes.
3. **Translation** is the process by which RNA decodes the genetic message and uses the information to build proteins.

Thus, information is stored in DNA, but is read and used by RNA to make proteins:

DNA $\longrightarrow$ RNA $\longrightarrow$ Proteins

16.9 REPLICATION OF DNA

Replication of DNA is an enzyme-catalyzed process that begins by a partial unwinding of the double helix. As the strands separate and the bases are exposed, new nucleotides line up on each strand in an exactly complementary manner, A to

T and G to C, and two new strands begin to grow. Each new strand is complementary to its old template strand, and two new identical DNA double helices are produced (Figure 16.10).

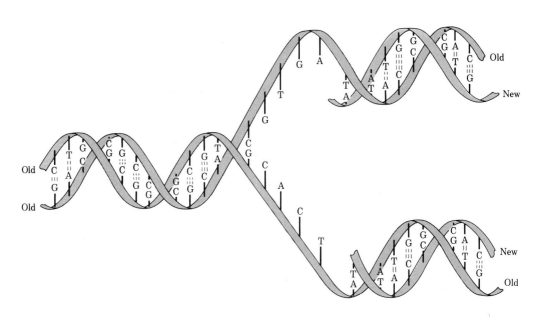

FIGURE 16.10
Schematic representation of DNA replication

Crick probably described the process best when he used the analogy of the two DNA strands fitting together like a hand in a glove. The hand and glove separate; a new hand forms inside the glove; and a new glove forms around the hand. Two identical copies now exist where only one existed before.

The process by which the individual nucleotides are joined to create new DNA strands is complex, involving many steps and different enzymes. Addition of new nucleotide units to the growing chain, which is catalyzed by the enzyme DNA polymerase, has been shown to occur by addition of a 5′-mononucleotide triphosphate to the free 3′-hydroxyl group of the growing chain, as indicated in Figure 16.11.

It is difficult to conceive of the magnitude of the replication process. The nucleus of a human cell contains 46 chromosomes, each of which consists of one very large DNA molecule. Current estimates of size place the molecular weight of a human DNA molecule as high as 1 trillion. A single molecule of human DNA is calculated to be about 1 m long and to contain 3 billion individual nucleotides. Regardless of the size of these massive molecules, the base sequence is faithfully copied during replication.

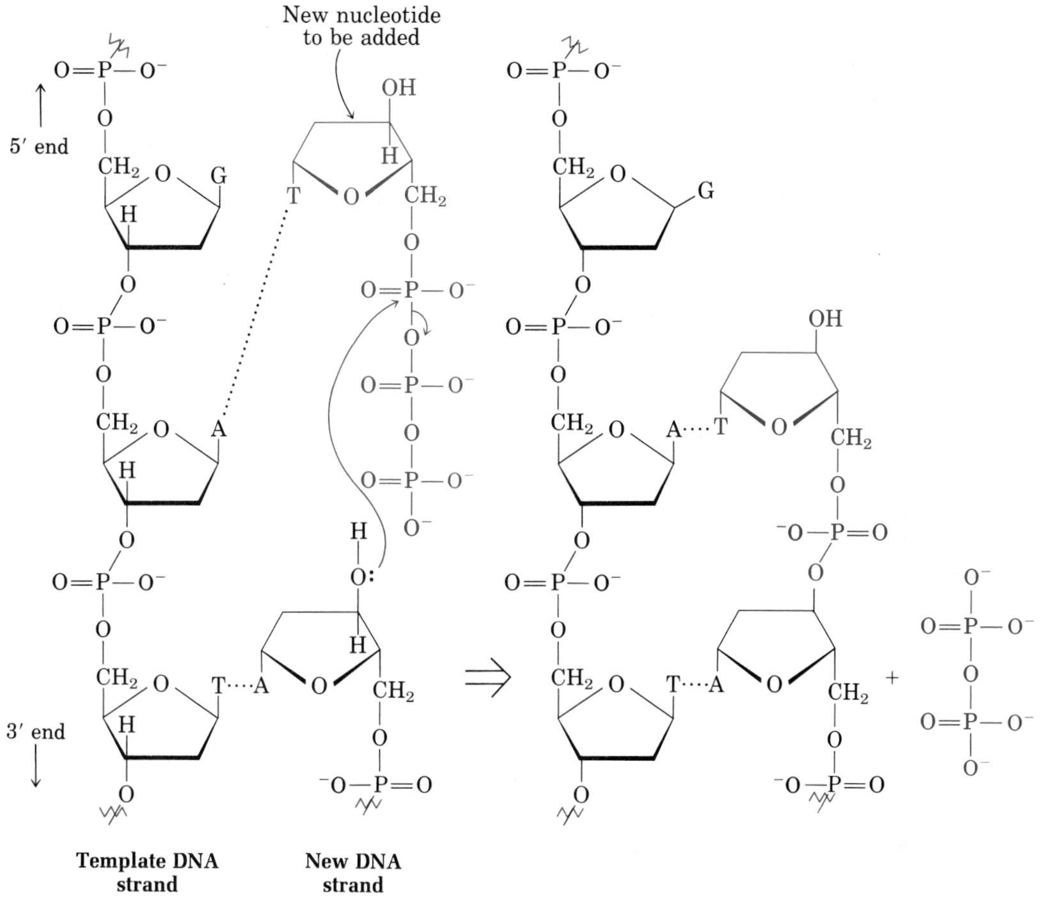

FIGURE 16.11
Addition of a new nucleotide to a growing DNA strand

16.10 STRUCTURE AND SYNTHESIS OF RNA: TRANSCRIPTION

Ribonucleic acid is structurally similar to DNA. Both are sugar–phosphate polymers and both have heterocyclic bases attached. The only differences are that RNA contains ribose rather than 2-deoxyribose, and contains uracil rather than thymine. Uracil in RNA forms strong hydrogen bonds to its complementary base, adenine, just as thymine does in DNA.

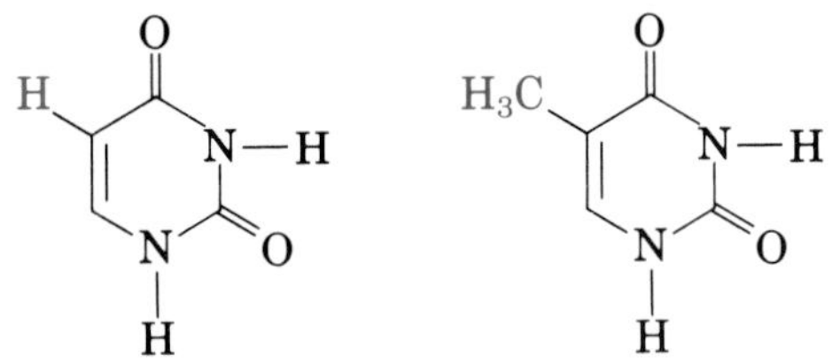

Uracil (in RNA)   Thymine (in DNA)

There are three major kinds of ribonucleic acid: **messenger RNA (mRNA)**, **transfer RNA (tRNA)**, and **ribosomal RNA (rRNA)**. All three are much smaller molecules than DNA, and all occur as single polyribonucleotide strands, rather than as double helices.

Molecules of RNA are synthesized in the nucleus of the cell by transcription of DNA. A small portion of the DNA double helix unwinds, and one of the two complementary DNA strands serves as a template for complementary ribonucleotides to line up. Bond formation then occurs in the $5' \rightarrow 3'$ direction, as with DNA replication. Unlike DNA replication, however, the completed RNA molecule does not remain in a double helix with DNA but separates and migrates from the cell nucleus. The DNA then rewinds to its stable double-helix conformation (Figure 16.12).

PROBLEM 16.7 Show how uracil can form strong hydrogen bonds to adenine.

PROBLEM 16.8 What RNA base sequence would be complementary to the following DNA base sequence?

G-A-T-T-A-C-C-G-T-A

16.11 RNA AND PROTEIN BIOSYNTHESIS: TRANSLATION

The primary cellular function of RNA is to direct biosynthesis of the thousands of diverse peptides and proteins required by an organism. These proteins in turn regulate all other biological processes. The mechanics of protein biosynthesis are directed by messenger RNA (mRNA) and take place on **ribosomes**, small granular particles in the cytoplasm of the cells. On the ribosome, mRNA serves as a template to pass on the genetic information it has transcribed from DNA.

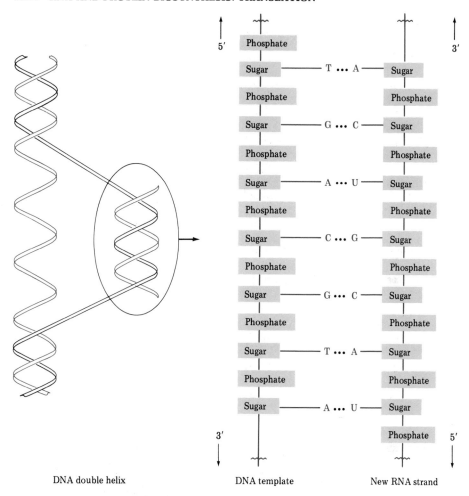

FIGURE 16.12
Synthesis of RNA using a DNA segment as template

The specific ribonucleotide sequence in mRNA forms a "code" that determines the order in which different amino acid residues are to be joined. Thus, each of the estimated 100,000 proteins in the human body is synthesized from a different mRNA that has been transcribed from a specific gene segment on DNA. Each "word" or **codon** along the mRNA chain consists of a series of three ribonucleotides that is specific for a given amino acid. For example, the series cytosine–uracil–guanine (C-U-G) on mRNA is a codon directing incorporation of the amino acid leucine into the growing protein. Similarly, guanine–adenine–uracil (G-A-U) codes for aspartic acid. Of the $4^3 = 64$ possible triads of the four bases in RNA, 61 code for specific amino acids (most amino acids are specified by more than one codon). The other 3 codons specify chain termination. Table 16.3 on page 480 shows the meaning of each codon.

TABLE 16.3   Codon assignments of base triads

First base (5' end)	Second base	Third base (3' end)			
		U	C	A	G
U	U	Phe	Phe	Leu	Leu
	C	Ser	Ser	Ser	Ser
	A	Tyr	Tyr	Stop	Stop
	G	Cys	Cys	Stop	Trp
C	U	Leu	Leu	Leu	Leu
	C	Pro	Pro	Pro	Pro
	A	His	His	Gln	Gln
	G	Arg	Arg	Arg	Arg
A	U	Ile	Ile	Ile	Met
	C	Thr	Thr	Thr	Thr
	A	Asn	Asn	Lys	Lys
	G	Ser	Ser	Arg	Arg
G	U	Val	Val	Val	Val
	C	Ala	Ala	Ala	Ala
	A	Asp	Asp	Glu	Glu
	G	Gly	Gly	Gly	Gly

The code expressed in mRNA is read by transfer RNA (tRNA) in a process called **translation**. There are at least 60 different tRNA's. Each specific tRNA acts as a carrier to bring a specific amino acid into place so that it may be transferred to the growing protein chain. A typical tRNA is roughly the shape of a cloverleaf, as shown in Figure 16.13. It consists of about 70–100 ribonucleotides and is bound to a specific amino acid by an ester linkage through the free 3'-hydroxyl on ribose at the 3' end of the tRNA. Each tRNA also contains in its structure a segment called an **anticodon**, a sequence of three ribonucleotides complementary to the codon sequence. For example, the codon sequence C-U-G present on mRNA would be "read" by a leucine-bearing tRNA having the complementary anticodon sequence G-A-C.

As each successive codon on mRNA is read, different tRNA's bring the correct amino acids into position for enzyme-mediated transfer to the growing peptide. When synthesis of the proper protein is completed, a "stop" codon signals the end and the protein is released from the ribosome. The entire process of protein biosynthesis is illustrated schematically in Figure 16.14 on page 482.

In summary, protein biosynthesis takes place in five discrete steps:

1. Messenger RNA, containing the genetic information transcribed from DNA, is synthesized in the nucleus and transported to ribosomes.

2. Individual amino acids are activated by binding to specific tRNA's.

3. Transfer RNA's containing the correct anticodon sequences line up at the proper complementary codon sequences on the 3' end of the mRNA chain and move the bound amino acid groups into position.

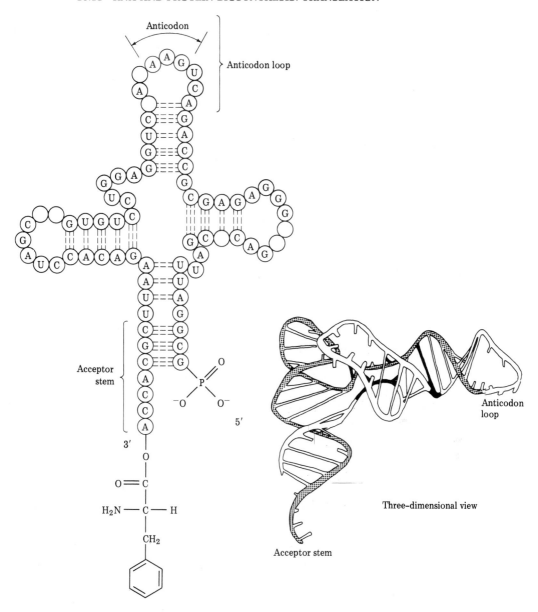

FIGURE 16.13
Structure of a tRNA molecule: The tRNA is a roughly cloverleaf-shaped molecule containing an anticodon triplet on one "leaf" and a covalently attached amino acid residue at its 3' end. The example shown is a yeast tRNA that codes for phenylalanine. (The nucleotides that are not specifically identified are chemically modified analogs of the four normal nucleotides.)

4. The polypeptide is produced as enzymes catalyze the addition of tRNA-bound amino acids to the growing peptide chain.

5. When the peptide is completed, a "stop" codon on mRNA halts the biosynthesis, and the peptide is released from the ribosome.

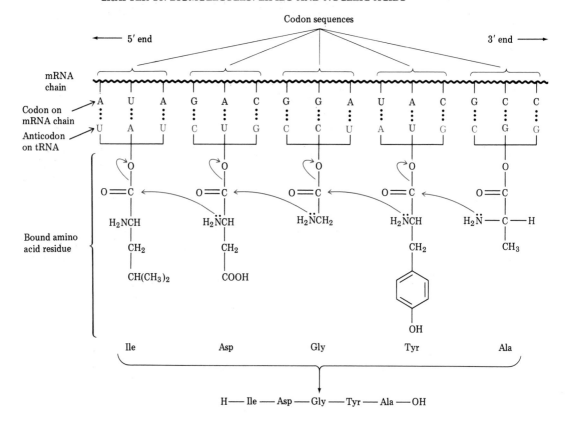

FIGURE 16.14
Schematic representation of protein biosynthesis: Messenger RNA, containing codon base sequences, is read by tRNA, containing complementary anticodon base sequences. Transfer RNA assembles proper amino acids into position for incorporation into the peptide.

PRACTICE PROBLEM   What amino acid sequence is coded for by the mRNA base sequence AUC-GGU?

Solution   Table 16.3 indicates that AUC codes for isoleucine, and that GGU codes for glycine. Thus, AUC-GGU codes for H-Ile-Gly-OH.

PROBLEM 16.9   List codon sequences for the following amino acids:

(a)   Ala   (b)   Phe   (c)   Leu   (d)   Val   (e)   Tyr

PROBLEM 16.10   What amino acid sequence is coded for by the following mRNA base sequence?

CUU-AUG-GCU-UGG-CCC-UAA

PROBLEM 16.11 What anticodon sequences of tRNA's are coded for by the mRNA in Problem 16.10?

PROBLEM 16.12 What was the base sequence in the original DNA strand on which the mRNA sequence in Problem 16.10 was made?

16.12 SEQUENCING OF DNA

> When we work out the structure of DNA molecules, we examine the fundamental level that underlies all processes in living cells. DNA is the information store that ultimately dictates the structure of every gene product, delineates every part of the organism. The order of bases along DNA contains the complete set of instructions that make up the genetic inheritance. (Walter Gilbert, Nobel Prize Lecture, 1980)

Deoxyribonucleic acid sequencing is carried out by a remarkably efficient and powerful method developed in 1977 by Allan Maxam and Walter Gilbert. Since molecules of DNA are so enormous—some molecules of human DNA contain several billion base pairs—the first problem in DNA sequencing is to find a method for reproducibly and selectively cleaving the DNA chain at specific points to produce smaller, more manageable pieces. This problem has been solved by the use of enzymes called **restriction endonucleases**. Each different restriction enzyme, of which more than 200 are available, cleaves a DNA molecule between two nucleotides at well-defined points along the chain where specific base sequences occur. Since the required sequence is usually four or more nucleotides long, it is unlikely to occur very often in the overall DNA chain.

By incubation of large DNA molecules with a given restriction enzyme, many different and well-defined segments of manageable length (100–200 nucleotides) are produced. If the original DNA molecule is incubated with another restriction enzyme having a different specificity for cleavage, still other segments are produced, whose sequences partially overlap those produced by the first enzyme. Sequencing of all the segments, followed by identification of the overlapping sections, then allows complete DNA structure determination in a manner similar to that used for protein sequencing (Section 15.7). For example, the restriction enzyme Alu I cleaves the linkage between G and C in the four-base sequence AG-CT; the enzyme Hpa II cleaves the C-C linkage in the four-base sequence C-CGG (Figure 16.15, page 484).

After restriction enzymes have cleaved DNA into smaller pieces (restriction fragments) the various double-stranded fragments are isolated, and each is radioactively tagged by enzymatically incorporating a labeled ^{32}P-containing phosphate group onto the 5'-hydroxyl of the terminal nucleotide. The fragments are then separated into two strands by heating, and the strands are isolated.

The heart of the sequencing problem is finding reaction conditions for obtaining specific DNA chain breakage next to each of the four nucleotide bases so that the restriction fragments can be further degraded and ultimately sequenced. This problem has been solved using two reagents, dimethyl sulfate and hydrazine.

Treatment of a restriction fragment with dimethyl sulfate, $(CH_3O)_2SO_2$, results in methylation (S_N2 reaction) of the purine bases A and G, but does not affect the

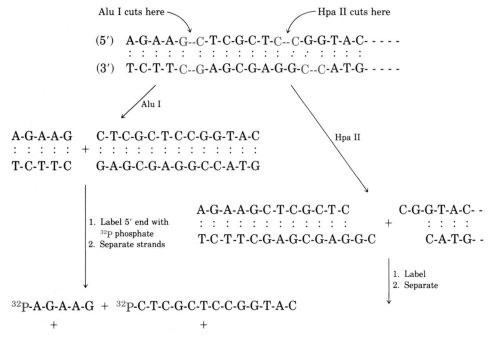

FIGURE 16.15
Cleavage of a DNA molecule with restriction enzymes: The enzyme Alu I cleaves at the sequence AG-CT; the enzyme Hpa II cleaves at C-CGG. After cleavage of the double-stranded DNA, the fragments are isolated, and each is labeled at its 5′ end by enzyme-catalyzed formation of a radioactively labeled ^{32}P-containing phosphate ester. The strands are then separated.

pyrimidine bases C and T. Deoxyadenosine is methylated at N3, and deoxyguanosine is methylated at N7.

Treatment of methylated DNA with an aqueous solution of the secondary amine piperidine then brings about destruction of the methylated nucleotides and specific opening of the DNA chain at both the 3' and 5' positions next to the methylated bases.

By working carefully, it's possible to find reaction conditions that are selective for cleavage either at A or at G. Thus, G methylates five times as rapidly as A, but the hydrolytic breakdown of methylated A occurs more rapidly than the breakdown of G if the methylated product is first heated with dilute acid prior to base treatment.

Breaking the DNA chain next to both pyrimidine nucleotides C and T can be accomplished by treatment of DNA with hydrazine, followed by heating with aqueous piperidine. Although conditions that are selective for cleavage next to T have not been found, a selective cleavage next to C can be accomplished by carrying out the hydrazine reaction in $2M$ NaCl.

In summary, four sets of reaction conditions have been devised for breaking a DNA chain at specific points:

1. **A > G:** Methylation, followed first by treatment with dilute acid and then by heating with aqueous piperidine, preferentially breaks the chain on both sides of A. (Some breakage also occurs next to G.)

2. **G > A:** Methylation, followed by heating with aqueous piperidine, preferentially breaks the chain on both sides of G. (Some breakage also occurs next to A.)

3. **C:** Treatment with hydrazine in $2M$ NaCl, followed by heating with aqueous piperidine, breaks the chain on both sides of C.

4. **C + T:** Treatment with hydrazine in the absence of NaCl, followed by heating with aqueous piperidine, breaks the chain next to *both* C and T.

After the restriction fragment has been broken down by selective cleavage reactions into a mixture of smaller pieces, the mixture is separated by electrophoresis (Section 15.3). When the mixture of DNA pieces is placed at one end of a strip of buffered gelatinous polyacrylamide and a voltage is applied across the ends of the strip, electrically charged pieces migrate along the gel. Each piece moves at a rate that depends both on its size and on the number of negatively charged phosphate groups (that is, the number of nucleotides) it contains. Smaller pieces move rapidly, and larger pieces move more slowly. The technique is so sensitive that up to 250 DNA pieces, differing in size by only one nucleotide, can be separated.

Once separation of the pieces has been accomplished, the position on the gel of each radioactive ^{32}P-containing piece is determined by exposing the gel to a photographic plate. Only the pieces containing the radioactively labeled 5'-phosphate end group are visualized; unlabeled pieces from the middle of the chain are present but do not appear on the photographic plate.

How can the cleavage, separation, and visualization techniques just discussed be used for DNA sequencing? Let's follow a DNA fragment through the series of steps to see how they ultimately lead to a sequence for the fragment.

1. A DNA molecule is incubated with a restriction enzyme, which cuts the chain at specific places and yields DNA fragments containing 100–200 nucleotide pairs.

2. The double-stranded DNA restriction fragments are radioactively labeled by incorporation of a ^{32}P-containing phosphate group at the 5'-hydroxyl of the terminal nucleotide.

3. The labeled restriction fragments are isolated, and each is separated into its two complementary strands. For example, imagine that we have now isolated a single-stranded DNA fragment of approximately 100 nucleotides with the following partial structure:

$$\text{(5' end)} \quad {}^{32}\text{P-C-T-C-A-G-T-A-C-C-G-} \text{- - -} \quad \text{(3' end)}$$

4. The labeled segment is subjected to four parallel sets of cleavage reactions under conditions that lead to (a) preferential splitting next to A, (b) preferential splitting next to G, (c) exclusive splitting next to C, and (d) splitting next to both T and C. *Mild reaction conditions are chosen so that only a few of the many possible splittings occur in each reaction.* In our example, the pieces shown in Table 16.4 would be produced.

TABLE 16.4   Splitting of a DNA restriction fragment under four sets of conditions^a

Cleavage conditions	Pieces produced		
Original DNA segment	^{32}P-C-T-C-A-G-T-A-C-C-G- - - -		
A > G	^{32}P-C-T-C		
	^{32}P-C-T-C-A-G-T	+	Larger pieces
G > A	^{32}P-C-T-C-A		
	^{32}P-C-T-C-A-G-T-A-C-C	+	Larger pieces
C	^{32}P-C-T		
	^{32}P-C-T-C-A-G-T-A		
	^{32}P-C-T-C-A-G-T-A-C	+	Larger pieces
C + T	^{32}P-C		
	^{32}P-C-T		
	^{32}P-C-T-C-A-G		
	^{32}P-C-T-C-A-G-T-A		
	^{32}P-C-T-C-A-G-T-A-C	+	Larger pieces

^{a}Only the pieces containing the radioactive end-label are considered. Other pieces are also produced but are not visualized.

5. Product mixtures from the four cleavage reactions are separated by gel electrophoresis, and the spots on the gel are visualized by exposure to a photographic plate. The location of each radioactive piece appears as a dark band on the photographic plate, but nonradioactive pieces are not visualized. The gel electrophoresis pattern shown in Figure 16.16 would be obtained in our hypothetical example.

6. The DNA sequence is then read directly from the gel. The band that appears farthest from the origin is the terminal mononucleotide (the smallest piece) and cannot be identified. Since the terminal mononucleotide appears only in the T + C column, however, it must have been produced by splitting *next to* a T or a C. Thus, the *second* nucleotide in the DNA fragment is either a T or a C. Since the smallest piece does not appear in the C column, however, the second nucleotide is not a C and must therefore be a T.

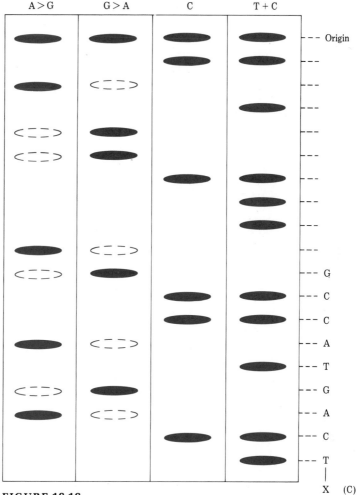

FIGURE 16.16
Representation of a gel electrophoresis pattern: The products of the four parallel cleavage experiments are placed at the top of the gel and a voltage is applied between top and bottom. Smaller products migrate along the gel at a faster rate and thus appear at the bottom. The DNA sequence can be read from the positions of the radioactive spots.

The second farthest band from the origin is a dinucleotide that appears in both C and T + C columns. This dinucleotide is produced by splitting next to the third nucleotide, which must therefore be a C. The third farthest band appears mainly in the A > G column, which means that the fourth nucleotide is an A. (There is also a faint band in the G > A column, since the specificity of these splittings is not perfect.)

Continuing in this manner, the entire sequence of the DNA fragment can be read from the gel simply by noting in what column the successively larger labeled poly-nucleotide pieces appear. Once read, the entire sequence can be checked by determining the sequence of the complementary strand. The identity of the 5′ terminal nucleotide can be determined by sequencing an overlapping segment produced by cleavage with another restriction enzyme.

The Maxam–Gilbert method of DNA sequencing is so efficient that fragments up to 150 nucleotides in length can be sequenced in a single day. So powerful is the method that some protein sequencing is now done by sequencing the DNA from which the protein's mRNA was transcribed. Such impressive achievements as the sequencing of the Epstein–Barr virus, which has 170,000 base pairs, are being recorded at an ever-increasing rate.

PROBLEM 16.13 Show the labeled products you would expect to obtain if the following DNA segment were subjected to each of the four cleavage reactions:

$$^{32}P\text{-A-A-C-A-T-G-G-C-G-C-T-T-A-T-G-A-C-G-A}$$

PROBLEM 16.14 Sketch what you would expect the gel electrophoresis pattern to look like if the DNA segment in Problem 16.13 were sequenced.

PROBLEM 16.15 Finish assigning the sequence to the gel electrophoresis pattern shown in Figure 16.16.

ADDITIONAL PROBLEMS

PROBLEM 16.16 Write representative structures for:

     (a) A fat   (b) A vegetable oil   (c) A steroid

PROBLEM 16.17 Write the structures of these molecules:

     (a) Sodium stearate   (b) Ethyl linoleate   (c) Glyceryl palmitodioleate

PROBLEM 16.18 Show the products you would expect to obtain from reaction of glyceryl trioleate with the following:

     (a) Excess Br_2 in CCl_4 (b) H_2/Pd
     (c) NaOH, H_2O (d) O_3, then Zn, CH_3COOH
     (e) $LiAlH_4$, then H_3O^+ (f) CH_3MgBr, then H_3O^+

PROBLEM 16.19 How would you convert oleic acid into these substances?

     (a) Methyl oleate   (b) Methyl stearate   (c) Nonanal   (d) Nonanedioic acid

PROBLEM 16.20 Eleostearic acid, $C_{18}H_{30}O_2$, is a rare fatty acid found in tung oil. On ozonolysis followed by treatment with zinc, eleostearic acid yields 1 part pentanal, 2 parts glyoxal, OHC—CHO, and 1 part 9-oxononanoic acid, $OHC(CH_2)_7COOH$. Propose a structure for eleostearic acid.

PROBLEM 16.21 Stearolic acid, $C_{18}H_{32}O_2$, yields oleic acid on catalytic hydrogenation over the Lindlar catalyst. Propose a structure for stearolic acid.

PROBLEM 16.22 Define the following terms:

     (a) Steroid   (b) DNA   (c) Base pair
     (d) Codon   (e) Lipid   (f) Transcription

PROBLEM 16.23 What DNA sequence is complementary to the following sequence?

G-A-A-G-T-T-C-A-T-G-C

PROBLEM 16.24 Draw the complete structure of the ribonucleotide codon UAC. For what amino acid does this sequence code?

PROBLEM 16.25 Draw the complete structure of the deoxyribonucleotide sequence from which the mRNA codon in Problem 16.24 was transcribed.

PROBLEM 16.26 What amino acids do the following ribonucleotide codons code for?

(a) AAU   (b) GAG   (c) UCC   (d) CAU   (e) ACC

PROBLEM 16.27 From what DNA sequences were each of the mRNA codons in Problem 16.26 transcribed?

PROBLEM 16.28 What anticodon sequences of tRNA's are coded for by each of the codons in Problem 16.26?

PROBLEM 16.29 Give an mRNA sequence that would code for synthesis of metenkephalin:

H-Tyr-Gly-Gly-Phe-Met-OH

PROBLEM 16.30 What amino acid sequence is coded for by the following mRNA base sequence?

CUA-GAC-CGU-UCC-AAG-UGA

PROBLEM 16.31 What anticodon sequences of tRNA's are coded for by the mRNA in Problem 16.30? What was the base sequence in the original DNA strand on which this mRNA was made? What was the base sequence in the DNA strand complementary to that from which this mRNA was made?

PROBLEM 16.32 Look up the structure of angiotensin II (Figure 15.2) and give an mRNA sequence that would code for its synthesis.

PROBLEM 16.33 Diethylstilbestrol (DES) exhibits estradiol-like activity even though it is structurally unrelated to steroids. Once used widely as an additive in animal feed, DES has been implicated as a causative agent in several types of cancers. Look up the structure of estradiol (Section 16.5) and show how DES can be drawn so that it is sterically similar to estradiol.

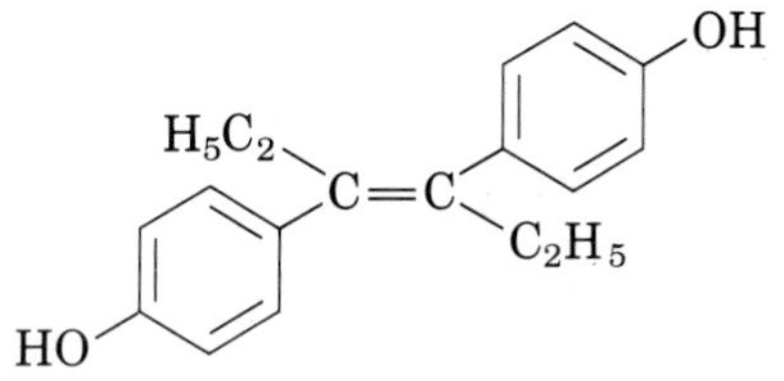

Diethylstilbestrol

PROBLEM 16.34 How many chiral centers are present in estradiol (Problem 16.33)? Label each of them.

PROBLEM 16.35   What products would you expect to obtain from reaction of estradiol (Problem 16.33) with these reagents?

(a) NaH, then CH$_3$I   (b) CH$_3$COCl, pyridine   (c) Br$_2$ (1 equiv)

PROBLEM 16.36   Look back at the conformation of cholesterol in Figure 16.5 and draw the following compound in its stable chair conformation:

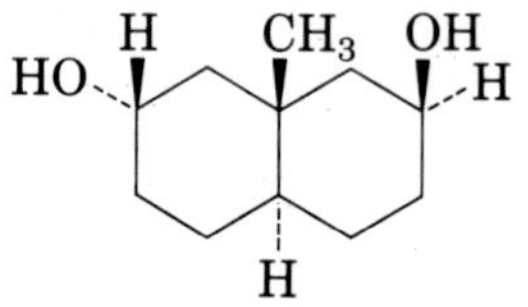

PROBLEM 16.37   As a general rule, equatorial alcohols react more rapidly with acid chlorides than axial alcohols. Predict the product obtained from reaction of the diol shown in Problem 16.36 with 1 equiv acetic anhydride.

Synthetic Detergents

Although soaps make life much more pleasant than it would otherwise be, they also have certain drawbacks. In hard water, which contains metal ions, soluble sodium carboxylates are converted into insoluble calcium and magnesium salts, leaving the familiar ring of scum around bathtubs and the "tattletale gray" on clothes.

These problems have been circumvented by synthesizing a class of synthetic detergents based on salts of long-chain alkylbenzenesulfonic acids. The operating principle of synthetic detergents is identical to the principle of soaps. The alkyl-benzene end of the molecule is lipophilic and attracts grease, but the sulfonate salt end is ionic and is attracted to water. Unlike soaps, however, sulfonate detergents do not form insoluble metal salts in hard water and do not leave an unpleasant scum.

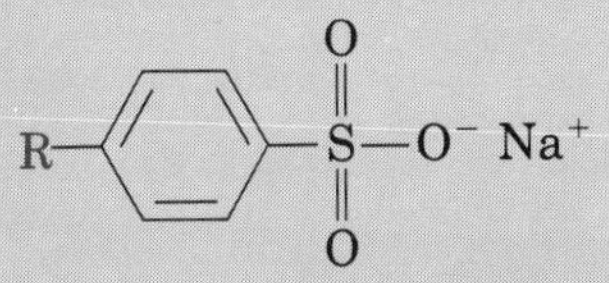

$$R-\!\!\!\left\langle\!\!\!\bigcirc\!\!\!\right\rangle\!\!\!-\overset{\overset{\displaystyle O}{\|}}{\underset{\underset{\displaystyle O}{\|}}{S}}-O^-\ Na^+$$

A synthetic detergent
(R = a mixture of C_{12} aliphatic chains)

Prostaglandins

Few compounds have caused as much excitement among medical researchers in the past decade as the **prostaglandins**. First isolated in the 1950s by Sune Bergstrom, Bengt Samuelsson, and their collaborators at the Karolinska Institute in Sweden, these simple lipids are synthesized in nature from the C_{20} fatty acid, arachidonic acid. The name prostaglandin derives from the fact that these compounds were first thought to be produced by the prostate gland, but they have subsequently been shown to be present in small amounts in all body tissues and fluids.

Prostaglandins are simple in structure. All have a cyclopentane ring with two long side chains, though they differ in the number of oxygen atoms and number of double bonds present. Prostaglandin E_1 (PGE_1) and prostaglandin $F_{2\alpha}$ ($PGF_{2\alpha}$) are representative structures:

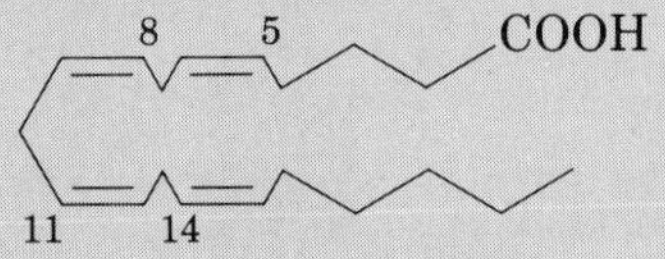

**Arachidonic acid,
(5Z,8Z,11Z,14Z)-eicosatetraenoic acid)**

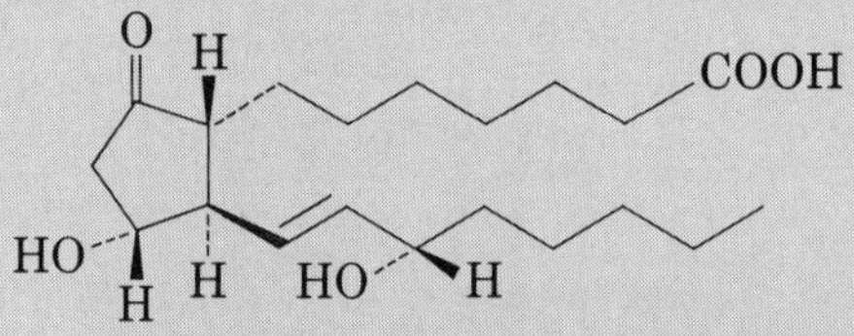

Prostaglandin E₁   **Prostaglandin F₂α**

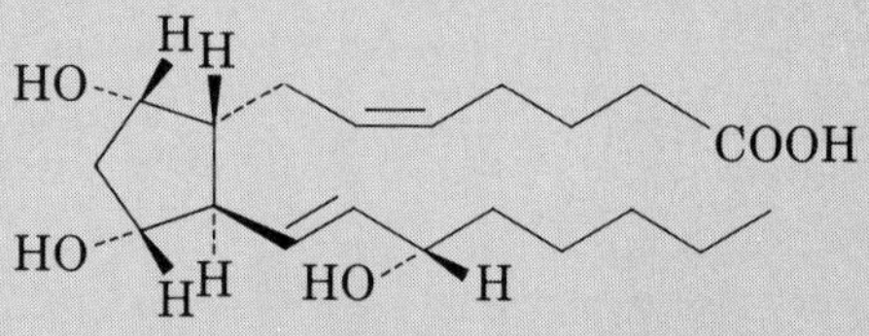

The several dozen known prostaglandins have an extraordinarily wide range of biological activities. Among their known actions are their abilities to affect blood pressure, to affect blood-platelet aggregation during clotting, to affect gastric secretions, to control inflammation, to affect kidney function, to affect reproductive systems, and to stimulate uterine contractions during childbirth. In addition, compounds that are closely related to the prostaglandins have still other effects. Recent interest has centered particularly on the thromboxanes, on prostacyclin, and on the leukotrienes, whose release in the body appears to trigger the asthmatic response.

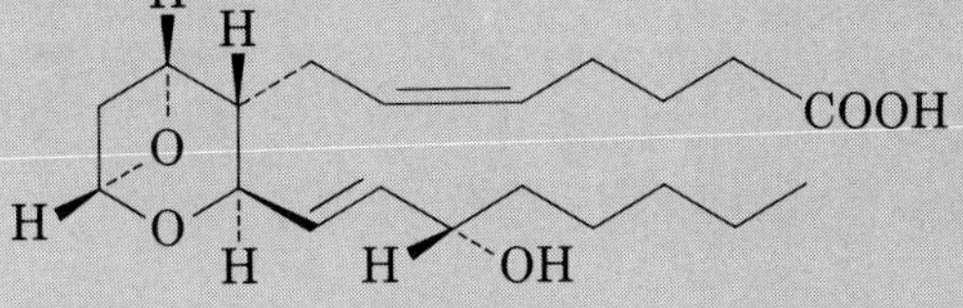

Thromboxane A$_2$

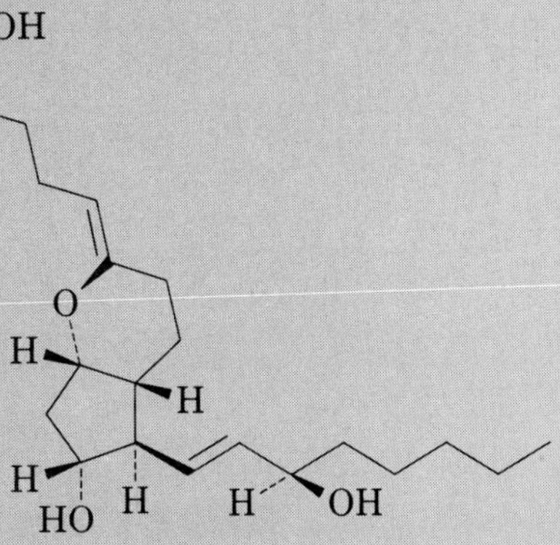

Prostacyclin

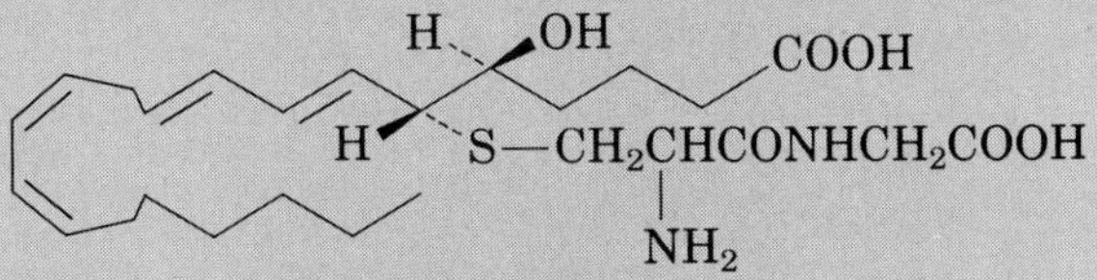

Leukotriene D$_4$

Prostaglandins are just beginning to be exploited in medicine, where their remarkable properties will surely lead to valuable new drugs.

Nomenclature of Polyfunctional Organic Compounds

Judging from the number of incorrect names that appear in the chemical literature, it's probably safe to say that relatively few practicing organic chemists are fully conversant with the rules of organic nomenclature. Simple hydrocarbons and monofunctional compounds present few problems; the basic rules governing the naming of such compounds are logical and easy to understand. However, problems are often encountered with polyfunctional compounds. Whereas most chemists could correctly identify hydrocarbon **1** as 3-ethyl-2,5-dimethylheptane, rather few could correctly identify polyfunctional compound **2**. Should we consider **2** as an ether? As an ethyl ester? As a ketone? As an alkene? It is, of course, all four, but it has only one correct name: ethyl 3-(4-methoxy-2-oxo-3-cyclohexenyl)propanoate.

$$CH_3CHCH_3$$
$$CH_3CH_2CHCH_2CHCH_2CH_3$$
$$CH_3$$

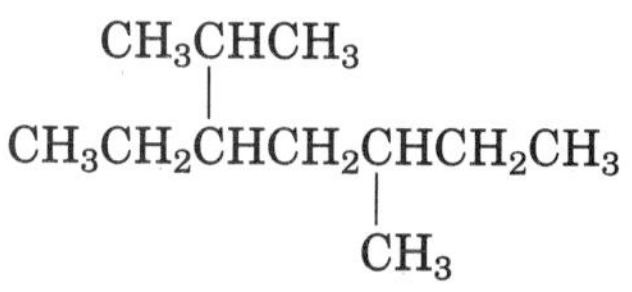

1. 3-Ethyl-2,5-dimethylheptane

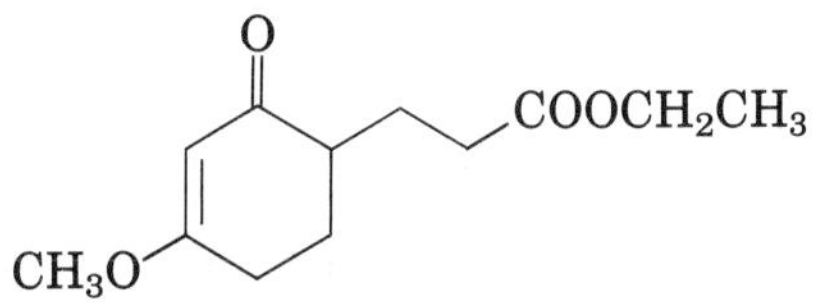

2. Ethyl 3-(4-methoxy-2-oxo-3-cyclohexenyl)propanoate

Naming polyfunctional organic compounds is really not much harder than naming monofunctional compounds. All that is required is a prior knowledge of monofunctional compound nomenclature and rigid application of a set of additional rules. In the following discussion, it's assumed that you have a good command of the rules of monofunctional compound nomenclature that are given throughout the text as each new functional group is introduced. A list of where these rules can be found is shown in Table A.1.

TABLE A.1 Where to find nomenclature rules for simple functional groups

Functional group	Text section	Functional group	Text section
Alkanes	2.3	Aldehydes	9.3
Cycloalkanes	2.11	Carboxylic acids	10.1
Alkenes	3.1	Acid halides	10.1
Alkynes	4.14	Acid anhydrides	10.1
Aromatic compounds	5.1	Amides	10.1
Alkyl halides	7.1	Esters	10.1
Ethers	8.1	Nitriles	10.1
Alcohols	8.1	Amines	12.1
Ketones	9.3		

The name of a polyfunctional organic molecule has four parts:

1. **Suffix:** the part that identifies the principal functional group class to which the molecule belongs

2. **Parent:** the part that identifies the size of the main chain or ring

3. **Substituent prefixes:** parts that identify what substituents are located on the main chain or ring

4. **Locants:** numbers that tell where substituents are located on the main chain or ring

To arrive at the correct name for a complex molecule, the above four name parts must be identified and then expressed in the proper order and format. Let's look at the four parts.

The Suffix: Functional Group Precedence

A polyfunctional organic molecule may contain many different kinds of functional groups, but for nomenclature purposes, we must choose just one suffix. It is not correct to use two suffixes; thus, keto ester **3** must be named either as a ketone with an *-one* suffix or as an ester with an *-oate* suffix, but can't be named as an *-onoate*. Similarly, amino alcohol **4** must be named either as an alcohol (*-ol*) or as an amine (*-amine*), but can't properly be named as an *-olamine*. The only exception to this rule is in naming compounds that have double or triple bonds. For example, the compound $H_2C{=}CHCH_2COOH$ is 3-butenoic acid, and $HC{\equiv}CCH_2CH_2CH_2CH_2OH$ is 5-hexyn-1-ol.

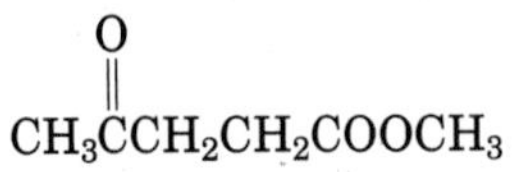

$$\overset{O}{\overset{\|}{CH_3CCH_2CH_2COOCH_3}}$$

3. Named as an ester with a keto (oxo) substituent
Methyl 4-oxopentanoate

$$\overset{OH}{\overset{|}{CH_3CHCH_2CH_2CH_2NH_2}}$$

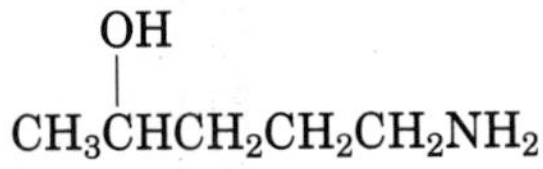

4. Named as an alcohol with an amino substituent
5-Amino-2-pentanol

How do we choose which suffix to use? Functional groups are divided into two classes, **principal groups** and **subordinate groups**, as shown in Table A.2. Principal groups are those that may be cited either as prefixes or as suffixes, whereas subordinate groups are those that may be cited only as prefixes. Within the principal groups, an order of precedence has been established. The proper suffix for a given compound is determined by identifying all the functional groups present and then choosing the principal group of highest priority. For example, Table A.2 indicates that keto ester **3** must be named as an ester rather than as a ketone, since an ester functional group is higher in priority than a ketone. Similarly, amino alcohol **4** must be named as an alcohol rather than as an amine. The correct name of **3** is methyl 4-oxopentanoate, and the correct name of **4** is 5-amino-2-pentanol. Further examples are shown below.

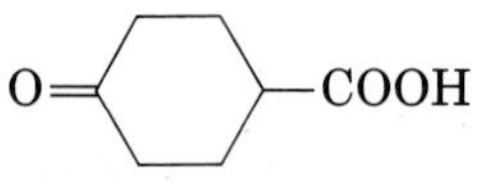

5. Named as a cyclohexanecarboxylic acid with an oxo substituent
4-Oxocyclohexanecarboxylic acid

TABLE A.2   Classification of functional groups for purposes of nomenclature[a]

Functional group class	Structure	Name when used as suffix	Name when used as prefix
Principal groups			
Carboxylic acids	—COOH	-oic acid -carboxylic acid	carboxy
Carboxylic anhydrides	$\overset{\text{O}}{\overset{\|}{\text{—C}}}$—O—$\overset{\text{O}}{\overset{\|}{\text{C}}}$—	-oic anhydride -carboxylic anhydride	
Carboxylic esters	—COOR	-oate -carboxylate	alkoxycarbonyl
Acyl halides	—COCl	-oyl halide -carbonyl halide	halocarbonyl (haloformyl)
Amides	—CONH$_2$	-amide -carboxamide	amido
Nitriles	—C≡N	-nitrile -carbonitrile	cyano
Aldehydes	—CHO	-al -carbaldehyde	formyl
	=O		oxo (either aldehyde or ketone)
Ketones	=O	-one	oxo
Alcohols	—OH	-ol	hydroxy
Phenols	—OH	-ol	hydroxy
Thiols	—SH	-thiol	mercapto, sulfhydryl
Amines	—NH$_2$	-amine	amino
Imines	=NH	-imine	imino
Alkenes	C=C	-ene	
Alkynes	C≡C	-yne	
Alkanes	C—C	-ane	
Subordinate groups			
Ethers	—OR		alkoxy
Sulfides	—SR		alkylthio
Halides	—F, —Cl, —Br, —I		halo
Nitro	—NO$_2$		nitro
Azides	N=N=N		azido
Diazo	=N=N		diazo

[a]The principal functional groups are listed in order of decreasing priority, but the subordinate functional groups have no established priority order. Principal functional groups may be cited either as prefixes or as suffixes; subordinate functional groups may be cited only as prefixes.

$$\underset{\underset{CH_3}{|}}{\overset{\overset{CH_3}{|}}{HOOC-C-CH_2CH_2CH_2COCl}}$$

6. Named as a carboxylic acid with a chlorocarbonyl substituent
5-Chlorocarbonyl-2,2-dimethylpentanoic acid

$$\underset{}{\overset{\overset{CHO}{|}}{CH_3CHCH_2CH_2CH_2COOCH_3}}$$

7. Named as an ester with an oxo substituent
Methyl 5-methyl-6-oxohexanoate

The Parent: Selecting the Main Chain or Ring

The parent or base name of a polyfunctional organic compound is usually quite easy to identify. If the group of highest priority is part of an open chain, we simply select the longest chain that contains the largest number of principal functional groups. If the highest-priority group is attached to a ring, we use the name of that ring system as the parent. For example, compounds **8** and **9** are isomeric aldehydo acids, and both must be named as acids rather than as aldehydes according to Table A.2. The longest chain in compound **8** has seven carbons, and the substance is therefore named 6-methyl-7-oxoheptanoic acid. Compound **9** also has a chain of seven carbons, but the longest chain that contains both of the principal functional groups has only three carbons. The correct name of this compound is 3-oxo-2-pentylpropanoic acid.

$$\underset{}{\overset{\overset{CHO}{|}}{CH_3CHCH_2CH_2CH_2CH_2COOH}}$$

8. Named as a substituted heptanoic acid
6-Methyl-7-oxoheptanoic acid

$$\underset{}{\overset{\overset{CHO}{|}}{CH_3CH_2CH_2CH_2CH_2CHCOOH}}$$

9. Named as a substituted propanoic acid
3-Oxo-2-pentylpropanoic acid

Similar rules apply for compounds **10–13**, which contain rings. Compounds **10** and **11** are isomeric keto nitriles, and both must be named as nitriles according to Table A.2. Substance **10** is named as a benzonitrile since the —CN functional group is a substituent on the aromatic ring, but substance **11** is named as an acetonitrile since the —CN functional group is on an open chain. The correct names are 2-acetyl-4-methylbenzonitrile (**10**) and (2-acetyl-4-methylphenyl)-acetonitrile (**11**). Compounds **12** and **13** are both keto acids and must be named as acids. The correct names are 3-(2-oxocyclohexyl)propanoic acid (**12**) and 2-(3-oxopropyl)cyclohexanecarboxylic acid (**13**).

10. Named as a substituted benzonitrile
2-Acetyl-4-methylbenzonitrile

11. Named as a substituted acetonitrile
(2-Acetyl-4-methylphenyl)acetonitrile

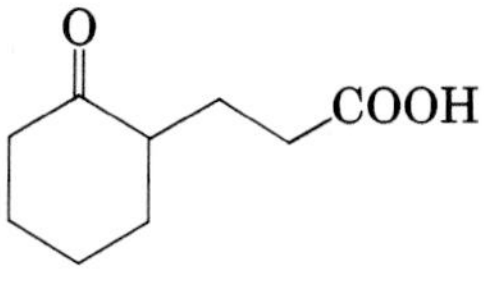

12. Named as a carboxylic acid
3-(2-Oxocyclohexyl)propanoic acid

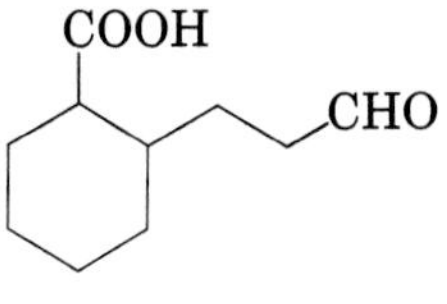

13. Named as a carboxylic acid
2-(3-Oxopropyl)cyclohexanecarboxylic acid

The Prefixes and Locants

With the suffix and parent name established, the next step is to identify and number all substituents on the parent chain or ring. These substituents include all alkyl groups and all functional groups other than the one cited in the suffix. For example, compound **14** contains three different functional groups (carboxyl, keto, and double bond). Since the carboxyl group is highest in priority, and since the longest chain containing the functional groups is seven carbons long, **14** is a heptenoic acid. In addition, the main chain has an oxo (keto) substituent and three methyl groups. Numbering from the end nearer the highest-priority functional group, we find that **14** is 2,5,5-trimethyl-4-oxo-2-heptenoic acid. Note that the final "e" of heptene is deleted in the word "heptenoic." This deletion only occurs when the name would have two adjacent vowels (thus, "heptenoic" has the final "e" deleted, but "heptenenitrile" retains the "e"). Look back at some of the other compounds we have considered to see other examples of how prefixes and locants are assigned.

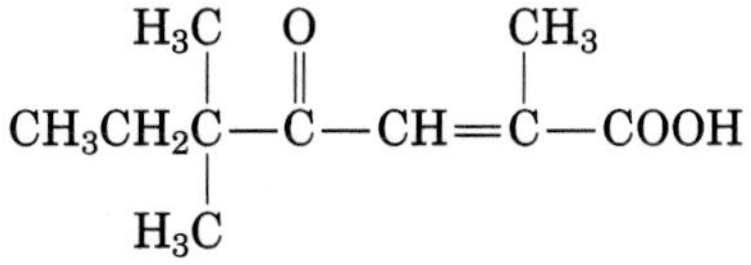

14. Named as a heptenoic acid
2,5,5-Trimethyl-4-oxo-2-heptenoic acid

Writing the Name

Once the name parts have been established, the entire name is written out. Several additional rules apply:

1. **Order of prefixes:** When the substituents have been identified, the main chain has been numbered, and the proper multipliers such as *di-* and *tri-* have been assigned, the name is written with the substituents listed in alphabetical, rather than numerical order. Multipliers such as *di-* and *tri-* are not used for alphabetization purposes, but the prefixes *iso-* and *tert-* are used.

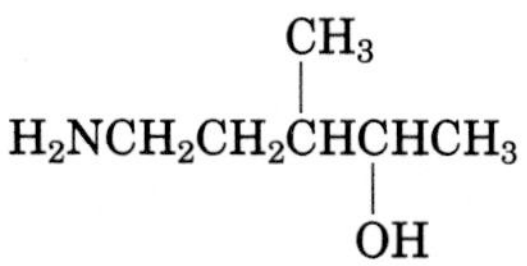

15. 5-Amino-3-methyl-2-pentanol (*NOT* 3-methyl-5-amino-2-pentanol)

2. **Use of hyphens; single- and multiple-word names:** The general rule is to determine whether the principal functional group is itself an element or compound. If it is either an element or a compound, then the name is written as a single word; if it is not, then the name is written as separate words. For example, methylbenzene (one word) is correct because the parent, benzene, is itself a compound. Diethyl ether, however, is written as two words because the parent, ether, is a class name rather than a compound name. Some further examples are shown below.

$$H_3C-Mg-CH_3 \qquad\qquad CH_3CHBrCOOH$$

16. Dimethylmagnesium   **17. 2-Bromopropanoic acid**
(one word, since magnesium is an element)   **(two words, since "acid" is not a compound)**

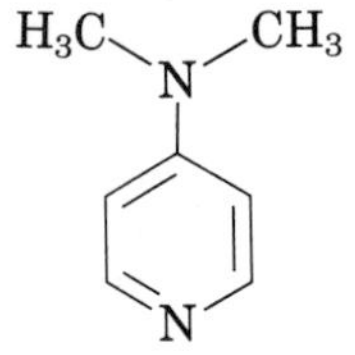

18. 4-(Dimethylamino)pyridine   **19. Methyl cyclopentanecarboxylate**
(one word, since pyridine is a compound)

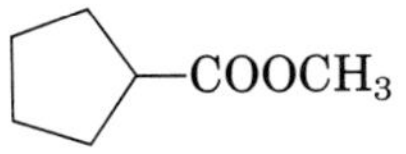

3. **Parentheses:** Parentheses are used to denote complex substituents when ambiguity would otherwise arise. For example, chloromethylbenzene has two substituents on a benzene ring, but (chloromethyl)benzene has only one complex substituent. Note that the expression in parentheses is not set off by hyphens from the rest of the name.

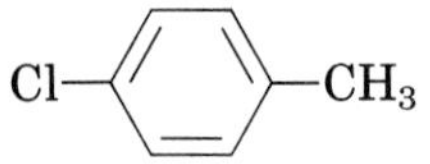

$$CH_3CHCH_2CH_3$$
$$HOOC-CHCH_2CH_2COOH$$

20. _p_-Chloromethylbenzene   **21. (Chloromethyl)benzene**   **22. 2-(1-Methylpropyl)pentanedioic acid**
(two substituents)   **(one complex substituent)**   **(The 1-methylpropyl group is a complex**
                                                                substituent on C2 of the main chain.)

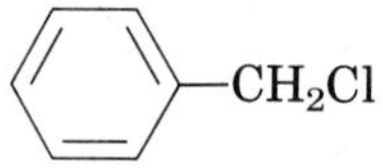

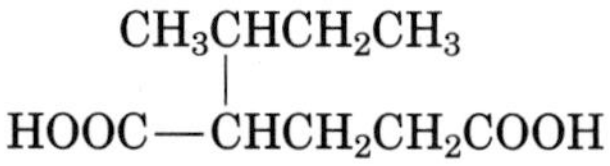

Additional Reading

Further explanations of the rules of organic nomenclature can be found in the following references:

1. O. T. Benfey, "The Names and Structures of Organic Compounds," Wiley, New York, 1966.

2. J. H. Fletcher, O. C. Dermer, and R. B. Fox, "Nomenclature of Organic Compounds: Principles and Practice," Advances in Chemistry Series No. 126, American Chemical Society, Washington, D.C., 1974.

3. International Union of Pure and Applied Chemistry, "Nomenclature of Organic Chemistry, Sections A, B, C, D, E, F, and H," Pergamon Press, Oxford, 1979.

4. J. G. Traynham, "Organic Nomenclature: A Programmed Introduction," Prentice-Hall, Englewood Cliffs, N.J., 1985.

Index

The references given in color refer to boldface entries in the text where terms are defined.